PLAYS FOR CHILDREN AND YOUNG ADULTS

GARLAND REFERENCE LIBRARY
OF SOCIAL SCIENCE
(VOL. 543)

PLAYS FOR CHILDREN AND YOUNG ADULTS
An Evaluative Index and Guide

RASHELLE S. KARP
JUNE H. SCHLESSINGER

Editorial Staff

Bernard S. Schlessinger, Coordinator
Karen Alstaetter
Janet Cockerham
Susan Halloran
Sharon Jennings
Mona Kerby
Susan Kleuser
Tracy Nelson
Toni Olshan
Selvin Royal
Melissa Stockton
Johanna Tunon
Vicky Walsh

GARLAND PUBLISHING, INC. • NEW YORK & LONDON
1991

Library of Congress Cataloging-in-Publication Data

Karp, Rashelle S.
    Plays for children and young adults : an evaluative index and
guide / Rashelle S. Karp, June H. Schlessinger.
        p.   cm. — (Garland reference library of social science ; v.
543)
    Includes index.
    ISBN 0–8240–6112–8 (alk. paper)
    1. Children's plays—Indexes. I. Schlessinger, June H.
II. Title. III. Series.
PN1627.K37   1991
016.812'540809282—dc20   90–44195
                                                                            CIP

Printed on acid-free, 250-year-life paper
Manufactured in the United States of America

To David,
who gracefully and lovingly
supported this venture

CONTENTS

PREFACE

Purpose of Work

The purpose of this book is to provide enough detailed and evaluative information about specific plays for children and young adults (ages 5–18) to enable those producing them to make effective decisions. To this end, 3,560 plays, playlets, choral readings, scenes, monologues, musical reviews, readers' theater, and skits appropriate for production by and/or for children and young adults that were published between 1975 and February 1989 have been thoroughly analyzed and evaluatively summarized.

Scope of the Work

We are especially grateful to the editors of the following companies for their cooperation in sending complimentary copies of their plays to our reviewers: I.E. Clark, Eldridge Publishing Company, Pioneer Drama Service, Anchorage Press, Dramatic Publishing Company, Coach House Press, and Baker's Plays. We have covered most of the plays of these companies.

Also included in this volume are appropriate plays listed in the H.W. Wilson *Play Index* (1978–1982 and 1983–1987), the catalog of Dramatists Play Service, all the plays published in *Plays: The Drama Magazine for Young People* (January 1975–February 1989), and Trefny and Palmer's *Index to Children's Plays in Collections, 1975–1984*. We have listed plays in anthologies and magazines, as well as individually published plays.

Each entry includes 1) grade level of the viewers and whether or not the play can be successfully produced by the indicated grade level; 2) a designation indicating whether the play has been negatively or positively reviewed (signified by a "+" or "-" after the grade level); 3) the play's author(s) (up to two are included); 4) the full title of the play; 5) a cast analysis; 6) the playing time (if available); 7) a brief description of the settings that would have to be reproduced on the stage; 8) the number of acts; 9) a brief plot summary; 10) an evaluation of the play; 11) royalty information (if available); 12) full bibliographic citation for the source document in which the play can be found; 13) a listing of subjects (up to three) that most accurately describe the main theme of the play; and 14) an indication of the type of play. In addition, when plays are adaptations of poems, short stories, other plays, or novels, the originals upon which they are based are identified.

Five indexes complete the volume: author/original title; cast; grade level; subject/play type; and playing time.

Logistics and Editorial Decisions

This has been an overwhelming project that has taken three long years to do. Our reviewers, most of whom have either drama or elementary/secondary education professional expertise, were highly conscientious. Each play has been read and evaluated by at least one reviewer and by at least one of the two coauthors. The plays were evaluated on the basis of their appropriateness for the targeted audience, and production considerations (i.e., will any special knowledge be required of the young actors to convincingly perform their parts, special purposes for which the play might be used, etc.). Those plays that received a negative evaluation from their first reviewer were read by at least two other reviewers, in addition to one of the coauthors, and only if all agreed was the negative evaluation carried forth.

Special notes are necessary on several headings:

Cast Analysis. The minimum number of males and females is listed. These numbers may not always agree with the publisher's catalogs, as the reviewers were told to carefully evaluate whether the cast members had to be male or female and how many cast members could be either male or female.

Acts. Actual acts, not scenes, are indicated; a play might contain several different scenes but only one act.

Settings. Settings are identified as briefly as possible, with only those specific settings that will have to be reproduced on stage being listed. If only props are needed, no setting is indicated.

Playing Time. Playing time is listed if it was given in the publisher's catalog, if it was listed on the play, or if one of the reviewers knew the playing time from actually viewing or performing the play.

Plot Summaries. Originally, plot summaries were quite long. We felt that it would be of great value to provide long plot summaries to give the maximum amount of information to potential producers. However, this resulted in a book which, when printed a year ago, was in excess of two volumes. Since the cost of such a work would have been prohibitive to many libraries, it was decided to edit the plot summaries to half their original length. Therefore, plot summaries give only the essential elements. We tried as much as possible to retain enough of the original detail to capture the spirit and tone of each play as well as its major themes.

Recommendation. The recommendations indicate what is uniquely positive or negative about the play, as well as any potentially controversial aspects and any potential production problems (e.g., staging, lighting, scene construction, etc.).

Subjects. It was extremely difficult to assign subjects to many of the plays. This is a problem common for all pieces of fiction and probably accounts, in part, for the scarcity of subject indexing for fiction. We tried to use the subject headings that were as specific as possible and that most closely resembled natural language.

Source. For plays that appear in more than one source, we chose the one that was either the most recent or that had the lowest royalty associated with it.

Original Authors/Original Titles. As with subjects, it was often difficult to identify whether or not a play had been adapted from a previously published work, especially since the original was usually not identified in the text of the play. Adaptations of folk tales and other forms of oral literature were also problematic. Although tremendous effort was expended to identify originals from which many of the plays were adapted, some have undoubtedly been missed. We welcome any additional information from the readers.

Indexes. Again, cost had to be weighed against comprehensiveness. Cross-references, which are undeniably useful and appropriate, are also very expensive, so we decided not to use them. We also welcome comments from readers about this decision.

In a project of this magnitude, many difficult editorial decisions must be made. The coauthors agonized over each decision and hope that the reading audience agrees with them.

Arrangement of the Work

The main text is arranged alphabetically by title. Each play has been assigned an identification number, to which the indexes refer.

ENTRY FORMAT

1. Identification number to which the indexes refer.
2. Grade level/range indicator. The grade level/range indicates the audience for which the play is most appropriate. An asterisk (*) following the grade level/range means that the play should be produced by groups older than the indicated audience.
3. (+/-). The overall review of the evaluator is indicated by a "+" or a "-" sign in parentheses.
4. Author(s). Up to two authors are listed, last name first. If the play is an adaptation of a poem, short story, other play, or novel, the authors of the original are identified in parentheses immediately following.
5. Title. The full title of the play is included. This is also the alphabetical access point. If the play is an adaptation of a poem, short story, other play, or novel, the original title is identified in parentheses immediately following.
6. Cast. Cast is broken down into females, males and unspecified. The abbreviations used are "m" for male, "f" for female, "u" for unspecified (either male or female), or "S" for several (when the number of a particular sex is not specified).
7. Acts. The number of acts is indicated, but scenes are not.
8. Settings. Specific settings that must be reproduced on the stage are listed. If no setting is necessary, that is indicated by "none"; the need for a bare stage is indicated by "bare stage"; if only props are needed, there is the word "props."
9. Playing Time. Playing time is indicated if it was listed in the publisher's catalog, if it was listed within the text of the play, or if the reviewer had viewed or produced the play him/herself. "NA" (not available) indicates that the playing time was unavailable.
10. Plot. A brief summary provides the essential details of the plot and enough of its periphery to provide a sense of the themes, tone, and spirit of the play.
11. Recommendation. The evaluation of the play includes those uniquely positive or negative elements that recommend it or make it inappropriate. In addition, any potentially controversial elements are identified, as are any potential production problems.
12. Royalty. Royalties were taken from the publisher's catalogs. They are for the highest royalty listed, as of 1988 (the date of the catalogs we used). In some cases, there may be additional royalties for the use of the music; these have not been indicated. Readers are cautioned that the royalties listed are only indicators; they should be confirmed with the publisher or from a new publisher's catalog. If the royalty was not available, it is listed as "NA" (not available). If there is no royalty, that is indicated as "None."
13. Source. A full bibliographic citation is provided. For plays that appear in more than one source, either the most recent appearance or the source which has the lowest royalty associated with it has been listed.
14. Subjects/Play Type. Up to three subjects are listed and one play type indicated.

CONTRIBUTORS/REVIEWERS

All of the contributors/reviewers have had professional experience in librarianship, elementary/secondary education, or theater production. They are also associated with either Clarion University of Pennsylvania, Texas Woman's University, or University of North Texas. They are listed, in alphabetical order, under the university with which they are affiliated.

Contributors/Reviewers Associated with Clarion University of Pennsylvania:

Ann P. Allan
Elizabeth Andrews
Jeffrey R. Bailey
Carole E. Bohn
Alan W. Buck
Carol Byrnes
Patricia Cantwell
Ann F. Cohen
Christy Coombs
Barbara Coopey
Linda Cornett
Jennifer Cousins
Nancy Cristiano
Judy L. Davis
Betty Detwiler
Susan J. DiMauro
Carole L. Dinco
Robert J. Doan
Kirk Doran
Sherry W. Dolloff
Judy Dorman
Barbara Nelson Estabrook
Clifford J. Farides
Deborah Gahm
Chandra Gigliotti
Richard Gittins
Lisa Graffius
Pat Griffith

Kathryn C. Grof-Tisza
Susan Halloran
Chris Harbison
David L. Hill
Lorraine L. Himber
Evelyn E. Hodgdon
Elizabeth Johnston
Karen Jordan
Carol J. Kearney
Cheryl Kirby
Rolaan Larson
Rick Lilla
Scott J. Litty
Stephanie B. Marcinko
Sharon Mathews
Althea S. McAllister
Laura J. McCluskey
Judy F. McConnell
Linda Mcdonald
Sandra McDowell
Nancy Miller
Dale Yvonne Motycka
Polly S. Mumma
Tracy L. Nelson
Toni Olshan
Karen L. O'Neil
Nancy Palma
Kristina Peters
Kathryn Pettorini
Jacqueline Pitman
Karen Reilly
Mary Rennie

Teri Repak
Kay M. Rhinehart
Kathleen M. Richards
Judith A. Ring
Pamela G. Ross
Donna J. Sallack
JoAnne Basar Schiefer
Lawrence S. Schwartz
Susan Serra
Ruth E. Shaw
Helen Sheehy
Mary Petersen Simpson
John Slonaker
Susan M. Snyder
Karen Kuti Sracic
Andrea J. Staples
Michelle Pehr Star
Margaret Stevens-Becksvoort
Charlotte R. Stonebraker
Dian Stratton
Mary R. Suggs
Karyl Sylken
Marsha Ann Tate
Sandra L. Thomas
Mary Van Milligan
Julie Weaver
Susan Weaver
Robin Wiley
Benjamin D. Williams
MLou Williams
Sarah M. Wright

**Contributors/Reviewers
Associated with Texas
Woman's University**

Yiyuk E. Alatorre
Diana Anderson
Margaret E. Anderson
Alan M. Berecka
Bo B. Bibb
Diane Blair
Roselyn R. Boateng
Danette L. Brandner
Laura A. Brooks
Margaret E. Coleman
Patricia A. Copppage
Christina Cowan
Virginia B. Dandy
Linda J. DePhillips
Diane M. Devine
Deanna A. Dodson
Sassi Domalapalli
Betty Dominquez
Marion A. Dorsey
Travis Dudley, Jr.
Gene D. Estes
Rebecca R. Feldman
Cynthia Ferguson
Kathryn B. Finley
Gary N. Fitsimmons
Barbara J. Glaus
Joe D. Gunter
Mohammad Hadavi
Dawn C. haden
Julie L. Hagood
Gail M. Haire
Genie T. Hammel
Ronald Heezen
Karen A. Hill
Peggy Hoffpauir
Nancy K. Howland
Barbara Huddleston
Sandra J. Jones
Ronald L. Keys
Edwin L. Kiser
Mary S. Kleuser
Mary B. Kraljic
Nancy A. Krueger
Velma M. Lingo
Merry E. Lowery
Donna J. Lyday
Lalisha Mack
E. Elaine Markley
Beverly R. Mathis
Deborah A. McCarthy
Marolyn McVey
Steven R. Mehal
Peggy A. Mills
Virginia Nichols

Jean Northington
William T. Parks
Erma Popek
Katherine Powell
Toni Prachick
Terry L. Praznik
Margaret J. Quartel
Doris J. Raby
Yvonne Reeder-Tinsley
Graciela Reyna
Wilma R. Richardson
Bickie Roberts
Fred A. Roberts
Barbara A. Robertson
Maria A. Robinson
Osbelia M. Rocha
Becky Rood
Jackie R. Rue
Judith K. Rusk
Joycelyn Schmid
Kathleen M. Seymour
James A. Shuff
Linda J. Skaggs
Kathleen Slaughter
Susan Steadman
Jennifer S. Stephens
Billy W. Stevens
Melissa Stockton
Scott Stockton
Paula F. Sutherland
Linda K. Swan
Kiem-Dung T. Ta
Laurene J. Teter
Jerri Thompson
Johanna Tunon
Linda Um Joachim
Sheldon Vik
Victoria I. Walsh
Betty Watkins
Billie J. White
Mary. L. Wiggins
Andrea L. Williams
Gloria Willingham
Leza Wilson
Connie Young

**Contributors/Reviewers
Associated with University of
North Texas**

Larry Adair
Jan Adams
Janet K. Alkire
Terri Allen
Monika Antonelli
Beverly Baker
Wanda Baldridge
Pam Barrett

Cheryl Beckley
Carisse Berryhill
Regina Billington
Lorraine Bingham
Lou B. Birdwell
Ruth Bison
Joe Blackburn
Mary J. Bloomquist
Debi Bly
Brenna Bonar
Kathryn Boone
Donna K. Brown
Risa L. Brown
Gina Mr. Brudi
Bill Buchner
Beth Bucy
Dorothy Buice
Phyllis Christensen
Janet S. Cockerham
Carolyn Courtney
Susan Cumings
Rita Curtis
Phyllis Daugherty
Mary Davis
Terri Decker
Pamela K. Drummond
Christopher J. Eatmon
Susan Elliot
Tracy Ellis
Dorothy S. Fesler
LaQuita Fields
Kathryn A. Findley
Linda Fleece
Gary D. Ford
Rita Foreman
Alice Fulbright
Rickey D. Fuller
Debby Funk
Janet Gillespie
Dorothy B. Glass
Linda Goodgron
Juanita Y. Grady
Karen Gretzler
Suzanne Grover
Nancy Hadley
Steve Hagstrom
Kelley Herbert
Susan Hidalgo
Ellen Hobbs
Shiela Holder
Frances Hollis
Diana Howard
Joseph Hu
Cynthia Hurt
Linda J. Ivy
Donna Jackson
Ellen Jeane
Donna Jobe

David Johnson
Angela Jones
John V. Jones, Jr.
Pamela M. Jones
Steven M. Jones
David Jordan
Yunfen G. Kao
Pamela J. Keesee
Berti Ketney
Chris King
Jo Klemm
Bobbie Klepper
Li-Chih Kuo
Charlotte Kuser
Karen L. Labuik
Mike Lauch
Glenn Lemieux
Linda Linderman
Brenda Lindsey
Lorraine Lord
Helen Mann
Janet L. McColloch
Mark McKenney
William R. Miller

Michael A. Moore
Patty Mount
Janice Nakashima
Marie Noe
Dorothy D. Nowlin
Bill Oates
John Parrett
Fredonia Paschall
Edith S. Pequeno
Beth Perry
Patricia F. Peters
James Phillips
Cherlyann Plemons
Tracey Preston
Luana Reed
Virginia Rey
Connie Rhoades
Sandra River
Carol Roberts
Alice Robledo
Connie Roe
Diane Roether
Cholly J. Rolater
Jessie Sacker

Sue Sappington
Brenda K. Scholl
Gail Schwamb
Melanie J. Scott
Paula Serna
Katherine St. Clair
Linda Talbert
Rebecca Taylor
Christine Tillery
Pamela Waller
Shirley Wallick
Rebecca Walls
Laurie S. Ward
Cheryl Weatherly
Cathy Webster
Holly L. Wells
John W. Wells
Sandra White
Nicki Wilcoxson
Susan Wilson
Beverly Wise
Lillian Withrow
Sherry Wosick

Plays for Children and Young Adults

1. 3-6. (+) Robinette, Joseph. **A*B*C [America before Columbus].** CAST: 1f, 1m, 28u. ACTS: 1. SETTINGS: Prehistoric world. PLAYING TIME: 60 min. PLOT: This 20,000 year history of America before Columbus depicts the lifestyle and inventions of prehistoric people. RECOMMENDATION: With a flexible cast of 7-30, this humorously teaches a great deal about prehistoric life. ROYALTY: $25. SOURCE: Robinette, Joseph. (1984). A*B*C (America before Columbus). Schulenburg, TX: I.E. Clark. SUBJECTS/PLAY TYPE: Prehistoric Age; Comedy.

2. 5-8. (-) Watson, Wenta Jean. **Abe and the runaways.** CAST: 4f, 7m. ACTS: 1. SETTINGS: Woods; log cabin; schoolhouse. PLAYING TIME: 20 min. PLOT: A teenaged Abe Lincoln helps two runaway slaves evade their owner. RECOMMENDATION: This has too much stereotyping and over used dialogue, and too many historical liberties and anachronisms. ROYALTY: Free to Plays subscribers. SOURCE: Kamerman, Sylvia E. (1983). Holiday plays round the year. Boston, MA: Plays, Inc. SUBJECTS/PLAY TYPE: Slavery; Lincoln, Abraham; Playlet.

3. 6-9. (-) Bradley, Virginia. **Abe Lincoln: Star center.** CAST: 1f, 9m, Su. ACTS: 1. SETTINGS: Stage; basketball court. PLAYING TIME: 25 min. PLOT: On the day before the big basketball game, Shad plays the role of Abraham Lincoln in a school play. When he refuses to take off his beard for the game, the other team members refuse to play if he wears it. At the last moment, he heeds the advice of his coach, his teacher, and his friend, and rips the beard from his chin. RECOMMENDATION: The thin, uninteresting plot is not improved by the complex staging which changes from a stage to a basketball court. ROYALTY: None. SOURCE: Bradley, Virginia. (1981). Holidays on stage. New York, NY: Dodd, Mead. SUBJECTS/PLAY TYPE: Lincoln, Abraham; Presidents' Day; Playlet.

4. 9-12. (+) Fisher, Aileen. **Abe's winkin' eye.** CAST: 4f, 4m. ACTS: 1. SETTINGS: Log cabin. PLAYING TIME: NA. PLOT: A cross section of life in Tom Lincoln's family is presented with special emphasis on the unique characteristics of Abe Lincoln's personality. RECOMMENDATION: This well depicts early pioneer family life. The language patterns should be carefully preserved both for the authenticity of the play and for their educational value. ROYALTY: None. SOURCE: Fisher, Aileen. (1986). Holiday programs for boys and girls. Boston, MA: Plays, Inc. SUBJECTS/PLAY TYPE: Lincoln, Abraham; Pioneer Life; Playlet.

5. 7-12. (-) Lerman, Louis. **The abolition flyer.** CAST: 1f, 4m, 1u. ACTS: 1. SETTINGS: None. PLAYING TIME: 20 min. PLOT: In this symbolic rendering of history, Levi Coffin, Arthur Tappan, William Lloyd Garrison, and Harriet Tubman meet in Cincinnati to discuss expansion of the Underground Railroad. The group boards the "Freedom Train" and travels South, picking up passengers as they go, but on the return trip North, the train is so filled that some must be turned away. They reach the stretch of rail between North Carolina and Tennessee, with slave-catchers right behind them, and the "Train" stalls and quits. The group calls out to the legendary John Henry, who appears, chops a hole through the mountain, and pushes the "Train" through to Freedom. RECOMMENDATION: The symbolic railroad will not be recognized as an allegory for the human train of people who helped the slaves escape to the North. John Henry's appearance trivializes the important role that Tubman and the Underground Railroad played in Black American History. This is trite, condescending, historically inaccurate, and inappropriate. ROYALTY: Free to Plays subscribers. SOURCE: Lerman, Louis. (1987, January/February). The abolition flyer. Plays: The Drama Magazine for Young People, pp. 57-62. SUBJECTS/PLAY TYPE: Underground Railroad; Black History; Abolition Movement; Reader's Theater.

6. 4-8. (+) Luftig, Richard. **Abracadabra.** CAST: 4f, 5m, 1u. ACTS: 1. SETTINGS: Living room; family room. PLAYING TIME: 20 min. PLOT: Sydney, a student at the Abra K. Dabra Magic School, is not good enough to earn a diploma. When he does magic tricks to impress Billy, a little boy who has not talked or laughed in a year, Sydney is so awful that Billy starts laughing, then begins to talk. Sydney learns that although he is not a good magician, he can perform magic of the heart. RECOMMENDATION: This works both as a comedy and as a serious presentation of the theme that laughter works miracles. ROYALTY: Free to Plays subscribers. SOURCE: Luftig, Richard. (1975, April). Abracadabra. Plays: The Drama Magazine for Young People, pp. 37-41. SUBJECTS/PLAY TYPE: Magic; Laughter; Comedy.

7. 10-12. (+) Mattera, John. **Abra-cadaver.** CAST: 2f, 3m, Su. ACTS: 1. SETTINGS: Living room. PLAYING TIME: NA. PLOT: Jack Marsh and his sister-in-law, Christine, plan to kill Jack's wife, Marie, during a magic act at a masquerade party. One plot twist reveals that Christine and Marie have plotted to kill Jack; another reveals that Jack has faked his death and conspired with the family lawyer to kill Marie and Christine. A final twist has Marie and the lawyer as the victors, with Christine and Jack both dead. However, there was a witness to their crime. RECOMMENDATION: This witty play relies heavily on plot twists and fast action, and should keep the audience guessing. ROYALTY: $20. SOURCE: Mattera, John. (1982). Abra-cadaver. Chicago, IL: Dramatic Pub. Co. SUBJECTS/PLAY TYPE: Murder; Mystery.

8. 4-12. (+) Gilfond, Henry. **Abraham Lincoln and the lady.** CAST: 1f, 1m, 2u. ACTS: 1. SETTINGS: Office. PLAYING TIME: 15 min. PLOT: Mrs. Harvey persuades Abraham Lincoln to build a northern hospital during the Civil War. RECOMMENDATION: The arguments for and against a northern hospital for northern soldiers are compelling, but the ending, where Lincoln asks Mrs. Harvey if she thinks he is handsome, does not make the symbolic point that it should, thereby spoiling the entire message about war. With some rewriting, and with directed discussion before and after, this high interest/low vocabulary drama might be

effective. **ROYALTY:** None. **SOURCE:** Gilfond, Henry. (1985). Holiday plays for reading. New York, NY: Walker. **SUBJECTS/PLAY TYPE:** Lincoln, Abraham; Civil War, American; Playlet.

9. 3-7. (+) Winther, Barbara. **Abu Nuwas. CAST:** 3f, 3m, Su. **ACTS:** 1. **SETTINGS:** Clearing. **PLAYING TIME:** 20 min. **PLOT:** In the first tale, farmer Haji complains to poet Abu Nuwas that someone stole his shoes. The suspects include Ali the cobbler, Ali's wife, and Haji's wife. Abu cleverly reveals the thief. In the next tale, Haji lends Abu a pot with a hole in it, hoping Abu will mend it for him. Instead, Abu returns a smaller, but usable pot, saying the big pot gave birth that night. Haji lends his friend a perfect pot, hoping to gain another undamaged pot, but Abu tells him that the large pot died during the night, and since he buried it for Haji, he has nothing to return. **RECOMMENDATION:** A delightful play, this displays a charm usually associated with McGuffy's Reader stories. **ROYALTY:** Free for amateur performance. **SOURCE:** Winther, Barbara. (1976). Plays from folktales of Africa and Asia. Boston, MA: Plays, Inc. **SUBJECTS/PLAY TYPE:** Folk Tales, Persia; Playlet.

10. 7-12. (+) Sawyer-Young, Kat. **Abused. CAST:** 1f. **ACTS:** 1. **SETTINGS:** None. **PLAYING TIME:** 1 min. **PLOT:** Karen admits that her father beats her, and asks what she can do about it. **RECOMMENDATION:** This should be followed up with information about dealing with abusive parents. **ROYALTY:** None. **SOURCE:** Sawyer-Young, Kat. (1987). Minute monologues for contemporary teens. Boston, MA: Baker's Plays. **SUBJECTS/PLAY TYPE:** Child Abuse; Monologue.

11. 7-12. (+) Sawyer-Young, Kat. **Accident. CAST:** 1m. **ACTS:** 1. **SETTINGS:** None. **PLAYING TIME:** 1 min. **PLOT:** Jeff gets angry at his friend, Feash, who is in a coma because of Jeff's irresponsible driving. **RECOMMENDATION:** Jeff's inability to realize that actions have consequences for which he must assume responsibility is well worth discussion. **ROYALTY:** None. **SOURCE:** Sawyer-Young, Kat. (1987). Minute monologues for contemporary teens. Boston, MA: Baker's Plays. **SUBJECTS/PLAY TYPE:** Responsibility; Monologue.

12. 9-12. (+) Kundrat, Theodore V. **Accidental journey. CAST:** 4f, 6m. **ACTS:** 1. **SETTINGS:** None. **PLAYING TIME:** 30 min. **PLOT:** Peter Piper has a run in with a burglar, during which Peter is bashed by his wife, Peggy. Peter's fleeting encounter with Death allows him to wander into several surreal situations where he meets Cleopatra, Helen of Troy, and Sappho. All three legendary beauties compete for Peter's affection. Having to choose between them, Peter pleads for life and for his Peggy, whom he admires because she behaves as his equal. Peter escapes Death and wakes up in Peggy's presence. **RECOMMENDATION:** Although easy to perform, strong elements of sexism and sexual tension form the bulk of the comedy. **ROYALTY:** $10. **SOURCE:** Kundrat, Theodore K. (1978). Accidental journey.

Chicago, IL: Coach House Press. **SUBJECTS/PLAY TYPE:** Marriage; Sex; Reader's Theater.

13. 9-12. (+) Ortwein, Terry. **Act three, scene five. CAST:** 3f, 1m, 1u. **ACTS:** 1. **SETTINGS:** Balcony. **PLAYING TIME:** 40 min. **PLOT:** Students rehearse the balcony scene from **Romeo and Juliet.** As they begin to understand the poetry, their ability to act out the scene improves. **RECOMMENDATION:** The difficulty with the language of Shakespeare is addressed, as are the abilities of the actors to convey emotions and understand what makes a good production. This would be ideal for students early in their dramatic careers. **ROYALTY:** $15. **SOURCE:** Ortwein, Terry. (1987). Act three, scene five. Boston, MA: Baker's Plays. **SUBJECTS/PLAY TYPE:** Shakespeare, William; **Romeo and Juliet;** Theater; Comedy.

14. 7-12. (+) Majeski, Bill. **Act your age! CAST:** 3f, 2m. **ACTS:** 1. **SETTINGS:** Living room. **PLAYING TIME:** 35 min. **PLOT:** Nancy has a crush on older Larry, her future brother-in-law, and tries to take Larry away from her sister, Sue, while Judd tries to capture Nancy's interest. Sue, her mother, and Larry conspire to turn Nancy away from Larry by playing up his "old" age, but to no avail. Judd finally gets Nancy's attention by tripping on his skateboard. **RECOMMENDATION:** This is mildly humorous but ageless in its appeal. **ROYALTY:** Free to Plays subscribers. **SOURCE:** Majeski, Bill. (1978, February). Act your age! Plays: The Drama Magazine for Young People, pp. 13-22. **SUBJECTS/PLAY TYPE:** Dating; Comedy.

15. 1-3*. (+) Breslow, Maurice & Posnick, Michael. **Adam and Eve and after. CAST:** 2f, 4m, 1u. **ACTS:** 1. **SETTINGS:** Bare stage, props. **PLAYING TIME:** NA. **PLOT:** The Biblical stories of Adam and Eve, Noah's Ark, Moses and the Pharaoh, Joshua and the Battle of Jerico, and David and Goliath are told. **RECOMMENDATION:** This uses pantomime, music, light effects, stage props, audience participation, and a singing narrator. It should be produced by talented young adults. **ROYALTY:** NA. **SOURCE:** Breslow, Maurice. (1982). Adam and Eve and after and Silver Bird and Scarlet Feather. Toronto: Playwrights Canada. **SUBJECTS/PLAY TYPE:** Bible Stories; Musical.

16. 7-12. (+) Smith, Beatrice S. **Adams for the Defense. CAST:** 2f, 3m, Su. **ACTS:** 1. **SETTINGS:** Sitting room. **PLAYING TIME:** 30 min. **PLOT:** John Adams witnesses the shooting of several patriots by a squad of British troops headed by Captain Preston, and is asked to defend Preston. His willingness to do so meets with opposition. Concerned for the safety of his family, he considers withdrawing from the case, but his wife convinces him to remain resolute and to defend the "rights of mankind." **RECOMMENDATION:** This glorifies John Adams, the values of justice and fair-mindedness he represented, and presents the concept that standing by principles can be difficult. **ROYALTY:** Free to Plays subscribers. **SOURCE:** Smith, Beatrice S.

(1976, May). Adams for the defense. Plays: The Drama Magazine for Young People, pp. 67-78. SUBJECTS/PLAY TYPE: Adams, John; Values; Playlet.

17. 9-12. (+) McDonough, Jerome. **Addict. CAST:** 5f, 5m, Su. **ACTS:** 1. **SETTINGS:** None. **PLAYING TIME:** 70 min. **PLOT:** Seven young people relate their experiences with drugs and alcohol. The human toll builds until the medical examiner reads the autopsy reports. As he calls their names, they lie down, upstage, in their own graves. Before the house lights come up, an announcer lists specific ways to get help. **RECOMMENDATION:** This very powerful piece should be included as part of a chemical abuse program on the secondary level. Issues raised in the performance require the services of trained professional counselors for further discussion and possible therapy. Parents might wish to attend a separate performance. The characters use current street lingo, which may need to be updated. **ROYALTY:** $35. **SOURCE:** McDonough, Jerome. (1985). Addict. Schulenburg, TX: I.E. Clark. **SUBJECTS/PLAY TYPE:** Drug Abuse; Tragedy.

18. 4-5. (+) Bland, Joellen. (Alger, Horatio, Jr.) **Adrift in New York.** (Adrift in New York) **CAST:** 2f, 6m. **ACTS:** 8. **SETTINGS:** Study. **PLAYING TIME:** 35 min. **PLOT:** A rich old man near death clings to the hope that he will see his son, who, at three years old, was kidnapped by a scheming nephew hoping to inherit the wealth. The son (now 18) comes back through a complicated chain of circumstances in which the villainy of the nephew is exposed. **RECOMMENDATION:** This classic rags to riches story reflects the social values and mores of the late 19th century. **ROYALTY:** Free to Plays Subscribers. **SOURCE:** Bland, Joellen. (1979, May). Adrift in New York. Plays: The Drama Magazine for Young People, pp. 13-24. **SUBJECTS/PLAY TYPE:** Values; Heroes; Melodrama; Adaptation.

19. 9-12. (+) Porter, Robert N. & Perry, Jack. (Alger, Horatio Jr.) **Adrift in New York.** (Adrift in New York) **CAST:** 11f, 5m, Su. **ACTS:** 2. **SETTINGS:** Mansion room. **PLAYING TIME:** 90 min. **PLOT:** Uncle John, head of the Linden family, writes two wills. One leaves the estate to his ward, Florence, and whomever she marries. The other leaves it to his long lost son, Harvey, who was kidnapped years ago. When he is certain Harvey is dead, John will sign the first will. His nephew, Curtis, who kidnapped Harvey, tries to convince Florence to marry him. She refuses and befriends a thief (Dodger), and Uncle John casts her out. Curtis arranges for Dodger to be shanghaied, but Dodger returns and brings back Curtis' deserted wife and baby. Dodger tells Florence that he loves her, and reveals his identity as the long lost son, Harvey. **RECOMMENDATION:** A real period piece with very appealing characters, the glimpses of American life at two levels of society are very realistic. The musical segments could be eliminated if desired. **ROYALTY:** $50. **SOURCE:** Porter, Robert N. & Perry, Jack. (1979). Adrift in New York. Denver, CO: Pioneer Drama Service. **SUBJECTS/PLAY TYPE:** Melodrama; Drug Abuse; Adaptation.

20. K-12. (+) Hendricks, William & Vogel, Cora. **Advent candle custom. CAST:** Su. **ACTS:** 1. **SETTINGS:** None. **PLAYING TIME:** 30 min. **PLOT:** This Advent program is a compilation of prayers, hymns, poems, and Bible readings from Isaiah and the Gospels. **RECOMMENDATION:** Recommended for a family to perform on the four Sundays of Advent and Christmas Day, or to be performed in church settings to celebrate Advent. **ROYALTY:** None. **SOURCE:** Hendricks, William & Vogel, Cora. (1983). Handbook of Christmas programs. Grand Rapids, MI: Baker Book House. **SUBJECTS/PLAY TYPE:** Christmas; Advent; Worship Program.

21. 4-7. (+) Hendricks, William & Vogel, Cora. **An Advent celebration. CAST:** Su. **ACTS:** 1. **SETTINGS:** None. **PLAYING TIME:** 30 min. **PLOT:** This Advent program takes readings from the Gospels to symbolize the light of God through the lighting of the candles. **RECOMMENDATION:** Because of the more familiar Bible passages interspersed with modern usage, this is recommended as part of a Sunday school class. **ROYALTY:** None. **SOURCE:** Hendricks, William & Vogel, Cora. (1983). Handbook of Christmas programs. Grand Rapids, MI: Baker Book House. **SUBJECTS/PLAY TYPE:** Christmas; Advent; Worship Program.

22. 5-6*. (+) Way, Brian. **Adventure faces. CAST:** 2f, 2m. **ACTS:** 1. **SETTINGS:** Bare stage. **PLAYING TIME:** 60 min. **PLOT:** "King" Charles, the carnival man, his wife, and daughter refuse to face their eviction from city land and the public's preferences for bingo and TV over live carnival entertainment. When the family's dearest friend turns out to be the "culprit" in the land sale, feelings of anger are expressed and resolved. **RECOMMENDATION:** This is a good presentation of emotions dealing with change: denial, fear, anger, and acceptance. Although recommended for 5th and 6th graders, the theme may be beyond them, and the need for them to participate in the carnival act may make them uncomfortable. **ROYALTY:** $20. **SOURCE:** Way, Brian. (1977). Adventure faces. Reston, VA: Educational Arts Association. **SUBJECTS/PLAY TYPE:** Change; Emotions; Friendship; Drama.

23. 5-11. (+) Deary, Terence. **Adventure Island. CAST:** 1m, 3u. **ACTS:** 1. **SETTINGS:** Ship; island. **PLAYING TIME:** 50 min. **PLOT:** Captain Spike and his crew, with the help of the children in the audience, attempt to outwit the villainous Black Jack when they are shipwrecked on Adventure Island. **RECOMMENDATION:** The script is amusing; the situations which the actors devise for the children to resolve are humorous. The play challenges children to make decisions and solve problems using their imagination. **ROYALTY:** None. **SOURCE:** Deary, Terence. (1977). Teaching through theatre. New York, NY: Samuel French. **SUBJECTS/PLAY TYPE:** Pirates; Participation Play.

24. 3-9. (+) Placek, Jeff. (Irving, Washington) **Adventure of the German student.** (Adventure of the German student) CAST: 1f, 6m. ACTS: 1. SETTINGS: Bare stage. PLAYING TIME: 15 min. PLOT: To justify owning a poltergeist charm, a man tells a ghost story about another man who had a one night romance with a woman who had been beheaded the night before. RECOMMENDATION: This might be a great hit at a slumber party or other spontaneous production outlets. ROYALTY: Free to Plays subscribers. SOURCE: Placek, Jeff. (1979, April). Adventure of the German student. Plays: The Drama Magazine for Young People, pp. 76-80. SUBJECTS/PLAY TYPE: Supernatural; Spirits; Playlet.

25. 4-6. (+) Placek, Jeff. (Doyle, Arthur Conan) **Adventure of the Norwood builder.** (Adventure of the Norwood builder) CAST: 2f, 6m. ACTS: 1. SETTINGS: Bare stage. PLAYING TIME: 15 min. PLOT: A young lawyer, John McFarlane, bursts in on Sherlock Holmes and explains that he has been accused of a murder he did not commit. He drew up a will for Jonas Oldacre, who appears to now be dead. Through his famous deductive reasoning, Holmes proves Jonas Oldacre is not dead. RECOMMENDATION: This provides an excellent opportunity to teach children deductive reasoning. The role of the Inspector also illustrates how important it is not to jump to conclusions. ROYALTY: Free to Plays subscribers. SOURCE: Placek, Jeff. (1983, October). The adventure of the Norwood builder. Plays: The Drama Magazine for Young People, pp. 69-79. SUBJECTS/PLAY TYPE: Mystery; Adaptation.

26. 7-12. (+) Walton, Charles. (Doyle, Arthur Conan) **The adventure of the six Napoleons.** (The adventure of the six Napoleons) CAST: 8m. ACTS: 1. SETTINGS: Study. PLAYING TIME: 30 min. PLOT: This is a faithful adaptation of the story by the same name. RECOMMENDATION: This retains the unique tone of Doyle's famous mysteries and characters. It is uncomplicated to produce as a stage play and could be done in class as as a round the table reading. ROYALTY: Free to Plays subscribers. SOURCE: Walton, Charles. (1981, November). The adventure of the six Napoleons. Plays: The Drama Magazine for Young People, pp. 69-80. SUBJECTS/PLAY TYPE: Mystery; Adaptation.

27. 9-12. (+) Kelly, Tim J. (Doyle, Arthur Conan) **The adventure of the speckled band.** (The adventure of the speckled band) CAST: 8f, 6m, 1u. ACTS: 2. SETTINGS: Reception hall. PLAYING TIME: NA. PLOT: In this classic Holmes tale, Grimesby Roylott, the ex-doctor who uses wild animals as watch dogs, is the evil villain. Shortly before one of his step daughters is to marry, she is seemingly frightened to death. The surviving sister brings Holmes and Watson onto the case just in time to prevent another murder. RECOMMENDATION: The many unusual characters will challenge and delight. ROYALTY: $35. SOURCE: Kelly, Tim J. (1981). The adventure of the speckled band. Schulenburg, TX: I.E. Clark. SUBJECTS/PLAY TYPE: Mystery; Murder; Adaptation.

28. 7-12. (+) Silva, Jerry. (Doyle, Arthur Conan) **The adventure of the speckled band.** (The adventure of the speckled band) CAST: 2f, 6m. ACTS: 1. SETTINGS: Bedroom; office. PLAYING TIME: 30 min. PLOT: This is a faithful adaptation of the classic Holmes mystery of murder in a locked room, perpetrated by a poisonous snake. RECOMMENDATION: If the reference to thievish gypsies were removed, this would be an excellent introduction to Doyle's writings, as actors and audience are inextricably caught up in Holmes' deductive reasoning. ROYALTY: Free to Plays subscribers. SOURCE: Silva, Jerry. (1978, March). The adventure of the speckled band. Plays: The Drama Magazine for Young People, pp. 73-80. SUBJECTS/PLAY TYPE: Mystery; Murder; Adaptation.

29. 3-9. (+) Bush, Max & Dielman, Dale. (Stevenson, Robert Louis) **The adventure of Treasure Island.** (Treasure Island) CAST: 2f, 8m. ACTS: 2. SETTINGS: Inn; ship; island. PLAYING TIME: 65 min. PLOT: Young Jim Hawkins longs to escape his mother's care, gets a treasure map, and sails for the treasure island with Capt. Smollett. The crew mutinies, captures Jim, and takes him to Skeleton Island, where the treasure is buried. Jim overcomes the pirates and locates the treasure. RECOMMENDATION: Suitable for young audiences and an older production team, this recreates the excitement of Stevenson's novel. Unfortunately, the character of John Silver, with a good heart but larcenous intentions, is not well developed. The chase and fight scenes on Skeleton Island may be difficult to stage. Controversial discussion questions could be raised among older viewers, such as how does greed differ between the pirates and Jim and his friends, or does Silver's interest in Jim have homoerotic tones? ROYALTY: $35. SOURCE: Bush, Max & Dielman, Dale. The adventure of Treasure Island. Chicago, IL: Dramatic Pub. Co. SUBJECTS/PLAY TYPE: Pirates; Treasure Hunting; Sea Tales; Adaptation.

30. 3-9. (+) Bradley, Alfred. (Bond, Michael) **The adventures of a bear called Paddington.** (A bear called Paddington) CAST: 2f, 8m. ACTS: 2. SETTINGS: Living room; kitchen; bathroom; antique shop; laundrette; hospital room; shop. PLAYING TIME: 65 min. PLOT: A stowaway bear from Darkest Peru is found at Paddington Station by the Brown family. They name him after the train station, take him into their home, and make him feel welcome. Paddington unsuccessfully tries to deal with everyday activities, and decides to return to Darkest Peru. As they search for him at the train station, they discover him asleep on a trolley, awaken him, and reassure him that he is wanted. Paddington agrees to return home with the Browns. RECOMMENDATION: The message about not judging others is well delivered, and audience participation is an important element. Each episode can be performed as a one act play. Some episodes require involved props and equipment. Due to the length of the play, actors older than the audience would be most appropriate, and smaller roles may be

doubled. ROYALTY: NA. SOURCE: Bradley, Alfred & Bond, Michael. (1974). The adventures of a bear called Paddington. London: Samuel French. SUBJECTS/PLAY TYPE: Bears; Mischief; Musical.

31. K-4. (+) Jackson, Richard Eugene. (Burgess, Thornton W.) **The adventures of Peter Cottontail.** (The adventures of Peter Cottontail) CAST: 8u. ACTS: 2. SETTINGS: Foxes' den; carrot patch; briar patch. PLAYING TIME: 60 min. PLOT: Peter Rabbit is chased by the persistent Reddy Fox, and must match wits to stay alive. RECOMMENDATION: The antics and humorous dialogue will delight young viewers. Junior high students may enjoy producing this for younger students. ROYALTY: $25. SOURCE: Jackson, Richard Eugene. (1981). The adventures of Peter Cottontail. Denver, CO: Pioneer Drama Service. SUBJECTS/PLAY TYPE: Animals; Comedy; Adaptation.

32. 7-12. (+) Endersby, Clive. **The adventures of Robin Hood.** (Robin Hood and his merry men) CAST: 3f, 8m, Su. ACTS: 1. SETTINGS: Woods; castle. PLAYING TIME: NA. PLOT: Robin Hood has several run-ins with the sheriff, emerging victorious. He meets Maid Marion and Prissy, tells them about his gang, and escorts them back to the castle. There, Robin Hood is caught, but Alan and Friar Tuck get away, disguise themselves, trick the sheriff into thinking that Robin has turned traitor, and beat the sheriff again. At the end, the king returns and pardons the Robin Hood gang. RECOMMENDATION: This uses audience participation appropriate for younger children, yet is too complicated to be understood by children younger than junior high level. It also has a lengthy, boring dialogue, too much explanatory narrative, and fails to capture the adventurous spirit of the original. ROYALTY: NA. SOURCE: Endersby, Clive. (1980). Young King Arthur/The adventures of Robin Hood. Toronto: Playwrights Canada. SUBJECTS/PLAY TYPE: Adventure; Legends, England; Adaptation.

33. 3-9*. (-) Bronson, Bernice M. & Lioce, Anthony R. Jr. **The adventures of Sherlock Holmes.** CAST: 8f, 9m, Su. ACTS: 1. SETTINGS: Apartment. PLAYING TIME: NA. PLOT: Sherlock Holmes solves four mysteries (the first three acted out in flashbacks), involving the actors and a large cast of children via audience participation. RECOMMENDATION: A detailed preface explains the necessary rehearsals to prepare the audience (up to 225 children) for participating. It is stressed that the adult actors must be skilled in improvising and involving the children. ROYALTY: $20. SOURCE: Bronson, Bernice M. & Lioce, Anthony R. Jr. (1979). The adventures of Sherlock Holmes. Boston, MA: Baker's Plays. SUBJECTS/PLAY TYPE: Audience Participation; Mystery.

34. 4-6. (+) Olfson, Lewy. (Twain, Mark) **Adventures of Tom Sawyer.** (Adventures of Tom Sawyer) CAST: 3f, 4m, Su. ACTS: 1. SETTINGS: None. PLAYING TIME: 15 min. PLOT: When Tom Sawyer gets into trouble with his aunt, his punishment is to whitewash her fence. He quickly cons several friends into helping so he can go

play. Later, when he tries to kiss Becky Thatcher, he is rejected. Feeling unhappy, he talks two friends into running away and by the time they return, the entire town thinks they have drowned. Eventually, the boys show up at their own funeral and realize how much everyone actually cares about them. RECOMMENDATION: Students will enjoy this easy excerpt from the popular classic which has been adapted for round the table reading. Well written dialogue enables the audience to visualize the setting, understand the characters, and experience the flavor of the original. ROYALTY: Free to Plays subscribers. SOURCE: Olfson, Lewy. (1977, April). Adventures of Tom Sawyer. Plays: The Drama Magazine for Young People, pp. 74-79. SUBJECTS/PLAY TYPE: Adventure; Deceit; Reader's Theater; Adaptation.

35. K-3. (+) **Advice.** CAST: 1u. ACTS: 1. SETTINGS: None. PLAYING TIME: NA. PLOT: Sitting on an ant hill is shown to be very uncomfortable. RECOMMENDATION: This funny poem may be performed alone or, as Bauer recommends, with other "Animal Antics." ROYALTY: NA. SOURCE: Bauer, Caroline Feller. (1987). Presenting reader's theater: Plays and poems to read aloud. New York, NY: H.W. Wilson SUBJECTS/PLAY TYPE: Ants; Ant Hills; Reader's Theater.

36. K-6. (+) Brock, James. (Aesopus) **Aesop's Fables.** (Aesop's Fables) CAST: 1f, 1m, Su. ACTS: 1. SETTINGS: Woods; meadow. PLAYING TIME: 45 min. PLOT: One of the children acting out Aesop's fables becomes upset because she can't have her own way. RECOMMENDATION: This teaches the morals of Aesop's fables in two ways: by having children act them out and by having one child behave like the fox in "The fox and the sour grapes." ROYALTY: $15. SOURCE: Brock, James. (1978). Aesop's fables. Denver, CO: Pioneer Drama Service. SUBJECTS/PLAY TYPE: Conceit; Sportsmanship; Fable; Adaptation.

37. K-6. (+) Mahlman, Lewis & Jones, David Cadwalader. (Aesopus) **Aesop's fables.** (Aesop's fables) CAST: 10u. ACTS: 1. SETTINGS: Puppet stage. PLAYING TIME: 15 min. PLOT: Three of Aesop's more popular fables are included. RECOMMENDATION: Puppeteers of at least upper elementary age should produce this collection. ROYALTY: Free to Plays subscribers. SOURCE: Mahlman, Lewis & Jones, David Cadwalader. (1981, February). Aesop's fables. Plays: The Drama Magazine for Young People, pp. 63-68 SUBJECTS/PLAY TYPE: Fables; Animals; Morality; Adaptation.

38. K-6. (+) Winther, Barbara. African trio. CAST: 2f, 5m, Su. ACTS: 1. SETTINGS: Bare stage, props. PLAYING TIME: 20 min. PLOT: This trio of compatible stories can be presented separately or in succession, with actors each taking multiple roles. In one, a boastful caterpillar outwits a hare, leopard, rhinoceros, and elephant, but is himself outwitted by a frog; the second story is a fanciful myth about a hare who climbs to heaven on a spiderweb and steals a piece of the sun for

the creatures on earth; the third features a sheltered princess, tricked by a servant girl into trading places. The servant girl marries a young tribal chieftain before the trick is discovered. **RECOMMENDATION:** This is a delightful group of tales to be presented for and by children, though adults would also enjoy acting. The characters may be presented by imagination and pantomime, or with colorful, elaborate costumes and settings. **ROYALTY:** Free for amateur performance. **SOURCE:** Winther, Barbara. (1976). Plays from folktales of Africa and Asia. Boston, MA: Plays, Inc. **SUBJECTS/PLAY TYPE:** Folk Tales, Africa; Playlet.

39. 6-8. (+) Bland, Joellen. (Henry, O.) **After twenty years.** (After twenty years) **CAST:** 3m. **ACTS:** 1. **SETTINGS:** Street. **PLAYING TIME:** 10 min. **PLOT:** Two friends vow upon separation to meet in 20 years at a designated location. One is a criminal; the other is a New York City policeman. At the appointed site, the criminal does not realize that the policeman he is talking to is his old pal. The policeman recognizes his friend as a wanted criminal and sadly, has him arrested. **RECOMMENDATION:** Although this is condensed and does not retain the polish of O. Henry's original, it could be used as an example of his famous surprise endings. **ROYALTY:** Free to Plays subscribers. **SOURCE:** Bland, Joellen. (1988, March). After twenty years. Plays: The Drama Magazine for Young People, pp. 55-57. **SUBJECTS/PLAY TYPE:** Suspense; Friendship; Adaptation.

40. 9-12. (+) Cope, Eddie. **Agatha Christie made me do it. CAST:** 5f, 6m. **ACTS:** 1. **SETTINGS:** Living room. **PLAYING TIME:** NA. **PLOT:** Hootspah, a dimwitted police detective, decides to "write a mystery play and make a lotta money" so he can quit the police force. He buys a book on Agatha Christie's writing technique and manages to write a murder mystery involving possible bigamy, amnesia, a missing body and murder weapon, numerous suspects, and the requisite surprise ending. **RECOMMENDATION:** While the characters are broadly drawn, the mystery has enough twists and turns to keep an audience interested. It humorously illustrates the essential elements of a murder mystery. **ROYALTY:** $50. **SOURCE:** Cope, Eddie. (1975). Agatha Christie made me do it. Schulenburg, TX: I.E. Clark. **SUBJECTS/PLAY TYPE:** Murder; Mystery; Comedy.

41. 9-12. (+) Handley, Oliver & Handley, Helen. **Age has nothing to do with it. CAST:** 2f, 3m. **ACTS:** 2. **SETTINGS:** Bare stage, props. **PLAYING TIME:** NA. **PLOT:** The relationships between men and women are examined in treatments of old age, middle age, and human nature as related to love. **RECOMMENDATION:** Some scenes are especially enchanting, as in the bedtime story between a gruff old man and his grandson. One possible drawback is that adults may appreciate the glimpses into human nature more than teenagers. Some characters would be better represented by mature actors. **ROYALTY:** $40. **SOURCE:** Handley, Oliver & Handley, Helen. (1986).

Age has nothing to do with it. Boston, MA: Baker's Plays. **SUBJECTS/PLAY TYPE:** Love; Relationships; Musical.

42. 8-12. (-) Martens, Anne Coulter. **The age of precarious. CAST:** 6f. **ACTS:** 1. **SETTINGS:** Patio. **PLAYING TIME:** 20 min. **PLOT:** Four girls try to undermine a friend's belief in astrology by showing her that the predictions of their horoscopes are silly. When the horoscopes start coming true they begin to question their own disbelief. **RECOMMENDATION:** The original conflict, whether to rent a lake cottage during the summer, might not be understood by high school students. The rest of the play involves patronizing attempts at humor, "girl talk," and irony. **ROYALTY:** Free to Plays subscribers. **SOURCE:** Martens, Anne Coulter. (1983, March). The age of precarious. Plays: The Drama Magazine for Young People, pp. 47-53. **SUBJECTS/PLAY TYPE:** Friendship; Astrology; Comedy.

43. 9-12. (-) Taikeff, Stanley. **Ah, Eurydice!** (Orpheus and Eurydice.) **CAST:** 1f, 2m. **ACTS:** 1. **SETTINGS:** Underworld. **PLAYING TIME:** NA. **PLOT:** A modern day Orpheus descends into the underworld to reclaim his bride, Eurydice, who died on their wedding day. Because of Orpheus' persuasive music, Pluto allows him to take Eurydice back, with the condition that Orpheus not look at Eurydice until they leave the underworld. When Eurydice appears she nags and demands a kiss. He turns and she melts away. He is eventually killed by a group of drunken women driving a car. **RECOMMENDATION:** The modern allusions (Eurydice teaches kindergarten in Yonkers), language (Orpheus passes "a guy chained to a rock"), and props (Pluto reclines on a beach chair) seem to trivialize the story. However, it might be used in the study of mythology to encourage students to research the allusions and then compare them. **ROYALTY:** $20. **SOURCE:** Taikeff, Stanley. (1977). Ah, Eurydice! New York, NY: Dramatists Play Service. **SUBJECTS/PLAY TYPE:** Mythology, Greek; Drama.

44. K-12. (+) Winther, Barbara. **Ah Wing Fu and the golden dragon. CAST:** 2f, 2m, Su. **ACTS:** 1. **SETTINGS:** Bare stage, backdrop. **PLAYING TIME:** 30 min. **PLOT:** Ah Wing Fu suddenly refuses to honor the protective Golden Dragon with fruit and flower offerings. The dragon, insulted, changes Fu into a butterfly, and sends winds, rains, and a tiger to batter him. Fu's family tries to save him, but the tiger turns on them. Fu offers himself as a sacrifice to save them, the Dragon notes penitence and restores him to his form and family. **RECOMMENDATION:** The action is painted with broad strokes, and will be especially successful if performed with dances, pantomimes, and acrobatics. Sound is important as musicians use cymbals, flute, and gongs to accent entrances, exits, etc. A giant paper mache head and several actors create the Golden Dragon. **ROYALTY:** Free for amateur performance. **SOURCE:** Winther, Barbara. (1976). Plays from folktales of Africa and Asia. Boston, MA: Plays, Inc. **SUBJECTS/PLAY TYPE:** Folktales, China; Selflessness; Playlet.

45. 4-7. (+) Rockwell, Thomas. AIII EEEEEEEEE! CAST: 10f, 11m, Su. ACTS: 2. SETTINGS: Bare stage, props. PLAYING TIME: NA. PLOT: Two mountain climbers discover demons in a cavern. They escape, but so do the demons. Tim, a small raggedy boy, leads the princess to safety while the populace is captured by ghouls and zombies. Tim and the princess disguise themselves as ghouls, the people are rescued, and the princess makes Tim her prince. The werewolf, who has been chained on stage, escapes and bites one of the children in the audience (actually a member of the cast, unknown to the audience). The play ends with a mob offstage chasing the werewolf. RECOMMENDATION: Children will love the chants of the demons ("Thumb and thigh, succulent fat hip, stuffed nose, creamed hearts and lips. Hoo hoo hoo!), the costumes, and the audience participation. The ingenious defeat of the demons is also invigorating: one of the demons is a "wound," whom they kill with penicillin, turning him into a scar. Production should be primarily by older children or adults, with younger children playing some of the parts. ROYALTY: NA. SOURCE: Rockwell, Thomas. (1980). How to eat fried worms, and other plays. New York, NY: Delacorte Press. SUBJECTS/PLAY TYPE: Monsters; Drama.

46. 7-12. (-) Kelly, Tim. Airline. CAST: 12f, 15m, 5u. ACTS: 3. SETTINGS: Apartment; office; dining room; airline terminal; airplane. PLAYING TIME: 120 min. PLOT: This concerns a very low budget airline and intertwined human dramas that unfold during one of its flights. RECOMMENDATION: This lacks any merit in terms of character, theme, plot, and language. ROYALTY: $35. SOURCE: Kelly, Tim. (1981). Airline. Denver, CO: Pioneer Drama Service. SUBJECTS/PLAY TYPE: Airlines; Comedy.

47. 8-12. (-) Murray, John. Airport adventure. CAST: 4f, 5m, Su. ACTS: 1. SETTINGS: Airport terminal. PLAYING TIME: 40 min. PLOT: A young couple posing as newlyweds are actually couriers with top secret plans for a nuclear bomb site. They are sabotaged in their attempt to deliver the plans to an agent in Switzerland. A clever imposter and her accomplice are arrested, and the couple continue their mission. RECOMMENDATION: The action is unbelievable, with too many unrelated subplots. Characters are outdated sexist stereotypes and with all the extraneous action, this would be difficult to stage. ROYALTY: Free to Plays subscribers. SOURCE: Murray, John. (1984). Mystery plays for young actors. Boston, MA: Plays, Inc. SUBJECTS/PLAY TYPE: Mystery; Secret Agents; Playlet.

48. 10-12. (-) Cope, Eddie & Cearley, Buster. Airport 1904. CAST: 3f, 3m. ACTS: 2. SETTINGS: Office. PLAYING TIME: NA. PLOT: A widow and her daughter try to save "America's first flying school" from bankruptcy and possession by a villain. They do with money they earn by curing the hero's sister of her inability to talk. RECOMMENDATION: The wit ends with the title. Each supposed comedic situation is either heterosexually or homosexually oriented. The play mocks people with mental and physical handicaps; the dialogue consists of obscene and absurd vocabulary. ROYALTY: $50. SOURCE: Cope, Eddie & Cearley, Buster. (1981). Airport 1904. Schulenburg, TX: I.E. Clark. SUBJECTS/PLAY TYPE: Musical; Flying; Melodrama.

49. 6-12. (+) Boiko, Claire. Al Adams and the wonderful lump. CAST: 5f, 4m, Su. ACTS: 1. SETTINGS: Living room; cave. PLAYING TIME: 30 min. PLOT: Ali Oompah frees his genies because magic does not work in the 20th century. However, the genies stay to help set up his carpet sales business. To sell flying carpets, Al rubs the magic lump (antigravity device), gets his wishes for fortune and success, and all is well. RECOMMENDATION: This delightful "fractured fairy tale" uses modern day conventions to liven up the old classic. ROYALTY: Free to Plays subscribers. SOURCE: Boiko, Claire. (1983, April). Al Adams and the wonderful lump. Plays: The Drama Magazine for Young People, pp. 44-52. SUBJECTS/PLAY TYPE: Magic; Genies; Comedy.

50. K-5*. (+) Glennon, William. (Galland, Antoine) Aladdin. (The 1001 nights) CAST: 4f, 5m, Su. ACTS: 3. SETTINGS: Street; exterior of house; palace interior; cave. PLAYING TIME: 95 min. PLOT: This faithfully traces the adventures of Aladdin just previous to and following his discovery of the lamp. RECOMMENDATION: Although suitable for young audiences, this should be performed by older students. The character of Zorah would give a would be villain a chance to shine. ROYALTY: $25. SOURCE: Glennon, William. (1965). Aladdin. Pittsburgh, PA: Pittsburgh Playhouse Press. SUBJECTS/PLAY TYPE: Magic Lamps; Folk Tales, Iran; Genies; Adaptation.

51. K-4*. (+) Goldberg, Moses. (Galland, Antoine) Aladdin. (The 1001 nights) CAST: 2f, 3m, Su. ACTS: 1. SETTINGS: Bare stage. PLAYING TIME: NA. PLOT: Disgusted with his wife's criticism of the way he peddles his wares, Burgundo decides to become an actor. His family agrees to participate in "The Story of Aladdin." The rest of the play centers on their preparation for, and finally their performance of this classic. RECOMMENDATION: The plot is exciting, the language is simple, and the audience has ample opportunity to get involved. ROYALTY: $25. SOURCE: Goldberg, Moses. (1977). Aladdin. New Orleans, LA: Anchorage Press. SUBJECTS/PLAY TYPE: Magic Lamps; Genies; Folk Tales, Iran; Adaptation.

52. 1-6. (+) Newman, Deborah. (Galland, Antoine) Aladdin. (The 1001 nights) CAST: 4f, 4m. ACTS: 1. SETTINGS: House room; palace room. PLAYING TIME: 20 min. PLOT: A magician lures Aladdin into a hole, abandons him, and tells his mother that he is dead. Aladdin escapes with the magic lamp, returns to his mother, and wishes that the Sultan's daughter marry him, which she does. The magician visits and tricks the sultana into giving him the lamp. Aladdin and his wife deceive the magician into drinking poison and they regain the lamp. RECOMMENDATION: The dialogue is short, and with its theme of magic and cleverness, this is a crowd pleaser. ROYALTY: NA. SOURCE:

Kamerman, Sylvia E. (1987). Plays from favorite folk tales. Boston, MA: Plays, Inc. SUBJECTS/PLAY TYPE: Folktales, Iran; Magic Lamps; Genies; Adaptation.

53. 3-6. (+) Porter, Robert Neil & Perry, Jack. (Galland, Antoine) **Aladdin.** (The 1001 nights) CAST: 7f, 4m. ACTS: 10. SETTINGS: Throne room; apron. PLAYING TIME: 60 min. PLOT: With the genie's help, young Aladdin foils the evil magician, wins the hand of the sultan's daughter, and lives happily ever after. RECOMMENDATION: The humor might be lost on younger children, but all ages can enjoy the fanciful characters. Songs can be spoken if musical accompaniment is unavailable. ROYALTY: $25. SOURCE: Porter, Robert Neil & Perry, Jack. (1979). Aladdin. Denver, CO: Pioneer Drama Service. SUBJECTS/PLAY TYPE: Magic Lamps; Folk Tales, Iran; Genies; Adaptation.

54. 1-8. (-) Thane, Adele. (Galland, Antoine) **Aladdin and his wonderful lamp.** (The 1001 nights) CAST: 4f, 6m, 1u. ACTS: 10. SETTINGS: Street; palace room. PLAYING TIME: 30 min. PLOT: Aladdin retrieves a lamp from a cave for a magician who promises riches. Aladdin angers the magician, who storms off without the lamp and swears revenge. The genie of the lamp makes Aladdin wealthy enough to win the sultan's daughter's hand in marriage. The magician, through trickery, obtains the lamp, transports the palace to an African desert, and enslaves Aladdin's family. In a dramatic moment, Aladdin regains the lamp, wishes for his family to be in their home, and for the magician to be trapped in the a mountain. RECOMMENDATION: This lacks the suspense of the original. The characters are not sufficiently developed and too much time is spent on irrelevant plot action to make it interesting. ROYALTY: None. SOURCE: Thane, Adele. (1983). Plays from famous stories and fairy tales. Boston, MA: Plays, Inc. SUBJECTS/PLAY TYPE: Genies; Magic Lamps; Folk Tales, Iran; Adaptation.

55. 7-12. (+) Denson, Wil & Cunningham, Michael. (Galland, Antoine) **Aladdin McFaddin.** (The 1001 nights) CAST: 5f, 5m, Su. ACTS: 1. SETTINGS: Desert; cave; castle. PLAYING TIME: 80 min. PLOT: Aladdin McFaddin loves Bessie Mae Moocho, the Sultan's daughter, but the cross Sultan thinks Aladdin isn't worthy. When the slimy villain, El Slippo Magish, gives him a magic ring, Aladdin uses it to prove his worth. Fortunes become reversed but magic rings, three slaves, a tenderhearted genie, and Alladin's quick thinking vanquish the villain and all ends happily. RECOMMENDATION: Full of broad humor, likeable characters, and splashy special effects, the plot moves quickly, and the exotic setting lends technicolor romance. ROYALTY: $50. SOURCE: Denson, Wil & Cunningham, Michael. Aladdin McFaddin. Schulenburg, TX: I.E. Clark. SUBJECTS/PLAY TYPE: Musical; Comedy; Folk Tales, Iran; Adaptation.

56. 1-6. (+) Landes, William-Alan. (Galland, Antoine) **Aladdin 'n his magic lamp.** (The 1001 nights) CAST: 2f, 5m, Su. ACTS: 2. SETTINGS: City streets; cave/oasis;

throne room; palace chamber; forest. PLAYING TIME: 60 min. PLOT: Aladdin wants to marry Princess Adora. Wazir the villain finds the Geni's magic lamp, but cannot enter the cave because because he is not honest. He sends Aladdin but becomes impatient and utters magic words that close the cave with Aladdin inside. Aladdin rubs the lamp, the Geni appears, and grants his wish to marry the Princess. Wazir plots to get the lamp back but ends up having a spell of goodness cast upon him. Aladdin and the Princess live happily ever after. RECOMMENDATION: Audience participation adds a spark of enthusiasm, and the animation of Aladdin's camel Nufsed (play on words) is most entertaining. Many lighting changes may be a problem for student production, but musical parts are easy. ROYALTY: $35. SOURCE: Landes, William-Landes. (1979). Aladdin 'n his magic lamp. Studio City, CA: Players Press. SUBJECTS/PLAY TYPE: Folk Tales, Iran; Genies; Magic Lamps; Adaptation.

57. 7-12. (+) Cheatham, Val R. (Galland, Antoine) **Aladdin strikes it rich.** (The 1001 nights) CAST: 2f, 1m, 3u. ACTS: 1. SETTINGS: Kitchen; cave. PLAYING TIME: 15 min. PLOT: An unemployed Aladdin receives help from a fast talking carpet salesman to find the magic lamp which grants his wishes for happiness and riches. RECOMMENDATION: This vaudevillian satire pokes fun at everyone with punchy one liners and puns. ROYALTY: Free to Plays subscribers. SOURCE: Cheatham, Val R. (1977, December). Aladdin strikes it rich. Plays: The Drama Magazine for Younger People, pp. 75-80. SUBJECTS/PLAY TYPE: Folk Tales, Iran; Magic Lamps; Skit; Adaptation.

58. 10-12. (+) Rimmer, David. **Album.** CAST: 2f, 2m. ACTS: 2. SETTINGS: Small room. PLAYING TIME: NA. PLOT: As four teenagers mature, they use the popular and the counter culture music of the 60s as reflections of their feelings. Peggy and Billy, who start out as the self assured, popular, mid-60s "straight" kids have difficulty adjusting to the cultural changes. Boo and Trish, who were always lonely in their individuality, find that the counter culture music and movements express their feelings and nonconformist ways. RECOMMENDATION: Through the use of popular music, the difficulties of fitting in, exploring different lifestyles, and experiencing sex are realistically expressed. The language is too raw for production in many high schools, but the writer offers alternative lines. The use of alcohol, allusions to other drugs, and a somewhat romanticized approach to teenage sex might upset some parents and teachers. ROYALTY: $50. SOURCE: Rimmer, David. (1980). Album. New York, NY: Dramatists Play Service. SUBJECTS/PLAY TYPE: Adolescent Problems; Drama.

59. K-5. (+) Bauer, Caroline Feller. (Hurwitz, Johanna) **Ali Baba and Princess Farrah.** (Ali Baba Bernstein) CAST: 1f, 1m, 3u. ACTS: 1. SETTINGS: Bedroom. PLAYING TIME: 10 min. PLOT: As they visit, Ali Baba persuades Valerie to kiss her pet frog in case it's a prince in disguise. When she does, he laughs at her. Valerie, in turn, convinces Ali Baba that he must kiss the

frog in case it is actually a princess. He does, and Valerie congratulates him on being a good sport. They go happily into the kitchen to eat a chocolate eclair. RECOMMENDATION: This delightful play shows how a friendship develops between two children because both are familiar with well known stories. This can either be acted or read aloud. ROYALTY: None. SOURCE: Bauer, Caroline Feller. (1987). Presenting reader's theater: Plays and poems to read aloud. New York, NY: H.W. Wilson. SUBJECTS/PLAY TYPE: Friendship; Reader's Theater; Adaptation.

60. K-4. (+) Mahlman, Lewis & Jones, David Cadwalader. (Galland, Antoine) **Ali Baba and the forty thieves.** (The 1001 nights) CAST: 6u. ACTS: 1. SETTINGS: Cave; living room; street; dock. PLAYING TIME: 25 min. PLOT: Ali Baba learns how to open the cave of the thieves and recovers his family's stolen fortune. His brother is caught by the thieves. Ali Baba saves him, but the two unwittingly lead the thieves to their home, where the thieves hide in empty oil jars, planning to rob the family again. Ali Baba's wife uncovers the plot, seals the jars, sets them sailing down the river, exposes the leader, and saves the family. RECOMMENDATION: Not as gory as the original, this adaptation, with its "open sesame" and "close sesame" refrain, will delight young audiences. Because of the length of some of the parts, it will have to be performed by older adolescents. ROYALTY: Free to Plays subscribers. SOURCE: Mahlman, Lewis & Jones, David Cadwalader. (1980). Folk tale plays for puppets. Boston, MA: Plays, Inc. SUBJECTS/PLAY TYPE: Thieves; Folk Tales, Iran; Greed; Puppet Play.

61. K-6. (+) Sanker, Joyce & Coates, Gary M. (Galland, Antoine). **Ali Baba and the thieves.** (The 1001 nights). CAST: 4f, 7m, Su. ACTS: 3. SETTINGS: Outside of two houses. PLAYING TIME: 60 min. PLOT: Ali Baba, a Persian wood-cutter, takes gold from a cache of robbers, who hide in oil barrels to kill him. Morgiana, a beautiful slave, discovers the ruse and kills the chief. She is rewarded with freedom. RECOMMENDATION: Creative, this would be a good introduction to a folk tales unit. Older elementary children should perform this for the younger ones. ROYALTY: $70. SOURCE: Sanker, Joyce. (1982). Ali Baba and the thieves. Franklin, OH: Eldridge Pub. Co. SUBJECTS/PLAY TYPE: Adventure; Folk Tales, Iran; Musical; Adaptation.

62. 9-12*. (+) Traylor, Gene. **Alias Jack the ripper.** CAST: 4f, 4m, Su. ACTS: 2. SETTINGS: Theater; offices; rooms in house; foggy street. PLAYING TIME: NA. PLOT: In the foggy streets of London, a gloved murderer brutally kills women; police have no clue or suspect. When a young singer, Taffy, is murdered, Rose dreams that Taffy seeks her help. Searching Taffy's apartment for clues, Rose is confronted by the alleged murderer. She is saved just in time by the police who kill the man. In the final scene, the real murderer is revealed to be a respected doctor, the dead man's twin brother. RECOMMENDATION: The serious drama is lightened by the humorous antics of an inexperienced police sergeant. Taffy must sing and some special effects

might be difficult to produce. ROYALTY: $50. SOURCE: Traylor, Gene. (1984). Alias Jack the Ripper. Chicago, IL: Dramatic Pub. Co. SUBJECTS/PLAY TYPE: Murder; Mystery; Drama.

63. 3-8. (+) Endersby, Clive. (Carroll, Lewis) **Alice.** (Alice's adventures in wonderland, and Through the looking glass) CAST: 5f, 3m, Su. ACTS: 1. SETTINGS: Bare stage, props. PLAYING TIME: 60 min. PLOT: Alice follows the White Rabbit through encounters with flowers, a caterpillar who mixes up nursery rhymes, the Mad Hatter and the March Hare, the Dormouse, the Cheshire Cat, Tweedledee and Tweedledum, and the Queen of Hearts. The rabbit reads the end of the book to find out how Alice escapes beheading. RECOMMENDATION: This must be presented by adults, since it relies on audience participation, puppets, and sophisticated special effects. It does justice to the original. ROYALTY: NA. SOURCE: Endersby, Clive. (1978). Alice and the wizard of Oz: Two plays for young audiences. Toronto: Playwrights Canada. SUBJECTS/PLAY TYPE: Fantasy; Adaptation.

64. 4-9. (+) Surette, Roy. (Carroll, Lewis) **Alice: a wonderland.** (Alice's adventures in wonderland, and Through the looking glass) CAST: 4f, 3m. ACTS: 2. SETTINGS: River side; drawing room; lawn. PLAYING TIME: NA. PLOT: When Alice chases a white rabbit down a hole, the Cheshire Cat directs her to the Mad Hatter's, whose chaotic tea party causes her to cry out to go home, which she does. Later, she goes through the drawing room mirror to rejoin the Wonderland characters and attend a croquet match with the Red Queen. During the match, Alice is accused of stealing royal tarts, placed on trial, and made a queen. While singing about that, Alice awakens to find herself again in the parlor. RECOMMENDATION: The use of dual roles and uncomplicated sets makes this within the production bounds of a limited group. The plot resembles the original, but familiarity with it would be helpful. Surette has updated the dialogue, and cut some scenes, but characters blend from both stories so nicely that one can almost imagine that the White Rabbit really did talk with Tweedledee and Tweedledum. ROYALTY: NA. SOURCE: Surette, Roy. (1983). Alice: a wonderland. Toronto, Canada: Playwrights Canada. SUBJECTS/PLAY TYPE: Dreams; Fantasy; Adaptation.

65. 7-12. (+) Snee, Dennis. (Carroll, Lewis) **Alice in America-land, or, through the picture tube and what Alice found there.** (Alice's adventures in wonderland, and Through the looking glass) CAST: 4f, 3m. ACTS: 2. SETTINGS: Living room; garden. PLAYING TIME: NA. PLOT: Instead of falling down a rabbit hole, Alice climbs through her TV set to confront advertising, consumerism, the nuclear age, the beauty industry, investigative journalism, the energy crisis, and government bureaucracy. Overwhelmed, she awakens to her normal world--or does she? RECOMMENDATION: The dialogue is witty and fast paced (to the point of leaving one breathless). Some subjects may be new to teenagers (i.e., EST and transcendental meditation). ROYALTY: $40. SOURCE:

Snee, Dennis. (1982). Alice in America-land, or, through the picture tube and what Alice found there. Boston, MA: Baker's Plays. SUBJECTS/PLAY TYPE: Satire; Adaptation.

66. 4-12*. Duffield, Brainerd. (Carroll, Lewis) **Alice in wonderland.** (Alice's adventures in wonderland.) CAST: 5f, 7m, Su. ACTS: 3. SETTINGS: Bare stage, raised platform. PLAYING TIME: NA. PLOT: Alice follows a talking rabbit down its hole, where she meets the Queen of Hearts, a poetry spouting mouse, and others, including the participants in an absurd tea party who befuddle her with their conversation, then direct her to the Queen of Hearts' croquet field. There she attempts croquet and engages in a dolorous conversation with a mock turtle. After further adventures she meets the Red and White Queens and toasts the marvels of wonderland. RECOMMENDATION: In this truly silly and fractured adaptation, the absurd characters with their loony wisdom are gone, replaced by meaningless charades. Where the original had an exuberant, hectic pace that carried the reader from one bizarre adventure to another, the progression here is simply chaotic. ROYALTY: $35. SOURCE: Duffield, Brainerd. (1978). Alice in wonderland. Elgin, IL: Performance Pub. Co. SUBJECTS/PLAY TYPE: Dreams; Fantasy; Adaptation.

67. 4-6. (+) Hill, Rochelle. (Carroll, Lewis) **Alice in wonderland.** (Alice's adventures in wonderland, and Through the looking glass) CAST: 3f, 7m, 1u. ACTS: 1. SETTINGS: Garden. PLAYING TIME: 25 min. PLOT: Alice dreams of a strange garden and its inhabitants: a rabbit who is late, a caterpillar who informs her she is in the Duchess' kitchen, a duchess making soup while holding a baby, a grinning Cheshire cat, the Mad Hatter at a tea party, the Queen of Hearts and her croquet game, and a Mock turtle with whom she discusses soup and lessons. Finally, Alice finds herself on trial. The presiding Queen of Hearts passes sentence that Alice should lose her head. Alice calls them all a "pack of cards" and is awakened by her mother. RECOMMENDATION: This preserves the dream like qualities of the original, and the language of 19th century England. But, would American children recognize a pinafore? Would they know that mad means crazy? Would they know what a hatter is? This might be most appropriate as a dramatization to follow a reading of the original. ROYALTY: Free to Plays subscribers. SOURCE: Hill, Rochelle. (1977, May). Alice in wonderland. Plays: The Drama Magazine for Young People, pp. 83-92. SUBJECTS/PLAY TYPE: Dreams; Fantasy; Adaptation.

68. 6-12. (+) Le Gallienne, Eva & Friebus, Florida. (Carroll, Lewis) **Alice in wonderland.** (Alice's adventures in wonderland, and Through the looking glass) CAST: 4f, 3m, Su. ACTS: 1. SETTINGS: Garden; living room pool; kitchen; courtroom; train; shop. PLAYING TIME: NA. PLOT: Alice is transported through a looking glass into a world filled with strange, nonsensical creatures. She meets the Duchess, whose baby turns into a pig; a mock turtle who went to sea school; a Cheshire Cat that is always smiling; a knight

with an upside down box on his back; and many more. Finally, Alice gives up on the craziness of this land, wakes up from the dream, and finds herself safe at home again. RECOMMENDATION: This would be a monumental undertaking, even for a professional company. The cast is huge and each character has a specialized costume. The sets are numerous and difficult to create. It would take long hours of rehearsals and a considerable budget to produce this, though it is well worth the effort. ROYALTY: $35. SOURCE: Le Gallienne, Eva & Friebus, Florida. (1976). Alice in Wonderland. Boston, MA: Baker's Plays. SUBJECTS/PLAY TYPE: Dreams; Fantasy; Adaptation.

69. 4-12. (-) Rochelle, R. (Carroll, Lewis) **Alice in wonderland.** (Alice's adventures in wonderland and Through the looking glass.) CAST: 3f, 7m, 1u. ACTS: 1. SETTINGS: Garden. PLAYING TIME: 25 min. PLOT: Alice falls asleep and dreams she falls down a rabbit hole where she encounters the Cheshire Cat, the Duchess, the Mad Hatter, the caterpillar, and the queen. RECOMMENDATION: This has an even more jumbled up sequence of events than the original, and it does not retain any of the charm and wonder that made Carroll's work a masterpiece. The sentences, words, and characters, taken out of context, are too confusing. ROYALTY: Free to Plays subscribers. SOURCE: Rochelle, R. (1984, March). Alice in Wonderland. Plays: The Drama Magazine for Young People, pp. 47-56. SUBJECTS/PLAY TYPE: Fantasy; Dreams; Adaptation.

70. 3-6. (+) Simms, Willard. (Carroll, Lewis) **Alice in Wonderland.** (Alice's adventures in wonderland and Through the looking glass.) CAST: 3f, 3u. ACTS: 1. SETTINGS: Bare stage. PLAYING TIME: 30 min. PLOT: While Alice dreams of Wonderland, her sister Sarah invites the audience to follow along. There they meet the worried rabbit, confused Dodo Bird, poetic caterpillar, and other characters. At a tea party, Alice is drawn into a trial and put on the witness stand. RECOMMENDATION: The audience participates in the action by assuming some of the minor roles. ROYALTY: $10. SOURCE: Simms, Willard. (1985). Alice in Wonderland. Denver, CO: Pioneer Drama Service. SUBJECTS/PLAY TYPE: Fantasy; Dreams; Adaptation.

71. K-6*. (+) Turner, Charles & Moore, Steven. (Carroll, Lewis) **Alice in Wonderland.** (Alice's adventures in Wonderland, and Through the looking glass) CAST: 4f, 2m, 18u. ACTS: 1. SETTINGS: Forest; croquet field; garden; courtroom. PLAYING TIME: NA. PLOT: Alice meets the White Rabbit who enters her room through a mirror. She falls through the mirror into the fantastical forest where she meets Dodo, Duck Gryphon, Mock Turtle, and Caterpillar. She attends the tea party and plays croquet with the queen. Alice escapes the sentence of "off with her head" by eating the magic mushroom which sends her home. RECOMMENDATION: Extensive sets, stage instructions, and dialogue make this difficult to produce. Also difficult will be the music and songs (which fit well with the storyline) and the elaborate costumes. ROYALTY: $60. SOURCE: Turner, Charles & Moore,

Steven. (1980). Alice in wonderland. Boston, MA: Baker's Plays. SUBJECTS/PLAY TYPE: Musical; Fantasy; Dreams; Adaptation.

72. 1-6. (+) Kelly, Tim. (Carroll, Lewis) **Alice's adventures in Wonderland.** (Alice's adventures in Wonderland and Through the looking glass) CAST: 10f, 12m, Su. ACTS: 2. SETTINGS: Bare stage, props. PLAYING TIME: 90 min. PLOT: Alice falls down the rabbit hole. On her way to the tart stealer's trial, she meets the caterpillar, Duchess and her baby/pig, and the Cheshire Cat who gives her directions to the Mad Hatter's tea party. An old knight gives Alice a ride to the eighth square where she receives her crown from the White Rabbit, then proceeds to the trial of the Knave of Hearts. During the course of the trial, Alice denounces it as a mockery. As the cards rush in to attack her, she wakes up next to her sister under the tree, where she had fallen asleep and dreamed the entire adventure. RECOMMENDATION: While the individual episodes are faithful to the original, their order and characters have been freely mixed. Due to its length, the role of Alice might be played by two actresses, alternating scenes. ROYALTY: $35. SOURCE: Kelly, Tim. (1978). Alice's adventures in Wonderland. Denver, CO: Pioneer Drama Service. SUBJECTS/PLAY TYPE: Fantasy; Animals; Dreams; Adaptation.

73. 5-10. (+) Macoby, Annie & Church, Jeff. **Alien equation.** CAST: 7f, 6m. ACTS: 1. SETTINGS: Classroom. PLAYING TIME: NA. PLOT: Max, class underachiever and on detention for misbehaving, discovers that his milk carton sculpture is actually a deuteron conductor that has drawn Al from earth's anti-matter twin. Max must help Al solve the Four Force equation to save him from "imploding." They accomplish this at a school dance, when a classmate discovers the needed link in music. RECOMMENDATION: Junior high actors should be the youngest age group to attempt this, but younger children will enjoy watching it. ROYALTY: NA. SOURCE: Macoby, Annie & Church, Jeff. (1986). Alien equation. Morton Grove, IL: Coach House Press. SUBJECTS/PLAY TYPE: Science Fiction; School; Science; Comedy.

74. 7-12. (+) McCusker, Paul. **Aliens.** CAST: 2u. ACTS: 1. SETTINGS: Bare stage, props. PLAYING TIME: 15 min. PLOT: Two aliens discuss the earthlings' custom of going to church on Sunday. They are confused by the contradictions when the humans sing about joy and love, but look bored; bow their heads to pray, but fix their hair and look around; and listen to the religious morals, then forget about them as soon as church is over. They decide not to waste time on such a contradictory people and they leave earth. RECOMMENDATION: This comedy with a message could be a useful church program or just a fun piece of entertainment. ROYALTY: NA. SOURCE: McCusker, Paul. (1984). Batteries not included. Boston, MA: Baker's Plays. SUBJECTS/PLAY TYPE: Church; Satire; Hypocrisy; Skit.

75. 1-9. (+) Guderjahn, Ernie. **Ali's flying rug.** CAST: 2m, Su. ACTS: 1. SETTINGS: Bare stage, props. PLAYING TIME: NA. PLOT: Ali, crooked rug salesman, is tricked into trading his entire rug shop for an old man's rug which he has been led to believe will fly. When he cannot make the rug fly, he returns it to the original owner and learns the supposedly mystical markings on the rug are actually spilled remnants of meals throughout the years. RECOMMENDATION: This is short and delightful. The part of Ali would have to be played by an older adolescent, but all other parts could be played by actors of any age. ROYALTY: NA. SOURCE: Guderjahn, Ernie. (1984). A children's trilogy. Studio City, CA: Player's Press. SUBJECTS/PLAY TYPE: Business; Thievery; Rugs; Comedy.

76. 9-12. (+) Tasca, Jules. **Alive and kicking.** CAST: 2f, 2m. ACTS: 2. SETTINGS: Living room. PLAYING TIME: NA. PLOT: When the Nix's youngest child marries, he brings his wife to his parent's home to live while he finishes college. A difficult relationship develops between mother and daughter-in-law, complicated by the mother's neurotic fixation on her own mortality. Things get easier when the young marrieds move to their own apartment and become parents themselves. RECOMMENDATION: This well done, bittersweet comedy highlights the wastefulness of obsessive worry in a gentle way. All the characters are likable and each portrays the needs of people at different stages of life. ROYALTY: $50. SOURCE: Tasca, Jules. (1983). Alive and kicking. Chicago, IL: Dramatic Pub. Co. SUBJECTS/PLAY TYPE: Family; Empty Nest; In-Laws; Comedy.

77. 3-6. (+) Boiko, Claire. **All about mothers.** CAST: 11f, 5m, Su. ACTS: 1. SETTINGS: Bare stage, props. PLAYING TIME: 15 min. PLOT: A fashion show format depicts stereotypical mothers from a variety of cultures and historical periods, each tinged with humor and irony and all pointing to the modern mother as the composite of all premium maternal qualities. A leopard-skin clad cave mother hums a version of "Hush little baby" with a Stone Age motif. Lotus Blossom, an Oriental mother, gazes into a crystal ball as she bakes fortune cookies for her family. The Victorian mother instructs her daughter in the fine art of fainting. Spotlighted is the modern mother, who enacts the roles of appointment secretary, judge for sibling grievances, handy-woman, and birthday party hostess. RECOMMENDATION: Intended as a Mother's Day salute, this can be adapted to feature many actors because of the flexibility of the chorus and narrator's parts. An imaginative director might want to expand upon the text to feature additional, original concepts of Mothers. Although stereotyped, this does not result in a sexist style. The potential is here for a rare, warm moment of insight into the mother child relationship. ROYALTY: None. SOURCE: Boiko, Claire. (1985). Children's plays for creative actors. Boston, MA: Plays, Inc. SUBJECTS/PLAY TYPE: Mother's Day; Mothers; Skit.

78. 7-12. (+) Fitzgerald, Neil C. **All alone at the top.** CAST: 3f, 5m. ACTS: 1. SETTINGS: Newspaper office. PLAYING TIME: 25 min. PLOT: Allison, school newspaper editor, must decide whether to fire her boyfriend, Steve, who has missed two deadlines, and whether to print an editorial that advocates having girls pay for prom expenses. RECOMMENDATION: This raises several questions of ethics and women's equality that would be excellent discussion openers. ROYALTY: Free to Plays subscribers. SOURCE: Fitzgerald, Neil C. (1984, May). All alone at the top. Plays: The Drama Magazine for Young People, pp. 1-9. SUBJECTS/PLAY TYPE: Ethics; Women's Rights; Playlet.

79. 4-6. (-) Phillips, Marguerite Kreger. **All because of a scullery maid.** CAST: 5f, 3m. ACTS: 1. SETTINGS: Sitting room. PLAYING TIME: 25 min. PLOT: A sequence of events involving hidden silhouettes and spying reveals that the scullery maid is a patriot who has helped the American Revolution. RECOMMENDATION: Even though adequately written, the plot is confusing. This will not be fun to memorize, nor will it be enjoyed by a young audience. ROYALTY: NA. SOURCE: Phillips, Marguerite Kreger. (1976, May). All because of a scullery maid. Plays: The Drama Magazine for Young People, pp. 49-58. SUBJECTS/PLAY TYPE: Patriotism; Revolution, U. S.; Playlet.

80. 3-6. (+) Merten, George. **All change for spring.** CAST: 1f, 3m, Su. ACTS: 1. SETTINGS: Forest. PLAYING TIME: NA. PLOT: A caterpillar and his friends are unhappy because he has not turned into a butterfly. They rejoice when the transformation finally occurs. RECOMMENDATION: This simple marionette dramatization should intrigue youngsters with its expressive characters and its informative context. ROYALTY: None. SOURCE: Merten, George. (1979). Plays for puppet performance. Boston, MA: Plays, Inc. SUBJECTS/PLAY TYPE: Caterpillars; Butterflies; Puppet Play.

81. 6-8. (+) Boiko, Claire. **All hands on deck.** CAST: 5f, 6m. ACTS: 1. SETTINGS: Parlor. PLAYING TIME: 30 min. PLOT: Daughters of an absent but fearless sea Captain while away afternoons under the tutelage of Aunt Patience. As she naps, they frolic in a fashion considered shameless by their contemporaries, dream of sea adventures and launch into a dramatic enactment of a pirate kidnapping. When they discover a real kidnap victim, an Indian prince, the girls become hostages in their own home, victims of the dastardly Captain Dread. Aunt Patience awakens, brandishes her cane, and attacks the pirate crew. Ironically, the reward given the sisters by the young Indian prince is a sacred elephant, the very animal to which their conduct was unfavorably compared by Aunt Patience. RECOMMENDATION: Contemporary women will be amused at this tale of the overpowering strength of the weaker sex. The fencing duel between Aunt Patience and Captain Dread is unforgettable. ROYALTY: None. SOURCE: Boiko, Claire. (1985). Children's plays for creative actors. Boston,

MA: Plays, Inc. SUBJECTS/PLAY TYPE: Pirates; Women's Rights; Playlet.

82. 7-9*. (+) Traylor, Gene & Elrod, James Michael. **All in disguise.** CAST: 2f, 4m, Su. ACTS: 1. SETTINGS: Bare stage, curtain, props. PLAYING TIME: NA. PLOT: A vagabond who lives by his wits gets entangled in the romance of two couples: a rich young girl who loves a poor student but is being forced to marry a rich old man, and the rich girl's maid, who falls in love with the vagabond's companion. Through a series of silly deceptions, where everyone is disguised as someone else, the loving couples are united and the vagabond is richly rewarded for his skill in causing a successful, but unintentional, happy ending. RECOMMENDATION: This is acted in a "tour de farce" commedia style, and attempts are made to merge this with more modern humor expressed in everyday language. ROYALTY: $20. SOURCE: Traylor, Gene & James Michael Elrod. (1981). All in disguise. Chicago, IL: Dramatic Pub. Co. SUBJECTS/PLAY TYPE: Mistaken Identity; Love; Comedy.

83. 6-10. (+) Kehret, Peg. **All mothers are clairvoyant.** CAST: 1u. ACTS: 1. SETTINGS: None. PLAYING TIME: NA. PLOT: A young adolescent bemoans how his/her mother can intuit all her children's activities, especially the illicit ones. RECOMMENDATION: Most children will be able to identify with this universal situation. ROYALTY: NA. SOURCE: Kehret, Peg. (1986). Winning monologs for young actors. Colorado Springs, CO: Meriwether Pub. SUBJECTS/PLAY TYPE: Mothers; Monologue.

84. 7-12. (+) Majeski, Bill. **The all night radio host.** CAST: Su. ACTS: 1. SETTINGS: Radio studio. PLAYING TIME: NA. PLOT: A radio talk show host gets calls from the past. Hannibal wants to know about using elephants for transportation, Paul Revere needs a good horse, Shakespeare reads a couple of lines from his newest play (and is panned), Lady Godiva can't find her horse, and King Solomon has wife trouble. RECOMMENDATION: Familiarity with each historical event is recommended. ROYALTY: Free to Plays subscribers. SOURCE: Majeski, Bill. (1978, October). The all-night radio host. Plays: The Drama Magazine for Young People, pp. 92- 96. SUBJECTS/PLAY TYPE: Comedy; Talk Shows; Skit.

85. 10-12. (+) Zodrow, John Rester. **All out.** CAST: 8f, 15m, Su. ACTS: 1. SETTINGS: TV studio. PLAYING TIME: NA. PLOT: In this disturbing, almost surrealistic play, contestants on a game show called "All Out" are subjected to a series of tests which increase in cruelty and shock (i.e., lasting five seconds in a torture device, hitting a loved one, asking a loved one to play Russian roulette). Eventually, the appalled host puts a stop to the bizarre action and speaks movingly about humanity and self respect. RECOMMENDATION: The nightmarish atmosphere of the play is heightened by ever present applause, the bizarre cheeriness of the announcer, and the "everyman" quality of the contestants as they are

cajoled or bullied into going "All Out" to win the grand prize in this fascinating excursion into the realm of human psychodrama. ROYALTY: NA. SOURCE: Zodrow, John Rester. (1981). All out. Chicago, IL: Dramatic Pub. Co. SUBJECTS/PLAY TYPE: Game shows; Greed; Drama.

86. 4-7. (+) Boiko, Claire. All points west. CAST: 2f, 11m, Su. ACTS: 1. SETTINGS: Bare stage, props. PLAYING TIME: 20 min. PLOT: The continuous banter of the characters examines the motives and expectations of westward pioneers. Jeb yearns to farm free, distant lands, while his wife trusts his vision and shares his dream; Cal flees the crowded city for the isolation of the West; Digger lusts after gold. As they reach their individual destinations, one traveller bemoans the end of the adventure. Prophetically, he is reassured by his father that the exploration of a vaster territory, space, challenges America. RECOMMENDATION: The parallels drawn between the motives and obstacles of space exploration and the early westward expansion are timely. ROYALTY: None. SOURCE: Boiko, Claire. (1985). Children's plays for creative actors. Boston, MA: Plays, Inc. SUBJECTS/PLAY TYPE: Westward Expansion, U.S.; Pioneers, U.S.; Space Exploration; Playlet.

87. 10-12. (+) Schaller, Mary W. All the world's a stage. CAST: Su. ACTS: 1. SETTINGS: Bare stage. PLAYING TIME: NA. PLOT: A modern student tells about Shakespeare's life, times, and work by interacting with some of Shakespeare's characters and showing representative scenes from some of his plays. RECOMMENDATION: This excellent introduction to Shakespeare and his work well highlights some of Shakespeare's most famous scenes. ROYALTY: $20. SOURCE: Schaller, Mary W. (1982). All the world's a stage. Woodstock, IL: Dramatic Pub. Co. SUBJECTS/PLAY TYPE: Shakespeare, William; Drama.

88. K-12. (+) Hendricks, William & Vogel, Cora. All three are empty. CAST: Su. ACTS: 1. SETTINGS: None. PLAYING TIME: 2 min. PLOT: This tells of the birth of Jesus, his crucifixion and resurrection, and relates all three to his victory over death and the sins of the world. RECOMMENDATION: Suitable for church or parochial school groups, this could be performed at a Christmas pageant or worship service. ROYALTY: NA. SOURCE: Hendricks, William & Vogel, Cora. (1978). Handbook of Christmas programs. Grand Rapids, MI: Baker Book House. SUBJECTS/PLAY TYPE: Christ, Jesus; Christmas; Worship Program.

89. 7-12. (+) Gleason, William. All through the house. CAST: 4f, 7m. ACTS: 2. SETTINGS: Parlor; ballroom. PLAYING TIME: NA. PLOT: A poker game is constantly interrupted by William's daughter, who begs for an expensive dress for the Christmas cotillion and by William's busy body mother-in-law who has promised that William will donate a bell for the church in her honor. William's good spirits and economic well being are shattered. To raise money, he sells his most prized possession, a watch. Mrs. Hawkins learns one of the cardplayers is wanted by the law and pandemonium erupts, but by Christmas morning all is resolved. RECOMMENDATION: A good nonreligious Christmas play, this has a bit of O. Henry's "Gift of the Magi" theme, and a good portion of humor. ROYALTY: $25. SOURCE: Gleason, William. All through the house. Chicago, IL: Dramatic Pub. Co. SUBJECTS/PLAY TYPE: Christmas; Gifts; Comedy; Drama.

90. 1-6. (+) Priore, Frank V. Allison and the magic street lamp. CAST: 1f, 2m, 1u. ACTS: 1. SETTINGS: Street. PLAYING TIME: 20 min. PLOT: Allison awakens an agitated genie from his 50 year slumber when she attempts to clean a dirty street lamp. She is granted three wishes, which, in her haste, she wastes. She cries as she realizes that she has thrown away the chance of a lifetime, and the genie, worried about being able to sleep through all the sobbing, gives her three consolation prizes. RECOMMENDATION: The characters in this updated version of classic folk tale motifs is excellent. It should be performed by older grades for the younger ones. ROYALTY: Free to Plays subscribers. SOURCE: Priore, Frank V. (1983). Allison and the magic street lamp. Boston, MA: Plays, Inc. SUBJECTS/PLAY TYPE: Genies; Folk Tale Motifs; Comedy.

91. 9-12. (+) Snee, Dennis. Almost the bride of Dracula or Why the Count remains a bachelor. CAST: 5f, 2m. ACTS: 1. SETTINGS: Castle room. PLAYING TIME: 25 min. PLOT: As his mother bemoans the fact that she has no grandchildren, Dracula reminisces, through monologues and flashbacks, about women he wished to marry: an Italian beauty, a spoiled rich girl, and a merry widow. It becomes obvious that he has had difficulty conveying the nature of his affection and interpreting the feelings of his girlfriends. He reconciles himself to a life of lonely bloodsucking. RECOMMENDATION: Although the plot is one that would amuse any group, the occasionally complex vocabulary is more suitable for older audiences. ROYALTY: $15. SOURCE: Snee, Dennis. (1980). Almost the bride of Dracula or Why the Count remains a bachelor. Boston, MA: Baker's Plays. SUBJECTS/PLAY TYPE: Love; Vampires; Dracula; Comedy.

92. 12. (-) Henley, Beth. Am I blue. CAST: 1f, 1m, Su. ACTS: 1. SETTINGS: Bar; street; living room. PLAYING TIME: NA. PLOT: Two teenagers, a boy and a girl, meet at a honky tonk New Orleans bar, go to the young girl's apartment, discover that they are both virgins, and begin a relationship. RECOMMENDATION: The New Orleans "French Quarter" setting will be unfamiliar to many adolescents, and they will find it difficult to identify with characters who make appointments with whores, refer to each other's behavior as sheeplike, and use words like "frankly." This dated play unsuccessfully attempts to show the stupidity of yielding to peer pressure and is basically out of the realm of most high schoolers' experience. ROYALTY: $25. SOURCE: Henley, Beth. (1982). Am I blue. New York, NY: Dramatists Play Service. SUBJECTS/PLAY TYPE: Peer Pressure; Drama.

93. 9-12*. (+) Shaffer, Peter. **Amadeus. CAST:** 6f, 12m, Su. **ACTS:** 2. **SETTINGS:** Apartment; palace; opera house; theater; residence; park; assembly hall. **PLAYING TIME:** NA. **PLOT:** The life of Wolfgang Amadeus Mozart is reviewed through the eyes of rival composer Antonio Salieri. Episodes show Salieri's jealousy at Mozart's success, his disgust with Mozart's promiscuous lifestyle, and Mozart's inexorable submission to insanity. At the conclusion, the audience is left to wonder how much the aging, decrepit Salieri was involved in Mozart's death. **RECOMMENDATION:** An undeniably excellent work, this extensive drama should be left to adult performers and producers, due to its great length, costuming requirements, and frequent scene changes. **ROYALTY:** $60. **SOURCE:** Shaffer, Peter. (1980). Amadeus. New York, NY: Harper & Row. **SUBJECTS/PLAY TYPE:** Mozart, Wolfgang Amadeus; Drama.

94. 5-8. (+) Bradley, Virginia. **Amateur night at Cucumber Center. CAST:** 3f, 4m, 4u. **ACTS:** 1. **SETTINGS:** Movie theater stage. **PLAYING TIME:** NA. **PLOT:** As the master of ceremonies presents a talent show, performers have little talent and most are pulled off the stage with a giant hook. **RECOMMENDATION:** To succeed, this requires quick ad-libbing and slapstick humor. **ROYALTY:** None. **SOURCE:** Bradley, Virginia. (1975). Is there an actor in the house? New York, NY: Dodd, Mead. **SUBJECTS/PLAY TYPE:** Revue; Variety Program.

95. 6-12. (+) Tasca, Jules & Drachman, Ted. **The amazing Einstein. CAST:** 2f, 3m, Su. **ACTS:** 1. **SETTINGS:** Two movable panels with a changeable sign. **PLAYING TIME:** NA. **PLOT:** Albert Einstein's life is portrayed in short scenes ranging from his high school days through World War II. His dedication to physics, pacifism, and his wife, Elsa, is strongly portrayed, as is his conflict in advocating development of the atomic bomb. Three experiments illustrating relativity are performed by the cast. **RECOMMENDATION:** The characterization is excellent, and the three experiments that Einstein does to explain his theories to the others are clearly staged. Pre- and post-performance questions and a suggested bibliography are appended. **ROYALTY:** Upon application. **SOURCE:** Tasca, Jules & Drachman, Ted. (1987). The amazing Einstein. Woodstock, IL: Dramatic Pub. Co. **SUBJECTS/PLAY TYPE:** Einstein, Albert; Relativity (Physics); Musical.

96. 9-12. (+) Kundrat, Theodore V. **The Amazon woman defeated. CAST:** 16f, 3m, 1u. **ACTS:** 1. **SETTINGS:** Bare stage, lectern. **PLAYING TIME:** 30 min. **PLOT:** King Eurythesus of Mycenae dispatches Hercules to capture a sacred girdle of the Amazons. Hercules takes along the fair haired Greek hero, Theseus, King of Athens. Hipolyta, sister of Amazon Queen Antiope, removes her girdle and taunts Hercules with it. Hercules kills her, the Greeks lay waste to the fortress, and Theseus takes Hipolyta captive. When the Amazons retaliate, Hipolyta is slain trying to defend Theseus, whom she loves. After her death, the Amazons swear peace and disband. **RECOMMENDATION:** The techniques of platform theater are experimental and some degree of sophistication is necessary; prior stage experience is suggested. The moral lies in the death of Hipolyta, epitomizing the futility of warfare between the sexes. **ROYALTY:** $10. **SOURCE:** Kundrat, Theodore V. (1978). The Amazon woman defeated. Chicago, IL: Coach House Press. **SUBJECTS/PLAY TYPE:** Amazons; Mythology, Greek; Reader's Theater.

97. 9-12. (+) Kundrat, Theodore V. **The Amazon woman victorious. CAST:** 15f, 4m, 1u. **ACTS:** 1. **SETTINGS:** None. **PLAYING TIME:** 30 min. **PLOT:** The last of the Scythian tribe, all women, band together and use both feminine wiles and fierce warrior tactics to slay their enemies and conquer new lands. They call themselves the Amazons and create a manless society, adopting the sacred girdle, a sign of the unmarried, as their symbol. This is the story of the formation of the unconquerable and indomitable Amazon warriors. **RECOMMENDATION:** Dynamic characters command the rapid pace of this production. The dialogue effectively communicates the magnificence and pride of the Amazons who strove to subjugate their male enemies and their own natural instincts. While audiences admire the Amazon strength of will, they may also sense the tragic future of a race founded on hatred of half the human race. Not for the novice performer. **ROYALTY:** $10. **SOURCE:** Kundrat, Theodore, V. (1978). The Amazon woman victorious. Chicago, IL: Coach House Press. **SUBJECTS/PLAY TYPE:** Amazons; Mythology, Greek; Reader's Theater.

98. 7-12. (+) Shamas, Laura Annawyn. **Amelia lives. CAST:** 1f. **ACTS:** 1. **SETTINGS:** Bare stage, props. **PLAYING TIME:** 75 min. **PLOT:** As her plane crashes, Amelia Earhart remembers events from her life, including her relationship with her alcoholic father, an unhappy childhood in which she questioned her self worth, her career as an aviatrix, and her reluctant marriage to publisher G.P. Putnam. The responsibilities of fame, contrasted against her desire to fly, provide the backdrop for her final flight in which she tried to "do something," rather than just be promoted. **RECOMMENDATION:** Amelia must be able to recall and convincingly deliver dialogue, letters, and her own comments. **ROYALTY:** NA. **SOURCE:** Shamas, Laura Annawyn. (1987). Amelia lives. Woodstock, IL: Dramatic Pub. Co. **SUBJECTS/PLAY TYPE:** Earhart, Amelia; Aviators; Monologue.

99. 9-12. (+) Muschell, David. **Amelia, once more. CAST:** 3f, 2m, 1u. **ACTS:** 1. **SETTINGS:** Dressing room. **PLAYING TIME:** NA. **PLOT:** Shelly Preston is skilled at "getting into" the character of the Crazed Amelia for her stage performance. When she begins having difficulty getting out of Amelia's character, she begs the director for a one night respite. Because of the success of the production, the director refuses. Shelly's boyfriend, the leading man, is also reluctant to allow her time off. By the time he recognizes the problem, it is too late, for Shelly becomes Amelia. The play closes as Shelly/Amelia begins her performance. **RECOMMENDATION:** The theme of mental instability is disturbing, and the open

ending is particularly effective. ROYALTY: $25. SOURCE: Muschell, David. (1985). Amelia, once more. Franklin, OH: Eldridge Pub. Co. SUBJECTS/PLAY TYPE: Mental Illness; Actors and Actresses; Drama

100. 5-8. (+) Winward, Marilyn & Bois, David. **America is...** CAST: 10u. ACTS: 1. SETTINGS: Bare stage, props. PLAYING TIME: 30 min. PLOT: This musical tribute to the United States includes songs and descriptive dialogue for each of ten regions. The segments are tied together by a narrator. Songs include, "This land is your land," "Dixie," "Give My Regards to Broadway," and "Moonlight Bay." RECOMMENDATION: This is an effective program for increasing awareness of American music and geography. It allows participation by all students and provides for either large or small groups. ROYALTY: $11. SOURCE: Winward, Marilyn & Bois, David. (1981). America is... Franklin, OH: Eldridge Pub. Co. SUBJECTS/PLAY TYPE: Geography, U.S.; Musical.

101. 3-8. (+) Lorenz, Ellen Jane. **America singing.** CAST: Su. ACTS: 1. SETTINGS: None. PLAYING TIME: 45 min. PLOT: This musical begins with a choral reading from Whitman's "Leaves of Grass," followed by Thanksgiving songs, Colonial music, America's first operas, Yankee Doodle, hymns, minstrel music, and other traditional American songs. The conclusion focuses on Katherine Bates' "America the Beautiful." RECOMMENDATION: The choral organization allows this to be adapted for any group size. ROYALTY: $25. SOURCE: Lorenz, Ellen Jane. (1975). America singing. Franklin, OH: Eldridge Pub. Co. SUBJECTS/PLAY TYPE: History, U.S.; Music, American; Musical.

102. 7-9. (+) Majeski, Bill. **America's new quiz whizzes.** CAST: 2f, 2m. ACTS: 1. SETTINGS: Kitchen. PLAYING TIME: NA. PLOT: Jim and Mary put all their resources into sending their children to Quiz College. Fred, their eldest son, enters with the news that he is going to quit Quiz College, become an engineer, and get married. The folks are crushed. But with some persuasion and help from the girlfriend's parents, they talk Fred into going back to school and making them all rich. RECOMMENDATION: The humor lies in the fact that the parents want their children to do the opposite of what real parents want their children to do. ROYALTY: None. SOURCE: Majeski, Bill. (1981). Easy skits, blackouts and pantomimes. Woodstock, IL: Dramatic Pub. Co. SUBJECTS/PLAY TYPE: Game Shows; Comedy; Skit.

103. 7-12. (+) Morris, Arlene J. **An American story: A documentary.** CAST: Su. ACTS: 1. SETTINGS: None. PLAYING TIME: 35 min. PLOT: Narrators review the American Revolution, settling of the West, the Civil War, Industrial Revolution, World War I, the establishment of the League of Nations, 19th amendment to the Constitution, the Depression, and other U.S. historic events. RECOMMENDATION: With quotes from famous speeches and period music, this adequately covers some of America's historical landmarks. ROYALTY: Free to Plays subscribers. SOURCE: Morris, Arlene J. (1980, May). An American story: A documentary. Plays: The Drama Magazine for Young People, pp. 68-76 SUBJECTS/PLAY TYPE: History, U. S.; Reader's Theater.

104. 7-12. (+) Rembrandt, Elaine. **Amos, man from Tekoah.** CAST: 5f, 9m. ACTS: 1. SETTINGS: Front of the Temple in Jerusalem. PLAYING TIME: 20 min. PLOT: Amos hears and sees the arrogant, spoiled ways of the people who claim to be very religious Jews and, in his anger, he tries to get them to see that they have strayed from what is right. As he warns that they will be punished for their evil ways, he is seized and taken away. RECOMMENDATION: This can be performed either at the pulpit or on an elaborate stage. The costumes can be contemporary or period, as long as the female actors are garishly overdressed. ROYALTY: None. SOURCE: Rembrandt, Elaine. (1981). Heroes, heroines & holidays-- Plays for Jewish youth. Denver, CO: Alternatives in Religious Education. SUBJECTS/PLAY TYPE: Amos; Bible Stories; Jewish Drama.

105. 6-12. (+) Kelly, Tim J. **Amy goes army.** CAST: 4f, Su. ACTS: 1. SETTINGS: Orderly room. PLAYING TIME: 30 min. PLOT: While visiting an Army base, Amy takes over her friend's post. Things go from bad to worse, as Amy messes up all of her duties until her friend returns and convinces everyone involved to forget the incident. RECOMMENDATION: Slapstick humor adds much to this takeoff on army life. ROYALTY: $10. SOURCE: Kelly, Tim J. (1982). Amy goes Army. Denver, CO: Pioneer Drama Service. SUBJECTS/PLAY TYPE: Military Service; Comedy.

106. 7-12. (+) Goldberg, Moses. **The analysis of Mineral #4.** CAST: 3f, 3m. ACTS: 1. SETTINGS: Chemistry lab. PLAYING TIME: NA. PLOT: Bunny and Aline are considered weird by the other kids in school, and Mickey ridicules them. Aline has episodes of precognition and decides that she must be an alien, finding this easier to accept than the idea that she doesn't fit in with her peers. Her chemistry teacher points out fallacies in her logic, and, in the process, proves that he values her as a person. RECOMMENDATION: This provides a valuable and lesson about tolerance and acceptance. The plot is a bit thin and the character personalities are one dimensional but there are some amusing, imaginative moments. ROYALTY: $25. SOURCE: Goldberg, Moses. (1982). The analysis of Mineral #4. New Orleans, LA: Anchorage Press. SUBJECTS/PLAY TYPE: Attitudes; Individuality; Comedy.

107. K-3. (+) Korty, Carol. **Anansi's trick does double work.** CAST: 5u. ACTS: 1. SETTINGS: None. PLAYING TIME: NA. PLOT: Anansi tells Goat, Warthog, Lion and Turkey he has dreamt that "Old Hag" will get them all unless they start being nice to each other. He tricks each one, in turn, except for Turkey, by doing something so foolish that they make fun of him. Then to prevent them from being caught by the Old Hag, he tells them they must do something nice for him. Each gives Anansi the goods that he had been taking to market. Turkey finds out about Anansi's trick and turns

the tables, fooling Anansi into returning everything. RECOMMENDATION: The appropriate repetition in the dialogue builds the suspense as Anansi "gets his due." ROYALTY: $25. SOURCE: Korty, Carol. (1975). Plays from African folktales. Boston, MA: Baker's Plays. SUBJECTS/PLAY TYPE: Folk Tales, Africa; Animals; Anansi; Playlet.

108. K-4. (+) Mahlman, Lewis & Jones, David Cadwalader. **Anansi and the box of stories. CAST:** 5u. **ACTS:** 1. **SETTINGS:** Throne room; forest. **PLAYING TIME:** 15 min. **PLOT:** Anansi, the spider man, asks the sky god for his box of stories so he can introduce stories to the world. The sky god says he will release the stories if Anansi brings him the leopard of horrible teeth, the hornets who sting like fire, and the fairy whom no man sees. Using his brains, Anansi accomplishes these tasks, receives the stories, and is told that because of his courage, the stories will be called spider stories. **RECOMMENDATION:** This captures the spirit and ambience of the African folk tale upon which it is based. It would be especially effective as an introduction to some of the Anansi tales, which have been published in beautiful picture books. **ROYALTY:** Free to Plays subscribers. **SOURCE:** Mahlman, Lewis & Jones, David Cadwalader. (1980). Folk tale plays for puppets. Boston, MA: Plays, Inc. **SUBJECTS/PLAY TYPE:** Folk Tales, Africa; Anansi; Puppet Play.

109. 3-6. (+) Winther, Barbara. **Anansi, the African spider. CAST:** 2f, 7m. **ACTS:** 3. **SETTINGS:** Forest. **PLAYING TIME:** 20 min. **PLOT:** Anansi the spiderman obtains the sky god's stories by tricking a crocodile with its greed, evicting hornets from their nests by appealing to their dissatisfaction, and making a monkey speechless by using its vanity. The sky king then tells two stories: the monkey who, because of his laziness, had to deliver a talking drum to the king; and the tall tale man, who is beaten at his own game as Anansi turns his tall tale against him. **RECOMMENDATION:** "He who dishes it out should be able to eat it" is the final moral which is delightfully acted out in this adaptation of some of the famous African Anansi folk tales. **ROYALTY:** Free for amateur performance. **SOURCE:** Winther, Barbara. (1976). Plays from folktales of Africa and Asia. Boston, MA: Plays, Inc. **SUBJECTS/PLAY TYPE:** Folk Tales, Africa; Anansi; Playlet.

110. 9-12*. (+) Bolton, Guy. (Maurette, Marcelle) **Anastasia.** (Anastasia) **CAST:** 5f, 8m. **ACTS:** 3. **SETTINGS:** Palace. **PLAYING TIME:** NA. **PLOT:** Anna claims she is Anastasia, the presumed murdered daughter of the Russian Tsar. Three Russian expatriots do not believe her claim, but cynically see an opportunity to become wealthy. They coach her, hoping to convince the rest of the royal family and the bankers who hold a fortune in trust for the real Anastasia. As time goes by, Anna remembers details which only Anastasia could have known, and she wins over part of the family. She is united with Dr. Serensky, who once had a romance with Anna and she decides to leave, flattered by the attentions of the doctor who loves her for who she is, not someone she once was. **RECOMMENDATION:** The

portrayal of the elderly Empress (Anna's alleged mother) is superb, and the closeness of the two women as healing forces for each other is touching. The characters, with their myriad motives, raise interesting issues for discussion about values and choices. Because of role length and character depth, production may need to be by adults, or by experienced actors. **ROYALTY:** NA. **SOURCE:** Bolton, Guy. (1955). Anastasia. New York, NY: Random House. **SUBJECTS/PLAY TYPE:** Revolution, Russia; Identity; Adaptation.

111. 11-12. (+) Taylor, Cecil P. **And a nightingale song. CAST:** 3f, 4m. **ACTS:** 2. **SETTINGS:** Living room. **PLAYING TIME:** NA. **PLOT:** Helen Stott, spinster older daughter, is the sensible strength of the Stott family: Mom, obsessively devoted to Catholicism; George (father), who ignores the crises around him by badly playing patriotic tunes on his piano; and Joyce, the lonely young sister who married her sweetheart, Eric, without really knowing him or herself. The foundations of their lives are shaken by the outbreak of World War II and Helen's love affair with a married soldier. When Helen moves away to make a weekend home for her lover, the family must learn to stand on its own. **RECOMMENDATION:** This is a touching, evocative story about a timeless subject: the bright glow of humanity often found in quiet strength sparked by the cataclysm of war. Taylor's dialogue is earthy and sparse, and the plotting of the action over several years is immediate, believable and interesting. **ROYALTY:** $75. **SOURCE:** Taylor, Cecil P. (1979). And a nightingale song. Woodstock, IL: Dramatic Pub. Co. **SUBJECTS/PLAY TYPE:** War; Drama.

112. 7-12. (+) Rembrandt, Elaine. **And brings us to this season: A Thanksgiving play. CAST:** 2f, 4m, 2u. **ACTS:** 1. **SETTINGS:** Kitchen; outside a synagogue. **PLAYING TIME:** 20 min. **PLOT:** A family realizes how important their live in grandfather is to them. **RECOMMENDATION:** This is relevant to today's busy lifestyles and truly shows the contributions and importance of older family members. **ROYALTY:** None. **SOURCE:** Rembrandt, Elaine. (1981). Heroes, heroines & holidays - Plays for Jewish youth. Denver CO: Alternatives in Religious Education. **SUBJECTS/PLAY TYPE:** Thanksgiving; Family; Grandparents; Skit.

113. 4-8. (-) Nolan, Paul T. **And Christmas is its name. CAST:** 9f, 16m. **ACTS:** 1. **SETTINGS:** Hospital corridor. **PLAYING TIME:** 25 min. **PLOT:** Jessica, handicapped and in a wheelchair, is visited by numerous Christmas spirits who share their faith in her ability to walk again. **RECOMMENDATION:** This is not be suitable for public school production because it focuses more on religion than Christmas. Also, it displays highly insulting stereotypes of disabled people. **ROYALTY:** Free to Plays subscribers. **SOURCE:** Kamerman, Sylvia. (1982). Christmas play favorites for young people. Boston, MA: Plays, Inc. **SUBJECTS/PLAY TYPE:** Christmas; Disabilities; Playlet.

114. 5-8*. (+) Weaver, Richard A. **And Jack fell down. CAST:** 1f, 2m, Su. **ACTS:** 1. **SETTINGS:** Puppet

stage. PLAYING TIME: 30 min. PLOT: Must puppets (perhaps representing mankind) be controlled by a masterful hand? One puppet believes he has feelings and can control his destiny without "strings". RECOMMENDATION: This very important story calls for audience members to form their own conclusions as to the ability of puppets (perhaps symbolizing themselves) to survive on their own. ROYALTY: $25. SOURCE: Weaver, Richard A. (1975). And Jack fell down. Schulenburg, TX: I.E. Clark. SUBJECTS/PLAY TYPE: Puppets; Self Determination; Drama.

115. 9-12. (+) Dee, Peter & Welch, John B. ...and stuff... CAST: 11f, 11m, Su. ACTS: 2. SETTINGS: In and around a high school. PLAYING TIME: 120 min. PLOT: This is a series of vignettes in which teens search for meaning in their lives. The topics range from use of drugs, to admiration of a father who is a widower, to despair. It culminates in making a music video. RECOMMENDATION: While sets can be simple or elaborate, many of the actors must be able to sing. The play addresses such issues as teen suicide, incest, prostitution, murder, divorce and sex. ROYALTY: $40. SOURCE: Dee, Peter & Welch, John B. (1985). ...and stuff... Boston, MA: Baker's Plays. SUBJECTS/PLAY TYPE: Adolescent Problems; Drama.

116. K-12. (+) Housman, Laurence. And the word was made flesh. CAST: 3u. ACTS: 1. SETTINGS: Bare stage, three posters. PLAYING TIME: 2 min. PLOT: This retells the story from the New Testament about God sending His only Son to redeem mankind. RECOMMENDATION: Suitable for church or parochial school groups for performance in a Christmas pageant or worship service. ROYALTY: NA. SOURCE: Hendricks, William & Vogel, Cora. (1978). Handbook of Christmas programs. Grand Rapids, MI: Baker Book House. SUBJECTS/PLAY TYPE: Christmas; Christ, Jesus; Worship Program.

117. 10-12*. (+) Willinger, David. Andrea's got two boyfriends. CAST: 1f, 3m. ACTS: 1. SETTINGS: School. PLAYING TIME: NA. PLOT: Based on the character of the author's real life retarded sister, Andrea, whose family sent her to Crystal Park institution. Her daily relationships with peers and her counselor are depicted. The purpose is to give a better understanding of retarded adults: their likes and dislikes, insecurities, frustrations, fears, angers and perspectives of sex, marriage, and love. This also provides insight into the challenge of resident counseling and caring. RECOMMENDATION: Created through interviews and the imaginative thought of the original players, the play deals with a sensitive issue which might embarrass young people because of their lack of understanding. The strong language and sexual gesturing may not be handled well except by mature audiences or those who have a some background in retardation. The author strongly advises all involved to gain first hand knowledge of retardation before production. ROYALTY: $25. SOURCE: Willinger, David. (1986). Andrea's got two boyfriends. New York, NY: Dramatists Play Service. SUBJECTS/PLAY TYPE: Mental Retardation; Psychology; Drama.

118. 3-6. (+) Baker, Charlotte. (Aesopus) Androcles and the lion. (Androcles and the lion) CAST: 5m, 2u. ACTS: 1. SETTINGS: Egyptian courtyard; wilderness; cave; prison cell; Roman Coliseum. PLAYING TIME: 20 min. PLOT: Androcles, a Roman slave and friend to all animals, seeks his freedom. He hides in the wilderness and befriends a lion by removing a thorn from its paw. Androcles is later caught by soldiers and awaits death in the Coliseum. When sent to his execution, Androcles is faced with a ferocious, starving lion, but the same one he befriended. Their loyalty to each other impresses the emperor, who rewards them with their freedom. RECOMMENDATION: This delightful and timeless story presents both major characters with sophistication, and empathetically describes thoughts and reasons for their behavior. ROYALTY: Free to Plays subscribers. SOURCE: Baker, Charlotte. (1978, January). Androcles and the lion. Plays: The Drama Magazine for Young People, pp. 43-48 SUBJECTS/PLAY TYPE: Fable; Lions; Friendship; Adaptation.

119. 7-9. (+) Barton, Dave & Bond, Matt. (Aesopus). Androcles and the lion. (Androcles and the lion) CAST: 18u. ACTS: 3. SETTINGS: Desert; Roman market; slave quarters; palace room; Roman arena. PLAYING TIME: 90 min. PLOT: A lion who has a thorn removed from his paw by Androcles returns the favor and saves his rescuer's life in the Circus Maximus arena of Caesar's Rome. RECOMMENDATION: This musical adaptation involves extensive period costuming and props and a large cast. ROYALTY: $60. SOURCE: Barton, Dave & Bond, Matt. (1978). Androcles and the lion. Denver, CO: Pioneer Drama Service. SUBJECTS/PLAY TYPE: Fable; Friendship; Lions; Musical; Adaptation.

120. K-6*. (+) Harris, Aurand. (Aesopus). Androcles and the lion. (Androcles and the lion) CAST: 1f, 4m, 1u. ACTS: 2. SETTINGS: Bare stage, props, backdrops. PLAYING TIME: NA. PLOT: Androcles, a slave, helps two lovers (Isabella and Lelio), who have been frightened by a lion, escape into the woods. He gains the lion's friendship before he is captured by his master, Pantalone. The lion is caught and also taken to Rome. It spots its old friend and jumps into the seats to attack Pantalone and his men. The emperor, so impressed by the strength of their friendship, grants their freedom and restores Isabella's dowry so she may wed Lelio. RECOMMENDATION: The plot ranges from comedy to drama, utilizing both suspense and irony. Much of the dialogue rhymes, and the audience is involved through occasional direct address. ROYALTY: Write Anchorage Press. SOURCE: Jennings, Coleman A. & Harris, Aurand. (1988). Plays Children Love. Volume II. New York, NY: St. Martin's Press. SUBJECTS/PLAY TYPE: Friendship; Fable; Lions; Adaptation.

121. 4-6. (-) Fisher, Aileen. Angel in the looking glass. CAST: 5f, 3m. ACTS: 2. SETTINGS: Sewing room. PLAYING TIME: NA. PLOT: A young girl dressed as an angel for a Christmas play wonders if people would act any differently if they believed she was a real angel. She decides to find out and knocks on three apartment doors

just when the inhabitants are hard pressed to make certain self sacrificing decisions. RECOMMENDATION: The changed behavior of the adults as a result of seeing the girl is totally unrealistic. ROYALTY: Free to Plays subscribers. SOURCE: Fisher, Aileen. (1986). Holiday programs for boys and girls. Boston, MA: Plays, Inc. SUBJECTS/PLAY TYPE: Family; Christmas; Angels; Drama.

122. K-8. (-) Minson, Maxine. **Angel in the park.** CAST: 4f, 7m, Su. ACTS: 1. SETTINGS: Bare stage, props. PLAYING TIME: 25 min. PLOT: A philanthropist disguises himself as a beggar in the city park at Christmas to reward some worthy soul for his or her goodness. He observes a pompous choral group, an ill tempered Santa Claus who brawls with the singers, and a thief. Discouraged, he meets Harriet Adams, a handicapped person who volunteers her time to entertain some orphans at the park. Her caring and unselfishness shine forth and she is rewarded for her true Christmas spirit. RECOMMENDATION: This has an unrealistic theme and overtones of handicapism, as Harriet Adams apparently is disabled only for the sake of evoking pity from the audience. ROYALTY: NA. SOURCE: Minson, Maxine. (1983). Angel in the park. Franklin, OH: Eldridge Pub. Co. SUBJECTS/PLAY TYPE: Christmas; Drama.

123. 7-12*. (+) Way, Brian. **Angel of the prisons.** CAST: 10f, 15m. ACTS: 2. SETTINGS: Street; prison; office. PLAYING TIME: NA. PLOT: Director Harry Caldwell and Producer John Snyder debate whether the life of Elizabeth Fry, 19th century prison reformer, would make good material for a movie. The debate turns into a reenactment of portions of her life, from her childhood, to her becoming a "plain" Quaker, through her marriage and various benevolent acts. RECOMMENDATION: The life of Elizabeth Fry is examined superficially, but with feeling. Used to complement a social studies unit on prison reform, this would also be appropriate material for younger audiences. ROYALTY: $45. SOURCE: Way, Brian. (1977). Angel of the prisons. Boston, MA: Baker's Plays. SUBJECTS/PLAY TYPE: Fry, Elizabeth; Prison Reform; Drama

124. 7-9. (+) Karshner, Roger. **Angela and Mary.** CAST: 2f. ACTS: 1. SETTINGS: None. PLAYING TIME: NA. PLOT: Angela consoles Mary, whose two year relationship with Roger has just ended because he was cheating on her with another girl. When a cute, new boy walks by, Mary starts to worry about how she looks and seems to forget all about Roger. RECOMMENDATION: This shows how quickly young love can end and be forgotten, but may be more appropriate for adults who realize this. ROYALTY: NA. SOURCE: Karshner, Roger. (1986). Scenes for teenagers. Toluce Lake, CA: Dramaline Pub. SUBJECTS/PLAY TYPE: Dating; Scene.

125. K-3. (+) Silverman, Eleanor. **Animal crackers.** CAST: 10u. ACTS: 2. SETTINGS: Zoo. PLAYING

TIME: NA. PLOT: The animals in the zoo decide that the walrus and the snake are "equals," just as humans are. RECOMMENDATION: Although it lacks a true climax and denouement, and seems to condone violence, children will enjoy the opportunity to dress as zoo animals, and the message of equality makes this versatile. ROYALTY: None. SOURCE: Silverman, Eleanor. (1983). Dramatics for children. Metuchen, NJ: Scarecrow Press. SUBJECTS/PLAY TYPE: Animals; Zoo; Equality; Skit

126. 10-12. (+) Hall, Peter & Peaslee, Richard. (Orwell, George) **Animal farm.** (Animal Farm) CAST: 15u. ACTS: 2. SETTINGS: None. PLAYING TIME: NA. PLOT: In this faithful retelling of the classic political allegory, the animals revolt against the farmer to bring about a socialist utopian society. The high minded commandments are all subverted and obliterated from history, as the social order reverts to its original status. RECOMMENDATION: The chilling tone and hard hitting message of the original story are well preserved in this innovative play, which uses a black background upon which animal cutouts (or people dressed as animals) move. The 37 "songs" which perfectly mirror the play's message, could either be taped or performed live. ROYALTY: Upon application. SOURCE: Hall, Peter. (1986). Animal farm. Chicago, IL: Dramatic Pub. Co. SUBJECTS/PLAY TYPE: Totalitarianism; Political Ideologies; Musical; Adaptation.

127. K-3. (+) Bauer, Caroline Feller. **Animal jokes.** CAST: 9u. ACTS: 1. SETTINGS: None. PLAYING TIME: NA. PLOT: Three jokes are told, one about how safe it is to swim in shark infested waters, another about waiting until goldfish have drunk all their water before giving them more, and a final one on how flashlights will protect you from tigers if you can run fast enough. RECOMMENDATION: Children will enjoy presenting these Vaudevillian flavored jokes for friends and parents, perhaps rounding out the performance with other "Animal Antics" material. ROYALTY: NA. SOURCE: Bauer, Caroline Feller. (1987). Presenting reader's theater: Plays and poems to read aloud. New York, NY: H.W. Wilson. SUBJECTS/PLAY TYPE: Animals; Jokes; Reader's Theater.

128. 1-3. (+) Jackson, R. Eugene & Alette, Carl. (Aesopus) **Animal krackers.** (Aesop's Fables) CAST: 14u. ACTS: 1. SETTINGS: Forest. PLAYING TIME: 60 min. PLOT: Twelve familiar fables are acted out by the forest animals for the amusement of the lion, who plans to eat them when they are finished. They prolong the fables as long as possible, then give the lion an acting award and encourage him to make a speech which affords them time to escape. RECOMMENDATION: This lively play has silly jokes and short musical numbers. Although all of the actors are on stage for the entire play, the speaking parts are short and the familiarity of the fables should allow for easy memorization. ROYALTY: $35. SOURCE: Jackson, R. Eugene & Alette, Carl. (1984). Animal krackers. Denver,

CO: Pioneer Drama Service. **SUBJECTS/PLAY TYPE:** Fable; Animals; Musical.

129. 1-6. (+) Turner, Jamie. (Montgomery, Lucy M.) **Anne of Green Gables.** (Anne of Green Gables) CAST: 6f, 3m, Su. ACTS: 1. SETTINGS: Kitchen. PLAYING TIME: 25 min. PLOT: A precocious young girl is brought from an orphanage to a farm, where she is accused of lying about a lost brooch, is swindled by a peddler, mistakenly dyes her hair green, and bakes a cake with cough syrup for the minister and his wife. RECOMMENDATION: This abridged version maintains the universal appeal of the original which examined the joys and frustrations of everyday living, the insecurities of youth, and the importance of family. ROYALTY: Free to Plays subscribers. SOURCE: Turner, Jamie. (1987, March). Anne of Green Gables. Plays: The Drama Magazine for Young People, pp. 54-64. **SUBJECTS/PLAY TYPE:** Adventure; Adaptation.

130. 10-12. (+) Gill, Barbara Gove. **The anniversary.** CAST: 6f, 5m, Su. ACTS: 3. SETTINGS: Living room. PLAYING TIME: 60 min. PLOT: Pat and Martha's children incorrectly assume that their parents are having affairs. In a delightful comedy of errors and misunderstandings, the children conspire to prevent the errant parents from splitting up. The alleged home breakers are innocent victims of the conspiracy and spend an anniversary party planned by the children stuffed in a closet, sleeping off spiked lemonade. When Pat and Mike leave for their anniversary cruise, Martha and Eric mysteriously reappear on the couch, dozing in a cozy embrace. RECOMMENDATION: This well constructed play is designed for little theater production. It has a range of possibilities for comedic effect, and the party scene offers a number of walk on roles. ROYALTY: $25. SOURCE: Gill, Barbara Gove. (1980). The anniversary. New York, NY: Eldridge Pub. Co. **SUBJECTS/PLAY TYPE:** Family; Misunderstandings; Comedy.

131. 7-12. (+) Fontaine, Robert. (Perrault, Charles) **Another Cinderella.** (Cinderella) CAST: 5f, 1m. ACTS: 2. SETTINGS: Shabby home. PLAYING TIME: 15 min. PLOT: This is an attempt to update the familiar classic with tongue in cheek characterizations and modern dialogue, although some lines will still have to be updated. RECOMMENDATION: Though the quality of the dialogue is uneven, this "fractured fairy tale" has Cinderella with the only foot big enough to fit the slipper, and will be great fun to produce and watch. ROYALTY: Free to Plays subscribers. SOURCE: Fontaine, Robert. (1978, February). Another Cinderella. Plays: The Drama Magazine for Young People, pp. 71-75. **SUBJECTS/PLAY TYPE:** Folk Tales, France; Adaptation; Skit.

132. 4-6. (+) Priore, Frank V. **Another routine day.** CAST: 2f, 5m. ACTS: 1. SETTINGS: Office. PLAYING TIME: 10 min. PLOT: Miss Keegan, secretary of the Parker Employment Agency, hopes for something unusual to happen. Big Bad Wolf, Jack (of the Beanstalk), and Cinderella come in. Miss Keegan helps them all, but tells her boss she's had just "another routine day." RECOMMENDATION: Children will enjoy the absurdity of the well known fairy tale characters as they appear in the modern everyday world. ROYALTY: Free to Plays subscribers. SOURCE: Priore, Frank V. (1981, October). Another routine day. Plays: The Drama Magazine for Young People, pp. 63-67. **SUBJECTS/PLAY TYPE:** Folk Tale Characters; Employment; Skit.

133. K-3. (+) Kennedy, X.J. **Ant.** CAST: 1u. ACTS: 1. SETTINGS: None. PLAYING TIME: NA. PLOT: Ants may be hard workers, but it is hard to tell by just watching and listening. RECOMMENDATION: Clever, this would be best used in conjunction with the other "Animal Antics" poems. ROYALTY: NA. SOURCE: Bauer, Caroline Feller. (1987). Presenting reader's theater: Plays and poems to read aloud. New York, NY: H.W. Wilson **SUBJECTS/PLAY TYPE:** Ants; Reader's Theater.

134. 6-9. (+) Eaton, Norman Bridge. **Anxious moments.** CAST: 1f, 2m. ACTS: 1. SETTINGS: Living room. PLAYING TIME: NA. PLOT: Margaret and her husband enlist the aid of a tree surgeon for an ailing elm tree. The couple becomes more and more emotional to the point of Margaret sobbing openly when Dr. Tinker announces that he will operate. All are relieved when the results of the operation are "a fine, healthy, bouncing baby bough." RECOMMENDATION: Although the characters are stereotypical, the ending is humorous and unexpected. This may be particularly amusing to children who have recently been enlightened to the reproductive differences between animals and plants. ROYALTY: None. SOURCE: Majeski, Bill. (1981). Easy skits, blackouts and pantomimes. Woodstock, IL: Dramatic Pub. Co. **SUBJECTS/PLAY TYPE:** Word Play; Trees; Comedy; Skit.

135. 12. (-) Gilsenan, Nancy. **Any famous last words?** CAST: 8f, 2m, 3u. ACTS: 2. SETTINGS: Hospital room. PLAYING TIME: NA. PLOT: Soon to go under anesthesia for minor surgery, successful playwright Lucy Sisson begins to question her writing ethics and has thoughts of not waking up. RECOMMENDATION: Dull characters, crude language, and cheap cracks at everyone from nuns to family make this a not so funny production. The intended theme is lost in the attempt to produce comedy. ROYALTY: $50. SOURCE: Gilsenan, Nancy. (1986). Any famous last words? Woodstock, IL: Dramatic Pub. Co. **SUBJECTS/PLAY TYPE:** Playwrights; Ethics, Literary; Comedy.

136. K-6. (+) Carlson, Bernice Wells. **Anyone could, but.** CAST: 2f, 6m, 1u. ACTS: 1. SETTINGS: Road. PLAYING TIME: NA. PLOT: The king wants to find someone in his kingdom who thinks of others. He places a stone in the middle of the road and watches for a person who will move it out of the way. Only one person moves the stone. RECOMMENDATION: As the author states, "if it's right, do it." ROYALTY: NA. SOURCE: Carlson, Bernice Wells. (1982). Let's find the big idea. Nashville, TN: Abingdon. **SUBJECTS/PLAY TYPE:** Individuality; Fable; Drama.

137. 6-12. (+) Hawse, Alberta. **Anything can happen on Christmas.** CAST: 5f, 3m. ACTS: 3. SETTINGS: Living room. PLAYING TIME: 60 min. PLOT: Adopted Erika looks for her birth mother with the help of her social science teacher, Rachel Duvall. Erika's adoptive parents feel betrayed and worry about losing Erika. Miss Duvall reveals that she is Erika's birth mother, explains why she gave Erika up for adoption, and why she decided to reveal herself at this time. After discussion, they begin to understand and respect each other's feelings and become friends. RECOMMENDATION: Emphasis lies in the adoptee's rights and open adoption records. The characters and their various viewpoints are realistically and poignantly developed. But due to the religious emphasis, this is only appropriate for church groups or parochial schools. ROYALTY: $30. SOURCE: Hawse, Alberta. (1983). Anything can happen on Christmas. Franklin, OH: Eldridge Pub. Co. SUBJECTS/PLAY TYPE: Christmas; Adoption; Christian Drama.

138. 1-3. (+) Boiko, Claire. **Anywhere and everywhere.** CAST: 3m, Su. ACTS: 1. SETTINGS: None. PLAYING TIME: 20 min. PLOT: Children explain many methods of transportation by chanting rhymes and imitating the movements of various modes of transportation. RECOMMENDATION: This involves movement around the stage, as well as a backstage crew to design the signs which are displayed as the action takes place. ROYALTY: None for amateur production. SOURCE: Boiko, Claire. (1981). Children's plays for creative actors. Boston, MA: Plays, Inc. SUBJECTS/PLAY TYPE: Transportation; Choral Reading.

139. 7-12. (+) Kral, Brian. **Apologies.** CAST: 4f, 2m. ACTS: 1. SETTINGS: Kitchen; bedroom. PLAYING TIME: NA. PLOT: The events leading up to Jennifer's suicide are chronicled in flashbacks. RECOMMENDATION: Unmistakable signs of a teenager in trouble are juxtaposed with her normal, pleasant life. This would be an excellent precursor to discussion about teenage suicide and how to prevent it. ROYALTY: $35. SOURCE: Kral, Brian. (1988). Apologies. New Orleans, LA: Anchorage Press, Inc. SUBJECTS/PLAY TYPE: Suicide; Drama.

140. 3-5. (-) Peterson, Andrew & Mahlman, Lewis. **Appearing knightly.** CAST: 1f, 4m, 2u. ACTS: 1. SETTINGS: Bare stage, props. PLAYING TIME: 20 min. PLOT: Sir Mordred kidnaps Princess Priscilla and promises her to an evil dragon if the dragon will kill Sir Robin. Sir Robin sets off to rescue the princess, not knowing that Mordred has sabotaged his lance. Robin notices the defective lance and the Wizard of the Forest gives him a magic sword. When Robin cuts the dragon down to size, Robin and Priscilla are betrothed. RECOMMENDATION: Although this is complete with villain, damsel in distress, knight in shining armor and dragon, it is quite discomforting. For example, Priscilla doesn't know if she should love the wimpy Robin, who refuses to fight just for the sport of it. The implications of a girl a month for the dragon are unpleasantly sexual and the jokes are too subtle to be appreciated by the age group for whom this was written. ROYALTY: Free to Plays subscribers. SOURCE: Peterson, Andrew & Mahlman, Lewis. (1988, November). Appearing knightly. Plays: The Drama Magazine for Young People, pp. 61-64. SUBJECTS/PLAY TYPE: Dragons; Knights; Puppet Play.

141. K-5. (+) Pyle, Howard. **The apple of contentment.** CAST: 4f, 4m, 1u. ACTS: 1. SETTINGS: Meadow. PLAYING TIME: 30 min. PLOT: Jovial, elf like Manikin Red Cap gives the mistreated Christine a seed from the apple of contentment. It grows into a large tree bearing one apple at a time, which only she can pick. The king promises that whoever picks an apple for him will become his queen. Christine presents the king with the desired apple, he makes her queen, and the Tree of Contentment follows them to their new home. RECOMMENDATION: This contains many humorous moments, such as evil sisters desperately trying to pick the apple from the unwilling tree. This should be performed by upper elementary actors. ROYALTY: Free to Plays subscribers. SOURCE: Thane, Adele. (1983). Plays from famous stories and fairy tales. Boston, MA: Plays, Inc. SUBJECTS/PLAY TYPE: Greed; Playlet.

142. 6-8. (-) Bradley, Virginia. **Apples for sale.** CAST: 4f. ACTS: 2. SETTINGS: Street. PLAYING TIME: NA. PLOT: A poor lady sells apples; a poor girl wants apples; a rich lady hates apples. Fate changes everything. The rich lady buys apples from the poor lady and gives them to the poor girl to eat. But now the poor lady is selling violets, not apples, and no one will buy violets. RECOMMENDATION: Dated language and too subtle humor make this unsuccessful. ROYALTY: None. SOURCE: Bradley, Virginia. (1975). Is there an actor in the house? New York, NY: Dodd, Mead. SUBJECTS/PLAY TYPE: Fate; Skit.

143. K-2. (-) Ratkowski, Thomas M. **Apples, oranges, strawberries.** CAST: 4f, 2m, 6u. ACTS: 1. SETTINGS: Street. PLAYING TIME: 15 min. PLOT: A fruit peddler's wares compete to look the freshest so they will be picked by the customer. As the peddler urges the customer to make her selection, the cart is upset and all the fruit spills on the street. The lady decides to serve fruit salad. RECOMMENDATION: The actors are dressed up as fruits, and at the end, they are all sprawled on top of each other. The idea has potential, but the dialogue is dated (hoot, man, rascal, tuckered out), the jokes are too sophisticated for the youngsters who would want to perform this, and fruit peddlers are now rare. ROYALTY: Free to Plays subscribers. SOURCE: Ratkowski, Thomas M. (1975, October). Apples, oranges, strawberries. Plays: The Drama Magazine for Young People, pp. 65-68. SUBJECTS/PLAY TYPE: Comedy; Fruit; Creative Dramatics.

144. 9-12. (+) Kehret, Peg. **Applying for a job.** CAST: 1u. ACTS: 1. SETTINGS: None. PLAYING TIME: NA. PLOT: A teen recounts his fears as he awaits a job interview. RECOMMENDATION: Many of the major concerns felt by people awaiting an interview are mentioned, but the monologue will especially appeal to

teenaged audiences. ROYALTY: NA. SOURCE: Kehret, Peg. (1986). Winning monologs for young actors. Colorado Springs, CO: Meriwether Pub. SUBJECTS/PLAY TYPE: Interviewing; Monologue.

145. K-12. (+) DeRooy, Henry M. **An appointment with God. CAST:** 5u. **ACTS:** 1. **SETTINGS:** None. **PLAYING TIME:** NA. **PLOT:** The Lord tells Simon that he will visit today. As Simon waits, he helps three needy people. That night, the Lord explains that he visited as the needy people and that Simon's help to others is the same as helping the Lord. **RECOMMENDATION:** This is simple and poignant. **ROYALTY:** NA. **SOURCE:** Altena, Hans. (1980). The playbook for Christian theater. Grand Rapids, MI: Baker Book House. **SUBJECTS/PLAY TYPE:** Kindness; Christian Drama.

146. 7-12. (+) Moeller, Ruby L. **April. CAST:** Su. **ACTS:** 1. **SETTINGS:** Bare stage, props. **PLAYING TIME:** NA. **PLOT:** This outline for an Easter program includes a short history of Easter and an Easter tableau featuring a cross, a resurrection poem, and two games, one with an Easter bonnet theme and the second with a Humpty Dumpty theme. A humorous poem about children's Easter gifts to mother is included. **RECOMMENDATION:** Much of the material is geared for an adult audience/cast: "Easter Bonnet Parade" calls for men as models and "An Easter Long Ago" is an adult's childhood remembrances. This would only be suitable for a group of Christians of various ages. The reading, "Easter," is an interesting historical synopsis of Christian Easter festivities. **ROYALTY:** NA. **SOURCE:** Moeller, Ruby L. (1975). Around the year programs. Boston, MA: Baker's Plays. **SUBJECTS/PLAY TYPE:** Easter; Playlet.

147. 2-4. (-) Thayer, Marjorie & Freeman, Don. **The April foolers. CAST:** 4f, 4m. **ACTS:** 2. **SETTINGS:** Street. **PLAYING TIME:** NA. **PLOT:** Children carefully plan an April Fools' joke, but become the victims themselves. **RECOMMENDATION:** The dialogue and parts are too long to be performed by younger children, but too didactic and moralistic to be of interest to older children. The presentation doesn't seem to "know" whether it is a picture book or a play to be performed. **ROYALTY:** NA. **SOURCE:** Thayer, Marjorie & Don Freeman. (1978). The April Foolers. Chicago, IL: Childrens Press. **SUBJECTS/PLAY TYPE:** April Fools' Day; Melodrama.

148. 3-5. (+) Marshall, Sheila L. **April's rebellion. CAST:** 7f, 8m, Su. **ACTS:** 1. **SETTINGS:** Forest. **PLAYING TIME:** 23 min. **PLOT:** Mother Nature is upset because the month of April refuses to cry, which leaves the earth with no rain. November gets her to cry by giving her an onion necklace. **RECOMMENDATION:** This skit is educational as each month threatens to abrogate its responsibilities (i.e., July won't allow fireworks, August won't allow picnics) to convince April of her duties. **ROYALTY:** Free to Plays subscribers. **SOURCE:** Marshall, Sheila L. (1977, April). April's rebellion. Plays: The Drama Magazine for Young People, pp. 43-48. **SUBJECTS/PLAY TYPE:** Calender; Months; Skit.

149. 7-12. (+) Boiko, Claire. **The Arabian knight. CAST:** 6f, 8m. **ACTS:** 5. **SETTINGS:** Throne room; desert. **PLAYING TIME:** NA. **PLOT:** A Sultan, trying to protect his daughters from modern ideas, sends them into the desert with an American Boy Scout. Returning to the palace, they have become liberated. This infuriates the Sultan, but his worries about his daughters not marrying because of their open-mindedness are put to rest when they are accepted as worthy wives. **RECOMMENDATION:** This clever and humorous treatment of equality for women entertainingly presents its message. The only drawback might be its obvious disdain for traditional Muslim customs concerning the proper behavior of women. **ROYALTY:** Free to Plays subscribers. **SOURCE:** Boiko, Claire. (1985, May). The Arabian knight. Plays: The Drama Magazine for Young People, pp. 10-20. **SUBJECTS/PLAY TYPE:** Women's Rights; Comedy.

150. 6-12. (+) Traktman, Peggy Simon. **Are there alligators in the sewers of the city of New York? CAST:** 1f, 3m. **ACTS:** 2. **SETTINGS:** Sidewalk; sewers. **PLAYING TIME:** NA. **PLOT:** Teenagers descend into the sewers of New York City in search of alligators. They encounter bank robber/snake charmer Ali Carpo who is hiding out after robbing a bank. He is protected by his three snakes and seems invincible but is finally scared by a large green alligator - actually the kids in costume. He exits from the sewer into the arms of the waiting police. **RECOMMENDATION:** The Halloween motif, the tough talking but not really despicable villain, and the clever ending will keep the audience thoroughly entertained. **ROYALTY:** $20. **SOURCE:** Traktman, Peggy Simon. (1980). Are there alligators in the sewers of the city of New York? Boston, MA: Baker's Plays. **SUBJECTS/PLAY TYPE:** Halloween; Adventure; Comedy.

151. 7-12. (+) Bradley, Virginia. **Arizona pilgrims. CAST:** 2f, 5m. **ACTS:** 1. **SETTINGS:** Shed. **PLAYING TIME:** NA. **PLOT:** On Thanksgiving, passengers are stranded after their small plane crashes in a sandstorm outside Phoenix. They find protection in an old shed, where indians rescue them. **RECOMMENDATION:** This serious play attempts to recreate a modern day setting of the first Thanksgiving. **ROYALTY:** None. **SOURCE:** Bradley, Virginia. (1981). Holidays on stage. New York, NY: Dodd, Mead. **SUBJECTS/PLAY TYPE:** Thanksgiving; Playlet.

152. 3-8. (+) Harris, Aurand. **Arkansaw bear. CAST:** 3f, 3m, 3u. **ACTS:** 1. **SETTINGS:** Bare stage. **PLAYING TIME:** NA. **PLOT:** A little girl has difficulty dealing with the impending death of her beloved grandfather. Her wish on a star brings a Mime and the world's greatest dancing bear. They help her understand that each of us will be remembered for what we teach the next generation, thereby becoming immortal. **RECOMMENDATION:** Use of bears, mime, and

circus symbolism help to tastefully explain death, but from a distance that children would be able to handle. Some of the more charming production touches (whistling, balloons, tree) and special effects might be difficult to achieve by a student theater group. ROYALTY: $35. SOURCE: Harris, Aurand. (1980). Arkansaw bear. New Orleans, LA: Anchorage Press, Inc. SUBJECTS/PLAY TYPE: Death; Drama.

153. 6-12. (+) Shaw, George Bernard. **Arms and the man.** CAST: 1f, 1m. ACTS: 1. SETTINGS: Terrace. PLAYING TIME: NA. PLOT: Major Petkoff and his wife discuss the latest requirements for being considered "civilized." Catherine insists that civilized people no longer shout at their servants. In turn, Major Petkoff informs his wife that civilized people no longer hang their wash to dry where visitors might see it. Catherine finds the idea absurd and comments that truly civilized people don't notice such things. RECOMMENDATION: This shows how modernization often proceeds at a pace faster than that to which people can adapt. It could be used as an analogy to today's technological revolution. ROYALTY: NA. SOURCE: Olfson, Lewy. (1980). Fifty great scenes for student actors. New York, NY: Bantam Books. SUBJECTS/PLAY TYPE: Modernization; Civilization; Scene.

154. 6-12. (+) Olfson, Lewy. (Verne, Jules) **Around the world in eighty days.** (Around the world in eighty days) CAST: 1f, 12m, 6u. ACTS: 1. SETTINGS: None. PLAYING TIME: 45 min. PLOT: Phileas Fogg wagers that he can go around the world in 80 days or less. Suspected of grand theft, he is pursued on his journey by the tenacious Detective Fix, who causes numerous delays. Fogg meets and becomes engaged to Princess Aouda of India. At the last minute, with the help of his manservant (heroic Passe Partout), Fogg arrives at the Reform Club with only seconds to spare, winning the prize. RECOMMENDATION: As an in class reading, this would hold the interest of the indicated audience. ROYALTY: Free to Plays subscribers. SOURCE: Olfson, Lewy. (1979). Around the world in eighty days. Plays: The Drama Magazine for Young People, pp. 70-80. SUBJECTS/PLAY TYPE: Adventure; Comedy; Reader's Theater. Adaptation.

155. 9-12. (+) Hulett, Michael. (Verne, Jules) **Around the world in eighty days.** (Around the world in eighty days) CAST: 4f, 12m, Su. ACTS: 1. SETTINGS: Foyer; train station; street; jungle; saloon; ship's deck. PLAYING TIME: 100 min. PLOT: Phileas Fogg bets his fortune that he can travel around the world in 80 days. Aided by his manservant, Passe Partout, and followed incognito by his fiancee Amanda, Fogg is also followed by Scotland Yard, which is convinced that he is a bankrobber. Fogg wins the wager, but realizes that time is not the most important aspect of life and he makes plans to marry Amanda the next day. RECOMMENDATION: For as few as seven actors or as many as the stage will allow, the main characters are endearing and well drawn. The six scene changes are challenging, but not impossible. ROYALTY: $35. SOURCE: Hulett, Michael.(1985). Around the world in

eighty days. Schulenberg, TX: I.E. Clark, Inc. SUBJECTS/PLAY TYPE: Adventure; Travel; Comedy; Adaptation.

156. 1-5. (+) Bradley, Alfred. (Bond, Michael) **The arrival of Paddington.** (The adventures of Paddington Bear) CAST: 3f, 2m, 2u. ACTS: 1. SETTINGS: Train station; living room. PLAYING TIME: NA. PLOT: Lovable Paddington shows up in a London train station as the Browns arrive home from a trip. They take the stowaway from darkest Peru home with them, where he begins a happy stay, despite his overflowing the bathtub. RECOMMENDATION: The slapstick antics of this bumbling bear are delightful again in this slightly British adaptation. ROYALTY: NA. SOURCE: Bradley, Alfred. (1977). Paddington on stage. Boston, MA: Houghton Mifflin. SUBJECTS/PLAY TYPE: Bears; Comedy; Adaptation.

157. 1-8. (+) Alderman, Elinor R. **As the bookworm turns.** CAST: 3f, 4m. ACTS: 1. SETTINGS: Living room. PLAYING TIME: 15 min. PLOT: The Bookworms are worried about their son because he hasn't been eating. As they discuss Junior's eating habits, they also discuss the relative nutritional merits of picture books (too rich), magazines (too unnutritious), and other types of reading/eating materials. They discover that Junior has been working overtime as an agent for the Bookworm Bureau of Investigation to uncover a gang of drugstore magazine rack-eating bookworms, and has been eating comic books away from home. RECOMMENDATION: This delightful Bookweek play has some sophisticated references (i.e. to Simon & Schuster) which will make it enjoyable for adults as well as children. ROYALTY: Free to Plays Subscribers. SOURCE: Alderman, Elinor R. (1980, November). As the bookworm turns. Plays: The Drama Magazine for Young People, pp. 33-38. SUBJECTS/PLAY TYPE: Reading; Book Week; Comedy.

158. 4-7. (-) Silverman, Eleanor. **As the globe trots.** CAST: 8f, 8m, 1u. ACTS: 2. SETTINGS: Doctor's office; dining room. PLAYING TIME: 10 min. PLOT: The butler did it with the help of the French maid and the cosmetics saleslady. But their narcotics smuggling ring in the Needlenose household is discovered by agents assigned to the case. RECOMMENDATION: This suffers from sexist and stereotypical roles and situations, as well as too many cast members. ROYALTY: NA. SOURCE: Silverman, Eleanor. (1983). Dramatics for children. Metuchen, NJ: Scarecrow Press. SUBJECTS/PLAY TYPE: Narcotics; Mystery; Comedy.

159. 8-10. (-) Olfson, Lewy. (Shakespeare, William) **As you like it.** (As you like it) CAST: 2f, 4m, 1u. ACTS: 1. SETTINGS: None. PLAYING TIME: NA. PLOT: Cousins Rosalind and Celia disguise themselves as a shepherd and a commoner in the forest. The man Rosalind loves professes his love for her while she is the "shepherd." They all reveal their true identities. RECOMMENDATION: Although this might be used as a brief introduction to Shakespeare, too much of the original is missing. ROYALTY: Free to Plays subscribers.

SOURCE: Olfson, Lewy. (1979, March). As you like it. Plays: The Drama Magazine for Young People, pp. 71-80. SUBJECTS/PLAY TYPE: Love; Reader's Theater; Adaptation.

160. 7-12. (+) Fisher, Aileen Lucia. **Ask Mr. Jefferson.** CAST: 2f, 3m, Su. ACTS: 1. SETTINGS: Library. PLAYING TIME: NA. PLOT: Students interview Thomas Jefferson about democracy and freedom in America. RECOMMENDATION: Jefferson answers the students' questions with phrases from our Constitution, providing a vivid and interesting dialogue. ROYALTY: Free to Plays subscribers. SOURCE: Fisher, Aileen Lucia. (1985). Year-round programs for young players. Boston, MA: Plays, Inc. SUBJECTS/PLAY TYPE: Jefferson, Thomas; Book Week; Constitution, U. S.; Playlet.

161. 11-12. (+) McDonough, Jerome. **Asylum.** CAST: 12u. ACTS: 1. SETTINGS: None. PLAYING TIME: 40 min. PLOT: A series of scenes that flow together explore the nature of normality and pose the thesis that individuals have a right to love as they see fit. RECOMMENDATION: Musical selections are the producer's prerogative although several are recommended. Roles are expandable and adaptable to either sex. The parts would challenge a young adult cast, especially if doubled, and the scenes could spark a great deal of discussion. ROYALTY: $20. SOURCE: McDonough, Jerome. (1975). Asylum. Schulenburg, TX: I.E. Clark, Inc. SUBJECTS/PLAY TYPE: Identity; Self Analysis; Drama.

162. 1-12. (+) Steinhorn, Harriet & Lowry, Edith. **At my bar mitzvah and his.** CAST: Su. ACTS: 1. SETTINGS: None. PLAYING TIME: 5 min. PLOT: A reader describes the traditional events of a young boy's bar mitzvah echoed by the chorus, which describes the same events during the holocaust. For example, the reader describes a young boy's acceptance of God; the chorus describes a young boy's questioning of God. RECOMMENDATION: Chilling contrasts sketch a technicolor picture of the horrors of the holocaust. ROYALTY: Free for amateur groups. SOURCE: Steinhorn, Harriet & Lowry, Edith. (1983). Shadows of the holocaust: Plays, readings, and program resources. Rockville, MD: Kar-Ben Copies, Inc. SUBJECTS/PLAY TYPE: Holocaust; World War II; Bar Mitzvah; Choral Reading.

163. 1-6. (+) Bauer, Caroline Feller. (Lowry, Lois) **At the airport.** (Switcharound) CAST: 2f, 1m, Su. ACTS: 1. SETTINGS: Airport terminal. PLAYING TIME: NA. PLOT: At the airport, J.P. walks behind his sister and mother, pretending not to know them. Sister and mother are called to the security checkpoint where J.P. is surrounded by security guards, examining the contents of his suitcase. His sister says that they have never seen J. P. before in their lives. RECOMMENDATION: This clever dramatization of a child's desire to be someone else cleverly turns the tables to make its important point. ROYALTY: NA. SOURCE: Bauer, Caroline Feller. (1987). Presenting reader's theater; Plays and poems to read aloud. New York, NY: H.W. Wilson Co. SUBJECTS/PLAY TYPE: Identity; Airports; Reader's Theater.

164. 4-6. (+) Postma, Janice. **At the name of Jesus.** CAST: Su. ACTS: 1. SETTINGS: None. PLAYING TIME: 60 min. PLOT: This explains the meanings of the names ascribed to Jesus in Luke, Matthew, John, Isaiah, Zachariah, Acts, and Numbers. RECOMMENDATION: This is recommended for its simple language, the lesson it teaches, and the symbolism of children placing the different names of Jesus on a banner. ROYALTY: None. SOURCE: Hendricks, William & Vogel, Cora. (1983). Handbook of Christmas programs. Grand Rapids, MI: Baker Book House. SUBJECTS/PLAY TYPE: Christmas; Worship Program.

165. 9-12. (+) Hatton, Thomas J. **Atalanta.** CAST: 7f, 7m, Su. ACTS: 2. SETTINGS: Throne room; forest. PLAYING TIME: NA. PLOT: A savage boar ravages the Greek countryside, tearing up crops and killing peasants. The king offers half his kingdom and the hand of his daughter in marriage to the man who can kill the beast. This seems perfect until the maiden Atalanta helps kill the boar, wins half the kingdom, and marries the man of her choice. RECOMMENDATION: A humorous look at an ancient story adapted to modern feminist times. The tongue in cheek production will work best with much dramatic action and emphasis on diction so the lines are heard clearly. ROYALTY: $35. SOURCE: Hatton, Thomas J. (1981). Atalanta. Chicago, IL: Dramatic Pub. Co. SUBJECTS/PLAY TYPE: Mythology, Greek; Comedy.

166. 9-12. (+) Charles, R.A. Jr. **Attic treasures.** CAST: 1f, 1m. ACTS: 1. SETTINGS: Attic. PLAYING TIME: 15 min. PLOT: As Liz rummages through the attic, she remembers her first love, her mother's death, and her strained relationship with her son. The play ends as she realizes that although memories can be painful, they also allow her to relive good times. RECOMMENDATION: The play uses an old man as the symbol of memory, who relates Liz's memories to her, and discusses the past's role in the present. Unfortunately, the play ends too abruptly to make its point well, and the scenes with the son are too vague to be clearly understood. With some additional text, this could be superb. ROYALTY: Free to Plays subscribers. SOURCE: Charles, R.A. Jr. (1982, January/ February). Attic treasures. Plays: The Drama Magazine for Young People, pp. 9-14. SUBJECTS/PLAY TYPE: Memories; Playlet.

167. K-3. (+) Stockdale, Marina Call & Griffith, Martha T. **Aubrey the snowflake.** CAST: Su. ACTS: 1. SETTINGS: Cloud; tree; freezer; heart. PLAYING TIME: 30 min. PLOT: Aubrey, an enthusiastic snowflake, prematurely jumps from his cloud onto a testy maple leaf, which warns him that he will melt unless he finds a cold place to wait for winter. Aubrey is blown into a passing ice cream truck, where two ice cream bars warn him of daily defrostings. Aubrey is then inhaled by the

ice cream man, and lodges in the man's cold heart, where he is lonely and sad. He is saved when the man sneezes and blows him back outside just as winter arrives. RECOMMENDATION: Children will love the brave, cheerful snowflake. Both dialogue and songs are simple and poetic. Though the main characters are few, speaking parts may be expanded to include about 35 children. ROYALTY: $25. SOURCE: Stockdale, Marina Call & Griffith, Martha T. (1987). Aubrey the snowflake. Schulenburg, TX: I.E. Clark. SUBJECTS/PLAY TYPE: Winter; Snow; Musical.

168. 12. (+) Moeller, Ruby L. **August. CAST:** 7f, 5m. ACTS: NA. SETTINGS: Bare stage, props. PLAYING TIME: NA. PLOT: Home is the theme for poetry, songs, discussion, skits, and word games. The comic skits give examples of homes inhabited by the self absorbed, the adulterer, and the insensitive. RECOMMENDATION: Intended for a women's club, this is inappropriate for most adolescents, particularly due to the comic treatment of infidelity. The word games are clever and tricky, but "Combination Salas" might offend audience members by selecting the person with the biggest ears, reddest hair, etc. ROYALTY: NA. SOURCE: Moeller, Ruby L. (1975). Around the year programs. Boston, MA: Baker's Plays. SUBJECTS/PLAY TYPE: Family; Comedy.

169. 7-12. (+) Pawloski, Thelma Rae. (Pawloski, Thelma Rae) **Auntie Luv and the Christmas orphans.** (The ugliest Christmas tree) CAST: 21f, 20m, Su. ACTS: 3. SETTINGS: Meeting room. PLAYING TIME: NA. PLOT: Orphans and Auntie Luv prepare for the Christmas open house. The local doctor and his wife attend, where the snobbish and prejudiced wife declares she is taking over the orphanage to change it into a school. The local townspeople generously open their hearts to adopt the orphans into their families. RECOMMENDATION: The theme seems more appropriate for a church production, and adult producers will fare better, as the cast involves many people of different ages. Many props are needed and many traditional carols are incorporated into this hefty Christmas production. ROYALTY: $50. SOURCE: Pawloski, Thelma Rae. (1986). Auntie Luv and the Christmas orphans. Franklin, OH: Eldridge Pub. Co. SUBJECTS/PLAY TYPE: Christmas; Orphans; Generosity; Musical.

170. 4-8. (+) Kehret, Peg. **Auras. CAST:** 1u. ACTS: 1. SETTINGS: None. PLAYING TIME: NA. PLOT: A young person explains his theory that people are surrounded by auras of color which reflect their personalities. RECOMMENDATION: Child molestation and death are hinted at, and the concept of people as colors is well developed. ROYALTY: NA. SOURCE: Kehret, Peg. (1986). Winning monologs for young actors Colorado Springs, CO: Meriwether Pub. SUBJECTS/PLAY TYPE: Personalities; Monologue.

171. 6-10. (+) Hark, Mildred & McQueen, Noel. **Author of liberty. CAST:** 2f, 6m. ACTS: 1. SETTINGS: Parlor. PLAYING TIME: 30 min. PLOT: In

conversations with Benjamin Franklin, John Adams, and other famous figures, Thomas Jefferson discusses the Declaration of Independence and the best strategy to use in getting it passed. RECOMMENDATION: Although a bit "sugary," this historical account is interesting. Many personal characteristics of Jefferson are illuminated, making him seem much more real. ROYALTY: Free to Plays subscribers. SOURCE: Hark, Mildred & McQueen, Noel. (1987, October). Author of liberty. Plays: The Drama Magazine for Young People, pp. 14-24. SUBJECTS/PLAY TYPE: Declaration of Independence, U. S.; Jefferson, Thomas; Playlet.

172. 8-12. (+) McDonough, Jerome. **B.A.T.S. CAST:** 7f, 3m. ACTS: 2. SETTINGS: Parlor. PLAYING TIME: 60 min. PLOT: The widow and the mistress of the late Angelo Baroni (former big time Chicago gangster), are dismayed when the new owner of the local cemetery plans to move it because Angelo and other family members are buried there. The ladies are successful in blocking the proposed move with the help of tenants of the Baroni house, including an extremely shy, would be terrorist, a man chasing woman, the surly butler/handy man who is Baroni's ex-hitman, and a newscaster who falls in love with Baroni's granddaughter. RECOMMENDATION: With a predictable plot, the action and dialogue of this zany, fast paced play are entertaining and humorous. Two temperamental elevators, one of which responds only to Country Western music and one which responds to Rock and Roll, produce door slamming, brake screeching, and crashing sounds available on a sound effects tape from the publisher. ROYALTY: NA. SOURCE: McDonough, Jerome. (1988). B.A.T.S. Schulenberg, TX: I.E. Clark SUBJECTS/PLAY TYPE: Satire; Redevelopment; Comedy.

173. K-4. (+) Mahlman, Lewis. Jones, David Cadwalader. **Baba Yaga. CAST:** 7u. ACTS: 1. SETTINGS: Cottage; kitchen; garden. PLAYING TIME: 25 min. PLOT: Maruska's mother sends her to buy mushrooms for dinner, warning her to stay away from witch Baba Yaga's house. She stops to pick flowers, loses the mushroom money, and since she has been bad, Baba Yaga catches her. Baba Yaga also captures a hedgehog, who relates the story of his enchantment at birth from a prince to an animal. Maruska asks so many questions that the witch becomes old (she ages ten years for every question), dies, and breaks the hedgehog/prince's spell. RECOMMENDATION: This delightful rendition is especially endearing because when the prince expectedly asks Maruska to marry him and live happily ever after, she unexpectedly tells him "one day, perhaps. But I'm still much too young." ROYALTY: Free to Plays subscribers. SOURCE: Mahlman, Lewis & Jones, David Cadwalader. (1980). Folk tale plays for puppets. Boston, MA: Plays, Inc. SUBJECTS/PLAY TYPE: Folk Tales, Russia; Witches; Puppet Play.

174. 5-7. (+) Priore, Frank V. **The babbling boom-box. CAST:** 1f, 5m. ACTS: 1. SETTINGS: Park. PLAYING TIME: 20 min. PLOT: Teenagers compare

"boom-boxes" until Clinton, the electronics wizard, arrives with "Barry," a giant portable radio that can tune in any station in the world, repair itself, and carry on conversations. "Barry" introduces a reluctant teenager to classical music, and the teen turns "Barry" on to rock music. RECOMMENDATION: Contemporary dialogue and theme will appeal since boom-boxes have a variety of regional names and since the electronics industry is so dynamic; directors will have to edit and update dialogue so this does not become dated. ROYALTY: Free to Plays subscribers. SOURCE: Priore, Frank V. (1985, May). The babbling boom-box. Plays: The Drama Magazine for Young People, pp. 55-60. SUBJECTS/PLAY TYPE: Radios; Boom-Boxes; Skit.

175. K-6*. (+) Holaman, Ken. (Herbert, Victor & MacDonough, Glen) **Babes in toyland.** (Babes in toyland.) CAST: 13f, 12m, Su. ACTS: 2. SETTINGS: Town square; forest; toymaker's workshop. PLAYING TIME: NA. PLOT: Villain Barnaby holds all the mortgages in Mother Goose Village, evicts Mother Goose from her shoe, contrives to drown Tom-Tom so that Contrary Mary will marry him instead, and bans every mention of Christmas. Tom-Tom seeks help from the Master Toymaker. He and Mary save the day and return to Mother Goose Village with a bag of gold and the Toymaker's blessing. RECOMMENDATION: In this wonderful adaptation, the lyrics and dancing are upbeat, and familiar storybook characters will entrance children. The costumes and sets are extravagant. It is suggested that the play be produced by adults for younger audiences. ROYALTY: $75. SOURCE: Holaman, Ken. (1988). Babes in toyland. New Orleans, LA: Anchorage Press, Inc. SUBJECTS/PLAY TYPE: Christmas; Mother Goose Characters; Musical; Adaptation.

176. K-12. (+) Jackson, R. Eugene & Alette, Carl. (Herbert, Victor & MacDonough, Glen) **Babes in toyland.** (Babes in toyland) CAST: 6f, 13m, 20u. ACTS: 2. SETTINGS: Town; toyland. PLAYING TIME: 75 min. PLOT: Alan is supposedly drowned and nursery rhyme characters are distressed. Alan's miserly Uncle Barnaby, who will inherit Alan's fortune, is glad to hear that Alan will no longer be competing for Mistress Mary's hand. Realizing they are to be victims of further plots, Alan and Mary escape to Toyland through the perilous Spider's Forest. They encounter further attempts on their lives by bumbling assassins. Inspector Marmaduke of the Toyland Police captures the villains. RECOMMENDATION: Although this features nursery rhyme characters, the level of dialogue, music, and action, if combined with creative scenery and costumes, will provide entertainment for audiences of all ages. ROYALTY: $75. SOURCE: Jackson, R. Eugene & Alette, Carl. (1987). Babes in toyland. Schulenburg, TX: I.E. Clark. SUBJECTS/PLAY TYPE: Christmas; Mother Goose Characters; Musical; Adaptation.

177. 1-8*. (+) Perry, Ruth & Smit, Ann. (Herbert, Victor & MacDonough, Glenn) **Babes in toyland.** (Babes in toyland) CAST: 14f, 10m, 6u. ACTS: 1. SETTINGS: Living room; ship deck; woods. PLAYING TIME: NA. PLOT: Mean Uncle Barnaby schemes to steal the toy factory from his orphaned niece and nephew, Jane and Alan. Barnaby plans to make real children into "special dolls" and sell them to Santa Claus. He has already kidnapped three of Widow Riper's children and shipped them on approval. Meanwhile, he orders Jane and Alan left in Spider Valley where he assumes they will die. They are saved by the Moth Queen. Barnaby is exposed, the children saved, and Alan and Jane are assured of their inheritance, the toyshop. RECOMMENDATION: This is an ambitious play with a large cast, many scene changes and several lengthy musical numbers. The nursery rhyme characters will be recognized and enjoyed by younger audiences. ROYALTY: $60. SOURCE: Perry, Ruth & Smit, Ann. (1978). Babes in toyland. Woodstock, IL: Dramatic Pub. Co. SUBJECTS/PLAY TYPE: Christmas; Nursery Rhyme Characters; Musical; Adaptation.

178. 8-12. (+) Davidson, Conrad E. **Baby.** CAST: 4f, 4m, 3u. ACTS: 1. SETTINGS: Bare stage, props. PLAYING TIME: NA. PLOT: Before birth, Coach tutors Baby on proper conduct. After birth, Baby cannot cope with Daddy's perpetual vocabulary lessons, Grandma's bad breath, or being tossed in the air. Coach, called back to help, assures Baby he can put up with his family, urges Baby to "give it to them with both barrels," and says he cannot help anymore as he has others to coach. RECOMMENDATION: Since this gently pokes fun at parenting, it may appeal more to parents. ROYALTY: $15. SOURCE: Davidson, C. E.(1983). Baby. New York, NY: Samuel French. SUBJECTS/PLAY TYPE: Satire; Babies; Comedy.

179. 7-12. (+) Sawyer-Young, Kat. **Baby.** CAST: 1f. ACTS: 1. SETTINGS: None. PLAYING TIME: 1 min. PLOT: Debbi is furious that her mother is having a fourth baby and vows never to have any herself. RECOMMENDATION: This humorously verbalizes the feelings of many teenagers. ROYALTY: None. SOURCE: Sawyer-Young, Kat. (1987). Minute monologues for contemporary teens. Boston, MA: Baker's Plays. SUBJECTS/PLAY TYPE: Motherhood; Monologue.

180. 1-8. (+) Whittaker, Violet. **Baby Moses.** CAST: 7u. ACTS: 4. SETTINGS: River; yard. PLAYING TIME: NA. PLOT: The story of how the baby Moses was saved, and why the Pharoah wished to kill all the Hebrew babies is told. The play ends, admonishing the audience to believe in Jesus if they wish to be protected by God the way Moses was. RECOMMENDATION: With detailed technical/production directions, this will be challenging and enjoyable to produce and watch. With some changes of the dialogue, this could easily be nondenominational. ROYALTY: NA. SOURCE: Whittaker, Violet. (1984). Puppet people scripts. Grand Rapids, MI: Baker Book House. SUBJECTS/PLAY TYPE: Moses; Christian Drama; Puppet Play.

181. 9-12. (+) Shamus, Laura Annawyn. (Fitzgerald, F. Scott) **Babylon revisited.** (Babylon revisited). CAST: 5f, 4m. ACTS: 1. SETTINGS: Living room; restaurant. PLAYING TIME: NA. PLOT: A man returns to Paris for

his nine year old daughter who has been living with her aunt and uncle since the death of her mother. He tries to convince them that he is no longer an alcoholic. Final arrangements are about to be made when the father learns he has to wait six more months to try to regain custody. He is left alone with his sorrow and guilt. RECOMMENDATION: Thought provoking, the problem of a child being separated from a parent has no time or place limitations. This also provides a thoughtful examination of the damage caused by alcoholism. ROYALTY: $20. SOURCE: Shamus, Laura Annawyn. (1984). Babylon revisited. Chicago, IL: Dramatic Pub. Co. SUBJECTS/PLAY TYPE: Parenthood; Alcoholism; Adaptation.

182. 7-10. (+) Dias, Earl J. **Bad day at Rock Bottom.** CAST: 4f, 6m. ACTS: 1. SETTINGS: Lobby. PLAYING TIME: 30 min. PLOT: Chief Big Elk and his daughter ask Sheriff Sam Strong to help find the people stealing sheep from the reservation. Investigation reveals that the culprits tried to frighten the Indians off their oil rich land. The Indians are given money to replace their goods, and the villains are arrested. RECOMMENDATION: A delightful spoof on an old western melodrama, the characters are individuals and the good guys aren't always good. Turns of events make the play very interesting. For example, Miss Lydia, who turns down all proposals of marriage, is left waiting at the altar while Maisie, the good hearted dance hall girl, marries the Sheriff. ROYALTY: Free to Plays subscribers. SOURCE: Dias, Earl J. (1979, January). Bad Day at Rock Bottom. Plays: The Drama Magazine for Young People, pp. 1-13. SUBJECTS/PLAY TYPE: Western; Melodrama.

183. 7-12. (+) McNally, Terrence. **Bad Habits.** CAST: 2f, 1m. ACTS: 1. SETTINGS: Park. PLAYING TIME: NA. PLOT: Nurse Benson, who is close to achieving "perfection" (a fully positive self image), and is certain she knows what is right for everyone, offers encouragement and advice to Nurse Hedges, who has feelings of inferiority and often snivels. She drives Hedges to try suicide. After a brief struggle, Nurse Benson subdues Nurse Hedges, pulls out a hidden cigarette, and prepares to smoke, revealing one bad habit she has yet to give up. RECOMMENDATION: If played for comedic effect, this scene entertainingly points out that that a few bad habits are all right. Timing is very important as the actresses play off each other. ROYALTY: NA. SOURCE: Handman, Wynn. (1980). Modern American scenes for student actors. New York, NY: Bantam Books. SUBJECTS/PLAY TYPE: Self Image; Scene.

184. 9-12. (-) Dresner, Harmon & Lubin, Shellen. **Bad news.** CAST: 6f, 4m. ACTS: 2. SETTINGS: Football stadium. PLAYING TIME: NA. PLOT: Chunk Brady, star player and captain of the football team, is flunking Spanish and may only play in the big game if he passes his midterm. Joy tutors him and her romantic inspiration helps him pass, but the Spanish instructor accuses him of cheating. Joy convinces the instructor to give Chunk the test again. Chunk once again passes, rushes in at halftime, and wins for Hinkson.

RECOMMENDATION: This collection of cliches and stereotypes contains no surprises. The dated slang, attitudes and wardrobe may evoke a response from those who grew up in the 40's and 50's, but will not hold much interest for a contemporary high school cast or audience. ROYALTY: Upon application. SOURCE: Dresner, Harmon & Lubin, Shellen. (1981). Bad news. Woodstock, IL: Dramatic Pub. Co. SUBJECTS/PLAY TYPE: Football; Colleges; Exams; Musical.

185. 6-8*. (+) Eminhizer, James A. Jr. & Hynes, Michael R. **The bad, the worse, and the broccoli, or the Green Baron's revenge.** CAST: 5f, 5m. ACTS: 1. SETTINGS: Health food bar. PLAYING TIME: 25 min. PLOT: Baron Von Broccoli wants to marry Sally Sweet so he can gain access to the water on her land for his broccoli fields. He hires a professional gunman, Caesar Salad to get rid of rival beau, Buffalo Bill. During their showdown, Caesar is shot. Before he dies, he tells Buffalo Bill of the Baron's plan. As the Baron and Buffalo fight, Sally frees herself and holds a gun on them. Buffalo Bill offers her a simple peaceful life and the Baron offers her 25 million dollars. The choice is easy: Sally chooses the Baron. RECOMMENDATION: The hardest part of producing this western wrapped in a vegetable motif will be casting; it will need at least high school age actors to carry the humor. ROYALTY: $30. SOURCE: Eminhizer, James A. & Hynes, Michael R. (1973). The bad, the worse, and the broccoli, or the Green Baron's revenge. Franklin, OH: Eldridge Pub. Co. SUBJECTS/PLAY TYPE: Western; Vegetables; Comedy.

186. 10-12. (+) Patrick, John. **A bad year for tomatoes.** CAST: 4f, 3m. ACTS: 2. SETTINGS: Living room. PLAYING TIME: NA. PLOT: TV actress Myra Marlowe hides in a Vermont village to write her autobiography. To rid her home of a procession of distractors, she invents a mad sister supposedly held in a locked room upstairs. The plan goes awry and Myra is accused of killing the nonexistent sister. Her agent returns in time to rescue her from the sheriff and to propose marriage. RECOMMENDATION: With dialogue that reads like a television sit-com, the humorous techniques are predictable, but because one joke follows on the heel of another, the listener may be forgiving. ROYALTY: $50. SOURCE: Patrick, John. (1975). A bad year for tomatoes. New York, NY: Dramatists Play Service. SUBJECTS/PLAY TYPE: Privacy; Stardom; Comedy.

187. K-5. (-) McDonough, Jerome. **The baddest angel band.** CAST: 10f, 4m, 14u. ACTS: 1. SETTINGS: None. PLAYING TIME: 30 min. PLOT: Three angels are sent to Earth at Christmas to find something redeeming about people. Although selfishness at first appears to be humans' primary characteristic, an emergency brings out the peoples' better sides. RECOMMENDATION: Children may find bits of the play funny, but they may not understand the whole. Frequent character and scene changes will be confusing for youngsters in the audience, and junior high or older will be bored with the simplistic plot and elementary humor. ROYALTY: $15. SOURCE: McDonough,

Jerome. (1985). The baddest angel band. Denver, CO: Pioneer Drama Service. SUBJECTS/PLAY TYPE: Christmas; Angels; Comedy.

188. 6-12. (+) Murray, John. **Badlands ballyhoo.** CAST: 3f, 7m, Su. ACTS: 1. SETTINGS: Restaurant. PLAYING TIME: 30 min. PLOT: Graveyard Gulch awaits new sheriff candidates. The first to arrive is Dead-Eye Dan, an arrogant show-off, who runs from town menace, Monster Malloy. The second candidate, Horace Whiffletree, a somewhat naive ornithologist, uses a secret technique of inner captivation he learned from his feathered friends and turns Malloy into a rooster. Horace pledges to clean up the town. RECOMMENDATION: This frolicsome, offbeat western features wonderful characterization. The numerous props needed for character development as well as background may cause some problems for smaller groups. ROYALTY: Free to Plays subscribers. SOURCE: Murray, John. (1976, January). Badlands ballyhoo. Plays: The Drama Magazine for Young People, pp. 21-32. SUBJECTS/PLAY TYPE: Western; Sheriffs; Comedy.

189. K-6. (+) Korty, Carol. (Tenenbaum, Samuel) **Bag of gold.** (Wise men of Chelm) CAST: 3u. ACTS: 1. SETTINGS: Bare stage, props. PLAYING TIME: NA. PLOT: Owners of a bag of gold stop at an inn. Fearing a robbery, they trade the gold for bags of air and proudly congratulate themselves for their shrewdness. RECOMMENDATION: Shrewd humor which allows the audience to feel superior, as well as hilarious physical comedy combine for an easily ad-libbed performance. ROYALTY: None. SOURCE: Korty, Carol. (1977). Silly soup: Ten zany plays. New York, NY: Charles Scribner's Sons. SUBJECTS/PLAY TYPE: Gold; Comedy; Skit; Adaptation.

190. 9-12. (+) Kinoy, Ernest & Marks, Walter. (Mitchell, Joseph) **Bajour.** (Based on **New Yorker** stories) CAST: 8f, 9m, Su. ACTS: 2. SETTINGS: Empty store; police station; kitchen; bedroom; museum. PLAYING TIME: NA. PLOT: An anthropology student lives with and studies a band of gypsies as they, unbeknownst to her, pull off a swindle (a "Bajour") involving her mother. The student and the policeman in charge of the case fall in love, and the stolen money is returned. RECOMMENDATION: The gypsies are unrelentingly, and without apology, the best thieves they can be. The musical is alive with much song and dance. Romantic interludes are best accomplished by older students. ROYALTY: NA SOURCE: Kinoy, Ernest & Walter Marks. (1976). Bajour. Chicago, IL: Dramatic Pub. Co. SUBJECTS/PLAY TYPE: Gypsies; Romance; Anthropology; Musical.

191. 2-6. (+) Biskin, Miriam. **The baker's dozen.** CAST: 3f, 3m, 3u. ACTS: 1. SETTINGS: Bakery. PLAYING TIME: 20 min. PLOT: A baker and his family are cursed by a witch, who demands 13 instead of 12 cookies when she orders a dozen. The friendly spirit of Kris Kringle shows the baker how to break the spell by treating the witch nicely. She is destroyed, and the man

has no more bad luck. RECOMMENDATION: This dual story of Christmas spirit and the origin of the term, a "baker's dozen" provides a good alternative to more well known Christmas stories. ROYALTY: Free to Plays subscribers. SOURCE: Biskin, Miriam. (1981, December). The baker's dozen. Plays: The Drama Magazine for Young People, pp. 61-66. SUBJECTS/PLAY TYPE: Christmas; Bakers; Generosity; Skit.

192. K-3. (+) Thane, Adele. **The baker's neighbor.** CAST: 6f, 4m, Su. ACTS: 1. SETTINGS: Street. PLAYING TIME: 15 min. PLOT: Manuel demands that Pablo pay for smelling his baked goods every day. A judge instructs Pablo to give his life savings to Manuel to count, pointing out that Manuel gets as much pleasure from counting money as Pablo gets from smelling the baked goods. He encourages Manuel to think more about making friends than making money. RECOMMENDATION: An interesting interlude here involves two of the characters playing a game where they decide what they'd like to be if they weren't a person. This, along with the message about the value of intangibles, will provoke discussion and new perceptions of reality. ROYALTY: NA. SOURCE: Kamerman, Sylvia E. (1987). Plays from favorite folk tales. Boston, MA: Plays, Inc. SUBJECTS/PLAY TYPE: Values; Folk Tale Motifs; Playlet.

193. 3-6. (+) Simon, Shirley. **The baking contest.** CAST: 6f, 3m, Su. ACTS: 1. SETTINGS: Palace courtyard. PLAYING TIME: 20 min. PLOT: An ordinary looking girl of good character and kind disposition triumphs over her two gorgeous, scheming cousins in a baking contest to determine the Prince's new bride. RECOMMENDATION: This simply, but effectively promotes self effacing honesty, hard work, and fair play. Although the bride is to be chosen on the basis of her good looks and cooking abilities, this can be forgiven, given the overall merit. ROYALTY: Free to Plays subscribers. SOURCE: Simon, Shirley. (1978, February). The baking contest. Plays: The Drama Magazine for Young People, pp. 65-70. SUBJECTS/PLAY TYPE: Values; Folk Tale Motifs; Playlet.

194. 6-10. (+) Kehret, Peg. **The bald eagle.** CAST: 1u. ACTS: 1. SETTINGS: None. PLAYING TIME: NA. PLOT: A young person describes the beauty and freedom of a bald eagle sighted in the wild. RECOMMENDATION: A touching view of our national bird, this could be used as part of a lesson on national symbols or wildlife conservation. ROYALTY: NA. SOURCE: Kehret, Peg. (1986). Winning monologs for young actors. Colorado Springs, CO: Meriwether Pub. SUBJECTS/PLAY TYPE: Bald Eagles; Wildlife Conservation; Patriotism; Monologue.

195. K-6. (+) Gotwalt, Helen Louise Miller. **The balky bike.** CAST: 5f, 10m. ACTS: 1. SETTINGS: Police station. PLAYING TIME: 25 min. PLOT: A bicycle at the police station will only move for a safe rider. The Bicycle Safety Squad recites the rules for safe biking, and it rolls. They leave the bike at the police station to be

used as a safety test for future bike riders. RECOMMENDATION: As a teaching tool for bicycle safety, this might work, if additional safety tips were added to the list. ROYALTY: Free to Plays subscribers. SOURCE: Gotwalt, Helen Louise Miller. (1977, March). The balky bike. Plays: The Drama Magazine for Young People, pp. 49- 57. SUBJECTS/PLAY TYPE: Bicycle Safety; Playlet.

196. 5-8. (+) Kelly, Tim. **The ballad of Gopher Gap.** CAST: 6f, 5m, Su. ACTS: 1. SETTINGS: Assay office. PLAYING TIME: 60 min. PLOT: Swindlers try to trick some visiting Easterners into investing in the Sperawampum Mine. A dashing hero, demure heroine, fearless newspaperwoman, and the local crazy lady save the money and the day. RECOMMENDATION: This has puns and corny jokes, some parody, and a generous amount of confusion and action. Some editing to eliminate offensive sexist comments is advised. ROYALTY: $25. SOURCE: Kelly, Tim. (1984). The ballad of Gopher Gap. Denver, CO: Pioneer Drama Service. SUBJECTS/PLAY TYPE: Comedy; Western; Comedy.

197. 10-12+. (+) Martin, Herb & Davis, Sheila. (Owen, Guy) **The ballad of the flim flam man.** (The ballad of the flim flam man) CAST: 6f, 11m, Su. ACTS: 2. SETTINGS: Bare stage. PLAYING TIME: NA. PLOT: Con-man Mordecai Jones and his accomplice, naive Curley Jones, pull off several scams, including a card trick, a traveling preacher impersonation, and a fake bond sale. Curley falls in love and wants to stop his life of crime, but is intrigued by Mordecai and his schemes. He decides to commit himself to Bonnie Lee and the straight life, and escapes punishment for his part in the scams by pointing out that everyone is equally guilty of greed. Mordecai Jones manages to avoid capture and continues his career as the flim flam man. RECOMMENDATION: The play requires actors who can sing and dance and keep up a fast patter of dialogue and "asides," but it could be performed by talented high school students. ROYALTY: NA. SOURCE: Martin, Herb & Davis, Sheila. (1977). The ballad of the flim flam man. Chicago, IL: Dramatic Pub. Co. SUBJECTS/PLAY TYPE: Greed; Con- Artists; Musical.

198. 3-6. (+) Asher, Sandra Fenichel. **The ballad of two who flew.** CAST: 4f, 9m, Su. ACTS: 1. SETTINGS: Courtyard. PLAYING TIME: 15 min. PLOT: America's first hydrogen air balloon voyage by Frenchman Jean Pierre Blanchard and Douffle, is described in ballad form by four narrators. A crowd, including four of our country's founding fathers, gives great significance to the flight, while the fear of the crowd witnessing the strange landing in New Jersey is allayed by Douffle. RECOMMENDATION: With its short dialogue, this will be within the abilities of most young actors, although the role of Monsieur Blanchard will be a challenge, as many of his lines are in French. ROYALTY: Free to Plays subscribers. SOURCE: Asher, Sandra Fenichel. (1976, March). The ballad of two who flew. Plays: The Drama Magazine for Young People, pp. 71-76. SUBJECTS/PLAY TYPE: Flight; Skit.

199. K-2*. (+) Way, Brian & Faulkes, Margaret. **Balloon faces.** CAST: 2f, 2m. ACTS: 1. SETTINGS: Bare stage. PLAYING TIME: NA. PLOT: A narrator guides the audience to the land of balloons to save them from deflating by making "magic music." RECOMMENDATION: Because the players must lead and maintain control of the audience participation, they should be adults experienced in experimental drama. ROYALTY: $20. SOURCE: Way, Brian & Faulkes, Margaret. (1977). Balloon faces. Boston, MA: Baker's Plays. SUBJECTS/PLAY TYPE: Balloons; Musical; Participation Play.

200. 9-12. (+) Brill, Michael Elliot. **Bamboozled!** CAST: 1f, 7m, 1u. ACTS: 1. SETTINGS: Street between two houses. PLAYING TIME: NA. PLOT: Brighella and Harlequin unsuccessfully try to help Leandro win Columbine away from the miser Pantalone, whom her father desires as a son-in-law. RECOMMENDATION: This hilarious comedy allows for acting spontaneity and will keep the audience in stitches. There are some substantial parts, so dedicated actors with good memories and a fine sense of timing are essential. ROYALTY: $35. SOURCE: Brill, Michael Elliot. (1985). Bamboozled. New Orleans, LA: Anchorage Press, Inc. SUBJECTS/PLAY TYPE: Slapstick; Harlequin Commedia; Farce.

201. 2-4. (-) Gotwalt, Helen Louise Miller. **Bandit Ben rides again.** CAST: 8f, 12m. ACTS: 1. SETTINGS: Ranch house. PLAYING TIME: NA. PLOT: Cowboys and Indians capture a bandit who is punished by being made into the TV bad man of the westerns. RECOMMENDATION: The number of songs make this a challenge for youngsters to perform, and stereotyped Indians, men and women, give this a sexist and racist tone. ROYALTY: Free to Plays subscribers. SOURCE: Gotwalt, Helen Louise Miller. (1986). Everyday Plays for Boys and Girls. Boston, MA: Plays, Inc. SUBJECTS/PLAY TYPE: Native Americans; Cowboys; Western; Playlet.

202. K-4. (+) Bauer, Caroline Feller. (Smith, William Jay) **Banjo tune.** (Banjo tune) CAST: 1m. ACTS: 1. SETTINGS: None. PLAYING TIME: 2 min. PLOT: A banjo player sings about his wife, locked in an old trunk in an attic. RECOMMENDATION: This is a lyrical, nonsensical choral reading, which includes audience participation and pantomime. ROYALTY: None. SOURCE: Bauer, Caroline Feller. (1987). Presenting reader's theater: Plays and poems to read aloud. New York, NY: H.W. Wilson. SUBJECTS/PLAY TYPE: Choral Reading; Adaptation.

203. 7-12. (+) Thomsen, John Graham. **Bar the door!** CAST: 3f, 4m, Su. ACTS: 1. SETTINGS: Living room. PLAYING TIME: NA. PLOT: Five teenagers cast a spell from an ancient book. Later, Arthur, one of the group, drowns. The others try to call back the dead and are successful. They are scared and refuse to let Arthur into the house. The doctor arrives shortly, carrying the dead Arthur in his arms and pronounces the time of death as

long ago. The teens are never sure what happened when they cast the spell, but decide to burn the book. **RECOMMENDATION:** Given an interest in the supernatural, an audience might be fascinated by this horror story. However, the language and slang are stilted and dated, and often the play fails to set a convincingly horrific tone. **ROYALTY:** $15. **SOURCE:** Thomsen, John Graham. (1978). Bar the door! Chicago, IL: Dramatic Pub. Co. **SUBJECTS/PLAY TYPE:** Supernatural; Thriller.

204. 7-9. (+) Kehret, Peg. **The bargain. CAST:** 1f. **ACTS:** 1. **SETTINGS:** None. **PLAYING TIME:** NA. **PLOT:** A young girl is convinced by her mother to join her in a painting project, a bargain at the two-for-one price. It turns out to be a very costly bargain, as usual, with the crafts being foisted upon a hapless grandmother, and a silent vow taken: never again! **RECOMMENDATION:** By relating this situation to other similar ones, young listeners learn to see through useless and costly "bargains." **ROYALTY:** NA. **SOURCE:** Kehret, Peg. (1986). Winning monologs for young actors. Colorado Springs, CO: Meriwether Pub. **SUBJECTS/PLAY TYPE:** Bargains; Monologue.

205. 7-12. (-) Murray, John. **Bargain day. CAST:** 1f. **ACTS:** 1. **SETTINGS:** Department store. **PLAYING TIME:** NA. **PLOT:** A housewife attends a department store sale and encounters one frustration after another while trying to make purchases. **RECOMMENDATION:** The housewife is unpleasantly stereotyped, the tone of the monologue is shrill, and the humor is forced. **ROYALTY:** None. **SOURCE:** Murray, John.(1982). Modern monologues for young people. Boston, MA: Plays, Inc. **SUBJECTS/PLAY TYPE:** Shopping; Monologue.

206. 1-3. (+) Blumenfeld, Lenore. **Barnaby the brave. CAST:** 2f, 8m, 2u. **ACTS:** 1. **SETTINGS:** Street. **PLAYING TIME:** 20 min. **PLOT:** Timid Barnaby travels to another town to find a job. He spends all night baking pies for triple wages, but his new employer gives him three pieces of advice as payment, instead of money. Barnaby reaches home, and when he breaks a loaf of bread as his employer instructed him, he finds that it is full of money. **RECOMMENDATION:** Barnaby is a likable ninny and his wife an excellent foil with her calm, matter of fact attitude. **ROYALTY:** Free to Plays subscribers. **SOURCE:** Blumenfeld, Lenore. (1982, October). Barnaby the brave. Plays: The Drama Magazine for Young People, pp. 44-50. **SUBJECTS/PLAY TYPE:** Folk Tale Motifs; Playlet.

207. 1-6*. (+) Pearson, Ken. **Barnji and the bear. CAST:** 5f, 7m, 1u. **ACTS:** 1. **SETTINGS:** Bare stage, props. **PLAYING TIME:** NA. **PLOT:** Barnji and his bear are shipwrecked in a storm. Barnji encounters Aki, a steward to the Danish king, who demands half ownership of the bear in exchange for food and shelter. When the king learns of Aki's behavior, he orders Aki to be Barnji's servant for one year. Leaving his bear with the king, Barnji sets out on a religious pilgrimage to Rome with a chest of gold from the king. This money is a great temptation to Aki, and his repeated plots to steal it make

up most of the action of the play. He returns to Denmark and the Norwegian king tries to convert Denmark to Christianity. Barnji persuades the two kings to declare a truce, and to allow religious freedom. The play ends with dancing, and plans for Barnji and an orphan girl to marry. **RECOMMENDATION:** Suggested by the Icelandic saga, "Autaun and the Bear," this is light, humorous, and uses audience participation to break up the length and provide a release of energy. The narrator interacts with the audience, making asides and encouraging children to boo the villain, give advice to the hero, and call for the magic bear. The role of the narrator is long and complex. **ROYALTY:** NA. **SOURCE:** Pearson, Ken. (1985). Barnji and the bear. Cheshire, England: New Playwrights Network. **SUBJECTS/PLAY TYPE:** Legends, Iceland; Fantasy.

208. K-3. (+) Gotwalt, Helen Louise Miller. **The bashful bunny. CAST:** 1f, 1m, 4u. **ACTS:** 1. **SETTINGS:** Woods. **PLAYING TIME:** 15 min. **PLOT:** When Peter Cottontail gets sick before the big egg hunt, his son must deliver the eggs. But Peter Junior is extremely shy and the thought of delivering the baskets in front of many people makes him very nervous. He meets an equally shy girl, Sherry, who is terrified that she has to recite a poem at the Easter Egg Hunt. Sherry helps Peter Junior by walking with him as he delivers eggs, and Peter Junior helps Sherry by standing where she can see him during her poem, wiggling his nose and flopping his ears. **RECOMMENDATION:** The two protagonists are especially concerned about their shyness because it has been mentioned on their report cards. This, along with realistic dialogue and an honest explanation of the characters' feelings, allows for very believable conflict and resolution. **ROYALTY:** Free to Plays subscribers. **SOURCE:** Gotwalt, Helen Louise Miller. (1987, April). The bashful bunny. Plays: The Drama Magazine for Young People, pp. 31- 37. **SUBJECTS/PLAY TYPE:** Easter; Shyness; Comedy.

209. K-5. (+) Ison, Colleen. **Basil is forgiven. CAST:** 1f, 1m, 5u. **ACTS:** 1. **SETTINGS:** Living/dining room. **PLAYING TIME:** NA. **PLOT:** Basil, the youngest of five children, isn't allowed to help with preparations for his mother's birthday party. In anger, he destroys the birthday cake. His siblings refuse to forgive him until their father reminds them that they have often been forgiven for the bad things that they have done. The play ends with Basil forgiven, and a reminder that God also forgives us. **RECOMMENDATION:** This does not downplay the severity of Basil's deed, but shows that after being punished, everyone should be forgiven. This well demonstrates the New Testament's concept of forgiving. Discussion questions are provided. **ROYALTY:** NA. **SOURCE:** Ison, Colleen. (1986). Goliath's last stand and fifteen more easy plays for children. Cincinnati, OH: Standard Pub. **SUBJECTS/PLAY TYPE:** Forgiveness; Christian Drama; Skit.

210. 3-6. (+) Gotwalt, Helen Louise Miller. **Baskets or bonnets. CAST:** 17f, 8m, 6u. **ACTS:** 1. **SETTINGS:** Park. **PLAYING TIME:** 15 min. **PLOT:** Mary Sunshine and Mother Nature prepare for Easter festivities. Pitter

and Patter, the boisterous raindrops, are forbidden to attend the Easter Parade. The cold, North Wind is restricted in favor of the warm West and South breezes. The North Wind snatches the new Easter bonnets from the heads of a group of festively attired children and the rabbits try to force the stolen hats over their long, floppy ears. Mother Nature chastises them and they realize that baskets are better for Easter duties than bonnets. As the North Wind returns the children's hats, the bunnies hide eggs. RECOMMENDATION: The large number of characters with small speaking parts (flowers, bunnies, etc.) lends a pageant like quality, making this ideal for production with large groups of young children. The theme emphasizes the idea that each individual plays a small but important role in life which he must perform to the best of his ability. ROYALTY: Free to Plays subscribers. SOURCE: Gotwalt, Helen Louise Miller. (1988, April). Baskets or bonnets. Plays: The Drama Magazine for Young People, pp. 44-49. SUBJECTS/PLAY TYPE: Easter; Comedy.

211. 7-12. (+) Britto, Betty. (Jarrell, Randall) The bat poet. (The bat poet) CAST: 12u. ACTS: 1. SETTINGS: Yard. PLAYING TIME: NA. PLOT: When Bat Poet, a free-spirited, nonconforming bat, stays awake one day, he describes, in poetry, his experiences and feelings. Technical poetic terms are introduced, and the attempt is made to show that emotion is the essence of poetry. RECOMMENDATION: A serious and sensitive attempt to explore the fundamental elements of poetry, this requires imaginative handling and talented acting. ROYALTY: NA. SOURCE: Britto, Betty. (1988). The bat poet. Schulenberg, TX: I.E. Clark. SUBJECTS/PLAY TYPE: Musical; Poetry; Adaptation.

212. 3-5. (+) Winther, Barbara. Bata, boy of ancient Egypt. CAST: 5f, 7m, 3u. ACTS: 1. SETTINGS: River. PLAYING TIME: 20 min. PLOT: As Bata seeks to learn the lessons of life, he is given a wife whose slip of the tongue reveals where Bata has hidden his soul, allowing his enemies to kill him. With the help of his brother, Bata comes back to life in the form of a bull, but again is captured and killed. The second time he returns to life beside the Nile River in the form of a papyrus plant. His wife, Lotus, in her remorse, asks to be with him and becomes a Lotus tree beside him. RECOMMENDATION: This adaptation of an Egyptian folk tale addresses the subjects of reincarnation and worship of Egyptian gods and goddesses. It could be used as an extension of a unit of study on religion/philosophy, literature, or social customs of the world. ROYALTY: Free to Plays subscribers. SOURCE: Winther, Barbara. (1978, May). Bata, boy of ancient Egypt. Plays: The Drama Magazine for Young People, pp. 42-48. SUBJECTS/PLAY TYPE: Reincarnation; Folk Tales, Egypt; Adaptation.

213. 7-12. (+) Winther, Barbara. Bata's lessons. CAST: 3f, 7m, Su. ACTS: 1. SETTINGS: Water and desert. PLAYING TIME: NA. PLOT: Bata dies while crossing the Nile to the land beyond and places his soul in the care of an acacia tree. Soldiers chop down the tree, kidnap Lotus, his wife, and make her queen of Egypt. The

gods reincarnate Bata two more times (as a bull and as a papyrus plant), but he is killed both times. Lotus, remorseful for not saving her husband, asks to be placed near him; thus, to this day, the lotus and papyrus are often seen growing side by side. RECOMMENDATION: A director with determination, imagination, and patience may find success in producing this somewhat brittle, symbolic story. Stage directions are complicated, the playwright has over peopled the Nile, and the main character's transformation into a bull may result in unwanted comedy. ROYALTY: Free for amateur performance. SOURCE: Winther, Barbara. (1976). Plays from folktales of Africa and Asia. Boston: Plays, Inc. SUBJECTS/PLAY TYPE: Folk Tales, Egypt; Playlet.

214. 10+. (+) Randazzo, Angela. Bats in the belfry. CAST: 8f, 6m, Su. ACTS: 2. SETTINGS: Parlor; dining room. PLAYING TIME: NA. PLOT: Four eccentric old ladies inform their unsuspecting niece, Pamela, that she is actually a black cat changed into a girl years ago by a warlock who is still around and up to no good. She refuses to believe them. On Halloween, the warlock appears, with plans to sacrifice Pamela's fiance in a Black Mass. White witches reverse the spells and render the warlock invisible and powerless. RECOMMENDATION: Reminiscent of Arsenic and Old Lace, this is a sophisticated and adroit mixture of the macabre and the humorous. The juxtaposition of the "normal" in the person of Pamela and the "strange" in the person of her four aunts is very effective and funny. The characters are appealing, if somewhat one dimensional and there is enough of the truly creepy to satisfy the horror fan. ROYALTY: $35. SOURCE: Randazzo, Angela. (1975). Bats in the belfry. Chicago, IL: Dramatic Pub. Co. SUBJECTS/PLAY TYPE: Halloween; Witches; Comedy.

215. K-5. (+) Ison, Colleen. The battle of the thoughts. CAST: Su. ACTS: 1. SETTINGS: Bare stage. PLAYING TIME: NA. PLOT: Two children with decisions to make think about their choices, as two armies, each representing their good and bad thoughts, symbolically fight with each other. In one case, the bad thoughts win; in the other, good thoughts win. The moral: if we listen to bad thoughts, it gets easier for them to win, but if we ask God for help, it is easier for good thoughts to win. RECOMMENDATION: The director might want to change the children's dilemmas to make them more relevant, but the vehicle of armies fighting concretely explains the battles that we all fight in our minds. The narrator tells the story as the children act it out. Discussion questions are provided. ROYALTY: NA. SOURCE: Ison, Colleen. (1986). Goliath's last stand: And fifteen more easy plays for children. Cincinnati, OH: Standard Pub. SUBJECTS/PLAY TYPE: Christian Drama; Good and Evil; Skit.

216. 1-8. (+) Givens, Shirley. Be on the winning team. CAST: 1f, 3m, 1u. ACTS: 6. SETTINGS: Living room; vacant lot; store. PLAYING TIME: NA. PLOT: Two boys accidentally break Mr. Cratchit's grocery store window. They agree to work off the debt. In spite of

Cratchit's sour disposition, they pray for him and work hard. When his window is vandalized, the boys clean it before Cratchit comes to work. He asks them why, and they tell him because they're Christians. He offers them permanent jobs, and they agree to work if he will start going to church. RECOMMENDATION: This well dramatizes the scripture passage about loving those who curse us and praying for those who persecute us. It would be an excellent Sunday school presentation. ROYALTY: NA. SOURCE: Whittaker, Violet. (1984). Puppet people scripts. Grand Rapids, MI: Baker Book House. SUBJECTS/PLAY TYPE: Christian Drama; Prayer; Puppet Play.

217. 10-12. (+) Anderson, Douglas. **The beams are creaking.** CAST: 2f, 8m. ACTS: 2. SETTINGS: Living room; cafe; prison cell; 15 suggestive locales. PLAYING TIME: NA. PLOT: As Hitler rises to power, Detrich Bonhoeffer, a German minister, becomes increasingly concerned about societal reorganization within Nazi Germany, the emergence of a dictatorship, persecution of the Jews, devastation of the war, and the control and interpretation of religious thought and doctrine. He participates in the resistance movement within Germany and in plots to kill Hitler. Although unsuccessful, Bonhoeffer is suspected of engineering the plot and is imprisoned. Evidence is later found to implicate him. The play concludes with members of the German Gestapo opening Bonhoeffer's cell door. RECOMMENDATION: With a flexible cast of up to 31, this combines white knuckle suspense with an inspiring climax, and is recommended for ambitious high school actors and directors. Dealing with the questions raised within the play and with settings comprising 15 "suggestive" locales presents a challenge. ROYALTY: NA. SOURCE: Anderson, Douglas. (1985). The beams are creaking. Boston, MA: Baker's Plays. SUBJECTS/PLAY TYPE: Germany; Church History; World War II; Drama.

218. 3-12. (+) Robinette, Joseph & Shaw, James R. (Jacobs, Joseph). **Beanstalk.** (Jack and the beanstalk) CAST: 4f, 5m. ACTS: 1. SETTINGS: Beanstalk. PLAYING TIME: 60 min. PLOT: Townspeople send Jack up the beanstalk to appease the giant Wog's hunger. Polly follows him. They learn that Wog is not mean, prevent Professor Hoodwink from swindling Jack out of the deed to his land, and abort Polly's arranged marriage to Ulysses L. Uppercrust III. Jack plans to turn the beanstalk into a tourist attraction as Polly and Wog plan to marry. RECOMMENDATION: Younger children may not be able to follow the different plots and may not fully understand the puns and one liners. Nevertheless, they would especially love Wog, his dog, and chicken. This should be staged by older students with musical talent. ROYALTY: $60. SOURCE: Robinette, Joseph & Shaw, James R. (1985). Beanstalk. Schulenburg, TX: I.E. Clark. SUBJECTS/PLAY TYPE: Animals; Comedy; Folk Tales, England; Musical; Adaptation.

219. 4-6. (+) Nolan, Paul T. **The beanstalk kid.** CAST: 5f, 3m. ACTS: 1. SETTINGS: Room in giant's castle. PLAYING TIME: 30 min. PLOT: Jack (grandson of the original Jack of the beanstalk) and Olaf climb the beanstalk to overcome the giant, return with the treasure, and be heros. The harmless giant has waited for Jack to take his youngest and very spoiled daughter, Gretchen. Olaf stays to become a giant and to be with Marsha, the older daughter. Jack and Gretchen return to the village with the treasure and two potted plants. Jack is finally a hero. RECOMMENDATION: Although the women are domineering and critical, and the men fools, the simple humor will amuse a young audience. ROYALTY: Free to Plays subscribers. SOURCE: Nolan, Paul T. (1976, October). The beanstalk kid. Plays: The Drama Magazine for Young People, pp. 1-10. SUBJECTS/PLAY TYPE: Folk Tale Motifs; Giants; Comedy.

220. 4-7. (+) Leonardi, Alfred. **The beanstalk trial.** CAST: 3f, 5m, 6u. ACTS: 1. SETTINGS: Bare stage. PLAYING TIME: 30 min. PLOT: Jack is tried for the murder of the Giant and the theft of his hen, gold, and harp. After several witnesses are called to the stand, Jack is acquitted and declared a hero. RECOMMENDATION: This ironic twist to the old tale is amusing and cleverly presented. An interesting question is introduced: was Jack justified in committing murder and thievery? ROYALTY: Free to Plays subscribers. SOURCE: Leonardi, Alfred. (1976, October). The beanstalk trial. Plays: The Drama Magazine for Young People, pp. 52-62. SUBJECTS/PLAY TYPE: Justice; Comedy.

221. 1-6. (+) Watts, Frances B. **The Bear's Halloween houseguests.** CAST: 3f, 1m, 3u. ACTS: 1. SETTINGS: Cave. PLAYING TIME: 20 min. PLOT: Hibernating Elmo and Beulah Bear are disturbed by Hannah and Hazel Witch and their cats who want to use the cave to brew their potions for Halloween. Instead of killing the witches, Beulah Bear helps one of the cats who has been hurt. Now, because a good deed has been performed in it, the cave cannot be inhabited by the witches, and the Bears finally hibernate. RECOMMENDATION: The lesson that kindness always has its rewards is well presented in this combination thriller/morality tale. ROYALTY: Free to Plays subscribers. SOURCE: Watts, Frances B. (1978, October). The Bear's Halloween houseguests. Plays: The Drama Magazine for Young People, pp. 49-54. SUBJECTS/PLAY TYPE: Halloween; Witches; Bears; Playlet.

222. 7-12. (+) Kelly, Tim J. (Doyle, Arthur Conan) **Beast of the Baskervilles.** (The hound of the Baskervilles.) CAST: 7f, 4m, Su. ACTS: 1. SETTINGS: Sitting room. PLAYING TIME: 30 min. PLOT: Incompetent Sir Henry is beset by exaggerated, stereotyped characters including the perfect butler, the beautiful fiancee, the clumsy serving girl, the escaped convict, and Sherlock Holmes. Other assorted servants, neighbors, and Holmes' talented landlady round out the cast. RECOMMENDATION: Quick moving, and full of asides and visual jokes, this parody would be fun to produce, but requires skillful direction and timing.

Victorian costumes would add an authentic touch, but are not necessary. ROYALTY: $15. SOURCE: Kelly, Tim J. (1984). Beast of the Baskervilles. Denver, CO: Pioneer Drama Service. SUBJECTS/PLAY TYPE: Comedy; Mystery; Adaptation.

223. 7-10. (-) Nicholson, Jessie. **A beau for Nora.** CAST: 7f, 7m. ACTS: 1. SETTINGS: Sitting room. PLAYING TIME: 40 min. PLOT: Nora, a gay nineties suffragette, has no beau. Five younger sisters do, but their father will not let them marry until Nora weds. Max, an eligible bachelor, desires a strong spirited woman for a wife, and sets his eye on Nora. They become engaged, and the siblings celebrate because they are free to marry. RECOMMENDATION: Marriage is treated as a simple, whimsical, sudden act, with women portrayed as silly and naturally inferior to men. ROYALTY: Free to Plays subscribers. SOURCE: Nicholson, Jessie. (1988, March). A beau for Nora. Plays: The Drama Magazine for Young People, pp. 21-32. SUBJECTS/PLAY TYPE: Marriage; Suffragist Movement; Feminism; Comedy.

224. 3-7. (+) Mahlman, Lewis. (de Beaumont, LePrince) **Beauty and the beast.** (Beauty and the beast). CAST: 10u. ACTS: 1. SETTINGS: Puppet stage. PLAYING TIME: 15 min. PLOT: When a vain prince is turned into a beast, a woman must agree to marry him to break the spell. The beast forces Beauty to live with him, and after some time, she agrees to marry him. RECOMMENDATION: This follows the plot of the original and could be performed live for extra impact. ROYALTY: Free to Plays subscribers. SOURCE: Mahlman, Lewis. (1977, January). Beauty and the beast. Plays: the Drama Magazine for Young People, pp. 81-86. SUBJECTS/PLAY TYPE: Folk Tales, France; Kindness; Puppet Play; Adaptation.

225. 9-12. (+) Kehret, Peg. **Beauty for sale.** CAST: 2f. ACTS: 1. SETTINGS: None. PLAYING TIME: NA. PLOT: Two youthful aspirants for instant glamour are introduced to the high pressure marketing world. The "guaranteed" promises of immediate movie star bodies are thrilling to one girl, but Shawna is skeptical. Dismayed, but undaunted, the friend dismisses Shawna's "poor judgment" and embarks on her own personal beauty quest. RECOMMENDATION: Young girls everywhere can relate to this, reliving their initial adventures in the exciting world of the mail-order "promised land." ROYALTY: NA. SOURCE: Kehret, Peg. (1986). Winning monologs for young actors. Colorado Springs, CO: Meriwether Pub. SUBJECTS/PLAY TYPE: Beauty; Monologue.

226. K-3. (+) Marks, Burton. **The Beauty potion.** CAST: 2f, 1m. ACTS: 1. SETTINGS: Bare stage, props. PLAYING TIME: NA. PLOT: Dora Dragon is upset because she feels ugly. Her fairy godmother gives her a magic potion to make her beautiful. Although it doesn't work, Dora is convinced that she is changed. Dracula Dragon, who looks just like Dora, convinces her of her beauty. RECOMMENDATION: This makes the point, "beauty is in the eye of the beholder," in an uncomplicated manner to which young children will

easily relate. ROYALTY: None. SOURCE: Marks, Burton. (1982). Puppet plays and puppet-making. Boston, MA: Plays, Inc. SUBJECTS/PLAY TYPE: Beauty; Dragons; Puppet Play.

227. 9-12. (+) Van Horn, Bill. **Beauty queen of Cabbage Corners.** CAST: 7f, 8m, Su. ACTS: 1. SETTINGS: Store front; porch. PLAYING TIME: 30 min. PLOT: Plain Phoebe Thrush wants to save enough money for an operation for her grandmother and to go to college. Her opportunity comes when a famous TV commentator and TV crew come to Cabbage Corners to interview Senator J.P. Martin. Since the town is so dull, Barbara Rivers, the TV commentator, livens it up by staging a robbery and holding a beauty contest which, after some very unusual events, Phoebe wins. RECOMMENDATION: This is full of adventure, action, and even some romance. It is pure entertainment. ROYALTY: Free to Plays subscribers. SOURCE: Van Horn, Bill. (1980, February). Beauty queen of Cabbage Corners. Plays: The Drama Magazine for Young People, pp. 1-12. SUBJECTS/PLAY TYPE: Mystery; Comedy.

228. 9-12. (+) Farquhar, George. (Nolan, Paul T.) **The beaux' stratagem.** (The beaux' stratagem.) CAST: 3f, 4m. ACTS: 1. SETTINGS: Chapel. PLAYING TIME: 25 min. PLOT: Two lovers who intended to marry each other for their respective fortunes, determine that they love each other enough to marry regardless of their financial situations. RECOMMENDATION: This play about love and marriage skillfully blends wit and sentiment. It is a comedy of manners, a stylized form of drama characterized by wit and brilliant dialogue which was popular in 17th century England. The plot reflects a cynical attitude toward society and life. ROYALTY: Free to Plays subscribers. SOURCE: Farquhar, George. (1978, November). The beaux' stratagem. Plays: The Drama Magazine for Young People, pp. 72- 79. SUBJECTS/PLAY TYPE: Marriage; Playlet.

229. 7-8. (+) Murray, John. **Bed and breakfast bedlam.** CAST: 6f, 6m. ACTS: 1. SETTINGS: Kitchen; dining room. PLAYING TIME: 30 min. PLOT: Lance and Jenny Peters, new owners of the Seaside Haven Hotel, await a visit from the Tour Allure Association. They serve a disastrous breakfast, then Lance helps prepare lunch for the inspectors, but accidentally substitutes red pepper for paprika. Hearing of a local robbery, the Peters' nephew, Tommy, looks for clues. After many instances of mistaken identity, the robber is discovered and all ends well. RECOMMENDATION: Interesting characters, fast moving plot, and good wholesome humor make this fun and snappy. Even the robber is likable. ROYALTY: Free to Plays subscribers. SOURCE: Murray, John. (1985, November). Bed and breakfast bedlam. Plays: The Drama Magazine for Young People, pp. 1-13. SUBJECTS/PLAY TYPE: Mystery; Family; Comedy.

230. 7-12. (+) Merritt, Eve. **Being human.** CAST: 3u. ACTS: 1. SETTINGS: Bare stage. PLAYING TIME: 10 min. PLOT: Three persons find themselves fastened to

one another by a large loop. Each pulls in his own direction, keeping the loop taut. Each has his own priority; one shelter, another food, another artistic expression. When each person stops pushing for his own agenda he finds he can step back, relax, and be freed. RECOMMENDATION: The short running time, small cast, and simplicity of set make this a good play for showcasing talent without a long lead time. The themes of cooperation and mutual understanding make this an excellent exercise for building ensemble. ROYALTY: Free to Plays Subscribers. SOURCE: Merritt, Eve. (1979, March). Being human. Plays: The Drama Magazine for Young People, pp. 13-15. SUBJECTS/PLAY TYPE: Cooperation; Individuality; Skit.

231. 3-12. (+) Pearson, Carol Lynn, & Redford, J.A.C. (Grimm Brothers) **Believe in make believe.** CAST: 5f, 2m, 5u. ACTS: 1. SETTINGS: Bare stage. PLAYING TIME: NA. PLOT: The performers avow their belief in make believe by singing, discussing it with the audience, and presenting tales collected by The Grimm Brothers. The action revolves around a king and queen's attempts to stop their daughter's crying. In between the scenes, the players present updated versions of "The Elves and the Shoemaker," and "The Bremen Town Musicians." In the last tale, "The Golden Goose," the simpleton makes the princess laugh and becomes her husband. RECOMMENDATION: This provides an opportunity for children to pretend and to participate. The tales should be known by the audience because there are no settings, few props, and only the basic outlines are presented. The play requires ad libbing, and two humorous speciality acts, selection of which is left to the director. ROYALTY: $35. SOURCE: Pearson, Carol Lynn & Redford, J.A.C. (1977). Believe in make believe. New Orleans, LA: Anchorage Press, Inc. SUBJECTS/PLAY TYPE: Folk Tales, Germany; Musical; Adaptation.

232. 6-10. (-) Boiko, Claire. (de Beaumont, LePrince). **Belinda and the beast.** (Beauty and the beast) CAST: 10f, 19m. ACTS: 1. SETTINGS: Cave; parlor. PLAYING TIME: 35 min. PLOT: Belinda, a librarian, is forced to live with the beast and his unkempt comrades. She rehabilitates them by starting a library. The beast survives a bullet because it was stopped by a copy of Shakespeare's "All's Well that Ends Well," and Belinda marries the beast. RECOMMENDATION: This unsuccessful parody suffers from irrelevant references to nuclear warfare ("first stage beast alert"); sexism; racism; insulting and unrealistic western dialect ("hot diggity dog") and outdated phrases ("ride like sixty"). ROYALTY: NA. SOURCE: Boiko, Claire. (1980). Dramatized parodies of familiar stories. Boston: Plays, Inc. SUBJECTS/PLAY TYPE: Librarians; Musical; Western; Parody.

233. 4-6. (+) Thane, Adele. (Longfellow, Henry Wadsworth) **The bell of Atri.** (The bell of Atri) CAST: 3m, Su. ACTS: 1. SETTINGS: Marketplace. PLAYING TIME: 15 min. PLOT: The king hangs a bell, to be rung by anyone who is wronged or mistreated. A hungry horse, Trojan, nibbles at the vines attached to the bell's rope. The bell rings and Peter, a stableboy, tells of Trojan's

abuse by his owner, Sir Rolfo, Knight of Atri, who no longer feeds or cares for him, but lives to count his bags of gold. The king, outraged, decrees that one half of the knight's gold be spent for Trojan's care, that henceforth Sir Rolfo will be known as Rolfo, the Unknightly, and that the day will be a holiday each year to celebrate the occasion of a poor creature that could not speak for itself. RECOMMENDATION: This faithful adaptation well teaches that compassion should be shown to both human and animal life. While the props and costumes are numerous, elaborate, and unusual, the play is worthy of the effort. ROYALTY: Free to Plays subscribers. SOURCE: Thane, Adele. (1981, October). The bell of Atri. Plays: The Drama Magazine for Young People, pp. 57-62. SUBJECTS/PLAY TYPE: Greed; Justice; Legends, Italy; Adaptation.

234. 9-12*. (+) Luce, William. **The belle of Amherst.** CAST: 1f. ACTS: 1. SETTINGS: Bare stage. PLAYING TIME: NA. PLOT: Emily Dickinson reflects on her life, including why she dresses strangely and stays at home; her relationships with her relatives, Preceptor (Thomas Higginson), and her suitors; and her feelings and frustrations about life and her poetry. RECOMMENDATION: Based on extensive research into Dickinson's letters, poetry, and biographies, this one person play draws a picture of the poet which is more realistic and less psychopathic than much of the literature about her suggests. Interspersed throughout are her poems which the actress recites as part of her stream-of-consciousness soliloquy. Running from childhood to death, this superb dramatic monologue is just within the grasp of a high school audience, but the actress will have to be a skilled adult. The set can be either a bare stage, or the various rooms of the Dickinson home, depending upon resources. ROYALTY: NA. SOURCE: Luce, William. (1976). The belle of Amherst. Boston, MA: Houghton Mifflin. SUBJECTS/PLAY TYPE: Dickinson, Emily; Monologue.

235. 7-12. (+) Kelly, Tim. **Belle of Bisbee.** CAST: 7f, 4m, Su. ACTS: 2. SETTINGS: Yard. PLAYING TIME: 60 min. PLOT: The school teacher heroine tries to save the school from being sold; the rock miner hero tries to help while courting her. The villain will stop at nothing, including blackmail, physical abuse of a woman, and hinted murder, to gain control of the school house for mineral rights to the land. Amelia saves the school house when she discloses she was married to the villain before he married the heroine, thus freeing the teacher to marry the hero. RECOMMENDATION: The actress who plays Amelia Dunk could "chew the scenery." She not only saves the situation, but she also literally knocks the stuffing out of the villain (a dummy). ROYALTY: $25.00. SOURCE: Kelly, Tim. (1985). Belle of Bisbee. Denver, CO: Pioneer Drama Service. SUBJECTS/PLAY TYPE: Swindlers and Swindling; Melodrama.

236. 6-12. (+) Murray, John. **The belles of Horsefly Gulch.** CAST: 4f, 7m. ACTS: 1. SETTINGS: Hillbilly cabin. PLAYING TIME: 25 min. PLOT: Widder Bronson tries to avoid eviction by snaring a husband. According to the code of the hills, the older daughter,

Hepzibah, must marry first. She is terribly unattractive; the younger sister, Marigold, is most attractive and has two suitors. All goes well, however, as one of Marigold's suitors prefers Hepzibah for her fine set of teeth, and all are married. RECOMMENDATION: The "hillbilly humor" provides numerous opportunities for slapstick and exaggerated antics. ROYALTY: Free to Plays subscribers. SOURCE: Murray, John. (1976, March). The belles of Horsefly Gulch. Plays: The Drama Magazine for Young People, pp. 25-37. SUBJECTS/PLAY TYPE: Matrimony; Mail Order; Hillbillies; Comedy.

237. K-3. (+) Carlson, Bernice Wells. (Aesopus). **Belling the cat.** (The mice in council) CAST: 5u. ACTS: 1. SETTINGS: Mouse hole. PLAYING TIME: NA PLOT: The littlest mouse suggests that they tie a bell around the cat to keep it from sneaking up and eating them. All agree to the idea, but no one will implement it. RECOMMENDATION: The mice realize that it's easier to suggest an idea than it is to carry it out. ROYALTY: SOURCE: Carlson, Bernice Wells. (1982). Let's find the big idea. Nashville: Abingdon. SUBJECTS/PLAY TYPE: Fable; Skit; Adaptation; Mice; Cats.

238. 1-6. (+) Cheatham, Val R. (Aesopus). **Belling the cat.** (The mice in council) CAST: 6u. ACTS: 1. SETTINGS: Barn interior. PLAYING TIME: 10 min. PLOT: To stop the cat from sneaking up and eating them, the animals decide to put a bell around his neck. As Oliver and Stanly flip a coin to see who will attach the bell, the cat appears. Thinking quickly, Godfeather Owl pleads with the cat to do anything but take their bell. As the cat grabs the bell, they escape. RECOMMENDATION: Stanly and Oliver are vulnerable and not too sure of themselves as they first win the audience's sympathy and later their cheers. This is an effective combination of an Aesop fable and an Uncle Remus solution. ROYALTY: Free to Plays subscribers. SOURCE: Cheatham, Val R. (1982, April). Belling the cat. Plays: The Drama Magazine for Young People, pp. 41-44. SUBJECTS/PLAY TYPE: Fable; Adaptation; Mice; Cats.

239. 12. (+) Gilsenan, Nancy. **Beloved friend.** CAST: 4f, 2m, Su. ACTS: 2. SETTINGS: Bare stage. PLAYING TIME: NA. PLOT: Sixteen year old Kristin (a wealthy white American) and 16 year old Rachel (a poor black Rhodesian) begin a friendship by mail that continues for 16 years, during which Kristin marries and has two children. Rachel becomes a teacher, fights and is taken prisoner in the Rhodesian civil war for black rights, at last becoming Rhodesian Minister of Education. In the final moving scene, Rachel and Kristin finally meet as Kristin is dying of multiple sclerosis. RECOMMENDATION: This masterpiece vividly portrays the growth and maturation of two equally striking women, tied together by a mutual consuming need for each other, and developed through the letters that they write. The glimpses of the horrors of civil war and the treatment of blacks in Rhodesia, juxtaposed against the comfortable upper middle class of America add to the excellence of this beautifully executed drama. ROYALTY: $60.

SOURCE: Gilsenan, Nancy. (1986). Beloved friend. Woodstock, IL: Dramatic Pub. Co. SUBJECTS/PLAY TYPE: Women; Friendship; Rhodesia, Civil War; Drama.

240. 4-8. (-) Sylvesper, Lloyd. **Bend, tear, and spindle.** CAST: 1f, 1m, 11u. ACTS: 2. SETTINGS: Living room. PLAYING TIME: NA. PLOT: A suburban couple, too old to adopt, become foster parents to eight children assigned to them by computer error. Pandemonium results when the social worker's boss shows up and the children try to avoid being found out. Ultimately they are returned to the juvenile center, but the couple continues as foster parents to five new children. RECOMMENDATION: This is an unrealistic scenario with stereotypical characters and sexism. It is fast moving, but talks down to the age level that might appreciate its humor. ROYALTY: $40. SOURCE: Sylvesper, Lloyd. (1978). Bend, tear, and spindle. Elgin, IL: Performance Pub. Co. SUBJECTS/PLAY TYPE: Foster Care; Comedy.

241. 7-12. (+) Boelt, Benn. **Beneath the cross.** CAST: 3f, 7m. ACTS: 1. SETTINGS: Bare stage. PLAYING TIME: 12 min. PLOT: This enactment of the crucifixion is similar to an Easter pageant presentation without the resurrection, as Mary Magdalene recounts the last moments of Jesus' life while they are acted on stage. RECOMMENDATION: Teenagers will find this a suitable Easter pageant presentation for church functions. ROYALTY: None. SOURCE: Altena, Hans.(1978). The playbook for Christian theatre. Grand Rapids, MI: Baker Book House. SUBJECTS/PLAY TYPE: Easter; Christian Drama.

242. 2-5. (+) Fisher, Aileen. **Benjy and his red flannels.** CAST: Su. ACTS: 1. SETTINGS: None. PLAYING TIME: 2 min. PLOT: Benjy sheds his long red underwear (in honor of spring), and saves a ship from crashing into a fallen bridge by flagging it with the underwear. RECOMMENDATION: This is a cheerful choral reading to welcome spring. ROYALTY: Free to Plays subscribers. SOURCE: Fisher, Aileen. (1986, March). Benjy and his red flannels. Plays: The Drama Magazine for Young People, pp. 52. SUBJECTS/PLAY TYPE: Spring; Choral Reading.

243. 9-12. (+) Pickering, Ken. Cole, Keith. **Beowulf: A rock musical.** (Beowulf) CAST: 3f, 4m, Su. ACTS: 2. SETTINGS: Tavern; lair; pit. PLAYING TIME: 100 min. PLOT: Beowulf slays the monster, Grendel. After Grendel's mother retaliates, Beowulf is forced to travel to her lair to destroy her. Many years later, Beowulf dies defending his castle from the dragon. RECOMMENDATION: The adaptation of the Beowulf legend as a rock musical makes it especially appealing to teenagers. The language and story remain true to the original throughout, while characters are given modern day personalities and reactions. While intended to be produced by high school aged children, this is extremely elaborate, with dance, music and song. ROYALTY: $75. SOURCE: Pickering, Ken and Cole, Keith. (1986). Beowulf: A rock musical. Schulenburg, TX: I.E. Clark.

SUBJECTS/PLAY TYPE: Vikings; Legends, England; Musical; Adaptation.

244. 7-12. (+) Murray, John. **Bermuda Triangle mystery.** CAST: 5f, 4m, 1u. ACTS: 1. SETTINGS: Ship. PLAYING TIME: 30 min. PLOT: As a luxury yacht passes through the Bermuda Triangle, passengers speculate on the cause of the mysterious disappearances of vessels in the area. Suddenly a freighter--reported missing five years before with the husband of one of the yacht's passengers on board--appears in the fog. Unexplainable events occur and make it appear that the yacht has passed into another dimension. RECOMMENDATION: This is a well written, suspense filled drama which will hold its audience spellbound. It should be fairly easy to produce, although there is some need for special effects. ROYALTY: None. SOURCE: Murray, John. (1985). Fifteen plays for teenagers. Boston, MA: Plays, Inc. SUBJECTS/PLAY TYPE: Science Fiction; Bermuda Triangle; Supernatural; Playlet.

245. 10-12. (+) Brooke, D. D.. (Fitzgerald, F. Scott) **Bernice bobs her hair.** (Bernice bobs her hair) CAST: 6f, 7m, Su. ACTS: 1. SETTINGS: Dance floor. PLAYING TIME: NA PLOT: Marjorie Harvey makes some cruel but accurate assessments about how Bernice, her visiting cousin, might make herself more vivacious. Bernice's efforts to take Marjorie's advice are so successful she attracts Warren, Marjorie's boyfriend. Marjorie dares Bernice to bob her hair; she does and is left looking quite plain. She leaves for home after cutting the sleeping Marjorie's hair. RECOMMENDATION: This faithful adaptation of the F. Scott Fitzgerald story of the same name requires all of the girls to wear their hair long for the production. The play deals with a rather limited milieu: the American upper class of the 1920s. ROYALTY: $20. SOURCE: Brooke, D. D. (1982). Bernice bobs her hair. Woodstock, IL: Dramatic Pub. Co. SUBJECTS/PLAY TYPE: Popularity; Fashion; Roaring 20's/Flappers; Adaptation.

246. K-12. (+) Robinson, Barbara. (Robinson, Barbara) **The best Christmas pageant ever.** (The best Christmas pageant ever) CAST: 15f, 12m ACTS: 1. SETTINGS: Living room; dining room; church interior. PLAYING TIME: 55 min. PLOT: Tryouts for the annual Christmas pageant are interrupted by the Herdmans, six kids who are constantly in trouble, and who win some of the parts in the pageant. Practices become very exciting, with much misbehavior, but the Herdmans are as profoundly affected by their parts in the pageant as the pageant has been altered by their presence. RECOMMENDATION: Anyone who has tired of the commercialization of Christmas will be touched by this faithful adaptation of the author's own prose. The play calls for a large cast of over 27, but no special effects are needed and informal staging is appropriate. ROYALTY: $35. SOURCE: Robinson, Barbara. (1983). The best Christmas pageant ever. New York: Samuel French, Inc. SUBJECTS/PLAY TYPE: Christmas; Comedy; Adaptation.

247. 9-12. (+) Sawyer-Young, Kat. **Best friends.** CAST: 2f. ACTS: 1. SETTINGS: Bedroom. PLAYING TIME: NA. PLOT: Kari and Tracy discuss the unfairness and unreasonableness of mothers. But their problems are forgotten as the girls decide to go to an ice cream shop and watch a boy with Matt Dillon lips. RECOMMENDATION: Teenage girls would be able to relate to the typical problems these girls have with their mothers. However, the overuse of the word "God" may be problematic. ROYALTY: NA. SOURCE: Sawyer-Young, Kat. (1986). Contemporary scenes for contemporary kids. Boston, MA: Baker's Plays. SUBJECTS/PLAY TYPE: Parents; Generation Gap; Scene.

248. 2-3. (+) Martin, Millie. **The best of the band.** CAST: Su. ACTS: 1. SETTINGS: Music classroom. PLAYING TIME: 10 min. PLOT: This choral reading features rhythm instruments, with two children playing sticks, drums, triangles, tamborines and cymbals. After first competing to see which instrument is the "best," the instruments finally agree with the children, who judge that they are best when played together. RECOMMENDATION: This short, excellent introduction to the rhythm instruments and the fun of music enables children to rotate roles, allowing each a chance to play the different instruments. ROYALTY: Free to Plays subscribers. SOURCE: Martin, Millie. (1981, March). The best of the band. Plays: The Drama Magazine for Young People, pp. 57-59. SUBJECTS/PLAY TYPE: Music; Unity; Choral Reading.

249. 1-6. (+) Sollid, Lynnette. (Houck, Oliver) **The best present of all.** (Ranger Rick's Nature Magazine) CAST: 7f, 5m, 4u. ACTS: 1. SETTINGS: Throne room. PLAYING TIME: 20 min. PLOT: The king wants to give the best present in the world to the children of the land. When he calls in the Royal Advisers, they tell him Princess Oriana wishes for a warm castle, but the advisers tell the King warmth takes energy which is costly, and they must choose the right source. Sources of energy--oil, gas, coal, water, atomic, geothermal, and solar energy--come to the throne room to tell about their origins, how skillful they are at producing heat, and the problems their consumption causes. The King decides to use geothermal and solar energy because they are permanent and will not destroy the land or the air. RECOMMENDATION: This imaginative play deals with the important theme of energy and its ecological effect as each energy source character offers scientific information without sounding like a textbook. Dialogue and costume design are significant, with oil and gas dressed as sheiks, and the atom nervous and talking rapidly. This would be especially worthwhile as an enrichment exercise. ROYALTY: Free to Plays subscribers. SOURCE: Sollid, Lynnette. (1977, May). The best present of all. Plays: The Drama Magazine

for Young People, pp. 37-43. SUBJECTS/PLAY TYPE: Ecology; Conservation; Adaptation.

250. 3-5. (+) Brown, Rochelle Theresa. **The best recipe for rice pudding. CAST:** 5f, 3m. **ACTS:** 1. **SETTINGS:** Kitchen. **PLAYING TIME:** 15 min. **PLOT:** Ms. Custard refuses to reveal her award winning recipe for rice pudding until Scrubwoman Katie, claiming that her own rice pudding recipe is better, makes so many blatant cooking errors that Ms. Custard becomes frustrated enough to show her the right way to cook the pudding. When she realizes that Katie now knows the recipe, it is too late. **RECOMMENDATION:** Dialogue is simple, and its repetition will please younger children. Designing and painting the kitchen setting could be a good art project, or the setting can be simplified enough to perform the play in a classroom. **ROYALTY:** Free to Plays subscribers. **SOURCE:** Brown, Rochelle Theresa. (1982, May). The best recipe for rice pudding. Plays: The Drama Magazine for Young People, pp. 45-48. **SUBJECTS/PLAY TYPE:** Trickery; Recipes; Comedy.

251. 7-9. (+) Kehret, Peg. **The best years. CAST:** 1f. **ACTS:** 1. **SETTINGS:** None. **PLAYING TIME:** NA. **PLOT:** A junior high girl involved in the misery of school lashes out, revealing the humiliating and misunderstood situations endured by kids: embarrassing locker room scenes, harassment over phone calls, terrible class pictures that must be taken, and teachers who just don't understand. **RECOMMENDATION:** This describes, in the vernacular of the young, the disheartening facts about school life that are so often dismissed by adults with the baffling statement, "These are the best years of your life, so enjoy!" **ROYALTY:** NA. **SOURCE:** Kehret, Peg. (1986). Winning monologs for young actors. Colorado Springs, CO: Meriwether Pub. **SUBJECTS/PLAY TYPE:** School; Monologue.

252. 7-12. (+) Sawyer-Young, Kat. **Betrayal. CAST:** 1f. **ACTS:** 1. **SETTINGS:** None. **PLAYING TIME:** 1 min. **PLOT:** Pam tells Lori that their relationship is over because Lori stole Pam's boyfriend. **RECOMMENDATION:** Friendship between women vs. their relationships with boys is well treated here. **ROYALTY:** None. **SOURCE:** Sawyer-Young, Kat. (1987). Minute monologues for contemporary teens. Boston, MA: Baker's Plays. **SUBJECTS/PLAY TYPE:** Dating; Friendship; Monologue.

253. 4-7. (+) Bradley, Virginia. **Better luck tomorrow, Mr. Washington. CAST:** 1f, 1m, Su. **ACTS:** 1. **SETTINGS:** Bedroom. **PLAYING TIME:** NA. **PLOT:** In a country inn, a guide shows a group of tourists where Washington supposedly slept. Martha and George enter and the tourists learn that only Martha got any sleep. **RECOMMENDATION:** This brief play will need clever thinking actors to make it come alive. **ROYALTY:** None. **SOURCE:** Bradley, Virginia. (1975). Is there an actor in the house? New York, NY: Dodd, Mead. **SUBJECTS/PLAY TYPE:** Comedy; Washington, George; Skit.

254. 1-5. (+) Fisher, Aileen Lucia. **Better than a calendar. CAST:** Su. **ACTS:** 1. **SETTINGS:** None. **PLAYING TIME:** 1 min. **PLOT:** Children volunteer to help a surprised mother with her tasks because it is Mother's Day. **RECOMMENDATION:** Older students should enjoy performing this brief choral reading for their younger peers. **ROYALTY:** Free to Plays subscribers. **SOURCE:** Fisher, Aileen Lucia. (1985, May). Better than a calendar. Plays: The Drama Magazine for Young People, pp. 51. **SUBJECTS/PLAY TYPE:** Mother's Day; Choral Reading.

255. K-8. (+) Presser, Elaine. **Betterworld. CAST:** 32u. **ACTS:** 2. **SETTINGS:** None. **PLAYING TIME:** 15 min. **PLOT:** A group of lost visitors encounter blue, green, red, and yellow soldiers in the Betterworld. The soldiers demonstrate, through a series of analogies, that their world is better because they believe in love and peace. The visitors are inspired to build a better world for themselves. **RECOMMENDATION:** The utopian world devoid of hatred makes for an effective play. **ROYALTY:** Free to Plays subscribers. **SOURCE:** Presser, Elaine. (1983, May). Betterworld. Plays: The Drama Magazine for Young People, pp. 43-50. **SUBJECTS/PLAY TYPE:** Peace; Playlet.

256. 5-8. (+) Bradley, Virginia. **Beware of the glump. CAST:** Su. **ACTS:** 2. **SETTINGS:** Street; yard. **PLAYING TIME:** NA. **PLOT:** All the townspeople fear Glump for different reasons, and each physically resembles the reason that he/she is afraid of Glump (e.g., huge floppy ears, enormous nose, red hair). **RECOMMENDATION:** This is a humorous play that will make the audience reflect on who they are and what they fear. **ROYALTY:** None. **SOURCE:** Bradley, Virginia. (1975). Is there an actor in the house? New York, NY: Dodd, Mead. **SUBJECTS/PLAY TYPE:** Fears; Relationships; Puppet Play.

257. 2-6. (-) Boiko, Claire. **Beware the genies! CAST:** 9f, 8m, Su. **ACTS:** 1. **SETTINGS:** Dump; cave; park. **PLAYING TIME:** 20 min. **PLOT:** While searching a polluted stream for a missing locket, Dan and Wendy discover three ecologically conscious genies in a bottle, who show the children visions from the past and future which demonstrate the progression of pollution, and plead for clean-ups. **RECOMMENDATION:** Overly didactic, gloomy, and childishly dramatized, this will insult rather than instruct. **ROYALTY:** Free to Plays subscribers. **SOURCE:** Boiko, Claire. (1979, January). Beware the genies! Plays: The Drama Magazine for Young People, pp. 59-64. **SUBJECTS/PLAY TYPE:** Ecology; Pollution; Genies; Playlet.

258. 7-12. (+) Nicol, Eric. **Beware the quickly who. CAST:** 10u. **ACTS:** 2. **SETTINGS:** None. **PLAYING TIME:** NA. **PLOT:** Johnny sets out to find his identity to avoid living in oblivion. As he searches, he meets with allusions to famous stories such as **Alice in Wonderland** and the Hobbit trilogy. Finally, he realizes that who you are is not as important as what you are.

RECOMMENDATION: As long as the wonderful allusions to classical literature are understood, this works well. ROYALTY: NA. SOURCE: Kids plays: Six Canadian plays for children. (1980). Toronto: Playwrights Press. SUBJECTS/PLAY TYPE: Identity; Drama.

259. 6-11. (+) Gotwalt, Helen Louise Miller. **Bewitched and bewildered. CAST:** 7f, 3m. **ACTS:** 1. **SETTINGS:** Living room. **PLAYING TIME:** 30 min. **PLOT:** When Emily Blake says Halloween is stupid, three witches come to Emily's house because they must get enough people to say Halloween is their favorite holiday so it won't take be taken off of the calendar. Since the truth is, Emily was not asked to the Halloween party by the boy she likes, the witches break the water pipes at school so that the party has to come to the only available place--Emily's house. They make up a love potion which causes the boy Emily likes falls to fall in love with her. **RECOMMENDATION:** For young teenagers suffering from the perils of teenage romance, this fantasy provides a lesson about "cutting off the nose to spite the face," as well as an "everybody lived happily ever" ending. **ROYALTY:** Free to Plays subscribers. **SOURCE:** Gotwalt, Helen Louise Miller. (1987, October). Bewitched and bewildered. Plays: The Drama Magazine for Young People, pp. 25-34. **SUBJECTS/PLAY TYPE:** Halloween; Witches; Comedy.

260. 9-12. (+) Watts, Irene N. **Beyond belief. CAST:** 1f, 2m. **ACTS:** 1. **SETTINGS:** Spire shaped structure; four triangular risers. **PLAYING TIME:** NA. **PLOT:** This collage of supernatural tales taken from classic authors deals with Satan, blood-thirsty men, graves, and dead people. **RECOMMENDATION:** Due to the morbid and occasionally gruesome subject matter, as well as many references to classical literature, this would only be appropriate for mature audiences. **ROYALTY:** NA. **SOURCE:** Watts, Irene N. (1981). Beyond belief. Toronto: Playwrights Canada. **SUBJECTS/PLAY TYPE:** Supernatural; Horror; Demons; Drama.

261. K-3. (+) Juster, Norton. (Juster, Norton) **Beyond expectations.** (The phantom tollbooth) **CAST:** 1m, 8u. **ACTS:** 1. **SETTINGS:** None. **PLAYING TIME:** NA. **PLOT:** Milo visits the Doldrums, where thinking and all other forms of activity are forbidden. With the help of a watchdog, he learns that he can use thought power to run his car and escapes the sleepy community. **RECOMMENDATION:** Adapted faithfully from the original novel, this would serve as a good introduction to the book itself, or to emphasize the importance of having an active mind. **ROYALTY:** NA. **SOURCE:** Bauer, Caroline Feller. (1987). Presenting reader's theater: Plays and poems to read aloud. New York, NY: H.W. Wilson. **SUBJECTS/PLAY TYPE:** Doldrums; Laziness; Reader's Theater; Adaptation.

262. 6-12. (-) Rybak, Rose Kacherian. **Bicentennial bonanza. CAST:** 4f, 15m, 4u. **ACTS:** 1. **SETTINGS:** TV studio. **PLAYING TIME:** 35 min. **PLOT:** Bicentennial bonanza is a TV game show which deals with American history. The emcee is assisted by Miss Liberty Belle, who selects the contestants (feminist Gloria Shiner, bank president Bob Caruthers, and librarian Bettina Bottingwell). All three miss their third question. The final contestant, a hippie named Harry, accidentally answers all three questions correctly and wins the $1776 jackpot. **RECOMMENDATION:** Originally intended to be produced for the 1976 bicentennial celebration, this unfortunately develops all of its humor from stereotyped characterizations of the contestants and from insultingly stereotyped questions. The play's exposition is clever, but its total dependence on insults renders it inappropriate. **ROYALTY:** Free to Plays subscribers. **SOURCE:** Rybak, Rose Kacherian. (1976, January). Bicentennial celebration. Plays: The Drama Magazine for Young People, pp. 69-78. **SUBJECTS/PLAY TYPE:** Game Shows; Independence Day, U.S.; Comedy.

263. 9-12. (+) Cook, Pat. **Big bucks. CAST:** 5f, 3m. **ACTS:** 2. **SETTINGS:** Living room. **PLAYING TIME:** NA. **PLOT:** Buck Fever's plantation is threatened by the construction of a new freeway past the house and by an IRS audit. When several bodies are dug up during construction, suspicion falls on each family member. Investigation reveals that the land was formerly an Indian burial ground, and an old treaty between the Indians and the U.S. government saves Buck's plantation. **RECOMMENDATION:** With all the action in one large living room and few costumes and properties needed, the play is easily produced. However, the Southern accent may be difficult to sustain through the whole play. The characters, the plot, and the dialogue are humorous in a very corny way, rather like a television sitcom. **ROYALTY:** $50. **SOURCE:** Cook, Pat. (1982). Big bucks. Chicago, IL: Dramatic Pub. Co. **SUBJECTS/PLAY TYPE:** Mystery; Comedy.

264. 1-3. (+) Martin, Judith. **Big burger. CAST:** 1f, 1m, 4u. **ACTS:** 1. **SETTINGS:** Bare stage. **PLAYING TIME:** 6 min. **PLOT:** As a family leaves on vacation, one child asks "how far is it?" They encounter a talking big burger sign, but are disappointed by the burgers. On their way again, they encounter a talking frozen custard sign. Will they stop again? **RECOMMENDATION:** The point that it's best not to digress from your goals is well made in this fantasy/comedy. **ROYALTY:** None. **SOURCE:** Martin, Judith. (1981). Everybody, everybody: A collection from the paper bag players. New York, NY: Elsevier/ Nelson Books. **SUBJECTS/PLAY TYPE:** Vacations; Determination; Comedy.

265. K-6. (+) Plescia, Gillian L. **Big cat, little cat, old man monkey. CAST:** 2m, 3u. **ACTS:** 1. **SETTINGS:** Bare stage, props. **PLAYING TIME:** 15 min. **PLOT:** Two cats arguing over who will get the larger rice cake have their dilemma solved by a wily and hungry monkey. **RECOMMENDATION:** This will be easily produced by fourth through sixth graders. **ROYALTY:** Free to Plays subscribers. **SOURCE:** Plescia, Gillian L. (1975, May). Big cat, little cat, old man monkey. Plays: The Drama Magazine for Young People, pp. 49-52.

SUBJECTS/PLAY TYPE: Cats; Sharing; Folk Tales, Japan; Playlet.

266. 3-6. (+) Bradley, Virginia. **The big red heart.** CAST: 3f, 3m. ACTS: 1. SETTINGS: Living room. PLAYING TIME: NA. PLOT: While the parents are away, Grimsley the grumpy babysitter stays with the Conroy children. When a Valentine arrives, they try to determine the sender, but without success. RECOMMENDATION: This is easily produced because there is one setting and the costumes are ordinary clothes. ROYALTY: None. SOURCE: Bradley, Virginia. (1981). Holidays on stage. New York, NY: Dodd, Mead. SUBJECTS/PLAY TYPE: Valentine's Day; Comedy.

267. 3-12. (+) Cable, Harold. (Perrault, Charles) **Big Red Riding Hood.** (Little Red Riding Hood) CAST: 3f, 3m. ACTS: 1. SETTINGS: Office; woods. PLAYING TIME: 30 min. PLOT: Granny and the Wolfe family battle for control of the goodies market as Granny feigns illness so Big Red will bake cookies for her, which she sells instead. When Red learns of Granny's deceit, she quits. But Grandpa convinces the Wolfes (who have the baking facilities) and Granny (whose grand-daughter has the recipes) to become partners in the race for Top Cookie. RECOMMENDATION: This wonderful takeoff on the original is so well constructed and so hilariously presents all the elements of the original (only slightly off-center), that it is a perfect choice for all ages (as long as it is produced by older adolescents). ROYALTY: Free to Plays subscribers. SOURCE: Cable, Harold. (1982, January/February). Big Red Riding Hood. Plays: The Drama Magazine for Young People, pp. 15- 24. SUBJECTS/PLAY TYPE: Comedy; Folk Tales, France; Farce; Business; Adaptation.

268. 1-4*. (+) Boiko, Claire. **The big shoo.** CAST: 1f, 8m, Su. ACTS: 1. SETTINGS: Cornfield. PLAYING TIME: 15 min. PLOT: Childhood friends contemplate the activities of Harvest Festival, especially the "Great Big Shoo," a crow-shooing contest between Tattersall, a friendly, ragged scarecrow loved and supported by the children and townspeople, and the Scarecrobot, Professor Pepper's automated atomic scarecrow. The crows reminisce about 30 years of familiarity and pranks shared with Tattersall and he is named the official scarecrow, but Scarecrobot is enlisted as the caller for the evening's square dances. RECOMMENDATION: The familiar scenario of the rejection of technological advancement in favor of faithful, reliable service is given a new twist when the technically superior Scarecrobot weeps nuts and bolts over his rejection. The audience shares his devastation at his first failure and seeks to console him by cheering his appointment to an alternate position. An elaborately constructed costume is necessary to do justice to the complexity of Scarecrobot's character, but the setting and other props are simple and require minimal effort. ROYALTY: None. SOURCE: Boiko, Claire. (1985). Children's plays for creative actors. Boston, MA: Plays, Inc. SUBJECTS/PLAY TYPE: Scarecrows; Technology; Playlet.

269. 10-12. (-) Murray, John. **Big top murders.** CAST: 5f, 7m. ACTS: 3. SETTINGS: Dressing room. PLAYING TIME: 35 min. PLOT: A high wire artist dies while performing her act, but it is learned that she died from snake venom poisoning, not her fall from the high wire. Hermione Finch uncovers the murderer as one of the co-owners of the circus who wanted it to fail so that he could get out of the business. RECOMMENDATION: The dialogue is stilted, the unlikely sequence of events is absurd, and characters are stereotyped and dated. ROYALTY: Free to Plays subscribers. SOURCE: Murray, John. (1985). Fifteen plays for teenagers. Boston, MA: Plays, Inc. SUBJECTS/PLAY TYPE: Circus; Murder; Mystery.

270. 6-10. (+) Witherell, James. **Bigfoot's revenge.** CAST: 4f, 3m, 1u. ACTS: 1. SETTINGS: General store. PLAYING TIME: 45 min. PLOT: In this frontier western melodrama, Eloise Goodhome and daughter Penelope own a stage stop and general store, which the villain, Judge Rapacity, wants to buy, as a railroad is to be built nearby. Otto, the judge's assistant, masquerades as Bigfoot and frightens Mrs. Goodhome into selling. Sweet Penelope and her friend, the real Bigfoot, unmask Otto, and the evil Judge Rapacity is arrested by a U.S. marshall. RECOMMENDATION: Different from most melodramas, all of the strong, positive characters are women, as is the hero. ROYALTY: $15. SOURCE: Witherell, James. (1983). Bigfoot's revenge. Denver, CO: Pioneer Drama Service. SUBJECTS/PLAY TYPE: Pioneer Life, U.S.; Bigfoot; Comedy; Melodrama.

271. 10-12. (+) Walden Theatre Young Playwrights 1985. **Bill number one: Quick turns on the carousel.** CAST: 5f, 3m, 1u. ACTS: 1. SETTINGS: Bare stage, props. PLAYING TIME: NA. PLOT: As a mime describes a carnival atmosphere, eight players simulate a carousel by using red streamers (anger) and blue streamers (sadness). They recite several monologues dealing with deep seated emotions. RECOMMENDATION: These well written monologues succinctly and effectively deal with teenage concerns like death, physical appearance, popularity, and sexual identity. This could be extremely useful for a drama class or as audition material. Some of the monologues are so deep that they would require a sophisticated high school audience to appreciate them. ROYALTY: $50. SOURCE: Walden Theatre Young Playwrights 1985. (1986). In sight. Woodstock, IL: Dramatic Pub. Co. SUBJECTS/PLAY TYPE: Adolescent Problems; Monologues.

272. 10-12. (-) Walden Theatre Young Playwrights, 1985. **Bill number three: Added attractions.** CAST: 1f, 3m, 7u. ACTS: 1. SETTINGS: Bare stage. PLAYING TIME: NA. PLOT: The players perform several monologues dealing with themes such as prejudice, helplessness, empathy, handicaps, selfishness, and complaining. RECOMMENDATION: Most of the material contained here is inferior. There are too many references to violence, including killing people and cruelty to animals. There is obscene language and

tastelessness, and the "cool" monologue is dated. ROYALTY: $50. SOURCE: Walden Theatre Young Playwrights, 1985. (1986). In sight. Woodstock, IL: Dramatic Pub. Co. SUBJECTS/PLAY TYPE: Emotions; Monologues.

273. 10-12. (+) Walden Theatre Young Playwrights, 1985. **Bill number two: Fun house reality. CAST:** 5f, 4m. ACTS: 1. SETTINGS: Bare stage. PLAYING TIME: NA. PLOT: The players perform several monologues which deal with fearful anticipation, the shame of family, inadequacy, punishment, daydreams, physical differences, loneliness, child abuse, suicide, and divorce. RECOMMENDATION: The easily identified experiences and characters are believable in this production, which might be especially beneficial for students who have shared these sorrows and can now realize that their experiences are not unique. Good class discussion could certainly be sparked by viewing this production. ROYALTY: $50. SOURCE: Walden Theatre Young Playwrights. (1986). In sight. Woodstock, IL: Dramatic Pub. Co. SUBJECTS/PLAY TYPE: Emotions; Monologues.

274. 4-6. (+) Mauro, Robert. **Billy Bart, scourge of the West. CAST:** 1f, 7m, Su. ACTS: 1. SETTINGS: Train crossing. PLAYING TIME: 25 min. PLOT: Because of his clothes, the townfolk have judged Billy Bart to be the scourge of the West. As he ties Miss Julie to the railroad tracks, he tries to convince her he is not really an evil villain. Famous figures appear, but none of them has the time or inclination to rescue Julie. Finally, Billy Bart unties Miss Julie, for he realizes she truly understands how he has been misjudged. RECOMMENDATION: In this old fashioned melodramatic spoof, Billy Bart is a humorously inconsistent villain and the personalities of the historical figures are humorously treated, as well. Corny dialogue is plentiful and slapstick humor abounds. ROYALTY: Free to Plays subscribers. SOURCE: Mauro, Robert. (1982, May). Billy Bart, scourge of the West. Plays: The Drama Magazine for Young People, pp. 49-55. SUBJECTS/PLAY TYPE: Melodrama; Comedy; Farce.

275. 5-9*. (+) Berger, Sidney. **Bird boy. CAST:** 2f, 7m, Su. ACTS: 1. SETTINGS: Indian village; secluded place; forest. PLAYING TIME: NA. PLOT: Little Wolf is a physically weak Indian boy about to undergo initiation rites into adulthood. When his friends intercede for him, an old woman grants him magic strength, but, still not strong enough to complete the tasks, he is banished from the tribe. The evil Great Eagle gives him wings in exchange for his spirit. Little Wolf realizes what a poor trade he has made when he finds he cannot land on earth. The audience joins in a chant to free him, and he returns to earth a much changed man. He and his tribe members learn to appreciate qualities other than physical strength. RECOMMENDATION: This has overtones of **Peter Pan**, with its flying actors and audience participation. It also has good special effects. It may require at least high school age people to handle the roles, and then under the tutelage of a mature and experienced director. ROYALTY: NA. SOURCE: Berger, Sidney. (1988). Bird boy. Schulenberg, TX: I.E.

Clark. SUBJECTS/PLAY TYPE: Native Americans; Drama.

276. 6-12. (+) Scandling, Mark. **The bird man. CAST:** 3f, 3m, 1u. ACTS: 1. SETTINGS: Bank. PLAYING TIME: 70 min. PLOT: Oscar (a former soldier) robs a bank and pulls a gun, demanding media attention and money to further the reparation fund for the thousands of birds destroyed by Army pilots. After taking several people hostage, Oscar realizes that he cannot escape and lets his pet bird go free. The post commander gives a check to help Oscar's fund, though the teller notices that it is unsigned. RECOMMENDATION: The troubled young man is well drawn and sympathetic, but army personnel are portrayed as uncaring and untrustworthy, making the play biased. ROYALTY: $30.00. SOURCE: Scandling, Mark. (1988). The bird man. Franklin, OH: Eldridge Pub. Co. SUBJECTS/PLAY TYPE: Ecology; Birds; Values; Drama.

277. 10-12. (+) Bennitt, Caroline. (Aristophanes) **Birds.** (Birds) CAST: 1f, 14m, 25u. ACTS: 2. SETTINGS: Utopia. PLAYING TIME: NA. PLOT: Two men fed up with the bureaucracy of the world ask the birds to help create a utopia world. RECOMMENDATION: This play is humorous, especially in the depictions of the ancient Roman gods, but it is corny in places. It will be a challenge to direct and perform because of the big cast (from 40 to 110 actors have been used in various productions). Some musical talent will be required, though this can be adapted to the situation at hand. The vocabulary, often from ancient mythology, may be troublesome. ROYALTY: NA. SOURCE: Bennitt, Caroline. (1979). Birds. London: Heinemann Educational Books. SUBJECTS/PLAY TYPE: Birds; Gods; Utopias; Adaptation.

278. 1-12. (+) Gotwalt, Helen Louise Miller. (Wiggin, Kate Douglas) **The Birds' Christmas carol.** (The Birds' Christmas carol) CAST: 10f, 8m, Su. ACTS: 4. SETTINGS: Street; bedroom. PLAYING TIME: 25 min. PLOT: Baby Carol, named for carolers, is born to the wealthy Bird family on a Christmas Eve in the late 1900s. Ten years later Carol is an invalid confined to bed and not expected to live. She plans what may be her last Christmas by inviting over the nine neighbor children from the poor Ruggles family. Mrs. Ruggles repairs her children's worn clothes and tries to teach them proper table manners before the party. The children have a wonderful time, and as the play ends, carolers sing outside the dying girl's window. RECOMMENDATION: This old fashioned, sentimental Christmas classic, filled with late 19th century costumes and settings, could be appreciated only during the holiday season. ROYALTY: Free to Plays subscribers. SOURCE: Kamerman, Sylvia E. (1983). Christmas play favorites for young people. Boston, MA: Plays, Inc. SUBJECTS/PLAY TYPE: Christmas; Playlet.

279. 9-12. (+) Majeski, Bill. **The birth of a salesman. CAST:** 6f, 6m. ACTS: 4. SETTINGS: Coffee shop. PLAYING TIME: 45 min. PLOT: After attending a

self assertiveness class, a young man is able to get a real estate sales position. But when he puts his assertiveness to work and criticizes the business and the real estate office owner (his girlfriend's father), he quickly learns that assertiveness does not mean abrasiveness. RECOMMENDATION: The message about being yourself rather than someone you think you should be is well presented. ROYALTY: Free to Plays subscribers. SOURCE: Majeski, Bill. (1983, November). The birth of a salesman. Plays: The Drama Magazine for Young People, pp. 21-32. SUBJECTS/PLAY TYPE: Family; Individuality; Playlet.

280. 3-4. (+) Olfson, Lewy. **A birthday anthem for America.** CAST: Su. ACTS: 1. SETTINGS: None. PLAYING TIME: 8 min. PLOT: A chorus pledges to conserve the land, support the democratic process, stamp out prejudice, and follow the ideals of the Constitution. RECOMMENDATION: This Bicentennial program captures the beauty of America and its people through rhyme and rhythm. The values of American ideology are well woven into the text, and the choral reading reaches a crescendo with the "promise" of the future. Although sentimental, this will inspire a sense of pride and patriotism. ROYALTY: Free to Plays subscribers. SOURCE: Olfson, Lewy. (1975, November). A birthday anthem for America. Plays: The Drama Magazine for Young People, pp. 77-78. SUBJECTS/PLAY TYPE: Patriotism; Independence Day, American; Choral Reading.

281. 5-9. (+) Wartski, Maureen Crane. **The birthday guests.** CAST: 3f, 3m. ACTS: 1. SETTINGS: Kitchen; living room. PLAYING TIME: 25 min. PLOT: Four members of the Phelps family miss the father and oldest son, who are away fighting in the Civil War. During a heavy fog, one officer from each side seeks food and shelter at the Phelps farmhouse. The tension of war is forgotten for a while when a truce is agreed upon by the two guests. After a congenial breakfast, during which the two realize they have many similarities, the fog lifts, they salute each other as friends, then depart in opposite directions to rejoin their men. RECOMMENDATION: The Civil War setting enhances the universal themes of brotherhood, peace, and friendship. Appropriate uniforms are needed for the officers. ROYALTY: Free to Plays Subscribers. SOURCE: Wartski, Maureen Crane. (1980, February). The birthday guests. Plays: The Drama Magazine for Young People, pp. 56-62. SUBJECTS/PLAY TYPE: Civil War, U.S.; Peace; Playlet.

282. 7-12. (+) Berghammer, Gretta & Caspers, Rod. (Wilde, Oscar) **The birthday of the infanta.** (Birthday of the infanta) CAST: 12u. ACTS: 1. SETTINGS: Bare stage, props. PLAYING TIME: NA. PLOT: To please the princess, Don Pedro brings her a horribly deformed child, whose ugliness makes her laugh. As she naps, the child fantasizes that he and the princess are in love. Tragically, he sees himself in a mirror, realizes what a horrid creature he is, and dies of a broken heart. When the princess awakens, she is furious that he cannot entertain her and commands that in the future, those who come to entertain her have no hearts to break.

RECOMMENDATION: This would be excellent as lead in to a unit about tolerance and the dignity of all human beings. This is meant to be performed as part of a trilogy by the authors which includes **The Happy Prince** and **The Devoted Friends** (entitled **Broken Hearts**). ROYALTY: NA. SOURCE: Jennings, Coleman A. & Berghammer, Gretta. (1986). Theatre for youth: Twelve plays with mature themes. Austin, TX: Univ. of Texas Press SUBJECTS/PLAY TYPE: Tolerance; Disabilities; Adaptation.

283. K-6*. (+) Walker, Stuart. (Wilde, Oscar) **The birthday of the infanta.** (The birthday of the infanta) CAST: 2f, 3m, 2u. ACTS: 1. SETTINGS: Bare stage, props. PLAYING TIME: NA. PLOT: The Chamberlain brings the Fantastic (a hunchbacked, disfigured little boy) to entertain the Princess. She laughs at his physical disabilities and disfigurement. The Fantastic sees himself, for the first time, in a mirror. His laughter at the ugly visage changes to agony and rage, he sobs uncontrollably and collapses. The Chamberlain finds the boy, dead, and advises Infanta that the Fantastic will dance no more as his heart is broken. The Infanta pronounces that future performers must have no hearts. RECOMMENDATION: This condensed version of Wilde's tragic short story follows the plot closely, but leaves out much background information on the King and many details of the birthday celebration. It presents the themes of the original well, and evokes the tragic emotions that should accompany its resolution. ROYALTY: NA. SOURCE: Jennings, Coleman A. & Harris, Aurand. (1988). Plays children love, Volume II. New York, NY: St. Martin's Press. SUBJECTS/PLAY TYPE: Cruelty; Disabilities; Adaptation.

284. 5-8. (+) Gotwalt, Helen Louise Miller. **A birthday pie for George.** CAST: 6f, 6m. ACTS: 1. SETTINGS: Living room. PLAYING TIME: 15 min. PLOT: George Washington Smith resents that he was named after the first President because they share the same birthday and his mother makes cherry pie for his party each year. As his guests arrive, he sneaks into the kitchen and hides the pies. After his mother sends his sister to buy a cake, George feels guilty, tells the truth, and resolves to live up to Washington's reputation for honesty. RECOMMENDATION: Many children will relate to George's problem. Although George's mother does indicate that she never knew how much a name might affect her child, her realization does not lead to a frank discussion between mother and child. Instead, George accedes to his mother's unrealistic wishes about his attitude. ROYALTY: Free to Plays subscribers. SOURCE: Gotwalt, Helen Louise Miller. (1988, January/February). A birthday pie for George. Plays: The Drama Magazine for Young People, pp. 39-43. SUBJECTS/PLAY TYPE: Washington, George; Birthday; Names; Playlet.

285. 9-12. (+) Schulman, Charlie. **The birthday present.** CAST: 3f, 4m, Su. ACTS: 3. SETTINGS: Living room; TV studio. PLAYING TIME: NA. PLOT: Wallace is a 10 year old loser whose father inoculates him as his birthday present just before "Daddy" is put into jail for

doing scientific experiments on people. Twenty years later an epidemic strikes, leaving all men sterile except Wallace, whose inoculation has immunized him. Wallace becomes a hero, makes money by artificially inseminating women, and calls himself the "Father of our country." RECOMMENDATION: Written by a 16 year old, this award winning play is short on characterization, but presents well the hypocrisies of people, the cruelty that sometimes exits within families, and the horrors of germ warfare. Because of the subject matter, it should be produced only by and for mature young adults. ROYALTY: NA. SOURCE: Lamb, Wendy. (1986). Meeting the winter bike rider and other prize winning plays. New York, NY: Dell. SUBJECTS/PLAY TYPE: Germ Warfare; Sterility; Satire.

286. 4-8. (+) Dixon, Michael B. & Patch, Jerry. **Bits and bytes.** CAST: 5u. ACTS: 1. SETTINGS: Computer store. PLAYING TIME: 60 min. PLOT: Happy, a young student, is introduced to the computer and its capabilities. She learns that while the computer is an excellent tool, it cannot replace people and learns a valuable lesson about installment buying. RECOMMENDATION: This excellent play teaches children about what a computer can and cannot do, and increases consumer awareness. The original cast may be expanded from 5 to 10 by using multiple casting. The play has been set to music, but the rhythm is such that the songs could be spoken. ROYALTY: $35. SOURCE: Dixon, Michael B. & Patch, Jerry. (1983). Denver, CO: Pioneer Drama Service. SUBJECTS/PLAY TYPE: Computers; Musical.

287. 7-12. (+) Jones, C. Robert. **The blabbermouth.** CAST: 5f, 3m. ACTS: 1. SETTINGS: Store. PLAYING TIME: NA. PLOT: Two teenagers and the leading citizen of the town learn about the values of compassion and good judgment when the careless repetition of information, even though true, nearly ruins the town's general store owner. RECOMMENDATION: This effectively and entertainingly demonstrates the value of good judgment, compassion, and community. ROYALTY: $15. SOURCE: Jones, C. Robert. (1983). The blabbermouth. Woodstock, IL: Dramatic Pub. Co. SUBJECTS/PLAY TYPE: Truth; Compassion; Values; Drama.

288. 9-12. (+) Sergel, Christopher. (Neihardt, John G.) **Black Elk speaks.** (Flaming rainbow) CAST: 3f, 11m. ACTS: 2. SETTINGS: Bare stage. PLAYING TIME: NA. PLOT: This powerful drama retells the chronology of events from Columbus' discovery of America to the Fetterman Massacre and Wounded Knee that ended forever the independence of a proud people. Using Black Elk's own poetic words, the proud heritage and dignity of Native Americans are tragically juxtaposed with their tragic fate at the hands of a callous, arrogant society. RECOMMENDATION: Representational plot and poetic dialogue make this a difficult presentation for adolescents. However, if the actors are given adequate background about the history of Native Americans, and have a sensitive director, this could be very successful. ROYALTY: $60. SOURCE: Sergel, Christopher. (1986).

Black Elk speaks. Woodstock, Il: Dramatic Pub. Co. SUBJECTS/PLAY TYPE: Native Americans; Adaptation.

289. 4-6. (-) Bland, Joellen. (Alcott, Louisa May) **The black sheep.** (Little men) CAST: 1f, 9m. ACTS: 1. SETTINGS: Parlor; schoolroom. PLAYING TIME: 30 min. PLOT: Professor and Jo Bhaer teach their boys lessons in honesty and kindness through a series of episodes. RECOMMENDATION: Although faithfully recreating the original plot, too much transitional material is missing, causing this play to become a series of melodramatic and undeveloped scenes. ROYALTY: Free to Plays subscribers. SOURCE: Bland, Joellen. (1983, November). The black sheep. Plays: The Drama Magazine for Young People, pp. 69-79. SUBJECTS/PLAY TYPE: Family; Orphans; Adaptation.

290. K-3. (+) McCaslin, Nellie. **The Blacksmith and the carpenter.** CAST: 3u. ACTS: 1. SETTINGS: Yard. PLAYING TIME: 10 min. PLOT: A rich man, who lives between a carpenter and a blacksmith, pays them to move so that he will have some quiet. They exchange houses and the rich man still has the noise. RECOMMENDATION: The old adage that money can't buy happiness is cleverly presented. ROYALTY: None SOURCE: McCaslin, Nellie. (1977). Puppet fun: Production, performance, and plays. New York, NY: D. McKay Co. SUBJECTS/PLAY TYPE: Money; Puppet Play.

291. 12. (+) Harnetiaux, Brian Patrick. **Bleeders.** CAST: 1f, 2m, Su. ACTS: 1. SETTINGS: Inner-city street. PLAYING TIME: NA. PLOT: An ex-hippie street poet and a middle-age suburban housewife (who is protesting the existence of an adult bookstore) meet. After a satirical exchange of words, the event that brought both to the store is revealed. The woman's husband was knifed as he was leaving the bookstore, and it was the poet who pulled the knife from the body, unintentionally causing the man to bleed to death. RECOMMENDATION: Although easy to produce, this play would be difficult for all but the most sophisticated older students to understand because of its depressing and ironic content. ROYALTY: $20. SOURCE: Harnetiaux, Bryan Patrick. (1987). Bleeders. Woodstock, IL: Dramatic Pub. Co. SUBJECTS/PLAY TYPE: Death; Hopelessness; Drama.

292. 9-12. (+) Foote, Horton. **Blind date.** CAST: 2f, 2m. ACTS: 1. SETTINGS: Living room. PLAYING TIME: NA. PLOT: Sarah Nancy visits her Aunt Delores, who introduces her to young men. The results are disastrous. Sarah Nancy cannot make conversation, so Delores gives her a list of questions to ask. She is painfully honest and blunt, is never gracious, and she retires to her room before the young men leave. A date arranged with Felix appears doomed as well, but when the two are finally left alone, they manage to co-exist comfortably. RECOMMENDATION: This period piece about social relationships for young people arranged by adults is one that teenagers would have difficulty relating to, although they might recognize the grown up who creates problems by trying too hard to help. ROYALTY:

NA. SOURCE: Foote, Horton. (1986). Blind date. New York, NY: Dramatist Play Service, Inc. SUBJECTS/PLAY TYPE: Dating; Comedy.

293. 7-12. (+) McCusker, Paul. **The blind date.** CAST: 1f, 2m. ACTS: 1. SETTINGS: Bare stage, props. PLAYING TIME: NA. PLOT: As two teenage boys talk while waiting for their dates, one ridicules the sensitivity of the other. Finally, only one of the two dates shows up because the other girl had a better offer. The girl who does come plays the flute, and so does the sensitive boy. The two go off, leaving the "cool" boy out in the cold. RECOMMENDATION: This cleverly presents the theme that being yourself is more valuable than trying to be "cool." Some of the dialogue may have to be updated. ROYALTY: NA. SOURCE: McCusker, Paul. (1984). Batteries not included. Boston: Baker's Plays. SUBJECTS/PLAY TYPE: Identity; Dating; Comedy; Skit.

294. 7-12. (+) Fuerstenberg, Anna. **Blind dates.** CAST: 3f, 2m, Su. ACTS: 1. SETTINGS: Bare stage, props. PLAYING TIME: NA. PLOT: This collection of fragmented scenes deals with everyday lives and decisions of high schoolers such as dating, sex, college, suicide, alcohol, schoolwork, drugs, how to treat your father's new girlfriend, peer pressure, homophobia, and parents' unemployment. RECOMMENDATION: The audience empathizes with the "sometimes confused, sometimes scared" positions of the characters until the very end. This is very adaptable to specific needs. ROYALTY: NA. SOURCE: Fuerstenberg, Anna. (1984). Blind dates. Ontario, Canada: Playwrights Canada. SUBJECTS/PLAY TYPE: Adolescent Problems; Attitudes; Drama.

295. 8-12. (+) Gilsenan, Nancy. **Blindspot.** CAST: 3f, 3m. ACTS: 1. SETTINGS: Living room. PLAYING TIME: NA. PLOT: When a young social worker cannot deal with a mentally retarded boy assigned to her, she leaves him with her two elderly aunts. They discover there is more awareness and potential for life in the boy than the psychologists admit. Unfortunately, the official diagnosis wins out over the loving one. RECOMMENDATION: This play's conclusion could stimulate hours of discussion on issues related to care for the mentally retarded and the elderly, gun control, and attitudes towards Native Americans. The aunts are endearing characters. Despite the attempt to confront many controversial issues in one short presentation, the drama is effective. ROYALTY: $20. SOURCE: Gilsenan, Nancy. (1981). Blindspot. Chicago, IL: Dramatic Pub. Co. SUBJECTS/PLAY TYPE: Mental Retardation; Elderly; Drama.

296. 4-6. (+) Guay, Georgette. **The bling said hello.** CAST: 2f, 1m. ACTS: 1. SETTINGS: Living room; bedroom; breakfast area; front porch; remote cliff. PLAYING TIME: 35 min. PLOT: An imaginative young girl and her policewoman mother, who live in an isolated small town in northern Canada, are visited by a sensitive and harmless alien being, the Bling. The editor of the local newspaper and his wife use the Bling to extort money from the citizens. After the girl befriends the Bling and learns of the editor's extortion scheme, she and her mother expose and capture the evil editor. The Bling departs. RECOMMENDATION: The fast moving plot reflects important themes including mother daughter relationships, female self reliance, and open-mindedness in judging others. The continuous action requires careful staging to insure easy flow. ROYALTY: NA. SOURCE: Guay, Georgette. (1980). Kids plays: six Canadian plays for children. Toronto, Canada: Playwrights Press. SUBJECTS/PLAY TYPE: Aliens; Science Fiction; Comedy.

297. 4-6*. (+) Guay, Georgette. **The bling said hello: You'll never be the same.** CAST: 2f, 1m, 7u. ACTS: 1. SETTINGS: Playground. PLAYING TIME: 40 min. PLOT: Sandy wants to be a ventriloquist, but her friends try to get her to join in "normal activities." She is torn between being a unique individual and wanting to belong. In a dream sequence, she visits Samenessness Land where all trees, flowers and people are the same. There, six "Sams" want to perform cloning surgery on her so she will look and act just like them. Bling, a fantasy friend from Ictarius, where everything is different, helps her to escape. She realizes she is much happier being herself, regardless of what her friends say. RECOMMENDATION: Accomplished performers may be needed to memorize the lines and portray the feelings and intensity of these scenes. Also needed is a synthesizer and musician for occasional background music. ROYALTY: NA. SOURCE: Guay, Georgette. (1979). The bling said hello: You'll never be the same. Toronto: Playwrights Canada. SUBJECTS/PLAY TYPE: Individuality; Friendship; Fantasy.

298. K-4. (+) Watts, Irene N. **A blizzard leaves no footprints.** CAST: 4f, 1m, 4u. ACTS: 1. SETTINGS: Tent; cave. PLAYING TIME: NA. PLOT: Two Eskimo children and their mother are visited in their igloo by Blizzard, who puts out their fire and steals the mother. The children, who regret not helping their mother, encounter many Eskimo legend adventures while trying to find her. They are reunited and promise to help in the future. RECOMMENDATION: The characters are solid, and the audience will relate to the plight of the two children feeling guilty about not doing their chores. Since audience participation is involved, actions are mimed and results will vary. The dialogue between the two siblings is natural and reflective of all brothers and sisters. This is best performed in the round. ROYALTY: NA. SOURCE: Watts, Irene N. (1978). A blizzard leaves no footprints; listen to the drum; patches; the rainstone: Four children's plays. Toronto: Playwrights Co-op. SUBJECTS/PLAY TYPE: Legends, Eskimo; Seasons; Playlet.

299. 9-12. (-) Andrukonis, Jim. **Blocky battles the books.** CAST: 3f, 3m. ACTS: 1. SETTINGS: Classroom. PLAYING TIME: 10 min. PLOT: Blocky, a former boxing champion, goes back to high school to get his diploma. He has trouble keeping up with his classmates, but with support and encouragement from his boxing coach and his girlfriend, he passes and gets his diploma.

RECOMMENDATION: The theme that a high school diploma can be achieved with hard work and determination is laudable, especially with this country's focus on adult education. However, Blocky is characterized as a moron, his classmates are a stereotyped female airhead (Buffy) and an obviously Jewish overachiever. This totally misses the mark as it makes fun of education, educators, and courageous adults who return to school. ROYALTY: Free to Plays subscribers. SOURCE: Andrukonis, Jim. (1988, October). Blocky battles the books. Plays: The Drama Magazine for Young People, pp. 59-63. SUBJECTS/PLAY TYPE: Adult Education; Skit.

300. 9-12. (+) Kelly, Tim. **Bloody Jack: a thriller based on the murders of Jack the Ripper.** CAST: 5f, 6m. ACTS: 2. SETTINGS: street corner; parlor. PLAYING TIME: NA. PLOT: This thriller offers audiences yet another theory on the identity of Jack the Ripper and the reason behind his horrible crimes. As the drama progresses, the audience realizes that each member of Dr. Sargents' household has both motive and opportunity for committing the crimes that have horrified and intrigued England for three months. The suspense builds as each character in turn takes on an aura of evil. It ends with a shocking denouement. RECOMMENDATION: Kelly exposes the complex natures of his characters with subtle developments in the plot and through the revelations that surface in conversational exchanges. The tension is tightly wound and the mechanism of the play finely crafted, so that if it were well acted it would be guaranteed to hold an audience spellbound. It would be a challenge for young actors but a very rewarding one if they could master the complexities of the characters. Before taking on the play, a class would need to examine the difficulties of creating a Victorian parlor setting. ROYALTY: $50. SOURCE: Kelly, Tim J. (1981). Bloody Jack: a thriller based on the murders of Jack the Ripper, in 2 acts. Schulenburg, TX: I.E. Clark. SUBJECTS/PLAY TYPE: Murder; Jack the Ripper; Thriller.

301. 1-3. (+) Martin, Judith. **Blown off the billboard.** CAST: 6u. ACTS: 1. SETTINGS: Bare stage. PLAYING TIME: 10 min. PLOT: A walking, talking pair of lips escape from a billboard during a gust of wind. The sign painters try to lure them back with a singing ice cream cone, but the lips, ice cream cone, and a bag of garbage all escape. RECOMMENDATION: This imaginative fantasy uses short songs and dances to liven it up and to tie it all together. ROYALTY: NA. SOURCE: Martin, Judith. (1981). Everybody, everybody: a collection from the paper bag players. NY: Elsevier/Nelson Books. SUBJECTS/PLAY TYPE: Billboards; Fantasy.

302. 4-6. (+) Miller, Kathryn Schultz. **Blue horses.** CAST: 2f, 2m. ACTS: 1. SETTINGS: Backyard. PLAYING TIME: 60 min. PLOT: Four children play a game of wishing upon a star and use their imaginations to act out their fantasies, discovering in the process that their fantasies are not as ideal as expected. RECOMMENDATION: The play can be useful to teach older children about accepting themselves as they

are. ROYALTY: $35. SOURCE: Miller, Kathryn Schultz. (1984). Blue horses. Morton Grove, IL: Coach House Press. SUBJECTS/PLAY TYPE: Wishes; Dreams; Self Knowledge; Drama.

303. K-2. (-) Lotspeich, Paulette W. **The Blue Jay disco show.** CAST: 8u. ACTS: 1. SETTINGS: None. PLAYING TIME: 10 min. PLOT: The Disco Hour show host interviews her guests, and breaks for commercials, in this satire of real celebrities and well known commercials. RECOMMENDATION: Because the celebrity and commercial parodies are based on older commercials, this very witty satire may not be understood by audiences who have probably never seen the originals upon which it is based. ROYALTY: Free to Plays subscribers. SOURCE: Lotspeich, Paulette W. (1980, November). The Blue Jay Disco Show. Plays: The Drama Magazine for Young People, pp. 67-69. SUBJECTS/PLAY TYPE: Comedy; Satire; Puppet Play.

304. 3-6*. (+) Martens, Anne Coulter. **The blue overalls angel.** CAST: 3f, 8m, Su. ACTS: 1. SETTINGS: Church stage; hillside. PLAYING TIME: 25 min. PLOT: As Scotty, a church janitor, fixes stage props in the church for a Christmas pageant, Jeanie, a seven year old unhappy orphan, enters looking for a Christmas angel. When she hears a young lady sing in the pageant rehearsal, she thinks she has found the angel. The singer and producer coldly rebuff the child. When Scotty intervenes on the child's behalf and reminds everybody of the true meaning of Christmas, the performer and producer change their attitudes and offer to help Jeanie. Scotty and his wife, who are childless, adopt her. RECOMMENDATION: This easily performed and simple Christmas play reminds viewers of less fortunate children and encourages the true spirit of love at Christmas time. Sentimental and symbolic, this would make a fine church-related program. ROYALTY: $3. SOURCE: Martens, Anne Coulter. (n.d.) The blue overalls angel. Franklin, OH: Eldridge Pub. Co. SUBJECTS/PLAY TYPE: Christmas; Drama.

305. K-5. (+) Mahlman, Lewis & Jones, David Cadwalder. **The blue willow.** CAST: 9u. ACTS: 1. SETTINGS: Bridge. PLAYING TIME: 15 min. PLOT: Two young lovers are separated by their feuding fathers, and fake their own deaths. After hearing the fathers wish they had heeded the children's wishes, the lovers reappear. The rich man to whom the father has betrothed his daughter is angry, but the fathers allow the children to marry. RECOMMENDATION: This provides a glimpse into ancient Chinese traditions, and without belittling them, allows modern thought to prevail. The biting dog, who is the basis of the fathers' feud, adds slapstick humor to this romantic adaptation. ROYALTY: Free to Plays subscribers. SOURCE: Mahlman, Lewis & Jones, David Cadwalder. (1980). Folk tale plays for puppets. Boston, MA: Plays, Inc. SUBJECTS/PLAY TYPE: Folk Tales, China; Love; Puppet Play.

306. 3-7. (-) Bredefeldt, Ghosta. **Blunder, bluebell, baby, and birdie.** CAST: 1f, 2m. ACTS: 1. SETTINGS: None. PLAYING TIME: NA. PLOT: Children's fears of

the dark, of parents' behavior, of being labeled a coward, of death, and of being left alone, are explored in this avant-garde presentation. RECOMMENDATION: Since actors must improvise to elicit audience participation, the play would best be performed by well prepared adults. The television scenes and language would need to be revised to eliminate the World War II references and Swedish slang. Even with these changes, the play is so nontraditional that its success would be highly doubtful. ROYALTY: NA. SOURCE: Bredefeldt, Ghosta. (1981). Blunder, bluebell, baby and birdie. New York, NY: Samuel French, Inc. SUBJECTS/PLAY TYPE: Loneliness; Drama.

307. 12. (+) Noojin, Randy. **Boaz.** CAST: 2m. ACTS: 1. SETTINGS: Living room. PLAYING TIME: 60 min. PLOT: Rich, a young loner, arrives at the ramshackle house of his apparently senile grandfather, Clayton. He tries in vain to communicate with Clayton, who simply offers things to eat and searches distractedly for various items. Rich's frustration mounts until he understands Clayton's desperation at being unable to give anyone anything. He pours out his heart to Clayton, accepts his offer of pie, asks him for help, and the two men communicate at last. RECOMMENDATION: This tour de force uses disjointed dialogue and lack of communication between two characters effectively to elicit feelings of intense frustration. Sometimes grimly humorous, sometimes painfully grating, the play climaxes in a moving scene of self revelation and compassion. Much profanity and discussion of two sensitive subjects, abortion and senility, make **Boaz** potentially controversial. ROYALTY: $20. SOURCE: Noojin, Randy. (1986). Boaz. Woodstock, IL: Dramatic Pub. Co. SUBJECTS/PLAY TYPE: South; Senility; Abortion; Drama.

308. 6-12*. (+) Gibson, William. **The body & the wheel.** CAST: 6f, 17m. ACTS: 2. SETTINGS: Ancient Rome. PLAYING TIME: NA. PLOT: This Easter play depicts well known scenes of the teachings of Christ. Albert Schweitzer's concept that Christ "laid hold of the wheel of the world" is dramatically emphasized by the physical movements of the players always moving in a circle. RECOMMENDATION: Even though this play is quite long, it has much action and presents an excellent religious and educational narrative. It requires some difficult techniques but most of the props are pantomimed. The production needs to be done by upper grades with children included as performers, most appropriately in a church setting. ROYALTY: $50. SOURCE: Gibson, William. (1975). The body & and the wheel. New York, NY: Dramatists Play Service, Inc. SUBJECTS/PLAY TYPE: Religious; Easter; Drama.

309. 7-9. (+) Belgrade Coventry Theatre in Education Company. **Bog deal.** CAST: 1f, 3m, 5u. ACTS: 2. SETTINGS: Divided stage - street scene with shops. PLAYING TIME: 360 min. PLOT: In two acts, set two weeks apart, this tells the story of a front man for an investor, who decides to personally buy up portions of property over several years. Through behind closed door agreements, he becomes rich from his investment at the expense of the homes of shop owners in an area of London. RECOMMENDATION: This exposes students to a depressing business world based on greed and back room agreements. The action revolves around undocumented economic development processes from 1950 to 1970 in England, and calls on students to make value judgments based on what they see. If supervised by well prepared educators, this could be a valuable expose of ethics in business. ROYALTY: NA. SOURCE: Belgrade Coventry Theatre in Education. (1980). Four junior programmes. London, England: Eyre Methuen. SUBJECTS/PLAY TYPE: Social Commentary; Urban Modernization; Exploitation; Participation Play.

310. 4-6. (+) Winther, Barbara. **The bogles of Dundee.** CAST: 3f, 4m, 3u. ACTS: 3. SETTINGS: Study. PLAYING TIME: 20 min. PLOT: Dr. Burns inherits his dead uncle's haunted house in Dundee, Scotland. The ghosts (bogles) are driven out when the house is cleaned, since bogles hate clean and bright areas. Dr. Burns looks forward to having his first dinner guest in his new home. RECOMMENDATION: Although the plot moves logically, the rather pat and "unhorrific" solution to the ghosts is a letdown. ROYALTY: Free to Plays subscribers. SOURCE: Winther, Barbara. (1984, March). The bogles of Dundee. Plays: The Drama Magazine for Young People, pp. 34-40. SUBJECTS/PLAY TYPE: Ghosts; Comedy.

311. 6-12. (+) Fenisong, Ruth. **The boiled eggs.** CAST: 1f, 6m. ACTS: 1. SETTINGS: Restaurant; courtroom. PLAYING TIME: 30 min. PLOT: A farmer, on his way to market to sell his cow, orders a meal of 10 boiled eggs at a restaurant and promises to pay after he sells his cow. The restauranteur agrees; she plans to charge the farmer for the eggs, the hens, and the unborn chicks. When the farmer returns, he refuses to pay his food bill of $1000 and goes to court. The farmer's lawyer arrives late, explaining that he has been boiling two bushels of corn for planting, showing that, just as boiled corn will not grow, boiled eggs will not hatch. The restauranteur not only loses the court case, but the restaurant as well when the eggs, which are rotten, explode. RECOMMENDATION: This farce will delight a young audience with its overdrawn characters, righteous resolution, and clever court argument. The dialogue is sometimes slow, but the play is well paced. ROYALTY: NA. SOURCE: Swortzell, Lowell. (1986). Six plays for young people from the federal theatre project (1936-1939). New York NY: Greenwood Press. SUBJECTS/PLAY TYPE: Restaurants; Swindlers and Swindling; Comedy.

312. 9-12. (+) DuBois, Graham. **Bonds of affection.** CAST: 3f, 3m, Su. ACTS: 1. SETTINGS: Room. PLAYING TIME: 30 min. PLOT: Shortly after the Battle of Gettysburg, a southern mother appeals to her old friend, President Lincoln, for safe passage for her family from Gettysburg back home. Her son, a bitter Confederate soldier, learns from Lincoln that bonds of affection can still exist between North and South. RECOMMENDATION: The play is suspenseful, and some of the conflict between North and South is

revealed, although sentimentality somewhat mars the overall effect. ROYALTY: Free to Plays subscribers. SOURCE: Kamerman, Sylvia E. (1983). Holiday plays round the year. Boston, MA: Plays, Inc. SUBJECTS/PLAY TYPE: Civil War, U.S.; Lincoln, Abraham; Drama.

313. 8-12. (+) Ferris, Monk. **Bone-Chiller! CAST:** 8f, 4m, Su. ACTS: 3. SETTINGS: Parlor/Library. PLAYING TIME: NA. PLOT: Family and friends arrive for the reading of Uncle Josiah's will. Much to their surprise, it is a rebus, with drawings for words. Many interesting facts and details are discovered about those present, as the rebus is solved. People disappear, scary noises are heard, and murders are committed as the friends unravel the will to find they have all inherited a great deal of money. RECOMMENDATION: Sophisticated excitement, intrigue, and lengthy dialogue make this play a choice for mature high school production. A copy of the will would be helpful to the audience. ROYALTY: $50. SOURCE: Ferris, Monk. (1985). Bone- Chiller!. New York, NY: Samuel French, Inc. SUBJECTS/PLAY TYPE: Murder; Rhebus; Wills; Mystery.

314. 1-6. (+) Purvin, George. Purvin, Nancy. **The boob in the tube. CAST:** 2f, 4m, Su. ACTS: 1. SETTINGS: Bedroom. PLAYING TIME: NA. PLOT: During spring break, George concentrates all his energy on watching television and becomes a couch potato. His family and friends provide him with a second chance to be himself. RECOMMENDATION: Written almost entirely in rhyme, the charming script has a timely moral, and uses everyone including the classroom teacher and principal (which should delight the children). There are several songs set to well known melodies. ROYALTY: $30. SOURCE: Purvin, George & Purvin, Nancy. (1986). The boob in the tube. Franklin, OH: Eldridge Pub. Co. SUBJECTS/PLAY TYPE: Television; Comedy.

315. 2-7. (+) Boiko, Claire. **The book that saved the earth. CAST:** 7u. ACTS: 1. SETTINGS: Library. PLAYING TIME: 20 min. PLOT: The Macronites invade Earth, landing in the Centerville Library. Their reading of Mother Goose Nursery Rhymes, with all the strange characters therein, makes them afraid to continue their invasion. RECOMMENDATION: The novel plot of this easy to produce play is filled with very humorous scenes. ROYALTY: Free to Plays subscribers. SOURCE: Boiko, Claire. (1984, November). The book that saved the Earth. Plays: The Drama Magazine for Young People, pp. 39-44. SUBJECTS/PLAY TYPE: Science Fiction; Books; Nursery Rhymes; Comedy.

316. 4-6. (+) Adelstein, Sheryl T. **The bookcase mystery. CAST:** 2f, 13u. ACTS: 1. SETTINGS: Classroom. PLAYING TIME: 20 min. PLOT: Common items found in a classroom (yardstick, chalk, eraser, etc.) steal a bookcase of books needed for the new school year. Each character gives a version of the mystery, which remains unsolved. Ms. Terry (mystery), the school teacher, discovers that they collectively stole because they were jealous of the books' knowledge. She asks

them to work as hard to make the school year successful as they did to steal the books. RECOMMENDATION: This is cleverly written with much word play (Scissors always gives "cutting answers;" Compass "gets the point" from Pencil; and Protractor sees a different "angle" to the mystery). ROYALTY: Free to Plays subscribers. SOURCE: Adelstein, Sheryl T. (1981, October). The bookcase mystery. Plays: The Drama Magazine for Young People, pp. 39-45. SUBJECTS/PLAY TYPE: School; Comedy.

317. 4-9. (+) Satchell, Mary. **Booker T. Washington. CAST:** 2f, 4m. ACTS: 1. SETTINGS: Sitting room. PLAYING TIME: 25 min. PLOT: Booker, age 13 and unschooled, works in the coal mines of West Virginia, but feels certain he will be a school principal someday. A black teacher helps him go to school while he works at the mine. When Booker wants to go to school at Hampton Institute in Virginia, his stepfather opposes him. His mother sells her favorite possession, a clock, so Booker will have money for school. RECOMMENDATION: This inspirational play about the childhood of Booker T. Washington could be presented during Black History Month. It is suitable for older students to perform before a younger audience. ROYALTY: Free to Plays subscribers. SOURCE: Satchell, Mary. (1989, January/February). Booker T. Washington. Plays: The Drama Magazine for Young People, pp. 61- 70. SUBJECTS/PLAY TYPE: Black Americans; Washington, Booker T.; Playlet.

318. K-6. (+) Chaloner, Gwen. **The bookworm. CAST:** 4f, 5m, 7u. ACTS: 1. SETTINGS: Library. PLAYING TIME: 20 min. PLOT: Betty seeks shelter from a rainstorm in the public library and meets a talking Bookworm. By introducing her to seven walking, talking reference books, Alice in Wonderland, Tom Sawyer, and other characters from children's literature, the Bookworm kindles Betty's interest in reading. RECOMMENDATION: Despite rather stilted language and a preachy tone, this offers a positive message regarding reading, and the Bookworm is a memorable fuddy duddy. ROYALTY: Free to Plays subscribers. SOURCE: Chaloner, Gwen. (1983, November). The bookworm. Plays: The Drama Magazine for Young People, pp. 45-50. SUBJECTS/PLAY TYPE: Library; Reading; Book Week; Skit.

319. 9-12. (+) Herron, Ralph. **Boom cake. CAST:** 6f, 6m, Su. ACTS: 2. SETTINGS: Beach house; office. PLAYING TIME: NA. PLOT: When Navy planes cause sonic booms that collapse her baking, Jo Ellen Miner sends an itemized bill to the government. Through a series of mix-ups, the bill becomes enlarged (i.e., 39 eggs become 39 dozen). An inspector from the Pentagon arrives at the Navy base, misunderstandings pile up until everyone is involved in a melee with the police. It is not explained how, but all the charges are dropped, Jo Ellen gets her supplies, and the inspector goes back to Washington in disgrace. RECOMMENDATION: Despite its being trite and predictable, this is entertaining. This musical has been successfully produced on small stages, but some juggling may be

required to construct the single set. This is geared for senior high acting groups, though slightly younger groups may be appropriate as an audience. ROYALTY: $75. SOURCE: Heron, Ralph. (1980). Boom cake. Elgin, IL: Performance Pub. SUBJECTS/PLAY TYPE: Musical; Bureaucracy; Navy, U.S.; Comedy.

320. 12. (-) Mattera, John. **Bored stiff. CAST:** 3f, 4m, Su. ACTS: 2. SETTINGS: Living room. PLAYING TIME: NA. PLOT: A husband considered dead reappears to murder the lawyer who helped him "die," and then married his widow. The wife and teenage daughter get involved with plans for murder too, and in the end, everyone dies. RECOMMENDATION: This plot is contrived and unnecessarily convoluted. The daughter falsely suggests to her mother that her father has forced himself on her sexually. The whole play is in bad taste and inappropriate for any audience. ROYALTY: $50. SOURCE: Mattera, John. (1987). Bored stiff. Woodstock, IL: Dramatic Pub. Co. SUBJECTS/PLAY TYPE: Mystery; Tragedy; Drama.

321. 7-12. (+) Nolan, Paul T. **Boshibari and the two thieves. CAST:** 3m. ACTS: 1. SETTINGS: Japanese house; orchard. PLAYING TIME: NA. PLOT: Two servants steal apples from their master's orchard but are caught because of their own pride and arrogance. One suggests that the other be tied to his jousting pole, and as he gloats, the master ties him up also. Confident that he has stopped them, the master leaves, only to return to an empty orchard. The thieves have fed each other. RECOMMENDATION: Because of Japanese customs and mannerisms, the Kyogen Farce requires much formality of movement and expression. Skill with the quarterstaff, a stout pole used in fighting, is necessary. ROYALTY: None for amateur performance. SOURCE: Nolan, Paul T. (1982). Folk tale plays round the world: a collection of royalty-free one-act plays about lands far and near. Boston, MA: Plays, Inc. SUBJECTS/PLAY TYPE: Japanese Kyogen Farce; Cunningness; Deceit; Adaptation.

322. 4-6. (+) Carney, Mary F. **The Boston machine.** CAST: 7f, 7m, Su. ACTS: 1. SETTINGS: Touring car. PLAYING TIME: NA. PLOT: Papa (Mr. Wellpepper) has just purchased an "infernal machine" and wants to take the family for a pleasant drive. The outing becomes complicated: the car is crowded with neighbors invited along. Papa is blamed for the problems that occur when the car runs out of gas and rain begins to fall. Somewhere in the fog, Papa takes a wrong turn and they end up back home. All blame Papa for ruining the day. RECOMMENDATION: This amusing piece has little plot, but the audience can sympathize with Papa. Proper costuming is a necessity. ROYALTY: $25. SOURCE: Carney, Mary F. (1979). The Boston machine. Franklin, OH: Eldridge Pub. Co. SUBJECTS/PLAY TYPE: Family; Comedy.

323. 9-12. (+) Roam, Pearl. **The Boston Massacre.** CAST: 2f, 30m, Su. ACTS: 1. SETTINGS: Courtroom. PLAYING TIME: 30 min. PLOT: The British troops involved in the Boston Massacre are put on trial. The facts indicate their lives had been threatened and they acted in self defense. But John Adams, their defense counsel, is threatened and pressured to hold back evidence. He refuses, imparting the most important lesson of the massacre, the need for integrity. RECOMMENDATION: The play may be useful to supplement classwork in history or civics, although its didactic tone and anti-climactic nature make it less than exciting. ROYALTY: Free to Plays subscribers. SOURCE: Roam, Pearl. (1981, February). The Boston Massacre. Plays: The Drama Magazine for Young People, pp. 22- 32. SUBJECTS/PLAY TYPE: Adams, John; Playlet.

324. 3-6. (-) Barbee, Lindsey. **The Boston tea party.** CAST: 4f, 3m. ACTS: 2. SETTINGS: Living room. PLAYING TIME: 20 min. PLOT: Six young people discuss the Boston tea party. RECOMMENDATION: This lacks much action or plot and somehow makes the Boston tea party seem boring. ROYALTY: None. SOURCE: Kamerman, Sylvia E. (1975). Patriotic and historical plays for young people. Boston, MA: Plays, Inc. SUBJECTS/PLAY TYPE: Boston Tea Party; Revolution, U. S.; Playlet.

325. K-5. (+) Ross, Laura. **The Boston tea party.** CAST: 6m, Su. ACTS: 3. SETTINGS: Meeting room; ship deck. PLAYING TIME: NA. PLOT: The colonists argue that the British government has no right to tax them since they have no representation in Parliament. In protest, they dump a shipload of tea into the Boston Harbor. RECOMMENDATION: As a narrator describes the events, the actors dramatize them with continuous movement and some short lines. Directions are included for making the buckram masks which the protesters wear. ROYALTY: None. SOURCE: Ross, Laura. (1975). Mask-Making with pantomime and stories from American history. New York, NY: Lothrop, Lee, & Shepard Co. SUBJECTS/PLAY TYPE: Revolution, U. S.; Pantomime.

326. 9-12. (+) Thane, Adele. (Stevenson, Robert Louis) **The bottle imp.** (The bottle imp.) CAST: 7f, 9m, 11u. ACTS: 1. SETTINGS: Garden; beach. PLAYING TIME: 30 min. PLOT: Keawe possesses a magic bottle whose imp grants wishes. But, if the bottle is possessed at death, the owner faces the flames of hell. Keawe receives his wishes and sells the bottle to Kokua. The bottle is sold to a shipmate. All is well until Kokua becomes seriously ill. Keawe buys the bottle back and requests that Kokua be healed. His wife helps him resell it. RECOMMENDATION: The many references to the flames of hell and the devil may make this unsuitable for younger children or religious groups. ROYALTY: Free to Plays Subscribers. SOURCE: Thane, Adele. (1980, February). The bottle imp. Plays: The Drama Magazine for Young People, pp. 70-80. SUBJECTS/PLAY TYPE: Adventure; Fantasy; Family; Adaptation.

327. 1-6. (-) Boelt, Martha Macdonald. **Bottom meets Mr. Shakespeare. CAST:** Su. ACTS: 4. SETTINGS: Puppet stage. PLAYING TIME: 15 min. PLOT: Bottom's mother sends him away to make his

fortune. He's no good at working, but does sing Hickory, Dickory, Dock; London Bridge; the Muffin Man; Froggie Went a Courtin'; and Old King Cole. Finally, Shakespeare gives him the part of Bottom in **A Midsummer Night's Dream**, he meets the queen, and becomes the court jester. RECOMMENDATION: This is an ineffective and confusing way to teach the songs, as well as introduce the plot to Shakespeare's play. ROYALTY: Free to Plays subscribers. SOURCE: Boelt, Martha Macdonald. (1983, April). Bottom meets Mr. Shakespeare. Plays: The Drama Magazine for Young People, pp. 62-66. SUBJECTS/PLAY TYPE: Shakespeare, William; Nursery Rhymes; Puppet Play.

328. K-4. (+) Smith, Robert B. **Bought me a cat.** CAST: Su. ACTS: 1. SETTINGS: Flannel board. PLAYING TIME: NA. PLOT: A man living alone in the country acquires pets, one at a time, to keep him company. RECOMMENDATION: This develops listening and memorization skills as the children tell the story back to the teacher. ROYALTY: NA. SOURCE: Smith, Robert B. (1984). Music dramas for children with special needs. Denton, TX: Troostwyk Press. SUBJECTS/PLAY TYPE: Memorization Skills; Musical; Drama.

329. 3-6. (+) Boiko, Claire. **The boy from next Tuesday.** CAST: 8f, 2u. ACTS: 1. SETTINGS: Park. PLAYING TIME: 20 min. PLOT: A boy from the future takes the children of the present 1,000 years into the polluted future, where people live underground and children can play outdoors for only a few minutes without wearing their helmets. Trees, sunshine, and flowers are only memories and water is like bitter medicine. RECOMMENDATION: The grim warning to today's children is clear: they must do something to protect the environment before it is too late. ROYALTY: Free to Plays subscribers. SOURCE: Boiko, Claire. (1981, February). The boy from next Tuesday. Plays: The Drama Magazine for Young People, pp. 53-58. SUBJECTS/PLAY TYPE: Ecology; Pollution; Playlet.

330. 6-8. (+) Christmas, Joyce. **The boy most likely to succeed.** CAST: 6f, 6m, 2u. ACTS: 1. SETTINGS: Living room. PLAYING TIME: 25 min. PLOT: A young boy, chosen as the most likely to succeed, dreams of various occupations (doctor, tycoon, reporter, etc.) as representatives of each profession emphasize the work required to obtain the necessary skills. RECOMMENDATION: This is moralistic, but a good introduction to a unit on preparation for work. ROYALTY: Free to Plays subscribers. SOURCE: Christmas, Joyce. (1981, May). The boy most likely to succeed. Plays: The Drama Magazine for Young People, pp. 1-11. SUBJECTS/PLAY TYPE: Careers; Comedy.

331. K-3. (+) Havilan, Amorie & Smith, Lyn. A boy named Abe. CAST: 2f, 3m, Su. ACTS: 1. SETTINGS: Log cabin; store. PLAYING TIME: NA. PLOT: Abraham Lincoln's voracious appetite for learning and his job in the town's general store are dramatized. The conclusion shows "Honest Abe" walking a great distance to return a penny he overcharged a customer.

RECOMMENDATION: The positive themes of truth and honesty are presented in an entertaining format and the play could be used in a social studies unit, a values clarification unit, or as a holiday play on Lincoln's Birthday or President's Day. It can be read or pantomimed. ROYALTY: NA. SOURCE: Havilan, Amorie & Smith, Lyn. (1985). A boy named Abe. Brandon, MS: Quail Ridge Press. SUBJECTS/PLAY TYPE: Lincoln, Abraham; Tripartite.

332. 4-9. (+) Priore, Frank V. **The boy who cried, "Martian!"** CAST: 3f, 2m. ACTS: 1. SETTINGS: Living room. PLAYING TIME: 20 min. PLOT: Gary, a science fiction fan, has cried, "Martian!" so often that nobody believes him when the real thing lands in the front yard. His older sister and her friend converse with the alleged aliens, but when they realize they actually are talking to Martians, they leave screaming. Gary tries to calm them, and the Martians conclude that earthlings regress as they grow older. RECOMMENDATION: The humor is subtle and children will love the word play and misunderstandings that develop. This could be modernized with the use of current musical hits. ROYALTY: Free to Plays subscribers. SOURCE: Priore, Frank V. (1982, January/February). The boy who cried, "Martian!" Plays: The Drama Magazine for Young People, pp. 71-77. SUBJECTS/PLAY TYPE: Comedy; Science Fiction; Skit.

333. 6-12. (+) Wiles, Julian. **The boy who stole the stars.** CAST: 2f, 2m, 3u. ACTS: 1. SETTINGS: Porch; front yard. PLAYING TIME: NA. PLOT: A boy and his grandparents must come to grips with the grandfather's impending death. The boy imagines a fight with a dragon of the sky to capture a star and give his grandfather more time. At the end of the summer, the boy has come to terms with death, and with himself. RECOMMENDATION: With sympathy for the characters and their situation, the play effectively examines acceptance of death, fear, friends who move away, love, and life, without being maudlin. ROYALTY: $35. SOURCE: Wiles, Julian. (1985). The boy who stole the stars. Woodstock, IL: Dramatic Pub. Co. SUBJECTS/PLAY TYPE: Death and Dying; Grandparents; Personal Relationships; Drama.

334. 3-8*. (+) Smalley, Webster. **The boy who talked to whales.** CAST: 3f, 7m, 1u. ACTS: 1. SETTINGS: Pier. PLAYING TIME: NA. PLOT: Jerry has befriended and learned to communicate with a large sperm whale, Ooka, in Puget Sound. Ooka becomes a major tourist attraction and is also noticed by the Secret Service who would like to use her as an underwater military spy. Jerry convinces Ooka to leave the area but first he teaches her to disable whaling boats with logs. This eventually leads to an international incident, but world nations must stop whaling before Jerry will ask Ooka (and the other whales that she has taught to use logs) to stop their actions. RECOMMENDATION: This story would appeal to children on several different levels. The interactions between the children, parents, and political and military authority figures point out the difficulty in communication that can occur between

idealistic, spontaneous children and adults who are sometimes calculating or hypocritical. The primary theme of the story—the sacredness of all forms of life--is well presented. The moral issue of choosing to perform a dishonest act to achieve a good end is briefly explored. The play requires a talented cast of older (grades 6-9) students. ROYALTY: $35. SOURCE: Smalley, Webster. (1981). The boy who talked to whales. New Orleans, LA: Anchorage Press, Inc. SUBJECTS/PLAY TYPE: Whales; Survival- Animals; Endangered Species; Drama.

335. 5-7. (+) Merten, Elizabeth. **The boy with green fingers. CAST:** 3f, 4m. **ACTS:** 2. **SETTINGS:** Puppet stage. **PLAYING TIME:** 15 min. **PLOT:** When a witch casts a spell on a baby, the gardener tries to make up for the witch's wrongdoings by presenting the child with the gift of "green fingers." The irate mother screams to no avail, but the child's ability to revive plants lands him a job at the palace grounds where he lives happily ever after. **RECOMMENDATION:** This whimsical hand puppet play is enjoyable and easy to produce. **ROYALTY:** NA. **SOURCE:** Merten, George. (1979). Plays for puppet performance. Boston: Plays, Inc. **SUBJECTS/PLAY TYPE:** Fantasy; Gardening; Puppet Play.

336. 9-12*. (+) Miller, Ev. **The boy with no name. CAST:** 4f, 2m. **ACTS:** 2. **SETTINGS:** Living room. **PLAYING TIME:** 90 min. **PLOT:** Eddy, 18, has a winning personality and the intellectual capacity of an eight year old. His mother, Kathy, consumed with guilt, perceives Eddy's condition to be God's punishment for premarital sex and realizes that it is her own increasingly irrational behavior that is causing her marital problems. She resorts to abusive behavior and the world of tranquilizers. A visit by her sister and niece triggers a family tragedy as Eddy is thought by Kathy to have attacked the niece. **RECOMMENDATION:** All audiences will be able to relate to this poignant, touching, and highly emotional play which offers valuable insight into some of the ordeals faced by the parents of retarded children. There is no fairy tale ending, and there are no "good and bad" guys, but there is a disquieting recognition at the end of the play that surely someone or something could have salvaged this family. **ROYALTY:** $35. **SOURCE:** Miller, Ev. (1985). The boy with no name. Denver, CO: Pioneer Drama Service. **SUBJECTS/PLAY TYPE:** Mental Retardations; Family Relationships; Drama.

337. 5-8. (+) Smith, Betty. **The boy, Abe. CAST:** 6f, 6m. **ACTS:** 1. **SETTINGS:** Classroom. **PLAYING TIME:** 20 min. **PLOT:** Abe Lincoln, 11, meets his new stepmother but resists her until she gives him two books (his very first), and insists that he be allowed to stay in school. He realizes that his new mother wants him to learn and because of this he is truly grateful. **RECOMMENDATION:** Believable characters, realistic dialogue, and an effective blend of fact and fiction make this better than average. **ROYALTY:** Free to subscribers of Plays. **SOURCE:** Kamerman, Sylvia E. (1983). Holiday plays round the year. Boston, MA: Plays, Inc. **SUBJECTS/PLAY TYPE:** Lincoln; Abraham; Playlet.

338. 4-8. (+) Hall, Margaret. **The Boyar's bride. CAST:** 1f, 5m. **ACTS:** 3. **SETTINGS:** Living room. **PLAYING TIME:** 15 min. **PLOT:** In this adaptation of a Rumanian folktale, a peasant's clever daughter wins herself a handsome, rich husband because she answers his riddles and outwits him with her own imaginative riddles. She also wins a cow and its future calves for her father. **RECOMMENDATION:** The themes of love for, and loyalty to, parents, and recognition of equality of men and women are presented subtly. Fairy tale elements contribute to the play's universal appeal. The surprise climax resolves the tension and ends the play as a happy love story. The pace is well suited to the action and dialogue. **ROYALTY:** Free to Plays subscribers. **SOURCE:** Hall, Margaret. (1985, January/February). The Boyar's bride. Plays: The Drama Magazine for Young People, pp. 33-36. **SUBJECTS/PLAY TYPE:** Folk Tales; Rumania; Riddles; Playlet.

339. 9-12. (+) Sabath, Bernard. **The boys in autumn. CAST:** 2m. **ACTS:** 2. **SETTINGS:** Yard. **PLAYING TIME:** NA. **PLOT:** Huck Finn and Tom Sawyer meet again, after Tom's lifelong search for his old buddy. Through conversation, the two (now old) men reveal their unsatisfied lives, renew their friendship, and vow to fulfill some of their childhood dreams. **RECOMMENDATION:** This is an excellent vehicle for presenting the ways in which we often get sidetracked from our dreams. The use of Twain's famous and familiar characters helps illuminate the tragedy of harsh reality, since their familiar youthful exploits do not have to be explained in detail in order to compare them with what the men have become. There is some explicit language. **ROYALTY:** $60. **SOURCE:** Sabath, Bernard. (1984). The boys in autumn. Woodstock, IL: Dramatic Publishing Co. **SUBJECTS/PLAY TYPE:** Old Age; Sawyer, Tom; Finn, Huckleberry; Drama.

340. 7-12. (-) Bradley, Virginia. **The bracelet engagement. CAST:** 4f, 2m. **ACTS:** 1. **SETTINGS:** Living room. **PLAYING TIME:** NA. **PLOT:** When a middle aged woman discovers that a playboy is toying with a young friend, she plots to expose him. **RECOMMENDATION:** The dated language and banal humor make this an unsuccessful play. **ROYALTY:** NA. **SOURCE:** Bradley, Virginia. (1977). Stage Eight: One-act plays. New York, NY: Dodd, Mead. **SUBJECTS/PLAY TYPE:** Family; Dating; Farce.

341. 4-6. (+) Olfson, Lewy. **The braggart's clever wife. CAST:** 1f, 2m, Su. **ACTS:** 1. **SETTINGS:** Living room. **PLAYING TIME:** NA. **PLOT:** A peasant couple who built their home on Magwitch's mountain learn he is coming. The wife, Miga, tells her husband, Johnkin, to dress in some of her clothes and wait. Magwitch enters and demands to see Johnkin, but Miga replies that her husband, the giant, is out and she needs to feed her "baby." Johnkin enters and chases Magwitch around the house, gurgling like a baby. Magwitch hastily leaves, telling Miga that she and her husband may stay there as long as they like. **RECOMMENDATION:** Everyone will enjoy this lively, high spirited play in which costuming and setting can be as simple or complex as desired.

ROYALTY: NA. SOURCE: Olfson, Lewy. (1975). You can put on a show. NY: Sterling Pub. Co. SUBJECTS/PLAY TYPE: Giants; Comedy.

342. 406. (+) Thane, Adele. (Grimm Brothers) **The brave little tailor.** (The brave little tailor) CAST: 5f, 7m, 11u. ACTS: 1. SETTINGS: Town square; forest. PLAYING TIME: 30 min. PLOT: A little peddler buys only one teaspoon of jam causing the jam peddler to leave in disgust, saying, "I'll come back on the day you marry the princess." Flies are attracted to the jam, but the tailor kills them all with one blow. He is so impressed with himself, he embroiders the words "Seven at One Blow" on a belt. Because of his bravery, the King asks him to kill two giants who menace the village, and promises the tailor half his kingdom and his daughter's hand in marriage, if he is successful. The tailor tricks the two giants into killing each other, the King honors his promise, and the jam peddler returns and is made official jam-maker for the kingdom. RECOMMENDATION: This version is altered slightly from the Grimms' original in that the tailor deliberately misleads people into thinking he killed seven men, not flies, and the princess knows she is falling in love with the tailor. The scenes of the dancing flies and moronic giants could be very funny. Also endearing are the version of "Pop Goes the Weasel," which the tailor sings, and a boasting song about their intelligence, which the giants sing to the tune of "Little Brown Jug." These could be sung, spoken or "rapped." This funny little play has merit on its own, but could also be used to teach the power of confidence and self esteem. ROYALTY: NA. SOURCE: Thane, Adele. (1983). Plays from famous stories and fairy tales. Boston, MA: Plays, Inc. SUBJECTS/PLAY TYPE: Folk Tales, Germany; Self Confidence; Giants; Adaptation.

343. 7-12. (-) O'Brien, John. **Break a leg.** CAST: 12f, 4m, Su. ACTS: 2. SETTINGS: Stage. PLAYING TIME: NA. PLOT: The Tilton High School seniors attempt a dress rehearsal for the class play. The rehearsal is chaotic as the cast members don't know their lines, people are missing, and the director is close to a nervous breakdown. The situation becomes progressively worse until it is apparent after the director's breakdown that this is really a "play" being performed and none of the events are "real." RECOMMENDATION: This play has a very confusing storyline which includes irrelevant characters who pointlessly wander in and out of the action, as well as humor which is so unsubtle, it is insulting to the audience. ROYALTY: $35. SOURCE: O'Brien, John. (1983). Break a leg. Woodstock, IL: Dramatic Pub. Co. SUBJECTS/PLAY TYPE: High School; Theater; Comedy.

344. 5-8. (+) Murray, John. **Break that record.** CAST: 9f, 10m, 4u. ACTS: 1. SETTINGS: TV studio. PLAYING TIME: 40 min. PLOT: Clint Fortune originates the concept for a TV show in which contestants break records by performing acts like leap frogging, walking backwards, and proposing marriage. One major event is the attempt by the justice of the peace Flammerton to steal a valuable diamond from the

sponsor of the show. Things don't go smoothly but the show is a big hit. RECOMMENDATION: The plot of this play is rather thin and some of the content will have to be updated. In spite of these drawbacks, the humor is pleasant and the premise interesting. ROYALTY: Free to Plays subscribers. SOURCE: Murray, John. (1977, December). Break that record. Plays: The Drama Magazine for Young People, pp. 15-30. SUBJECTS/PLAY TYPE: Television; Comedy.

345. 4-12. (+) Gleason, William. (Perrault, Charles) **Breaker calling Cinderella.** (Cinderella) CAST: 9f, 4m. ACTS: 2. SETTINGS: Dining room; porch. PLAYING TIME: NA. PLOT: In this modern day Cinderella story, the prince, Billy Bob, is an attractive, wealthy rancher and oil well owner who returns to his hometown to settle down. He is intrigued by a voice on the CB known only as Silver Princess. In a chance encounter the two fall in love, not knowing each other's true identity. Billy Bob has to fight off the advances of Silver Princess's ugly stepsisters and pushy stepmother before the inevitable happy ending. RECOMMENDATION: The special appeal of this play may be past its peak because CB's are not as popular as they once were. ROYALTY: $35. SOURCE: Gleason, William. (1977). Breaker calling Cinderella. Chicago, IL: Dramatic Publishing Co. SUBJECTS/PLAY TYPE: Folk Tales, France; CB Radios; Comedy; Adaptation.

346. 9-12. (+) Snee, Dennis. **Breaking up is hard to do.** CAST: 3f, 4m, 1u. ACTS: 1. SETTINGS: Bare stage. PLAYING TIME: 35 min. PLOT: A narrator discusses the nature of human relationships using three couples: 70 year olds married for fifty years; 30 year olds dating for a few years; and teenagers who have known each other for three months. RECOMMENDATION: The themes of love, human relationships, and the universality of male female relationships are ideal for student audiences. ROYALTY: $15. SOURCE: Snee, Dennis. (1976). Breaking up is hard to do. Boston, MA: Baker's Plays. SUBJECTS/PLAY TYPE: Relationships, Male Female; Comedy.

347. 9-12. (+) Sawyer-Young, Kat. **Breakup.** CAST: 1f, 1m. ACTS: 1. SETTINGS: Hallway. PLAYING TIME: NA. PLOT: Jealous that her boyfriend, Kevin, is flirting with her best friend, Dawn dumps him and refuses to listen to his weak explanations. RECOMMENDATION: Modifying the explicit language would not interfere with the presentation of these common feelings among steadies. ROYALTY: NA. SOURCE: Sawyer-Young, Kat. (1986). Contemporary scenes for contemporary kids. Boston, MA: Baker's Plays SUBJECTS/PLAY TYPE: Dating; Jealousy; Scene.

348. 2-6. (+) Hark, Mildred & McQueen, Noel. (Grimm Brothers) **The Bremen town musicians.** (The Bremen town musicians) CAST: 8u. ACTS: 1. SETTINGS: Road; forest. PLAYING TIME: 15 min. PLOT: Four animals (Donkey, Hound, Cat, and Cock) run away from their respective homes because their masters no longer want the old animals. They form a musical band and head for Bremen to look for work.

Hungry and tired, they approach a house where four robbers sit inside at a table laden with delicious food. The animals frighten away the robbers by making loud music and the animals enjoy the food. The animals congratulate themselves, sleep, go into Bremen, become musicians, and live in the house that suits them all. RECOMMENDATION: This is a faithful adaptation of the old familiar folk tale of the same name. It should be easy and fun to produce. ROYALTY: Free to Plays subscribers. SOURCE: Hark, Mildred & McQueen, Noel. (1981, October). The Bremen town musicians. Plays: The Drama Magazine for Young People, pp. 51-56. SUBJECTS/PLAY TYPE: Aging; Robbers; Folk Tales, Germany; Adaptation.

349. 1-5*. (+) Peterson, Gary & Nestor, Larry. (Grimm Brothers) The Bremen town musicians. CAST: 1f, 9m, Su. ACTS: 1. SETTINGS: Barnyard; street; pirate's cove. PLAYING TIME: 60 min. PLOT: After trying unsuccessfully to warn the local townspeople about robbers, Rooster, Donkey, Dog and Cat, four would-be musicians, cleverly manage to capture the band of pirates who have stolen the Brementown treasure chest. RECOMMENDATION: Purists may object to this cavalier adaptation of the Grimm Brothers tale. The story takes on a nautical flavor as pirates share equal billing with the heroic animal musicians. Children will enjoy the talking animals and the songs. ROYALTY: $35. SOURCE: Peterson, Gary, & Nestor, Larry. (1983). Denver, CO: Pioneer Drama Service. SUBJECTS/PLAY TYPE: Animals; Pirates; Adaptation.

350. 4-6. (+) Sills, Paul. (Grimm Brothers) The Bremen town musicians. (The Bremen town musicians) CAST: 6u. ACTS: 1. SETTINGS: None. PLAYING TIME: NA. PLOT: An ass, hound, cat, and cock escape their masters who want to kill them because they are old and cannot work as well as they used to. As they search for food at a cottage which has a light on, they see two thieves eating. The animals jump through the window, making animal sounds, scare the thieves away, and then make the cottage their new home. RECOMMENDATION: Although the dialogue is lengthy and often stilted, the personification of the animals is engaging. The plot elicits sympathy for the characters and for the theme that aging does not make one useless. ROYALTY: Write Samuel French. SOURCE: Jennings, Coleman A. and Harris, Aurand. (1988). Plays children love, Volume II. New York, NY: St. Martin's Press. SUBJECTS/PLAY TYPE: Aging; Folk Tales, Germany; Adaptation.

351. K-3. (-) Creegan, George R. The Brementown litterbug. CAST: 5u. ACTS: 1. SETTINGS: Yard. PLAYING TIME: 10 min. PLOT: A dog and rooster try to scare a witch out of the neighborhood because her yard is full of weeds and trash. After they succeed, they realize the ghost who helped them is real, rather than a person disguised as a ghost. RECOMMENDATION: This play has dubious value. The message is that if people have different values from those of the community, it is all right to persecute them. ROYALTY: Free to Plays subscribers. SOURCE: Creegan, George R.

(1988, May). The Brementown litterbug. Plays: The Drama Magazine for Young People, pp. 61- 63. SUBJECTS/PLAY TYPE: Discrimination; Puppet Play.

352. 1-6. (+) Jackson, R. Eugene. (Harris, Joel Chandler) Brer Rabbit's big secret. (Uncle Remus: His songs and his sayings) CAST: 5u. ACTS: 2. SETTINGS: Field; swamp; Goober Patch; road. PLAYING TIME: 60 min. PLOT: Brer Bear, Brer Fox, and Brer Wolf plot to catch and eat Brer Rabbit. After an unsuccessful attempt they decide that Brer Rabbit must have some sort of "lucky charm." He does--a rabbit's foot. One day, Brer Rabbit loses his rabbit's foot and Brer Bear finds it. The three now figure luck has run out and they will catch him. But they soon learn that Brer Rabbit does not rely just on good luck but also on his brain. RECOMMENDATION: Set in the deep South, the play uses the dialect of the original, which may be difficult to recreate. One scene centers around the well known "tar baby." ROYALTY: $40. SOURCE: Jackson, R. Eugene. (1979). Brer Rabbit's big secret. Denver, CO: Pioneer Drama Service. SUBJECTS/PLAY TYPE: Animals; Bears; Musical.

353. 9-12. (+) Kelly, Tim. Bride of Frankenstein. CAST: 7f, 7m, Su. ACTS: 2. SETTINGS: Cliff house. PLAYING TIME: 90 min. PLOT: Dr. Frankenstein comes to California to find a male surfer's brain for his Monster, and a female swimmer's brain for the Monster's Bride. Count Dracula and his two brides make an unexpected visit and pose a threat to Dr. Frankenstein's work. RECOMMENDATION: The contemporary language, setting, comical dialogue, and plot make this enjoyable. ROYALTY: $35. SOURCE: Kelly, Tim. (1976). Bride of Frankenstein. Denver, CO: Pioneer Drama Service. SUBJECTS/PLAY TYPE: Horror; Comedy.

354. 11-12. (+) Olfson, Lewy. The bride of Gorse-Bracken Hall. CAST: 2f, 3m. ACTS: 1. SETTINGS: Parlor. PLAYING TIME: 15 min. PLOT: In this broad spoof of a British gothic romance, a naive young governess prepares to marry the wheelchair bound lord of the manor amidst exaggerated stereotypical characters. Everyone doubts whether the wedding should occur except for the bride. The others all know the dark secret of the manor: the groom is a merman. After discovering the secret, the bride goes on with the marriage because, as she says, "no one's perfect." RECOMMENDATION: Students will enjoy the farcical parody in this play. The widely bizarre events and characters here are distinctive, even down to their unusual names, and the dialogue is wonderfully tongue in cheek. ROYALTY: Free to Plays subscribers. SOURCE: Olfson, Lewy. (1975, February). The bride of Gorse-Bracken Hall. Plays: The Drama Magazine for Young People, pp. 35-40. SUBJECTS/PLAY TYPE: Romance; Comedy; Satire.

355. 7-12. (+) Sodaro, Craig. The brides and the lumberjacks. CAST: 9f, 7m, Su. ACTS: 3. SETTINGS: Lumber camp. PLAYING TIME: 35 min. PLOT: Owners of two lumber camps vie for workers and business. One

unethical owner, Barnsnaggle, writes for brides for his lumberjacks, but the other owner (Pickett) exchanges the letters so that his camp will get the brides. Trouble erupts, including the return of Barnsnaggle's wife whom he left for dead to get her money. But, since the cook has gone to cooking school and become a gourmet, and the lumberjacks show potential for civilization, the brides agree to stay and all ends well. RECOMMENDATION: With clever one liners, exaggerated characterization, and interesting, well developed personalities, this mixed up story provides humorous, innocent fun. ROYALTY: Free to Plays subscribers. SOURCE: Sodaro, Craig. (1983, April). The brides and the lumberjacks. Plays: The Drama Magazine for Young People, pp. 1-12. SUBJECTS/PLAY TYPE: Lumberjacks; Marriage; Comedy.

356. 10-12. (+) Ainsworth, Ford. (Asbjornsen, P.C.) The bridge. (The three billy-goats gruff) CAST: 6u. ACTS: 1. SETTINGS: Bridge. PLAYING TIME: NA. PLOT: Three trolls on the bridge assert the primacy of superstition over reason. Three starving billy goats approach the bridge. Hero and Credo grovel to be allowed to cross the bridge to green lush pastures, but Solo, a goat in search of Truth, refuses to humble himself. Both Hero and Credo offer themselves as sacrifices, weasel their way out of their promises, and are allowed to cross anyway. The trolls tell Solo that the Waters of Truth in the stream will produce madness, ostracism from the herd, and probably death. After a brief skirmish, Solo drinks from the stream and can no longer see or hear the trolls. When he tells Hero and Credo that the trolls are gone, they think he is crazy, and he is separated from them forever. RECOMMENDATION: This powerful play deals with truth, the weaknesses of society, and man's ability to recognize and cope with them. Societal verities, human qualities, and characteristics are portrayed as being both positive and negative factors either facilitating or inhibiting recognition of and/or dealing with truth. Skillfully written, this thought provoking piece can be recommended for production only by and for mature students because of the subtle questions it raises and its likelihood of being misunderstood. ROYALTY: $20. SOURCE: Ainsworth, Ford. (1982). The bridge. Schulenburg, TX: I.E. Clark. SUBJECTS/PLAY TYPE: Fable; Animals; Folk Tales, Norway; Adaptation.

357. K-3. (+) Gamarra, Pierre & Henderson, Paulette. The bridge over the river Clarinette. CAST: 1f, 3m, 3u. ACTS: 1. SETTINGS: None. PLAYING TIME: NA. PLOT: Poor townspeople, thinking that it is a bargain to buy a much needed bridge from the devil for the price of giving up their speech, belatedly realize how much they have overpaid. RECOMMENDATION: A good demonstration of the need for foresight and communication, this play will also entertain young children. ROYALTY: NA. SOURCE: Bauer, Caroline Feller. (1987). Presenting reader's theater: Plays and poems to read aloud. New York, NY: H.W. Wilson. SUBJECTS/PLAY TYPE: Bridges; Devils; Reader's Theater.

358. 3-8. (+) Tesh, Jane. The brightest star. CAST: 7f, 9m, 6u. ACTS: 1. SETTINGS: Bare stage, backdrop. PLAYING TIME: 10 min. PLOT: Tiny, a small star, can't keep up with her ambitious classmates. She is woefully behind in shining, sparkling, and twinkling. However, since she is good and kind, she is chosen by the angels to lead the Shepherd and Wise Men to the manger site at Jesus' birth. RECOMMENDATION: Because this deals with the religious significance of Christmas, it is recommended for church schools rather than public schools. Some vocabulary might be difficult for elementary children. ROYALTY: Free to Plays subscribers. SOURCE: Tesh, Jane. (1987, December). The brightest star. Plays: The Drama Magazine for Young People, pp. 46-50. SUBJECTS/PLAY TYPE: Christmas; Playlet.

359. K-3. (+) Bauer, Caroline Feller. Bringing news from home. CAST: 2u. ACTS: 1. SETTINGS: None. PLAYING TIME: NA. PLOT: A steward stretches out the story of a disaster at his master's home by starting with small details and gradually revealing the important facts. RECOMMENDATION: If acted in hyperbole, this will provide sidesplitting humor for young audiences. ROYALTY: NA. SOURCE: Bauer, Caroline Feller. (1987). Presenting reader's theater: Plays and poems to read aloud. New York, NY: H.W. Wilson. SUBJECTS/PLAY TYPE: Disaster; Messengers; Reader's Theater.

360. 7-12. (+) Cheatham, Val R. Broadway hit. CAST: 3f, 5m. ACTS: 1. SETTINGS: Backstage. PLAYING TIME: 20 min. PLOT: Moss, the play director, struggles to get his play underway amidst problems from a union conscious cleaning lady, a lyricist and a composer who are constantly bickering, and two vain, demanding leading characters. Even worse, on opening night, the two leading characters elope, and the small town aspiring starlet and the director must take the two leading roles. RECOMMENDATION: This slapstick spoof on the world of Broadway theater is entertaining. Although the author makes no attempt at depth of character, plot, or dialogue, the characters reveal basic human frailties in an amusing way. ROYALTY: Free to Plays subscribers. SOURCE: Cheatham, Val R. (1981, March). Broadway hit. Plays: The Drama Magazine for Young People, pp. 65-70. SUBJECTS/PLAY TYPE: Theater; Skit.

361. 1-3. (+) Gotwalt, Helen Louise Miller. The broken broomstick. CAST: 14u. ACTS: 1. SETTINGS: Woods. PLAYING TIME: 15 min. PLOT: On Halloween night, the Little Witch breaks her broomstick. When she can't fix it, wise Mr. Owl helps her get a new one. RECOMMENDATION: The entire class may participate if desired. ROYALTY: NA. SOURCE: Gotwalt, Helen Louise Miller. (1985). First plays for children: A collection of little plays for the youngest players. Boston, MA: Plays, Inc. SUBJECTS/PLAY TYPE: Halloween; Witches; Skit.

362. 7-12. (+) Nolan, Paul T. (Kleist, Heinrich) **The broken jug.** (The broken jug) CAST: 3f, 5m. ACTS: 1. SETTINGS: Courtroom. PLAYING TIME: 30 min. PLOT: A valuable jug has been broken and the owner takes her grievance to an extremely nervous and badly bruised judge. He is nervous because he is concealing the fact that he is the guilty party. He is bruised because of his hasty escape from the scene of a crime. Justice prevails and the guilty judge must pay for the broken jug and his unethical behavior. RECOMMENDATION: Even the youngest will realize early on that the judge is guilty, and will enjoy watching his flimsy excuses for postponing the case. ROYALTY: Free to Plays subscribers. SOURCE: Nolan, Paul T. (1977, March). The broken jug. Plays: The Drama Magazine for Young People, pp. 70-80. SUBJECTS/PLAY TYPE: Farce; Justice; Adaptation.

363. 3-6. (-) Blumenfeld, Lenore. **Bronco Bess goes whaling.** CAST: 2f, 2m, 1u. ACTS: 1. SETTINGS: Ship. PLAYING TIME: 30 min. PLOT: Bronco Bess meets the captain of a whaling ship (who can't swim and can't bear to kill a whale). Cap'n gives the ship to a cabin boy, and leaves with Bess to help her save her ranch. RECOMMENDATION: This suffers from boring dialogue, insulting western drawls, predictable "ship's talk" (e.g., landlubber, lollygaggin', etc.), and a totally unimaginative plot. ROYALTY: Free to Plays subscribers. SOURCE: Blumenfeld, Lenore. (1978, October). Bronco Bess goes whaling. Plays: The Drama Magazine for Young People, pp. 55-64. SUBJECTS/PLAY TYPE: Sea Stories; Comedy.

364. 6-12*. (+) Feltch, Mark. **The Bronx bomber.** CAST: 4m, Su. ACTS: 1. SETTINGS: Basketball court. PLAYING TIME: NA. PLOT: In 1922, two young men compete in a one-on-one basketball game in front of 4,000 people. Frankie wins and Pete spends the next 55 years planning revenge. Just as the basketball court is about to be torn down, a local wino finds Frankie penniless in a drunk tank. In the rematch, Frankie collapses. After he recovers, the men become friends. Frankie never knew that Pete lost his friends and the respect of the community when he lost the 1922 basketball game. RECOMMENDATION: This movingly provides insight into a variety of issues: the elderly, resentments, competition, and friendship. ROYALTY: $15. SOURCE: Feltch, Mark. (1977). The Bronx bomber. Woodstock, IL: Dramatic Pub. Co. SUBJECTS/PLAY TYPE: Basketball; Elderly; Competition; Drama.

365. 7-12. (-) Gotwalt, Helen Louise Miller. **The broomstick beauty.** CAST: 4f, 2m. ACTS: 1. SETTINGS: Cave. PLAYING TIME: 20 min. PLOT: A young witch tries to become beautiful to catch her man. When she leaves her makeup bag, her friends have a permanent and a facial. RECOMMENDATION: This is too outdated and boring, not to mention that it gives the impression that looks are the only factor in a lasting relationship. ROYALTY: Free to Plays subscribers. SOURCE: Gotwalt, Helen Louise Miller. (1984, October). The broomstick beauty. Plays: The Drama Magazine for Young People, pp. 12-20. SUBJECTS/PLAY TYPE: Halloween; Witches; Comedy.

366. 7-12. (+) Sawyer-Young, Kat. **Brother.** CAST: 1m. ACTS: 1. SETTINGS: None. PLAYING TIME: 1 min. PLOT: Mike is furious because his brother didn't return the car in time for Mike's date. RECOMMENDATION: This well describes the aggravation of older siblings with younger ones. ROYALTY: None. SOURCE: Sawyer-Young, Kat. (1987). Minute monologues for contemporary teens. Boston: Baker's Plays. SUBJECTS/PLAY TYPE: Siblings; Monologue.

367. 7-9. (+) Sawyer-Young, Kat. **Brotherly love.** CAST: 2m. ACTS: 1. SETTINGS: Bathroom. PLAYING TIME: NA. PLOT: David mercilessly teases his brother because he spends so much time combing his hair. Sean forces him to apologize, but the apology seems insincere. RECOMMENDATION: Sibling rivalry is demonstrated in a harsh, rather intimidating manner. Discretion is advised; this should perhaps only be used where the students have a relatively solid sense of security. ROYALTY: NA. SOURCE: Sawyer-Young, Kat. (1986). Contemporary scenes for contemporary kids. Boston, MA: Baker's Plays. SUBJECTS/PLAY TYPE: Sibling Rivalry; Self Concept; Scene.

368. 7-12. (+) McCusker, Paul. **Brothers.** CAST: 2f. ACTS: 1. SETTINGS: Living room. PLAYING TIME: NA. PLOT: After a bachelor's party, two brothers reminisce about growing up and how the older brother always took care of the younger one. RECOMMENDATION: This is touching, and if the references to accepting Christ were removed, it could provide secular entertainment. ROYALTY: None with purchase of script. SOURCE: McCusker, Paul. (1982). Souvenirs: Comedies and dramas for Christian fellowship. Boston, MA: Baker's Plays. SUBJECTS/PLAY TYPE: Love; Siblings; Skit.

369. 10-12. (+) Kelly, Tim. **The brothers O'Toole.** CAST: 10f, 7m, Su. ACTS: 2. SETTINGS: Combined city hall/store/library. PLAYING TIME: 90 min. PLOT: The town of Aspiration is besieged by a bandit, Rawhide, who robs the stage and prevents the delivery of merchandise to the local store. When the first of the two unmarried O'Toole brothers arrives, he receives the amorous attentions of the store proprietress, Cassandra. When the second brother, Terence, arrives, he is mistaken for Rawhide and arrested. Things are straightened out and Rawhide is asked to become a bandit again for the tourist trade. When the marriage minded women get serious about weddings, the brothers O'Toole use the distractions created by Rawhide's activities to leave the would-be brides at the altar. RECOMMENDATION: Humorous dialogue and lively action combine with a variety of character types to provide an entertaining play. The use of one actor for both of the O'Toole parts is a challenge, but attracts attention. ROYALTY: $25. SOURCE: Kelly, Tim. (1975). The brothers O'Toole. Denver, CO: Pioneer Drama Service. SUBJECTS/PLAY TYPE: Western; Comedy.

370. 5-12. (+) Van Horn, Bill. **Buck, a tale of the frozen North.** CAST: 3f, 4m, 1u. ACTS: 1. SETTINGS: Outpost; hideout. PLAYING TIME: 30 min. PLOT: Sergeant Dobetter of the Mounties is sent to bring back the insidious Dirty Dan McGinty. After he realizes that his fiance has been kidnapped under his nose by Dirty Dan, Dobetter goes to rescue her and is himself captured. Buck, his loyal dog, leads the other Mounties in a successful rescue. But when they fall again into one of Dirty Dan's traps, Dobetter is the hero. RECOMMENDATION: The humor is blatant and the division between good and evil is very clearly defined. ROYALTY: Free to Plays Subscribers. SOURCE: Van Horn, Bill. (1979, March). Buck, a tale of the frozen North. Plays: The Drama Magazine for Young People, pp. 1-11. SUBJECTS/PLAY TYPE: Comedy; Melodrama.

371. 5-9. (+) Campbell, Paddy L. **Buckskin and Chapperos.** CAST: 3f, 4m. ACTS: 1. SETTINGS: Farmyard; saloon; street. PLAYING TIME: NA. PLOT: Eccentric, old Uncle Gillie builds a time machine so that he and his nephew can travel back to the Old West, where Gillie lost his gold to Bad Bob. With a few hitches (i.e., when they arrive, they're out of sync and have to figure out how to make everyone come alive) they succeed. They relive the past as Bad Bob steals the gold, and dies in a gunfight. Just in time, they return home. Gillie's nephew asks why Gillie didn't recover his gold and Gillie answers that you can't change history. RECOMMENDATION: This lighthearted comedy pokes fun at all the stereotypes of the Old West with classic puns. Delightfully superficial, yet sophisticated, this would be an excellent opener for a more lengthy play. ROYALTY: NA. SOURCE: Campbell, Paddy L. (1984). Buckskin and chapperos; Madwitch: two plays for children. Toronto, Canada: Playwrights. SUBJECTS/PLAY TYPE: Old West; Time Travel; Comedy.

372. 6-9. (+) Hark, Mildred & McQueen, Noel. **Bud for president.** CAST: 2f, 3m, 1u. ACTS: 1. SETTINGS: Living room. PLAYING TIME: 30 min. PLOT: Fred Sanders and his son, Bud, work toward an election day victory, each with his own style. Fred supports a personal friend, whom he feels can solve the problems in the community. Bud feels a group effort is necessary. Fred becomes aware that Bud's editorial is helpful in getting Jim Faraday elected because it influences the community. RECOMMENDATION: This introduces children to politics and civic involvement. It points out the importance of independent thought and community involvement. ROYALTY: Free to Plays subscribers. SOURCE: Hark, Mildred, & McQueen, Noel. (1980, November). Bud for president. Plays: The Drama Magazine for Young People, pp. 23-32. SUBJECTS/PLAY TYPE: Politics; Family; Playlet.

373. 5-9. (+) Wheetley, Kim. **The buffalo and the bell.** CAST: 2u. ACTS: 1. SETTINGS: Curtain. PLAYING TIME: NA. PLOT: Three villains trick Pandi into selling his buffalo for less than it is worth by convincing him it is a goat. He, in turn, tricks the villains out of additional money and is no longer considered a simpleminded farmer. RECOMMENDATION: An Indonesian play based on traditional puppet and masked theater customs, this uses Indonesian conventions of martial arts stance and shadow puppeteering. The use of an "orchestra" allows for more children to be included in production. ROYALTY: Write to Dramatic Publishing. SOURCE: Jennings, Coleman A. & Harris, Aurand. (1981). Plays children love. New York, NY: Doubleday. SUBJECTS/PLAY TYPE: Folk Tales, Indonesia; Trickery; Shadow Puppet Play.

374. 1-6. (-) Sodaro, Craig. **Buffalo Bill's wild west show.** CAST: 9f, 4m, 11u. ACTS: 1. SETTINGS: Bare stage, backdrops. PLAYING TIME: 20 min. PLOT: A series of vignettes at a Wild West show feature Calamity Jane and Buffalo Bill, who tell a fractured tale about how the West was won. RECOMMENDATION: Characters are one-dimensional and the antics are not really funny, nor are they effective parody. This mediocre piece will have limited appeal. ROYALTY: Free to Plays subscribers. SOURCE: Sodaro, Craig. (1987, May). Buffalo Bill's wild west show. Plays: The Drama Magazine for Young People, pp. 35-40. SUBJECTS/PLAY TYPE: Western; Comedy.

375. K-3. (+) Kusking, Karla. **A bug.** CAST: 2u. ACTS: 1. SETTINGS: None. PLAYING TIME: NA. PLOT: A tale of "survival of the fittest," this short poem about bugs ends on a humorous note. RECOMMENDATION: Children will enjoy performing this well done tale of bugs' cannibalistic eating habits, perhaps in combination with others of Bauer's "Animal Antics." ROYALTY: NA. SOURCE: Bauer, Caroline Feller. (1987). Presenting reader's theater: Plays and poems to read aloud. New York, NY: H.W. Wilson. SUBJECTS/PLAY TYPE: Bugs; Insects; Reader's Theater.

376. 1-3. (+) Martin, Judith. **The Building and the statue.** CAST: 2m, 3u. ACTS: 1. SETTINGS: Bare stage, props. PLAYING TIME: 5 min. PLOT: The mayor and governor argue about which to tear down for a new road: a historical building or a statue of the governor. Their argument ends in a car accident, as the building and the statue leave to find a more peaceful location. RECOMMENDATION: The clash between the need to modernize big cities while maintaining the majesty of old landmarks is well documented. This could provoke much directed discussion. ROYALTY: None. SOURCE: Martin, Judith. (1981). Everybody, everybody: a collection from the paper bag players. New York, NY: Elsevier/Nelson Books. SUBJECTS/PLAY TYPE: Modernization; Comedy.

377. K-6. (+) Korty, Carol. (Tenenbaum, Samuel) **Building the house.** (Wise men of Chelm) CAST: 5u. ACTS: 1. SETTINGS: House. PLAYING TIME: NA. PLOT: A group of friends construct a house, but are dissatisfied because it's too dark. Slowly, they dismantle it, until they are standing outside, exclaiming that it is the sunniest house they ever saw. RECOMMENDATION: This uses pantomime and physical comedy. It may spark discussion about attitudes and how people view the

world. ROYALTY: None. SOURCE: Korty, Carol. (1977). Silly soup: Ten zany plays. New York, NY: Charles Scribner's Sons. SUBJECTS/PLAY TYPE: Comedy; Attitudes; Skit; Adaptation.

378. 5-12. (+) McCusker, Paul. **The bum.** CAST: 3u. ACTS: 1. SETTINGS: Park. PLAYING TIME: NA. PLOT: As two people discuss Scriptures, they decide how to help a hurt bum. They tell him that God loves him and walk away, convinced they did the Christian thing. RECOMMENDATION: The irony is well presented. If the references to Christianity were changed to references about humanity, this could be used for a secular message. ROYALTY: None with purchase of script. SOURCE: McCusker, Paul. (1982). Souvenirs: Comedies and dramas for Christian fellowship. Boston, MA: Baker's Plays. SUBJECTS/PLAY TYPE: Kindness; Hypocrisy; Skit.

379. 6-12. (+) Osterberg, Susan Snider & Jackson, R. Eugene. (Osterberg, Susan Snider) **Bumper snickers.** (Things that stick to bumpers) CAST: Su. ACTS: 2. SETTINGS: Street Corner. PLAYING TIME: 45 min. PLOT: Dialogue in several of the skits centers on the theme of a bumper sticker or series of stickers. It would be possible to do this using just the dialogue written for one set of bumper stickers that express a single theme (i.e. safe driving habits, good health, etc.). The play is intended to build upon puns developed from each sticker slogan. RECOMMENDATION: Although quite funny, subtitles, double meanings, and sexual overtones in some of the dialogue are not appropriate for certain age levels. ROYALTY: $35. SOURCE: Osterberg, Susan Snider & Jackson, R. Eugene. (1978). Bumper snickers. Schulenburg, TX: I.E. Clark. SUBJECTS/PLAY TYPE: Bumper Stickers; Comedy.

380. 12*. (+) Bond, Edward. **The bundle.** CAST: 4f, 23m. ACTS: 2. SETTINGS: River bank; court house. PLAYING TIME: NA. PLOT: This is an imagined episode in the life of the great Haiku poet, Basho. He sets off on a journey for truth during the starvation years in Japan and encounters a Ferryman and an abandoned child, Wang. Wang saves his mother and father from death by selling himself to Basho as an indentured slave. At the end of the indenture, Wang goes through the countryside creating social unrest against landowners, leaving his parents to be questioned about his actions. The ferryman is forced to set a trap for Wang to save his wife's life but he cannot betray the boy and warns Wang, forfeiting his wife's life. The play ends with Basho in confusion and Wang philosophical. RECOMMENDATION: The play is very philosophical, and the imagery and complex messages could only be properly conveyed by professional actors. While the settings are simple, the huge cast could also pose a problem. The humanity of the Ferryman and his wife are displayed beautifully, but the many deep meanings would be very difficult to portray, and difficult for adolescent audiences to understand. ROYALTY: $60. SOURCE: Bond, Edward. (1981). The bundle. Chicago, IL: Dramatic Pub. Co. SUBJECTS/PLAY TYPE: Humanity; Japan; Basho. Drama.

381. 1-6. (-) Gotwalt, Helen Louise Miller. **Bunnies and bonnets.** CAST: 9f, 6m, Su. ACTS: 1. SETTINGS: Waiting room. PLAYING TIME: 20 min. PLOT: Typical stage mothers take their children, dressed up in rabbit costumes, to audition for a TV Easter show. The TV Producer tells them there has been a mistake and that he needs Easter bonnets instead. The Easter bunny appears and gives everyone an Easter egg, which, after being consumed, changes the griping children into "nice" children, and the nasty producer into a cheerful, accommodating man. RECOMMENDATION: The transformations are hard to swallow in this overdone and very patronizing piece. ROYALTY: Free to Plays subscribers. SOURCE: Gotwalt, Helen Louise Miller. (1983, April). Bunnies and bonnets. Plays: The Drama Magazine for Young People, pp. 35- 43. SUBJECTS/PLAY TYPE: Easter; Comedy.

382. 3-6. (-) McGowan, Jane. **Bunnies and bonnets.** CAST: 12f, 6m. ACTS: 1. SETTINGS: Waiting room. PLAYING TIME: 20 min. PLOT: Dressed in bunny costumes, various performers crowd a TV producer's waiting room, hoping to be cast in an Easter special. Their disappointment at the producer's announcement that he is casting a bonnet show rather than a bunny show is dispelled when the real Easter Bunny shows up and solves everyone's problems. RECOMMENDATION: Annoyingly noisy rather than humorously chaotic, the play presents only stereotyped characters: pushy stage mothers, a much put-upon secretary, bragging actors and a harried male executive. The ending is painfully pat. ROYALTY: Free to subscribers of Plays. SOURCE: Kamerman, Sylvia E. (1983). Holiday plays round the year. Boston, MA: Plays, Inc. SUBJECTS/PLAY TYPE: Easter; Show Business; Fantasy.

383. 11-12. (+) Poston, Dick. **Burlesque humor revisited: A history-like comedy run-down from the world of burlesque condensed into twelve classic sketches.** CAST: Su. ACTS: 2. SETTINGS: Bare stage, props. PLAYING TIME: NA. PLOT: This historical review of burlesque humor is portrayed in 12 sketches which treat the human condition in various settings. Frustration, misinterpretation, and wordplay occur throughout, presented by the same three characters: a comic, a straight man, and a lady. Included are famous acts like, "Who's on First," "Niagara Falls," "Wall Street," "Cleaning and Dyeing," and "The Farmhouse Scene." RECOMMENDATION: Due to the ribald humor and adult language in some of the sketches, this should be edited for younger audiences. Young adults would most appreciate the timing and "patter" so common to burlesque humor. Sketches could be performed individually or as a set, and could be performed by three or more people, to allow more participants. ROYALTY: $15 each skit. SOURCE: Poston, Dick. (1977). Burlesque humor revisited: A history-like comedy run-down from the world of burlesque condensed into twelve classic sketches. New York, NY: Samuel French. SUBJECTS/PLAY TYPE: Burlesque; Comedy.

384. 5-7. (-) Gersbach, Jo. **Business ventures.** CAST: 7f, 6m, 12u. ACTS: 1. SETTINGS: Bare stage. PLAYING TIME: 15 min. PLOT: Four friends pretend to start four businesses for fun and to make pretend money. They enact the experiences of selling, doctoring, and waitressing. RECOMMENDATION: The practitioners of the occupations are depicted as incompetent and insulting to their customers, the problems of business are not realistically depicted, many of the references are outdated, and the lessons are too heavy handed. ROYALTY: Free to Plays subscribers. SOURCE: Gersbach, Jo. (1978, May). Business ventures. Plays: The Drama Magazine for Young People, pp. 65-70. SUBJECTS/PLAY TYPE: Business; Comedy.

385. 7-12. (+) Sawyer-Young, Kat. **Busted.** CAST: 1m. ACTS: 1. SETTINGS: None. PLAYING TIME: 1 min. PLOT: Brian explains that he takes drugs to escape his unreasonable parents. RECOMMENDATION: This describes the teenager's feelings well, and is realistic in its approach to the unanswered parental question, "What should we do about it?" ROYALTY: None. SOURCE: Sawyer-Young, Kat. (1987). Minute monologues for contemporary teens. Boston, MA: Baker's Plays. SUBJECTS/PLAY TYPE: Drugs; Substance Abuse; Monologue.

386. 2-4. (+) Gotwalt, Helen Louise Miller. **The busy barbers.** CAST: 23f, 14m. ACTS: 1. SETTINGS: Barber shop. PLAYING TIME: 15 min. PLOT: Three barbers cheerfully cut children's hair, when a new slick and tricky barber promises to give haircuts that will make each child look like someone else. The children give it a try, but then regret it. When the mothers arrive, they do not know which child is whose and demand that the barber undo his magic. RECOMMENDATION: This is a humorous play with songs and lines that are easy for children to learn, and sets and props that can be simply constructed. ROYALTY: Free to Plays subscribers. SOURCE: Gotwalt, Helen Louise Miller. (1960). First plays for children: A collection of little plays for the youngest players. Boston, MA: Plays, Inc. SUBJECTS/PLAY TYPE: Children; Magic; Musical; Skit.

387. 10-12. (+) Majeski, Bill. **But I don't want to get involved.** CAST: 3f, 3m, 8u. ACTS: 1. SETTINGS: Kitchen; courtroom. PLAYING TIME: NA. PLOT: Henry Walters "happens" to take his binoculars into the kitchen and looks out the window into the bedroom of the adjacent apartment. He witnesses a couple fighting and then sees the woman, Felicia, fatally shoot her husband. Only after being urged to do so by his wife, Henry tells the police. At the coroner's inquest, Felicia is acquitted because of Henry's testimony and a slick defense attorney. In a surprise ending, the defense attorney confronts Henry and Felicia with his knowledge of their affair and their murder conspiracy, and he demands blackmail money. RECOMMENDATION: The plot and clever, surprise ending are entertaining; the characters are entirely believable. However, the themes of an unhappy marriage, infidelity, and getting away with murder may pose problems for some high school

productions. ROYALTY: $30. SOURCE: Majeski, Bill. (1988). But I don't want to get involved. Franklin, OH: Eldridge Pub. Co. SUBJECTS/PLAY TYPE: Mystery; Murder; Drama.

388. 9-12. (+) Cottrell, Susan C. **But listen.** CAST: 2f, 2m. ACTS: 1. SETTINGS: Apartment. PLAYING TIME: NA. PLOT: Helen, who handles incoming calls for superior court, deals with all callers in a clipped, bureaucratic fashion. While showing Kim, a trainee, how to transfer callers and put them on hold (her standard responses), she receives a bomb threat. Her methodically uninvolved procedures to determine which department the caller wants and then putting him "on hold" several times frustrates and enrages the would-be bomber. When Helen goes on her coffee break, Kim listens to the man's problem and suggests a solution. He tells her there really is no bomb. RECOMMENDATION: If Helen's character is played "dead-pan," this play will be hilarious. ROYALTY: $15. SOURCE: Cottrell, Susan. (1976). But listen. Woodstock, IL: The Dramatic Pub. Co. SUBJECTS/PLAY TYPE: Telephone Operators; Bureaucracy; Communication; Comedy.

389. 12+. (+) Kelly, Tim J. **The butler did it.** CAST: 5f, 5m. ACTS: 3. SETTINGS: House. PLAYING TIME: NA. PLOT: In this spoof on English mystery plays, Miss Marple, a mystery buff, invites a group of detective writers to her eerie Ravenswood Manor for the weekend. She has arranged for an "imaginative" weekend with the authors who assume the identities of fictional characters in order to solve a make believe crime. However, when a man is found murdered in the wine cellar, the writers try to solve the case before anyone else is murdered. Each member of the group turns out to be someone other than who they say they are. The killer is unmasked by one of the writers who is really a police detective. RECOMMENDATION: This fairly complicated plot requires the audience to follow several story threads simultaneously: the make believe murder mystery, the real murder mystery, and the undercurrents between the principal characters which reveal to the audience that all is not as it seems. If the roles are played straightforwardly by the actors, allowing the humor to emerge, it should be very successful. The sets and special effects will require skill. ROYALTY: $40. SOURCE: Kelly, Tim J. (1977). The butler did it. Boston, MA: Baker's Plays. SUBJECTS/PLAY TYPE: Mystery; Comedy.

390. 9-12. (+) Kelly, Tim & Christianson, Arne. (Kelly, Tim) **The butler did it, singing.** (The butler did it) CAST: 5f, 5m, Su. ACTS: 2. SETTINGS: Sitting room. PLAYING TIME: NA. PLOT: Miss Maple, an eccentric dowager, invites a group of detective writers to a spooky house on an isolated island so they can impersonate their fictional heroes or heroines. The festivities are interrupted when the guests discover a dead man on the sitting room floor. The detective writers attempt to solve the crime, but bungle the job. In the end, everyone has a guilty secret to confess, and the real killer turns out to be the one least suspected. RECOMMENDATION: This quick comedy relies heavily on exaggeration for laughs.

Every aspect is to be overdone: the spooky set, the acting, the death scene, and the ineptness of the characters. The song lyrics are quite funny. ROYALTY: $75. SOURCE: Kelly, Tim. (1986). The butler did it, singing. Boston, MA: Baker's Plays. SUBJECTS/PLAY TYPE: Comedy; Musical; Mystery; Adaptation.

391. 10-12. (+) Gibson, William. **The butterfingers angel, Mary & Joseph, Herod the nut, & the slaughter of 12 hit carols in a pear tree.** CAST: 4f, 6m, 4u. ACTS: 2. SETTINGS: Barn. PLAYING TIME: NA. PLOT: In this dramatization of the traditional story of the birth of Christ, Mary and Joseph are portrayed as ordinary people who are confused and surprised by the situation in which they find themselves. RECOMMENDATION: The perspective this play offers on Mary and Joseph's role in, and understanding of Christ's birth is both comic and thought provoking at the same time. The occasional use of strong language and the liberties taken in developing the character and motives of Mary and Joseph might be a problem for some people. ROYALTY: $50. SOURCE: Gibson, William. (1975). The butterfingers angel, Mary & Joseph, Herod the nut, & the slaughter of 12 hit carols in a pear tree. New York, NY: Dramatists Play Service, Inc. SUBJECTS/PLAY TYPE: Christmas Story; Comedy.

392. 5-10. (+) Barasch, Shirley. **A button for my yarmulke.** CAST: 3f, 6m, Su. ACTS: 1. SETTINGS: Room; grocery store; street; synagogue. PLAYING TIME: NA. PLOT: David, 14, is about to graduate from the Jewish Institute and his mother insists that he wear his great-great grandfather's old and tattered yarmulke on graduation day. In an effort to make the cap more palatable for the reluctant David, he and the rabbi search the neighborhood for a fancy button with which to adorn it. During their search for a button, David learns the value of tradition as sentimental storekeepers give him teffilin, an old talis, and an ancient sheet of music, each representing a part of his proud heritage. RECOMMENDATION: Knowledge of Jewish culture would help with understanding the play, but is not an absolute necessity since the message, about tradition, is universal. ROYALTY: NA. SOURCE: Barasch, Shirley. (1986). A button for my yarmulke. Morton Grove, IL: The Coach House Press, Inc. SUBJECTS/PLAY TYPE: Jewish Culture; Jewish Drama.

393. 5-12. (+) Norquist, Richard & Zimmerman, Gary. **Buttonnose.** CAST: 8f, 11m, Su. ACTS: 2. SETTINGS: Ghost town; hayloft; gypsy camp. PLAYING TIME: NA. PLOT: On a trip out west with her parents, Roberta falls asleep in a ghost town and awakens 100 years in the past. She meets a young man, helps to bring two bank robbers to justice, becomes an honorary gypsy, and joins in the town's 4th of July celebration. Falling asleep again, she awakens in the present. RECOMMENDATION: The play's length and frequent musical numbers would make it quite demanding. The stereotypical depiction of the gypsies is also problematic. However, children should enjoy the premise of time travel and the play's response to Roberta's question, "Can dreams be real?" ROYALTY: Upon application. SOURCE: Norquist, Richard &

Zimmerman, Gary. (1977). Buttonnose. Woodstock, IL: Dramatic Pub. Co. SUBJECTS/PLAY TYPE: Fantasy; Time Travel; Old West; Musical.

394. 7-10. (+) Sodaro, Craig. **Cabin under siege.** CAST: 3f, 3m. ACTS: 1. SETTINGS: Cabin living room. PLAYING TIME: 25 min. PLOT: Retired Judge Crenshaw and his wife are visited by his niece and her roommate at their secluded mountain home. They are confronted by a convicted felon, out to revenge his brother's death following a jail term handed down by the judge. After the felon is overpowered, a policeman shows up to take him in. But the policeman is actually the felon and vice versa. In a struggle, the real bad guy is knocked out with a frying pan, the policeman comes to, and all is set right. RECOMMENDATION: This has a cleverly executed plot, the twist at the end is unexpected, and the use of a heroine instead of a hero is refreshing. Producers should be aware that there is much violence and fear portrayed here. ROYALTY: Free to Plays subscribers. SOURCE: Sodaro, Craig. (1988, May). Cabin under siege. Plays: The Drama Magazine for Young People, pp. 1-8. SUBJECTS/PLAY TYPE: Mystery; Playlet.

395. 4-8. (+) Kehret, Peg. **Cafeteria lunches.** CAST: 1u. ACTS: 1. SETTINGS: None. PLAYING TIME: NA. PLOT: A child ridicules the inedible state of most cafeteria lunches. RECOMMENDATION: Most school children will appreciate the humor in this monologue, especially those who don't "brown bag" it. ROYALTY: NA. SOURCE: Kehret, Peg. (1986). Winning monologs for young actors. Colorado Springs, CO: Meriwether Pub. SUBJECTS/PLAY TYPE: School Cafeteria; Monologue.

396. 7-12. (+) Fratti, Mario. **The cage.** CAST: 1f, 1m. ACTS: 1. SETTINGS: Bare stage, props. PLAYING TIME: NA. PLOT: Christiano bars himself in his family's apartment, because he fears he might kill his family and people who are hypocritical. Realizing that he has lost his sense of perception and self control, he withdraws into himself. RECOMMENDATION: This is an ideal piece to use for sharpening young actors' and actresses' skills at expressing the subtleties of human expression. ROYALTY: NA. SOURCE: Olfson, Lewy. (1980). Fifty great scenes for student actors. New York, NY: Bantam Books. SUBJECTS/PLAY TYPE: Social Interaction; Behavior; Scene.

397. 9-12. (+) Campton, David. **Cagebirds.** CAST: 8f. ACTS: 1. SETTINGS: Room. PLAYING TIME: NA. PLOT: Six women, each a bird analogy representing a stereotype of a particular kind of modern woman, are caught up in their own selfish thoughts and ignore the plight of the group as a whole--namely, their imprisonment. This continues until the Wild One is added to the cage and attempts to organize the flock. She picks the lock and tries to persuade the others to flee with her. Her arguments finally rally them to action, but the action is to murder her. The irony of "man's" condition, objectified by this play, is that freedom for the individual is possible only through communality. RECOMMENDATION: The distinct types represented

by each caged "bird" are not immediately recognizable and the interrupted monologues are confusing until the listener realizes the author's intent. Until the arrival of the Wild One, the action is minimal and stagnant. Overall, the playwright's approach to his theme is effective. The play should elicit lively discussion from high school students, especially those concerned about their own freedoms within the confines of school and family. ROYALTY: $20. SOURCE: Campton, David. (1976). Cagebirds. Woodstock, IL: Dramatic Pub. Co. SUBJECTS/PLAY TYPE: Birds; Alienation; Drama.

398. 10-12. (+) Wouk, Herman. (Wouk, Herman) **The Caine mutiny court-martial.** (The Caine mutiny) CAST: 19m. ACTS: 2. SETTINGS: Court-martial room. PLAYING TIME: NA. PLOT: Lt. Maryk is charged with mutiny after relieving Capt. Queeg of his duties on the night of a violent storm. Lt. Greenwald has been appointed to defend Maryk, but the odds of finding his client not guilty are tied up in respect and tradition. His aim is to prove that the Captain is a psychopath during crises. As the trial progresses, witnesses reveal the weakness of the Captain, and Maryk is acquitted. RECOMMENDATION: The actual court-martial in the novel is a single chapter, but the adaptation stands on its own. The portrayal of Lt. Greenwald is more poignant, but much of the same dialogue is used and it follows the novel's details quite closely. ROYALTY: $50. SOURCE: Wouk, Herman. (1983). The Caine mutiny court-martial. New York, NY: Samuel French. SUBJECTS/PLAY TYPE: Court-Martial; Navy; Betrayal; Adaptation.

399. 12. (+) Mooney, Vicki. **Cake and sippin' whiskey.** CAST: 6f, 3m. ACTS: 2. SETTINGS: Porch; kitchen. PLAYING TIME: NA. PLOT: Bunce Morgan returns from WWII to his fiance, the beautiful but spoiled Starlene Giddens who, the night before, was seduced by Bunce's best friend, Jake Weaver. At the homecoming party everyone drinks too much, Jake and Bunce go hunting, and Jake accidently shoots Bunce, who is blinded. Starlene tells Bunce the shooting was deliberate. Jake is a victim of Starlene's lies and is forced to leave town. RECOMMENDATION: The adult language, sensitive material, and overt sexual actions here make this inappropriate for young actors. However, the emotions and the consequences of Starlene's lying are strongly depicted, and the southern dialogue and stereotypes are vivid and consistent. ROYALTY: $50. SOURCE: Mooney, Vicki. (1983). Cake and sippin' whiskey. Chicago, IL: Dramatic Pub. Co. SUBJECTS/PLAY TYPE: Lying; Friendship; Drama.

400. 4-12. (+) Gleason, William. **The Calamityville terror.** CAST: 7f, 4m. ACTS: 2. SETTINGS: Room. PLAYING TIME: NA. PLOT: Mrs. Stowe rents the Barclay Estate for her girls' school, and agrees to allow Mr. Barclay's insane sister, Elsie, to continue to reside there. The young woman went mad the evening her parents were murdered and Mrs. Stowe suspects that Elsie was the culprit. The students befriend Elsie, which worries Mrs. Stowe but delights Mr. Barclay, who, in fact, had murdered his parents, convinced his distraught sister that she had done the deed, and keeps her

drugged and crazed. The hired man and Elsie's new friends interfere with the brother's attempt to have Elsie committed, and expose him as the murderer. RECOMMENDATION: Only two easily rigged special effects are needed to make the production effective and no special costuming is required. The drama is high on suspense and on opportunities for melodramatic acting. ROYALTY: $50. SOURCE: Gleason, William. (1981). The Calamityville terror. Chicago, IL: Dramatic Pub. Co. SUBJECTS/PLAY TYPE: Murder; Insanity; Drama.

401. K-3*. (+) Hurt, Mary Leonard. **The calendar court.** CAST: 1f, 1m, 22u. ACTS: 1. SETTINGS: Ballroom. PLAYING TIME: 15 min. PLOT: Bewildered and confused, Little Miss 1977 wanders into the ballroom of the Calendar Court of Father Time. Father Time arrives, and everyone anxiously awaits the arrival of the New Year. Miss 1977 realizes that she is the New Year for whom they have all been waiting. Since she is still confused, the twelve months who are present explain what makes up a calendar year and what happens in each month. RECOMMENDATION: This should be produced by middle or high school students for elementary students. Some minor changes are needed to update it. ROYALTY: Free to Plays subscribers. SOURCE: Hurt, Mary Leonard. (1977, January). The calendar court. Plays: The Drama Magazine for Young People, pp. 41-46. SUBJECTS/PLAY TYPE: Calendar; Months; Holidays; Skit.

402. 4-12. (-) Gilfond, Henry. **A call to duty.** CAST: 2f, 7m, 2u. ACTS: 1. SETTINGS: Sitting room. PLAYING TIME: 15 min. PLOT: George Washington reluctantly accepts the presidency after his unanimous election. RECOMMENDATION: None of the pros and cons of Washington's decision is presented here and the constant intrusions of ladies who want him to dance the minuet trivialize the entire drama. ROYALTY: None. SOURCE: Gilfond, Henry. (1985). Holiday plays for reading. New York, NY: Walker. SUBJECTS/PLAY TYPE: Washington, George; Presidency, American; Drama.

403. 4-6. (+) Stahl, Le Roy. **Calling all cars!** CAST: 1f, 3m, Su. ACTS: 1. SETTINGS: Office. PLAYING TIME: NA. PLOT: Mr. Smuggins, President of Smuggins' Automotive Works, wants to build a better car. Mr. Hartburn, the company inventor, shows Mr. Smuggins and Mr. Bemis, the company superintendent, his latest blueprints and announces that the new car will not use gasoline, making it the most economical car ever. The only difficulty is that the car won't run. RECOMMENDATION: This is a drawn out joke with a snappy punchline. The audience must be mature enough to understand the joke, as well as how an automobile operates. ROYALTY: None. SOURCE: Majeski, Bill. (1981). Easy skits, blackouts and pantomimes. Woodstock, IL: Dramatic Pub. Co. SUBJECTS/PLAY TYPE: Comedy; Automobiles; Skit.

404. 6-8. (+) Bradley, Virginia. **Callyope, the crying comic.** CAST: 8m. ACTS: 5. SETTINGS: Curtain; circus; field. PLAYING TIME: NA. PLOT: When Callyope

runs away and learns to laugh, he becomes Callyope the laughing comic. RECOMMENDATION: While no stage scenery is required, attention should be given to the costumes and the acting in this lengthy play. ROYALTY: None. SOURCE: Bradley, Virginia. (1975). Is there an actor in the house. New York, NY: Dodd, Mead. SUBJECTS/PLAY TYPE: Circus; Friends; Comics; Skit.

405. 4-9. (+) Kilcup, Rick. **Camel Lot. CAST:** 1f, 6m, 1u. ACTS: 3. SETTINGS: Throne room. PLAYING TIME: 15 min. PLOT: A fire breathing dragon threatens to destroy the kingdom of King Arthuritis until Peter Peasants learns the dragon is two men in costume working for Sir William, who is trying to steal the kingdom. When Sir Lanceaflop fails to kill the dragon, Peter hits it with a wooden sword and the men inside topple over, revealing the charade. The princess finishes them off with karate and plans happily to marry Peter. RECOMMENDATION: The modern touches to this classic formula are hilarious, and the creativity allowed for the costuming will make this a great production for even the largest groups. ROYALTY: Free to Plays subscribers. SOURCE: Kilcup, Rick. (1982, January/February). Camel Lot. Plays: The Drama Magazine for Young People, pp. 39-46. SUBJECTS/PLAY TYPE: Dragons; Comedy.

406. 9-12. (+) Sandock Frank. **Campaign fever.** CAST: 5f, 5m, Su. ACTS: 1. SETTINGS: Art room; bare stage, props. PLAYING TIME: 35 min. PLOT: Susan, a candidate for senior class president, and her campaign manager, are distressed to find out that Steve, captain of the basketball team, has entered the race. The election ends in a tie between them. Absent students are asked to vote to break the tie, including the basketball team, which was away at a game. Susan wins the election when Steve supports her, and asks for Steve's help in carrying out her duties. RECOMMENDATION: With realistic characters and dialogue, this lesson on fair play is subtly conveyed. With its modern school setting, it should be easily produced, although some of the dialogue may be too lengthy for younger performers. ROYALTY: Free to Plays subscribers. SOURCE: Sandock, Frank. (1982, November). Campaign fever. Plays: The Drama Magazine for Young People, pp. 1-11. SUBJECTS/PLAY TYPE: Elections; Playlet.

407. 4-6. (+) Sawyer-Young, Kat. **Campout. CAST:** 2m. ACTS: 1. SETTINGS: Yard. PLAYING TIME: NA. PLOT: On a backyard campout, Adam and Josh tell ghost stories. Josh's story about a man hunting for his lost liver frightens them so much that they race to the house to spend the night. RECOMMENDATION: The characters effectively portray a common and delightful children's activity that has the expected result. ROYALTY: NA. SOURCE: Sawyer-Young, Kat. (1986). Contemporary scenes for contemporary kids. Boston, MA: Baker's Plays. SUBJECTS/PLAY TYPE: Camping Out; Ghost Stories; Scene.

408. 9-12. (+) Scanlan, Michael. **Candid. CAST:** 3f, 3m. ACTS: 1. SETTINGS: Dining room; living room; bedroom; auditorium. PLAYING TIME: NA. PLOT: T.J.

presents a photo essay in slides to his teacher, Mrs. Paschal. What starts as an assignment for school turns into a documentary on the disintegration of T.J.'s family, precipitated by the mother's desertion. RECOMMENDATION: Many teenagers in the audience will empathize with T. J. The play is rather brief and should be easy for young adults to perform. The dialogue and situation are direct, honest and sometimes painfully true to life. ROYALTY: $15. SOURCE: Scanlan, Michael. (1986). Candid. Boston, MA: Baker's Plays. SUBJECTS/PLAY TYPE: Family; Desertion; Drama.

409. 9-12. (+) Harris, Aurand. (Shaw, George Bernard) **Candida.** (Candida) CAST: 2f, 3m. ACTS: 1. SETTINGS: Drawing room. PLAYING TIME: NA. PLOT: Candida Morell returns home to her husband, Reverend Morell, bringing a young poet named Eugene, who is secretly in love with her. Eugene tells Morell that he doesn't deserve Candida, and Morell becomes despondent. In the end, Candida chooses Morell over Eugene. Based on George Bernard Shaw's original work, the entire play dwells on the relationship between Eugene, the man of emotion, and Morell, the man of rhetoric, as they fight for Candida's affection. RECOMMENDATION: It is questionable whether there is enough content to keep an audience interested. Because of the abridgment of Shaw's original work, characters develop too rapidly. ROYALTY: $15. SOURCE: Harris, Aurand. (1979). Candida. Boston, MA: Baker's Plays. SUBJECTS/PLAY TYPE: Emotion; Love; Adaptation.

410. 3-7. (+) Gersbach, Jo. **A candle lights the way.** CAST: 5f, 3m. ACTS: 1. SETTINGS: Living room. PLAYING TIME: 15 min. PLOT: Mrs. Lankford, a widow, is sad because none of her family can come home for Christmas. Bessie, the maid, places a wreath with a candle in the window which attracts the attention of the Jordan family, traveling during the severe snow storm, who are invited to stay for Christmas. RECOMMENDATION: The theme of Christmas spirit is warmly presented and appropriate to the age group and the season. ROYALTY: Free to Plays subscribers. SOURCE: Gersbach, Jo. (1978, December). A candle lights the way. Plays: The Drama Magazine for Young People, pp. 41-46. SUBJECTS/PLAY TYPE: Christmas; Drama.

411. 7-12. (+) Fitzgerald, Neil C. **Can't anyone hear me? CAST:** 3f, 1m. ACTS: 1. SETTINGS: Office. PLAYING TIME: 15 min. PLOT: A teenage girl having problems with a teacher is sent to the high school counselor. The counselor senses the deeper family roots of the problems and suggests family counseling, which is resisted by the father. The relationship between the student and teacher is resolved, but questions remain about the family's future. The author suggests discussion after the play and includes 14 questions to facilitate dialogue. RECOMMENDATION: The plot, setting, and characters portraying the situation of many contemporary families may trigger disturbing personal responses in most viewers, which would generate discussion for a forum dealing with family problems.

ROYALTY: Free to Plays subscribers. SOURCE: Fitzgerald, Neil C. (1984, April). Can't anyone hear me? Plays: The Drama Magazine for Young People, pp. 36-42. SUBJECTS/PLAY TYPE: Family; Drama.

412. K-6. (+) Merton, George. **Captain Blackpatch.** CAST: 1f, 6u. ACTS: 1. SETTINGS: Bare stage, props. PLAYING TIME: NA. PLOT: When a fisherman disappears during a fierce storm, his son meets the dead Captain Blackpatch, who has shanghaied the father to become part of his undersea crew. The father saves the Captain's dog (really an octopus), from an attacking swordfish, and father and son are set free in gratitude. RECOMMENDATION: This has all the mystery, horror, and comic relief of a great pirate story, and is simple enough for even the youngest. ROYALTY: Free for amateur performance. SOURCE: Merten, George. (1979). Plays for puppet performance. Boston, MA: Plays, Inc. SUBJECTS/PLAY TYPE: Pirates; Puppet Play.

413. 5-7. (+) Gotwalt, Helen Louise Miller. **Captain castaway's captives.** CAST: 4f, 8m, 5u. ACTS: 1. SETTINGS: Ship's deck. PLAYING TIME: 30 min. PLOT: Captain Castaway and his crew must abduct students with English grades of C or below and march them down the plank if a grammatical or literary inconsistency is detected. Six student prisoners, aided by Lady Dorinda, discover that the Captain cannot spell and challenge him to a spelling bee. When he loses, prisoners and crew maroon him on a desert island with spelling books and writing paper. RECOMMENDATION: This creative idea would make an excellent English class project. Videotaped, it could provide an entertaining introduction to the study of correct English usage. ROYALTY: Free to Plays subscribers. SOURCE: Gotwalt, Helen Louise Miller. (1986, May). Captain Castaway's captives. Plays: The Drama Magazine for Young People, pp. 61-70. SUBJECTS/PLAY TYPE: Grammar; Skit.

414. 7-12. (+) Kelly, Tim J. **Captain Fantastic!** CAST: 12f, 7m, Su. ACTS: 3. SETTINGS: Newspaper office; Rat Hole Club. PLAYING TIME: NA. PLOT: The Editor of the Paul Bunyan High School Newspaper, Waldo, is a "comic book buff," who receives a knock out blow that turns his world into comic book action, where he is Captain Fantastic and his enemies are comic book sinister forces. Captain Fantastic struggles against the forces and wins, as does Waldo in his personal life after awakening. RECOMMENDATION: This is an entertaining farce about comic book heroes which will appeal to anyone who has read many comic books. ROYALTY: $40. SOURCE: Kelly, Tim J. (1979). Captain Fantastic! Boston, MA: Baker's Plays. SUBJECTS/PLAY TYPE: Comic Books; School Newspapers; Farce.

415. 1-6. (+) Kelly, Tim. **Captain Nemo and his magical marvelous submarine machine.** CAST: 7f, 6m, 1u. ACTS: 2. SETTINGS: Seashore; path; cave; submarine interior. PLAYING TIME: 60 min. PLOT: Barnacle Bess spots some pirates on shore and calls for the aid of Captain Nemo. Together they encounter the pirates and their two children hostages. The Sea Witch plots to take over Captain Nemo's submarine. When the children are released, the pirates promise to be nice, but the Sea Witch convinces them differently. A dramatic encounter takes place aboard the submarine, and goodness prevails. RECOMMENDATION: Captain Nemo and his slick weapons, used for good, would keep a younger viewing audience's attention. The plot is well developed and is easy to follow, as is the dialogue. ROYALTY: $25. SOURCE: Kelly, Tim. (1978). Captain Nemo and his magical marvelous submarine machine. Denver, CO: Pioneer Drama Service. SUBJECTS/PLAY TYPE: Submarines; Comedy.

416. 7-12. (+) Bland, Joellen. (Verne, Jules) **Captain Nemo and the mysterious island.** (The mysterious island) CAST: 6m. ACTS: 1. SETTINGS: None. PLAYING TIME: 30 min. PLOT: Several men, imprisoned by Confederate troops, escape in a gas filled balloon to an uninhabited island, where a mysterious being helps by providing supplies and saving them from pirates. He is Captain Nemo of the Nautilus legend. Before he dies, Nemo helps them to escape from the island before a volcano destroys it. RECOMMENDATION: This action-packed adventure will surely capture the interests of young adults. It is an adequate adaptation and should inspire some students to read the original. ROYALTY: Free to Plays subscribers. SOURCE: Bland, Joellen. (1981, March). Captain Nemo and the mysterious island. Plays: The Drama Magazine for Young People, pp. 71-80. SUBJECTS/PLAY TYPE: Adventure; Science Fiction; Reader's Theater.

417. 3-6. (+) Boiko, Claire. **Captain Scrimshaw's treasure.** CAST: 2f, 4m. ACTS: 1. SETTINGS: Parlor. PLAYING TIME: 30 min. PLOT: Captain Amos Scrimshaw, recently deceased, leaves his entire $20,000 fortune to his best friend. Three of the four people waiting for the reading of the will contemplate their claim, while Johnny Pauper regrets the captain's death. A butler, Codfish Jones (actually Captain Scrimshaw in disguise), greets the fortune seekers at the door. The will is read and the fortune seekers find that the fortune is hidden somewhere in the parlor and they must seek it. Johnny discovers the treasure, but claims he'd rather have the Captain back alive. He is rewarded when the Captain rips off his disguise, revealing his identity to his one true friend, Johnny. RECOMMENDATION: The suspense of this delightful mystery is enhanced by the riddle of the clues, the mad dash of the hunt and the personality build up of each character before the curtain. The actual hunt may be confusing to an audience as they try to discern the thoughts and actions of each character. ROYALTY: Free to Plays subscribers. SOURCE: Boiko, Claire. (1976, January). Captain Scrimshaw's treasure. Plays: The Drama Magazine for Young People, pp. 33-40. SUBJECTS/PLAY TYPE: Mystery; Friendship; Playlet.

418. 7-12. (+) Hamlett, Christina. **Captain Sebastien--and Thaddeus Lord.** CAST: 2f, 3m. ACTS: 1. SETTINGS: Ship quarters. PLAYING TIME: 20 min. PLOT: Thaddeus Lord, a count, and a pirate change places to thwart a disastrous planned marriage, but the

fat, ugly bride to be runs off to marry someone else. In order not to disgrace the family, Lillian substitutes for the sister who has run off, and the Captain and Lillian fall in love. British ships approach to fight the pirate ship and the players decide to pass the Captain off as Lillian's fiance. The Captain miraculously finds Thaddeus Lord's papers and adopts this identity. **RECOMMENDATION:** While this play ends happily, it would be more suitable for the upper grades since a kiss is called for between the Captain and Lillian, but the kiss could be omitted and would be less objectionable to the junior high set. A strong and convincing Captain is needed, since he humorously addresses the audience and involves them in the plot by asking rhetorical questions. **ROYALTY:** Free to Plays subscribers. **SOURCE:** Hamlett, Christina. (1983, October). Captain Sebastien--and Thaddeus Lord. Plays: The Drama Magazine for Young People, pp. 1-10. **SUBJECTS/PLAY TYPE:** Marriage; Sea Captains; Comedy.

419. 7-12. (+) DeBoy, David. **Captain's outrageous.** CAST: 2f, 4m. ACTS: 2. SETTINGS: Hospital room. PLAYING TIME: NA. PLOT: While hospitalized with ulcers, Captain O'Michaels tries to re-establish a relationship with his son by threatening to sue his hospital roommate, a prominent white bread manufacturer who also happens to be his son's most important client. RECOMMENDATION: This wonderful light comedy illustrates the difficulty of intergenerational communication in a hilarious way complete with romance, chase scenes, slapstick comedy, and an equally funny resolution. **ROYALTY:** $50. **SOURCE:** DeBoy, David. (1986). Captain's outrageous. Woodstock, IL: Dramatic Pub. Co. **SUBJECTS/PLAY TYPE:** Family; Relationships; Comedy.

420. 9-12. (+) Bruce, Mark. **Car crazy.** CAST: 1f, 1m. ACTS: 1. SETTINGS: Bare stage. PLAYING TIME: 15 min. PLOT: A young boy obsessed with his brand new car continually polishes it, drives at the high speed of 10 miles per hour, and puts cloths on the seats in order to protect them from possible stains. Heather, his girlfriend, is upset when the car stalls because Jack is driving too slowly up a hill and she gets out to walk away. Jack leaves the car to follow her, forgetting to put on the emergency brake, and the car rolls down the hill and crashes, leaving Jack with nothing more than a heap of shattered fiberglass. RECOMMENDATION: Anyone who has ever had the pleasure of owning a new car should certainly be able to relate to this play. The humor is satirical and will be especially appreciated by those of this age who are either anticipating or enjoying the purchase of their own car. **ROYALTY:** Free to Plays subscribers. **SOURCE:** Bruce, Mark. (1982, March). Car crazy. Plays: The Drama Magazine for Young People, pp. 61-66. **SUBJECTS/PLAY TYPE:** Dating; Automobiles; Skit.

421. 7-12. (+) Campton, David. **Cards, cups and crystal ball.** CAST: 5f. ACTS: 1. SETTINGS: Sitting room. PLAYING TIME: NA. PLOT: Three sisters, Flora, Nora, and Dora, who are charlatans, inherit the family ability to predict the future. The mysterious Lady M visits

for a consultation. She tried to manipulate the future by committing murder and other heinous crimes, but pays for her misdeeds when she falls down the stairs after tripping over a misplaced coal scuttle. **RECOMMENDATION:** This is an inoffensive little play, even if it is silly and predictable. It would be good for a beginning acting class exercise, but the all female cast makes it very limited. It does not reach tragedy, or even melodrama. **ROYALTY:** $20. **SOURCE:** Campton, David. (1987). Cards, cups and crystal ball. Woodstock, IL: Dramatic Pub. Co. **SUBJECTS/PLAY TYPE:** Fortune Telling; Mystery; Melodrama.

422. K-7. (+) Kilcup, Rick. **The care and feeding of a dragon.** CAST: 2f, 1m, 10u. ACTS: 1. SETTINGS: Throne room. PLAYING TIME: 15 min. PLOT: A dragon tells the king and queen he plans to eat the princess in 24 hours. The knights prove too cowardly to protect her, and the royal wizard's new wand isn't working right. The princess comes to her own rescue by appeasing his hunger with spaghetti prepared by the royal chef, who is delighted that the dragon likes the spaghetti and agrees to work on a chili recipe. RECOMMENDATION: The royal chef, Sir Noodles, has served spaghetti 36 times in a row as he has tried to perfect the recipe. This will delight youngsters, especially when he starts a three month term of chili dinners in order to perfect this recipe too. **ROYALTY:** Free to Plays subscribers. **SOURCE:** Kilcup, Rick. (1988, May). The care and feeding of a dragon. Plays: The Drama Magazine for Young People, pp. 29- 33. **SUBJECTS/PLAY TYPE:** Dragons; Food; Comedy.

423. 7-12. (+) Bradley, Virginia. **The carousel and the cold fried egg.** CAST: 4f, 8m, Su. ACTS: 1. SETTINGS: Porch; fairground. PLAYING TIME: NA. PLOT: Letty Simms refuses to marry pig farmer Lucius McNeil and heads for the fair. During her ride on the ferris wheel, it stops. Lucius begins to climb after her and she realizes she loves him. RECOMMENDATION: The play's slight humor and country bumpkin characters will appeal to teenage audiences, but will require some creative stage sets. **ROYALTY:** NA. **SOURCE:** Bradley, Virginia. (1977). Stage eight: One act plays. New York, NY: Dodd, Mead. **SUBJECTS/PLAY TYPE:** Family; Dating; Comedy.

424. 5-8. (+) Benz, Jewel. **Carriage Trade.** CAST: 5f, 3m, Su. ACTS: 1. SETTINGS: Driveway; garage sale. PLAYING TIME: NA. PLOT: Karen and Sue hold a garage sale and agree to take care of Herbie's baby brother so Herbie can play baseball. A customer, Mrs. Hustlebustle, loses an earring and, while Karen is searching for it, the baby carriage with Herbie's baby brother in it is sold. Both the earring and the baby are recovered. RECOMMENDATION: This illustrates how young people can get things confused in their attempts to be helpful, with both the lost baby and earring portraying the world of mishaps that cause anxiety until they are resolved--at which time they become funny. Simple, realistic and funny, this play could be produced within an elementary school classroom. **ROYALTY:** $25. **SOURCE:** Benz, Jewel. (1975). Carriage trade. Franklin,

OH: Eldridge Pub. Co. SUBJECTS/PLAY TYPE: Garage Sales; Kidnapping; Comedy.

425. 5-8. (+) Boiko, Claire. **Carry on, Maid Marian!** (Robin Hood) CAST: 8f. ACTS: 1. SETTINGS: Forest; throne room. PLAYING TIME: 40 min. PLOT: In this play within a play, women's roles, plot, and characters are reversed when the merry men of Sherwood Forest all become ill, and all is left up to Maid Marian and the merry maids. They proceed to steal the Queen's treasury and give it to the poor, and plan to create a charter of English rights for all which they will call the Magna Carta. RECOMMENDATION: Women's lib frees the women of Sherwood Forest from boredom and drudgery in the farcical adaptation of one Robin Hood tale. Although the women are complete bunglers, they do accomplish their goal in spite of stereotypical female handicaps. Popular tunes add to the overall gaiety of this piece. ROYALTY: Free to Plays subscribers. SOURCE: Boiko, Claire. (1977, April). Carry on, Maid Marian! Plays: The Drama Magazine for Young People, pp. 13-22. SUBJECTS/PLAY TYPE: Musical; Comedy; Women's Rights; Adaptation.

426. 5-8. (+) Fisher, Aileen. **The carved symbol.** CAST: 1m, 4u. ACTS: 1. SETTINGS: Bare stage, props. PLAYING TIME: 5 min. PLOT: Four children discuss, in rhyme, the chair in which George Washington sat during the drafting of the Constitution. The chair is the allegorical symbol of the nation; its carved symbol of a rising sun represents the rise of democracy in this new country. RECOMMENDATION: This dramatic choral reading is quite appropriate as a testimony to the spirit and symbol of the U.S. Constitution and those who had the vision to write it. The rhyme and lofty words echo well the significance of the actions described. ROYALTY: Free to Plays subscribers. SOURCE: Fisher, Aileen. (1975, May). The carved symbol. Plays: The Drama Magazine for Young People, pp. 91-92. SUBJECTS/PLAY TYPE: Constitution, U.S.; Choral Reading.

427. 7-12. (+) Murray, John. **A case for two detectives.** CAST: 1m. ACTS: 1. SETTINGS: Living room. PLAYING TIME: 30 min. PLOT: A murder case is solved in two different ways and with two different conclusions by two private detectives: the cerebral Quentin Van Quentin and tough guy Rivets O'Neill. In the surprise ending, both are wrong; the butler did it. RECOMMENDATION: The performer has an opportunity to stretch in his/her craft. Since appreciation of the piece is predicated on the audience's recognition of the parodied mystery story conventions, some of the humor may escape less experienced audiences. ROYALTY: Free to Plays subscribers. SOURCE: Murray, John. (1982). Modern Monologues for Young People. Boston, MA: Plays, Inc. SUBJECTS/PLAY TYPE: Detectives; Mystery; Comedy; Monologue.

428. 6-9. (+) Murray, John. **A case for two spies.** CAST: 4f, 6m, 1u. ACTS: 1. SETTINGS: Hotel lobby. PLAYING TIME: 25 min. PLOT: In this spoof of TV spy shows, a scientific formula and its inventor have disappeared. Bumbling, incorrect assumptions, and character misjudgments about suspects abound. RECOMMENDATION: This humorous play may have limited appeal because younger actors and audiences probably won't be familiar with the shows or cartoon actors that are the object of the fun. Dialogue (as with other Murray plays of this vein) convey multiple meanings but tend toward adult sophisticated humor. ROYALTY: Free to Plays subscribers. SOURCE: Murray, John. (1985). Fifteen plays for today's teenagers. Boston, MA: Plays, Inc. SUBJECTS/PLAY TYPE: Spies; Satire.

429. 7-12. (-) Allred, Jan. **A case of belonging.** CAST: 3f, 2m. ACTS: 1. SETTINGS: Bare stage. PLAYING TIME: NA. PLOT: An angel, a devil, and a representative of "Limbo" argue over who shall have the rights to a newly dead person. Each tries unsuccessfully to lift the body, which is finally lifted by an IRS representative who claims ownership on the basis of tax evasion. RECOMMENDATION: Although the premise is humorous enough and the arguments presented sometimes are clever, mostly this play is boring, unsuccessfully slapstick, and vaguely sexist. ROYALTY: $15. SOURCE: Allred, Jan. (1978). A case of belonging. Elgin, IL: Performance Pub. Co. SUBJECTS/PLAY TYPE: Taxes; Comedy.

430. 6-9. (-) Bryan, Linda L. **A case of cleanser: A juvenile mystery farce in one act.** CAST: 9f, 4m. ACTS: 1. SETTINGS: Bare stage, props. PLAYING TIME: 30 min. PLOT: Rocky, a former fight manager, blackmails his grandmother, Madeleine, for the murder of her husband, but she outwits him by giving him counterfeit money. Madeleine's granddaughters find their dead grandfather's diary, in which he has plotted revenge on his wife. RECOMMENDATION: This farce features funny stereotypes, with mediums, mothers, crooks, ghosts, and the old lady. Frequent entrances and cross-action provide much action, but some may find that the story has too many elements to develop them all well in the time provided. Also, the relationship between the girls and their grandmother is flat with no emotion shown over the grandmother's shady past or blighted future. ROYALTY: $5. SOURCE: Bryan, Linda L. (1978). A case of cleanser: a juvenile mystery farce in one act. Denver, CO: Pioneer Drama Service. SUBJECTS/PLAY TYPE: Mystics; Ghosts; Comedy; Farce.

431. 7-12. (+) Murray, John. **A case of mistaken identity.** CAST: 4f, 4m. ACTS: 1. SETTINGS: Living room. PLAYING TIME: 25 min. PLOT: A young wife, Mary, alone in the new house, receives a hysterical phone call from a woman warning that someone wants to kill her. Fred, a stranger, forces his way into the house and demands money stolen from a bank, which he thinks she has hidden somewhere. The police arrest Fred, leaving Mary with Noel, a psycho who thinks she is the dead wife of his brother, the bank robber. More complications and fast action arise, culminating when the money is found in an old stuffed teddy bear. RECOMMENDATION: This packs a great deal into one short play, which is complete with scary

thunderstorms, eerie foreshadowings, the requisite menaced woman, mistaken identification of the villain, and, of course, a psycho. If well cast, it will be a thriller. ROYALTY: Free to subscribers. SOURCE: Murray, John. (1988). A case of mistaken identity. Boston, MA: Plays, Inc. SUBJECTS/PLAY TYPE: Mystery; Suspense; Drama.

432. 4-7. (+) Boiko, Claire. **The case of the bewitched books. CAST:** 7f, 3m, 12u. ACTS: 1. SETTINGS: Library. PLAYING TIME: 20 min. PLOT: The witch, two stepsisters, and wicked queen of folk tale fame cast a spell on the children's reading room in the public library, turning the villains of the stories into heroines. They soon realize that great villains make terrible heroines. RECOMMENDATION: The audience will need to be familiar with the original tales to understand the humor in this absolutely delightful excursion. ROYALTY: Free to Plays subscribers. SOURCE: Boiko, Claire. (1978, November). The case of the bewitched books. Plays: The Drama Magazine for Young People. pp. 51-57. SUBJECTS/PLAY TYPE: Folk Tale Characters; Censorship; Comedy.

433. 1-6. (+) Durden, Mae. **The case of the Easter villains. CAST:** Su. ACTS: 1. SETTINGS: Puppet stage. PLAYING TIME: 20 min. PLOT: The day before Easter, Ally Alligator and Mostly Pig blacken the Easter eggs. At midnight, the Easter Bunny and Mrs. Easter ask all the bunnies to help by withdrawing all their eggs from bank and painting them; Easter is saved. Ally and the pig are punished by having to learn techniques of landscaping and flood control. The play ends with a parade. RECOMMENDATION: Depending upon the abilities of the producers, the puppets can be simply decorated socks, or they can be quite elaborate. ROYALTY: Free to Plays subscribers. SOURCE: Durden, Mae. (1976, April). The case of the Easter villains. Plays: The Drama Magazine for Young People, pp. 74-78. SUBJECTS/PLAY TYPE: Easter; Puppet Play.

434. 5-8. (+) Wallace, Ruth. **The case of the frustrated corpse. CAST:** 2f, 2m. ACTS: 1. SETTINGS: Living room. PLAYING TIME: NA. PLOT: A corpse which talks to the audience when no one else is on stage, lies on a sofa with a dagger in his chest. The maid dusts the living room but doesn't acknowledge him. The wife moves his feet off the sofa, but also doesn't notice that he has been stabbed. A detective arrives to investigate a crime--not the murder, but the alleged burglary of the wife's pearls, which are found in the sofa. Everyone leaves and the corpse wonders when someone will notice that he is dead. RECOMMENDATION: The audience will delight in this very clever vignette. This would make an excellent filler during a scene change for a longer play. ROYALTY: Free to Plays subscribers. SOURCE: Wallace, Ruth. (1977, October). The case of the frustrated corpse. Plays: The Drama Magazine for Young People, pp. 78-80. SUBJECTS/PLAY TYPE: Comedy; Skit.

435. 3-8. (+) Gotwalt, Helen Louise Miller. **The case of the giggling goblin. CAST:** 7f, 11m, Su. ACTS: 1. SETTINGS: Bare stage, props. PLAYING TIME: 20 min. PLOT: Gladys Goblin is branded a public nuisance by the citizens of Hauntsville because she giggles. She is to be banished from Halloween until some improvements can be seen. However, when men arrive to dynamite the mine, Gladys gives a long, piercing laugh and scares them away. Gladys is a hero, and the charges against her are dropped. RECOMMENDATION: The length and difficulty of dialogue requires that this be performed by older students for the younger ones. The names of the characters are especially funny. ROYALTY: Free to Plays subscribers. SOURCE: Gotwalt, Helen Louise Miller. (1987, October). The case of the giggling goblin. Plays: The Drama Magazine for Young People, pp. 39-45. SUBJECTS/PLAY TYPE: Halloween; Goblins; Comedy.

436. 6-9. (+) Alexander, Sue. **The case of the kidnapped nephew. CAST:** 3f, 5m, 1u. ACTS: 1. SETTINGS: Courtroom. PLAYING TIME: NA. PLOT: Timothy Crane, secretary for writer Pamela Madison, is on trial for kidnapping Pamela's nephew, Brian Farley. Although his attorney struggles to prove him innocent, a crucial slip during the cross examination gives Brian away. RECOMMENDATION: A mystery play interestingly solved in a courtroom, this will hold children's interest with its fast action, dialogue, and plot. Audiences will enjoy solving this whodunit before the culprit is actually identified, and young actors will have fun producing this simple drama, despite their level of inexperience. ROYALTY: NA. SOURCE: Alexander, Sue. (1980). Whatever happened to Uncle Albert and other puzzling plays. New York, NY: Houghton Mifflin. SUBJECTS/PLAY TYPE: Court Trials; Kidnapping; Mystery.

437. 2-6. (+) Smith, Gary H. **Case of the missing homework: A melodrama for young actors. CAST:** 8f, 7m, Su. ACTS: 3. SETTINGS: Living room; schoolroom; office. PLAYING TIME: NA. PLOT: Priscilla finishes her final homework assignment, which will determine whether she receives the highest total score in her class. Priscilla's jealous brother steals the assignment and gives it to her rival, with whom he wants to go steady. An imbecile of a detective, Foulfellow Fern, is hired to discover the identity of the thief, which he accomplishes by accident. Priscilla is vindicated and still becomes the best student. RECOMMENDATION: This play is witty, humorous, and would be a good tool for demonstrating a melodrama. Some may be offended by the disrespectful depiction of people in authority, but other than that, this production will be uncomplicated and enjoyable for upper elementary actors to stage for younger audiences or their peers. Card-cued audience participation also adds flavor to the production. ROYALTY: $30. SOURCE: Smith, Gary H. (1976). Case of the missing homework: A melodrama for young actors. Franklin, OH: Eldridge Pub. Co. SUBJECTS/PLAY TYPE: Family; School; Grades; Comedy.

438. 7-12. (+) Huff, Betty Tracy. **The case of the missing masterpiece. CAST:** 6f, 4m. ACTS: 1. SETTINGS: Artist's studio. PLAYING TIME: 25 min.

PLOT: Uncle Henry, an artist, has been murdered during a botched attempt to acquire a stolen Rembrandt painting. However, because the painting has not been found, the murderer is still lurking around the scene of the crime looking for it. Henry's nieces and a detective solve the murder and the mystery of the stolen painting when they discover a pair of gloves with paint on them. Since all the suspects had been wearing gloves, they know that the murderer is the only one without gloves. RECOMMENDATION: The usual gathering of suspects is a familiar (but necessary) touch in order to solve the mystery in this short whodunit. If the audience is observant, they might be able to solve the mystery before the concluding scene. ROYALTY: Free to Plays subscribers. SOURCE: Huff, Betty Tracy. (1977, April). The case of the missing masterpiece. Plays: The Drama Magazine for Young People, pp. 23-32. SUBJECTS/PLAY TYPE: Murder; Mystery.

439. 6-9. (+) Willment, Frank. **The case of the missing motive.** CAST: 4f, 4m. ACTS: 1. SETTINGS: Library. PLAYING TIME: 30 min. PLOT: Oscar Bannister, a wealthy philanthropist, is poisoned at his dinner party by one of his guests. The murderer is revealed to be Agatha Pritchett, a retired school teacher who loves mysteries. RECOMMENDATION: This play has all the elements of a well written mystery: poison, several suspects with seemingly no motives, and a mysterious message. The solution to the murder is not easily discerned and keeps the audience guessing. ROYALTY: Free to Plays subscribers. SOURCE: Willment, Frank. (1980, November). The case of the missing motive. Plays: The Drama Magazine for Young People, pp. 11-22. SUBJECTS/PLAY TYPE: Mystery; Playlet.

440. 4-8. (-) Lawrence, James E. **The case of the phantom baseball.** CAST: 13f, 4m. ACTS: 3. SETTINGS: Living room. PLAYING TIME: 90 min. PLOT: Sam Shovel, private eye, has been called in by Elizabeth Cantrell, a rich and elderly widow, to prove she is a clairvoyant. Every time her grandson hits a home run, the ball disappears from the park and "reappears" to smash through a window in her home. Shovel discovers that Doris Cantrell and Captain Danner have staged the baseball scheme to make Elizabeth appear crazy so they can get her money. Elizabeth decides at the end that a close relationship with one's family is more important than mystical powers. RECOMMENDATION: The plot has more potential than it delivers. The humor is overdone, but may be appreciated. ROYALTY: $25. SOURCE: Lawrence, James E. (1978). The case of the phantom baseball. Denver, CO: Pioneer Drama Service. SUBJECTS/PLAY TYPE: Mystery; Swindlers And Swindling; Clairvoyance; Comedy.

441. 7-12. (+) Willment, Frank. **The Case of the Punjabi Ruby.** CAST: 4f, 5m. ACTS: 1. SETTINGS: Jewelry shop. PLAYING TIME: 30 min. PLOT: A gem auction at Madame Martine's jewelry store is interrupted by a robbery. All five witnesses are suspects. Inspector Conlon, his retired seventh grade teacher, Miss Agatha Pritchett, and the robbery suspects, recreate the crime. Miss Agatha exposes Madame Martine as Molly Martin, her gum chewing ex-student, who is the thief of the Punjabi ring. RECOMMENDATION: The audience will enjoy matching wits with Miss Agatha, as she and Inspector Conlon recreate the crime in this well constructed whodunit, with humorously stereotypical characters. ROYALTY: Free to Plays subscribers. SOURCE: Willment, Frank. (1977, January). The case of the Punjabi ruby. Plays: The Drama Magazine for Young People, pp. 11-22. SUBJECTS/PLAY TYPE: Robbers; Mystery.

442. 10-12. (+) Martens, Anne Coulter. **The case of the silent dog.** CAST: 4f, 7m, Su. ACTS: 1. SETTINGS: Airport; living room. PLAYING TIME: 30 min. PLOT: Two bank robbers attempt a getaway at a local airport. One of the robbers accidentally gets his flight bag containing the loot switched with that of a young woman returning home to work in the very bank that was robbed. Her homecoming is disrupted by the bank robbers who return to reclaim their lost loot. Their escape is foiled by the clever detective work of the young woman and her neighbor. RECOMMENDATION: The "family-next-door" and the bumbling bank robbers add a comic sense of believability to the situations, as the mild suspense holds the interest in spite of the play's mostly predictable events. ROYALTY: Free to Plays subscribers. SOURCE: Martens, Anne Coulter. (1977, March). The case of the silent dog. Plays: The Drama Magazine for Young People, pp. 15-24. SUBJECTS/PLAY TYPE: Bank Robbery; Mystery.

443. 4-6. (+) Brooks, Courtaney. **The case of the stolen dinosaur.** CAST: 2f, 8m, 1u. ACTS: 1. SETTINGS: Bare stage. PLAYING TIME: NA. PLOT: Three brave children and an assortment of other eccentric characters, including Sir Thad, Lady Maude, and Waldo Perfecto, rescue the children's pet, the only living dinosaur in the world, who has been stolen and spirited away to Hawaii. RECOMMENDATION: Children will love this comic mystery which has all of the elements of farce and magic with a final and heroic rescue of the dinosaur. ROYALTY: NA. SOURCE: Brooks, Courtaney. (1983). The case of the stolen dinosaur. Claremont, CA: Belnice Books. SUBJECTS/PLAY TYPE: Dinosaurs; Comedy; Mystery.

444. 3-7. (+) Kilcup, Rick. **The case of the vanishing cluckers.** CAST: 2f, 3m, 12u. ACTS: 1. SETTINGS: Chicken coop; kitchen. PLAYING TIME: 15 min. PLOT: Several members of the Cluck and Crow Glee Club have mysteriously disappeared just before the start of the Barnyard Talent Contest. The famous canine private eye, Harlow Hound, called in to solve the mystery, allows himself to be "chicken napped" by Colonel Beauregard Fox, a scheming southern-fried chicken chef. However, it is the singing chickens themselves who really save the day for the Glee Club. RECOMMENDATION: Elementary age children would have fun with this funny and fast plot of singing chickens and a fast-food fox. The characters are exaggerated for comic effect but this is appropriate for this play. Dialogue isn't too creative, but does add to the

humor. **ROYALTY:** Free to Plays Subscribers. **SOURCE:** Kilcup, Rick. (1980, February). The case of the vanishing cluckers. Plays: The Drama Magazine for Young People, pp. 39-44. **SUBJECTS/PLAY TYPE:** Chickens; Foxes; Mystery; Comedy.

445. 6-10. (+) Henderson, Nancy. (Thayer, Ernest L.) **Casey at the bat.** (Casey at bat.) **CAST:** 9m, 10u. **ACTS:** 1. **SETTINGS:** Baseball diamond. **PLAYING TIME:** 8 min. **PLOT:** This poetic pantomime follows the story of Thayer's famous poem. **RECOMMENDATION:** Because it requires mostly males, this play might be difficult to perform in class, but the crowd of undetermined size alleviates this problem. **ROYALTY:** Permission required if performed outside of the classroom. **SOURCE:** Henderson, Nancy. (1978). Celebrate America: a baker's dozen of plays. New York, NY: Julian Messner. **SUBJECTS/PLAY TYPE:** Baseball; Pantomime; Adaptation.

446. 10-12. (+) Schnessel, S. Michael. **Cassie's miracle. CAST:** 5f, 7m, Su. **ACTS:** 1. **SETTINGS:** Ghetto apartment. **PLAYING TIME:** 60 min. **PLOT:** Cassie, a poor widow, is told on Christmas Day that she must find another place to live because her landlord can no longer afford to keep up the building. Later in the day, Cassie sees a beautiful impression of Jesus Christ in her window, and radio evangelist Rev. Cannon helps sell tickets to see the miracle, in hopes of saving the building. Unfortunately, the visitors steal all of Cassie's belongings. However, another miracle saves Cassie, when her landlord finds her a new home where she can live for free. **RECOMMENDATION:** The story of Cassie is moving, as we feel both her pain and her strong faith. Written for a racially mixed cast, this can be adapted to any group, although the religious content makes it inappropriate for public schools. **ROYALTY:** $35. **SOURCE:** Schnessel, S. Michael. (1982). Cassie's miracle. Schulenburg, TX: I.E. Clark. **SUBJECTS/PLAY TYPE:** Christmas; Faith; Christian Drama.

447. 7-11. (+) Dias, Earl J. **Cast up by the sea. CAST:** 3f, 5m. **ACTS:** 3. **SETTINGS:** Living room. **PLAYING TIME:** 25 min. **PLOT:** A family is forced to accept the marriage of their daughter to a man she does not love in order to avoid financial ruin. Unbeknownst to them, he is causing their troubles in order to compel their beautiful daughter to marry him before her true love returns from the sea. Her beau, now rich, returns and exposes the plot. **RECOMMENDATION:** This melodrama, with its overdone characters portraying good and evil, will be great for those willing to "ham it up." **ROYALTY:** Free to Plays subscribers. **SOURCE:** Dias, Earl J. (1986, January/February). Cast up by the sea. Plays: The Drama Magazine for Young People, pp. 10-20. **SUBJECTS/PLAY TYPE:** Family; Comedy; Melodrama.

448. 2-5. (+) Nicholson, Jessie. **A castle in Spain. CAST:** 4f, 4m, Su. **ACTS:** 1. **SETTINGS:** Barn interior. **PLAYING TIME:** 30 min. **PLOT:** A starving artist and his five children make their home in a barn where the artist continues painting Spanish castles, which do not sell. The children dress up like ghosts, and a famous

bullfighter mistakes one for his dead daughter. When he realizes she is not really a ghost, he is relieved, buys the father's newest painting and provides enough wealth for the artist and the family to move to Spain. **RECOMMENDATION:** This presents a loving family whose positive outlook in the face of dire circumstances is endearing. The ending is a bit contrived, but if the audience can suspend disbelief, it could work. **ROYALTY:** Free to Plays subscribers. **SOURCE:** Nicholson, Jessie. (1988, January/February). A castle in Spain. Plays: The Drama Magazine for Young People, pp. 1-10. **SUBJECTS/PLAY TYPE:** Artists; Ghosts; Families; Playlet.

449. 5-8. (+) Sroda, Anne. **The Castlebury clock. CAST:** 4f, 6m, Su. **ACTS:** 1. **SETTINGS:** Garden. **PLAYING TIME:** 20 min. **PLOT:** A wicked wizard, G. Whiz, threatens to harm the king and his subjects if he is not allowed to marry the king's daughter. The king's plans to protect the Princess Gloxina offend G. Whiz, who casts a spell on the town to make everyone sleep for 500 years. Walter, a modern man, stumbles upon the castle 500 years later, and awakens the townspeople when he moves the hands of the clock. He is convinced that he must marry Gloxinia in order to save her from G. Whiz. G. Whiz returns, only to discover that his plan has backfired, and leaves confused and angry. The townspeople live happily ever after. **RECOMMENDATION:** Young viewers will be attracted to this play, as it incorporates many of the elements found in familiar fairy tales: magic, royalty, and a happing ending. The traditional conflict of good vs. evil, with good emerging triumphant, is well-done. **ROYALTY:** Free to Plays subscribers. **SOURCE:** Sroda, Anne. (1976, March). The Castlebury clock. Plays: The Drama Magazine for Young People, pp. 47-53. **SUBJECTS/PLAY TYPE:** Magic; Fantasy; Melodrama.

450. K-8. (+) Christmas, Joyce S. **The cat and the electronic fiddle. CAST:** 2f, 2m, 8u. **ACTS:** 1. **SETTINGS:** Field. **PLAYING TIME:** 20 min. **PLOT:** Jinx attracts all the other cats in the neighborhood to form a rock band. As they prepare, all the characters from the nursery rhyme come through. Jinx fails to inspire the group, and goes home to the security of regular meals and dishes of milk. Jinx and the "laughing dog" resolve to go on the road as a dog and cat rock duo. **RECOMMENDATION:** The contemporary rock theme mixed with nursery rhyme characters and their familiar lines can provide a bridge for bringing together very young and older students. **ROYALTY:** Free to Plays Subscribers. **SOURCE:** Christmas, Joyce S. (1979, March). The cat and the electronic fiddle. Plays: The Drama Magazine for Young People, pp. 55-60. **SUBJECTS/PLAY TYPE:** Rock Music; Nursery Rhyme Characters; Comedy.

451. 4-8. (+) Kehret, Peg. **The cat door. CAST:** 1u. **ACTS:** 1. **SETTINGS:** None. **PLAYING TIME:** NA. **PLOT:** A child details the frisky escapades of a pet cat. **RECOMMENDATION:** Any audience member with a pet will see the humor in this short piece. **ROYALTY:** NA. **SOURCE:** Kehret, Peg. (1986). Winning monologs

for young actors. Colorado Springs, CO: Meriwether Pub. SUBJECTS/PLAY TYPE: Cats; Monologue.

452. 4-8. (+) Solly, Bill. **The cat in the castle.** CAST: 2f, 2m, 3u. ACTS: 1. SETTINGS: Throne room; moat; dungeon; belfry. PLAYING TIME: NA. PLOT: Two cats announce, and then re-enact, the tale of their great adventure of escaping the fiery yawn of the Pterodactyl and the ire of the Queen who hates cats. RECOMMENDATION: The songs included are entertaining and a clear message is presented to the children: make friends by showing them attention. ROYALTY: $25. SOURCE: Solly, Bill. (1985). The cat in the castle. Boston, MA: Baker's Plays. SUBJECTS/PLAY TYPE: Cats; Friendship; Musical.

453. K-3. (+) Creegan, George R. **The cat who roared.** CAST: 6u. ACTS: 1. SETTINGS: Forest. PLAYING TIME: 5 min. PLOT: Kopper Kat wants to be a mountain lion and succeeds in developing a ferocious roar which frightens away her friends. She is glad when she regains her own voice and, consequently, her old friends. RECOMMENDATION: This very short and simple little fable is simply delicious. The young child will understand Kopper Kat's desire to be big and powerful, and her relief to be herself again. ROYALTY: Free to Plays Subscribers. SOURCE: Creegan, George R. (1979, April). The cat who roared. Plays: The Drama Magazine for Young People, pp. 69-70. SUBJECTS/PLAY TYPE: Fables; Animals; Puppet Play.

454. 1-8. (+) Whittaker, Violet. (Applegarth, Margaret T.) **Catarina's ten fingers.** (At the foot of the rainbow) CAST: Su. ACTS: 2. SETTINGS: Outside. PLAYING TIME: NA. PLOT: Catarina attends Sunday school nine times before her family moves to a village without a Sunday school. She tells the children her nine stories, each named for one of her ten fingers. When a missionary arrives and tries to tell Bible stories, the children already know them. So, the tenth finger is called the Go ye finger, named for what Catarina has done, spreading the word of Jesus. RECOMMENDATION: This simple but charming story does not have to be set in Puerto Rico, as written, but could be set in any community without a church nearby. It neatly tells how even a child can teach the Bible. ROYALTY: NA. SOURCE: Whittaker, Violet. (1984). Puppet people scripts. Grand Rapids, MI: Baker Book House. SUBJECTS/PLAY TYPE: Puppet Play; Christian Drama; Adaptation.

455. 4-9. (+) Shore, Maxine. **Catastrophe Clarence.** CAST: 6m. ACTS: 1. SETTINGS: Astronomy observatory. PLAYING TIME: 20 min. PLOT: While visiting his astronomer uncle, a boy and his friend become involved in trying to save the earth from a deadly meteor. RECOMMENDATION: Simple production specifications complement this humorous, suspenseful, and adventurous play. The small, entirely male cast could be a deterrent for some. ROYALTY: Free to Plays subscribers. SOURCE: Kamerman, Sylvia E. (1981). Space and science fiction plays for young

people. Boston, MA: Plays, Inc. SUBJECTS/PLAY TYPE: Science Fiction; Space; Drama.

456. 8-12. (+) Urdahl, Richard. **Caught in the middle of the fourth.** CAST: 1f, 2m. ACTS: 1. SETTINGS: None. PLAYING TIME: NA. PLOT: A mother is caught in the middle of a generational argument between her father and her son. The son feels she never lets him do anything and there are too many rules. Her father feels that she is too lenient with the boy. Tension builds within her until her primal scream for help ends the skit. RECOMMENDATION: Although targeted for a Christian audience and intended as a reminder of the fourth commandment, this skit does not preach and would have appeal to broader audiences. Teenagers could use this production as a performance or as a reading to touch off a group talk on the subjects of communication and the generation gap. ROYALTY: $10. SOURCE: Urdahl, Richard. (1984). Don't listen to us, Lord...we're only praying. Boston, MA: Baker's Plays. SUBJECTS/PLAY TYPE: Generation Gap; Communication; Christian Drama.

457. 6-8. (+) Olfson, Lewy. **Cause for celebration.** CAST: 3f, 2m, Su. ACTS: 1. SETTINGS: Living room. PLAYING TIME: 15 min. PLOT: On the Fourth of July, 2076, Tammy and Scott Martin and their children, David and Nora, prepare for a Tricentennial celebration dressed as famous historical people. As they are about to leave, Nora says that she is not going because it is "immoral" to celebrate a country that has so many problems. David makes fun of the plant she is planning on entering in a competition because it is a living plant and not made of aluminum or styrofoam. She defends it, saying that her plant may not be perfect, but it is growing and she has hope for its future. Nora's mother applies Nora's defense of her plant to a defense of the United States: it may not be perfect, but it is still progressing. Nora changes her outlook on the celebration and agrees to go. RECOMMENDATION: This presents humorous but thought provoking ideas about what the future will hold and well illustrates the need for all of us to be involved in the affairs of our country. ROYALTY: Free to Plays subscribers. SOURCE: Olfson, Lewy. (1976, January). Cause for celebration. Plays: The Drama Magazine for Young People, pp. 79-84. SUBJECTS/PLAY TYPE: Independence Day, U.S.; Comedy.

458. 10-12. (+) Kelly, Tim J. **The cave.** CAST: 12u. ACTS: 1. SETTINGS: Bare stage. PLAYING TIME: NA. PLOT: This is about humanity's struggle against fear and character faults. The cast enters, wondering what it is expected to perform and looking for a "director." They decide to pantomime a scene from their great success which makes fun of the public's appetite for morbid events. Finding cards bearing the words sea, cave and future, they choose the perceived safety of the cave, but a creature enters the cave and attacks them. They vote to leave the cave to try to live "outside." RECOMMENDATION: Dialogue is witty and often caustic in this intriguing, abstract production. The mood

is somber to begin with but lifts at the end. Characters evolve from fearful and aggressive to a willingness to risk leaving the cave and looking for something better. ROYALTY: $15. SOURCE: Kelly, Tim J. (1977). The cave. New York, NY: Dramatists Play Service, Inc. SUBJECTS/PLAY TYPE: Fear Of The Unknown; Risk Taking; Philosophy; Drama.

459. 7-10. (+) Garver, Juliet. **Cave man, brave man.** CAST: 3f, 2m. ACTS: 2. SETTINGS: Cave. PLAYING TIME: 25 min. PLOT: A Stone Age artist becomes a hero by drawing animals on the cave walls. After each drawing is finished, whatever has been drawn is magically caught by one of the cave hunters. RECOMMENDATION: Teenage students will appreciate the attempts at modern day humor in a caveman setting. The only drawback to this otherwise insightful drama is the sexist tone with which problems in marriage, dating, male/female roles, and what's really important in life are examined. ROYALTY: Free to Plays subscribers. SOURCE: Garver, Juliet. (1986, May). Cave man, brave man. Plays: The Drama Magazine for Young People, pp. 17-26. SUBJECTS/PLAY TYPE: Cave Drawings; Stone Age; Comedy.

460. 8-12. (+) Heuer, John. **Cavern of the jewels.** CAST: 4f, 4m, 1u. ACTS: 2. SETTINGS: Forest; cavern; mansion; dungeon. PLAYING TIME: NA. PLOT: A brother and sister on a berry picking outing meet two forest gnomes who are decorating the forest using the magical properties of jewels. The children's greedy, cruel parents find out about the jewels and throw one of the gnomes into their dungeon. The children are forced to tell where the jewels are kept, and the parents and an equally greedy Reverend seize the treasure. The gnomes call on a water spirit, who defeats the father in a sword fight, recovers the jewels, and turns the father into a sand turtle. RECOMMENDATION: Although this fairy tale play is enjoyable, it is only suitable for older children because it is too long, the parents are excessively cruel (treating their children as despised servants), there are sexual innuendos woven throughout, the stage setting is fairly complicated, and the costumes must be carefully done. In the hands of a good group of actors, this play could be a modern day fairy tale that really succeeds in demonstrating the corrupting force that wealth has, even on supposedly holy people. ROYALTY: $35. SOURCE: Heuer, John. (1976). Cavern of the jewels. New York, NY: Dramatists Play Service. SUBJECTS/PLAY TYPE: Greed; Cruelty; Drama.

461. 7-12. (+) Freistadt, Berta. **The celebration of Kokura.** CAST: 7f, Su. ACTS: 1. SETTINGS: Bare stage. PLAYING TIME: NA. PLOT: Told in a stylized format by two narrators and various people who come onto the stage, this is the story of the bombing of Hiroshima and Nagasaki. The experiences of women who survived because they were in the nearby town of Kokura are related in rhythmic verse, as is the history of the atomic bomb. RECOMMENDATION: This easily produced play will chillingly and realistically depict the ironies and paradoxes of a weapon of destruction whose justification was peace. ROYALTY: NA. SOURCE: Lowe, Stephen.

(1985). Peace plays. New York, NY: Methuen. SUBJECTS/PLAY TYPE: Atomic Bomb; Hiroshima; Kokura; Choral Reading.

462. 4-7. (-) Kehret, Peg. **Cemeteries are a grave matter.** CAST: 3f, 3m, Su. ACTS: 1. SETTINGS: Living room; street. PLAYING TIME: NA. PLOT: The McNutts, a family of morticians, battle against a group that is for cremation and against burials. Daughter Jenny, 17, becomes emotionally attached to male corpses, which gives her the strength of purpose to fight Daniel, the rich and hypocritical advocate of cremation. The McNutts win the right to continue with burials and Jenny turns her attentions to a live suitor. RECOMMENDATION: This is a very weak comedy, with poor humor, one dimensional characters and stilted dialogue. The plot does provide a vehicle for criticizing the hypocrisy that can accompany self-serving wealth, but it does so by creating a distasteful situation with too much emphasis on necrophilia. ROYALTY: $15. SOURCE: Kehret, Peg. (1975). Cemeteries are a grave matter. Chicago, IL: Dramatic Pub. Co. SUBJECTS/PLAY TYPE: Funeral Customs; Necrophilia; Comedy.

463. 3-8*. (+) Watts, Irene N. **A chain of words.** CAST: 2f, 3m, Su. ACTS: 1. SETTINGS: Village; farm; cottage; plains. PLAYING TIME: NA. PLOT: Six Japanese folk tales illustrate typical themes such as greed, cruelty, kindness, and forgiveness in ways similar to Western folk tales. Unlike many Western folktales, the greedy or foolish person in these stories often becomes good in the end and is spared from death. RECOMMENDATION: These fascinating tales are based on the traditional Japanese Kabuki style of drama and must be presented in that style to be effective. They should be uncluttered in both costuming and setting, and a chorus is needed. Musical instruments such as a flute, a gong, cymbals, and a Japanese drum, will add to the effect. Young children will enjoy the tales, but they should be presented by older children, perhaps 9-12 graders, to create the proper atmosphere. ROYALTY: NA. SOURCE: Watts, Irene N. (1978). A chain of words. Vancouver, Canada: Talonbooks. SUBJECTS/PLAY TYPE: Folk Tales, Japan; Musical.

464. 1-8. (+) Whittaker, Violet. **Chaluba, the African god carver.** CAST: 5m, Su. ACTS: 7. SETTINGS: Forest; village courtyards. PLAYING TIME: NA. PLOT: Chaluba, the idol maker, decides that wooden idols are not as powerful as the god who makes the hands that carve the idols. Exiled because of his blasphemy, he goes in search of God and learns to read. When he returns to his village, the villagers give him a recently acquired Bible, in the reading of which he finds God. RECOMMENDATION: The message of the play is that all who search for God will find him. The section in which the children are told that Chaluba became a Christian could be deleted to make this nondenominational. ROYALTY: NA. SOURCE: Whittaker, Violet. (1984). Puppet people scripts. Grand Rapids, MI: Baker Book House. SUBJECTS/PLAY TYPE: Religious Drama; God; Puppet Play.

465. 9-12. (-) Krawitz, H. Michael. **The chance of a lifetime or How the unicorn lost his spot.** CAST: 2f, 2m, 3u. ACTS: 1. SETTINGS: Wharf. PLAYING TIME: 25 min. PLOT: A male unicorn, who is waiting for his wife to arrive before he enters Noah's Ark is tempted by a female animal of unidentified species named Marilyn. While he deliberates, the Ark leaves. He and Marilyn are left on the wharf to face the Great Flood. RECOMMENDATION: Very loosely based on the story of Noah's Ark, this is intended to illustrate the dilemma of a person who cannot make up his mind. The characters are not convincing; the theme and the plot are not decisively drawn; and the language is frequently in very questionable taste, unrealistic, and not really entertaining. The play would offend people on religious as well as aesthetic grounds. ROYALTY: $15. SOURCE: Krawitz, H. Michael. (1981). The chance of a lifetime. Schulenburg, TX: I.E. Clark. SUBJECTS/PLAY TYPE: Cartoon; Noah's Ark; Drama.

466. 3-6. (+) Gabriel, Michelle. **Chanukah story.** CAST: 3m, 6u. ACTS: 1. SETTINGS: Outdoors. PLAYING TIME: 10 min. PLOT: This depicts the origin of the Jewish festival, Chanukah, when King Antiochus was driven away by Judah Maccabee, and the Temple menorah, with enough oil only for one day, remained burning for eight days. RECOMMENDATION: This puppet play explains the story of Chanukah and emphasizes that Chanukah is celebrated as struggle for religious freedom. ROYALTY: None. SOURCE: Gabriel, Michelle. (1978). Jewish plays for Jewish days. Denver, CO: Alternatives in Religious Education, Inc. SUBJECTS/PLAY TYPE: Chanukah; Jewish Drama; Puppet Play.

467. 7-12. (+) Watts, Frances B. **The charge of the bathtub brigade.** CAST: 3f, 3m, 1u. ACTS: 1. SETTINGS: Living room. PLAYING TIME: 20 min. PLOT: Hal loves Sal, but a parade of tenants through the living room to the adjoining bathroom in Sal's boarding house doesn't allow for privacy. Hal becomes desperate, but only after a fight which involves all the tenants does he find the "privacy" to propose. RECOMMENDATION: The actors do not speak in this "different" play; the "Reader" therefore must convincingly deliver the rhymed verse script, with the actors timing their actions to the script, and piano music setting the mood and tone. ROYALTY: $3. SOURCE: Watts, Frances B. (n.d.) The charge of the bathtub brigade. Franklin, OH: Eldridge Pub. Co. SUBJECTS/PLAY TYPE: Pantomimes; Dating; Melodrama.

468. 3-12. (+) McDonough, Jerome. (Dickens, Charles) **Charles Dickens' a Christmas carol.** (A Christmas carol) CAST: 8f, 7m, Su. ACTS: 1. SETTINGS: None. PLAYING TIME: 35 min. PLOT: Concise and faithful to the Dickens' classic, the visits by the spirits successfully touch Scrooge's hard heart, enabling him to alter in turn his relations with his nephew, clerk, and humankind in general, and to effect a brighter future for Tiny Tim. RECOMMENDATION: The simple script and staging of this wonderful classic makes for a remarkably easy but effective road show. The script contains wonderful production notes that allow for expansion or contraction of staging and music. ROYALTY: $15. SOURCE: McDonough, Jerome. (1976). Charles Dickens' a Christmas carol. Schulenburg, TX: I.E. Clark. SUBJECTS/PLAY TYPE: Christmas; Cyclorama.

469. 6-10. (+) Way, Brian. (Dickens, Charles) **Charles Dickens' Oliver Twist.** (Oliver Twist) CAST: 13f, 17m, Su. ACTS: 2. SETTINGS: Theater-in-the-round with platforms, tables, and chairs. PLAYING TIME: NA. PLOT: Oliver Twist runs away from his apprenticeship to an abusive undertaker, meets up with a gang of pickpockets, and is accused of theft. A witness clears him, and he is taken in by Mr. Brownlow, the victim of the theft, but the gang kidnaps him and forces him into burglary, during which he is shot and captured. Rose Maylie, the burglary victim, nurses Oliver and protects him from further kidnappings by the gang. She and Mr. Brownlow learn of Monks, who has stolen Oliver's inheritance and all evidence of his identity. RECOMMENDATION: While well written, this adaptation suffers from typical Dickensian melodramatic situations and several stereotyped characters. A professional group of actors could turn it into a captivating performance for a young audience, but performed by children, it could become overly sentimental and trite. On the other hand, there are some glorious villains, who, if well acted, might turn the production into a delight. The drama group must possess actors capable of memorizing a great many lines. ROYALTY: NA. SOURCE: Way, Brian. (1977). Charles Dickens' Oliver Twist. Boston, MA: Baker's Plays. SUBJECTS/PLAY TYPE: Thieves; London; Adaptation.

470. 9-12. (+) Nolan, Paul T. (Thomas, Brandon) **Charley's Aunt.** (Charley's Aunt) CAST: 3f, 5m. ACTS: 1. SETTINGS: Garden/patio. PLAYING TIME: 30 min. PLOT: Two young Oxford scholars are in desperate need of a chaperone. One of them, Charley, arranges for his rich Aunt, recently returned from Brazil, to be present when they propose to their sweethearts. When the Aunt cannot make it, they convince their older friend, Lord Babberly, to act as Charley's Aunt. Deception and farce follow to win the hearts of their ladies (and more importantly the consent to marry). RECOMMENDATION: In this excellent adaptation of Brandon Thomas' grander work, the part of Jack's father and Lord Babberly are combined into one character. Scenery is simple but the more authentic the Victorian costumes, the better. Older groups may even want to try the original version. ROYALTY: Free to Plays subscribers. SOURCE: Nolan, Paul T. (1985, January/February). Charley's Aunt. Plays: The Drama Magazine for Young People, pp. 67-79. SUBJECTS/PLAY TYPE: Dating; Marriage; Comedy; Adaptation.

471. 9-12. (+) Rogers, David & Strouse, Charles. (Keyes, Daniel) **Charlie and Algernon.** (Flowers for Algernon) CAST: 4f, 6m. ACTS: 2. SETTINGS: Playground; hospital room; bakery; office; computer room. PLAYING TIME: NA. PLOT: This is a faithful

adaptation of the original. RECOMMENDATION: The pathos and tragedy of the original are movingly recreated here. The cast will have to be quite talented, and some sexual scenes may have to be changed. ROYALTY: Upon application. SOURCE: Roger, David & Strouse, Charles. (1981). Charlie and Algernon. Woodstock, IL: Dramatic Pub. Co. SUBJECTS/PLAY TYPE: Love; Mental Retardation; Adaptation.

472. 4-8. (+) George, Richard. (Dahl, Roald) **Charlie and the chocolate factory.** (Charlie and the chocolate factory) CAST: 9f, 10m, Su. ACTS: 1. SETTINGS: Home; factory. PLAYING TIME: NA. PLOT: The world's greatest chocolate maker, Willy Wonka, conducts a contest, the winner of which will take over Wonka's candy-making operation. The five semi-finalists and their parents are invited to tour Mr. Wonka's factory. One contestant, the pure but poor Charlie Bucket, proves his mettle and is given the chocolate factory. RECOMMENDATION: The play carefully follows the storyline of this popular children's classic. In fact, Roald Dahl praises the adaptation in the introductory notes. There are good, clear suggestions for simple staging putting the production well within the reach of upper elementary children to produce. ROYALTY: $50. SOURCE: George, Richard. (1976). Charlie and the chocolate factory. Chicago, IL: Dramatic Pub. Co. SUBJECTS/PLAY TYPE: Fantasy; Adaptation.

473. 4-7*. (-) George, Richard R. (Dahl, Roald) **Charlie and the great glass elevator.** (Charlie and the great glass elevator) CAST: 5f, 16m, Su. ACTS: 2. SETTINGS: Glass elevator; White House; spaceship; Ground Control. PLAYING TIME: NA. PLOT: Charlie Bucket and his family go for a joy ride with Willy Wonka in the Great Glass Elevator. Using the elevator like a spaceship, they repel an alien invasion and salvage an American orbiter. RECOMMENDATION: Many of the actors will deliver long speeches. Mr. Dahl claims this play is easier to produce than **Charlie and the Chocolate Factory,** but the play itself is lacking in many aspects. The U.S. President is presented as a fool while the Russian Premier and the Chinese Assistant Premier are so poorly caricatured that the play borders on being offensive to ethnic minorities. ROYALTY: $50. SOURCE: George, Richard R. (1984). Charlie and the great glass elevator. Woodstock, IL: Dramatic Pub. Co. SUBJECTS/PLAY TYPE: Space; Fantasy; Adaptation.

474. 8-11. (-) Garver, Juliet. **Charlie and the six chicks.** CAST: 10f, 2m. ACTS: 1. SETTINGS: Living Room. PLAYING TIME: 35 min. PLOT: A teenager is invited by six girls to the Senior Prom, and each girl thinks she is his only date. Realizing his predicament, he tries to invent excuses not to attend the dance, but to no avail. His female cousin, whom he has not seen in several years, appears and advises him to tell each date the truth about the others. They all decide to dump him, and he takes his cousin instead. RECOMMENDATION: The situations are contrived, the solution unrealistic, and the characters flat. ROYALTY: Free to Plays subscribers. SOURCE: Garver, Juliet. (1980, April). Charlie and the six chicks. Plays: The Drama Magazine for Young People, pp. 9-21. SUBJECTS/PLAY TYPE: Dating; Comedy.

475. 3-6*. (+) Robinette, Joseph. (White, E. B.) **Charlotte's web.** (Charlotte's web) CAST: 5f, 4m, 10u. ACTS: 2. SETTINGS: Farmyard; barn; county fair. PLAYING TIME: NA. PLOT: Wilbur, a pig, is adopted by a young farm girl and enjoys his life in her uncle's barnyard with his many animal friends, including a spider, Charlotte, who lives above Wilbur's pen. Wilbur is devastated, however, to discover that he will be slaughtered in the fall. Charlotte exerts all her wisdom and skill to prevent this from happening, eventually succeeding, but then she must die herself. RECOMMENDATION: This adaptation of E. B. White's famous children's book is faithful to the original in both spirit and detail. The book's message about the importance of friendship and the inevitability of change is transferred gracefully, along with the charming animal characters. However, the play has many long speeches which would make many of the roles too difficult for younger children to enact. ROYALTY: $50. SOURCE: Robinette, Joseph. (1983). Charlotte's web. Woodstock, IL: Dramatic Pub. Co. SUBJECTS/PLAY TYPE: Fantasy; Animals; Adaptation.

476. 11-12. (+) Weaver, Richard A. **The chastening.** CAST: 3m. ACTS: 1. SETTINGS: Park. PLAYING TIME: 25 min. PLOT: George relives his youth and treatment by his father, reflecting on his relationship with his own son. RECOMMENDATION: In this thought provoking presentation, many subjects are covered, including discipline, child abuse, neglect, and drug abuse. High school students could likely identify with the action. The play is recommended for senior high production due to the content. ROYALTY: $25. SOURCE: Weaver, Richard A. (1975). The chastening. Schulenburg, TX: I.E. Clark. SUBJECTS/PLAY TYPE: Family Relationships; Drama.

477. 9-12. (+) Mitchell, Ken. **Chautauqua girl.** CAST: 3f, 3m. ACTS: 1. SETTINGS: Tent show. PLAYING TIME: NA. PLOT: Nora Cross and her Chautauqua troupe are in Vancouver, B.C., to perform their variety show. Although the rest of the troupe is delayed due to a train derailment, the group continues their show without the regular performers, improvising and substituting Nora and even the new tent boy. Nora first receives a letter from her fiance asking her to return home immediately, then an ultimatum. Nora rebels, takes off her engagement ring, and sends it back to him. She decides to stay with the show "perhaps forever." RECOMMENDATION: This is well structured, with a good story line, a touch of romance, entertaining subplots, and never ending action. Lack of stage directions in the text leaves room for personalized innovation, but also tends to be confusing. Some minor plot inconsistencies would also need to be remedied. The entire cast will need to have musical ability. ROYALTY: NA. SOURCE: Mitchell, Ken. (1982). Chautauqua girl. Toronto, Canada: Playwrights Canada. SUBJECTS/PLAY TYPE: Vaudeville; Canada; Musical.

478. 7-12. (+) Hatton, Thomas J. **Checkmate. CAST:** 2f, 2m. ACTS: 1. SETTINGS: Living room. PLAYING TIME: 25 min. PLOT: Tom Jordan loses chess matches repeatedly to Hamilton Worthington, the President of the college chess club, and is refused membership. But Tom can get in if he gets Worthington a date with Heather Howard, Tom's girlfriend. Tom, Heather, and her friend Debbie, plot to distract Worthington during the crucial match so that Tom will win. The distractions succeed, Worthington forfeits the game, and Tom is admitted to the chess club. RECOMMENDATION: If the audience accepts the hero's obsession with gaining admittance to the chess club, they may find the plot amusing. ROYALTY: Free to Plays subscribers. SOURCE: Hatton, Thomas J. (1981, April). Checkmate. Plays: The Drama Magazine for Young People, pp. 1-10. SUBJECTS/PLAY TYPE: Dating; Chess; Comedy.

479. 6-12. (-) Dias, Earl J. **Chef's special. CAST:** 5f, 4m. ACTS: 1. SETTINGS: Room. PLAYING TIME: 30 min. PLOT: A French chef moves to a small town inn to work and write a gourmet cookbook. The new found prosperity of the inn is jeopardized when the chef's manuscript is stolen. The Chief of Police, Stella Steele, uses her photographic memory and woman's intuition to solve the case. RECOMMENDATION: Though much of this whodunit relies on cliches and stereotypes, the characters of the police chief and sergeant are refreshingly cast as women, in a statement against gender biases on the job. ROYALTY: Free to Plays subscribers. SOURCE: Dias, Earl J. (1978, January). Chef's special. Plays: The Drama Magazine for Young People, pp. 13-25. SUBJECTS/PLAY TYPE: Mystery; Sexism; Drama.

480. 10-12. (+) Frayn, Michael. (Chekhov, Anton Pavlovich) **The cherry orchard.** (The cherry orchard) CAST: 5f, 5m, 4u. ACTS: 4. SETTINGS: Nursery; roadside; drawing room. PLAYING TIME: NA. PLOT: Russian aristocrat Madame Ranyevskaya returns from Paris to discover that her Russian estate, including the cherry orchard, is being auctioned to cover her debts. Still living in the past, Madame Ranyevskaya gives a ball on the evening of the auction. Lopakhin, a former peasant and now a merchant, announces that he has purchased the estate and will cut down the orchard to build summer cottages. The family prepares to leave, aware that this is the end of their static aristocracy. RECOMMENDATION: This classic Russian play requires background preparation to understand. There is very little action, with no heroes or heroines. ROYALTY: NA. SOURCE: Frayn, Michael. (1978). The cherry orchard. New York, NY: Samuel French. SUBJECTS/PLAY TYPE: Russian Literature; Family; Tragicomedy; Adaptation.

481. 1-3. (+) Martin, Judith. **The Chicken and the egg. CAST:** 10u. ACTS: 1. SETTINGS: Bare stage. PLAYING TIME: 5 min. PLOT: The chickens and the eggs argue which came first and ask, "Won't you please help us out?" RECOMMENDATION: A familiar question is argued here by a flexible cast. The audience participation at the end could be part of a social studies or English writing unit. ROYALTY: None. SOURCE: Martin, Judith. (1981). Everybody, everybody: A collection from the paper bag players. New York, NY: Elsevier/Nelson Books. SUBJECTS/PLAY TYPE: Chickens; Comedy.

482. 11-12*. (+) Medoff, Mark Howard. **Children of a lesser god. CAST:** 4f, 3m. ACTS: 2. SETTINGS: None. PLAYING TIME: NA. PLOT: James, a teacher at a school for the deaf, falls in love with and marries one of the students, Sarah. He wants to bring Sarah, who only "signs," into the hearing world, but she thinks learning to read lips and speaking is somehow a refutation of her true identity. The couple struggles, wanting to communicate better while not wanting to change or be changed by each other. RECOMMENDATION: Although this play would be educational for high school students, some schools might be hesitant to sponsor it because of its presentation of a teacher courting and then marrying a student. Most of the cast must be proficient in sign language, although the audience doesn't need to know sign language because most of the signing is interpreted. The set requires only a few props and no backdrops. ROYALTY: $50. SOURCE: Medoff, Mark Howard. (1980). Children of a lesser god. Clifton, NJ: James T. White & Co. SUBJECTS/PLAY TYPE: Communication; Hearing Impairment; Drama.

483. 5-10. (-) Kane, Eleanora Bowling. **The children of Chocolate Street. CAST:** 8f, 2m. ACTS: 1. SETTINGS: Store. PLAYING TIME: 15 min. PLOT: Two children and a fairy become a mean candy store owner's conscience and force her to "get the Christmas spirit" and give away all of her stock. RECOMMENDATION: There really is no need for the candy store owner to give away all of her stock; the recipients are not too poor to pay, nor have they done anything to deserve the giveaway. People can't be forced to "get the Christmas spirit." ROYALTY: Free to Plays subscribers. SOURCE: Kane, Eleanora Bowling. (1982, December). The children of Chocolate Street. Plays: The Drama Magazine for Young People, pp. 60-64. SUBJECTS/PLAY TYPE: Christmas; Comedy.

484. 9-12. (+) Martin, Eller. **Children of the Southern Pacific. CAST:** 1f, 1m. ACTS: 1. SETTINGS: Grassy area. PLAYING TIME: NA. PLOT: Lucy, a homeless woman sleeping near a Southern Pacific Railroad billboard, is awakened by Jack, another homeless drifter, and confides to him that her goal is to rejoin her children. Impressed with Jack's experience and knowledge, she decides she wants to go with him, but Jack tells her she should go her own way, back to her children. RECOMMENDATION: The play is short and requires little or no scenery or props. Its themes of false hope and weakness are sobering but skillfully presented. ROYALTY: $20. SOURCE: Martin, Eller. (1987). Children of the Southern Pacific. Woodstock, IL: Dramatic Pub. Co. SUBJECTS/PLAY TYPE: Goals; False Hope; Homelessness.

485. 6-12. (+) Brooks, Jeremy & Mitchell, Adrian. (Thomas, Dylan) **A child's Christmas in Wales.** (A

child's Christmas in Wales) CAST: 7f, 19m, Su. ACTS: 2. SETTINGS: Bare stage. PLAYING TIME: NA. PLOT: Dylan Thomas, as narrator and boy child, relives his family Christmas in the 1920s, including the visit of the drunken postman, who is offered a friendly drink at every home; the Christmas dinner with his relatives at his home, when the turkey burns and firemen arrive; pudding and post-dinner entertainment with riddles; sledding and stone-skimming with friends and cousins at the seaside; and Christmas cake, ghost stories and songs in the glow of the gaslight. RECOMMENDATION: The commentary by Thomas is poetic prose and the scenes are elegiac and evoke memories in the viewers. The play succeeds because the point of view, that of an observant, verbal young boy, is maintained throughout, as the viewers experience his relationships with his close friends and relatives. ROYALTY: Upon application. SOURCE: Brooks, Jeremy & Mitchell, Adrian. (1984). A child's Christmas in Wales. Chicago, IL: Dramatic Pub. Co. SUBJECTS/PLAY TYPE: Welsh Customs; Christmas; Musical; Adaptation.

486. 1-6. (+) Book of praise for children, 1881. A child's offering. CAST: Su. ACTS: 1. SETTINGS: None. PLAYING TIME: 2 min. PLOT: This is a simple prayer about the kind of gifts a child can bring to the Christ child: obedience and love. RECOMMENDATION: This recitation is recommended because of the underlying message of obedience and the simplicity of the language. ROYALTY: None. SOURCE: Hendricks, William and Vogel, Cora. (1983). Handbook of Christmas programs. Grand Rapids, MI: Baker Book House. SUBJECTS/PLAY TYPE: Christmas; Choral Reading; Christian Drama.

487. K-4. (+) Martin, Judith & Ashwander, Donald. Chills and fever. CAST: 2f, 1m, 8u. ACTS: 1. SETTINGS: Bedroom. PLAYING TIME: 30 min. PLOT: A sick girl refuses to take her medicine and is visited by giant embodiments of three symptoms: Headache, Itchy Spots, and Runny Nose. She asks the audience how to get rid of them and they tell her to take her medicine. After doing so, the symptoms disappear, and she leaves to go play baseball. RECOMMENDATION: The personified cold symptoms are delightful. However, the chant repeated several times by the audience, "Take your medicine, take your pill," could reinforce an attitude of drug dependence; the instant recovery is also misleading. This may be useful to initiate discussion about what drugs can and cannot do. ROYALTY: NA. SOURCE: Martin, Judith & Ashwander, Donald. (1985). Reasons to be cheerful: A revue for children. New York, NY: The Paper Bag Players, Inc. SUBJECTS/PLAY TYPE: Drugs; Medicine; Colds; Musical Revue.

488. 2-6. (+) Swortzell, Lowell. The Chinese Cinderella. CAST: 3f, 5m, Su. ACTS: 1. SETTINGS: Bare stage, props. PLAYING TIME: NA. PLOT: Pearl Blossom, a young Chinese woman, has a wicked stepmother and stepsisters as in "Cinderella." Doves and a cow help Pearl Blossom do her housework in time to attend the royal procession where the richest man in

China sees her and asks to marry her. RECOMMENDATION: A young child could read the long statements of the stage manager, or an older child could take this part. The royal procession, which uses dance, acrobatics, and other physical movements, and which could involve a large number of children, is especially appealing. ROYALTY: Write the author. SOURCE: Jennings, Coleman A. & Harris, Aurand. (1988). Plays children love, Volume II. New York, NY: St. Martin's Press. SUBJECTS/PLAY TYPE: Kindness; Playlet.

489. K-3*. (+) Campbell, Paddy. Chinook. CAST: Su. ACTS: 1. SETTINGS: None. PLAYING TIME: NA. PLOT: Children must defeat the ice woman in order to bring spring to the land. Chinook, the spring wind, finally melts the ice woman's hold on the earth. RECOMMENDATION: This involves audience participation, as the participants help the actors melt ice, do fire dances, build bridges, climb mountains, etc. The theatre in the round format works very well. ROYALTY: NA. SOURCE: Kids plays: six Canadian plays for children. (1980). Toronto, Canada: Playwrights Press. SUBJECTS/PLAY TYPE: Seasons; Winter; Spring; Participation Play.

490. 7-12. (+) Stuckey, June. The choice. CAST: 3f, 9m. ACTS: 1. SETTINGS: Bare stage, props. PLAYING TIME: NA. PLOT: A gang of teenagers is arrested for vandalizing the town's nativity scene statues on Christmas Eve. When the local minister visits the gang in jail, some of the gang members feel remorse, and decide that the gang will use the high school's theater costumes and take the place of the damaged statues. RECOMMENDATION: This play should be well received by an audience expecting a Christian religious theme. General audiences may find the play overly dogmatic and condescending. ROYALTY: None. SOURCE: Stuckey, June. (1981). The choice. Boston, MA: Baker's Plays. SUBJECTS/PLAY TYPE: Christmas; Vandalism; Christian Drama.

491. 4-7. (+) Werner, Sally. The choosing of Easter Rabbit. CAST: 1f, Su. ACTS: 1. SETTINGS: Woods. PLAYING TIME: 10 min. PLOT: A group of rabbits, aware that the Easter Fairy is coming that night to choose the Easter Rabbit, become selfishly concerned with being chosen, except for Raggedy Rabbit, who is more concerned with helping animals in need. The Easter Fairy appears, reveals that she was disguised as the animals helped by Raggedy, and chooses Raggedy to be the Easter Rabbit. The other rabbits, ashamed, become helpers. RECOMMENDATION: The play lends itself to creativity in ad lib scenes and in scenes calling for strutting. The plot is delightful and thinly veiled, allowing for younger audiences to anticipate the outcome. The message could be portrayed as a theme or a moral, depending on the intent of the producer. The play is especially suitable for church environments. ROYALTY: Free to Plays subscribers. SOURCE: Werner, Sally. (1984, April). The choosing of Easter Rabbit. Plays: The Drama Magazine for Young People, pp. 43-46. SUBJECTS/PLAY TYPE: Easter; Skit.

492. 3-6*. (+) Miller, Kathryn Schultz. **Choosing sides for basketball.** CAST: 2f, 2m. ACTS: 1. SETTINGS: Gym. PLAYING TIME: NA. PLOT: Adult actors playing children agonize over whether they'll be chosen for a basketball game. Childhood personalities and insecurities as well as problems with parents are treated until all are chosen for the game. RECOMMENDATION: This is quick moving and thought provoking. ROYALTY: $20. SOURCE: Miller, Kathryn Schultz. (1981). Choosing sides for basketball. Boston, MA: Baker's Plays. SUBJECTS/PLAY TYPE: Basketball; Childhood Anxieties; Drama.

493. 12. (+) Horovitz, Israel. **The Chopin playoffs.** CAST: 3f, 5m. ACTS: 1. SETTINGS: Rooms; stores; auditorium. PLAYING TIME: NA. PLOT: Two teenage Jewish boys, Stanley and Irving, both accomplished pianists and both rivals for the love of the same gentile girl (Fern Fipps) would do about anything to win Fern's love. From humorous verbal attacks to actual physical abuse, the boys are ready to annihilate one another until Fern agrees to marry the one who wins the Drinkwater Music Competition. Because of their common heritage, Fern's obvious lack of intelligence, and their parents' opposition to Fern, the boys deliberately lose the competition, and leave Fern for another. RECOMMENDATION: If one could look beyond the cursing, lewd language, and the stereotyping of Jews, Jewish families, and gentile girls, this play might be quite humorous. True understanding of the humor and the reasons behind the boys' actions could only come with the wisdom of age and total familiarity with Jewish culture, so that the play would be appropriate for an adult Jewish community theater presentation only. ROYALTY: $50. SOURCE: Horovitz, Israel. (1987). The Chopin playoffs. New York, NY: Dramatists Play Service, Inc. SUBJECTS/PLAY TYPE: Teen Rivalry; Pianists; Jews; Comedy.

494. 4-6. (+) Duvall, Lucille. **The chosen one.** CAST: 3f, 4m, Su. ACTS: 1. SETTINGS: Cottage. PLAYING TIME: NA. PLOT: Little Felix, the son of a shepherd, is devastated when his beloved sheep Beppo gets loose one stormy Christmas Eve, but Beppo comes back and Felix is granted two wishes. RECOMMENDATION: The play contains French words which are not always defined. It is best used with actors who can memorize lengthy parts and when a long play is needed. ROYALTY: None. SOURCE: Kamerman, Sylvia E. (1975). A treasury of Christmas plays. Boston, MA: Plays, Inc. SUBJECTS/PLAY TYPE: Holidays; Christmas; Religion; Drama.

495. K-12. (+) Hendricks, William & Vogel, Cora. **Christmas.** CAST: Su. ACTS: 1. SETTINGS: None. PLAYING TIME: 6 min. PLOT: Selected verses from a traditional Irish carol tell of the angels informing the shepherd of Jesus' birth in Bethlehem, and urging the shepherd to go pay homage to Jesus. RECOMMENDATION: Suitable for church or parochial school groups, this could be a performance at a Christmas pageant or worship service. ROYALTY: NA. SOURCE: Hendricks, William and Vogel, Cora. (1978). Handbook of Christmas programs. Grand Rapids, MI: Baker Book House. SUBJECTS/PLAY TYPE: Choral Reading; Christmas; Worship Program.

496. K-12. (+) Hendricks, William & Vogel, Cora. **Christmas.** CAST: Su. ACTS: 1. SETTINGS: None. PLAYING TIME: 1 min. PLOT: Based on the Gospel of Luke, this deals with Mary, the mother of Christ, and the Angel Gabriel. RECOMMENDATION: This traditional Hereford carol is suitable for church or parochial school groups for performance at a Christmas pageant or worship service. ROYALTY: NA. SOURCE: Hendricks, William & Vogel, Cora. (1978). Handbook of Christmas programs. Grand Rapids, MI: Baker Book House. SUBJECTS/PLAY TYPE: Virgin Mary; Gabriel; Christmas; Worship Program.

497. K-12. (+) Shawnee CRC Club. **Christmas.** CAST: 13u. ACTS: 1. SETTINGS: None. PLAYING TIME: NA. PLOT: The story of Christmas is told through choral readings and traditional songs. RECOMMENDATION: Using the language of the Bible, this is a lovely Christmas devotional, suitable for church use. ROYALTY: NA. SOURCE: Altena, Hans. (1980). The playbook for Christian theater. Grand Rapids, MI: Baker Book House. SUBJECTS/PLAY TYPE: Christmas; Christian Drama.

498. 1-6. (+) Fisher, Aileen Lucia. **Christmas all around.** CAST: Su. ACTS: 1. SETTINGS: Bare stage. PLAYING TIME: 1 min. PLOT: In this narrative poem, boys and girls alternate reciting verses about the sights, smells, and anticipation of Christmas. RECOMMENDATION: This would be appropriate for children to recite, or if it seems too long for first graders, they might act out the verses while an adult recites the poem. ROYALTY: Free to Plays subscribers. SOURCE: Fisher, Aileen Lucia. (1985). Year-round programs for young players. Boston, MA: Plays, Inc. SUBJECTS/PLAY TYPE: Christmas; Choral Reading.

499. K-6. (+) Martin, Judith & Ashwander, Donald. **Christmas all over the place.** CAST: 6f, 3m, Su. ACTS: 1. SETTINGS: Bare stage. PLAYING TIME: NA. PLOT: Two families who are close friends, plan to send Christmas presents to each other and, to ensure arrival, decide to deliver the gifts in person. Each family takes an airplane and arrives at the other family's home to find that no one is there. The Huffenpuffs call their own home and the Wigglebees answer. Each family decides to celebrate Christmas at the other's home and they agree to try to get together the next year. RECOMMENDATION: This comedy successfully portrays a simple Christmas theme through a light and humorous plot, and conversational dialogue with simple props and no costumes. ROYALTY: $10. SOURCE: Martin, Judith & Ashwander, Donald. (1977). Christmas all over the place. New Orleans, LA: Anchorage Press, Inc. SUBJECTS/PLAY TYPE: Christmas; Comedy; Skit.

500. 1-12*. (+) Kurtz, Jack. **Christmas and the gargoyle who wouldn't say thank you.** CAST: 1f, 3m. ACTS: 1. SETTINGS: Bare stage. PLAYING TIME: NA. PLOT: Timmy and his friends enjoy playing in old Mr. Magruder's ruined garden, although the crochety man is forever chasing them out. One winter day, Timmy accidentally digs up a rose bush, angering Mr. Magruder. He buys a replacement rose bush, which Magruder merely throws away. When Christmas arrives, Timmy gives the old man a small gift, which apparently goes unacknowledged, but changes the lives of all concerned. RECOMMENDATION: Originally designed as a read-aloud skit, this sermon is entertaining for all age groups. Younger children will enjoy hearing this story read by older teens or adults, while learning the lesson of forgiveness and understanding. Due to the religious themes, this is best suited for a church oriented program. ROYALTY: None for the first performance. SOURCE: Kurtz, Jack. (1979). Gargoyles, plastic balls and soup. Boston, MA: Baker's Plays. SUBJECTS/PLAY TYPE: Christmas; Love; Gifts; Reader's Theater.

501. 5-8. (+) Newman, Deborah. (Dickens, Charles) **Christmas at the Cratchits.** (A Christmas carol) CAST: 4f, 4m. ACTS: 1. SETTINGS: Rooms. PLAYING TIME: 15 min. PLOT: The Cratchit family, although poor, derives Christmas joy from being together and sharing family love. RECOMMENDATION: The intimate view of the Cratchit family and their feelings is warm and endearing. ROYALTY: Free to Plays subscribers. SOURCE: Newman, Deborah. (1986, December). Christmas at the Cratchits. Plays: The Drama Magazine for Young People, pp. 43-47. SUBJECTS/PLAY TYPE: Christmas; Adaptation.

502. 8-10. (-) Miller, Patsy & Thurston, Cheryl Miller. **Christmas at the O.K. Corral.** CAST: 3f, 7m, 2u. ACTS: 1. SETTINGS: Corral. PLAYING TIME: 30 min. PLOT: Bad guys try to stop Christmas by stealing the presents. RECOMMENDATION: The settings, names and theme of this play are overused, and it gives the impression that Christmas is just about receiving gifts. ROYALTY: Free to subscribers of Plays. SOURCE: Kamerman, Sylvia E. (1983). Holiday plays round the year. Boston, MA: Plays, Inc. SUBJECTS/PLAY TYPE: Christmas; Western; Drama.

503. 2-9. (+) Galvin, Randy. **Christmas attitudes: skits and scenes about people and their attitudes about Christmas.** CAST: 2f, 2m, 2u. ACTS: 1. SETTINGS: Bare stage, props. PLAYING TIME: 60 min. PLOT: Seven skits showing various whimsical attitudes toward Christmas are connected by short introductory narration. Scenes include an overview of the selling and singing aspects of the holiday, a man depressed over being too skinny to play Santa Claus, an expensive automated Santa machine, a mimed snowball battle, Santa being prosecuted in court, a mimed shopping mall battle, and a day in the life of a Christmas present. RECOMMENDATION: All the skits are secular, although the Christmas content makes this most appropriate for church groups. The wide age appeal of the skits makes this appropriate for upper level children to present to their peers or to younger children. ROYALTY: $35. SOURCE: Galvin, Randy. (1988). Christmas attitudes: skits and scenes about people and their attitudes about Christmas. Schulenburg, TX: I.E. Clark. SUBJECTS/PLAY TYPE: Christmas; Comedy; Skit.

504. K-12. (+) Longfellow, Henry Wadsworth. **Christmas bells.** CAST: 4u. ACTS: 1. SETTINGS: None. PLAYING TIME: 3 min. PLOT: As children ring bells to symbolize the saying "Peace on earth, good will to men," they rejoice that right will prevail. RECOMMENDATION: Suitable for church or parochial school groups for performance at a Christmas pageant or worship service, this could also be performed as a recitation by one child. ROYALTY: NA. SOURCE: Hendricks, William & Vogel, Cora. (1978). Handbook of Christmas programs. Grand Rapids, MI: Baker Book House. SUBJECTS/PLAY TYPE: Christmas; Worship Program.

505. 1-3. (+) Fisher, Aileen. **The Christmas cake.** CAST: 1f, 2m, 1u. ACTS: 1. SETTINGS: Kitchen. PLAYING TIME: 10 min. PLOT: As Mrs. McGilly dashes out the door, she tells Mr. McGilly to put her freshly made cake in the oven. Mr. McGilly forgets, but since his wife forgot to put the cherries in the cake, absentmindedness saves the day. RECOMMENDATION: Brief and told in rhyme, with no serious message and with little plot, this play is strictly for entertainment. ROYALTY: NA. SOURCE: Fisher, Aileen. (1986). Holiday programs for boys and girls. Boston, MA: Plays, Inc. SUBJECTS/PLAY TYPE: Christmas; Comedy.

506. 4-9. (+) Miller, Ev. **Christmas Cameo.** CAST: 3f, 2m. ACTS: 1. SETTINGS: Mortuary; apartment. PLAYING TIME: 30 min. PLOT: Two retirees, living together although unmarried, are forced to eat at funeral receptions to augment their food budget. They meet Tammy, a young, rich teenager who has a cynical view of life and Christmas in particular. Tammy plans her own kidnapping to gain the attention and affection of her parents, and forces the retirees to accept her into their home while waiting for the ransom. The retirees wrestle with the problem of accepting the hoax (and the needed money) or of exposing Tammy's plot to her parents. Tammy's parents deliver the ransom and apologize for their actions toward Tammy, who discovers, with her parents, the importance of love and the family unit. The two retirees now have sufficient money to marry. RECOMMENDATION: This is warm and funny, has a surprise ending, and portrays two situations which give food for thought (i.e. the unmarried state of the two retirees, as well as the problem of neglectful parents). Characterization is good; each character has a fully developed and understandable personality which softens the dual themes. ROYALTY: $15. SOURCE: Miller, Ev. (1985). Christmas cameo. Denver, CO: Pioneer Drama Service, Inc. SUBJECTS/PLAY TYPE: Christmas; Elderly; Retirement; Family Relationships; Comedy.

507. 3-6*. (-) Novakov, George J. Jr. **The Christmas caper.** CAST: 13f, 2m, Su. ACTS: 1. SETTINGS: Santa's workshop; cave. PLAYING TIME: 25 min. PLOT: Gretsel, a wicked boy, kidnaps Santa Claus and plans to take his place delivering gifts on Christmas Eve. The elves enlist the help of the Dew Fairy in rescuing Santa, but her magic wand is out of commission. The Dew Fairy realizes that all Gretsel needs is love and attention. Gretsel releases Santa and allows the Dew Fairy to change him into a reindeer so he can take the ailing Rudolph's place. RECOMMENDATION: Aimed at children but with humor which turns on what amounts to in-jokes for adults, the play is an unsuccessful mixture of **A Midsummer Night's Dream, The Year Without Santa Claus,** and **The Grinch Who Stole Christmas.** ROYALTY: One amateur production free. SOURCE: Novakov, George G. Jr. (1979). The Christmas caper. Franklin, OH: Eldridge Pub. Co. SUBJECTS/PLAY TYPE: Christmas; Comedy.

508. K-6. (+) McMaster, Beth & Beck, Dick. **Christmas cards.** CAST: 4u. ACTS: 1. SETTINGS: Royal hall. PLAYING TIME: 30 min. PLOT: The king of the land of Christmas Cards cannot make decisions, which is ruining his business of making Jack-in-the-box toys. The Queen hires a seamstress to sew a cloak of wisdom for the king by reading the Book of Knowledge as she sews, but one of the Jacks replaces the Book of Knowledge with a TV Guide, so that the king can only answer questions with titles of TV programs or characters. The queen and king decide to return the cloak but, through a series of questions for which the audience provides the answers, deduce which Jack is the saboteur. The queen tricks the Jack into thinking his cloak is no good, and the king takes the true cloak of wisdom and is able to make decisions. RECOMMENDATION: This musical will require a high energy level for the four actors performing the several roles, and full attention from the audience since character changes are made in full view. The audience participation segment is clever and the theme of good vs. bad is universal. Older audiences will appreciate the references to the television programs and the ways they are incorporated into the king's answers. ROYALTY: NA. SOURCE: McMaster, Beth & Beck, Dick. (1981). Happy holly/ Christmas cards. Toronto, Canada: Simon & Pierre Pub. SUBJECTS/PLAY TYPE: Christmas; Jealousy; Wisdom; Musical.

509. 10-12. (+) Gaines, Frederick. (Dickens, Charles) **A Christmas carol.** (A Christmas carol) CAST: 12f, 27m, 10u. ACTS: 1. SETTINGS: Streets; office; house; bedroom; stairway. PLAYING TIME: NA. PLOT: This adaptation comes alive on a simply mounted stage with platforms. RECOMMENDATION: This fine, well articulated, and stylish production provides a vivid interpretation of Dickens' classic. Simple set designs allow for low budget performances. ROYALTY: Contact publisher for permission. SOURCE: Donahue, John Clark & Jenkins, Linda Walsh. (1975). Plays from the Children's Theatre Company of Minneapolis. St. Paul, MN: North Central Pub. Co. SUBJECTS/PLAY TYPE: Christmas; Adaptation.

510. 6-12. (+) Hackett, Walter. (Dickens, Charles) **A Christmas carol.** (A Christmas carol) CAST: 5f, 19m. ACTS: 2. SETTINGS: Bare stage, props. PLAYING TIME: 30 min. PLOT: An old man's miserly ways are changed when he is visited by the ghost of his dead partner and the three spirits of Christmas. RECOMMENDATION: This is an easily produced and faithful adaptation of the classic Christmas tale. ROYALTY: Free to Plays subscribers. SOURCE: Hackett, Walter. (1987, December). A Christmas carol. Plays: The Drama Magazine for Young People, pp. 53-64. SUBJECTS/PLAY TYPE: Christmas; Adaptation.

511. 3-6. (+) Holloway, Sister Marcella Marie & Joyce, Sister Mary Ann. (Dickens, Charles) **A Christmas carol.** CAST: 12f, 11m, Su. ACTS: 1. SETTINGS: Office; bedroom. PLAYING TIME: 75 min. PLOT: A faithful adaptation of the original story. RECOMMENDATION: This adaptation has small speaking parts for a number of younger children, and the adults could be played by older children or adults, so everyone could have a chance to participate. There are several opportunities for a chorus of children to perform. ROYALTY: $35. SOURCE: Holloway, Sister Marcella Marie & Joyce, Sister Mary Ann. (1975). A Christmas carol. Denver, CO: Pioneer Drama Service. SUBJECTS/PLAY TYPE: Christmas; Musical; Drama.

512. 9-12. (+) Kamerman, Sylvia E. (Dickens, Charles) **A Christmas carol.** CAST: 4f, 9m, 3u. ACTS: 1. SETTINGS: Bare stage. PLAYING TIME: NA. PLOT: A miserly old businessman celebrates Christmas for the first time in his life after being visited by three ghosts during the night. RECOMMENDATION: As delightful as ever, this timeless Christmas favorite is fun for older children to perform; performers might prefer this to a full staged version since no care must be given to special visual effects. ROYALTY: None. SOURCE: Kamerman, Sylvia E. A treasury of Christmas plays. Boston, MA: Plays, Inc. SUBJECTS/PLAY TYPE: Christmas; Adaptation.

513. 9-12. (+) Thane, Adele. (Dickens, Charles) **A Christmas carol.** (A Christmas carol) CAST: 7f, 12m, Su. ACTS: 1. SETTINGS: Office. PLAYING TIME: 30 min. PLOT: The classic tale is faithfully retold. RECOMMENDATION: This well introduces youngsters to Dickens' classic, and the only negative is that we miss Scrooge alone in bed in his cold lonely house. ROYALTY: Free to Plays subscribers. SOURCE: Thane, Adele. (1982, December). A Christmas carol. Plays: The Drama Magazine for Young People, pp. 69-79. SUBJECTS/PLAY TYPE: Christmas; Adaptation.

514. 7-12. (+) Vance, Robert. (Dickens, Charles) **A Christmas carol.** (A Christmas carol) CAST: 10f, 16m. ACTS: 2. SETTINGS: Street; cemetery; office; bedroom; kitchen. PLAYING TIME: 50 min. PLOT: The classic tale is faithfully retold. RECOMMENDATION: This adaptation follows the original plot very closely as it illustrates clearly the importance of concern and involvement of individuals in the lives of others. Notes are included for casting and for performance "in the

round." ROYALTY: $25. SOURCE: Vance, Robert. (1961). Charles Dickens' a Christmas carol. Morton Grove, IL: The Coach House Press Inc. SUBJECTS/PLAY TYPE: Christmas; Adaptation.

515. 7-12. (+) Vance, Robert. (Dickens, Charles) A Christmas carol. (A Christmas carol) CAST: 10f, 16m. ACTS: 2. SETTINGS: Street; cemetery; office; bedroom; kitchen. PLAYING TIME: 50 min. PLOT: A miserly old man celebrates Christmas for the first time in years after being reminded by spirits of his past and warned about a lonely future. RECOMMENDATION: This underscores the responsibility of all people for improving the lives of others and that anyone can change character if he/she wishes. This classical adaptation, while lengthy, is faithful to the original. With doubling, the cast could be reduced to 16 males and 8 females. ROYALTY: $45. SOURCE: Way, Brian. (1977). The Christmas carol. Boston, MA: Baker's Plays. SUBJECTS/PLAY TYPE: Christmas; Greed; Adaptation.

516. 7-12. (+) Horovitz, Israel. (Dickens, Charles) A Christmas carol, Scrooge and Marley. (A Christmas carol) CAST: 7f, 15m, Su. ACTS: 2. SETTINGS: Office; living room; bedroom. PLAYING TIME: NA. PLOT: This is the well known Christmas Carol of Dickens, with the added device of Jacob Marley as part of each scene and as speaker to the audience. He is seen dragging his chains as he appears to Ebenezer Scrooge to try to change his old partner's way. RECOMMENDATION: Always appealing, the classic Christmas tale is adapted here for more mature audiences and will require an efficient director to handle the special effects, as well as a cast that can handle the sophisticated dialogue. ROYALTY: NA. SOURCE: Horovitz, Israel. (1979). Christmas carol, Scrooge and Marley. New York, NY: Dramatists Play Service, Inc. SUBJECTS/PLAY TYPE: Christmas; Greed; Redemption; Adaptation.

517. K-4. (+) Bennett, Rowena. Christmas cheer. CAST: Su. ACTS: 1. SETTINGS: None. PLAYING TIME: 5 min. PLOT: Children list the activities of Christmas. RECOMMENDATION: This would be an effective holiday program. ROYALTY: Free to Plays subscribers. SOURCE: Bennett, Rowena. (1986, December). Christmas cheer. Plays: The Drama Magazine for Young People, pp. 42. SUBJECTS/PLAY TYPE: Christmas; Choral Reading.

518. 7-12. (+) Olfson, Lewy. Christmas coast to coast. CAST: 4f, 4m, 5u. ACTS: 1. SETTINGS: Living room. PLAYING TIME: 25 min. PLOT: One Christmas season, John Lannan, a newspaper reporter, is selected to appear on the television program, "American at Home." Arriving home early, he discovers his wife planning to fill the house with all of the items and people from the twelve days of Christmas song. Not only does the expense of the project overwhelm him, but when the TV crew arrives early, everything is pandemonium as they begin a broadcast about a "quiet old-fashioned Christmas." RECOMMENDATION: This could have been more successful, if the humor had not relied mostly on an exasperated husband who is furious that his

airheaded wife has spent so much money. ROYALTY: Free to Plays subscribers. SOURCE: Olfson, Lewy. (1987, December). Christmas coast to coast. Plays: The Drama Magazine for Young People, pp. 12-20. SUBJECTS/PLAY TYPE: Christmas; Comedy.

519. 3-5. (+) Mills, Grace Evelyn. Christmas comes to Hamelin. CAST: 13f, 12m, 14u. ACTS: 3. SETTINGS: Town hall; orphanage. PLAYING TIME: 20 min. PLOT: With the help of a stranger, the citizens of Hamelin, once devastated by the Pied Piper, set aside their grief at the loss of their children in favor of the Christmas joy that an odd assortment of orphans can bring to them. RECOMMENDATION: An okay storyline has a happy ending that points out all children are lovable, regardless of individual traits. Scenery and costumes are fairly easy, and there are no special effects. However, there are numerous difficult phrases and expressions that might need to be simplified, and the size of the cast (40+) could be unwieldy. ROYALTY: Free to Plays subscribers. SOURCE: Kamerman, Sylvia E. (1982). Christmas play favorites for young people. Boston, MA: Plays, Inc. SUBJECTS/PLAY TYPE: Christmas; Orphans; Drama.

520. 7-12. (+) Jackson, Eugene. Christmas crisis at Mistletoe Mesa. CAST: 4f, 6m. ACTS: 1. SETTINGS: Town square. PLAYING TIME: 40 min. PLOT: The hero, Happy Holiday, develops amnesia caused by a blow to the head, and is tricked by Mama Grunch and her son, Ebenezer, into signing over the deed to the town and adjacent gold mine. The villainous Grunches ban Christmas festivities, and when Santa Claus arrives, they lock him in the hotel outhouse. Happy receives another blow on the head, regains his memory, rids the town of the villains, and all ends well. RECOMMENDATION: This slapstick, westernized takeoff of "A Christmas Carol" will add an interesting slant to the usual dramatic holiday fare. It is possible to have the Bully, the Chief, and Santa Claus all played by one actor, if necessary for comic relief. ROYALTY: $35. SOURCE: Jackson, Eugene. (1980). Christmas crisis at Mistletoe Mesa. Denver, CO: Pioneer Drama Service. SUBJECTS/PLAY TYPE: Christmas; Western; Fantasy; Melodrama.

521. K-3. (+) Ison, Colleen. Christmas day for Jessica May. CAST: 3f, 2m, Su. ACTS: 1. SETTINGS: Bedroom; nativity scene. PLAYING TIME: NA. PLOT: Jessica is a spoiled brat who thinks of Christmas only in terms of the presents she gets. After attending a Christmas play, she learns about the real meaning of Christmas, and changes from a person who only wants, into a person who gives. RECOMMENDATION: A chorus narrates this play in interesting rhyme, as the cast acts out what the chorus says. This is not overly didactic, nor is it overly sentimental, making it effective for today's sophisticated children. Discussion questions are provided. ROYALTY: NA. SOURCE: Ison, Colleen. (1986). Goliath's last stand: and fifteen more easy plays for children. Cincinnati, OH: Standard Pub. SUBJECTS/PLAY TYPE: Christmas; Skit.

522. K-12. (+) Van Halsema, Thea B. A Christmas devotional. CAST: Su. ACTS: 1. SETTINGS: None.

PLAYING TIME: 20 min. PLOT: The theme focuses on each person's spiritual preparation for the birth of Christ by compiling Bible readings from the Old and the New Testaments. RECOMMENDATION: This would be most appropriate as part of a worship service or a church related class because of the Bible passages used. ROYALTY: None. SOURCE: Hendricks, William & Vogel, Cora. (1983). Handbook of Christmas. Grand Rapids, MI: Baker Book House. SUBJECTS/PLAY TYPE: Christmas; Worship Program.

523. 3-7. (-) Baker, Charles. **The Christmas doubters.** CAST: 4f, 5m. ACTS: 1. SETTINGS: Living room. PLAYING TIME: 20 min. PLOT: Mr. Jameson's daughters grudgingly agree to put the Christmas presents under the tree while their father sleeps so that he can still believe in Santa Claus. They are visited by St. Nick and his modern elves, and then by Mr. Smithers, who has dressed up like Santa Claus at their father's request. When father and mother come downstairs, the whole family is left pondering the sugar plum that the real Santa Claus left. RECOMMENDATION: Although the plot is reasonable, this falls flat because its exposition is just too dry and unconvincing. ROYALTY: Free to Plays subscribers. SOURCE: Baker, Charles. (1984, December). The Christmas doubters. Plays: The Drama Magazine for Young People, pp. 49-54. SUBJECTS/PLAY TYPE: Christmas; Playlet.

524. 4-6. (+) Hark, Mildred & McQueen, Noel. **Christmas Eve letter.** CAST: 4f, 3m, Su. ACTS: 1. SETTINGS: Living room. PLAYING TIME: 30 min. PLOT: As the Stevens family trims the Christmas tree, everyone is excited except Ginny, who has the family puzzled about her strange behavior. She is sad and withdrawn because there isn't a Santa Claus. Mr. Johnson, editor of the town newspaper, drops by and answers Ginny's letter written to him with a rewriting of the **New York Sun** letter of 1897. Ginny happily looks forward to the Christmas holiday, which she now understands better. RECOMMENDATION: The upbeat and positive philosophical editorial relays the message of joy and hope living in the hearts and minds of mankind. ROYALTY: None. SOURCE: Kamerman, Sylvia E. (1988). The big book of Christmas plays. Boston, MA: Plays, Inc. SUBJECTS/PLAY TYPE: Christmas; Santa Claus; Playlet.

525. 1-3. (+) Thane, Adele. (Howells, William Dean) **Christmas every day.** (Christmas every day) CAST: 4f, 5m. ACTS: 5. SETTINGS: Living room. PLAYING TIME: 25 min. PLOT: A little girl's wish of Christmas everyday comes true, but becomes a nightmare when everyone starts hating it because of the cost involved in buying gifts, the effort of preparing every day, etc. RECOMMENDATION: In keeping with Howells' cynical attitude toward the materialistic nature of the holiday, this presents the problems of greed and its consequences. ROYALTY: Free to Plays subscribers. SOURCE: Thane, Adele. (1983, December). Christmas every day. Plays: The Drama Magazine for Young People, pp. 55- 62. SUBJECTS/PLAY TYPE: Christmas; Adaptation.

526. K-12. (+) Phillips, Brook. **Christmas everywhere.** CAST: Su. ACTS: 1. SETTINGS: None. PLAYING TIME: 5 min. PLOT: This choral reading is presented by a speaking choir to describe the true meaning of Christmas. RECOMMENDATION: Suitable for church or parochial school groups for performance at a Christmas pageant or worship service. ROYALTY: NA. SOURCE: Hendricks, William & Vogel, Cora. (1978). Handbook of Christmas programs. Grand Rapids, MI: Baker Book House. SUBJECTS/PLAY TYPE: Christmas; Choral Reading; Worship Program.

527. 4-6. (+) Postma, Janice. (Phillips, Brook) **Christmas everywhere.** (Christmas everywhere) CAST: Su. ACTS: 1. SETTINGS: None. PLAYING TIME: 90 min. PLOT: This is a compilation and explanation of Christmas customs from the countries of France, Mexico, Norway, Sweden, Germany, Switzerland, England, and the United States. The customs of gift giving, Christmas tree trimming, the Yule log, mistletoe, and Santa Claus are explained as they have originated in each of these countries. The explanations are interspersed with Bible readings from the Gospel according to St. Luke. RECOMMENDATION: This is recommended because of the explanations of the Christmas customs which allow children to understand how present day customs evolved. ROYALTY: None. SOURCE: Hendricks, William & Vogel, Cora. (1983). Handbook of Christmas programs. Grand Rapids, MI: Baker Book House. SUBJECTS/PLAY TYPE: Christmas; Worship Program.

528. 6-8. (+) Little, Lynnette. **Christmas for Carol.** CAST: 2f, 3u. ACTS: 1. SETTINGS: Bedroom; living room. PLAYING TIME: 20 min. PLOT: All Christmas means to 10 year old Carol is lots of presents, but her widowed mother is too poor to buy her the things she wants. Following a bedtime story on Christmas Eve, Carol is visited by three ghosts who show her how selfish and insensitive she has been in the past and how things will be in the future if she doesn't change. Like Scrooge in Dickens' tale, Carol realizes the real meaning of Christmas is not the number of presents but the amount of love shared with someone who cares. RECOMMENDATION: Realistic characters and up-to-date language characterize this modern day version of Dickens' famous work. The contrast between: 1) past Christmases filled with poverty, but a loving mother and 2) future Christmases filled with wealth, but a mother who leaves Carol alone on Christmas day in order to go skiing, is readily understood by younger audiences. ROYALTY: Free to Plays subscribers. SOURCE: Little, Lynnette. (1979, December). Christmas for Carol. Plays: The Drama Magazine for Young People, pp. 35-42. SUBJECTS/PLAY TYPE: Christmas; Family; Playlet.

529. 7-12. (+) Olfson, Lewy. (Hugo, Victor) **Christmas for Cosette.** (Les Miserables) CAST: 4f, 4m, Su. ACTS: 1. SETTINGS: Inn; marketplace. PLAYING TIME: NA. PLOT: This is an adaptation of an episode in Victor Hugo's **Les Miserables**, written for a round the table reading rather than a performance. Jean Valjean, an escaped convict who has remained virtuous and

humane, rescues an abused eight year old child from servitude at an inn. The child, Cosette, meets Valjean, a kindly, ragged old man, in the marketplace. Valjean accompanies the child back to the inn where she works, and he stays the night there, observing the cruelty that she endures at the hands of the innkeepers. Although he is dressed in rags, Valjean has earned money with which he pays for his lodging and buys a beautiful doll for Cosette. In the morning, he asks the innkeepers if he may take the child with him, but the greedy, opportunistic couple, convinced that Valjean is a wealthy man in disguise, refuse to part with Cosette for less than fifteen hundred francs. Valjean pays the innkeepers and leaves with the child, promising her a better life. RECOMMENDATION: This treatment of the Hugo classic is warm and memorable. ROYALTY: Free to Plays Subscribers. SOURCE: Olfson, Lewy. (1980, December). Christmas for Cosette. Plays: The Drama Magazine for Young People, pp. 71-79. SUBJECTS/PLAY TYPE: Christmas; Adaptation.

530. K-1. (+) Fisher, Aileen Lucia. **Christmas fun.** CAST: Su. ACTS: 1. SETTINGS: Bare stage. PLAYING TIME: 1 min. PLOT: This is a short adaptation of "Hickory Dickory Dock," except the children watch the clock, waiting for Santa to come. RECOMMENDATION: This poem would be good for a very young group of children to recite for a Christmas program. ROYALTY: Free to Plays subscribers. SOURCE: Fisher, Aileen Lucia. (1985). Year-round programs for young players. Boston, MA: Plays, Inc. SUBJECTS/PLAY TYPE: Christmas; Choral Reading.

531. K-3. (+) Havilan, Amorie & Smith, Lyn. **The Christmas gift.** CAST: 1f, 4m, Su. ACTS: 1. SETTINGS: Hillside; stable. PLAYING TIME: NA. PLOT: On a clear night near Bethlehem in Judea, as shepherds sleepily watch their sheep, they see a bright star above them and an angel appears, telling them that a baby has been born who will someday be King. They follow the star to Bethlehem and a stable where they find baby Jesus lying in a manger. Soon after, three royal kings appear, each bringing gifts for the baby. The kings and shepherds kneel together to worship the Holy Child, knowing this child is a gift from God to establish good will among men and to bring peace on earth. RECOMMENDATION: This very simple rendition of the traditional Christmas tale may be performed as a pantomime, using a narrator when the acting involves very young children or as a musical, by inserting the suggested carols at the given cues. ROYALTY: NA. SOURCE: Havilan, Amorie & Smith, Lyn. (1985). Easy plays for preschoolers to third graders. Brandon, MS: Quail Ridge Press. SUBJECTS/PLAY TYPE: Christian Drama; Tripartite.

532. 3-6. (+) Gozzi, Joan Daniels. **Christmas goes modern.** CAST: 5f, 6m, Su. ACTS: 1. SETTINGS: North Pole. PLAYING TIME: 10 min. PLOT: The mayor of the North Pole wants a new improved North Pole. He also wants to modernize Christmas by making the colors orange and blue and getting rid of mistletoe, snow, evergreen wreaths, and Santa's ho-ho's. He also wants to change Santa's red velvet suit to plaid and his sleigh and reindeer to a Cadillac with rear wheel suspension. Santa and the citizens protest and Santa becomes mayor. Tradition prevails and they have an old-fashioned Christmas. RECOMMENDATION: This is a wonderfully modern play whose upbeat dialogue will enable audiences to relate to the theme. ROYALTY: Free to Plays subscribers. SOURCE: Gozzi, Joan Daniels. (1980, December). Christmas goes modern. Plays: The Drama Magazine for Young People, pp. 55- 61. SUBJECTS/PLAY TYPE: Christmas; Comedy.

533. 4-6. (+) Very, Alice. **Christmas in old Boston.** CAST: 5f, 4m, Su. ACTS: 1. SETTINGS: Living room. PLAYING TIME: 10 min. PLOT: The Parsley children are not allowed to celebrate Christmas, but must card and spin wool. Revelers come while their father is out, but are run off. When Master Parsley returns, he brings with him a newspaper containing a sermon on the "Lawfulness and the Right Manner of Keeping Christmas." He also brings small dolls for the girls. The girls sing Christmas carols at the door and the play ends with the rest of the family joining in. RECOMMENDATION: Much explanation may be needed in order for children to understand the archaic language, culture, and customs presented here. It would be an appropriate concluding activity for a study unit on Puritanism, early colonial history, or Christmas. ROYALTY: Free to Plays subscribers. SOURCE: Very, Alice. (1975, December). Christmas in old Boston. Plays: The Drama Magazine for Young People, pp. 53-56. SUBJECTS/PLAY TYPE: Christmas; Puritans; Playlet.

534. 4-7. (+) Clapp, Patricia. **Christmas in old New England.** CAST: 3f, 3m. ACTS: 1. SETTINGS: Living room. PLAYING TIME: 20 min. PLOT: The Puritan injunction against the celebration of Christmas in the Colonies has been repealed, allowing a family to pursue traditional holiday festivities. RECOMMENDATION: The reasons for the Puritans' law prohibiting Christmas are not given, and only the superficial rituals of the holiday are presented. The play does succeed in recreating the excitement of the holiday, even if it is couched in terms of presents and food. ROYALTY: Free to Plays subscribers. SOURCE: Clapp, Patricia. (1983, December). Plays: The Drama Magazine for Young People, pp. 35-41. SUBJECTS/PLAY TYPE: Christmas; Puritans; Playlet.

535. 6-12. (+) Cheatham, Val R. **Christmas in Oz: A musical fantasy.** CAST: Su. ACTS: 3. SETTINGS: Forest; kitchen. PLAYING TIME: 45 min. PLOT: This is a sequel to Baum's classic with the Christmas themes of goodness and sharing. Miss Gulch has just purchased the mortgage on Aunt Em and Uncle Henry's farm. To save the farm, Dorothy puts on her red slippers, falls asleep, and awakens in Oz to search for the Wizard. A "Closed for Christmas" sign posted on the Wizard's door discourages the group, but they decide to celebrate Christmas in Oz. When they give the Wicked Witch the slippers as a present, she is so overcome with emotion, she gives them back to Dorothy so she can return to Kansas. All ends well when everyone decides the best

way to celebrate Christmas is to share it with others. RECOMMENDATION: The Oz characters and settings should make this play comfortable for players and audiences alike. The Christmas message of sharing and kindness is clear. The music is nice, appropriate for middle school to high school singers, and somewhat reminiscent of the original movie score. ROYALTY: $80. SOURCE: Cheatham, Val R. (1983). Christmas in Oz: a musical fantasy. Franklin, OH: Eldridge Pub. Co. SUBJECTS/PLAY TYPE: Fantasy; Christmas; Musical.

536. 6-12. (+) Kehret, Peg. **Christmas is now.** CAST: 5f, 6m, 6u. ACTS: 1. SETTINGS: Church. PLAYING TIME: 25 min. PLOT: As the kids rehearse the Christmas pageant, Mary says the play and Christmas have lost relevance. The director disagrees and takes her on a city tour: she meets a couple whose college aged son is flying home for Christmas with money he earned for the ticket, visits a nursing home where carolers give an elderly woman pleasure, watches people bringing food to share with the less fortunate at Christmas, and meets a crisis center volunteer who foregoes Christmas Eve with her family to be available if someone needs her. After the trip, the narrator reads the script as people Mary and the director visited file in to illustrate that the love of Christmas is still relevant. RECOMMENDATION: This is an excellent Christmas play for children to view because it has such a contemporary message about love and the relevance of Christmas. It would be a good choice for a youth group to perform. ROYALTY: NA. SOURCE: Kehret, Peg. (1976). Christmas is now. Franklin, OH: Eldridge Pub. Co. SUBJECTS/PLAY TYPE: Christmas; Love; Drama.

537. 2-6. (+) Richard, Gail J. **Christmas magic.** CAST: 2f, 5m. ACTS: 1. SETTINGS: Toy store. PLAYING TIME: 15 min. PLOT: A brother and sister, whose father is sick and unable to buy them presents for the holiday, enter a toy store on Christmas Eve after closing. There, they witness an annual event of magic when the toys come to life and discover that no one has bought them. When the children feel sorry for the homeless toys, Santa Claus sends them their favorites and promises the other toys that he will take care of them also. RECOMMENDATION: This is a charming story and will be enjoyed by all who, deep down inside, believe that a toy must be very sad when no child takes it home. Although the ending is rather predictable, this one will give the proverbial heartstrings a good, hard yank. In addition, many of the actors will have ample opportunity to show off with some "robot" miming. ROYALTY: Free to Plays subscribers. SOURCE: Richard, Gail J. (1982, December). Christmas magic. Plays: The Drama Magazine for Young People, pp. 37-40. SUBJECTS/PLAY TYPE: Christmas; Toys; Playlet.

538. K-3. (+) Kreft, Clara. **A Christmas medley.** CAST: 3f, 4m, Su. ACTS: 1. SETTINGS: Santa's workshop. PLAYING TIME: 30 min. PLOT: Just before Christmas, Santa and his helpers are visited by several characters from Nursery Rhyme Land, who perform variations on "Mary had a little lamb" and several other nursery rhymes. The cast also sings "Jolly old St.

Nicholas" and "Rudolph the red-nosed reindeer." RECOMMENDATION: This is a very simple vehicle for allowing young children to perform nursery rhymes and to sing Christmas carols. The plot is entirely based on the nursery rhymes, which are told with a Christmas twist. ROYALTY: NA. SOURCE: Kreft, Clara. (n.d.). A Christmas medley. Franklin, OH: Eldridge Pub. Co. SUBJECTS/PLAY TYPE: Christmas; Nursery Rhymes; Musical.

539. 5. (+) Hoffman, E.T.A. (Hoffman, E.T.A.) **The Christmas nutcracker.** (Nutcracker) CAST: 4f, 6m, 3u. ACTS: 1. SETTINGS: Room. PLAYING TIME: 30 min. PLOT: This play retells the old German folk tale in which a young girl helps the King of Toys defeat the King Mouse. RECOMMENDATION: Although the stage directions call for some sophisticated special effects (black-outs, etc.), the magical Christmas tale is well adapted. ROYALTY: Free to Plays subscribers. SOURCE: Kamerman, Sylvia E. (1976). On stage for Christmas. Boston, MA: Plays, Inc. SUBJECTS/PLAY TYPE: Christmas; Folk Tales, Germany; Adaptation.

540. 7-12. (+) Gotwalt, Helen Louise Miller. **The Christmas oboe.** CAST: 2f, 5m. ACTS: 1. SETTINGS: Living room. PLAYING TIME: 25 min. PLOT: When Charlie Reynolds pretends to have lost his oboe so he can take Mary to the Christmas dance on the same night of an oboe music competition, family harmony is disrupted. When Willie Reynolds and Eddie Bates (both age 12) play detective and open a package Mary has attempted to leave unobtrusively for Charlie, another oboe (Mary's) is discovered. Charlie confesses he hid his oboe in a suitcase. Mrs. Reynolds is dismayed because she has just given that suitcase to a poor family desperately trying to get their child a musical instrument. All is saved when a new oboe from Uncle Milton is delivered. RECOMMENDATION: This is a cute drama, in which mixups and well meaning people provide the dramatic tension. The pat ending is a little anticlimactic but, overall, the story does have some interest. ROYALTY: Free to Plays subscribers. SOURCE: Gotwalt, Helen Louise Miller. (1987, December). The Christmas oboe. Plays: The Drama Magazine for Young People, pp. 21-30. SUBJECTS/PLAY TYPE: Christmas; Playlet.

541. 1-5. (+) Jennings, Coleman & Harris, Aurand. **A Christmas pageant.** CAST: 1f, 8m, Su. ACTS: 1. SETTINGS: Room; stable; hillside. PLAYING TIME: NA. PLOT: The Angel Gabriel appears to a young girl, Mary, to announce that she has been chosen by God to be the mother of His son. Joseph and Mary travel to Bethlehem, where Mary gives birth to her baby, wraps him in swaddling clothes and lays him in a manger. Shepherds seek out the baby; three kings, having observed an unusual star in the heavens, follow it from their homes in the East until they come to the house where the child sleeps. RECOMMENDATION: This traditional Christmas drama needs very little introduction to the cast, and chorus members can provide background music by singing traditional hymns. Costumes should fit the parts that are being played, and

can easily be constructed from available materials. ROYALTY: None. SOURCE: Jennings, Coleman & Harris, Aurand. (1981). Plays children love. New York, NY: Doubleday Co. Inc. SUBJECTS/PLAY TYPE: Christmas; Christ Child; Christian Drama.

542. 4-12. (+) Hamlett, Christina. **Christmas partners.** CAST: 5f, 2m. ACTS: 1. SETTINGS: Living room; office. PLAYING TIME: 20 min. PLOT: Lucy and Tracy ask Grandma Claus how she and Grandpa got started in the Christmas business. Kristine Claus was running the Christmas Agency one year when everyone left her stranded with the night's deliveries. In desperation she hired Nicholas, who had just arrived by plane and was in need of a job. Although accustomed to a gentleman's life, he agreed to give it a try and has been at it ever since. In a final, humorous twist, Nicholas remembers the past differently, telling his granddaughters that it was he who hired Kristine, much to his wife's amusement. RECOMMENDATION: This clever portrayal of Grandma Claus in her earlier days as the modern executive running the Christmas Agency, and Grandpa Claus as the rich, suave gentleman has enough sophistication to appeal to high school age actors and actresses (for the parts of Kristine and Nicholas Kringle), although a younger audience of upper elementary aged students will enjoy this, too. ROYALTY: $20. SOURCE: Hamlett, Christina. (1987). Christmas partners. Franklin, OH: Eldridge Pub. Co. SUBJECTS/PLAY TYPE: Christmas; Santa Claus; Comedy.

543. 6-8. (+) McSweeny, Maxine. **The Christmas party.** CAST: 7f, 5m. ACTS: 1. SETTINGS: Store; post office. PLAYING TIME: NA. PLOT: A family running a country store and post office are unable to have their traditional Christmas party because their business has been very slow since the farmers, their customers, have had a bad crop year. A creditor comes to close the store but cannot, since it also serves as the local post office. Despite their misfortune, the family decides to have a party without the usual refreshments. During the party, the owner's children find an old box of wood tops which the agent excitedly takes towards payment, stating that he has a market for them. The owner and his friends whittle more tops, relieved to be able to earn money during a bad business year. RECOMMENDATION: This touching play involves the audience in a family's and a community's suffering through economically hard times. The ending happily promises that the future will be better. However, for this play to interest and emotionally involve the audience, the actors must have some ability. ROYALTY: NA. SOURCE: McSweeny, Maxine. (1977). Christmas plays for young players. South Brunswick, Canada: A.S. Barnes. SUBJECTS/PLAY TYPE: Christmas; Drama.

544. 6-12. (+) Gotwalt, Helen Louise Miller. **A Christmas promise.** CAST: 3f, 3m. ACTS: 1. SETTINGS: Living room. PLAYING TIME: 25 min. PLOT: The mother, father, and older sister of a teenage boy promise that he will take three different girls to the same dance. However, the son has his own date.

RECOMMENDATION: The play is fast paced; however, it resolves a bit too easily and has little to do with Christmas. ROYALTY: Free to Plays subscribers. SOURCE: Gotwalt, Helen Louise Miller. (1984, December). A Christmas promise. Plays: The Drama Magazine for Young People, pp. 1-11. SUBJECTS/PLAY TYPE: Dating; Comedy.

545. K-12. (+) Hendricks, William & Vogel, Cora. **Christmas prophecy.** CAST: 7u. ACTS: 1. SETTINGS: Bare stage, posters. PLAYING TIME: 5 min. PLOT: This describes various prophecies concerning the coming of Christ in the scriptures: the Gospel of John, Genesis 3:15, Genesis 12:3, Psalm 16:10, Isaiah 7:14 and Isaiah 9:6. RECOMMENDATION: This is suitable for church or parochial school groups for performance at a Christmas pageant or worship service. ROYALTY: NA. SOURCE: Hendricks, William & Vogel, Cora. (1978). Handbook of Christmas programs. Grand Rapids, MI: Baker Book House. SUBJECTS/PLAY TYPE: Christ, Jesus; Christmas; Worship Program.

546. 8-10. (-) Newman, Deborah. **The Christmas question.** CAST: 1m, Su. ACTS: 1. SETTINGS: Bare stage, props. PLAYING TIME: 30 min. PLOT: A reporter tries to find the best part of Christmas by asking Santa (whose answer is the children's faces), a caroler (the Christmas tree), another caroler (sound of music), a dancer (it makes you believe in the best), another dancer (thinking of other people). The reporter concludes that the best part of Christmas is that its spirit is forever. RECOMMENDATION: Although a bit heavy-handed (and the process of asking the same question repeatedly becomes boring), the true spirit of Christmas is described. ROYALTY: Free to Plays subscribers. SOURCE: Newman, Deborah. (1984, December). The Christmas question. Plays: The Drama Magazine for Young People, pp. 45-48. SUBJECTS/PLAY TYPE: Christmas; Playlet.

547. 5-8. (-) Hark, Mildred & McQueen, Noel. **Christmas recaptured.** CAST: 4f, 4m. ACTS: 1. SETTINGS: Living room. PLAYING TIME: 30 min. PLOT: When Jean gets 14 handkerchiefs for Christmas, dad gets three awful ties, Bobby's train set won't work, Dave loses Mom's necklace, and Mom complains that her blouse is one whole size too large, it seems that the Christmas spirit must be recaptured in this household. Aunt Matilda shows up and begins to turn things around. RECOMMENDATION: This play is rather dull. The theme and plot are good but too common. The action is very predictable. We've all heard too many "tie" jokes about Christmas. ROYALTY: Free to Plays subscribers. SOURCE: Kamerman, Sylvia E. (1978). On stage for Christmas. Boston, MA: Plays, Inc. SUBJECTS/PLAY TYPE: Christmas; Skit.

548. 4-12. (-) Boiko, Claire. **The Christmas revel.** CAST: 8f, 8m, Su. ACTS: 1. SETTINGS: Great hall. PLAYING TIME: 35 min. PLOT: On Christmas Eve in old England, the queen declares a contest in which the girl and boy who bring and most eloquently describe a doll will each receive a bag of gold. A stranger helps

Betsy and Nan to win the prize, as he most eloquently describes their doll. The stranger turns out to be a young William Shakespeare. RECOMMENDATION: While dolls will not interest older students, the play's difficult old English dialogue would be best understood by them. Also, sexism (where the girls bring the doll but only the boys speak), the implausible appearance of a young Shakespeare, and the overall lack of a real plot combine to make this very boring. Also, the time is out of place, in that William Shakespeare was a grown man in Queen Elizabeth's reign. ROYALTY: Free to Plays subscribers. SOURCE: Kamerman, Sylvia E. (1983, December). The Christmas revel. Plays: The Drama Magazine for Young People, pp. 9-20. SUBJECTS/PLAY TYPE: Christmas; Shakespeare, William; Dolls; Playlet.

549. 7-10. (+) Gill, Barbara Gove. **Christmas revisited.** CAST: 4f, 3m. ACTS: 1. SETTINGS: Living room. PLAYING TIME: NA. PLOT: Disenchanted with Christmas, modern teenagers wonder if the scene of Bethlehem ever really happened. Miraculously, their television becomes a time machine and a young shepherd boy appears and tells them what he has just seen in Bethlehem. Mary arrives next, and shares with them what it was like to be a young, frightened girl who was visited by an angel and found herself pregnant and unmarried in an era when that was punishable by death. The young people are amazed at this occurrence and wonder if it was all a dream. RECOMMENDATION: The many religious references make this play suitable only for a church environment, and the playwright includes a suggested program of carols, scripture readings, and prayers to precede the play if desired. The demonstration of the living conditions and customs of ancient Israel, as well as its depiction of teenagers as the protagonists in the original episode make this Christmas production especially appropriate for its intended audience and performers. ROYALTY: NA. SOURCE: Gill, Barbara Gove. (1981). Christmas revisited. Franklin, OH: Eldridge Pub. Co. SUBJECTS/PLAY TYPE: Christmas; Christian Drama.

550. K-4. (+) Seymeyn, Dorothy. **Christmas rhythms.** CAST: Su. ACTS: 1. SETTINGS: None. PLAYING TIME: 30 min. PLOT: This describes events that followed Caesar's decree that all must return to their birthplace to be counted. As each character readies for the trip, the actors simulate noises of preparation (hammering, baling hay, coins jangling, etc.). For Mary and Joseph, the trip is from Nazareth to Bethlehem, where Jesus is born. RECOMMENDATION: Suitable for church or parochial school groups for performance at a Christmas pageant or worship service, this can be livened by singing all the verses of each of the songs. ROYALTY: NA. SOURCE: Hendricks, William & Vogel, Cora. (1978). Handbook of Christmas programs. Grand Rapids, MI: Baker Book House. SUBJECTS/PLAY TYPE: Christmas; Worship Program.

551. K-3. (+) Fisher, Aileen Lucia. **Christmas shoppers.** CAST: 1u. ACTS: 1. SETTINGS: None. PLAYING TIME: NA. PLOT: This is a recitation on Christmas and its feelings of merriment.

RECOMMENDATION: This is appropriate for young children to recite for a Christmas program at school. ROYALTY: Free to Plays subscribers. SOURCE: Fisher, Aileen Lucia. (1985). Year-round programs for young players. Boston, MA: Plays, Inc. SUBJECTS/PLAY TYPE: Christmas; Choral Reading.

552. 5-12. (+) Hark, Mildred & McQueen, Noel. **Christmas shopping early.** CAST: 3f, 3m, Su. ACTS: 1. SETTINGS: Living room. PLAYING TIME: 35 min. PLOT: A family's attempts to follow the older son's lead in computerizing Christmas for maximum efficiency leads to chaos and the realization that there is "no such thing as a high tech Christmas." RECOMMENDATION: This is a rather simple, unexciting sit-com which, although believable, may be too bland to hold an audience's interest. ROYALTY: Free to Plays subscribers. SOURCE: Kamerman, Sylvia E. (1983, December). Christmas shopping early. Plays: The Drama Magazine for Young People, pp. 1-8. SUBJECTS/PLAY TYPE: Christmas; Family; Comedy.

553. 9-12. (+) Dias, Earl J. **Christmas spirit.** CAST: 4f, 4m, Su. ACTS: 1. SETTINGS: Living room. PLAYING TIME: 20 min. PLOT: Sally Gillum feels lonely living in a small New England town after having lived in New York. Her father, a writer, finds the town refreshing and writes a story describing the town's virtues. On Christmas Eve, the townspeople thank him, and Sally realizes that in order to have friends, she must be friendly. RECOMMENDATION: Although this is neither action packed nor friendly, teenagers will enjoy its brief and slight romantic subplot. Dias effectively presents a young woman's watershed moment as she realizes that small town citizens can be bright and cultured, too. ROYALTY: None if performed by an amateur group and no admission is charged. SOURCE: Kamerman, Sylvia E. (1975). A treasury of Christmas plays. Boston, MA: Plays, Inc. SUBJECTS/PLAY TYPE: Christmas; Drama.

554. 7-12. (+) Dias, Earl J. **The Christmas starlet.** CAST: 5f, 6m. ACTS: 1. SETTINGS: Living room. PLAYING TIME: 30 min. PLOT: A broadway actress comes home for the holidays. Her family and friends discover, to their dismay, that fame has gone to the young actress' head. RECOMMENDATION: This play has a good lesson for young people although it is for the older set because of the theme. ROYALTY: Free to Plays subscribers. SOURCE: Kamerman, Sylvia E. (1978). On stage for Christmas. Boston, MA: Plays, Inc. SUBJECTS/PLAY TYPE: Christmas; Drama.

555. 4-6. (+) Kehret, Peg. **Christmas surprise.** CAST: 1f. ACTS: 1. SETTINGS: None. PLAYING TIME: NA. PLOT: A child expresses the disappointment resulting from having peeked at her Christmas gifts. RECOMMENDATION: Whether they celebrate Christmas or not, all children will be able to relate to the disappointment of having spoiled a surprise. ROYALTY: NA. SOURCE: Kehret, Peg. (1986). Winning monologs for young actors. Colorado Springs, CO: Meriwether Pub. SUBJECTS/PLAY TYPE: Christmas; Surprises; Monologue.

556. 2-4. (+) Fisher, Aileen Lucia. **The Christmas tablecloth.** CAST: 3f, 2m. ACTS: 1. SETTINGS: Living room. PLAYING TIME: 10 min. PLOT: On Christmas day, a family eagerly awaits visitors, so that the 40 year tradition of having Christmas visitors sign an heirloom tablecloth will not be broken. It is snowing so hard, the only visitor that day is a hungry cat. The family uses the cat's pawprint as a signature. RECOMMENDATION: Although the language is a bit dated, with some rewriting, this would be a cozy story. ROYALTY: Free to Plays subscribers. SOURCE: Fisher, Aileen. (December, 1986). The Christmas tablecloth. Plays: The Drama Magazine for Young People, pp. 29-32. SUBJECTS/PLAY TYPE: Christmas; Traditions; Playlet.

557. 2-4. (-) Oberacker, Shirley C. **A Christmas tale.** CAST: 6f, 6m, Su. ACTS: 1. SETTINGS: House interior. PLAYING TIME: NA. PLOT: This is a choral recitation and pantomime in which the Easter Bunny meets Santa on Christmas Eve, and the two decide to exchange Easter and Christmas gift giving. RECOMMENDATION: The silly premise of this play does not satisfy any Christmas spirit, and there is too much scenery to justify the short length of the program. ROYALTY: Free to Plays subscribers. SOURCE: Kamerman, Sylvia E. (1978). On stage for Christmas. Boston, MA: Plays, Inc. SUBJECTS/PLAY TYPE: Christmas; Pantomime; Choral Reading.

558. 1-3. (+) Porter, Robert Neil. **Christmas tea.** CAST: 2f, 1m, 1u. ACTS: 1. SETTINGS: Play-room. PLAYING TIME: 15 min. PLOT: Two dolls, Miss Molly Dressup and Miss Old Fashioned Alice, try to make Teddy Bear behave as they do (prim and proper) and join in their tea party. Alice threatens to lock Teddy out, claiming that Santa delivered him by mistake one Christmas. When Santa arrives, the toys discover that Alice was actually delivered by mistake, but they gracefully assert their friendship for her anyway. RECOMMENDATION: Young children will enjoy watching the dolls come to life, and the action when Teddy chases the dolls will help maintain their attention. It could be a useful presentation to illustrate the theme, "judge not, that ye be not judged." Most of the lines are short and could be easily memorized by the children. ROYALTY: $5. SOURCE: Porter, Robert Neil. (1966, in reprint). Christmas tea. Denver, CO: Pioneer Drama Service. SUBJECTS/PLAY TYPE: Friendship; Christmas; Fantasy.

559. 1-3. (+) Fisher, Aileen. **A Christmas tree for Kitty.** CAST: 4f, 2m, Su. ACTS: 1. SETTINGS: None. PLAYING TIME: 10 min. PLOT: Jannis and Todd decorate a Christmas tree for their cat, Kitty. A friend thinks it's for her newborn sister, Kitty. RECOMMENDATION: This Christmas mix up includes a good portrayal of how to share. ROYALTY: Free to Plays subscribers. SOURCE: Fisher, Aileen. (1986). Holiday programs for boys and girls. Boston, MA: Plays, Inc. SUBJECTS/PLAY TYPE: Christmas; Sharing; Family; Comedy.

560. 5-8. (+) Gotwalt, Helen Louise Miller. **The Christmas umbrella.** CAST: 6f, 7m, 10u. ACTS: 1. SETTINGS: Santa's workshop; living room. PLAYING TIME: 20 min. PLOT: Santa mistakenly delivers a box of umbrellas to the Umberto family instead of the requested toys. Meanwhile, father is unable to find Christmas trees to distribute to the neighbors. The children open the box with the umbrellas and are disappointed, but the mother suggests decorating one with Christmas ornaments. When neighbors arrive for trees, they are given decorated umbrellas instead. In exchange, they give gifts to the Umbertos. RECOMMENDATION: This engaging play relates the true meaning of Christmas love and sharing in a positive and humorous manner. The concept of decorating and sharing umbrellas for Christmas seems far fetched but works well in expressing the theme. The scene changes would not be difficult. ROYALTY: Free to Plays subscribers. SOURCE: Gotwalt, Helen Louise Miller. (1986). Special plays for holidays. Boston, MA: Plays, Inc. SUBJECTS/PLAY TYPE: Christmas; Santa Claus; Drama.

561. 2-6. (+) McGowan, Jane. **The Christmas umbrella.** CAST: 7f, 7m, 10u. ACTS: 1. SETTINGS: Santa's workshop; living room. PLAYING TIME: 20 min. PLOT: A mixup at the North Pole sends an Italian family a package of umbrellas instead of the children's requested toys. In the holiday spirit, the Umbertos make due with what they were given and enjoy a rich experience of love. RECOMMENDATION: This play, which requires 24 children, should prove to be an excellent class project. The grandmother's telling of an old Italian Christmas tale provides some exposure to ethnic traditions and folklore. The combination of Santa Claus, "invisible" elves, and old European culture makes for an unusual but interesting blend. ROYALTY: Free to Plays subscribers. SOURCE: McGowan, Jane. (1982, December). The Christmas umbrella. Plays: The Drama Magazine for Young People, pp. 45-52. SUBJECTS/PLAY TYPE: Christmas; Drama.

562. K-12. (+) Havergal, Frances Ridley. **A Christmas verse.** CAST: Su. ACTS: 1. SETTINGS: None. PLAYING TIME: 1 min. PLOT: This simple Christmas play reflects the meaning of Christmas as it describes the birth of Christ and the importance of understanding the meaning of the religious symbols. RECOMMENDATION: Although this could only be performed in a church setting, it is nicely done and offers a broad view of Christmas tradition. ROYALTY: None. SOURCE: Hendricks, William & Vogel, Cora. (1983). Handbook of Christmas programs. Grand Rapids, MI: Baker Book House. SUBJECTS/PLAY TYPE: Christmas; Choral Reading.

563. 7-12. (+) Bailey, Anne Howard. **The Christmas visitor.** CAST: 3f, 4m, Su. ACTS: 1. SETTINGS: Living room. PLAYING TIME: 30 min. PLOT: On Christmas Eve the Remingtons receive an unexpected visitor who helps them rekindle their love for each other.

RECOMMENDATION: How wonderful to give older children an opportunity to think about how easily love can drift from our relationships. This is an excellent vehicle for discussion about marital relationships. ROYALTY: Free to Plays subscribers. SOURCE: Kamerman, Sylvia E. (1978). On stage for Christmas. Boston, MA: Plays, Inc. SUBJECTS/PLAY TYPE: Family; Christmas; Marriage; Drama.

564. 6-12. (+) McCallum, Phyllis. (Alcott, Louisa May) **Christmas with Little women.** (Little women) CAST: 7f, 2m. ACTS: 2. SETTINGS: Parlor. PLAYING TIME: 45 min. PLOT: Two Christmases a year apart illustrate the changes in the lives of the March girls as they prepare for Amy's trip to Europe, Meg's marriage to John, and their father's return from the Civil War. RECOMMENDATION: Fans of the original will thoroughly enjoy this dramatization of some of the classic's most memorable moments. Those not familiar with novel may find the number of events a bit overwhelming in so short a play, despite the skillful weaving of these events and the way in which the dialogue captures the spirit of the original. Although older students will have more facility with the acting, this play, like the original, will appeal to a large age group. ROYALTY: $5. SOURCE: McCallum, Phyllis. (1980). Christmas with Little women. Denver, CO: Pioneer Drama Service. SUBJECTS/PLAY TYPE: Christmas; Drama; Adaptation.

565. 4-6. (+) Hamlett, Christina. (Dickens, Charles) **Christmas with the Cratchits.** (A Christmas carol) CAST: 3f, 3m, 2u. ACTS: 1. SETTINGS: Living room. PLAYING TIME: NA. PLOT: Robin Bleach, host of "Lifestyles of the Poor and Obscure," arrives at the Cratchits to show how the very poor celebrate Christmas Eve. He finds the Cratchits celebrating their winning the lottery. Bob Cratchit plans to tell Scrooge what he thinks of him and quit his job. Little Tim Cratchit reminds his family that money cannot buy the most important things in life. Then the lottery commission calls to inform them their ticket was a forgery; they're not rich. When Scrooge arrives, he tells Cratchit that he has had a dream that convinced him to change his mean ways. He offers Cratchit a partnership in the firm and, in turn, receives an invitation to Christmas dinner. RECOMMENDATION: This is an amusing adaptation that preserves the spirit of the original. A good classroom play with simple props and costumes. ROYALTY: $25. SOURCE: Hamlett, Christina. (1988). Christmas with the Cratchits. Franklin, OH: Eldridge Pub. Co. SUBJECTS/PLAY TYPE: Christmas; Adaptation.

566. 3-5*. (-) Swortzell, Lowell & Van Fossen, David. **Christopher Columbus.** CAST: 8f, 10m, Su. ACTS: 1. SETTINGS: Shops; palace; ship's deck; boulder. PLAYING TIME: NA. PLOT: This musical interpretation of the discovery of the New World by Columbus spans a period of 32 years. Christopher Columbus dreams of sailing the world, inspired by a sailor recently returned from a voyage, and a scholar, who presents him with a book about the travels of Marco Polo. The play continues through Columbus' pleas to Queen Isabella for money to finance a voyage to the New World. After a long wait, she finally agrees. RECOMMENDATION: Most of the characters are undeveloped, flat, and colorless, due in large part to the absence of descriptive notes and directions. The 14 musical numbers may enliven the action. This play is historically accurate. ROYALTY: NA. SOURCE: Swortzell, Lowell & Van Fossen, David. (1981). Christopher Columbus. Denver, CO: Pioneer Drama Service. SUBJECTS/PLAY TYPE: Columbus, Christopher; Musical.

567. 4-8. (+) Hendricks, William & Vogel, Cora. **Christ's birth: the central date in history.** CAST: 5u. ACTS: 1. SETTINGS: Platform. PLAYING TIME: 10 min. PLOT: This exercise describes the birth of Christ and explains the origin of B.C. and A.D. in terms of Christ's birth. RECOMMENDATION: Suitable for church or parochial school groups for performance at a Christmas pageant or worship service, this could also be used to supplement the teaching of early Roman history. Producers should be aware that this does not explain the other abbreviations: B.C.E. and A.C.E. ROYALTY: NA. SOURCE: Hendricks, William & Vogel, Cora. (1978). Handbook of Christmas programs. Grand Rapids, MI: Baker Book House. SUBJECTS/PLAY TYPE: Christ, Jesus; Calendar; Choral Reading.

568. 1-6. (+) Norwaish, Tammy. (Perrault, Charles) **Cinder Dweller.** (Cinderella) CAST: Su. ACTS: 3. SETTINGS: House; teepee. PLAYING TIME: 15 min. PLOT: Wishful Spirit tells the story of a beautiful Indian maiden who lives with her mean step-squaw, Mighty Pain in Neck, and her two wicked stepsisters, Thundering Mouth and Swamp Face. Because she slept by the ashes of the campfire and wore rags, she was called Cinder Dweller. The stepsisters are invited to a Royal Pow wow. Chief Charming is looking for a bride. This is the story of Cinderella in a Native American setting. RECOMMENDATION: This is a very funny adaptation, and students of all ages will enjoy it. The mock Indian names and the funny lines make this quite enjoyable. ROYALTY: Free to Plays subscribers. SOURCE: Norwaish, Tammy. (1987, October). Cinder Dweller. Plays: The Drama Magazine for Young People, pp. 51-56. SUBJECTS/PLAY TYPE: Puppet Play; Adaptation.

569. 1-6. (+) Boiko, Claire. (Perrault, Charles) **Cinder Riley.** (Cinderella) CAST: 5f, 2m, Su. ACTS: 1. SETTINGS: Kitchen. PLAYING TIME: 20 min. PLOT: Introduced by a leprechaun and the audience cheering and applauding, the tale is set in Ireland. In contrast to the original, Cinder Riley is a princess who longs to be a kitchen maid. Her stepmother and stepsisters want her to marry an ugly king, but she wants to marry a poor lad. The Fairy Godmother saves the day, arranging for Cinder Riley to marry her lad and the stepmother to marry the ugly king. RECOMMENDATION: In this thought provoking piece, viewers must redefine the necessary ingredients for true love and happiness. It is emphasized that attraction is not solely based on wealth, power, or physical beauty, but upon goodness and pureness of

heart. Creative viewers may extend the idea of reversing the plot or characterization to other classic tales with amusing, provocative results. ROYALTY: Free to Plays subscribers. SOURCE: Boiko, Claire. (1985, March). Cinder Riley. Plays: The Drama Magazine for Young People, pp. 37-42. SUBJECTS/PLAY TYPE: Folk Tales, France; Romance; Comedy; Adaptation.

570. 3-8*. (+) Fox, Phyllis Ward. (Perrault, Charles) Cinderella. (Cinderella) CAST: 5f, 2m. ACTS: 2. SETTINGS: Street; home; room. PLAYING TIME: 90 min. PLOT: This is the classic Cinderella tale with a twist. The white rabbit from Alice in Wonderland gets lost in this story by mistake and helps the fairy godmother help Cinderella. RECOMMENDATION: The sophisticated costuming, lengthy parts, and the six musical numbers would make this play difficult to produce even for high school students. A wide range of ages should enjoy watching it, however. The dialogue between the fairy godmother and the rabbit alludes to other well known children's stories and is especially amusing. The action is fast paced, the story line is crisp, and the song lyrics and dialogue are catchy. ROYALTY: $35. SOURCE: Fox, Phyllis Ward. (1978). Cinderella. Chicago, IL: Coach House Press. SUBJECTS/PLAY TYPE: Folk Tales, France; Stepsisters; Musical; Adaptation.

571. 7-12. (-) Springer, William J. (Grimm Brothers) Cinderella? (Cinderella) CAST: 7f, 3m, Su. ACTS: 1. SETTINGS: House; palace. PLAYING TIME: 40 min. PLOT: As Cinderella's fairy godmother (Tuesday) narrates, the traditional plot unfolds. RECOMMENDATION: Written as a spoof of the "Dragnet" series, this Cinderella spin off is cleverly written, though more conservative viewers may not approve of various innuendos. ROYALTY: $30. SOURCE: Springer, William J. (1978). Cinderella. Franklin, OH: Eldridge Pub. Company SUBJECTS/PLAY TYPE: Comedy; Fantasy; Dragnet; Adaptation

572. 2-3*. (+) Glennon, William. (Perrault, Charles) Cinderella. (Cinderella) CAST: 6f, 4m, Su. ACTS: 3. SETTINGS: Yard; palace. PLAYING TIME: 90 min. PLOT: In this version of the well known tale, a jester plays the major role, serving as go between for Cinderella and the fairy godmother, and as matchmaker for Cinderella and the Prince. RECOMMENDATION: Young audiences will be entertained, but this should be produced by junior high or high school aged actors. ROYALTY: $25. SOURCE: Glennon, William. (1982). Cinderella. Morton Grove, IL: Coach House Press, Inc. SUBJECTS/PLAY TYPE: Folk Tales, France; Stepsisters; Adaptation.

573. K-6. (+) Netzel, Sally. (Perrault, Charles) Cinderella. (Cinderella) CAST: 8f, 5m, Su. ACTS: 2. SETTINGS: Market square; room; ballroom. PLAYING TIME: 60 min. PLOT: This is a faithful retelling of the original classic. RECOMMENDATION: This is unique because of the humor found throughout the play, which enhances the original theme. Older elementary children might enjoy producing this for younger ones. ROYALTY:

$25. SOURCE: Netzel, Sally. (1981). Cinderella. Schulenburg, TX: I.E. Clark. SUBJECTS/PLAY TYPE: Folk Tales, France; Stepsisters; Adaptation.

574. 1-6. (+) Thane, Adele. (Perrault, Charles) Cinderella. (Cinderella) CAST: 7f, 7m, Su. ACTS: 1. SETTINGS: Kitchen; ballroom. PLAYING TIME: 35 min. PLOT: This is a faithful retelling of the classic story. RECOMMENDATION: Each character is individualized with specific traits but broadly sketched, allowing for as much or as little depth as desired. ROYALTY: Free to Plays subscribers. SOURCE: Thane, Adele. (1977, May). Cinderella. Plays: The Drama Magazine for Young People, pp. 51-60. SUBJECTS/PLAY TYPE: Folktales, France; Stepsisters; Adaptation.

575. K-4*. (+) Hotchner, Steve & Hotchner, Kathy. (Perrault, Charles) Cinderella, Cinderella. (Cinderella) CAST: 5f, 3m. ACTS: 1. SETTINGS: Bare stage. PLAYING TIME: NA. PLOT: This is a simplified version of Perrault's classic tale. RECOMMENDATION: Children from the audience are involved in the action of this wonderful rendition. One finds the fairy godmother's lost wand under his/her seat, and many come up on stage to help Cinderella clean, dance at the ball, and go to the wedding. Although staging is minimal, the play must be produced by older actors. ROYALTY: $25. SOURCE: Hotchner, Steve & Hotchner, Kathy. Cinderella, Cinderella. Woodstock, IL: Dramatic Pub. Co. SUBJECTS/PLAY TYPE: Folk Tales, France; Participation Play; Stepsisters; Adaptation.

576. 1-5*. (+) Fendrich, Shubert. (Perrault, Charles) Cinderella goes disco. (Cinderella) CAST: 2f, 2m, 7u. ACTS: 1. SETTINGS: None. PLAYING TIME: NA. PLOT: A modern day Cinderella is convinced her frazzled fairy godmother can do magic after hearing "Beauty and the Beast" and "Sleeping Beauty." She allows the fairy to outfit her for the disco dance and of course she wins the prince's heart while "getting down" under the strobe lights. RECOMMENDATION: There are references here that would have to be updated and even very young children may find Persephone, the fairy godmother, silly. Otherwise, this is recommended for offering three familiar fairy tales combined in a production that is short enough for young children. Also, the play uses audience participation on and off the stage: this is sure to keep the children intrigued. The performance itself requires a teenaged or young adult cast and Persephone, in particular, must have a personality which elicits a positive, trusting response from young children. ROYALTY: NA. SOURCE: Fendrich, Shubert. (1979). Cinderella goes disco. Denver, CO: Pioneer Drama Service. SUBJECTS/PLAY TYPE: Folk Tales, France; Comedy; Participation Play; Adaptation.

577. 1-8*. (+) Homer, Frances. (Perrault, Charles) Cinderella of loveland. (Cinderella) CAST: 12f, 6m, Su. ACTS: 3. SETTINGS: Kitchen; palace room. PLAYING TIME: NA. PLOT: This traditional retelling has added a few characters for variety: a talking cat named Ashes, a

beautiful but vain princess from a neighboring land, and the prince's court jester, Biff. RECOMMENDATION: This humorous, lively adaptation is recommended for production by an adult group for young people because of its difficult timing and dancing requirements. ROYALTY: $25. SOURCE: Homer, Frances. (1961). Cinderella of loveland. Chicago, IL: Dramatic Pub. Co. SUBJECTS/PLAY TYPE: Folk Tales, France; Cinderella; Adaptation.

578. 7-12. (+) Koste, Virginia Glasgow. The Cinderella syndrome. CAST: 5f. ACTS: 1. SETTINGS: Room, fireplace. PLAYING TIME: 30 min. PLOT: The young and beautiful Cinderella has a chance to go to a ball given by the prince, who hopes to find a wife. In this play, instead of the stepmother and stepsisters being mean to Cinderella, they are kind and concerned, wanting Cinderella to go to the ball because she is so beautiful. Cinderella, feeling sorry for herself as she is only a stepdaughter, sends her stepfamily off to the ball. Her godmother then appears with a dress and shoes designed especially for this occasion. Cinderella prepares for the ball, knowing this is her destiny. RECOMMENDATION: A delightful comedy, the traditional story is presented in a more believable manner, not relying so much on "magical" powers, but on kindness and self worth. Instead of an evil vs. good plot, this concerns itself more with self actualization and responsibility. ROYALTY: NA. SOURCE: Koste, Virginia Glasgow. (1983). The Cinderella syndrome. Boston, MA: Baker's Plays. SUBJECTS/PLAY TYPE: Responsibility; Identity; Folk Tales, France; Adaptation.

579. 7-12. (+) Chase, Jerry. (Perrault, Charles) Cinderella wore combat boots. (Cinderella) CAST: 5f, 2m. ACTS: 1. SETTINGS: Throne room; cottage. PLAYING TIME: NA. PLOT: An aging King decides that his 38 year old son must marry. He holds a ball so the prince can find a bride. The prince is convinced that girls are "sissies," until he meets the beautiful and natural Cinderella in her gown and combat boots (a gift from her father). The stroke of midnight catches her with one boot off, letting the Prince see how comfortable it is. She runs off and he is left with the boot. He travels the kingdom, trying to find out the mysterious owner. Of course, the wicked stepsisters claim it is theirs, but can't fit it, and the Prince finds Cinderella at last. RECOMMENDATION: In this hilarious adaptation, the evil characters are joyously overplayed. For example, the stepsisters require acetylene torches and hammers to make themselves up for the ball. The script encourages audience participation, as does the storyteller who introduces the characters, interacts with them, and generally adds to the fun. ROYALTY: $20. SOURCE: Chase, Jerry. (1980). Cinderella wore combat boots. New York, NY: Dramatists Play Service. SUBJECTS/PLAY TYPE: Folk Tales, France; Audience Participation; Adaptation.

580. 7-12. (-) Nolan, Paul T. Cinderfellow. CAST: 4f, 6m. ACTS: 1. SETTINGS: Throne room. PLAYING TIME: 25 min. PLOT: The king searches for an appropriate husband for the princess, one with feet big enough to fill the king's incredibly large shoes. One by one, potential suitors drop out because of various foot problems. Finally, only the maligned Cinderfellow is left who, they discover, is actually the long lost son of the real Cinderella. Now he can marry the princess, who is delighted because he is cute. RECOMMENDATION: The clever situation is overshadowed by humor stretched too thin to be funny. The characters are flat, stereotyped, and cry too much. The princess is more interesting: she is usually irritated. The audience will be irritated, too. ROYALTY: Free to Plays subscribers. SOURCE: Nolan, Paul T. (1986, April). Cinderfellow. Plays: The Drama Magazine for Young People, pp. 18-26. SUBJECTS/PLAY TYPE: Folk Tales, France; Marriage; Comedy.

581. 3-7. (+) Gotwalt, Helen Louise Miller. Circus daze. CAST: 3f, 12m. ACTS: 1. SETTINGS: Circus tent; office. PLAYING TIME: 25 min. PLOT: A group of children are caught sneaking into a circus tent in search of an old family friend. They talk to the circus owner about joining the circus, but decide circuses are not much fun after all, because most of the stunts are more dangerous than exciting. RECOMMENDATION: The right group could make this a three ring spectacle. However, sexist stereotyping would have to be deleted, some updated dialogue would have to be added, and acrobatic skills are required to maintain the interest. ROYALTY: Free to Plays subscribers. SOURCE: Gotwalt, Helen Louise Miller. (1986, May). Circus daze. Plays: The Drama Magazine for Young People, pp. 37-44. SUBJECTS/PLAY TYPE: Circus; Comedy.

582. 7-12. (+) Kraus, Joanna Halpert. Circus home. CAST: 3f, 10m. ACTS: 2. SETTINGS: Circus stage; house. PLAYING TIME: NA. PLOT: Benjie, a huge young man whose father and peers consider him a freak, leaves home to join a traveling circus and finds acceptance and love. When he averts a near tragedy during a performance, his father is able to accept him as somebody unique and capable of wonderful things. RECOMMENDATION: This is a good presentation to demonstrate to young adults how each of us is different and unique. ROYALTY: NA. SOURCE: Kraus, Joanna Halpert. (1979). Circus family. Rowayton, CT: New Plays, Inc. SUBJECTS/PLAY TYPE: Circus; Family; Drama.

583. 2-5. (+) Paston, Bryna N. & Tolins, Selma. The circus secret. CAST: 6f, 4m, 16u. ACTS: 1. SETTINGS: Bare stage. PLAYING TIME: 20 min. PLOT: Margie, an almost 11 year old girl, decides she is too grown up for the circus. When she develops a friendship with Sir Clown, she discovers the many talented folk of the circus world and realizes that no one is ever too old for the circus. RECOMMENDATION: This musical contains an assortment of circus performers who will captivate, interest, and entertain. Although Margie seems too easily swayed in her opinion, the strong character of Sir Clown helps audiences overlook this. ROYALTY: Free to Plays subscribers. SOURCE: Paston, Bryna N. & Tolins, Selma. (1977, November). The circus secret. Plays: The Drama Magazine for Young People, pp. 59-64. SUBJECTS/PLAY TYPE: Circus; Clowns; Musical.

584. 2-6. (+) Sanker, Joyce & Coates, Gary M. **Ciro's circus.** CAST: 10f, 13m. ACTS: 3. SETTINGS: Dressing room. PLAYING TIME: 60 min. PLOT: A brother and sister run away with the circus, hiding in a large trunk. The boy becomes a clown and his sister, the circus seamstress. When the performance is about to begin, their guardian and a policeman appear to take them home. But the juggler notices that the guardian can juggle, so she becomes his new partner, and all join the circus. RECOMMENDATION: The believable characters involve the audience in their plight and in the metamorphosis of the old woman from a cruel to a compassionate person. The setting is important to the play and is easily staged. ROYALTY: $50. SOURCE: Sanker, Joyce. (1984). Ciro's circus. Franklin, OH: Eldridge Pub. Co. SUBJECTS/PLAY TYPE: Adventure; Circus; Performing Arts; Musical.

585. K-12. (-) Goldstein, Benjamin & Namanworth, Phillip. **Clap your hands. CAST:** 20u. ACTS: 1. SETTINGS: Bare stage. PLAYING TIME: NA. PLOT: Ageless Looice sings, dances, and runs for president so that a selfish senator doesn't take over and exploit all the imaginary creatures, animals, and storybook characters in the world. When Looice is disqualified from the race because he has no age, he takes on the job of Santa's helper. His friend, the penguin, becomes president, ushering in a government of love and generosity. RECOMMENDATION: Intended to be a musical for all ages, this is not appropriate for any age. Political and environmental comments, dated slang, and bad puns are juxtaposed with sickeningly sweet "kiddie" imagery. Crammed with rainbows, jellybeans, laughing clouds, Santa Claus, and much, much more, the resulting mishmash is nauseating. ROYALTY: $50. SOURCE: Goldstein, Benjamin & Namanworth, Phillip. (1982). Clap your hands. Chicago, IL: The Dramatic Pub. Co. SUBJECTS/PLAY TYPE: Satire; Government; Musical.

586. 7-12. (+) Huff, Betty Tracy. **Clarabelle the clock watcher. CAST:** 7f, 5m, 1u. ACTS: 1. SETTINGS: Clock. PLAYING TIME: 25 min. PLOT: Clarabelle, a girl from a noble family, sets out to recover her family's fortune by working as a clock watcher. She outwits her ex-love, Percival Dillberry (who caused her family's poverty by stealing her father's "diamond-studded portfolio") and recovers the family's stolen property. Both Clarabelle's and the town's future are ensured. RECOMMENDATION: Although melodramatic, this makes several astute observations about the working conditions in Europe in 1900. The play is entertaining, especially the villains who dance with the clock's moving dancers. Some of the player's costumes would need special attention. ROYALTY: Free to Plays subscribers. SOURCE: Huff, Betty Tracy. (1981, March). Clarabelle the clock watcher. Plays: The Drama Magazine for Young People, pp. 1-10. SUBJECTS/PLAY TYPE: Clocks; Melodrama.

587. 7-12. (-) Hamlett, Christina. **Classified romance. CAST:** 1f, 2m. ACTS: 1. SETTINGS: Hotel room. PLAYING TIME: 20 min. PLOT: A count visiting in America places a newspaper ad, "Bewitched Frog Seeks Princess," in the personals. His ad is answered by a lonely girl and their phone conversation comprises the play. RECOMMENDATION: The phone conversation approaches wittiness and sensitivity, but never quite gets there. A teenage audience would not identify with the characters. Since the two hang up with no plans to meet, there is no conclusion. ROYALTY: Free to Plays subscribers. SOURCE: Hamlett, Christina. (1984, March). Classified romance. Plays: The Drama Magazine for Young People, pp. 57-63. SUBJECTS/PLAY TYPE: Dating; Romance; Playlet.

588. 3-6. (+) Boiko, Claire. **A clean sweep. CAST:** 9f, 9m, 6u. ACTS: 1. SETTINGS: Bare stage, props. PLAYING TIME: 15 min. PLOT: As the Old Year sweeps out the past months, they come across specific holidays, each of which provides a poetic memory. Christmas, too, is swept away, and the New Year prepares for the coming year, which is ushered in by "Auld Lang Syne." RECOMMENDATION: A wonderful short play in which the passing of an old year is portrayed charmingly. Most roles consist of short dialogue, so this would make an appropriate show for inexperienced actors to perform in an assembly or for a parents' program. ROYALTY: None. SOURCE: Boiko, Claire. (1981). Children's plays for creative actors: A collection of royalty-free plays for boys and girls. Boston, MA: Plays, Inc. SUBJECTS/PLAY TYPE: Calendar; Holidays; Choral Reading.

589. K-6. (+) Gotwalt, Helen Louise Miller. **Clean sweep. CAST:** 3f, 3m. ACTS: 1. SETTINGS: Living room. PLAYING TIME: 20 min. PLOT: Six children look for Mother's Day gift ideas until they stumble upon treasure hunt clues, left by their Aunt Grace, which lead them through the house, requiring them to clean up various messes as they go. The house is left neat as a pin and they find a jewelry set thoughtfully purchased by their aunt to give to their mother the next day. RECOMMENDATION: A delightful piece, this encourages thoughtful, non-monetary gifts as Mother's Day presents. Older elementary students should take on acting and production requirements, but children as young as kindergarten will understand and enjoy the plot. ROYALTY: Free to Plays subscribers. SOURCE: Gotwalt, Helen Louise Miller. (1987, May). Clean sweep. Plays: The Drama Magazine for Young People, pp. 55-60. SUBJECTS/PLAY TYPE: Mother's Day; Treasure Hunt; Playlet.

590. 7-12. (+) Dias, Earl J. **The cleanest town in the west. CAST:** 3f, 6m. ACTS: 1. SETTINGS: Soda bar; dining room. PLAYING TIME: 30 min. PLOT: Red Gulch's lazy sheriff and inept deputy try to prove that two suspicious strangers held up the stage coach, but the most unlikely characters prove to be guilty. RECOMMENDATION: What seems to be a simple stagecoach holdup is complicated because the characters are other than what they appear to be. The language is "pseudo" Texan and a bit patronizing. The characters are stereotyped; however, the suspicious stranger quotes Chaucer and Shakespeare (for which the cast and audience may need background), and the weak

female turns out to be the robber. The clean up of crime is inappropriately equated with the prohibition of alcohol. Scenes would easily be staged, but costuming may be difficult. ROYALTY: Free to Plays subscribers. SOURCE: Dias, Earl J. (1987, January/February). The cleanest town in the west. Plays: The Drama Magazine for Young People, pp. 10-20. SUBJECTS/PLAY TYPE: Old West; Mysteries; Comedy.

591. 9-12.*(+) Berger, Maurice. **Cleft for me.** CAST: 4f, 7m, Su. ACTS: 1. SETTINGS: Bare stage, rock. PLAYING TIME: 30 min. PLOT: A man hears tapping from behind a rock and tries to get help for the person he assumes is trapped inside a cave. What arrives to supposedly rescue the person are instead self-serving onlookers and, in the ensuing action, the person behind the rock is forgotten. When the do-gooders leave to attend another public "tragedy," the hero moves the rock away and frees the person, only to meet with great hostility. The hero himself enters the cave and pulls the rock across the opening. RECOMMENDATION: Entertaining while making a statement, this is a comment on the social psychology within contemporary America, real vs. stated goals. This excellent play is not for younger audiences, but for those mature enough to see beyond its superficial comedic aspects. ROYALTY: $15. SOURCE: Berger, Maurice. (1967, in reprint). Cleft for me. Denver, CO: Pioneer Drama Service. SUBJECTS/PLAY TYPE: Social Psychology; Satire.

592. K-6. (-) Korty, Carol. **Clever Clyde.** CAST: 5u. ACTS: 1. SETTINGS: Bare stage, props. PLAYING TIME: NA. PLOT: An overzealous trainer does not realize that his dog, Clyde, cannot perform any of his tricks, and continues to praise him. RECOMMENDATION: The physical comedy here can be adapted to almost any level of acting or acrobatic skill. This would be a good short piece during a scene change for a longer play. ROYALTY: None. SOURCE: Korty, Carol. (1977). Silly soup: Ten zany plays. New York, NY: Charles Scribner's Sons. SUBJECTS/PLAY TYPE: Comedy; Skit; Adaptation.

593. 1-6. (+) Feather, Jean. **The clever cobbler.** CAST: 3f, 6m. ACTS: 1. SETTINGS: Cottage room. PLAYING TIME: 15 min. PLOT: A cobbler, unable to earn a living, is persuaded by his wife to become an astrologer. People ask for his assistance, and he always seems to know the answer, for which he is paid well. The Sultan asks his help in finding 40 chests of gold, which he accidentally locates. He is rewarded with a chest of gold and the position of chief astrologer to the Sultan. RECOMMENDATION: In this clever tale, luck and mistaken meanings humorously lead to fame and fortune. Children of all ages will enjoy this production, although the acting should be left to upper elementary children, who can best deal with the comedic timing. ROYALTY: NA. SOURCE: Kamerman, Sylvia E. (1987). Plays from favorite folk tales. Boston, MA: Plays, Inc. SUBJECTS/PLAY TYPE: Folk Tale Motifs; Astrology; Playlet.

594. 4-6. (+) Winther, Barbara. **The clever dog of Hawaii.** CAST: 2f, 1m, 7u. ACTS: 1. SETTINGS: Taro field. PLAYING TIME: 20 min. PLOT: Three evil spirits steal the haughty queen's conch shell horn. A clever dog helps the stepsister retrieve the horn, making life easier for her and the dog's master. RECOMMENDATION: Although this is quite good, it could be difficult to create the setting and atmosphere necessary for the play to come alive. ROYALTY: Free to Plays subscribers. SOURCE: Winther, Barbara. (1980, April). The clever dog of Hawaii. Plays: The Drama Magazine for Young People, pp. 43-48. SUBJECTS/PLAY TYPE: Folk Tales, Hawaii; Dogs; Playlet.

595. 4-6. (+) Carlson, Bernice Wells. **Clever, eh?** CAST: 3f, 3m. ACTS: 1. SETTINGS: Road; dining room. PLAYING TIME: 10 min. PLOT: A woodcutter overcharges two desperate French refugees for some wood. He tells his story to the innkeeper, who then overcharges him, and returns the money to the refugees. RECOMMENDATION: "Cheating is not the same as being clever," is presented here in a nonpatronizing manner, as the cheater receives his justice from people who are truly clever. ROYALTY: NA. SOURCE: Carlson, Bernice Wells. (1982). Let's find the big idea. Nashville, TN: Abingdon. SUBJECTS/PLAY TYPE: Cheating; Fable.

596. 4-7. (+) Sills, Paul. (Grimm Brothers) **The clever Elsie.** (The clever Elsie) CAST: 2f, 3m. ACTS: 1. SETTINGS: Peasant cottage; cornfield. PLAYING TIME: NA. PLOT: Clever Elsie is the only daughter of peasants who are anxious to see her married. A young man, John, asks for Elsie's hand, but discovers that, although clever, she is quite lazy. While she sleeps in the fields, John spreads a net covered with bells over her. On awakening, she asks John who she is. He claims not to know her, and Elsie goes in search of herself and leaves the country. The moral is well-illustrated: it is better to be industrious than clever. RECOMMENDATION: As with many folk tales, this one perpetuates the notion of women as chattel. The way in which the "moral" is stated will either make audiences groan or amuse them as a humorous philosophical malaprop. ROYALTY: NA. SOURCE: Sills, Paul. (1981). More from story theatre. New York, NY: Samuel French. SUBJECTS/PLAY TYPE: Folk Tales, Germany; Fools And Simpletons; Playlet.

597. 2-5. (+) Bauman, A. F. **Close encounter of a weird kind.** CAST: 2f, 3m, 3u. ACTS: 1. SETTINGS: Earth living room. PLAYING TIME: 15 min. PLOT: While their parents are gone, three children are visited by aliens who ask them a riddle: what keeps things hot and cold. The children give the aliens a thermos. RECOMMENDATION: This is filled with humor and suspense. With simple costumes and stage settings, it is easily produced. ROYALTY: Permission necessary for non-amateur productions. SOURCE: Kamerman, Sylvia E. (1981). Space and science fiction plays for young people. Boston, MA: Plays, Inc. SUBJECTS/PLAY TYPE: Science Fiction; Comedy.

598. 12. (+) Miller, Ev. **Close the door so it can't get in your room.** CAST: 10f, 11m, Su. ACTS: 2. SETTINGS: Classroom. PLAYING TIME: 100 min. PLOT: A first year teacher is disillusioned by students and other teachers who seem to care little for education. At the last moment, he chooses to teach "one more year." RECOMMENDATION: This play is a teacher's view of school life, best appreciated by adults working in education. The novice teacher's victories are small and have little to do with his subject, English. The play is fairly honest, but finding an appropriate audience might be difficult. ROYALTY: $50. SOURCE: Miller, Ev. (1986). Close the door so it can't get in your room. Schulenburg, TX: I.E. Clark, Inc. SUBJECTS/PLAY TYPE: School; Teaching; Drama.

599. 4-8*. (+) Way, Brian. **The clown.** CAST: 2f, 2m. ACTS: 1. SETTINGS: Circus arena. PLAYING TIME: 60 min. PLOT: When Clown, famous for a complicated trick involving a 20-foot ladder and two buckets of water, is pushed into retirement, a reporter and photographer want to do a film about his life. They involve the audience in the project. After the project's completion, Clown retires, but becomes ringmaster, fulfilling his greatest dream. RECOMMENDATION: This must be presented by adults or young adults because of its excellent audience participation and improvisation. Characters are well developed and enhance the theme of never giving up. The "in-the-round" setting provides the circus mood. ROYALTY: $20. SOURCE: Way, Brian. (1977). The clown. Boston, MA: Baker's Plays. SUBJECTS/PLAY TYPE: Clowns; Circus; Retirement; Drama.

600. 6-10. (+) Murray, John. **Clown-a-rama.** CAST: 5f, 4m. ACTS: 1. SETTINGS: Gym. PLAYING TIME: 30 min. PLOT: Two rival groups of students prepare for a clowning competition, while the play explores typical boy/girl relationships, peer pressure, malicious pranks, blackmail, and sabotage. Woven into the dialogue is some history of clowning and the circus, and a subtle commentary regarding parental sensitivity towards their children's career choices. RECOMMENDATION: Some sexist stereotypes and outdated dialogue require editing. Trampoline and juggling skills are needed. ROYALTY: Free to Plays subscribers. SOURCE: Murray, John. (1985). Fifteen plays for today's teenagers. Boston, MA: Plays, Inc. SUBJECTS/PLAY TYPE: Peer Pressure; Clowns; Comedy.

601. K-4*. (+) Bain, Reginald F. (Jacobs, Joseph) **Clowns' play.** (Jack and the beanstalk) CAST: 4f, 4m. ACTS: 1. SETTINGS: Bare stage. PLAYING TIME: 35 min. PLOT: A group of clowns is informed by the Bumblebee Barnstormers, a traveling troupe of actors, that the troupe's van has broken down. The clowns improvise and perform the famous children's story, **Jack and the Beanstalk,** themselves. RECOMMENDATION: Great fun for both the performers and the audience, this allows many opportunities for audience response. The character, Scrappy (Jack), should be a proficient mime, potentially a casting problem. ROYALTY: $35. SOURCE: Bain,

Reginald F. (1981). Clowns' play. Woodstock, IL: The Dramatic Pub. Co. SUBJECTS/PLAY TYPE: Clowns; Folk Tales, England; Adaptation.

602. K-12. (+) Gleason, William. **The Clumsy Custard horror show and ice cream clone review.** CAST: 3f, 9m, Su. ACTS: 2. SETTINGS: Castle courtyard; dungeon; bedroom; cave. PLAYING TIME: NA. PLOT: A familiar plot of good guys vs. bad guys is imbedded in a story of a princess kidnapped by bad guys, then rescued by a handsome prince. They fall in love and live happily ever after. Freshness is provided by an unusual cast of fantasy characters, including the Clumsy Custard, played by three people in one costume. RECOMMENDATION: This requires a great deal of audience participation, so it might help to have some "plants" in the audience to encourage interaction. The actors will need to be from the upper grades. ROYALTY: $50. SOURCE: Gleason, William. (1979). The clumsy custard horror show and ice cream clone review. Chicago, IL: Dramatic Pub. Co. SUBJECTS/PLAY TYPE: Fantasy; Comedy; Drama.

603. 1-6. (+) Bland, Joellen. **The cobbler who became an astrologer.** (The cobbler's dilemma) CAST: 3f, 8m. ACTS: 1. SETTINGS: Street; throne. PLAYING TIME: 20 min. PLOT: A cobbler, at the insistence of his greedy wife, professes to be an astrologer and, through luck, he solves three mysteries. When the king rewards him with riches, he discovers that fear of failure outweighs the rewards of success, and that peace and comfort are rewards in themselves. He gives the reward to his wife so she can take a trip around the world. RECOMMENDATION: The solved mysteries are ingenious and interesting. The shrewish wife could be changed to avoid the sexism that this implies. This might be used to provoke discussion about fears of failure and taking risks. ROYALTY: Free to Plays subscribers. SOURCE: Bland, Joellen. (1987, May). The cobbler who became an astrologer. Plays: The Drama Magazine for Young People, pp. 49-54. SUBJECTS/PLAY TYPE: Folk Tales, Italy; Adaptation.

604. K-3. (+) Uchida, Yoshiko. **Cockroach.** CAST: 3u. ACTS: 1. SETTINGS: None. PLAYING TIME: NA. PLOT: A person, after squashing a cockroach, wonders if there are now orphans living under his stove. RECOMMENDATION: Cleverly done, this will work well with other related poems. ROYALTY: NA. SOURCE: Bauer, Caroline Feller. (1987). Presenting reader's theater: Plays and poems to read aloud. New York, NY: H.W. Wilson. SUBJECTS/PLAY TYPE: Cockroaches; Reader's Theater.

605. 9-12. (+) Conley, Pauline C. **The code breaker.** CAST: 2f, 2m, 1u. ACTS: 1. SETTINGS: None. PLAYING TIME: NA. PLOT: A young scientist, one of four teenagers living in a futuristic enclosed world controlled by computers, wanders into the unknown outside world. He tries to convince his companions there is another reality, but they regard his discoveries as threatening. He escapes before he can be punished and his friend, Bernice, plans to join him later.

RECOMMENDATION: Easily produced, this will be of interest to teenagers because of its futuristic theme of a life controlled not by parents, but by computers. The plot builds a level of tension that is guaranteed to keep audiences captivated. ROYALTY: $35. SOURCE: Conley, Pauline C. (1983). The code breaker. New Orleans, LA: Anchorage Press, Inc. SUBJECTS/PLAY TYPE: Future; Science Fiction; Computers; Drama.

606. 9-12. (+) Jackson, Richard Eugene. **Coffey Pott meets the wolf man.** CAST: 8f, 4m. ACTS: 3. SETTINGS: Study. PLAYING TIME: 90 min. PLOT: Coffey and Sugar Pott, the daughters of a former detective, visit the old family home, a run down Victorian mansion which is being used by Teen Films, Inc., to shoot a Wolf Man movie. Although the role of Wolf Man is played by Mike, another Wolf Man mysteriously carries off the leading lady and director. Coffey and Sugar keep their own identities secret and discover that the Schmittle family (Mama, Siegfried, and Hans) are causing the problems because Hans played the Wolf Man part in the "old" days and wants his part back. RECOMMENDATION: In this unique Halloween production, both humor and suspense are neatly interwoven, and characterizations are designed to be an attainable challenge for inexperienced teen actors. ROYALTY: $25. SOURCE: Jackson, Richard Eugene. (1982). Coffey Pott meets the wolf man. Schulenburg, TX: I.E. Clark. SUBJECTS/PLAY TYPE: Mystery; Werewolves; Film Production; Comedy.

607. 7-9. (+) Karshner, Roger. **Colin and Ernie.** CAST: 2m. ACTS: 1. SETTINGS: None. PLAYING TIME: NA. PLOT: Two new boys have problems meeting friends. Colin thinks that it is Ernie's fault, but Ernie tells him that he must make the first move. RECOMMENDATION: Although the language is raw, this handles well the feelings of being placed in unfamiliar circumstances. ROYALTY: NA. SOURCE: Karshner, Roger. (1986). Scenes for teenagers. Toluce Lake, CA: Dramaline Pub. SUBJECTS/PLAY TYPE: Social Grace; Scene.

608. K-1. (+) Alexander, Sue. **Come quick!** CAST: 2u. ACTS: 1. SETTINGS: Living room. PLAYING TIME: NA. PLOT: A little boy tries to pull a series of April Fool's jokes on his father, but his father turns them around. RECOMMENDATION: April Fool plays are rare, and this one successfully illustrates the spirit of the holiday. Speaking parts are easily learned and may be changed slightly as children act and react to the play. ROYALTY: None. SOURCE: Alexander, Sue. (1977). Small plays for special days. New York, NY: Seabury Press. SUBJECTS/PLAY TYPE: April Fool's Day; Comedy.

609. 4-6. (+) Henderson, Nancy. **Come to the fair.** CAST: 10f, 10m, 7u. ACTS: 1. SETTINGS: County fair. PLAYING TIME: 12 min. PLOT: Eleven year old Bedelia Wiggins is sad because her quilt did not win a prize. Her spirits are lifted, however, when her mother lets her go to the lemonade social. RECOMMENDATION: This is an enjoyable play with clowns, singing, and dancing, but the large cast might

cause some problems. ROYALTY: Permission required if performed outside of the classroom. SOURCE: Henderson, Nancy. (1978). Celebrate America: a baker's dozen of plays. New York, NY: Julian Messner. SUBJECTS/PLAY TYPE: Fairs; Drama.

610. K-12. (-) Calvin College Chapel Service. **Come, thou long-expected Jesus.** CAST: Su. ACTS: 1. SETTINGS: None. PLAYING TIME: 15 min. PLOT: This service excerpts Bible readings from the Confrontation and the Conquest. RECOMMENDATION: This would need to be part of a longer church worship service, since it would otherwise read as disjointed Bible passages. ROYALTY: None. SOURCE: Hendricks, William & Vogel, Cora. (1983). Handbook of Christmas programs. Grand Rapids, MI: Baker Book House. SUBJECTS/PLAY TYPE: Christmas; Liturgy; Worship Program.

611. 9-12. (+) Kelly, Tim. **The comedian.** CAST: 6f, 6m, Su. ACTS: 1. SETTINGS: Bare stage, props. PLAYING TIME: NA. PLOT: In this play within a play, an amateur cast rehearses the drama of St. Genesius' betrayal and murder in the court of Emperor Diocletian during the persecution of the Christians. RECOMMENDATION: This intense drama will be a challenge to its cast members because each has a dual role, in the present and ancient past, and the changes between the past and present occur abruptly. It clearly and quickly provides an historic perspective on the horror of the Christian persecutions. ROYALTY: NA. SOURCE: Kelly, Tim. (1984). The comedian. Boston, MA: Baker's Plays. SUBJECTS/PLAY TYPE: St. Genesius; Christian Persecutions; Play Rehearsals; Drama.

612. 10-12. (+) Pickett, C. B. (Shakespeare, William) **The comedy of errors.** (The comedy of errors) CAST: 5f, 12m, Su. ACTS: 1. SETTINGS: Platform. PLAYING TIME: 35 min. PLOT: In this modern adaptation of one of Shakespeare's funniest plays, twin brothers, both named Antipholus, and their attendants, twins named Dromio, are involved in a case of mistaken identity. As youngsters, the twins are separated in a shipwreck. Twenty years later, one pair go in search of their brothers, and when they end up with their twin's wives, the results are hilarious. Both sets of twins are reunited and all ends happily. RECOMMENDATION: With zany characters, exaggerated costuming, and modern background music, this will delight high school audiences, especially those studying Shakespeare. Although the stage directions are somewhat complex and the language archaic, the simple set design and use of pantomime make this possible to perform. ROYALTY: $15. SOURCE: Pickett, C. B. (1986). The comedy of errors. Schulenburg, TX: I.E. Clark. SUBJECTS/PLAY TYPE: Farce; Comedy; Mistaken Identity; Twins; Adaptation.

613. 9-12. (+) Singleton, Robert M. (Shakespeare, William) **The comedy of errors.** (The comedy of errors) CAST: 5f, 11m. ACTS: 1. SETTINGS: None. PLAYING TIME: NA. PLOT: This one act adaptation centers around two sets of identical twins who were separated in childhood but whose paths cross

repeatedly, with wives, husbands, masters, and servants continually mistaking each other's identities. When the father of one set of twins is about to be executed, the brothers encounter one another, the order for execution is countermanded, and all ends well. RECOMMENDATION: The contemporary language and the rapid pace of the action will hold a student audience's interest and may even stimulate interest in a genuine Shakespeare comedy. High school drama students should be able to present this play so their fellow students will find the absurd situations truly amusing. ROYALTY: $15. SOURCE: Singleton, Robert M. (1977). The comedy of errors. Chicago, IL: Dramatic Pub. Co. SUBJECTS/PLAY TYPE: Twins; Mistaken Identity; Comedy; Adaptation.

614. 4-12. (-) Burchett, Jack. **Comic country Christmas.** CAST: 6f, 5m, 2u. ACTS: 1. SETTINGS: Living room. PLAYING TIME: 45 min. PLOT: As the Smiths await the arrival of their children and grandchildren, they reminisce about Christmas, 1955, when their youngest son, Ernest, hid "Santa Claus" in their attic. In reality, Santa was a bank robber who thought he had a perfect hideaway. Shaken because his partner was arrested and the stolen money recovered, the gangster decided to turn himself in and begin a new life by allowing Mr. Smith to collect the reward money and provide a "good" Christmas for his family. The last scene updates the audience with the homecoming of the younger generations of Smiths. RECOMMENDATION: This unbelievable plot and superficial Christmas message are too contrived. Plodding dialogue and "hick" accents simply accentuate its flaws. ROYALTY: NA. SOURCE: Burchett, Jack (1988). Comic country Christmas. Franklin, OH: Eldridge Pub. Co. SUBJECTS/PLAY TYPE: Family; Comedy; Christmas; Comedy.

615. K-2. (+) Fleischman, Paul. **The common egret.** CAST: 2u. ACTS: 1. SETTINGS: None. PLAYING TIME: NA. PLOT: Two readers refute the belief that "common egrets" are merely "common." RECOMMENDATION: Poetically written, this short production, when read with precise timing, will make a lovely presentation for parents. ROYALTY: NA. SOURCE: Bauer, Caroline Feller. (1987). Presenting reader's theater: Plays and poems to read aloud. New York, NY: H.W. Wilson Co. SUBJECTS/PLAY TYPE: Egrets; Reader's Theater.

616. 7-9. (-) Kurtz, Jack. **The complaint booth.** CAST: 10f, 11m, 15u. ACTS: 1. SETTINGS: Booth. PLAYING TIME: NA. PLOT: A variety of characters come to the complaint booth for help with myriad problems, which can all be resolved in this fantasyland, where Christmas is celebrated every day. The story ends vaguely, drawing to an unrelated conclusion about being happy with who we are. RECOMMENDATION: Although imaginatively written, the ending is almost in contradiction with the presentation. The point, whatever it is, is lost. ROYALTY: NA. SOURCE: Kurtz, Jack. (1978). Without bathrobes: Alternatives in drama for youth: three one-act chancel comedies. New York, NY:

Baker's Plays. SUBJECTS/PLAY TYPE: Christmas; Christian Drama; Satire.

617. 4-6. (+) Valdes, Carolyn J. **A computerized Christmas.** CAST: 6f, 8m, 4u. ACTS: 1. SETTINGS: Shopping center; workroom; clubhouse. PLAYING TIME: NA. PLOT: In the year 2002, children give their Christmas wishes to a computer while Santa, Mrs. Claus, and their elves are prisoners on the North Star. The kidnapper, Grumpenkrause, has computerized Christmas and Christmas gifts. Seven children rescue Santa, return him to the North Pole, and restore the traditional Christmas. RECOMMENDATION: This underscores the values inherent in Christmas, while at the same time providing a setting and situation to which children can relate. The cold and impersonal Christmas computer will captivate the audience, and Santa and Mrs. Claus' plight will draw their sympathy. While the sets and music are complex, detailed suggestions are given which simplify the production. ROYALTY: $30. SOURCE: Valdes, Carolyn J. (1979). A computerized Christmas. Franklin, OH: Eldridge Pub. Co. SUBJECTS/PLAY TYPE: Christmas; Computers; Drama.

618. K-3. (+) Marks, Burton. **The Concert.** CAST: 3u. ACTS: 1. SETTINGS: Bare stage, props. PLAYING TIME: NA. PLOT: Madame Macarone is introduced, and sings terribly. She leaves the stage, thanking the audience for their applause. RECOMMENDATION: This clever spoof of people who are too self important will delight the audience as they groan to the horrible music. ROYALTY: None. SOURCE: Marks, Burton. (1982). Puppet plays and puppet-making. Boston, MA: Plays, Inc. SUBJECTS/PLAY TYPE: Concerts; Self Importance; Puppet Play.

619. 9-11. (+) Miller, Ev. **The concrete ark.** CAST: 5f, 6m. ACTS: 1. SETTINGS: Living room. PLAYING TIME: NA. PLOT: A brilliant, eccentric professor prepares for his predicted end of the world by constructing a large fall out shelter and selecting 10 individuals he judges to be virtuous enough to restart a more humane society. Put into a state of suspended animation by the professor, they awaken 12 years later as the only survivors in a ravaged world. In a power struggle between the professor and his politician friend, the professor is devastated, and half the group is killed. However, the play ends on a hopeful note with the wedding of the youngest couple. RECOMMENDATION: The intriguing premise provides the opportunity to speculate about the future. The dialogue and interplay among the characters are believable. ROYALTY: $15. SOURCE: Miller, Ev. (1982). The concrete ark. Chicago, IL: Dramatic Pub. Co. SUBJECTS/PLAY TYPE: Survival; Betrayal; Plague; Drama.

620. 7-12. (-) McCusker, Paul. **The condensed Bible.** CAST: 2u. ACTS: 1. SETTINGS: Bible bookstore. PLAYING TIME: NA. PLOT: A teenager enters the Bailey Brothers' Bible bookstore looking for a simple condensed Bible. The irreverent shopowner tries to sell

him several absurd editions. The teenager becomes angry and leaves. RECOMMENDATION: This begins promisingly, but instead of developing an ending to match the witty repartee, the audience is left dissatisfied, as the teenager just disappears. With an ending, this could have been excellent. ROYALTY: NA. SOURCE: McCusker, Paul. (1984). Batteries not included. Boston, MA: Baker's Plays. SUBJECTS/PLAY TYPE: Bibles; Comedy; Skit.

621. 12*. (+) Carri'ere, Jean-Claude & Brook, Peter. (Attar, Farid Uddi) **The conference of the birds.** (The conference of the birds) CAST: 3f, 15m, 18u. ACTS: 1. SETTINGS: Bare stage. PLAYING TIME: NA. PLOT: The unhappy birds of the world decide to find their Great King. They meet many characters along the way who tell them stories and illustrate the illusory nature of all earthly attachments. Some of the birds succumb to fear and doubt; some die. Survivors find the King, and learn that the meaning of life he represents exists within each of them. RECOMMENDATION: This dramatized Zen poem would be a beautiful and intense theatrical experience if produced by a professional company for a mature audience. It is far too difficult a play for student actors to attempt and probably too subtle and demanding an artistic event for a school age audience. ROYALTY: $60. SOURCE: Carri'ere, Jean-Claude. (1982). The conference of the birds. Chicago, IL: Dramatic Pub. Co. SUBJECTS/PLAY TYPE: Wisdom; Enlightenment; Drama.

622. 7-12. (+) Sawyer-Young, Kat. **Confrontation.** CAST: 1m. ACTS: 1. SETTINGS: None. PLAYING TIME: 1 min. PLOT: Chris tries to explain to his father that he's not into sports and doesn't have a girlfriend, but is not gay. RECOMMENDATION: This effectively reflects the clash between traditional and modern values. ROYALTY: None. SOURCE: Sawyer-Young, Kat. (1987). Minute monologues for contemporary teens. Boston, MA: Baker's Plays. SUBJECTS/PLAY TYPE: Stereotypes; Monologue.

623. 9-12. (+) Kelly, Tim. (Twain, Mark) **A Connecticut Yankee in King Arthur's court.** (A Connecticut Yankee in King Arthur's court) CAST: 7f, 6m, Su. ACTS: 1. SETTINGS: Camelot. PLAYING TIME: 60 min. PLOT: Hank, a stage crew member for a high school production of "Knights of the Round Table," becomes an unwilling time traveler after colliding with a fellow student's fist. The play follows the plot of the original story until Morgan Le Fey stabs Hank, just as he regains consciousness. A new girl arrives in school, and everyone is amazed when he knows her name, because he recognizes her as one of the ladies-in-waiting of King Arthur's court. He refuses to explain, knowing that no one would believe him. RECOMMENDATION: Many details from the original have been left out, the language and mannerisms of the modern characters have been updated, and the ending takes only minutes as opposed to 13 centuries. There are two fight scenes in which Hank uses karate, giving the director an opportunity to inject extra action if desired. ROYALTY: $25. SOURCE: Kelly, Tim. (1983). A Connecticut Yankee in King Arthur's court.

Denver, CO: Pioneer Drama Service. SUBJECTS/PLAY TYPE: Comedy; Time Travel; Adaptation.

624. 6-9. (+) Olfson, Lewy. (Twain, Mark) **A Connecticut Yankee in King Arthur's court.** (A Connecticut Yankee in King Arthur's court) CAST: 3f, 6m, 1u. ACTS: 1. SETTINGS: None. PLAYING TIME: 15 min. PLOT: A Connecticut Yankee goes back in time to the court of King Arthur. His scientific knowledge allows him to perform "magic" which impresses Arthur but threatens Merlin, who uses his own magic to send the Yankee back to his own time. RECOMMENDATION: This is sufficiently close to Twain's original that it serves as a good introduction to the intriguing and amusing story. ROYALTY: Free to Plays subscribers. SOURCE: Olfson, Lewy. (1985, December). A Connecticut Yankee in King Arthur's court. Plays: The Drama Magazine for Young People, pp. 47-54. SUBJECTS/PLAY TYPE: Reader's Theater; Time Travel; Social Justice; Adaptation.

625. 1-6. (-) Horn, Bill Van. **Constitution!** CAST: 40u. ACTS: 1. SETTINGS: Bare stage. PLAYING TIME: 25 min. PLOT: A convention is called to revise the Articles of Confederation, and the delegates plod through trite logistics. The Constitution is written and each of the actors speaks an excerpted line. RECOMMENDATION: The intent seems to be to show some of the difficult compromises made in drafting the Constitution. However, this is too bogged down with trite dilemmas and never really does explain any of the decisions that were made. ROYALTY: Free to Plays subscribers. SOURCE: Horn, Bill Van. (1988, April). Constitution! Plays: The Drama Magazine for Young People, pp. 35-43. SUBJECTS/PLAY TYPE: Constitution, U.S.; Playlet.

626. 9-12. (+) Brown, Carol J. **The Constitution is born.** CAST: 14m. ACTS: 1. SETTINGS: Bare stage. PLAYING TIME: 25 min. PLOT: Fifty-five delegates representing the thirteen colonies meet in Independence Hall in Philadelphia to discuss the proposed Constitution of the United States. RECOMMENDATION: This historically accurate play presents the issues of a strong central government versus individual state's rights. The lesson about compromise is especially valuable. ROYALTY: Free to Plays subscribers. SOURCE: Brown, Carol. (1986, December). The Constitution is born. Plays: The Drama Magazine for Young People, pp. 49-54. SUBJECTS/PLAY TYPE: Constitutional Convention, U.S.; Franklin, Benjamin; Reader's Theater.

627. 6-9. (+) Nicholson, Jessie. **Conversation piece.** CAST: 4f, 3m, 2u. ACTS: 1. SETTINGS: Living room. PLAYING TIME: 25 min. PLOT: Mrs. Holmes needs something to place over her mantel. As Mother's Day approaches, her four children and their dad bring home their ideas of a mantelpiece: driftwood, stuffed eagle, antlers, and a bearskin rug. Mrs. Holmes keeps the driftwood. RECOMMENDATION: Although not a total loss, the characters here are not always believable, nor are the gifts they provide for their mother. Reflecting an

outlook that everything is perfect, this is rather saccharine, slow moving, and forgettable. ROYALTY: Free to Plays subscribers. SOURCE: Nicholson, Jessie. (1988, May). Conversation piece. Plays: The Drama Magazine for Young People, pp. 9-18. SUBJECTS/PLAY TYPE: Mother's Day; Comedy.

628. 7-12. (+) Valency, Maurice Jacques. **Conversation with a sphinx.** CAST: 5f, 1m, 1u. ACTS: 1. SETTINGS: Bare stage, props. PLAYING TIME: NA. PLOT: A pragmatic, realistic, and unsuperstitious Oedipus meets the Sphinx on his way to Thebes. The Sphinx foretells Oedipus' famous future in which he kills his father and marries his mother, and tries to convince Oedipus not to go. Oedipus does not believe the Sphinx, answers the requisite riddle in order to continue his journey, and moves on to meet his fate. RECOMMENDATION: This is an excellent literary drama that could be used with a unit on mythology. It would be fairly simple to produce, and different students could take turns being the Sphinx and reciting parts of Oedipus' story. Although it varies some from the original, the author's liberty can be excused, since the imagery, symbolism, and metaphor of the original are superbly presented in this riveting adaptation. ROYALTY: $25. SOURCE: Valency, Maurice Jacques. (1980). Conversation with a sphinx. New York, NY: Dramatists Play Service. SUBJECTS/PLAY TYPE: Mythology, Greek; Oedipus; Drama.

629. 7-9. (-) Donahue, John Clarke. **The cookie jar.** CAST: 4f, 8m, 20u. ACTS: 1. SETTINGS: Giant mixing bowl. PLAYING TIME: NA. PLOT: The evil Stale Cake Company attempts to win the people of Cookie Land with cheap gimmicks, but is stopped by the Matchbox House people and won over to the side of good. RECOMMENDATION: The dated language, convoluted plot, and elaborate production requirements make this very unsuccessful. ROYALTY: NA. SOURCE: Donahue, John Clarke. (1975). The cookie jar and other plays. Minneapolis, MN: Univ. of Minnesota Press. SUBJECTS/PLAY TYPE: Social Criticism; Fantasy; Musical; Drama.

630. 2-9. (+) Marks, Burton. **The Cooking lesson.** CAST: 1u. ACTS: 1. SETTINGS: Bare stage, props. PLAYING TIME: NA. PLOT: Mr. Dingleberry attempts to make spinach and mushroom ice cream, only to end up with candy, which he hands out to the audience. RECOMMENDATION: The message seems to be that foods that are not generally liked may be better than one thinks. ROYALTY: None. SOURCE: Marks, Burton. (1982). Puppet plays and puppet-making. Boston, MA: Plays, Inc. SUBJECTS/PLAY TYPE: Foods; Puppet Play.

631. 6-9. (+) Boiko, Claire. **Cool Casey's Christmas.** CAST: 4f, 6m, 3u. ACTS: 1. SETTINGS: Fast food restaurant. PLAYING TIME: 30 min. PLOT: Casey enters a contest in which, if he resists the Christmas spirit until midnight on Christmas Eve, he will win his dream: a date with Marianne Marvel, Miss Adolescent America. If he can't hold out, his friend Mike will win $100. Casey loses the contest when he offers cocoa to a shivering Santa. The power of Christmas is reaffirmed when moments later, Marianne returns to reward Casey's kindness with a date. RECOMMENDATION: The teenagers are likable, although slightly dated; the beauty queen could be changed to a rock or television star. This is a light weight comedy with opportunities for tongue in cheek humor. ROYALTY: NA. SOURCE: Boiko, Claire. (1988). Cool Casey's Christmas. Franklin, OH: Eldridge Pub. Co. SUBJECTS/PLAY TYPE: Christmas; Dating; Santa Claus; Comedy.

632. 5-12. (+) Gleason, William & Leslie, Diane. **The coolest cat in town.** CAST: 3f, 6m, Su. ACTS: 2. SETTINGS: School dance; park bench. PLAYING TIME: NA. PLOT: Junior Bumpers wants to be a rock musician but his parents are strongly opposed because Junior's uncle mysteriously disappeared at the peak of his musical career. The uncle's frozen body is discovered during a high school prom. A "frigidologist" is brought in to thaw the body, and Junior and Uncle Billy Dee pair up to find superstardom. RECOMMENDATION: This is a fun production and students will identify with the conflict between Junior and his parents over his choice not to go to college. ROYALTY: Upon application. SOURCE: Gleason, William, & Leslie, Diane. (1979). The coolest cat in town. Chicago, IL: Dramatic Pub. Co. SUBJECTS/PLAY TYPE: Careers; Rock Musical; Drama.

633. 4-7. (+) Deverell, Rex. **The Copetown city kite crisis.** CAST: 4f, 3m. ACTS: 1. SETTINGS: Town square. PLAYING TIME: NA. PLOT: Residents of Copetown discover that its economic base, the town kite factory, is creating a pollution problem. They must decide which is more important: a clean environment or financial stability. RECOMMENDATION: In this thought provoking play, the characters have to evaluate their lifestyles and how it effects their environment. The play is also recommended for its dramatization of the decision making processes. ROYALTY: NA. SOURCE: Deverell, Rex. (1980). Kids plays: Six Canadian plays for children. Toronto, Canada: Playwrights Press, Inc. SUBJECTS/PLAY TYPE: Science; Environment; Decision Making; Drama.

634. 9-12. (+) Truss, Jan. **Cornelius dragon.** CAST: 2f, 2m, Su. ACTS: 1. SETTINGS: Bare stage, props. PLAYING TIME: NA. PLOT: Cornelius Horatio Dragon, a first generation Canadian embarrassed by his European immigrant parents, runs away, assuming the ordinary name of Jim Black. He is robbed and used as a clown in the circus. His circus friends heckle an oddly dressed Arathusa and ask Cornelius to help throw her out. Instead, Cornelius affirms his identity and joins Arathusa as the two travel "home." RECOMMENDATION: This is an excellent portrayal of the loneliness and self hate that many immigrants feel as they try to assimilate into a new culture. With symbolism, as well as brutal honesty, the drama poignantly shows one adolescent's painful attempts to forge his own identity. This might be especially useful as part of a unit about cultural pride, or as part of a unit dealing with the immigrants to this country during and

after World War II. Some swearing might have to be changed, and some acrobatic ability is also required. ROYALTY: NA. SOURCE: Doolittle, Joyce. (1984). Eight plays for young people. Edmonton, Canada: NeWest Pub. SUBJECTS/PLAY TYPE: Identity; Immigrants; Drama.

635. 9-12. (+) Miranda, Julian E. **Cornerstone of civil rights. CAST:** 4f, 13m, Su. **ACTS:** 1. **SETTINGS:** Meeting room. **PLAYING TIME:** 20 min. **PLOT:** At a meeting in Jamestown (1619), English settlers discuss rights for Englishmen exclusively. Jamestown settlers from other nations insist on their rights and refuse to work until they are granted. Without shipbuilders, carpenters, glassmakers, and other artisans, the English cannot survive. They grant the immigrants civil rights, just as the first ships of black slaves arrive. **RECOMMENDATION:** This effectively presents, at a child's level of comprehension, the paradox of the early settlers who, while insisting on their own freedoms, began a system of inequalities from which we still suffer. A reference to the early slaves who didn't fight against their captivity could be deleted to more accurately represent their predicament. **ROYALTY:** Free to Plays subscribers. **SOURCE:** Miranda, Julian E. (1975, March). The cornerstone of civil rights. Plays: The Drama Magazine for Young People, pp. 31. **SUBJECTS/PLAY TYPE:** Civil Rights; Playlet.

636. 10-12. (+) Majeski, Bill. **Corn's-a-poppin'. CAST:** 10f, 8m, 8u. **ACTS:** 2. **SETTINGS:** Gym. **PLAYING TIME:** 90 min. **PLOT:** A group of theater students hope to solve Venerable University's money troubles by staging **Romeo and Juliet**. They rehearse in the gym, which has also been rented to a therapy group. Characters from the two groups have odd interactions, and unlikely coincidences save the school. **RECOMMENDATION:** Recommended for a large cast mostly interested in having fun, the plot is silly but fast paced. **ROYALTY:** $25. **SOURCE:** Majeski, Bill. (1981). Corn's-a-poppin'. Denver, CO: Pioneer Drama Service. **SUBJECTS/PLAY TYPE:** College Life; Therapy Groups; Comedy.

637. 10-12. (+) Moon, Gerald. **Corpse! CAST:** 1f, 3m. **ACTS:** 2. **SETTINGS:** Two apartments. **PLAYING TIME:** NA. **PLOT:** Destitute, Evelyn Farrant contracts to kill Rupert, heir to the Farrant fortune, and take his place. Through a series of plot twists, it is discovered that Major Powell is actually Evelyn and Rupert's father, a criminal who deserted their mother. Evelyn is revealed to be insane, with plans to kill both brother and father. Evelyn fences with and kills his father minutes before the arrival of a constable, who discovers Major Powell's body hidden in a cupboard. **RECOMMENDATION:** This clever play requires a talented lead actor since he will actually play two parts, one of which is an actor playing two parts. Evelyn must deliver several long speeches; many are quotes from Shakespeare's plays. He also hints quite broadly that he is gay or bisexual. The staging could be complicated as the author suggests a revolving stage to accommodate many scene changes. For an experienced theater department, this offers a showcase

for a gifted lead actor and a challenge to a backstage crew. ROYALTY: $50. SOURCE: Moon, Gerald. (1985). Corpse! London, England: Samuel French. SUBJECTS/PLAY TYPE: Twins; Murder; Comedy; Thriller.

638. 3-8. (+) Kehret, Peg. **Cotton candy. CAST:** 1u. **ACTS:** 1. **SETTINGS:** None. **PLAYING TIME:** NA. **PLOT:** A youngster humorously expounds on the various ways to eat cotton candy, and offers several cautions. **RECOMMENDATION:** Amusingly written, this simple piece will evoke chuckles from any carnival sweet fancier. **ROYALTY:** NA. **SOURCE:** Kehret, Peg. (1986). Winning monologs for young actors. Colorado Springs, CO: Meriwether Pub. **SUBJECTS/PLAY TYPE:** Candy; Monologue.

639. 9-12. (-) Snee, Dennis. (Stoker, Bram) **The count will rise again or Dracula in Dixie.** (Dracula) **CAST:** 5f, 6m. **ACTS:** 2. **SETTINGS:** Sitting room. **PLAYING TIME:** NA. **PLOT:** Count Dracula visits the South where he brings two beautiful belles under his spell. An assortment of Southern gentlemen attempt to foil the vampire, who is finally defeated when he kills himself rather than acquiesce to the man hungry female sheriff. **RECOMMENDATION:** Most of the characters are stereotypes, and a good deal of the dialogue consists of one liners. Neither plot nor humor is strong enough to sustain the play through two acts. **ROYALTY:** $40. **SOURCE:** Snee, Dennis. (1980). The count will rise again or Dracula in Dixie. Boston, MA: Baker's Plays. **SUBJECTS/PLAY TYPE:** Comedy; Horror; Adaptation.

640. 9-12. (+) Nelson, Ken & Dyville, Jack. (Dickens, Charles) **A country Christmas carol.** (A Christmas carol) **CAST:** 11f, 15m, Su. **ACTS:** 2. **SETTINGS:** Saloon; office. **PLAYING TIME:** 90 min. **PLOT:** In this Westernized version of Dickens' classic, "Greedy and Rotten" Scrooge is a rich bad guy with an office above Sadie Sasparilla's Saloon. He has treated everyone badly since he inherited the business from Boss Marley. The Ghost of Boss Marley returns and with help, acts out scenes from Christmas past, present, and future, reforming Scrooge. At the end, Belle marries the new Scrooge, who helps the Crachit family. **RECOMMENDATION:** Even though this resorts to silly cowboy stereotypes and outrageous Western drawl, it is amusing. **ROYALTY:** $35. **SOURCE:** Nelson, Ken. (1985). A country Christmas carol. Schulenbug, TX: I.E. Clark, Inc. **SUBJECTS/PLAY TYPE:** Christmas; Musical; Adaptation.

641. 10-12. (+) Kelly, Tim J. **Country gothic. CAST:** 9f, 5m, Su. **ACTS:** 1. **SETTINGS:** Meeting house. **PLAYING TIME:** NA. **PLOT:** A young bridegroom comes to an isolated farming community on his wedding day, only to discover that he is intended as a human sacrifice to insure a good crop. **RECOMMENDATION:** This begins with a cozy scene from American country life, and is shockingly transformed into a scene of betrayal and death. The shock is effective, though the violence of the ending may be considered excessive by some. **ROYALTY:** $15. **SOURCE:** Kelly, Tim J. (1977). Country

gothic. Boston, MA: Baker's Plays. **SUBJECTS/PLAY TYPE:** Country; Human Sacrifice; Horror.

642. K-4. (+) Carlson, Bernice Wells. **The country mouse and the city mouse. CAST:** 5u. **ACTS:** 1. **SETTINGS:** Woods. **PLAYING TIME:** 10 min. **PLOT:** A country and city mouse visit each other, and both decide they prefer their own habitats. **RECOMMENDATION:** "What's good for you may be misery for someone else" is once again effectively dramatized in this familiar tale. **ROYALTY:** NA. **SOURCE:** Carlson, Bernice Wells. (1982). Let's find the big idea. Nashville, TN: Abingdon. **SUBJECTS/PLAY TYPE:** Fable; Skit.

643. 3-5. (+) Gotwalt, Helen Louise Miller. **The country store cat. CAST:** 6f, 5m, 15u. **ACTS:** 1. **SETTINGS:** Store. **PLAYING TIME:** NA. **PLOT:** A storekeeper tries to get rid of his cat because it cannot catch the mice which ravage the store supplies. Two children discover that the cat is too nearsighted to catch the mice and provide it with glasses. **RECOMMENDATION:** This nostalgic, humorous piece cleverly uses music and a talking cat to entertain and teach the qualities inherent in a "country store." **ROYALTY:** Free to Plays subscribers. **SOURCE:** Gotwalt, Helen Louise Miller. (1985). First plays for children. Boston, MA: Plays, Inc. **SUBJECTS/PLAY TYPE:** Cats; Musical.

644. 9-12. (+) Jones, Carolyn. **Coup d'etat. CAST:** 2f, 8m, 12u. **ACTS:** 1. **SETTINGS:** Office; living room. **PLAYING TIME:** NA. **PLOT:** A revolution in the Central American country of St. Passis will adversely affect the lives of Juan and his family by eliminating his father's job. To save the family, Juan goes to the capital where the revolution has been quelled and the king has returned to his throne to hear a series of zany reorganization options. As the play closes, Juan is in control. **RECOMMENDATION:** The play is a satire of Latin American politics, with the characters all stereotypes. The audience needs to be knowledgeable enough in world politics to understand the satire. **ROYALTY:** NA. **SOURCE:** Lamb, Wendy. (1987). The ground zero club and other prize winning plays. New York, NY: Dell Pub. Co. Inc. **SUBJECTS/PLAY TYPE:** Politics; Revolution; Satire.

645. K-8. (+) Olfson, Lewy. **A couple of right smart fellers. CAST:** 4m. **ACTS:** 1. **SETTINGS:** Yard. **PLAYING TIME:** 12 min. **PLOT:** Two brothers live in the country and outsmart a couple of city dwellers who try to purchase a valuable chair for a trifling sum. **RECOMMENDATION:** Zeke and Zack's cleverness is both surprising and humorous; their fake naivete will make audiences roll with laughter. **ROYALTY:** Free to Plays subscribers. **SOURCE:** Olfson, Lewy. (1983, May). A couple of right smart fellers. Plays: The Drama Magazine for Young People, pp. 37-42. **SUBJECTS/PLAY TYPE:** Swindlers and Swindling; Comedy.

646. 9-12. (+) Graczyk, Ed. (Crane, Stephen) **Courage. (The red badge of courage) CAST:** 1f, 8m, Su.

ACTS: 2. **SETTINGS:** Bare stage, props. **PLAYING TIME:** NA. **PLOT:** A young man, poised between childhood and adulthood, enlists in the army. In the first battle he runs away, but he becomes a hero during the second skirmish. **RECOMMENDATION:** To present its message about maturing, this adaptation has the young man talk and argue with his conscience and the devious part of his soul, represented by the boy. Much of the setting and atmosphere of battle is accomplished by shining slides of toy soldiers and battle scenes on the backdrop, making production a challenge to the actors rather than the stage crew. **ROYALTY:** NA. **SOURCE:** Jennings, Coleman A. & Berghammer, Gretta. (1986). Theatre for youth: Twelve plays with mature themes. Austin, TX: Univ. of Texas Press. **SUBJECTS/PLAY TYPE:** Manhood; War; Adaptation.

647. 4-6. (+) Chaloner, Gwen. **The court of King Arithmetic. CAST:** 5f, 8m, 10u. **ACTS:** 1. **SETTINGS:** Throne room. **PLAYING TIME:** 25 min. **PLOT:** Two children destroy their math homework and are brought before the king for punishment. The court decides to remove numbers from their lives, but only after their value has been shown. When they realize how important numbers are, the children agree to make arithmetic their best friend. **RECOMMENDATION:** This would be excellent for a math class as it attempts to answer the eternal question of "What good is math for me?" It is not patronizing, ends satisfactorily and even teaches a bit about the mechanics of arithmetic calculations. **ROYALTY:** Free to Plays subscribers. **SOURCE:** Chaloner, Gwen. (1977, April). The court of King Arithmetic. Plays: The Drama Magazine for Young People, pp. 57-62. **SUBJECTS/PLAY TYPE:** Arithmetic; Skit.

648. 7-12. (+) Bucci, Mark. (Cameron, Eleanor) **The court of the stone children. CAST:** 9f, 4m. **ACTS:** 2. **SETTINGS:** Courtyard; apartment. **PLAYING TIME:** NA. **PLOT:** Lonely Nina becomes involved with a 19th century French family through paintings of it in a San Francisco museum. She helps the curator solve a mystery involving the mistaken identity of one of the painting's characters and subsequent present day confusion about historical events surrounding the family. **RECOMMENDATION:** This quiet, intellectual play has enough mystery to create tension and keep the audience interested, although it may be a bit too long for one sitting. The parts are expandable for larger casts. **ROYALTY:** $35. **SOURCE:** Bucci, Mark. (1978). The court of the stone children. Chicago, IL: Dramatic Pub. Co. **SUBJECTS/PLAY TYPE:** Friendship; Mystery; Time Travel; Drama.

649. 8-12. (+) Nolan, Paul T. **The Courters. CAST:** 1f, 5m. **ACTS:** 1. **SETTINGS:** City square. **PLAYING TIME:** 25 min. **PLOT:** Flavio and Isabella are afraid they can't marry because their guardians are planning to marry, leaving Flavio without an inheritance and Isabella without a dowry. Flavio and a friend discourage the guardians from marrying, pitting one against the other, and arranging for each to make a fool of himself in front of the other. The older generation joins the wedding

party for Flavio and Isabella. RECOMMENDATION: The foolishness of the two older men seems a bit contrived, yet the play examines the nature of pride and the nature of people effectively. ROYALTY: None for amateur performances. SOURCE: Nolan, Paul T. (1982). Folk tale plays round the world: A collection of royalty-free one-act plays about lands far and near. Boston, MA: Plays, Inc. SUBJECTS/PLAY TYPE: Marriage; Pride; Comedy; Comedia dell'Arte, Italian.

650. 7-12. (+) Muschell, David. **The courtesy chip.** CAST: 9f, 9m. ACTS: 3. SETTINGS: Street; living room; business office. PLAYING TIME: NA. PLOT: Sam Marko, operator of a successful futuristic grocery business, has been robbed by two Biomats, human looking robots. Sam is not fond of Biomats until he encounters a female, Mary Forten. Sam marries Mary but they are the target of public censure that hurts Sam's business. Although Sam and Mary try selling Biomats, they decide to return to the grocery business. RECOMMENDATION: The complex themes dealing with love, prejudice, and technology will appeal to more mature students, and the roles within the play can easily be switched to either sex, with the possibility of doubling several characters. ROYALTY: $35. SOURCE: Muschell, David. (1987). The courtesy chip. Franklin, OH: Eldridge Pub. Co. SUBJECTS/PLAY TYPE: Fantasy; Science Fiction; Drama.

651. 10-12. (+) Foote, Horton. **Courtship.** CAST: 5f, 3m. ACTS: 1. SETTINGS: Veranda; music/sitting room. PLAYING TIME: NA. PLOT: The efforts of two daughters to understand their family are frustrating because their parents try to insulate them from the realities of adult relationships. The daughters resist the parents' inability to adjust to change with tactics that the powerless have always used when opposing the powerful: covert operations, including deception. RECOMMENDATION: An elegiac tone pervades as this looks back with love and forgiveness. Thus, no matter how thick and intractable the tension between controlling parent and freedom seeking young adult, one has a sense that the drama is part of a much larger pattern and that the characters, despite this brief struggle, will adapt and be absorbed into the larger history of the family. The message is positive: beyond the sorrow is survival; even an individual's death is assimilated into the communality of the whole. ROYALTY: $50. SOURCE: Foote, Horton. (1984). Courtship. New York, NY: Dramatists Play Service. SUBJECTS/PLAY TYPE: Courtship; Parenting; Drama.

652. 1-6. (+) Bealmear, J.H. **The covetous councilman.** CAST: 2f, 2m. ACTS: 1. SETTINGS: House. PLAYING TIME: 15 min. PLOT: After leaving their savings with a councilman for safekeeping, a carpenter and his wife are swindled. The mayor's wife overhears their pleadings and, in disguise, she pretends to consider leaving some jewels in his care when the couple reappears to ask for their money again. To show his trustworthiness before the second woman, the councilman returns the money. She then reveals her identity, and announces that she will tell her husband of

his activities, and he will not be promoted. RECOMMENDATION: This charming story teaches the value of honesty. While younger children will enjoy watching, the acting and production will have to be left to an older group, due to the length of the dialogue. ROYALTY: NA. SOURCE: Kamerman, Sylvia E. (1987). Plays from favorite folk tales. Boston, MA: Plays, Inc. SUBJECTS/PLAY TYPE: Folk Tale Motifs; Honesty; Playlet.

653. 4-8. (+) Hearn, Sneed. **The cowboys' birthday bash.** CAST: 3f, 3m. ACTS: 1. SETTINGS: Living room. PLAYING TIME: NA. PLOT: Mrs. Woods, her daughter, and Daphne, the school teacher, prepare for the annual cowboys' birthday party. After the party begins, the Sheriff arrests the outlaw, mean Windy Billy, for bank robbery. One of the gang proves that Billy could not have robbed the bank since he was handing out presents at an orphans' party at the time of the robbery. Billy decides his mean reputation has been ruined and he can no longer lead the gang. He becomes a school teacher and marries Mrs. Woods' daughter. Daphne takes over as gang leader, becoming Dangerous Daphne. RECOMMENDATION: Young play viewers who delight in silliness will enjoy this hilarious horse opera, though actors of at least junior high school age will have the greatest success with the "hammed up" comedy. ROYALTY: $25. SOURCE: Hearn, Sneed. (1987). The cowboys' birthday bash. Franklin, OH: Eldridge Pub. Co. SUBJECTS/PLAY TYPE: Western; Birthdays; Comedy.

654. 7-12. (-) Huff, Betty Tracy. **Cracker barrel circus.** CAST: 10f, 7m, Su. ACTS: 1. SETTINGS: General store. PLAYING TIME: 30 min. PLOT: Sebastian Skinflindt, the meanest man in town, attempts to foreclose mortgages on the heroine's farm and on the Prancing Sisters' Circus. With the help of Clyde Cumbersome, Skinflindt's employee, the circus performers perform in Skinflindt's store to raise money for the mortgages. While trying to stop the show, Skinflindt accidentally reveals that the mortgages are illegal and the day is saved. RECOMMENDATION: This comedy-satire has more cliches than genuine humor. The complex staging would present problems. ROYALTY: Free to Plays subscribers. SOURCE: Huff, Betty Tracy. (1975, December). Cracker barrel circus. Plays: The Drama Magazine for Young People, pp. 1-12. SUBJECTS/PLAY TYPE: Mortgages; Swindlers and Swindling; Comedy.

655. 7-12. (+) Kelly, Tim. (Wells, H. G) **Crazy, mixed-up island of Dr. Moreau.** (The island of Dr. Moreau) CAST: 9f, 5m, Su. ACTS: 1. SETTINGS: Lobby. PLAYING TIME: 25 min. PLOT: Dr. Moreau, a mad scientist, turns animals into half animal/half people creatures. He is visited by four shipwrecked show business people, who take to the creatures and invite them to go into show business. The beast-people gladly accept, and escape with the show people on a mail boat. RECOMMENDATION: This parody has a few well timed lines, and the visual effect of the beast people's animal mannerisms could be amusing. Many of the

jokes are corny and rely on puns. ROYALTY: $15. SOURCE: Kelly, Tim. (1977). Crazy, mixed-up island of Dr. Moreau. Boston, MA: Baker's Plays. SUBJECTS/PLAY TYPE: Parody; Science Fiction; Comedy.

656. 7-12. (+) Booth, Richard. **The creature in the crawlspace. CAST:** 4f, 6m, 2u. **ACTS:** 3. **SETTINGS:** Living room; laboratory. **PLAYING TIME:** NA. **PLOT:** The Clervals move into the isolated estate left by their scientist brother and experience vampires and murders. The "dead" brother, disfigured by experiments, is really living under the floor and appears just in time to save his little daughter. In the ensuing fight the vampire vanishes in smoke and the creature dies. All seems well until a few days later on Halloween, when another murder is committed and a new boarder arrives at the estate, Mr. Canis Lupus, the werewolf. **RECOMMENDATION:** Despite a weak ending, this is intriguing, due to its broad use of special effects. Production should be left to older high school students or adults. However, younger high schoolers will appreciate this accurate vampire drama, with its frequent references to Bram Stoker's classic. **ROYALTY:** $35. **SOURCE:** Booth, Richard. (1988). The creature in the crawlspace. Franklin, OH: Eldridge Pub. Co. **SUBJECTS/PLAY TYPE:** Vampires; Horror; Monsters; Drama.

657. 7-9*. (+) De Long, J.R. **The creep show. CAST:** 9f, 14m, 5u. **ACTS:** 2. **SETTINGS:** Movie theater. **PLAYING TIME:** NA. **PLOT:** Aunt Kadittlehopper accompanies six teenagers to an old horror movie, where they all enter the movie screen. They encounter Kernal Hybrid, who has an insane plan to steal all the popcorn in the world and replace it with his Jumbo Pop. Auntie recognizes him as her suitor of 50 years earlier, and ruins his plans by insisting that they marry. The teenagers find themselves back in the theater, wondering if they were dreaming, when Auntie walks down the aisle with the Kernal. **RECOMMENDATION:** Although a junior high audience may enjoy this corny, pun filled comedy, they will be unable to fulfill the setting, costuming, and special effect requirements. An adult group should manage the actual production. **ROYALTY:** $35. **SOURCE:** De Long, J.R. (1988). The creep show. Franklin, OH: Eldridge Pub. Co. **SUBJECTS/PLAY TYPE:** Mystery; Comedy.

658. 9-12. (-) Jackson, Richard Eugene. **The creepy castle hassle. CAST:** 6f, 6m. **ACTS:** 3. **SETTINGS:** Castle interior. **PLAYING TIME:** NA. **PLOT:** Professor Valkenstein and his students get lost in Scotland's countryside and are refused accommodations in a castle owned by Dr. Zono, a "mad" German scientist. Two students enter anyway and get lost in the secret rooms of the castle. The others return to find them, while Inspector Donally and Sergeant Abernathy show up to investigate grave robberies. These have been committed by Igor, a servant, and Mrs. Potter, the housekeeper, to provide subjects for Dr. Zono, who now wants the live brain juices of the two lost students for his research. Mrs. Potter is murdered and all must remain until the crime is solved. Igor is accidentally given some of Dr. Zono's

brain juices, making him smarter. He reveals Dr. Zono's plans and admits to killing Mrs. Potter, who was often cruel to him. **RECOMMENDATION:** Although this has character and possibilities, it is marred by gratuitous sexual stereotyping throughout. **ROYALTY:** $40. **SOURCE:** Jackson, Richard Eugene. (1975). The creepy castle hassle. Elgin, IL: Performance Pub. Co. **SUBJECTS/PLAY TYPE:** Castles; Mystery; Mad Scientists; Comedy.

659. 4-12. (-) Gilfond, Henry. **A crisis in the newspaper office. CAST:** 7u. **ACTS:** 1. **SETTINGS:** Office. **PLAYING TIME:** 15 min. **PLOT:** The school newspaper staff discusses whether or not to write editorials about the candidates for the upcoming mayoral election. They decide they are too young to presume to know about politics and instead, write about the need for adults to vote and their willingness to help adults get to the polls. **RECOMMENDATION:** The students "cop out" here, as they become the seen, but not heard, children of the past. **ROYALTY:** None. **SOURCE:** Gilfond, Henry. (1985). Holiday plays for reading. New York, NY: Walker. **SUBJECTS/PLAY TYPE:** Election Day; Voting; Playlet.

660. 3-6. (+) Fisher, Aileen. **Crispus Attucks. CAST:** Su. **ACTS:** 1. **SETTINGS:** None. **PLAYING TIME:** NA. **PLOT:** This recounts the history of Crispus Attucks, who escaped from slavery and became a seaman. In 1770 Boston, fighting against British enforcement of the stamp tax laws, he became the first black to die fighting for American Independence. **RECOMMENDATION:** This valuable poem enlightens young people about the role Black Americans played in America's fight for independence. With much room for artistic license, this could easily be incorporated into a larger production. **ROYALTY:** NA. **SOURCE:** Kamerman, Sylvia E. (1987). Plays of Black Americans: Episodes from the Black experience in America, dramatized for young people. Boston, MA: Plays, Inc. **SUBJECTS/PLAY TYPE:** Black Americans; Boston Massacre; Attucks, Crispus; Choral Reading.

661. K-4. (+) Boiko, Claire. **The crocus who couldn't bloom. CAST:** 9f, 10m. **ACTS:** 1. **SETTINGS:** Garden. **PLAYING TIME:** 20 min. **PLOT:** The precise pageantry of nature is revealed as Mother and Father Nature perform their autumn chores. The final autumn chore is planting the Crocus, whose sprouting will announce the arrival of Spring. Gertie, the human gardener, is needed to rescue Crocus from the grip of a deadly weed. Spring proceeds according to plan, covering the earth with flowers and butterflies, symbolically portraying a message of rebirth and new life. **RECOMMENDATION:** Young audiences will admire the drive and purpose of the creatures of nature, recognize the value of these characteristics in human beings as well, and extend the evident need for teamwork to their own environments. **ROYALTY:** None. **SOURCE:** Boiko, Claire. (1985). Children's plays for creative actors. Boston, MA: Plays, Inc. **SUBJECTS/PLAY TYPE:** Spring; Seasons; Playlet.

662. 7-12. (+) Bennett, Gordon. **The crooked town.**
CAST: 3u. ACTS: 1. SETTINGS: Bare stage. PLAYING
TIME: 12 min. PLOT: A peddler gives an ugly, crooked
town two gifts: a mirror, with which the people can
improve themselves; and a kazoo, with whose music they
can find happiness. The action is interpreted religiously.
RECOMMENDATION: This has well-paced lines and
would be a valuable church performance. ROYALTY:
None. SOURCE: Altena, Hans. (1978). The playbook for
christian theatre. Grand Rapids, MI: Baker Book House.
SUBJECTS/PLAY TYPE: Morality; Reader's Theater.

663. 7-12. (+) Hamlett, Christina. **Cross purposes.**
CAST: 2f, 2m. ACTS: 1. SETTINGS: Living room.
PLAYING TIME: 30 min. PLOT: Two brothers, Eric and
Milo (who is a vampire) meet Eric's fiance and her
mother. Milo explains his eccentric behavior by claiming
to be an actor. RECOMMENDATION: This delightful
comedy, in which the characteristics of vampires are
humorously revealed through the character's dialogue
and actions, will be a treasure to perform. It ends with
Eric wondering whether his children will be human or
vampire. ROYALTY: Free to Plays subscribers.
SOURCE: Hamlett, Christina. (1983, April). Cross
purposes. Plays: The Drama Magazine for Young People,
pp. 25-33. SUBJECTS/PLAY TYPE: Vampires; Comedy.

664. K-6*. (+) Way, Brian. **The crossroads. CAST:**
3f, 3m. ACTS: 2. SETTINGS: Crossroad with a signpost.
PLAYING TIME: 50 min. PLOT: An old tramp is
studying the signpost at a crossroad, when the Spirit of
the Signpost asks him to help her protect the crossroad
from the Mighty Monster of the West, the Proud Bird of
the East, the Queen of the North, and the Scientist of the
South, all of whom would like to control the world. To
ensure peace, the tramp must get the instruments of
power from each. He is successful and they all live in
harmony. RECOMMENDATION: This is more
concerned with the mechanism by which the tramp
succeeds in obtaining a part of each of the warring
protagonists than it is with universal messages or
themes. It demands a great deal of audience
participation, so should be staged by adults or young
adults for small groups of children. ROYALTY: $40.
SOURCE: Way, Brian. (1977). The crossroads. Boston,
MA: Baker's Plays. SUBJECTS/PLAY TYPE: Ethics;
Human Behavior; Peace; Participation Play.

665. 2-4. (+) Carlson, Bernice Wells. **Crowded?**
CAST: 2f, 2m, 4u. ACTS: 1. SETTINGS: Room.
PLAYING TIME: 7 min. PLOT: When a farmer's wife
complains that the room is too small for her to rock their
baby to sleep, the Rabbi first sends all of the farm
animals in and then removes them, so the couple can
see how much space they really have.
RECOMMENDATION: Children will enjoy this
favorite classic in which the audience is invited to state
the moral of the play at the end. ROYALTY: None.
SOURCE: Carlson, Bernice Wells. (1982). Let's find the
big idea. Nashville, TN: Abingdon Press.
SUBJECTS/PLAY TYPE: Folk Tales, Jewish; Fable.

666. 4-6. (-) Boiko, Claire. **The crowning of Miss
Primavera.** CAST: 13f, 9m, 2u. ACTS: 1. SETTINGS:
Auditorium. PLAYING TIME: 25 min. PLOT: A
Bluebird, the Chickadee family, and four cheerleaders
gather for the crowning of Miss Primavera, the most
Spring-like month. At the end of the competition, Miss
Primavera is crowned by Superspring, a Batman like
hero. All gather to sing to Miss Primavera.
RECOMMENDATION: Most children will find the
thin plot too silly to be interesting. This may also be
difficult to stage as it calls for a cast of 24, and it is
necessary for cast members to sing. ROYALTY: Free to
Plays subscribers. SOURCE: Boiko, Claire. (1979, April).
The crowning of Miss Primavera. Plays: The Drama
Magazine for Young People, pp. 49-53.
SUBJECTS/PLAY TYPE: Spring; Musical; Comedy.

667. 3-5. (+) Boiko, Claire. **Crunch, the energy-
eating dragon. CAST:** 2f, 5m, Su. ACTS: 1. SETTINGS:
Throne room. PLAYING TIME: NA. PLOT: The royal
kingdom is threatened by Crunch, a dragon who feeds on
energy power. The royal janitor saves the kingdom by
shrinking the dragon and requiring an energy diet for
both the palace and the dragon.
RECOMMENDATION: This clever and humorous
lead-in to a study of energy conservation can be
produced simply in a classroom with many students
participating. ROYALTY: Free to Plays subscribers.
SOURCE: Boiko, Claire. (1979, November). Crunch, the
energy-eating dragon. Plays: The Drama Magazine for
Young People, pp. 31-37. SUBJECTS/PLAY TYPE:
Energy Conservation; Dragons; Comedy.

668. 7-9. (+) Sawyer-Young, Kat. **Crush. CAST:** 2f.
ACTS: 1. SETTINGS: Outside school. PLAYING TIME:
NA. PLOT: After school, two girls talk about a boy whose
eyes remind them of Elvis Presley, even though Elvis
makes them both sick. They suggest possible names for
the boy's R initial and giggle about being married to him,
while wondering if he is already married.
RECOMMENDATION: This is an excellent portrayal
of how girls talk about boys. One section, with sexual
overtones, may be inappropriate. ROYALTY: NA.
SOURCE: Sawyer-Young, Kat. (1986). Contemporary
scenes for contemporary kids. Boston, MA: Baker's Plays.
SUBJECTS/PLAY TYPE: Infatuation; Love; Scene.

669. 7-12. (+) Higbee, Rand. **CRUSH! CAST:** 4f, 2m,
2u. ACTS: 1. SETTINGS: Library. PLAYING TIME: NA.
PLOT: Tom, a college freshman, daydreams about
Rhonda, a library clerk, as he spends his Friday night in
the library studying. When Tom finally decides to ask
Rhonda out, she has gone off duty.
RECOMMENDATION: Up-to-date language and
modern situations make this lighthearted comedy
realistic. It has several fight scenes with one including
mock gun play. ROYALTY: $30. SOURCE: Higbee,
Rand. (1988). Crush! Franklin, OH: Eldridge Pub. Co.
SUBJECTS/PLAY TYPE: Dating; Comedy.

670. 9-12. (+) Kelly, Tim. **Cry of the banshee. CAST:**
8f, 5m, Su. ACTS: 3. SETTINGS: Isolated estate.

PLAYING TIME: 120 min. PLOT: Since the 1500s, the Whitman family has been under a curse in which, every 100 years, a banshee wails and another Whitman dies. Family members, friends, a parapsychologist, and a detective gather at Whitman Manor to hear the banshee's wail. The niece is found dead in the wine cellar, and the amusingly bumbling private eye and the observant ghost hunter solve the mystery, explaining that the family horse trainer is an ancient spirit under the spell of a gypsy. The power of love proves stronger than the power of hate and the spirit of the curse disappears. RECOMMENDATION: The plot is predictable and the characters too stereotyped to sustain the suspense, but the characters are so excessive that the dialogue and action lend themselves to the caricature of melodrama. ROYALTY: $35. SOURCE: Kelly, Tim. (1977). Cry of the banshee. Denver, CO: Pioneer Drama Service. SUBJECTS/PLAY TYPE: Mystery; Melodrama.

671. 7-12. (+) Martens, Anne Coulter. **A cue for Cleopatra.** CAST: 6f, 6m, Su. ACTS: 1. SETTINGS: Stage. PLAYING TIME: 35 min. PLOT: A high school student mistakes a grouchy old woman's car for that of his girlfriend's and is caught driving it. In order to hide from the old woman, he puts on the Cleopatra costume being used in a play. A comical version of **Antony and Cleopatra** ensues, following which the old woman apologizes for not believing the boy's story, and agrees to help the school by selling them some of her land so they can enlarge the baseball field. RECOMMENDATION: Although the old woman is horribly stereotyped, and the high schoolers use some outdated slang, the campy **Antony and Cleopatra** redeems this. The director may need to rewrite some of the dialogue. ROYALTY: Free to Plays subscribers. SOURCE: Martens, Anne Coulter. (1983, April). A cue for Cleopatra. Plays: The Drama Magazine for Young People, pp. 13-24. SUBJECTS/PLAY TYPE: Theater; Comedy.

672. 8-12. (+) Callanan, Cecelia C. **Cupid and Company.** CAST: 2f, 2m. ACTS: 2. SETTINGS: Office. PLAYING TIME: 20 min. PLOT: The office of Cupid and Company is visited separately by each member of a couple who seeks to buy insurance on their romantic relationship. They run into each other at the insurance office and decide they are so right for one another no policy is needed. RECOMMENDATION: The premise of insurance for love is no more disturbing than the premise of insurance for death. This is a well-done analogy, although it is a bit cruel to insurance agents, who are portrayed as heartless and exploitive. ROYALTY: Free to Plays subscribers. SOURCE: Callanan, Cecelia C. (1986, January). Cupid and Company. Plays: The Drama Magazine for Young People, pp. 21-26. SUBJECTS/PLAY TYPE: Valentine's Day; Insurance; Satire.

673. 7-12. (-) Martens, Anne Coulter. **The cupid computer.** CAST: 6f, 6m, 6u. ACTS: 1. SETTINGS: Hall; classroom. PLAYING TIME: 25 min. PLOT: A math teacher and several students at one high school program a computer to make matches with students from another high school for the Valentine's Dance. A student

changes the program and dates are mismatched. After several humorous mixups, the students go to the dance and have a great time. RECOMMENDATION: The computer technology used in the play is dated, the humor is condescending, and the dialogue is not believable. ROYALTY: Free to Plays subscribers. SOURCE: Martens, Anne Coulter. (1984, January/February). The cupid computer. Plays: A Drama Magazine for Young People, pp. 1-12. SUBJECTS/PLAY TYPE: Valentine's Day; Computer Dating; Comedy.

674. 1-6. (+) Fisher, Aileen Lucia. **Cupid in earmuffs.** CAST: 6f, 2m, 7u. ACTS: 1. SETTINGS: Schoolyard. PLAYING TIME: NA. PLOT: On Valentine's Day, Cupid cannot bring enough love and friendship potion to earth because of all the heavy clothing he must wear, including a pair of heart shaped earmuffs. Things go well, however, until Margie and Pam become upset because they did not receive Valentines from each other. Cupid uses his heart shaped earmuffs to settle this most serious of problems. RECOMMENDATION: Cupid might need some help learning all the lines, but the rest of the parts are quite short. The parts of the helpers and the children could be split to create a small part for each child in a class. The director will need to offer an explanation of several items in the dialogue. ROYALTY: Free to Plays subscribers. SOURCE: Fisher, Aileen Lucia. (1985). Cupid in earmuffs. Year-round programs for young players. Boston, MA: Plays, Inc. SUBJECTS/PLAY TYPE: Valentine's Day; Cupid; Comedy.

675. 7-12. (+) Gotwalt, Helen Louise Miller. **Cupid on the loose.** CAST: 2f, 3m. ACTS: 1. SETTINGS: Park. PLAYING TIME: 20 min. PLOT: A grown-up tells Henry that he is Cupid and, when Henry demands proof, he shoots Sylvia with his slingshot, causing her to fall in love with Henry. The policeman who was called to arrest Cupid is then matched with his sweetheart by Cupid, and the couples leave as Cupid sings a song about his powers. RECOMMENDATION: The physical comedy, as the women are slingshot-struck, will delight youngsters, even if the rest of the play is a bit syrupy and dull. ROYALTY: Free to Plays subscribers. SOURCE: Gotwalt, Helen Louise Miller. (1982, January/February). Cupid on the loose. Plays: The Drama Magazine for Young People, pp. 25-32. SUBJECTS/PLAY TYPE: Valentine's Day; Cupid; Comedy.

676. 4-8. (+) Boiko, Claire. **Cupivac.** CAST: 6f, 10m, 8u. ACTS: 1. SETTINGS: Bare stage, backdrop. PLAYING TIME: 20 min. PLOT: An attempt at computer matchmaking mismatches all the famous applicants (i.e., Cleopatra and Scrooge, Snow White and the Jolly Green Giant). When Cupid pairs the computer technicians with Cinderella's wicked stepmother and stepsisters, the technicians quickly reverse their enthusiasm for computerized matchmaking and call for a reinstatement of Cupid's humanistic approach. RECOMMENDATION: This diatribe against computerized matchmaking will entertain the imaginative youngster with its absurd coupling of mythical and legendary figures. Youthful viewers can be

lead to explore the power of imagination, emotion, and empathy over convenience and practicality in building relationships. The names of local personages may be included to increase the absurdity of the contrived matches. ROYALTY: None. SOURCE: Boiko, Claire. (1985). Children's plays for creative actors. Boston, MA: Plays, Inc. SUBJECTS/PLAY TYPE: Love; Computer Dating; Comedy.

677. 1-6. (-) Gotwalt, Helen Louise Miller. **The curious quest.** CAST: 3f, 6m. ACTS: 1. SETTINGS: Living room. PLAYING TIME: 20 min. PLOT: Eight students are practicing a fairy tale play about what is valuable. When it doesn't ring true, they write another play about what is important to an American citizen, using the concept of weighing freedoms on the scales of justice. Freedom of speech, freedom of religion, and freedom to travel are all presented, but the scales are tipped by the right to vote. RECOMMENDATION: The exposition of our democratic freedoms is a laudable goal, but this drags in the beginning and continues to lose interest as the teenagers bore the audience with their work on their new production. ROYALTY: Free to Plays subscribers. SOURCE: Gotwalt, Helen Louise Miller. (1975, March). The curious quest. Plays: The Drama Magazine for Young People, pp. 61- 68. SUBJECTS/PLAY TYPE: Patriotism; Voting; Playlet.

678. 9-12. (+) Patrick, John. **The curious savage.** CAST: 6f, 5m. ACTS: 3. SETTINGS: Living room. PLAYING TIME: NA. PLOT: Mrs. Savage's insanely greedy stepchildren want the $10 million which she inherited from her husband. She wants to use the money to fulfill others' dreams and wishes. The children commit her to a sanitarium to obtain the money, but are foiled by the compassion and love the sanitarium residents feel for Mrs. Savage and each other. RECOMMENDATION: The gentle innocence of the residents is contrasted with the harshness of a world in which money is all important. The director will need to ensure that the action and players are not exaggerated for comedic effect, since personalities are more important here than comic relief. The final scene is a delightful fantasy, which, if carefully lighted, concludes the play with great poignancy. ROYALTY: $35. SOURCE: Patrick, John. (1979). The curious savage. New York, NY: Dramatist Play Service, Inc. SUBJECTS/PLAY TYPE: Greed; Drama.

679. 9-12. (+) Hamlett, Christina. **The curse of Cassandra.** CAST: 1f, 1m. ACTS: 1. SETTINGS: Living room. PLAYING TIME: 25 min. PLOT: This zany plot of love involves Wayne, his new and old girlfriends, and a "fortune-telling" computer date, Petra, who succeeds in sending Wayne back to Jamie, his old girlfriend, who always believed in him and supported him. RECOMMENDATION: A little far fetched at times, this is a comedic fantasy to which many can relate. ROYALTY: Free to Plays subscribers. SOURCE: Hamlett, Christina. (1985, January/February). The curse of Cassandra. Plays: The Drama Magazine for Young People, pp.17-24. SUBJECTS/PLAY TYPE: Fortune Telling; Romance; Computer Dating; Comedy.

680. 7-12. (-) Murray, John. **The curse of Demon Creek.** CAST: 6f, 5m. ACTS: 3. SETTINGS: Garage; shack. PLAYING TIME: 30 min. PLOT: Two cousins visit the gold mine which one of them inherited. The ghost of a deceased miner convinces one cousin to shoot the other, then kills the survivor. The ghost's wife kills the cousins' wives when they come looking for their husbands. After discovering the gold is actually fool's gold, the ghosts realize that their mine is safe forever. RECOMMENDATION: The plot here is not only predictable but it ploddingly repeats itself three times. ROYALTY: Free to Plays subscribers. SOURCE: Murray, John. (1984, January/ February). The curse of Demon Creek. Plays: The Drama Magazine for Young People, pp. 13- 25. SUBJECTS/PLAY TYPE: Ghost Story; Greed; Playlet.

681. 10-12. (+) Mulligan, Robert S. (Shelley, Mary) **The curse of Frankenstein.** (Frankenstein) CAST: 6f, 8m. ACTS: 1. SETTINGS: Drawing room. PLAYING TIME: NA. PLOT: In this spoof, the creature (a midget named Milo whose greatest problem is trying to reach his victims' necks) has already been created when the play begins. Reactions by the characters which are opposite to those in the original story bring about much of the humor. RECOMMENDATION: Similarities between this and Mel Brooks' **Young Frankenstein** abound, with this more silly and less satirical than the movie. Unfortunately, all the women act sex-starved. Attempts to adapt or edit these portrayals will be difficult since they are such a recurring theme, and leaving them as written may prove embarrassing or offensive. ROYALTY: $40. SOURCE: Mulligan, Robert S. (1985). The curse of Frankenstein. Boston, MA: Baker's Plays. SUBJECTS/PLAY TYPE: Satire; Comedy; Adaptation.

682. 8-10. (+) Gotwalt, Helen Louise Miller. **The curse of hag hollow.** CAST: 4f, 2m. ACTS: 1. SETTINGS: Cave. PLAYING TIME: 25 min. PLOT: Three witch sisters need a slave to do their cooking and cleaning, so the youngest, Vanilla, kidnaps a husky female who turns out to be a boy, Terry, in a Halloween costume. The witches are horrified because the situation fulfills an ancient prophesy, forcing them to be Terry's slaves forever. Terry wants a girl, Drusilla, to like him. The witches retrieve Drusilla, but don't tell Terry that they think she is their renegade sister, who has been pretending to be human. Drusilla and Terry are returned to their homes, and the audience is left wondering if the witches were right about the "bewitching" Drusilla. RECOMMENDATION: This utterly "haunting" tale has a delightfully imaginative plot and fast paced dialogue. ROYALTY: Free to Plays subscribers. SOURCE: Gotwalt, Helen Louise Miller. (1986, October). The curse of Hag Hollow. Plays: The Drama Magazine for Young People, pp. 13-23. SUBJECTS/PLAY TYPE: Witches; Halloween; Comedy.

683. 5-8. (+) Silverman, Eleanor. **The curse of McNamara's castle.** CAST: 6f, 7m, 3u. ACTS: 3. SETTINGS: Lawyer's office; peddler's home; castle. PLAYING TIME: 10 min. PLOT: Kathleen and James inherit the haunted family castle, in which two people

have been murdered. They catch the ghost, who is actually their lawyer looking for an alleged treasure. They find the treasure, amidst much ghostly noise. RECOMMENDATION: The plot is carried by the mood, and the settings follow through on the frightening theme. Children will especially enjoy the suggestion (by the ghostly noises at the ending) that there may actually be a ghost. ROYALTY: NA. SOURCE: Silverman, Eleanor. (1983). Dramatics for children. Metuchen, NJ: Scarecrow Press. SUBJECTS/PLAY TYPE: Ghosts; Castles; Treasure; Mystery.

684. 8-12. (+) Sodaro, Craig. **Curse of the Pharaoh's cat.** CAST: 4f, 3m. ACTS: 1. SETTINGS: Office. PLAYING TIME: 25 min. PLOT: Professor Milliken finds a small golden artifact called the Pharaoh's cat which, legend says, will bring misfortune to whomever finds it. Professor Milliken is killed by someone who appears to be the mummy of Ramses III, but his secretary and a journalism student discover that the murder was committed by jewel thieves posing as graduate students working with Professor Milliken's niece. The cat remains safe because the Professor had encased it in a ceramic teardrop and given it to his secretary as an amulet. RECOMMENDATION: This mystery has enough plot turns to keep audiences off guard. The setting of Egyptology is both mystery and history. ROYALTY: Free to Plays subscribers. SOURCE: Sodaro, Craig. (1986, November). Curse of the Pharaoh's cat. Plays: The Drama Magazine for Young People, pp. 13-21. SUBJECTS/PLAY TYPE: Mystery; Egyptology; Playlet.

685. 3-8. (+) Cheatham, Val R. **Curses! foiled again!** CAST: 1f, 3m, Su. ACTS: 1. SETTINGS: Bare stage, backdrop. PLAYING TIME: 15 min. PLOT: Dastardly Nasty Colfax tries to discredit hero Bruce Goodguy so Colfax can marry Nell Truehart himself. The villain is thwarted, and Bruce and Nell live happily ever after. RECOMMENDATION: A good pianist is mandatory for the full effect, and the two narrators have a substantial amount of dialogue. ROYALTY: Free to Plays subscribers. SOURCE: Cheatham, Val R. (1977, February). Curses! foiled again! Plays: The Drama Magazine for Young People, pp. 67-70. SUBJECTS/PLAY TYPE: Swindlers and Swindling; Melodrama.

686. 7-9. (+) Karshner, Roger. **Curt and Marcie.** CAST: 1f, 1m. ACTS: 1. SETTINGS: None. PLAYING TIME: NA. PLOT: Siblings Marcie and Curt discuss college plans. Curt feels it is their obligation to follow the family tradition (boys go to Yale and girls to Smith); Marcie would like to go to a junior college and study retailing. Curt argues with her, but Marcie remains adamant. RECOMMENDATION: Although this is aimed at an upper middle class audience, it does convey the need to make individual decisions. ROYALTY: NA. SOURCE: Karshner, Roger. (1986). Scenes for teenagers. Toluce Lake, CA: Dramaline Pub. SUBJECTS/PLAY TYPE: Values; Individuality; College; Scene.

687. 6-12. (+) Sodaro, Craig. **Curtain call.** CAST: 4f, 3m. ACTS: 1. SETTINGS: Cafe. PLAYING TIME: NA. PLOT: Grams, a former star in the Western Theater Circuit, and her now deceased son, founded the Bar None Cafe. Her grandson and his wife are eager to leave the town and start a business elsewhere, but Grams does not want to sell the cafe. When a prospective buyer arrives to close the deal, Grams pulls out a rifle and plays her finest role. The cafe remains in her hands. RECOMMENDATION: The characterization is engaging and realistic, the language simple and straight forward. ROYALTY: $20. SOURCE: Sodaro, Craig. (1984). Curtain call. Chicago, IL: Dramatic Pub. Co. SUBJECTS/PLAY TYPE: Nostalgia; Family; Drama.

688. 9-12. (+) Johnston, Gregory. **Curtain going up!** CAST: 10f, 7m, 1u. ACTS: 3. SETTINGS: Bare stage. PLAYING TIME: NA. PLOT: This light comedy deals with a new drama teacher producing her first high school play. She must contend with jealousy, parent and peer pressures, and the beginning of a personal romance. RECOMMENDATION: As this shows how allegedly insurmountable teenage problems often solve themselves, it hilariously sets up scenarios in which easily identifiable types interact. ROYALTY: $35. SOURCE: Johnston, Gregory. (1980). Curtain Going Up! New York, NY: Samuel French. SUBJECTS/PLAY TYPE: Theater; Comedy.

689. 7-12. (+) Deary, Terence. **The custard kid.** CAST: 2f, 2m. ACTS: 1. SETTINGS: Western town; courtroom. PLAYING TIME: 60 min. PLOT: The Custard Kid and Calamity Kate have identical monogrammed suitcases. When Custard picks up Calamity's, Sheriff Doris Dillon arrests him for stealing. Custard loses a fast draw contest and must go to trial, with the audience as witnesses and jury members. RECOMMENDATION: An entertaining story, this is enhanced with appropriate "mood" music, songs, and dancing, and is an effective way to teach accurate observation and to examine values of right and wrong, justice and mercy. ROYALTY: None. SOURCE: Deary, Terence. (1977). Teaching through theatre. New York, NY: Samuel French. SUBJECTS/PLAY TYPE: Old West; Justice; Comedy; Participation Play.

690. 3-5. (-) Boiko, Claire. (Perrault, Charles) **Cybernella or the triumph of technological true love.** (Cinderella) CAST: 11f, 9m, Su. ACTS: 1. SETTINGS: Living room; discotheque. PLAYING TIME: 30 min. PLOT: The Peacocks are unable to keep their hired help so they purchase an attractive robot maid named Cybernella. When the prince of disco holds a bash to choose his dancing partner, the Peacock sisters hope to catch his eye. Cybernella zooms in on a motorcycle and the prince is mesmerized, not surprising since the prince turns out to be a robot too. RECOMMENDATION: This is dated by its 70s jargon and disco setting. The parts that aren't dated are trite, and the remainder is simply annoying. ROYALTY: None. SOURCE: Boiko, Claire. (1980). Dramatized

parodies of familiar stories. Boston: Plays, Inc. SUBJECTS/PLAY TYPE: Robots; Parody; Adaptation.

691. 9-12. (+) Bland, Joellen. (Rostand, Edmond) **Cyrano de Bergerac.** (Cyrano de Bergerac) CAST: 1f, 9m. ACTS: 1. SETTINGS: Theater stage. PLAYING TIME: 30 min. PLOT: Cyrano, an accomplished poet and swordsman, loves beautiful Roxane, but feels he is too ugly to win her. He helps his handsome friend, Christian, to win Roxane's love by writing romantic letters and speeches for him. Christian is killed in battle and Roxane mourns for 15 years before she learns that Cyrano authored the words that caused her to love Christian. Sadly, Cyrano is accidentally killed, and dies in Roxane's arms. RECOMMENDATION: This retains much of the original's beauty of language. Although the ending is sad, it does not leave one with a feeling of hopelessness. Rather, it is a story of love between the three main characters, each of whom demonstrates unselfish caring for others. ROYALTY: Free to Plays subscribers. SOURCE: Bland, Joellen. (1984, January/February). Cyrano de Bergerac. Plays: The Drama Magazine for Young People, pp. 57-68. SUBJECTS/PLAY TYPE: Love; Reader's Theater; Adaptation.

692. 8-12. (+) Harris, Aurand. (Rostand, Edmond.) **Cyrano de Bergerac.** (Cyrano de Bergerac.) CAST: 5f, 11m. ACTS: 1. SETTINGS: Theater; garden; battlefield; convent. PLAYING TIME: NA. PLOT: Cyrano de Bergerac is described as an extraordinary poet, scientist, swordsman, and musician, who has an extraordinarily large nose. Cyrano loves Roxane, but believes she could never return his love. He helps his friend Christian, who is infatuated with Roxane, to write poetic letters of love, and Roxane and Christian marry. Christian and Cyrano are sent off to war, where Cyrano writes daily letters for Christian, until Christian dies in battle. Cyrano returns home, visiting Roxane weekly at her convent home until, near death, he admits he wrote all of Christian's messages. Roxane proclaims her love as he dies in her arms. RECOMMENDATION: In this excellent adaptation, the plot has been abridged into one act without sacrificing the integrity of the original story. The characters are developed into full interesting individuals, the dialogue is alive and full of action, and the theme is simple, logical, and realistic. ROYALTY: $15. SOURCE: Harris, Aurand. (1979). Cyrano de Bergerac. Boston, MA: Baker's Plays. SUBJECTS/PLAY TYPE: Love; Adaptation.

693. 9-12*. (+) Leonard, Hugh. **Da.** CAST: 3f, 5m. ACTS: 2. SETTINGS: Kitchen; seafront; hillside. PLAYING TIME: NA. PLOT: Charlie, in his forties, comes home after his father's death. He experiences flashbacks and actively converses with the characters in his imagination in an attempt to reconcile with a difficult past. Charlie exhorts his ghostly Da to leave him in peace, but learns that one cannot easily escape the past. RECOMMENDATION: A fascinating mental drama, this tale of a young man's examination of the past will intrigue mature high schoolers. Several Britishisms, oaths, and sexual references may need to be amended to

make this more appropriate for young American audiences. Because of its extensive length, adults should produce this. ROYALTY: $50. SOURCE: Leonard, Hugh. (1978). Da. New York, NY: Samuel French. SUBJECTS/PLAY TYPE: Aging; Adoption; Reminiscences; Drama.

694. 4-8. (+) Hatton, Thomas J. **Daedalus and Icarus.** CAST: 3f, 4m. ACTS: 2. SETTINGS: Outside Labyrinth; inside Labyrinth. PLAYING TIME: 10 min. PLOT: Icarus tells his father, Daedalus (architect of the Labyrinth), of his desire to go surfing, just as Theseus, prince of Athens, and Ariadne, daughter of King Minos, arrive, bemoaning the plan to sacrifice Theseus to the Minotaur. Daedalus tells Theseus how to escape, for which Minos punishes Daedalus and Icarus by throwing them into the Labyrinth. They escape, using wings, Daedalus' latest invention, but Icarus ignores his father's warning, flies too close to the sun, and loses his wings. He saves himself by using his own invention, a parachute. RECOMMENDATION: This humorous and upbeat treatment of a Greek myth will appeal to all. Absurdity is created by the use of contemporary language, expressions, and activities. ROYALTY: Free to Plays subscribers. SOURCE: Hatton, Thomas J. (1985, January/February). Daedalus and Icarus. Plays: The Drama Magazine for Young People, pp. 59-63. SUBJECTS/PLAY TYPE: Mythology, Greek; Daedalus; Icarus; Skit.

695. 2-5. (+) Smith, Gladys V. **The dancing dame's lost shoes.** CAST: 6f, 8m, 3u. ACTS: 1. SETTINGS: Street; cobbler's shop. PLAYING TIME: 15 min. PLOT: Mother Goose characters go on a scavenger hunt for the Dancing Dame's lost shoes and the master's lost fiddlesticks. They are rewarded with a pie or a pair of shoes. RECOMMENDATION: This is a lively and entertaining use of familiar characters in an unfamiliar situation. ROYALTY: Free to Plays subscribers. SOURCE: Smith, Gladys V. (1980, March). The dancing dame's lost shoes. Plays: The Drama Magazine for Young People, pp. 39-44. SUBJECTS/PLAY TYPE: Mother Goose Characters; Shoes; Nursery Rhyme Characters; Playlet.

696. K-6. (+) Osterman, Marilyn & Kluge, Marilyn. **The dancing spider.** CAST: 15u. ACTS: 1. SETTINGS: Jungle. PLAYING TIME: 45 min. PLOT: This West African folk tale examines the values of industry, generosity, and cooperation. Ananse, a lazy but lovable spider, and other small jungle animals, gather food and deal with large jungle animals such as the lion by working together. The play teaches that, by cooperating, small people can solve big problems. RECOMMENDATION: The animal characters, simple dialogue and music, and an easily understood moral make this especially enjoyable to younger children. The number of players adapts easily to the size of the group. ROYALTY: $25. SOURCE: Osterman, Marilyn & Kluge, Marilyn. (1981). The dancing spider. Chicago, IL: Dramatic Pub. Co. SUBJECTS/PLAY TYPE: Folk Tales, West Africa; Musical.

697. K-6. (+) Martin, Judith & Ashwander, Donald. **Dandelion.** CAST: Su. ACTS: 1. SETTINGS: Bare stage, props. PLAYING TIME: NA. PLOT: A series of nine scenes, skits, and songs presents a highly simplified version of the natural history of the world. RECOMMENDATION: This imaginative revue presents a complex subject at the most basic level, with songs and visual props that even very young children can enjoy. ROYALTY: NA. SOURCE: Martin, Judith & Ashwander, Donald. (1984). Dandelion. New York, NY: Paper Bag Players. SUBJECTS/PLAY TYPE: Evolution; Musical.

698. 5-10. (+) Boiko, Claire. **Danger in hyperspace.** CAST: 8f, 10m. ACTS: 4. SETTINGS: Bedroom; laboratory. PLAYING TIME: 30 min. PLOT: Two high school boys find themselves transported to another dimension to stop an evil genius who is playing with the space-time continuum. They keep him from becoming master of the universe by erasing information from a computer disk. When he tries to take revenge, help arrives from the 11th dimension in the form of a guardian angel who sends all the boys back home. RECOMMENDATION: This intriguing excursion, where shadows are three dimensional, and where plane geometry allows people to move through new dimensions, will both excite and satisfy all science fiction buffs. The cast can be any mixture of males and females. ROYALTY: Free to Plays subscribers. SOURCE: Boiko, Claire. (1986, January/February). Danger in hyperspace. Plays: The Drama Magazine for Young People, pp. 33- 41. SUBJECTS/PLAY TYPE: Science Fiction; Playlet.

699. 1-8. (+) Whittaker, Violet. **Daniel.** CAST: 4m, 1u. ACTS: 6. SETTINGS: Lion's den; living room. PLAYING TIME: NA. PLOT: Daniel is trapped by rival officers and spends the night in the lion's den. God prevents him from being injured, the officers are punished, and the audience is instructed to know God better and pray more so that they will be blessed. RECOMMENDATION: The need for prayer as a sign of commitment to God is presented nondenominationally. Directors may want to delete the irrelevant comment by Daniel that he is a eunuch. ROYALTY: NA. SOURCE: Whittaker, Violet. (1984). Puppet people scripts. Grand Rapids, MI: Baker Book House. SUBJECTS/PLAY TYPE: Bible Stories; Puppet Play.

700. K-3. (-) Silverman, Eleanor. **Daniel Boone and the Indians.** CAST: 2m, 4u. ACTS: 1. SETTINGS: Woods; Indian camp. PLAYING TIME: NA. PLOT: Daniel and his friend are captured by Indians, but they escape. RECOMMENDATION: This has no point and its stereotyping of Indians as evil makes it strongly insulting. ROYALTY: None. SOURCE: Silverman, Eleanor. (1983). Dramatics for children. Metuchen, NJ: Scarecrow Press. SUBJECTS/PLAY TYPE: Native Americans; Skit.

701. 5-7. (+) Satchell, Mary. **Daniel Hale Williams, pioneer surgeon.** CAST: 4f, 5m. ACTS: 1. SETTINGS: Doctor's office; parlor. PLAYING TIME: 20 min. PLOT: The real life, historical surgeon Daniel Hale Williams is initially introduced as an apprentice to a physician, but he achieves his goal of attending medical school. As a practicing physician, he is instrumental in founding an interracial hospital and nursing school, and is instrumental in the development of heart surgery. RECOMMENDATION: This is of manageable length and, with its theme of perseverance, could be used to introduce children to the important figures in black history. ROYALTY: NA. SOURCE: Kamerman, Sylvia E. (1987). Plays of black Americans. Boston: Plays, Inc. SUBJECTS/PLAY TYPE: Black Americans; Medical History; Williams, Daniel Hale; Playlet.

702. 9-12. (-) Filichia, Peter. (Shakespeare, William) **A Danish soap.** (Hamlet) CAST: 6f, 7m. ACTS: 1. SETTINGS: Heaven; psychiatrists' office; living room; hospital room. PLAYING TIME: NA. PLOT: Shakespeare's soul is restless because people on Earth have forgotten his works. He asks to be returned to Earth to re-establish himself as a modern screenwriter. His friends in heaven put on a soap opera version of **Hamlet** to convince the starkeeper to allow Shakespeare a day on Earth, where the focus is on a television parody of **Hamlet.** RECOMMENDATION: Neither Shakespeare's supposedly 16th century dialogue nor the soap opera format is very convincing or entertaining. The promise of this comedy is lost in uninspired word plays and heavy handed allusions to **Hamlet.** ROYALTY: $10. SOURCE: Filichia, Peter. (1978). A Danish soap. Boston, MA: Baker's Plays. SUBJECTS/PLAY TYPE: Soap Operas; Comedy.

703. 3-6. (+) Harder, Eleanor. (Harder, Eleanor) **Darius the dragon.** (Darius and the Dozer Bull) CAST: 1f, 3m, 5u. ACTS: 2. SETTINGS: Cave; street; park; jail cell. PLAYING TIME: NA. PLOT: Darius, a 1,300 year old dragon writing his memoirs, chases a yellow bulldozer (which has slammed into his cave) into city traffic, where he is rescued from almost certain death by Jennifer, 10. They learn that the inner city park is about to be turned into a parking lot. When a protest march led by Darius gets out of hand, the old dragon is arrested and jailed. Darius manages to escape banishment to Yellowstone National Park, melts the "dozer Bull" in a breath of fire, and the two generations agree they must work together to preserve the park. RECOMMENDATION: The serious theme of preserving the environment does not overpower the well constructed story line. Children will enjoy making the simple cut out props and scenery. ROYALTY: NA. SOURCE: Harder, Eleanor. (1983). Darius the dragon. Denver, CO: Pioneer Drama Service. SUBJECTS/PLAY TYPE: Ecology; Dragons; Comedy.

704. 7-12. (+) Sawyer-Young, Kat. **Date.** CAST: 1f. ACTS: 1. SETTINGS: None. PLAYING TIME: 1 min. PLOT: Stephanie tries to talk about her date on the phone, but keeps getting interrupted by family members. RECOMMENDATION: The universal complaint about lack of privacy will be appealing to teenagers. ROYALTY: None. SOURCE: Sawyer-Young, Kat. (1987). Minute monologues for contemporary teens.

Boston, MA: Baker's Plays. **SUBJECTS/PLAY TYPE:** Privacy; Dating; Monologue.

705. 8-12. (+) Hammett, Christina. **Dateline: Romance. CAST:** 1f, 2m. **ACTS:** 1. **SETTINGS:** Restaurant. **PLAYING TIME:** 10 min. **PLOT:** Hilary and Eric meet in a quiet French cafe on their computer arranged date, and Hilary confesses that she's a reporter for the **Tribune**, writing a story about people who use computer dating services. Eric then confesses they would have met anyway; he also works for the **Tribune** and had a friend set up their meeting through the dating service. They laugh and decide to share a dish of ice cream. **RECOMMENDATION:** Lighthearted conversation along with Eric's effective jokes about dinner make this a delightful curtain raiser or an introduction to role acting for a drama class. **ROYALTY:** Free to Plays subscribers. **SOURCE:** Hamlett, Christina. (1987, April). Dateline: romance. Plays: The Drama Magazine for Young People, pp. 51-54. **SUBJECTS/PLAY TYPE:** Computer Dating; Blind Dates; Comedy.

706. 9-12. (+) Levy, Maya. **Daughters. CAST:** 9f. **ACTS:** 9. **SETTINGS:** Bare stage, props. **PLAYING TIME:** NA. **PLOT:** In this anthology of monologues about the trials and tribulations of growing up female, each monologue presents a unique insight into girls' lives, how they perceive themselves, their relationships with their parents and peers, and how they react to the roles that are expected of them as female adolescents. Most of the girls are "black sheep" by traditional standards. **RECOMMENDATION:** Although heavy with psychological undertones and often depressing, this is a sensitive glimpse at the awkwardness and pain of growing up. Due to the sometimes negative, sometimes shocking themes, it would be advisable for the producer to use discretion in selecting an audience. With a focus on characterization, settings are sparse, but the speeches are fairly long; they may be difficult to master for some teenagers. **ROYALTY:** $40. **SOURCE:** Levy, Maya. (1985). Daughters. Boston, MA: Baker's Plays. **SUBJECTS/PLAY TYPE:** Mothers and Daughters; Women; Monologue.

707. 7-9. (+) Karshner, Roger. **David and Clark. CAST:** 2m. **ACTS:** 1. **SETTINGS:** None. **PLAYING TIME:** NA. **PLOT:** David and Clark have acne, which distresses them. Clark thinks it's due to nature and puberty, but David has it figured to be McDonald's food (greaseballs). After discussing curative methods they have tried, they leave to get a hot fudge sundae. **RECOMMENDATION:** Although the language is raw, this is quite humorous and easy to identify with. **ROYALTY:** NA. **SOURCE:** Karshner, Roger. (1986). Scenes for teenagers. Toluce Lake, CA: Dramaline Pub. **SUBJECTS/PLAY TYPE:** Acne; Scene.

708. K-6. (+) Gotwalt, Helen Louise Miller. **The day and the man. CAST:** 15u. **ACTS:** 1. **SETTINGS:** Bare stage. **PLAYING TIME:** 5 min. **PLOT:** As February 12th is spelled, each letter is associated with a historical fact about Abraham Lincoln. **RECOMMENDATION:** The lines here are not long and focus appropriately on

wisdom, equality, liberty, and friendship. **ROYALTY:** Free to Plays subscribers. **SOURCE:** Gotwalt, Helen Louise Miller. (1982, January/February). The day and the man. Plays: The Drama Magazine for Young People, pp. 69-70. **SUBJECTS/PLAY TYPE:** Lincoln, Abraham; Choral Reading.

709. 7-12. (+) Huff, Betty Tracy. **A day at the store. CAST:** 8f, 7m, Su. **ACTS:** 1. **SETTINGS:** Store. **PLAYING TIME:** 30 min. **PLOT:** Gloria Treadworthy, daughter of the owner of a failing dry goods store, foils the sabotage efforts of C. P. Frillington, the competition. **RECOMMENDATION:** This lighthearted story, set at the turn of the century, is complete with overdone references to typical melodramatic conventions, and exaggerated good and evil characters. **ROYALTY:** Free to Plays subscribers. **SOURCE:** Huff, Betty Tracy. (1986, March). A day at the store. Plays: The Drama Magazine for Young People, pp. 23- 36. **SUBJECTS/PLAY TYPE:** Comedy; Melodrama.

710. 7-12. (+) Mitchell, W. O. (Mitchell, W. O.) **The day Jake made her rain.** (Jake and the Kid) **CAST:** 2f, 2m, Su. **ACTS:** 1. **SETTINGS:** Farmyard. **PLAYING TIME:** NA. **PLOT:** During a serious drought, Jake brags that he is able to make rain. The desperate farmers call his bluff, and Jake is forced to make a "rain machine." On the appointed day, Jake turns the machine on and, to the town's (and Jake's) surprise, it rains. **RECOMMENDATION:** In this adaptation of one of Mitchell's famous "prairie plays," the dialect, feelings, and characters of the genre are well captured. Because of the dialect, more experienced actors might be required, but a good high school cast could manage this. **ROYALTY:** NA. **SOURCE:** Doolittle, Joyce. (1984). Eight plays for young people. Edmonton, Canada: NeWest Pub. **SUBJECTS/PLAY TYPE:** Depression; Drought; Rainmaking; Adaptation.

711. 2-4. (+) Fisher, Aileen. **Day of destiny. CAST:** 10u. **ACTS:** 1. **SETTINGS:** Ship's deck. **PLAYING TIME:** 20 min. **PLOT:** Christopher Columbus's crew loses faith in their leader and plot to throw him overboard. Columbus is sure they are close to land because birds are flying close to the ship, and he convinces the sailors to continue for two more days. As the play ends, Columbus stands on deck, confident that the land of promise is near. **RECOMMENDATION:** This could supplement the study of Christopher Columbus and the discovery of the New World. It is suspenseful, and, although the characters are not explored in depth, it presents a convincing picture of a man whose faith in himself and his mission was all consuming. **ROYALTY:** Free to Plays subscribers. **SOURCE:** Fisher, Aileen. (1988, October). Day of destiny. Plays: The Drama Magazine for Young People, pp. 45-50. **SUBJECTS/PLAY TYPE:** Exploration; Columbus, Christopher; Playlet.

712. 5-9. (+) Kehret, Peg. **Day of liberation. CAST:** 1u. **ACTS:** 1. **SETTINGS:** None. **PLAYING TIME:** NA. **PLOT:** A boy has just had his braces taken off, and he joyfully outlines the things he can do now: eat corn on the

cob, smile openly, and kiss girls. RECOMMENDATION: The ecstatic emotions of a boy freed from three years of braces are captured cleverly and amusingly. This could easily be adapted for a female player. ROYALTY: NA. SOURCE: Kehret, Peg. (1986). Winning monologs for young actors. Colorado Springs, CO: Meriwether Pub. SUBJECTS/PLAY TYPE: Braces; Monologue.

713. 9-12. (-) Frost, Warren. **The day Paul Newman came to call.** CAST: 2f, 3m. ACTS: 1. SETTINGS: Dining room. PLAYING TIME: NA. PLOT: Two sisters live together, one in an imaginary world where she thinks that movie stars are coming to visit her. On her way to the mental institution, she imagines the psychiatrist is Paul Newman. The audience learns that the mental problems are inherited, and the sane sister will soon fall prey to the same hallucinations. RECOMMENDATION: The subject matter of mental illness is exploited, rather than explained here, and little is to be gained from this presentation. ROYALTY: $20. SOURCE: Frost, Warren. (1983). The day Paul Newman came to call. Chicago, IL: Dramatic Pub. Co. SUBJECTS/PLAY TYPE: Mental Illness; Comedy.

714. K-6. (+) DuVal, Martha. **The day the clowns lost their smiles.** CAST: 2f, Su. ACTS: 1. SETTINGS: Circus ring. PLAYING TIME: 30 min. PLOT: All but the clowns are caught up in the excitement of opening day. The circus crew works to determine why the clowns look so sad and finally cheer them up. RECOMMENDATION: Although this is long, it presents unique opportunities for creative expression. ROYALTY: Free to Plays subscribers. SOURCE: DuVal, Martha. (1980, May). The day the clowns lost their smiles. Plays: The Drama Magazine for Young People, pp. 61-63. SUBJECTS/PLAY TYPE: Clowns; Circus; Creative Dramatics.

715. 7-12. (+) Madden, David. **The day the flowers came.** CAST: 2f, 4m, Su. ACTS: 1. SETTINGS: Living room. PLAYING TIME: NA. PLOT: J.D. Hindle awakens with a hangover and learns through a newspaper article that his family has supposedly been killed in a hurricane. His reactions to well meaning friends and delivery men who bring condolences are presented, but it turns out that he dreamed the tragedy. RECOMMENDATION: This is an interesting study of an individual's response to personal tragedy. The reactions of denial and regret are well done and thought provoking. ROYALTY: $15. SOURCE: Madden, David. (1975). The day the flowers came. Chicago, IL: Dramatic Pub. Co. SUBJECTS/PLAY TYPE: Family Relationships; Death; Drama.

716. 7-12. (+) Martens, Anne Coulter. **The day the President called...and called...and called.** CAST: 16u. ACTS: 1. SETTINGS: Living room. PLAYING TIME: NA. PLOT: Pam, a teenager, is hit on the head by the President's golf ball. He tries to call her to apologize but encounters difficulties because Pam's grandmother is deaf and does not hear the phone, and Pam's sister believes it is her boyfriend, and refuses to answer the phone to teach him a lesson. Eventually the President is able to get through. RECOMMENDATION: With its light plot, the play will need a sparkling cast to make the most of the "slapstick" ad lib scenes. ROYALTY: NA. SOURCE: Martens, Anne Coulter. (1976). The day the President called...and called ...and called. Boston, MA: Baker's Plays. SUBJECTS/PLAY TYPE: Situational Comedy; Comedy.

717. 9-12. (+) Bethencourt, João. **The day they kidnapped the Pope.** CAST: 2f, 5m, Su. ACTS: 2. SETTINGS: Living room; kitchen. PLAYING TIME: NA. PLOT: The Pope is kidnapped by a taxi driver, Sam, who demands that the world not kill anyone for 24 hours by way of ransom. The Rabbi comes to play chess with the Pope, then turns the family in for the reward and the house becomes the scene of a siege, until the United Nations votes on a 24-hour peace declaration. Although the Rabbi and a pompous Cardinal nearly foil Sam's plans, the Day of Peace is won, the Pope absolves Sam and decorates him for his efforts. RECOMMENDATION: Not only is this play a commentary on the world situation, but it is also an endearing look at ecumenical cooperation, although with potentially prejudicial overtones. Sara Leibowitz is a delightful Jewish mother and the dialogue and repartee are witty and engaging. The sets are simple and the offstage parts would need an experienced hand to make the timing work, but could be recorded. ROYALTY: $50. SOURCE: Bethencourt, João. (1979). The day they kidnapped the Pope. Chicago, IL: Dramatic Pub. Co. SUBJECTS/PLAY TYPE: Politics; Catholics; Jews; World Affairs; Comedy.

718. K-4*. (+) Edwards, Tony. **The day they lost Raggety Ruth.** CAST: 5f, 4m. ACTS: 1. SETTINGS: Play room. PLAYING TIME: NA. PLOT: Mandy's three dolls, Raggety Ruth, Tin Soldier, and Clown are excited about moving day, which is on Mandy's birthday. As a gift, Mandy receives a beautiful doll, Pretty Priscilla who, in a fit of jealous rage, locks Raggety Ruth in a closet. The family moves without the doll and the new family that moves in wants to throw her away. Raggety Ruth sets out to find Mandy again and, eventually, she returns to her friends. She shows Priscilla the folly of her jealousy and the dolls live together in peace. RECOMMENDATION: This charming story reassures young audiences that moving is a happy event, but also shows that people can love more than one person at a time. Written in England, this has some slang and terms that may need to be altered for American audiences. ROYALTY: NA. SOURCE: Edwards, Tony. (1985). The day they lost Raggety Ruth. Cheshire, England: The New Playwrights' Network. SUBJECTS/PLAY TYPE: Moving; Jealousy; Dolls; Fantasy.

719. 10-12. (+) Wilson, Lanford. **Days ahead.** CAST: 1m. ACTS: 1. SETTINGS: Victorian room. PLAYING TIME: NA. PLOT: An insane man tells the empty walls his fears that his lover and he will be separated, as he reads his diary aloud. He rejoices that he is older and surer now, and could deal with the possibility that she may choose to leave. As he talks, he produces a fork and

begins to scrape away gently and methodically at the wall. Waiting for the wall to give way, he murmurs that, now, he and his love will have wonderful times together. RECOMMENDATION: This has the chilling appeal of Poe and could be staged and acted by high school students, although the actor will need to have extraordinary powers of memorization. ROYALTY: NA. SOURCE: Wilson, Lanford. (1981). The rimers of Eldritch and other plays. New York, NY: Hill & Wang. SUBJECTS/PLAY TYPE: Horror; Psycho-Drama; Mental Illness; Monologue.

720. 10-12. (+) Murray, John. **The dazzling diamond caper.** CAST: 6f, 7m, Su. ACTS: 1. SETTINGS: Hotel lobby; manager's office. PLAYING TIME: 45 min. PLOT: Two jewel thieves switch briefcases with a diamond courier in a hotel lobby. The courier is suspected of being a thief, and is in even more trouble when a dead man who looks like the accused courier is found in a hotel room closet. The villain, one of two thieves who has murdered his accomplice, has his plan foiled when characters from the two subplots enter the main plot just long enough to provide clues about the masquerading thief and assist in his capture. RECOMMENDATION: The story is humorous but reminiscent of identical plots in plays, paperback novels, and TV shows. Some of the dialogue and action need to be updated for contemporary teenagers. Fans of the author will forgive the lack of originality in the plot. ROYALTY: Free to Play subscribers. SOURCE: Murray, John. (1985). Fifteen plays for today's teenagers. Boston, MA: Plays, Inc. SUBJECTS/PLAY TYPE: Mystery; Murder; Crime; Comedy.

721. 7-9. (+) Murray, John. **Dead of night.** CAST: 3f, 3m. ACTS: 1. SETTINGS: Living room. PLAYING TIME: 30 min. PLOT: Hector Styles is killed and the suspect is his nephew and heir, Clay. An antique dealer discovers a tape recorded message by Mr. Styles claiming his nephew is trying to poison him. But the recorder, a gift from Clay, arrived after his uncle's death. Mr. Styles' attorney incriminates himself, then confesses details of his plot to frame Clay and gain control of the estate. RECOMMENDATION: Additional characters would have broadened the suspect list, but would also have lengthened the playing time. Traditional male-female role models are maintained as the male saves the female; however, both share equally in solving the mystery. The scant cast is permitted no character growth, but the plot is logically developed and proceeds to a satisfactory conclusion. ROYALTY: Free to Plays subscribers. SOURCE: Murray, John. (1988, November). Dead of night. Plays: The Drama Magazine for Young People, pp. 10-20. SUBJECTS/PLAY TYPE: Mystery; Murder; Playlet.

722. 9-12. (+) McCusker, Paul. **Dear diary.** CAST: 2f. ACTS: 1. SETTINGS: None. PLAYING TIME: NA. PLOT: As two rival teenage girls read what they are writing in their diaries, one takes to heart the preacher's sermon about how loving God depends on loving others. She tries to make up with her rival, who thinks that she is plotting to discredit her by being nice.

RECOMMENDATION: This could work as well if the characters were boys and the dating incidents involved girls. ROYALTY: None with purchase of script. SOURCE: McCusker, Paul. (1982). Souvenirs: Comedies and dramas for Christian fellowship. Boston, MA: Baker's Plays. SUBJECTS/PLAY TYPE: Love; Christian Drama.

723. 4-6*. (+) Raspanti, Celeste. **Dear Mister Noah.** CAST: 6f, 6m, Su. ACTS: 1. SETTINGS: Noah's Ark. PLAYING TIME: 55 min. PLOT: The audience visits Noah's Ark as the animals converse. Mr. Fox causes dissension among the animals by accusing mouse of stealing provisions which he has stolen himself. This deception sets him apart from the other animals when they leave the ark for dry land. RECOMMENDATION: The production is too long for the younger children (who would enjoy it) to produce. Many will enjoy familiar fables retold by the animals themselves. ROYALTY: $25. SOURCE: Raspanti, Celeste. (1975). Dear Mister Noah. Chicago, IL: Dramatic Pub. Co. SUBJECTS/PLAY TYPE: Noah's Ark; Fable; Comedy.

724. 8-12. (+) Alberts, David. **Death by arrangement.** CAST: 4f, 7m. ACTS: 3. SETTINGS: Study. PLAYING TIME: NA. PLOT: Murder suspects gather in a lawyer's study to be questioned. After much interrogation, the inspector is about to implicate the murderer when the real inspector arrives. The imposter, brandishing a pistol, backs toward the door, and demands blackmail payments from all for the damaging information he now has. After he is subdued, the audience learns that all the suspects are guilty of a murder conspiracy and have cleverly framed the imposter. RECOMMENDATION: The clear writing style and fluid dialogue sustain interest and make this mystery's surprising twists and turns entertaining and easy to follow. It will challenge high school actors and entertain audiences of young adults and adults. No one will guess the ending. ROYALTY: $50. SOURCE: Alberts, David. (1981). Death by arrangement. Boston, MA: Baker's Plays. SUBJECTS/PLAY TYPE: Murder; Mystery.

725. 10-12. (+) Freed, Paul. **Death by chocolate.** CAST: 6f, 6m. ACTS: 2. SETTINGS: Office. PLAYING TIME: NA. PLOT: Three mysterious deaths occur at a health resort, two caused by poisonous chocolates, and one presumed to be a suicide. The mystery is solved by a mystery playwright and the health club playboy, who find that the author and his "fat" daughter did it in the drawing room. RECOMMENDATION: This is a very funny play with many twists and turns to keep the audience in stitches. There are a few lines about the butler's love affair and his illegitimate daughter which could cause some problems. ROYALTY: $40. SOURCE: Freed, Paul. (1985). Death by chocolate. Boston, MA: Baker's Plays. SUBJECTS/PLAY TYPE: Comedy; Health Clubs; Mystery.

726. 7-12. (-) Levin, Victor. **Death in Scarsdale.** CAST: 2f, 3m. ACTS: 1. SETTINGS: Living room. PLAYING TIME: NA. PLOT: The deceased describes the unrequited love and subsequent failed marriage that

caused him to commit suicide. RECOMMENDATION: The play's setting in Scarsdale, NY, does not take the place of more detailed characterization (unless the audience is intimately familiar with the Jewish "Scarsdale scene"). The play also suffers from obscure literary references, difficult words (e.g., misogynist), and allusions to marital problems probably too complex to be understood by teenagers. Finally, although it tries not to, the drama glorifies suicide as a romantic solution to problems. ROYALTY: $20. SOURCE: Levin, Victor. (1983). Death in Scarsdale. Chicago, IL: Dramatic Pub. Co. SUBJECTS/PLAY TYPE: Love; Drama.

727. 7-12. (+) Linney, Romulus. (Rowlandson, Mary) **The death of King Philip.** (The sovereignty and goodness of God) CAST: 2f, 2m. ACTS: 1. SETTINGS: Bare stage, props. PLAYING TIME: NA. PLOT: Mary Rowland's famous and moving narrative of her captivity during the Indian wars is the basis of this account of the death of the Wampanoag Indian Chief, King Philip and the horrible tragedy of war. The spirit of her original recordings of conversations with Indian leaders is well retained, including the Biblical references and the sometimes ambiguous understanding of the situation that characterized it. RECOMMENDATION: Written in a highly stylized form, this superb drama will not be easy to understand unless the audience has some knowledge of the Indian wars and the truth about the white man's role in them. ROYALTY: NA. SOURCE: Linney. Romulus. (1984). The death of King Philip. New York, NY: Dramatists Play Service, Inc. SUBJECTS/PLAY TYPE: Native Americans; Philip, King; Adaptation.

728. 7-8. (-) Garver, Juliet. **Debbie and the dating machine.** CAST: 6f, 4m. ACTS: 1. SETTINGS: Office. PLAYING TIME: 30 min. PLOT: Debbie, a shy college freshman who works in the campus computer dating center, gets advice from Charlie, the computer, then discovers the voice of the computer is really a young technician sent to program the machine. The discovery leads to romance for Debbie and newly discovered confidence in herself. RECOMMENDATION: In this sexist and highly offensive romantic drama, the image of women as only needing romance is sickeningly presented. ROYALTY: Free to Plays Subscribers. SOURCE: Garver, Juliet. (1979, May). Debbie and the dating machine. Plays: The Drama Magazine for Young People, pp. 1-12. SUBJECTS/PLAY TYPE: Dating; Romance; Playlet.

729. 7-9. (+) Paston, Bryna N. & Tolins, Selma. **Debbie's dilemma.** CAST: 8f, 5m, Su. ACTS: 1. SETTINGS: Gymnasium; election room. PLAYING TIME: 20 min. PLOT: Two of Debbie's best friends compete for Athlete of the Year; her vote will determine the winner. The audience is asked to determine how she voted. RECOMMENDATION: Although circumstances involved in the play's decision making are somewhat unrealistic, it does provide an excellent vehicle for discussion on decision making and personal responsibility in making choices. Easy to produce in a classroom setting, it could be used in an election year in

a government class. ROYALTY: Free to Plays subscribers. SOURCE: Paston, Bryna N. & Tolins, Selma. (Nov., 1979). Debbie's dilemma. Plays: The Drama Magazine for Young People, pp. 23- 30. SUBJECTS/PLAY TYPE: Friendship; Decision Making; Voting; Playlet.

730. 7-12. (+) Moeller, Ruby L. **December.** CAST: 5f, Su. ACTS: NA. SETTINGS: Bare stage, props. PLAYING TIME: NA. PLOT: The histories of seven Christmas songs are told; three games are played; and three poems read. In a final candlelight service, ten candles are lit in succession as a reader reads the Ten Commandments for Christmas. A prayer and two carols complete the presentation. RECOMMENDATION: Although this is confusing and disjointed, it might be useful for Christian religious schools or Christian Sunday School Christmas programs. Unfortunately, the games used have nothing to do with the theme. But "The Ten Commandments for Christmas" contains some nice sentiment for the season, and the histories of the carols are interesting. ROYALTY: NA. SOURCE: Moeller, Ruby L. (1975). Around the year programs. Boston, MA: Baker's Plays. SUBJECTS/PLAY TYPE: Christmas; Musical.

731. 6-12. (+) Way, Brian. **The decision.** CAST: 2f, 2m, Su. ACTS: 1. SETTINGS: Bare stage. PLAYING TIME: 55 min. PLOT: Hassan, the elder son of the ruling family of the backward country of Xavia, returns after being away for many years and encourages the ideas and ways of life of a more progressive society. After a logical debate, the people vote to implement the changes. Then they realize that important elements of their lifestyles and beliefs will change, and they reverse themselves. RECOMMENDATION: While enacting a debate of progress vs. tradition, this entertains the audience with a view of a mythical primitive society. Audience participation is encouraged. The elder son has very extensive dialogue and should be played by an older, more experienced actor, though the other roles could easily be handled by mature junior or senior high actors. It would best be performed as theater in the round. ROYALTY: $20. SOURCE: Way, Brian. (1977). The decision. Boston: Baker's Plays. SUBJECTS/PLAY TYPE: Modernization; Tradition; Drama.

732. 11-12. (+) Forsyth, James. **Defiant island.** CAST: 3f, 12m, Su. ACTS: 3. SETTINGS: Ship deck; salon; chapel; citadel. PLAYING TIME: NA. PLOT: The tragic life of Henry Christophe, self proclaimed king of Haiti from 1811-1820, is depicted as this chronicles his problems of uniting a people dominated by voodoo into a working, fighting force. His dreams for the island are beautiful, but doomed, and in the end, his people rebel against him. Unable to rally his people into a fighting force to combat approaching ships, he kills himself, never to know that the ships were friendly. RECOMMENDATION: This does not always portray Christophe's life accurately. However, the intense conflict and the description of Haiti and its people are well done. This will make great demands on the cast, but the audience will quickly sympathize with the characters

because each is so well developed. ROYALTY: $60. SOURCE: Forsyth, James. (1975). Defiant island. Chicago, IL: The Dramatic Pub. Co. SUBJECTS/PLAY TYPE: Black History; Haiti; Christophe, Henry; Drama.

733. 7-12. (+) Murray, John. **Den mother.** CAST: 1f. ACTS: 1. SETTINGS: None. PLAYING TIME: NA. PLOT: Mrs. Harlow, elected den mother of the month, tries to cope with nine rowdy, uncooperative boys who wreak havoc on her house, a son who refuses to take part in the cub scout meeting, and an unhelpful husband. RECOMMENDATION: While dealing with so many imaginary characters may offer a technical challenge for a young actress in the classroom, this hilarious farce's frantic tone and easily recognized situations make it a delight. ROYALTY: None. SOURCE: Murray, John. (1982). Modern monologues for Young People. Boston, MA: Plays, Inc. SUBJECTS/PLAY TYPE: Cub Scouts; Comedy; Monologue.

734. 7-9. (+) Cable, Harold. **A deputy for Broken Bow.** CAST: 5f, 4m, 8u. ACTS: 1. SETTINGS: Main street. PLAYING TIME: 35 min. PLOT: Tom Feeble is the incredibly stupid hero, made deputy sheriff at the request of his grandma. Sheriff Kindly is really the villain, Hughie the Hood, who steals jewels from widows. Sheriff Kindly hopes to dazzle the lovely young heroine Nell who is unimpressed and devoted to Tom. Tom captures Hughie the Hood and becomes a hero, the new sheriff and Nell's betrothed. RECOMMENDATION: This comic melodrama is more ridiculous than most and should be played solely for laughs. ROYALTY: Free to Plays subscribers. SOURCE: Cable, Harold. (1985, April). A deputy for Broken Bow. Plays: The Drama Magazine for Young People, pp. 22-30. SUBJECTS/PLAY TYPE: Melodrama; Western; Comedy.

735. 10-12*. (+) Marchant, William. **The desk set.** CAST: 8f, 8m. ACTS: 3. SETTINGS: Office. PLAYING TIME: NA. PLOT: Life is going smoothly in the reference department of a TV network until the boss' nephew, an efficiency engineer, installs computers. Bunny Watson, head of Reference, defends human competency against machine efficiency. When the computer accidently fires everyone in the building, pandemonium reigns. Quickly forgiven by the staff, the nephew explains that no job loss will occur and that the electronic brain was installed only to assist, and not to replace human counterparts. RECOMMENDATION: This is fast paced, with lively dialogue and a still pertinent view of computerization. The timing required by the situations makes this most appropriate for adult actors. ROYALTY: $50. SOURCE: Marchant, William. (1984). The desk set. New York, NY: Samuel French. SUBJECTS/PLAY TYPE: Librarians; Computers; Comedy.

736. 9-12. (+) Hamlett, Christina. **Desperately seeking princess.** CAST: 1f, 2m. ACTS: 1. SETTINGS: Hotel room; living room. PLAYING TIME: NA. PLOT: Freddie and Cindy meet over the telephone as the result of a newspaper personal ad..."Bewitched frog seeks princess." The conversation is progressing when the two

are interrupted and Cindy hangs up before giving her name to Freddie whom she has learned is a count. RECOMMENDATION: The bittersweet twist of the plot makes this appealing. The language is conversational and the lines should be easily remembered. The small cast and simple sound effects and props make this a good choice for one act group interpretation exercises, as well as for competition. ROYALTY: Free to Plays subscribers. SOURCE: Hamlett, Christina. (1987). Humorous plays for teenagers. Boston, MA: Plays, Inc. SUBJECTS/PLAY TYPE: Telephone Calls; Romance; Comedy.

737. 7-12. (-) Kelly, Tim J. **Destiny.** CAST: 5f, 5m. ACTS: 2. SETTINGS: None. PLAYING TIME: NA. PLOT: Destiny Mink, a gorgeous, high powered female executive who, as Peggy (a poor and ugly child with a huge nose), was spurned by the handsome but shallow Rake Carbuncle, is blackmailed by her plastic surgeon's nurse (who uses little Peggy's old nose as evidence). Eventually she is reunited with her childhood love, Rake, after sending his crazy wife, Clover, to jail for attempted murder. RECOMMENDATION: The joke in this play wears fairly thin early on. The characters, meant to be caricatures, elicit no sympathy and provide little humor. Rake's obtuseness is overdone, Destiny's character is inconsistent in all of her manifestations, and the final scene is hurried and absurd. ROYALTY: $40. SOURCE: Kelly, Tim J. (1985). Destiny. Boston, MA: Baker's Plays. SUBJECTS/PLAY TYPE: Beauty; Mistaken Identity; Farce.

738. 5-8. (+) Hamlett, Christina. **Details at 11...: A news spoof.** CAST: 7f, 7m, 2u. ACTS: 1. SETTINGS: Newsroom. PLAYING TIME: NA. PLOT: The six o'clock news team reports on stories involving characters from folk tales and children's stories. Highlights include interviews with the police chief investigating Humpty Dumpty's fall, a witness to Alice's disappearance with the White Rabbit, and others. RECOMMENDATION: This is a funny, fast paced and clever spoof of TV news. The stories are recounted in authentic "newscast" style, with many puns and jokes. It would be an excellent classroom or variety show skit. ROYALTY: $20. SOURCE: Hamlett, Christina. (1988). Details at 11...: A news spoof. Franklin, OH: Eldridge Pub. Co. SUBJECTS/PLAY TYPE: Folk Tale Characters; Comedy; Skit.

739. 9-12. (+) Bradbury, Ray. **A device out of time.** CAST: 3m. ACTS: 1. SETTINGS: Street; room. PLAYING TIME: NA. PLOT: Colonel Freeleigh relives the Civil War at Shiloh, and brings it to life so vividly that one of the boys in the audience momentarily experiences its intensity. Freeleigh also describes a bison stampede and the bizarre and tragic death of a Chinaman during a magic show. Then he falls asleep. RECOMMENDATION: The actor who plays the Colonel would have to be a professional or an extremely talented amateur to bring his scenes to life. ROYALTY: $25. SOURCE: Bradbury, Ray. (1986). A device out of time. Woodstock, IL: Dramatic Pub. Co. SUBJECTS/PLAY TYPE: Civil War, U.S.; Drama.

740. 9-12*. (+) Van Horn, Bill. **The devil's work indeed.** CAST: 14f, 8m, Su. ACTS: 1. SETTINGS: Interior of a home. PLAYING TIME: 60 min. PLOT: Seven young girls assume trance-like states and are considered bewitched. The devil is blamed and an expert on witchcraft is called in. The girls become caught up in treachery and name individuals in the town who have bewitched them. Tension mounts as the accused witches are brought before two judges, creating strange reactions among the girls. The play ends tragically and abruptly. RECOMMENDATION: Maintaining the emotional tension would be demanding not only for the director and actors, but also for the audience. Audiences should be prepared beforehand, by their study of American history, to be aware of the drama's historical and social context. Two reference works are cited in the notes which might prove useful in discussions of the Salem witch trials. ROYALTY: $15. SOURCE: Van Horn, Bill. (1979). The devil's work indeed. Denver, CO: Pioneer Drama Service. SUBJECTS/PLAY TYPE: Salem Witch Trials; Puritans; Drama.

741. 7-12. (+) Murray, John. **The Devonshire demons.** CAST: 4f, 4m, 1u. ACTS: 3. SETTINGS: Living room. PLAYING TIME: 40 min. PLOT: Three couples visit Devonshire Downs, the ancestral home of the mysterious Cedric Johnson who reportedly dabbled in the occult. Now, the only occupant of the dark mansion is a malevolent housekeeper who cares for some curiously lifelike dolls and a six-foot tall snake plant. Two couples are consumed by forces within the house and a young man and his associate find that diabolical forces roam the moors outside. The wife of the last young man survives--as a vampire. RECOMMENDATION: This drama of the supernatural has all the necessary bloodcurdling touches. The only thing it lacks is a plot. Since the structure of the drama is made of three set pieces, one for each doomed couple, it is difficult to maintain interest in the rather underdeveloped characters' fate. However, the two constants, the house and its keeper, are creepy enough to keep the audience's attention. ROYALTY: Free to Plays subscribers. SOURCE: Murray, John. (1985). Fifteen plays for todays teenagers. Boston, MA: Plays, Inc. SUBJECTS/PLAY TYPE: Demons; Halloween; Drama.

742. 5-9. (+) Berghammer, Gretta & Caspers, Rod. (Wilde, Oscar) **The devoted friends.** (The devoted friends) CAST: 1f, 1m, 8u. ACTS: 1. SETTINGS: Bare stage, props. PLAYING TIME: NA. PLOT: A wise barkeeper tells three travelers a story about a rich miller who unscrupulously took advantage of the good little Hans, rationalizing his behavior as friendship. Finally, little Hans drowned after fetching the doctor for the miller, and the miller was angry because the broken wheelbarrow he was going to give to little Hans is useless now. RECOMMENDATION: This effectively portrays the evils of the self righteous, who twist lofty ideals until they become tortuous and cruel. The miller's assessment that little Hans knows the practice of friendship, but not the theory, is perhaps the climax of this morality tale. ROYALTY: NA. SOURCE: Jennings, Coleman A. and Berghammer, Gretta. (1986). Theatre for youth: Twelve

plays with nature themes. Austin, TX: Univ. of Austin Press. SUBJECTS/PLAY TYPE: Friendship; Adaptation.

743. 9-12. (+) Majeski, Bill. **The diabolical daydreams of Danny Dawson.** CAST: 3f, 7m, Su. ACTS: 2. SETTINGS: Conference room; psychiatrist's office; living room. PLAYING TIME: NA. PLOT: Danny is shy, polite, talented, and not progressing in his advertising career or romance. By daydreaming that he is nasty, aggressive, and successful, he escapes this situation, but the daydreaming and a colleague who plots against him, only make matters worse. The company psychiatrist and Danny's understanding girlfriend help him to achieve a satisfactory balance and a happy ending. RECOMMENDATION: The important issues of self concept and ambition are explored in a humorous way. A "villain" lends an air of comic melodrama to the plot and provides just enough tension to move the story along. All the scenes are on stage simultaneously as lighting controls the scene changes, including the switch to Danny's fantasy world. ROYALTY: $35. SOURCE: Majeski, Bill. (1981). The diabolical daydreams of Danny Dawson. Chicago, IL: Dramatic Pub. Co. SUBJECTS/PLAY TYPE: Daydreams; Self Concept; Ambition; Comedy.

744. 9-12. (-) Shenk, Marcia Ann. **Diary.** CAST: 1f, 1m. ACTS: 1. SETTINGS: Living room/kitchen. PLAYING TIME: NA. PLOT: Jenny, a young girl, discovers a handsome stranger in her apartment and tries to find out who he is and how he got there. Instead, he tells her things about her personal life that could only have come from her diary in which she writes to an imaginary friend, Gene. The stranger admits he is Gene and has come to earth to be with her. In total disbelief, Jenny asks him to leave or else she will. Gene warns that if she leaves he will vanish forever. Jenny leaves the apartment, then returns to find it empty. She laughs about her weird dream, then notices the blue mug from which Gene had drunk, now lying in pieces on the kitchen floor. RECOMMENDATION: Although the characters are believable and Jenny's experience bizarre, there is no indication that she has learned anything from her experience. The plot is supposed to be suspenseful, but the audience will not have any problem unraveling it, and will know who the young man is long before Jenny. Finally, the situation of a strange man in a young girl's apartment, and her rather lackadaisical attitude toward it is not realistic for today's society. ROYALTY: $15. SOURCE: Shenk, Marcia Ann. (1975). Diary. New York, NY: Samuel French. SUBJECTS/PLAY TYPE: Fantasy; Diaries; Drama.

745. 8-12. (-) Birnkrant, Samuel. **Diary of Adam and Eve.** CAST: 1f, 1m. ACTS: 1. SETTINGS: Garden. PLAYING TIME: 30 min. PLOT: Adam and Eve gradually come to respect each other, with the evolution shared with the audience as each writes in a diary and speaks the entries aloud. RECOMMENDATION: The stage setting is simple to create, but the play itself moves slowly and the occasional spots of humor rely a great deal on sexual stereotypes. ROYALTY: $10. SOURCE: Birnkrant, Samuel. (1977). Diary of Adam and Eve.

Denver, CO: Pioneer Drama Service. **SUBJECTS/PLAY TYPE**: Creation; Love; Comedy.

746. 2-12*. (+) Morley, John. **Dick Whittington. CAST**: 4f, 13m, Su. **ACTS**: 2. **SETTINGS**: Street; marketplace; stores; mansion; hillside; ship; harem tent; hall. **PLAYING TIME**: 150 min. **PLOT**: London is overrun by rats, and King Rat plans to become Lord Major. His only rivals are Dick Whittington and his cat, Tommy, who are working for the wealthy merchant, Fitzwarren. Dick is framed by King Rat and drummed out of town for stealing money, but the Fairy of the Bells helps Dick win back his good name. He sails for Morocco, survives a shipwreck, wins a duel with King Rat, comes home a wealthy man to marry lovely Alice Fitzwarren, and becomes the new Lord Mayor of London. **RECOMMENDATION**: This contains many of the traditional elements of British pantomime: slapstick humor, audience participation, and much singing and dancing. Some editing of both dialogue and musical numbers would be possible without detracting from the play, if a shorter production is desired. Designed to appeal to a wide range of ages, the plot will attract children, but much of the humor will only be understood by adults. Only adults should attempt to produce this very detailed dramatic performance, although some children may be cast as extras. **ROYALTY**: NA. **SOURCE**: Morley, John. (1986). Dick Whittington. New York, NY: Samuel French. **SUBJECTS/PLAY TYPE**: Comedy; Folk Tales, England; Pantomime.

747. 1-3. (+) Hume, Pat & Dorsey, Don M. (Johnson, Richard) **Dick Whittington and his amazing cat.** (Dick Whittington and his amazing cat) **CAST**: 4f, 9m, Su. **ACTS**: 1. **SETTINGS**: Road; doorway; kitchen; hall; dock. **PLAYING TIME**: NA. **PLOT**: Dick Whittington befriends a talking cat while on a journey to London to seek his fortune. He finds employment in the house of Mr. Fitzwarren, owner of a merchant vessel about to embark on a voyage. Each member of the household contributes to the trip and Dick is forced to give his beloved cat. The cat saves an Oriental monarch from starvation when he takes on the voracious mice in the kingdom. In gratitude the Caliph sends gold and jewels to Dick. **RECOMMENDATION**: Although neither the settings, language nor plot seem to fit the suggested time frame of the 1930s, the story is quite entertaining. The set requirements are considerable and might make this too expensive for a student group. **ROYALTY**: $25. **SOURCE**: Hume, Pat, & Dorsey, Don M. (1980). Dick Whittington and his amazing cat. New Orleans, LA: Anchorage Press, Inc. **SUBJECTS/PLAY TYPE**: Adventure; Cats; Folk Tales, England; Musical; Adaptation.

748. 4-6. (+) Thane, Adele. **Dick Whittington and his cat. CAST**: 4f, 3m, Su. **ACTS**: 1. **SETTINGS**: Kitchen. **PLAYING TIME**: 25 min. **PLOT**: Dick Whittington, a poor urchin boy, runs away to London to make his fortune. He finds employment as a kitchen boy in an alderman's house, but his sleeping place in the attic is full of rats. He saves a cat from being drowned and it eats all the rats in the attic, and becomes his best friend. Dick's master takes the cat on a trading journey overseas, and Dick is afraid he will never see her again. However, when Dick's master returns, he brings Dick a chest of gold from the King of Barbary because the cat has rid the King's palace of all the rats. Dick has made his fortune, and it is predicted he will one day be Mayor of London. **RECOMMENDATION**: Staging calls for many off-stage voices and noises, and one character must sing. This would be a logical choice for a class studying the middle ages or English history. **ROYALTY**: Free to Plays subscribers. **SOURCE**: Thane, Adele. (1975, April). Dick Whittington and his cat. Plays: The Drama Magazine for Young People, pp. 42-51. **SUBJECTS/PLAY TYPE**: Folktales, England; Cats; Playlet.

749. K-12. (+) Scholey, Arthur. (Dickens, Charles) **The Dickens Christmas carol show.** (A Christmas Carol) **CAST**: 8f, 10m. **ACTS**: 2. **SETTINGS**: Office; home; schoolroom; ballroom; orphanage; dining room; parlor; cemetery; street. **PLAYING TIME**: 25 min. **PLOT**: This is a faithful musical adaptation. **RECOMMENDATION**: Musicians and a fiddler are needed to produce this. It is also recommended that the upper grades produce for the lower grades, although some parts might be played by younger actors. **ROYALTY**: $35. **SOURCE**: Scholey, Arthur. (1979). The Dickens Christmas carol show. New Orleans, LA: Anchorage Press. **SUBJECTS/PLAY TYPE**: Christmas; Musical; Adaptation.

750. 7-12. (+) Miller, Ev. **Dickerson for Senate! CAST**: 4f, 5m, Su. **ACTS**: 2. **SETTINGS**: Bare stage, props. **PLAYING TIME**: NA. **PLOT**: High principled Brian Dickerson has no chance to win his party's primary or election to the U.S. Senate. Mr. Arian and Mr. Burroughs, representing good and evil, function as catalysts for changing this situation. They engage in a game where each seeks to influence Dickerson's decisions regarding sacrificing his principles for the sake of winning. Burroughs brings evidence used by Dickerson to secure the nomination at the cost of his opponent's political death. This is repeated as the general election approaches. Arian, however, reminds Dickerson that each human must choose between good and evil and building or destroying lives. Dickerson destroys the evidence, and his chances of winning the election, and Mr. Arian wins the "game." **RECOMMENDATION**: This describes the intricacies of politics and exposes the nature of political manipulation. Either as a play about the political process or about morality, it attracts the attention of the audience, and is recommended for the information it conveys and the questions it raises. Some regional biases which are not essential to the plot may be deleted. **ROYALTY**: $35. **SOURCE**: Miller, Ev. (1983). Dickerson for Senate! Franklin, OH: Eldridge Press. **SUBJECTS/PLAY TYPE**: Ethics, Political; Drama.

751. 8-12. (-) Stearns, Mary. **Diet begins tomorrow.**
CAST: 5f. ACTS: 1. SETTINGS: Sleeping porch.
PLAYING TIME: NA. PLOT: Four matronly women
decide to lose weight. Ann secretly couples dieting with
exercise, since she has a black maid who is a wonderful
cook. Unfortunately, her three friends arrive as she is
exercising, so she rolls under the bed to avoid discovery.
The friends find the exercise plans on the desk, Marge
begins to demonstrate them, and spots Ann hiding
under the bed. After a good laugh, they all decide to
begin their diet "tomorrow." RECOMMENDATION:
The play's theme, dieting, and its dialogue appear more
suited for an adult audience. However, the antics
included within the plot (e.g. hiding under the bed) are
more appropriate for younger audiences. The extreme
stereotype of the black maid, who speaks in old south
black dialect is an unforgiveable affront, as is the
portrayal of her very proper, very pompous employer.
ROYALTY: NA. SOURCE: Stearns, Mary. (n.d.). Diet
begins tomorrow. Franklin, OH: Eldridge Pub. Co.
SUBJECTS/PLAY TYPE: Dieting; Comedy.

752. 4-12. (+) Gilfond, Henry. **The difference a
valentine makes.** CAST: 2f, 3m, 1u. ACTS: 1.
SETTINGS: Living room. PLAYING TIME: 15 min.
PLOT: Mom and 10 year old Billie get Valentine's cards.
Sara, 16, who hasn't gotten one from her boyfriend,
proclaims that the whole idea is childish. But when her
card finally arrives, she is delighted.
RECOMMENDATION: The message that little
considerations from others are paramount is well
presented in this high interest/low vocabulary skit.
ROYALTY: None. SOURCE: Gilfond, Henry. (1985).
Holiday plays for reading. New York, NY: Walker.
SUBJECTS/PLAY TYPE: Valentine's Day; Skit.

753. 7-12. (+) Sawyer-Young, Kat. **Different. CAST:**
1f. ACTS: 1. SETTINGS: None. PLAYING TIME: 1 min.
PLOT: Anna, an immigrant, asks her American friends
to help her assimilate. RECOMMENDATION: This will
provoke much discussion about the problems of
immigrants. ROYALTY: None. SOURCE: Sawyer-
Young, Kat. (1987). Minute monologues for
contemporary teens. Boston, MA: Baker's Plays.
SUBJECTS/PLAY TYPE: Immigrants; Language
Barriers; Monologue.

754. 7-12. (+) Atkin, Flora B. **Dig n' tell. CAST: 8u.**
ACTS: 1. SETTINGS: Archaeological dig. PLAYING
TIME: NA. PLOT: Archaeologists enact Jewish folktales
that are inspired by the various objects they find during a
Middle Eastern archaeological dig. The stories illustrate
the folly of greed and stupidity, and extoll virtue.
RECOMMENDATION: This is a unique way to use
storytelling as the folktales are acted out dramatically
and humorously. The play requires some singing and
dancing. Some of the vocabulary may need to be
explained in the program. ROYALTY: NA. SOURCE:
Atkin, Flora B. (1978). Dig n' tell. Rowayton, CT: New
Plays for Children. SUBJECTS/PLAY TYPE: Folk Tales,
Jewish; Archaeology; Drama.

755. 7-12. (+) Murray, John. **Dig that Mastodon!**
CAST: 7f, 5m, Su. ACTS: 1. SETTINGS: Living room.
PLAYING TIME: 35 min. PLOT: When Dwight Reed
unearths some Mastodon bones, tourists and the media
descend on his family and disrupt their lives. They are
happy to be forgotten when someone else finds
Stegosaurus bones. RECOMMENDATION: The
theme and plot are within the comprehension level of
the intended audience. The materials necessary can
easily be obtained at a minimum expenditure.
ROYALTY: None. SOURCE: Murray, John. (1979).
Fifteen plays for teenagers. Boston, MA: Plays, Inc.
SUBJECTS/PLAY TYPE: Family; Media; Comedy.

756. 7-9. (+) Plotz, Rob. **Dingaling. CAST: 9f, 4m.**
ACTS: 1. SETTINGS: Office. PLAYING TIME: NA.
PLOT: An inept young man who takes a job as a
telephone solicitor for vacuums makes customers angry,
but gives the impression of doing a fine job. When the
boss tries to promote him to demonstrator, the young
man quits rather than face the customers he spoke to.
His replacement encounters the irate customers who
were   offended   by   the   first   solicitor.
RECOMMENDATION: The solicitor's part is quite
lengthy, but this is hilarious. ROYALTY: $25. SOURCE:
Plotz, Rob. (1983). Dingaling. Franklin, OH: Eldridge Pub.
Co. SUBJECTS/PLAY TYPE: Salespeople; Comedy.

757. 7-9. (+) Karshner, Roger. **Dino and Susan.**
CAST: 1f, 1m. ACTS: 1. SETTINGS: None. PLAYING
TIME: NA. PLOT: Dino tells Susan that Chris, a
classmate, committed suicide by shooting himself. They
question why this happened to someone who seemed so
happy, and wonder what kinds of problems Chris was
holding inside. Dino and Susan agree that
communication is important. RECOMMENDATION:
This effectively makes a point about the importance of
communication. ROYALTY: NA. SOURCE: Karshner,
Roger. (1986). Scenes for teenagers. Toluce Lake, CA:
Dramaline Pub. SUBJECTS/PLAY TYPE: Suicide;
Scene.

758. K-4*. (+) Hotchner, Steve & Hotchner, Kathy.
The dinosaur play. CAST: 2f, 2m, 1u. ACTS: 1.
SETTINGS: Swamp. PLAYING TIME: 25 min. PLOT: A
narrator takes the audience back in time to prehistory,
where the children are introduced to different kinds of
dinosaurs that may be the "right" mother for an
unidentified dinosaur egg. In the end, the egg receives
an inappropriate mother (because the right one is not
available) and an appropriate (but reluctant) father.
RECOMMENDATION: Children will enjoy being able
to help the abandoned egg find a mother in this
charming, cute play. Older actors are necessary to guide
the children's participation. ROYALTY: $25. SOURCE:
Hotchner, Steve, & Hotchner, Kathy. (1977). The
dinosaur play. Chicago, IL: Dramatic Pub. Co.
SUBJECTS/PLAY TYPE: Dinosaurs; Audience
Participation; Extinction; Skit.

759. 7-12. (+) McDonough, Jerome. **Dirge. CAST: 5f,**
6m, Su. ACTS: 1. SETTINGS: Small town jail. PLAYING

TIME: NA. PLOT: A young man is in jail awaiting his execution. Flashbacks explain that the young man accidentally stabbed his girlfriend's mother while trying to defend her, but no one believes this, and the only person who knows the truth, the girlfriend, is too afraid to speak up. Since no one will listen to him, the young man is taken away to be hanged. RECOMMENDATION: This engrosses the audience with the action while encouraging consideration of how such a miscarriage of justice could come about. ROYALTY: $15. SOURCE: McDonough, Jerome. (1975). Dirge. Boston, MA: Baker's Plays. SUBJECTS/PLAY TYPE: Justice; Capital Punishment; Drama.

760. 9-12. (+) Van Horn, Bill. **Dirty Dan strikes again! CAST:** 6f, 10m, Su. ACTS: 1. SETTINGS: Outpost. PLAYING TIME: 30 min. PLOT: Multiple problems exist for lovely Louella Lovelace as she prepares for her wedding. Her fiance, Richard Dobetter, is off searching for Jacques LeSprat, and the dastardly Dirty Dan has sworn to marry her himself. When Dobetter arrives, he is injured when fat LeSprat falls on him. Lovely Louella exposes the disguised Dirty Dan and holds him hostage with an unloaded gun, but to no avail. The townspeople rush off to find silver, the church is buried by an avalanche, and the expected guests do not arrive. But the wedding is finally performed, and Dirty Dan serves as the flower girl. RECOMMENDATION: The diverse characters are bound together by a smooth plot. Action packed and hilarious scenes will hold the audience's attention, and the dialogue is natural and funny. ROYALTY: $30. SOURCE: Van Horn, Bill. (1987). Dirty Dan strikes again! Franklin, OH: Eldridge Pub. Co. SUBJECTS/PLAY TYPE: Police; Northwest Mounted Police; Melodrama.

761. 8-12*. (+) Kelly, Tim. **Dirty work in high places.** CAST: 9f, 8m, 5u. ACTS: 2. SETTINGS: Cottage interior; executive suite; street. PLAYING TIME: NA. PLOT: The villain, "Gentle Grimes," seeks to oust Grandpa, Grandma, Baby Bob, and Baby Alice from their humble cottage in order to build high rise apartments, but also wants to marry their granddaughter, Little Saccharin. Simultaneously, he works to retain his mayoral office in spite of street protests and rallies led by the Widow Aged, and to sell a smog machine to an underdeveloped country under the guise of assisting it to enter the "modern world." Dauntless Crusader, a consumer advocate, exposes Gentle Grimes and loses his heart to Little Saccharin. RECOMMENDATION: This delightful melodrama, focusing upon unscrupulous contemporary business and political practices, would be difficult to stage but will be worth the effort. It requires a large theater group with varied talents, and a director with experience, patience, and attention to detail. The many diverse characters are often on stage at the same time. ROYALTY: $40. SOURCE: Kelly, Tim. (1976). Dirty work in high places. Boston, MA: Baker's Plays. SUBJECTS/PLAY TYPE: Swindlers and Swindling; Ethics, Business; Satire; Melodrama.

762. 6-8. (+) Tyo, John & Tyo, Anna. **Disco stars.** CAST: 3f, 4m, Su. ACTS: 1. SETTINGS: School gym. PLAYING TIME: 30 min. PLOT: Juan and Debbie practice for a disco dance contest; the winners appear on Rick Clark's television show. Kim and Mike have also entered the contest but claim falsely that they are not practicing. Kim and Mike win the dance competition but Rick Clark picks Juan and Debbie to appear on his show because they are hard workers. RECOMMENDATION: This discusses the value of hard work and truthfulness. The subject, disco dancing, is dated but the play could be easily updated by substituting a different type of dancing. This could also be used to showcase dancers. ROYALTY: Free to Plays Subscribers. SOURCE: Tyo, John & Tyo, Anna. (1979, April). Disco stars. Plays: The Drama Magazine for Young People, pp. 1-11. SUBJECTS/PLAY TYPE: Dancing; Playlet.

763. 9-12*. (+) Way, Brian. **Discovery and survival.** CAST: 3f, 4m. ACTS: 2. SETTINGS: Bare stage. PLAYING TIME: NA. PLOT: A series of scenes depicts the hope and despair of the human spirit through various events in human history. They range from a war zone, to prison, to slavery, and to the invention of Braille and the telegraph. RECOMMENDATION: While the emphasis is on the indomitable human spirit, the situations which are dramatized will fascinate high school audiences and provoke thought and discussion. This should be produced by adults. ROYALTY: $20. SOURCE: Way, Brian. (1977). Discovery and survival. Boston, MA: Baker's Plays. SUBJECTS/PLAY TYPE: Human Spirit; Experimental Theater; Drama.

764. 9-12. (+) Leonard, Jim Jr. **The diviners. CAST:** 5f, 6m. ACTS: 2. SETTINGS: Bare stage, props. PLAYING TIME: NA. PLOT: Buddy is a simple minded boy with the ability to divine water with a stick, though he has an unbearable fear of water, refusing to wash in it. C.C., an itinerant ex-preacher, looks for work at Buddy's father's farm. He tries to eliminate Buddy's fear of water and takes him out to the river, where the interfering townswomen mistake the act as a baptism. Angered at the intrusion, C.C. loses his grip on Buddy, who drifts out into the river and drowns. RECOMMENDATION: This is a touching, thought provoking story. Throughout, the warmth and honesty of the characters infect the audience with the goodness in people. Lighting is essential to create the flowing river and to convey atmosphere. ROYALTY: $50. SOURCE: Leonard, Jim. (1980). The diviners. New York, NY: Samuel French. SUBJECTS/PLAY TYPE: Mental Retardation; Drama.

765. 4-6. (+) Sawyer-Young, Kat. **Divorce. CAST:** 2f. ACTS: 1. SETTINGS: Front porch. PLAYING TIME: NA. PLOT: Fearing her parents might divorce, Ann confides in Beth, a child of divorced parents. Beth advises Anne not to worry, tells her what divorce has meant to her, then expresses her own desires to have her parents get back together again. RECOMMENDATION: In a serious, sensitive scene,

two girls discuss the fears, the benefits, and the hopes that a divorce can bring: fear that they were the cause, benefits in that they can celebrate Christmas twice, and hope that reconciliation is possible. ROYALTY: NA. SOURCE: Sawyer-Young, Kat. (1986). Contemporary scenes for contemporary kids. Boston, MA: Baker's Plays. SUBJECTS/PLAY TYPE: Divorce; Scene.

766. 7-12. (+) Sawyer-Young, Kat. **Divorce. CAST:** 1m. ACTS: 1. SETTINGS: None. PLAYING TIME: 1 min. PLOT: Rick describes his feelings about his parents' deteriorating relationship. RECOMMENDATION: This will be therapeutic for children and might help divorcing parents to be more careful about their children's feelings. ROYALTY: None. SOURCE: Sawyer-Young, Kat. (1987). Minute monologues for contemporary teens. Boston, MA: Baker's Plays. SUBJECTS/PLAY TYPE: Divorce; Monologue.

767. 9-12. (+) Murray, John. **Do or diet. CAST:** 1u. ACTS: 1. SETTINGS: None. PLAYING TIME: NA. PLOT: A middle aged woman leads a weekly meeting of the Calorie Counters, reporting on the members' progress, weighing dieters, and providing menu suggestions about which she knows nothing. When she is told that her "never fail scale" is 10 pounds light, she screams her "think thin - live thin - be thin" motto, as she voluntarily steps down from her position. RECOMMENDATION: This might be particularly effective at a Weight Watcher's meeting, in lieu of the usual "inspirational" speeches. ROYALTY: None. SOURCE: Murray, John. (1982). Modern monologues for young people. Boston, MA: Plays, Inc. SUBJECTS/PLAY TYPE: Comedy; Dieting; Monologue.

768. 7-12. (+) McNair, Rick. **Doctor Barnardo's pioneers. CAST:** 2f, 3m. ACTS: 1. SETTINGS: Office, ship, farmyard, porch. PLAYING TIME: NA. PLOT: Two preteens are sent to the famous English Barnardo School for orphans, then to Canadian foster homes to work for their keep. The sister and brother are shuffled to several homes, some pleasant and some cruel. Neither is able to fulfill career aspirations, but they do succeed in making a living and a life for themselves in the new world. RECOMMENDATION: The Barnardo School was an attempt to gainfully employ children who lived on the streets of London in the late 1800s. Although begun for humanitarian reasons, the cruelty that the children often suffered, as well as the success that some of them found, is well portrayed here. With doubling and tripling, the cast could be minimal, but a cast of 24 would be most comfortable for an amateur crew. ROYALTY: NA. SOURCE: Doolittle, Joyce. (1984). Eight plays for young people. Edmonton, Canada: NeWest Pub. SUBJECTS/PLAY TYPE: Orphans; Barnardo School; Drama.

769. 1-12. (+) Fricker, Olga. (Lofting, Hugh) **Doctor Dolittle.** (The voyages of Doctor Dolittle) **CAST:** 3f, 4m, Su. ACTS: 3. SETTINGS: Parlor; shore. PLAYING TIME: 75 min. PLOT: Dr. Dolittle, his friend Matthew, and his animal family are introduced to the audience.

Since the animals love and trust Dr. Dolittle, they teach him how to talk to them, after which their adventures begin. He goes to Africa (with a few of the animals) to help sick monkeys. Once the animals have recovered, he returns home accompanied by Pushmi-Pullyu. They join a circus, but become quickly disillusioned, and at the end of the play, Dr. Dolittle buys the circus. RECOMMENDATION: Fricker's adaptation of her brother's book is as delightful as the original. ROYALTY: $35. SOURCE: Fricker, Olga. (1976). Doctor Dolittle. Woodstock, IL: Dramatic Pub. Co. SUBJECTS/PLAY TYPE: Animals; Adaptation.

770. 3-8. (+) Marrapodi, Betty. **Doctor Hoo. CAST:** 8u. ACTS: 1. SETTINGS: Office. PLAYING TIME: 20 min. PLOT: Animals, hurt or defeated by various types of pollution, come to Dr. Hoo's medical clinic and talk about pollution's dangerous effects. RECOMMENDATION: This examines air and water pollution, insecticide poisoning, dumping of dangerous waste materials, and the destruction of animal species and entire forests from the unusually thought provoking viewpoint of animals and fish. The characters, the plot, and the language are handled well and are appropriate for children. ROYALTY: $10. SOURCE: Marrapodi, Betty. (1973). Doctor Hoo. Schulenburg, TX: I.E. Clark. SUBJECTS/PLAY TYPE: Ecology: Human Survival; Animal Survival; Comedy.

771. 9-12. (+) Bland, Joellen. (Moliere) **A doctor in spite of himself.** (A doctor in spite of himself) **CAST:** 3f, 5m. ACTS: 1. SETTINGS: Woods; furnished room. PLAYING TIME: 30 min. PLOT: A man of riches and power tries to marry his daughter off to a wealthy man 30 years her senior. The daughter, in love with a penniless man, loses her voice, and her father sends his servants to find a doctor who will cure her. They come upon a woodcutter's wife, who tells them her husband is a doctor, but will not admit it unless he is beaten. They find the woodcutter, beat him, and press him into service as a doctor. A humorous set of events take place. The daughter finally marries her true love who inherits a fortune, and the woodcutter returns to his wife, vowing to be a better husband and father. RECOMMENDATION: This does not do justice to the original; it neither conveys the spirit, the satiric messages, nor the plot, and it employs a trite ending and pallid characterizations. ROYALTY: Free to Plays subscribers. SOURCE: Bland, Joellen. (1982, April). A doctor in spite of himself. Plays: The Drama Magazine for Young People, pp. 70-80. SUBJECTS/PLAY TYPE: Farce; Doctors; Adaptation.

772. 10-12. (-) Malkin, Michael R. (Moliere) **The doctor in spite of himself.** (A doctor in spite of himself) **CAST:** 3f, 8m. ACTS: 3. SETTINGS: Woods; living room; garden. PLAYING TIME: NA. PLOT: A disgruntled wife takes revenge on her husband by convincing others that he is a doctor. Instead of "getting his just rewards" for impersonating a doctor, the husband becomes rich and famous through his clever use of bogus "hocus pocus" and connivery. RECOMMENDATION: Malkin tries unsuccessfully to

capture the wry humor and shrewd satire of Moliere's original. The adaptation includes subtle sexual innuendos (which probably will not be understood by adolescents), overt sexual behavior, and scenes where action critical to the plot is not detailed. ROYALTY: $25. SOURCE: Malkin, Michael R. (1981). The doctor in spite of himself. Chicago, IL: Dramatic Pub. Co. SUBJECTS/PLAY TYPE: Doctors; Farce; Adaptation.

773. 7-12. (+) Sawyer-Young, Kat. **Dog.** CAST: 1m. ACTS: 1. SETTINGS: None. PLAYING TIME: 1 min. PLOT: James talks about how great his dead dog was. RECOMMENDATION: This describes effectively the memories of a dog, and teaches how to deal positively with death. ROYALTY: None. SOURCE: Sawyer-Young, Kat. (1987). Minute monologues for contemporary teens. Boston, MA: Baker's Plays. SUBJECTS/PLAY TYPE: Death; Dogs; Monologue.

774. 1-6. (+) Hamlett, Christina & Simpson, Wayne. **Dogs! A tail wagging musical.** CAST: 5f, 6m, Su. ACTS: 2. SETTINGS: Animal shelter. PLAYING TIME: 60 min. PLOT: Ralph and Angel care for seven homeless dogs in a city animal shelter. Angel uses "heart talk" to communicate with the dogs, and learns each one's special story and how they all wonder why humans are so uncaring. Mrs. Kimble, resident of a retirement home nearby, offers them all a home as time is running out. RECOMMENDATION: Very young children will empathize with the plight of the homeless dogs in this production written for older actors. Music and supportive lyrics are included and since all the action takes place in a city animal shelter, the set is inexpensive. ROYALTY: $80. SOURCE: Hamlett, Christina. (1988). Dogs! A tail wagging musical. Franklin, OH: Eldridge Pub. Co. SUBJECTS/PLAY TYPE: Pets; Dogs; Animal Shelter; Musical.

775. 7-12. (+) Boiko, Claire. **A dog's best friend.** CAST: 5f, 6m, 3u. ACTS: 1. SETTINGS: Pet shop. PLAYING TIME: 15 min. PLOT: Wolfington T. Bowser owns a people shop to which several dogs come with various problems and questions about their people. RECOMMENDATION: In this caricature of dog owners and their peculiarities, the dialogue is clever, witty, and the potential for comedic acting is wide open. The lighthearted humor is carried out through setting, names of characters, and costumes. The producer should note that a French accent is necessary for two of the female characters. ROYALTY: Free to Plays subscribers. SOURCE: Boiko, Claire. (1982, April). A dog's best friend. Plays: The Drama Magazine for Young People, pp. 59-62. SUBJECTS/PLAY TYPE: Dogs; Pets; Comedy.

776. 4-8. (+) Kehret, Peg. **Dogs, Orion and buttons.** CAST: 1u. ACTS: 1. SETTINGS: None. PLAYING TIME: NA. PLOT: Describing the wonders in life opened up to him by taking time to notice details, a youngster expounds on the value of observation. RECOMMENDATION: Simply, honestly, and without preaching, this encourages us to pay attention to life's details. ROYALTY: NA. SOURCE: Kehret, Peg. (1986).

Winning monologs for young actors. Colorado Springs, CO: Meriwether Pub. SUBJECTS/PLAY TYPE: Observation; Hobbies; Monologue.

777. 10-12. (+) Dee, Peter. **Doing poetry with Helen, Veronica, Sonny, and poor dead Charlie.** CAST: 2f, 2m. ACTS: 1. SETTINGS: Bare stage, props. PLAYING TIME: NA. PLOT: Teenagers hold their regular group meeting to read poetry they have written, the first meeting without their friend Charlie, who committed suicide six days earlier. As the group reads poems which deal with old age, discovery, AIDS, and death, Charlie (as a ghost) reacts to them and comments about himself. The climax of the poetry reading is Veronica's response to Charlie's death. RECOMMENDATION: Through extraordinarily moving poetry and brutally honest displays of emotion, this provides an excellent vehicle for a discussion of any of the topics presented. The author suggests that the poems might be presented individually. Explicit and graphic language and sexual allusions may be a problem for some, but they cannot be removed without destroying the impact of this play for mature, well read audiences and actors. ROYALTY: NA. SOURCE: Dee. Peter. (1986). Doing poetry with Helen, Veronica, Sonny and poor dead Charlie. Boston, MA: Baker's Plays. SUBJECTS/PLAY TYPE: Suicide; Poetry; Drama.

778. 1-6. (-) Clark, Mary Margaret. **The doll with the blue bonnet.** CAST: 10f, 11m, 8u. ACTS: 3. SETTINGS: Meadow. PLAYING TIME: NA. PLOT: This adaptation of a Tejas Indian legend centers around the belief that sacrificing prized possessions to the rain god will bring rain. When Little Princess, an Indian girl, and Billy Jones, a young pioneer, become friends, they exchange gifts, a token of friendship and a peace offering. Billy's gift is a doll wearing a blue bonnet made of materials gathered from the land. Because the doll becomes Little Princess' most cherished possession, it is burned as a sacrifice to the rain god. Not realizing its significance, Billy becomes upset with his friend for throwing away his gift. His unhappiness changes to wonder when the next day he sees a meadow full of blue flowers wearing "bonnets." RECOMMENDATION: This might have been intended to teach how Indians and pioneers lived during the early days of settling, but it is hopelessly sentimental, historically inaccurate, and very stereotyped. This will require much preparation time, but it is too sappy to be worth the effort. ROYALTY: $30. SOURCE: Clark, Mary Margaret. (1976). The doll with the blue bonnet. Franklin, OH: Eldridge Pub. Co. SUBJECTS/PLAY TYPE: Texas, History; Legends, Native American; Tejas Indians; Musical.

779. 7-12*. (+) McDonough, Jerome. **Dolls.** CAST: 9f, 5m, Su. ACTS: 1. SETTINGS: High school. PLAYING TIME: NA. PLOT: This strong play focuses upon the disastrous consequences of teenage sex and drug abuse: unwanted pregnancy, disease (i.e. AIDS), child abuse, and addiction. Teenagers, either alone or in small groups, relate or portray their reactions to and the consequences of their sexual encounters. An ensemble of actors is used to dispel myths, reinforce major points,

separate the revelations, and provide transition. Functioning as a backdrop for the characters, slides are projected, depicting stages of conception and fetal development. At intervals the slides change and an off-stage narrator describes each new stage of development. RECOMMENDATION: This is a very believable peer oriented look at the myths surrounding teenage sexuality as well as a very frank presentation of the consequences of sexual activity and drug use at this early age. A parental permission form is provided for use in obtaining parental approval for a son/daughters' participation in the play, a rationale for presenting the play, and a series of suggestions on how to prepare the community. **Dolls** will prompt many questions from all who are involved. ROYALTY: NA. SOURCE: McDonough, Jerome. (1988). Dolls. Schulenburg, TX: I. E. Clark. SUBJECTS/PLAY TYPE: Pregnancy, Teenage; Drug Abuse; Sexual Diseases; Drama.

780. 9-12. (+) Kundrat, Theodore V. (Ibsen, Henrik) **A doll's house: A modern version for Reader's Theatre.** (A doll's house) CAST: 2f, 2m. ACTS: 1. SETTINGS: Bare stage. PLAYING TIME: 60 min. PLOT: A domestic quarrel results in the wife's traumatic awakening to the realization that both her father and husband have treated her as a doll rather than a person. She slams the door on eight years of marriage to "seek her true identity" as a person. RECOMMENDATION: The original play more vividly developed the characters and their relationships, but the impact of this version is essentially the same. ROYALTY: $15. SOURCE: Kundrat, Theodore V. (1979). A doll's house: A modern version for Readers Theatre. Chicago, IL: Coach House Press. SUBJECTS/PLAY TYPE: Marriage; Blackmail; Domestic Problems; Reader's Theater; Adaptation.

781. 4-9. (+) Hischak, Thomas. **The dolls of Poplar House.** CAST: 10f. ACTS: 1. SETTINGS: Living room; attic. PLAYING TIME: NA. PLOT: The girls of Poplar House orphanage are devastated that the Poplar House dolls, collected over many years, are about to be sold to pay for electricity. Mrs. Woods, a bitter, wealthy woman, is convinced by the innocent chidings of the youngsters to donate the needed money. In the process of becoming a nicer person she decides to adopt one of the orphans. RECOMMENDATION: With its message that "something human is dearer to me than the wealth of all the world," this sensitive and lovely drama is appealingly presented and easily resolves itself. Because of the use of dolls and the girls' attachment to them, the play might not appeal to boys unless some of the dolls are changed to be more masculine. Making the dolls will be a challenge. ROYALTY: $15. SOURCE: Hischak, Thomas. (1979). The dolls of Poplar House. Chicago, IL: Dramatic Pub. Co. SUBJECTS/PLAY TYPE: Orphans; Dolls; Drama.

782. K-6. (+) Ashby, Sylvia. **Don Coyote.** CAST: Su. ACTS: 1. SETTINGS: Desert. PLAYING TIME: 60 min. PLOT: A boastful, incorrigible young coyote tries to persuade an animal to race against him in the annual Golden Gourd Race, which he wins every year. He tricks Uncle Armadillo into the race, but the animals, tired of

Don Coyote's trickery and deceit, "fix" the race so Uncle Armadillo wins. Unfortunately, even after Don Coyote is the victim, he remains mischievous. RECOMMENDATION: A very humorous play, this uses a wide age range of children, depending on individual acting ability and number of lines per character. The character of Don Coyote must sing well, for this is his only admirable talent. There are a number of Spanish words in the dialogue which would be an excellent reinforcement for a school teaching the language but they can be minimized without any sacrifice in quality. ROYALTY: $25. SOURCE: Ashby, Sylvia. (1979). Don Coyote. Schulenburg, TX: I.E. Clark. SUBJECTS/PLAY TYPE: Animals; Folk Tale Motifs; Comedy.

783. 6-7. (+) Miller, Jane V. **Don't be just a file clerk.** CAST: 2f, 2m, Su. ACTS: 1. SETTINGS: Office. PLAYING TIME: 15 min. PLOT: Mr. Brown visits a job placement agency, whose vice president, Vance, inflates Brown's resume. He offers Brown several gentrified position openings, and refers him to aptitude testing. When a call comes in announcing an opening for a gifted executive, Vance leaves for the interview, and Brown takes Vance's place. RECOMMENDATION: This hilarious spoof of our penchant for "gentrifying" job names and inflating resumes would be an excellent introduction to the real world of interviewing and job placement. ROYALTY: Free to Plays subscribers. SOURCE: Miller, Jane V. (1975, February). Don't be just a file clerk. Plays: The Drama Magazine for Young People, pp. 73-78. SUBJECTS/PLAY TYPE: Farce; Resumes; Jobs; Skit.

784. 11-12*. (+) Gilsenan, Nancy. **Don't count on forever.** CAST: 9f, 8m. ACTS: 2. SETTINGS: Living room; office; bathroom hallway; apartment. PLAYING TIME: NA. PLOT: Lisa, a senior and head of the high school yearbook, is popular and well adjusted, until her father suddenly moves out to live with another woman. Lisa and her mother struggle toward acceptance and find ways to go on. In her commencement speech, Lisa tells her fellow graduates that they should throw away bad memories and hold on to the good ones. RECOMMENDATION: Lisa is a believable character and her struggle to accept her family's situation is well developed; much of the audience may be able to identify with it. The humor, as Lisa directs weird members of her yearbook staff, adds comic relief to this thought provoking piece. ROYALTY: $50. SOURCE: Gilsenan, Nancy. (1983). Don't count on forever. Chicago, IL: Dramatic Pub. Co. SUBJECTS/PLAY TYPE: Family; Divorce; Drama.

785. 1-6*. (-) Pearson, Carol Lynn Wright & Redford, J.A.C. (Aesopus) **Don't count your chickens until they cry wolf.** (Aesop's fables) CAST: Su. ACTS: 1. SETTINGS: Bare stage, blocks. PLAYING TIME: NA. PLOT: This is a musical retelling of several familiar Aesop's fables. The fables, linked by songs, illustrate the dangers of laziness, vanity, dishonesty, and other frailties of human nature. RECOMMENDATION: The author fails to unify the wide array of fables and characters into

a cohesive unit. Without adequate transitions, the audience is unable to discern when each fable has concluded, and many of the "morals" presented may not be clearly understood. The song lyrics are bright and energetic and some witty remarks are also interspersed within an otherwise disjointed play. ROYALTY: $25. SOURCE: Pearson, Carol Lynn Wright & Redford, J.A.C. (1979). Don't count your chickens until they cry wolf. New Orleans, LA: Anchorage Press. SUBJECTS/PLAY TYPE: Fables; Adaptation.

786. K-3*. (-) Sullivan, Jessie P. **Don't do it just because someone else does!** CAST: 2u. ACTS: 1. SETTINGS: Puppet stage. PLAYING TIME: NA. PLOT: Two children discuss the danger of following the lead of their popular smoking classmates. They decide that before they can convince the smokers to stop, they must first convert them to Christianity. RECOMMENDATION: The implication that only Christians can behave responsibly is abhorrent, and defeats the whole intent of Thessalonians 5:21, the point of this skit. ROYALTY: None. SOURCE: Sullivan, Jessie P. (1978). Puppet scripts for children's church. Grand Rapids, MI: Baker Book House. SUBJECTS/PLAY TYPE: Peer Pressure; Christian Drama; Puppet Play.

787. 6-8. (+) Bradley, Virginia. **Don't fall asleep coach, you might possibly dream.** CAST: 9m. ACTS: 1. SETTINGS: Office. PLAYING TIME: NA. PLOT: A football coach has a nightmare in which his team shrinks and melts away after a rain. RECOMMENDATION: A successful production of this brief skit requires extra large costumes and very small players. ROYALTY: None. SOURCE: Bradley, Virginia. (1975). Is there an actor in the house? New York, NY: Dodd, Mead. SUBJECTS/PLAY TYPE: Football; Skit.

788. 10-12. (+) Urdahl, Richard. **Don't listen to us, Lord...we're only praying.** CAST: 2f, 3m. ACTS: 1. SETTINGS: Conference room. PLAYING TIME: NA. PLOT: The Bishop's Committee needs to find jobs for 12 recent seminary graduates. The new committee chairman wants to call for resignations and reassignments; the Bishop is reluctant. The committee agrees to pray for a solution to the problem and, amazingly, the phone begins to ring, bringing news of the deaths of some targeted retirees. The Bishop becomes nervous about this coincidence and adjourns the meeting for fear that the Lord is listening too carefully to their prayers. RECOMMENDATION: This explores the question of religious faith and the power of prayer. Due to its religious nature, audiences should be chosen carefully, but a young adult Sunday school class might enjoy viewing/ producing/reading this as a supplement to a Bible study group. ROYALTY: $10. SOURCE: Urdahl, Richard. (1984). Don't listen to us, Lord...we're only praying. Boston: Baker's Plays. SUBJECTS/PLAY TYPE: Faith; Prayer; Christian Drama.

789. 5-12. (+) Murray, John. **Don't pet my rock.** CAST: 6f, 10m, Su. ACTS: 1. SETTINGS: Ballroom. PLAYING TIME: 35 min. PLOT: A young couple searches for the half-million dollar Slope Diamond which was stolen while on exhibit during the national pet rock show. Audrey's pet rock, thought to be a piece of the sphinx and capable of speaking, draws media attention and is switched with the Slope Diamond by the unsuspecting thieves trying to make a getaway. In the search, numerous "rock" puns and satirical comments are made. RECOMMENDATION: This zany play has some subtle social messages for those who know a little history, literature, and geology, and who remember the pet rock craze of several years ago. Teenagers who have not been exposed to these subjects will probably laugh anyway and may even start another pet rock trend. This should be performed by high school students or adult amateurs because of the long dialogue for most of the parts. ROYALTY: Free to Plays subscribers. SOURCE: Murray, John. (1985). Fifteen plays for today's teenagers. Boston, MA: Plays, Inc. SUBJECTS/PLAY TYPE: Satire; Pet Rocks; Comedy.

790. 9-12. (+) Cope, Eddie. **Don't print that! Or, 10 nights in a newsroom.** CAST: 6f, 4m, 4u. ACTS: 3. SETTINGS: Newspaper office. PLAYING TIME: 90 min. PLOT: A villainous mayor tries to take over a small-town newspaper that is crusading against corruption at city hall. The newspaper staff refuses to be bought, threatened, or seduced from doing its job. RECOMMENDATION: The dialogue is often more snappy than funny, but if the cast has fun with the play (which is likely), the audience will probably enjoy itself too. High school students may not appreciate the brisk word play as much as an older audience. ROYALTY: $35. SOURCE: Cope, Eddie. (1983). Don't print that! Or, ten nights in a newsroom. Schulenburg, TX: I.E. Clark. SUBJECTS/PLAY TYPE: Newspaper; Corruption, Political; Loyalty; Melodrama.

791. 9-12. (+) Kelly, Tim J. **Don't rock the boat.** CAST: 13f, 12m, Su. ACTS: 3. SETTINGS: Cruise ship. PLAYING TIME: 90 min. PLOT: An aspiring young ship captain conducts his first cruise, which is punctuated with strange passengers and hilarious episodes. Three young singers impersonate an older, well known trio, but during the performance, rich Mrs. Wither's jewels are stolen. Pirates storm the ship and, not until the ship's nurse dopes the pirates, can both hijacking and robbery problems be solved. Running the ship ashore, the Captain is aided by maritime high school students and is rewarded by the Commodore with a new position. RECOMMENDATION: The outrageous characterizations in this comedy will allow for flamboyant acting. Musical/dance numbers are optional but add extra flavor. ROYALTY: $35. SOURCE: Kelly, Tim J. (1983). Don't rock the boat. Franklin, OH: Eldridge Pub. Co. SUBJECTS/PLAY TYPE: Pirates; Cruises; Comedy.

792. 8-12. (-) Slattery, Margaret E. **Don't send for Hector.** CAST: 4f, 5m. ACTS: 1. SETTINGS: Newspaper office. PLAYING TIME: 30 min. PLOT: Situations go from bad to disastrous as students left in charge of a local newspaper lose accounts and readers. They call in Hector the genius to solve their problems, even though his costs border on extortion. Hector "fixes" everything, but instead of collecting his fees, he meets the girl of his

dreams. RECOMMENDATION: Although the conflict is humorous and well developed, Hector's solutions are sexist and anti-educational; the boys on the paper are portrayed as controlling the actions of one of the female reporters. These flaws make a potentially good play into an insulting one. ROYALTY: Free to Plays subscribers. SOURCE: Slattery, Margaret E. (1983, March). Don't send for Hector. Plays: The Drama Magazine for Young People, pp. 12- 22. SUBJECTS/PLAY TYPE: Newspapers; Comedy.

793. 1-3*. (-) Sucke, Greer. **Don't sleep under the mapou tree. CAST:** 2f, 4m. ACTS: 2. SETTINGS: Tree; crossroads. PLAYING TIME: 45 min. PLOT: Two plays are included, based on Haitian folklore. The first details the efforts of a werewolf to summon a warlock to banish the Sun. The sun is trapped inside the Mapou Tree and villagers outsmart both warlock and werewolf to free it. The second concerns a boy named Bouki who is asked to travel to Port-au-Prince to sell yams, and encounters Legba, the god of the crossroads, and other magical creatures on his trip. RECOMMENDATION: Written to be performed in a workshop by professional actors with children from the audience participating, this may be inappropriate for the indicated grade level due to its frightening characters and storylines. ROYALTY: $15. SOURCE: Sucke, Greer. (1980). Don't sleep under the mapou tree. Denver, CO: Pioneer Drama Service. SUBJECTS/PLAY TYPE: Folk Tales, Haiti; Participation Play.

794. 8-12. (+) Majeski, Bill. **Don't try to Hyde from me, Dr. Jekyll. CAST:** 6f, 3m, Su. ACTS: 2. SETTINGS: Clinic; home. PLAYING TIME: NA. PLOT: A young doctor Jekyll experiments with a pill to cure nervousness and shyness, but it turns him into a wild stand-up comic, "Mr. Hyde." Reggie wants to frame the doctor in order to steal his fiancee but, after he takes the pill, betrays himself. RECOMMENDATION: Much of the humor here relies on sophomoric jokes and suggestive character names. The allusion to a known literary work and the idea of hidden personalities should intrigue the audience. ROYALTY: $35. SOURCE: Majeski, Bill. (1977). Don't try to Hyde from me, Dr. Jekyll. Chicago, IL: Dramatic Pub. Co. SUBJECTS/PLAY TYPE: Personalities; Comedy.

795. 7-12. (-) Brother, Eric & Shaw, Mark. **Donna's angel. CAST:** 3f, 4m. ACTS: 1. SETTINGS: High school auditorium. PLAYING TIME: 30 min. PLOT: Donna consoles Jimmy, who feels he is to blame for losing the football game. Brian, the quarterback, also feels Jimmy is to blame, and tries to pick a fight. Donna settles things temporarily by getting the two to agree that whoever gets a date with Rhonda Ravelli for the prom wins, with the loser acting as chauffeur. Donna hopes to go with Jimmy, and does, because Jimmy loses the bet, and wins Donna's heart. RECOMMENDATION: This play illustrates how confusing teenage relationships can be. However, although written in 1981, it simply does not have a contemporary tone. ROYALTY: Free to Plays subscribers. SOURCE: Brothers, Eric and Shaw, Mark. (1981, November). Donna's angel. Plays: The Drama

Magazine for Young People, pp. 23- 32. SUBJECTS/PLAY TYPE: Romance; Wishes; Comedy.

796. 7-9. (+) Karshner, Roger. **Donny and Fred. CAST:** 2m. ACTS: 1. SETTINGS: None. PLAYING TIME: NA. PLOT: A recovered teenage alcoholic successfully convinces his friend to stop drinking because he cares. RECOMMENDATION: Although the language is raw, the boys' interaction is realistic and the situation of a friend trying to help another through alcoholism is important for teens to see. ROYALTY: NA. SOURCE: Karshner, Roger. (1986). Scenes for teenagers. Toluca Lake, CA: Dramaline Pub. SUBJECTS/PLAY TYPE: Alcoholism; Scene.

797. 7-9. (+) Karshner, Roger. **Donny and Harry. CAST:** 2m. ACTS: 1. SETTINGS: None. PLAYING TIME: NA. PLOT: Donny and Harry, teen alcoholics, meet for the first time at an alcoholic meeting. Donny, a recovering alcoholic, tries to help Harry, who is just now quitting and whose mother is also in Alcoholics Anonymous. Harry realizes by talking to Donny that he is not alone and that he can quit. RECOMMENDATION: This draws a very realistic picture of teenage alcoholism and its cure. Some of the language is raw, but can be omitted without affecting the message. ROYALTY: NA. SOURCE: Karshner, Roger. (1986). Scenes for teenagers. Toluca Lake, CA: Dramaline Pub. SUBJECTS/PLAY TYPE: Alcoholism; Scene.

798. 2-5. (+) Clapp, Patricia. **The do-nothing frog. CAST:** 6f, 9m, 1u. ACTS: 1. SETTINGS: Shop. PLAYING TIME: 15 min. PLOT: In a store for the future where children can browse to find their future careers, each child chooses a career that will make the world a better place to live except one who wants to be a do-nothing frog. The storekeeper and the other children convince him that his career is unworthy and he comes up with the alternative of being a zookeeper. RECOMMENDATION: Although this has very little dialogue to memorize, no costuming, and few props, the children are not characterized realistically. The play gives us a view of the future society as a structured utopia where everyone will be a smiling productive member. Being a frog may be more appealing. ROYALTY: Free to Plays subscribers. SOURCE: Clapp, Patricia. (1978, April). The do-nothing frog. Plays: The Drama Magazine for Young People, pp. 53-58. SUBJECTS/PLAY TYPE: Careers; Social Studies; Conformity; Skit.

799. 9-12. (+) Murray, John. **The door. CAST:** 2f, 1m. ACTS: 1. SETTINGS: Living room. PLAYING TIME: 25 min. PLOT: A young nurse becomes nervous after she is hired by an old woman, Mrs. Merlin, to care for her invalid husband, Paul, yet is not allowed to see him. While Mrs. Merlin prepares tea, the nurse finds a magazine that looks new, but is actually 10 years old; she decides that Paul has been dead for 10 years. She tries to escape from the house, but Mrs. Merlin agrees to let the nurse meet Paul. A feeble old man comes out of the bedroom and horrifies Nurse Withers by telling her that it was actually Mrs. Merlin who died 10 years ago. RECOMMENDATION: The suspense builds quickly,

the dialogue is purposeful and believable, and the full bodied plot will allow the cast to perform well with or without much experience. ROYALTY: Free to Plays subscribers. SOURCE: Murray, John. (1986, October). The door. Plays: The Drama Magazine for Young People, pp. 24- 30. SUBJECTS/PLAY TYPE: Supernatural; Mystery; Horror; Playlet.

800. 7-12. (+) Zeder, Susan L. **Doors. CAST:** 1f, 3m, Su. **ACTS:** 1. **SETTINGS:** Boy's room. **PLAYING TIME:** NA. **PLOT:** Jeff, 11, confides to a friend that he cannot stand his parents' constant arguing. He imagines how he would like his parents to act, but inevitably, arguing enters into the fantasy. Jeff faces reality when mom and dad announce they are getting a divorce; he accepts the situation and comforts his hurt mother. RECOMMENDATION: This shows the real hurt of a child whose parents fight, and portrays the tension of a dissolving marriage as it successfully brings a common "social problem" into focus on stage. Dialogue for the "arguments" is not supplied, but should be improvised by the actors to fit the audience. ROYALTY: $35. SOURCE: Zeder, Susan L. (1985). Doors. New Orleans, LA: Anchorage Press, Inc. SUBJECTS/PLAY TYPE: Divorce; Family Relations; Drama.

801. 1-8*. (+) Hotchner, Steve & Hotchner, Kathy. (Baum, Lyman Frank) **Dorothy and the Wizard of Oz.** (The wonderful Wizard of Oz) **CAST:** 3f, 1m, 3u. **ACTS:** 1. **SETTINGS:** Bare stage. **PLAYING TIME:** 35 min. **PLOT:** The audience plays the Munchkins, as the Wicked Witch of the West plots to get Dorothy's magic slippers. Dorothy finds her way back to Kansas with some help from the Wizard. RECOMMENDATION: Children will be very excited to have the cast coming into the audience and performing the play in their midst. Because of the audience participation, it is recommended that the play be produced by older actors. The music is original. ROYALTY: $25. SOURCE: Hotchner, Steve and Kathy Hotchner. (1979). Dorothy and the Wizard of Oz. Chicago, IL: Dramatic Pub. Co. SUBJECTS/PLAY TYPE: Participation Play; Oz; Musical; Adaptation.

802. 3-7. (+) Nolan, Paul T. **The Double Nine of Chih Yuan. CAST:** 2f, 3m, Su. **ACTS:** 1. **SETTINGS:** Bare Stage. **PLAYING TIME:** 20 min. **PLOT:** Why the Chinese celebrate the ninth day of the ninth month, called the Double Nine, and why kites are part of that celebration is explained here. An old man comes to Chin Yuan's farm, which represents China, and tells the family he will lead them to safety from the killing frost of winter. A doll is left behind, because it is not alive. A turtle, which is living, is flown on the kite to be above the frost. When the family returns after the frost, they find all is well with the children's possessions. Through this experience, China learns to prepare for winter and kites become part of the celebration of its arrival. RECOMMENDATION: With beautiful, poetic language, this not only tells the story of a Chinese custom, but also demonstrates the wisdom of thinking positively, and the necessity of foresight. ROYALTY: None for amateur performance. SOURCE: Nolan, Paul T. (1982). Folk tale plays round

the world: A collection of royalty-free, one-act plays about lands far and near. Boston: Plays, Inc. SUBJECTS/PLAY TYPE: Mythology, China; Allegory.

803. 7-9. (-) Karshner, Roger. **Doug and Doris. CAST:** 1f, 1m. **ACTS:** 1. **SETTINGS:** None. **PLAYING TIME:** 5 min. **PLOT:** Doug, a fan of older films, and Doris, who likes modern movies, fight about which is better with no resolution, because all they do is knock the other type without successfully defending their favorite. RECOMMENDATION: This inane fight has no point, and its language is unsuitable. ROYALTY: NA. SOURCE: Karshner, Roger. (1986). Scenes for teenagers. Toluca Lake, CA: Dramaline Publications. SUBJECTS/PLAY TYPE: Movies; Scene.

804. K-3. (+) Bauer, Caroline Feller. **Down with president stomach. CAST:** 10u. **ACTS:** 1. **SETTINGS:** None. **PLAYING TIME:** NA. **PLOT:** The body parts decide the stomach is too greedy to be president, and they petition God to make a change. But when He tells them to choose a replacement, the body parts realize they can't function when the stomach doesn't work, and re-elect it unanimously. RECOMMENDATION: The functions of various body parts are reviewed quite well, although some groups may be displeased with the religious slant. ROYALTY: NA. SOURCE: Bauer, Caroline Feller. (1987). Presenting reader's theater: Plays and poems to read aloud. New York, NY: H.W. Wilson. SUBJECTS/PLAY TYPE: Body; Stomach; Reader's Theater.

805. 4-8. (+) Cheatham, Val R. **Dr. Frankenstein and friends. CAST:** 3f, 5m, Su. **ACTS:** 1. **SETTINGS:** Living room. **PLAYING TIME:** 15 min. **PLOT:** Dr. Frankenstein, Wolfman, Dracula, Tombstone, Vampira, and Happy Medium gather on a stormy evening to discuss television commercials which make monsters look like silly superstitions. Some children accidentally enter the house, believe they are in a wax museum and are too afraid to stay. The monsters decide to turn the house into a wax museum of horrors. RECOMMENDATION: The monsters reveal themselves as slightly neurotic rather than sinister, and they provide a perfect setup for puns, plays on words, and graveyard humor. The ending is a salute to pragmatism and the need to adapt to changing times. ROYALTY: Free to Plays subscribers. SOURCE: Cheatham, Val R. (1975, November). Dr. Frankenstein and friends. Plays: The Drama Magazine for Young People, pp. 61- 66. SUBJECTS/PLAY TYPE: Monsters; Wax Museums; Farce; Skit.

806. 7-12. (+) Van Horn, Bill. **Dr. Frankenstein's space operation. CAST:** 4f, 4m, 4u. **ACTS:** 1. **SETTINGS:** Space ship. **PLAYING TIME:** 30 min. **PLOT:** Dracula, Frankenstein's monster, robots, clones, and the respective progeny of Drs. Frankenstein and Von Helsing are caught up in a futuristic plot for world domination. By setting Dr. Frankenstein's life-making machine to "subtract," the evil doers are destroyed. RECOMMENDATION: Familiarity with the Frankenstein and Dracula stories is necessary in order to

fully appreciate the humor in this satire/melodrama. **ROYALTY:** Free to Plays subscribers. **SOURCE:** Van Horn, Bill. (1983, March). Dr. Frankenstein's space ship. Plays: The Drama Magazine for Young People, pp. 1-11. **SUBJECTS/PLAY TYPE:** Science Fiction; Comedy.

807. 7-10. (+) Miller, Ev. (Hawthorne, Nathaniel) **Dr. Heidegger's experiment.** (Dr. Heidegger's experiment) **CAST:** 1f, 4m. **ACTS:** 1. **SETTINGS:** Study. **PLAYING TIME:** NA. **PLOT:** Dr. Heidegger, a scientist, invites four friends who have become unsuccessful to participate in an experiment in which they are offered a chance at renewed youth, in exchange for their promises to act better. As they become younger and younger, the wisdom that their sad lives have taught is forgotten, and they are as foolish as ever. **RECOMMENDATION:** Although this neither projects the atmosphere of the original, nor reveals Dr. Heidegger faithfully, the essential theme--the unfortunate constancy of human nature, is clearly presented. It could serve either as a dramatic production in its own right or as a worthwhile and accessible introduction to a story whose ambiance and language might seem formidable to younger readers. **ROYALTY:** $20. **SOURCE:** Miller, Ev. (1986). Dr. Heidegger's experiment. Franklin, OH: Eldridge Pub. Co. **SUBJECTS/PLAY TYPE:** Fountain of Youth; Old Age; Science Fiction; Adaptation.

808. 7-12. (+) Bland, Joellen. (Stevenson, Robert Louis) **Dr. Jekyll and Mr. Hyde.** (The strange case of Dr. Jekyll and Mr. Hyde) **CAST:** 6m. **ACTS:** 1. **SETTINGS:** Laboratory. **PLAYING TIME:** 35 min. **PLOT:** In nineteenth century England, Dr. Henry Jekyll is involved in chemical experiments that induce alter egos and dramatically alter the person physically as well as emotionally. As the play develops, Hyde's menacing character grows increasingly more sinister. In a climactic scene, Jekyll strikes the final blow for decency by forcing Hyde to drink poison that destroys them both. **RECOMMENDATION:** Bland has successfully adapted the story of Jekyll and Hyde for the stage. The malevolence of Hyde's character aids in conveying and sustaining a sense of impending doom, while the concept of dual personality is well established through the technique of flashbacks. This play would be a welcome supplement to any English curriculum, for children, like adults, will be fascinated by the macabre that dominates Stevenson's tale. **ROYALTY:** Free to Plays subscribers. **SOURCE:** Bland, Joellen. (1981, May). Dr. Jekyll and Mr. Hyde. Plays: The Drama Magazine for Young People, pp 64-76. **SUBJECTS/PLAY TYPE:** Horror; Monsters; Good and Evil; Adaptation.

809. 7-12*. (-) Oakley, G. William. (Stevenson, Robert Louis) **Dr. Jekyll and Mr. Hyde.** (The strange case of Dr. Jekyll and Mr. Hyde) **CAST:** 4f, 4m. **ACTS:** 1. **SETTINGS:** Drawing room in late Victorian London. **PLAYING TIME:** NA. **PLOT:** Dr. Henry Jekyll's chemical experiments concerning the good and the evil parts of human nature in general have been ongoing, and the British police are closing in on Dr. Jekyll for the crimes of his chemically induced other personality, Mr. Edward Hyde. **RECOMMENDATION:** This play is

supposed to be a comedy, but its supposedly humorous parts are not funny. It trivializes the conflict between good and evil that is such a vital part of the work from which this play is adapted and its portrayal of the multiple personality of Dr. Jekyll is so unrealistic that it is absolutely unbelievable. **ROYALTY:** NA **SOURCE:** Oakley, G. William. (1981). Dr. Jekyll and Mr. Hyde. Denver, CO: Pioneer Drama Service. **SUBJECTS/PLAY TYPE:** Comedy; Melodrama; Good and evil; Adaptation.

810. 2-4. (-) Hark, Mildred. McQueen, Noel. **Dr. Manners. CAST:** 4f, 3m. **ACTS:** 1. **SETTINGS:** Doctor's office. **PLAYING TIME:** 10 min. **PLOT:** Several children visit Dr. Manners and Nurse Polite with different cases of impoliteness and are urged to look at themselves as they would be with a helping of Politeness. Dr. Manners explains that it is important to have your heart in the right place. **RECOMMENDATION:** It is easy to see the faults of others; this play allows the audience to see what their own rudeness can look like to others. However, it is very dated, very patronizing, and very insulting to the audience's intelligence. **ROYALTY:** Free to Plays subscribers. **SOURCE:** Hark, Mildred & McQueen, Noel. (1978, May). Dr. Manners. Plays: The Drama Magazine for Young People, pp. 59-64. **SUBJECTS/PLAY TYPE:** Manners; Rudeness; Playlet.

811. 5-6. (+) Bland, Joellen. (Stoker, Bram) **Dracula.** (Dracula.) **CAST:** 5f, 6m, **ACTS:** 1. **SETTINGS:** Castle room; Vault room; Hospital. **PLAYING TIME:** 35 min. **PLOT:** Dracula desires to move from Transylvania to England and invites an English lawyer named Harker to his castle to help with arrangements. Harker suspects that Dracula may be a vampire, escapes, has a breakdown, and is hospitalized. Harker's wife works at a sanitarium where her friend Lucy has been hospitalized for loss of blood. Dracula victimizes Lucy, changing her into a vampire. The cured Harker vows to destroy Dracula and other vampires. Dracula attempts to victimize Harker's wife, is surrounded with crosses just in time, and falls out the window into the sunlight. Once again, good conquers evil. **RECOMMENDATION:** Some of the props and effects may be difficult, but this excellent adaptation follows the original very closely, and is well worth the extra effort. **ROYALTY:** Free to Plays subscribers. **SOURCE:** Bland, Joellen. (1980, October). Dracula. Plays: The Drama Magazine for Young People, pp. 69-80. **SUBJECTS/PLAY TYPE:** Horror; Vampires; Adaptation.

812. 9-12. (+) Hotchner, Stephen. (Stoker, Bram) **Dracula.** (Dracula.) **CAST:** 14f, 5m, Su. **ACTS:** 3. **SETTINGS:** Castle; home; forest. **PLAYING TIME:** 90 min. **PLOT:** Jonathan Harker sells British real estate to Count Dracula, unaware that he is allowing the infamous bloodsucking vampire to spread his evil beyond the borders of Transylvania. When Harker discovers the truth, he joins Dr. Van Helsing in an attempt to destroy Dracula. Harker's wife, Mina, is next on Dracula's list. **RECOMMENDATION:** This engrossing adaptation of the horror story may be too scary for young viewers. Sound effects, special lighting, and special make-up add greatly to the mood of this play, which should have no

trouble holding the attention of the audience. ROYALTY: $35. SOURCE: Hotchner, Stephen. (1978). Dracula. Denver,CO: Pioneer Drama Service. SUBJECTS/PLAY TYPE: Horror; Vampires; Adaptation.

813. 10-12*. (-) Johnson, Crane. (Stoker, Bram) **Dracula.** (Dracula) CAST: 4f, 3m, ACTS: 2. SETTINGS: Study. PLAYING TIME: NA. PLOT: Professor von Helsing is engaged to cure Renfield's morbid and insane behavior and, as an afterthought, to cure Lucy's recent episodes of sleepwalking. After discovering that Lucy has become a vampire, von Helsing destroys her and Count Dracula in the traditional way, but not before Renfield is killed by the Count. RECOMMENDATION: This adaptation is long on pseudo-intellectual speeches and very short on action, or anything else of interest. The flavor, mood, or characterizations of the original have not been retained in this boring melodrama. ROYALTY: $35. SOURCE: Johnson, Crane. (1976). Dracula. New York: Dramatists Play Service. SUBJECTS/PLAY TYPE: Vampires; Horror; Adaptation.

814. 7-12*. (-) Mattera, John. (Stoker, Bram) **Dracula.** (Dracula.) CAST: 6f, 8m, Su. ACTS: 3. SETTINGS: Castle; clinic; crypt. PLAYING TIME: NA. PLOT: Jonathan Harker arrives at Count Dracula's castle on business to learn Dracula is after his lovely fiancee, Lucy. Dracula fails and is killed by an imbecile. Lovely Lucy regains her senses and embraces her true love, Harker, who has been turned into a vampire. RECOMMENDATION: Anyone who has seen a B-grade Dracula movie has also seen this play. The scenes and dialogue are standard and predictable. Because of its difficult sets, costumes, and individual performances, it would be difficult for adolescents to produce. ROYALTY: $35. SOURCE: Mattera, John. (1980). Dracula. Chicago, IL: Dramatic Pub. Co. SUBJECTS/PLAY TYPE: Horror; Vampires; Adaptation.

815. 4-12. (+) Kelly, Tim J. **The Dracula kidds, or, the house on Blood Pudding Lane.** CAST: 12f, 7m, Su. ACTS: 2. SETTINGS: Sitting room. PLAYING TIME: NA. PLOT: In this highly entertaining play, the "kidds" from Kidd Academy find a house full of surprises when they spend their spring break at a haunted mansion. Among the students is Maureen Haywood, author of a book that debunks the Dracula theory. A furious Count Dracula appears to demand that Maureen retract her book and apologize. What follows is one suspenseful yet funny scene after another, as the students turn detective and unravel the mystery behind the appearance of Count Dracula. RECOMMENDATION: This comic thriller, with its creepy characters and spooky stage effects, is sure to delight audiences of all ages, and is especially recommended for young people in grades 4 through 12. High school students will find the play simple and fun to produce. ROYALTY: $35. SOURCE: Kelly, Tim J. (1986). The Dracula kidds, or, the house on Blood Pudding Lane. Schulenburg, TX: I.E. Clark. SUBJECTS/PLAY TYPE: Mystery; Comedy; Vampires; Farce.

816. 7-12. (+) Majeski, Bill. **Dracula returns.** CAST: 4f, 3m, 4u. ACTS: 1. SETTINGS: Meeting room; street corner; castle foyer. PLAYING TIME: 35 min. PLOT: Transylvania is in an economic slump because Dracula is dead. Some citizens meet with Tommy and plan a promotion to revive the economy. Nancy is writing a magazine article about the return of Dracula, which occurs every 193 years. Tommy and Nancy decide to stage Dracula's return as a publicity stunt. Carefully planted rumors about Dracula sightings convince the townspeople of his return. But, an attempted hijacking of a bloodmobile, which was not planned, make Tommy and Nancy suspect the real Dracula has returned. The vampire is revealed to be Lady Dowagell, a leading citizen and a descendent of Dracula, and tourists crowd into Transylvania as the economy flourishes. RECOMMENDATION: This wonderfully capitalistic spoof will keep audiences rolling in the aisles over hilarious publicity schemes, bungled photography attempts, a terrorized victim who uses charades to name his attacker, and puns popping out throughout. ROYALTY: Free to Plays subscribers. SOURCE: Majeski, Bill. (1977, May). Dracula returns. Plays: The Drama Magazine for Young People, pp. 25-36. SUBJECTS/PLAY TYPE: Supernatural; Vampires; Farce.

817. 9-12. (+) Kelly, Tim. (Stoker, Bram) **Dracula: The vampire play.** (Dracula) CAST: 11f, 6m. ACTS: 3. SETTINGS: Sitting room. PLAYING TIME: NA. PLOT: Dr. Quincy's niece is ill with some disease that defies diagnosis until Professor Van Helsing examines her and claims that she and others are the victims of Dracula. When Dracula is confronted, the vampire spends too much time away from his castle, can't reach his coffin before sunrise, and vanishes before their eyes. RECOMMENDATION: The characterization is well done and never trite; the eerie lighting and convoluted plots are captivating. This does require an attentive audience to fully understand the somewhat difficult vocabulary and the subtle clues uncovered in the different plots. ROYALTY: $50. SOURCE: Kelly, Tim. (1978). Dracula: The vampire play. Schulenburg, TX: I. E. Clark. SUBJECTS/PLAY TYPE: Vampires; Horror; Adaptation.

818. 5-6. (+) Saunders, Dudley F. **Dracula's treasure.** CAST: 2f, 6m, 1u. ACTS: 1. SETTINGS: House. PLAYING TIME: NA. PLOT: A father and his two children move to an old country house whose former owner has mysteriously disappeared. People appear and disappear through secret panels, an empty coffin is found in a secret room and Dracula is often seen lurking near the children. The police officer is really a thief, the housekeeper is the real police officer, there is a search for hidden treasure, and the children are saved from Dracula by a protective statue--or are they? RECOMMENDATION: The plot is convoluted and there are some portions of the play that seem unnecessary but, overall, the play would be enjoyable for older elementary school children. The subject matter might be frightening for very young children, since it is unclear whether the children are saved from Dracula at

the end. ROYALTY: $25. SOURCE: Saunders, Dudley F. (1975). Dracula's treasure. New Orleans, LA: Anchorage Press, Inc. SUBJECTS/PLAY TYPE: Horror; Mystery.

819. 3-5. (+) Kraus, Joanna Halpert. **The Dragon hammer.** CAST: 1f, 2m, 8u. ACTS: 1. SETTINGS: Mountain. PLAYING TIME: NA. PLOT: In this Korean fairy tale, the kind and righteous boy, Bang-Su, finds the Goblins' magic Dragon Hammer and outwits them to keep it. RECOMMENDATION: Clear dialogue and avoidance of overt moralizing or stereotyping, along with ample production notes, make this adaptation an easily produced introduction to Asian folklore. ROYALTY: NA. SOURCE: Kraus, Joanna Halpert. (1977). The dragon hammer and the tale of Oniroku. Rowayton, Conn. : New Plays. SUBJECTS/PLAY TYPE: Folk Tales, Korean; Playlet.

820. 7-12. (+) Meili, Janet. **The dragon meets his match.** CAST: 3f, 3m. ACTS: 1. SETTINGS: Room; cave. PLAYING TIME: 20 min. PLOT: Young Princess Olivia persuades Myron the Dragon to kidnap her instead of Elder Princess Blanche, so Sir Henry can rescue and marry her. Thinking Myron made a mistake, Blanche goes to the dragon's cave. Olivia is such a pain to the dragon he agrees to return her so Blanche can wait for Sir Henry but Sir William passes by the cave first and rescues Blanche. That leaves Sir Henry for Lady Olivia and all's well. RECOMMENDATION: In this medieval fantasy, the characters, plot, and conflict are believable and consistent in their speech and action. Costuming for the period would be the most involved aspect of this production but it is still easily done. ROYALTY: Free to Plays Subscribers. SOURCE: Meili, Janet. (1980, February). The dragon meets his match. Plays: The Drama Magazine for Young People, pp. 23-29. SUBJECTS/PLAY TYPE: Fantasy; Dragons; Comedy.

821. 2-4*. (+) Grecian, Phil. **The dragon of Nitt.** CAST: 2f, 5m, 1u. ACTS: 1. SETTINGS: Village square; forest; cave; witch's lair. PLAYING TIME: 70 min. PLOT: Abercrombie the carpenter ventures through Fantasy Forest to recover a box which contains the secret to happiness, stolen by Hecate witch. With the help of his daughter, a dog and a dragon, this unlikely group of heroes manages to vanquish the witch, only to discover that happiness was always theirs. RECOMMENDATION: This charming fantasy will delight children with its friendly and perceptive dragon, animated tree, and a nasty witch who is transformed by the power of friendship. Although the play may be a bit lengthy for the very young, it moves along at a good pace and has a message for everyone. It would be best produced by older students for younger students. Special effects and specially designed costuming is essential to create the mood. ROYALTY: $35. SOURCE: Grecian, Phil. (1986). The dragon of Nitt. Morton Grove, IL: Coach House Press, Inc. SUBJECTS/PLAY TYPE: Dragons; Happiness; Fantasy.

822. 4-7. (+) Stehling, D.M. **Dragons.** CAST: 5u. ACTS: 1. SETTINGS: Bare stage. PLAYING TIME: 5 min. PLOT: As a student reads from a file that describes a dragon, a dragon enters the stage behind him and demonstrates the described characteristics. RECOMMENDATION: Designed for creative dramatics, this could be useful in speech and drama classes where students practice monologues, or as practice for pantomime. ROYALTY: Free to Plays subscribers. SOURCE: Stehling, D.M. (1982, November). Dragons. Plays: The Drama Magazine for Young People, pp. 63-64. SUBJECTS/PLAY TYPE: Comedy; Dragons; Creative Dramatics.

823. K-2. (+) Lobel, Arnold. **Dragons and giants.** CAST: 5u. ACTS: 1. SETTINGS: None. PLAYING TIME: NA. PLOT: Frog and Toad test their courage by climbing a mountain, facing a snake and dodging a hawk, but end up proclaiming their bravery from under their beds. RECOMMENDATION: A clever adaptation of the children's story, this would work well as a reader's theater or as a stage production. ROYALTY: NA. SOURCE: Bauer, Caroline Feller. (1987). Presenting reader's theater: plays and poems to read aloud. NY: H.W. Wilson Co. SUBJECTS/PLAY TYPE: Frogs and Toads; Reader's Theater; Bravery; Adaptation.

824. 4-6. (+) Mauro, Robert. **The dragon's secret.** CAST: 1f, 2m, 1u. ACTS: 1. SETTINGS: Forest. PLAYING TIME: 10 min. PLOT: A young boy, named Lance-A-Little, wants to become a knight and faces his challenge--a dragon. The dragon, Grendal, claims he is a victim of rumor and prejudice, and has been falsely accused for the town's recent misfortunes. Lance returns and admits he did not kill the dragon because he felt Grendal was not the cause of their problems. The elders congratulate Lance on his decision and reveal that it was all a test of his judgment. Lance is knighted and becomes Sir Lance-A-Lot. RECOMMENDATION: Lance is the likable character who carries the message that a true hero must have heart as well as muscle. He risks disgrace to follow his beliefs, but is ultimately and justly rewarded for his action. ROYALTY: Free to Plays Subscribers. SOURCE: Mauro, Robert. (1980, April). The dragon's secret. Plays: The Drama Magazine for Young People, pp. 59-62. SUBJECTS/PLAY TYPE: Knights; Dragons; Leaders; Skit.

825. 2-3. (+) Howard, Helen L. **The dragon's trick.** CAST: 2f, 4m. ACTS: 1. SETTINGS: Town square. PLAYING TIME: 15 min. PLOT: In this adaptation of a Mexican folktale, a dragon digs a deep hole in the town square and takes away the dirt in a sack. The village mayor accidentally falls into the hole. Indignantly, he orders the hole filled and falls into the hole the workmen have dug to fill the first hole. The events reoccur. Exasperated, the Mayor offers a gold piece to anyone who can solve the mystery of the holes. Brave Pepe confronts the dragon and threatens to cut off his tail if he does not return the sack of dirt. The fearful dragon complies and Brave Pepe wins the gold. RECOMMENDATION: The dragon is a silly character who is supposedly fierce, but exhibits cowardice and vanity when threatened with the loss of his "beautiful tail." This, combined with the quandary over the holes, makes for an amusing story. Unfortunately, however,

insinuations are made that the Mexican workmen are stereotypically lazy; when asked to fill the holes, they complain of the heat and ask to do it "manana." ROYALTY: Free to Plays subscribers. SOURCE: Howard, Helen L. (1981, January). The dragon's trick. Plays: The Drama Magazine for Young People, pp. 45-48. SUBJECTS/PLAY TYPE: Folk Tales, Mexico; Comedy; Skit.

826. 6-8. (+) Sills, Paul. **The dream of good fortune.** CAST: 2f, 4m. ACTS: 1. SETTINGS: Bare stage, props. PLAYING TIME: NA. PLOT: The appearance of an angel sends Luqman Ali, a poor dung sweeper, to Cairo to find a fortune. Upon arrival, he is given advice that sends him home again, to discover a treasure hidden under his own stove. RECOMMENDATION: This wonderful story has proven successful as a book, **The Treasure.** Performing without benefit of props, scenery, or narrator might prove difficult, and numerous chaotic stage directions will require attentive direction and practice. The irony is presented simply and delightfully. ROYALTY: NA. SOURCE: Sills, Paul. (1981). More from story theatre. NY: S. French SUBJECTS/PLAY TYPE: Fortunes; Dreams; Playlet.

827. 12. (-) Rogers, June Walker and Rogers, David. (Shakespeare, William) **The dream on Royal Street.** (Midsummer Night's Dream) CAST: 8f, 12m, Su. ACTS: 2. SETTINGS: Hotel lobby; garden; banquet room. PLAYING TIME: NA. PLOT: Egeus, the owner of the Royal Street Hotel wants his daughter, Hermia, to marry Demetrius, his assistant. However, Hermia doesn't love Demetrius; Helena, the switchboard operator, does. It is Mardi Gras night and the entertainer's manager, Puck, thinks he can play cupid and solve the love problems at the hotel. After much confusion, all is well. RECOMMENDATION: This is an attempt to modernize Shakespeare's **Midsummer Night's Dream** by setting it in a modern day New Orleans hotel during Mardi Gras, adding some modern plot twists and modernizing the language. However, the mix of modern and medieval fails to do justice to either of the two stories. Also, the sexism in the original has been sensationalized here to the point of depravity, as Helena asks Demetrius to beat her and treat her like a dog so that her love will grow for him. ROYALTY: Upon application. SOURCE: Rogers, June Walker and David Rogers. (1981). The dream on Royal Street. Chicago, IL: Dramatic Pub. Co. SUBJECTS/PLAY TYPE: Love; Musical; Adaptation.

828. 7-12. (-) Bland, Joellen. (Collins, Wilkie) **The dream woman.** (Moonstone) CAST: 2f, 5m. ACTS: 1. SETTINGS: Stable; kitchen. PLAYING TIME: 20 min. PLOT: A doctor tells a story about a man's eerie dream: his estranged wife appears at his bedside with a knife, intending to kill him. The poor man does not know if his wife is alive or dead and stays constantly awake, trying to avoid the dream and watching for the woman. RECOMMENDATION: Although the ghostly story is very well told, complete with horrific descriptions of the wife/apparition, the excellent buildup falls flat with an anticlimactic ending and with none of the mysteries

solved, or even mentioned, except as part of the buildup to the climax. As a ghost story for late night slumber parties or campfires, this is fine. As a satisfying play, this is very disappointing. ROYALTY: Free to Plays subscribers. SOURCE: Bland, Joellen. (1985, March). The dream woman. Plays: The Drama Magazine for Young People, pp. 56-64. SUBJECTS/PLAY TYPE: Ghost Story; Horror; Adaptation.

829. 7-9. (+) Kennedy, Eddie. **Dreamwalk.** CAST: 2f, 2m. ACTS: 1. SETTINGS: Lounge. PLAYING TIME: NA. PLOT: A young cancer patient confides in her friend (another patient) that the visits from her family and friends seem less and less natural as her disease progresses. Her sister arrives, and the two women discuss the wall that has grown between them and the changes that a devastating disease can cause in love and friendship. The young woman and her friend meet again after visiting hours and acknowledge that some things, like the nearness of death, must be confronted alone. RECOMMENDATION: This easy to produce play deals sensitively with the problems that a major illness presents to the patient, the patient's family and friends. This production could be a starting point for a classroom discussion on dealing with illness in one's own life or in the life of a friend or family member. ROYALTY: $20. SOURCE: Kennedy, Eddie. (1983). Dreamwalk. Woodstock, IL: Dramatic Pub. Co. SUBJECTS/PLAY TYPE: Cancer; Death; Family; Drama.

830. 7-12. (+) Gilsenan, Nancy. **A dress for Sadie Redwing.** CAST: 4f, 2m. ACTS: 1. SETTINGS: Ranch house; kitchen; living room. PLAYING TIME: NA. PLOT: A 13 year old girl, visiting her relatives on a South Dakota ranch, is confronted with the evidence of racial prejudice in her otherwise kind and forthright relations. When a Blackfoot mother stops at the house to beg for a dress for her dying daughter, the girl gives her the dress she was going to wear to a barn dance. RECOMMENDATION: A subtle but vivid dramatization of the prejudices shown toward North American Indians, this play should stir much discussion in the classroom. Sensitive acting skills are required for all parts. ROYALTY: $20. SOURCE: Gilsenan, Nancy. (1980). A dress for Sadie Redwing. Chicago, IL: Dramatic Pub. Co. SUBJECTS/PLAY TYPE: Prejudice; Native Americans; Drama.

831. 9-12. (+) Hellesen, Richard. **Drive-in.** CAST: 3f, 4m. ACTS: 1. SETTINGS: Drive-in movie. PLAYING TIME: NA. PLOT: In three cars at a drive-in are: a boy and a girl; two young women; and three young men. Barb and Jim have had a fight and are telling their respective companion(s) their sides of the story. The action moves between the cars. RECOMMENDATION: The drive-in setting will appeal to high school audiences of today even though there are very few drive-ins left. The dialog which is key to the whole play could easily be transferred to a more contemporary setting. The interweaving of the young women's and men's conversations to allow the audience to hear both sides of the fight at once is a plus. ROYALTY: $15. SOURCE: Hellesen, Richard. (1984).

Drive-in. Boston: Baker's Plays. SUBJECTS/PLAY TYPE: Dating; Drama.

832. 6-10. (+) Kehret, Peg. **The driver's test is a piece of cake.** CAST: 1u. ACTS: 1. SETTINGS: None. PLAYING TIME: NA. PLOT: The anxieties surrounding the driver's test are humorously and realistically outlined by a young teen. RECOMMENDATION: Nervousness combined with a false bravado is typical of most young people in stressful positions, and provides most of the humor in this sketch. ROYALTY: NA. SOURCE: Kehret, Peg. (1986). Winning monologs for young actors. Colorado Springs, CO: Meriwether Pub. SUBJECTS/PLAY TYPE: Driving (Test); Monologue.

833. 7-12. (+) Murray, John. **The driving lesson.** CAST: 1u. ACTS: 1. SETTINGS: None. PLAYING TIME: NA. PLOT: A young wife's attempts to learn to drive are accompanied by all the usual first driver mishaps. RECOMMENDATION: The wife is stereotyped as a mindless female; if this were changed to a son or daughter learning from a mother or father, it would be hilarious, especially when the poor policeman has to jump out of the way of an inexperienced parallel parker. ROYALTY: None. SOURCE: Murray, John. (1982). Modern monologues for young people. Boston: Plays, Inc. SUBJECTS/PLAY TYPE: Comedy; Driver's Education; Monologue.

834. 12. (+) Hull, Raymond. **The drunkard's revenge.** CAST: 2f, 3m, Su. ACTS: 2. SETTINGS: Hotel lobby. PLAYING TIME: 90 min. PLOT: Edward Middleton, reformed drunkard, is connived into purchasing a beverage he thinks is endorsed by the Temperance League, but is actually 60 proof. Edward's son returns from the gold mines, and swears obedience to his father, who is getting drunker by the day and is about to lose the hotel. After a succession of melodramatic events, the play ends happily with the villains thwarted. RECOMMENDATION: Some knowledge of the early temperance movement is required to fully appreciate this. The parody of melodrama and the political and social innuendos might appeal more to adults. ROYALTY: $25. SOURCE: Hull, Raymond. (1982). The drunkard's revenge. Denver, CO: Pioneer Drama Service. SUBJECTS/PLAY TYPE: Temperance; Gold Rush; Comedy.

835. 6-12. (-) Fendrich, Shubert & Mohr, Christopher. **Ducktails and bobbysox.** CAST: 13f, 8m. 1u. ACTS: 2. SETTINGS: Malt shop; press box. PLAYING TIME: NA. PLOT: Rival groups, the Schoolies and the Yellow Jackets, battle at the Victor Malt Shop. Alex, star football quarterback, can't compete in the Homecoming game because Wheels, leader of the motorcycle gang, ties him up. At the conclusion, Alex is freed and enters the game in the final minutes to salvage a victory. RECOMMENDATION: This is completely predictable, cliched, and the song lyrics are trite. ROYALTY: NA. SOURCE: Fendrich, Shubert & Mohr, Christopher. (1980). Ducktails and bobbysox. Denver, CO: Pioneer Drama Service. SUBJECTS/PLAY TYPE: Comedy.

836. 9-12*. (-) Mayhew, John F. **Dues for Kate O'Donnell.** CAST: 3f, 4m, 4u. ACTS: 1. SETTINGS: Theater. PLAYING TIME: NA. PLOT: Kate (a 67 year old amateur playwright) feels that Homer (a professional playwright) stereotypes the elderly in his newest play. He disagrees, and rejects her play (because it really isn't very good), but recognizes her insight. He hires her as his assistant, in return for which he will teach her to make her words "soar." RECOMMENDATION: In its attempt to deal with so many issues: the plight of the elderly in society; the personal agony of playwriting; the difficulties of play production; and literary technique, this does not do justice to any of them. There is no real character development, a great deal of the humor depends upon the audience recognizing allusions to works of famous playwrights, and in the end, the audience is left thinking "so what?" ROYALTY: $20. SOURCE: Mayhew, John F. (1987). Dues for Kate O'Donnell. Woodstock, IL: Dramatic Pub. Co. SUBJECTS/PLAY TYPE: Elderly; Social Issues; Play Writing; Comedy.

837. 10-12. (+) Harnetiaux, Bryan Patrick. **Dumb luck.** CAST: 4f, 6m, Su. ACTS: 2. SETTINGS: Apartment. PLAYING TIME: NA. PLOT: When Sally wins a million dollars in a magazine contest, her life turns into a comic nightmare, replete with unwanted fame, unwanted suitors, an inept friend turned manager, greedy relatives, crazy accidents, and a magazine editor who wants to use her as a feminist symbol. Sally remains good humored and ingenious through it all and keeps her sense of integrity intact. RECOMMENDATION: There is enough general craziness to thrill high school students as they easily assimilate the play's message of basic human integrity. ROYALTY: $50. SOURCE: Harnetiaux, Bryan Patrick. (1981). Dumb luck. Chicago, IL: Dramatic Pub. Co. SUBJECTS/PLAY TYPE: Integrity; Comedy.

838. 1-4. (+) Thane, Adele. (Grimm Brothers) **Dummling and the golden goose.** (The Golden Goose) CAST: 9f, 15m, 4u. ACTS: 1. SETTINGS: Country road; Inn. PLAYING TIME: 25 min. PLOT: Poor Dummling, verbally abused by his mother, brothers, and sisters, is asked by an old man for a handout. He gives the old man what he has and, in return, the old man tells Dummling to find the Golden Goose in the gnarled oak tree. He does, and sets out to see the king. Everyone who tries to take a feather from the goose, or touches someone who tried, sticks to the person in front, forming a parade. When Dummling reaches the king, he finds that there is a contest to make the princess, who has never smiled, laugh. When the princess sees Dummling and his procession she laughs and the two are betrothed. RECOMMENDATION: This play teaches the moral that giving is good and that those who give will also receive. The message is delivered through the use of rhythmic dialogue, excellent development of action, and a nondidactic tone. ROYALTY: None. SOURCE: Thane, Adele. (1983). Plays from Famous Stories and Fairy Tales. Boston, MA: Plays, Inc. SUBJECTS/PLAY TYPE: Folk Tales, Germany; Generosity; Adaptation.

839. 2-7*. (+) Barton, Dave & Bond, Matt. **Earthlings.** CAST: 2f, 3m. ACTS: 1. SETTINGS: Bare stage. PLAYING TIME: NA. PLOT: Five actors sing, dance, and role play to teach the audience about six ecological issues: litter, graffiti, vandalism, pollution, smog and endangered species. RECOMMENDATION: This musical addresses ecological issues without giving much substantive information. The generic quality has prevented the play from becoming too outdated. Production would probably demand junior high school or older actors, or exceptionally talented children. ROYALTY: $25. SOURCE: Barton, Dave & Bond, Matt. (1978). Earthlings. Boston, MA: Baker's Plays. SUBJECTS/PLAY TYPE: Ecology; Pollution; Musical.

840. K-8*. (+) Kral, Brian. (Asbjornsen and Moe) **East of the sun, west of the moon.** (East of the sun, west of the moon) CAST: 3f, 4m, Su. ACTS: 3. SETTINGS: Castle; cottage; wilderness. PLAYING TIME: NA. PLOT: A poor family sells their daughter, Karin, to a bear-like man who promises them an annual payment. The bear is actually a young man under the spell of trolls, which can be broken only by a young girl's devotion. Karin betrays the bear and he is whisked away by two troll women. She finds her Bear lover with the help of the four winds and three hags, and frees him from the spell. RECOMMENDATION: Moral persistence and devotion winning over greed and evil is the theme. The production calls for some elaborate visual and sound effects and intricate props and settings so it may be beyond the capacity of many young people's theater groups. ROYALTY: $35. SOURCE: Kral, Brian. (1987). East of the sun, west of the moon. New Orleans, LA: Anchorage Press, Inc. SUBJECTS/PLAY TYPE: Folk Tales, Norway; Adaptation.

841. 2-4. (+) Spamer, Claribel. **Easter baskets.** CAST: Su. ACTS: 1. SETTINGS: Shop. PLAYING TIME: 10 min. PLOT: The Easter Bunny and his elves, busy coloring eggs for Easter, find that they are short on time and eggs, and ask Gracie Goose and the other Geese to provide extra eggs. The Rainbow Fairy helps color them and the Easter Bunny leaves to make his deliveries. RECOMMENDATION: This play briefly discusses the principle of sharing and thinking of others. ROYALTY: Free to Plays Subscribers. SOURCE: Spamer, Claribel. (1979, April). Easter baskets. Plays: The Drama Magazine for Young People, pp. 45-48. SUBJECTS/PLAY TYPE: Easter; Comedy.

842. 4-6. (-) Spamer, Claribel. **The Easter Bunny's contest.** CAST: 8u. ACTS: 1. SETTINGS: Clearing. PLAYING TIME: 10 min. PLOT: The Easter Bunny calls all the bunny rabbits together to choose one for a special assignment, and Little Bunny's special talents are recognized at last. RECOMMENDATION: The moral is presented too simplistically and the intended humor falls short of the mark. ROYALTY: Free to Plays subscribers. SOURCE: Spamer, Claribel. (1980, April). The Easter Bunny's contest. Plays: The Drama Magazine for Young People, pp. 31-34. SUBJECTS/PLAY TYPE: Easter; Rabbits; Playlet.

843. 4-6. (+) Pratt, Hal. **Easter Ernie's pot of gold.** CAST: 6m, Su. ACTS: 1. SETTINGS: Shoe shop. PLAYING TIME: 20 min. PLOT: Ernie the shoemaker loves to paint his shoes bright colors, but no one will buy them. He must sell one pair before Easter day, or he will have to make only brown and black shoes. He decides to help out the Easter Bunnies by painting eggs and, on Easter morning, discovers that the bunnies have bought all his shoes to wear in the Easter parade. RECOMMENDATION: Ernie is a sympathetic character to whom children will easily relate. Appropriate for older children to perform for younger ones. ROYALTY: Free to Plays subscribers. SOURCE: Pratt, Hal. (1985, April). Easter Ernie's pot of gold. Plays: The Drama Magazine for Young People, pp. 45-49. SUBJECTS/PLAY TYPE: Easter; Comedy.

844. 3-5. (+) Sroda, Anne. **The Easter geese.** CAST: 6f, 3m, 4u. ACTS: 1. SETTINGS: Lawn. PLAYING TIME: 15 min. PLOT: A gaggle of geese, picketing the Easter Rabbit's factory because he does not use goose eggs, meet two rabbit employees who complain that the Easter Rabbit doesn't pay enough lettuce leaves. The Easter Rabbit arrives, expecting the mayor to proclaim him Man of the Year, but the group mistakes him for a reporter and tells him their complaints. When the mayor arrives for the presentation, the Easter Rabbit delights everyone by announcing raises for his employees and a decision to include goose eggs in production. RECOMMENDATION: With visual comedy, the theme that cooperative action brings results is conveyed. This play could be used as holiday entertainment or for discussion on teamwork, including work with other "ethnic" groups. ROYALTY: Free to Plays subscribers. SOURCE: Sroda, Anne. (1976, April). The Easter geese. Plays: The Drama Magazine for Young People, pp. 39-44. SUBJECTS/PLAY TYPE: Easter; Labor Relations; Skit.

845. K-6. (-) Very, Alice. **Easter puzzle.** CAST: 3f, 3m, 3u. ACTS: 1. SETTINGS: Living room. PLAYING TIME: 15 min. PLOT: Children try to solve a riddle about a house with no windows and no doors as they look for Easter eggs. RECOMMENDATION: This slow moving play in rhyme has rhymes too sophisticated for young children and a plot too insulting for older children. ROYALTY: Free to Plays subscribers. SOURCE: Very, Alice. (1978, March). Easter puzzle. Plays: The Drama Magazine for Young People, pp. 59-62. SUBJECTS/PLAY TYPE: Easter; Skit.

846. 2-6*. (+) Shore, Susan. (Jackson, Maud C.) **Easter shoes.** (Easter shoes) CAST: 4f, 3m. ACTS: 1. SETTINGS: Living room. PLAYING TIME: 20 min. PLOT: Jennifer and Justin visit grandparents for Easter. Her grandmother is dismayed by Jennifer's self interest in her new clothes. A poor migrant worker steals Jennifer's shoes so his daughter can attend church. Jennifer's attitude is changed by her participation in the church pageant, cast as an angel wearing a simple robe and sandals. When the migrant worker's daughter tries to return the shoes after church, Jennifer encourages her to keep them and promises other help. RECOMMENDATION: The religious theme makes

this unsuitable for a public school environment, but suitable for a Christian church or private school. Although the language is at a second grade level, this play would work better if staged by the older elementary grades for all the elementary grades. ROYALTY: $15.00 SOURCE: Shore, Susan. (1988). Easter shoes. Franklin, OH: Eldridge Pub. Co. SUBJECTS/PLAY TYPE: Selflessness; Easter; Christian Drama.

847. K-3. (+) Silverman, Eleanor. **The Easter wish.** CAST: 2u. ACTS: 1. SETTINGS: Bare stage. PLAYING TIME: NA. PLOT: A fairy godmother turns a torn stuffed rabbit into the Easter Rabbit. RECOMMENDATION: Children will enjoy the creative activities, as well as the story. ROYALTY: None. SOURCE: Silverman, Eleanor. (1983). Dramatics for children. Metuchen, NJ: Scarecrow Press. SUBJECTS/PLAY TYPE: Easter; Puppet Play.

848. 7-12. (+) Hamlett, Christina. **Eat, drink, and be scary.** CAST: 8f, 5m. ACTS: 1. SETTINGS: Restaurant. PLAYING TIME: 20 min. PLOT: Elise brings someone her mother thinks is her fiance to their family restaurant which features characters from horror shows. After misunderstandings are solved, it turns out that Evan Steelburg (of "Back to the Suture") wants to make a movie at the restaurant, not marry Elise. RECOMMENDATION: This is clever as the horror characters interact with each other. The punch line is a great and unexpected end. ROYALTY: Free to Plays subscribers. SOURCE: Hamlett, Christina. (1988, October). Eat, drink, and be scary. Plays: The Drama Magazine for Young People, pp. 12-20. SUBJECTS/PLAY TYPE: Witches; Spielberg, Steven; Halloween; Comedy.

849. 7-12. (-) Gleason, William. **Ed Opus Rex or What really happened to teen angel.** CAST: 1f, 6m, 14u. ACTS: 1. SETTINGS: Parking lot. PLAYING TIME: NA. PLOT: In this comedy, a broad parody of Sophocles, Ed Opus moves to West Thebes where he gains respect and popularity by outsmarting gang leader Ritzo Sphinx. Later, the two discover they are actually brothers. Ritzo is one half of a split personality, and the other half is the missing "good guy," Teen Angel. All ends well. RECOMMENDATION: The humor is very dated. Even more disturbing is the supposedly humorous section where the hero is beaten up by a gang as they ask him riddles, each of which ends with an answer which elicits some sort of physical abuse. Blind people are ridiculed and given stereotyped "special gifts" (such as soothsaying), the dialect sometimes borders on racist and, at other times, reverts to translations of ancient Roman philosophy or the King James Bible. There really is nothing funny here. ROYALTY: $20. SOURCE: Gleason, William. (1976). Ed Opus Rex. Chicago, IL: Dramatic Pub. Co. SUBJECTS/PLAY TYPE: Musical; Comedy.

850. 10-12. (+) McDonough, Jerome. **Eden.** CAST: 1f, 2m, Su. ACTS: 1. SETTINGS: Bare stage. PLAYING TIME: 60 min. PLOT: Corrupt government and a greedy

corporation develop a synthetic child and try to force it on the populace in place of real children. Conflicts arise between those in favor of and those opposed to the synthetic child idea. When inoculation becomes mandatory, the plot culminates in the capture and inoculation of the last holdout. It is played against the death of a real child from the dance of life, which represents birth and blossoming of human children in contradiction with assembly-line production of Genofacts. RECOMMENDATION: This cross between Swift's **Modest Proposal** and Levin's **The Stepford Wives** is highly recommended for its quick action and deep message. ROYALTY: $25. SOURCE: McDonough, Jerome. (1978). Eden. Schulenburg, TX: I.E. Clark. SUBJECTS/PLAY TYPE: Future; Corruption; Science Fiction; Drama.

851. 8-12. (+) Purkey, Ruth Angell. **The Eden echo.** CAST: 4f, 1m. ACTS: 1. SETTINGS: Garden terrace. PLAYING TIME: NA. PLOT: In a world of women, even the word "men" is forbidden. An avenging creator has eradicated all men because of their war-like nature and invention of the H bomb. Still, two old ladies remember how much more interesting life was with men around. A young woman captures what she thinks is a groundhog but what is actually the last surviving man, who has been hidden in a state of suspended animation. After she finds out what he is, they go off, probably to begin Man's second chance on earth. RECOMMENDATION: This futuristic variation of the Biblical story of the creation of man is a simple play, filled with quiet, gentle humor. It would spark discussions on stereotypes, alternate futures, or the nature of youth. ROYALTY: $15. SOURCE: Purkey, Ruth Angell. (1976). The Eden echo. Boston, MA: Baker's Plays. SUBJECTS/PLAY TYPE: Women; Future; Comedy.

852. 7-9. (+) Karshner, Roger. **Edna and Joyce.** CAST: 2f. ACTS: 1. SETTINGS: None. PLAYING TIME: NA. PLOT: Edna and Joyce were both molested by their father when they were younger, but Joyce has recovered because she has been able to talk about it. Joyce tells Edna that if she talks about her hurt, she will feel better. RECOMMENDATION: Dealing successfully with a very powerful subject, this play probably should not be used without experienced professional supervision. ROYALTY: NA. SOURCE: Karshner, Roger. (1986). Scenes for teenagers. Toluce Lake, CA: Dramaline Publications. SUBJECTS/PLAY TYPE: Sexual Abuse; Scene.

853. 7-9. (+) Kehret, Peg. **The efficient baby-sitter.** CAST: 1m. ACTS: 1. SETTINGS: None. PLAYING TIME: NA. PLOT: During a young boy's first job as a baby-sitter, the children threw their Spaghettios around the kitchen, decided to play hide and seek, and used the opportunity to go back into the house and lock him out. In spite of these problems, Mrs. Anderson asks him to baby-sit again, but the boy decides it isn't worth the trouble. RECOMMENDATION: This is great fun, and casting a boy as a baby-sitter is refreshingly nonsexist. ROYALTY: NA. SOURCE: Kehret, Peg. (1986). Winning

monologs for young actors. Colorado Springs, CO: Meriwether Publishing. **SUBJECTS/PLAY TYPE:** Babysitting; Monologue.

854. 10-12. (+) Kelly, Tim J. (Collins, Wilkie) **Egad, the woman in white: an astonishing and inspiring melodrama.** (The woman in white) **CAST:** 10u. **ACTS:** 2. **SETTINGS:** Library; corridor; cell; path; church room. **PLAYING TIME:** NA. **PLOT:** An evil villain marries a young heiress against her will, and then seals her in a madhouse so he can steal her fortune. Episodes of murder, blackmail, betrayal, lying, and cheating all climax as the villain is brought to justice when he is burnt to death in the fire he set to kill the heiress. **RECOMMENDATION:** This hilarious melodrama can be cast to fit the available actors and will be fun as everyone "hams it up." **ROYALTY:** $35. **SOURCE:** Kelly, Tim J. (1975). Egad, the woman in white: an astonishing and inspiring melodrama. NY: Samuel French. **SUBJECTS/PLAY TYPE:** Melodrama; Comedy; Romance; Adaptation.

855. 9-12. (+) Roose-Evans, James. (Hanff, Helene) **Eighty Four, Charing Cross Road.** (84, Charing Cross Road) **CAST:** 3f, 1m, 5u. **ACTS:** 2. **SETTINGS:** Apartment; bookstore. **PLAYING TIME:** NA. **PLOT:** This entire play is the written communication between a New York book collector, Helene Hanff, and a bookstore in England over a 20 year period. Book orders develop into a friendship with genuine caring on both sides. Miss Hanff sends gifts of rationed items to England and the bookstore staff reciprocates with special books for her. Letters chronicle the history of the time and the changes in the lives of Miss Hanff and the staff of the book shop. When Helene is finally able to visit England, the shop has closed, and her faithful correspondent has died. **RECOMMENDATION:** This faithful adaptation of Hanff's book poignantly shows the power of written words and the development of a friendship against the backdrop of 20 years of history. **ROYALTY:** NA. **SOURCE:** Roose-Evans, James. (1983). 84, Charing Cross Road. NY: Samuel French. **SUBJECTS/PLAY TYPE:** Friendship; Adaptation.

856. 10-12. (+) Rudolph, Grace. **Elders' statements: Almost a home. CAST:** 3f, 2m, 1u. **ACTS:** 1. **SETTINGS:** Motel. **PLAYING TIME:** NA. **PLOT:** An elderly man and woman escape from a nursing home and steal a car. Thinking they are in New Hampshire after driving 3,420 miles, they end up at a motel only a block from the nursing home. A nurse from the home spots her stolen car, confronts the two in the motel room, and returns them to the home. **RECOMMENDATION:** This delightfully naughty tale realistically depicts the elderly as having the same desires for freedom and independence as other age groups. Although the play was written for elderly actors, high school actors will enjoy developing the characters. **ROYALTY:** $10. **SOURCE:** Rudolph, Grace. (1984). Elders' statements: One-act plays and monologues. Boston, MA: Baker's Plays. **SUBJECTS/PLAY TYPE:** Comedy; Elderly; Stealing.

857. 7-10. (+) Rybak, Rose Kacherian. **Election day in Spooksville. CAST:** 5f, 11m, 2u. **ACTS:** 2. **SETTINGS:** Meeting hall. **PLAYING TIME:** 50 min. **PLOT:** Frank N. Stein, Jr. returns to Spooksville and challenges Lucifer's 300 year reign as mayor. As head of the Reform Party, Frank desires to change Spooksville from a place of horror to a respectable suburban town. But love enters the picture as the would-be reformer falls prey to Vampira, the incumbent's daughter. She helps him realize that the ways of Spooksville run deep in his blood. He concedes the election and Spooksville is saved from becoming modern. **RECOMMENDATION:** This is a perfect play for combining Halloween with Social Studies. It touches on the function of the town hall meeting as it relates to the political process, and its humor keeps it from being overly didactic. Names such as Frank N. Stein, Mummy Fide, and Jack L. Hyde are examples of typical word play through-out the script. **ROYALTY:** Free to Plays subscribers. **SOURCE:** Rybak, Rose Kacherian. (1984, November). Election day in Spooksville. Plays: The Drama Magazine for Young People, pp. 23-34. **SUBJECTS/PLAY TYPE:** Halloween; Political Processes; Comedy.

858. 9-12. (+) Pomerance, Bernard. **The Elephant Man. CAST:** 6f, 12m, Su. **ACTS:** 1. **SETTINGS:** Office; store; lecture room; fairgrounds; station; hospital room. **PLAYING TIME:** NA. **PLOT:** Deformed and hideous, the Elephant Man is treated as a freak. Society allows him no peace or human dignity until Dr. Treves discovers his condition and responds with compassion, but inhumanely uses Merrick as a subject of scientific instruction and experimentation. **RECOMMENDATION:** Taken from Sir Frederick Treves' (1923) and Ashley Montague's (1973) monographs, this splendid drama causes one to seriously think of human dignity. If Merrick is actually portrayed as a deformed man, the actor must endure the possible consequences of prolonged walking and/or sitting in the bent, crippled positions required. **ROYALTY:** NA. **SOURCE:** Pomerance, Bernard. (1979). The Elephant Man. NY: Samuel French, Inc. **SUBJECTS/PLAY TYPE:** Merrick, John; Dignity; Elephantitis; Drama.

859. 1-8. (+) Whittaker, Violet. **Elisha is used of God. CAST:** Su. **ACTS:** 10. **SETTINGS:** River; living room; throne room. **PLAYING TIME:** NA. **PLOT:** After Elijah dies, Elisha takes over Elijah's job. In a series of ten scenes, Elisha brings water to a barren land, helps King Jehoshaphat defeat the Moabites, saves a widow's sons from being taken as slaves, gives an old woman a son and brings the boy back to life after he has died, performs many other miracles, and finally convinces the king to believe in God. **RECOMMENDATION:** This rather dull but adequate recitation of some of Elisha's heroic exploits will, in the superman tradition, help children to see the power of God. **ROYALTY:** NA. **SOURCE:** Whittaker, Violet. (1984). Puppet people scripts. Grand Rapids, MI: Baker Book House. **SUBJECTS/PLAY TYPE:** Elisha; Bible Stories; Puppet Play.

860. 8-12. (+) Garver, Juliet. **Elizabeth. CAST:** 1f. **ACTS:** 1. **SETTINGS:** Bare stage, props. **PLAYING TIME:** 15 min. **PLOT:** The courtship and marriage of Elizabeth Barrett to Robert Browning are dramatized in monologue, interspersed with E. Browning's poetry. Elizabeth explains her relationship with her father and his disapproval of Robert; her relationship with Robert and how they met secretly; her happiness because Robert encouraged her creativity; and her grief because her father would not accept the marriage and disowned her. **RECOMMENDATION:** This very dramatic monologue would be suitable for a dramatic reading competition. **ROYALTY:** Free to Plays subscribers. **SOURCE:** Garver, Juliet. (1977, October). Elizabeth. Plays: The Drama Magazine for Young People, pp. 71- 77. **SUBJECTS/PLAY TYPE:** Browning, Elizabeth Barrett; Monologue.

861. 3-6. (+) Thane, Adele. (Grimm, Jacob Ludwig Carl, and Grimm, Wilhelm Carl) **The elves and the shoemaker.** (The elves and the shoemaker.) **CAST:** 7f, 6m, 3u. **ACTS:** 1. **SETTINGS:** Shoemaker's shop. **PLAYING TIME:** 30 min. **PLOT:** It is three days before Christmas and Johann, the shoemaker, has no money to buy gifts for the village children. At night he cuts out a small pair of shoes from his last piece of scrap, lays them on the counter, and goes to bed. At midnight, three poorly dressed elves come to the shop and complete the shoes, which the shoemaker and his wife, Frieda, find the next day. When the Duke and his family come to the shop and see the lovely shoes, the Duke buys them and orders more. The shoemaker cuts the shoes out, goes to bed, and the elves help again. When the shoemaker sells the shoes, he has enough money to buy more leather, to buy gifts for the village children, and to make clothes and shoes for the elf benefactors. **RECOMMENDATION:** This well known story makes an excellent Christmas play. Liberal ad-libbing, traditional Christmas melodies with new lyrics, and pantomime, all add to the general mirth and good will. **ROYALTY:** None. **SOURCE:** Thane, Adele. (1983). Plays from Famous Stories and Fairy Tales. Boston: Plays, Inc. **SUBJECTS/PLAY TYPE:** Christmas; Folk Tales, Germany; Adaptation.

862. 7-12. (+) Nolan, Paul T. (Fulda, Ludwig) **Emma and the professor's coat.** (The fur coat) **CAST:** 2f, 2m, 3u. **ACTS:** 1. **SETTINGS:** Study. **PLAYING TIME:** 25 min. **PLOT:** Max, a scholar in his early 30s, and his wife, Emma, have separated after four years of marriage. Max discusses their separation in a logical, scientific manner, predicting that life will be sad and dull for Emma while he will be free to enjoy complete harmony. To his dismay, the opposite occurs. Before it is too late, he discovers the real meaning of marriage, and the couple reunites. **RECOMMENDATION:** Although the play ends with the unrealistic reunion of a separated couple, it does reveal the maturation process, during which each spouse defines his/her responsibilities to the relationship in a changing society. **ROYALTY:** Free to Plays subscribers. **SOURCE:** Nolan, Paul T. (1976, March). Emma and the professor's coat. Plays: The Drama Magazine for Young

People, pp. 87-95. **SUBJECTS/PLAY TYPE:** Marriage; Adaptation.

863. 2-6. (-) Boettcher-Tate, Karen. **Emma Lou and the Big Ragout. CAST:** 7f, 3m, 6u. **ACTS:** 2. **SETTINGS:** Throne room; forest. **PLAYING TIME:** NA. **PLOT:** Because Princess Emma Lou Shankpump has only three days to become engaged or her father will lose his throne. Miss Glorious Lovoone, owner of the local charm school, escorts the princess to see Big Ragout, who can give her the charm necessary to win Prince Bucky. On their journey, Emma Lou and Glorious meet a number of exotic creatures. When Big Ragout disappointingly proves to be a horrible, insulting creature, Emma Lou discovers that she doesn't need more charm. Prince Bucky has always loved her, but was too shy to say so. **RECOMMENDATION:** Little in this play makes it appropriate for elementary children. The characters are totally unbelievable, even as fairy tale figures. Emma Lou wavers between being a modern teenager and a medieval maid. Miss Glorious, of the charm school, is painted as the antithesis of charm, primarily on the basis of her ungrammatical speech. The resolution defies belief, while it shows that violence and insults can get you what you want. The negative theme of materialism is especially prominent at the end when Ragout promises Glorious a new wardrobe, Porche (sic), a large screen TV, a VCR, a personal computer and a Doberman-Pinscher. **ROYALTY:** NA. **SOURCE:** Boettcher-Tate, Karen. (1987). Emma Lou and the Big Ragout. Denver, CO: Pioneer Drama Services **SUBJECTS/PLAY TYPE:** Marriage; Comedy.

864. 3-12. (+) Bayer, Harold. (Andersen, Hans Christian) **The emperor's new clothes.** (The emperor's new clothes) **CAST:** 2f, 5m, 1u. **ACTS:** 1. **SETTINGS:** Bare stage. **PLAYING TIME:** 50 min. **PLOT:** Skim and Scram have run out of food, wine and money. They convince a merchant to pay handsomely for an invisible powder which they claim, when added to water, produces the best wine imaginable. They then introduce themselves to the vain emperor as the former tailors of a fictitious rival emperor, and convince him to hire them to make clothes out of cloth which is invisible to anyone who is stupid or unfit for his position. Of course, no one is able to see the suit, but no one except a child will say so, since that would be an admission of stupidity. Skim and Scram leave with their money, and the emperor tries to be happy about his lovely new clothes. **RECOMMENDATION:** The fast paced, witty dialogue and four songs make this an entertaining play. This sophisticated version will be appreciated by a wide range of ages, although it must be performed by older children because of its lengthy dialogue. **ROYALTY:** NA. **SOURCE:** Bayer, Harold. (1982). Motley tales: a collection of folk and fairy tales with music. Boston, MA: Baker's Plays. **SUBJECTS/PLAY TYPE:** Folk Tales, Denmark; Vanity; Clothes; Adaptation.

865. 2-4*. (+) Cole, Sharon A. (Andersen, Hans Christian) **The emperor's new clothes.** (The emperor's new clothes) **CAST:** 3f, 8m, 3u. **ACTS:** 1. **SETTINGS:**

Palace. **PLAYING TIME:** 60 min. **PLOT:** When clever but greedy Snip and Tuck appeal to Emperor Velvet's vanity, they are hired to weave him a fine suit of new clothes. They convince the emperor that the clothes are under a magical spell and anyone who can't see them is a fool. A hilarious scene results when the gullible emperor appears in a royal procession wearing the invisible suit of clothes. The emperor learns a lesson about selfishness and pride the hard way, and the swindling tailors end up in the royal dungeon. **RECOMMENDATION:** This well loved classic tale continues to entertain and amuse. Humorous characters such as Prince Terry Cloth and Princess Polly Ester, and dialogue which plays off names like Sir Yesir add to the fun and laughter. Casting is flexible so that many roles may be played by males or females (adult or children). **ROYALTY:** $25. **SOURCE:** Cole, Sharon A. (1980). The emperor's new clothes. Schulenburg, TX: I.E. Clark. **SUBJECTS/PLAY TYPE:** Clothes; Vanity; Folk Tales, Denmark; Adaptation.

866. K-6. (+) Kase, Judith B.. (Andersen, Hans Christian) **The emperor's new clothes.** (The emperor's new clothes) **CAST:** 2f, 3m, 7u. **ACTS:** 2. **SETTINGS:** Bare stage, props. **PLAYING TIME:** NA. **PLOT:** This is a humorous but faithful adaptation of Hans Christian Andersen's beloved story. **RECOMMENDATION:** This play's humor offers something for every age range. For the younger group, the fun can be found in a scene where the two weavers are trapped in a huge bag. For the older group, it is the story itself. Yet for others, it may be found in the monologue of the stage coordinator. Although the cast should be in fourth grade and up, the audience could include children in kindergarten on up. **ROYALTY:** $25. **SOURCE:** Kase, Judith B. (1979). The emperor's new clothes. New Orleans, LA: The Anchorage Press, Inc. **SUBJECTS/PLAY TYPE:** Clothes; Folk tales, Denmark; Vanity; Adaptation.

867. 3-6. (+) Lynch-Watson, Janet. (Andersen, Hans Christian) **The emperor's new clothes.** (The emperor's new clothes) **CAST:** Su. **ACTS:** 5. **SETTINGS:** Palace; attic; market. **PLAYING TIME:** 25 min. **PLOT:** A selfish emperor changes suits four times a day, while the queen wears patched old clothes. The queen finally orders some new clothes from a catalog. Two swindlers fool the emperor by telling him that they are going to make him clothes from material that has magical powers. Because the emperor was told that the clothes will be invisible to anyone who is either unfit for his job or very silly, no one will tell the emperor that he is naked, except for a young boy. **RECOMMENDATION:** The humor and whimsy of the original story are well preserved in this shadow puppet play. Production notes and patterns are included. **ROYALTY:** NA. **SOURCE:** Lynch-Watson, Janet. (1980). The shadow puppet book. NY: Sterling Pub. Co. **SUBJECTS/PLAY TYPE:** Folk Tales, Denmark; Vanity; Clothes; Shadow Puppet Play.

868. 4-12. (+) DiFonso, Don. (Andersen, Hans Christian) **The emperor's nightingale.** (The nightingale). **CAST:** 2f; 4m; 6u. **ACTS:** 2. **SETTINGS:** Throne room; kitchen; bedroom; forest. **PLAYING TIME:** 90 min. **PLOT:** The Emperor is a sad, unsympathetic man since his wife died in childbirth and he lost his daughter to bandits. He requests that the nightingale living in his garden be brought to him to sing. Plum Blossom, a kitchen servant, finds the nightingale and brings it to the palace. As the bird sings, the Emperor's health improves. Lord Chamberlain, the Emperor's cousin, and his devious wife, Lady Ming, set their sights on being the next emperor and queen. They secretly send the Emperor a mechanical nightingale that will sing at any time. When the mechanical nightingale breaks, the emperor's health fails, and soon he is on his death bed. Plum Blossom goes to the forest and returns with the real nightingale. As she sings, the Emperor's health quickly improves. He notices that the locket Plum Blossom wears matches the locket he inherited from his grandfather, and the emperor realizes she is his long lost daughter. Mindful of how poorly he has ruled his people, the Emperor promises to be more merciful and understanding. **RECOMMENDATION:** This delightful adaptation of the well known folk tale would serve as an interesting introduction to the study of ancient China or Asian history. **ROYALTY:** $50. **SOURCE:** DiFonso, Don and Barasch, Shirley. (1984). The Emperor's nightingale. Denver, CO: Pioneer Drama Service. **SUBJECTS/PLAY TYPE:** Folk Tales, Denmark; Musical; Nightingales; Adaptation.

869. 3-6. (+) Mahlman, Lewis. (Andersen, Hans Christian) **The emperor's nightingale.** (The nightingale) **CAST:** 8u. **ACTS:** 1. **SETTINGS:** Forest; bedroom. **PLAYING TIME:** 15 min. **PLOT:** The emperor receives a nightingale and a mechanical bird as gifts. Though the nightingale sings more beautifully, the emperor is able to keep the mechanical bird captive, and he banishes the real nightingale. On his deathbed, the emperor calls for the nightingale. The nightingale strikes a deal with death to prolong the life of the emperor on the condition that the emperor agrees to give the bird her freedom if she sings for him occasionally. **RECOMMENDATION:** In this skillful but short adaptation, formal language matches the courtliness of the setting. A fisherman poetically introduces each scene in the Greek style, although the reason for banishing the nightingale is never made clear because some of the story has been condensed. The scene in which the nightingale bargains with death is easily understood. Scenery and costuming for the puppets require skill. Some background of Oriental culture and royalty would help in understanding the plot. **ROYALTY:** Free to Plays subscribers. **SOURCE:** Mahlman, Lewis. (1978, April). The emperor's nightingale. Plays: The Drama Magazine for Young People, pp. 59-62. **SUBJECTS/PLAY TYPE:** Folk Tales, Denmark; Death; Puppet Play; Adaptation.

870. 5-12. (+) Thane, Adele. (Andersen, Hans Christian) **The emperor's nightingale.** (The nightingale) **CAST:** 5f, 7m, 2u. **ACTS:** 1. **SETTINGS:** Garden. **PLAYING TIME:** 25 min. **PLOT:** In this humorous retelling of the classic fairy tale, the Chinese emperor is pleased and soothed by his own living nightingale's song until he receives a mechanical bird from the emperor of Japan. The new bird supplants the

nightingale until it breaks and can't be repaired. The emperor is heart broken and falls ill. When death seems imminent, the real nightingale returns. The emperor is overjoyed and revives, resolving to never take the nightingale for granted again. RECOMMENDATION: Humorous asides deflate the king's pompous statements and the courtly language used throughout this delightful adaptation. Particularly notable here is the excellent use of language which allows this to rise above the traditional retelling of the story. ROYALTY: None. SOURCE: Thane, Adele. (1983). Plays from Famous Stories and Fairy Tales. Boston: Plays, Inc. SUBJECTS/PLAY TYPE: Comedy; Folk Tales, Denmark; Nightingales; Adaptation.

871. 1-3. (+) Bauer, Caroline Feller. **The emperor's prized possession. CAST:** 2f, 3m, Su. **ACTS:** 1. **SETTINGS:** Outside a palace wall. **PLAYING TIME:** 6 min. **PLOT:** The emperor wishes to give his cat a very important sounding name. Each time he chooses one (Sky, Cloud, Wind, Wall, Mouse), a member of his family or the Prime Minister points out a flaw. The emperor finally is led to the inevitable choice of the name "Cat." **RECOMMENDATION:** The audience participates as the voice of the cat. The characters can be portrayed stiffly or with an older group performing, very broadly and comically. The themes of pride and of trying to make something more important than it really is can generate interesting discussion. **ROYALTY:** None. **SOURCE:** Bauer, Caroline Feller. (1987). Presenting reader's theater: plays and poems to read aloud. New York, NY: H. W. Wilson and Company. **SUBJECTS/PLAY TYPE:** Pride; Values; Reader's Theater.

872. 3-6. (+) Jones, David Cadwalader. **The enchanted well. CAST:** 6u. **ACTS:** 1. **SETTINGS:** Bare stage, props. **PLAYING TIME:** 15 min. **PLOT:** While helping her mother get water from the well, Meg accidentally hits Boggart, the well's echo. In retaliation, Boggart takes her voice away. Trying to help, a witch tells Meg to bring the bucket from the well, but not to spill any of the water on the way. Because Meg does spill water, and now can't stop talking, the witch says that the only solution is to out-talk the Boggart. Meg returns to the well and talks nonstop to Boggart. Finally, he gets tired of echoing her and releases the spell. **RECOMMENDATION:** This delightful tale about clumsiness, echoes, and filibustering is on target with its humor and its characterizations. **ROYALTY:** Free to Plays subscribers. **SOURCE:** Jones, David Cadwalader. (1975, April). The enchanted wall. Plays: The Drama Magazine for Young People, pp. 61-65. **SUBJECTS/PLAY TYPE:** Folk Tales, Scotland; Echoes; Puppet Play.

873. 12. (+) Jacobson, Ruth. **Encounter. CAST:** 1f, 2m. **ACTS:** 1. **SETTINGS:** Bare stage. **PLAYING TIME:** NA. **PLOT:** Three strangers find themselves trapped in a mysterious, bare room. As the two men and one woman try to understand their situation, their initial wariness of one another fades, and they find a release from fear and confinement in mutual affection.

RECOMMENDATION: Adult language and subject matter may make this play unsuitable for high school audiences, but very appropriate for experimental theatre or for interpretation in a theater class. ROYALTY: $20. SOURCE: Jacobson, Ruth. (1986). Encounter. Woodstock, IL: Dramatic Pub. Co. SUBJECTS/PLAY TYPE: Human Relations; Playlet.

874. 7-12. (-) McCusker, Paul. **An encounter at the library. CAST:** 1f, 1m. **ACTS:** 1. **SETTINGS:** Bare stage, props. **PLAYING TIME:** NA. **PLOT:** In ecstasy because Dave sat down next to her in the library, Carole sings an exuberant song and tells Dave she's not busy on Friday night. **RECOMMENDATION:** This play is patronizing, unfunny, and Dave's ending line "Gee I should read Shakespeare more often!" seems to make little sense. **ROYALTY:** NA. **SOURCE:** McCusker, Paul. (1984). Batteries not included. Boston: Baker's Plays. **SUBJECTS/PLAY TYPE:** Romance; Comedy.

875. 6-12. (+) McCusker, Paul. **An encounter in the park. CAST:** 2m. **ACTS:** 1. **SETTINGS:** Bare stage, props. **PLAYING TIME:** NA. **PLOT:** Now destitute, a once famous Christian writer, a playwright, and a musician explain that because their fellow Christians copied their works instead of buying them, they have no money. The play ends with a plea for people to observe copyright laws. **RECOMMENDATION:** Even if the questionable references and appeals to Christians were deleted, this would be a didactic admonition about copyright laws. **ROYALTY:** NA. **SOURCE:** McCusker, Paul. (1984). Batteries not included. Boston, MA: Baker's Plays. **SUBJECTS/PLAY TYPE:** Copyright; Skit.

876. 9-12. (+) DuBois, Graham. **The end of the road. CAST:** 4f, 3m. **ACTS:** 1. **SETTINGS:** Living room. **PLAYING TIME:** 30 min. **PLOT:** During the Revolutionary War, a family living near Valley Forge faces a crisis when it appears that they have unknowingly harbored a traitor. **RECOMMENDATION:** This offers clear conflict and sufficient suspense to keep the audience involved from beginning to end. **ROYALTY:** Free to Plays subscribers. **SOURCE:** Kamerman, Sylvia E. (1983). Holiday plays round the year. Boston, MA: Plays, Inc. **SUBJECTS/PLAY TYPE:** Revolutionary War, U.S.; Espionage; Family; Playlet.

877. 10-12. (+) Rudolph, Grace. **Enid Murphy's eyes and ears on the world. CAST:** 2f. **ACTS:** 1. **SETTINGS:** Living room. **PLAYING TIME:** NA. **PLOT:** Eighty year old Enid lives by herself in a house that she can no longer clean, so 60 year old Hilda comes in weekly to help. They gossip about some of Hilda's other senior clients while griping and sniping at each other. On her way out, Hilda informs Enid that the Friendly Circle is having their Christmas meeting at Enid's house and that she is bringing a hideous Christmas tree to decorate Enid's living room. Smarting at this trick, Enid calls another friend to verify this information and invites her for lunch. **RECOMMENDATION:** This easily staged vignette centers upon two slightly stereotypical old women, but it makes the more important point that everyone needs companionship. **ROYALTY:** $10. **SOURCE:** Rudolph,

Grace. (1984). Elders' statements: One-act plays and monologues. Boston, MA: Baker's Plays. SUBJECTS/PLAY TYPE: Aging; Christmas; Comedy.

878. 6-9. (-) Hark, Mildred & McQueen, Noel. **Enter George Washington. CAST:** 3f, 2m. **ACTS:** 1. **SETTINGS:** Living room. **PLAYING TIME:** 25 min. **PLOT:** A young boy's role in a play about George Washington changes his views of this national hero. **RECOMMENDATION:** The sudden change in Albert's attitude toward his sister and his new found appreciation of the father of our country seem forced. The language is stilted and the humor is rather flat. **ROYALTY:** Free to Plays subscribers. **SOURCE:** Hark, Mildred & McQueen, Noel. (1982, January/ February). Enter George Washington. Plays: The Drama Magazine for Young People, pp. 47-54. **SUBJECTS/PLAY TYPE:** Washington, George; Playlet.

879. 10-12. (+) Stein, Joseph. (Reiner, Carl) **Enter laughing.** (Enter laughing) **CAST:** 4f, 11m. **ACTS:** 2. **SETTINGS:** Machine shop; office; theater; dressing room; phone booth; kitchen; restaurant; cemetery. **PLAYING TIME:** NA. **PLOT:** David Kolowitz, a machine shop apprentice and aspiring young actor, finagles free acting lessons while dodging his parents' hopes for his future as a druggist. He overcomes numerous humorous obstacles, including an abundance of pretty women, and earns his night onstage along with the approval of his parents. **RECOMMENDATION:** Youths will relate to this young man who follows his dreams and exaggerates his prowess as a lover. However, frequent scene changes require an energetic stage crew, and the part of David is demanding, as he appears in all 17 scenes. **ROYALTY:** NA. **SOURCE:** Stein, Joseph. (1984). Enter laughing: A comedy in two acts. New York, NY: Samuel French. **SUBJECTS/PLAY TYPE:** Comedy; Careers; Jewish Family; Adaptation.

880. 1-8. (+) Steinhorn, Harriet & Lowry, Edith. **The escape. CAST:** 5f, 4m, Su. **ACTS:** 1. **SETTINGS:** Concentration camp barracks. **PLAYING TIME:** 10 min. **PLOT:** When the women in a Polish concentration camp (1943) are to be deported, they give Rachel a comb, pants, and sweater so that she can try to escape. However, at the last minute, Rachel joins the others, saying that if she were discovered missing, they would be killed, and she couldn't allow that to happen. The play ends as they all sing "Ani Maamin." **RECOMMENDATION:** The heroism and selflessness of the Jewish prisoners are starkly contrasted against the brutality of the Nazis and futility of the Jews' belief that they might survive. The theme of heroic human dignity is tragically, but effectively, delivered. **ROYALTY:** Free for amateur groups. **SOURCE:** Steinhorn, Harriet & Lowry, Edith. (1983). Shadows of the Holocaust: Plays, readings, and program resources. Rockville, MD: Kar-Ben Copies, Inc. **SUBJECTS/PLAY TYPE:** Holocaust; Concentration Camps; World War II; Drama.

881. 7-12. (+) Davis, Ossie. **Escape to freedom. CAST:** 2f, 5m. **ACTS:** 1. **SETTINGS:** Cabin; backyard; farmyards; ship's hulk. **PLAYING TIME:** NA. **PLOT:** Having been born a slave, Frederick Douglass suffers years of cruelty. In spite of immense odds, he learns to read, and this skill enables him to escape to freedom in the North. **RECOMMENDATION:** This not only depicts the history accurately, but skillfully weaves emotion and spirit into the story via dialogue and song. Skillful acting and directing are necessary. **ROYALTY:** NA. **SOURCE:** Davis, Ossie. (1978). Escape to freedom. New York, NY: Viking Press. **SUBJECTS/PLAY TYPE:** Slavery; Douglass, Frederick; Drama.

882. 6-10. (+) Boiko, Claire. **Escape to the blue planet. CAST:** 3f, 2m, 6u. **ACTS:** 1. **SETTINGS:** Backyard on earth; throne room on another planet. **PLAYING TIME:** 35 min. **PLOT:** A case of mistaken identity causes a young man and his cousin to be transported to another planet. **RECOMMENDATION:** The humorous, believable story uses common objects as realistic "space" props. **ROYALTY:** Free to Plays subscribers. **SOURCE:** Kamerman, Sylvia E. (1981). Space and science fiction plays for young people. Boston, MA: Plays, Inc. **SUBJECTS/PLAY TYPE:** Science Fiction; Adventure; Comedy.

883. 8-12. (+) Raymond, Martha H. **Esmeralda or the emeralds. CAST:** 3f, 4m, Su. **ACTS:** 1. **SETTINGS:** Park; gazebo. **PLAYING TIME:** NA. **PLOT:** Harry and Herbie, two bumbling con men, accidentally meet their former victim, Reginald Trueheart, and his young love Esmeralda, at the gazebo. The con men hide their stolen goods in the gazebo and Reginald accidentally discovers it. A struggle ensues and Esmeralda knocks out the crooks, but proclaims Reginald the hero. She points out he is entitled to the rewards, and her Uncle Charlie allows Esmeralda and Reginald to marry. **RECOMMENDATION:** This could be entertaining if the actors played up the humor. The sets and costumes as described are fairly complex, but can be simplified. The romantic scenes may be a problem with younger grades. **ROYALTY:** $20. **SOURCE:** Raymond, Martha H. (1986). Esmeralda or the emeralds. Franklin, OH: Eldridge Pub. Co. **SUBJECTS/PLAY TYPE:** Romance; Melodrama; Comedy.

884. 10-12. (+) Rahmann, Pat. **Essentials. CAST:** 1f, 1m. **ACTS:** 1. **SETTINGS:** Kitchen. **PLAYING TIME:** NA. **PLOT:** Walter values order and cleanliness while his wife, Margaret, is concerned with the welfare of all living things including her dog, birds, spider, and a goat hidden in the basement. Before leaving for work in the morning, Walter compiles a list of chores for Margaret, including calling an exterminator for the cockroaches. Margaret objects to killing them and is unmoved by Walter's concern for details and appearances. **RECOMMENDATION:** The contrast between Margaret's and Walter's outlooks is successfully and comically developed in their breakfast table conversation. The witty treatment of two distinct personalities bound not only by expectations of marriage but also by their apparent love for each other is appealing. **ROYALTY:** $15. **SOURCE:** Rahmann, Pat.

(1976). Essentials. Boston, MA: Baker's Plays. SUBJECTS/PLAY TYPE: Marriage; Pets; Personality Conflicts; Comedy.

885. 6-12. (+) Foley, Irene M. **Esteban's balloons.** CAST: 5f, 5m, Su. ACTS: 1. SETTINGS: Street. PLAYING TIME: NA. PLOT: Three teenage boys have to find summer jobs. After considering their options, they decide to sell balloons at the local street fair. When their supplier decides to go into business for himself, they have to hustle to find balloons. Since they show initiative, they are offered summer jobs as messengers on Wall Street. RECOMMENDATION: This is an interesting lesson in capitalism, with some innocent romance thrown in. The director may want to change the characters from Hispanics to generic kids. ROYALTY: $15. SOURCE: Foley, Irene M. (1986). Esteban's balloons. Chicago, IL: Dramatic Pub. Co. SUBJECTS/PLAY TYPE: Employment; Entrepreneurs; Drama.

886. 9-12. (+) Murray, John. **Even a child can do it.** CAST: 1u. ACTS: 1. SETTINGS: None. PLAYING TIME: NA. PLOT: A man tries to put together an "easy-to-assemble" chaise lounge and decides that the "child" who allegedly could do it would need a degree in mechanical engineering. RECOMMENDATION: The idea is old, but this still works, especially if the physical humor and pantomime are exaggerated. ROYALTY: None. SOURCE: Murray, John. (1982). Modern monologues for young people. Boston, MA: Plays, Inc. SUBJECTS/PLAY TYPE: Kits; Comedy; Construction; Monologue.

887. 8-10. (-) Dubois, Graham. **Every day is Thanksgiving.** CAST: 5f, 4m. ACTS: 1. SETTINGS: Living room. PLAYING TIME: 30 min. PLOT: The boys are unhappy about a mother's demand that they escort the new girl in town to a masquerade dance, until they meet her. She is beautiful, likes football, and comes from France. One lucky boy gets to take her to the dance and he learns about Europe. RECOMMENDATION: This is replete with paper thin characters, a totally predictable outcome, stereotyped references to women, unresolved conflicts, and patronizing lessons about foreigners in the "wonderful" U.S.A. ROYALTY: Free to Plays subscribers. SOURCE: Dubois, Graham. (1983, November). Every Day is Thanksgiving. Plays: The Drama Magazine for Young People, pp. 13-20. SUBJECTS/PLAY TYPE: Thanksgiving; Dating; Comedy.

888. K-3. (+) King, Peggy Cameron. **Every season has a reason.** CAST: 4f, 4m, 8u. ACTS: 1. SETTINGS: None. PLAYING TIME: 10 min. PLOT: The value of each season is introduced first by a cast member who dislikes it, and then by a cast member who likes it. RECOMMENDATION: This is a positive use of the comparison and contrast method of discovery. The rhyming dialogue would also be appropriate for a first attempt at memorization of play material. ROYALTY: Free to Plays subscribers. SOURCE: King, Peggy Cameron. (1981, May). Every season has a reason. Plays: The Drama Magazine for Young People, pp. 42-44. SUBJECTS/PLAY TYPE: Seasons; Choral Reading.

889. 1-3. (+) Martin, Judith. **Everybody, everybody.** CAST: 3f, 3m. ACTS: 4. SETTINGS: Bare stage, props. PLAYING TIME: 10 min. PLOT: Instead of arguing about food, kissing, songs, the merits of being fat or thin, or how to fight, the picnickers keep their own opinions, sing a song, and shake hands. RECOMMENDATION: The four skits deal humorously with common issues for youngsters. Paper bags are the only costumes necessary. ROYALTY: None. SOURCE: Martin, Judith. (1981). Everybody, everybody: a collection from the paper bag players. NY: Elsevier/Nelson Books. SUBJECTS/PLAY TYPE: Friends; Opinions; Comedy.

890. 9-12. (+) Huff, Betty Tracy. **Everybody loves Gladys.** CAST: 5f, 5m, Su. ACTS: 1. SETTINGS: Office. PLAYING TIME: 35 min. PLOT: The head of the Widget Can Opener Company, Mr. Morton, receives a sickly looking plant, Gladys the aspidistra, from his best customer, Mr. Norris, with a plea to revive her. A plant expert's prescription is to give the plant love, conversation, and quiet music. When Beatrice, an industrial spy for a rival company, tells Mr. Norris that Mr. Morton has failed, Norris decides not to place his order with Widget. But Beatrice's activities are discovered, including her directive to play loud rock music. The plant expert concludes that Gladys droops because she is sad that Gladys' favorite secretary, Sally, has an allergy to her. When Sally discovers that her allergy is not to Gladys, but to fish plant food, Gladys is happy, so Mr. Norris is happy and doubles his Widget order. RECOMMENDATION: This comedy, revolving around an unlikely plot, would provide excellent light entertainment. ROYALTY: Free to Plays subscribers. SOURCE: Huff, Betty Tracy. (1975, May). Everybody loves Gladys. Plays: The Drama Magazine for Young People, pp. 1-12. SUBJECTS/PLAY TYPE: Plants; Comedy.

891. 11-12. (+) Egermeier, Virginia. **Everyman, everywoman.** (Everyman) CAST: 5f, 4m, 10u. ACTS: 1. SETTINGS: Bare stage. PLAYING TIME: NA. PLOT: In this fine adaptation of the classic 15th century morality play, Everyman, Death, the five wits (hearing, sight, smell, touch, taste), knowledge, discretion, strength, beauty, and worldly goods cannot help the man nearing death. Only good deeds and repentance for sins will allow him to enter heaven. RECOMMENDATION: This allegorical drama effectively delivers its theme about life, death, and life after death without sectarian references. ROYALTY: NA. SOURCE: Egermeier, Virginia. Everyman, everywoman. (1982). Woodstock, IL: Dramatic Pub. Co. SUBJECTS/PLAY TYPE: Morality Play; Allegory; Death; Drama.

892. 11-12. (-) Foster, Christine. Cohen, Phyllis. **Everything but anchovies.** CAST: 2f, 2m. ACTS: 1. SETTINGS: Game show; woods. PLAYING TIME: NA. PLOT: Four students quarrel after being defeated on a game show and end up on the edge of a woods, where their abominable actions toward each other involve drugs, sex, and alcohol. They return home with their problems and frustrations still unresolved. RECOMMENDATION: This deals with the serious

subjects of alcohol, drugs, and broken homes, but the teens frequently burst into songs which are inconsistent with the weighty problems. ROYALTY: NA. SOURCE: Foster, Christine and Cohen, Phyllis. (1984). Everything but anchovies. Toronto: Playwrights Canada. SUBJECTS/PLAY TYPE: Friendship; Drug Abuse; Peer Pressure; Drama.

893. 7-12. (+) Kelly, Tim. **Everything's Jim Dandy.** CAST: 3f, 3m. ACTS: 2. SETTINGS: Living room. PLAYING TIME: NA. PLOT: Jim Dandy, an endearingly irresponsible rodeo cowboy learns that responsibility, in the form of marriage and a secure job, is not so scary as it originally seemed. RECOMMENDATION: Humor and originality makes this play successful and the rodeo star's carefree personality is a vivid portrayal of youth and spirit. Teenagers will identify with the well drawn characters in this poignant story about growing up and will understand the important, but not didactic theme. ROYALTY: $35. SOURCE: Kelly, Tim. (1981). Everything's Jim Dandy. Schulenburg, TX: I.E. Clark. SUBJECTS/PLAY TYPE: Maturation; Responsibility; Drama.

894. K-3. (-) Dannecker, Hazel. **Everywhere Christmas.** CAST: 10u. ACTS: 1. SETTINGS: None. PLAYING TIME: 15 min. PLOT: Children dressed in native costumes from Holland, France, Norway, Brazil, Germany, Sweden, Mexico, England and the United States recite verses describing Christmas customs in their countries. The recitation concludes as all the children sing "Joy to the World." Inclusion of a short carol from each country is an option. RECOMMENDATION: Although any number of children could have a part, and the format is appropriate for young children, the verses are awkward and poorly written. It could be used in private or church schools, but many religious references preclude its use in public schools. ROYALTY: None. SOURCE: Dannecker, Hazel. (n.d.) Everywhere Christmas. Franklin, OH: Eldridge Pub. Co. SUBJECTS/PLAY TYPE: Christmas; Choral Reading.

895. 1-6. (+) Very, Alice. **Everywhere Christmas.** CAST: 8f, 11m, Su. ACTS: 1. SETTINGS: Living room. PLAYING TIME: 15 min. PLOT: While two children wait by the fireplace, hoping Santa will bring their gifts, an old man asks for money and the children give him their only penny. They hear the sound of sleigh bells and Santa Claus arrives with children from all over the world, who describe how they celebrate Christmas in their cultures. RECOMMENDATION: Short, rhyming dialogue will be easy to memorize as Christmas in different European cultures is entertainingly described. ROYALTY: NA. SOURCE: Very, Alice. (1986, December). Everywhere Christmas. Plays: The Drama Magazine for Young People, pp. 33-36. SUBJECTS/PLAY TYPE: Christmas; Playlet.

896. 6-12. (+) Belgrade Coventry Theatre in Education Company. **Example: The case of Craig and Bentley.** CAST: 7f, 12m. ACTS: 2. SETTINGS: Bare stage, props. PLAYING TIME: NA. PLOT: Derek Bentley, a gullible young man with a low IQ, is talked into helping Chris Craig with a number of petty thefts. One night they are caught and Craig shoots and kills a policeman. Both are charged with murder and convicted, but Craig, who is 16, is sentenced to prison while Bentley, who is 19, is sentenced to death despite questions regarding his involvement in the actual shooting. Despite appeals on his behalf, Derek Bentley is executed. RECOMMENDATION: This play explores the topic of capital punishment thoroughly and would be excellent as an opener for further discussion on how laws have changed, as well as how laws and court procedures in the U.S. differ from those in Britain. The authors recommend that this play be produced in the morning with an afternoon workshop session to elaborate on the issues. The cast size can be as few as four males and two females. ROYALTY: NA. SOURCE: Schweitzer, Pam. (1983). Theatre in education: four secondary programs. London: Methuen. SUBJECTS/PLAY TYPE: Capital Punishment; Justice; Drama.

897. 5-8. (+) Krushel, Kenneth. **The exploits of Mullah Nasrudin.** CAST: 3f, 7m, Su. ACTS: 1. SETTINGS: Bazaar; home; desert; court. PLAYING TIME: 25 min. PLOT: Mullah Nasrudin, noted for solving the most puzzling problems, has been asked by his nephew, Rumi, to help him win the hand of Princess Esmeralda. The Emperor seeks Mullah's advice concerning a suitable husband for his daughter. Mullah weaves an extraordinary tale about a monster, Great Eye, who will be slain by a brave warrior, a suitable husband for Princess Esmeralda. Mullah, Hassein, and Rumi appear at the Emperor's court with a bag supposedly containing the eyes of Great Eye, actually two stones. The Emperor becomes quite skeptical. Mullah convinces the Emperor of their value and of Rumi's bravery. He allows Rumi to marry his daughter. RECOMMENDATION: Although somewhat predictable, this adaptation of a Turkish folk tale is quite entertaining. The important role of the monster is, for the most part, left to the imagination, and therefore does not overwhelm the other characters, or excessively frighten young audiences. ROYALTY: Free to Plays subscribers. SOURCE: Krushel, Kenneth. (1976, March). The exploits of Mullah Nasrudin. Plays: The Drama Magazine for Young People, pp. 39-46. SUBJECTS/PLAY TYPE: Folk Tale, Turkish; Adaptation.

898. K-4. (+) Boiko, Claire. **The exterior decorator.** CAST: 1f, 3m, 16u. ACTS: 1. SETTINGS: Bare stage, props. PLAYING TIME: 15 min. PLOT: It is March, the scene is outdoors, Madame Jacques Frost suffers depression caused by the drab colors, miserable weather and boredom of late winter. Monsieur Jacques Frost calls Dr. Equinox who prescribes a radical change: spring colors, blue sky, sunlight and fresh breezes. When the transformation is complete the set is brighter, lighter and more cheerful. Madame Frost is cured. The playlet ends with airy music played by four robins. RECOMMENDATION: Directors don't need to worry about children forgetting their lines as the story line is clear and could be ad-libbed. Some musical recordings are required. ROYALTY: None. SOURCE: Boiko, Claire.

(1985). Children's plays for creative actors. Boston, MA: Plays, Inc. **SUBJECTS/PLAY TYPE:** Seasons; Playlet.

899. 11-12. (+) Mastrosimone, William. **Extremities.** CAST: 3f, 1m. ACTS: 2. SETTINGS: Living room. PLAYING TIME: NA. PLOT: Raul has been watching a farmhouse where three young women live. One day when Marjorie is there alone, he breaks in and attempts to rape her. She sprays him with an aerosol can, ties him up, stuffs him into the fireplace and threatens to burn him alive. Her roommates come home and turn against her when Raul contends she "came on to him." By threatening castration, Marjorie gets Raul to admit his attack, as well as several rape-murders in the past. As Patricia and Terry go for help, he crawls back into the fireplace to await his fate. Marjorie weeps. RECOMMENDATION: **Extremities** is an explosive, contemporary, psychological drama exploring societal attitudes about rape. It has received very favorable reviews and enjoyed considerable success off-Broadway. The dialogue and situations are intended for mature adult audiences. The essential question posed by this play requires considerable moral sophistication: having succeeded in turning a violent attack to one's own advantage, is one justified in exacting retribution, or does the common bond of shared humanity suggest mercy toward the attacker? ROYALTY: $60. SOURCE: Mastrosimone, William. (1978). Extremities. New York: Samuel French. SUBJECTS/PLAY TYPE: Rape; Drama.

900. 4-7. (+) Fisher, Aileen Lucia. **The fable of three brothers.** CAST: 4m. ACTS: 1. SETTINGS: Bare stage. PLAYING TIME: NA. PLOT: An aging father decides to apportion his estate to his three sons as a test to see who will show the most wisdom in running it. Two of the sons ravage the land, but the third practices sound ecological techniques and is praised. RECOMMENDATION: This presents the issues of ecology to children. ROYALTY: NA. SOURCE: Fisher, Aileen Lucia. (1985). The fable of three brothers. Boston, MA: Plays, Inc. SUBJECTS/PLAY TYPE: Ecology; Skit.

901. 10-12*. (+) Deary, Terence. **The factory.** CAST: 5u. ACTS: 1. SETTINGS: Factory. PLAYING TIME: 60 min. PLOT: Workers and management at the United Badge Company clash over pay and productivity. RECOMMENDATION: This study of industrial relations through craft work and role playing explores themes surrounding profit, loss, and the implications of overproduction, and would be a valuable exposure to the subject of labor relations. ROYALTY: None. SOURCE: Deary, Terence. (1977). Teaching through theatre. London: Samuel French. SUBJECTS/PLAY TYPE: Labor Relations; Drama.

902. 7-12. (+) Parks, Richard D. **The facts of life.** CAST: 5f, 2m, Su. ACTS: 2. SETTINGS: Lounge; cafeteria; room; street. PLAYING TIME: 90 min. PLOT: Based on episodes from a popular television series, a group of boarding school girls learn to face the responsibilities of growing up and to accept differences among themselves. RECOMMENDATION: This

humorously depicts problems of youth. ROYALTY: $35. SOURCE: Parks, Richard D. (1981). The facts of life. Denver, CO: Pioneer Drama Service. SUBJECTS/PLAY TYPE: Friendship; School; Comedy.

903. 9-12. (+) McDonald, Alice. **The fairest flower of the south or To know her is to love her.** CAST: 6f, 3m. ACTS: 2. SETTINGS: Drawing room. PLAYING TIME: 45 min. PLOT: Villainous Horton Smedley tries to court Mrs. Mason-Dixon and Miss Aura-Lee simultaneously. When Beauregard Mason-Dixon rescues Aura-Lee and his mother from Mr. Smedley, Aura-Lee's father is hit on the head. This causes the old man to regain his senses and remember where he has hidden the family gold. As a result, Beauregard and Aura-Lee will live happily ever after. RECOMMENDATION: Although melodramatic, the play has amusing dialogue. A cast capable of hamming it up might have fun with it. ROYALTY: $20. SOURCE: McDonald, Alice. (1977). The fairest flower of the South or To know her is to love her. Denver, CO: Pioneer Drama Service. SUBJECTS/PLAY TYPE: Civil War, U.S.; Southern Life; Melodrama.

904. 1-8. (+) Whittaker, Violet. **The faithful lighthouse keeper.** CAST: 4u. ACTS: 3. SETTINGS: Lighthouse. PLAYING TIME: NA. PLOT: In this parable about being faithful to God, an old lighthouse keeper turns on his lights during a storm, even though everyone says he's not needed anymore. When his lights save a man's life, he is praised for his steadfast faithfulness. RECOMMENDATION: The lighthouse keeper's faithfulness is to be compared to the faithfulness of a Christian's witnessing, in the church-setting discussion which should follow this presentation. ROYALTY: NA. SOURCE: Whittaker, Violet. (1984). Puppet people scripts. Grand Rapids, MI: Baker Book House. SUBJECTS/PLAY TYPE: Christian Drama; Parable; Faithfulness; Puppet Play.

905. 9-12. (+) Kelly, Tim. (Poe, Edgar Allan) **The fall of the house of Usher.** (The fall of the house of Usher) CAST: 10f, 6m, 10u. ACTS: 2. SETTINGS: Tavern; apartment; burial vault. PLAYING TIME: NA. PLOT: On a dark, stormy night, a stranger and his ill female companion stop at an inn for carriage repairs. The stranger tells of odd events occurring at the House of Usher, such as peculiar symptoms exhibited by a brother and sister. Dr. Fortunato warns that the burial vault should not be sealed if one of the siblings appears to die. Madelaine does die, and is buried; however, she regains consciousness and makes her way into brother Roderick's apartment, where he dies of shock. RECOMMENDATION: Although the tavern setting and strange "storyteller" are not part of Edgar Allan Poe's original work, they do add an interesting dimension. ROYALTY: $35. SOURCE: Kelly, Tim. (1979). The fall of the house of Usher. Schulenburg, TX: I.E. Clark. SUBJECTS/PLAY TYPE: Horror; Drama.

906. 7-12. (+) Sergel, Christopher. (Gore, Christopher) **Fame.** (Fame) CAST: 15f, 9m, Su. ACTS: 2. SETTINGS: School. PLAYING TIME: NA. PLOT: Beginning with

auditions for the New York School of Performing Arts, the play follows four young people through painful events, and shows how they become stronger, more mature dancers, actors, and musicians. RECOMMENDATION: This lively play, with its excellent stage settings and lighting effects, shows the non-glamorous parts of life before fame. ROYALTY: $60. SOURCE: Sergel, Christopher. (1985). Fame. Woodstock, IL: Dramatic Pub. Co. SUBJECTS/PLAY TYPE: Actors and Actresses; Adaptation.

907. 10-12. (+) Ward, Muriel. A family affair. CAST: 4f, 5m. ACTS: 1. SETTINGS: Living room. PLAYING TIME: 35 min. PLOT: When Steve's college friend visits, Steve's sisters, Barbie and Joanie, compete for Dick's attention, make fools of themselves, and alienate their boyfriends, Jerry and Tom. However, when Steve introduces his friend, Lila, to Dick and the couple are very compatible, Joanie and Barbie hastily make up with their boyfriends. RECOMMENDATION: This lighthearted tale about teenage infatuations is believable until the two sisters pretend to faint. While the resolution is rather weak, this would be a good play to introduce improvisation. ROYALTY: Free to Plays subscribers. SOURCE: Ward, Muriel. (1986, October). A family affair. Plays: The Drama Magazine for Young People, pp. 1-12. SUBJECTS/PLAY TYPE: Dating; Comedy.

908. 7-12. (-) Gregg, Andy. The family jewels. CAST: 6f, 4m. ACTS: 1. SETTINGS: Dining room. PLAYING TIME: NA. PLOT: Lord and Lady Twitchwell find themselves in financial difficulties and have invited millionaires from Germany, the Orient, France, Texas, and Arabia (each of whom is impersonating one of the other millionaires) to bid on their family jewels. Meanwhile, a hired detective is watching for a famous British jewel thief. The thief turns out to be Lady Twitchwell, herself, who switched the family jewels with jelly beans. RECOMMENDATION: The humor in this comedy is based on national stereotypes. For example, the Britains are bumbling, the Texan is loud and brash, and the Frenchwoman is sexy. Because the impersonations are signaled by switching the costumes and accents, the play might be confusing to the audience. ROYALTY: $15. SOURCE: Gregg, Andy. (1984). The family jewels. Chicago, IL: Dramatic Pub. Co. SUBJECTS/PLAY TYPE: Mystery; Comedy.

909. 10-12. (-) Dean, Darryl. Family reunion. CAST: 5f, 6m. ACTS: 2. SETTINGS: Street corner. PLAYING TIME: NA. PLOT: An urban Black family struggles with economic and social pressures which force the respectable, loving father to leave home and earn money as a bootlegger. The teenage son is knifed in a street gang fight. After the son and father are helped by a neighborhood doctor, the family is reunited and takes pride from learning that they are related to the famous Haitian revolutionary, Toussaint L'Overture. RECOMMENDATION: The complex pressures of urban life for a poor Black family are dealt with in a simplistic and contrived way which jeopardizes the author's theme of strength being derived from courage and pride. ROYALTY: $35. SOURCE: Dean, Darryl. (1979). Family reunion. Chicago, IL: Dramatic Pub. Co. SUBJECTS/PLAY TYPE: Families; Street gangs; Black Pride/Identity; Drama.

910. 7-12. (+) Stevens, John A. The family trees. CAST: 1f, 2m. ACTS: 1. SETTINGS: Woodlots. PLAYING TIME: NA. PLOT: Silvia, the forest spirit, describes a two century feud between two woodcutter families, one which practices ecology and conservation, and one which doesn't. The flagrant users suffer because of their practices, and earn less money than the conservationists. The play concludes with a plea for sound ecology. RECOMMENDATION: This complicated production uses flashbacks, musical duets, addresses to the audience, and educational vignettes about ecology and the dangers of cutting down entire forests. It is quite effective and, didactically, gets its point across. ROYALTY: NA. SOURCE: Stevens, John A. (1982). The family trees. Toronto: Playwrights Canada. SUBJECTS/PLAY TYPE: Ecology; Conservation; Trees; Musical Drama.

911. 10-12. (+) Rudolph, Grace. The fan. CAST: 1m. ACTS: 1. SETTINGS: Bare stage, props. PLAYING TIME: NA. PLOT: A priest sits at a table mulling over the changes he's seen in priestly camaraderie and describes several amusing episodes in his life. RECOMMENDATION: Although intriguing, this monologue would be difficult for a young amateur to perfect, and therefore may work better as a read aloud episode, leading to a church related discussion of changing values and religious views. ROYALTY: $10. SOURCE: Rudolph, Grace. (1984). Elders' statements: One-act plays and monologues. Boston, MA: Baker's Plays. SUBJECTS/PLAY TYPE: Catholicism; Priests; Humor; Monologue.

912. K-12. (+) Haraszthy, Jan. The fantastic happy landing. CAST: 13f, 12m. ACTS: 2. SETTINGS: Office; throne room; trial room. PLAYING TIME: 60 min. PLOT: Because he doesn't like school, Willy is called to the principal's office. While waiting for his father to arrive, Willy and the school janitor, who experiments with time travel, travel together to King Arthur's court. Not wanting to fight a dragon, they travel again and come to the Land of Gazwah, where thinking is forbidden. Upon returning to the present, Willy realizes that thinking and learning are important, and he tells his father and the principal that he will change, because he now realizes school is important. RECOMMENDATION: Younger children will enjoy this comic but didactic fantasy. ROYALTY: $25. SOURCE: Haraszthy, Jan. (1975). The fantastic happy landing. Chicago, IL: Dramatic Pub. Co. SUBJECTS/PLAY TYPE: School; Time travel; Comedy.

913. 3-5. (+) Reid, Sally. (Dahl, Roald) Fantastic Mr. Fox. (Fantastic Mr. Fox) CAST: 7f, 9m, 26u. ACTS: 1. SETTINGS: Woods; tunnel; chicken coop; storehouse. PLAYING TIME: NA. PLOT: Trapped underground by three furious farmers, a family of foxes and their animal friends almost starve before Mr. Fox outwits the farmers

by tunneling under their storehouses to steal food. RECOMMENDATION: The simple plot is enlivened with much action that sends the actors into the aisles as the animals try to escape from the angry farmers. ROYALTY: $50. SOURCE: Reid, Sally. (1986). Fantastic Mr. Fox. Woodstock, IL: Dramatic Pub. Co. SUBJECTS/PLAY TYPE: Animals; Melodrama; Adaptation.

914. 9-12*. (+) Scott, Dennis. **The fantasy of Sir Gawain & the Green Knight.** (Sir Gawain & the Green Knight) CAST: 2f, 4m, Su. ACTS: 1. SETTINGS: Bare stage. PLAYING TIME: NA. PLOT: Gawain is King Arthur's only knight brave enough to accept the Green Knight's challenge. Sir Gawain passes three ritual tests on his journey to find the Green Knight. When a magic belt from the Lady Allison, Bercilak's wife, saves Gawain, Bercilak reveals that he is the Green Knight and commends Gawain on his love of life, while reminding him that no man is perfect. RECOMMENDATION: The beautiful verse captures the mystery and beauty of the original 14th century poem. It could be a Christmas play or a winter-spring pageant. ROYALTY: $35. SOURCE: Scott, Dennis. (1978). The fantasy of Sir Gawain & the Green Knight. New Orleans, LA: Anchorage Press, Inc. SUBJECTS/PLAY TYPE: Knights of the Round Table; Honor; Verse Play.

915. 7-12. (-) Hatton, Thomas J. **Far trek. CAST:** 1f, 2m, 4u. ACTS: 1. SETTINGS: Control room. PLAYING TIME: 10 min. PLOT: In this pep rally skit, the crew of the spaceship Extraprize outwits the evil Mad Scientist and foils his plan to prevent the school from winning their game. RECOMMENDATION: The humor is weak, and the connection between a takeoff on the popular Star Trek series and winning a school game is farfetched. ROYALTY: Free to Plays subscribers. SOURCE: Hatton, Thomas J. (1981, November). Far trek. Plays: The Drama Magazine for Young People, pp. 65-67. SUBJECTS/PLAY TYPE: Pep Rallies; Skit.

916. 8-12. (+) Malkind, Margaret. **Farewell forsaken corners. CAST:** 7f, 6m. ACTS: 1. SETTINGS: Parlor. PLAYING TIME: 30 min. PLOT: Almaretta, eager to impress her new roommates, fabricates a story about a brother kidnapped by pirates. In the end Almaretta earns the respect and position she longed for in the beginning by telling the truth and doing good deeds. RECOMMENDATION: Humorous conversations provide insight into the daily lives of young working women in the 1830s. Their actions and attitudes might seem severe and contrived, yet perhaps not far removed from today's realities. ROYALTY: Free to Plays subscribers. SOURCE: Malkind, Margaret. (1978, May). Farewell, forsaken corners. Plays: The Drama Magazine for Young People, pp. 11-21. SUBJECTS/PLAY TYPE: Honesty; Relationships; Melodrama.

917. 8-12. (+) Ainsworth, Ford. (Shaw, Bernard) **Farewell to Galatea.** (Pygmalion) CAST: 4f, 2m. ACTS: 1. SETTINGS: Studio. PLAYING TIME: 35 min. PLOT: A young artist creates an ideal woman but finds that her perfection is not so desirable after all. This is also the story of the problematic nature of having wishes granted. RECOMMENDATION: The age old themes of love, and who is worthy of love, are treated entertainingly. ROYALTY: $15. SOURCE: Ainsworth, Ford. (1978). Farewell to Galatea: A comedy in one act. Schulenberg, TX: I.E. Clark. SUBJECTS/PLAY TYPE: Love; Pygmalion; Mythology; Comedy.

918. 8-12. (+) Schaaf, Albert K. **The fast food fiasco.** CAST: 5f, 4m. ACTS: 1. SETTINGS: Newspaper office. PLAYING TIME: 30 min. PLOT: The school newspaper staff is about to receive a junk food dinner, and student reporter Carol is expecting Mrs. Armstrong, a health food and physical fitness expert for an interview. Because Carol is competing for the Armstrong Award, she wants to impress Mrs. Armstrong. But after Carol takes a brave stand against Mrs. Armstrong's intolerance of other people's preferences, she learns it was all a test and wins the award. RECOMMENDATION: Funny and up-to-date dialogue punctuates this hilarious, fast moving high school comedy. Mrs. Armstrong's insults and intolerance and Carol's stand in defense of her friends are indicative of each character's definite personality. ROYALTY: Free to Plays subscribers. SOURCE: Schaaf, Albert K. (1980, January). The fast food fiasco. Plays: The Drama Magazine for Young People, pp. 1-10. SUBJECTS/PLAY TYPE: Nutrition; Honesty; Comedy.

919. 8-12. (+) McLean, Arthur. **The fast runner.** CAST: 2f, 2m. ACTS: 1. SETTINGS: Porch. PLAYING TIME: 20 min. PLOT: While Granny and Grandpaw wait for Lanta, their 17 year old granddaughter, to come home for supper, they discuss her excessive pride in her ability to run fast; they want to see her married and settled. When a sinister old man asks to race with Lanta, she agrees. Although Granny pleads with Lanta not to race, the girl ignores her. When Lanta finishes the race and stops at the porch, sure she has won, the old man opens the front door, swings a sickle in the air, and Lanta falls to the porch floor, dead. RECOMMENDATION: This mountain morality play would intrigue older teenagers and spark discussions about mortality. ROYALTY: $10. SOURCE: McLean, Arthur. (1980). The fast runner. Denver, CO: Pioneer Drama Service. SUBJECTS/PLAY TYPE: Death; Drama.

920. K-6. (+) Smith, Robert B. **The fast white rabbit and the slow green turtle. CAST:** Su. ACTS: 1. SETTINGS: Flannel board. PLAYING TIME: 5 min. PLOT: When a rabbit and turtle have a race, the speedy rabbit dallies and stops to rest, while the persistent turtle passes him to win the race. RECOMMENDATION: Children will enjoy participating in the story by cheering, playing musical instruments, and acting out the race. They will use their imagination in this musical drama emphasizing rhythm and instrumental accompaniment. ROYALTY: NA. SOURCE: Smith, Robert B. (1984). Music dramas for children with special needs. Denton, TX: Troostwyk Press. SUBJECTS/PLAY TYPE: Memorization Skills; Animals; Musical; Drama.

921. 9-12. (+) Reale, William. **Fast women.** CAST: 1f, 2m. ACTS: 1. SETTINGS: Running track. PLAYING TIME: NA. PLOT: George and Marianne are both runners. George is intimidated by Marianne and believes that he is destined always to come in fifth. When Marianne tells him that she came in fifth in the Nationals, he identifies with her, and they begin to date. RECOMMENDATION: In spite of the fair amount of profanity here, young people will gain insight into their own experiences from this very short and easily produced drama. ROYALTY: $10. SOURCE: Reale, William. (1983). Fast women. New York: Dramatists Play Service. SUBJECTS/PLAY TYPE: Dating; Athletics; Drama.

922. 7-12. (-) **The fastest thimble in the West.** (Brave little tailor) CAST: 15f, 21m, Su. ACTS: 1. SETTINGS: Living room; saloon. PLAYING TIME: 45 min. PLOT: Two-Bits and Henry defeat Brute McGurk in battle, receive a $5,000 reward and save their orphanage from foreclosure by mean, miserly Grudge. They are amazed to discover that the orphan, Two-Bits, is actually Grudge's nephew and heir to his fortune. RECOMMENDATION: Patronizing portrayals of orphans, an absurdly simplistic and unreal plot, and the use of sophisticated business terminology, make this play unacceptable. ROYALTY: NA. SOURCE: Boiko, Claire. (1980). Dramatized parodies of familiar stories. Boston: Plays, Inc. SUBJECTS/PLAY TYPE: Western; Musical; Parody.

923. 7-12. (+) Clark, I. E. **The fate of Fayette.** CAST: Su. ACTS: 3. SETTINGS: Historical sites. PLAYING TIME: NA. PLOT: This pageant of the development of Fayette County (TX) from the years 1816 to 1986 includes the settling of colonies, the Texas Revolution, Texas' involvement in the Civil War, industrial progress, the Depression years and Fayette County today. RECOMMENDATION: Each of the many 3-20 minute episodes could be produced separately, reducing the number of cast members. Abundant historical information complemented by humor and wit could help students enjoy their history. Some episodes include music and dancing. ROYALTY: NA. SOURCE: Clark, I. E. (1985). The fate of Fayette. Schulenburg, TX: I.E. Clark. SUBJECTS/PLAY TYPE: Texas, History; Skit.

924. 7-12. (+) Tyler, Mel. **Father and child doing well.** CAST: 2f, 2m. ACTS: 1. SETTINGS: Street corner. PLAYING TIME: NA. PLOT: When a nurse is collecting money for the hospital where she works, a man promises to donate $5.00 if she agrees to be his nurse if he's ever hospitalized. After his donation is made, she tells him that she works in a maternity hospital. RECOMMENDATION: This is very witty, although old fashioned. ROYALTY: None. SOURCE: Majeski, Bill. (1981). Easy skits, blackouts and pantomimes. Woodstock, IL: Dramatic Pub. Co. SUBJECTS/PLAY TYPE: Comedy; Donations; Nurses; Skit.

925. 7-10. (+) Garver, Juliet. **Father of the year.** CAST: 9f, 2m. ACTS: 1. SETTINGS: Living room. PLAYING TIME: 30 min. PLOT: A man named Father of the Year feels obliged to make many types of charitable donations his family can't afford. RECOMMENDATION: This lighthearted domestic drama is interesting because of the family life theme and the twists in the plot. The pleasant resolution with the family helping the Father of the Year cope with his new found fame, endears the characters to the audience. ROYALTY: Free to Plays subscribers. SOURCE: Garver, Juliet. (1979, January). Father of the year. Plays: The Drama Magazine for Young People, pp. 14-24. SUBJECTS/PLAY TYPE: Family; Fame; Playlet.

926. 7-10. (+) Gotwalt, Helen Louise Miller. **Father talks turkey.** CAST: 4f, 2m, 1u. ACTS: 1. SETTINGS: Living room. PLAYING TIME: 30 min. PLOT: Mr. Marston takes charge of his family's Thanksgiving dinner after their cook quits, and he forgets to order the food. Luckily, their former cook, Frieda, appears with turkey dinner and all the trimmings. Although Frieda has her own television cooking show, she dramatically tells them that, since they taught her about the American Thanksgiving custom when she emigrated from Europe, she will always cook for them at Thanksgiving. RECOMMENDATION: Although the stereotyped character and dialogue of the cook may not succeed with all audiences, it is ironic that the redeeming feature of this sit-com is in the heavily-accented theme delivered by the patriotic, yet unrealistic, cook. ROYALTY: Free to Plays subscribers. SOURCE: Gotwalt, Helen Louise Miller. (1988, November). Father talks turkey. Plays: The Drama Magazine for Young People, pp. 1-9. SUBJECTS/PLAY TYPE: Thanksgiving; Comedy.

927. K-2. (+) Boiko, Claire. **Father Time's garden.** CAST: 1f, 1m, 21u. ACTS: 1. SETTINGS: Garden. PLAYING TIME: 15 min. PLOT: Father Time gives the audience a tour of his garden, which is complete with impatient seconds waiting to grow into minutes, hours, days of the week, years, and decades. RECOMMENDATION: The novel manner of presentation, and the music, will help preschool and early primary level children increase their understanding of time. ROYALTY: Free to Plays subscribers. SOURCE: Boiko, Claire. (1979, January). Father Time's garden. Plays: The Drama Magazine for Young People, pp. 50-54. SUBJECTS/PLAY TYPE: Time; Skit.

928. 10-12. (-) McDonough, Jerome. **Faugh.** CAST: 8f, 3m. ACTS: 1. SETTINGS: Lobby. PLAYING TIME: 60 min. PLOT: Faugh, a run-down dormitory at Watkins College, is going to be closed by the granddaughter of the founder of the college. The housemother and an extremely strange assortment of residents (including a music major composing an opera for sand crabs and a computer nerd who thinks the computer is in love with him) manage to work together to save Faugh from being closed. RECOMMENDATION: The humor in this play inappropriately revolves around the exploitation of a schizophrenic student. The outcome is too predictable, and the dialogue is boring. ROYALTY: $25. SOURCE:

McDonough, Jerome. (1986). Faugh. Schulenberg, TX: I. E. Clark. **SUBJECTS/PLAY TYPE:** College Life; Comedy.

929. 1-7*. (+) Graham, Wanda. **Feast of phantom.** **CAST:** 2m, 1u. **ACTS:** 1. **SETTINGS:** Bare stage, props. **PLAYING TIME:** NA. **PLOT:** Miss Peach, a schoolteacher, tries to teach her raucous and irreverent student, Freddie Fluke, the importance of conserving energy resources, especially fossil fuels. Freddie seems more interested in fast cars, girls and mayhem. When Freddie's behavior gets very out of control, the referee/stage manager blows his whistle and action freezes. Eventually, the "conservation" lesson is learned. **RECOMMENDATION:** The use of comedy to pad what could be a very dull lesson works well in this play. This would make an excellent school assembly program. **ROYALTY:** NA. **SOURCE:** Graham, Wanda. (1981). Feast of phantom. Toronto: Playwrights Canada. **SUBJECTS/PLAY TYPE:** Energy Conservation; Fossil Fuels; Comedy.

930. 7-9. (+) Sodaro, Craig. (Hawthorne, Nathaniel) **FeatherTop.** (Feathertop.) **CAST:** 5f, 3m, Su. **ACTS:** 2. **SETTINGS:** Farm. **PLAYING TIME:** NA. **PLOT:** Mistress Goodkin is more interested in appearances and titles than in her daughter Polly's love for Kit the dairyman. The local witch creates FeatherTop and passes him off as a nobleman. His title and fortune blind Mistress Goodkin to his obvious shortcomings as Polly's suitor. When Polly is kidnapped, Kit saves her and the virtues of true love become obvious to all. **RECOMMENDATION:** This is a rather heavy handed adaptation of Hawthorne's short story "Feathertop: A Moralized Legend." Its many additional characters and twists of plot detract from Hawthorne's far simpler tale. **ROYALTY:** NA. **SOURCE:** Sodaro, Craig. (1987). FeatherTop. Woodstock, IL: Dramatic Pub. Co. **SUBJECTS/PLAY TYPE:** Love; Social Class; Family; Adaptation.

931. 7-9. (+) Moeller, Ruby L. **February. CAST:** 4f, 4m, Su. **ACTS:** 1. **SETTINGS:** Bare stage, props. **PLAYING TIME:** NA. **PLOT:** A series of skits, songs, poems and games about Valentine's Day and winter explain the origin of Valentine's Day. A tableau of costumed couples pose while love songs are sung. The program closes with two games: Air Mail Delivery (a Valentine relay race) and Heart Clap (similar to musical chairs). **RECOMMENDATION:** The main focus of the program, "The Origin of the Valentine," is informative and interesting and would appeal to anyone over ten years of age. However, the poems are old fashioned and rather maudlin, making them unsuitable for children. The games are clever adaptations of familiar favorites that sound like fun for any age. **ROYALTY:** NA. **SOURCE:** Moeller, Ruby L. (1975). Around the year programs. Boston, MA: Baker Plays. **SUBJECTS/PLAY TYPE:** Valentine's Day; Holiday Program.

932. 4-6. (+) Gotwalt, Helen Louise Miller. **A February failure. CAST:** 2f, 1m, Su. **ACTS:** 1. **SETTINGS:** Classroom. **PLAYING TIME:** 15 min.

PLOT: Harry has a bad day: sleeping late, being late for school, forgetting his homework. This leads to the play's premise: even Abraham Lincoln had to cope with a series of failures, but he overcame them and achieved greatness. **RECOMMENDATION:** The idea that failures can be overcome is an appropriate theme for a Lincoln's Birthday presentation. Although the point is over emphasized and the student teacher roles are stereotypes, the play contains valuable information about Lincoln's life. **ROYALTY:** Free to Plays subscribers. **SOURCE:** Gotwalt, Helen Louise Miller. (1986). Special plays for the holidays. Boston, MA: Plays, Inc. **SUBJECTS/PLAY TYPE:** Lincoln, Abraham; Failure; Playlet.

933. 4-7. (+) Marshall, Sheila L. **February on trial. CAST:** 2f, 4m, Su. **ACTS:** 1. **SETTINGS:** Courtroom. **PLAYING TIME:** 20 min. **PLOT:** Following the court testimony by Edison, Lincoln, Washington, Miss Valentine, the Groundhog, and others who celebrate birthdays or special days during the shortest month of the year, the judge notes that February is a vital month that marks great moments. He officially declares that February does its fair share of the year's work. **RECOMMENDATION:** The personification of the months makes the subject matter quite interesting. **ROYALTY:** Free to Plays subscribers. **SOURCE:** Marshall, Sheila L. (1983, January February). February on trial. Plays: The Drama Magazine for Young People, pp. 63-69,96. **SUBJECTS/PLAY TYPE:** February; Comedy.

934. 1-6. (+) Fisher, Aileen. **February spelldown. CAST:** 5f, 5m. **ACTS:** 1. **SETTINGS:** Bare stage. **PLAYING TIME:** 3 min. **PLOT:** Ten youngsters enter one by one and stand in line to say a sentence beginning with one letter of VALENTINES. Each sentence expresses a different aspect of the holiday. **RECOMMENDATION:** The spelldown conveys the spirit of Valentine's Day in a tender way. However, because the language is literary, it may be too sophisticated for younger audiences, while the juvenile format is too young for older audiences. **ROYALTY:** NA. **SOURCE:** Fisher, Aileen. (1986, January/February). February spelldown. Plays: The Drama Magazine for Young People, pp. 66. **SUBJECTS/PLAY TYPE:** Valentine's Day; Choral Reading.

935. 7-12. (+) Dias, Earl J. **Feudin' fun. CAST:** 3f, 5m, Su. **ACTS:** 2. **SETTINGS:** Cabin. **PLAYING TIME:** 25 min. **PLOT:** Two hillbilly families are feuding when a handsome stranger arrives at the Hogwash cabin. He is from the rival Fudge family but, before that is revealed, he endears himself to the Hogwash daughter, Lulu. Lulu helps him show that the families have no reason to feud. All ends happily as Lulu marries the stranger and Lulu's father weds the Fudge matriarch. **RECOMMENDATION:** Although the characters are stereotypical, they convey several important messages: feuding and unfounded prejudice is wrong; and, once people put aside their prejudices, they might find friendship and love. **ROYALTY:** Free to Plays subscribers. **SOURCE:** Dias, Earl J. (1985, March). Feudin' fun. Plays: The Drama Magazine for Young

People, pp. 23-32. **SUBJECTS/PLAY TYPE**: Feuds; Comedy.

936. 10-12. (+) Kaufman, Leslie. **Field day. CAST**: 2m. **ACTS**: 1. **SETTINGS**: Bare stage, props. **PLAYING TIME**: NA. **PLOT**: Two men, identified only as #1 and #2, land in a minefield behind enemy lines. Number one is frightened, questions the mission, and refuses to move. Number two is a dedicated soldier. Although both think the enemy is aware of their position, Number one still refuses to move. Number two threatens to carry Number one in order to conclude the mission. Suddenly, Number two realizes he is walking through a live minefield, and he becomes the frightened one. **RECOMMENDATION**: This story about the tragedy of war is thought provoking. The purple lighting makes it quite dramatic. Potential directors should be aware of descriptions of sexual intercourse contained in the dialogue. **ROYALTY**: NA. **SOURCE**: Lamb, Wendy. (1987). The ground zero club and other prize winning plays. New York, NY: Dell Pub. Co., Inc. **SUBJECTS/PLAY TYPE**: War; Fear; Drama.

937. 1-3. (+) Rosen, Michael. **Fifteen seconds. CAST**: 1f, 1u. **ACTS**: 1. **SETTINGS**: None. **PLAYING TIME**: NA. **PLOT**: A balky child eventually puts on his shoes, after being coerced by his mother. **RECOMMENDATION**: Parents and children alike will recognize this humorously familiar scene. **ROYALTY**: NA. **SOURCE**: Bauer, Caroline Feller. (1987). Presenting reader's theater: Plays and poems to read aloud. New York, NY: H.W. Wilson. **SUBJECTS/PLAY TYPE**: Shoes; Stubbornness; Reader's Theater.

938. 11-12. (+) Patricia, Nicholas A. **The fifth sun. CAST**: 1f, 5m, 8u. **ACTS**: 2. **SETTINGS**: Bare stage, props. **PLAYING TIME**: NA. **PLOT**: This is the life of Oscar Arnulfo Romero, Archbishop of San Salvador, assassinated on March 24, 1980. Episodes expose the turmoil faced by Romero as he struggles to reconcile his duties both to the church and to his country. His beliefs and actions are likened to a Mayan/Nahuan sacrificial myth, in which an unselfish man gives his life for the well-being of the world. While working to protect his people from the Communist threat, Romero is killed by an assassin. **RECOMMENDATION**: While Romero's life is interesting and relevant to political realities, the symbolism and imagery may be too heavy for young audiences. The emphasis given to Christian philosophy within this play recommends it to church related groups. **ROYALTY**: $60. **SOURCE**: Patricia, Nicholas. (1986). The fifth sun. Woodstock, IL: Dramatic Pub. Co. **SUBJECTS/PLAY TYPE**: Romero, Oscar Arnulfo; San Salvador; Politics; Drama.

939. 5-12. (+) Franzen, Jon. Siebert, Kathy. **The fig connection. CAST**: 2f, 7m, 7u. **ACTS**: 1. **SETTINGS**: Alley; park; office; laboratory. **PLAYING TIME**: NA. **PLOT**: When Russians try to capture Sir Isaac Newton, or at least steal his manuscript about gravity, British detectives and a constable thwart their attempts. **RECOMMENDATION**: This slapstick spy spoof moves at a frantic pace, with a great deal of bumbling and silliness. Current political events should be considered. The actors must be able to sing, and one actor must be a good piano player. **ROYALTY**: $15. **SOURCE**: Franzen, Jon, & Siebert, Kathy. (1977). The fig connection. Woodstock, IL: Dramatic Pub. Co. **SUBJECTS/PLAY TYPE**: Espionage; Comedy.

940. 7-12. (+) Sawyer-Young, Kat. **Fight. CAST**: 1m. **ACTS**: 1. **SETTINGS**: None. **PLAYING TIME**: 1 min. **PLOT**: JoJo decides to round up his gang to fight Deeno. Deeno wants revenge because JoJo "came on to" Deeno's girlfriend when JoJo was "high." **RECOMMENDATION**: The futility of violence and how it gets out of hand are well presented here. **ROYALTY**: None. **SOURCE**: Sawyer-Young, Kat. (1987). Minute monologues for contemporary teens. Boston: Baker's Plays. **SUBJECTS/PLAY TYPE**: Violence; Gangs; Monologue.

941. 7-12. (+) Murray, John. **The final curtain. CAST**: 5f, 6m, Su. **ACTS**: 1. **SETTINGS**: Drawing room. **PLAYING TIME**: 30 min. **PLOT**: When an actor is murdered, a detective and his wife who are attending the play solve the murder. The doorman, wronged by the leading man, killed him by putting cyanide in his stage ice cubes. **RECOMMENDATION**: Suspense builds until the detective's wife solves the case. The interviews of suspects are short enough not to be boring, but long enough to cast doubt on each suspect's professed innocence. **ROYALTY**: Free to Plays subscribers. **SOURCE**: Murray, John. (1987, May). The final curtain. Plays: The Drama Magazine for Young People, pp. 23-34. **SUBJECTS/PLAY TYPE**: Mystery; Murder; Playlet.

942. 6-9. (+) Sayre, George Wallace. **Final edition. CAST**: 2f, 6m. **ACTS**: 1. **SETTINGS**: Newsroom. **PLAYING TIME**: 30 min. **PLOT**: A day in the life of an editor is chronicled as the audience witnesses the unfolding details of a boat company scandal. **RECOMMENDATION**: The suspense grows stale after the first scene, as most of the action is conveyed by telephone and personal conversations. However, insight is given into the newspaper industry and the importance of freedom of the press. **ROYALTY**: Free to Plays subscribers. **SOURCE**: Sayre, George Wallace. (1981, March). Final edition. Plays: The Drama Magazine for Young People, pp. 11-22. **SUBJECTS/PLAY TYPE**: Newspapers; Freedom of the Press; Playlet.

943. 9-12. (+) Lang, William. **Final play. CAST**: 1f, 3m. **ACTS**: 1. **SETTINGS**: Room. **PLAYING TIME**: NA. **PLOT**: Three soldiers are imprisoned in a room kept under surveillance by a representative of "the people." The representative never personally appears, but she issues directives regarding the men's interactions. The resultant total mindless submissiveness causes the men to assume childish behaviors and begin to kill each other. **RECOMMENDATION**: This poignantly illustrates the possible plight of prisoners of war. Some of the language and subject matter may be objectionable. **ROYALTY**: $20. **SOURCE**: Lang, William. (1977). Final play. Chicago, IL: Dramatic Pub. Co. **SUBJECTS/PLAY TYPE**: Prisoners Of War; Torture; Mind Control; Drama.

944. 9-12. (+) Schaller, Mary W. **The final trial of Richard III.** CAST: 5f, 17m, Su. ACTS: 1. SETTINGS: Courtroom. PLAYING TIME: NA. PLOT: King Richard III is the defendant in a courtroom trial occurring 500 years after his death. His lawyer is charity, the prosecution is history, the judge is time. Does Richard deserve his cold-blooded reputation, or was he caught in the transition of times? Or was he a reflection of his period and the victim of a Tudor writer's smear campaign? The audience listens to the testimony, weighs the evidence, and renders the verdict. RECOMMENDATION: This play is extremely clever. Its outcome depends on whether the director chooses to portray Richard as guilty by having the lines delivered with cynicism and double meanings or whether the director chooses to make Richard appear not guilty by having all his lines delivered with openness and directness. ROYALTY: $50. SOURCE: Schaller, Mary W. (1986). The final trial of Richard III. Chicago, IL: Dramatic Pub. Co. SUBJECTS/PLAY TYPE: Richard III, King; Trial; Comedy; Drama.

945. 1-7. (+) Lynch, May. **Finn McCool.** CAST: 6f, 5m. ACTS: 1. SETTINGS: Cabin. PLAYING TIME: 15 min. PLOT: Two competitive giants, Cuhullin and Finn McCool, boast of their strength. Cuhullin stalks Finn, but Finn's wife, Una, sets a trap for Cuhullin. She convinces Cuhullin that he really is a weakling because he can't eat bread (with skillets hidden in it) or squeeze water from stone as her "baby," Finn in disguise, can. Defeated, Cuhullin gives up his aggressive chase. RECOMMENDATION: This captivating folk tale portrays women as being the stronger sex due to their cleverness. ROYALTY: NA. SOURCE: Kamerman, Sylvia. (1987). Plays from favorite folk tales. Boston, MA: Plays, Inc. SUBJECTS/PLAY TYPE: Legends, Ireland; Competition; Giants; Playlet.

946. K-8. (+) Englehardt, James F. & Weiss, Carol. (Andersen, Hans Christian) **The fir tree.** (The fir tree) CAST: 2f, 3m. ACTS: 2. SETTINGS: Forest; living room. PLAYING TIME: 75 min. PLOT: Hans Christian Andersen narrates this tale of the young fir tree who cannot wait to grow tall, and the young boy Eric, who can not wait to grow up, both refusing to appreciate their lives until these goals are met. Although the fir tree is cut down before he can grow tall, he reveals to Eric the importance of appreciating all the simple pleasures life brings. RECOMMENDATION: This delightful musical adaptation should appeal to a varied age group, although it is recommended that the older children act out the parts because each part is doubled. The use of simple props to illustrate the wind, the sun, and the stream and the use of puppets for the lesser parts are clever. The song lyrics are simple without being silly or juvenile. ROYALTY: $50. SOURCE: Englehardt, James F. & Weiss, Carol. (1986). The fir tree. Morton Grove, IL: Coach House Press. SUBJECTS/PLAY TYPE: Musical; Christmas; Folk Tales, Denmark; Adaptation.

947. 2-6. (+) Winther, Barbara. **Fire demon and south wind.** CAST: 1f, 10m, 6u. ACTS: 1. SETTINGS: Countryside. PLAYING TIME: 20 min. PLOT: After South Wind convinces Fire Demon to eat the Silver Palace, the villagers rebuild it, and protect the Palace with a well, as suggested by the King. After the Palace is destroyed again, the villagers use a steam breathing dragon for protection. The third time, the king asks for the villagers' advice. They build a stone monster which cannot be consumed by fire, and the Fire Demon is defeated. RECOMMENDATION: This visually imaginative play requires much preparation. Papier-mache masks, drums, and cymbals are advised. The pidgin English of the Orientals might need to be changed to avoid the insulting stereotype. ROYALTY: Free to Plays subscribers. SOURCE: Winther, Barbara. (1975, October). Fire demon and south wind. Plays: The drama magazine for young People, pp. 47-52. SUBJECTS/PLAY TYPE: Folk Tales, Korea; Playlet.

948. 7-12. (+) Kehret, Peg. **The fire drill.** CAST: 1f. ACTS: 1. SETTINGS: None. PLAYING TIME: NA. PLOT: In a familiar school scene, the fire drill, the teachers try to monitor the exercise seriously. The students comply only after collecting decorated books, meeting friends for the trip outside, making locker stops, and gossiping. RECOMMENDATION: This is an especially candid look at the "what's the big deal" philosophy of this age group. ROYALTY: NA. SOURCE: Kehret, Peg. (1986). Winning monologs for young actors. Colorado Springs, CO: Meriwether Pub. SUBJECTS/PLAY TYPE: Fire Drills; Monologue.

949. 2-7. (+) Hagy, Loleta. **Fire in a paper.** CAST: 5f. ACTS: 1. SETTINGS: Room. PLAYING TIME: 20 min. PLOT: A Chinese lady, concerned that her two daughters-in-law are excessively frivolous, allows them to visit their home village only if they bring back two gifts: fire wrapped in paper, and wind wrapped in paper. Their gifts are a paper lantern, a fan, and a treat of kumquats. The mother-in-law is pleased and promises to visit their home village often with them. RECOMMENDATION: This play teaches a lesson on responsibility and duty through the device of a suspenseful plot. Younger children will enjoy the play, but upper elementary students probably will need to be the actors, due to the difficulty of the simulated Chinese speech. ROYALTY: NA. SOURCE: Kamerman, Sylvia E. (1987). Plays from favorite folk tales. Boston, MA: Plays, Inc. SUBJECTS/PLAY TYPE: Folk Tales, China; Responsibility; Playlet.

950. 7-12. (+) Clark, Barrett H. **Fires at Valley Forge.** CAST: 8m. ACTS: 1. SETTINGS: Bare stage. PLAYING TIME: 30 min. PLOT: Four young farm boys bring provisions and a message of hope over a treacherous journey to Valley Forge. When the boys meet General Washington, they learn that their words are more valuable than the provisions they bring to the weary soldiers. RECOMMENDATION: The rhetoric gets a little heavy handed but the important message is told in an interesting way. ROYALTY: Free to Plays subscribers. SOURCE: Clark, Barrett H. (1984, January/February). Fires at Valley Forge. Plays: The Drama Magazine for Young People, pp. 26- 34.

SUBJECTS/PLAY TYPE: Valley Forge; Washington, George; Revolution, U.S.; Playlet.

951. 9-12. (+) Orkow, Ben. **The first actress.** CAST: 2f, 17m. ACTS: 3. SETTINGS: Courtyard; jail; theater; London. PLAYING TIME: NA. PLOT: Felicia disguises herself as a boy and joins the Globe Theatre troupe, working for Richard Burbage and William Shakespeare. Her secret is revealed when the troupe plays before the queen. But the royal prohibition against women actors is ignored, as long as Felicia gives up acting and returns to "women's work." RECOMMENDATION: What might Shakespeare's plays have been like if real women were allowed to play the parts in Elizabethan England? What might Shakespeare and Burbage have thought of the idea? These are two of the questions raised by the play along with illustrating the difficulty women have breaking into all male occupations. The dialogue is authentic, the plot plausible, and the characters interesting. ROYALTY: $35. SOURCE: Orkow, Ben. (1976). The first actress. New York, NY: Dramatists Play Service. SUBJECTS/PLAY TYPE: Shakespeare, William; Elizabethan England; Women's Rights; Comedy.

952. 1-6. (+) Kundrat, Theodore V. **The first Christmas.** CAST: 4f, 8m, 1u. ACTS: 1. SETTINGS: None. PLAYING TIME: 30 min. PLOT: On their first Christmas, a boy does not believe that an angel would come down to earth; the girl does. One evening, the girl hears a little rose calling her. She brings the flower back to bed with her. Later in the night the rose wakes her to hear the angels. When their father takes the children to see the baby Jesus, the little girl places her rose in the crib, and it turns into an angel. RECOMMENDATION: Recommended for church groups, this reader's theater or radio play does not have to be memorized, and there are no settings. ROYALTY: $10. SOURCE: Kundrat, Theodore V. (1978). The first Christmas. Chicago, IL: Coach House Press. SUBJECTS/PLAY TYPE: Christmas; Radio Plays; Reader's Theater.

953. 2-5. (+) Baker, Charles. **The first Christmas tree.** CAST: Su. ACTS: 1. SETTINGS: Forest. PLAYING TIME: 10 min. PLOT: A tree's kindness to forest animals transforms it from a scrawny tree into the first Christmas tree. RECOMMENDATION: This pleasantly reflects the value of kindness to others and the true spirit of Christmas. ROYALTY: Free to Plays subscribers. SOURCE: Baker, Charles. (1983, December). The first Christmas tree. Plays: The Drama Magazine for Young People, pp. 51-54. SUBJECTS/PLAY TYPE: Christmas; Puppet Play.

954. 4-6. (+) Capell, Loretta C. **The first Christmas tree.** CAST: 3f, 2m, Su. ACTS: 1. SETTINGS: Woods. PLAYING TIME: NA. PLOT: Young Johann's selflessness on a bitter cold Christmas Eve brings a memorable holiday for all his family as the Christ child brings an everlasting gift to their home. RECOMMENDATION: With great sensitivity, this story (appropriate for church groups only) explains that the true meaning of Christmas can only be felt when we consider other's needs before our own. ROYALTY: Free to Plays subscribers. SOURCE: Kamerman, Sylvia E. (1975). A treasury of Christmas plays. Boston, MA: Plays, Inc. SUBJECTS/PLAY TYPE: Christmas; Playlet.

955. 7-12. (+) McCusker, Paul. **The first church of the elite saints.** CAST: 3f, 1m, 3u. ACTS: 1. SETTINGS: Church. PLAYING TIME: NA. PLOT: As Bupkus, a doorkeeper trainee, learns how to screen church worshippers according to their status in life, he decides to give up the distasteful job. RECOMMENDATION: Although a bit heavy handed, and perhaps a bit too judgmental, this does show the hypocrisy of external piety when the spirit is not pious. If the specific references to churches were changed, this would be appropriate for any religious group. ROYALTY: None with purchase of script. SOURCE: McCusker, Paul. (1982). Souvenirs: comedies and dramas for Christian fellowship. Boston, MA: Baker's Plays. SUBJECTS/PLAY TYPE: Hypocrisy; Skit.

956. 8-10. (+) Kehret, Peg. **First date.** CAST: 1f. ACTS: 1. SETTINGS: None. PLAYING TIME: NA. PLOT: All of a girl's daydreaming about her fantastic first date with the boy of her dreams comes to a crashing halt when Herbert calls, instead of Kurt. The magic of the first date doesn't happen, and the night comes to a merciful end as Herbert is stymied by the good night kiss. RECOMMENDATION: This monologue will resurrect the experience of the "first date" for many, even though it may best be forgotten. ROYALTY: NA. SOURCE: Kehret, Peg. (1986). Winning monologs for young actors. Colorado Springs, CO: Meriwether Pub. SUBJECTS/PLAY TYPE: Dating; Monologue.

957. 9-12. (+) Murray, John. **First day of school.** CAST: 1u. ACTS: 1. SETTINGS: None. PLAYING TIME: NA. PLOT: A new teacher has problems applying her modern methods on her first day in the classroom. RECOMMENDATION: Educators and would-be educators will delight in this hilarious "expose" of the teacher's dilemma. ROYALTY: None. SOURCE: Murray, John. (1982). Modern monologues for young people. Boston, MA: Plays, Inc. SUBJECTS/PLAY TYPE: Teachers; Comedy; Monologue.

958. 3-8. (+) Mark, William. **The first Leon.** CAST: 6f, 6m, Su. ACTS: 1. SETTINGS: Living room; soup kitchen; street. PLAYING TIME: 45 min. PLOT: It is Christmas, and seven year old Kimmy and her sister and mother miss their father. Jailed through misunderstandings for not meeting support payments, Leon disappears upon his release. While helping her mother and sister feed the homeless in a soup kitchen on Christmas Eve, Kimmy gives her "wish" list to a sidewalk Santa. A "real" Santa, a wealthy man whose daughter is dead, overhears and sets out to find the father Kimmy desperately wants home for Christmas. The story concludes with Kimmy's wish coming true. RECOMMENDATION: This delightful, heart warming story reflects many family situations, and tastefully handles the problems of non-support payments and single parent families. The theme of helping others is

important, as feeding the homeless in a soup kitchen is the mother's way of teaching her children the true meaning of Christmas. ROYALTY: $40. SOURCE: Mark, William. (1988). The first Leon. Franklin, OH: Franklin Pub. Co. SUBJECTS/PLAY TYPE: Christmas; Single Parent Family; Drama.

959. 3-5. (+) Minter, Jan. **First manned flight to Venus. CAST:** 3u. **ACTS:** 1. **SETTINGS:** Space capsule; mission control. **PLAYING TIME:** 20 min. **PLOT:** The first manned flight to Venus is prevented from landing by Venu, the small Venus native, who can exercise complete control over the spacecraft. After exchanging a Venus rock for a tape player, Venu releases the spacecraft after extracting a promise that it will not land because it would upset the ecological balance on Venus. **RECOMMENDATION:** This will hold the interest of the young audience as it imparts a brief message about the importance of conservation. **ROYALTY:** Free to Plays subscribers. **SOURCE:** Minter, Jan. (1980, March). First manned flight to Venus. Plays: The Drama Magazine for Young People, pp. 31-38. **SUBJECTS/PLAY TYPE:** Science Fiction; Conservation; Playlet.

960. 9-12. (+) Kelly, Tim J. **First on the rope. CAST:** 5f. **ACTS:** 1. **SETTINGS:** Mountain; wilderness. **PLAYING TIME:** 25 min. **PLOT:** Four female rock climbers on the verge of being the first women to conquer a mountain discover that their Indian guide already climbed it with her mother years ago. **RECOMMENDATION:** This play lacks any moral character. The four spoiled, self-centered girls are condescending, vicious and unsportsmanlike when they discover their guide had succeeded in their goal years ago. Showing no remorse after the guide's accident (in which she appears to have died), they even contemplate covering up the whole incident. Even when the guide returns at the end, the girls decide to move on without blaming themselves in any way for the near tragedy. The play could be used for a discussion about ethics. **ROYALTY:** $15. **SOURCE:** Kelly, Tim J. (1982). First on the rope. Schulenburg, TX: I.E. Clark. **SUBJECTS/PLAY TYPE:** Mountain Climbing; Drama.

961. 12*. (+) Kirby, Michael. **First signs of decadence. CAST:** 3f, 2m. **ACTS:** 3. **SETTINGS:** Living room. **PLAYING TIME:** 90 min. **PLOT:** First Signs is alternative theater with a "pattern" rather than a plot. In 1931 Berlin, two actors, two financial investors, and the author meet. Throughout the casual conversation, strong implications surface. For example, the psychoanalyst/investor is interested in human behavior and animal experimentation; the female is probably Jewish, and other subtle, sinister signs emerge. These patterns are the essence of the presentation. This is modern, non-traditional theater. **RECOMMENDATION:** Although the playwright recommends non-preparation of an audience for this "happening," the prefaces, stage scheme, and timing illustration give perspective for the play. The minimal plot content leads to intellectualizing, reminiscent of the happening experience presentations of the early 60s,

whose sole purpose was the performance and not the play as literature. This work would be appreciated by mature, prepared audiences. **ROYALTY:** $50. **SOURCE:** Kirby, Michael. (1986). First signs of decadence. Schulenburg, TX: I.E. Clark. **SUBJECTS/PLAY TYPE:** Avant-Garde; Nazis; Alternative Theater.

962. 1-4*. (+) Slavit, Norma. **The first snowflake. CAST:** 12u. **ACTS:** 1. **SETTINGS:** Sky; clouds. **PLAYING TIME:** 12 min. **PLOT:** At the beginning of the world as the first snowflakes prepare to come to earth, they discuss the fun they will bring to children. The north and south winds help, and a thermometer featuring a change in temperature demonstrates the relationship between temperature and snow. **RECOMMENDATION:** Much of the play depends on the children rolling snowballs, knocking on windows, and other snow activities. The cast is expandable. This is a fine seasonal play for stage or classroom. **ROYALTY:** Free to Plays subscribers. **SOURCE:** Slavit, Norma. (1981, January). The first snowflake. Plays: The Drama Magazine for Young People, pp. 65-69. **SUBJECTS/PLAY TYPE:** Winter; Snow; Creative Dramatics.

963. 3-6. (+) Fisher, Aileen. **First Thanksgiving. CAST:** 4f, 4m. **ACTS:** 1. **SETTINGS:** None. **PLAYING TIME:** 5 min. **PLOT:** In this choral reading, the eight characters, lined across a stage, interchange rhymed lines. The reading depicts the story of the American pilgrims and the first Thanksgiving at Plymouth Rock. **RECOMMENDATION:** Because of the short reading time and the number of characters, the play would be useful for a history lesson, especially if performed the day before the holidays as a break from routine. **ROYALTY:** Free to Plays subscribers. **SOURCE:** Fisher, Aileen. (1984, November). First Thanksgiving. Plays: The Drama Magazine for Young People, pp. 38. **SUBJECTS/PLAY TYPE:** Thanksgiving; Choral Reading.

964. 9-12. (+) Murray, John. **The fish story. CAST:** 1f. **ACTS:** 1. **SETTINGS:** None. **PLAYING TIME:** NA. **PLOT:** A woman causes all sorts of problems when her husband takes her fishing. **RECOMMENDATION:** Although dated and dependent on classic stereotypical foolishness of a woman for its humor, this is hilarious. **ROYALTY:** None. **SOURCE:** Murray, John. (1982). Modern monologues for young people. Boston, MA: Plays, Inc. **SUBJECTS/PLAY TYPE:** Fishing; Comedy; Monologue.

965. 4-9. (+) Young, Alida E. (Grimm Brothers) **A fish story.** (The fisherman and his wife) **CAST:** 1f. **ACTS:** 1. **SETTINGS:** Pier. **PLAYING TIME:** 10 min. **PLOT:** A flounder caught by the narrator's husband convinces him to throw it back. The fish then grants every request that the couple makes: a new mobile home, a stone castle, and, for the wife, the title of "Supermarket queen for a day." The husband becomes disenchanted and begins to pout. When the wife asks the fish for everything to be back as it was, the stone house crashes down, nearly injuring the husband. The wife vows never

to wish for anything again. RECOMMENDATION: In this contemporary takeoff on the classic folk tale, the wife tells her updated side of the story. It would be funny if the audience knows the original, and it could be used with a classroom unit on folk tales. ROYALTY: Free to Plays subscribers. SOURCE: Young, Alida E. (1981, March). A fish story. Plays: The Drama Magazine for Young People, pp. 60-63. SUBJECTS/PLAY TYPE: Greed; Folk Tales, Germany; Adaptation; Comedy; Monologue.

966. K-3. (+) McCaslin, Nellie. (Grimm Brothers) **The fisherman and his wife.** (The fisherman and his wife) CAST: 1f, 2m. ACTS: 1. SETTINGS: Lakeside; home. PLAYING TIME: 10 min. PLOT: A poor fisherman catches a flounder that was once a prince but is now under a spell. The fish promises to grant the fisherman's wishes, if he lets him go. The fisherman's wife asks for increasingly extravagant gifts until the fish becomes angry and revokes all the gifts he has granted. RECOMMENDATION: This dramatizes the exploitation of the kindness of others, as the reader sympathizes with the fisherman who must request favors of the fish to please his demanding wife. ROYALTY: None. SOURCE: McCaslin, Nellie. (1977). Puppet fun: Production, performance, and plays. NY: D. McKay Co. SUBJECTS/PLAY TYPE: Greed; Folk Tales, Germany; Adaptation; Puppet Play.

967. 1-5. (+) Swortzell, Lowell. (Grimm Brothers) **The fisherman and his wife.** (Fisherman and his wife) CAST: 1f, 2m, Su. ACTS: 1. SETTINGS: Bare stage, props. PLAYING TIME: NA. PLOT: A fisherman catches a wish granting fish, frees it in exchange for having his wishes granted, and tells his wife the fantastic story. She greedily asks for a cottage to replace their hut, a mansion to replace the cottage, and a castle to replace the mansion. The fish becomes angrier with each demand. When she asks to be able to make the sun rise and set and the moon to come up, the fish returns the wife to her hut "as a reward for greed that has no end." RECOMMENDATION: In this faithful adaptation the characters are succinctly described through cleverly written dialogue. ROYALTY: Write to Plays, Inc. SOURCE: Jennings, Coleman A. and Harris, Aurand. (1981). Plays children love. New York, NY: Doubleday, Inc. SUBJECTS/PLAY TYPE: Folk Tales, Germany; Greed; Wishes; Adaptation.

968. 9-12. (+) Cook, Michael. **The fisherman's revenge.** CAST: 2f, 3m. ACTS: 1. SETTINGS: Cottage; Courtroom. PLAYING TIME: NA. PLOT: A poor Canadian fisherman and his daughter try to scrape a living from the barren Newfoundland waters, while a hen-pecked merchant and his greedy wife rehash their soured marriage. A lawsuit arises over an unpaid bill and a skirmish results. The court's judgment is that the fisherman will pay his debt, as the merchant and wife assume more traditional family roles and attempt to live a less greedy life. RECOMMENDATION: Although the plot is a simple one and can be easily performed by high school students, the audience and the actors need to be aware of the regional, local, and cultural issues of

Maritime Canada. The play includes mature themes of promiscuity and adultery. ROYALTY: NA. SOURCE: Cook, Michael. (1984). The fisherman's revenge. Toronto: Playwrights Union of Canada. SUBJECTS/PLAY TYPE: Love; Marriage; Canada; Drama.

969. 7-9. (+) Sawyer-Young, Kat. **Fishing.** CAST: 2m. ACTS: 1. SETTINGS: Outside. PLAYING TIME: NA. PLOT: With typical sibling rivalry, two brothers "egg" each other on with name calling and exaggeration while they fish. Not until the scene ends does the audience realize they were fishing in the swimming pool. RECOMMENDATION: This is a concise scene whose value lies in the use of pantomime which stimulates the audience to imagine what the boys are doing and helps create the surprise ending. ROYALTY: NA. SOURCE: Sawyer-Young, Kat. (1986). Contemporary scenes for contemporary kids. Boston, MA: Baker's Plays. SUBJECTS/PLAY TYPE: Sibling Rivalry; Pantomime; Scene.

970. 7-9. (+) Martens, Anne Coulter. **Fit to be tied.** CAST: 4f, 3m. ACTS: 1. SETTINGS: Living room. PLAYING TIME: 35 min. PLOT: Faye's little brother handcuffs her to her former boyfriend, Jeff. When her new boyfriend and a prospective employer come to see her, she tries to hide the handcuffs and Jeff. All ends well when Faye gets both the job and Jeff, the boyfriend she really likes. RECOMMENDATION: Although the characters are somewhat dated and the plot hackneyed, this is a typical teenage fantasy, especially for the younger ages. ROYALTY: Free to Plays subscribers. SOURCE: Martens, Anne Coulter. (1977, October). Fit to be tied. Plays: The Drama Magazine for Young People, pp. 27-38. SUBJECTS/PLAY TYPE: Dating; Comedy.

971. 7-12. (-) Bradley, Virginia. **Five times Sue is Julia Bates.** CAST: 4f, 2m. ACTS: 1. SETTINGS: Living room. PLAYING TIME: NA. PLOT: A young girl attempts to unite an estranged family by hinting of buried treasure in the old family home. RECOMMENDATION: The resolution is realistically disappointing: no found treasure and no loving reunions. ROYALTY: NA. SOURCE: Bradley, Virginia. (1977). Stage eight: One-act plays. New York: Dodd, Mead. SUBJECTS/PLAY TYPE: Family; Comedy.

972. 7-12. (+) Nord, Myrtle. **Five under cover.** CAST: 1f, 6m. ACTS: 2. SETTINGS: Bare stage, props. PLAYING TIME: 25 min. PLOT: Based on the heroics of patriots during the American Revolution, this is the story of how patriot spies sent messages about the British army movements. RECOMMENDATION: This will be an excellent introduction to the American Revolution and the sacrifices that people made for it. ROYALTY: NA. SOURCE: Nord, Myrtle. (1983, April). Five under cover. Plays: The Drama Magazine for Young People, pp. 53-60. SUBJECTS/PLAY TYPE: Revolution, U.S.; Playlet.

973. 9-12. (+) Durkin, Patricia. **Fixed up.** CAST: 1f, 1m. ACTS: 1. SETTINGS: Prom. PLAYING TIME: NA. PLOT: A boy and a girl on a blind date at their prom discuss their insecurities and fears about the future and

the innocence and happiness of children. After they chastise each other for not appreciating themselves enough, they leave in search of ice cream. RECOMMENDATION: Common fears about college and graduation are exposed, as are the ways in which many people downgrade themselves. Ending on a positive note, this dramatically but realistically depicts a common prom night experience. ROYALTY: NA. SOURCE: Lamb, Wendy. (1986). Meeting the winter bike rider and other prize winning plays. New York, NY: Dell SUBJECTS/PLAY TYPE: Proms; Graduation; Drama.

974. K-6. (+) Korty, Carol. (Tenenbaum, Samuel) The flagpole. (Wise men of Chelm) CAST: 3u. ACTS: 1. SETTINGS: Bare stage. PLAYING TIME: NA. PLOT: Two friends practice moving a flagpole by carrying a tall person. He is so heavy that they realize they will not be able to carry the real flagpole the next day. When the person walks away, they are happy as they decide to let the real flagpole walk on its own, too. RECOMMENDATION: This is a sure tension easer for children in need of a break from more serious pursuits. ROYALTY: None. SOURCE: Korty, Carol. (1977). Silly soup: Ten zany plays. New York, NY: Charles Scribner's Sons. SUBJECTS/PLAY TYPE: Comedy; Flagpoles; Skit; Adaptation.

975. 3-7*. (+) Wilson, Alice. Flashback!. CAST: 6u. ACTS: 1. SETTINGS: Bare stage. PLAYING TIME: NA. PLOT: In this flashback through childhood, six people enact various experiences common to all children: sibling rivalries, hassles with parents, school anxieties, and friendships. RECOMMENDATION: This must be choreographed in a professional manner for trained actors/dancers but can be performed with a minimum of props and scenery. Because there is no continuous story line but rather a series of vignettes, attention should be paid to the timing, clarity, and precision of the pantomimes that bring the scenes to life. ROYALTY: $20. SOURCE: Wilson, Alice. (1979). Flashback! New Orleans, LA: Anchorage Press. SUBJECTS/PLAY TYPE: Adolescent Problems; Musical Comedy.

976. 7-12. (+) Sawyer-Young, Kat. Flat. CAST: 1f. ACTS: 1. SETTINGS: None. PLAYING TIME: 1 min. PLOT: Anita complains about not having developed breasts yet. RECOMMENDATION: When Anita asks whether parental permission is necessary for a "boob job," everyone will laugh with her. ROYALTY: None. SOURCE: Sawyer-Young, Kat. (1987). Minute monologues for contemporary teens. Boston: Baker's Plays. SUBJECTS/PLAY TYPE: Breasts; Monologue.

977. 5-7. (+) Bradley, Virginia. Flat, flat, flat. CAST: 11u. ACTS: 2. SETTINGS: Castle; field. PLAYING TIME: NA. PLOT: A tyrant imprisons his subjects and destroys all books that don't say the world is flat. His subjects believe that the world is round, and the tyrant eventually falls off his own flat world. RECOMMENDATION: This illustrates that one's own beliefs are sometimes wrong, and that we shouldn't force

our opinions on others. ROYALTY: None. SOURCE: Bradley, Virginia. (1975). Is there an actor in the house? New York: Dodd, Mead. SUBJECTS/PLAY TYPE: Truth; Geography; Beliefs; Puppet Play.

978. 9-12*. (+) Johnston, Carol. (Feydeau, George) A flea in her ear. (A flea in her ear) CAST: 5f, 8m, Su. ACTS: 3. SETTINGS: Living room; Hotel. PLAYING TIME: NA. PLOT: A wife sets a trap at a hotel for her husband who she thinks is cheating on her. She has a friend write a liaison note for her, but the friend's husband sees it and thinks the worst. He decides to go to the hotel to kill both his wife and her "lover." Many people end up getting involved: the first wife and husband, the maid, and the porter, who looks just like the originally suspected husband. After much action and silly confusion, the truth comes out and the play ends happily. RECOMMENDATION: This lively play is entertaining with light humor and laughable characters. The dialogue is short and flows easily; two characters must speak some Spanish. ROYALTY: $50. SOURCE: Johnston, Carol. (1975). A flea in her ear. Woodstock, IL: Dramatic Pub. Co. SUBJECTS/PLAY TYPE: Paris; Romance; Comedy; Farce.

979. 7-12. (+) Saul, Oscar. Lantz, Louis. Flight. CAST: 11f, 52m. ACTS: 2. SETTINGS: Bare stage, backdrops. PLAYING TIME: NA. PLOT: This documentary drama, which begins with the Lindbergh flight across the Atlantic, and continues in flashbacks, shows key historical events that relate mankind's fascination with flying. Act I includes the discovery of fire, the story of the Ebony Horse, da Vinci's first experiments with flight, the first balloon flight, and Lillenthal and his glider. Act II includes the Wright Brothers' airplane, the first mail flight, and the first around the world flight. The play ends with a stirring account of Lindbergh's plane being sighted over France. RECOMMENDATION: This ambitious play has believable dialogue, except for the Indian speech which will require editing. It would keep the interest of history students or those interested in aviation. ROYALTY: Write to publisher. SOURCE: Swortzell, Lowell. (1986). Six plays for young people from the Federal Theatre Project (1936-1939). NY: Greenwood Press. SUBJECTS/PLAY TYPE: Aviation; Docu-drama.

980. 7-12. (+) Murray, John. Flight international. CAST: 6f, 7m, Su. ACTS: 1. SETTINGS: Airport. PLAYING TIME: 35 min. PLOT: In this mystery, a group of American teenage athletes is traveling to England to an international competition. One member of the group steals a valuable emerald necklace from a jeweler traveling on the same plane. The remainder of the play describes how the other teenagers identify the thief with the help of astrology. RECOMMENDATION: The lively conversations of the teenage athletes have a genuine ring to them. Added to an intriguing mystery and a wide range of comedy situations, this is a winner. ROYALTY: Free to Plays subscribers. SOURCE: Murray, John. (1984, April). Flight international. Plays: The Drama Magazine for Young People, pp. 1-14. SUBJECTS/PLAY TYPE: Mystery; Comedy; Playlet.

981. 5-8. (+) Huff, Betty Tracy. **Flora of the flower shop.** CAST: 6f, 5m. ACTS: 1. SETTINGS: Flower shop. PLAYING TIME: 30 min. PLOT: A lovely florist is threatened by a cold villain who will foreclose the mortgage on her flower shop if she does not marry him. She falls in love with a stunt pilot who saves her, and they plan to marry. RECOMMENDATION: This old fashioned melodrama is recommended for its witty dialogue, continuous action, and audience participation. The exaggerated acting style and flowery language are very entertaining. ROYALTY: Free to Plays subscribers. SOURCE: Huff, Betty Tracy. (1976, October). Flora of the flower shop. Plays: The Drama Magazine for Young People, pp. 27-36. SUBJECTS/PLAY TYPE: Comedy; Melodrama.

982. 9-11. (-) McDonald, Alice. **Flora, the fur trader's daughter, or: She had nothing to hide.** CAST: 4f, 4m. ACTS: 1. SETTINGS: Trading post--1880. PLAYING TIME: 45 min. PLOT: This is a typical melodrama of the old West involving Indians, settlers, traders and robbers. Furs and supplies are stolen, captives are taken, beauty tips are exchanged, villains are captured, and heroes are made. RECOMMENDATION: This is suitable only, perhaps, for high school literature and drama students looking at a history of cultural bias and how it is still conveyed. Stilted, demeaning dialogue portrays Indians as simpletons, save for their ability to hunt. The trader is billed as barely intelligent enough to run a store and raise a daughter, yet slick enough to outfox Indians but not the villain. ROYALTY: $5. SOURCE: McDonald, Alice. (1983). Flora, the fur trader's daughter, or: She had nothing to hide. Denver, CO: Pioneer Drama Service. SUBJECTS/ PLAY TYPE: Old West; Indians; Melodrama.

983. 6-12. (+) Daane, Joy. **Flossie's final fling.** CAST: 4f, 4m. ACTS: 3. SETTINGS: Living room. PLAYING TIME: 30 min. PLOT: Grandma is coming to visit and everyone thinks she's coming home to die because of a dog-shredded letter with words like "Will" and "dying" in it. A healthy granny shows up on a bicycle, takes charge, brightens the family's lives and granny and Will peddle off to Niagara Falls. RECOMMENDATION: Clever dialogue and distinctive characters make this an enjoyable comedy with the valuable theme that happiness lies in taking control of one's life and working for what you want. ROYALTY: $25. SOURCE: Daane, Joy. (1977). Flossie's final fling. Franklin, OH: Eldridge Pub. Co. SUBJECTS/PLAY TYPE: Elderly; Self Esteem; Comedy.

984. 4-12. (+) Gilfond, Henry. **A flower for Johnny Reb.** CAST: 4f, 1m. ACTS: 1. SETTINGS: Living room; cemetery. PLAYING TIME: 15 min. PLOT: Peggy puts flowers at her father's grave and at the grave of the soldier who killed him. Although her mother is angry at first, she realizes the folly of continuing to hate. RECOMMENDATION: This high interest\low vocabulary drama shows the tragedy of war and the even more tragic consequences of bearing grudges. ROYALTY: None. SOURCE: Gilfond, Henry. (1985).

Holiday plays for reading. New York: Walker. SUBJECTS/PLAY TYPE: Memorial Day; War; Drama.

985. 3-6. (+) Albert, Laura. **The flower that grew overnight.** CAST: 1f, 2m. ACTS: 1. SETTINGS: Bare stage. PLAYING TIME: 10 min. PLOT: The day before Mother's Day Sam decides to secretly grow a flower to give to his mother the next day. He learns that orange juice helps him to grow, so he waters the flower seed with juice. When the flower doesn't grow right away, Sam is disappointed, but his father buys a flower to replace the seed. His father's subterfuge works, and Sam's mother is very happy when he gives her the flower. RECOMMENDATION: This charming play leaves the audience with a warm, pleasant feeling. ROYALTY: Free to Plays subscribers. SOURCE: Albert, Laura. (1976, May). The flower that grew overnight. Plays: The Drama Magazine for Young People, pp. 59-62. SUBJECTS/PLAY TYPE: Mother's Day; Comedy; Skit.

986. 10-12. (+) Smith, David Fielding. **A flurry of birds.** CAST: 5f, 20m, 1u. ACTS: 2. SETTINGS: Town; clearing; dooryard; tavern; bedroom; shed; river; road. PLAYING TIME: NA. PLOT: In this story of the events in Concord on the eve and first day of the American Revolution, the war is explored through the lives of individuals. Each of the men called to do his duty responds willingly. After the battle, two of the town's men have lost their lives for the freedom of their families, and the audience is shown that freedom is worth whatever it costs. RECOMMENDATION: A product of both fact and imagination, the historical elements are sound; but the language is modernized. This effectively recaptures the historical facts, though the time is somewhat telescoped. ROYALTY: $50. SOURCE: Smith, David Fielding. (1975). A flurry of birds. Boston, MA: Baker's Plays. SUBJECTS/PLAY TYPE: Patriotism; Revolution, U.S.; Drama.

987. 6-8. (-) Majeski, Bill. **A flutter of lace.** CAST: 4f, 5m. ACTS: 1. SETTINGS: Bare stage. PLAYING TIME: 10 min. PLOT: Three brief skits are based on a girl dropping her handkerchief to attract her man. In each skit, the man is distracted and injured. The narrator concludes that modern romances are not based on falling handkerchiefs. He drops his own and is approached by a young woman. He concludes that times haven't changed as much as he thought. RECOMMENDATION: These pointless tales of aborted romance ending in injury are followed by the equally pointless scene in which traditional male and female roles are reversed. The conclusion, that things have not changed, is supported neither by the content of the play nor by history. ROYALTY: Free to Plays subscribers. SOURCE: Majeski, Bill. (1981, February). A flutter of lace. Plays: The Drama Magazine for Young People, pp. 59-62. SUBJECTS/PLAY TYPE: Comedy; Courtship; Skit.

988. 12. (+) Rodgers, Richard. Hart, Lorenz. **Fly with me.** CAST: 4f, 6m, Su. ACTS: 2. SETTINGS: Classroom; garden. PLAYING TIME: NA. PLOT: Columbia, a futuristic college, offers outrageous courses such as

safebreaking and lying with a straight face. The plot centers around the love class and the New Love Law which prohibits kissing and hugging. The students revolt and break the New Love Law. RECOMMENDATION: This spoof on college life and life in the Soviet Union is designed for an older audience that would pick up on the word play and innuendos. Interspersed throughout are songs and dances. Actors of considerable talent would be needed to make this play a success. ROYALTY: Upon application. SOURCE: Rodgers, Richard and Hart, Lorenz and Hammerstein, Oscar. (1982). Fly with me. Chicago, IL: Dramatic Pub. Co. SUBJECTS/PLAY TYPE: College Life; Love; Musical; Comedy.

989. 3-8. (+) Winther, Barbara. **The flying horse machine.** CAST: 5f, 5m, 6u. ACTS: 1. SETTINGS: Courtyard. PLAYING TIME: 30 min. PLOT: Maroudah, the evil magician, asks to marry the king's daughter, Princess Fahan. Her brother objects. Maroudah becomes angry and tricks the prince into riding his flying machine but doesn't tell him how to land. The prince figures it out in time to save the princess. The magician starts to cast a vengeful spell, but the two act insane, frightening him into jumping on his flying horse, never to return. RECOMMENDATION: Based on the short story, "Ebony Horse," this play might present some scenery and special effects difficulties. However, it captures the mood of the original. Directors might want to change the insanity part to something less prejudicial. ROYALTY: Free to Plays subscribers. SOURCE: Winther, Barbara. (1977, January). The flying horse machine. Plays: The Drama Magazine for Young People, pp. 33-40. SUBJECTS/PLAY TYPE: Fantasy; Folk tales; Persia; Playlet.

990. 5-12*. (+) Harris, Aurand. (Vikramaditya of Ujjain) **The flying prince.** CAST: 5f, 7m, Su. ACTS: 2. SETTINGS: Road; mountain; palace; cave. PLAYING TIME: NA. PLOT: Enroute to her wedding, Manorama is captured by the bandit Badri. The prince-bridegroom becomes a bird and rescues her. Badri's servant, Pandu, steals the prince's human body and delays his turning back into a prince. The prince finally does resume human form, and the wedding takes place. RECOMMENDATION: A delightful excursion into legends and folklore of ancient India, this simple tale makes unfamiliar cultural traditions easily accessible. It is filled with colorful adventures and transformations which will delight children of any age. ROYALTY: $35. SOURCE: Harris, Aurand. (1985). The flying prince. New Orleans, LA: Anchorage Press, Inc. SUBJECTS/PLAY TYPE: Folk Tales, India; Adaptation.

991. 8-12. (+) Carmichael, Fred. **Foiled by an innocent maid or, the curse of the iron horse.** CAST: 4f, 2m. ACTS: 1. SETTINGS: Living room. PLAYING TIME: 45 min. PLOT: Poor, innocent Hope Faithwell, and a baby rescued from a train wreck, seek refuge in the house of a mother and daughter mourning a baby's death caused by the same wreck. Since neither the mother nor daughter can bear the sight of an infant, the stage is set for innumerable humorous episodes in which Faith must hide the child yet attend to its needs.

After a web is untangled, it is discovered the baby is heir to a fortune, the deliveryman who has amnesia is its father, and Faith is in love with both of them. RECOMMENDATION: Combining a fast pace, twisting plot and double edged humor, this melodrama is consistently humorous and exciting. Stage gimmicks add comic tension, while the writing will keep both audience and actors eager to hear the next line. ROYALTY: $10. SOURCE: Carmichael, Fred. (1977). Foiled by an innocent maid or the curse of the iron horse. New York, NY: Samuel French. SUBJECTS/PLAY TYPE: Swindlers and Swindling; Melodrama.

992. 5-12. (+) Winther, Barbara. **Follow the river Lai.** CAST: 6f, 6m, Su. ACTS: 1. SETTINGS: Forest. PLAYING TIME: 25 min. PLOT: At a Buddhist temple, Tu Khiem saves a girl from jail by bribing a guard. To repay him, the girl tells him where to find the Land of Bliss, which he has been searching for. Tu Khiem wishes to return to visit his friend, but learns that years have passed in the Land of Bliss, and now it is the girl's son who lives there. The son helps him escape pursuing soldiers and Tu Khiem learns about the dangers of a life of disillusionment. RECOMMENDATION: This sad play will strike familiar chords in older viewers who know "Rip Van Winkle. Strong, sentimental feelings will still be kindled by this Vietnamese telling. ROYALTY: Free for amateur productions. SOURCE: Winther, Barbara. (1976). Plays from folktales of Africa and Asia. Boston: Plays, Inc. SUBJECTS/PLAY TYPE: Folktales, Vietnam; Playlet.

993. K-3. (+) Ison, Colleen. **Following Jesus.** CAST: Su. ACTS: 1. SETTINGS: Bare stage. PLAYING TIME: NA. PLOT: The failings of Jesus' disciples are retold. The story ends with the reminder that Jesus loved the disciples anyway, and that people should put their failures behind them. RECOMMENDATION: In this play meant for church groups, failures are described as needing to be overlooked, and replaced with forward thinking. The narrator will need to be an adult. Discussion questions are provided. ROYALTY: NA. SOURCE: Ison, Colleen. (1986). Goliath's last stand: And fifteen more easy plays for children. Cincinnati: Standard Pub. SUBJECTS/PLAY TYPE: Christian Drama; Jesus' Disciples; Skit.

994. 1-4*. (+) Urquhart, John & Grauer, Rita. **Fool of the world.** (The fool of the world and his flying ship) CAST: 3f, 1m, Su. ACTS: 1. SETTINGS: None. PLAYING TIME: NA. PLOT: In this adaptation of the Russian folktale, a young peasant overcomes many obstacles to build a flying ship and win the hand of a princess in marriage. RECOMMENDATION: This delightful folktale relies upon the imagination of the audience to enhance the story. Costuming and scenery may be minimal, but simple music is required to carry out the mood and illusion. ROYALTY: $25. SOURCE: Urquhart, John & Graver, Rita. (1987). Fool of the world. New Orleans, LA: Anchorage Press, Inc. SUBJECTS/PLAY TYPE: Folk Tales, Russia; Adaptation.

995. 2-5. (+) Bauer, Caroline Feller. **Fooling the king.** CAST: 1f, 2m, 4u. ACTS: 1. SETTINGS: Castle. PLAYING TIME: 5 min. PLOT: A bored king proclaims that anyone who can fool him will win a bag of gold. Wise men come to try to fool the king with new riddles, but all fail. A little girl finally wins the gold when she fools the king into thinking that he promised her the gold last week. RECOMMENDATION: Audiences will enjoy their participation and hearing new riddles. This can be either acted or read aloud. ROYALTY: None. SOURCE: Bauer, Caroline Feller. (1987). Presenting reader's theater: Plays and poems to read aloud. New York, NY: H. W. Wilson Co. SUBJECTS/PLAY TYPE: Riddles; Trickery; Reader's Theater.

996. 9-12. (+) Simon, Neil. **Fools: a comic fable.** CAST: 3f, 7m. ACTS: 2. SETTINGS: Village square. PLAYING TIME: NA. PLOT: An eager young school teacher tries to rid a remote village of a 200 year old curse of stupidity. To do so, he must educate Sophia, the beautiful young daughter of the town physician, within 24 hours, or the teacher himself will become stricken with stupidity. Although the task is overwhelming, he perseveres until he has broken the curse. RECOMMENDATION: This wonderful comedy combines humor, romance, and a message about tolerance into one delightful package. ROYALTY: $60. SOURCE: Simon, Neil. (1981). Fools: a comic fable. NY: Samuel French. SUBJECTS/PLAY TYPE: Wisdom; Stupidity; Comedy.

997. 11-12. (+) Walden, William. **A foot in the door.** CAST: 2f, 3m. ACTS: 2. SETTINGS: Living room. PLAYING TIME: NA. PLOT: A pollster interviews a young widow and quickly becomes involved with her personal life. The pollster is revealed to be a private investigator whose loyalties shift to the young widow as he discovers more about the mysterious circumstances under which her husband died. RECOMMENDATION: This adult play has enough twists and sophistication to challenge worldly, capable students. Its single setting and contemporary costuming present no serious technical problems. ROYALTY: $50. SOURCE: Walden, William. (1984). A foot in the door. Schulenberg, TX: I. E. Clark. SUBJECTS/PLAY TYPE: Mystery; Murder; Drama.

998. 6-8. (+) Gotwalt, Helen Louise Miller. **Football hero.** CAST: 3f, 3m, Su. ACTS: 1. SETTINGS: Dance. PLAYING TIME: 25 min. PLOT: Stan invites Margie to the dance to get her to write his English composition on Thanksgiving so he can remain on the football team. Margie refuses to help him. Stan apologizes sincerely and realizes that he has truly enjoyed her company. Convinced by his sincerity, Margie decides to help him and Stan begins to see the real meaning of Thanksgiving. RECOMMENDATION: This fairly accurate portrayal of teenage problems and relationships presents the value of liking a person for himself rather than for what he can do for you. Also included is the serious meaning of Thanksgiving without being "cute" or "corny." ROYALTY: Free to Plays subscribers. SOURCE: Gotwalt, Helen Louise Miller. (1980, November). Football hero. Plays: The Drama Magazine for Young People, pp. 1-10. SUBJECTS/PLAY TYPE: Dating; Thanksgiving; Playlet.

999. 7-12. (-) Murray, John. **For art's sake.** CAST: 1f. ACTS: 1. SETTINGS: Bare stage. PLAYING TIME: NA. PLOT: A woman visiting an art museum with her husband pretends that she is an art expert, with ridiculous results. RECOMMENDATION: While the topic of pretentious art critics potentially could be very humorous, insufficient and weak humor lead to an equally weak ending. ROYALTY: None. SOURCE: Murray, John. (1982). Modern monologues for young people. Boston: Plays, Inc. SUBJECTS/PLAY TYPE: Comedy; Art; Monologue.

1000. K-3*. (+) Watson, Sally Passmore. **For the love of a worm.** CAST: 3f, 4m. ACTS: 1. SETTINGS: Forest. PLAYING TIME: 45 min. PLOT: Jennifer, a young girl, must do a good deed to see the Star Queen. She accomplishes this by saving a worm, Ooie Gooie, from being eaten by a black widow spider, Slinky Stinky, and a purple-feathered Ring Digger bird, Aurora Bell. Assisting her is Leafy Limb, a magic apple tree, who allows Ooie Gooie to escape by hiding him within Dapple Apple, a happy apple. RECOMMENDATION: Funny names and a series of "near misses" in which Ooie Gooie is nearly made into "green worm jam" will keep younger children on the edge of their seats. ROYALTY: $15. SOURCE: Watson, Sally Passmore. (1978). For the love of a worm. Denver, CO: Pioneer Drama Service. SUBJECTS/PLAY TYPE: Wishes; Worms; Friendship; Drama.

1001. 1-6. (-) Gotwalt, Helen Louise Miller. **The forgetful Easter rabbit.** CAST: 7f, 8m, Su. ACTS: 1. SETTINGS: Forest. PLAYING TIME: 15 min. PLOT: A group of children set out to find and punish the Easter rabbit for not giving them Easter baskets. Just as they put the hapless rabbit into the stewpot, Lady Forget-Me-Not reminds the children that they, too, forget to do things (return library books, their chores, etc.) and she cures the rabbit's forgetfulness with her forget-me-not tea. RECOMMENDATION: The greedy, self-centered, and cruel children are not in keeping with the holiday spirit, making the play especially inappropriate for a holiday based on a religious event. ROYALTY: Free to Plays subscribers. SOURCE: Gotwalt, Helen Louise Miller. (1982, April). The forgetful Easter rabbit. Plays: The Drama Magazine for Young People, pp. 29-35. SUBJECTS/PLAY TYPE: Easter; Forgetfulness; Playlet.

1002. K-3. (+) Ross, Brenda. **The forgetful Santa.** CAST: 2u. ACTS: 1. SETTINGS: North Pole. PLAYING TIME: 5 min. PLOT: Just before Christmas, Santa Claus forgets what to do. Worried, the Snow Queen thinks that if the children remind Santa Claus that they love him, he will remember about Christmas. When she leads the audience in saying "we love you," Santa Claus remembers and leaves for his annual trip. RECOMMENDATION: The simple plot, appropriate dialogue, and audience participation help children identify with the characters, whose personalities are easily recognizable from the costuming and stage props. ROYALTY: Free to Plays subscribers. SOURCE: Ross, Brenda. (1978, December). The forgetful Santa. Plays: The Drama Magazine for Young People, pp. 53-54. SUBJECTS/PLAY TYPE: Christmas; Puppet Play.

1003. 4-7*. (+) Falls, Gregory A. (Key, Alexander) **The forgotten door.** (The forgotten door) CAST: 2f, 5m. ACTS: 1. SETTINGS: Exterior; cave; forest; house; yard; juvenile court. PLAYING TIME: NA. PLOT: A young boy from outer space falls to earth. He can understand what people and animals are thinking and, because he is strange, people are hostile. Brought to Juvenile Court, the boy convinces the kindly country magistrate of his unearthly but benign powers and wins her friendship. Just in time to escape military curiosity, he is drawn up into the safety of his alien world. RECOMMENDATION: This adaptation includes humor, adventure, fantasy, and the important message that it is up to everyone to bring peace to the world. ROYALTY: $35. SOURCE: Falls, Gregory. (1986). The forgotten door. New Orleans, LA: Anchorage Press, Inc. SUBJECTS/PLAY TYPE: Science Fiction; Values; Adaptation.

1004. 7-10. (+) Sodaro, Craig. **Forlorn at the fort.** CAST: 4f, 2m, 1u. ACTS: 1. SETTINGS: Empty stage. PLAYING TIME: 25 min. PLOT: In this real melodrama, the audience is invited to sigh, boo, and cheer for the heroine, villain, and hero, respectively. Beautiful Penelope must marry villainous Ebenezer or her mother will lose the hotel homestead since the villain has secured the deed to the hotel. Calamity Jane arrives and must save the day over and over as the villain repeatedly gains the upper hand. The hero and Calamity finally dispose of the villain. RECOMMENDATION: The audience gets into the action and everyone will thoroughly enjoy this play, which might even be a good fund raiser. ROYALTY: Free to Plays subscribers. SOURCE: Sodaro, Craig. (1981, February). Forlorn at the fort. Plays: The Drama Magazine for Young People, pp. 39-46. SUBJECTS/PLAY TYPE: Comedy; Melodrama.

1005. 5-8. (+) Mauro, Robert. **Formula for romance.** CAST: 2f, 2m. ACTS: 1. SETTINGS: Two rooms. PLAYING TIME: 15 min. PLOT: Sue and Bill want to date each other, but they don't know how to start. Sue gets advice from Rhonda. Bill gets advice from Pete. When Sue and Bill discover that Rhonda and Pete have dated and broken up, they discard the lists of suggestions provided by Rhonda and Pete, and talk to each other honestly. RECOMMENDATION: The parallel action and matching dialogue of this fast paced and humorous boy meets girl sketch creates a sense of the ludicrous. Recommended especially for Valentine's Day. ROYALTY: Free to Plays subscribers. SOURCE: Mauro, Robert. (1985, January/February). Formula for romance. Plays: The Drama Magazine for Young People, pp. 53-58. SUBJECTS/PLAY TYPE: Dating; Valentine's Day; Skit.

1006. 9-12. (+) Rogers, June Walker. (Cohan, George M.) **Forty-five minutes from Broadway.** (Forty-five minutes from Broadway) CAST: 6f, 7m, Su. ACTS: 2. SETTINGS: Stage; estate exterior; and interior. PLAYING TIME: NA. PLOT: A high school drama club is trying to decide what musical to perform. When the student director falls and hits his head, he dreams George M. Cohan's original production, **Forty-five Minutes from Broadway**, a comic musical melodrama about inherited money and marrying for money or love. Upon his recovery, the student announces that Cohan's musical will be their spring show. RECOMMENDATION: As a play within a play, the work is familiar and lively. ROYALTY: NA. SOURCE: Rogers, June Walker. (1978). Forty-five minutes from Broadway. Chicago, IL: Dramatic Pub. Co. SUBJECTS/PLAY TYPE: Comedy; Broadway; Musical.

1007. 12*. (+) Margulies, Donald. **Found a peanut.** CAST: 2f, 6m. ACTS: 1. SETTINGS: Yard. PLAYING TIME: NA. PLOT: Several city children engage in the cruelty, competition, and occasional flashes of insight and communication common to childhood. RECOMMENDATION: This interesting play about the foibles of childhood is not intended for children and is to be played by actors in their 20s and 30s. ROYALTY: $50. SOURCE: Margulies, Donald. (1984). Found a peanut. New York: Dramatists Play Service. SUBJECTS/PLAY TYPE: Childhood; Drama.

1008. 9-12. (+) McElrath, William N. **Four fishers of men.** CAST: 3f, 11m. ACTS: 1. SETTINGS: Lake; town; table; prison; tomb. PLAYING TIME: NA. PLOT: Peter, Andrew, James, and John retell various stories from the New Testament as they reflect on Jesus' influence on their lives. RECOMMENDATION: This is an effective play for church groups that requires good actors because much of the action is pantomimed without the aid of any scenery. It calls for contemporary language and modern clothing. ROYALTY: NA. SOURCE: McElrath, William N. (1978). Four fishers of men. Nashville, TN: Broadman Press. SUBJECTS/PLAY TYPE: Apostles; New Testament; Easter; Drama.

1009. 8-10. (+) Priore, Frank. **Fourteen ninety two blues.** CAST: 1f, 10m, 1u. ACTS: 1. SETTINGS: Ship's deck; dock. PLAYING TIME: 20 min. PLOT: A contemporary Columbus has modern day problems: the men insist on being paid; Columbus receives a summons because his ships are docked in a no docking zone; and Mrs. Columbus wants her husband to stay home and make money. After Columbus leaves, he encounters an Indian in a canoe and they discuss their goals (India and California), exchange pleasantries about how they acquired their vessels, and the play ends. RECOMMENDATION: This clever, imaginative play looks at how a historical figure might fare if placed in modern times. ROYALTY: Free to Plays subscribers. SOURCE: Priore, Frank V. (1983, October). 1492 Blues. Plays: The Drama Magazine for Young People, pp. 61-68. SUBJECTS/PLAY TYPE: Columbus Day; Columbus, Christopher; Comedy.

1010. 9-12. (+) McCusker, Paul. **The fourth of July.** CAST: 2m. ACTS: 1. SETTINGS: None. PLAYING TIME: NA. PLOT: As two young men discuss what is wrong with America, they decide that celebrating the Fourth of July doesn't condone the country's problems but rather, affirms their own commitment to working for its progress. RECOMMENDATION: This is an interesting presentation of the issues of free speech and patriotism. ROYALTY: NA. SOURCE: McCusker, Paul. (1982). Souvenirs: comedies and dramas for Christian fellowship. Boston: Baker's Plays. SUBJECTS/PLAY TYPE: Independence Day, U.S.; Skit.

1011. 1-3. (+) Cohen, Veronika & Smith, Robert B. (Aesopus) **The fox-the crow-the cheese.** (A fox and a raven) CAST: Su. ACTS: 1. SETTINGS: Forest. PLAYING TIME: NA. PLOT: A hungry fox must outsmart a crow to get some cheese. RECOMMENDATION: This short play will improve children's listening skills by its substitution of the character's names throughout the story with various human and instrumental sounds. The entire class will be actively involved either through character portrayals or making the sounds. ROYALTY: None. SOURCE: Cohen, Veronika & Smith, Robert B. (1984). Music dramas for children with special needs. Denton, TX: Troostwyk Press. SUBJECTS/PLAY TYPE: Fable; Trickery; Adaptation.

1012. 11-12*. (+) Cooper, Susan & Cronyn, Hume. **Foxfire.** CAST: 2f, 4m. ACTS: 2. SETTINGS: Cabin. PLAYING TIME: 120 min. PLOT: A mountain woman, Annie Nations, struggles against change by refusing to sell her home, an act which she believes will allow her dead husband's spirit to leave her. All but one of her children, Dillard, have left home. Annie must help Dillard avoid the pitfalls of stardom when his wife leaves him. During an argument with her husband's spirit, Annie realizes times change, and she decides to sell her house to a developer and move with Dillard. RECOMMENDATION: Production of this play will be costly and time-consuming. The musical segments will need a lot of work, and the score must be requested separately from the publisher. Mature young adults should enjoy watching this tale of a strong mountain woman as portrayed by a cast of adults. ROYALTY: $60. SOURCE: Cooper, Susan. (1983). Foxfire. New York, NY: Samuel French. SUBJECTS/PLAY TYPE: Family Issues; Aging; Rural Life; Drama.

1013. 7-12. (+) Hayes, Theresa. **Fractured families.** CAST: 7f, 8m, 4u. ACTS: 3. SETTINGS: Hallway; classroom; gym. PLAYING TIME: 90 min. PLOT: Highschoolers and their parents attend a "love" rap session, intended to teach them how to communicate with each other to prevent teen suicide. They learn about the principles of "GET REAL" (grow up, ease up, timing, repeat, earning, asking and assuming, and listen) as communication techniques. Each family discusses its problems, and resolves them using the learned techniques. RECOMMENDATION: This excellent description of a well known communication technique uses real family problems (divorce, death, nagging, etc.) to show how communication can help. The dialogue is realistic but, if this is to be performed in a secular institution, some religious references may need editing. Discussion questions are provided at the end of the play. ROYALTY: NA. SOURCE: Hayes, Theresa. (1986). Getting your act together. Cincinnati, OH: Standard Pub. Co.

SUBJECTS/PLAY TYPE: Communication; Christian Drama.

1014. 10-12. (+) Gilsenan, Nancy. **Fragile unions.** CAST: 2f, 1m. ACTS: 1. SETTINGS: Bowling alley. PLAYING TIME: NA. PLOT: Two best friends, whose husbands are coworkers and members of the same union (on strike now for three months) meet for their weekly bowling match. Dianne tells Mindy she can't bowl with her anymore. When Mindy's husband arrives, he violently proclaims that Dianne and her husband, Norm, are "dead" because Norm has crossed the union's picket line. RECOMMENDATION: This moving drama illustrates the bitterness and hatred that can develop between decent people during a union strike. The termination of a deep friendship because of political commitments works beautifully as a tragic device. This play would work very well as part of a social studies unit on the labor movement and related issues. ROYALTY: $20. SOURCE: Gilsenan, Nancy. (1984). Fragile unions. Chicago, IL: Dramatic Pub. Co. SUBJECTS/PLAY TYPE: Labor Unions; Friend-ship; Drama.

1015. 4-9. (+) Bland, Joellen. (Shelley, Mary Wollstonecraft) **Frankenstein.** (Frankenstein) CAST: 2f, 9m. ACTS: 1. SETTINGS: None. PLAYING TIME: 20 min. PLOT: During a discovery expedition, a ship's crew take aboard Dr. Frankenstein. He says he created a monster whose very existence has been a torment to him, killing his brother, best friend, and wife. Dr. Frankenstein dies, urging the captain to kill the creature if it appears. Soon after, it does appear, but only to lament the Doctor's death and to indicate that all it ever wanted was love and kindness. With no reason to live, the creature leaves the ship to end its lonely, miserable life. RECOMMENDATION: This is abbreviated, but faithful to the original story, even using some of the original dialogue. Designed for round-the-table reading, the poignant conflict between Dr. Frankenstein and his creation reflects the universal need for love, compassion and acceptance. Ironically, each character realizes this at the other's expense when the creature, rejected by his creator, seeks to destroy everything the doctor cares most about. The play imparts the theme with subtlety and skill. ROYALTY: Free to Plays subscribers. SOURCE: Bland, Joellen. (1981, October). Frankenstein. Plays: The Drama Magazine for Young People, pp. 71-80. SUBJECTS/PLAY TYPE: Reader's Theater; Horror; Adaptation.

1016. 10-12. (+) Gialanella, Victor. (Shelley, Mary Wollstonecraft) **Frankenstein.** (Frankenstein) CAST: 3f, 9m. ACTS: 2. SETTINGS: Sitting room; bedroom; laboratory; graveyard; cottage; woods. PLAYING TIME: NA. PLOT: In the mid-1800s, Victor Frankenstein, a wealthy, aristocratic scientist, attempts to discover the secret of life by experimenting on corpses obtained by grave robbing. He creates a monster whose pain and torment eventually destroy Victor's life, and the lives of the people around him. RECOMMENDATION: The subject matter and creepy atmosphere will make this play ideal for a Halloween presentation. Characters are not subtle, and so are suitable for amateurs to play. However, the many required scene changes and special effects may make production technically very challenging. **ROYALTY:** $50. **SOURCE:** Gialenella, Victor. (1982). Frankenstein. New York, NY: Dramatists Play Service. **SUBJECTS/PLAY TYPE:** Halloween; Horror; Adaptation.

1017. 9-12. (-) Mattera, John & Barrows, Stephen A. (Shelley, Mary Wollstonecraft) **Frankenstein.** (Frankenstein) **CAST:** 1f, 3m, 3u. **ACTS:** 1. **SETTINGS:** Bedroom. **PLAYING TIME:** NA. **PLOT:** Based on Mary Shelley's novel, this play is extremely abridged. In a surprise ending, it was Dr. Frankenstein's best friend, not the creature, who killed the victims. **RECOMMENDATION:** Characters who do not come to life, a very abridged plot, plus a very unsatisfactory "trick" ending, result in a very poor adaptation of a very good novel. **ROYALTY:** $20. **SOURCE:** Mattera, John & Barrows, Stephen A. (1981). Frankenstein. Chicago, IL: Dramatic Pub. Co. **SUBJECTS/PLAY TYPE:** Halloween; Horror; Adaptation.

1018. 9-12. (+) Nowlan, Alden & Learning, Walter. (Shelley, Mary Wollstonecraft) **Frankenstein.** (Frankenstein) **CAST:** 2f, 6m, 8u. **ACTS:** 3. **SETTINGS:** Hall; laboratory; cottage; bedroom; ship. **PLAYING TIME:** NA. **PLOT:** This adaptation is true to the original novel. Central to this emphasis is the love/hate relationship between the creature and his creator. **RECOMMENDATION:** The intent to stay true to Shelley's original work combined with three acts to develop characterization and plot help to make this a very successful adaptation. The set designs are simple enough (with the possible exception of the final boat scene) to be designed by high school students and the love/hate relationship between Frankenstein and his creature provides enough energy to keep an audience keenly interested. **ROYALTY:** $60. **SOURCE:** Nowlan, Alden & Learning, Walter. (1981). Frankenstein. Wood-stock, IL: Dramatic Pub. Co. **SUBJECTS/PLAY TYPE:** Abandonment; Halloween; Jealousy; Adaptation.

1019. 9-12. (+) O'Neal, Christopher. (Shelley, Mary) **Frankenstein: The monster play.** (Frankenstein) **CAST:** 6f, 3m, Su. **ACTS:** 3. **SETTINGS:** Parlor; lab. **PLAYING TIME:** 120 min. **PLOT:** Dr. Frankenstein brings his creation to life with dire consequences for himself and his family who are unable to accept the misshapen monster. **RECOMMENDATION:** A faithful adaptation of Mary Shelley's novel, the play would provide an excellent creative technical experience for students with some background in stagecraft. **ROYALTY:** $35. **SOURCE:** O'Neal, Christopher. (1980). Frankenstein: The monster play. Schulenburg, TX: I.E. Clark. **SUBJECTS/PLAY TYPE:** Monsters; Misunderstanding; Tragedy; Adaptation.

1020. 9-12. (+) Kelly, Tim. **The Frankensteins are back in town.** **CAST:** 14f, 8m, 3u. **ACTS:** 3. **SETTINGS:** School; manor. **PLAYING TIME:** NA. **PLOT:** Baroness von Frankenstein arrives in Withering Heights and enrolls Shelley and Victor Frankenstein, direct descendants of the monster and his bride, in school. The play includes typical high school situations, as well as a few scenes that are characteristic of the Frankenstein horror movies. In the resolution, not only have Shelley and Victor been accepted

by the student body, but Victor is running for student senate president and Shelley has made the football team. **RECOMMENDATION:** The zany characters and the comical scenes throughout will make the play particularly enjoyable. Although some of the dialogue is outdated, the author proposes in the production notes that terms may be changed to give the play a contemporary flavor. This could be useful as a program on the acceptance of handicapped or special students into the mainstream. **ROYALTY:** $35. **SOURCE:** Kelly, Tim. (1980). The Frankensteins are back in town. Schulenburg, TX: I.E. Clark. **SUBJECTS/PLAY TYPE:** Disabilities; Halloween; Monsters; Comedy.

1021. 11-12. (-) Cope, Eddie. **Frankenstein's centerfold.** **CAST:** 9f, 3m. **ACTS:** 2. **SETTINGS:** Hotel. **PLAYING TIME:** NA. **PLOT:** In this cross between **Frankenstein** and **My Fair Lady,** Dr. Victor Frankenstein IV and his assistant, Igor, construct a beautiful young woman who they hope will win the Miss North American Co-ed Scholarship Pageant. Their plans are complicated by a seductive female Russian spy who wants the blueprints for their creation, and by the creation herself, who is a slow and literal minded learner. **RECOMMENDATION:** The premise is clever, but the slapstick comedy isn't especially funny. A few instances of bedroom humor may make the play unsuitable for some schools or grades. **ROYALTY:** $35. **SOURCE:** Cope, Eddie. (1984). Frankenstein's centerfold. Schulenburg, TX: I.E. Clark. **SUBJECTS/PLAY TYPE:** Creation; Beauty Contests; Comedy.

1022. 9-12. (+) Weinstein, Robert. **Free choice. CAST:** 2f, 7m, Su. **ACTS:** 1. **SETTINGS:** Office. **PLAYING TIME:** NA. **PLOT:** Arthur Conn meets with Mr. DeVille to determine whether Conn's soul should go to heaven or hell. When DeVille discusses the immoral life Conn has led, Conn first denies it all, giving excuses, but then admits he cheated his brother out of his thriving business and is responsible for his brother's suicide. When the pitiful Conn is given the option to face his brother (who has forgiven him) and live in heaven, or to "writhe in pain" forever in hell, he chooses hell. **RECOMMENDATION:** Set in the limbo between heaven and hell, this captures a tone which is more moralistic than religious. Conn's final decision to face his punishment by choosing hell poignantly conveys the message that actions have inescapable consequences. By producing this play on a gloomy, bare stage, the production crew can further enhance the dark truths portrayed in this gripping drama. **ROYALTY:** $20. **SOURCE:** Weinstein, Robert. (1986). Free choice. Franklin, OH: Eldridge Pub. Co. **SUBJECTS/PLAY TYPE:** Morals; Consequences; Drama.

1023. 9-12. (+) Isom, Joan Shaddox. **Free spirits. CAST:** 10f, 4m. **ACTS:** 1. **SETTINGS:** Dining room; woods; jail. **PLAYING TIME:** 30 min. **PLOT:** Unhappy teenagers decide to rough it as free spirits in the woods near a small town. However, they soon find that only two of them are willing to work to provide necessities (build the shack, cook meals, etc.). The townspeople have the teens arrested as a bunch of undesirable hippies and their parents get them released. They return home, and admit living on one's own is not as easy as they thought. RECOMMENDATION: This seems to favor societal norms and downplays the value of protest. However, if produced as a lighthearted parody, it might be acceptable. ROYALTY: Free to Plays subscribers. SOURCE: Isom, Joan Shaddox. (1975, March). Free Spirits. Plays: The Drama Magazine for Young People, pp. 16-30. SUBJECTS/PLAY TYPE: Hippies; Communes; Playlet.

1024. 7-12. (+) Cope, Eddie. **Freebies. CAST:** 6f, 3m. ACTS: 1. SETTINGS: Newspaper office. PLAYING TIME: NA. PLOT: The new male editor of a newspaper women's department prohibits the previous practice of accepting "free samples" in exchange for free publicity in the newspaper. At first, the reporters (all women) are angry, but after returning from their first real reporting assignment, they realize that it is more interesting to find their scoops than to receive them. RECOMMENDATION: Although this easy to produce play contains an interesting moral dilemma, it is so full of sexist remarks and sexism (only a man is considered appropriate as the editor of the women's section) that it is highly offensive. With some updating, nonsexist recasting, and a rewrite of the last scene in which one male editor proves his superiority by pummeling the other male editor, the play would be acceptable and entertaining. ROYALTY: $15. SOURCE: Cope, Eddie. (1982). Freebies. Schulenburg, TX: I.E. Clark. SUBJECTS/PLAY TYPE: Newspapers; Morals; Bribery; Comedy.

1025. 5-8. (+) Rembrandt, Elaine. (Steinberg, Judah) **The freedom birds: A Passover tale.** (The breakfast of the birds) CAST: 2f, 3m, 3u. ACTS: 1. SETTINGS: Home. PLAYING TIME: 20 min. PLOT: Two birds share their ideas on freedom with the Hebrew children of parents who are slaves in Egypt. The father learns of Moses, who claims he will ask the Pharaoh to give freedom to their people. As Moses leads the Israelites out of bondage, they find freedom is not such an easy course and they begin to starve. The birds see their plight and sacrifice themselves to keep the Hebrews from turning back. RECOMMENDATION: This is a simplified, but unusually altered version of the Passover story which can be performed on a basic or elaborate set. Good production suggestions are offered. ROYALTY: None. SOURCE: Rembrandt, Elaine. (1981). Heroes, heroines & holidays - plays for Jewish youth. Denver, CO: Alternatives in Religious Education, Inc. SUBJECTS/PLAY TYPE: Passover; Jewish Drama; Adaptation.

1026. 9-12. (+) Rozell, O.B. **The freeway. CAST:** 6f, 2m, 1u. ACTS: 1. SETTINGS: Porches; lawn. PLAYING TIME: NA. PLOT: Lena (black) and Maude (white) are neighbors and lifelong friends. Their families are gone and they keep each other company in their "golden years." Their friendship has erased the prejudice their southern backgrounds encouraged. When the highway department routes a freeway through their homes, both try to deal with it as their families suggest. As their children move them out, Maude dies, and Lena mourns her dual losses. RECOMMENDATION: Full of symbolism, this play focuses on differences between black and white, new ways

and old ways, and the young and elderly. It presents a powerful message. The script offers a challenging showcase for the two actors who play Lena and Maude. This play offers good, nonstereotypical roles for black actors. ROYALTY: $25. SOURCE: Rozell, O.B. (1976). The freeway. Schulenburg, TX: I.E. Clark. SUBJECTS/PLAY TYPE: Elderly; Friendship; Drama.

1027. 8-12. (+) Nolan, Paul T. (de Beton, Noel) **The French Cabinetmaker.** (Crispin Medecin) CAST: 4f, 3m, Su. ACTS: 1. SETTINGS: Cabinetmaker's shop. PLAYING TIME: 20 min. PLOT: Angelica has two suitors, Andre and Crispin. Andre, the unwanted suitor, is trapped in the house and, to hide from Angelica's papa, he is disguised as a table. Angelica encourages her papa to saw and hammer on the table to repair it. There are several such amusing incidents until Crispin is left as the lone suitor and Angelica's papa grants his blessing to the marriage. RECOMMENDATION: Although the plot revolves around the sexist view of women as being preoccupied with marriage, the slapstick comedy is hilarious. Much is lost in this abridgement of the original, but as a comedy it stands well on its own merits. ROYALTY: None for amateur performance. SOURCE: Nolan, Paul T. (1982). Folk tale plays round the world: A collection of royalty-free, one-act plays about lands far and near. Boston, MA: Plays, Inc. SUBJECTS/PLAY TYPE: Romance; Marriage; Comedy; Farce.

1028. 11-12. (+) Sterling, Pam. **Friday's child. CAST:** 2f, 6m. ACTS: 1. SETTINGS: Alley; apartment; forest. PLAYING TIME: NA. PLOT: Tommy, an Irish Catholic, wants to defend his motherland by helping rid it of occupying British soldiers. A young terrorist kills a British soldier, is captured, and implicates Tom in the crime. Tom's own terrorist attempt is foiled by Tara, who holds the bomb as it explodes. RECOMMENDATION: An effective, even handed play, this condemns violence, even as it impartially describes the sources from which it springs. Although not easy to produce, the sensitive portrayal of the Irish conflict makes this worthwhile. ROYALTY: NA. SOURCE: Sterling, Pam. (1982). Friday's child. Morton Grove, IL: Coach House Press, Inc. SUBJECTS/PLAY TYPE: War; Ireland; Drama.

1029. 1-6*. (+) Ryan, Josephine. **A friend for Christmas. CAST:** 4f, 4m, Su. ACTS: 1. SETTINGS: School room. PLAYING TIME: NA. PLOT: Timmy, age 7, wants a puppy for Christmas, but his teacher, neighbors and schoolmates think he should be happy with his new baby brother. Timmy decides he will trade his brother for a puppy, but his plan does not work. Just when he decides that he is being selfish, and that he should give the baby a big brother (himself) for Christmas, Santa leaves a puppy for Timmy. As evidence that Timmy has learned a lesson of love, he whispers to the puppy, "Hush, puppy. You'll wake the baby." RECOMMENDATION: This would be suitable as a Christmas presentation or a lesson on the subject of a new baby in the house. ROYALTY: NA. SOURCE: Ryan, Josephine. (1982). A friend for Christmas. Ontario, Canada: Playwrights Canada. SUBJECTS/PLAY TYPE: Christmas; Siblings; Drama.

1030. K-12. (+) Hendricks, William & Vogel, Cora. **The friendly beasts. CAST:** Su. **ACTS:** 1. **SETTINGS:** None. **PLAYING TIME:** 2 min. **PLOT:** This choral reading tells the story of the birth of Christ from the perspective of the barn animals. **RECOMMENDATION:** Suitable for church or parochial school groups, this 12th century carol would be especially pleasing at a Christmas pageant or worship service. **ROYALTY:** NA. **SOURCE:** Hendricks, William & Vogel, Cora. (1978). Handbook of Christmas programs. Grand Rapids, MI: Baker Book House. **SUBJECTS/PLAY TYPE:** Christmas; Christ, Jesus; Worship Program.

1031. 7-12. (-) Campbell, Louis H. **The frightful fate of Wilhelmina Worthington or, treed by a coon hound. CAST:** 2f, 4m, 1u. **ACTS:** 1. **SETTINGS:** Kitchen/sitting room. **PLAYING TIME:** 35 min. **PLOT:** The hero Dan Dogood, who loves the heroine, Wilhelmina, has gone to the big city to prove that the villain, Lucas Letch, is cheating Wilhelmina's parents on their mortgage. The deceitful Lucas tries to trick Wilhelmina into marriage in exchange for the mortgage, but she outwits him. The villainous plot is discovered in the nick of time, and everyone is saved. **RECOMMENDATION:** This mediocre melodrama has a predictable plot and an inconsistently applied dialect: too much in places, missing in others. **ROYALTY:** $20. **SOURCE:** Campbell, Louis H. (1984). The frightful fate of Wilhelmina Worthington or, treed by a coon hound. Franklin, OH: Eldridge Pub. Co. **SUBJECTS/PLAY TYPE:** Mortgages; Marriage; Melodrama.

1032. K-4. (+) Mahlman, Lewis & Jones, David Cadwalader. (Grimm Brothers) The frog prince. (The frog prince) **CAST:** 1f, 2m. **ACTS:** 1. **SETTINGS:** Garden; dining room; bedroom. **PLAYING TIME:** 20 min. **PLOT:** A prince comes to claim a princess as his wife but, before he does so, a wizard turns him into a frog. He remains a frog until the spoiled princess performs three good deeds. **RECOMMENDATION:** The action and humor in this play make it very appealing to children. **ROYALTY:** Free to Plays subscribers. **SOURCE:** Mahlman, Lewis, & Jones, David Cadwalader. (1974). Puppet plays for young players. Boston, MA: Plays, Inc. **SUBJECTS/PLAY TYPE:** Folk Tales, Germany; Puppet Play; Adaptation.

1033. 4-6. (+) Mamet, David. (Grimm Brothers) **The frog prince.** (The frog prince) **CAST:** 2f, 2m. **ACTS:** 1. **SETTINGS:** Woods. **PLAYING TIME:** 20 min. **PLOT:** An arrogant and self-centered prince is turned into a frog and, until a pure and honest woman of her own free will plants a selfless kiss upon his lips, he will remain a frog. After many exciting adventures, a milkmaid kisses him goodbye and he is restored to his human form. He questions whether he deserved all of the misfortune brought on by his arrogance, but when tested, he proves how much he has changed. **RECOMMENDATION:** In this different view of the old fairy tale, the prince pays a heavy price for his selfishness. After the production, the audience should be given an opportunity for discussion. **ROYALTY:** Write to publisher. **SOURCE:** Mamet, David. (1986). Three children's plays. New York, NY: Grove Press, Inc. **SUBJECTS/PLAY TYPE:** Folk Tales, Germany; Selfishness; Values; Playlet.

1034. 5-8. (+) Nolan, Paul T. (Grimm Brothers) **The frog who wouldn't be kissed.** (The frog prince) **CAST:** 4f, 3m. **ACTS:** 1. **SETTINGS:** Woods. **PLAYING TIME:** 20 min. **PLOT:** Lyman, a poetry reading student who sees himself as the class "frog," refuses to cast the deciding vote in the election for class princess. Two candidates try to bribe him to vote. When the third candidate, Nora, approaches Lyman and asks him to be her date to the dance, Lyman figures she is also just trying to get his vote. He rudely turns her down, saying nobody had the time of day for him until he had the vote that would decide the election. Then he learns that Nora had withdrawn from the election and wanted Lyman as a date on his own merits. They make plans to be each other's dates. **RECOMMENDATION:** This reinforces the Shakespearean line quoted within it, "to thine own self be true." Although the dialogue is rather syrupy and reminiscent of a Brady Bunch rerun, the play is quick and may command attention if the audience recognizes some of the intended symbolism and the quotations from Shakespeare. **ROYALTY:** Free to Plays subscribers. **SOURCE:** Nolan, Paul T. (1975, October). The frog who wouldn't be kissed. Plays: The Drama Magazine for Young People, pp. 28-36. **SUBJECTS/PLAY TYPE:** Folk Tales, Germany; Friendship; Adaptation.

1035. 10-12. (+) Shrevelove, Burt & Sondheim, Stephen. (Aristophanes) **The frogs.** (The frogs) **CAST:** 4f, 10m, Su. **ACTS:** 1. **SETTINGS:** Poolside. **PLAYING TIME:** NA. **PLOT:** In this modern, freely adapted version of the Aristophanes comedy, Dionysus and Xanthias try to bring Bernard Shaw back to earth so he can write plays for the theater which, according to Dionysus, is in bad shape. In Hades, a contest of words is held between Shaw and Shakespeare. Shakespeare wins, and Pluto, the ruler of Hades, allows Shakespeare to return to earth with Dionysus instead of Shaw. **RECOMMENDATION:** This is a freewheeling, rather bawdy spectacle filled with slapstick humor, literary allusions, and flamboyant stage and lighting effects. The cast size is expandable. **ROYALTY:** Upon application. **SOURCE:** Shrevelove, Burt & Sondheim, Stephen. (1975). The frogs. Chicago, IL: Dramatic Pub. Co **SUBJECTS/PLAY TYPE:** Mythology, Greek; Playwrights; Musical; Comedy.

1036. 10-12. (+) Ibsen, Henrik. **from A doll's house. CAST:** 1f, 1m. **ACTS:** 1. **SETTINGS:** Living room. **PLAYING TIME:** NA. **PLOT:** Mr. Krogstad asks Nora to use her influence with her husband to save his job, threatening to reveal her secret debts if she does not. Nora threatens to kill herself, but Krogstad regains his control over her by taunting her about her reputation. **RECOMMENDATION:** This riveting excerpt from Ibsen's original should delight any teenage acting group. **ROYALTY:** NA. **SOURCE:** Olfson, Lewy. (1980). Fifty great scenes for student actors. New York, NY: Bantam Books. **SUBJECTS/PLAY TYPE:** Debt; Blackmail; Scene.

1037. 12. (+) Gazzo, Michael V. **from A hatful of rain. CAST:** 1f, 1m. **ACTS:** 1. **SETTINGS:** Bare stage, props. **PLAYING TIME:** NA. **PLOT:** Celia, a young woman in the early stages of pregnancy, is angry at her husband, Johnny, who stayed out all night. As he attempts to smooth things over, she tries to keep her composure, while telling him it's over between them. When Johnny gives her a gift for the baby, she reacts as he had calculated, and tells him she won't leave him. RECOMMENDATION: Only for acting students or students studying drama, this strong scene is an exercise in the evolution of emotions in a character. Dialogue is simple and moves evenly throughout. One gets a sense of much more moving underneath the surface. ROYALTY: NA. SOURCE: Handman, Wynn. (1980). Modern American scenes for student actors. New York, NY: Bantam Books. SUBJECTS/PLAY TYPE: Emotions; Manipulation; Scene.

1038. 8-12. (+) Gazzo, Michael V. **from A hatful of rain.** CAST: 2m. ACTS: 1. SETTINGS: Living room. PLAYING TIME: NA. PLOT: Johnny, a drug addict, tries unsuccessfully to borrow $20 from his brother, Polo. He admits he owes a dealer several hundred dollars and tells Polo that the dealer and his men are coming today to collect. Polo advises Johnny to run away, but Johnny refuses and decides to wait for the dealer and his thugs to arrive and fight to the end. RECOMMENDATION: This shows some of the feelings of desperation that a drug addict can have. If played properly, this powerful scene can lead to further discussion and would be excellent for use in a drug resistance program. It may be suitable for a younger audience, provided there is adult supervision and explanation as well as further discussion. ROYALTY: NA. SOURCE: Handman, Wynn. (1980). Modern American scenes for student actors. New York, NY: Bantam Books. SUBJECTS/PLAY TYPE: Addiction; Drug Abuse; Scene.

1039. 10-12. (+) O'Neill, Eugene. **from A moon for the misbegotten.** CAST: 1f, 1m. ACTS: 1. SETTINGS: Yard. PLAYING TIME: NA. PLOT: In this coarse view of family life, an abusive father rages at his spunky daughter, who has just helped the last of her brothers escape their father's wrath. The two reminisce about some of their disreputable business dealings, and conclude by expressing pride in each other's abilities. RECOMMENDATION: Although this scene from O'Neill's play does not depict the most savory of lifestyles, it could serve as either a practice scene for young teenaged actors, or as a supplement to a discussion on child abuse. ROYALTY: NA. SOURCE: Olfson, Lewy. (1980). Fifty great scenes for student actors. New York, NY: Bantam Books. SUBJECTS/PLAY TYPE: Child Abuse; Family; Scene.

1040. 9-12. (+) Hansberry, Lorraine. **from A raisin in the sun.** CAST: 1f, 1m. ACTS: 1. SETTINGS: Living room. PLAYING TIME: NA. PLOT: In a discussion between a disillusioned black female medical student and her male Nigerian friend, it is revealed that the student is upset that her brother lost the family's money and that she wants to give up her struggle for education. Her friend tells her to continue; he is full of hope. He asks her to return to Nigeria with him, and leaves her to think about it. RECOMMENDATION: In this strong scene, the dialogue swings like a pendulum between the two characters' feelings of disillusionment and hope about the black community and youth in general. ROYALTY: NA. SOURCE: Handman, Wynn. (1980). Modern American scenes for student actors. New York, NY: Bantam Books.

SUBJECTS/PLAY TYPE: Emotions; Disillusionment; Hope; Scene.

1041. 9-12. (+) Sommer, Edith. **from A room full of roses.** CAST: 2f. ACTS: 1. SETTINGS: Living room. PLAYING TIME: NA. PLOT: Bridget, 15, has recently been reunited with her mother, Nancy, after living with her father for eight years. Bridget wants to hate her mother but, deep inside, she yearns for her mother's love. Nancy wants to win her daughter's affections, but Bridget's tough act proves hard to get past. After an argument and some serious discussion, Bridget discovers that her mother really does care for her and, in confusion, runs upstairs to sort out her feelings. RECOMMENDATION: This illustrates the feelings of hurt and rejection that can affect children of divorced parents, and points out that parents may not be as uncaring as a young person may feel they are. It would provide a good opportunity for students to discuss ways in which children of divorced parents can express their feelings to their parents, as well as ways in which parents can let their children know that they care about them. ROYALTY: NA. SOURCE: Handman, Wynn. (1980). Modern American scenes for student actors. New York, NY: Bantam Books. SUBJECTS/PLAY TYPE: Mothers and Daughters; Divorce; Scene.

1042. 12. (+) Inge, William. **from A social event.** CAST: 1f, 1m. ACTS: 1. SETTINGS: Bedroom. PLAYING TIME: NA. PLOT: A young, married actor couple, whose feelings are hurt because they have not been invited to the funeral of the year by the widow, are discussing their situation. They are embarrassed and feel slighted. He suggests they give food poisoning as an excuse for their absence; she refuses. RECOMMENDATION: This could be a fun scene to play if the actors have a grasp on the irony and play up the little eccentricities these young actors might have. ROYALTY: NA. SOURCE: Handman, Wynn. (1980). Modern American scenes for student actors. New York, NY: Bantam Books. SUBJECTS/PLAY TYPE: Vanity; Scene.

1043. 9-12. (+) Williams, Tennessee. **from A streetcar named Desire.** CAST: 2f. ACTS: 1. SETTINGS: Bedroom. PLAYING TIME: NA. PLOT: Blanche Dubois, about thirty, goes to New Orleans to live with her sister, Stella, and her husband, Stanley. The night before, Stanley hosted a poker game that turned violent, and he smashed some furniture and slapped Stella. He immediately apologizes and reconciles with Stella, but Blanche doesn't know this. The next morning, Blanche, near hysteria, attempts to convince Stella to leave this "beast" and go off with her to seek a better life. But Stella is deeply in love with Stanley and is happy and content with her present situation and refuses to go. RECOMMENDATION: This illustrates how different viewpoints alter perceptions of a situation. The exciting dialogue will hold the audience's attention if delivered well. Although this scene was written in 1947, and some of the dialogue has become dated, it can be adapted with little difficulty to modern times if desired. ROYALTY: NA. SOURCE: Handman, Wynn. (1980). Modern American scenes for student actors. New York, NY: Bantam Books. SUBJECTS/PLAY TYPE: Wife Abuse; Scene.

1044. 11-12. (+) Wilde, Oscar. **from A woman of no importance.** CAST: 2m. ACTS: 1. SETTINGS: None. PLAYING TIME: NA. PLOT: Gerald, an unsophisticated young man, converses with Lord Illingworth who, although highly sophisticated, has become callous to the problems in people's lives. Illingworth feels that society is everything because, without it, one is at a loss "fitting in." RECOMMENDATION: The epigrammatic dialogue keeps the interactions light, frivolous, and reflective of high society at that time. ROYALTY: NA. SOURCE: Olfson, Lewy. (1980). Fifty great scenes for student actors. New York, NY: Bantam Books. SUBJECTS/PLAY TYPE: Society; Class Consciousness; Scene.

1045. 7-10. (+) Foote, Horton. **from A young lady of property.** CAST: 2f. ACTS: 1. SETTINGS: Front porch. PLAYING TIME: NA. PLOT: Wilma, 15, inherited the property owned by her mother. She and her friend Arabella have written to a Hollywood agent and asked for screen tests. While discussing their futures, both girls decide that neither of them really wants to go to Hollywood, and they decide to stay in their hometown, marry, raise a family, and remain friends forever. RECOMMENDATION: This scene was written in the early 1950s, and the attitudes of that time are reflected here. A normal life for a girl is described as marrying and having children. Only boys could ask for a date and propose marriage. This would be suitable for a skit on life in the 1950s, but otherwise it is outdated. ROYALTY: NA. SOURCE: Handman, Wynn. (1980). Modern American scenes for student actors. New York, NY: Bantam Books. SUBJECTS/PLAY TYPE: Life Stages; Scene.

1046. 10-12. (+) Shepard, Sam. **from Action.** CAST: 1u. ACTS: 1. SETTINGS: None. PLAYING TIME: NA. PLOT: The actor tells a story about three moths who attempt to understand a candle flame. The first moth looked at the flame but could not understand it. The second moth touched the flame with the tip of his wings, but the heat drove him off. The third moth threw himself on the flame and embraced it, thus being the only one who really understood it. RECOMMENDATION: From a play which makes a statement about the 1970s, this speech identifies the feelings people have when trying to decide between the emptiness of inaction or the possible consequences of action. ROYALTY: NA. SOURCE: Handman, Wynn. (1980). Modern American scenes for student actors. New York, NY: Bantam Books. SUBJECTS/PLAY TYPE: Understanding; Commitment; Scene.

1047. 10-12. (+) Miller, Arthur. **from All my sons.** CAST: 2f. ACTS: 1. SETTINGS: Backyard. PLAYING TIME: NA. PLOT: Ann prepares to marry Chris Keller, son of a businessman. Ann's neighbor, Sue, wants Ann and Chris to move away after they are married so Chris won't be around to support her husband's idea of giving up his medical practice to do research. Sue considers Chris a phony and a crook just like his father, who was recently acquitted on charges of supplying flawed equipment to the military. RECOMMENDATION: This scene from Miller's wartime drama deals with the effects of idealism on others. Also, jealousy of socially prominent or more

controversial person, is alluded to and could provide material for further discussion. ROYALTY: NA. SOURCE: Handman, Wynn. (1980). Modern American scenes for student actors. New York, NY: Bantam Books. SUBJECTS/PLAY TYPE: Relationships; Idealism; Scene.

1048. 10-12. (+) Miller, Arthur. **from All my sons.** CAST: 1m. ACTS: 1. SETTINGS: None. PLAYING TIME: NA. PLOT: Chris tells Ann about his experiences in combat in World War II and how he felt guilty for being alive when so many others had not survived. His guilt is compounded because he works for his father whose manufacturing business prospered because of the war. RECOMMENDATION: This speech allows the actor to express inner conflicts and explore feelings of guilt and love. Miller expresses universal truths concerning war and its consequences. ROYALTY: NA. SOURCE: Handman, Wynn. (1980). Modern American scenes for student actors. New York, NY: Bantam Books. SUBJECTS/PLAY TYPE: War; Veterans; Scene.

1049. 9-12. (+) Mosel, Tad. (Agee, James) **from All the way home.** (A death in the family) CAST: 2m. ACTS: 1. SETTINGS: Room. PLAYING TIME: NA. PLOT: As two brothers, Jay and Ralph, sit together, Ralph, an alcoholic, drinks continuously. Throughout his conversation, he exposes his feelings of insecurity, inferiority, and jealousy of his brother. Ralph asks Jay, a former alcoholic, how drinking used to make him feel. Jay states that being drunk made his problems disappear temporarily, but inevitably increased them. Then Jay reveals that he stopped drinking by making a vow to kill himself if he ever got drunk again. He decided to stay sober for his children. Sadly, Ralph, a father also, is too weak to take his brother's vow to stop drinking but states that he will "vow to think on it!" RECOMMENDATION: The characters and the dialogue are very convincing. This could effectively be used with other scenes in a program dealing with other social problems, as part of an anti-drug assembly, or in a high school drama class. ROYALTY: NA. SOURCE: Handman, Wynn. (1980). Modern American scenes for student actors. New York, NY: Bantam Books. SUBJECTS/PLAY TYPE: Alcoholism; Scene.

1050. 9-12. (+) Mosel, Tad. (Agee, James) **from All the way home.** (A death in the family) CAST: 2f. ACTS: 1. SETTINGS: Dining room; kitchen. PLAYING TIME: NA. PLOT: Mary learns that her husband was involved in a serious car accident. She and her Aunt Hannah wait for a call from Hannah's husband, who was called to the scene by the police. Mary and Hannah both realize that Mary's husband is probably dead, but as they talk, they avoid directly discussing that topic. RECOMMENDATION: This is a very powerful and moving scene in which the unspoken carries the most importance. The characters, in their own ways, are trying to prepare themselves for what they both feel is inevitable. This scene would be perfect for opening a discussion on how to cope with the death of a loved one. ROYALTY: NA. SOURCE: Handman, Wynn. (1980). Modern American scenes for student actors. New York, NY: Bantam Books. SUBJECTS/PLAY TYPE: Death; Scene.

1051. 12. (+) Hellman, Lillian. **from Another part of the forest.** CAST: 1f, 1m. ACTS: 1. SETTINGS: Living room. PLAYING TIME: NA. PLOT: A couple converses prior to their meeting his family, who disapprove of her bad reputation. After he says the wrong thing and her temper flares, he tries to calm her down. RECOMMENDATION: This is a good study to show a quick change of emotions between two characters. It discusses "whoring," a word essential to the development of the characters. ROYALTY: NA. SOURCE: Handman, Wynn. (1980). Modern American scenes for student actors. New York, NY: Bantam Books. SUBJECTS/PLAY TYPE: Prejudice; Morality; Scene.

1052. 8-12. (+) Anthony, C.L. **from Autumn Crocus.** CAST: 2f. ACTS: 1. SETTINGS: None. PLAYING TIME: NA. PLOT: While traveling, Fanny falls in love with a married man. Fanny's companion, Edith, tries to talk her out of a rash decision. RECOMMENDATION: This short scene raises moral questions about extramarital affairs, which could lead to thought provoking discussion. ROYALTY: NA. SOURCE: Olfson, Lewy. (1980). Fifty great scenes for student actors. New York, NY: Bantam Books. SUBJECTS/PLAY TYPE: Affairs, Extramarital; Scene.

1053. 8-12. (+) McNally, Terrence. **from Bad habits.** CAST: 1f, 1m. ACTS: 1. SETTINGS: Poolside. PLAYING TIME: NA. PLOT: April and Roy Pitts are two actors who have gone to a center for couples having marital problems. As they lie beside the pool working on their suntans, they exchange barbs about their careers and each other. RECOMMENDATION: This scene is designed purely for enjoyment as the two actors exchange personal insults. It includes some possibly objectionable language. ROYALTY: NA. SOURCE: Handman, Wynn. (1980). Modern American scenes for student actors. New York, NY: Bantam Books SUBJECTS/PLAY TYPE: Marital Problems; Egos; Comedy; Scene.

1054. 9-12. (+) Hauptman, William. **from Comanche cafe.** CAST: 2f. ACTS: 1. SETTINGS: Cafe. PLAYING TIME: NA. PLOT: In the 1930s, Ronnie, a young waitress at the Comanche Cafe, reveals her dream of leaving Oklahoma, the heart of the Dust Bowl. She tells her friend her distorted view of all the sections of the U.S. she intends to visit. For example, she will go to California because the movie stars walk into the drugstores and it never rains there. RECOMMENDATION: Many high school students could identify with this excellent monologue because they are so often dissatisfied with life in their own communities and want to explore. Many of them also share Ronnie's belief that life must be more glamorous or exciting in another location. ROYALTY: NA. SOURCE: Handmann, Wynn. (1980). Modern American scenes for student actors. New York, NY: Bantam Books. SUBJECTS/PLAY TYPE: Depression, American; Aspirations; Scene.

1055. 8-12. (+) Shakespeare, William. **from Cymbeline.** CAST: 1f, 1m. ACTS: 1. SETTINGS: Woods. PLAYING TIME: NA. PLOT: An unfaithful husband sends his servant, Pisanio, to kill his wife, Imogene. Pisanio tries to lure her into the woods by showing her a letter that states she was unfaithful to her husband. They both know that the letter is false, but Imogene realizes that life without her husband would be miserable, and she asks to be killed. Instead, Pisanio helps her to dress up as a man for a planned escape. RECOMMENDATION: The characters are both selfless and caring, and the language is faithful to the original. ROYALTY: NA. SOURCE: Olfson, Lewy. (1980). Fifty great scenes for student actors. New York, NY: Bantam Books. SUBJECTS/PLAY TYPE: Fidelity; Marriage; Scene.

1056. 10-12. (+) James, Henry. **from Daisy Miller.** CAST: 2m. ACTS: 1. SETTINGS: None. PLAYING TIME: NA. PLOT: Eugenio has been arranging meetings between Giovanelli and a young American heiress, Daisy Miller. He plans to press Giovanelli for money once he's married to Daisy. Without his help, Eugenio tells Giovanelli, there would be no chance for a marriage. Both Eugenio and Giovanelli are accomplished manipulators, and the naivete of American tourists makes it easy for them to play out their games. RECOMMENDATION: The dramatization of James's own novel is true to the original idea, as the two characters bargain for the future of the young heiress. ROYALTY: NA. SOURCE: Olfson, Lewy. (1980). Fifty great scenes for student actors. New York, NY: Bantam Books. SUBJECTS/PLAY TYPE: Social Mores; Expatriate Literature; Scene.

1057. 11-12. (+) Miller, Arthur. **from Death of a salesman.** CAST: 2m. ACTS: 1. SETTINGS: Bedroom. PLAYING TIME: NA. PLOT: Bif and Happy reminisce in their childhood bedroom. Neither brother is happy with his life. Bif feels that he never really grew up and Happy is not satisfied with his position at work. They discuss their father's disappointment in them and each blames the other for past failures. Bif wants Happy to join him on a ranch so, together, they can be successful. Happy almost acquiesces, but decides that first, he must best his present boss. Happy decides to join Biff after he is a success at his present job. RECOMMENDATION: The two characters show a deep sense of frustration and longing for success. The emotional drain of failure comes through in the dialogue, first as the two try to see where they failed, and then as each tries to put a better face on the future. ROYALTY: NA. SOURCE: Olfson, Lewy. (1980). Fifty great scenes for student actors. New York, NY: Bantam Books. SUBJECTS/PLAY TYPE: Frustration; Failure; Scene.

1058. 11-12. (+) Morley, Robert & Langley, Noel. **from Edward, my son.** CAST: 2m. ACTS: 1. SETTINGS: Office. PLAYING TIME: NA. PLOT: Harry Soames, released from jail, returns to his former place of employment to inquire about his old job. The two men discuss Soames' children and how they are being cared for. A significant moment occurs when Soames reveals that he sees his crime as no different than what other men get away with every day. The scene ends with Arnold putting Soames off as to their next meeting. As Soames leaves, he casts an insult at Arnold's character. RECOMMENDATION: Actors for this study of contrasting characters will need to project tension, wariness, and emotional sensitivity. ROYALTY: NA. SOURCE: Olfson, Lewy. (1980). Fifty great scenes for student actors. New York, NY: Bantam Books. SUBJECTS/PLAY TYPE: Ethics, Business; Scene.

1059. 12. (+) Stein, Joseph. (Reiner, Carl) **from Enter laughing (1963).** (Enter laughing) CAST: 1f, 1m. ACTS: 1. SETTINGS: Dressing room. PLAYING TIME: NA. PLOT: An aspiring actor flirts with an ingenue who considers herself far above him. When he showers her with compliments, she teases him with romantic poetry, and he clumsily responds with four lines from **Gunga Din.** He totally misses being her leading man and the scene ends with him as a tragic clown. RECOMMENDATION: This farce needs a seasoned director's polish in order to evoke the intended humor. Not for amateurs, this should only be used by students for practicing ranges of emotions. The leading lady must disrobe and dress before an audience. ROYALTY: NA. SOURCE: Handman, Wynn. (1980). Modern American scenes for student actors. New York, NY: Bantam Books. SUBJECTS/PLAY TYPE: Aspirations; Vanity; Scene.

1060. 10-12. (+) Mowatt, Anna Cora. **from Fashion.** CAST: 1f, 1m. ACTS: 1. SETTINGS: Sitting room. PLAYING TIME: NA. PLOT: In an argument between a husband and wife, the lifestyles of the rich and famous are satirized, as the wife is shown to be a slave to style and appearances. The husband represents the voice of rationality, as he mocks the shortcomings of living in this fashion. RECOMMENDATION: A razor sharp examination of fashion worshippers, this will generate discussion of the fashionable lifestyle. ROYALTY: NA. SOURCE: Olfson, Lewy. (1980). Fifty great scenes for student actors. New York, NY: Bantam Books. SUBJECTS/PLAY TYPE: Fashion; Marriage; Scene.

1061. 10-12. (-) Fornes, Maria Irene. **from Fefu and her friends.** CAST: 1f. ACTS: 1. SETTINGS: None. PLAYING TIME: NA. PLOT: At a reunion at Fefu's house, Paula talks about the resentment she felt when she had to work each summer while her friends vacationed in Europe. She tries to present her feelings rationally, but breaks down and has to leave. RECOMMENDATION: This will provide the actress with opportunity to begin speaking in a calm, rational manner and gradually lose control. ROYALTY: NA. SOURCE: Handman, Wynn. (1980). Modern American scenes for student actors. New York, NY: Bantam Books. SUBJECTS/PLAY TYPE: Friendship; Economic Classes; Scene.

1062. 9-12. (+) Feiffer, Jules. **from Feiffer's people.** CAST: 2m. ACTS: 1. SETTINGS: Street corner. PLAYING TIME: NA. PLOT: Harry, a young successful executive, meets his older, former co-worker, Eddie, on the street. A pompous Eddie gives Harry many unsolicited tips on getting ahead in the business world. When Harry admits that he is doing very well, Eddie asks about Harry's paycheck and becomes envious of his lifestyle. At the end of the scene, the positions are reversed and Eddie asks advice of Harry. RECOMMENDATION: This could be read in a psychology class or combined with other scenes depicting personality characteristics. ROYALTY: NA. SOURCE: Handman, Wynn. (1980). Modern American

scenes for student actors. New York, NY: Bantam Books. SUBJECTS/PLAY TYPE: Personality Traits; Scene.

1063. 5-12. (+) Rembrandt, Elaine. **From freedom to independence.** CAST: 3m, Su. ACTS: 1. SETTINGS: Bare stage. PLAYING TIME: 15 min. PLOT: Ancient Israelites and modern Israelis discuss oppression and the miracle that brought them freedom. Moses and Ben Gurion are paralleled as heroes of the Jewish people. RECOMMENDATION: This effectively pulls together Biblical times and modern day. ROYALTY: None. SOURCE: Rembrandt, Elaine. (1981). Heroes, heroines & holidays - plays for Jewish youth. Denver, CO: Alternatives in Religious Education, Inc. SUBJECTS/PLAY TYPE: Jewish Drama; Ben Gurion; David; Reader's Theater.

1064. 11-12. (+) Dean, Philip Hayes. **from Freeman.** CAST: 2m. ACTS: 1. SETTINGS: Kitchen. PLAYING TIME: NA. PLOT: Two black men converse. Rex, a doctor, congratulates his brother, Freeman, on the birth of his new son and offers to drive him to his new job. When Freeman denigrates his boss, Rex tells his brother just to do his job so that he can support his family. Freeman maintains that his brother has sold out to make a big salary. Finally, Rex asks his brother what skill he really possesses, and Freeman admits that he must take the job as a janitor. Freeman then says that the brothers' friendship is over. RECOMMENDATION: This could be used in an advanced level psychology or sociology class to stimulate a discussion of interpersonal relationships. This includes vulgar racist, and antihomosexual remarks. ROYALTY: NA. SOURCE: Handman, Wynn. (1980). Modern American scenes for student actors. New York, NY: Bantam Books. SUBJECTS/PLAY TYPE: Black Americans; Relationships; Scene.

1065. 6-12. (+) Dean, Phillip Hayes. **from Freeman.** CAST: 1f, 1m. ACTS: 1. SETTINGS: Living room. PLAYING TIME: NA. PLOT: Freeman dreams of great things for the future but is insufficiently educated and lacks the credentials necessary for advancement. He tells his wife, Osa Lee, who is happy in her secure, middle-class world, of his plans to build an expensive home and hire servants. When Osa Lee asks where the money would come from, Freeman only replies, "I'll get it." RECOMMENDATION: This would be useful to urge students to continue their education. ROYALTY: NA. SOURCE: Handman, Wynn. (1980). Modern American scenes for student actors. New York, NY: Bantam Books. SUBJECTS/PLAY TYPE: Aspirations; Education; Careers; Scene.

1066. 7-10. (+) Werfel, Franz. **from Goat song.** CAST: 1f, 1m. ACTS: 1. SETTINGS: Farmhouse. PLAYING TIME: NA. PLOT: When Mirko questions the fidelity of his betrothed, Stanja, she asks him about the small stone hut with the smoking chimney that he neglected to show her on his tour of his farm. Mirko realizes that he has not dared, for 20 years, to ask his father about its existence. RECOMMENDATION: This historical piece presents an enlightening view of social attitudes in Slavic countries.

ROYALTY: NA. SOURCE: Olfson, Lewy. (1980). Fifty great scenes for student actors. New York, NY: Bantam Books. SUBJECTS/PLAY TYPE: Marriage; Slavic Lifestyles; Scene.

1067. 6-12. (+) Douglas, Barry. **From hearse to eternity.** CAST: 1f, 3m. ACTS: 1. SETTINGS: Bare stage, props. PLAYING TIME: 20 min. PLOT: On their first day, two hearse drivers bungle the job, as they lose the funeral procession, and then can't find the directions to the cemetery. Bickering as to who's at fault, they hear a voice from the coffin. Expecting to find the old lady they were to bury, they find a young girl, who believes she is in heaven. She soon realizes that she hasn't been buried yet, has come out too early, and now cannot enter heaven to be with her husband. When a man runs up and apologizes for being late, the girl recognizes the man as her husband and discovers that she is indeed in a "heaven on earth." RECOMMENDATION: The quarrelsome hearse drivers keep the dialogue light and moving throughout the unlikely situation in which these two dolts find themselves. ROYALTY: Free to Plays subscribers. SOURCE: Douglas, Barry. (1976, January). From hearse to eternity. Plays: The Drama Magazine for Young People, pp. 13-20. SUBJECTS/PLAY TYPE: Heaven; Death; Comedy.

1068. 10-12. (-) Feiffer, Jules. **from Hold me.** CAST: 1m. ACTS: 1. SETTINGS: None. PLAYING TIME: NA. PLOT: A man talks about his life in four serio-comic monologues. "I Used to Read Them Ads" is about how his popularity increased when he changed brands of soap and toothpaste. In "Bread Crumbs," he reveals how his bad sense of direction caused him to leave a trail of bread crumbs everywhere he went. The problem of losing socks in the laundromat is discussed in "More Socks." And, in "Joey Wants to Scream," the man explains how he mentally announced his way through life. RECOMMENDATION: Using situations which are familiar to many people, these monologues express some of the humor and irony which can be found in our daily lives. ROYALTY: NA. SOURCE: Handman, Wynn. (1980). Modern American scenes for student actors. New York, NY: Bantam Books. SUBJECTS/PLAY TYPE: Popularity; Advertising; Laundromats; Scene.

1069. 9-12. (+) Feiffer, Jules. **from Hold me!** CAST: 2f. ACTS: 1. SETTINGS: Bare stage. PLAYING TIME: NA. PLOT: In the first monologue, a woman says her talking allows men to discover she is brighter than they, and they avoid her. Attracted to a man, she speaks more slowly and helps him to make one intelligent remark after another. Pleased with himself, he enjoys her companionship. Next, a woman admits that she was tired of her husband's companionship when he announced that he was going on a business trip. As time passed in his absence, she saw old friends and went out constantly. Then she tired of her friends and remembered why she had married Frank. She slept on his side of the bed and in the fourth week, she fell madly in love with him. But when he returned from his trip, she couldn't wait for him to take another trip, so she could love him again. RECOMMENDATION: These stories reveal the pain and confusion that real people

suffer. They would be very useful to read before a discussion of the roles of men and women in a psychology, sociology, or American history class. ROYALTY: NA. SOURCE: Handman, Wynn. (1980). Modern American scenes for student actors. New York, NY: Bantam Books. SUBJECTS/PLAY TYPE: Male and Female Roles; Scene.

1070. 9-12. (+) Bullins, Ed. **from House party.** CAST: 1f. ACTS: 1. SETTINGS: Bare stage. PLAYING TIME: NA. PLOT: A black woman tells about her hard life in modern day Harlem. She stood in line to get food stamps; she fought those who tried to cut into the food line, only to find that the food ran out, making people so angry they talked about stealing. She recalls past riots in Harlem and how most of the money of Harlem residents is spent in bars and liquor stores. She sadly notes that the church, once a powerful social institution in the black community, has lost influence among young blacks. Finally, she indicates the black community is being destroyed by liquor and dope. With relief, she mentions that she sent her son, Jimmy, to Texas for the summer. RECOMMENDATION: This is a moving portrayal of the problems which many blacks face in urban America. ROYALTY: NA. SOURCE: Handman, Wynn. (1980). Modern American scenes for student actors. New York, NY: Bantam Books. SUBJECTS/PLAY TYPE: Black Americans; Scene.

1071. 12. (+) van Druten, John. **from I am a camera.** CAST: 1f, 1m. ACTS: 1. SETTINGS: Dressing room. PLAYING TIME: NA. PLOT: Two people converse for the first time after a quarrel. Sally, who is hung over, tells Christopher that she has outgrown him and is leaving him. RECOMMENDATION: This scene could be used as an exercise to show Sally's change of character. The actress must dress before an audience. ROYALTY: NA. SOURCE: Handman, Wynn. (1978). Modern American scenes for student actors. New York, NY: Bantam Books. SUBJECTS/PLAY TYPE: Relationships; Scene.

1072. 10-12. (+) Van Druten, John. **from I am a camera.** CAST: 1f, 1m. ACTS: 1. SETTINGS: Apartment. PLAYING TIME: NA. PLOT: Chris and Sally say goodbye as Sally leaves for the Riviera to do a picture, and Chris leaves to write a novel. They part sadly, knowing they'll miss each other. RECOMMENDATION: In this scene, the emotions of friendship are explored. The excerpt is fairly short, though the female role has some short soliloquies. ROYALTY: NA. SOURCE: Olfson, Lewy. (1980). Fifty great scenes for student actors. New York, NY: Bantam Books. SUBJECTS/PLAY TYPE: Friendship; Scene.

1073. 9-12. (+) Patrick, Robert. **from Kennedy's children.** CAST: 1f. ACTS: 1. SETTINGS: Bar. PLAYING TIME: NA. PLOT: Wanda relives in great detail the day President Kennedy was assassinated. She was pasting captions on the bottoms of photos for "Salon Hair Styles" and regretting her tawdry affair with the stockroom fellow. The sales manager burst in and told all the employees to turn on the radio because the president had been shot in Dallas. Their hopes were raised by some broadcasts and dashed by others. A bawling, middle-aged man rushed into the office and screamed that it was a communist plot and the end of the world. In fact, the broadcasts indicated there might be a plot to kill all the top level politicians. As some stations kept predicting the president's recovery, all the church bells in New York started ringing. RECOMMENDATION: Reading this scene in an American history class would spark excellent class discussion, and it could also be effectively read in an English class to discuss the role of heroes as guides for our own lives. ROYALTY: NA. SOURCE: Handman, Wynn. (1980). Modern American scenes for student actors. New York, NY: Bantam Books. SUBJECTS/PLAY TYPE: Kennedy, Assassination; Scene.

1074. 9-12. (+) Shepard, Sam. **from La turista.** CAST: 1f, 2m. ACTS: 2. SETTINGS: Hotel room. PLAYING TIME: NA. PLOT: This is a conversation between two severely sunburned Americans on vacation in Mexico. The man has also fallen victim to dysentery. He describes spontaneous combustion as the worst level of sunburn. A young Mexican beggar boy enters the room and they hide from him. RECOMMENDATION: Although very abstract, Shepard's view of man and the universe might be appreciated by sophisticated audiences, especially if the scene is followed by directed discussion. ROYALTY: NA. SOURCE: Handman, Wynn. (1980). Modern American scenes for student actors. New York, NY: Bantam Books. SUBJECTS/PLAY TYPE: Sunburn; Scene.

1075. 11-12. (+) Shepard, Sam. **from La Turista.** CAST: 1f. ACTS: 1. SETTINGS: Bare stage. PLAYING TIME: NA. PLOT: Salem vividly recalls an occurrence when she was 10 years old. Her family had just travelled two hours in total silence. When they arrived home, Salem, her father, mother, sisters, and brothers started into the house. On the very top porch step Salem spit and her father stepped in it. Everyone immediately began to talk. In a show of authority, her father took off his belt and struck her across the ankles and knees. She collapsed on the porch. Silence descended. Her father put his belt back on and the procession went in the front door. Salem remained lying on the front porch, rubbing her injuries, and enjoying her solitude. RECOMMENDATION: This scene clearly depicts a dysfunctional family; the father's authority is maintained through violence. It could be read in a sociology class to stimulate discussion of child abuse or the roles of family members. ROYALTY: NA. SOURCE: Handman, Wynn. (1980). Modern American scenes for student actors. New York, NY: Bantam Books. SUBJECTS/PLAY TYPE: Family Relationships; Child Abuse; Scene.

1076. 11-12. (+) Stairs, Barrie. **from Lamp at midnight.** CAST: 2m. ACTS: 1. SETTINGS: Office. PLAYING TIME: NA. PLOT: Galileo hopes to get the Cardinal's stamp of approval on his new system of astronomy. When Cardinal Bellarmin decrees that this new theory of astronomy will destroy all that the church stands for, Galileo must submit to Church theology, and give up his own theory. RECOMMENDATION: The emotions that pass between the two men are highly charged because each is steeped in his own beliefs. ROYALTY: NA. SOURCE: Olfson, Lewy. (1980). Fifty great scenes for student actors. New York, NY: Bantam Books.

SUBJECTS/PLAY TYPE: Galileo; Theology, Catholic; Catholic Church; Scene.

1077. 9-12. (-) Frings, Ketti. (Wolfe, Thomas) **from Look homeward, angel.** (Look homeward, angel) CAST: 1f, 1m. ACTS: 1. SETTINGS: Bare stage. PLAYING TIME: NA. PLOT: A mother tells her son to disregard being spurned by his girlfriend and reminds him he soon will be leaving for college. He angrily says his mother's whole life has been dedicated to her boarders, tells her of his resentment of them and her, and says goodbye. RECOMMENDATION: This would be an excellent vehicle for young people to act out feelings of resentment. Both characters allow plenty of room for experimenting with feelings. Dialogue is fitting for both characters, sharp and professional. Eugene has a few long speeches. ROYALTY: NA. SOURCE: Handman, Wynn. (1980). Modern American scenes for student actors. New York, NY: Bantam Books. SUBJECTS/PLAY TYPE: Resentment; Leaving Home; Family Relationships; Scene.

1078. 9-12. (+) Wilson, Lanford. **from Ludlow fair.** CAST: 2f. ACTS: 1. SETTINGS: Bedroom. PLAYING TIME: NA. PLOT: In this stream-of-consciousness monologue, plain, shy Agnes admits that she is very nervous about going out to lunch with Charles. She is curling her hair just for him and will order whatever he does at the restaurant. She considers the pros and cons of his appearance and states that she desires to be married and have children. RECOMMENDATION: Many teenagers could identify with Agnes's desire to be popular and to be loved. This could be used by high school drama classes or as audition material for females. It could also be used in a home economics, sociology, or psychology class to stimulate a discussion on male-female relationships or personality traits. ROYALTY: NA. SOURCE: Handman, Wynn. (1980). Modern American scenes for student actors. New York, NY: Bantam Books. SUBJECTS/PLAY TYPE: Relationships; Scene.

1079. 8-12. (+) Anderson, Maxwell. **from Mary of Scotland.** CAST: 2f. ACTS: 1. SETTINGS: None. PLAYING TIME: NA. PLOT: Mary, Queen of Scots, speaks with Elizabeth I of England, her captor, and refuses to abdicate her throne. RECOMMENDATION: The powerful emotion and political rivalry depicted here will make this short dialogue a challenge for practicing actors. ROYALTY: NA. SOURCE: Olfson, Lewy. (1980). Fifty great scenes for student actors. New York, NY: Bantam Books. SUBJECTS/PLAY TYPE: Elizabeth I; Mary, Queen of Scots; Scene.

1080. 11-12. (+) Sexton, Anne. **from Mercy Street.** CAST: 1f. ACTS: 1. SETTINGS: Bare stage. PLAYING TIME: NA. PLOT: Tormented, Daisy searches for inner peace; she feels her soul is diseased. She is tired of being a woman and begs Jesus to release her from her body and give her back her soul. She also pleads with Him for forgiveness because she did not help some people who burned to death in a fire. RECOMMENDATION: This scene, written with the flowing imagery of a poem, could be riveting for a sophisticated audience. References to Daisy's flirtation with her own father and other references to Jesus and God could create problems. ROYALTY: NA. SOURCE: Handman, Wynn. (1980). Modern American scenes for student actors. New York, NY: Bantam Books. SUBJECTS/PLAY TYPE: Guilt; Scene.

1081. 11-12. (+) Williams, Tennessee. **from Orpheus descending.** CAST: 2f, 1m. ACTS: 1. SETTINGS: Room. PLAYING TIME: NA. PLOT: In the first monologue, Carol tells Val about her frustration with corrupt Southern society, her efforts to aid poor black farmers, the abuse she suffered, and the current apathy toward fighting social problems. In the second monologue, Lady tells Val that, in her youth, her family had a fig tree which seemed barren and dying. Suddenly it bore a small green fig and she was so overjoyed, she decorated the tree with Christmas ornaments. After years of being barren herself, now-pregnant Lady announces excitedly to Val that she, too, has beaten death. RECOMMENDATION: Tennessee Williams' two monologues portray vividly the desire of two women to feel alive and conquer death. The first monologue could be used effectively in an American history class to discuss race relations in the South before the 1960s. ROYALTY: NA. SOURCE: Handman, Wynn. (1980). Modern American scenes for student actors. New York, NY: Bantam Books. SUBJECTS/PLAY TYPE: Aspirations; Black History; Scene.

1082. 10-12. (+) Williams, Tennessee. **from Orpheus descending.** CAST: 1f, 1m. ACTS: 1. SETTINGS: Store. PLAYING TIME: NA. PLOT: A soda shop owner talks to a clerk who has just had a complaint registered against him. She threatens to fire him for behaving suggestively, but she calms down and they discuss relationships briefly. RECOMMENDATION: This short scene dealing with the physical aspect of human relationships would make an interesting repertoire addition. ROYALTY: NA. SOURCE: Olfson, Lewy. (1980). Fifty great scenes for student actors. New York, NY: Bantam Books. SUBJECTS/PLAY TYPE: Relationships; Trust; Scene.

1083. 7-12. (+) Gilbert, William Sullivan. **from Patience.** CAST: 1f, 1m. ACTS: 1. SETTINGS: None. PLAYING TIME: NA. PLOT: Patience is a young, humble dairy maid and Grosvenor is a young poet, the personification of perfection. The two fall in love, but resolve to part as the only solution to their dilemma: to monopolize Grosvenor with a relationship would be selfish, though there is no selfishness in Patience's love. As Grosvenor bids farewell, Patience convinces him that although she may not love him, there is no impropriety in his loving her. RECOMMENDATION: The point is made but, unfortunately, the music for this operetta, which allowed the profound subject to be effectively treated in a flippant manner, is not included. ROYALTY: NA. SOURCE: Olfson, Lewy. (1980). Fifty great scenes for student actors. New York, NY: Bantam Books. SUBJECTS/PLAY TYPE: Idealism; Love; Scene.

1084. 4-12. (+) Inge, William. **from Picnic.** CAST: 2f. ACTS: 1. SETTINGS: Porch; front yard. PLAYING TIME: NA. PLOT: Millie is delighted to have a date with muscular Hal for the Labor Day picnic. Her sister, Madge,

is unhappy to have a date with boring Alan Seymour. The two girls discuss their dates and rumors about another girl. RECOMMENDATION: This interesting scene illustrates sibling rivalry and how discussion between two siblings often only hints at signs of caring or support. ROYALTY: NA. SOURCE: Handman, Wynn. (1980). Modern American scenes for student actors. New York, NY: Bantam Books. SUBJECTS/PLAY TYPE: Sibling Rivalry; Scene.

1085. 10-12. (+) Jerome, Helen. **from Pride and prejudice.** CAST: 2f. ACTS: 1. SETTINGS: Parlor. PLAYING TIME: NA. PLOT: Lady Catherine confronts Elizabeth Bennet about Elizabeth's engagement to her nephew. She expects Elizabeth to shrink from her haughty accusations and entanglements with Darcy. Instead, Elizabeth banters with, and soon infuriates, the older woman. Elizabeth does not concede, and Lady Catherine is shocked at being bested by a younger woman. RECOMMENDATION: The language is true to the spirit and tone of Austen's original, as two strong characters battle for their pride. ROYALTY: NA. SOURCE: Olfson, Lewy. (1980). 50 great scenes for student actors. New York, NY: Bantam Books. SUBJECTS/PLAY TYPE: Vanity; Class Consciousness; Scene.

1086. 8-12. (+) Shakespeare, William. **from Romeo and Juliet.** CAST: 2f. ACTS: 1. SETTINGS: None. PLAYING TIME: NA. PLOT: In an exchange between Juliet and her nurse, we learn that Romeo has just slain Juliet's cousin Tybalt in a duel. RECOMMENDATION: While offering an authentic excerpt of Shakespearean drama, this short scene also presents an interesting dilemma on loyalty. ROYALTY: NA. SOURCE: Olfson, Lewy. (1980). Fifty great scenes for student actors. New York, NY: Bantam Books. SUBJECTS/PLAY TYPE: Loyalty; Scene.

1087. 8-12. (+) Rattigan, Terence. **from Separate tables.** CAST: 2f. ACTS: 1. SETTINGS: None. PLAYING TIME: NA. PLOT: Sibyl is comforted by Miss Cooper, a hotel employee, after learning the shocking truth about the Major, a hotel guest with whom she'd been friends. RECOMMENDATION: Though short, there are powerful emotions conveyed in this scene which will challenge practicing young actors. ROYALTY: NA. SOURCE: Olfson, Lewy. (1980). Fifty great scenes for student actors. New York, NY: Bantam Books. SUBJECTS/PLAY TYPE: Self Acceptance; Scene.

1088. 11-12. (+) Levinson, Alfred. **from Socrates wounded.** CAST: 2f. ACTS: 1. SETTINGS: Yard. PLAYING TIME: NA. PLOT: After a battle, Socrates returns home a hero. Xanthippe, Socrates' wife, does not think of him as a war hero so much as just her husband: a man with all the faults of other men. Hera and Xanthippe exchange anecdotes about their husbands and gossip about their lives. RECOMMENDATION: In modern, clever dialogue, the two women complain about their lives. ROYALTY: NA. SOURCE: Olfson, Lewy. (1980). Fifty great scenes for student actors. New York, NY: Bantam Books. SUBJECTS/PLAY TYPE: Greece, Ancient; Philosophy; Scene.

1089. 7-12. (+) Hellman, Lillian. from The autumn garden. CAST: 2f. ACTS: 1. SETTINGS: Living room. PLAYING TIME: NA. PLOT: Sophie comes to the U. S. to live with her aunt and uncle, Nina and Nick. She is unhappy and wants to go home to France. The previous night, Nick got drunk and made advances toward her before falling asleep on her bed. Sophie tries to use this incident to blackmail Nina for enough money to return to France. Nina agrees to give her the money but wishes to call it a gift, while Sophie insists on calling it blackmail money. They debate this use of terminology to no obvious conclusion. RECOMMENDATION: This realistic scene illustrates how the need for self-respect can affect actions. Young Sophie harbors no illusions about her life and only wants to go back to France, but middle-aged Nina wishes to maintain the illusion of a perfect marriage. ROYALTY: NA. SOURCE: Handman, Wynn. (1980). Modern American scenes for student actors. New York, NY: Bantam Books. SUBJECTS/PLAY TYPE: Self-Respect; Illusions; Scene.

1090. 12. (+) Hellman, Lillian. from The autumn garden. CAST: 2f. ACTS: 1. SETTINGS: None. PLAYING TIME: NA. PLOT: Sophie, a young French girl, has been compromised by Mr. Deney. Since Mrs. Deney and her husband have reconciled, the wife hopes to assuage her conscience by paying Sophie $5,000. Sophie calls it blackmail money, since she needs to feel vindicated. Sophie and Mrs. Deney banter about the money and the seriousness of the conflict. The scene ends angrily, but with Sophie gaining the upper hand. RECOMMENDATION: The characters are very much Hellman creations. Sophie is at once naive and cunning when she sets Mrs. Deney up and gains the advantage. ROYALTY: NA. SOURCE: Olfson, Lewy. (1980). Fifty great scenes for student actors. New York, NY: Bantam Books. SUBJECTS/PLAY TYPE: Social Conflict; Scene.

1091. 10-12. (+) Hellman, Lillian. from The autumn garden. CAST: 1f, 1m. ACTS: 1. SETTINGS: None. PLAYING TIME: NA. PLOT: Constance and Ned have always loved each other, but neither said so. Now that their lives have passed by, they blame their failures on the fact that they've lied to themselves for too long. Constance proposes to Ned, but he turns her down and they resign themselves to separate lives. RECOMMENDATION: Although a little weak by itself, this may serve as a good practice scene for a drama group. ROYALTY: NA. SOURCE: Olfson, Lewy. (1980). Fifty great scenes for student actors. New York, NY: Bantam Books. SUBJECTS/PLAY TYPE: Marriage; Loneliness; Scene.

1092. 12. (+) Albee, Edward. from The ballad of the sad cafe. CAST: 1f, 1m. ACTS: 1. SETTINGS: Porch. PLAYING TIME: NA. PLOT: A young man proposes marriage to a very cool and distant young woman. He explains he is a reformed man, with some money and property. She accepts, but obviously the property has won her over, not the man. RECOMMENDATION: The pauses, gestures, and other body language make this scene strong. ROYALTY: NA. SOURCE: Handman, Wynn. (1980). Modern American scenes for student actors. New York, NY: Bantam Books. SUBJECTS/PLAY TYPE: Love; Materialism; Marriage; Scene.

1093. 11-12. (+) de Beaumarchais, Pierre-Augustin Caron. from The barber of Seville. CAST: 2m. ACTS: 1. SETTINGS: None. PLAYING TIME: NA. PLOT: A Count has fallen in love with a physician's young ward. Rosine is kept locked away by the doctor, who seeks to marry her himself. Figaro gains access to the doctor's house disguised as a servant, and helps the Count pursue Rosine. RECOMMENDATION: Figaro, as a comical master of all trades, and Rosine's craftiness in getting past her guardian will interest students. ROYALTY: NA. SOURCE: Olfson, Lewy. (1980). Fifty great scenes for student actors. New York, NY: Bantam Books. SUBJECTS/PLAY TYPE: Satire; Women's Rights; Scene.

1094. 12. (+) Perelman, S.J. from The beauty part (1961). CAST: 1f, 1m. ACTS: 1. SETTINGS: Living room. PLAYING TIME: NA. PLOT: A young man tells his artistic, shallow girlfriend of his intentions to become an artist, because he thinks that will please her. When she finds he is penniless, she drops him because she is interested only in money. RECOMMENDATION: The dialogue defines the characters and their relationships well. ROYALTY: NA. SOURCE: Handman, Wynn. (1980). Modern American scenes for student actors. New York, NY: Bantam Books. SUBJECTS/PLAY TYPE: Shallowness; Materialism; Scene.

1095. 9-12. (+) Tesich, Steve. from The carpenters. CAST: 1f, 1m. ACTS: 1. SETTINGS: Kitchen. PLAYING TIME: NA. PLOT: In this conversation, a man is positive his son has a bomb in the basement and he believes that his whole family is against him. His wife informs him he is ruining the family routine now that he is allowed to come home on weekdays. RECOMMENDATION: This scene is best suited for mature audiences, followed by directed discussion. ROYALTY: NA. SOURCE: Handman, Wynn. (1980). Modern American scenes for student actors. New York, NY: Bantam Books. SUBJECTS/PLAY TYPE: Family; Generation Gap; Scene.

1096. 11-12. (+) Bagnold, Enid. from The chalk garden. CAST: 2f. ACTS: 1. SETTINGS: Living room. PLAYING TIME: NA. PLOT: A governess and her young charge pry into each other's lives and secrets. The governess has been tried for murder, while the youngster was allegedly an assault victim. They both wish to keep their own secrets. RECOMMENDATION: The scene is intense. What might pass for banter in another play has great depth here. ROYALTY: NA. SOURCE: Olfson, Lewy. (1980). Fifty great scenes for student actors. New York, NY: Bantam Books. SUBJECTS/PLAY TYPE: Relationships; Allegory; Scene.

1097. 10-12. (+) Maugham, W. Somerset. from The circle. CAST: 1f, 1m. ACTS: 1. SETTINGS: Parlor. PLAYING TIME: NA. PLOT: A spoiled young woman asks her preoccupied husband for a divorce, but he refuses. He claims to still love her and says divorce would ruin his career. RECOMMENDATION: This excerpt from a British social drama is packed with emotional fireworks, despite its restraint. It portrays the strain in a dissolving marriage and would be an excellent choice as a practice skit for a teenaged acting troupe or as part of a discussion on marital problems. ROYALTY: NA. SOURCE: Olfson, Lewy. (1980). Fifty great scenes for student actors. New York, NY: Bantam Books. SUBJECTS/PLAY TYPE: Divorce; Scene.

1098. 12. (+) Miller, Arthur. from The crucible. CAST: 1f, 1m. ACTS: 1. SETTINGS: Dark stage. PLAYING TIME: NA. PLOT: To win Proctor, Abigail, 17, has had his wife brought to trial for witchcraft. Abigail and Proctor meet outside in the dark, as he tries to persuade her to withdraw the charges. She angrily refuses, claiming that the hypocrites have won him over. Although Procter warns her he will tell of their adultery in court, Abigail still refuses to recant. RECOMMENDATION: This is an excellent study of a tortured man and his former paramour during the Salem witch trials. ROYALTY: NA. SOURCE: Handman, Wynn. (1980). Modern American scenes for student actors. New York, NY: Bantam Books. SUBJECTS/PLAY TYPE: Guilt; Love; Scene.

1099. 11-12. (+) Hochhuth, Rolf. from The deputy. CAST: 2m. ACTS: 1. SETTINGS: Reception room. PLAYING TIME: NA. PLOT: At the Papal Legation, the Nuncio is upset because the Pope refuses to stand against Hitler and against the persecution and murder of the Jews. After trying to communicate his feelings to a young priest new to Rome, the Nuncio reaches a point of no return on his stance opposing the Vatican. RECOMMENDATION: This scene demonstrates the frustration that is felt by an honorable person who sees basic values challenged by an uncaring religious leader. ROYALTY: NA. SOURCE: Olfson, Lewy. (1980). Fifty great scenes for student actors. New York, NY: Bantam Books. SUBJECTS/PLAY TYPE: Jews, Persecution; Catholic Church, Concorda; Values; Scene.

1100. 11-12. (+) Sheridan, Richard Brinsley. from The duenna. CAST: 2m. ACTS: 1. SETTINGS: Piazza. PLAYING TIME: NA. PLOT: Ferdinand and Isaac discuss Clara, the girl Ferdinand loves. When Ferdinand learns that Isaac has just left Clara in the arms of her true love, Antonio, the two men discuss why Clara would want to marry Antonio, and they part as enemies because of Isaac's interference. RECOMMENDATION: The scene is taut with emotion and the language is appropriate to the time period. ROYALTY: NA. SOURCE: Olfson, Lewy. (1980). Fifty great scenes for student actors. New York, NY: Bantam Books. SUBJECTS/PLAY TYPE: Lover's Triangle; Scene.

1101. 9-12. (+) Zindel, Paul. from The effect of gamma rays on man-in-the-moon marigolds. CAST: 2f. ACTS: 1. SETTINGS: Garage. PLAYING TIME: NA. PLOT: Tillie prepares for the high school's science fair to display her project, some Man-in-the-Moon Marigolds. Ruth, Tillie's jealous older sister, wants her to fail and tries to make Tillie feel insecure about herself and their mother, an eccentric who wears outlandish outfits. As the fair draws near, Ruth shows her insecurity as she begs Tillie to give

her a pet rabbit that belongs to both girls, and Tillie agrees. RECOMMENDATION: This could prompt discussions about sibling rivalry, self esteem, and jealousy, if references to boiling the skin off a cat for a science project don't sidetrack the audience. ROYALTY: NA. SOURCE: Handman, Wynn. (1980). Modern American scenes for student actors. New York, NY: Bantam Books. SUBJECTS/PLAY TYPE: Sibling Rivalry; Insecurity; Self Esteem; Scene.

1102. 9-12. (+) Ribman, Ronald. (Turgenev, Ivan) from The journey of the fifth horse. (Diary of a superfluous man) CAST: 1f, 1m. ACTS: 1. SETTINGS: Park. PLAYING TIME: NA. PLOT: A lonely young woman, filled with childish romantic fantasies, attempts to get a lonely man to take part in one of her fantasies. He refuses to play the role and doesn't understand her pain. RECOMMENDATION: This emotionally powerful scene depicts the futility of some relationships, as well as the treatment of women in 19th century Russia. ROYALTY: NA. SOURCE: Handman, Wynn. (1978). Modern American scenes for student actors. New York, NY: Bantam Books. SUBJECTS/PLAY TYPE: Frustration; Isolation; Women's Rights; Scene.

1103. 8-12. (+) Parker, Dorothy & D'Usseau, Arnaud. from The ladies of the corridor. CAST: 2f. ACTS: 1. SETTINGS: None. PLAYING TIME: NA. PLOT: Despondently, Lulu waits for Paul to come to dinner, when Connie arrives and tries to cheer her out of her depression. RECOMMENDATION: This short, poignant scene will provide excellent practice for young actors. ROYALTY: NA. SOURCE: Olfson, Lewy. (1980). Fifty great scenes for student actors. New York, NY: Bantam Books. SUBJECTS/PLAY TYPE: Depression; Scene.

1104. 11-12. (+) Ibsen Henrik. from The master builder. CAST: 2m. ACTS: 1. SETTINGS: None. PLAYING TIME: NA. PLOT: Before he dies, Mr. Brovik wishes to see his son, Ragnar, become a well married, successful architect. Mr. Solness, who worked his way up in Brovik's company, is dismayed because he wishes to keep the reins of power in his own hands. RECOMMENDATION: This offers good dialogue that gets quickly to the theme of the scene. ROYALTY: NA. SOURCE: Olfson, Lewy. (1980). Fifty great scenes for student actors. New York, NY: Bantam Books. SUBJECTS/PLAY TYPE: Family Relationships; Power Struggles; Scene.

1105. 9-12. (+) Simon, Neil. from The odd couple. CAST: 2m. ACTS: 1. SETTINGS: Apartment. PLAYING TIME: NA. PLOT: Best friends share an apartment because they are separated from their wives. Felix is nervous and meticulous, while Oscar is laid back and sloppy. Felix, who loves to cook, brings a plate of spaghetti into the dining room. The two have an argument that ends with bickering, spaghetti on the wall, hurt feelings, and Felix leaving. RECOMMENDATION: The contrasting personalities of Felix and Oscar would provide laughs for a teenage audience, who would be able to relate this scene to experiences in their own lives. This contains some questionable language, as well as a reference to phenobarbital. **ROYALTY:** NA. **SOURCE:** Handman, Wynn. (1980). *Modern American scenes for student actors.* New York, NY: Bantam Books. **SUBJECTS/PLAY TYPE:** Relationships; Scene.

1106. 11-12. (+) Lowell, Robert. **from The old glory.** **CAST:** 5m. **ACTS:** 1. **SETTINGS:** Ship's deck. **PLAYING TIME:** NA. **PLOT:** The captain of a 19th century ship converses with his young, puritanical bosun, John Perkins. He tries to get Perkins to accept all of his own prejudices and beliefs, such as raising American slaves to white man's level by intermarriage, and deeming education as unnecessary. Perkins, on the other hand, is upset by Jefferson's affair with a black woman, favors abolition of slavery, and dislikes both Spaniards and Catholics. Finally, the captain dictates that the young man take up smoking, stop worrying about his family, and support the new president, Thomas Jefferson. **RECOMMENDATION:** This historically accurate scene, descriptively written in verse, presents many of the social and political biases of Americans in the early 1800s through lively, well drawn characters. **ROYALTY:** NA. **SOURCE:** Handman, Wynn. (1980). *Modern American scenes for student actors.* New York, NY: Bantam Books. **SUBJECTS/PLAY TYPE:** Slavery; Prejudice; Scene.

1107. 11-12. (+) Vanbrugh, Sir John. **from The relapse.** **CAST:** 2m. **ACTS:** 1. **SETTINGS:** None. **PLAYING TIME:** NA. **PLOT:** Brothers, Foppington and Fashion, whose frivolity and decadence reflect their society, talk of love affairs and women, neither of which Foppington esteems highly. An argument over Fashion's request for 500 pounds from his brother ends with Foppington's verbal slap at his brother. **RECOMMENDATION:** The dialogue should be delivered with British accents and the characters will need to be careful not to be overly foppish and effeminate. **ROYALTY:** NA. **SOURCE:** Olfson, Lewy. (1980). *Fifty great scenes for students.* New York, NY: Bantam Books. **SUBJECTS/PLAY TYPE:** Satire; Scene.

1108. 6-8. (+) Sherwood, Robert. **from The road to Rome. CAST:** 1f, 1m. **ACTS:** 1. **SETTINGS:** None. **PLAYING TIME:** NA. **PLOT:** In an ethical debate, Hannibal is persuaded by his Roman lover, Amytis, to spare Rome, not as a bribe to her, but to prove that he is a great man who believes that destruction is a waste. **RECOMMENDATION:** The theme of pacifism comes through in this short skit, despite the melodrama. **ROYALTY:** NA. **SOURCE:** Olfson, Lewy. (1980). *50 great scenes for student actors.* New York, NY: Bantam Books. **SUBJECTS/PLAY TYPE:** Ethics; Hannibal; Rome; Scene.

1109. 10-12. (+) Behrman, S.N. **from The second man.** **CAST:** 2f, 2m. **ACTS:** 3. **SETTINGS:** Apartment. **PLAYING TIME:** NA. **PLOT:** In a confusing love quadrangle, a widow loves a writer, and a scientist loves a lady named Miss Grey. The widow and writer await the arrival of the scientist and Miss Grey. When the scientist discovers Miss Grey's scarf in the writer's apartment, they discuss how confusing emotions can be and conclude by agreeing that it would be nice if people were more like science: predictable. **RECOMMENDATION:** This play would appeal to young adults due to its exploration of the

emotional relationship between friends and romantic partners, a situation with which the audience could easily identify. **ROYALTY:** NA. **SOURCE:** Olfson, Lewy. (1980). *Fifty great scenes for student actors.* New York, NY: Bantam Books. **SUBJECTS/PLAY TYPE:** Affairs; Relationships; Scene.

1110. 11-12. (+) Bergman, Ingmar. **from The seventh seal. CAST:** 2m. **ACTS:** 1. **SETTINGS:** Church. **PLAYING TIME:** NA. **PLOT:** Squire Jons enters the church and finds a painter at work on a fresco that represents the Dance of Death. The painter wants to frighten people. Asked if he is attempting to make people atone and seek the church's teachings, the painter answers that he paints life as it is. The painter feels he will eventually die of plague, which he then describes, causing Jons to think about frightening aspects of life and death. **RECOMMENDATION:** This gloomy scene, as it delineates the possibilities for death and sin, is emotional and dark drama. **ROYALTY:** NA. **SOURCE:** Olfson, Lewy. (1980). *Fifty scenes for student actors.* New York, NY: Bantam Books. **SUBJECTS/PLAY TYPE:** Middle Ages; Crusades; Scene.

1111. 10-12. (+) Rattigan, Terrance. **from The Sleeping Prince. CAST:** 1f, 1m. **ACTS:** 1. **SETTINGS:** Apartment. **PLAYING TIME:** NA. **PLOT:** A young actress and a prince discuss the end of their affair. They acknowledge the childishness of the situation, but part fondly and maturely. **RECOMMENDATION:** This short scene will be a challenge to perform without lapsing into over exaggeration. **ROYALTY:** NA. **SOURCE:** Olfson, Lewy. (1980). *Fifty great scenes for student actors.* New York, NY: Bantam Books. **SUBJECTS/PLAY TYPE:** Royalty; Relationships; Scene.

1112. 9-12. (+) Simon, Neil. **from The star-spangled girl. CAST:** 1f, 2m. **ACTS:** 1. **SETTINGS:** Apartment. **PLAYING TIME:** NA. **PLOT:** In this soliloquy, Sophie tells her neighbor Norman that she is tired of his attention. He tried to carry her suitcase, but dropped it down five flights of stairs. Then he left chocolate bars in her mailbox which melted and ruined three letters. After recounting several of these disastrous episodes, Sophie tells Norman to leave her "ay-lone." **RECOMMENDATION:** This humorous scene focuses on the universal theme of a man falling so hard for a beautiful girl that he is willing to do anything to win her love. Sophie must be played with a convincing Southern accent. **ROYALTY:** NA. **SOURCE:** Handman, Wynn. (1980). *Modern American scenes for student actors.* New York, NY: Bantam Books. **SUBJECTS/PLAY TYPE:** Love; Romance; Scene.

1113. 7-12. (+) Serling, Rod. **from The strike. CAST:** 2m. **ACTS:** 1. **SETTINGS:** Battlefield post. **PLAYING TIME:** NA. **PLOT:** Major Gaylord has sent 20 of Lt. Jones' men to locate and determine the strength of the enemy. When Lt. Jones learns about the order and that the men have probably been captured or killed, he wants to form a second patrol to look for them. When Major Gaylord refuses, Jones tries to make Major Gaylord feel guilty about his decision and change his mind, but he fails. **RECOMMENDATION:** This scene by the well known host of TV's "Twilight Zone" points out the emotional stress involved in wartime decisions. The two points of view reveal that personal convictions are sometimes set aside in desperate situations. ROYALTY: NA. SOURCE: Handman, Wynn. (1980). Modern American scenes for student actors. New York, NY: Bantam Books. SUBJECTS/PLAY TYPE: War; Guilt; Scene.

1114. 10-12. (+) Saroyan, William. from The time of your life. CAST: 1f, 1m. ACTS: 1. SETTINGS: Bar. PLAYING TIME: NA. PLOT: Two strangers in a bar discuss the disappointments they have dealt with in former relationships and how life mostly consists of waiting. They part, but remain joined by a emotional bond. RECOMMENDATION: Many poignant subjects are blended together: unhappy relationships, loneliness, and love. ROYALTY: NA. SOURCE: Olfson, Lewy. (1980). Fifty great scenes for student actors. New York, NY: Bantam Books. SUBJECTS/PLAY TYPE: Loneliness; Relationships; Scene.

1115. 10-12. (+) Shakespeare, William. from The two gentlemen of Verona. CAST: 2m. ACTS: 1. SETTINGS: None. PLAYING TIME: NA. PLOT: The scene opens with a play on words shared by two clowning servants. Each tries to outdo the other in stretching a point to reach a joke and they become excited over a rhymed letter and the questions it poses. At scene's end, one learns that the other has failed to inform him he is wanted at the gate by his master. RECOMMENDATION: Witty repartee between the two servants is matched by their grasp of a bit of comedy and a joke, and results in a light, frivolous scene. ROYALTY: NA. SOURCE: Olfson, Lewy. (1980). Fifty great scenes for student actors. New York, NY: Bantam Books. SUBJECTS/PLAY TYPE: Comedy; Scene.

1116. 12. (+) Coward, Neil. from The vortex. CAST: 2f. ACTS: 1. SETTINGS: Bedroom. PLAYING TIME: NA. PLOT: Helen attempts to comfort her hysterical friend, Florence, over the loss of a man named Tom. They discuss the "other woman" and the past life that has made her frivolous. Helen, the more stable of the two, wishes that Florence was more capable of emotion and real love, but knows she will never change. RECOMMENDATION: The dialogue, while seemingly frivolous, is emotionally charged, reflecting a decadent society concerned only with its own pleasure. ROYALTY: NA. SOURCE: Olfson, Lewy. (1980). Fifty great scenes for student actors. New York, NY: Bantam Books. SUBJECTS/PLAY TYPE: Social Conflict; Vanity; Scene.

1117. 11-12. (+) Anouilh, Jean. from The waltz of the toreadors. CAST: 2m. ACTS: 1. SETTINGS: Study. PLAYING TIME: NA. PLOT: The General complains about his wife who is always "ill," his shallow daughters, and a life which he now sees as futile and set against him. RECOMMENDATION: This serious satire of marriage and the passage of time will be better understood if the entire play is read. ROYALTY: NA. SOURCE: Olfson, Lewy. (1980). Fifty great scenes for student actors. New York, NY: Bantam Books. SUBJECTS/PLAY TYPE: Satire; Marriage; Life; Scene.

1118. 10-12. (+) Congreve, William. from The way of the world. CAST: 1f, 1m. ACTS: 1. SETTINGS: Sitting room. PLAYING TIME: NA. PLOT: Mr. Mirabell and Mrs. Millament discuss conditions for their marriage. Mrs. Millament insists upon having a continuous courtship, respect in public, freedom of speech, and privacy after their wedding. Mr. Mirabell agrees, as long as she has no women friends and refrains from using facial masks or alcohol. Though somewhat displeased with the arrangements, they plan to wed. RECOMMENDATION: This skit broaches the subject of marriage and prenuptial agreements using the elegant but circuitous language of the 18th century. ROYALTY: NA. SOURCE: Olfson, Lewy. (1980). Fifty great scenes for student actors. New York, NY: Bantam Books. SUBJECTS/PLAY TYPE: Marriage; Prenuptial Agreements; Scene.

1119. 12. (+) Boothe, Clare. from The women. CAST: 2f. ACTS: 1. SETTINGS: Beauty salon. PLAYING TIME: NA. PLOT: Olga, a manicurist, talks as Mary tries to read. Olga tells Mary about an extra-marital affair Stephen Haines is having with Olga's friend, Crystal Allen. At scene's end, we learn that Mary is, in fact, Mrs. Stephen Haines and has just learned of her husband's affair. RECOMMENDATION: The dialogue is carried almost solely by Olga, who must convey a lack of intelligence in a gossipy manner. ROYALTY: NA. SOURCE: Olfson, Lewy. (1980). Fifty great scenes for student actors. New York, NY: Bantam Books. SUBJECTS/PLAY TYPE: Affairs, Extramarital; Social Conflict; Gossip; Scene.

1120. 10-12. (-) Chin, Frank. from The year of the dragon. CAST: 1m. ACTS: 1. SETTINGS: None. PLAYING TIME: NA. PLOT: From a play dealing with the problems of Chinese-American families struggling for identity, this is an interchange between Fred, 40, and his father, 60. Fred tries to help his father understand him by relating an incident in which Fred met a former classmate. RECOMMENDATION: Fred's speech reveals the anguish and sense of loss he feels when he realizes his father's dominance and his own insecurity have caused him to waste his life. ROYALTY: NA. SOURCE: Handman, Wynn. (1980). Modern American scenes for student actors. New York, NY: Bantam Books. SUBJECTS/PLAY TYPE: Chinese-Americans; Fathers and Sons; Scene.

1121. 10-12. (+) Albee, Edward. from The zoo story. CAST: 1u. ACTS: 1. SETTINGS: Bench. PLAYING TIME: NA. PLOT: Jerry meets a stranger in Central Park and tells him his story. His mother ran off with another man when he was ten and she died a year later. Two weeks afterwards, his dad died in an automobile accident. He moved in with his dour aunt, and she dropped dead on the afternoon of his high school graduation. RECOMMENDATION: Jerry's speech expresses the agitation and bitterness of a young man about to take his own life. The dialogue is stark and realistic. ROYALTY: NA. SOURCE: Handman, Wynn. (1980). Modern American scenes for student actors. New York, NY: Bantam Books. SUBJECTS/PLAY TYPE: Family Relationships; Death; Scene.

1122. 8-10. (+) Albee, Edward. **from The zoo story.** CAST: 2m. ACTS: 1. SETTINGS: Park. PLAYING TIME: NA. PLOT: Jerry, a "permanent transient," has decided he wishes to die and walks to Central Park, where he meets Peter. Jerry starts an argument with Peter in an attempt to get Peter to fight and, he hopes, kill him. Jerry has tossed a knife in Peter's direction and, as Peter holds the knife for self defense purposes, Jerry intentionally impales himself on the knife and dies. RECOMMENDATION: The scene is compellingly and energetically written. The unusual nature of this "suicide" is thought provoking and should be a source of further discussion. ROYALTY: NA. SOURCE: Handman, Wynn. (1980). Modern American scenes for student actors. New York, NY: Bantam Books. SUBJECTS/PLAY TYPE: Suicide; Death; Scene.

1123. 11-12. (+) Glaspell, Susan. **from Trifles.** CAST: 2f. ACTS: 1. SETTINGS: Kitchen. PLAYING TIME: NA. PLOT: Mrs. Hale and Mrs. Peters have come to the farmhouse following the murder of farmer John Wright. Wright's wife is suspected, and the women discuss a connection between the dead bird kept by the farmer's wife, and the dead farmer. Their conversation includes macabre details of other deaths or murders, discussed in hushed tones of conspiracy and secrecy, and the scene ends with the women blaming themselves for not calling on Mrs. Wright. RECOMMENDATION: There is much mystery here as clues to a murder are sought in the stark and cold setting. ROYALTY: NA. SOURCE: Olfson, Lewy. (1980). Fifty great scenes for student actors. New York, NY: Bantam Books. SUBJECTS/PLAY TYPE: Family Conflict; Murder; Scene.

1124. 11-12. (+) Chekov, Anton. **from Uncle Vanya.** CAST: 2f. ACTS: 1. SETTINGS: None. PLAYING TIME: NA. PLOT: Yelena (the wife of Sonya's father) and Sonya talk about the doctor, whom they both love. Each woman speaks of her unhappiness, but neither communicates her true feelings. The two try to come to an understanding and apologize for past mistakes and emotional upheaval. They seek to be honest about their feelings, but neither can bear the feeling of love the other feels for the doctor. RECOMMENDATION: In this emotionally taut scene, the two women converse without actually communicating. ROYALTY: NA. SOURCE: Olfson, Lewy. (1980). Fifty great scenes for student actors. New York, NY: Bantam Books. SUBJECTS/PLAY TYPE: Communication; Scene.

1125. 10-12. (+) Chekov, Anton. **from Uncle Vanya.** CAST: 1f, 1m. ACTS: 1. SETTINGS: Courtyard. PLAYING TIME: NA. PLOT: Yelena and Astrov are parting forever. Although once strongly attached to one another, they could never wed, since Yelena was already married. Astrov now realizes the destructive influences Yelena and her husband had on him and the town, and he is glad they are leaving. RECOMMENDATION: Although brief, this segment contains powerful emotions, and should make an excellent practice piece for young actors. ROYALTY: NA. SOURCE: Olfson, Lewy. (1980). Fifty great scenes for student actors. New York, NY: Bantam Books. SUBJECTS/PLAY TYPE: Affairs, Extramarital; Departures; Scene.

1126. 10-12. (+) Heller, Joseph. **from We bombed in New Haven.** CAST: 2m. ACTS: 1. SETTINGS: Bare stage. PLAYING TIME: NA. PLOT: An authoritarian, paranoid Major tells his subordinate Captain Starkey to locate a deserter named Henderson so he can kill him. Starkey, a compassionate man, questions this order and threatens to quit. The major, who is confident of his authority, calls Starkey's bluff, and the captain reluctantly enforces the order. RECOMMENDATION: In this brief but powerful anti-war protest, the audience would become emotionally involved because the actors step out of their parts to address them directly. Strongly expressed emotions of anxiety, weariness, despair, shame, and resentment will encourage students to examine their own moral values. This could open a discussion of the Holocaust in an American, European, or World History class. ROYALTY: NA. SOURCE: Handman, Wynn. (1980). Modern American scenes for student actors. New York, NY: Bantam Books. SUBJECTS/PLAY TYPE: War; Values; Scene.

1127. 10-12. (+) Milner, Ronald. **from Who's got his own.** CAST: 1m. ACTS: 1. SETTINGS: None. PLAYING TIME: NA. PLOT: Tim returns home for the funeral of his abusive father. He talks to his mother about his feelings of hatred for his father and describes an incident of abuse from his childhood. RECOMMENDATION: As an early work in the black theater movement of the 1960s, this play helped raise the consciousness of both black and white audiences. The scene focuses on Tim's rage and the embarrassment and guilt he felt because of his father's abuse of him and his mother. ROYALTY: NA. SOURCE: Handman, Wynn. (1980). Modern American scenes for student actors. New York, NY: Bantam Books. SUBJECTS/PLAY TYPE: Black Americans; Child Abuse; Fathers and Sons; Scene.

1128. K-5*. (+) Sullivan, Jessie P. **The fruit of the spirit.** CAST: 2u. ACTS: 1. SETTING: Puppet stage. PLAYING TIME: NA. PLOT: Two children discuss the pleasure they derive from knowing Galatians 5:22-23. RECOMMENDATION: Although didactic and overly cheerful, this is adequate for a church production. ROYALTY: None. SOURCE: Sullivan, Jessie P. (1978). Puppet scripts for children's church. Grand Rapids, MI: Baker Book House. SUBJECTS/PLAY TYPE: Christian Drama; Love; Puppet Play.

1129. K-12. (-) Gunnink, Ida. **The fullness of time.** CAST: Su. ACTS: 1. SETTINGS: None. PLAYING TIME: 30 min. PLOT: This compilation of Bible readings from the Book of Psalms and the Gospels according to saints Luke and Matthew concerns the spiritual preparation for the birth of the Christ child. RECOMMENDATION: This is recommended as a part of a worship service or presentation during a church related class. ROYALTY: None. SOURCE: Hendricks, William & Vogel, Cora. (1983). Handbook of Christmas programs. Grand Rapids, MI: Baker Book House. SUBJECTS/PLAY TYPE: Christmas; Worship Program.

1130. 9-12. (+) Wilson, Pat. **Funeral tea.** CAST: 5u. ACTS: 1. SETTINGS: Parlor. PLAYING TIME: NA.

PLOT: Four people gather for tea after the cremation of a relative. When it is time to scatter the ashes, they make the devastating discovery that they don't have them, and are convinced that the tea they have just been drinking was actually made from the ashes. Comedy and confusion reign until the caterer appears with the jar of ashes, which resembles the tea jar. The mourners regain their composure and leave. The caterer decides to make a cup of tea and discovers they have taken the tea jar, leaving the ashes. RECOMMENDATION: This wryly humorous play could be performed by either men or women using a Cockney or otherwise British accent. ROYALTY: $15. SOURCE: Wilson, Pat. (1972 female version; 1974 male version; still in reprint). Funeral tea. Elgin, IL: Performance Pub. SUBJECTS/PLAY TYPE: Cremation; Funerals; Comedy.

1131. K-5*. (+) Hotchner, Bill & Roser, Bill. **The further adventures of Maide Marian.** CAST: 2f, 3m, 1u. ACTS: 3. SETTINGS: Forest; tree house. PLAYING TIME: 35 min. PLOT: When Robin Hood is bewitched by the Ditheroo, Maide Marian seeks out this evil creature to destroy it, but becomes its victim. Robin, hiding in his tree house, beset with Ditheroo-induced terrors, finally gathers courage to emerge. He attacks the Ditheroo and destroys its spells. RECOMMENDATION: This musical includes several scenes that depend on audience participation. The direct interaction with the actors should intrigue youngsters. ROYALTY: $35. SOURCE: Hothcher, Steve & Roser, Bill. (1977). The further adventures of Maide Marian. Chicago, IL: Dramatic Pub. Co. SUBJECTS/PLAY TYPE: Robin Hood; Sherwood Forest; Enchantment; Musical.

1132. 4-7. (+) Deverell, Rex. **The gadget.** CAST: 2f, 3m. ACTS: 1. SETTINGS: Factory. PLAYING TIME: NA. PLOT: Ivan, boy inventor, enjoys creating harmless but useful inventions from junk. Ivan wants to dismantle his latest invention, a machine which jumps around and eats things, because it doesn't do anything worthwhile. Gump, an adult wheeler-dealer, buys the gadget and uses questionable advertising tactics to sell it. When one of the gadgets destroys a nearby lake by drinking the water and killing the fish, Ivan and his friends trick the gadgets into eating one another. RECOMMENDATION: Character development is secondary to the play's themes about the dangers of machines and slick advertising. Wonderfully shrewd dialogue, quick repartee, and a delightful plot, along with sharp comments on societal problems make the play enjoyable. ROYALTY: NA. SOURCE: Deverell, Rex. (1979). The gadget. Toronto, Canada: Playwrights Canada. SUBJECTS/PLAY TYPE: Consumerism; Advertising; Ecology; Drama.

1133. 5-7. (+) Murray, John. **The gala garage sale.** CAST: 4f, 2m, Su. ACTS: 1. SETTINGS: Garage. PLAYING TIME: 20 min. PLOT: Jane Griggin has inherited her Uncle's estate, but has no fortune with which to maintain the family home. Sue and Tom Parker, who come to Jane's garage sale, sympathize with her and search for clues to the missing fortune. Professor Grobble realizes that the initials AU on a chest that belonged to her uncle represent the chemical symbol for gold. Further examination reveals that the hinges and all the metal work on the chest have been formed from gold. Jane is thrilled since two other trunks also display the AU monogram, and now she will be able to keep her uncle's home. RECOMMENDATION: This points up the stereotype of women's shopping, while presenting a treasure hunt puzzle. Although there is little character development, the three couples' affectionate banter is natural and realistic. ROYALTY: Free to Plays subscribers. SOURCE: Murray, John. (1988, November). The gala garage sale. Plays: The Drama Magazine for Young People, pp. 33-41. SUBJECTS/PLAY TYPE: Mystery; Comedy.

1134. 10-12. (+) Johnson, Robert & Scott, Charles. **The game.** CAST: 4f, 13m, Su. ACTS: 2. SETTINGS: Bare stage, backdrops. PLAYING TIME: NA. PLOT: Two university student groups, the R.S.V.P.s (Radical Students Volunteering for Peace) and the S.S.T. (Students Serving Truth), are at odds. Their leaders, J.J. and Bill, each try to win Leslie, the university president's daughter. Violence seems imminent when demonstrations are accompanied by counter demonstrations. J.J. wins Leslie and becomes a hero when he disarms a bomb that is planted in the administration building. The students realize that peace is better than violence. RECOMMENDATION: Some knowledge of the 1960s would be helpful, as this offers insights into this era of dissent. Some obscenities can easily be edited. ROYALTY: $59. SOURCE: Johnson, Robert and Scott, Charles. (1976). The game. Franklin, OH: Eldridge Pub. Co. SUBJECTS/PLAY TYPE: Comedy; Protests; 1960s, U.S.; Musical.

1135. 9-12. (+) Hark, Mildred & McQueen, Noel. **A game of hearts.** CAST: 2f, 3m. ACTS: 1. SETTINGS: Living room. PLAYING TIME: 30 min. PLOT: Bud's sudden interest in weddings on Valentine's Day upsets and alarms his family. They suspect he plans to marry Sally, and possibly elope. The fact is that Bud and Sally are going to a Valentine dance dressed in his parent's wedding clothes, the very costumes his parents were going to wear to the party. They are so relieved after hearing Bud's explanation they decide to stay home and play a game of hearts. RECOMMENDATION: In this comedy of misunderstandings, characters and dialogue are very realistic. This is a situation to which most family members could relate. ROYALTY: Free to Plays subscribers. SOURCE: Hark, Mildred & McQueen, Noel. (1980, February). A game of hearts. Plays: The Drama Magazine for Young People, pp. 13-22. SUBJECTS/PLAY TYPE: Valentine's Day; Comedy.

1136. 8-12. (+) Garver, Juliet. **The game of life.** CAST: 1f, 2m. ACTS: 1. SETTINGS: Restaurant. PLAYING TIME: NA. PLOT: Adam Wilson and his father, a recent widower, differ over Adam's college plans. Adam wants to study art; his father wants him to play football. Adam confides in Mandy, his girlfriend. Adam wins an art scholarship, but decides to compromise by playing football for a couple of years and taking the few art classes offered at that college, giving his father time to adjust. Later, he can attend art college. Adam wins Mandy's admiration by making a difficult decision. RECOMMENDATION: Adam is an endearing character because of his sensitivity and concern for his father, and shows maturity by compromising his own desires for his father's needs. This playlet would be an excellent choice to generate discussion on sexism or over domineering parents, in either a junior or senior high setting. ROYALTY: $4. SOURCE: Garver, Juliet. (1986). One-act dramas. Franklin, OH: Eldridge Pub. Co. SUBJECTS/PLAY TYPE: Family; Careers; Football; Drama.

1137. 9-12. (+) Riley, Lew. **Game show.** CAST: 5f, 5m. ACTS: 2. SETTINGS: Backstage; game show set. PLAYING TIME: NA. PLOT: Five minutes before going on the air, William Baron, the producer of a game show, decides to reject one of the contestants. In her place, Kathy Burns, the show's production assistant, is rushed onto stage, where she learns she will be competing against her ex-fiance, Steve Nystrom. Another contestant helps her out and afterwards, the two go on a date. RECOMMENDATION: Although some of the language and situations may be inappropriate for a school audience, a more adult audience may be appreciative. With the current popularity of game shows, the audience will be easily caught up in the humor of this spoof. ROYALTY: NA. SOURCE: Riley, Lew. (1986). Game show. Woodstock, IL: Dramatic Pub. Co. SUBJECTS/PLAY TYPE: Game Shows; Values; Comedy.

1138. K. (+) Gotwalt, Helen Louise Miller. **Garden hold-up.** CAST: 1f, 7m, 10u. ACTS: 2. SETTINGS: Garden. PLAYING TIME: 15 min. PLOT: After gardeners plant their spring seeds, their garden is threatened by some young animals who later realize their selfishness. RECOMMENDATION: Despite the obvious attempt to teach children a moral, the use of rhyme, repetition, and song provides a good vehicle for beginning actors. This could work nicely into a spring or summer program on the theme of gardens in literature and/or the theme of the interdependence of man and nature. ROYALTY: Free to Plays subscribers. SOURCE: Gotwalt, Helen Louise Miller. (1985). First plays for children: A collection of little plays for the youngest players. Boston, MA: Plays, Inc. SUBJECTS/PLAY TYPE: Gardening; Morality.

1139. 7-12. (+) Wilson, David Henry. **Gas and candles.** CAST: 1f, 2m. ACTS: 2. SETTINGS: Apartment. PLAYING TIME: NA. PLOT: A poor, hungry, elderly British couple try to get food by pretending they have been taken hostage by Irish terrorists in own apartment. This unorthodox plea for help serves only to get them placed in a psychiatric hospital by the police who had come to rescue them. RECOMMENDATION: Although this is billed as a comedy, the sad and depressing nature of the couple's plight seems to dominate in spite of some clever dialogue. The play might have had more appeal if it had been either a comedy or an insightful drama about the plight of the elderly. ROYALTY: $50. SOURCE: Wilson, David Henry. (1985). Gas and candles. Chicago, IL: Dramatic Pub. Co. SUBJECTS/PLAY TYPE: Elderly; Family Relationships; Poverty; Comedy.

1140. 3-7. (+) Nolan, Paul T. **The Gates of Dinklesbuehl.** CAST: 1f, 7m, Su. ACTS: 1. SETTINGS:

Street. PLAYING TIME: 25 min. PLOT: During the Thirty Years' War, the Swedes prepare to destroy the German city of Dinklesbuehl. The children, hearing that the Swedish general's son has died, meet the army at the gate and offer to replace his son with whomever he selects. The general is so overwhelmed that he spares the city. RECOMMENDATION: This juxtaposes the innocent wisdom of children with the jaded deliberations of adults, as a young heroine saves a city from destruction. ROYALTY: None for amateur performance. SOURCE: Nolan, Paul T. (1982). Folk tale plays from round the world: A collection of royalty-free, one-act plays about lands far and near. Boston, MA: Plays, Inc. SUBJECTS/PLAY TYPE: Dinkelsbuehl Kinder-zeche; Thirty Years' War; Playlet.

1141. 10-12. (+) Majeski, Bill. (Henry, O.) **A gazebo for my lady.** (Lost on dress parade) CAST: 2f, 3m. ACTS: 1. SETTINGS: Office; street; restaurant; home. PLAYING TIME: NA. PLOT: At the turn of the century, a young architect falls for a rich young woman who tries to pass herself as one of the working class. The young man has just been fired by the miserly head of a firm that specializes in architectural cliches. When all the characters meet in a restaurant, where the young man now works as a waiter, true love and architectural integrity triumph. RECOMMENDATION: A light play with many humorous moments, this love story could be very enjoyable although some of the allusions to architectural styles and ornamentation may be lost on a young audience, and the period costumes may pose difficulties for the average school drama club. ROYALTY: $15. SOURCE: Majeski, Bill. (1978). A gazebo for my lady. Chicago, IL: Dramatic Pub. Co. SUBJECTS/PLAY TYPE: Architecture; Comedy; Adaptation.

1142. 9-12. (-) Riley, Lew. **The General is coming! The General is coming!** CAST: 7f, 12m, Su. ACTS: 2. SETTINGS: Army orderly room. PLAYING TIME: NA. PLOT: As the company tries to get ready for inspection, everything goes wrong: the motor pool sergeant, General "Mad Dog" Madigan is missing, his wife is on the warpath, and Private Brooks' family is coming to visit her. Brooks has been coached to announce the General's arrival very loudly and has been warned the General doesn't like women soldiers. When he arrives, Brooks is unable to speak and the General catches everyone unprepared. Then Brooks' family arrives. Her father, Senator Brooks, greets the General, asks his daughter how she likes army life, and remarks on the fine company she belongs to. The General, lobbying for his third star, is forced to agree with the Senator and ends up promoting the commander and letting the entire company off the hook. RECOMMENDATION: This is not suitable for high school production because of its acceptance of drunkenness and gambling as harmless behavior, and its suggestive sexual situations. ROYALTY: $50. SOURCE: Riley, Lew. (1983). The General is coming! The General is coming! Chicago, IL: Dramatic Pub. Co. SUBJECTS/PLAY TYPE: Military Life; Comedy.

1143. 10-12. (+) Rudolph, Grace. **Generation gaps.** CAST: 1f. ACTS: 1. SETTINGS: Bare stage. PLAYING

TIME: NA. PLOT: An elderly bag lady looks for a suitable dress for her daughter. She chats with the audience about women's lot in life, using the examples of underachievement she's seen in her own life. RECOMMENDATION: This focuses on women's rights and briefly discusses euthanasia. It could prompt some interesting discussions from a high school audience. ROYALTY: $10. SOURCE: Rudolph, Grace. (1984). Elders' statements: One-act plays and monologues. Boston, MA: Baker's Plays. SUBJECTS/PLAY TYPE: Women's Rights; Aging; Achievement; Monologue.

1144. 3-6. (+) Gotwalt, Helen Louise Miller. **The gentle giant-killer.** CAST: 10f, 7m, Su. ACTS: 1. SETTINGS: Office. PLAYING TIME: 25 min. PLOT: Jack the Giant-Killer of fairy tale fame seeks work at the Busy Bee Employment Agency. After the initial shock of meeting the famous giant-killer, the Busy Bee staff find a job for Jack rescuing an English class from the clutches of a giant who has been inflicting difficulties on them. The children explain their difficulties in understanding grammar to Jack, who slays the giant and leaves behind a magic formula for learning the parts of speech: a song. RECOMMENDATION: The play has a simple and direct theme: rhyming and making up songs about a subject help people remember. As reinforcement, there are many rhyming sequences that would complement a unit on the parts of speech or on folk tales. ROYALTY: Free to Plays subscribers. SOURCE: Gotwalt, Helen Louise Miller. (1986). Everyday plays for boys and girls. Boston, MA: Plays, Inc. SUBJECTS/PLAY TYPE: Folk Tale Motifs; School; Grammar; Comedy.

1145. 7-12. (-) Hayes, Theresa. **Gentlemen prefer ladies (and vice versa).** CAST: 11f, 9m, Su. ACTS: 2. SETTINGS: Kitchen; classroom; McDonalds; living room. PLAYING TIME: 90 min. PLOT: Melissa, a high school student, dresses like a "tramp." When her friend is raped by some boys that they both are friendly with, Melissa realizes she shouldn't dress so immodestly. In a church counseling session, she and her friends discuss rape, pornography, immodest dress, the sexual revolution, and premarital sex. Passages from the Bible are read and then interpreted to support the church's views. Discussion questions are provided at the end of the play. RECOMMENDATION: Although the counsellors state that Janice was not responsible for her rape, the didactic theme is that anyone who dresses immodestly is wrong and will be punished. The play also claims that sexual freedom causes more babies, more abortions, more unwed mothers, more mothers on welfare, and, because of that, more child abuse. This will undoubtedly appeal to those who agree with the religious dogma, and the realistic dialogue may convince some adolescents to listen. However, the play never does deal with the rape, and the teenagers pray for Janice to get better at the same time that they say that God forgives the rapists even though they were wrong. This belittles the crime of rape, and perpetuates the myth that women cause their own sexual assaults. ROYALTY: NA. SOURCE: Hayes, Theresa. (1986). Getting your act together. Cincinnati, OH: Standard Pub. Co. SUBJECTS/PLAY TYPE: Rape; Dress; Christian Drama.

1146. 3-6. (+) Bauman, A. F. **George and his good wife, Elsie.** CAST: 2f, 2m, Su. ACTS: 1. SETTINGS: Cottage; road. PLAYING TIME: 10 min. PLOT: George, who seems to unable to do anything right, has a good wife, Elsie, who thinks he can do no wrong. George sets out to sell his cow, but he trades so poorly, he is left with only a coin. Returning home with this coin, he meets Jack, who bets him $100 that Elsie will be very angry. However, when Elsie displays only pleasure with George and his exchange, Jack must pay $100, and Elsie praises George for his cleverness. RECOMMENDATION: Extra parts can be created by having children, instead of props, play the parts of the animals being traded in this humorous adaptation of a Norwegian folk tale. ROYALTY: Free to Plays subscribers. SOURCE: Bauman, A.F. (1979, January). George and his good wife, Elsie. Plays: The Drama Magazine for young People, pp. 55-58. SUBJECTS/PLAY TYPE: Folk Tales, Norway; Comedy.

1147. K-3. (+) McCaslin, Nellie. **George the timid ghost.** CAST: 2u. ACTS: 1. SETTINGS: Bare stage. PLAYING TIME: 5 min. PLOT: George the ghost is trying to learn how to scare people. When he hears footsteps, he becomes so frightened he doesn't know what to do. The audience is asked to finish the story. RECOMMENDATION: The audience participation here is so simple that even the youngest actors will be able to coordinate it. ROYALTY: None. SOURCE: McCaslin, Nellie. (1977). Puppet fun: production, performance, and plays. New York, NY: D. McKay Co. SUBJECTS/PLAY TYPE: Ghosts; Puppet Play.

1148. 5-8. (+) Priore, Frank V. **George Washington and the public relations man.** CAST: 1f, 4m. ACTS: 1. SETTINGS: Office. PLAYING TIME: 15 min. PLOT: George Washington is overwhelmed by paper work and the duties he must perform as president. In his closet he finds a man from 1984 who shows him a lighter, calculator, money, and tells him all sorts of historical data, then leaves through the closet just as he arrived. George wonders if it was all a dream, but when he sees the calculator, George knows that it really happened. RECOMMENDATION: This light hearted view of history would be an amusing addition to a unit of George Washington or as a celebration of President's Day. ROYALTY: Free to Plays subscribers. SOURCE: Priore, Frank V. (1984, January/February). George Washington and the public relation man. Plays: The Drama Magazine for Young People, pp. 51-56. SUBJECTS/PLAY TYPE: Washington, George; President's Day; Skit.

1149. 4-8. (+) Hark, Mildred & McQueen, Noel. **George Washington Carver.** CAST: 3f, 7m. ACTS: 1. SETTINGS: Bare stage. PLAYING TIME: 40 min. PLOT: This play outlines Carver's childhood with Sue and Mose Carver, who recognized his exceptional talent with plants and encouraged his schooling; his completion of a Master's of Science degree after years of hard work and many jobs; and his decision to go back to help other poor, struggling students in Tuskegee. Two reporters interview Carver in the third scene, and depict him as a venerable old man of many accomplishments, who generously served humanity. RECOMMENDATION: This would make a good general introduction to the character and accomplishments of Carver, with its appeal slanted towards a younger audience. ROYALTY: NA. SOURCE: Kamerman, Syliva E. (1987). Plays of black Americans. Boston: Plays, Inc. SUBJECTS/PLAY TYPE: Carver, George Washington; Black Americans; Playlet.

1150. 6-8. (+) Fisher, Aileen. **George Washington farmer.** CAST: 1m. ACTS: 1. SETTINGS: Bare stage. PLAYING TIME: NA. PLOT: This choral reading tells the story of George Washington's life before he became President. RECOMMENDATION: Although there is nothing new here, the simple presentation style makes it a more interesting way to learn about George Washington's life. ROYALTY: Free to Plays subscribers. SOURCE: Kamerman, Sylvia E. (1975). Patriotic and historical plays for young people. Boston, MA: Plays, Inc. SUBJECTS/PLAY TYPE: Washington, George; Choral Reading.

1151. 7-12. (+) Robert, Harvey. **George Washington swept here.** CAST: 8f, 9m, Su. ACTS: 2. SETTINGS: Bedroom; schoolroom; tavern; wilderness. PLAYING TIME: 90 min. PLOT: This examines the human side of George Washington and presents an amusing glimpse of what life at home with the Washingtons might have been like. RECOMMENDATION: This is written for adult groups, but with a few minor changes it is also appropriate for younger audiences. It is funnier if the viewer knows the true historical version. It does not pretend to be a factual presentation of this period in history, but aims to amuse. ROYALTY: $25. SOURCE: Robert, Harvey. (1975). George Washington swept here. Schulenburg, TX: I.E. Clark. SUBJECTS/PLAY TYPE: Washington, George; Comedy.

1152. 9-12. (+) Robinette, Joseph. **Get Bill Shakespeare off the stage.** CAST: 3f, 3m, 10u. ACTS: 2. SETTINGS: School; home. PLAYING TIME: NA. PLOT: Fran Caldwell, the young, new drama teacher, wants to do excerpts from Shakespeare instead of the usual "light comedy" for the traditional school play. After meeting resistance from the school board, parents, and students, she agrees to do the mindless comedy that is preferred. However, the students have come to appreciate Shakespeare and go on to perform the excerpts much to her delight and surprise. RECOMMENDATION: The issue of the essence of fine drama and of the rewards of student participation in dramatic productions is presented through the point of view of students, teachers, and parents. Subplots address the concerns of each of these groups and the inter- actions are handled with sensitivity. The characters are well developed and the dialogue is believable and entertaining. ROYALTY: $35. SOURCE: Robinette, Joseph. (1980). Get Bill Shakespeare off the stage. Woodstock, IL: Dramatic Pub. Co. SUBJECTS/PLAY TYPE: High School; Theater; Comedy.

1153. 3-12. (+) Avery, Helen P. (Wilde, Oscar) **The ghost of Canterville Hall.** (The Canterville ghost) CAST: 4f, 4m, 4u. ACTS: 2. SETTINGS: Hall; balcony. PLAYING TIME: NA. PLOT: When a British couple is run out of their family mansion by a 16th century ghost, they sell it to

an American family delighted with the thought of having their own ghost. The children have fun trying to scare the ghost, and the parents try to reason with the ghost to keep him from haunting. The ghost finally finds peace and leaves when the adolescent daughter trusts him and risks her life to save his soul. RECOMMENDATION: Children will delight in the ghost and the reactions of the other characters to him. Adults will also be struck by the contrast between the players' attitudes toward him. There is a moral to the story: the daughter who exemplifies morality finally suceeds in helping the ghost because she is sincere and courageous. ROYALTY: $25. SOURCE: Avery, Helen P. (1977). The ghost of Canterville Hall. New Orleans, LA: Anchorage Press, Inc. SUBJECTS/PLAY TYPE: Ghost Stories; Haunted Houses; Comedy; Adaptation.

1154. 5-10. (+) Hamlett, Christina. **The ghost of Hemsptead House.** CAST: 2f, 4m. ACTS: 1. SETTINGS: Sheriff's office. PLAYING TIME: 20 min. PLOT: This is a farce about a movie maker who inadvertently has a whole town believing that the "old haunted house" is really haunted. But as the curtain falls, all is explained except for the one piece of evidence that started the whole ruckus, and suspicions run higher than ever. RECOMMENDATION: Older children and young teenagers will have a great time "hamming it up" in this play which would be enjoyed by even younger audiences. ROYALTY: Free to Plays subscribers. SOURCE: Hamlett, Christina. (1983, March). The ghost of Hemstead House. Plays: The Drama Magazine for Young People, pp. 35-40. SUBJECTS/PLAY TYPE: Mystery; Ghosts; Comedy.

1155. 4-8. (+) Alexander, Sue. **The ghost of Plymouth castle.** CAST: 2f, 3m, 2u. ACTS: 1. SETTINGS: Parlor. PLAYING TIME: NA. PLOT: Lady Plymouth will inherit Plymouth Castle if she can stay alone in the castle for four more nights. Unfortunately, she is frightened every evening by an apparent ghost, so Blaylock Jones and Datson are called in. Meanwhile, Lady Plymouth's cousin, Kevin, and his fiancee, Prunella, stop for a visit and the audience learns that the castle will go to Kevin if Lady Plymouth fails to stay the entire 44 days. That night, Jones and Datson sneak in through a window and catch the "ghost," Prunella, whose violet perfume has given her away. RECOMMENDATION: Children will enjoy helping solve the mystery of the ghost of Plymouth Castle, as the characters, plot, and dialogue of this playlet are simple, yet full of energy. This would make a clever Halloween production for young, inexperienced actors. ROYALTY: NA. SOURCE: Alexander, Sue. (1980). Whatever happened to Uncle Albert and other puzzling plays. New York, NY: Houghton Mifflin. SUBJECTS/PLAY TYPE: Detectives; Ghosts; Inheritances; Mystery.

1156. 9-12*. (+) Pielmeier, John. **A ghost story.** CAST: 1f, 2m. ACTS: 1. SETTINGS: Cabin. PLAYING TIME: NA. PLOT: Oswald and Hackett meet during a blizzard when they take shelter in a cabin. They converse until a strange woman named Soma appears in the doorway. The three then tell each other ghost stories, with Soma telling the goriest one about a man who drank blood. When they lie down to sleep, Soma slits Oswald's throat as Hackett watches. He explains that this has not yet happened, but someday it will because he has dreamed it so often. RECOMMENDATION: A fascinating horror tale, this may not be appropriate because of its excessive gore and a drug reference. With some editing, this could be used as Halloween entertainment for high school audiences. ROYALTY: NA. SOURCE: Pielmeier, John. (1984). Haunted lives. New York, NY: Dramatists Play Service, Inc. SUBJECTS/PLAY TYPE: Horror; Murder; Blood; Drama.

1157. 4-7. (+) Nicholson, Jessie. **The ghost walks tonight.** CAST: 3f, 8m, 1u. ACTS: 1. SETTINGS: Living room. PLAYING TIME: 20 min. PLOT: Three boys bet they can spend Halloween night in a haunted house. While their friends dress up in costumes to try to scare them out of the house, two robbers with a sack of stolen money hide out in the house. When one of the boys finds the sack of money, they realize that the men are robbers and they bring a police officer to the house and the robbers are arrested. The boys and their friends then share the reward. RECOMMENDATION: This combines suspense with comedy to tell a good, old fashioned ghost story, but much of the dialogue will need to be modernized (i.e. lam outa here; what ails you). ROYALTY: Free to Plays subscribers. SOURCE: Nicholson, Jessie. (1988, October). The ghost walks tonight. Plays: The Drama Magazine for Young People, pp. 36-44. SUBJECTS/PLAY TYPE: Halloween; Robbers; Ghost Stories; Playlet.

1158. 6-10. (+) Kelly, Tim J. **Ghostchasers!** CAST: 14f, 12m, 1u. ACTS: 2. SETTINGS: Reception area; office. PLAYING TIME: 90 min. PLOT: When patients at the asylum, engaged in "fantasy therapy," take over, confusion reigns. The mix-ups bring a poltergeist, unknown relative, burglar, ghostchasers, reporter, and unexpected strangers together. RECOMMENDATION: This play is based on the popular movie, **Ghostbusters**, which, in itself may make it popular with young students. However, it may be more fun to produce than to watch, since there is so much confused action, and so many mistaken identities, that it is hard to follow at times. ROYALTY: $35. SOURCE: Kelly, Tim J. (1986). Ghostchasers! Denver, CO: Pioneer Drama Service. SUBJECTS/PLAY TYPE: Ghosts; Comedy.

1159. 9-12. (+) Marschalk, Raymond J. Sr. (Bronte, Emily) **The ghostly affair at Wuthering Heights.** (Wuthering Heights) CAST: 4f, 4m. ACTS: 3. SETTINGS: Estate. PLAYING TIME: NA. PLOT: In a sequel to the lives of Catherine and Heathcliff of the original classic, Jane and Peter Earnshaw, newlyweds and descendents of the two ghosts, inherit the estate of Wuthering Heights. The ghosts haunt Wuthering Heights. Jane tries to convince Peter that a wedding is the only solution to the haunting. Heathcliff and Catherine are present during the planning, and comment throughout. More extraordinary events occur, and finally the wedding ceremony takes place and the ghosts are united. RECOMMENDATION: This has a believable plot, albeit somewhat outrageous, with characters' actions parallel to the original. It would be beneficial for the audience to know the original story, but this play could stand alone. Themes of morality and love

make this more suitable for an older audience or a high school cast which has read "Wuthering Heights." Production would require much time and many rehearsals. ROYALTY: $35. SOURCE: Marschalk, Raymond J. Sr. (n.d.). The ghostly affair at Wuthering Heights. Franklin, OH: Eldridge Pub. Co. SUBJECTS/PLAY TYPE: Ghosts; Love; Comedy; Adaptation.

1160. 12. (+) Kundrat, Theodore V. (Ibsen, Henrik) **Ghosts.** CAST: 2f, 3m. ACTS: 3. SETTINGS: None. PLAYING TIME: 100 min. PLOT: Complex relationships in the family of deceased, unsavory, Captain Alving provide the foundation for a story of deceit. The captain, mistakenly regarded as a pillar of society, was a drunkard and debaucher. His wife tries to quiet rumors of his lifestyle by endowing an orphanage in his memory. He inflicts pain from beyond the grave because his son suffers from inherited syphilis and cannot marry his true love because she is in reality his half sister. Two characters outside the family help to explain the sequence of events that ultimately ends in tragedy. RECOMMENDATION: This adaptation has two major drawbacks: the language is awkward and the dialogue does not flow smoothly. Ibsen is quite heavy for adults and the play may be too long to hold student's interest. However, using a reader's theater style of presentation could eliminate distraction and allow for concentration on the many possible themes that could spark discussion including the meaning of the title, the symbolism of the orphanage burning, and the criticisms the author was leveling at his society. The play includes an excellent essay on the concept of reader's theater by the author of the adaptation. ROYALTY: $15. SOURCE: Kundrat, Theodore V. (1978). Ghosts. Chicago, IL: Coach House Press, Inc. SUBJECTS/PLAY TYPE: Deceit;, Tragedy; Reader's Theatre.

1161. 6-9. (+) Priore, Frank V. **Ghosts are revolting!** CAST: 2f, 6m. ACTS: 1. SETTINGS: Lobby. PLAYING TIME: 20 min. PLOT: When the ghosts go on strike (i.e. Clank, is tired of rattling chains and wants to make noise with a "boom box"; MacGregor wants to haunt a castle with central heat), their demands are met so that people will attend the ghostless parties. Halloween is saved for all. RECOMMENDATION: This humorous, updated ghost story is traditional with haunting, rattling chains, and Scottish castles, but is also modern with ghosts wanting boom boxes, designer sheets, and good music. ROYALTY: Free to Plays subscribers. SOURCE: Priore, Frank V. (1986, October). Ghosts are revolting! Plays: The Drama Magazine for Young People, pp. 57-63. SUBJECTS/PLAY TYPE: Halloween; Ghosts; Comedy.

1162. 3-6. (+) Pendleton, Edrie. **Ghosts in the library.** CAST: 9f, 7m. ACTS: 1. SETTINGS: Library. PLAYING TIME: 30 min. PLOT: While visiting their grandparents, four bored children are told to use any book in the library but they ask their grandparents' permission to go to the movies instead. When the room is empty, characters such as Sherlock Holmes, Becky Sharp from **Vanity Fair**, D'Artagnan from **The Three Musketeers**, David Copperfield, and Jo from **Little Women** enter. As they discuss the children's dislike for reading, the children return to find the candles burning and the books from which the characters came. They glance through the books, each finding one to his/her liking. RECOMMENDATION: This dramatizes attitudes of many children towards books, and tries to personify the opinions that classic literary characters might have about them. Unfortunately, the discussions of the literary characters are too judgmental (comic books are horrible, movies leave nothing to the imagination). Although the play is at a 3-6 grade performance/audience level, the selected books are suitable for high school readers. This will not convince anyone to read, nor will it entertain with its overly didactic and condescending dialogue. ROYALTY: Free to Plays subscribers. SOURCE: Pendleton, Edrie. (1988, November). Ghosts in the library. Plays: The Drama Magazine for Young People, pp. 42-50. SUBJECTS/PLAY TYPE: Book Week; Reading; Drama.

1163. 2-5. (+) Gilfond, Henry. **The ghosts of Halloween. CAST:** 10u. **ACTS:** 1. **SETTINGS:** Living room. **PLAYING TIME:** 15 min. **PLOT:** As the announcer sets the scene, one of a group of teenagers in a haunted house sees three ghosts. As he runs away, his friends laugh and tell the "ghosts" to take off their sheets. When the ghosts do not comply, the rest of the group runs away. RECOMMENDATION: As the tables are turned on the would-be pranksters, the announcer asks the audience whether the ghosts are real, or whether the first victim of the joke has taken his revenge in this high interest\low vocabulary skit. ROYALTY: None. SOURCE: Gilfond, Henry. (1985). Holiday plays for reading. New York, NY: Walker. SUBJECTS/PLAY TYPE: Halloween; Skit.

1164. 4-6. (+) Fisher, Aileen. **Ghosts on guard. CAST:** 3f, 4m. **ACTS:** 1. **SETTINGS:** Living room. **PLAYING TIME:** 15 min. **PLOT:** On Halloween, nasty Mrs. Briggs dresses up Mr. Briggs as a ghost and insists he scare away the children before they soap the windows. Instead, Mr. Briggs captures the children and makes friends with them. RECOMMENDATION: This slightly dated, lengthy play is told in rhyme. Still, it is suitable for Halloween programs. ROYALTY: NA. SOURCE: Fisher, Aileen. (1986). Holiday programs for boys and girls. Boston, MA: Plays, Inc. SUBJECTS/PLAY TYPE: Halloween; Comedy.

1165. 7-10. (+) Hamlett, Christina. **Ghostwriter or ghost? CAST:** 1f, 2m. **ACTS:** 1. **SETTINGS:** Library. **PLAYING TIME:** 10 min. **PLOT:** For many years, Bernie has been Roger's ghostwriter. Now that Roger is going to marry Cynthia, who is wealthy and loves his books, Roger will stop writing and will live off Cynthia's money so she will not find out he is not the author of his books. Bernie decides to get even with Roger. He dresses up as Captain Drake, the hero of all the books, and surprises Cynthia, who thinks he is a ghost. Cynthia is very taken with "Captain Drake" after talking to him and dumps Roger for Bernie. RECOMMENDATION: This has witty dialogue, well defined individual personalities, and derives its major appeal from an ironic twist in fate, as the "shadow" man takes his rightful place in the forefront. ROYALTY: Free to Plays subscribers. SOURCE: Hamlett, Christina. (1986, May). Ghostwriter or ghost? Plays: The Drama Magazine

for Young People, pp. 10-16. SUBJECTS/PLAY TYPE: Ghostwriters; Romance; Comedy.

1166. K-2. (+) Hoff, Syd. **Giants. CAST:** 6u. **ACTS:** 1. **SETTINGS:** Bare stage. **PLAYING TIME:** NA. **PLOT:** Five schoolchildren pretend to be giants when the teacher (the giant) arrives. Thinking the children are also giants because they are on stools (to be of equal height) the "giant" decides not to eat them. The children awaken the sleeping giant and advise him that they have been shrunk by a giant shrinker. The giant runs for his life. RECOMMENDATION: The believable characterization would be exciting to this age group, and the physical movements involved would be fun and easily done. ROYALTY: Write Scott Meredith Literary Agency. SOURCE: Jennings, Coleman A. & Harris, Aurand. (1988). Plays children love, Volume II. New York, NY: St. Martin's Press. SUBJECTS/PLAY TYPE: Giants; Playlet.

1167. 9-12. (+) DeWyze, Virginia. **The gift. CAST:** 5f, Su. **ACTS:** 1. **SETTINGS:** Living room; hotel suite; pawn shop. **PLAYING TIME:** 30 min. **PLOT:** This play centers around the disappearances and reappearances of a distinctive little wooden box. It was first given as a wedding present to Kimberly Prescott by her uncle, who intended for it to be passed on to Kimberly's daughter, Julie, upon her marriage. By error, it is sent to a church bazaar in a box of miscellaneous items, and it finds many homes until it finally is presented to Julie as a wedding present, just as her uncle intended. RECOMMENDATION: This comprises six monologues. The entire play can be done as a monologue, or it can be presented by two to five women. If desired, non-speaking roles can be cast to expand the number of players. Because of the length of the monologues, it would be enjoyed more by older students. Suggestions for script changes are included if the director wants this to be a Christmas play. ROYALTY: $10. SOURCE: DeWyze, Virginia. (1983). The gift. Denver CO: Pioneer Drama Service. SUBJECTS/PLAY TYPE: Gifts; Christmas; Irony; Monologue.

1168. 7-11. (+) Duffield, Brainerd. (Henry, O.) **Gift of the magi.** (The gift of the magi) **CAST:** 3f, 1m. **ACTS:** 1. **SETTINGS:** Apartment. **PLAYING TIME:** NA. **PLOT:** Because a poor young married couple in 19th century New York City cannot afford to buy each other Christmas presents, each sells a prized possession to purchase a gift for the other. The husband pawns his heirloom watch to buy his wife hair combs and his wife sells her long hair to buy him a chain for his watch. Their gifts confirm their love for each other. RECOMMENDATION: This is a well written, faithful adaptation whose dialogue is succinct and faithful to the the original story. ROYALTY: $10. SOURCE: Duffield, Brainerd. (1976). Gift of the magi. Boston, MA: Baker's Plays. SUBJECTS/PLAY TYPE: Gifts; Love; Christmas; Adaptation.

1169. 5-12. (+) Hischak, Thomas. (Henry, O.) **The gift of the magi.** (The gift of the magi) **CAST:** 1f, 1m. **ACTS:** 1. **SETTINGS:** Apartment. **PLAYING TIME:** 35 min. **PLOT:** In this faithful adaptation, two young newly-weds sacrifice their proudest possessions to give each other the perfect Christmas present, only to discover the sacrifice of each eliminates the ability to use the other's gift. RECOMMENDATION: The good production notes and excellent dialogue make this play highly recommended. ROYALTY: $15. SOURCE: Hischak, Thomas. (1983). The gift of the magi. Denver, CO: Pioneer Drama Service. SUBJECTS/PLAY TYPE: Christmas; Comedy; Gifts; Adaptation.

1170. 5-12. (+) Martens, Anne Coulter. (Henry, O.) **The gift of the magi.** (The gift of the magi) CAST: 5f, Su. ACTS: 1. SETTINGS: Apartment; shops. PLAYING TIME: 25 min. PLOT: A newly married couple finds they don't have the money to buy each other Christmas gifts. He pawns his heirloom watch to buy her hair combs. She cuts off her long hair and sells it to buy him a new watch chain. Their gifts are useless but their love is confirmed. RECOMMENDATION: The play is faithful to O. Henry's classic short story and is a fine choice for the holiday season. ROYALTY: $20. SOURCE: Martens, Anne Coulter. (1963). The gift of the Magi. Woodstock, IL: Dramatic Pub. Co. SUBJECTS/PLAY TYPE: Christmas; Gifts; Love; Adaptation.

1171. 10-12. (+) Loos, Anita. (Colette) **Gigi.** (Gigi) CAST: 5f, 2m. ACTS: 2. SETTINGS: Living room; boudoir. PLAYING TIME: NA. PLOT: Gigi, an impetuous 16 year old, is raised by a mother who sacrifices her family responsibilities to become an actress and socialize with ordinary men, rather than gentry. A grandmother and great aunt Alicia conspire to train her for a more respectable future. Gigi, always one step ahead of her family, stuns her relatives when she evokes more than a declaration of love from their well to do friend, Gaston Lachaille, and receives a proposal of marriage. RECOMMENDATION: Gigi has entertained audiences as a novel, a play, and a musical with great success for many years. The characters have a most appealing style and personality, and the dialogue flows with wit and humor. ROYALTY: $50. SOURCE: Loos, Anita. (1981). Gigi. New York, NY: Samuel French, Inc. SUBJECTS/PLAY TYPE: Marriage; Romance; Comedy.

1172. 9-12. (+) Morton, Richard. **The gigolo of Jerome Avenue.** CAST: 1f, 1m. ACTS: 1. SETTINGS: Living room. PLAYING TIME: NA. PLOT: Lou Brill (the "gigolo of Jerome Avenue" as he was called in high school), now in his 60s, pays a visit to high school friend, Fiona Krempel. They reminisce and he asks her to marry him. Fiona, in love with Lou in high school, tells him of the pain he caused when he asked her to the high school prom, and she sat in her new dress waiting for him all night. Lou urges her to forget the past and to marry him. She tells him to "get lost." RECOMMENDATION: Missed opportunities, misunderstandings, and the lack of communication encountered in life strongly effect the future. The message is poignantly delivered that if Lou and Fiona had talked to each other more and had been less concerned with themselves, this scene might never have taken place. ROYALTY: NA. SOURCE: Morton, Richard. (1983). The gigolo of Jerome Avenue. Woodstock, IL: Dramatic Pub. Co. SUBJECTS/PLAY TYPE: High School; Drama.

1173. 1-3. (+) Laurie, Rona. (Potter, Beatrix) **Ginger and Pickle's village shop.** (Tales of Beatrix Potter) CAST: 3f, 3m, 10u. ACTS: 1. SETTINGS: Store; parlor. PLAYING TIME: NA. PLOT: A dog and cat run a general store and let customers buy on credit. Eventually, the taxes are due and the dog needs his license, but there is no money, so the store closes. Both find productive lives elsewhere. Meanwhile, Sally Henny-Penny reopens the store with much more merchandise, but she insists on cash. RECOMMENDATION: Along with amusing the audience, this also teaches a lesson about credit buying and the business world. ROYALTY: NA. SOURCE: Laurie, Rona. (1980). Children's plays from Beatrix Potter. London, England: F. Warne. SUBJECTS/PLAY TYPE: Animals; Adaptation.

1174. K-3. (+) Mahlman, Lewis & Jones, David Cadwalader. (Jacobs, Joseph) **The gingerbread boy.** (Johnny-Cake.) CAST: 8u. ACTS: 1. SETTINGS: Kitchen; woods; river. PLAYING TIME: 15 min. PLOT: A childless woman bakes a gingerbread boy, who runs away. He escapes being eaten by a cow, chickens, horse, farmer, hen, and fox, and then returns home, having learned not to run away again. RECOMMENDATION: This is a delightful rendition of the famous English folk tale, complete with the gingerbread son, and other musical parts. ROYALTY: Free to Plays subscribers. SOURCE: Mahlman, Lewis & Jones, David Cadwalder. (1980). Folk tale plays for puppets. Boston, MA: Plays, Inc. SUBJECTS/PLAY TYPE: Folk Tales, England; Runaways; Puppet Play.

1175. K-6. (+) Solomon, Olivia. (Jacobs, Joseph) **The gingerbread boy.** (Johnny-Cake) CAST: 1f, 1m, 8u. ACTS: 3. SETTINGS: Bare stage, backdrop. PLAYING TIME: NA. PLOT: After a gingerbread boy is baked by an old woman, he tempts his fate by teasing a rooster, cat, dog, horse, cow, old man, and old woman, into chasing him. He skillfully outruns them, but is cleverly duped by the wily fox. The gingerbread boy is resurrected to take a bow and sing the closing song with the rest of the characters. RECOMMENDATION: The characters here are introduced in a song/dance parade of familiar choral tunes and farewell music. The saucy gingerbread boy leads all on a merry chase and in the end succumbs to his fate, but his resurrection for a bow adds a cheery note to a rather sad ending. ROYALTY: NA. SOURCE: Solomon, Olivia. (1983). Five folk comedies for today's juvenile stage. Tuscaloosa, AL: Portals. SUBJECTS/PLAY TYPE: Folk Tales, England; Vanity; Musical.

1176. 7-12. (+) Huff, Betty Tracy. **The girl and gold mine.** CAST: 4f, 6m. ACTS: 1. SETTINGS: Campsite. PLAYING TIME: 30 min. PLOT: Dastardly and rich Jasper Mudhaven offers to buy Smedley's barren gold mine so that he can pay the mortgage on his house. Unknown to Smedley, but known to Jasper, is the whereabouts of the undiscovered gold vein in the mine. "Blazing saddles" type Indians, a sheriff who turns out to be one of the character's lost father, and revelations of true love all become important before Smedley foils Jasper's plans. RECOMMENDATION: This has all the requisite pieces for a melodrama, with the addition of delightful satire. Overacting and exaggerated costuming will enhance the likeable scripts. **ROYALTY:** Free to Plays subscribers. **SOURCE:** Huff, Betty Tracy. (1983, January-February). The girl and gold mine. Plays: The Drama Magazine for Young People, pp. 21-30. **SUBJECTS/PLAY TYPE:** Family; Playlet.

1177. 7-12. (+) Kehret, Peg. **The girl that I marry.** **CAST:** 1m. **ACTS:** 1. **SETTINGS:** None. **PLAYING TIME:** NA. **PLOT:** A young man explains what he wants in a wife: a woman who likes football, loves dogs, and ignores housework. Until he can find one woman who fits these conditions, he will not marry. **RECOMMENDATION:** This enjoyable view of marriage will amuse teenagers and could be adapted to a female viewpoint, if needed. **ROYALTY:** NA. **SOURCE:** Kehret, Peg. (1986). Winning monologs for young actors. Colorado Springs, CO: Meriwether Pub. **SUBJECTS/PLAY TYPE:** Marriage; Monologue.

1178. 3-6. (+) Hall, Margaret. **The girl who used her wits.** **CAST:** 4f, 1m. **ACTS:** 1. **SETTINGS:** Chinese garden; country road. **PLAYING TIME:** 13 min. **PLOT:** In this traditional style folk tale, two wives ask their mother-in-law if they may return to their hometown for a visit. She decides they may go only if they can bring back fire wrapped in paper and wind wrapped in paper. They meet a poor peasant girl named Indigo who figures out the solutions to the two tasks. As a result, the unmarried third son decides to marry Indigo, who is poor but very beautiful and very witty. **RECOMMENDATION:** The suspense and humor at the end, as well as rich vocabulary, make this appealing. **ROYALTY:** NA. **SOURCE:** Hall, Margaret. (1981, March). The girl who used her wits. Boston, MA: Plays, Inc. **SUBJECTS/PLAY TYPE:** Folk Tales, China; Playlet.

1179. 7-12. (+) Miller, Ev. **The girl who was asked to turn blue. CAST:** Su. **ACTS:** 1. **SETTINGS:** Bare stage. **PLAYING TIME:** NA. **PLOT:** Tracey Logan, 16, finds herself in a world where everyone is completely blue, has numbers instead of names, lives in cells with groups of no more than 999, and looks to Number One (the High Priest and Keeper of the Holy Cabinet) for wisdom and guidance. At one time, this society was similar to ours, but now everyone is the same because "differences only cause problems...and we do not want problems." Tracey is given two choices: maintain her individuality and become an outcast or turn blue and become accepted by those her own age. The choice is the director's, as to which ending (or both endings) the audience will see. **RECOMMENDATION:** This would be exellent for dealing with society, individuality, and conformity. By using both endings, much discussion can take place and many questions can be raised about the pros and cons of being an individual and of a society that expects complete conformity. **ROYALTY:** $15. **SOURCE:** Miller, Ev. (1986). The girl who was asked to turn blue. Woodstock, IL: Dramatic Pub. Co. **SUBJECTS/PLAY TYPE:** Conformity; Individuality; Science Fiction.

1180. 10-12. (+) Patrick, John. **The girls of the garden club. CAST:** 17f, 2m. **ACTS:** 3. **SETTINGS:** Living room. **PLAYING TIME:** NA. **PLOT:** Rhoda Greenleaf wants a

greenhouse and her husband says she will get one when she is elected President. Rhoda decides that becoming President of the Garden Club will suffice. The winner of the Garden Club Flower Show is entitled to be its next president. To ensure winning the show, Rhonda orders rare bulbs from Burma. But on the day of the show, the exotic Burmese plant and Rhonda consume too much wine. The plant reacts better to the alcohol than Rhoda, and it talks itself into being a first prize winner. **RECOMMENDATION:** The plot is a simple comedy, with expected plans going awry, witty dialogue, and humorous characters. The sexual exchanges between the characters might be controversial for school children a tone of both sexism and anti-semitism surfaces in some of the lines. **ROYALTY:** $50. **SOURCE:** Patrick, John. (1977). The girls of the garden club. New York, NY: Dramatists Play Service. **SUBJECTS/PLAY TYPE:** Gardening; Battle of the Sexes; Comedy.

1181. 9-12. (+) Sterling, Pamela. **Give me liberty!** **CAST:** 2f, 4m. **ACTS:** 1. **SETTINGS:** Tavern; office; army camp; home. **PLAYING TIME:** NA. **PLOT:** A young black slave girl disguises herself as a boy in order to joint the Continental Army. But after being shot, she gets help from a doctor she met in a tavern. Confusion results when the doctor's daughter thinks that the girl soldier will propose marriage to her. All ends well when the girl reveals her true identity. **RECOMMENDATION:** An excellent historical play, this production touches on the aspects of freedom, both from the standpoints of black slaves and women in the 1700s. This play could be staged around Independence Day or could be used as a supplement to a history unit. **ROYALTY:** $35. **SOURCE:** Sterling, Pamela. (1984). Give me liberty! Morton Grove, IL: Coach House Press. **SUBJECTS/PLAY TYPE:** Revolution, U.S.; Slavery; Drama.

1182. 7-12. (+) Fendrich, Shubert & Cohan, George M. **Give my regards to Broadway. CAST:** 11f, 4m, Su. **ACTS:** 2. **SETTINGS:** Theater; battleground; hospital. **PLAYING TIME:** 90 min. **PLOT:** A struggling company stages a broadway musical with the help of a talented ingenue and a rich bookie. Crises occur as a temperamental star tries to steal the lead from the new young actress and when members of the mob try to rub out the bookie. Eventually, the production is a success, the director proposes to the ingenue, and the hoodlum discovers he has musical talent. **RECOMMENDATION:** This interesting period piece can be produced with few scenery changes, and limited props. All actors must be able to sing and some dancing is necessary, but the dialogue and music should be manageable for junior and senior high actors. **ROYALTY:** $75. **SOURCE:** Fendrich, Shubert & Cohan, George M. (1981). Give my regards to Broadway. Denver, CO: Pioneer Drama Service. **SUBJECTS/PLAY TYPE:** Patriotism; Musical.

1183. 1-3. (+) Gotwalt, Helen Louise Miller. (Grimm Brothers) **The glass slippers.** (Cinderella) **CAST:** 5f, 7m, 8u. **ACTS:** 1. **SETTINGS:** Cobbler's shop. **PLAYING TIME:** 20 min. **PLOT:** The Cinderella story is told from the viewpoint of the cobblers who made the glass slippers. The only additions to the original story are the four cobblers, of whom one is obsessed with making shoes out of glass. RECOMMENDATION: While the rhyming, sing-songy lines of the play would make it easy for children to memorize, these characteristics also may make the dialogue seem forced and artificial. On the other hand the play is simple and short, and would be quite easy to produce with younger children. ROYALTY: Free to Plays subscribers. SOURCE: Gotwalt, Helen Louise Miller. (1986). Everyday plays for boys an girls. Boston, MA: Plays, Inc. SUBJECTS/PLAY TYPE: Folk Tales, France; Adaptation.

1184. 7-12. (+) By some very talented young playwrights. **Glimpses. CAST:** 3f, 3m. **ACTS:** 3. **SETTINGS:** Bare stage. **PLAYING TIME:** NA. **PLOT:** This is a collection of 32 scenes, dramatic monologues, and short playlets concerning human problems such as death, suicide, inadequacy, parents, siblings, and dating as seen from various teenager's viewpoints. RECOMMENDATION: Appealing both to produce and watch, **Glimpses** offers an effective balance between painful topics and humorous tones which will make them especially appealing to teenagers. The pieces are brief, from one paragraph to three pages long and could be learned easily. Staging depends on props and lighting, and not all scenes need to be performed, allowing a unique opportunity for a cast to customize their production. Some explicit language may be deleted. **ROYALTY:** $50. **SOURCE:** Glimpses. (1982). Woodstock, IL: Dramatic Pub. Co. **SUBJECTS/PLAY TYPE:** Adolescent Problems; Monologue; Comedy; Playlet.

1185. 5-11. (+) Deary, Terence. **Glorygum. CAST:** 2f, 2m. **ACTS:** 1. **SETTINGS:** Classroom; spacecraft. **PLAYING TIME:** 60 min. **PLOT:** The commander of a spacecraft tells the children he needs their help to create a story for the last three inhabitants of Glorygum, the planet from which all storybook characters come. They are the only characters left there because no one has made up a story for them yet. RECOMMENDATION: Children are encouraged to give free rein to their imaginations by the Glorygummers in this fun project that stimulates creativity. **ROYALTY:** None. **SOURCE:** Deary, Terence. (1977). Teaching through theatre. New York, NY: Samuel French. **SUBJECTS/PLAY TYPE:** Science Fiction; Imagination; Participation Play.

1186. 8-12. (+) Shiras, Frank. (Anonymous) **Go ask Alice.** (Go ask Alice) **CAST:** 15f, 8m. **ACTS:** 2. **SETTINGS:** Bedroom; bathroom; store; waiting room. **PLAYING TIME:** NA. **PLOT:** Lonely and insecure Alice becomes trapped in a drug scene because of an acid party. She almost frees herself but continues to be plagued by "friends" still on drugs. Alice has flashbacks and tries to stop them with sleeping pills. She overdoses, and dies. RECOMMENDATION: The confusion, loneliness and rebellion of adolescence powerfully depicted here would help some teenagers think realistically about their own situations. **ROYALTY:** $50. **SOURCE:** Shiras, Frank. (1976). Go ask Alice. Woodstock, IL: Dramatic Pub. Co. **SUBJECTS/PLAY TYPE:** Drug Abuse; Drama.

1187. 6-12. (+) Priore, Frank V. **Go, go, go, UFO! CAST:** 10f, 5m. **ACTS:** 2. **SETTINGS:** Living room. **PLAYING TIME:** NA. **PLOT:** A teacher and her four female students from Venus are marooned on Earth when their spaceship breaks down. They seek refuge in the home of a suburban New Jersey family, the Holloways. As suspicions are confirmed about the "aliens," one of the students decides to remain on Earth. Mr. Holloway is glad to send his brother-in-law to Venus in her place until it is discovered that the only problem with the spaceship is that the parking brake was left on. RECOMMENDATION: Lines with double meanings, a stereotypical suspicious neighbor, and a British UFO investigator will add to the fun of this comedy which should be performed by high schoolers. **ROYALTY:** $35. **SOURCE:** Priore, Frank V. (1984). Go, go, go, UFO! Chicago, IL: The Dramatic Pub. Co. **SUBJECTS/PLAY TYPE:** Science Fiction; Fantasy; Comedy.

1188. 4-6. (+) Cheatham, Val R. **Go west, young man. CAST:** 1f, 11m, 1u. **ACTS:** 1. **SETTINGS:** Wagon train camp. **PLAYING TIME:** 20 min. **PLOT:** A narrator's comments about the Old West provide the transitions between scenes in which a mild mannered school teacher from the East captures the villain, and "gets his girl." RECOMMENDATION: Western dialect and stop action for interpretations by the narrator increase the interest for this humorous and lively play which requires the acting skill of children in upper elementary grades. **ROYALTY:** Free to Plays subscribers. **SOURCE:** Cheatham, Val R. (1983, November). Go west, young man. Plays: The Drama Magazine for Young People, pp. 51-56. **SUBJECTS/PLAY TYPE:** Old West; Wagon Trains; Comedy.

1189. K-4*. (+) Sullivan, Jessie P. **God answers prayers. CAST:** 2u. **ACTS:** 1. **SETTINGS:** Puppet stage. **PLAYING TIME:** NA. **PLOT:** Mortimer is worried that he will fail a spelling test because he feels he does not have time to study. Mathilda says God will help him if he studies and prays, supporting her view with Mark 9:23. Mortimer decides to study and pray. RECOMMENDATION: This deals with a common worry of children, and proposes a proactive solution. It illustrates to children how the Bible can positively influence their lives. **ROYALTY:** None. **SOURCE:** Sullivan, Jessie P. (1978). Puppet scripts for children's church. Grand Rapids, MI: Baker Book House. **SUBJECTS/PLAY TYPE:** Christian Drama; School; Studying; Puppet Play.

1190. 10-12. (+) Urdahl, Richard. **God can take care of Himself...but what about our kids? CAST:** 1f, 1m. **ACTS:** 1. **SETTINGS:** Room. **PLAYING TIME:** NA. **PLOT:** An invitation to dinner from an unmarried couple sparks an intense conversation between an husband and wife about who is happier: married or unmarried couples. Their conversation leads into issues such as the reasons for marrying. One spouse believes that the children would be confused if their parents weren't married. The discussion ends with each agreeing to think about the other's point of view. RECOMMENDATION: This brings up a valid topic in today's society: unmarried couples. The question of morality is approached from several points of view, making it an excellent discussion starter. For a church youth group, this would be appropriate for a class supplement or a small production. ROYALTY: $10. SOURCE: Urdahl, Richard. (1984). Don't listen to us, Lord...we're only praying. Boston, MA: Baker's Plays. SUBJECTS/PLAY TYPE: Marriage; Cohabitation; Christian Drama.

1191. K-3*. (-) Sullivan, Jessie P. **God doesn't want us to worry.** CAST: 2u. ACTS: 1. SETTINGS: Puppet stage. PLAYING TIME: NA. PLOT: Mathilda is worried about her performance in an upcoming play because during rehearsal she dropped a prop on her foot. Mortimer convinces her not to worry because God will take care of her. The play doesn't go as planned, as another actor drops a prop on Mathilda's foot. Mortimer tells her that God had taken care of her by preparing her for the accident. RECOMMENDATION: The logic here is absurd. ROYALTY: None. SOURCE: Sullivan, Jessie P. (1978). Puppet scripts for children's church. Grand Rapids, MI: Baker Book House. SUBJECTS/PLAY TYPE: Christian Drama; Puppet Play.

1192. K-5*. (+) Sullivan, Jessie P. **God hates lying.** CAST: 2u. ACTS: 1. SETTINGS: Puppet stage. PLAYING TIME: NA. PLOT: Mortimer confesses to Mathilda that his bad habit of lying is really beginning to bother him, especially since Proverbs 6:16-19 states that God hates lying. Mathilda suggests that he ask God's forgiveness and pray to Him every time he is tempted to lie, and he is able to break the habit. RECOMMENDATION: Delightful and uplifting, the characters here are "real" in their actions and feelings. ROYALTY: None. SOURCE: Sullivan, Jessie P. (1978). Puppet scripts for children's church. Grand Rapids, MI: Baker Book House. SUBJECTS/PLAY TYPE: Lying; Truth; Christian Drama; Puppet Play.

1193. K-2*. (+) Sullivan, Jessie P. **God wants us to be unselfish.** CAST: 2u. ACTS: 1. SETTINGS: Puppet stage. PLAYING TIME: NA. PLOT: Two friends are talking about being selfish. The female character is concerned with being a "good big sister." Bible quotes are used to help solve the problems of selfishness with the main theme of "give, and it shall be given unto you." RECOMMENDATION: This may abe enjoyable and appropriatre for church-related groups. ROYALTY: None. SOURCE: Sullivan, Jessie P. (1978). Puppet scripts for children's church. Grand Rapids, MI: Baker Book House. SUBJECTS/PLAY TYPE: Christian Drama; Siblings; Puppet Play.

1194. 1-5. (-) Cieslinksi, L. John. **God's greatest hits.** CAST: Su. ACTS: 1. SETTINGS: Bare stage, props. PLAYING TIME: 55 min. PLOT: This play combines Bible stories with hymns and spirituals. The stories include the Creation, Adam and Eve, Noah and the Ark, the Tower of Babel, Moses and Pharaoh, David and Goliath, Daniel in the Lion's Den, Jonah and the Whale, and the Patience of Job. Songs range from "Kumbaya" to "Rise and Shine" to "When the Saints Go Marchin' In." RECOMMENDATION: Although it is a nice idea, this play doesn't work. The songs are not integrated with the text, but are simply put into the scenes. The music appears to be the author's favorites, but does not seem to be appropriate. Older children may enjoy the humor, but the songs may bore them. Younger children will have trouble with the play's length. ROYALTY: NA. SOURCE: Cieslinski, L. John. (1988). God's greatest hits. Franklin, OH: Eldridge Pub. Co. SUBJECTS/PLAY TYPE: Bible Stories; Comedy; Musical.

1195. 7-12. (+) Rembrandt, Elaine. **God's wide spaces.** CAST: 5f, 3m, 1u. ACTS: 1. SETTINGS: Kitchen. PLAYING TIME: 20 min. PLOT: A group of men and women share the problems of life in a kibbutz in Merhavia. One member of the group is an optimist who continues to voice her belief that the people and their country will "grow and flourish." This character is revealed as the real life Golda Meir. RECOMMENDATION: This excellent fictional scenario is set in a real place, and involves a notable Israeli heroine of humble beginnings. The true identity of Golda's character is not revealed until the very end, which lends a most dramatic effect. ROYALTY: None. SOURCE: Rembrandt, Elaine. (1981). Heroes, heroines & holidays - plays for Jewish youth. Denver, CO: Alternatives in Religious Education, Inc. SUBJECTS/PLAY TYPE: Meir, Golda; Israel; Drama.

1196. K-3. (+) Silverman, Eleanor. **Godzilla meets Old Stormalong.** CAST: 3u. ACTS: 1. SETTINGS: Ocean. PLAYING TIME: NA. PLOT: Stormalong outwits Godzilla in a clam eating contest by putting tobacco in the clams to make Godzilla sick. RECOMMENDATION: This whimsical "good conquers evil" tale is delightfully appealing. ROYALTY: NA. SOURCE: Silverman, Eleanor. (1983). Dramatics for children. Metuchen, NJ: Scarecrow Press. SUBJECTS/PLAY TYPE: Monsters; Skit.

1197. 7-12. (+) Martens, Anne Coulter. **The go-go gophers.** CAST: 7f, 7m, Su. ACTS: 1. SETTINGS: Music room. PLAYING TIME: 40 min. PLOT: Three members of the football team paint the rival football team's bench and hide from the other team's coach by impersonating "J.J. and the Gophers" rock band. When the screen hiding the record player to which the boys are pantomiming is knocked over, the coach realizes that no harm was done and he allows the boys to wash the paint off and stay on the team. RECOMMENDATION: Although the language and plot here are slightly dated, the theme of the play (the absurdity of high school rivalries) is commendable, and the message that good music transcends the generation gap is effectively and amusingly portrayed. ROYALTY: Free to Plays subscribers. SOURCE: Martens, Anne Coulter. (1978, January). The go-go gophers. Plays: The Drama Magazine for Young People, pp. 27-38. SUBJECTS/PLAY TYPE: Rock Music; Sportsmanship; Comedy.

1198. 9-12. (-) Ohlson, Thomas. **Gold, frankincense, Christmas tree ornaments, and myrrh.** CAST: 1f, 4m. ACTS: 2. SETTINGS: Bare stage, props. PLAYING TIME: NA. PLOT: Two sorcerers and their servant travel back in time to Jerusalem, one week before the birth of Jesus. Intent upon making the event a "money making proposition," they do not recognize Jesus's parents, and rudely dismiss them. Later, the sorcerer is healed by Josh (Jesus), but again does not recognize him. The sorcerer departs, leaving "Josh" a Christmas tree ornament. RECOMMENDATION: By attempting to incorporate too much material into one play, the author has created a very garbled, incomprehensible version of the Christmas story. The jumps between the past and present are illogical and serve only to confuse the audience, while the moments of humor often come at strangely inappropriate times. Parts must be doubled and tripled, with actors changing costumes and characters before the audience. ROYALTY: $40. SOURCE: Ohlson, Thomas. (1981). Gold, frankincense, Christmas tree ornaments, and myrrh. Boston, MA: Baker's Plays. SUBJECTS/PLAY TYPE: Christmas; Christ, Jesus; Nativity; Drama.

1199. 7-12. (+) Anderson, Robert. **The gold mine at Jeremiah Flats.** CAST: 3f, 4m. ACTS: 1. SETTINGS: Living room; gold mine. PLAYING TIME: 30 min. PLOT: To help Mrs. Allspent pay the mortgage, the dastardly banker, Mr. Quickbuck, suggests that they let evil Jack Turmoil purchase their gold mine, although the mine is flooded with water. When Jack causes an explosion to kill Goodworthy, the mine is drained. Mr. Goodworthy then finds gold in the mine, and sends Turmoil to jail. RECOMMENDATION: This melodramatic spoof should be overplayed to complement the characters' funny one liners. ROYALTY: Free to Plays subscribers. SOURCE: Anderson, Robert A. (1986, November). The gold mine at Jeremiah Flats. Plays: The Drama Magazine for Young People, pp. 23-32. SUBJECTS/PLAY TYPE: Gold; Mortgages; Melodrama.

1200. 5-7. (+) Reay, Nina. **Gold rush days.** CAST: 2f, 4m, 2u. ACTS: 1. SETTINGS: Camp. PLAYING TIME: 10 min. PLOT: Two prospectors, their burro, and the Nelson family camp together overnight. When an outlaw attempts to steal their gold dust and valuables, Alexander Hilton, the burro, comes to their rescue and foils Pistol Pete's plan. RECOMMENDATION: The action and characters are interesting, especially the biscuit-loving burro. ROYALTY: Free to Plays subscribers. SOURCE: Reay, Nina. (1977, February). Gold rush days. Plays: The Drama Magazine for Young People, pp. 43-46. SUBJECTS/PLAY TYPE: Gold Prospecting; Playlet.

1201. 6-12. (+) Asher, Sandra Fenechel. (Tenenbaum, Samuel) **The golden cow of Chelm.** (Wise men of Chelm) CAST: 6u. ACTS: 1. SETTINGS: Road; village green. PLAYING TIME: 20 min. PLOT: A group of foolish villagers purchase a skinny cow from a stranger because they think it will produce gold. When it doesn't, the stranger tells them to stop feeding it so it will stop giving milk and give gold instead. The cow almost starves and still gives no gold. The villagers feel guilty, feed the cow, and decide they should have bought a goose that lays golden eggs. RECOMMENDATION: This wonderful adaptation of a Jewish folk tale recaptures all the foolishness and irony of the original, with understated humor and wonderfully synchronized dialogue. ROYALTY: Free to Plays subscribers. SOURCE: Asher, Sandra Fenechel. (1980, October). The golden cow of Chelm. Plays: The Drama Magazine for Young People, pp. 57-62. SUBJECTS/PLAY TYPE: Folk Tales, Jewish; Comedy.

1202. 7-9. (+) Jackson, Richard Eugene. **A golden fleecing.** CAST: 4f, 3m, 1u. ACTS: 2. SETTINGS: Saloon; mine shaft. PLAYING TIME: 60 min. PLOT: The play's seven characters struggle for control of Cactus Bob's Saloon and a gold mine. In the end, the good ones win. RECOMMENDATION: This is an enjoyable brief return to the type of American morality play that was popular on the silent screen, and might well be a useful part of a unit on motion pictures as part of our national culture. ROYALTY: $25. SOURCE: Jackson, Richard Eugene. (1980). A golden fleecing. Denver, CO: Pioneer Drama Service. SUBJECTS/PLAY TYPE: Western; Melodrama.

1203. K-6. (+) Ringwood, Gwen. (Grimm Brothers) **The golden goose.** (The golden goose) CAST: 6f, 8m. ACTS: 1. SETTINGS: Forest. PLAYING TIME: 30 min. PLOT: Simple Wit shares his food with an old man who rewards him with a magic goose. As Simple travels along, everyone who touches the goose becomes stuck to it. The mayor's daughter, Christella, who has never smiled in her life, laughs at the long line of people stuck together and Simple wins her hand in marriage. The spell on the goose is broken. The Wits want Simple to come back and take care of them but he is off on his new life with Christella. RECOMMENDATION: In this delightful com- posite of themes and plots from several well known folk tales, the stage manager lends a narrative touch of comedy and encourages the audience to participate. ROYALTY: NA. SOURCE: Ringwood, Gwen. (1979). The golden goose. Toronto, Canada: Playwrights Co-op. SUBJECTS/PLAY TYPE: Sharing; Folk Tales, Germany; Greed; Adaptation.

1204. K-1. (+) Sills, Paul. (Grimm Brothers) **The golden goose.** (The golden goose) CAST: 4f, 7m, 1u. ACTS: 1. SETTINGS: Bare stage, props. PLAYING TIME: NA min. PLOT: Three sons, out to make their fortunes, must pass a test of generosity. The first two sons fail when they refuse to share their food. The simpleton shares his food and is rewarded with a golden goose. Everyone who touches the goose is stuck to it, and when she sees the hilarious parade, the king's solomn daughter is filled with laughter. The king gives the simpleton his daughter's hand in marriage and the simpleton gives the goose to the king. RECOMMENDATION: This effectively uses recorded music, pantomime, and easy but hilarious physical comedy. It will be a pleasure to produce. ROYALTY: Write to Samuel French. SOURCE: Jennings, Coleman & Harris, Aurand. (1988). Plays children love volume II. New York, NY: St. Martin's Press. SUBJECTS/PLAY TYPE: Folk Tales, Germany; Greed; Sharing; Skit.

1205. 11-12*. (+) Wiles, John. (Aeschylus) **The golden masque of Agamemnon.** (Oresteia) CAST: 22f, 20m. ACTS: 2. SETTINGS: Bare stage, tower. PLAYING TIME: 120 min. PLOT: A composite of several Agamemnon legends, this play follows his struggles in the Trojan War. Sacrificing one of his daughters to curry favor with the gods, Agamemnon arouses the wrath of his wife. When he returns home following the war, she murders him in his bath. Their son, Orestes, avenges his father by murdering his mother, and is pursued by the Furies, who wish to punish him for matricide. Eventually, Athena frees him from their threats, as he had acted according to divine law, and he is forgiven. RECOMMENDATION: This play is a very good study of Greek mythology, but is appropriate only for an audience of mature teens because of its convoluted, symbolic plot, its highly formalized characters, and the dialogue, which would be difficult to absorb by any audience unfamiliar with classical Greek drama. ROYALTY: NA. SOURCE: Wiles, John. (1978). The golden masque of Agamemnon. London, England: Heinemann Educational Books Ltd. SUBJECTS/PLAY TYPE: Agamemnon Cycle; Mythology, Greek; Adaptation.

1206. K-3. (+) Silverman, Eleanor. **The golden touch.** CAST: 1f, 1m, 2u. ACTS: 4. SETTINGS: None. PLAYING TIME: 5 min. PLOT: Greedy King Midas asks for the golden touch, turns his daughter into gold, and realizes his folly. RECOMMENDATION: Although "bare bones," this gets its message across. ROYALTY: None. SOURCE: Silverman, Eleanor. (1983). Dramatics for children. Metuchen, NJ: Scarecrow Press. SUBJECTS/PLAY TYPE: Greed; Mythology, Greek; Skit.

1207. 6-12*. (+) Hewett, Dorothy. **Golden valley.** CAST: 7m, 1u. ACTS: 2. SETTINGS: Bare stage, backdrops. PLAYING TIME: NA. PLOT: Set in Australia, this fantasy centers around four elderly animal/people: Aunt Jane, the crane; Aunt Em, the wombat; Uncle Nee, the possum; and Uncle Di, the mopoke. They decide to adopt a girl, Marigold, to replace Jenny, their girl who ran away years before. Evil Jack Swannell, the family's landlord, threatens to evict them for not paying their rent, but Marigold, aided by Tib, the cat-witch, and Nim, the mysterious runaway boy, is saves them. RECOMMENDATION: Although this fantasy could be quite difficult to produce, due to its length, the dual personalities of the characters, and the staging intricacies, this is a fascinating mystical tale of life in the Australian outback. A cyclorama stage is recommended, with a few basic props, to create an outdoor effect. Some terms may need to be clarified for American audiences. ROYALTY: NA. SOURCE: Hewett, Dorothy. (1985). Golden valley; song of the seals. Sydney, Australia: Currency Press Pty. Ltd. SUBJECTS/PLAY TYPE: Australia; Animals; Fantasy; Musical.

1208. 3-5. (-) Nolan, Paul T. (Moe, Jorgen & Abjornsen, Peter) **The golden voice of little Erik.** CAST: 3f, 6m, Su. ACTS: 1. SETTINGS: Street. PLAYING TIME: 15 min. PLOT: The mistreated sheriff's apprentice has just been paid three pennies for three years of work. As he leaves, the sheriff cautions him not to sing because his voice is terrible. Although he only has three pennies, he gives them away to three beggars and is granted three wishes. He wishes for a good voice that will make everyone happy and willing to give him things. He makes everyone so happy that the town appoints him sheriff and makes the sheriff his apprentice. RECOMMENDATION: This patronizing play has none of the charm of the original. Youngsters would do better to read the original. ROYALTY: None for amateur performance. SOURCE:

Nolan, Paul T. (1982). Folk tale plays round the world: A collection of royalty-free, one-act plays about lands far and near. Boston, MA: Plays, Inc. SUBJECTS/PLAY TYPE: Charity; Folk Tales, Norway; Adaptation.

1209. K-3. (+) Harder, Eleanor. **Goldilocks and the Christmas bears.** CAST: 5f, 3m, Su. ACTS: 2. SETTINGS: Forest. PLAYING TIME: 50 min. PLOT: Goldilocks returns to the forest to visit the hibernating three bears and bring them Christmas presents. The other animals are apprehensive about waking the Bears, but Goldilocks insists that they cannot sleep through Christmas. She teaches the bears and other forest animals about the meaning of Christmas. RECOMMENDATION: Young children will enjoy this performance which should be done by older students or adults. The songs are not the traditional Christmas songs, but have been composed by the author. ROYALTY: $35. SOURCE: Harder, Eleanor. (1981). Goldilocks and the Christmas bears. Chicago, IL: Dramatic Pub. Co. SUBJECTS/PLAY TYPE: Christmas; Musical.

1210. K-6*. (+) Hills, Richard. **Goldilocks and the three bears.** CAST: 6f, 9m, Su. ACTS: 2. SETTINGS: Castle interior; woods; park. PLAYING TIME: NA. PLOT: The princess awaits her prince while the king awaits the fortune which will accompany him. (The Kingdom of Beardom is broke.) Enter the wicked witch, who casts a spell, making a wedding nearly impossible. Goldilocks, with the help of Fairy Light, convinces the audience that if they really believe and wish hard enough, they can bring the prince and princess together. The audience succeeds, the kingdom is saved, and the prince and princess live happily ever after. RECOMMENDATION: Bearing no resemblance to the original; this is a hodge podge of characters from nursery rhymes and fairy tales. The addition of 26 song and dance numbers, 10 scene changes, and audience participation make this an elaborate and very busy production. It would work well as a community project, where both adults and children could be cast. ROYALTY: NA. SOURCE: Hills, Richard. (1984). Goldilocks and the three bears. MacClesfied, England: New Playwrights' Network. SUBJECTS/PLAY TYPE: Nursery Rhymes, Folk Tale Characters; Musical.

1211. 3-6. (+) Kilcup, Rick. **Goldilocks strikes again.** CAST: 3f, 5m, 1u. ACTS: 1. SETTINGS: Cottage. PLAYING TIME: 25 min. PLOT: While Mama, Papa, and Baby Bear are out jogging, McEvil Weasel sneaks into their house and makes it appear that Goldilocks is guilty of breaking and entering. Detectives Grinn and Bearit are investigating when Goldilocks arrives and is accused of the crime. RECOMMENDATION: This is a clever spoof of the **Three Bears** story. The Bear family relationships and the familiarity of the story provide wit and charm and several modern twists make it enjoyable. ROYALTY: Free to Plays subscribers. SOURCE: Kilcup, Rick. (1978, May). Goldilocks strikes again. Plays: The Drama Magazine for Young People, pp. 73-80. SUBJECTS/PLAY TYPE: Animals; Folk Tales, England; Comedy; Skit.

1212. K-5. (+) Ison, Colleen. **Goliath's last stand.** CAST: 2m, Su. ACTS: 1. SETTINGS: Bare stage, props.

PLAYING TIME: NA. PLOT: The story of David and Goliath is told. RECOMMENDATION: This is a contemporary piece with modern dialogue and easy audience participation. Discussion questions are provided. ROYALTY: NA. SOURCE: Ison, Colleen. (1986). Goliath's last stand: And fifteen more easy plays for children. Cincinnati, OH: Standard Pub. SUBJECTS/PLAY TYPE: Bible Story; Participation Play; Christian Drama; Skit.

1213. 2-8*. (+) Jennings, Coleman A. & Harris, Aurand. Golliwhoppers! CAST: 9u. ACTS: 4. SETTINGS: None. PLAYING TIME: NA. PLOT: This comprises four tales of early America. In "Big Jesse Frebold Ebenser Chopalong" (backwoods tall tale), Jesse and Amelia are without meat or gunpowder. Jesse goes to chop a tree to make a barrel for his wife. Along the way, he kills geese, deer, a snake, rabbits, a bear, and fish, all with no gun. They have food and clothing to last them a long time. In "The Sun Snatchers" (an Indian legend), Native Americans find themselves cold and in the dark because the sun has been stolen. As they run toward where they believe the sun to be, they encounter several players playing a game with the sun. The main runner asks to play, then steals the sun and runs home. It is too hot with the sun so close to the Earth, but the Raven helps by placing it higher in the sky. In "The Knee-high Man" (a black cante-fable), the Knee-high Man (a puppet) walks through the swamp asking Wild Boar, Alligator, and Owl how he can become taller. The first two cannot help, but the Owl tells him he has nothing to fear. Since he is small enough to hide, he can climb high in the trees to see what is around him; he is fine just as he is. In "Goll-Gollee-Gee" (an Appalachian Mountain ballad), a stingy, old woman whose health and eyesight begin to fail, hires Lazey Lou and tells her not to look up the chimney where the old woman has hidden her money. Lazey Lou finds the money bag, steals it and runs. She goes out by the cow, who needs to be milked, the horse, who needs to be rubbed, and the tree, whose apples need to be picked, saying to all that she has no time. The cow, horse and tree all reveal Lazy Lou's hiding place. The old woman retrieves her money, returns home and hires another maid, Rudey Rue, who does the same thing. After retrieving her money a second time, the old woman hires yet a third maid, Sukey Sue. She too finds the money bag and, unable to put it back, she drops it on the floor and runs, stopping to milk the cow, rub the horse, and pick the apples. None of the three tell on her, so the old woman goes on, searching until she collapses. When a man takes her home, she finds her bag, then calls for Sukey Sue to pay her. RECOMMENDATION: Each tale is brimming with pantomime, singing, dancing, and audience interaction, and contains the regional flavor of its place of origin, while subtly offering lessons on such topics as morality and self acceptance. ROYALTY: NA. SOURCE: Jennings, Coleman A. & Harris, Aurand. (1988). Plays children love, Volume II. New York, NY: St. Martin's Press. SUBJECTS/PLAY TYPE: Folk Tales, Native American; Folk Tales, Black Americans; Folk Tales, American; Musical.

1214. 12. (+) Taylor, Cecil P. Good. CAST: 4f, 6m. ACTS: 2. SETTINGS: Bare stage. PLAYING TIME: NA. PLOT: Professor John Halder's decision to join the Nazi party is not based on any ideological commitment but rather on the immediate emotional gratification of being welcomed as a valuable comrade, and the probability of personal advancement. A humanist, he justifies his participation as a way of moderating the policies of the "real" Nazis. He deludes himself with visions of joining his Jewish friend in jail. He continues to see his role in book burnings and finally in Auschwitz as somehow different from the role of other Nazi's. The pressures on him are personified by the entire cast interacting with him in one long conversation in which his ailing mother, wife, mistress, Nazi officials, and Hitler himself participate. RECOMMENDATION: Successful production of this excellent play will challenge even the most practiced and sophisticated high school casts. Some of the songs are in German and Yiddish. The continuous interaction between the central character and the rest of the cast, a constantly interrupted and resumed conversation among 10 individuals, is extremely demanding. ROYALTY: $75. SOURCE: Taylor, Cecil P. (1983). Good. Chicago, IL: Dramatic Pub. Co. SUBJECTS/ PLAY TYPE: Holocaust; Nazi Germany; Anti-Semitism; Rationalization; Drama.

1215. K-3. (+) Bauer, Caroline Feller. A good buy. CAST: 1f, 1m, 3u. ACTS: 1. SETTINGS: Bare stage, props. PLAYING TIME: 5 min. PLOT: Goya's wife instructs him to sell the donkey and buy a new one. On his way to market, Goya reflects on his donkey's faithfulness. At the auction, the auctioneer impresses the audience with the donkey's exceptional looks. Goya buys back his own animal. His wife is surprised to see their old donkey back, but Goya and the donkey are pleased. RECOMMENDATION: This valuable tool for praising friendship and service present the themes subtly. ROYALTY: None. SOURCE: Bauer, Caroline Feller. (1987). Presenting reader's theater: Plays and poems to read aloud. New York, NY: H. W. Wilson Co. SUBJECTS/PLAY TYPE: Friendship; Loyalty; Folk Tales, Persia; Reader's Theater.

1216. K-2. (+) Alexander, Sue. Good day, giant. CAST: 2u. ACTS: 1. SETTINGS: Forest. PLAYING TIME: NA. PLOT: An ogre and a giant are sad on Valentine's Day. Since they've eaten up most of the people in the neighborhood, they haven't received any cards. Both decide to surprise each other with Valentine cards. RECOMMENDATION: This is brief, simple to produce, and quite funny. ROYALTY: None. SOURCE: Alexander, Sue. (1977). Small plays for special days. New York, NY: Seabury Press. SUBJECTS/PLAY TYPE: Valentine's Day; Giants and Ogres; Fantasy; Comedy.

1217. 6-9. (+) Winther, Barbara. The good deeds of Pacca. CAST: 2f, 5m, 3u. ACTS: 1. SETTINGS: Jungle. PLAYING TIME: 20 min. PLOT: The old Sakkar tells a story to the Prince about Pacca, an excellent archer who wanted to join the Royal Guard but could not because he was too small. When Pacca meets Katti (a tall man who complains of his lot in life) he suggests that Katti join the guard and says that Pacca himself will go along as Katti's page to do all the archery, and that they share the pay equally. After Pacca enables Katti to become famous, Katti decides that he no longer needs Pacca. When monkeys attack, Katti is unable to perform so he runs off and returns to his old job. Pacca saves the day by leading the guards against the attacking monkeys. Impressed by Pacca's performance, the Queen rewards him with a commission. Once in the guard, Pacca offers to take Katti on as his page and share the wages equally. RECOMMENDATION: Based on Indian folk tales which are, in turn, based on Buddhist sacred writings, this morality play with pantomime and chanting could be used to study world cultures. ROYALTY: Free to Plays subscribers. SOURCE: Winther, Barbara. (1977, December). The good deeds of Pacca. Plays: The Drama Magazine for Young People, pp. 56-62. SUBJECTS/PLAY TYPE: Folk Tales, India; Fable.

1218. 10-12. (+) Barbie, Richard A. **Good King Hal.** CAST: 15f, 14m. ACTS: 2. SETTINGS: Throne room; tavern; road; battlefields. PLAYING TIME: NA. PLOT: Hal, the young Prince of Wales, disgraces his family with wild, drunken living. Through a strange turn of events he becomes king (King Henry V), matures, gives up his wayward past, and eventually leads England to victory in a war with France. RECOMMENDATION: Full of action and humor, the plot will certainly entertain high school students, although the somewhat Shakespearean language style and rhythm may cause some difficulty. The costumes, props, scenes, and musical talent needed for a successful performance will be challenging. ROYALTY: Upon application. SOURCE: Barbie, Richard A. (1981). Good King Hal. Chicago, IL: Dramatic Pub. Co. SUBJECTS/PLAY TYPE: Henry V, King of England; Comedy; Musical.

1219. 4-8. (+) Kehret, Peg. **Goodbye Grandma.** CAST: Su. ACTS: 1. SETTINGS: None. PLAYING TIME: NA. PLOT: When Kevin's grandmother enters a nursing home because she can no longer care for herself, Kevin has a difficult time because they had a very close relationship and he sadly remembers the way things used to be. RECOMMENDATION: Young children will relate to Kevin's sorrows at the loss of his grandmother in this monologue with an important theme. The monologue could easily be adapted to a female speaker. ROYALTY: NA. SOURCE: Kehret, Peg. (1986). Winning monologs for young actors. Colorado Springs, CO: Meriwether Pub. SUBJECTS/PLAY TYPE: Aging; Monologue.

1220. 2-6. (+) Brandt, Dorothy. **Goodbye to litter.** CAST: 17u. ACTS: 1. SETTINGS: Park. PLAYING TIME: 15 min. PLOT: The Garden Club cannot concentrate on meditation because of all the litter. Although the litter tries to stage an uprising, the Club members clean it up. RECOMMENDATION: With dialogue and action appropriate for even the youngest actors, this play is a good lesson about ecology. ROYALTY: Free to Plays subscribers. SOURCE: Brandt, Dorothy. (1977, February). Goodbye to litter. Plays: The Drama Magazine for Young People, pp. 53-57. SUBJECTS/PLAY TYPE: Ecology; Litter; Skit.

1221. 3-12*. (+) Kinoy, Ernest. **Goodbye to the clown.** CAST: 3f, 3m. ACTS: 1. SETTINGS: Office; dining room. PLAYING TIME: NA. PLOT: Peggy, 9, has trouble at

school and home because she blames her difficult behavior on a "clown," an imaginary playmate. No one except Peggy and the audience can see the clown. Peggy's insistence on its reality is very upsetting to her mother, but slowly Peggy realizes that the clown has been a substitute for her dead father. With this, the clown is no longer needed and he says goodbye. RECOMMENDATION: This superb drama tackles difficult subjects. Peggy's relationship with the clown will be recognized by all children who have or have had imaginary playmates, and the clown's natural departure when Peggy doesn't need him anymore will reassure children and parents. This would be especially effective as a clinical experience for children who have to deal with death, or as an adult play. It probably should be performed for younger children only if a skilled educator can lead a follow up discussion. ROYALTY: NA. SOURCE: Kinoy, Ernest. (1954). Goodbye to the clown. New York, NY: Samuel French. SUBJECTS/PLAY TYPE: Death; Imagination; Drama.

1222. 7-12. (+) Hamlett, Christina. **Gopher junction.** CAST: 1f, 7m. ACTS: 4. SETTINGS: Street. PLAYING TIME: 20 min. PLOT: A sheriff sets out to arrest a gang of criminals and receives help from a mysterious female double agent who marries him. RECOMMENDATION: As the sheriff and Miss Purity bring the events to life through their cleverness and attraction towards each other, this is not as predictable as it first seems. ROYALTY: Free to Plays subscribers. SOURCE: Hamlett, Christina. (1985, May). Gopher junction. Plays: The Drama Magazine for Young People, pp. 1-9. SUBJECTS/PLAY TYPE: Comedy; Adventure; Melodrama.

1223. 10-12. (+) Gilsenan, Nancy. **Gorilla bold.** CAST: 4f, 8m. ACTS: 2. SETTINGS: Living room; newspaper office. PLAYING TIME: NA. PLOT: The **Weekly Bugle** is stationed in the living room of corporate dropouts, Hank and Jackie Kiley, and is published with the help of their three reluctant teenaged children and Jackie's newly divorced mother. When Jackie's investigative reporting wins them a coveted prize, the town's corporate newspaper forces them out of business. Their dream does not die though, as they make plans to start a radio station. RECOMMENDATION: This is a delightful play suitable for older teenaged actors to produce for their peers or for adults. The dialogue of the teenagers is especially funny. They bewail the loss of their old consumer oriented life style, while their parents, busily involving them all in a worthwhile venture, ignore their complaints. ROYALTY: $50. SOURCE: Gilsenan, Nancy. (1986). Gorilla bold. Woodstock, IL: Dramatic Pub. Co. SUBJECTS/PLAY TYPE: Entre- preneurship; Newspapers; Life Styles; Comedy.

1224. K-3. (+) Ison, Colleen. **Gossiping.** CAST: 4u. ACTS: 1. SETTINGS: Bare stage. PLAYING TIME: NA. PLOT: The new person at school is rumored to be a stupid crybaby. The new arrival's first friend decides against the friendship after hearing the rumors. Then she realizes that the new kid's behavior is strange only because of fear. The friend decides not to listen to gossip any more. RECOMMENDATION: This focuses on gossip and the problems of jumping to conclusions on the basis of circumstantial evidence. Discussion questions are provided. ROYALTY: NA. SOURCE: Ison, Colleen. (1986). Goliath's last stand: And fifteen more easy plays for children. Cincinnati, OH: Standard Pub. SUBJECTS/PLAY TYPE: Gossip; Truth; Skit.

1225. 11-12*. (+) Pielmeier, John. **A gothic tale.** CAST: 1f, 2m. ACTS: 1. SETTINGS: Tower room. PLAYING TIME: NA. PLOT: Morten wins the drunken Isaac in a card game, Isaac having bet himself when all his money was gone. Morten keeps Isaac locked in the tower and Morton's lonely mistress, Eliza, visits, telling Isaac about her life. Soon Isaac falls in love with the woman. She promises to release him, but never returns after leaving to fetch the key. Isaac dies, and Morten locks the body in a cupboard with five other bodies. RECOMMENDATION: While intriguing, this may be too mature for most high school audiences, due to the brief nudity and the macabre ending. The production could be a unique Halloween presentation. ROYALTY: NA. SOURCE: Pielmeier, John. (1984). Haunted lives. New York, NY: Dramatists Play Service, Inc. SUBJECTS/PLAY TYPE: Horror; Captivity; Love; Drama.

1226. 3-6. (+) Boiko, Claire. (Thayer, Ernest Lawrence) **Gracie at the bat.** (Casey at the bat) CAST: 1f, 17m, 6u. ACTS: 1. SETTINGS: Baseball diamond. PLAYING TIME: 15 min. PLOT: The Mudville baseball team is playing the Center City team. In the bottom of the ninth the score is 4 to 2, with Mudville trailing. One by one, the Mudville players have to leave the game. With two on base, their last player comes to bat. When the player removes the baseball hat, everyone is surprised to see a girl. Gracie hits a home run and Mudville wins the game. RECOMMENDATION: This clever takeoff on "Casey at the bat" relies on a chorus for most of the dialogue. ROYALTY: Free to Plays subscribers. SOURCE: Boiko, Claire. (1977, March). Gracie at the bat. Plays: The Drama Magazine for Young People, pp. 65-69. SUBJECTS/PLAY TYPE: Baseball; Skit; Adaptation.

1227. 10-12. (+) Fontaine, Robert. **Graduation address.** CAST: 2f, 2m. ACTS: 1. SETTINGS: Living room. PLAYING TIME: 10 min. PLOT: The valedictorian tries out his "address" on his fellow classmates. As he presents his speech, each sentence is evaluated and subsequently removed from the address. RECOMMENDATION: The play provides an amusing look at one of education's most prestigious traditions, the valedictory speech. ROYALTY: Free to Plays subscribers. SOURCE: Fontaine, Robert. (1981, May). Graduation address. Plays: The Drama Magazine for Young People, pp. 61-63. SUBJECTS/PLAY TYPE: Comedy; Graduation; Speeches; Valedictorian Speeches; Skit.

1228. 6-8. (+) Tesh, Jane. **Grammar gulch.** CAST: 10f, 6m, 9u. ACTS: 1. SETTINGS: Playground. PLAYING TIME: 20 min. PLOT: Dirty "Done Got" Dan McGee and his Ain't Gang steal all the verbs from the Grammar Gulch bank. Sam and Kathy, who have just had a grammar test, take Sam's own collection of verbs to search for Sheriff Noun and his deputy pronouns. Sam and Kathy find the outlaws instead and order them to "freeze" (one of Sam's

verbs) until the sheriff arrives. RECOMMENDATION: This is a clever way to reinforce the parts of speech. ROYALTY: Free to Plays subscribers. SOURCE: Tesh, Jane. (1985, April). Grammar Gulch. Plays: The Drama Magazine for Young People, pp. 39-44. SUBJECTS/PLAY TYPE: Language Arts, Parts of Speech; Comedy.

1229. 2-9*. (+) Robbins, Norman. **The grand old Duke of York.** CAST: 5f, 7m, Su. ACTS: 2. SETTINGS: Street; woods; castle throne room; hill. PLAYING TIME: NA. PLOT: Favorite nursery rhyme characters battle to keep evil Baron Snatcher from ousting the ineffectual, but good Duke of York. Colin, the gypsy boy, aided by the prophesies of Mother Shipton, stops the Baron and the evil fairy, Maleficent, with a powerful talisman. The side of good is secured by the Duke, who ends the crisis by rescuing his long lost son, Colin. Beaten, Maleficent has a change of heart and offers to rebuild the city, while Colin and his fiancee, Melody, are married. RECOMMENDATION: This British pantomime is written on a story book level for young audiences, andd more mature audiences will enjoy the quick repartee and innuendos. Some British terms may require clarification for American audiences. ROYALTY: NA. SOURCE: Robbins, Norman. (1981). The grand old Duke of York. New York, NY: Samuel French. SUBJECTS/PLAY TYPE: Melodrama; Satire; Nursery Rhyme Characters; Musical.

1230. 3-6. (+) Lasky, Mark A. & Landes, William-Alan. **Grandpa's bedtime story.** CAST: 3f, 2m, 14u. ACTS: 2. SETTINGS: Bedroom; throne room; castle; cave; forest road; dungeon. PLAYING TIME: NA. PLOT: Grandpa tells Johnny a bedtime story about folk tale characters who, dissatisfied with the progress of the story, demand that Johnny and his Grandfather join in the action. They defeat the wicked witch, her helpers, a dragon, and a giant, and rescue the princess before Johnny's parents come home. RECOMMENDATION: Children will like seeing familiar characters in unexpected situations as they enjoy the audience participation. ROYALTY: $25. SOURCE: Lasky, Mark & Landes William-Alan. (1979). Grandpa's bedtime story. Studio City, CA: Players Press. SUBJECTS/PLAY TYPE: Comedy; Folk Tale Motifs; Fantasy.

1231. 9-12. (-) Martens, Anne Coulter. **Granny from Killarney.** CAST: 4f, 2m. ACTS: 1. SETTINGS: Living room. PLAYING TIME: 30 min. PLOT: Larry O'Dell, 17, is eagerly awaiting an acceptance letter from Albion College. He spends the afternoon of St. Patrick's Day with Susanne, his girlfriend, and Trish, his 15 year old sister, making shamrocks for a school dance. A woman identifying herself as his great great grandmother discloses that she is a leprechaun, and grants Larry three wishes, to be renewed each St. Patrick's Day. Larry squanders all three wishes. Granny returns and bargains for her last wish to negate Larry's third wish, thus restoring a verbal relationship between Larry and Susanne, and giving Larry a second chance to restate his last wish. Larry wants Granny to return to Ireland as his last wish. RECOMMENDATION: This play includes over manipulated, convoluted series of events. Audiences would find the plot far fetched, the characters unrealistic, and the dialogue dated and trite. ROYALTY: Free to Plays subscribers. SOURCE: Martens, Anne Coulter. (1988, March). Granny from Killarney. Plays: The Drama Magazine for Young People, pp. 10-20. SUBJECTS/PLAY TYPE: St. Patrick's Day; Skit.

1232. 1-3. (+) Bennett, Rowena. **Granny Goodman's Christmas.** CAST: 5f, 4m, Su. ACTS: 1. SETTINGS: Kitchen. PLAYING TIME: NA. PLOT: Granny catches an elf in a rat trap and the offended elfman ransacks Granny's kitchen a few days before Christmas, destroying all the cakes and cookies she had planned to give as gifts. RECOMMENDATION: Charmingly written in rhyme, the dialogue may be challenging, but the actors and audience will surely enjoy themselves. ROYALTY: None. SOURCE: Kamerman, Sylvia E. (1975). A treasury of Christmas plays. Boston, MA: Plays, Inc. SUBJECTS/PLAY TYPE: Fantasy; Christmas; Playlet.

1233. 2-5. (+) Wilson, Pat Lay. (Aesopus) **The grasshopper and the ant.** (The grasshopper and the ant) CAST: 2f, 2m, 12u. ACTS: 1. SETTINGS: Meadow. PLAYING TIME: 10 min. PLOT: Hopalong Grasshopper realizes the value of work when his plan to convince friends to share their winter lodging with him backfires. RECOMMENDATION: This charming adaptation features lovely songs, set to familiar tunes. ROYALTY: Free to Plays subscribers. SOURCE: Wilson, Pat Lay. (1979, November). The grasshopper and the ant. Plays: The Drama Magazine for Young People, pp. 49-52. SUBJECTS/PLAY TYPE:
Animals; Musical; Adaptation.

1234. 8-10. (+) Mauro, Robert A. **The great American game show.** CAST: 6f, 5m. ACTS: 1. SETTINGS: TV studio. PLAYING TIME: 25 min. PLOT: With hints from mystery guests and Uncle Sam (the TV program host), famous historical panelists guess the identity of Francis Scott Key, Susan B. Anthony, and Harriet Beecher Stowe. RECOMMENDATION: While watching the show, the audience will guess themselves, learning a bit of history and laughing from the puns. ROYALTY: Free to Plays subscribers. SOURCE: Mauro, Robert. (1981, February). The great American game show. Plays: The Drama Magazine for Young People, pp. 33-38. SUBJECTS/PLAY TYPE: Key, Francis Scott; Anthony, Susan B.; Stowe, Harriet Beecher; Comedy.

1235. 9-12. (+) Tyler, Mel & Wilson, Marriott. **The great beyond.** CAST: 1f, 1m. ACTS: 1. SETTINGS: Parlor. PLAYING TIME: NA. PLOT: Mr. Benson goes to a spiritualist to communicate with his late wife, and learns that his wife is wandering in space, unable to get to heaven. The contact between the spiritualist and Mrs. Benson can only be restored if Mr. Benson pays more money, and this continues until Mrs. Benson is supposedly just five feet from the Gates of Heaven. Mr. Benson jumps up and starts out the door, refusing to pay more to help his wife, saying "if she can't jump five feet, she can go to...." And the stage fades to black. RECOMMENDATION: This pokes fun at the legitimacy of spiritualism, and most will find the situation amusing. ROYALTY: None. SOURCE: Majeski, Bill. (1981). Easy skits, blackouts and

pantomimes. Woodstock, IL: Dramatic Pub. Co. SUBJECTS/PLAY TYPE: Comedy; Spiritualism; Skit.

1236. 7-12. (+) Olfson, Lewy. (Shakespeare, William) **Great Caesar's ghost!** (Julius Caesar) CAST: 4u. ACTS: 1. SETTINGS: Office. PLAYING TIME: 10 min. PLOT: On March 15th, Julius Caesar, best selling author of **The Gallic Wars**, tries, with Irving the Soothsayer, to discern the meaning of the message revealed in the crystal ball, while Marc Antony delivers fractured fragments of his famous lines. As Caesar and Marc Antony leave for the Forum, Caesar's secretary and the soothsayer exchange witticisms about the importance Caesar places on the cryptic message, "Beware the Ides of March." RECOMMENDATION: This spoof would be an ideal advanced study project to supplement serious study of the original work. ROYALTY: Free to Plays subscribers. SOURCE: Olfson, Lewy. (1989, March). Great Caesar's ghost! Plays: The Drama Magazine for Young People, pp. 51-54. SUBJECTS/PLAY TYPE: Julius Caesar; Ides of March; Farce.

1237. 6-9. (-) Harrison, Robyn. **The great Christmas strike.** CAST: 3f, 7m, 8u. ACTS: 2. SETTINGS: Fireplace; classroom. PLAYING TIME: 20 min. PLOT: Some of the symbols of Christmas (Santa, Rudolph, snowflakes, stockings, and sugarplums) decide they have been treated unjustly for many years and go on strike. A group of students, after acknowledging their past selfishness, contrives a story of a family in need following an auto accident, which restores everyone's perception of the real meaning of Christmas. RECOMMENDATION: The complaints and complainers elicit no sympathy, nor are they tempered by humor. The ending is contrived and this is too juvenile to appeal to older ages, but is too advanced to be understood by younger ages (i.e. with such concepts as equal opportunity, cloning, and individualism). ROYALTY: $30. SOURCE: Harrison, Robyn. (1983). The great Christmas strike. Franklin, OH: Eldridge Pub. Co. SUBJECTS/PLAY TYPE: Christmas; Selfishness; Strikes; Drama.

1238. 1-8. (+) Bufton, Mary. **Great day in Starflake county court.** CAST: 6f, 6m, Su. ACTS: 1. SETTINGS: Courtroom. PLAYING TIME: 40 min. PLOT: Shortly after Christmas, Santa Claus stands trial for breaking and entering, unfair interstate trade practices, illegal parking, unfair wages, and flying with no flight plan. After listening to witnesses both for and against, the jury finds Santa not guilty. RECOMMENDATION: Similar to the trial in **Miracle on Thirty-Fourth Street**; the issue is whether or not Santa should be allowed to continue in his present job. ROYALTY: NA. SOURCE: Bufton, Mary. (1977). Great day in Starflake county court. Franklin, OH: Eldridge Pub. Co. SUBJECTS/PLAY TYPE: Christmas; Santa Claus; Comedy.

1239. 4-6. (+) Smith, Gary H. **The great discovery.** CAST: 9m. ACTS: 1. SETTINGS: Beach. PLAYING TIME: 20 min. PLOT: As Columbus and his inept men land at the New World, they are confronted by sophisticated natives who, they insist, are possessed. The natives want to interview the Spaniards for the local newspaper and are interested in working out treaties and trade agreements. The Spaniards finally leave in frustration and the natives go fishing, having successfully secured a few more years of peace and freedom. RECOMMENDATION: This spoof humorously portrays Native Americans in unusual, non-historical, and nonstereoptyed roles. ROYALTY: $25. SOURCE: Smith, Gary H. (1975). The great discovery. Franklin, OH: Eldridge Pub. Co. SUBJECTS/PLAY TYPE: Native Americans; Columbus, Christopher; Comedy.

1240. 8-12. (+) Field, Barbara. (Dickens, Charles) **Great expectations.** (Great expectations) CAST: 5f, 8m. ACTS: 2. SETTINGS: Stage, platform and scaffolding. PLAYING TIME: NA. PLOT: This faithfully follows the plot of the original. **RECOMMENDATION: Great Expectations** contains marvelous characters and the theme that honesty and generosity of heart are worth far more than riches and a facade of superiority. This rather superficial and necessarily condensed adaptation still manages to convey some of the human drama. Production requires a demanding amount of memorization for the main characters and requires close attention to the subtleties of personality. ROYALTY: $50. SOURCE: Field, Barbara. (1984). Great expectations. New York, NY: Dramatists Play Service. SUBJECTS/PLAY TYPE: Values; Wealth; Family; Drama.

1241. 7-12. (+) Snapper, Dave. **The great fire.** CAST: 1m, 3u. ACTS: 1. SETTINGS: Fire station. PLAYING TIME: 12 min. PLOT: The town firemen know the detailed history of past fires and have the latest equipment. However, when Mr. Vogel reports that his barn is burning, they are too busy remininscing to help. RECOMMENDATION: For church groups, this explicates James 2:14-17. ROYALTY: None. SOURCE: Altena, Hans. (1978). The playbook for Christian theatre. Grand Rapids, MI: Baker Book House. SUBJECTS/PLAY TYPE: Fire; Morality; Comedy.

1242. 5-9. (+) Winther, Barbara. **The great hurricane.** CAST: 5u. ACTS: 1. SETTINGS: Bare stage, backdrop. PLAYING TIME: 20 min. PLOT: When tigre threatens the lives of all the animals, gallinita (chicken), conejo (rabbit), and coqui (treefrog) cleverly outwit the boasting tigre by convincing him that he must be tied to a tree in order to withstand the coming hurricane winds. RECOMMENDATION: Colorful Spanish words give this classic theme an Hispanic flavor. ROYALTY: Free to Plays subscribers. SOURCE: Winther, Barbara. (1979, March). The great hurricane. Plays: The Drama Magazine for Young People, pp. 49-54. SUBJECTS/PLAY TYPE: Animals; Spanish/English Plays; Folk Tale Motifs.

1243. 1-3. (+) Brown, Rochelle Theresa. **The great mitten caper.** CAST: 1f, Su. ACTS: 1. SETTINGS: Yard. PLAYING TIME: 15 min. PLOT: Three kittens who do not want to wear their mittens pretend to soil their mittens, and volunteer to wash them in hot water so they will shrink and be unwearable. When their mother learns that the kittens were being teased because they wore mittens, she decides that they now will wear gloves. RECOMMENDATION: Children who know the rhyme will be able to predict the actions; this will make it even more fun. ROYALTY: Free to Plays subscribers. SOURCE: Brown, Rochelle Theresa. (1984, January/February). The great kitten caper. Plays: The Drama Magazine for Young People, pp. 47-50. SUBJECTS/PLAY TYPE: Comedy; Animals; Skit.

1244. 3-5. (+) Wilson, Patti & Smith, Sandra. **Great moments in history.** CAST: 4f, 3m. ACTS: 1. SETTINGS: Bank. PLAYING TIME: 15 min. PLOT: Julius Caesar, Michelangelo, and Ben Franklin approach a loan officer to obtain money to finance their memorable contributions to history. RECOMMENDATION: This historical comedy requires some previous knowledge of the characters. ROYALTY: Free to Plays subscribers. SOURCE: Wilson, Patti & Smith, Sandra. (1980, March). Great moments in history. Plays: The Drama Magazine for Young People, pp. 59-63. SUBJECTS/PLAY TYPE: Caesar, Julius; Franklin, Ben; Michelangelo; Skit.

1245. 1-6. (+) Riekens, Deloney M. **The great Mother Goose cook-off.** CAST: 3f, 6m, Su. ACTS: 2. SETTINGS: Bakery. PLAYING TIME: 12 min. PLOT: Mother Goose, who owns a bakery, has a cook-off with valuable prizes. Old Mother Hubbard laments that she cannot enter because her cupboard is bare. Other Mother Goose characters help her by entering baked goods under Old Mother Hubbard's name. RECOMMENDATION: Costuming is quite elaborate and the dialogue includes references to Mother Goose rhymes. ROYALTY: Free to Plays subscribers. SOURCE: Riekens, Deloney M. 1985, March). The great Mother Goose cook-off. Plays: The Drama Magazine for Young People, pp. 35-36. SUBJECTS/PLAY TYPE: Nursery Rhyme Characters; Comedy.

1246. 5-8. (+) Kilcup, Rick. **The great omelet caper.** CAST: 11u. ACTS: 1. SETTINGS: Shop. PLAYING TIME: 20 min. PLOT: As a promotion for their new omelet shop, Wiley and Sly capture Humpty Dumpty, whom they plan to make into a large omelet. The Prince and the Princess rescue him, and discover that Humpty is already hard boiled. RECOMMENDATION: Full of puns and double entendres, this is a delightful new twist for familiar characters. ROYALTY: Free to Plays subscribers. SOURCE: Kilcup, Rick. (1979, February). The great omelet caper. Plays: The Drama Magazine for Young People, pp. 57-63. SUBJECTS/PLAY TYPE: Fantasy; Nursery Rhyme Characters; Skit.

1247. 6-9. (-) Cheatham, Val R. & Sondergard, Sid. (Aesopus) **The great race.** (The hare and the tortoise) CAST: 15u. ACTS: 2. SETTINGS: Forest. PLAYING TIME: 90 min. PLOT: In this musical adaptation, Fox decides to win big money by entering Crow in the race, forcing Chicken (Little) to help him fix the race so that Hare will win. His plan is ruined when Hare does not cooperate and Crow throws the race to collect on his bet that Tortoise would win. Smokey the Bear; Stanley (Laurel) and Oliver (Hardy) as mice trying to bell the Cat; the Lion as King of the Forest with his Owl advisers; and many others join the fun. RECOMMENDATION: The idea of bringing together characters from several fables as well as from the popular media is good; this, however, this is too dated. Children will not understand and may be bored by references to outdated topics such as be-bop music and Muhammed Ali. ROYALTY: $60. SOURCE: Cheatham, Val R. & Sondergard, Sid. (1979). The great race. Franklin, OH: Eldridge Pub. Co. SUBJECTS/PLAY TYPE: Fable; Races; Adaptation.

1248. 7-12. (+) Winther, Barbara. **The great Samurai sword. CAST:** 4f, 4m, Su. ACTS: 1. SETTINGS: Bare stage, props. PLAYING TIME: 20 min. PLOT: Naoto protests the arranged wedding between him and Osada by neglecting his sword practice and ordering Osada to borrow money to pay his gambling debts. Instead, Osada, a swordswoman herself, asks for the ancestral samurai sword, and says that her husband must win it from her before he can sell it. She bests him in a tournament. Five years later, when Naoto returns from intensive training for a rematch, Osada returns the sword, saying it has served its purpose. RECOMMENDATION: This humorous kabuki-style tale requires Japanese costumes, Oriental music, and stylized presentation. ROYALTY: Free for amateur performance. SOURCE: Winther, Barbara. (1976). Plays from folktales of Africa and Asia. Boston, MA: Plays, Inc. SUBJECTS/PLAY TYPE: Folk Tales, Japan; Kabuki Theater; Samurai; Playlet.

1249. 4-12. (+) Acord, Jan. (Hearn, Lafcadio) **The great wave. (The Great wave) CAST:** 37u. ACTS: 1. SETTINGS: Bare stage, backdrop. PLAYING TIME: 15 min. PLOT: Old and wise Hamaguchi lives high on a hill above the sea. While inspecting the excellent rice crop, an earthquake occurs. He orders the crop burned so that the villagers below will rush up the hill to fight the fire. In this way, the villagers are saved from the tidal wave that follows the earthquake. Hamaguchi is honored. RECOMMENDATION: Inspired by the classic Japanese Noh theater, this contains dance, music, and a theme of personal sacrifice for the common good. ROYALTY: Free to Plays subscribers. SOURCE: Acord, Jan. (1975, April). The great wave. Plays: The Drama Magazine for Young People, pp. 81-84. SUBJECTS/PLAY TYPE: Folk Tales, Japan; Adaptation.

1250. 3-6. (+) Bradley, Virginia. **The greater miracle. CAST:** 2f, 2m. ACTS: 1. SETTINGS: Living room. PLAYING TIME: 25 min. PLOT: A grandfather explains the history and meaning of Hanukkah to his grandchildren. RECOMMENDATION: The action described in Grandpa Kramer's lengthy monologue is pantomimed. ROYALTY: None. SOURCE: Bradley, Virginia. (1981). Holidays on stage. New York, NY: Dodd, Mead. SUBJECTS/PLAY TYPE: Hanukkah; Pantomime.

1251. 9-12. (+) Williams, Jaston & Sears, Joe. **Greater Tuna. CAST:** 5f, 14m. ACTS: 2. SETTINGS: Bare stage, props. PLAYING TIME: NA. PLOT: Life in Tuna, Texas is depicted through the broadcasts of the local radio station, OKKK, which include trivial news events, absurd theater reviews, and eccentric citizens. Announcers Arles and Thurston sign off with the OKKK motto: "If you can find someplace you like better than Tuna...then MOVE!" RECOMMENDATION: The radio station as a device to link the stories is imaginative and effective. The characters are lively and distinctive, and many serious issues such as racism and censorship are addressed so flamboyantly that the audience is forced to take a close look at them. Some use of questionable language. Cast can vary from 2 to 19. ROYALTY: $50. SOURCE: Williams, Jaston & Sears, Joe. (1983). Greater Tuna. New York, NY: Samuel French, Inc. SUBJECTS/PLAY TYPE: Satire; Radio; Small-Town Life; Comedy.

1252. 4-6. (-) Murray, John. **The greatest Christmas gift. CAST:** 9f, 5m, 7u. ACTS: 1. SETTINGS: Village square; peasant cottage; castle room. PLAYING TIME: 30 min. PLOT: Three Irish sisters, with the help of a magical man (Willy Wisp) and three leprechauns, take on an evil witch to find the greatest Christmas gift, love. RECOMMENDATION: The contrived plot is not helped by the lame dialogue and weak characterization. ROYALTY: Free to Plays subscribers. SOURCE: Kamerman, Sylvia E. (1976). On stage for Christmas. Boston, MA: Plays, Inc. SUBJECTS/PLAY TYPE: Christmas; Leprechauns; Fantasy.

1253. 3-10. (+) Nersesian, Robert. **The greatest girls' softball team of Sussex County. CAST:** 11f, 1m. ACTS: 1. SETTINGS: Softball diamond. PLAYING TIME: NA. PLOT: Dabney and Shelia, members of the winless Al's Pizza Pounders girls' softball team fight when Shelia taunts Dabney with her "secret." Before the big game, Stoner, the team dreamer, talks with her imaginary friend, the "Goddess of Softball," who tells her that Dabney has problems and that she should look out for new talent. The new talent turns out to be Sievers, who was allowed to join the softball team even though he is a boy. When Sievers, who knew Dabney from another school, reveals the secret that Dabney's father is in prison, Dabney wants to quit the team, but Stoner implores her to stay. In return for Stoner's friendship, Dabney teaches her some softball moves which enable Stoner to make the winning play. The stage action freezes as Dabney, looking up to a place we cannot see, says "Dad, we won." RECOMMENDATION: This movingly and realistically explores the value of friendship, with comedic interspersions (i.e. a hilarious imitation of Howard Cosell, slapstick physical comedy, and one liners). The role reversals are quite refreshing. ROYALTY: $30. SOURCE: Nersesian, Robert. (1987). The greatest girls' softball team of Sussex County. Franklin, OH: Eldridge Pub. Co. SUBJECTS/PLAY TYPE: Friendship; Values; Comedy; Drama.

1254. 7-12. (+) Dias, Earl J. **Greed for gold. CAST:** 3f, 5m. ACTS: 1. SETTINGS: Hotel lobby; shack. PLAYING TIME: 30 min. PLOT: Darwin Doom and his sidekick, Jasper Scroggs, plot to sell worthless land along Furnace Creek to the townspeople by saying that there is gold in the creek. To bait the trap, Doom gets people to believe that the sheriff is trying to discourage townspeople from buying the land so he can have it all himself. When Stella Sweet, the sheriff's daughter, catches Doom and Scroggs salting the creek with gold nuggets, they kidnap her to their hideout. The sheriff and two Indian friends find the hideout in time to save the villains from total annihilation at the hands of "sweet Stella," who has been secretly taking a correspondence course in the martial arts. RECOMMENDATION: The characters, whose dialogue alternates between hilarious one liners and sophisticated speeches, fit right into the classic melodramatic mold. ROYALTY: Free to Plays subscribers. SOURCE: Dias, Earl J. (November, 1976). Greed for gold. Plays: The Drama Magazine for Young People, pp. 1-12. SUBJECTS/PLAY TYPE: Comedy; Western; Melodrama.

1255. 1-6. (+) Gotwalt, Helen Louise Miller. **The greedy goblin.** CAST: 3f, 5m, 1u. ACTS: 1. SETTINGS: Living room. PLAYING TIME: NA. PLOT: The day before Halloween, a goblin steals every pumpkin pie in town. The police can't solve the case, but the children set a trap, catch the goblin, and extract a promise that the pies will be returned. RECOMMENDATION: This salute to children's superior imagination has contemporary language and uncomplicated props and scenery. It is recommended that the older grades produce the play for younger grades. ROYALTY: Free to Plays subscribers. SOURCE: Gotwalt, Helen Louise Miller. (1986). Special plays for holidays. Boston, MA: Plays, Inc. SUBJECTS/PLAY TYPE: Halloween; Drama.

1256. K-1. (+) De Regniers, Beatrice Schenk. **The greedy man's week.** CAST: 2u. ACTS: 1. SETTINGS: None. PLAYING TIME: NA. PLOT: Two readers describe the enormous amounts of food a man eats during the week, and his appropriately enormous weekend stomach ache. RECOMMENDATION: Peers and parents alike will enjoy this funny dialogue as read by two youngsters. ROYALTY: NA. SOURCE: Bauer, Caroline Feller. (1987). Presenting reader's theater: Plays and poems to read aloud. New York, NY: H.W. Wilson Co. SUBJECTS/PLAY TYPE: Greed; Food; Reader's Theater.

1257. 9-12. (+) Kelly, Tim J. (Wallace, Edgar) **The Green Archer.** (The Green Archer) CAST: 6f, 6m. ACTS: 2. SETTINGS: Sitting room/library/office. PLAYING TIME: NA. PLOT: Evil Garre Castle is haunted by the ghost of the Green Archer and is inhabited by the vengeful and terminally ill Abel Bellamy, who has kept his sister-in-law imprisoned in the dungeon for eight years. Rather than face death, Abel plots to destroy the castle and the lives of his enemies. His scheme is foiled by the Green Archer (his nephew in disguise), who rescues everyone. RECOMMENDATION: This dramatization of the 1924 best selling thriller is faithful to the suspense laden atmosphere of the original. Although minor changes are made in plot to simplify it for the stage (i.e. flooding the dungeons with gas, not water), and some of the characters are also changed, it remains mysterious, and the characters remain chillingly evil. ROYALTY: $40. SOURCE: Kelly, Tim J. (1980). The Green Archer. Boston, MA: Baker's Plays. SUBJECTS/PLAY TYPE: Mystery; Thriller; Adaptation.

1258. 4-7. (+) Murray, John. **Green thumb from outer space.** CAST: 3f, 7m, 4u. ACTS: 1. SETTINGS: Farm. PLAYING TIME: 35 min. PLOT: A middle aged science teacher/part-time farmer is visited by an alien on a mission to save Earth from a serious food shortage with "dabble dust," which produces giant vegetables. The dust not only makes the teacher's vegetables huge, but they also begin to speak and walk, enabling the teacher to win a blue ribbon in the local Harvest Festival as well as to save her job. RECOMMENDATION: The conflict between the main character and her adversary adds a degree of tension and suspense. While the plot lacks depth, the humorous events are appealing. ROYALTY: Free to Plays subscribers. SOURCE: Murray, John. (1980, October). Green thumb from outer space. Plays: The Drama Magazine for Young People, pp. 1-14. SUBJECTS/PLAY TYPE: Fantasy; Vegetables; Gardening; Comedy.

1259. 9-12. (+) DuBois, Graham. **The greeneyed monster.** CAST: 2f, 9m. ACTS: 2. SETTINGS: Living room. PLAYING TIME: 25 min. PLOT: Two brothers on a football team cannot take their girlfriends to the Thanksgiving dance because of the team's curfew. Tom suggests that, if they make their girlfriends think that other girls are after them, the girls won't mind skipping one dance. They find one girl willing to pretend to be "after them," but the other girl has to be played by a boy dressed up as a girl. The ruse is discovered, but all ends well. The football coach agrees to extend the curfew until 10:00. The brothers take their girlfriends to the dance and stay till ten, and their co-conspirators (who are not on the team) escort the girls after the 10:00 curfew. RECOMMENDATION: In this comedy of errors, much humor derives from the devices of cross dressing and mistaken identities. Its more serious side considers dating relationships and jealousy. ROYALTY: Free to Plays subscribers. SOURCE: DuBois, Graham. (1986, November). The green-eyed monster. Plays: The Drama Magazine for Young People, pp. 1-12. SUBJECTS/PLAY TYPE: Dating; Jealousy; Comedy.

1260. 9-12. (+) Way, Brian. **Gringling Gibbons and the Plague of London.** 2f, 9m. ACTS: 2. SETTINGS: Living room. PLAYING TIME: 25 min. PLOT: While waiting out a London air-raid in a bomb shelter, a mother explains to her son why a carved wooden box is always lovingly carried to the shelter with them. The story takes them back to the early struggles of the famous young carver, Gringling Gibbons, during 17th century London at the time of the Great Plague and the Great Fire. Gibbons' struggles against poverty, crime and the plague bring him to such places as a dungeon in Newgate Prison and the court of King Charles II and put him in touch with people as diverse as a thieving sailor and Dr. Christopher Wren. Gibbons' honesty and fine workmanship finally bring him much deserved recognition. RECOMMENDATION: A masterful tool for teaching history and a riveting play, this may be too demanding for high school production. However, it is an exquisite play for junior and senior high audiences. ROYALTY: $45. SOURCE: Way, Brian. (1977). Gringling Gibbons and the Plague of London. Boston, MA: Baker's Plays. SUBJECTS/PLAY TYPE: Gibbons, Gringling; Artists; Drama.

1261. 9-12. (+) Sodaro, Craig. (Irving, Washington) **The groom's ghost.** (The groom's ghost) CAST: 4f, 3m, 4u. ACTS: 1. SETTINGS: Parlor. PLAYING TIME: 25 min. PLOT: A young woman meets her bridegroom for the first time, two weeks before the wedding. Because of circumstances, the "bridegroom" never is able to tell her that he is really the servant of the count to whom she is betrothed, and that the count has died. Two weeks later, the young couple is married. RECOMMENDATION: This is an interesting, classic tale of social status and marriage in 1890s Germany. ROYALTY: Free to Plays subscribers. SOURCE: Sodaro, Craig. (1984, October). The groom's ghost. Plays: The Drama Magazine for Young People, pp. 56-64. SUBJECTS/PLAY TYPE: Family; Marriage; Ghosts; Adaptation.

1262. 7-10. (+) Majeski, Bill. **Gross encounters of the worst kind.** CAST: 9f, 5m, Su. ACTS: 1. SETTINGS: Living room; soda shop; courtroom. PLAYING TIME: NA. PLOT: Just when 17 year old Trish is so bored by life that her parents call in the school's therapist, a young alien from outer space lands in her yard looking for a typical American teenager to bring back to his planet for study. He finds Trish, falls in love with her, but by mistake returns to his planet with Trish's grandmother. After much confusion the grandmother is returned. Trish and her alien part, but Trish no longer suffers from boredom. RECOMMENDATION: Although this spoof on a popular 1970s movie is corny and predictable, junior high students might enjoy it. ROYALTY: $15. SOURCE: Majeski, Bill. (1978). Gross encounters of the worst kind. Chicago, IL: Dramatic Pub. Co. SUBJECTS/PLAY TYPE: Aliens; UFOs; Boredom; Comedy.

1263. 10-12. (+) Schulman, Charlie. **The ground zero club.** CAST: 3f, 2m, 3u. ACTS: 1. SETTINGS: Bare stage, backdrops. PLAYING TIME: NA. PLOT: As a security guard is told a nuclear war has begun, Sal, a 25 year old punker, and Angela, his Catholic school girlfriend, enter arguing. Sal tells Angela and the guard that he belongs to the Ground Zero Club, and all members are supposed to meet before a nuclear war for a tremendous party. Bob and Feonna, dressed from a night out, come to the deck so that Feonna can kill herself, but the guard stops her. Bob reveals that they were celebrating his new position in the government Office of Defense. Each person decides to give up a bad habit, then Sal takes an overdose when Angela dumps him. They mourn their wasted lives as a tourist looks through a telescope at the missile approaching the Statue of Liberty. The tourist is killed, but the bomb does not go off. The guard feels love for the first time, Sal lies unconscious, Bob leaves for Washington, and Feonna invites Angela to live with her, leaving the guard to clean up the mess. RECOMMENDATION: Mature audiences may appreciate the bitter slapstick of this modern drama, which could initiate a serious discussion on the consequences of nuclear war and the need to live for the day. ROYALTY: NA. SOURCE: Lamb, Wendy. (1985). Ground zero club and other prize winning plays. New York, NY: Dell Pub. Co. SUBJECTS/PLAY TYPE: Nuclear Weapons; Warfare; Death; Drama.

1264. 4-6. (+) Bradley, Virginia. **A groundhog by any other name.** CAST: 5m, Su. ACTS: 1. SETTINGS: Bare stage, props. PLAYING TIME: NA. PLOT: When Rinehart the Rabbit is chased by a dog, he hops into Grover Groundhog's burrow and pledges his friendship to the disinterested groundhog. On February 2, Grover doesn't

wake up, so Rinehart tucks in his ears and poses as the groundhog for the humans of Punxsutawney, PA. RECOMMENDATION: This gently humorous play requires strong actors in the roles of the rabbit and the groundhog. Animal costumes will also enhance the play. ROYALTY: None. SOURCE: Bradley, Virginia. (1981). Holidays on stage. New York, NY: Dodd, Mead. SUBJECTS/PLAY TYPE: Groundhog Day; Comedy.

1265. 10-12. (+) Stein, Mark. **The Groves of academe.** CAST: 2m. ACTS: 1. SETTINGS: Office. PLAYING TIME: NA. PLOT: Bill Groves, a young assistant professor of English, has his hands full with Paul, one of his students, who attacks academics and their work. During their many discussions, Groves' patience and real wisdom allows Paul to see that the scholarly approach does have some value. Paul writes an excellent term paper but, at the end of the semester, Groves is denied tenure because he has been teaching rather than publishing. RECOMMENDATION: This successfully captures many of the problems and joys of academic life. Its brevity, simple setting and many humorous lines should make it interesting to produce or watch. ROYALTY: $20. SOURCE: Stein, Mark. (1982). The Groves academe. New York, NY: Dramatists Play Service. SUBJECTS/PLAY TYPE: Education; Academic Life; Friendship; Comedy.

1266. 7-12. (+) Hutson, Natalie Bovee. **The grumble group.** CAST: 3f, 2m. ACTS: 1. SETTINGS: Bus stop. PLAYING TIME: NA. PLOT: Four senior citizens sit at a bus stop complaining until Mrs. Grandy, an elderly lady with a positive outlook on life, joins them. She tells the group a little about herself and how she likes to ride the bus and watch the world go by. She gets the group to think about what they do instead of don't like. By the time the bus arrives, the original group has made plans to share some of their interests with each other to help pass the time while they wait for the bus the next day. RECOMMENDATION: The senior citizens may be stereotyped as complainers, but the theme is quite positive. ROYALTY: NA. SOURCE: Hutson, Natalie Bovee. (1984). The grumble group. Stevensville, MI: Educational Service. SUBJECTS/PLAY TYPE: Bus Stops; Attitudes; Comedy.

1267. K-4*. (+) Goldstein, Benjamin & Namanworth, Phillip. **Guess again.** CAST: 3f, Su. ACTS: 1. SETTINGS: Street. PLAYING TIME: NA. PLOT: Alone, Jane closes her eyes and dreams that she is a space child named Guess Again who also eagerly searches for friends. When she is denied entrance to Imaginary Land because she doesn't know the magic words, Guess Again asks colors, letters, numbers, and the four seasons for help. They reveal the necessary words and, as Guess Again enters Imaginary Land, Jane awakes to meet two new friends. RECOMMENDATION: This musical play includes fifteen songs, some of which have been used on Sesame Street. The children will like the spaceship, colorful costumes of fantasy creatures, rainbows, backdrop made up of stars and planets, and the fantasy theme. ROYALTY: NA. SOURCE: Goldstein, Benjamin. (1982). Guess again. Chicago, IL: Dramatic Pub. Co. SUBJECTS/PLAY TYPE: Dreams; Imagination; Fantasy.

1268. 7-12. (-) Majeski, Bill. **Guess who's coming to Earth? or Gross encounters of the worst kind.** CAST: 4f, 2m, 10u. ACTS: 2. SETTINGS: Living room; soda shop; alien room. PLAYING TIME: NA. PLOT: Trish is dissatisfied with her life. An alien being arrives to bring a typical teenager back to his planet. He falls in love with Trish and attempts to take her back to his planet, but being somewhat mistake prone, takes her grandmother instead. It ends with the return of the grandmother and a happy, although shortlived, reuniting of the alien and Trish who look forward to occasional visits as they lead their separate lives. RECOMMENDATION: There is very little originality here. The characters are shallow stereotypes that do not develop and the plot is overdeveloped at the expense of the humor. ROYALTY: $35. SOURCE: Majeski, Bill. (1979). Guess who's coming to earth tonight or Gross encounters of the worst kind. Woodstock, IL: Dramatic Pub. Co. SUBJECTS/PLAY TYPE: UFOs; Romance; Aliens; Comedy.

1269. 8-12. (+) Barbee, Lindsey. **A guide for George Washington.** CAST: 3f, 3m. ACTS: 4. SETTINGS: None. PLAYING TIME: 25 min. PLOT: On Christmas eve in 1776, Washington and his men cross the Delaware to catch the Hessians off guard. RECOMMENDATION: Told in verse and suitable for stage production or reading in the round, the stilted language may cause some students to lose interest in this fictionalized drama. ROYALTY: None. SOURCE: Kamerman, Sylvia E. (1975). Patriotic and historical plays for young people. Boston, MA: Plays, Inc. SUBJECTS/PLAY TYPE: Washington, George; Drama.

1270. 8-12. (+) Garver, Juliet. **Gun laws, anyone?** CAST: 1f, 1m. ACTS: 1. SETTINGS: Cafeteria. PLAYING TIME: NA. PLOT: A boy whose brother has been accidentally shot while hunting asks if he may join a girl in the school cafeteria. When the girl speaks out strongly against guns, the two discuss gun control and agree to meet again. RECOMMENDATION: Snappy and well synchronized dialogue conveys strong ideas about guns and violence. ROYALTY: $4. SOURCE: Garver, Juliet. (1986). One-act dramas. Franklin, OH: Eldridge Pub. Co. SUBJECTS/PLAY TYPE: Gun Control; Debates; Drama.

1271. K-2. (+) Albert, Rollin'. **Gusty goat.** CAST: 3f, 5m, Su. ACTS: 1. SETTINGS: Farmyard. PLAYING TIME: 10 min. PLOT: Farm animals work and play together until a crafty wolf lures a young calf inside his grab bag. The goat is not fooled by the wolf's disguise and rescues the calf. The wolf is encircled by all the animals and forced to leave the farm. RECOMMENDATION: This wryly humorous skit may be used as part of a class creative dramatics project since it offers many opportunities to practice movement, dance, and pantomime. The dialogue fits each particular animal, allowing the students opportunity to perform animal sounds. ROYALTY: Free to Plays subscribers. SOURCE: Albert, Rollin'. (1977, April). Gusty goat. Plays: The Drama Magazine for Young People, pp. 69-73. SUBJECTS/PLAY TYPE: Friendship; Cooperation; Creative Dramatics.

1272. 4-6. (+) Bradley, Virginia. **Gwendolyn Gloria Gertrude McFee.** CAST: 19f. ACTS: 1. SETTINGS: Bare stage. PLAYING TIME: NA. PLOT: Gwendolyn, from the ages of 3 to 6, runs the gamut of vocational choices and finally decides to be a little girl. RECOMMENDATION: This rhyme would be especially appropriate for Girl Scouts or Camp Fire Girls. ROYALTY: None. SOURCE: Bradley, Virginia. (1975). Is there an actor in the house? New York, NY: Dodd, Mead. SUBJECTS/PLAY TYPE: Careers; Skit.

1273. 7-12. (+) Eisenberg, Mike. **Hackers.** CAST: 1f, 3m. ACTS: 1. SETTINGS: Computer center. PLAYING TIME: NA. PLOT: Mary has created the "Checkmate 6," a chess-playing computer program which she is preparing to take to Europe for international matches. For his program, Martin theorizes that, with the proper programming and controlled circumstances, it will be impossible to differentiate Martin, the man, from Martin, the computer and, in a climatic scene, they become indistinguishable. While Martin wonders if the world really wants machine to replace man, Mary learns that the chess association has disqualified "Checkmate 6" for being a machine. Both Mary and Martin discard their projects and rejoin the world of the living. RECOMMENDATION: Convincing, individual, and dynamic characters explore controversial questions dealing with the relationships between humans and computers. ROYALTY: $50. SOURCE: Eisenberg, Mike. (1986). Hackers. New York, NY: Samuel French. SUBJECTS/PLAY TYPE: Computer Programmers; Computers; Comedy.

1274. 3-5. (+) Henderson, Nancy. **Hail the lucky year.** CAST: 3f, 5m, 6u. ACTS: 1. SETTINGS: Street; throne room. PLAYING TIME: 12 min. PLOT: A petty, jealous god makes much trouble for mankind in this pantomimed retelling of an ancient Chinese New Year legend. RECOMMENDATION: This play enjoyably depicts Chinese mythology. ROYALTY: Free for classroom production. SOURCE: Henderson, Nancy. (1978). Celebrate America: A baker's dozen of plays. New York, NY: Julian Messner. SUBJECTS/PLAY TYPE: Chinese Customs; New Year, Chinese; Pantomime.

1275. 6-8. (+) Hamlett, Christina. **Hairum-Scarum.** CAST: 7f. ACTS: 1. SETTINGS: Salon. PLAYING TIME: 15 min. PLOT: A quiet afternoon at the Fantastic Frills hairstyling salon is interrupted by a procession of storybook characters, in person and on the phone, with "hairy" problems (i.e. Rapunzel wants to try "one of those cute, short styles") At last everyone is satisfied and calm returns to the salon. RECOMMENDATION: This well paced short vignette revolves around a series of puns and would be an excellent opener for a longer play. ROYALTY: Free to Plays subscribers. SOURCE: Hamlett, Christina. (1987). Humorous plays for teenagers. Boston, MA: Plays, Inc. SUBJECTS/PLAY TYPE: Hair; Comedy.

1276. 2-5. (+) Carlson, Bernice Wells. **Half of the reward.** CAST: 1f, 2m, 4u. ACTS: 3. SETTINGS: Palace. PLAYING TIME: 10 min. PLOT: An honest peasant is forced to promise the Czar's servant half of the reward he will receive for returning a lost gem. The peasant asks for fifty lashes as his reward and then explains to the Czar that he was being forced to share the reward.

RECOMMENDATION: This clever adaptation of an old fable moves quickly and flows well. ROYALTY: None. SOURCE: Carlson, Bernice Wells. (1982). Let's find the big idea. Nashville, TN: Abingdon Press. SUBJECTS/PLAY TYPE: Folk Tale Motifs; Fable.

1277. 2-5. (+) Gotwalt, Helen Louise Miller. **The half pint cowboy.** CAST: 22u. ACTS: 1. SETTINGS: Ranch. PLAYING TIME: 15 min. PLOT: When the little cowboy is left behind, as usual, while the bigger cowboys chase cattle rustlers and head off an Indian war party, he helps a hurt Indian boy, son of the Chief. Cattle rustlers come to the ranch and the cowboy is saved by the Chief and his braves who have come looking for the Indian boy. The big cowboys return to find the cattle rustlers tied up and the Chief ready to smoke the peace pipe. RECOMMENDATION: Although universally positive human traits are considered in the theme of this play, there is also stereotyping of "cowboys and Indians" dialect. The play calls for all male characters, but any or all roles could be played by females. ROYALTY: Free to subscribers of Plays. SOURCE: Gotwalt, Helen Louise Miller. (1960). First plays for children: A collection of little plays for the youngest players. Boston, MA: Plays, Inc. SUBJECTS/PLAY TYPE: Cowboys; Indians; Skit.

1278. 6-8. (+) Satchell, Mary. **The hall of Black American Heroes.** CAST: 10f, 12m. ACTS: 1. SETTINGS: Exhibition hall. PLAYING TIME: 30 min. PLOT: A group of reluctant students on a museum tour visit the Hall of American Black Heroes. After the guide has identified the portraits of seven heroes, the lights fade. When the lights come up again, real characters are on stage, to portray and tell about Crispus Attucks, Sojourner Truth, Harriet Tubman, Frederick Douglass, Jackie Robinson, Wilma Rudolph, and Sugar Ray Leonard. The students discover that history can be relevant, interesting, and exciting. RECOMMENDATION: It is easy to identify with the students in the tour as they complain about not going to the park or skating rink. It is to be hoped that it is just as easy to be lured into the history lesson. ROYALTY: Free to Plays subscribers. SOURCE: Satchell, Mary. (1985, January/February). The Hall of Black American Heroes. Plays: The Drama Magazine for Young People, pp. 44-52. SUBJECTS/PLAY TYPE: Black Americans; Drama.

1279. 4-6. (+) Burchard, Rachael C. **Hallelujah hopscotch.** CAST: 8f, 4m, Su. ACTS: 2. SETTINGS: Yard. PLAYING TIME: 90 min. PLOT: Two small girls dream of meeting fairies while one rebellious fairy dreams of playing with real children. They overcome the conventions of their distinct worlds through perseverance and imagination. RECOMMENDATION: Without being overly didactic, a moral is clearly presented: unthinking obedience to authority and conformity to convention limits one's existence. The rhyming dialogue of the fairy kingdom is appealing, and cast size is flexible. ROYALTY: $35. SOURCE: Burchard, Rachael C. (1986). Hallelujah hopscotch. Morton Grove, IL: Coach House Press, Inc. SUBJECTS/PLAY TYPE: Conformity; Beliefs; Fairies; Musical.

1280. 3-5. (+) Lahr, Georgiana Lieder. **Halloween cats leave home.** CAST: 7f, 2m, 18u. ACTS: 1. SETTINGS: Forest. PLAYING TIME: 15 min. PLOT: Seven witches who have lost their cats learn from the Chipmunks and Blue Jays that the cats have run away to the Enchanted Forest because they feel overworked and under appreciated. Master Owl advises them to negotiate. He mediates on the witches' behalf, and the cats unanimously accept their terms. The play ends as the Halloween party begins. RECOMMENDATION: This teaches the importance of negotiation. ROYALTY: Free to Plays subscribers. SOURCE: Lahr, Georgiana Lieder. (1981, October). Halloween cats leave home. Plays: The Drama Magazine for Young People, pp. 46-50. SUBJECTS/PLAY TYPE: Labor Relations; Negotiation; Comedy; Skit.

1281. K-3*. (+) Peltola, Irma I. **Halloween parade.** CAST: 3f, 3m, Su. ACTS: 1. SETTINGS: Cornfield; street. PLAYING TIME: 10 min. PLOT: A melancholy scarecrow and sympathetic pumpkin tell their fondest wish of being in the Halloween parade to a friendly witch, who grants it. RECOMMENDATION: This simple plot provides a narrative context for the traditional Halloween costume parade. The wistful scene between the unhappy scarecrow and his equally sad but consoling friend, the pumpkin, is very effective. The play also contains good, eerie music. ROYALTY: Free to Plays subscribers. SOURCE: Peltola, Irma I. (1982, October). Halloween parade. Plays: The Drama Magazine for Young People, pp. 51-54. SUBJECTS/PLAY TYPE: Halloween; Fantasy.

1282. 1-3. (+) Spamer, Claribel. **Halloween secret.** CAST: 4f, 4m. ACTS: 1. SETTINGS: Cornfield. PLAYING TIME: 10 min. PLOT: Having anxiously waited for her first Halloween flight, Little Witch worries that her clumsiness will prevent her from accompanying the older witches. She reveals to sympathetic pumpkins her fear that the dark causes her clumsiness. The pumpkins suggest that the witches take them on their flight to light the way. The older witches carve scary faces on their large pumpkins, while Little Witch realizes that a small pumpkin is sometimes better, and she chooses Little Pumpkin for her lantern. RECOMMENDATION: While she succeeds in alleviating her fear of the dark, Little Witch's failure to fully overcome it is realistic and adds to the value of this play that teaches children there is no shame in being scared. ROYALTY: Free to Plays subscribers. SOURCE: Spamer, Claribel. (1980, October). Halloween secret. Plays: The Drama Magazine for Young People, pp. 39-42. SUBJECTS/PLAY TYPE: Halloween; Fear; Comedy.

1283. K-3. (+) Creegan, George. **A Halloween to remember.** CAST: 7u. ACTS: 1. SETTINGS: Forest. PLAYING TIME: 15 min. PLOT: Early on Halloween evening, Old Tree warns the forest animals about Twitch, a nervous witch who eats forest animals on Halloween. The animals put Jack-O-Lantern on a large stump to scare Twitch. He shows his illuminated face as Twitch comes near, and Twitch flees into the forest, thinking the place is haunted. The animals decide to have a Jack-O-Lantern every Halloween. RECOMMENDATION: This ghost story is delightful, but songs and dialogue may need to be changed to update the play. ROYALTY: Free to Plays subscribers. SOURCE: Creegan, George. (1978, October). A Halloween to remember. Plays: The Drama Magazine for Young People, pp. 73-77. SUBJECTS/PLAY TYPE: Witches; Halloween; Ghost Story.

1284. 3-6. (+) Smiley, Holli Lynn. **Ham it up, Leo.** CAST: 2u. ACTS: 1. SETTINGS: Bare stage. PLAYING TIME: 10 min. PLOT: An aggressive lion tamer pushes his luck a bit too far and gets tamed by the lion. RECOMMENDATION: An abundance of physical stage directions gives children a chance to ad lib and interpret. This also provides a chance for good interplay between two strong lead characters. ROYALTY: Free to Plays subscribers. SOURCE: Smiley, Holli Lynn. (1982, January/February). Ham it up, Leo. Plays: The Drama Magazine for Young People, pp. 66-68. SUBJECTS/PLAY TYPE: Comedy; Lion Tamers; Skit.

1285. 4-6. (-) Thornton, Jane Foster. (Browning, Robert) **Hamelin pays the piper.** (The pied piper of Hamelin) CAST: 5f, 7m, 7u. ACTS: 1. SETTINGS: Living room; office; town square. PLAYING TIME: 20 min. PLOT: The town of Hamelin, infested by rats, offers a purse of gold and the princess to anyone who can get rid of them. The Pied Piper charms the rats away with his flute. The townspeople try to trick the Piper out of his reward, but the princess warns him. He begins to leave town with the children, but the townspeople stop him by granting his reward. The town regains its children and is freed from the rats. RECOMMENDATION: This adaptation changes the ending so that all can end happily. Unfortunately, it also changes the reasons for nonpayment to focus on the trickery and evil of women (who suggest the deceit) as well as the cavalier disposal of the princess as a bride to a stranger. This does not do justice to the original, nor does it stand on its own merit. ROYALTY: Free to Plays subscribers. SOURCE: Thornton, Jane Foster. (1977, April). Hamelin pays the piper. Plays: The Drama Magazine for Young People, pp. 33-42. SUBJECTS/PLAY TYPE: Fantasy; Adaptation.

1286. 7-9. (+) Olfson, Lewy. (Shakespeare, William) **Hamlet.** (Hamlet) CAST: 2f, 7m, 3u. ACTS: 1. SETTINGS: Palace. PLAYING TIME: NA. PLOT: The original plot is preserved. Prince Hamlet, as commanded by his father's ghost, attempts to avenge his father's murder. He feigns insanity as part of his plot to catch the murderous present king, Claudius, who has married Hamlet's mother. Using a play that re-enacts the crime, Hamlet startles Claudius into a confession. Tragedy strikes when Hamlet's love interest, Ophelia, commits suicide, and several accidental murders occur as Hamlet wreaks vengeance. At the conclusion, Hamlet, too, is slain after achieving his goal of killing Claudius. RECOMMENDATION: This read aloud version of **Hamlet** preserves much of Shakespeare's dialogue, but in a more easily read format. ROYALTY: Free to Plays subscribers. SOURCE: Olfson, Lewy. (1980, November). Hamlet. Plays: The Drama Magazine for Young People, pp. 70-80. SUBJECTS/PLAY TYPE: Revenge; Adaptation.

1287. K-5. (+) Martin, Judith. **Hands off! Don't touch.** CAST: Su. ACTS: 1. SETTINGS: Forest. PLAYING TIME: NA. PLOT: A butterfly catcher reaches to pick a beautiful flower but it sings the "Hands Off! Don't Touch" song and while the audience repeats it, the flower slips away. The same events are repeated for a butterfly, and then for the man who encounters a hungry lion. RECOMMENDATION: The themes of "do unto others" and "leave wildlife as you find it" run throughout this production in which the actions and the audience participation are delightful. ROYALTY: Write to Paper Bag Players, Inc. SOURCE: Jennings, Coleman & Harris, Aurand. (1981). Plays children love. New York, NY: Doubleday Co., Inc. SUBJECTS/PLAY TYPE: Environment; Ecology; Participation Play.

1288. 5-8. (+) Nicholson, Jessie. **The handwriting on the wall.** CAST: 4f, 4m. ACTS: 2. SETTINGS: Parlor. PLAYING TIME: 25 min. PLOT: The ghosts of George and Martha Washington help two teenagers and their twin brother and sister save their mother's country inn from a villainous judge. Although Washington had never slept there when he was alive, as the teens had hinted in their publicity, George's ghost helps the twins find a secret passage, drops a button as proof that he had been there, and carves his name on a desk, using his sword. RECOMMENDATION: In this light hearted and imaginative ghost story, the dialogue is witty, and George uses a number of puns and other kinds of word play. ROYALTY: Free to Plays subscribers. SOURCE: Nicholson, Jessie. (1983, January/ February). The handwriting on the wall. Plays: The Drama Magazine for Young People, pp. 48-56. SUBJECTS/PLAY TYPE: Washington, George; Washington, Martha; Ghosts; Comedy.

1289. 3-6. (+) Dexter, Harriet. (Dodge, Mary Mapes) **Hans Brinker.** (Hans Brinker or The silver skates) CAST: 3f, 7m, 1u. ACTS: 1. SETTINGS: None. PLAYING TIME: NA. PLOT: Since Raff Brinker was injured ten years ago, his family has found living difficult. As Christmas approaches, Hans Brinker decides to try one more time to get medical help for his father. At the same time, he earns some extra money to buy skates so that he and his sister can enter a race. She wins, but Hans gives up his chance to win because he helps a friend by giving him the strap off his skate. In the happy ending, the doctor Hans reaches operates successfully on Raff, the family's savings are restored, and Hans agrees to train as the doctor's assistant. RECOMMENDATION: This round the table reading captures the essence of the classic children's story. The narrator's bridges, which link the segments of dialogue, are especially effective. ROYALTY: Free to Plays subscribers. SOURCE: Dexter, Harriet. (1983, January/February). Hans Brinker. Plays: The Drama Magazine for Young People, pp. 57-62. SUBJECTS/PLAY TYPE: Family; Adaptation.

1290. 3-5. (+) Thane, Adele. (Grimm Brothers) **Hansel and Gretel.** (Hansel and Gretel) CAST: 3f, 3m, Su. ACTS: 1. SETTINGS: Cottage; forest. PLAYING TIME: 30 min. PLOT: Though Hansel and Gretel work hard, their family has little to eat. After spilling their milk, they decide to help by picking strawberries but time catches them in the forest after dark. As they sleep, a visit from the Sandman assures them of happy dreams and protection. However, upon awakening they find themselves in the custody of a wicked witch who threatens to eat them. It is only by their own cunning in dealing with the witch that they are able to turn her into a gingerbread cookie and escape. Just as they are freed, they are found by their parents. RECOMMENDATION: This is a delightful, loose adaptation of the classic tale. ROYALTY: Free to Plays subscribers. SOURCE: Thane, Adele. (1978, May). Hansel and Gretel. Plays: The Drama Magazine for Young People, pp. 49-58. SUBJECTS/PLAY TYPE: Folk Tales, Germany; Witches; Adaptation.

1291. 4-6. (+) Kundrat, Theodore V. (Grimm Brothers) **Hansel and Grethel.** (Hansel and Gretel) CAST: 6u. ACTS: 1. SETTINGS: None. PLAYING TIME: 30 min. PLOT: Hansel and Grethel live near the woods with their poverty-stricken father and stepmother. The stepmother plots to dispose of the children by losing them in the woods. Later, lost in the woods, Hansel and Grethel chance upon a witch's cottage made of candy and pastry. Famished, they eat some of the house until the Witch appears and entices them inside. There, she traps Hansel in a cage and forces Grethel to help her fatten him up. When Hansel is fat, the witch heats her oven to roast him, but resourceful Grethel manages to push the witch into the oven instead. When the children discover that their stepmother has died, the three are happy and rich with the witch's money. RECOMMENDATION: Realistic dialogue adds to the suspense of this effective adaptation. ROYALTY: $10. SOURCE: Kundrat, Theodore V. (n.d.) Hansel and Grethel. Morton Grove, Il: The Coach House Press, Inc. SUBJECTS/PLAY TYPE: Folk Tales, Germany; Witches; Reader's Theater.

1292. 4-6. (+) Cheatham, Valerie R. **Hansel, Gretel, and friends.** CAST: 4f, 2m, 1u. ACTS: 1. SETTINGS: Kitchen; forest. PLAYING TIME: 15 min. PLOT: Hansel and Gretel are forced to make brooms for their father's failing business. Hungry, Hansel goes to the forest to pick some strawberries. Their mother sends Gretel after him, who drops bread crumbs along the way so she won't get lost. They encounter their fairy godmother, who appears to be a bit confused because she is looking for Cinderella. After the godmother goes off in search of Cinderella, the witch appears and produces a fabulous gingerbread house in order to the capture the children. But when she discovers their father is a broom maker, the witch decides to give them the house in return for a broom so she can fly away and retire. RECOMMENDATION: This parody of the folk tale uses modern language mixed with some modern concerns to provide humor which is obvious from the beginning. There are several repeated lines which children will immediately learn. Since it requires only a very simple set, the play could be performed easily on a rainy day in place of recess. ROYALTY: Free to Plays subscribers. SOURCE: Cheatham, Val R. (1976, November). Hansel, Gretel, and friends. Plays: The Drama Magazine for Young People, pp. 73-78. SUBJECTS/PLAY TYPE: Comedy; Witches; Folk Tales, Germany; Skit.

1293. K-3. (+) Havilan, Amorie & Smith, Lyn. **Hanukkah.** CAST: 6m, 1u. ACTS: 1. SETTINGS: Temple. PLAYING TIME: NA. PLOT: Judah Maccabee defeats the Syrians and liberates the temple which has been defiled with Syrian idols. After the temple is restored, he and Aaron pour oil from the only bottle left into the first cup of the candelabrum to start the rededication ceremony. The bit of oil which should have only been enough for one day burns for eight, letting all of Jerusalem know that a miracle has occurred. RECOMMENDATION: This explains simply, but movingly, the child's version of the "Festival of Lights." Good for a synagogue or community theater, it can be performed dramatically or as a pantomime. ROYALTY: NA. SOURCE: Havilan, Amorie & Smith, Lyn. (1985). Easy plays for preschoolers to third graders. Brandon, MS: Quail Ridge Press. SUBJECTS/PLAY TYPE: Hanukkah; Tripartite.

1294. K-6*. (+) Ashby, Sylvia. (Grimm Brothers) **Happily ever after.** (Tales told by the Brothers Grimm) CAST: Su. ACTS: 3. SETTINGS: Bare stage, props and backdrop. PLAYING TIME: 65 min. PLOT: The Grimm Brothers describe their folk tale work briefly, and then tell three stories. In "Prince Bristlebeard," a snobby princess is married to a beggar as punishment for having insulted all her princely suitors. Humbled by the experience, she happily learns that her husband is really a prince in disguise. "Luck Child" is about a peasant baby destined to marry the King's daughter. The King does all he can to destroy the boy, but despite an attempted drowning, murderous thieves, and a vicious giant, the child eventually grows up to wed the princess and become King. "Two Eyes," a middle daughter, is ill-used by her mother and sisters. But with the help of a fairy godmother, Two Eyes' life is improved by a magic goat, which brings her food, and a beautiful gold and silver tree, which attracts a prince. She marries the prince and leaves her old life of misery. RECOMMENDATION: The tales represent themes commonly found in Grimms' fairy tales: the ugliness of pride, the evil of prejudice, and the inevitable triumph of good. Production is extremely versatile, as the entire play can be performed by 6-30 players, with men and women switching roles to add humor if desired. While children of all ages may watch, production is more within the reach of high school students or adults. ROYALTY: $20. SOURCE: Ashby, Sylvia. (1988). Happily ever after. Schulenburg, TX: I.E. Clark. SUBJECTS/PLAY TYPE: Folk Tales, Germany; Grimm Brothers; Adaptation.

1295. 11-12. (+) Kelly, Tim. **Happily never after.** CAST: 8f, 3m, 1u. ACTS: 1. SETTINGS: None. PLAYING TIME: 30 min. PLOT: As lovebirds seek marital counseling, characters from "The Frog and the Princess," "Snow White," " Sleeping Beauty," and "Cinderella" determine that unrealistic role expectations, stereotyping, social distinctions, and bigotry cause strife between spouses, relatives, and generations. RECOMMENDATION: As folk tale characters provide comic relief, this may be viewed as hokey or meaningful, depending upon the audience. Some might call this a soap opera with folk tale imagery and an **Our Town** setting. ROYALTY: $10. SOURCE: Kelly, Tim. (1975). Happily never after. Denver, CO: Pioneer Drama Service. SUBJECTS/PLAY TYPE: Marriage; Situation Comedy.

1296. 2-6. (+) Sroda, Anne. **The happiness box.** CAST: 4f, 1m. ACTS: 1. SETTINGS: Street. PLAYING TIME: 15 min. PLOT: Three women are waiting to buy trinkets from a peddler. A fourth woman convinces them that they are wasting their money on trash and should spend on practical items for their households. When the peddler realizes why the women will not buy his trinkets, he shows them that impractical items can make people happy and are not always foolish investments. RECOMMENDATION: As the play ends with a poem about "hyacinths for the soul," the message that frivolity has its place is prettily delivered. ROYALTY: Free to Plays subscribers. SOURCE: Sroda, Anne. (1975, October). The happiness box. Plays: The Drama Magazine for Young People, pp. 53-58. SUBJECTS/PLAY TYPE: Frivolity; Playlet.

1297. 9-12. (+) Mullin, Molly Ann. **Happy birthday, girl.** CAST: 1f, 1m. ACTS: 1. SETTINGS: Living room. PLAYING TIME: NA. PLOT: Janice, a socially isolated career woman in her late twenties, is alone on her birthday. Suddenly, a stranger appears in her apartment. He seems to know everything about Janice, even the green dress she wants for her birthday, which he magically produces. Gradually, Janice's feelings change from suspicion to trust as their conversation shifts to her inability to make friends. As they talk, she realizes that she alienates herself and is not happy being a loner. When a friend from works telephones her to ask her out, she hesitates, but then accepts his offer. RECOMMENDATION: The terse dialogue in this brief play leads quickly to a surprisingly sensitive and insightful discussion of loneliness, isolation as a result of career priorities, and self defeating habits. The only weak points are some clumsy allusions that the mysterious stranger is an angel and some rather forced jokes. ROYALTY: $15. SOURCE: Mullin, Molly Ann. (1985). Happy birthday, girl. Boston, MA: Baker's Plays. SUBJECTS/PLAY TYPE: Career Women, Friendship; Angels; Drama.

1298. 1-12. (+) Nolan, Jeannette Covert. **Happy Christmas to all.** CAST: 3f, 3m. ACTS: 1. SETTINGS: Library. PLAYING TIME: 20 min. PLOT: When Clement Moore returns from buying the Christmas dinner turkey, the children give him a kitten for Christmas. Moore gives them a Christmas poem: " 'Twas the night before Christmas...." The next year, the family surprises him by having it printed in the newspaper. Dr. Moore fears that such an unscholarly publication may ruin his reputation, but Mrs. Moore gently suggests that he may be remembered longer for this short poem than for all the books he has written. RECOMMENDATION: This provides warm insight into the life of the author Dr. Clement Clarke Moore, and whether or not the action is totally accurate, it leaves a warm feeling. ROYALTY: None. SOURCE: Kamerman, Sylvia E. (1988). The big book of Christmas plays. Boston, MA: Plays, Inc. SUBJECTS/PLAY TYPE: Christmas; Moore, Clement Clarke; Playlet.

1299. 7-12. (-) Fendrich, Shubert & Fendrich, Steven. **Happy days.** CAST: 10f, 6m, Su. ACTS: 2. SETTINGS: Burger joint. PLAYING TIME: 90 min. PLOT: When Richie tutors the new transfer student, Gloria, Lori Beth, his girlfriend, gets the wrong idea. The Appleton sisters, Hilda and Cynthia, plan to turn Arnold's restaurant into a chic boutique until Cynthia discovers that Al (the owner) is, in truth, her long lost sailor love. Lori Beth finds out the real story about Gloria and they become good friends, singing with the rest of the cast "It happened in the Fifties, Rock n' Roll!" RECOMMENDATION: Based on the television series, all the Fifties Rock n' Roll nostalgia in the world will not rescue this trite and predictable production. No audience should be expected to suspend disbelief to this extent. ROYALTY: $75. SOURCE: Fendrich, Shubert & Fendrich, Steven. (1982). Happy days. Denver, CO: Pioneer Drama Service. SUBJECTS/PLAY TYPE: Television Drama; 1950s, U.S.; Musical Comedy.

1300. 9-12. (+) Gleason, William. **Happy daze.** CAST: 6f, 6m, Su. ACTS: 2. SETTINGS: None. PLAYING TIME: NA. PLOT: A lonely teenager retreats into a 1950s fantasy world where he is popular. When he can no longer find happiness in his imaginary popularity, he returns to real life and learns to cope with being a teenager. RECOMMENDATION: Teenagers with an interest in the 1950s should both enjoy seeing and portraying these characters. Although the theme is obvious, it is not heavy handed. ROYALTY: $35. SOURCE: Gleason, William. (1977). Happy daze. Woodstock, IL: Dramatic Pub. Co. SUBJECTS/PLAY TYPE: Teenagers; 1950s, U.S.; Comedy.

1301. K-6. (+) McMaster, Beth. **Happy holly.** CAST: 2f, 3u. ACTS: 1. SETTINGS: Bare stage, props. PLAYING TIME: NA. PLOT: An efficiency expert steals Santa's map and the elves' thinking caps, so that he can do Christmas his own way. When the thinking caps are retrieved, the expert is exposed, and forced to wear happy holly, which makes him a more agreeable person. RECOMMENDATION: With rhymes, music and picturesque exclamations (i.e. painted peppermints!), this is a nice, uplifting, and secular Christmas play. ROYALTY: NA. SOURCE: McMaster, Beth. (1981). Happy holly/Christmas cards. Toronto, Canada: Simon & Pierre. SUBJECTS/PLAY TYPE: Christmas; Musical.

1302. 7-12. (+) Taylor, Cecil P. **Happy lies.** CAST: 4f, 2m, Su. ACTS: 1. SETTINGS: Bedrooms; kitchen. PLAYING TIME: NA. PLOT: Derek, who is justifiably frustrated by his family life (his father has left them for another woman, his mother doesn't want him to visit the father, the father thinks he's not friendly enough to his girlfriend), turns his attention to Kamala, a crippled Indian girl. The two correspond and Derek tries to get her a wheelchair so she can go to school. At first she refuses a wheelchair, still holding on to the hope that she will walk. Finally, she faces reality, builds her own wheelchair, and the play ends with her wheeling the mile to school. RECOMMENDATION: The audience should be familiar with India's culture and caste system, as well as Britain's relationship with India. Kamala's fight to maintain her independence and dignity will generate discussion about the problems of disabled people. ROYALTY: NA.

SOURCE: Taylor, Cecil P. (1983). Live theatre: Four plays for young people. London, England: Methuen. SUBJECTS/PLAY TYPE: Disabilities; Drama.

1303. 3-7. (+) Berghammer, Gretta & Caspers, Rod. (Wilde, Oscar) **The happy prince.** (The happy prince) CAST: 4f, 4m, 5u. ACTS: 1. SETTINGS: Bare stage, props. PLAYING TIME: NA. PLOT: The statue of the Happy Prince cries because he can see all the misery of the city. He convinces a little swallow to delay its trip south and help some of the poor people by presenting them with the jewels and gold that decorate the statue. When the swallow stays too long and tells the prince that it is dying, the prince's lead heart breaks. Both the prince and the dead swallow are placed in the trash, but are reincarnated as angels in heaven. RECOMMENDATION: This adaptation movingly recreates Wilde's story about the injustice of wealth and poverty living side by side. This is meant to be performed as part of a trilogy which includes "The Devoted Friends," and "Birthday of the Infanta." ROYALTY: NA. SOURCE: Jennings, Coleman A. & Berghammer, Gretta. (1986). Theatre for youth: Twelve plays with mature themes. Austin, TX: Univ. of Austin Press. SUBJECTS/PLAY TYPE: Poverty; Philanthropy; Adaptation.

1304. 3. (+) Golden, Edward. (Wilde, Oscar) **The happy prince.** (The happy prince) CAST: 4f, 8m, 5u. ACTS: 1. SETTINGS: Bare stage, backdrops. PLAYING TIME: 20 min. PLOT: A swallow is going to Egypt for the winter to be with his friends, when he pauses to rest overnight under a statue of the Happy Prince, which has human emotions. The statue begs him to run errands of generosity, and the swallow delivers the statue prince's jewels to poverty-stricken people. After the Prince has nothing left to give and Winter has set in, the swallow dies and the Prince's heart breaks. The townspeople decide the statue has become unsightly and have it removed. When it is melted down, the statue's heart refuses to melt and is thrown in a garbage heap with the dead swallow. The narrator concludes by stating that Paradise would be ruled in "love and kindness" by the Prince, and that there the swallow would sing forever. RECOMMENDATION: This endearing adaptation poignantly offers a very selfless view of love. ROYALTY: Free to Plays subscribers. SOURCE: Golden, Edward. (1988, November). The happy prince. Plays: The Drama Magazine for Young People, pp. 52-60. SUBJECTS/PLAY TYPE: Reader's Theater; Poverty; Philanthropy; Adaptation.

1305. 5-8. (+) Majeski, Bill. **Happy Valentine's Day.** CAST: 1f, 2m. ACTS: 1. SETTINGS: Shop. PLAYING TIME: 12 min. PLOT: When Ed Nensil goes into a card shop for a Valentine card for his girlfriend, "Dr." Lovelace tries to sell him weird Valentines. In a turnabout, Ed helps Dr. Lovelace and his secretary to get together. RECOMMENDATION: With the interest that middle school children find in romance, this play will be a hit with its cynical one liners and elements of very humorous farce. ROYALTY: Free to Plays subscribers. SOURCE: Majeski, Bill. (1979, February). "Happy Valentine's day." Plays: The Drama Magazine for Young People, pp. 53-56. SUBJECTS/PLAY TYPE: Valentine's Day; Skit.

1306. 10-12. (+) Fendrich, Shubert & Fendrich, Steven. **Happy valley high.** CAST: 10f, 6m. ACTS: 2. SETTINGS: Auditorium; soda shop. PLAYING TIME: 120 min. PLOT: The Happy Valley High football team hopes Al, their new coach, will reverse their losing record. Chances look even better when Olie joins the football team and his sister becomes a cheerleader. Soon, an undercurrent of intrigue develops when another new student, Cathy Rogers, tries to get information on the team's playbook for her old boyfriend at a rival high school. Instead, Cathy falls in love with Olie and helps Happy Valley to a win. In a subplot of lost love, Al, the new coach, and Cynthia, Olie and Betty's mother, find each other again after 15 years and rekindle their affections. RECOMMENDATION: This fifties musical moves a little slowly and the plot is transparent. Perhaps by omitting some of the more trite musical interludes, it could be an amusing presentation. ROYALTY: NA. SOURCE: Fendrich, Shubert & Fendrich, Steven. (1988). Happy valley high. Denver, CO: Pioneer Drama Service. SUBJECTS/PLAY TYPE: High School; 1950s, U.S.; Comedy; Musical.

1307. 7-12. (+) Caruso, Joseph G. **Happyville.** CAST: 3f, 3m, Su. ACTS: 2. SETTINGS: Yard. PLAYING TIME: 40 min. PLOT: Happyville is terrified of Shootin' Sam because there is no marshall. When a pretty sharpshooter hillbilly, Hawkeye Hannah, arrives to eliminate the problem, she is surprised to find that Shootin' Sam is a "hansome hunk of a man" and her heart melts. Should she save the town, or win Sam's heart? She does both by turning the duel into a shooting match in which the winner becomes sheriff. She lets Sam win and he can no longer be "bad" because he now has responsibilities of sheriff. RECOMMENDATION: In this happy comedy, the cast will use old fashioned western drawl to portray the characters. ROYALTY: $25. SOURCE: Caruso, Joseph G. (1981). Happyville. Schulenburg, TX: I.E. Clark. SUBJECTS/PLAY TYPE: Western; Comedy.

1308. 3-7. (+) McDonough, Jerome. **Hark, Harold the angel sings.** CAST: 1f, Su. ACTS: 1. SETTINGS: None. PLAYING TIME: 25 min. PLOT: When the sheep in the meadow try to find Christmas, Harold, a female angel, comes to help, but fouls up everything she tries to do. After imaginary trips to many places, the animals find they have been part of the holiday all along. RECOMMENDATION: This would be impressively performed by using a living cyclorama made up of all chorus members not actively involved in each scene. This has good plays on words and the animal names are quite original. ROYALTY: $15. SOURCE: McDonough, Jerome. (1985). Hark, Harold the angel sings. Denver, CO: Pioneer Drama Service. SUBJECTS/PLAY TYPE: Christmas; Cyclorama.

1309. K-12. (+) Doddridge, Philip. (Watson, Jeannette Grace) **Hark, the glad sound.** (A chronicle of Christmas) CAST: Su. ACTS: 1. SETTINGS: None. PLAYING TIME: 2 min. PLOT: The Savior's coming is anticipated. RECOMMENDATION: Suitable for church or parochial school groups, this would be a joyful choral reading for a Christmas pageant or worship service. ROYALTY: NA. SOURCE: Hendricks, William & Vogel, Cora. (1978).

Handbook of Christmas programs. Grand Rapids, MI: Baker Book House. SUBJECTS/PLAY TYPE: Christmas; Christ, Jesus; Worship Program.

1310. 4-5. (+) Ross, Laura. **Harriet Tubman, conductor of the freedom train.** CAST: 3f, 3m, Su. ACTS: 1. SETTINGS: Bare stage, backdrop. PLAYING TIME: NA. PLOT: This dramatizes one of the journeys which Tubman made with slaves who wished to be free. RECOMMENDATION: The use of pantomime and masks will help to inspire the actors with the courageousness of Tubman, who founded the Freedom Train. ROYALTY: None. SOURCE: Ross, Laura. (1975). Mask-Making with pantomime and stories from American history. New York, NY: Lothrop, Lee, & Shepard Co. SUBJECTS/PLAY TYPE: Black Americans; Underground Railroad; Tubman, Harriet; Pantomime.

1311. 3-5. (+) Fisher, Aileen. **Harriet Tubman, the second Moses.** CAST: 4f, 3m, Su. ACTS: 1. SETTINGS: Bare stage. PLAYING TIME: 30 min. PLOT: Narrators and the person who plays Harriet Tubman describe her life as a slave (from childhood to adulthood), her decision to create the underground railroad, and her perilous trips as a leader of groups traveling north to freedom. RECOMMENDATION: The use of 3rd person and 1st person narration is a strong and very effective technique which touches the heart of the reader. The narration of Harriet Tubman from a child's point of view especially helps arouse the audience's empathy. ROYALTY: Free to Plays subscribers. SOURCE: Fisher, Aileen. (1988, January/February). Harriet Tubman, the second Moses. Plays: The Drama Magazine for Young People, pp. 35-38. SUBJECTS/PLAY TYPE: Black Americans; Tubman, Harriet; Underground Railroad; Choral Reading.

1312. K-4. (-) Fisher, Aileen Lucia. **Harvest feast.** CAST: Su. ACTS: 1. SETTINGS: None. PLAYING TIME: 2 min. PLOT: The pilgrims prepare for Thanksgiving. RECOMMENDATION: Although the spirit of Thanksgiving is well captured here, the poem's setting in colonial times and some sophisticated language may make comprehension difficult. ROYALTY: Free to Plays subscribers. SOURCE: Fisher, Aileen Lucia. (1985). Year-round programs for young players. Boston, MA: Plays, Inc. SUBJECTS/PLAY TYPE: Thanksgiving; Choral Reading.

1313. 7-12. (+) Garver, Juliet. **Harvey the hypochondriac.** CAST: 2f, 3m. ACTS: 1. SETTINGS: Living/dining room. PLAYING TIME: 15 min. PLOT: Harvey's obsession with a healthy lifestyle comes to an embarrassing climax when he makes everyone at a dinner party uncomfortable. He and his girlfriend argue, but both regret it. After Abby botches her attempt to show Henry how obsessive he is, the two agree to compromise. RECOMMENDATION: It is difficult to see what Abby sees in Henry, but she does explain that he has been particularly obnoxious lately. The humor here is quite effective (especially Henry's mistaking a veterinarian for an M.D.) and it would make an excellent curtain raiser. ROYALTY: Free to Plays subscribers. SOURCE: Garver, Juliet. (1987, November). Harvey the hypochondriac.

Plays: The Drama Magazine for Young People, pp. 49-55. SUBJECTS/PLAY TYPE: Allergies; Hypochondriac; Health Consciousness; Skit.

1314. K-3*. (+) Way, Brian. **The hat.** CAST: 2f, 2m. ACTS: 1. SETTINGS: None. PLAYING TIME: 40 min. PLOT: Peter who lives with his mother, a milliner, delivers a hat to magic man, Mr. Hump. Delighted, Mr. Hump tries it on but is then unable to get it off. Peter fetches his mother, who comes with her crystal ball. At first, she is unable to do more than change the hat's color, but by combining all the colors, they finally remove it. RECOMMENDATION: Young children will especially like this play since they are able to participate in the storytelling. The performance in the round gives the children an added sense of being a part of the action. Not only are primary colors used for color recognition, but also for what action or images these colors can create in a person's imagination. ROYALTY: $15. SOURCE: Way, Brian. (1977). The hat. Boston, MA: Baker's Plays. SUBJECTS/PLAY TYPE: Colors; Comedy.

1315. 9-12. (+) Purkey, Ruth Angell. **The haunted carousel: A whirligig through time and space.** CAST: 8f, 6m, Su. ACTS: 1. SETTINGS: Park. PLAYING TIME: 30 min. PLOT: A woman's son disappears as he rides the polar bear on a park carousel during the 1890s. The son, the mother, and the polar bear all surface in various ways during the 1920s, 1950s, and into the future. RECOMMENDATION: For advanced audiences, this hauntingly travels through time and space, keeping viewers captivated. ROYALTY: $15. SOURCE: Purkey, Ruth Angell. (1982). The haunted carousel: a whirligig through time and space. Schulenburg, TX: I.E. Clark. SUBJECTS/PLAY TYPE: Mystery; Supernatural; Drama.

1316. 4-6. (+) Bradley, Virginia. **The haunted house.** CAST: 6m, Su. ACTS: 2. SETTINGS: Haunted house. PLAYING TIME: NA. PLOT: Mr. Sly agrees to imprison people in the ghosts' haunted house. But when Mr. Sly refuses to give the ghosts their part of the profit, they add Sly to their collection of people in the haunted house. RECOMMENDATION: This skit is brief, easy to produce, uses few props and is especially appropriate for Halloween. ROYALTY: None. SOURCE: Bradley, Virginia. (1975). Is there an actor in the house? New York, NY: Dodd, Mead. SUBJECTS/PLAY TYPE: Halloween; Pantomime.

1317. 6-10. (+) Miller, Kathryn Schultz. **Haunted houses.** CAST: 2f, 2m, Su. ACTS: 1. SETTINGS: Mansion. PLAYING TIME: 35 min. PLOT: Four teenage friends at an old mansion tell ghost stories, and in the process, reveal much about themselves. RECOMMENDATION: The simple stories interestingly express teenage feelings about parents, siblings, and identity. ROYALTY: $20. SOURCE: Miller, Kathryn Schultz. (1986). Haunted houses. Morton Grove, IL: The Coach House Press, Inc. SUBJECTS/PLAY TYPE: Identity; Emotions; Drama.

1318. 10-12. (+) Murray, John. **The haunting of Hathaway house.** CAST: 7f, 6m, 1u. ACTS: 1. SETTINGS: Drawing room. PLAYING TIME: 30 min. PLOT: Three scenes develop separate murder mysteries to confirm that Hathaway house is haunted. First, a greedy nephew plots the death of his grieving aunt, who acts as if her husband is still living. Next, mistaken for the spurned admirer of the young woman for whom the house was built, a widow avenges her husband's death by killing the person she thinks killed him. Finally, a greedy brother conducts a mock seance to rid the house of ghosts. The audience is led to believe that the people currently in the house are returning from previous lives as inhabitants or previous inhabitants. It's hard to tell the real ghosts. **RECOMMENDATION:** The well written, fast moving, and suspenseful plot twists keep the audience on the edge of their seats. **ROYALTY:** Free to Plays subscribers. **SOURCE:** Murray, John. (1985). Fifteen plays for today's teenagers. Boston, MA: Plays, Inc. **SUBJECTS/PLAY TYPE:** Murder; Mystery; Drama.

1319. 3-6. (+) Gotwalt, Helen Louise Miller. **Haunts for hire. CAST:** 6f, 8m. **ACTS:** 1. **SETTINGS:** Office. **PLAYING TIME:** 30 min. **PLOT:** The high school drama club is raising money for the scholarship fund by haunting for money. A representative of the AF of G (Amalgamated Federation of Ghosts) advises that they join. When they decline, the ghosts pull some real haunts, and the police threaten to close the drama club. The club decides to join the AF of G and an agreement is reached where the club does the bookings and the ghosts do the hauntings. **RECOMMENDATION:** This very clever portrayal of unions, disguised as a ghost story would be excellent as a Halloween play, or as an introduction to the labor movement. **ROYALTY:** Free to Plays subscribers. **SOURCE:** Gotwalt, Helen Louise Miller. (1975, October). Haunts for Hire. Plays: The Drama Magazine for Young People, pp. 37-46. **SUBJECTS/PLAY TYPE:** Halloween; Labor Unions; Comedy.

1320. 9-12. (+) Kelly, Tim J. (Taylor, Tom) **Hawkshaw the detective.** (The ticket-of-leave man) **CAST:** 6f, 5m, Su. **ACTS:** 2. **SETTINGS:** Tea room; attic; office. **PLAYING TIME:** 120 min. **PLOT:** Innocent Bob from the country, falls under the influence of "the Tiger" and wrongfully goes to jail for 5 years. Upon release, the Tiger ruins each of Bob's jobs by disclosing his jail stint. Finally, Bob agrees to help Tiger rob a safe, but really he is setting them up to be caught by Hawkshaw, the detective. They are caught, Bob's good name is restored, and the play ends happily. **RECOMMENDATION:** This humorous melodrama with exaggerated characters does not contain the slapstick dialogue with double meanings that often make such plays more silly than funny. There is a subtle moral message that something for nothing is not easily come by, and that those who are willing to cut you in on such a good deal usually do it for their benefit, but at your expense. **ROYALTY:** $25. **SOURCE:** Kelly, Tim J. (1976). Hawkshaw the detective. Denver CO: Pioneer Drama Service. **SUBJECTS/PLAY TYPE:** Theft and Deception; Counterfeiting; Comedy; Adaptation.

1321. 3-6. (-) Uitvlugt, J.W.F. **He is altogether lovely. CAST:** Su. **ACTS:** 1. **SETTINGS:** None. **PLAYING TIME:** 30 min. **PLOT:** An educated scientist does not understand the meaning of Christmas until people working at many types of jobs present the word of the Lord through a compilation of the Bible passages from the Books of Isaiah, Psalms, and Corinthians. **RECOMMENDATION:** The mix of mundane ordinary dialogue and lengthy Biblical passages does not fit together well. **ROYALTY:** None. **SOURCE:** Hendricks, William & Vogel, Cora. (1983). Handbook of Christmas programs. Grand Rapids, MI: Baker Book House. **SUBJECTS/PLAY TYPE:** Christmas; Worship Program.

1322. 3-7. (+) Moessinger, William. **He won't be home for Christmas. CAST:** 6f, 9m, Su. **ACTS:** 1. **SETTINGS:** Store; Santa's workshop; home. **PLAYING TIME:** NA. **PLOT:** Tommy Benson wants his father, who is working in Alaska, to come home for Christmas. He sends a letter to Santa asking for his help. Convinced that there is no Santa, Tommy pulls off the department store Santa's beard. The real Santa learns what happened and makes sure Mr. Benson gets home on Christmas day. **RECOMMENDATION:** This delightfully stresses family love and the Christmas spirit. There are several choral singing parts and solos for Tommy and his mom. **ROYALTY:** Free to Plays subscribers. **SOURCE:** Kamerman, Sylvia E. (1978). On stage for Christmas. Boston, MA: Plays, Inc. **SUBJECTS/PLAY TYPE:** Christmas; Musical; Playlet.

1323. 6-8. (+) Merten, George. **A head for Peppino. CAST:** 1f, 1m, 2u. **ACTS:** 1. **SETTINGS:** Puppet stage. **PLAYING TIME:** 15 min. **PLOT:** An inane magician tries unsuccessfully to make a puppet's face look like that of a human being. **RECOMMENDATION:** The magician's tragically humorous magical efforts make this a roaring success. **ROYALTY:** None. **SOURCE:** Merten, George. (1979). Plays for puppet performance. Boston, MA: Plays, Inc. **SUBJECTS/PLAY TYPE:** Magic; Comedy; Puppet Play.

1324. 4-8. (+) Van Horn, Bill. (Irving, Washington) **The headless horseman rides again.** (The legend of Sleepy Hollow) **CAST:** 6f, 5m. **ACTS:** 1. **SETTINGS:** School. **PLAYING TIME:** 30 min. **PLOT:** In this sequel to the original, the children, aware of Icabod's earlier encounter with the ghost, are frightened by the reoccurrences of these strange happenings. The situation is resolved with the ghost finally being laid to rest, and Icabod and Katie planning to marry. **RECOMMENDATION:** Familiarity with the original will enhance enjoyment, as this prolongs the delicious horror story. **ROYALTY:** $10. **SOURCE:** Van Horn, Bill. (1981). The headless horseman rides again. Denver, CO: Pioneer Drama Service. **SUBJECTS/PLAY TYPE:** Ghosts; Crane; Icabod; Adaptation.

1325. K-4*. (+) Lauck, Carol. **Heads and tales. CAST:** 2f, 3m. **ACTS:** 1. **SETTINGS:** Library. **PLAYING TIME:** NA. **PLOT:** TJ is having trouble writing a story for homework. In a dream he meets his imagination and a Professor who show him how to free his imagination. TJ does well and earns his storytelling pom-pom. When he awakens, he still has his pom-pom and knows what story he will write. **RECOMMENDATION:** A delightful children's play with a message that people who don't use their imagination are almost as sad as people who don't smile. **ROYALTY:** NA. **SOURCE:** Lauck, Carol. (1978). Heads and tales. New York, NY: Samuel French, Inc. **SUBJECTS/PLAY TYPE:** Homework; Imagination; Fantasy.

1326. 7-12. (+) McCusker, Paul. **Heart Hart's heart-to-heart show.** CAST: 1f. ACTS: 1. SETTINGS: Bare stage, props. PLAYING TIME: NA. PLOT: A love advisor humorously answers questions from her TV viewers. For example, when asked how far a couple should go on a date, she answers "Baltimore." RECOMMENDATION: This is too cliched and includes overused humor. ROYALTY: NA. SOURCE: McCusker, Paul. (1984). Batteries not included. Boston, MA: Baker's Plays. SUBJECTS/PLAY TYPE: Love; Dating; Comedy.

1327. 2-5. (+) Carlson, Bernice Wells. **The heart of a monkey.** CAST: 2u. ACTS: 1. SETTINGS: Beach. PLAYING TIME: 5 min. PLOT: A monkey's fast thinking saves his life when he accepts an invitation to visit a shark's home and learns that the shark plans to kill him for his heart. RECOMMENDATION: This is a short, humorous dialogue. ROYALTY: None. SOURCE: Carlson, Bernice Wells. (1982). Let's find the big idea. Nashville, TN: Abingdon Press. SUBJECTS/PLAY TYPE: Animal Tales; Fable.

1328. 7-12. (-) Sawyer-Young, Kat. **Heartbreak.** CAST: 1m. ACTS: 1. SETTINGS: None. PLAYING TIME: 1 min. PLOT: Ryan is shocked to discover that a woman he likes is old enough to be his mother, but he bounces back by asking whether her children are girls. RECOMMENDATION: This does a poor job of reflecting the problems of age differences. ROYALTY: None. SOURCE: Sawyer-Young, Kat. (1987). Minute monologues for contemporary teens. Boston, MA: Baker's Plays. SUBJECTS/PLAY TYPE: Dating; Generation Gap; Monologue.

1329. K-3. (+) Tesh, Jane. **Heartland.** CAST: 9f, 5m. ACTS: 1. SETTINGS: Bare stage, props. PLAYING TIME: 10 min. PLOT: When Jack Frost and the frost fairies steal all the valentines from the Valentine Orchard, they admit the crime to Benny of the Double Dare Detective Agency, explaining that they took the valentines because they never received any. Benny mentions the lovely designs that Jack Frost creates and how he could use them to decorate the Valentines. Jack and Farmer Brown become partners and everyone sings the ending to the tune of "My Bonnie Lies Over the Ocean." RECOMMENDATION: The device of growing valentines, whose verses comprise much of the play's text, in an orchard may be unrealistic, but it works well in this fluffy piece. ROYALTY: Free to Plays subscribers. SOURCE: Tesh, Jane. (1989, February). Heartland. Plays: The Drama Magazine for Young People, pp. 31-34. SUBJECTS/PLAY TYPE: Valentine's Day; Skit.

1330. 5-7. (+) Fisher, Aileen. **Hearts, tarts, and valentines.** CAST: 3f, 6m, Su. ACTS: 1. SETTINGS: Kingdom. PLAYING TIME: 20 min. PLOT: The King of Hearts and the King of Diamonds feud over a lace handkerchief. The townspeople restore friendship between the two royal houses by sending "words of friendship from the heart" on lace cards to the kings on February 14. RECOMMENDATION: The theme is not overly didactic, and the versed dialogue and puns add a light touch. ROYALTY: Free to Plays subscribers. SOURCE: Fisher, Aileen. (1986). Holiday programs for boys and girls. Boston, MA: Plays, Inc. SUBJECTS/PLAY TYPE: Nursery Rhyme Characters; Valentine's Day; Playlet.

1331. 1-3. (+) Tutt, Barbara. **A heart-warming tale.** CAST: 2f, 1m, 5u. ACTS: 1. SETTINGS: Courtyard. PLAYING TIME: 15 min. PLOT: The Knave of Hearts who stole the tarts returns on Valentine's Day to apologize for what he has done. It happens to be the same day that the Queen of Hearts is interviewing for a new Knave of Hearts. The Queen of Clubs helps him apologize, the Queen of Hearts forgives him, and the Knave regains his job. RECOMMENDATION: Children would be interested in the card characters as well as the familiar nursery rhyme. The play succeeds in treating the theme of penitence lightly but effectively. ROYALTY: NA. SOURCE: Tutt, Barbara. (1986, January/February). A heart-warming tale. Plays: The Drama Magazine for Young People. pp. 61-65. SUBJECTS/PLAY TYPE: Nursery Rhyme Characters; Valentine's Day; Skit.

1332. 8-10. (+) Bailey, Craig C. **Heaven sent.** CAST: 1f, 1m, 1u. ACTS: 1. SETTINGS: Bedroom. PLAYING TIME: NA. PLOT: Stuart, 16, lacks self confidence. Repudiated by his girlfriend in favor of another boy, Stuart is visited by his SAFLITON, Supernatural Advisor for Life, Cassandra. Smart, modern, and chic, Cassandra does not fit into Stuart's preconceived notion of a godmother. A series of magical antics, hard questions, and finally Cassandra's disgust with his self pity help Stuart realize that faith and a belief in one's self are the first steps towards accomplishing anything. RECOMMENDATION: Teens will easily relate to Stuart's feelings of inadequacy, and the lesson is presented in a nonthreatening, nondidactic manner. ROYALTY: NA. SOURCE: Bailey, Craig. (1988). Heaven sent. Franklin, OH: Eldridge Pub. Co. SUBJECTS/PLAY TYPE: Self Respect; Self Confidence; Fantasy.

1333. 4-8. (-) Benson, Islay. **Heavy hangs the mortgage.** CAST: 6f, 5m. ACTS: 1. SETTINGS: Kitchen. PLAYING TIME: 30 min. PLOT: Villainous Despard demands the mortgage payment by the Overthrotes, or else. Two charlatans convince the Overthrotes to give them a small amount of money with the promise that they will receive a much greater amount of money in the future. At the last minute, poor but honest Tom Smith rushes in to save the Overthrote family by exposing the charlatans, and announcing that scientists have discovered uranium on his farm which makes him a wealthy man. He helps pay the mortgage and marries Guinevere Overthrote. RECOMMENDATION: Even the great cast of characters cannot carry the weak plot and unbelievable situations. ROYALTY: Free to Plays subscribers. SOURCE: Benson, Islay. (1980, May). Heavy hangs the mortgage. Plays: The Drama Magazine for Young People, pp. 47-53. SUBJECTS/PLAY TYPE: Mortgages; Swindlers and Swindling; Melodrama.

1334. 9-12. (+) Kundrat, Theodore V. (Ibsen, Henrik) **Hedda Gabler.** (Hedda Gabler) CAST: 3f, 3m, 1u. ACTS: 4. SETTINGS: Bare stage. PLAYING TIME: 90 min. PLOT: A distillation of the original, the major plot and character elements remain intact, with only Berte the maid dropped. RECOMMENDATION: This is one of several Ibsen commentaries on the modern woman that generated much debate in the feminist age. The language is Americanized (Jorge becomes George and Madame Hedda is Mrs. Hedda), but the self destructive Hedda remains brightly alive and speaks provokingly to high school students. The production normally should be the work of adults, but the reader's theater concept places fewer demands on the performers and opens the production to interested high school students. The stage directions appear to be intended to reinforce the characters' alienation from one another or their efforts to "make connection." ROYALTY: NA. SOURCE: Kundrat, Theodore V. (1979). Hedda Gabler. Chicago, IL: Coach House Press. SUBJECTS/PLAY TYPE: Women; Marriage; Behavior; Adaptation.

1335. K-12. (+) Baldwin, John. (Spyri, Johanna Heusser) **Heidi.** (Heidi) CAST: 8f, 3m, 1u. ACTS: 2. SETTINGS: Mountain. PLAYING TIME: 60 min. PLOT: Heidi, a small girl living in the mountains with her grandfather, is taken away to be the companion of a young invalid in Frankfurt. Heidi does much good for Clara but begins to pine for her home. Clara's father returns to his home after an absence and, realizing what is wrong with Heidi, helps her to return to her beloved mountains and grandfather. RECOMMENDATION: This faithful adaptation omits Heidi's early years with her grandfather but amply includes the original action and charm. ROYALTY: $25. SOURCE: Baldwin, John. (1980). Heidi. Denver, CO: Pioneer Drama Service. SUBJECTS/PLAY TYPE: Orphans; Adaptation.

1336. 1-6*. (+) Pugh, Ann & Utter, Betty. (Spyri, Johanna) **Heidi.** (Heidi) CAST: 6f, 7m, Su. ACTS: 2. SETTINGS: Swiss village; drawing room; railroad station; street. PLAYING TIME: NA. PLOT: When Heidi, an orphan, is placed in the care of her hermit grandfather she discovers the beauty of the Swiss Alps and the old man discovers joy in life. Then, to the dismay of her grandfather and her friend Peter, the goat boy, Heidi is forced to move to Frankfurt to become companion of the invalid Clara. The housekeeper in the Frankfurt home mistreats the little Swiss girl, but Clara and her absent minded tutor defend Heidi and assure her she will live again on the mountain with her grandfather. Heidi is returned to those who love her and Clara's health is restored as well. RECOMMENDATION: This is a pallid adaptation of the Johanna Spyri children's classic. Still, the nasty Fraulein Rottenmeier and the loving, exuberant Heidi hold one's attention. ROYALTY: $60. SOURCE: Pugh, Ann & Utter, Betty. (1979). Heidi. Schulenburg, TX: I.E. Clark. SUBJECTS/PLAY TYPE: Switzerland; Orphans; Adaptation.

1337. 3-12. (+) Thane, Adele. (Spyri, Johanna) **Heidi.** (Heidi) CAST: 7f, 4m. ACTS: 4. SETTINGS: Hut; drawing room. PLAYING TIME: 35 min. PLOT: This is a faithful

adaptation of the original, although it more resembles the Shirley Temple movie than the book. RECOMMENDATION: All of the melodrama and overdone sentimentality is recaptured here, as Heidi is perpetually good and long-suffering, and as Clara becomes strong enough to walk again. ROYALTY: Free to Plays subscribers. SOURCE: Thane, Adele. (1988, May). Heidi. Plays: The Drama Magazine for Young People, pp. 43-52, 75. SUBJECTS/PLAY TYPE: Orphans; Adaptation.

1338. 9-12. (+) Huff, Betty Tracy. **The heiress of Harkington Hall.** CAST: 7f, 4m. ACTS: 1. SETTINGS: Hall. PLAYING TIME: 40 min. PLOT: Daffodil, an imposter posing as the heiress of Harkington Hall, is being courted by the sinister Smedley, posing as Lord Lambastingly, in order to win Daffodil and her money. Meanwhile, Rose, a young, sweet, orphan maid, falls in love with the real Lord Lambastingly. After much scheming by Daffodil and Smedley to claim the fortune, a letter reveals that the true heir can be identified by a shilling worn on an "icky string." Because Rose has a shilling like this, she is proclaimed the true heiress and Wentworth, the old family retainer, is revealed to be her long lost father. Rose makes plans to marry Lambastingly. RECOMMENDATION: In this lively satirical comedy of a Gothic melodrama, the characters are drawn with exaggerated perfection, the comic asides are hilarious, and the silly action matches the dialogue well. ROYALTY: Free to Plays subscribers. SOURCE: Huff, Betty Tracy. (1975, April). The heiress of Harkington Hall. Plays: The Drama Magazine for Young People, pp. 1-11. SUBJECTS/PLAY TYPE: Melodrama; Romance; Inheritance; Satire.

1339. 4-7. (-) Rockwell, Thomas. **The heiress, or the croak of doom.** CAST: 3f, 7m. ACTS: 3. SETTINGS: Madhouse. PLAYING TIME: 30 min. PLOT: Two boys, who supposedly are a werewolf and a vampire, try to drive Helen crazy in order to obtain the multimillion dollar Farkus peanut fortune to which she is heiress. The boys release balloons from under her bed, paint her feet red and green, and make her believe that she has pulled an arm off a person. When she brings her uncle in to show him, nothing can be found. This convinces both of them that she is insane and she commits herself to an asylum, where the boys have disguised themselves as a humpbacked carpenter and her humpbacked doctor. Eventually, the boys are foiled and Helen receives her inheritance. However, the boys escape and Helen is left in despair, as she wonders what they might try next. RECOMMENDATION: This has unpleasant stereotypes, unmysterious happenings, and a trite, over used plot. It also leaves much unresolved, as the victimized girl is left to ponder the horrors of her unknown, but probably terrible, future. ROYALTY: NA. SOURCE: Rockwell, Thomas. (1980). How to eat fried worms, and other plays. New York, NY: Delacorte Press. SUBJECTS/PLAY TYPE: Comedy; Family; Drama.

1340. 1-9*. (+) Keller, Martha V. & Murray, Elaine P. **Hello, Mr. Appleseed.** CAST: 3f, 5m. ACTS: 1. SETTINGS: Cabin. PLAYING TIME: 45 min. PLOT: Young Molly has been telling Nathaniel of the visits Johnny Appleseed made to her frontier family and the stories he told. A knock is heard and it is Johnny Appleseed. During supper and afterwards there are fleeting glimpses of an Indian at the window. Johnny and the father investigate but find no one. After everyone has gone to bed, Johnny is wakened by his friend, White Feather who tells him that some animals need his help. When they come back, White Feather is invited in to meet the family. Molly takes on the responsibility of caring for some orphaned bobcat kittens and Johnny Appleseed answers the call to move on. RECOMMENDATION: This is a useful play to introduce the character of Johnny Appleseed and the nature of frontier life. The action and dialogue are basically realistic. However the Indian is disturbingly stereotyped. ROYALTY: $15. SOURCE: Keller, Martha V. & Murray, Elaine P. (1978). Hello, Mr. Appleseed. Denver, CO: Pioneer Drama Service. SUBJECTS/PLAY TYPE: Appleseed, Johnny; Chapman, John; Colonial America; Drama.

1341. 9-12. (+) Grote, David G. (Andreyev, Leonid Nikolaevich) Help. (Love of One's Neighbor) CAST: 11f, 3m, Su. ACTS: 1. SETTINGS: Amusement park. PLAYING TIME: NA. PLOT: A large crowd gathers in an amusement park to see if a man on the tall observation tower will jump, so that they can say they were present when the tragedy occurred. The man calls for help, but no one in the crowd notices or has time. RECOMMENDATION: The characters are represented as stereotypes, easily recognized. The actors use props and mime to develop their characterizations, and the play is recommended for its excellent portrayal of modern society. ROYALTY: $15. SOURCE: Grote, David G. (1980). Help. Schulenburg, TX: I.E. Clark. SUBJECTS/PLAY TYPE: Satire; Drama.

1342. 4-6. (+) Bradley, Virginia. Help! CAST: 3u. ACTS: 3. SETTINGS: Meadow; forest; mountain. PLAYING TIME: NA. PLOT: Two friends go to a meadow and get stung by bees; they go to a forest and get poison ivy; finally they go to a mountain and fall off. All these bad things happen because of their carelessness. RECOMMENDATION: This easy pantomime teaches the importance of safety. ROYALTY: None. SOURCE: Bradley, Virginia. (1975). Is there an actor in the house? New York, NY: Dodd, Mead. SUBJECTS/PLAY TYPE: Ecology; Safety; Pantomime.

1343. 9-12. (+) Kelly, Tim. Help! I'm trapped in a high school! CAST: 19f, 11m. ACTS: 2. SETTINGS: Classroom; office; living room. PLAYING TIME: 90 min. PLOT: Incorrigible students are imprisoned in a high school with a drill instructor for a principal. A group of "good" students and two student teachers have been erroneously sent to the school for incorrigibles. During a series of humorous escape attempts, one of the teachers establishes a rapport with the "bad" students, and one of the "good" students helps to focus public attention on the prison like atmosphere of the school. RECOMMENDATION: This fast paced comedy requires assured actors with presence and timing. Costuming requires that "bad" students are identified by their unconventional dress and hair styles, which allows for creativity. Teachers and administrators may find this offensive, however, as they are portrayed as

crooks and know nothings, with the exception of Miss Nolan. ROYALTY: $50. SOURCE: Kelly, Tim. (1988). Help! I'm trapped in a high school! Denver, CO: Pioneer Drama Service. SUBJECTS/PLAY TYPE: High School; Comedy.

1344. 5-10. (+) Kehret, Peg. Help! Send candy bars. CAST: 1u. ACTS: 1. SETTINGS: None. PLAYING TIME: NA. PLOT: A youngster bemoans the lack of sweets and snacks in the house since his/her mother has gone on a diet. RECOMMENDATION: A clever dramatization, this short monologue should capture feelings familiar in many households. ROYALTY: NA. SOURCE: Kehret, Peg. (1986). Winning monologs for young actors. Colorado Springs, CO: Meriwether Pub. SUBJECTS/PLAY TYPE: Snacks; Dieting; Monologue.

1345. K-3. (+) Silverman, Eleanor. (Cleary, Beverly) Henry and Ribsy. (Henry and Ribsy) CAST: 2f, 2m, 4u. ACTS: 3. SETTINGS: Street; telephone booth; bus. PLAYING TIME: NA. PLOT: Henry takes a stray dog home with him on the bus, causing great consternation for the bus riders and driver. RECOMMENDATION: The humor in this adaptation of a Beverly Cleary episode will be a hit. ROYALTY: NA. SOURCE: Silverman, Eleanor. (1983). Dramatics for children. Metuchen, NJ: Scarecrow Press. SUBJECTS/PLAY TYPE: Dogs; Comedy; Skit; Adaptation.

1346. 6-10. (+) Foon, Dennis. Heracles. CAST: 2m, 3u. ACTS: 1. SETTINGS: Platform; tapestry. PLAYING TIME: NA. PLOT: The three fates tell Iolaus of the birth, life, and death of his uncle, Heracles, when he comes to the funeral pyre to collect the hero's bones which will help him defeat the king's army. Iolaus is sent away without the bones to fight as a man in a world now ruled by men. The fates continue weaving and chanting the story. RECOMMENDATION: The success of the play will depend on casting, as there is very little scenery or props to aid in characterization. The dialogue is clear and expressive. ROYALTY: NA. SOURCE: Foon, Dennis. (1978). Heracles. Vancouver, Canada: Talonbooks. SUBJECTS/PLAY TYPE: Mythology, Greek; Drama.

1347. 4-8. (-) Bradley, Virginia. Here lies McClean. CAST: 2f, 3m, 2u. ACTS: 4. SETTINGS: Cottage. PLAYING TIME: NA. PLOT: Pretending to be a ghost, a traveling actor aids the caretaker's wife by frightening her husband into moving away. RECOMMENDATION: The plot and the characters are confusing and do not fit together well; parts of the plot may too complex for the intended age group. ROYALTY: None. SOURCE: Bradley, Virginia. (1975). Is there an actor in the house? New York, NY: Dodd, Mead. SUBJECTS/PLAY TYPE: Cemeteries; Ghosts; Comedy.

1348. 3-6. (+) Bradley, Virginia. Herlock Sholmes. CAST: 1f, 8m. ACTS: 1. SETTINGS: Bare stage. PLAYING TIME: NA. PLOT: This a play on words as the title indicates. The detective and his men are called to a "dead party" but think they are looking for a "dead body." A comical search for clues produces fun for the bored party guests. RECOMMENDATION: The characters are delightfully bumbling, the funny fast paced plot is enjoyable, and the theme is original. ROYALTY: None. SOURCE: Bradley, Virginia. (1975). Is there an actor in the house? New York, NY: Dodd, Mead. SUBJECTS/PLAY TYPE: Detectives; Murder; Comedy.

1349. 7-10. (+) Cheatham, Val R. **The hero. CAST:** 2f, 8m, Su. ACTS: 1. SETTINGS: Street. PLAYING TIME: 35 min. PLOT: Prior to the American Centennial, Waverly, VA receives a check for $1,103.44 from the estate of the town's founder. The townspeople are to celebrate the Centennial and commemorate unremembered war hero Frederick Schmidt. They write to Schmidt and he replies that he will march in the parade, even though he is 108 years old. He shows up in the uniform of a British Redcoat which angers the people, until Schmidt explains that he had earned the gratitude of the town's founder by not shooting him during a battle. He continues that America is the only country where a former enemy could become a citizen with the same right as any other. RECOMMENDATION: This lacks full credibility, as very few people live to the age of 108 while passing themselves off as being thirty years younger. However, the characters are interesting, and the ending provides both a surprise and a stirring statement about the meaning of democracy. ROYALTY: Free to Plays subscribers. SOURCE: Cheatham, Val R. (1976, April). The hero. Plays: The Drama Magazine for Young People, pp. 15-22. SUBJECTS/PLAY TYPE: Patriotism; Revolution, U.S.; Playlet.

1350. 8-12. (+) Albert, Rollin'. **Hero here at Heorot.** CAST: 3f, 5m, Su. ACTS: 1. SETTINGS: Bare stage. PLAYING TIME: 15 min. PLOT: Beowulf, a 1960s style hippy, is summoned to help Hrothguano, the King of Denmark, slay a terrible monster. They go to the swamp to duel with Grendel, but the monster is aided by his mother in the fight. In the end, Beowulf saves Denmark by slaying Grendel and making a business deal with Grendel's mother to make and sell love beads. RECOMMENDATION: Much of the humor in this spoof of the classic is based on literary puns. Only a well read group of students will recognize the very humorousliterary allusions. ROYALTY: Free to Plays subscribers. SOURCE: Albert, Rollin'. (1976, February). Hero here at Heorot. Plays: The Drama Magazine for Young People, pp. 49-54. SUBJECTS/PLAY TYPE: Beowulf; Comedy.

1351. 7-12. (-) Hawse, Alberta. **Herod is alive and well.** CAST: 4f, 2m. ACTS: 3. SETTINGS: Living room. PLAYING TIME: NA. PLOT: The Hudson family celebrates Christmas and worries about the "unsaved" girl their college aged son, Larry, is bringing home. They spend their time trying to convert Adrian and watching their younger son Ricky and his friends rehearse the extended version of the Christmas story that they will perform at school. The Hudsons find out that the play will not be staged due to a complaint, but they continue to practice, having faith that God will allow the show to go on, and Adrian is finally converted. RECOMMENDATION: This excessively didactic and insulting religious drama uses its dialogue to criticize

secular schools and learning as being heathen. Only certain church groups agreeing with every aspect of this play's dogma will find any use for it. ROYALTY: NA. SOURCE: Hawse, Alberta. (1975). Herod is alive and well. Franklin, OH: Eldridge Pub. Co. SUBJECTS/PLAY TYPE: Christmas; Christian Drama.

1352. K-4. (+) Bauer, Caroline Feller. **Hershele gets a meal. CAST:** 1f, 2m, 1u. ACTS: 1. SETTINGS: Dining room. PLAYING TIME: 5 min. PLOT: Hershele Ostropoler comes to an inn late at night for his evening meal only to find that serving hours are over. Hershele says he will be like his father who "did what he had to do." Frightened, the innkeeper and his wife promptly bring Hershele some food. They learn when he finishes that he only meant that he'd have to go to bed hungry. RECOMMENDATION: The sinister implications of Hershele's first response to the innkeeper will keep viewers in delightful suspense and his second answer will cause much laughter. This can either be acted or read aloud. ROYALTY: None. SOURCE: Bauer, Caroline Feller. (1987). Presenting reader's theater: Plays and poems to read aloud. New York, NY: H.W. Wilson Co. SUBJECTS/PLAY TYPE: Folk Tales, Jewish; Reader's Theater.

1353. 9-12. (+) Magpie Company. **Hey Mum, I own a factory.** CAST: Sf, Sm. ACTS: 1. SETTINGS: Factory; living room. PLAYING TIME: NA. PLOT: The failing Protectaware company is saved by a sit down strike staged by its predominantly female employees. The company is bought by the women on a co-op basis, but, clinging to old stereotypes, they elect a man as manager. The co-op does so well that the manager convinces the women to sell the company, promising that they will all keep their jobs. Six months after the sale, all employees except the male manager have been fired. RECOMMENDATION: This is an excellent portrayal of women's problems caused by societal stereotypes and women's own inability to rise above them. Some rewriting will be necessary in order to update the dialogue and Americanize it. This would be especially helpful as part of a unit on women's rights, alternative business structures, or even capitalism. ROYALTY: Write to author. SOURCE: Lonie, John. (1985). Learning from life. Sydney, Australia: Currency Press. SUBJECTS/PLAY TYPE: Women's Rights; Co-ops; Drama.

1354. 7-12. (-) Fendrich, Shubert. **Hey, teach! CAST:** 11f, 6m. ACTS: 2. SETTINGS: Classroom. PLAYING TIME: 90 min. PLOT: Ms. Audrey Douglas, a new journalism teacher at Central High, insists that all her students do some work on the school paper to pass the course. She runs into trouble when she lets the paper expose the bad conditions in the cafeteria and when she gives a failing grade to a star basketball player. But all works well in the end for Ms. Douglas and the "good" people involved in various subplots. RECOMMENDATION: The characters are stereotyped and contrived; too much of the plot is pat and unrealistic. ROYALTY: $35. SOURCE: Fendrich, Shubert. (1977). Hey, teach! Denver, CO: Pioneer Drama Service. SUBJECTS/PLAY TYPE: High School; Teachers; Drama.

1355. 4-6. (-) Bradley, Virginia. **Hibernian picnic.** CAST: 1m, Su. ACTS: 1. SETTINGS: Open stage. PLAYING TIME: NA. PLOT: As the curtain opens, the Irish are eating and laughing at their picnic. A man named Smith enters but is forced to leave. He returns with a placard saying O'Smith and he is again turned away. When he returns with an American flag, he is allowed to join the celebration. RECOMMENDATION: This brief pantomime seems pointless and confusing. ROYALTY: None. SOURCE: Bradley, Virginia. (1975). Is there an actor in the house? New York, NY: Dodd, Mead. SUBJECTS/PLAY TYPE: Irish Americans; Pantomime.

1356. 8-12. (-) Carlin, Matthew. **Hide and seek.** CAST: 8f, 4m. ACTS: 1. SETTINGS: Library. PLAYING TIME: 60 min. PLOT: Rich, eccentric Hiram Collingsworth is dead, and all his potential heirs (also possible murderers) have been summoned. During the night, Collingsworth's daughter, Melissa, has been plotting with her sister Katherine's fiance, Michael, to take over the Collingsworth business and fortunes. However, as it turns out, Collingsworth is only pretending to be dead, and with the help of Katherine and a London detective, Melissa and Michael are tricked into confessing. They are sent away, and Collingsworth, Katherine and the detective live happily ever after. RECOMMENDATION: Although the audience may be fairly sure of the villains' identities early on, the manner in which the mystery is solved could hold attention. Unfortunately, the stereotyped language and actions of the black maid and the Italian cook mar what could have been an entertaining play. ROYALTY: $25. SOURCE: Carlin, Matthew. (1985). Hide and seek. Schulenberg, TX: I.E. Clark. SUBJECTS/PLAY TYPE: Mystery; Comedy.

1357. 8-12. (+) Sternfield, Allen. **Hide and seek.** CAST: 2f, 3m. ACTS: 1. SETTINGS: Dining room, kitchen. PLAYING TIME: NA. PLOT: After 35 years, Sam and his son, Peter, visit the home of a childhood friend. In the course of the conversation between the visitors and the friend's family, Sam discovers that the idyllic memories of his youth were based on misconceptions, and that the friend's family both envied and despised his parents and him. He also discovers that his friend, Richard, and another childhood friend died tragically at the age of nine in a plunge down a grain elevator shaft. As the memories become more unpleasant, it becomes apparent that the now elderly family wishes to keep Peter to replace their lost child. Sam carries Peter from the room and the scene ends with a little boy and a man looking at an empty house that they have never entered; the occupants are now forgotten ghosts. RECOMMENDATION: This finely honed ghost story is guaranteed to keep adult and teenage audiences on the edge of their seats. The parts are challenging but within the capacities of high schoolers to perform. ROYALTY: $15. SOURCE: Sternfield, Allen. (1975). Hide and seek. Chicago, IL: Dramatic Pub. Co. SUBJECTS/PLAY TYPE: Ghosts; Memories; Drama.

1358. 4-6. (+) Boiko, Claire. **Hiding Mr. Hale.** CAST: 3f, 5m, Su. ACTS: 1. SETTINGS: Schoolhouse. PLAYING TIME: 20 min. PLOT: Nathan Hale is in danger of being captured by the British. A clever school mistress and her pupils try to outwit the Redcoats by having Hale pretend to be a student. Hale sits on the dunce stool, facing the wall, with the dunce cap on his head. When the Redcoats search the room, the children distract the soldiers with various antics. The Redcoats leave without discovering Hale. RECOMMENDATION: The interaction between the children, the school mistress, and the Redcoats is humorous and enjoyable. The play retains the language of the period and gives insight into what everyday life was like during the American Revolution. ROYALTY: Free to Plays subscribers. SOURCE: Boiko, Claire. (1977, October). Hiding Mr. Hale. Plays: The Drama Magazine for Young People, pp. 47-52. SUBJECTS/PLAY TYPE: Revolution, U.S.; Comedy.

1359. 12. (+) Denholtz, Elaine. **The high chairs.** CAST: 4f, 3m. ACTS: 2. SETTINGS: Kitchen. PLAYING TIME: NA. PLOT: Flo (early forties) is married, has two children, and is the daughter of elderly parents who live with her family. She devotes herself to the care of this demanding old couple who become increasingly helpless and finally die from eating a whole box of their favorite treat, chocolate covered ants. Flo is consumed with guilt, and she finds herself growing more like her mother everyday. In the final scene, her own children mistake her for their grandmother. RECOMMENDATION: The themes of this play--euthanasia, sexuality, financial security, old age, middle age, funerals, and guilt--are adult and depressing, even though there are attempts at some humor. ROYALTY: $35. SOURCE: Denholtz, Elaine. (1975). The high chairs. New York, NY: Dramatic Pub. Co. SUBJECTS/PLAY TYPE: Family; Elderly; Death; Drama.

1360. 4-7. (+) Watts, Frances B. **High fashion from Mars.** CAST: 2f, 2m, 6u. ACTS: 1. SETTINGS: Office. PLAYING TIME: 10 min. PLOT: A movie producer harasses his designers about their Martian costumes until a real Martian takes the producer to Mars to be a model for a movie about Earth. RECOMMENDATION: This is short, entertaining, and easy to produce. ROYALTY: Free to Plays subscribers. SOURCE: Kamerman, Sylvia E. (1981). Space and science fiction plays for young people. Boston, MA: Plays, Inc. SUBJECTS/PLAY TYPE: Science Fiction; Comedy.

1361. 3-6. (+) Majeski, Bill. **High fashion in the bird world.** CAST: 1f, 1u. ACTS: 1. SETTINGS: Bare stage. PLAYING TIME: NA. PLOT: Momma Bird complains that her feathers are drab and her life as a mother is boring, while her husband is colorful and his life is exciting. She wishes to travel and her husband, who understands her plight, agrees to take her on a trip. RECOMMENDATION: This humorous monologue would be a good vehicle for an expressive young actress. Using the bird world, it successfully satirizes human behavior. ROYALTY: Free to Plays subscribers. SOURCE: Majeski, Bill. (1978, May). High fashion in the bird world. Plays: The Drama Magazine for Young People, pp. 71-72. SUBJECTS/PLAY TYPE: Birds; Satire; Monologue.

1362. 9-12. (+) Dias, Earl J. **High, high society.** CAST: 4f, 7m. ACTS: 1. SETTINGS: Drawing room. PLAYING TIME: 25 min. PLOT: The newly rich and pretentious Mrs.

Waters plans to have her daughter marry a French count, but a down to earth friend from back home suspects the Count is nothing more than a con man. The truth comes out that evening at a formal dinner party, to Mrs. Water's embarrassment and her daughter Seraphina's delight. As the Count is carried off to jail, the young woman accepts the marriage proposal of the man she has really loved all along. When he casually states that he is related to English nobility, the mother couldn't be happier. RECOMMENDATION: The intentionally formal language and frequent asides to the audience add to the melodramatic flavor of this 1870 romantic drawing room comedy. The large cast of characters have distinct personalities and humorous dialogue. Increasing action keeps the play moving through the climax. Fairly elaborate settings and costume changes add interest. ROYALTY: Free to Plays subscribers. SOURCE: Dias, Earl J. (1979, December). High, high society. Plays: The Drama Magazine for Young People, pp. 23-34. SUBJECTS/PLAY TYPE: Romance; Status Seeking; Comedy.

1363. 9-12. (+) Irvin, Jeff. **High noon in Gloomtown.** CAST: 3f, 7m, 3u. ACTS: 1. SETTINGS: Bar. PLAYING TIME: 45 min. PLOT: In this simple, but highly amusing melodrama, the hero (Green) must rescue the heroine (Nell) from evil Bart, who plots to steal Nell's family land from her drunken father and turn Nell into a floozy barmaid. RECOMMENDATION: With its clever verse narrative, exaggerated comedic acting, and audience participation, this will entertain all. The stage is in darkness while voices are piped through to the audience. ROYALTY: NA. SOURCE: Irvin, Jeff. (1987). High noon in Gloomtown. Schulenburg, TX: I.E. Clark. SUBJECTS/PLAY TYPE: Western; Comedy; Melodrama.

1364. 7-12. (-) Dias, Earl J. **High wind on the prairie.** CAST: 2f, 6m, ACTS: 1. SETTINGS: Living room. PLAYING TIME: 30 min. PLOT: Cynthia is about to be forced to marry a greedy cattle baron who is going to foreclose on the mortgage to her parent's ranch. Her missing fiance appears in time to stop the marriage, repay the money he owes her father, and reveal that the oil deposits on the property. A drifter is really a petroleum chemist and asks Cynthia to marry him. She agrees and spurns her fiance, since she feels that he has become too involved with another woman. RECOMMENDATION: Although this has a twist at the end, the characters are stereotyped and unexciting. ROYALTY: Free to Plays subscribers. SOURCE: Dias, Earl J. (1982, March). High wind on the prairie. Plays: The Drama Magazine for Young People, pp. 1-12. SUBJECTS/PLAY TYPE: Mortgages, Swindlers and Swindling, Melodrama.

1365. 3-5. (+) Howard, Helen L. (Wilder, Laura Ingalls) **The highback comb.** (Little house on the prairie) CAST: 4f, 4m. ACTS: 3. SETTINGS: Store; woods. PLAYING TIME: 15 min. PLOT: Laura and Mary Ingalls raise money to buy "Ma" a comb for Mother's Day. They lose the money when two boys, dressed as wolves, scare them. The boys find the money, deliver it to the store, and then bring the comb to the Ingall's house. RECOMMENDATION: This is pleasant, but rather pat. ROYALTY: Free to Plays subscribers. SOURCE: Howard,

Helen L. (1986, May). The highback comb. SUBJECTS/PLAY TYPE: Independence Day, Generosity, Mother's Day. Adaptation.

1366. 7-12. (+) Nolan, Paul T. **The highland fling.** CAST: 4f, 4m, Su. ACTS: 1. SETTINGS: Countryside. PLAYING TIME: 25 min. PLOT: Two feuding Scottish clans, are taught a lesson in tolerance by a wise old man who suggests a dance contest between the fiercely competitive rivals. Each clan takes a turn but the old man decides that he can only choose the winner by watching the two best dancers from each clan. The two youngest members of each clan dance together, and the judge' decides that both clans are at their best when joined together. The clan members agree and shake hands. RECOMMENDATION: This will be difficult to produce because of the Scottish dialect, the folk dances, and the traditional Scottish costumes, but the effort is worth it. ROYALTY: None for amateur performance. SOURCE: Nolan, Paul T. (1982). Folk tale plays round the world: a collection of royalty-free, one-act plays about lands far and near. Boston, MA: Plays, Inc. SUBJECTS/PLAY TYPE: Folktale, Scottish, Cooperation Musical.

1367. 9-12. (-) Murray, John. **The highway restaurant.** CAST: 1u. ACTS: 1. SETTINGS: None. PLOT: A family on a car trip is ready for dinner, but can't agree on where to stop. RECOMMENDATION: The plot is predictable and the language dated and cliched. ROYALTY: None. SOURCE: Murray, John. (1982). Modern monologues for young people. Boston: MA: Plays, Inc. SUBJECTS/PLAY TYPE: Vacation, Comedy Monologue.

1368. 9-12. (+) Van Horn, Bill. **The hillbillies and the robots.** CAST: 9f, 4m, 11u. ACTS: 1. SETTINGS: Store. PLAYING TIME: 30 min. PLOT: Two generations of feuding hillbillies, two scientists, and a stodgy army colonel and his soldiers stop a group of robots-gone-wild at the space research center. RECOMMENDATION: The large cast and number of costumes might be difficult, but this is hilarious. ROYALTY: Free to Plays subscribers. SOURCE: Kamerman, Sylvia E. (1981). Space and science fiction plays for young people. Boston, MA: Plays, Inc. SUBJECTS/PLAY TYPE: Science Fiction, Comedy.

1369. 7-12. (+) Huff, Betty Tracy. **Hillbilly blues.** CAST: 11f, 12m, Su. ACTS: 1. SETTINGS: Barn. PLAYING TIME: 40 min. PLOT: Two feuding mountain families try to settle their differences with a music contest which is reluctantly judged by a a talent scout from a record company. Chad, one of the feuding family members, is in love with Donna Sue, a member of the rival family. When the talent scout's assistant flirts with Chad in an attempt to make her love interest, the scout, jealous, Donna Sue is angry. After the contest, the assistant explains her actions, Donna Sue and Chad reconcile their mutual attraction. The feuding stops when it is suggested that the families enter a joint record contract. ROYALTY: Free to Plays subscribers. SOURCE: Huff, Betty Tracy. (1980, January). Hillbilly blues. Plays: The Drama Magazine for Young People, pp. 17-26. SUBJECTS/PLAY TYPE: Family, Feuds; Comedy.

1370. 3-6. (+) Roseberry, Sherry. **Hillbilly love is homegrown.** CAST: 6f, 5m, 1u. ACTS: 1. SETTINGS: Front of a cabin. PLAYING TIME: NA min. PLOT: The unscrupulous land developer Conrad Mason, tries to trick the Dudleys, a family of hillbillies, into selling their land. The Dudley's headstrong daughter, Liz, decides Conrad is "Mr. Right," much to the chagrin of her milquetoast boyfriend, Homer. Conrad's scheme is discovered, and Homer wins Liz over with a display of "manly forcefulness." RECOMMENDATION: The characters are motivated stereotypes and the action is choppy; but the slapstick and sight gags may be entertaining if they are performed. zestfully ROYALTY: $30. SOURCE: Roseberry, Sherry. (1988). Hillbilly love is homegrown. Franklin, OH: Eldridge Pub. Co. SUBJECTS/PLAY TYPE: Comedy, Hillbillies, Musical. Melodrama.

1371. 7-12. (+) Majeski, Bill. **The hip hypnotist.** CAST: 5f, 4m, Su. ACTS: 1. SETTINGS: Soda shoppe; living/family room. PLAYING TIME: NA. PLOT: As teenagers grapple with who will take whom to the prom, self important Bob invites everyone to a party, and specifically invites Nancy, whom he is sure will succumb to his "machoism". At the party, a "hypnotist" chooses Nancy as his subject and asks her to approach the boy with whom she would most like to be. Nancy pretends to be hypnotized, starts toward Bob, but then goes to Dave. Bob is flabbergasted, Dave is the hero, and all ends well. RECOMMENDATION: Adolescents will identify with this light-hearted look at their own foibles. ROYALTY: $25. SOURCE: Majeski, Bill. (1977). The hip hypnotist. Franklin, OH: Eldrige Pub. Co. SUBJECTS/PLAY TYPE: Dating, Youth, Psychology; Comedy.

1372. 5-12. (+) Wintermute, John B.. **Hiriam, the innkeeper.** CAST: 1f, 2m, 1u. ACTS: 1. SETTINGS: Church sanctuary. PLAYING TIME: NA. PLOT: A minister is interrupted by an old man who is revealed to be Hiriam, the innkeeper who turned the Holy Family away 2000 years ago. Hiriam has been looking for the Holy Family ever since to make amends. The minister explains to Hiriam that although Christ died on the Cross, He continues to live in people's hearts, and that the innkeeper can make amends through prayer and sharing Him with others. Hiriam goes into the congregation (audience) where he touches people in the pews. They in turn, touch others, sharing the message of love. RECOMMENDATION: The theme of Christ being alive is shared in a meaningful, heartfelt way. ROYALTY: NA. SOURCE: Wintermute, John B. (1988). Hiriam, the innkeeper. Franklin, OH: Eldridge Pub. Co. SUBJECTS/PLAY TYPE: Christmas.Christian drama.

1373. 7-12. (+) Vandersall, Bernice. **Hisses and kisses: a burlesque melodrama in pantomime.** CAST: 2f, 2m, 16u. ACTS: 1. SETTINGS: None.. PLAYING TIME: NA. PLOT: As a narrator reads the story, Manuel chases a servant girl, Maggie, insisting that if she doesn't marry him, he will lock her in the smokehouse. Maggie's true love rescues her and they gallop off into the sunset. RECOMMENDATION: The humor here lies in the literal interpretation of emphasized words through the actors' pantomime. ROYALTY: None. SOURCE: Majeski, Bill.

(1981). Easy skits, blackouts and pantomimes. Woodstock, IL: Dramatic Pub. Co. SUBJECTS/PLAY TYPE: Romance, Semantics, Comedy. Pantomime.

1374. 5-8. (+) Ryback, Rose Kacherian. **History hits the jackpot.** CAST: 5f, 15m, ACTS: 1. SETTINGS: T.V. studio. PLAYING TIME: 35 min. PLOT: Historical characters and well-known contemporary entertainment personalities provide an American history lesson within the framework of a quiz show. RECOMMENDATION: This humorous and informative play puts historical facts into a context that is enjoyable and easy to remember. The characterizations are natural and entertaining. ROYALTY: Free to Plays subscribers. SOURCE: Ryback, Rose Kacherian. (1976, October). History hits the jackpot. Plays: The Drama Magazine for Young People, pp. 17-26. SUBJECTS/PLAY TYPE: U.S. History.Comedy.

1375. 10-12*. (+) Maganza, Dennis M.. (Fielding, Henry.) **The history of Tom Jones** A. (The history of Tom Jones.) CAST: 8f, 8m, ACTS: 2. SETTINGS: Bare stage, platforms. PLAYING TIME: NA. PLOT: Tom Jones, a foundling taken in by the good squire Allworthy, is a headstrong youth ruled by passion. He falls in love with Sophia Western, whose father has betrothed her to Allworthy's calculating nephew, Blifil. Jones quarrels with Blifil, and Sophia, to avoid marriage to Blifil, flees. The second act of the play follows Jones and Sophia's parallel journeys to London, their pursuit by Blifil and Squire Western, the near hanging of Tom, the dramatic revelation of his true identity, his reconciliation with Allworthy, and, finally, his reunion with Sophia. RECOMMENDATION: This is true to the spirit of the original. Funny and complex, it will hold the attention of the audience, and provide a challenge for the actors. ROYALTY: $50. SOURCE: Maganza, Dennis M. (1986). The history of Tom Jones. Schulenburg, TX: I. E. Clark. SUBJECTS/PLAY TYPE: Comedy, Class Struggle, Marriage. Adaptation.

1376. 9-12. (+) Munoz, Luis. (Maganza, Dennis) **The history of Tom Jones** B. (The history of Tom Jones) CAST: 7f, 8m, Su. ACTS: 1. SETTINGS: Single unit set. PLAYING TIME: 35 min. PLOT: Born illegitimately, Tom Jones became the ward of Squire Allworthy. Tom loves Sophia, the daughter of Squire Western, but Western will not let the two marry. Tom fights and appears to kill a man. Hastily sentenced to hang, Tom is saved from death by the appearance of his mother.. RECOMMENDATION: This skillful adaptation possesses the humor and plot complexities of Fielding's original, but can be acted in less time and has been expurgated of its bawdier intonations. ROYALTY: $20. SOURCE: Munoz, Luis. (1987). The history of Tom Jones. Schulenberg, TX: I.E. Clark. SUBJECTS/PLAY TYPE: Marriage, Comedy, Class Struggle. Adaptation.

1377. 9-12. (-) Gleason, William. **Hit and misdemeanor.** CAST: 8f, 7m, 4u. ACTS: 2. SETTINGS: TV detective show. PLAYING TIME: NA. PLOT: During the filming of a TV detective show, someone attempts to murder the two female stars. Rivalries, jealousies, and secret love affairs are exposed in real, mostly unpleasant roles as an investigation occurs. Throughout the confusion, as a TV drama becomes entwined with reality, the director--a disembodied voice--comments on the action. RECOMMENDATION: While within in the abilities of high schoolers, the dialogue is trite and the characters are predictable. ROYALTY: $50. SOURCE: Gleason, William. (1984). Hit and misdemeanor. Wood-stock, IL: Dramatic Pub. Co. SUBJECTS/PLAY TYPE: Murder.Mystery.

1378. 7-12. (+) Fletcher, Lucille. **The hitchhiker.** CAST: 8f, 4m, ACTS: 1. SETTINGS: Bare stage.PLAYING TIME: NA. PLOT: Ronald Adams sets off to drive by himself from Brooklyn to California. He first sees the hitchhiker while crossing the Brooklyn Bridge and then sees him repeatedly on the trip. After six days he is so spooked that to get hold of himself he tries to call his mother. A stranger answers the phone and reports that his mother has been hospitalized since the death of her oldest son Ronald, who was killed six days earlier in an accident on the Brooklyn Bridge. RECOMMENDATION: Originally written as a radio play for Orson Welles, this thriller falls flat as a visual performance. ROYALTY: $20. SUBJECTS/PLAY TYPE: Ghosts; Supernatural; Radio Play; Thriller.

1379. 7-12. (+) McCusker, Paul. **The hitchhiker.** CAST: 2u. ACTS: 1. SETTINGS: Bare stage, props. PLAYING TIME: NA. PLOT: A jaded motorist picks up a hitchhiker. The two discuss Christmas, with the motorist talking about the trappings of the holiday and how fake and shortlived they are. The hitchhiker tells him that he can't focus on temporary things, but should focus on the eternal aspects of Christmas, the Christ child. The motorist asks the hitchhiker to spend Christmas with him and his family and to share his perspectives with them. RECOMMENDATION: With gentle humor and cutting truth, this demonstrates that the spirit of Christmas cannot be overlooked. Appropriate for church groups. ROYALTY: NA. SOURCE: McCusker, Paul. (1984). Batteries not included. Boston, MA: Baker's Plays. SUBJECTS/PLAY TYPE: Christian Drama; Christmas; Skit.

1380. K-12*. (+) Duffield, Brainerd & Morres, John. (Tolkien, J.R.R.) The hobbit. (The hobbit) CAST: 1f, 4m, 19u. ACTS: 2. SETTINGS: Living room; campfire; cave; dragon's lair. PLAYING TIME: NA. PLOT: Gandolf the wizard, and a dozen dwarves coerce the Hobbit, Bilbo Baggins, into accompanying them on a mission to slay the dragon Smaug and reclaim their ancestral land. The adventures enroute include battling trolls and goblins, and discovering a magic ring. Although a reluctant adventurer, Bilbo proves that "Hobbits may be heroes, too." RECOMMENDATION: This faithful, although much condensed, adaptation of the classic Tolkien tale will be greatly enjoyed by children as well as by Tolkien's adult fans. ROYALTY: $60. SOURCE: Duffield, Brainerd & John Morris. (1977). The hobbit. Boston, MA: Baker's Plays. SUBJECTS/PLAY TYPE: Fantasy; Adaptation.

1381. 6-8. (+) Martens, Anne Coulter. **Hobgoblin house.** CAST: 7f, 5m. ACTS: 1. SETTINGS: Garage. PLAYING TIME: 30 min. PLOT: The Vinson children and friends are having a Halloween party. Marilyn's aunt forbids her to attend the Vinsons' Halloween party because the aunt is suspicious of young people. Marilyn comes to the party anyway, leaving a note for her aunt which states that she has run away. After reading it, the aunt regrets her behavior and allows Marilyn to join the party. RECOMMENDATION: This promotes understanding between generations and the interaction between the young people is realistic. However, the sometimes unnatural dialogue and characterizations may need some rewriting to be totally successful. ROYALTY: Free to Plays subscribers. SOURCE: Martens, Anne Coulter. (1976, October). Hobgoblin house. Plays: The Drama Magazine for Young People, pp. 37-46. SUBJECTS/PLAY TYPE: Generation Gap; Halloween; Drama.

1382. 4-8. (-) Winther, Barbara. **The Hodja speaks.** CAST: 1f, 4m, 1u. ACTS: 1. SETTINGS: Turkish dining room. PLAYING TIME: 20 min. PLOT: Hodja, the classic wise-fool of folklore, stars in two separate stories. In the first, he has a silence contest with his wife to see who must feed the donkey. The Hodja wins, but at great personal expense and embarrassment when he allows a thief to get away rather than speak. In the second, Hodja bets a neighbor that he can spend the night outside without freezing. The neighbor claims Hodja lost the bet because he was warmed by the heat of a candle in a neighbor's window. The Hodja graphically refutes this argument by inviting the neighbor to dinner, which he is trying to cook with a small candle. RECOMMENDATION: Well phrased dialogue contributes to the overall mood of these timeless fables. ROYALTY: Free to Plays subscribers. SOURCE: Winther, Barbara. (1982, May). The Hodja speaks. Plays: The Drama Magazine for Young People, pp. 39-44. SUBJECTS/PLAY TYPE: Folk Tales, Turkey; Tricksters; Playlet.

1383. 9-12. (+) Nowell, Janie B. & Gitter, Marshall. **Hoedown heaven.** CAST: 3f, 4m. ACTS: 2. SETTINGS: Cafe. PLAYING TIME: 90 min. PLOT: The day of the Hoedown brings romance, crime, and plans for the future into the lives of small town folk. Clem gets his big chance to call dances when the real caller gets sick, Sari (his girl) makes her singing debut, and Rooster tries to stage an illegal cock fight. The chickens are cooked by mistake, Clem overcomes his stuttering, and the cafe owner decides to turn her place into Hoedown Heaven, a dancehall where Clem and Sari can perform. RECOMMENDATION: This pleasant, amusing musical is recommended as a light piece that would be relatively easy to stage. However, singing ability is necessary for all players. ROYALTY: $40. SOURCE: Nowell, Janie B. & Gitter, Marshall. (1982). Hoedown heaven. Denver, CO: Pioneer Drama Service. SUBJECTS/PLAY TYPE: Western; Square Dancing; Musical.

1384. 9-12. (+) Lieblich, Lilian. **Hole in the Ground.** CAST: 2f, 2m. ACTS: 1. SETTINGS: Family room/den. PLAYING TIME: 60 min. PLOT: An overheard argument, the absence of Eliot's wife, and a large hole in the yard make Dixie, Eliot's nosey neighbor, suspicious. Where is Chris? Suspicions turn to fear late at night, when Dixie sees Eliot pull a large bloody sack out of a crate and bury its contents. The police are called. Chris is discovered to be visiting her mentally ill sister, a family secret. Buried had been a buffalo head, bought for the horns. RECOMMENDATION: A guaranteed "hit," this combines suspense, dialogue which will make the audience roar with laughter, and just enough action to keep it moving. ROYALTY: $25. SOURCE: Lieblich, Lilian. (1980). Hole in the ground. Denver, CO: Pioneer Drama Service. SUBJECTS/PLAY TYPE: Mystery; Comedy.

1385. 7-10. (-) Kurtz, Jack. **The holiday. CAST**: 1f, 3m, 5u. **ACTS**: 1. **SETTINGS**: Bare stage. **PLAYING TIME**: NA. **PLOT**: A museum guide tells a tourist group the story of a hypothetical rainy country, its ruler, and its people, who base the value of the person on the kind of raincoat worn. Action comes from the selfish residents of the country, who resent the the wise, aging ruler's edicts, which parallel the Ten Commandments and crimp the residents' selfish lifestyles. They depose the King and continue their greedy, self centered lives. The play ends with the tour guide telling the story to the next group of tourists. RECOMMENDATION: This unsuccessful satire of Christian belief is not resolved and it delivers a defeatist message about the inherent evil of mankind. ROYALTY: NA. SOURCE: Kurtz, Jack. (1978). Without bathrobes: Alternatives in drama for youth: Three one-act chancel comedies. Boston, MA: Baker's Plays. SUBJECTS/PLAY TYPE: Christian Drama; Satire.

1386. 3-6. (+) Gabriel, Michelle. **The holiday machine. CAST**: 1f, 1m, 12u. **ACTS**: 1. **SETTINGS**: Room. **PLAYING TIME**: 15 min. **PLOT**: A boy and a girl discover a computer that answers all their questions about Simchat Torah, a period of joy and enjoyment. RECOMMENDATION: This play, a spoof on computer technology, also provides all the information on the symbols and significance of Simchat Torah. ROYALTY: None. SOURCE: Gabriel, Michelle. (1978). Jewish plays for Jewish days. Denver, CO: Alternatives in Religious Instruction, Inc. SUBJECTS/PLAY TYPE: Simchat Torah; Jewish Drama.

1387. 7-12. (+) Hawse, Alberta. **Holly day's inn: a Christmas drama. CAST**: 7f, 5m, Su. **ACTS**: 3. **SETTINGS**: Hamburger shop. **PLAYING TIME**: 70 min. **PLOT**: Hollister Day, kindhearted Christian proprietor of a small hamburger stand at a crossroads, keeps his shop open on Christmas Eve. He is visited by a steady stream of unhappy people, including his wife, who are at their own personal crossroads. A confused young pastor and his wife, the bewildered children of quarreling parents, the quarreling parents, and a bevy of other shop patrons pop in and out, laughing, crying, and fighting. They minister to each other in various ways and lives are changed. RECOMMENDATION: The major plot is addressed more to older youth and adults, but the mini-Christmas pageant embedded in the play and performed by children will appeal to younger audiences. This is unsuitable for public school use, as it is fundamentalist Christian. Some of the language is slightly dated, and the plot resolution is extremely sentimentalized. ROYALTY: NA. SOURCE: Hawse, Alberta. (1977). Holly Day's inn: A Christmas

drama. Franklin, OH: Eldridge Pub. Co. SUBJECTS/PLAY TYPE: Christmas; Christian Drama.

1388. 7-12. (+) Hawse, Alberta. **Holly's Christmas detour. CAST**: 6f, 4m, Su. **ACTS**: 2. **SETTINGS**: Hotel lobby. **PLAYING TIME**: 70 min. **PLOT**: Bad weather forces Hollister Day, a devout Christian, to take a detour and stop at a small motel on Christmas Eve. His detour had a purpose, however, as he helps motel guests on their own personal detours to get their lives back on track. RECOMMENDATION: The sometimes warm, sometimes prickly interaction among the guests and staff of Martin's Motel is lively and fast paced. The play requires child and adult actors and will appeal to a wide age range. The heavy Christian emphasis precludes public school use. ROYALTY: NA. SOURCE: Hawse, Alberta. (1987). Holly's Christmas detour. Franklin, OH: Eldridge Pub. Co. SUBJECTS/PLAY TYPE: Christmas; Christian Drama.

1389. 7-12. (+) Hawse, Alberta. **Holly's Christmas runaway. CAST**: 8f, 6m, Su. **ACTS**: 3. **SETTINGS**: Hamburger shop. **PLAYING TIME**: 70 min. **PLOT**: Teenaged Brenda runs away from home because she feels unloved. She and her drug using boyfriend stop at a small cafe when their car breaks down. The Christian owners of the cafe and their friends convince Brenda not to leave with her boyfriend and to contact her father instead. The story also includes a retired hypochondriac, whom the Christians also help, and a nativity tableau. RECOMMENDATION: Although heavy handed, the themes of Christian love and communication are clearly presented. Due to the religious emphasis, this is appropriate for church groups or parochial schools only. ROYALTY: $50. SOURCE: Hawse, Alberta. (1980). Holly's Christmas runaway. Franklin, OH: Eldridge Pub. Co. SUBJECTS/PLAY TYPE: Christmas; Runaways; Christian Drama.

1390. 7-12. (-) Gotwalt, Helen Louise Miller. **Home for Christmas. CAST**: 3f, 3m. **ACTS**: 2. **SETTINGS**: Living room. **PLAYING TIME**: 30 min. **PLOT**: The Fairchild family is in an uproar; Christmas is nearly here, but all the usual celebrations are complicated by Cousin Ruth and her twins, who are staying with the family until they can find their own apartment. The children plot on their own to find an apartment for Ruth by having Sandy Fairchild date the son of a local apartment supervisor. When Sandy's boyfriend stops to visit, he is so angered at her "unfaithfulness" that he refuses to share his surprise at first. Finally, he forgives them and reveals that he has located an apartment for Cousin Ruth. With this settled, the Fairchilds are all happy at the conclusion, even when they receive a letter from another relative needing to live with them over Christmas. RECOMMENDATION: Although the author points out at the conclusion that the most important part of Christmas is for families to be together, the rest of this play is trite and unbelievable. The characters are superficial at best and display so much selfishness that they overwhelm the theme of togetherness. ROYALTY: Free to Plays subscribers. SOURCE: Gotwalt, Helen Louise Miller. (1986, December). Home for Christmas. Plays: The Drama Magazine for Young People, pp. 21-28. SUBJECTS/PLAY TYPE: Christmas; Family; Playlet.

1391. 9-12. (+) Martens, Anne Coulter. (Douglas, Lloyd C) **Home for Christmas.** (Home for Christmas) CAST: 13f, 9m, Su. ACTS: 2. SETTINGS: Living room. PLAYING TIME: 55 min. PLOT: A family gathers at the old homestead for the first Christmas together in many years. All but one of the grown children are unaware that their mother is suffering from a terminal disease. At first the eldest, wealthy and sophisticated daughter resents having to spend her holiday in a crude country setting, and her hostility alienates a former friend and saddens her siblings and her teenage daughter. When the elderly school marm of their youth appears to lead the family in a Christmas recitation, the warm memories of childhood flood over the daughter and she reaches out in love and friendship and helps to create a joyous last Christmas for her mother. RECOMMENDATION: A meaningful Christmas story is conveyed in this easy to produce play expressing selfless love and sharing as the true meaning of the holiday. Each character is well developed as a distinct, if somewhat idealized, personality. The overall tone is sentimental but appropriate for the season. One female actor must know how to play the piano. ROYALTY: $25. SOURCE: Martens, Anne Coulter. (1982). Home for Christmas. Chicago, IL: The Dramatic Pub. Co. SUBJECTS/PLAY TYPE: Christmas; Family; Drama.

1392. 7-12. (-) Murray, John. **Home movies.** CAST: 1m. ACTS: 1. SETTINGS: None. PLAYING TIME: NA. PLOT: A man and his wife invite friends to see their home movies, which are, of course, awful. RECOMMENDATION: This is a tired, overworked plot of little interest to modern audiences, who are accustomed to video movies. ROYALTY: None. SOURCE: Murray, John. (1982). Modern monologues for young people. Boston, MA: Plays, Inc. SUBJECTS/PLAY TYPE: Home Movies; Comedy; Monologue.

1393. 4-6. (+) Miller, Rory. **Home sweet haunt.** CAST: 3f, 3m, Su. ACTS: 1. SETTINGS: Living room. PLAYING TIME: 10 min. PLOT: A homeless witch discovers a house that has just the right amount of cobwebs, but whose ghostly owners, Lenny and Penny, are not so sure that they welcome her. The witch, however, has a magical way of making herself indispensable, and when the ghosts throw a party, she uses her bag of tricks to prove what an asset she can be by "curing" the ghoulish guests of their various ills. Lenny and Penny are so dazzled by their uninvited guest's talents that she is asked to become a permanent part of this haunted household. RECOMMENDATION: "Home, Sweet Haunt" conjures up everyone's favorite generic monsters--Wolfman, Spiderwoman, vampires, monsters, and witches. It would be particularly appropriate for Halloween. ROYALTY: Free to Plays subscribers. SOURCE: Miller, Rory. (1979, October). Home, sweet haunt. Plays: The Drama Magazine for Young People, pp. 51-54. SUBJECTS/PLAY TYPE: Halloween; Monsters; Fantasy.

1394. 7-12. (+) Murray, John. **Home sweet home computer.** CAST: 1m. ACTS: 1. SETTINGS: None. PLAYING TIME: NA. PLOT: Bill brings home a new home computer, but his family is unimpressed by its functions, or more appropriately, its disfunctions. RECOMMENDATION: This is a mildly amusing look at the unrealistic expectations people have for their new technological "toys." ROYALTY: None. SOURCE: Murray, John. (1982). Modern monologues for young people. Boston, MA: Plays, Inc. SUBJECTS/PLAY TYPE: Comedy; Modern Technology; Computers; Monologue.

1395. 7-12. (+) Rembrandt, Elaine. **Home to stay.** CAST: 2f, 8m, Su. ACTS: 1. SETTINGS: Wall; temple. PLAYING TIME: 20 min. PLOT: A modern day reporter, tourists, and soldiers discuss the Western Wall in Israel and the special meanings it has for them. They discuss the changes that have taken place over hundreds of years in Jerusalem and the impact the Wall has had on the Jews. RECOMMENDATION: The old stories of Jeremiah and Eleazar Ben Yair are blended nicely with the more recent ones of soldiers who fought to liberate Jerusalem. ROYALTY: None. SOURCE: Rembrandt, Elaine. (1981). Heroes, heroines & holidays - plays for Jewish youth. Denver, CO: Alternatives in Religious Education, Inc. SUBJECTS/PLAY TYPE: Israel; Jewish Drama; Skit.

1396. K-12. (+) Clark, Perry. (Hamner, Earl Jr) **The homecoming.** (The homecoming) CAST: 9f, 13m, Su. ACTS: 2. SETTINGS: Porch; kitchen; barn; restaurant counter; pool hall; parlor. PLAYING TIME: NA. PLOT: One Christmas Eve during the Depression, the Spencer family is waiting for Mr. Spencer to return from his out-of-town job. Although busy preparing for Christmas, the family still worries. The oldest son searches for his father. He stops at the pool hall, a church, and the Staples Sisters' home but does not find his father. Finally, Mr. Spencer arrives and Christmas begins. RECOMMENDATION: This adaptation faithfully follows the original story. The characters will be familiar to many as the Walton Family, and it is similar to the TV movie of the same name. ROYALTY: $50. SOURCE: Clark, Perry. (1976). The homecoming. Woodstock, IL: The Dramatic Pub. Co. SUBJECTS/PLAY TYPE: Christmas; Adaptation.

1397. K-6. (+) Watson, Sally Passmore. **The honey and the scarf.** CAST: 2f, 4m, 7u. ACTS: 1. SETTINGS: Meadow. PLAYING TIME: NA. PLOT: With the help of a bee and a cricket, Blossom, a worm, takes care of nature's spring and summer flowers. Winter comes, and not understanding, Blossom tries to save the flowers but fails. She must protect herself from the cold, the "Winter Witch." Understanding comes, however, with spring. Blossom turns into a beautiful butterfly, and a new worm appears to take Blossom's place, nurturing once again newly emerging flowers. RECOMMENDATION: This deals explicitly and bluntly with nature's cycle of life and death. Blossom is a lovable worm with endearing qualities in conflict with "Winter Witch" and the spirit "Wind." It would be best staged with older elementary children performing the major roles. ROYALTY: NA. SOURCE: Watson, Sally Passmore. (1978). The honey and the scarf. El Cerrito, CA: Theater World Pub. Co. SUBJECTS/PLAY TYPE: Nature; Friendship; Seasons; Skit.

1398. 5-7. (+) Henderson, Nancy. **Honor the brave.** CAST: 5f, 2m. ACTS: 1. SETTINGS: Cemetery. PLAYING TIME: 10 min. PLOT: Two Vietnam veterans go to a cemetery on Memorial Day, where they meet the sister of a dead friend and discover the true meaning of Memorial Day. RECOMMENDATION: This is solemn and thought provoking. ROYALTY: Permission required if performed outside of the classroom. SOURCE: Henderson, Nancy. (1978). Celebrate America: a baker's dozen of plays. New York, NY: Julian Messner. SUBJECTS/PLAY TYPE: Memorial Day; Vietnam War; Soldiers; Drama.

1399. 7-12. (+) Jennings, Coleman A. **The honorable Urashimo Taro.** CAST: 3f, 6m, Su. ACTS: 1. SETTINGS: Dock, underwater. PLAYING TIME: NA. PLOT: Urashimo Taro and his son save a turtle from being killed. In appreciation, the turtle brings Taro to meet the sea Princess, and to see the beauty of the ocean. While under the sea, Taro saves the inhabitants by killing the sea scorpion, and he becomes a celebrated hero. When he returns to earth, he realizes that he has been under the sea for 80 years, and his son is now a grandfather. Taro is horrified, but declines the turtle's offer of immortality under the sea. He wants to live his last years with his family, saying that with a son and grandchildren his life is beginning anew. RECOMMENDATION: This fantasy would have to be performed with highly stylized dance and body movements, since the settings cannot be fabricated. It is a mature rendition of the classic folk tale, and although the theme about living and learning is not as clear as it could be, it does get delivered. ROYALTY: NA. SOURCE: Jennings, Coleman A. & Berghammer, Gretta. (1986). Theatre for youth: Twelve plays with mature themes. Austin, TX: Univ. of Texas Press. SUBJECTS/PLAY TYPE: Folk Tales, Japan; Immortality; Drama.

1400. K-4*. (+) Ahl, Mary. **Hoppily ever after or the prince and the frog princess.** CAST: 5f, 5m. ACTS: 1. SETTINGS: Castle. PLAYING TIME: 30 min. PLOT: Determined to rid his wife and himself of their sons' constant bickering, the king orders his sons each to shoot an arrow in opposite directions and tells them they must marry the girl they find at the end of the arrow. Alexander, the Crown prince, is forced to marry Francine, a frog girl, because his arrow landed in her pond. Mortified by the idea initially, Alexander grows to love the frog princess for who she is. This love transforms Francine into a human princess. RECOMMENDATION: Although the lines are too long for very young children to memorize, the plot of the story is delightful, making it very appropriate for younger ages. ROYALTY: $15. SOURCE: Ahl, Mary. (1977). Hoppily ever after or the prince and the frog princess. Chicago, IL: Dramatic Pub. Co. SUBJECTS/PLAY TYPE: Folk Tale Motifs; Marriage; Comedy.

1401. 7-12. (+) Reines, Bernard J. **Horace Mann, American educator.** CAST: 3f, 14m. ACTS: 3. SETTINGS: Drawing room. PLAYING TIME: 30 min. PLOT: Horace Mann's struggle to improve public education is traced through his appointment as the Secretary of Massachusetts State Board of Education, his defense of his programs during times of budget cuts, his initiation of "normal" schools to educate teachers, and finally his decision to resign and run for the U.S. House of Representatives. RECOMMENDATION: In this portrayal of a great and selfless man, the issues of public education and the need to support education with tax dollars are well presented. Other notable historical figures, including George Emerson and Edmund Dwight, add to the historical accuracy. This would be an excellent introduction to our educational system; it would also be a facilitator of discussions about the ways in which federal budgets have recently been cut. ROYALTY: Free to Plays subscribers. SOURCE: Reines, Bernard J. (1987, November). Horace Mann, American educator. Plays: The Drama Magazine for Young Adults, pp. 23-32. SUBJECTS/PLAY TYPE: Mann, Horace; Education, History; Education Week; Drama.

1402. 6-9. (+) Gotwalt, Helen Louise Miller. **Horn of plenty.** CAST: 4f, 6m. ACTS: 1. SETTINGS: Living room. PLAYING TIME: 35 min. PLOT: In a Thanksgiving mix-up, the police are called to the Hill household where a robbery seems to have occurred. Young Tony Hill confesses to selling his personal belongings to pay for a sousaphone he has lost. The sousaphone is returned in time for the Thanksgiving day parade, and Tony discovers his old tuba was one used by John Philip Sousa, a "horn of plenty." RECOMMENDATION: Sorting out the mix-up of a suspected robbery adds excitement and interest and results in a satisfying conclusion. Tony's romance with his girlfriend adds further appeal. This can be used for the Thanksgiving holiday or as a lead in to a discussion and study of musical instruments and the music of Sousa. ROYALTY: Free to Plays subscribers. SOURCE: Gotwalt, Helen Louise Miller. (1979, November). Horn of plenty. Plays: The Drama Magazine for Young People, pp. 11-22. SUBJECTS/PLAY TYPE: Thanksgiving; Sousa, John Philip; Playlet.

1403. 9-12. (+) Kelly, Tim J. **Horror high, or, It came from the student lounge.** CAST: 6f, 6m, 8u. ACTS: 2. SETTINGS: School. PLAYING TIME: NA. PLOT: One stormy night Marcus, an inmate from the asylum, escapes and stalks Toombs High School to seek revenge. In order to smoke him out of the high school, the students re-enact the prom night that was Marcus's breaking point. But not everyone present is whom they appear to be; a new student is actually an art thief, the inmate thought to be Marcus is a harmless patient, and the hospital intern is the demented Marcus in disguise. Identities are clarified, inmates are captured, and Toombs High School returns back to normal. RECOMMENDATION: This is a clever spoof of the popular teen "chop-chop" movie. Several plots work together to keep the action fast paced and frantic. Add to this, slapstick humor, witty dialogue, and ludicrous characters, and the result is a very funny play. ROYALTY: $40. SOURCE: Kelly, Tim J. (1982). Horror high, or, It came from the student lounge. Boston, MA: Baker's Plays. SUBJECTS/PLAY TYPE: High School; Horror; Comedy.

1404. 7-12. (+) Gotwalt, Helen Louise Miller. **Horrors, incorporated.** CAST: 2f, 3m, Su. ACTS: 1. SETTINGS: Office. PLAYING TIME: 30 min. PLOT: Ghosts, goblins, witches, and other specters are striking at Horrors, Inc., a thousand year old business where monsters and horrors are manufactured. The beleaguered owner, Monster X, needs a new product to save his business. The Mad Scientist has developed a magic Elixir, but it has not been tested on humans. Two teenagers come to the office to rent Halloween costumes and are threatened with the magic Elixir. They use quick wits and humor to solve the business problems of Horror, Inc. and avoid the Elixir. RECOMMENDATION: All will relish this slapstick comedy. ROYALTY: Free to Plays subscribers. SOURCE: Gotwalt, Helen Louise Miller. (1981, October). Horrors, incorporated. Plays: The Drama Magazine for Young People, pp. 24-32. SUBJECTS/PLAY TYPE: Halloween; Monsters; Comedy.

1405. 7-10. (+) Dias, Earl J. **Horse sense.** CAST: 4f, 2m, 1u. ACTS: 1. SETTINGS: Workshop. PLAYING TIME: 25 min. PLOT: Paul Revere's horse tells the story of Revere's family and their commitment to liberty, as he recreates the events that led up to Revere's famous midnight ride. RECOMMENDATION: The horse's comments add comic relief to this part fact/part fictional account. The bitter debates about the Revolution are well presented here, as is a more personal look at the hero. ROYALTY: Free to Plays subscribers. SOURCE: Dias, Earl J. (1975, October). Horse Sense. Plays: The Drama Magazine for Young People, pp. 69-78. SUBJECTS/PLAY TYPE: Revere, Paul; Comedy.

1406. 9-12. (+) Kelly, Tim J. **Hospital.** CAST: 25u. ACTS: 2. SETTINGS: Hospital. PLAYING TIME: 90 min. PLOT: Bedside Manor, the hospital run by Dr. Jekyll, whose major philosophy is "keep 'em laughing," is being evaluated by the Board of Health as a new set of interns arrives along with a television crew, a gypsy, and an undercover cop. The villain conniving to get the hospital closed is Dr. Fred, a phony psychiatrist. The plot is uncovered, and all ends well. RECOMMENDATION: This fast moving comedy is full of puns and "bad" jokes and contains several odd characters and mini-plots. The cast would need to concentrate to keep all of the lines and actions straight, but it would be fun to produce. ROYALTY: $35. SOURCE: Kelly, Tim J. (1982). Hospital. Denver, CO: Pioneer Drama Service. SUBJECTS/PLAY TYPE: Medicine; Doctors; Comedy.

1407. 9-12. (+) Murray, John. **Hot line to destruction.** CAST: 6f, 4m. ACTS: 1. SETTINGS: Office. PLAYING TIME: 35 min. PLOT: On an unusual night at Tele-teen, the private secretary at the Bardian Embassy tries to call the police to report an attempted assassination of the Bardian ambassador, but she reaches Tele-Teen instead. The secretary says that she is being followed and does not have time to recall the police so she asks Tele-Teen to call them and warn the ambassador. The would-be assassin learns of the call, cuts Tele-Teen's telephone lines, and locks them in the building. Through their ingenuity, the teens do contact the police and save the ambassador. The assassin then tries to kill the teens because they have learned his identity, but is thwarted. RECOMMENDATION: Adventure, mystery and humor combine here to allow a wide latitude of emotive acting. ROYALTY: Free to Plays subscribers. SOURCE: Murray, John. (1975, May). Hot line to destruction. Plays: The Drama Magazine for Young People, pp. 13-28. SUBJECTS/PLAY TYPE: Hotlines; Mystery; Playlet.

1408. 7-12. (-) Foley, Irene. **Hotel Atlantic.** CAST: 3f, 6m. ACTS: 2. SETTINGS: Hotel lobby. PLAYING TIME: 30 min. PLOT: The planned reopening of an old Victorian hotel is almost destroyed by the "unregistered" guest/ghost of Robert Louis Stevenson, who scares away the chef. Stevenson saves the gala event by helping to cook the meal, then he plays matchmaker for the two protagonists. Finally, he leaves a copy of **Treasure Island**, inscribed with "I'm moving on." RECOMMENDATION: This is a trite little romance whose cliches and stereotyped characters are not saved by the irrelevant and insulting use of the ghost of a famous author. With no redeeming qualities, this play is not appropriate for any audience wishing to be entertained. ROYALTY: Free to Plays subscribers. SOURCE: Foley, Irene. (1985, March). Hotel Atlantic. Plays: The Drama Magazine for Young People, pp. 1-11. SUBJECTS/PLAY TYPE: Mystery; Ghosts; Stevenson, Robert Louis; Comedy.

1409. 7-12. (+) Gotwalt, Helen Louise Miller. **Hotel Santa Claus.** CAST: 4f, 10m, Su. ACTS: 1. SETTINGS: Living room. PLAYING TIME: 30 min. PLOT: Joyce and Woody Pendleton spend the Christmas holidays with their Aunt Crystal who lives in a hotel. Unknown to them, Crystal works as a typist because she hopes to meet Gordon Hayes, an important producer casting a play for which she wants to audition. On Christmas Eve the city is snowed in, so Jody and Woody relieve their boredom by following their family motto, C.I.F.O.--"Christmas is for others." They throw a party for everyone stranded in the hotel lobby. When Aunt Crystal arrives home and discovers the surprise impromptu party she sings for the party and is discovered by Santa, who is actually Gordon Hayes, the famous producer. RECOMMENDATION: Family tradition and unknown identities are the key elements in this play. Although it is a bit confusing at times, if acted well, the subtle humor will be apparent. ROYALTY: Free to Plays subscribers. SOURCE: Gotwalt, Helen Louise Miller. (1987, December). Hotel Santa Claus. Plays: The Drama Magazine for Young People, pp. 1-11. SUBJECTS/PLAY TYPE: Christmas; Playlet.

1410. 5-12. (+) Bland, Joellen. (Doyle, Arthur Conan) **The hound of the Baskervilles.** (The hound of the Baskervilles) CAST: 2f, 6m. ACTS: 1. SETTINGS: None. PLAYING TIME: 30 min. PLOT: Holmes solves the case of a mysterious hound who apparently has killed several members of the Baskerville family. A naturalist living across the moor is discovered to be a Baskerville family member intent on getting the family fortune. He is foiled in his attempt to kill Sir Henry Baskerville. RECOMMENDATION: Though the use of Watson as both narrator and actor is somewhat confusing, this preserves the mystery and flavor of the original and successfully simplifies it for a young audience. ROYALTY: Free to Plays subscribers. SOURCE: Bland, Joellen. (1979, October). The hound of the Baskervilles. Plays: The Drama Magazine for Young People, pp. 69-80. SUBJECTS/PLAY TYPE: Mystery; Inheritances; Reader's Theater; Adaptation.

1411. 8-12. (+) Kelly, Tim. (Doyle, Arthur Conan) **The hound of the Baskervilles.** (The hound of the Baskervilles) CAST: 5f, 5m. ACTS: 2. SETTINGS: Sitting room. PLAYING TIME: NA. PLOT: Sherlock Holmes and Watson are called to the moors to solve the mystery of threats to Sir Henry, and to identify the Hound of Baskervilles. Leaving Watson alone in the house, Holmes moves about the moor secretly. Suspicion falls on all characters, but Holmes solves the puzzle. RECOMMENDATION: The writing is suspenseful and sharp as the dialogue moves quickly and smoothly between characters. The reparte could well evoke chuckles, where warranted, to ease the suspense. Holmes glides through this piece as shrewdly as ever and Watson's character behaves as expected. ROYALTY: $35. SOURCE: Kelly, Tim. (1976). The Hound of the Baskervilles. New York, NY: Samuel French. SUBJECTS/PLAY TYPE: Mystery; Inheritances; Curses; Adaptation.

1412. 10-12. (+) Leslie, F. Andrew. (Doyle, Arthur Conan) **The hound of the Baskervilles.** (The hound of the Baskervilles) CAST: 3f, 6m. ACTS: 2. SETTINGS: Room; drawing room. PLAYING TIME: NA. PLOT: Holmes and Watson are visited by Dr. James Mortimer, who informs them of the bizarre death of the owner of Baskerville Hall in Devonshire. Holmes sends Watson back to the Hall with Mortimer and the new inheritor, Sir Henry Baskerville. Mr. and Mrs. Barrymore; Mrs. Barrymore's brother, Laura Lyons; and Mr. and Mrs. Stapleton are the pieces of the puzzle that Watson must investigate and report upon to Holmes. A ghostly, ferocious hound and a deadly moor are key elements of the murder mystery. Holmes arrives from his surprising vantage point in time to resolve the case and save Sir Henry for a future romance. RECOMMENDATION: This adaptation retains the distinctive atmosphere of Doyle's Holmes mysteries. The essentials of the plot and character are retained without complex dialogue or staging. Because there are few major characters, memorization of the 73 page script by the actors will be a challenge. ROYALTY: $35. SOURCE: Leslie, F. Andrew. (1981). The hound of the Baskervilles. New York, NY: Dramatists Play Service. SUBJECTS/PLAY TYPE: Inheritances; Curses; Mystery; Adaptation.

1413. 8-12. (+) Gotwalt, Helen Louise Miller. **The hound of the Maskervilles.** CAST: 7f, 7m, Su. ACTS: 1. SETTINGS: Clearing. PLAYING TIME: 35 min. PLOT: The witches of Hag Hollow are to entertain Lady Maskerville, one of Britain's most famous ghosts, who is in the United States as a Foreign Exchange Ghost. Upon the arrival of the Lady and her entourage, the witches learn of the Mayor's plan to use their property for road construction. Prior to this, the town's bank has been robbed by two gunmen, Bingo and Bongo. As the witches tend to reception details, Lady Maskerville takes a nap in her coffin, only to be awakened by the two bank robbers. Because Lady Maskerville threatens that her dog, Fang, will eat them, Bingo and Bongo reluctantly agree to stay and help at her reception. In the end, Fang is the hero, the land is saved, the robbers are put away, and Lady Maskerville has a lovely reception. RECOMMENDATION: The dialogue and story line are easy to follow. The costuming is quite elaborate and Fang

is supposed to be a real dog. ROYALTY: Free to Plays subscribers. SOURCE: Gotwalt, Helen Louise Miller. (1985, October). The hound of the Maskervilles. Plays: The Drama Magazine for Young People, pp. 9-20. SUBJECTS/PLAY TYPE: Witches; Robbery; Comedy.

1414. 9-12. (+) Albert, Rollin'. **Hounded by basketballs.** CAST: 1f, 7m. ACTS: 1. SETTINGS: Bare stage, props. PLAYING TIME: 35 min. PLOT: Surelocked Home and Dr. Whatsis, the famous detective team, are consulted by Mrs. Berylium Vizcaya, whose husband is missing. When a cab brings his body to Home's residence, the questions now are, who killed Lod Vizcaya and when did he die, because if he died after midnight, his inheritance will go to his wife. However, if he died before midnight, his money will go to Herr Stomp and his Peppy Poopie Puppy Palace, a pack of killer dogs. Home discovers that Lady Vizcaya and the cabbie are the murderers. Lady Vizcaya, attempting to escape dies in the swamp; the cabbie is arrested by Inspector Lestrade; and Herr Stomp inherits the fortune. RECOMMENDATION: This uproarious spoof will require a director and actors with good comic timing. ROYALTY: Free to Plays subscribers. SOURCE: Albert, Rollin'. (1976, April). Hounded by basketballs. Plays: The Drama Magazine for Young People, pp. 1-14 SUBJECTS/PLAY TYPE: Mystery; Holmes, Sherlock; Comedy.

1415. 9-12. (+) Thane, Adele. (Hawthorne, Nathaniel) **The House of the Seven Gables.** CAST: 7f, 10m, Su. ACTS: 1. SETTINGS: Gallows; variety shop; garden; parlor. PLAYING TIME: 35 min. PLOT: This is a faithful adaptation of Hawthorne's famous story about the Pyncheon family, cursed in 1692 by Matthew Maule. In 1850, Clifford Pyncheon returns to Seven Gables after 30 years in prison, though he is innocent of his uncle's murder. Clifford's cousin believes Clifford knows about a treasure that their uncle left. In the end, Phoebe Pyncheon, a country cousin, and Thomas Holgrave, a boarder at Seven Gables, fall in love, and Holgrave reveals that he is really Thomas Maule, descendant of Matthew. The curse turns out to be a family disease, and the treasure is a now worthless deed to land in Maine which had been bought over from England 150 years earlier. RECOMMENDATION: In this good introduction to the classic, language is sufficiently Victorian, but players should be able to learn their parts. Production requires some unusual items, such as a harpsichord, and a stage large enough to place a gallows and garden in front of the curtain. ROYALTY: Free to Plays subscribers. SOURCE: Thane, Adele. (1985, April). The House of the Seven Gables. Plays: The Drama Magazine for Young People, pp. 52-63. SUBJECTS/PLAY TYPE: Witchcraft; Adaptation.

1416. 10-12. (+) Bullins, Ed. **House party.** CAST: 1m. ACTS: 1. SETTINGS: None. PLAYING TIME: NA. PLOT: A black man tells how his life used to be when he was an author. The more he wrote, the more he had to write. His girl wouldn't answer when he called her, his mother stopped speaking to him, and his father turned his back on him. So he locked up the room where he used to write, got a job at the post office, and married his girl. Now everyone is happy but him. RECOMMENDATION:

As this scene shows how a man gave up his dreams to please other people, the dialogue reveals his disillusionment with a mundane life. ROYALTY: NA. SOURCE: Handman, Wynn. (1980). Modern American scenes for student actors. New York, NY: Bantam Books. SUBJECTS/PLAY TYPE: Writers; Black Americans; Scene.

1417. 7-10. (-) Donahue, John Clarke. **How could you tell?** CAST: 19f, 21m. ACTS: 1. SETTINGS: Circus tent; room; pier; raft; land. PLAYING TIME: NA. PLOT: Disillusioned circus performers quit, as the heed a mysterious stranger's advice. Later, they find a new circus life. RECOMMENDATION: Overused dialogue, complex plot and very elaborate production requirements make this play unsuccessful. ROYALTY: NA. SOURCE: Donahue, John Clarke. (1975). The cookie jar and other plays. Minneapolis, MN: University of Minnesota Press. SUBJECTS/PLAY TYPE: Circus; Social Criticism; Fantasy; Drama.

1418. 4-8. (+) Bradley, Virginia. **How did we manage before the postman came?** CAST: 1f, 10m, 1u. ACTS: 1. SETTINGS: Store; kitchen. PLAYING TIME: NA. PLOT: In this comedy about the history of mail service, Father Time takes the audience through the mail services of cavemen, Wild West cowboys, and finally today. RECOMMENDATION: Actually three plays in one, this very funny story gives children a history lesson as well as a chance to have fun with colorful characters from the past. ROYALTY: None. SOURCE: Bradley, Virginia. (1975). Is there an actor in the house? New York, NY: Dodd, Mead. SUBJECTS/PLAY TYPE: Mail; Cowboys; Cavemen; Comedy.

1419. 6-10. (+) Cook, Pat. **How does a thing like that get started?** CAST: 4f, 7m. ACTS: 1. SETTINGS: Park. PLAYING TIME: NA. PLOT: A small town is turned upside down when several false rumors circulate. One story involving a sick mare gets twisted into an incident having the town's mayor on his deathbed. Another case involves an elopement that was joked about but never took place. The story concludes with everyone in town bickering over the truth which is told when the subjects of the gossip confront each other. RECOMMENDATION: A likable play that contains some funny, but corny word plays, this points out the confusion that can result if people are more interested in the titillation than truth. ROYALTY: $15. SOURCE: Cook, Pat. (1987). How does a thing like that get started? Boston, MA: Baker's Plays. SUBJECTS/PLAY TYPE: Gossip; Misunderstandings; Rumors; Comedy.

1420. 5-8. (+) Pierce, Carl Webster. **How does your garden grow?** CAST: 1f, 2m. ACTS: 1. SETTINGS: Radio studio. PLAYING TIME: NA. PLOT: As a stylishly dressed horticulturist tells the listening audience a tale about growing a fanciful plant which is a cross between potatoes, onions, lettuce, and parsley, she demonstrates a real discrepancy between her dress and the way she describes herself to the radio audience. RECOMMENDATION: Recommended with reservation, this short skit would be an interesting exercise for testing the listening skills of a student audience. However, the content and theme of misrepresenting oneself may seem boring to a young audience. ROYALTY: None. SOURCE: Majeski, Bill. (1981). Easy skits, blackouts and pantomimes. Woodstock, IL: Dramatic Pub. Co. SUBJECTS/PLAY TYPE: Comedy; Horticulture; Skit.

1421. K-12. (+) Chesterton, Frances. **How far is it to Bethlehem?** CAST: 2u. ACTS: 1. SETTINGS: None. PLAYING TIME: 2 min. PLOT: Two travelers speculate about the object of their travels: the newborn Christ child. RECOMMENDATION: This is suitable for church or parochial school groups for performance at a Christmas pageant or worship service. ROYALTY: NA. SOURCE: Hendricks, William & Vogel, Cora. (1978). Handbook of Christmas programs. Grand Rapids, MI: Baker Book House. SUBJECTS/PLAY TYPE: Christ, Jesus; Christmas; Worship Program.

1422. K-12. (+) Clough, Judith L. **How far is it to Bethlehem?** CAST: 2f, 6m, Su. ACTS: 1. SETTINGS: Yard; room; heaven; field; stable. PLAYING TIME: 45 min. PLOT: The title question is asked from four different perspectives: by Mary and Joseph as they pack for their trip to Bethlehem; by the wise men of Chaldea as they discuss the special star and what it means; in heaven, as the angels prepare to proclaim Christ's birth; and on a hill near Bethlehem, where shepherds hear the good news. The play ends with the traditional nativity scene. RECOMMENDATION: New Testament accuracy is sacrificed in order to portray the traditional Christmas story, since the wise men were not present on the night of Jesus' birth, but arrived two years later to worship him. However, this play has merit for a church presentation because it shows the kinds of feelings and thoughts that might have been in the hearts and minds of those who witnessed the birth of Christ. ROYALTY: NA. SOURCE: Clough, Judith L. (1987). How far is it to Bethlehem? Franklin, OH: Eldridge Pub. Co. SUBJECTS/PLAY TYPE: Christmas; Christ, Jesus; Christian Drama.

1423. 5-10. (+) Kehret, Peg. **How I almost made one thousand dollars.** CAST: 1u. ACTS: 1. SETTINGS: None. PLAYING TIME: NA. PLOT: A youngster explains how he failed as a zip code directory salesman. RECOMMENDATION: Many will be able to empathize with the hazards of "get rich quick" schemes. ROYALTY: NA. SOURCE: Kehret, Peg. (1986). Winning monologs for young actors. Colorado Springs, CO: Meriwether Pub. SUBJECTS/PLAY TYPE: Money Making; Salesmen; Monologue.

1424. 9-12. (+) Mauro, Robert. **How I bought my first car.** CAST: 1f, 2m. ACTS: 1. SETTINGS: Bare stage, props. PLAYING TIME: 10 min. PLOT: Slides of Corvettes and Porsches illustrate the beginning of Sandy's first person account as she describes her first dream car she hopes to purchase with summer wages earned at a local fast food restaurant. Sandy's dreams of affluence are dispelled by the prices given by Big Bill and Happy Harry, whose sly deceits and hard sell techniques focus upon unusual "extras" (i.e., no windows for people who like to "feel the wind in their faces," four tires "filled with air"). The ironic climax of Sandy's comparison shopping spree occurs when she questions the integrity of Happy Harry and is threatened with a termination of her allowance if she doesn't purchase the car: Happy Harry is her father. RECOMMENDATION: The use of slides projected on the backdrop adds humor to this satirical play. The intricacies of the deceitful "hard sell" scheme are exposed, and the wary attitude of the consumer is applauded. The dilapidated condition of "the lemon," Sandy's first exposure to a used car, is truly funny. ROYALTY: Free to Plays subscribers. SOURCE: Mauro, Robert. (1988, April). How I bought my first car. Plays: The Drama Magazine for Young People, pp. 61-64. SUBJECTS/PLAY TYPE: Car Salesmen; Automobiles; Comedy.

1425. 7-12. (+) Leech, Michael T. (Tolstoy, Leo) **How much land does a man need?** (How much land does a man need?) CAST: Su. ACTS: 1. SETTINGS: None. PLAYING TIME: NA. PLOT: A greedy man dies while trying to increase his property as the title's question is answered: "six feet, from his head to his heels." RECOMMENDATION: The irony of this Tolstoy masterpiece is abridged, but not lost in this round the table reading. ROYALTY: Free for Plays subscribers. SOURCE: Leech, Michael (1977, January). How much land does a man need? Plays: The Drama Magazine for Young People, pp. 87-95. SUBJECTS/PLAY TYPE: Greed; Reader's Theater; Adaptation.

1426. K-3. (+) Twerfoo, Gustav A. & Smith, Robert B. **How music came into the world.** CAST: Su. ACTS: 1. SETTINGS: Jungle; pond. PLAYING TIME: NA. PLOT: A wise old owl must judge a vocal competition between an elephant, frog, and a dog. The owl concludes that the three sound better when they sing together. RECOMMENDATION: This West African folk tale explains the origin of music with simple and difficult versions of songs to be chosen to suit the performers' abilities. Audience participation is encouraged. ROYALTY: NA. SOURCE: Smith, Robert B. & Flohr, John W. (1984). Music dramas for children with special needs. Denton, TX: Troostwyk Press. SUBJECTS/PLAY TYPE: Folk Tales, Africa; Musical; Skit.

1427. 3-5. (+) Bartlett, Nicholas. **How now brown cow.** CAST: 10f, 15m. ACTS: 1. SETTINGS: Farmyard; jungle. PLAYING TIME: NA. PLOT: Brown Cow, self appointed mother of the farm yard, is unable to organize her fellow farm animals to celebrate the Eve of St. Francis. A passing swallow persuades the group to follow her to India, where they encounter jungle creatures and Brown Cow intimidates a Great Snake who has been terrorizing the countryside. Returning to the farm, they find that the farmer is starting a new day. RECOMMENDATION: The vivid personalities and relationships of the animals in this large cast are cleverly developed. Humorous songs, set to familiar tunes are interspersed throughout the play. Distinctly British, both in humor and language, this may need some editing for American children. ROYALTY: NA. SOURCE: Bartlett, Nicholas. (1979). Four short plays. London, England: Heinemann Educational Books. SUBJECTS/PLAY TYPE: Animals; Comedy; St. Francis Day; Musical.

1428. K-4*. (+) Young, Richard T. **How reading came back to Nowhere.** CAST: 3f, 5m, Su. ACTS: 1. SETTINGS: Town; library. PLAYING TIME: 60 min. PLOT: The citizens of Nowhere cannot read because they are not allowed to have books, by order of King Maestro Mean. When Parsley wanders into Nowhere carrying a book, the Nowhereians beg her to teach them to read. She does so, but is soon captured by the king. Due to the ineptness of the king's guards, she escapes, and uses a long lost book to expose Mean's fraudulent claim to the throne. Mean is deposed, and the name of the town is changed to Somewhere, where everyone's favorite pastime is reading. RECOMMENDATION: This play entertainingly reinforces the importance of learning to read. ROYALTY: $25. SOURCE: Young, Richard T. (1988). How reading came back to Nowhere. Schulenburg, TX: I.E. Clark. SUBJECTS/PLAY TYPE: Reading; Illiteracy; Comedy.

1429. 3-6. (+) Kelly, Tim. **How Santa got his Christmas tree.** CAST: 1f, 1m, 7u. ACTS: 1. SETTINGS: Workshop. PLAYING TIME: 30 min. PLOT: Problems at Santa's workshop arise when Stingy doesn't use enough glue for quality toys, and Sneaky steals toys from the other helpers. Santa is forced to banish them from his village. In revenge, Stingy and Sneaky steal Santa's Christmas tree and hold stolen toys for ransom. When Santa wants to rename Sneaky and Stingy and plans to give them another chance, they confess to their crime, and return everything. RECOMMENDATION: Humor and audience participation will enhance interest while also showing the folly of revenge. ROYALTY: $15. SOURCE: Kelly, Tim. (1985). How Santa got his Christmas tree. Denver, CO: Pioneer Drama Service. SUBJECTS/PLAY TYPE: Christmas; Revenge; Comedy.

1430. K-3. (+) Havilan, Amorie & Smith, Lyn. **How tall is a year?** CAST: 30u. ACTS: 1. SETTINGS: None. PLAYING TIME: 20 min. PLOT: Graduating students discuss whom they met during the school year: the librarian, policeman, fireman, and the bus driver, and they list what they learned: how to tie their shoes, brush their teeth, swimming, and how to recognize letters, numbers, colors, and animals. RECOMMENDATION: A possible presentation for parent-teacher night or an end of the school year program, this talks about growth of learning throughout the school year. ROYALTY: NA. SOURCE: Havilan, Amorie & Smith, Lyn. (1985). Easy plays for preschoolers to third grade. Brandon, MS: Quail Ridge Press. SUBJECTS/PLAY TYPE: School; Learning; Skit.

1431. K-5. (+) Bauer, Caroline Feller. (Kipling, Rudyard) **How the camel got his hump.** (Just so stories) CAST: 1m, 7u. ACTS: 1. SETTINGS: Desert. PLAYING TIME: 15 min. PLOT: At the beginning of the world, all animals worked except the camel, who only made a noise that sounded like "hump." When the djinn of the deserts confronts the camel, he only "humps." The djinn thinks magic thoughts, and as the camel "humps," so does his back. For failing to work and obtain food for the first three days of the world, the hump on his back provided the camel with needed food for that length of time. And so it is to this day. RECOMMENDATION: A delightful and timeless "why" story, this uses some of the original's vocabulary and phrasing, which adds to its charm. ROYALTY: None. SOURCE: Bauer, Caroline Feller. (1987). Presenting reader's theater: plays and poems to read aloud. New York, NY: H.W. Wilson Co. SUBJECTS/PLAY TYPE: Laziness; Reader's Theater; Adaptation.

1432. K-6. (+) Harris, Aurand. (Kipling, Rudyard) **How the camel got his hump.** (Just so stories) CAST: 1f, 1m, 4u. ACTS: 1. SETTINGS: Bare stage. PLAYING TIME: NA. PLOT: A magician performs some magic tricks and then tells a story about a camel who refuses to help a caveman, his dog, and horse. The magician gives the camel a hump on his previously "humpless" back, since the camel refused to share the responsibility of working with others. RECOMMENDATION: The magic tricks are entertaining, as is the audience involvement. Providing music gives a role to children who aren't acting. ROYALTY: Write Anchorage Press. SOURCE: Jennings, Coleman A. & Harris, Aurand. (1988). Plays children love, Volume II. New York, NY: St. Martin's Press. SUBJECTS/PLAY TYPE: Magic; Camels; Playlet.

1433. K-6. (+) Harris, Aurand. (Kipling, Rudyard) **How the first letter was written.** (Just so stories) CAST: 4f, 3m, Su. ACTS: 1. SETTINGS: Bare stage. PLAYING TIME: NA. PLOT: After performing magic tricks, a magician tells of a young cavegirl who accompanies her father as he fishes. When a stranger appears, the cavegirl attempts to communicate with him by drawing a picture. Realizing only that he has been directed to go somewhere, the stranger goes to the fishing camp where he is almost killed by the other cavemen. When the girl and her father return, she tells her people that she sent the stranger with her "letter." RECOMMENDATION: Magic and music combine to provide an acting role for everyone in this imagined history of writing. ROYALTY: Write to Anchorage Press. SOURCE: Jennings, Coleman A. & Harris, Aurand. (1988). Plays children love, Volume II. New York, NY: St. Martin's Press. SUBJECTS/PLAY TYPE: Magic; Communication; Playlet.

1434. 1-3. (+) Mahlman, Lewis. **How the little dipper came to be.** CAST: 6u. ACTS: 5. SETTINGS: House; woods. PLAYING TIME: 15 min. PLOT: Clara enters the mysterious woods at night to get water for her sick mother. She shares her cool water with an old man and a poor dog. Each time she shares, the dipper becomes more valuable, turning to silver and then gold. When she gives her mother the remaining water, the dipper flies from her hand and forms the starry Little Dipper in the sky. Lady Night tells Clara that she has been rewarded for her kindness, and that her family will never be in need again. The Little Dipper will always exist to symbolize Clara's kindness. RECOMMENDATION: This modern "porquois" story is uplifting and romantic. ROYALTY: Free to Plays subscribers. SOURCE: Mahlman, Lewis. (1984, November). How the Little Dipper came to be. Plays: The Drama Magazine for Young People, pp. 45-48. SUBJECTS/PLAY TYPE: Kindness; Little Dipper; Puppet Play.

1435. 9-12. (+) Seay, James L. & Puras, Ed. **How the west was fun.** CAST: 7f, 5m, Su. ACTS: 3. SETTINGS: Dance hall. PLAYING TIME: NA. PLOT: Curley, a young naive cowboy, loves Miss Lilly, a dance hall girl who only has eyes for Sgt. Tyree Turwilliger of the U. S. Cavalry. When Curley buys a love potion from a quack Indian medicine man, all the dance hall girls drink some. While Curley is out of the room, a telegram arrives, announcing that Curley is now a millionaire, and all the girls immediately fall in "love" with him, leaving Curley and the Indian amazed at the potion's effectiveness. RECOMMENDATION: This entertaining spoof, with its themes of unrequited love and the power of money includes songs integral to the plot. The pace never lags and puns abound. ROYALTY: $50. SOURCE: Seay, James L. & Puras Ed. (1983). How the west was fun. Elgin, IL: Performance Pub. Co. SUBJECTS/PLAY TYPE: Cowboys; Western; Love Potions; Musical; Comedy.

1436. 3-5*. (+) Nobleman, Roberta. **How the world was made.** CAST: 1f, 1m, 20u. ACTS: 1. SETTINGS: Outdoors. PLAYING TIME: NA. PLOT: In the Cheyenne legend of earth's creation, Maheo, the All Spirit, creates water and swimming animals. At the animals' request, Maheo creates land, plant life, and finally man and woman. RECOMMENDATION: This delightful introduction to mythology requires pantomime and fourth grade reading skills. ROYALTY: NA. SOURCE: Nobleman, Roberta. (1979). Mime and masks. Rowayton, CT: New Plays Books. SUBJECTS/PLAY TYPE: Creation; Legends, Native American; Pantomime.

1437. 9-12. (+) Irvin, Jeff. **How timely Nick and Betty Brown formed a conglomerate.** CAST: 2f, 5m, Su. ACTS: 1. SETTINGS: Boxing ring. PLAYING TIME: 45 min. PLOT: In this 1920s melodrama, Sam the Axe threatens to kill sweet Betty Brown if she does not pay off her dead father's gambling debt within one week. Timely Nick Crocker comes to Betty's rescue when he takes the $1000 prize in a boxing match with Masher Maloney. Sam the Axe is arrested for bank robbery, and Betty and Nick use the prize money to start the Betty Crocker conglomerate. RECOMMENDATION: Although the characters' heavy use of alcohol may offend some, this is fun filled, with rhyming narration, audience participation, and exaggerated acting by comical characters. ROYALTY: $20. SOURCE: Irvin, Jeff. (1987). High noon in styrofoam with timely Nick and Betty Brown. Schulenburg, TX: I.E. Clark. SUBJECTS/PLAY TYPE: Comedy; Melodrama.

1438. 4-8. (+) Boiko, Claire. **How to catch a ghost.** CAST: 5f, 7m, Su. ACTS: 1. SETTINGS: Night exterior. PLAYING TIME: 20 min. PLOT: Taro, a small boy, descends upon a temple graveyard garden equipped to capture ghosts with arrows, a net, and flypaper. His friends discover Taro entangled in flypaper and explain to him that Obon's ghosts are welcome ones. They help him to entice the ghosts through dancing, singing, and gifts. It is only then that Taro is able to experience for himself the meaning of Obon and its friendly spirits. The play is highlighted by the music of flutes, xylophones, drums and wood blocks. RECOMMENDATION: This remarkably different ghost story is a refreshing change. Told with an Oriental flare, the unique story will help students catch a glimpse of Japanese culture through kimonos, kites, crickets, music, and a chanting chorus. **ROYALTY:** Free to Plays subscribers. **SOURCE:** Boiko, Claire. (1979, October). How to catch a ghost. Plays: The Drama Magazine for Young People, pp. 37-41. **SUBJECTS/PLAY TYPE:** Ghosts; Halloween; Obon Drama.

1439. K-6. (+) Rockwell, Thomas. **How to eat fried worms. CAST:** 2f, 6m, 5u. **ACTS:** 3. **SETTINGS:** Bare stage, three sections. **PLAYING TIME:** NA. **PLOT:** Tom's friends are discussing the time Tom was kept in for not eating his dinner. When Billy says he would eat one bite of anything before he would get sent to his room, Tom dares Billy to eat one worm a day for fifteen days. Over this time period, the boys try all kinds of tricks to make Billy lose the bet. Billy wins, and even develops a taste for worms, thanks to his mother, who created all types of worm recipes to help him. **RECOMMENDATION:** The whimsy and pleasant grossness, along with the clever design of the stage setting to indicate passage of time and change of scenes, make this a zany, delightful play. **ROYALTY:** NA. **SOURCE:** Rockwell, Thomas. (1980). How to eat fried worms, and other plays. New York, NY: Delacorte Press. **SUBJECTS/PLAY TYPE:** Bets; Dares; Worms; Comedy.

1440. K-6. (+) Rockwell, Thomas. **How to eat like a child and other lessons in not being a grown-up. CAST:** 2f, 6m, 5u. **ACTS:** 3. **SETTINGS:** Bare stage, three sections. **PLAYING TIME:** NA. **PLOT:** This comprises 22 "lessons" about being a child from a child's point of view. In a fast paced series of vignettes, one small group after another is spotlighted. For example, Corey the comedian is telephoning: "Hello. Is your refrigerator running? You'd better go catch it." Rachel poses an eternal question, "Would you rather freeze to death or be burned alive?" In a whole group sketch, parent language is translated. For example, "we'll see" means, "No." Other sketches include "How to deal with injustice," and "How to act after being sent to your room." The closing song, like the opening one, reiterates familiar vagaries of childhood. **RECOMMENDATION:** This is a truly funny play where the realistic characters, dialogue and situations provide the basis of humor. A close adaptation of the book, the play could foster dialogue between the generations. All age groups can identify with each of the sketches and because of the various types of presentations, cast and audience interest is maintained. **ROYALTY:** NA. **SOURCE:** Ephron, Delia & Forster, John & Kahan, Judith. (1986). How to eat like a child and other lessons in not being grown-up. New York, NY: Samuel French. **SUBJECTS/PLAY TYPE:** Parent-Child Relationships; Behavior; Musical; Comedy.

1441. 1-3*. (+) Sullivan, Jessie P. **How to have a happy family. CAST:** 2u. **ACTS:** 1. **SETTINGS:** Puppet stage. **PLAYING TIME:** NA. **PLOT:** Two friends discuss how one gets angry too easily at her little sister and is at a loss for what to do. Psalm 133:1 is used to help solve the problem of family unity with the main theme of "...how good and pleasant it is for brethren to dwell together in unity." **RECOMMENDATION:** The emotions are universal and the solution plausible, but this is only suitable for church groups. **ROYALTY:** None. **SOURCE:** Sullivan, Jessie P. (1978). Puppet scripts for children's church. Grand Rapids, MI: Baker Book House. **SUBJECTS/PLAY TYPE:** Christian Drama; Siblings; Temper; Puppet Play.

1442. K-3*. (+) Sullivan, Jessie P. **How to lose your life to Jesus. CAST:** 2u. **ACTS:** 1. **SETTINGS:** Puppet stage. **PLAYING TIME:** NA. **PLOT:** Mortimer stops Mathilda to find out why she is rushing past him to help a sick neighbor. At Mortimer's request, Mathilda explains the lesson of Matthew 10:39, inspiring him to "lose his life to Jesus." **RECOMMENDATION:** The concept of giving up a personal desire for Jesus is simply explained, but often repeated, making this play very didactic. **ROYALTY:** None. **SOURCE:** Sullivan, Jessie P. (1978). Puppet scripts for children's church. Grand Rapids, MI: Baker Book House. **SUBJECTS/PLAY TYPE:** Christian Drama; Kindness; Puppet Play.

1443. K-5*. (+) Sullivan, Jessie P. **How to read the Bible. CAST:** 2u. **ACTS:** 1. **SETTINGS:** Puppet stage. **PLAYING TIME:** NA. **PLOT:** Two children decide that to understand the Bible better, they should find one that is written at their reading level, pray before reading it, try to figure out what God is saying, believe it, and then do it. **RECOMMENDATION:** Although simply presented, the concepts of II Timothy 3:16 are quite sophisticated and valuable. This could be used for any church related group. **ROYALTY:** None. **SOURCE:** Sullivan, Jessie P. (1978). Puppet scripts for children's church. Grand Rapids, MI: Baker Book House. **SUBJECTS/PLAY TYPE:** Christian Drama; Bible; Puppet Play.

1444. K-3. (+) Fisher, Aileen. **How to spell a patriot. CAST:** 16u. **ACTS:** 1. **SETTINGS:** None. **PLAYING TIME:** 5 min. **PLOT:** Sixteen children, each holding one letter of George Washington's name, appear on stage, and each recites a couplet relating their letter to some character trait of George Washington. **RECOMMENDATION:** This presents a good opportunity for younger children to participate in a program, as each has only two lines to memorize. The couplets are appropriately simple and patriotic. **ROYALTY:** Free to Plays subscribers. **SOURCE:** Fisher, Aileen. (1987, January/February). How to spell a patriot. Plays: The Drama Magazine for Young People, pp. 54- 55. **SUBJECTS/PLAY TYPE:** Washington, George; Patriotism; President's Day; Choral Reading.

1445. 4-12. (+) Gilfond, Henry. **How wise the fool! CAST:** 2f, 9m, Su. **ACTS:** 1. **SETTINGS:** Town square. **PLAYING TIME:** 15 min. **PLOT:** A small town routs an army by convincing the soldiers that the populace is all fools, and therefore not worth conquering. **RECOMMENDATION:** This is the author's view of the origin of April Fool's Day. Although it may not be historically accurate, this high interest/low vocabulary skit stands well on its own. **ROYALTY:** None. **SOURCE:** Gilfond, Henry. (1985). Holiday plays for reading. New York, NY: Walker. **SUBJECTS/PLAY TYPE:** April Fool's Day; Skit.

1446. 7-12. (+) Garver, Juliet. **A howling success.** CAST: 5f, 4m, 2u. ACTS: 1. SETTINGS: Living room. PLAYING TIME: 30 min. PLOT: The Allen family reacts unfavorably to the news that Cousin Lyle plays a dog on Broadway, until they find out how profitable his talent really is. RECOMMENDATION: This contemporary satire features dynamic and credible, though somewhat stereotypical characters, such as the constantly hungry teenage boy, the egocentric actor, the star struck teenage girl, the slightly morbid 10 year old, and the cynical father. The theme of "it's not what you do, it's how much you get paid for it", is a worthy object of satire. ROYALTY: Free to Plays subscribers. SOURCE: Garver, Juliet. (1978, April). A howling success. Plays: The Drama Magazine for Young People, pp. 11-20. SUBJECTS/PLAY TYPE: Satire; Comedy.

1447. 3-7. (+) Woster, Alice. **Hubbub on the bookshelf.** CAST: 3f, 6m. ACTS: 1. SETTINGS: Bookshelf. PLAYING TIME: 25 min. PLOT: Bookworms accustomed to a bland diet of stationery undergo personality changes determined by the books they eat. It is decided that they must eat a little of each book, in order to have a healthy balanced diet. RECOMMENDATION: Though some of the dialogue could be improved, an interesting premise and vivid characterizations make this quite entertaining. Also, the lesson that books are full of variety is well taught. ROYALTY: Free to Plays subscribers. SOURCE: Woster, Alice. (1978, February). Hubbub on the bookshelf. Plays: The Drama Magazine for Young People, pp. 41-51. SUBJECTS/PLAY TYPE: Literature; Comedy.

1448. 6-12. (-) Harris, Aurand. (Twain, Mark) **Huck Finn's story.** (The adventures of Huckleberry Finn) CAST: 4f, 4m. ACTS: 1. SETTINGS: Bare stage. PLAYING TIME: NA. PLOT: Huck escapes from his father, who is holding him for ransom, and finds Jim, who has run away from Miss Watson. They meet two scoundrels who almost succeed in selling Jim, but word comes that Jim has been set free by Miss Watson. Huck heads West. RECOMMENDATION: Although well adapted, Jim's dialogue and dialect, while true to the Twain novel, would undoubtedly offend black students. ROYALTY: $35. SOURCE: Harris, Aurand. (1988). Huck Finn's story. New Orleans, LA: Anchorage Press, Inc. SUBJECTS/PLAY TYPE: Slavery; Adventure; Adaptation.

1449. 7-12. (+) DuBois, Graham. (Twain, Mark) **Huckleberry Finn.** (The adventures of Huckleberry Finn) CAST: 1f, 4m, 1u. ACTS: 1. SETTINGS: None. PLAYING TIME: 25 min. PLOT: Huckleberry Finn is kidnapped by his father and taken to a remote cabin as a captive. Pap Finn tries to gain access to Huck's money, but Huck is rescued by his friend Joe. Huck kills a pig and leaves a bloody trail so that his father will think that Huck has been killed by thieves. While hiding on Jackson Island, Huck runs into his friend, Jim, a slave, who confesses that he has run away from his owner. To find out the local gossip, Huck disguises himself as a girl and visits an old woman in town. She realizes he is a boy in disguise and hints to him of the search for Jim. Huck takes the information back to Jim and they begin their escape which leads to many

adventures on the Mississippi River. RECOMMENDATION: This round the table reading gives a good sense of the original. ROYALTY: Free to subscribers. SOURCE: DuBois, Graham. (1984, May). Huckleberry Finn. Plays: The Drama Magazine for Young People, pp. 56-64. SUBJECTS/PLAY TYPE: Adventure; Con-Artists; Adaptation.

1450. 7-12. (+) DuBois, Graham. (Twain, Mark) **Huckleberry Finn.** (The adventures of Huckleberry Finn) CAST: 1f, 4m, 1u. ACTS: 1. SETTINGS: None. PLAYING TIME: 25 min. PLOT: Twain's well known characters, Huck Finn and Tom Sawyer, decide to float down the river on a raft for the summer. Their adventures include saving the inheritance of three sisters from two con-artists posing as their long lost uncles. RECOMMENDATION: This musical adaptation bears little resemblance to Twain's novel of the same name. If the audience can accept this playwright's version, it may work as a musical production. ROYALTY: $60. SOURCE: Caruso, Joseph George. (1986). Huckleberry Finn. Denver, CO: Pioneer Drama Service. SUBJECTS/PLAY TYPE: Comedy; Con-Artists; Adventure; Musical.

1451. 7-10. (-) DuBois, Graham. **The humblest place.** CAST: 3f, 6m, Su. ACTS: 1. SETTINGS: Yard. PLAYING TIME: NA. PLOT: A successful old innkeeper ignores all signs telling him that the world's savior is to be born in his very own inn; he even thinks his own wife's faith is ludicrous. RECOMMENDATION: This tedious narrative lacks sensitivity throughout and ends abruptly with no real focus. ROYALTY: Free to Plays subscribers. SOURCE: Kamerman, Sylvia E. (1975). A treasury of Christmas plays. Boston, MA: Plays, Inc. SUBJECTS/PLAY TYPE: Christmas; Christian Drama.

1452. 7-12. (+) Dotterer, Dick. **The Humpty Dumpty complex.** CAST: 5f, 6m. ACTS: 2. SETTINGS: Family room. PLAYING TIME: NA. PLOT: When Robyn wishes he had a guardian angel, Stephen, who is invisible to everyone but Robyn, appears to help her. Receiving permission from his superiors to be mortal for one day, he arranges to be Robyn's date for the Harvest Festival. When the boy Robyn likes sees her with Stephen, he is jealous and declares that he cares for Robyn. The time comes for Stephen to return to his angel status and all ends well. RECOMMENDATION: This combination of familiar themes and recognizable ploys will interest young preteens and high schoolers. ROYALTY: $40. SOURCE: Dotterer, Dick. (1981). The Humpty Dumpty complex. Boston, MA: Baker's Plays. SUBJECTS/PLAY TYPE: Dating; Guardian Angels; Drama.

1453. 1-6. (+) Pratt, Hal. (Asbjornsen, Peter & E. Moe) **The hungry troll.** (Three billy boats gruff) CAST: 4u. ACTS: 1. SETTINGS: Bridge. PLAYING TIME: 5 min. PLOT: After a hungry troll tries unsuccessfully to eat several goats that go over the bridge, he decides that living on the hill and eating grass would be an improvement over his present situation. RECOMMENDATION: This amusing puppet play will capture the interest of young children, as the clever dialogue and absorbing new twist teach a lesson about changing viewpoints and thereby improving one's life. ROYALTY: Free to Plays subscribers. SOURCE: Pratt, Hal. (1985, March). The hungry troll. Plays: the Drama Magazine for Young People, pp. 44-46. SUBJECTS/PLAY TYPE: Fantasy; Puppet Play; Folk Tales, Norway; Adaptation.

1454. 7-12. (+) Jackson, Richard Eugene & Ellis, David. (Carroll, Lewis) **The hunting of the Snark.** (The hunting of the Snark) CAST: 9u. ACTS: 1. SETTINGS: Spaceship; planet Snark. PLAYING TIME: 60 min. PLOT: A captain, a beaver, a butcher, a banker, and a lawyer embark on a fantasy space trip to capture an unseen animal named the Snark. After a bumpy ride the crew arrives on the Snark's rugged planet, and encounter wild beings such as the shrieking Jub Jub bird, and the terrifying Bandersnatch. The unfortunate Butcher vanishes once he finds the Snark because it is of the dreaded Boojum variety. The play ends as the remaining crew vow not to give up the search. RECOMMENDATION: Adapted from Lewis Carroll's nonsense poem of the same name, this modernized version captures the essence of the original, although several characters have been combined or eliminated. ROYALTY: $60. SOURCE: Jackson, Richard Eugene & Ellis, David. (1987). The hunting of the Snark. Schulenburg, TX: I.E. Clark. SUBJECTS/PLAY TYPE: Fantasy; Adventure; Space Travel; Adaptation.

1455. 3-6. (+) Pratt, Hal. (Carroll, Lewis) **Hunting the Snark.** (The hunting of the Snark) CAST: 1f, 3m, 4u. ACTS: 1. SETTINGS: Bare stage, backdrop. PLAYING TIME: 15 min. PLOT: Benjamin Bunny convinces Eric Bunny to search for a nonexistent snark, who is clever as a fox, brave as a lion, and fast as a horse or rabbit. In his search, Benjamin is chased by a fox, runs away from a lion, and chases a horse. The children to whom the snark belongs tell Benjamin that there is no such thing as a snark. Eric laughs at Benjamin's gullibility until an offstage voice identifies himself as a friendly snark and invites Benjamin for a carrot flavored soda. Puppets sing verses to the tunes of "We're Off to See the Wizard" and "Home on the Range." RECOMMENDATION: The animal characters play jokes and make mistakes, but good wins over bad as simple sentence structure and rhyming lines contribute to ease of production. ROYALTY: Free to Plays subscribers. SOURCE: Pratt, Hal. (1984, May). Hunting the snark. Plays: The Drama Magazine for Young People, pp. 73-75. SUBJECTS/PLAY TYPE: Animals; Jokes; Puppet Play; Adaptation.

1456. 4-8. (+) Kelly, Tim J. **Hurricane Smith and the garden of the golden monkey.** CAST: 11f, 11m, Su. ACTS: 2. SETTINGS: Open stage. PLAYING TIME: 120 min. PLOT: When a movie director is stranded at her school, a student screenwriter asks the director to read a script she has written. It is about Hurricane Smith, an adventurer who is given a golden monkey which may be a clue to the fate of his missing father. Hurricane and an intrepid photographer, Linda, fly to the Amazon to seek out the Garden of the Golden Monkey and discover the secret of the Cobra people. They encounter a treacherous trader, the evil cobra woman, a nursemaid gorilla, and finally, the story behind the father's disappearance. The tale is filled with tacky sensationalism: just the thing the movie

director has been looking for. RECOMMENDATION: If this script within a script is played for laughs and for exaggerated effects, the cast will have fun hamming it up while portraying the larger than life motion picture characters. ROYALTY: $35. SOURCE: Kelly, Tim J. (1985). Hurricane Smith and the Garden of the Golden Monkey. Denver, CO: Pioneer Drama Service. SUBJECTS/PLAY TYPE: Adventure; Jungle; Comedy.

1457. 9-12. (+) Kelly, Tim. (Kelly, Tim) **Hurricane Smith: The musical.** (Hurricane Smith and the garden of the golden monkey) CAST: 15m, Su. ACTS: 2. SETTINGS: Stage. PLAYING TIME: 90 min. PLOT: Gloria, an aspiring screenwriter, coaxes Eddie, a low grade film director, to look at a script for a musical adventure called "Hurricane Smith." The entire script is re-enacted in order to convince Eddie of the story's film potential. Hurricane Smith, a world adventurer, gets in and out of danger until the final curtain. RECOMMENDATION: This musical adventure of bad movies has many characters that, when played with exaggeration, will get many laughs. The minimal staging and props make this a good choice for a drama department on a limited budget or as a traveling production for a competition. ROYALTY: $90. SOURCE: Kelly, Tim. (1988). Hurricane Smith: the musical. Denver, CO: Pioneer Drama Service. SUBJECTS/PLAY TYPE: Comedy; Adventure; Adaptation.

1458. 7-12. (-) Keller, Teddy. **The hypocritical oafs.** CAST: 3f, 3m. ACTS: 1. SETTINGS: Hospital. PLAYING TIME: 30 min. PLOT: Incompetent doctors and nurses perform operations using carpenter's and plumber's tools, as they exchange bad puns. A nurse attempts to get an alcoholic doctor and his lecherous colleague removed, but with the help of a wisecracking orderly, they outsmart her. RECOMMENDATION: This gives six characters an excuse to stand around and tell bad jokes and puns. The dialogue is extremely sexist and totally mindless. ROYALTY: $15. SOURCE: Keller, Teddy. (1985). The hypocritical oafs. Boston, MA: Baker's Plays. SUBJECTS/PLAY TYPE: Hospitals; Doctors; Nurses; Farce.

1459. 7-12. (+) Moloney, Louis. Saldaña, Johnny. **I didn't know that!** CAST: 2f, 3m. ACTS: 1. SETTINGS: Bare stage. PLAYING TIME: 40 min. PLOT: Collected pieces of information from popular compilations of first facts, world records, and oddities, are presented with action and music. RECOMMENDATION: This is a very interesting and clever way for people of all ages to learn about many interesting facts of life, curiosities, etc. ROYALTY: NA. SOURCE: Moloney, Louis & Saldaña, Johnny. (1980). I didn't know that! New Orleans, LA: Anchorage Press. SUBJECTS/PLAY TYPE: Family; World Records; First Facts; Comedy.

1460. 7-12. (+) Fisher, Aileen Lucia. **I have a dream.** CAST: 2f, 8m, Su. ACTS: 1. SETTINGS: Bare stage, props. PLAYING TIME: 20 min. PLOT: As a master of ceremonies narrates Martin Luther King's life, a series of short skits re-enact events such as the Montgomery bus boycott, the march preceding King's "I Have a Dream" speech, the march to gain the right to vote, and finally a news bulletin announcing King's assassination. The play ends with the music "We Shall Overcome." RECOMMENDATION: Slides of Martin Luther King Jr. would enhance this production, as would a more thorough presentation of Dr. King's accomplishments. ROYALTY: Free to Plays subscribers. SOURCE: Fisher, Aileen Lucia. (1986, January/February). Plays: The Drama Magazine for Young People, pp. 27-32. SUBJECTS/PLAY TYPE: King, Martin Luther Jr.; Civil Rights; Black Americans; Playlet.

1461. K-12. (+) Hendrick, William & Vogel, Cora. I have a little secret. CAST: Su. ACTS: 1. SETTINGS: None. PLAYING TIME: 1 min. PLOT: This recitation reflects the idea of keeping a secret, whether keeping the secret of a gift or keeping the secret of the birth of Christ, until it is time to announce the news. RECOMMENDATION: This may be part of a Christmas devotional program. ROYALTY: None. SOURCE: Hendrick, William & Vogel, Cora. (1983). Handbook of Christmas programs. Grand Rapids, MI: Baker Book House. SUBJECTS/PLAY TYPE: Christmas; Choral Reading.

1462. 10-12. (+) Haynes, Harold J. & Gordon, John J. I just wanna tell somebody. CAST: 7f, 12m, 3u. ACTS: 2. SETTINGS: None. PLAYING TIME: NA. PLOT: After Tony is physically abused by his unemployed father, he dreams of an imaginary courtroom where children bring their abusive parents to trial. Neglect, physical abuse, emotional abuse, and sexual abuse are all represented. RECOMMENDATION: This powerful drama is highly recommended for mature teenagers and adults. The emotional subject matter of child abuse is presented frankly, but without sensationalism. Audiences should be prepared in advance, and some group processing is recommended after viewing. This may be staged as a musical. ROYALTY: $50. SOURCE: Haynes, Harold J. & Gordon, John J. (1987). I wanna tell somebody. Schulenburg, TX: I.E. Clark. SUBJECTS/PLAY TYPE: Child Abuse; Drama.

1463. K-4. (+) Nobleman, Roberta. I know an old lady who swallowed a fly. CAST: 1f, 10u. ACTS: 1. SETTINGS: Kitchen. PLAYING TIME: NA. PLOT: Based on the song with the same title, this pantomime involves an old lady who is so hungry that she swallows a fly and other assorted animals. At the end, the old woman dies. RECOMMENDATION: While some actors pantomime, others sing the song and play simple musical instruments such as triangles, bells, and sticks. ROYALTY: NA. SOURCE: Nobleman, Roberta. (1979). Mime and masks. Rowayton, CT: New Plays Books. SUBJECTS/PLAY TYPE: Comedy; Animals; Pantomime.

1464. 9-12. (+) Erhard, Tom. I know I saw gypsies. CAST: Su. ACTS: 1. SETTINGS: Bare stage. PLAYING TIME: 45 min. PLOT: This is an avant garde poetic dramatization of the hopes and fears that adolescents face, including depression, euphoria, anger, losing weight, belonging, popularity, loneliness, love, rejection, death, and incarceration. RECOMMENDATION: This will be more appropriate for mature audiences, but all high

schoolers will identify with the emotions which are very effectively captured in these challenging roles. ROYALTY: $25. SOURCE: Erhard, Tom. (1982). I know I saw gypsies. Woodstock, IL: Dramatic Pub. Co. SUBJECTS/PLAY TYPE: Fears; Hopes; Drama.

1465. 9-12. (-) Stahl, Le Roy. I object! CAST: 1f, 4m. ACTS: 1. SETTINGS: Courtroom. PLAYING TIME: NA. PLOT: The defendant in a lawsuit is clearly lying on the stand, but the judge overrules all of the plaintiff's attorney's objections because the defendant, a pretty young girl, is flirting with the judge. RECOMMENDATION: The plot and theme are dated, vaguely vaudevillian at best, and blatantly sexist. The defendant is a bimbo who obviously caused a major auto accident, but escapes prosecution by using her "feminine wiles," making this more offensive than humorous. ROYALTY: None. SOURCE: Majeski, Bill. (1981). Easy skits, blackouts and pantomimes. Woodstock, IL: Dramatic Pub. Co. SUBJECTS/PLAY TYPE: Legal System; Skit.

1466. K-3*. (+) Miller, Kathryn Schultz & Miller, Barry. I think I can. CAST: 2f, 2m. ACTS: 1. SETTINGS: Play area. PLAYING TIME: 45 min. PLOT: Becky overcomes her fear of speaking in front of her class by imagining herself in a variety of nontraditional roles. RECOMMENDATION: Brimming with opportunities for audience participation, this requires that the four main characters play multiple roles and sing. ROYALTY: $15. SOURCE: Miller, Kathryn Schultz & Miller, Barry. (1975). I think I can. Denver, CO: Pioneer Drama Service. SUBJECTS/PLAY TYPE: Animals; Comedy; Confidence; Musical.

1467. 7-9. (+) Kehret, Peg. I thought Ellen was my friend. CAST: 1f. ACTS: 1. SETTINGS: None. PLAYING TIME: NA. PLOT: A young girl experiences her first awkward attempts at finding a best friend and confidante and sharing her innermost thoughts. Feelings of deep hurt, betrayal and emotional upheaval are endured, as Ellen, the best friend, trades friendship for peer success. Spurned and disillusioned, the girl realizes that Ellen was not a good choice. RECOMMENDATION: This accurately depicts the emotional problems associated with the need to confide in someone who will be a bridge between parents and the society of the young. ROYALTY: NA. SOURCE: Kehret, Peg. (1986). Winning monologs for young actors. Colorado Springs, CO: Meriwether Pub. SUBJECTS/PLAY TYPE: Friendship; Monologue.

1468. 6-12. (+) Murray, John. I want to report a murder. CAST: 4f, 4m, Su. ACTS: 1. SETTINGS: Living room. PLAYING TIME: 30 min. PLOT: Lottie suspects one of her boarders of murder when a maid fleetingly sees a lifeless body in his room. When the police investigate, they find the dismembered parts of a dummy, which is part of the boarder's stage act. After the police leave, the maid picks up the dummy's head, finds stolen diamonds in it, and confronts the thief, who tries to strangle her with a telephone cord. In the nick of time, the police, acting on a hunch, return to save her. RECOMMENDATION: This has a high level of suspense and intrigue, a continuous unfolding of events, a simple but effective plot, and a sequence of events which build tension until the effectively timed climax. ROYALTY: Free to Plays subscribers. SOURCE: Murray, John. (1987, April). I want to report a murder. Plays: The Drama Magazine for Young People, pp. 12-22. SUBJECTS/PLAY TYPE: Mystery; Jewel Thieves; Playlet.

1469. 7-10. (+) Wilson, Pat. **I wish I'd never asked them to come.** CAST: 10f. ACTS: 1. SETTINGS: Sitting room/study. PLAYING TIME: NA. PLOT: Confusion and uproar reign supreme at a private girls' school reunion, as eight returning graduates show how much they've changed. The Bishop's wife spurns her old classmates, but the tables are turned when she snubs Molly for getting tangled up with the police, only to learn that Molly is the Duchess she is to entertain that evening. RECOMMENDATION: Distinctly European in its storyline and approach, this comedy of errors should entertain, though some Britishisms may need to be clarified. Only determined young actors should attempt this, due to its verbosity, but staging should pose no problems. ROYALTY: $15. SOURCE: Wilson, Pat. (1977). I wish I'd never asked them to come. Elgin, IL: Performance Pub. Co. SUBJECTS/PLAY TYPE: School; Reunions; Teachers; Comedy.

1470. 3-5. (-) Bromley, Marie. **I wonder who frightened them.** CAST: 3u. ACTS: 1. SETTINGS: Dark room. PLAYING TIME: 10 min. PLOT: Two burglars robbing an abandoned house meet a ghost. In a case of mistaken identity, the Ghost confuses the robbers and they respond in a humorous, bungling fashion. RECOMMENDATION: This has too much dialogue and not enough action. Production would be difficult, as it takes place in the dark. (The puppets use flashlights.) ROYALTY: Free to Plays subscribers. SOURCE: Bromley, Marie. (1979, October). I wonder who frightened them. Plays: The Drama Magazine for Young People, pp.61-64. SUBJECTS/PLAY TYPE: Comedy; Ghost Stories; Puppet Play.

1471. 1-3. (+) Martin, Judith. **I won't take a bath.** CAST: 2f, 1m, 2u. ACTS: 1. SETTINGS: Bare stage, props. PLAYING TIME: 5 min. PLOT: The talking bathtub and bar of soap beg Peter to take his bath, but he stubbornly refuses until his mother walks in. RECOMMENDATION: With rhyme, Peter shows his dismay and Peter's mother shows that she empathizes with his distaste of baths. It's nice to remind children that parents were young once, too. ROYALTY: None. SOURCE: Martin, Judith. (1981). Everybody, everybody: A collection from the paper bag players. New York, NY: Elsevier/Nelson Books. SUBJECTS/PLAY TYPE: Baths; Comedy.

1472. 12. (+) Jacobs, J. T. **Ice milk.** CAST: 5f, 10m. ACTS: 2. SETTINGS: Hospital rooms; nurse's lounge; living room. PLAYING TIME: NA. PLOT: Mrs. Mandell has just died in a nursing home. Through flashbacks to his youth, Mr. Mandell remembers how they met while working at a nursing home, and how the various patients there influenced their lives. The play ends with Mr. Mandell's determination to adjust to life without his wife. RECOMMENDATION: This is a moving commentary on

how the aged are treated. Through narrative poetry and graphic scenes depicting life in a nursing home, the problems of old age are compared to the problems of youth. Although the acting is within the ability of adolescents, this would probably be better for more mature audiences. ROYALTY: $50. SOURCE: Jacobs, J.T. (1984). Ice milk. Chicago, IL: Dramatic Pub. Co. SUBJECTS/PLAY TYPE: Death; Elderly; Nursing Homes; Drama.

1473. 9-12. (+) Carroll, John R. **If it don't hurt, it ain't love.** CAST: 2f, 2m. ACTS: 1. SETTINGS: Hospital room. PLAYING TIME: NA. PLOT: Cathy knows and accepts the fact that she is dying, but her mother refuses to believe it. When Cathy falls in love with a hospital orderly who openly discusses her illness and her impending death, Cathy's mother forbids them to see each other. After Cathy dies, her mother and the orderly realize that they wasted Cathy's last days in needless arguments. They comfort each other as they discuss their own memories of Cathy. RECOMMENDATION: The need for communication and acceptance among families and friends of terminally ill patients is stressed as the characters come to understand that they must make the most of every moment. ROYALTY: NA. SOURCE: Carroll, John R. (1979). If it don't hurt, it ain't love. Boston, MA: Baker's Plays. SUBJECTS/PLAY TYPE: Death; Love; Drama.

1474. 5-12. (+) Tulloch, Richard. **If only we had a cat.** CAST: 1f, 1m, 5u. ACTS: 1. SETTINGS: Bedroom. PLAYING TIME: NA. PLOT: Dr. Stoner (an 80 year old botanist and university professor) breaks her hip getting off a student's motorcycle. She is forced into a retirement home to recuperate. While there, she and a male resident try to regain their dignity and sense of self worth by getting a cat. Because they do not have permission from the home, the animal shelter refuses their request. But the home's staff finally learns to respect them. RECOMMENDATION: Although some of the Australian slang would have to be changed, this is a realistic and poignant portrayal of the plight of senior citizens who because of their age, are expected to be childlike. This should be performed by grades 9-12 for their peers, or for the younger grades. ROYALTY: Write to author. SOURCE: Lonie, John. (1985). Learning from life. Sydney, Australia: Currency Press. SUBJECTS/PLAY TYPE: Elderly; Self Esteem; Drama.

1475. 4-6. (+) Bradley, Virginia. **If the rabbit pickets, you're doing something wrong.** CAST: 2f, 3m, Su. ACTS: 1. SETTINGS: Garden. PLAYING TIME: NA. PLOT: A boy spends his whole life trying to make his garden grow, but nothing ever happens because he always forgets to plant the seeds. RECOMMENDATION: In this cute play, the ending is predictable, but the anticipation only adds to the fun. Lines and props are simple but effective. ROYALTY: None. SOURCE: Bradley, Virginia. (1975). Is there an actor in the house? New York, NY: Dodd, Mead. SUBJECTS/PLAY TYPE: Gardening; Comedy.

1476. P-2. (+) De Regniers, Beatrice Schenk. **If we walked on our hands.** CAST: 6u. ACTS: 1. SETTINGS: None. PLAYING TIME: NA. PLOT: Several readers list how strange the world would be if we did certain things differently, such as sending children to work while parents played. **RECOMMENDATION**: A fun nonsense recitation, young children will enjoy performing this for parents or peers. **ROYALTY**: NA. **SOURCE**: Bauer, Caroline Feller. (1987). Presenting reader's theater: Plays and poems to read aloud. New York, NY: H.W. Wilson Co. **SUBJECTS/PLAY TYPE**: Nonsense; Reader's Theater.

1477. 4-6. (-) Bradley, Virginia. **If you recognize me, don't admit it. CAST**: 1f, 3m, Su. **ACTS**: 6. **SETTINGS**: Bare stage. **PLAYING TIME**: NA. **PLOT**: In this opposites sketch, Santa Claus goes to the South Pole; the mother tells the child to feel free to skip school; etc. There are six specified scenes and the author suggests writing others. **RECOMMENDATION**: This play does not fit together and leaves the audience waiting for an ending or some sort of closure. **ROYALTY**: None. **SOURCE**: Bradley, Virginia. (1975). Is there an actor in the house? New York, NY: Dodd, Mead. **SUBJECTS/PLAY TYPE**: Opposites; Comedy.

1478. 2-6. (+) Winther, Barbara. **Ijapa, the tortoise. CAST**: 2f, 4m, Su. **ACTS**: 1. **SETTINGS**: Village; bush. **PLAYING TIME**: 20 min. **PLOT**: To provide food for his family, lazy but shrewd Ijapa approaches the village as a dancing palm tree. The frightened villagers flee, leaving behind their delicious yams, which the tortoise gathers and takes home. The village priest then fixes the yams so they will stick to the hand of the thief. The next day, when Ijapa becomes the dancing palm again, he is caught as the yams stick to his hands. Next, Ijapa trespasses on the Bush Spirits' land to plant corn. When confronted, Ijapa tells Bush Spirit that he was told to plant by a powerful ancestor. The Bush Spirits play along and tell him that "they will do as he does," as the corn is planted quickly. The next day there are ears of corn. Ijapa's wife picks an ear, but discards it in the river as it is spoiled. The Bush Spirits do as Ijapa's wife does and they discard all the corn into the river. **RECOMMENDATION**: These two wonderful tales are told with lively descriptions (if Ijapa doesn't find food his tortoise wife will "flip onto her back and wave her feet" while his children "pull in their heads and refuse to speak"); simple dialogue; and well drawn characterizations. The irony of each vignette is carefully and effectively portrayed. **ROYALTY**: Free to Plays subscribers. **SOURCE**: Winther, Barbara. (1977, October). Ijapa, the tortoise. Plays: The Drama Magazine for Young People, pp. 57-64. **SUBJECTS/PLAY TYPE**: Folk Tales, Nigeria; Tortoises; Fable.

1479. 10-12. (+) Higgins, Colin & Cannan, Denis. (Turnbull, Colin) **The Ik.** (The Mountain People) **CAST**: 5f, 7m, Su. **ACTS**: 1. **SETTINGS**: Huts. **PLAYING TIME**: NA. **PLOT**: When their land was designated as a national park by the British Administrators in 1946, the Ik were forced to become farmers in a barren mountainous territory, changing from a nomadic lifestyle to one based on farming. Unfortunately, the tribe was not trained to farm and the area to which they were moved got little rain. In 1964, Colin Turnbull checked on the progress that these people had made. He found a tragic and brutal combination of cruelty, starvation, and lingering tribal

customs, all of which are chillingly depicted by the playwright. **RECOMMENDATION**: Based on the actual relocation of the Ik, a nomadic hunter gatherer tribe in northern Uganda, this stark drama presents the dark side of the human condition, when all means of self support have been destroyed. Potential producers should be aware that this is a very disturbing piece. **ROYALTY**: $60. **SOURCE**: Higgins, Colin & Coleman, Denis. (1984). The Ik. Chicago, IL: Dramatic Pub. Co. **SUBJECTS/PLAY TYPE**: Displacement; Adaptation.

1480. 11-12. (+) Colley, Peter. **I'll be back before midnight. CAST**: 2f, 2m. **ACTS**: 2. **SETTINGS**: Living room. **PLAYING TIME**: NA. **PLOT**: Greg and Jan come to a large isolated farmhouse so Jan can recover from her recent breakdown. Soon, they are joined by Greg's sister, Laura (Greg has invited her knowing that Jan doesn't like her) and they are visited frequently by their only neighbor, a large folksy farmer, George. Rumor of a murder in the house and Jan's growing realization that Greg and Laura are plotting to kill her (the evil extent of the plan slowly becomes terrifyingly clear) lead to a series of bizarre happenings and a final climactic scene which leaves only Jan still alive. **RECOMMENDATION**: This "thriller" succeeds admirably from the first revelation to the final twist. The characters remain true throughout, and the horrific plot twists just keep on coming as the suspense builds steadily. Hints of incest might be controversial. **ROYALTY**: $50. **SOURCE**: Colley, Peter. (1985). I'll be back before midnight. Boston, MA: Baker's Plays. **SUBJECTS/PLAY TYPE**: Murder; Drama.

1481. 7-12. (-) Christmas, Joyce S. **I'll make you a star. CAST**: 3f, 3m. **ACTS**: 1. **SETTINGS**: Talent agency. **PLAYING TIME**: 15 min. **PLOT**: Newcomer Mary "Sweet" agrees to work as a secretary for Max Buffalo's talent agency on one condition: that he assign her to any part for which she's suited. In a series of supposedly humorous antics, other actors enter the talent agency to convince Max to get parts for them. **RECOMMENDATION**: References to "The Gong Show" and Fonzie, along with stereotyped characters and dated dialogue, make this shallow and inappropriate. **ROYALTY**: Free to Plays subscribers. **SOURCE**: Christmas, Joyce S. (1979, November). I'll make you a star. Plays: The Drama Magazine for Young People, pp. 67-72. **SUBJECTS/PLAY TYPE**: Talent Agencies; Show Business; Comedy.

1482. 1-6. (+) Miller, Kathryn Schultz & Miller, Barry Ingram. **I'm a celebrity. CAST**: 2f, 2m, Su. **ACTS**: 1. **SETTINGS**: Classroom; library; playground. **PLAYING TIME**: 60 min. **PLOT**: Harold Dorfmiller is ridiculed by fellow students because he dreams and escapes to other worlds through books. At the end of the play, the other students have joined him. Five songs included in the script may be live or taped. **RECOMMENDATION**: Although this admirably deals with the identity problems of teenagers, the sudden change of attitudes toward Harold seems unrealistic. **ROYALTY**: $25. **SOURCE**: Miller, Kathryn Schultz, and Miller, Barry Ingram. (1981). I'm a celebrity. Schulenburg, TX: I.E. Clark. **SUBJECTS/PLAY TYPE**: Identity; Musical.

1483. 10-12. (+) Miller, Ev. **I'm a stranger here myself.**
CAST: 6f, 4m, Su. ACTS: 2. SETTINGS: Kitchen;
classroom; living room; park. PLAYING TIME: NA.
PLOT: Casey O'Hara has a father who wants him to be a
jock, and a mother who does not like Mark, his best friend.
Casey is confused and easily swayed in the wrong
direction by Mark. Family problems, Lori, and having the
lead in the class play, help Casey realize what is important
and send him in a separate direction from Mark.
RECOMMENDATION: Some might find this play in bad
taste for school production because of the references to
alcohol and sex. However, family problems, emotions, and
solutions are dealt with realistically and openly.
ROYALTY: $35. SOURCE: Miller, Ev. (1983). I'm a
stranger here myself. Chicago, IL: Dramatic Pub. Co.
SUBJECTS/PLAY TYPE: Alcohol Abuse; Family; Drama.

1484. K-3. (+) Ison, Colleen. **I'm nice to everybody.**
CAST: 1f, 4u. ACTS: 1. SETTINGS: Bare stage. PLAYING
TIME: NA. PLOT: Tony claims that he is nice to everyone
until his friend points out the people to whom he is mean.
Tony then says he's nice to everyone except for the people
he knows. He realizes the folly of this and decides to be
nice to everyone. RECOMMENDATION: The examples
of nastiness could be changed to suit any situation in this
easily understood presentation about treatment of others.
Discussion questions are provided. ROYALTY: NA.
SOURCE: Ison, Colleen. (1986). Goliath's last stand: And
fifteen more easy plays for children. Cincinnati, OH:
Standard Pub. SUBJECTS/PLAY TYPE: Behavior; Skit.

1485. 4-8. (+) Kehret, Peg. **I'm not my brother, I'm me.**
CAST: 1m. ACTS: 1. SETTINGS: None. PLAYING TIME:
NA. PLOT: A young boy recounts the trouble he has in
school, due to the well known reputations of his two older
brothers: one an over achiever, and one a prankster. When
the prankster brother goes away to college and shapes up
into a good student, he tells his younger brother that his
life improved when he stopped trying to live up to his
older brother. The young boy decides to do the same.
RECOMMENDATION: This is an apt choice for a unit on
self awareness. ROYALTY: NA. SOURCE: Kehret, Peg.
(1986). Winning monologs for young actors. Colorado
Springs, CO: Meriwether Pub. SUBJECTS/PLAY TYPE:
Siblings; Peer Pressure; Monologue.

1486. 10-12. (+) Gardner, Herb. **I'm not Rappaport.**
CAST: 2f, 5m. ACTS: 2. SETTINGS: Bench. PLAYING
TIME: NA. PLOT: Midge and Nat, both 80, meet each day
at the same park bench. Midge tells Nat exciting fantasies
about his past and desperately dodges his daughter who
wants to put him in an old age home. Nat quietly works at
night as an apartment super, hoping that if he keeps a low
profile, he won't be forced into retirement. Midge tries to
finesse Nat out of being fired when the apartment goes
condo, he impersonates a gangster to help a young girl
welch on her cocaine debts, and he attacks a young punk
who has demanded protection money from them. All of
his acts of heroism are unsuccessful, and, broken, he
agrees to his daughter's demands. However, Nat, who
claims to hate Midge's fantasies, asks him what else he did
besides waiting tables, and the play ends with a happy
and rejuvenated Midge settling in to tell more stories.

RECOMMENDATION: This superb and poignant
statement on the plight of the elderly combines forceful
confrontations with satirical humor, to address such issues
as forced retirement, homelessness, the inadequacies of
social security, the elderly's need to be helped but not
smothered, and the victimization of the old merely
because their bodies don't work well. It will require skilled
actors (adults would be best), some knowledge of the
beginnings of unionization, and familiarity with the
sincere sentiments of those Americans who were involved
in the communist movement during the Hitler/Stalin era.
This is powerful drama with a very timely message.
ROYALTY: NA. SOURCE: Gardner, Herb. (1987). I'm not
Rappaport. New York, NY: Samuel French.
SUBJECTS/PLAY TYPE: Elderly; Drama.

1487. 10-12. (+) Allman, Sheldon & Pickett, Bob. **I'm
sorry, the bridge is out, you'll have to spend the night.**
CAST: 12f, 7m. ACTS: 2. SETTINGS: Castle. PLAYING
TIME: NA. PLOT: Naive tourists, John and Mary, are
stranded outside of Dr. Frankenstein's castle on a rainy,
dreary night. Frankenstein wants to transplant John's brain
but his other house guests including Count Dracula, his
wife Natasha, the Wolfman, and assorted vampires all
have other plans for John and Mary. Nevertheless, they
survive the night. RECOMMENDATION: The predictable
and corny dialogue depends on animated and fast paced
delivery. The play also requires a rather elaborate set
design. ROYALTY: Upon application. SOURCE: Allman,
Sheldon & Pickett, Bob. (1988). I'm sorry, the bridge is out,
you'll have to spend the night. Chicago, IL: Dramatic Pub.
Co. SUBJECTS/PLAY TYPE: Comedy; Frankenstein;
Haunted Castles; Musical.

1488. 1-4. (+) Wolkstien, Diane. **I'm Tipingee, she's
Tipingee, we're Tipingee, too.** CAST: 4f, 1m, 2u. ACTS: 1.
SETTINGS: Well. PLAYING TIME: 10 min. PLOT: When
a wicked stepmother agrees to trade her daughter,
Tipingee, to an old man, she instructs him to go to the
water well the next day and collect the girl in the red
dress. Tipingee overhears the plans, and arranges for her
friends all to wear red dresses the next day, so that he
cannot pick her out in the crowd. This continues for
several days, until, frustrated, the man takes the
stepmother away instead. RECOMMENDATION: This
enchanting Haitian folk tale has clear, concise dialogue,
which can easily be memorized by young actors, while the
emphasis on movement and action creates a dynamic
environment for both actors and audience. ROYALTY:
NA. SOURCE: Bauer, Caroline Feller. (1987). Presenting
reader's theater: Plays and poems to read aloud. New
York, NY: H.W. Wilson Co. SUBJECTS/PLAY TYPE:
Trickery; Folk Tales, Haiti; Reader's Theater.

1489. 7-12. (+) Bland, Joellen. (Moliere) **The imaginary
invalid.** (The imaginary invalid.) CAST: 3f, 6m. ACTS: 1.
SETTINGS: Sitting room. PLAYING TIME: 30 min.
PLOT: Argan, a hypochondriac, arranges the marriage of
his daughter to a man she has never met. The daughter
resists the arrangement as she has fallen in love with
another man. Argan's wife, with the help of a crooked
lawyer, schemes to have her husband send his disobedient
daughter to a convent, thereby also gaining the daughter's

generous dowry. At the suggestion of his maidservant and his brother, Argan feigns death, enabling him to learn of his wife's deceitfulness as she speaks with unconcern over his "death," and hear his daughter's grief as she cries sorrowfully. The father sits up, embraces his devoted daughter, and consents to the marriage of her choice. RECOMMENDATION: This classic might work better with the upper grades since romance, and satire are prominent in the drama. Toinette, the maidservant, often addresses the audience directly, thereby drawing them into the action. ROYALTY: Free to Plays subscribers. SOURCE: Bland, Joellen. (1985, May). The imaginary invalid. Plays: The Drama Magazine for Young People, pp. 65-76. SUBJECTS/PLAY TYPE: Hypochondriacs; Reader's Theater; Marriage; Adaptation.

1490. 10-12. (+) Wolman, Diana. **The imaginary trial of George Washington - The father of our country takes the stand.** CAST: 3f, 15m, Su. ACTS: 1. SETTINGS: Courtroom. PLAYING TIME: 30 min. PLOT: As George Washington defends himself against the charge of treason, patriots witness for Washington, and provide insight into the American Revolution. RECOMMENDATION: This allows students to visualize the courage and sacrifice that many of our heroic figures experienced, and is recommended for any high school American history class. ROYALTY: Free to Plays subscribers. SOURCE: Kamerman, Sylvia E. (1987). Patriotic and historical plays for young people. Boston, MA: Plays, Inc. SUBJECTS/PLAY TYPE: Colonial America; Washington, George; Drama.

1491. 9-12. (+) Olfson, Lewy. (Wilde, Oscar) **The importance of being Earnest.** (The importance of being Earnest) CAST: 4f, 5m. ACTS: 3. SETTINGS: Drawing room; garden. PLAYING TIME: 30 min. PLOT: Jack Worthington maintains two identities. His other persona is an older brother called Earnest. As Earnest, he meets and falls in love with Gwendolen. Gwendolen's first cousin, Algernon, learns of Jack's double life and Jack's lovely ward, Cecily (who knows of Earnest only through Jack's stories). Algernon poses as Earnest and visits Cecily. They fall in love. Now both women think they are to marry men named Earnest. The mistaken identities are straightened out and a mystery about Jack's birth is solved revealing that his name really is Earnest and he is actually Algernon's older brother. RECOMMENDATION: This adaptation combines economy of dialogue with a slightly less involved plot than the original, resulting in a fast moving comedy of manners. In the process, it manages to keep just enough of the original intact to allow the plot to resolve itself without confusion. ROYALTY: Free to Plays subscribers. SOURCE: Olfson, Lewy. (1986, April). The importance of being Earnest. Plays: The Drama Magazine for Young People, pp. 53-63. SUBJECTS/PLAY TYPE: Comedy; Romance; Mistaken Identity; Adaptation.

1492. 9-12. (-) Hamlett, Christina. (Wilde, Oscar) **The importance of being Ernestine.** (The importance of being Ernest) CAST: 4f, 3m, 2u. ACTS: 1. SETTINGS: Apartment. PLAYING TIME: 25 min. PLOT: Ernestine, (alias Jacqueline) is in love with Ben, her best friend's cousin. Her studious country cousin, Cecil, believes that "Ernestine" is Jacqueline's sister. Elissa (Ernestine's best friend) becomes curious about Cecil and visits him in the country, introducing herself as Ernestine, Jacqueline's sister. She and Cecil fall in love. Ernestine (Jacqueline) arrives at the estate, followed by Ben. Much confusion results as to who is the real Ernestine. Ellisa admits to pretending to be Ernestine to meet Cecil, and Jacqueline admits to taking Ernestine as her stage name. Agatha (Ben's mother) arrives to take Ben away and meets the housekeeper, whom she recognizes as the one who mistakenly left a baby, Agatha's niece, in a handbag 22 years earlier. The baby in the handbag turns out to be Jacqueline, making her Elissa's sister and Ben's cousin. Agatha withdraws her objection to Ben and Jacqueline's marriage, so both couples are happy. Best of all, as a baby, Jacqueline was named after her mother, Ernestine. RECOMMENDATION: The wit of the original play has not survived in this bland adaptation. It is logically written, so that the tangle of identities becomes clear at the end, but the characters and dialogue are not interesting. ROYALTY: $25. SOURCE: Hamlett, Christina. (1988). The importance of being Ernestine. Franklin, OH: Eldridge Pub. Co. SUBJECTS/PLAY TYPE: Comedy; Romance; Adaptation.

1493. 7-12. (+) Naylor, Phyllis Reynolds. **An impromptu noel.** CAST: 1f, 5m. ACTS: 1. SETTINGS: Hotel room. PLAYING TIME: 12 min. PLOT: Four high school band members are snowbound in an unfamiliar city on Christmas Eve. Their dismay turns into happiness as they share their music with other stranded travelers and people who must work on Christmas Eve. RECOMMENDATION: This will come alive if musicians are in the cast. It is more appropriate for church groups than for public school productions. ROYALTY: None. SOURCE: Altena, Hans (1978). The playbook for christian theatre. Grand Rapids, MI: Baker Book House. SUBJECTS/PLAY TYPE: Christmas; Drama.

1494. K-12. (+) Zeder, Suzan L. **In a room somewhere.** CAST: 2f, 3m. ACTS: 1. SETTINGS: Bare stage, props. PLAYING TIME: NA. PLOT: Characters are suddenly zapped out of their present situations into the "room" where they discover (with the help of a mysterious guide) the inner healing of the child within all of us. The audience is invited to bring to the "room" their own personal transactions and take from the "room" the healing power present. RECOMMENDATION: This fast moving modified transactional analysis will surely touch the inner child in all who produce or view this magnificent piece of art. The play is a personal invitation to all participants to understand their own negative behaviors and heal themselves. Production is suitable for upper grades only. ROYALTY: $35. SOURCE: Zeder, Suzan L. (1988). In a room somewhere. New Orleans, LA: Anchorage Press. SUBJECTS/PLAY TYPE: Musical; Transactional Analysis; Behavior; Drama.

1495. 11-12. (+) Storey, David. **In celebration.** CAST: 2f, 5m. ACTS: 2. SETTINGS: Living room. PLAYING TIME: NA. PLOT: The Shaws' grown sons return to the family home in an English mining town to celebrate their parents' 40th wedding anniversary. The facade of the happily reunited family is soon shattered as the brothers acrimoniously reminisce among themselves about the poverty of their childhood and their mother's resentment of her first, prenuptial pregnancy. The brother's own resentments and disappointments come pouring out after the celebration dinner. RECOMMENDATION: British slang and accents, the allusions to social class, the sophisticated treatment of the themes of guilt and atonement, may make this excellent play difficult for American students to present successfully. It would be best produced by students in a preprofessional theatrical program. ROYALTY: $60. SOURCE: Storey, David. (1979). In celebration. Chicago, IL: Dramatic Pub. Co. SUBJECTS/PLAY TYPE: Family Relationships; Marriage; Celebrations; Drama.

1496. 3-5. (-) LaRue, Sydney. **In celebration of Christopher Columbus.** CAST: 1f, 2m. ACTS: 1. SETTINGS: City square. PLAYING TIME: 10 min. PLOT: Christopher Columbus uses modern language to discuss his discovery of the New World. RECOMMENDATION: The weak attempts at humor make this play unsuccessful as does the confusing vehicle of putting Columbus into modern day, looking back at his discovery. ROYALTY: Free to Plays subscribers. SOURCE: LaRue, Sydney. (1979, October). In celebration of Christopher Columbus. Plays: The Drama Magazine for Young People, pp. 65-68. SUBJECTS/PLAY TYPE: Columbus, Christopher; Skit.

1497. 6-12. (+) Nolan, Paul T. **The in-group.** CAST: 12u. ACTS: 1. SETTINGS: Bare stage, platform, props. PLAYING TIME: 30 min. PLOT: The three players seated on the stools are members of an exclusive group. They speak only to each other and look down on the other groups of players who are seated on the floor. They do not laugh, cry, or do anything except congratulate each other on being members of the "in-group." Number Three is the first one to notice activities of the other groups and question his membership in the "in-group." He slowly decides to leave the group in spite of warnings from the other two. After his departure, a member of another group joins the "in-group" but another leaves. The play continues in this manner until only one member of the original group is left. Finally, this member is drawn into the other groups to experience the fun of living with others. RECOMMENDATION: An excellent vehicle to show that life, with failures, successes, happiness, and tears is more desirable than being isolated and protected. This fine dramatic selection could serve as a springboard for discussion of cliques and individualism. ROYALTY: Free to Plays subscribers. SOURCE: Nolan, Paul T. (1976, May). The in-group. Plays: The Drama Magazine for Young People, pp. 27-37. SUBJECTS/PLAY TYPE: Cliques; Individualism; Playlet.

1498. K-5. (+) Pugh, Shirley. **In one basket (tale of a mouse, the rich man, three wishes, Gustav).** CAST: Su. ACTS: 1. SETTINGS: None. PLAYING TIME: NA. PLOT: In "Tale of a mouse," Lana, a mouse, asks the sun, a cloud, the wind, and a wall to marry her. When they all say that a mouse is her best choice, she agrees to marry Stanley, the mouse, who has always loved her. In "The rich man," a very rich man offers his blacksmith and goldsmith neighbors money to move from their homes so he can buy peace and quiet. Each moves, but into the other's house. In "The three wishes," a fairy grants a husband and wife three wishes. The wife wishes for a pudding. The husband, angered by her wish, wishes the pudding on to her nose. The final joint wish is to remove the pudding from her nose. They decide that they are most content when there are no wishes. Finally, in "Gustav," a widow's dull son sells her butter to a rock, thinking he is selling it to the town. However, finding gold under the rock where two robbers have hidden it, Gustav takes the gold to his mother. A neighbor who tries to outwit Gustav must pay one hundred gold pieces to the widow because Gustav's sad story made him laugh, which he didn't believe would happen. RECOMMENDATION: These delightful short dramatizations are executed in a story theater form which allows the characters to be both narrators and characters. The dialogue is brief, and the props can be imaginary. ROYALTY: Write to Anchorage Press. SOURCE: Jennings, Coleman A. & Harris, Aurand. (1981). Plays children love. New York, NY: Doubleday Co., Inc. SUBJECTS/PLAY TYPE: Values; Reader's Theater.

1499. K-12*. (+) Doyle, Sharon Elizabeth. **In other words.** CAST: 2f, 4m, Su. ACTS: 1. SETTINGS: None. PLAYING TIME: NA. PLOT: Communication is analyzed and explored through four vignettes during which the letters of the alphabet and words are mimed; a baby learns the steps in communication; cavemen discover language; and students prepare for a song and dance competition. RECOMMENDATION: This educational play requires performers who know and trust each other's movements; who are talented in mime; and who are able to "physicalize psychology." The author/director offers three pages of suggestions to prepare the ensemble for production. Yet she concludes that "the best thing that can be done with **In Other Words** is to have fun with it." Given talent, time, and a patient director, experienced high school students could perform this challenging piece. ROYALTY: $20. SOURCE: Doyle, Sharon Elizabeth. (1979). In other words. New Orleans, LA: Anchorage Press, Inc. SUBJECTS/PLAY TYPE: Communication; Pantomime; Alphabet; Drama.

1500. 1-7. (+) Havens, Betty. **In Search of the golden teardrop.** CAST: 14f, 3m, 8u. ACTS: 1. SETTINGS: None. PLAYING TIME: 35 min. PLOT: Princess Beatrice drops a golden teardrop into a pond and it is lost. The King and Queen offer a reward for its recovery. George and the Minstrel outwit King Neptune, and recover the teardrop. Of course, they are welcomed as heroes when they return. But all George wants is a big dinner. RECOMMENDATION: Upper grades should produce this for lower grades, as the wonderful adventures include talking water, rapids, and danger. ROYALTY: $15. SOURCE: Havens, Betty. (1977). In search of the golden teardrop. Schulenburg, TX: I.E. Clark. SUBJECTS/PLAY TYPE: Adventure; Folk Tale Motifs; Self Confidence; Comedy; Drama.

1501. 9-12. (+) Fendrich, Shubert. **In St. Louis, at the fair.** CAST: 10f, 5m, 2u. ACTS: 2. SETTINGS: Dining room. PLAYING TIME: 90 min. PLOT: When the new French chef fails to appear, cowboy Louie is mistaken for the chef. After burning, curdling, and ruining the fancy French sauces, he and the waitresses decide to serve what they know best: good, old fashioned American. Outside the kitchen, the waitresses fall in love with Johnny and Dick, who work at the fair exhibits, and Louie finds Flo. Together they sing the title reprise as the curtain falls. RECOMMENDATION: The thirteen musical selections require a cast with vocal talent. A happy, nostalgic glimpse at the time in America when coffee cost 3 cents a cup. ROYALTY: $50. SOURCE: Fendrich, Shubert. (1978). In St. Louis, at the fair. Denver, CO: Pioneer Drama Service. SUBJECTS/PLAY TYPE: St. Louis; Fairs; Musical; Comedy.

1502. K-12. (+) Hendricks, William & Vogel, Cora. **In the town.** CAST: 2f, 2m. ACTS: 1. SETTINGS: None. PLAYING TIME: 7 min. PLOT: Mary and Joseph struggle to find lodging on the eve of Christ's birth. RECOMMENDATION: Adapted from a 15th century French carol, this is suitable for performance at a Christmas pageant or worship service. The dialogue between Mary and Joseph is touching. ROYALTY: NA. SOURCE: Hendricks, William & Vogel, Cora. (1978). Handbook of Christmas programs. Grand Rapids, MI: Baker Book House. SUBJECTS/PLAY TYPE: Christmas; Christ, Jesus; Virgin Mary; Worship Program.

1503. K-12. (+) Silesius, Angelus. **In thine own heart.** CAST: Su. ACTS: 1. SETTINGS: None. PLAYING TIME: 1 min. PLOT: This delivers themes symbolic of the Christmas season: Christ's birth and that belief in Christ makes a person complete. RECOMMENDATION: This recitation would be effective for any church related program. ROYALTY: None. SOURCE: Hendricks, William & Vogel, Cora. (1983). Handbook of Christmas programs. Grand Rapids, MI: Baker Book House. SUBJECTS/PLAY TYPE: Christmas; Choral Reading.

1504. K-3*. (+) Bauer, Caroline Feller. (Milne, A. A.) **In which Tigger comes to the forest and has breakfast.** (The house at pooh corner) CAST: 1m, 7u. ACTS: 1. SETTINGS: Forest homes. PLAYING TIME: 20 min. PLOT: Tigger visits Pooh, and Pooh has a terrible time feeding him until Kanga discovers that Tigger likes Roo's medicine, Extract of Malt. RECOMMENDATION: Tigger's constant bouncing and moving about help keep the action dynamic as Pooh demonstrates the qualities of kindness, concern and consideration. This can be either acted or read aloud. ROYALTY: NA. SOURCE: Bauer, Caroline Feller. (1987). Presenting reader's theater: Plays and poems to read aloud. New York, NY: H.W. Wilson Co. SUBJECTS/PLAY TYPE: Food; Reader's Theater; Adaptation.

1505. K-12. (+) Rossetti, Christina. **Incarnate lover.** CAST: Su. ACTS: 1. SETTINGS: None. PLAYING TIME: 2 min. PLOT: This describes love as the meaning of Christmas. RECOMMENDATION: Suitable for church or parochial school groups for presentation at a Christmas

pageant or worship service. ROYALTY: NA. SOURCE: Hendricks, William & Vogel, Cora. (1978). Handbook of Christmas programs. Grand Rapids, MI: Baker Book House. SUBJECTS/PLAY TYPE: Choral Reading; Love; Christmas; Worship Program.

1506. 9-12. (+) Hackett, Walter. **Incident at Valley Forge.** CAST: 2f, 6m. ACTS: 4. SETTINGS: Bare stage. PLAYING TIME: 30 min. PLOT: General Greene discourages three soldiers from deserting the troops at Valley Forge. RECOMMENDATION: This provides insight into how the soldiers dealt with food rationing and loneliness. Not spectacular, but informative. ROYALTY: Free to Plays subscribers. SOURCE: Kamerman, Sylvia E. (1975). Patriotic and historical plays for young people. Boston, MA: Plays, Inc. SUBJECTS/PLAY TYPE: Valley Forge; Greene, Nathaniel; Revolutionary War, U.S.; Playlet.

1507. 6-10. (+) Kelly, Tim J. **The incredible bulk at Bikini Beach.** CAST: 10f, 6m, 1u. ACTS: 1. SETTINGS: Restaurant. PLAYING TIME: 30 min. PLOT: A stormy night on the beach unites gangsters, the richest girl in town and her boyfriend (who is also the incredible bulk), a famous doctor, a ghost, and a parapsychologist. They part company when the incredible bulk unblocks the road. RECOMMENDATION: While weak in plot and characterization, young students may enjoy the conglomeration of odd characters. Most lines are short, and related only to one of the many subplots. This may make it good for inexperienced actors. ROYALTY: $15. SOURCE: Kelly, Tim J. (1980). The incredible bulk at Bikini Beach. Denver, CO: Pioneer Drama Service. SUBJECTS/PLAY TYPE: Ghosts; Monsters; Incredible Hulk; Comedy.

1508. 7-12*. (+) Nowlan, Alden & Learning, Walter. (Doyle, Arthur Conan) **The incredible murder of Cardinal Tosca.** (The incredible murder of Cardinal Tosca) CAST: 2f, 12m, Su. ACTS: 2. SETTINGS: Church; Sherlock Holmes and Dr. Watson's lodgings; morgue; thieves' den. PLAYING TIME: NA. PLOT: Sherlock Holmes, Cardinal Tosca, and Dr. Watson save the world from Professor Moriarty's evil plan to use a Satanic cult to murder the Emperor of Austria. RECOMMENDATION: This captures the spirit of the original and the characters of Holmes, Watson and Moriarty. It is a complicated production, however, and best suited for a little theater production. ROYALTY: $60. SOURCE: Nowlan, Alden, & Learning, Walter. (1981). The incredible murder of Cardinal Tosca. Chicago, IL: Dramatic Pub. Co. SUBJECTS/PLAY TYPE: Mystery; World War I; Adaptation.

1509. 9-12. (+) Miller, Ev. **The incredible years.** CAST: 3f, 7m, 1u. ACTS: 2. SETTINGS: Home; waiting room; hospital room. PLAYING TIME: 120 min. PLOT: Woody, a young son in the Jansky family, and the character around whom the play develops, is initiated into some of the moral and emotional complexities of adult life with the help of his parents and his dying uncle. RECOMMENDATION: Issues of sibling rivalry, conflict between teenagers and adults, and the impact of impending death of a loved one are timeless. The characters (with the exception of the aunt, who is an unfortunate caricature) are well developed. ROYALTY: $35. SOURCE: Miller, Ev. (1980). The incredible years. Denver, CO: Pioneer Drama Service. SUBJECTS/PLAY TYPE: Family Relationships; Behavior; Values; Drama.

1510. 7-9. (+) Marcell, Raleigh Jr. (Poe, Edgar Allan) **The infamous soothing system of Professor Maillard.** (The system of Doctor Tarr and Professor Fether) CAST: 14u. ACTS: 1. SETTINGS: Office; ballroom. PLAYING TIME: NA. PLOT: The hero visits Professor Maillard's asylum to learn about his system, in which inmates are allowed to wander about unsupervised. A party, apparently attended by asylum workers, is in progress and the hero converses with Maillard and the guests. The play concludes with the realization by the audience that the inmates have arisen and imprisoned their doctors. RECOMMENDATION: Although the surprise ending is predictable, this could be used effectively to illustrate how Poe created and explored an aura of mystery and menace in his literary works. ROYALTY: $15. SOURCE: Marcell, Raleigh Jr. (1981). The infamous soothing system of Professor Maillard. Schulenburg, TX: I.E. Clark. SUBJECTS/PLAY TYPE: Science Fiction; Satire; Adaptation.

1511. 7-12. (-) Sodaro, Craig. (Harte, Bret) **Ingenue of the Sierras.** (Ingenue of the Sierras) CAST: 3f, 5m, Su. ACTS: 1. SETTINGS: Living room. PLAYING TIME: 25 min. PLOT: A young girl claims to have run away from home to meet her outlaw fiance. When he shows up to get her, they are forced to marry on the spot. During the wedding, the stage is robbed and the outlaw turns out to be the leader of the gang. However, the young girl turns out not to be who she says she is, but is instead a gold-digger. The outlaw leader gets his comeuppance. RECOMMENDATION: This has too many sexist remarks and characterizations, along with a confusing and unsatisfying end. ROYALTY: Free to Plays subscribers. SOURCE: Sodaro, Craig. (1986, January). Ingenue of the Sierras. Plays: The Drama Magazine for Young People, pp. 1-9. SUBJECTS/PLAY TYPE: Adventure; Marriage; Comedy.

1512. 7-12. (-) Sawyer-Young, Kat. **Innocent.** CAST: 1m. ACTS: 1. SETTINGS: None. PLAYING TIME: 1 min. PLOT: Roger lends his coat to John, who scrapes a teacher's car while riding his skateboard. Now, Roger has to convince the principal that it was John, and not he, who did it. RECOMMENDATION: It is unclear why John has not come forward, and the case of mistaken identity wears thin. ROYALTY: None. SOURCE: Sawyer-Young, Kat. (1987). Minute monologues for contemporary teens. Boston, MA: Baker's Plays. SUBJECTS/PLAY TYPE: Mistaken Identity; Monologue.

1513. 10-12. (+) Archibald, William. (James, Henry) **The innocents: A new play.** (The turn of the screw) CAST: 4f, 2m. ACTS: 2. SETTINGS: Living room. PLAYING TIME: NA. PLOT: Two precocious orphans living in their absent uncle's large country home are victimized by two servants in ways left to the imagination. A sensitive young governess assumes care of the children after the servants' deaths, and fights the evil influence the servants, now ghosts, have on the children. The little girl is taken from the house to safety, but the young boy dies in the governess's arms as he denounces the evil ghost. RECOMMENDATION: This Jamesian thriller starts out simply, but quickly and effectively moves into the realm of human cruelty and evil. ROYALTY: NA. SOURCE: Archibald, William. (1979). The innocents: A new play. New York, NY: Samuel French. SUBJECTS/PLAY TYPE: Ghost Stories; Adaptation.

1514. 2-8. (+) Boiko, Claire. **The insatiable dragon.** CAST: 1f, 6m, Su. ACTS: 1. SETTINGS: Kitchen. PLAYING TIME: 15 min. PLOT: Wang, the magician, has promised dragons named "fire," to four people. Li-Ping's dragon will turn the night into day; San-Su's will bring the June sun to warm her house in December; Soba's will turn his meals into feasts fit for an emperor; and Lum-Fu's will melt stone hearts into tears of silver. Before Wang can give the people fire, they need sticks to carry it to their homes. They leave in search of sticks; Wang's apprentice stays to guard the fire. Though warned not to feed it, let it out of its bowl, or let its siblings into the room, Chu-Chu is conned into doing all these things by the clever fire, which then grows larger. Wang and the four return, douse the fire with water until it returns to its bowl, and light their sticks. RECOMMENDATION: This tells a fascinating story as it teaches children the dangers of fire and some fire fighting techniques. The dragons are cleverly represented by hand puppets. ROYALTY: None. SOURCE: Boiko, Claire. (1981). Children's play for creative actors. Boston, MA: Plays, Inc. SUBJECTS/PLAY TYPE: Fire; Folk Tales, China; Playlet.

1515. 9-12. (+) Scanlan, Michael. **Inside out.** CAST: 4f, 2m. ACTS: 1. SETTINGS: None. PLAYING TIME: 15 min. PLOT: Two teens repeat phrases that they hear often from their parents (i.e. don't do this, don't do that). Soon, Jacqueline and her alter ego, Jackie, argue about what Jacqueline should/shouldn't do. Astonishing her best friend, Jackie accepts a date with Chuck, a guy with a bad reputation. On the date, Jacqueline and Chuck find they are both confused about who they are. They try to help each other. RECOMMENDATION: The outstanding dialogue perfectly imitates young peoples' language and mannerisms. ROYALTY: $15. SOURCE: Scanlan, Michael. (1984). Inside/out. Hollywood, CA: Samuel French. SUBJECTS/PLAY TYPE: Problem Solving; Behavior; Playlet.

1516. 4-10. (-) Purvin, George. **The inside story of Christmas past.** CAST: 3f, 9m, Su. ACTS: 1. SETTINGS: Santa's workshop. PLAYING TIME: NA. PLOT: Santa becomes ill because his computer predicts he cannot produce enough toys for an over-populated world. In spite of strike threats, the elves hire women, children, the aged in nursing homes, and juvenile delinquents. Santa fills all the orders, and respect among the groups develops. RECOMMENDATION: This Christmas social commentary misses the mark. Conflicts like Santa's providing "toys for the Arab and toys for the Jew," and the annoying rhymes as dialogue make this insulting to any group. ROYALTY: $30. SOURCE: Purvin, George. (1985). The inside story of Christmas past. Franklin, OH: Eldridge Pub. Co. SUBJECTS/PLAY TYPE: Christmas; Santa Claus; Elves; Comedy.

1517. 7-12. (+) Leech, Michael T. (Gogol, Nikolai V.) **The inspector general.** (The inspector general) CAST: 3f, 11m, Su. ACTS: 1. SETTINGS: Living room; hotel room. PLAYING TIME: 30 min. PLOT: Anton, the mayor of a small Russian village, learns that the Inspector General plans a surprise inspection and will be traveling incognito. The town officials soon learn that a civil servant, Khlestakhov, has been in town for a few days. Assuming Khlestakhov is the inspector general they treat him lavishly, offering bribes, and engaging him to Anton's daughter. After Khlestakhov leaves, the townspeople discover that he was an imposter; the real Inspector General has just arrived and wishes to see them immediately. RECOMMENDATION: Surprisingly faithful to the plot of Gogol's classic, this retains much of the satire of the original plot and characters. ROYALTY: Free to Plays subscribers. SOURCE: Leech, Michael T. (1975, November). The inspector general. Plays: The Drama Magazine for Young People, pp. 82-96. SUBJECTS/PLAY TYPE: Comedy; Mistaken Identity; Satire; Adaptation.

1518. 7-12. (+) Mauro, Robert A. **Inspector Rousseau strikes again.** CAST: 3f, 3m. ACTS: 1. SETTINGS: Living room. PLAYING TIME: 30 min. PLOT: World famous Inspector Rousseau attempts to solve a murder by accusing all the members of the household, but he discovers he is at the wrong address and there is no murder. RECOMMENDATION: The misunderstandings and misadventures in this Pink Panther style comedy are hilarious. The inspector must have a French accent. ROYALTY: Free to Plays subscribers. SOURCE: Mauro, Robert A. (1979, November). Inspector Rousseau strikes again. Plays: The Drama Magazine for Young People, pp. 1-10. SUBJECTS/PLAY TYPE: Mystery; Detectives; Comedy.

1519. 7-12. (-) Murray, John. **An international affair.** CAST: 3f, 2m, Su. ACTS: 1. SETTINGS: Art gallery. PLAYING TIME: 25 min. PLOT: Peter Van Loon and an art gallery director smuggle semiconductor chips in the bases of the artist's statues. When the director is fired, Van Loon must steal the last statue alone. Pretending to impersonate himself, he asks to take the statue to Amsterdam. When Gretel begins to think he is a fake, Van Loon disappears. He returns posing as himself. He takes the statue to the director's office, hides it in his coat, and claims he was attacked and that the statue stolen by the imposter. Fran, a newspaper reporter, is suspicious. She examines Van Loon's coat, finds the statue and the semiconductor chips, and has Van Loon arrested. RECOMMENDATION: The plot is contrived, confusing and totally unbelievable. Van Loon is unable to carry out his plan because he makes so many mistakes in his conversation that it would be impossible not to suspect him of something. ROYALTY: Free to Plays subscribers. SOURCE: Murray, John. (1989, March). An international affair. Plays: The Drama Magazine for Young People, pp.

1-9. SUBJECTS/PLAY TYPE: Mystery; Artwork; Smuggling; Playlet.

1520. 7-12. (+) Sawyer-Young, Kat. **Interview.** CAST: 1f. ACTS: 1. SETTINGS: None. PLAYING TIME: 1 min. PLOT: As Cindy interviews for a job, she seems almost too good to serve up fries at McDonald's. RECOMMENDATION: This could be used to discuss interviewing strategies. ROYALTY: None. SOURCE: Sawyer-Young, Kat. (1987). Minute monologues for contemporary teens. Boston, MA: Baker's Plays. SUBJECTS/PLAY TYPE: Interviewing; Monologue.

1521. 10-12. (+) Cervantes, Madolin. **Interview with God.** CAST: 3m. ACTS: 1. SETTINGS: Bedroom; throne. PLAYING TIME: NA. PLOT: The essence of man, hell, heaven, creation of the world, and the reasons for evil are examined as God and Gabriel try to convince a newly dead man that God exists. RECOMMENDATION: This is an extremely moving and revealing theological discussion. Some updating of the language, as well as a change of dialect for Gabriel will be needed. Potential producers should be aware that the author pokes fun at several religious dogmas (i.e., original sin, the seven day creation story) and religions (i.e., Episcopalian). ROYALTY: $10. SOURCE: Cervantes, Madolin. (1977). Interview with God. Boston, MA: Baker's Plays. SUBJECTS/PLAY TYPE: Heaven; Hell; Drama.

1522. 7-12. (+) Murray, John. **The introduction.** CAST: 1f. ACTS: 1. SETTINGS: Bare stage, props. PLAYING TIME: NA. PLOT: Mrs. Allen too loquaciously introduces a guest speaker at a meeting of a women's literary society, and uses up the guest's time slot. RECOMMENDATION: While the character is stereotypical and exaggerated, the digressions she makes are so hilarious that the play works very well. Anyone who has ever sat through a long winded introduction will enjoy this outrageous sketch. ROYALTY: None. SOURCE: Murray, John. (1982). Modern monologues for young people. Boston, MA: Plays, Inc. SUBJECTS/PLAY TYPE: Comedy; Meetings; Monologue.

1523. 4-8. (+) Kehret, Peg. **Inventions I intend to make.** CAST: 1u. ACTS: 1. SETTINGS: None. PLAYING TIME: NA. PLOT: A youngster describes inventions he hopes to design, including a pet fur yarn maker, a detachable floor scrubber, and an automatic food finder. RECOMMENDATION: Humorously written, this will charm an audience with its realistic view from a child's imagination. ROYALTY: NA. SOURCE: Kehret, Peg. (1986). Winning monologs for young actors. Colorado Springs, CO: Meriwether Pub. SUBJECTS/PLAY TYPE: Inventions; Monologue.

1524. 9-12. (+) Majeski, Bill. **The invisible lady of Barnaby Tech.** CAST: 11f, 10m. ACTS: 2. SETTINGS: Living room; lab; soda shop; meeting room. PLAYING TIME: NA. PLOT: Karina, while searching for a cream to get rid of wrinkles stumbles upon one that makes her temporarily invisible. While invisible, she helps Professor Millbrook keep his job and she also helps Wendell, a shy intellectual, defeat the "big man on campus." Wendell becomes too popular and overconfident, but reality returns when Karina's invisibility cream is finished. **RECOMMENDATION:** It will be a challenge for the cast to make it appear that they are being manipulated by an invisible woman. Millbrook, in a speech that is to demonstrate his controversial nature, makes a statement about dwarves that may have to be changed. **ROYALTY:** $35. **SOURCE:** Majeski, Bill. (1981). The invisible lady of Barnaby Tech. Chicago, IL: Dramatic Pub. Co. **SUBJECTS/PLAY TYPE:** Invisibility; Colleges and Universities; Comedy.

1525. 9-12. (+) Cope, Eddie. **The invisible man.** **CAST:** 7f, 4m. **ACTS:** 3. **SETTINGS:** Hotel lobby. **PLAYING TIME:** NA. **PLOT:** When six coeds manage an isolated hotel as a home economics project, unique characters visit to investigate its history and a rumor of hidden gold. The most mysterious is the Invisible Man. The story unravels with thrilling events and murder. **RECOMMENDATION:** Only the concept of an invisible man comes from the story by the same title by H. G. Wells. Loaded with mystery, suspense, and laughter, the play uses wonderful special effects for the scenes with the Invisible Man, and allows for much acting creativity which will challenge the student actors and producers. **ROYALTY:** $35. **SOURCE:** Cope, Eddie. (1980). The invisible man. Schulenburg, TX: I.E. Clark. **SUBJECTS/PLAY TYPE:** Mystery; Drama.

1526. 7-10. (+) Kelly, Tim. (Wells, H.G.) **The invisible man.** (The invisible man) **CAST:** 8f, 7m, Su. **ACTS:** 1. **SETTINGS:** Inn lobby. **PLAYING TIME:** 30 min. **PLOT:** The village inn lodgers are wary of Mr. Griffin, whose face is covered with bandages and dark glasses to hide the fact that he is invisible. A scientist arrives to talk with him, but Griffin runs away. Later, he is captured by the police. In a surprise ending, one of the servants drinks Mr. Griffen's potion and becomes invisible herself, starting the confusion all over again. **RECOMMENDATION:** The short, to the point dialogue of this hilarious melodrama makes it an appropriate choice for less-experienced actors. Many of the minor roles can be switched to male parts if desired, and any number of extras can be inserted as villagers. Timing is critical. **ROYALTY:** $15. **SOURCE:** Kelly, Tim. (1977). The invisible man. Denver, CO: Pioneer Drama Service. **SUBJECTS/PLAY TYPE:** Comedy; Invisibility; Adaptation.

1527. 7-12. (+) Olfson, Lewy. (Wells, H. G.) **The invisible man.** (The invisible man.) **CAST:** 4f, 7m, 1u. **ACTS:** 1. **SETTINGS:** Town. **PLAYING TIME:** NA. **PLOT:** While working with the color of various substances, Griffin makes himself invisible. He staggers into the Coach and Horses Inn late one night in February, and requests a room with a stout door, fire and food. He does not want anyone to know his secret. When Dr. Cuss discovers the secret, Griffin kills him, and eludes capture by the townsmen. Later that night, Griffin comes face to face with Kemp, a scientist and old school mate. Griffin wants Kemp to keep his secret, but Kemp refuses and helps the townspeople kill Griffin. **RECOMMENDATION:** This faithful adaptation, although short, will appeal to youngsters' imagination and desires

for spooky stories. **ROYALTY:** Free to Plays subscribers. **SOURCE:** Olfson, Lewy. (1978, October). The invisible man. Plays: The Drama Magazine for Young People, pp. 81-91. **SUBJECTS/PLAY TYPE:** Science Fiction; Reader's Theater; Adaptation.

1528. 5-9. (-) Thane, Adele. (Gilbert, William S. & Sullivan, Arthur) **Iolanthe or the peer and the peri.** (The peer and the peri) **CAST:** 6f, 5m, Su. **ACTS:** 1. **SETTINGS:** Fairy grove; yard. **PLAYING TIME:** 35 min. **PLOT:** The Queen of fairies pardons Iolanthe for marrying a mortal. Iolanthe's 25-year exile from her husband over, she admits that she has a half-mortal son, Strephon, who is desperately in love with Phyllis, a ward of Lord Chancellor, Iolanthe's former husband. He forbids Strephon to marry Phyllis, who witnesses Iolanthe consoling Strephon and, not believing that Iolanthe is his mother, breaks the engagement. Strephon becomes the leader of Parliament, is reunited with Phyllis, tells her that his mother is a fairy, and learns the truth about his father. Lord Chancellor still forbids the marriage, instead announcing his intention to marry Phyllis himself. Iolanthe tells him that Strephon is their son. The Fairy Queen appears to take Iolanthe's life, the penalty for her communication with her ex-husband. However, the sister fairies announce their marriages to the mortal Peers. When the fairy Queen herself marries a mortal, she changes Fairy Law to state "death to fairies that do NOT marry mortals." The group flies off to Fairy Land. **RECOMMENDATION:** Without the original stupendous music and lyrics, this is boring. **ROYALTY:** Free to Plays subscribers. **SOURCE:** Thane, Adele. (1975, October). Iolanthe or the peer and the peri. Plays: The Drama Magazine for Young People, pp. 83- 96. **SUBJECTS/PLAY TYPE:** Musical; Adaptation.

1529. 10-12. (+) Rudolph, Grace. **Irma. CAST:** 2f. **ACTS:** 1. **SETTINGS:** Bare stage, props. **PLAYING TIME:** NA. **PLOT:** Irma cuts her long hair and asks for approval from Gladys. The focus shifts, as Irma reminisces about her love for her two husbands and children, and the hardships she endured for that love. **RECOMMENDATION:** Reminiscent of **I Remember Mama,** young actors will enjoy the challenge of playing an elderly character in this simply written sketch. **ROYALTY:** $10. **SOURCE:** Rudolph, Grace. (1984). Elders' statements: One-act plays and monologues. Boston, MA: Baker's Plays. **SUBJECTS/PLAY TYPE:** Family; Elderly; Love; Drama.

1530. 5-8. (+) Martens, Anne Coulter. **Is Cupid stupid? CAST:** 4f, 3m, Su. **ACTS:** 1. **SETTINGS:** Card store. **PLAYING TIME:** 25 min. **PLOT:** Needing money to buy a bracelet for a demanding and unappreciative girl, a boy is hired by a card store to play Cupid at party. He accidentally shoots an arrow at the woman who hired him. She demands that he be arrested, but a young girl working in the card shop helps him hide. Cupid surrenders, the lady realizes he did not shoot her intentionally, and Cupid realizes the girl he really likes is the undemanding one from the card shop. **RECOMMENDATION:** Lively dialogue and fast moving action complement the corny valentine rhymes which Cupid tries to sell to the card store owner for the coming holiday. **ROYALTY:** Free to Plays subscribers. **SOURCE:** Martens, Anne Coulter. (1988,

January/ February). Is Cupid stupid? Plays: The Drama Magazine for Young People, pp. 11-19. **SUBJECTS/PLAY TYPE:** Valentine's Day; Comedy.

1531. 7-12*. (-) Sodaro, Craig. **Is there a ghost in the house?** **CAST:** 4f, 2m, 2u. **ACTS:** 1. **SETTINGS:** Living room. **PLAYING TIME:** 30 min. **PLOT:** Three members of a high school science club try to prove the scientific impossibility of ghosts by spending the night in an allegedly haunted house. Their encounter with its eccentric inhabitant and an inept cat burglar are among the night's events which change their opinions about the supernatural. **RECOMMENDATION:** The play's trite jokes and predictable plot place it far below the level of sophistication of today's high school students. The characters are one dimensional at best, and the humor depends entirely upon the nervous hysteria of two minor characters, who have little more to do than jump, stutter and shriek. **ROYALTY:** Free to Plays subscribers. **SOURCE:** Sodaro, Craig. (1982, October). Is there a ghost in the house? Plays: The Drama Magazine for Young People, pp. 1-11. **SUBJECTS/PLAY TYPE:** Ghosts; Halloween; Comedy.

1532. 7-12. (+) Rybak, Rose Kacherian. **Is there life after high school?** **CAST:** 9f, 12m, 13u. **ACTS:** 1. **SETTINGS:** Registration area. **PLAYING TIME:** 40 min. **PLOT:** As recent High School graduates make choices about their futures, Jody decides to attend college, but does not know what to study. Juan wants to go to college but his family wants him to get a job. A musical duet splits up when one wants to make it big in the music business, while the other wants to go to college and study music education. Another teen does not want to assume adult responsibilities. In the end, the teenagers find solutions. **RECOMMENDATION:** This is a funny play about a very real and important time for teenagers. Each character is introduced and isolated in the play, so most do not interact with the others. Yet there is a connection among them because they all must make the same kinds of decisions. **ROYALTY:** Free to Plays subscribers. **SOURCE:** Rybak, Rose Kacherian. (1980, May). Is there life after high school? Plays: The Drama Magazine for Young People, pp. 1-11. **SUBJECTS/PLAY TYPE:** Careers; Comedy.

1533. 4-8. (+) Lane, Marion. **Is there life on other planets?** **CAST:** 6u. **ACTS:** 1. **SETTINGS:** Conference room. **PLAYING TIME:** NA. **PLOT:** Scientists discuss the possibility of life on another planet--earth. **RECOMMENDATION:** This is short, easy to produce, and the surprise ending is a delight. **ROYALTY:** None. **SOURCE:** Kamerman, Sylvia E. (1981). Space and science fiction plays for young people. Boston, MA: Plays, Inc. **SUBJECTS/PLAY TYPE:** Science Fiction; Scientists; Skit.

1534. 4-6. (-) Way, Brian. **The Island.** **CAST:** 2f, 2m. **ACTS:** 1. **SETTINGS:** Bare stage, backdrop. **PLAYING TIME:** NA. **PLOT:** A conquering army takes command of a peaceful island. The head of the army, Adamson, and the head of the island, Headman, discuss the rules for occupation. Especially upsetting to Headman is the new rule prohibiting an upcoming festival which is central to the lives of islanders. Adamson's wife is appalled by the senseless brutality of the occupation and offers to help persuade her husband to allow the festival. Adamson allows the festival to proceed. The audience is then supplied with materials and, divided into groups of five, and they make one mask for each group. Then, singing a song which was learned during the play, the audience dances out of the theater. **RECOMMENDATION:** Issues including witchcraft, conscience, martial law, the occupation of another land, and the enslavement of a people are all raised here, but never explored. The point of the play seems to be to encourage us to learn about other cultures, but it is very superficial. **ROYALTY:** $20. **SOURCE:** Way, Brian. (1977). The island. Boston, MA: Baker's Plays. **SUBJECTS/PLAY TYPE:** War; Drama.

1535. 10-12*. (+) Kligman, Paul. **It all ends up in a shopping bag.** **CAST:** 6f, 15m. **ACTS:** 2. **SETTINGS:** Bare stage. **PLAYING TIME:** NA. **PLOT:** Returning home from his father's funeral, a grown son reminisces about his father, a Russian Jewish immigrant to Canada in the early part of this century. The scenes move from the grocery store run by the father and his friend, to the variety of marginal and failed businesses that followed this first enterprise. The father antagonizes some people and is cheated by others, he bullies his wife and his children, but in the end the story is of a courageous and tenacious man who struggled against anti-semitism and poverty to earn money for himself and his family. **RECOMMENDATION:** The Jewish idioms may be unfamiliar to some audiences, but the family orientation is timeless, as are the courage and stubbornness of the main characters. Some of the parts are extremely long, and it is questionable whether high school students would be capable of mastering them. The play might be best produced for a Jewish Community Center or for an audience familiar with Jewish culture. **ROYALTY:** $50. **SOURCE:** Kligman, Paul. (1982). It all ends up in a shopping bag. Chicago, IL: Dramatic Pub. Co. **SUBJECTS/PLAY TYPE:** Immigrants; Jews; Anti-semitism; Family; Depression, U.S.; Drama.

1536. 10-12. (+) Taylor, Renee & Bologna, Joseph. **It had to be you.** **CAST:** 1f, 2m. **ACTS:** 2. **SETTINGS:** TV studio; apartment. **PLAYING TIME:** NA. **PLOT:** Theda Blau explains how she met and fell in love with Vito Pignoli, a director and producer of commercials. Although it was love at first sight for Theda, convincing Vito that he loved her was a challenge. Luring him up to her apartment, she seduced him, but disgusted, he tried to leave, fell, and hurt his back, forcing him to remain at Theda's. She convinced him to call his estranged son and to face some unpursued goals in his life. They began to write a play together. By dawn, Vito declared his love for her. **RECOMMENDATION:** This has some very funny lines, and Theda's ability to draw out the sensitive nature of Vito is rewarding to read. The excellent multi-dimensional characters may be too challenging for all but the most gifted high schoolers. **ROYALTY:** $60. **SOURCE:** Taylor, Renee & Bologna, Joseph. (1984). It had to be you. New York, NY: Samuel French. **SUBJECTS/PLAY TYPE:** Love; Comedy.

1537. 1-10. (+) Pugh, Ann. (Browning, Robert) **It happened in Hamelin.** (Pied Piper of Hamelin.) **CAST:** 4f,

7m, Su. ACTS: 1. SETTINGS: Stage; public square; woods; cave. PLAYING TIME: 90 min. PLOT: The selfish and bombastic Mayor of Hamelin is concerned that his corrupt government will be jeopardized if the rat problem in the city isn't solved. The scatter-brained wizardess fails to eliminate the rodents, so the town employs the Pied Piper. When he accomplishes his task but is unable to collect payment, the piper spirits away the children of the town. There is a happy ending when the villagers learn the value of honesty. RECOMMENDATION: This uses catchy verses but casting requires musical ability, so junior high schoolers should produce this for younger audiences. ROYALTY: $50. SOURCE: Pugh, Ann. (1973). It happened in Hamelin. Schulenburg, TX: I.E. Clark. SUBJECTS/PLAY TYPE: Rats; Musical; Comedy; Adaptation.

1538. 9-12. (+) Cornish, Roger N. **It hardly matters now.** CAST: 2f, 1m. ACTS: 1. SETTINGS: Living room. PLAYING TIME: 20 min. PLOT: May, an attractive well dressed divorcee, visits her two old college friends, Herb and Carrie, who have been married for 44 years. Carrie has always joked with Herb about how she and May flipped a silver dollar to see who would marry him. May lets it slip that the joke was really the truth. Initially, Herb is hurt and May decides to leave, but the two women realize that true love and friendship depend on honesty. RECOMMENDATION: The performance is brief and episodic; character development must be immediately and precisely achieved. The themes that the past can haunt, that there is no age limit on heartache or bruised feelings, and that friendship can weather any misunderstanding are delivered in a nonmoralizing manner. ROYALTY: $10. SOURCE: Cornish, Roger N. (1978). It hardly matters now. Denver CO: Pioneer Drama Service. SUBJECTS/PLAY TYPE: Elderly; Friendship; Drama.

1539. 9-12. (+) Perry, E. Eugene. **It works for everybody else!** CAST: 5f, 2m. ACTS: 1. SETTINGS: Living room; porch and yard. PLAYING TIME: NA. PLOT: Feeling unappreciated and neglected by her family, a mother stages a strike, pickets in the front yard, and demands more help from her husband and children. RECOMMENDATION: Realistic dialogue and an easily identifiable stay at home mother who feels unappreciated provide a novel treatment of the subject matter. ROYALTY: NA. SOURCE: Perry, R. Eugene. (1984). It works for everybody else. Studio City, CA: Players Press. SUBJECTS/PLAY TYPE: Women's Rights; Family; Comedy.

1540. 3-6*. (+) Clark, I.E. & Carter, Kit. **It's a dungaree world.** CAST: 6f, 2m, 16u. ACTS: 2. SETTINGS: Playroom; forest; jungle. PLAYING TIME: 100 min. PLOT: When dolls come alive, Suzette is arrested by Skoolies and taken to the Concentration Campus, an institution for dolls who do not study their lessons. Bill and Betty, aided by numerous characters such as the pink elephant turned blue and the friendly fairy, reach the Skoolie Cave and ask for Suzette's release. But Pirates, in need of a substitute mother, demand Suzette for themselves. A battle between mother and Skoolies ensues, but they negotiate a short-lived truce. The fight renewed, they are stopped by an invisible wall put up by the wicked

witch. All is resolved by the appearance of the rooster shouting that it is five o'clock and time for the dolls to become lifeless again. RECOMMENDATION: Despite a preachy tone, this is rather clever. Some imagery needs to be changed (punishment at a "Concentration Campus" is probably inappropriate), but with judicial editing, this is suitable for an adult cast to perform for a young audience. ROYALTY: $60. SOURCE: Clark, I.E. & Carter, Kit. (1974). It's a dungaree world. Schulenburg, TX: I.E. Clark. SUBJECTS/PLAY TYPE: Dolls; Musical; Comedy.

1541. 7-12. (-) Murray, John. **It's a mystery to me.** CAST: 1m. ACTS: 1. SETTINGS: Bare stage. PLAYING TIME: NA. PLOT: Tom quits his job to write a murder mystery novel, but his overly helpful family creates endless disturbances which culminate in a visit from a policeman who is investigating rumors of bloody bodies. RECOMMENDATION: The humor is weak, based upon a frivolous treatment of mental illness which is offensive and stereotypical. ROYALTY: None. SOURCE: Murray, John. (1982). Modern monologues for young people. Boston, MA: Plays, Inc. SUBJECTS/PLAY TYPE: Mental Illness; Comedy; Interruptions; Monologue.

1542. 5-8. (-) Martens, Anne Coulter. **It's a woman's world.** CAST: 5f, 3m, Su. ACTS: 1. SETTINGS: Dining room. PLAYING TIME: 35 min. PLOT: Roles are reversed here, as men stay at home and women work. Some men question this inequality and two high schoolers decide to be equal. RECOMMENDATION: The roles of the men as women are insultingly overdone. ROYALTY: Free to Plays subscribers. SOURCE: Martens, Anne Coulter. (1978, October). It's a woman's world. Plays: The Drama Magazine for Young People, pp. 31-42. SUBJECTS/PLAY TYPE: Sexual Equality; Skit.

1543. K-3. (+) Hark, Mildred & McQueen, Noel. **It's about time.** CAST: 1f, 1m, Su. ACTS: 1. SETTINGS: Bedroom. PLAYING TIME: 25 min. PLOT: As a young boy dreams, clocks of various types come to life to teach him the value of time. RECOMMENDATION: This will be effective for those young enough to enjoy the animation and dramatics of the personified clocks, but old enough to understand the theme of not wasting time. ROYALTY: Free to Plays Subscribers. SOURCE: Hark, Mildred & McQueen, Noel. (1979, April). It's about time. Plays: The Drama Magazine for Young People, pp. 65-69. SUBJECTS/PLAY TYPE: Time; Skit.

1544. 3-5. (+) Kelly, Tim J. **It's Bigfoot.** CAST: 17u. ACTS: 1. SETTINGS: Lodge. PLAYING TIME: 30 min. PLOT: The daughters of a rustic lodge owner create Bigfoot to keep father's business from floundering. The ensuing publicity brings a T.V. news crew, the "Save Bigfoot Foundation," an advertising executive (who wants Bigfoot to sell shampoo), a Canadian Royal Mountie, and a hunter with his Indian guide (who wants to stuff the creature). When the daughters' scheme is revealed, the real "Lady Bigfoot" appears and carries the Mountie (with whom she has been smitten) into the forest. The guests rush off after them. RECOMMENDATION: This has delightful slapstick comedy, timeless humor, wonderful sarcasm, and fast paced action. The director will have to be careful not to portray negative stereotypes of Native Americans. **ROYALTY:** $20. **SOURCE:** Kelly, Tim J. (1978). It's Bigfoot. Denver, CO: Pioneer Drama Service. **SUBJECTS/PLAY TYPE:** Bigfoot; Slapstick; Comedy.

1545. 7-12. (+) Murray, John. **It's magic. CAST:** 1m. **ACTS:** 1. **SETTINGS:** Bare stage. **PLAYING TIME:** NA. **PLOT:** A pompous magician tries to entertain a high school assembly crowd, but all his tricks fail because of his clumsy assistant. **RECOMMENDATION:** A mildly amusing look at failed special effects, this suffers from weak tension build-up and an unconvincing character. It might, however, be an amusing production for a school talent show. **ROYALTY:** None. **SOURCE:** Murray, John. (1982). Modern monologues for young people. Boston, MA: Plays, Inc. **SUBJECTS/PLAY TYPE:** Comedy; Magicians; Monologue.

1546. K-4*. (+) Sullivan, Jessie P. **It's no fun to be criticized! CAST:** 2u. **ACTS:** 1. **SETTINGS:** Puppet stage. **PLAYING TIME:** NA. **PLOT:** A child prays to avoid hating another who has said unkind things about her. **RECOMMENDATION:** This teaches the meaning of Matthew 7:1. **ROYALTY:** None. **SOURCE:** Sullivan, Jessie P. (1978). Puppet scripts for children's church. Grand Rapids, MI: Baker Book House. **SUBJECTS/PLAY TYPE:** Forgiveness; Christian Drama; Puppet Play.

1547. K-2. (+) Heidacker, Nadine. (Andersen, Hans Christian) **It's perfectly true.** (It's perfectly true) **CAST:** 9u. **ACTS:** 1. **SETTINGS:** Barnyard. **PLAYING TIME:** 10 min. **PLOT:** A simple story becomes blown out of proportion by gossips. **RECOMMENDATION:** Younger children will find the simple story both entertaining and educational. **ROYALTY:** Free to Plays subscribers. **SOURCE:** Heidacker, Nadine. (1980, March). It's perfectly true. Plays: The Drama Magazine for Young People, pp. 64-66. **SUBJECTS/PLAY TYPE:** Gossip; Folk Tales, Denmark; Adaptation; Puppet Play.

1548. K-6. (+) Mc Donough, Jerome. **It's so sad, so sad, when an elf goes bad. CAST:** 12u. **ACTS:** 1. **SETTINGS:** Santa's place. **PLAYING TIME:** 30 min. **PLOT:** Santa puts Emmy, his smallest and most accident-prone elf, in charge of Ralph, a reindeer forced into retirement. The pair take revenge on Santa by turning him into a destructive monster who destroys the presents in one home. When the children see the mess on Christmas morning, they are so heartbroken that Emmy and Ralph repent. They fix all the broken presents and learn that "no matter what anybody's done to you, getting even just makes you sad all over again." **RECOMMENDATION:** The dialogue is so realistic that the audience will be sobbing along with the actors. **ROYALTY:** $15. **SOURCE:** McDonough, Jerome. (1979). It's so sad, so sad, when an elf goes bad. Schulenburg, TX: I.E. Clark. **SUBJECTS/PLAY TYPE:** Christmas; Revenge; Drama.

1549. 11-12. (+) Nolan, Paul T. **It's your move. CAST:** 4f, 5m. **ACTS:** 1. **SETTINGS:** Sidewalk. **PLAYING TIME:** 30 min. **PLOT:** While playing checkers, two senior citizens decide to be philosophers and share their wisdom with the younger generation. They observe two partners argue and compromise; then two college girls argue, but solve their problems. The senior citizens observe that there is much foolishness in the world, but that through compromise, problems can be solved. **RECOMMENDATION:** This would be especially suitable in a social studies class, as it stresses the importance of compromise. **ROYALTY:** Free to Plays subscribers. **SOURCE:** Nolan, Paul T. (1977, February). It's your move. Plays: The Drama Magazine for Young People, pp. 33-42. **SUBJECTS/PLAY TYPE:** Compromise; Playlet.

1550. 4-6. (+) Shippee, Harlan. (Jacobs, Joseph) **Jack and his magic trash can.** (Jack and the beanstalk) **CAST:** 2f, 4m, 1u. **ACTS:** 1. **SETTINGS:** House; used car lot; moon. **PLAYING TIME:** 15 min. **PLOT:** Jack and his mother have nothing to eat, so Jack goes to trade his car for money to buy food. Instead, he ends up with a magic trash can that takes him to the moon where he rescues the king and the princess from the terrible Moon Monster, brings them home and marries the princess while his mother marries the king. **RECOMMENDATION:** Upper elementary grades could design and make the puppets to produce this for the younger grades. **ROYALTY:** Free to Plays subscribers. **SOURCE:** Shippee, Harlan. (1981, December). Jack and his magic trash can. Plays: The Drama Magazine for Young People, pp. 67-71. **SUBJECTS/PLAY TYPE:** Spoof; Folk Tales, England; Puppet Play; Adaptation.

1551. 2-6. (+) Mahlman, Lewis & Jones, David Cadwalader. (Jacobs, Joseph) **Jack and the beanstalk.** (Jack and the beanstalk) **CAST:** 5f, 3m, 1u. **ACTS:** 1. **SETTINGS:** Garden; fair; kitchen. **PLAYING TIME:** 15 min. **PLOT:** A poor boy plants magic beans which produce a stalk that he climbs. He saves a hen that lays golden eggs and rescues a princess from a giant. **RECOMMENDATION:** Humor adds to this fine adaptation of the classic fairy tale. **ROYALTY:** Free to Plays subscribers. **SOURCE:** Mahlman, Lewis & Jones, David Cadwalader. (1974). Puppet plays for young players. Boston, MA: Plays, Inc. **SUBJECTS/PLAY TYPE:** Puppet Play; Folk Tales, England; Giants; Adaptation.

1552. K-5. (+) McCallum, Phyllis. (Jacobs, Joseph) **Jack and the beanstalk.** (Jack and the beanstalk) **CAST:** 4f, 3m, 1u. **ACTS:** 1. **SETTINGS:** Cottage; castle. **PLAYING TIME:** 45 min. **PLOT:** A faithful dramatization of the classic tale. **RECOMMENDATION:** Fantasy, magic, and suspense are appealing here. This would also work well as a puppet or marionette show. **ROYALTY:** $15. **SOURCE:** McCallum, Phyllis. (1975). Jack and the beanstalk. Denver, CO: Pioneer Drama Service. **SUBJECTS/PLAY TYPE:** Folk Tales, England; Giants; Magic; Adaptation.

1553. 3-7. (+) Rafferty, Robert. (Jacobs, Joseph) **Jack and the beanstalk.** (Jack and the beanstalk) **CAST:** 4f, 4m, 1u. **ACTS:** 1. **SETTINGS:** Bare stage. **PLAYING TIME:** NA. **PLOT:** A faithful adaptation of the original. **RECOMMENDATION:** This combines the fun of telling and acting; the beanstalk may be created with lighting effects. **ROYALTY:** $15. **SOURCE:** Rafferty, Robert. (1979).

Jack and the beanstalk. Elgin IL: Performance Pub. Co. SUBJECTS/PLAY TYPE: Folk Tales, England; Giants; Magic; Adaptation.

1554. K-6. (+) Solomon, Olivia. (Jacobs, Joseph) **Jack and the beanstalk.** (Jack and the beanstalk) CAST: 2f, 2m. ACTS: 1. SETTINGS: Cottage; giant's home. PLAYING TIME: NA. PLOT: The poetically inclined Jack swears to avenge his dead father who was robbed by a giant, but first he plans to sell the family cow to save them from starvation. He returns with three beans and falls asleep while writing a poem about them. The beans grow into a magic beanstalk, which Jack climbs until he comes to a castle. The giant's wife answers his knock, and warns Jack that her husband may eat him. Despite almost being discovered, Jack recovers his father's stolen treasure, and escapes down the beanstalk, with the giant in hot pursuit. Cutting down the beanstalk, Jack puts an end to the giant, and is free to write his poems. Jack asserts at the end that it is easier to kill giants than it is to create poetry. RECOMMENDATION: Solomon has expanded on Jack's capricious nature through her portrayal of him as a poet, which, combined with humor and levity, serves to lighten the critical moments. Because there are only four parts, the actors must have strong powers of memorization, although much of the action is pantomimed. ROYALTY: NA. SOURCE: Solomon, Olivia. (1983). Five folk comedies for today's juvenile stage. Tuscaloosa, AL: Portals. SUBJECTS/PLAY TYPE: Folk Tales, England; Revenge; Giants; Playlet.

1555. 3-5. (+) Thane, Adele. (Jacobs, Joseph) **Jack and the magic beanstalk.** (Jack and the beanstalk) CAST: 4f, 5m, Su. ACTS: 1. SETTINGS: Yard; giant's kitchen. PLAYING TIME: 30 min. PLOT: Living in abject poverty, Jack sells the cow to a kindly woman for a handful of beans. The woman tells Jack about how his father was once rich. Jack's mother throws the beans away in disgust when he returns home, and a giant beanstalk grows. Climbing to its top, Jack finds a giant's castle and steals back his father's treasures. The giant chases him, but Jack chops down the beanstalk when he reaches the bottom, killing the pursuing giant. The old woman appears, returns the cow, and everyone celebrates. RECOMMENDATION: This tells us that Jack is not an opportunist, but rather, a son avenging his father's sufferings. The giant's wife speaks of being beaten by her husband, but this could be eliminated. This would be a good choice for an inexperienced cast. ROYALTY: None. SOURCE: Thane, Adele. (1983). Plays from famous stories and fairy tales. Boston, MA: Plays, Inc. SUBJECTS/PLAY TYPE: Giants; Folk Tales, England; Adaptation.

1556. 1-6+. (+) Landes, William-Alan. (Jacobs, Joseph) **Jack n' the beanstalk.** (Jack and the beanstalk) CAST: 6f, 7m, Su. ACTS: 2. SETTINGS: Road; castle; clouds. PLAYING TIME: 60 min. PLOT: Jack sells the family cow for magic beans. When they sprout he climbs them to the giant's castle where he recovers his family's treasure and kills the giant. To warm up the audience before the story begins, the narrator tells offbeat renditions of "Humpty Dumpty," "Old King Cole," and "Little Miss Muffet."

RECOMMENDATION: Strengths here are the audience participation directed by the storyteller, the humor resulting from the unexpected variation on the introductory Mother Goose rhymes, and the adherence to the classic story. The language, number of scenes, and musical requirements preclude production by younger children. ROYALTY: $35. SOURCE: Landes, William-Alan. (1979). Jack n' the beanstalk. Studio City, CA: Players Press. SUBJECTS/PLAY TYPE: Folk Tales, England; Musical.

1557. 5-8. (+) Kilcup, Rick. (Jacobs, Joseph) **Jackie and the cornstalk.** (Jack and the beanstalk) CAST: 2f, 3m, 2u. ACTS: 3. SETTINGS: Cottage; cloud. PLAYING TIME: 15 min. PLOT: Jackie is a girl who climbs a cornstalk produced by magic seeds. She foils an ogre's plot to kidnap and barbecue a prince. They escape the ogre, climb down the cornstalk, and the sheriff chops it down and leads off a sorrowful ogre. RECOMMENDATION: The interactions between the characters are clever. The Prince is an endearing wimp who dreads his fate with regal reluctance. Even though Jackie is the heroine, she does not solve the problem of the escape which weakens the play. References to modern technology add clever humor. ROYALTY: Free to Plays subscribers. SOURCE: Kilcup, Rick. (1986, April). Jackie and the cornstalk. Plays: The Drama Magazine for Young People, pp. 27-32. SUBJECTS/PLAY TYPE: Comedy; Folk Tales, England; Giants; Adaptation.

1558. 10-12. (+) Cohen, Burt. **Jackie Lantern's Hallowe'en revenge.** CAST: 2f, 3m. ACTS: 2. SETTINGS: Farmhouse; porch. PLAYING TIME: NA. PLOT: As Mother good-naturedly tries to shoot her daughter, Betsey, Father ruminates in his front porch rocker. The sheriff arrives with vague accusations of some unspecified crime, further confusing the already ambiguous family relationships. Father attempts to drown his son, Tom, to protect the family's good name. As all try to reconstruct the still unknown crime, each family member thinks of past "crimes" that might make them guilty. As Mother reveals to Betsey and Tom that they were kidnapped from their real parents, the sheriff discovers that he has been sent, not to accuse anyone in the family, but to protect them from the returned kidnapper. RECOMMENDATION: About the ambiguities of love and hate, right and wrong, and the absurdities associated with these concepts, this will be difficult to produce, and the cartoon-like, hillbilly ambience adds to the challenge. For sophisticated high school casts and adults, the humorous language and thought-provoking themes make it worth the effort. ROYALTY: $50. SOURCE: Cohen, Burt. (1986). Jackie Lantern's Hallowe'en revenge. New York, NY: Dramatists Play Service. SUBJECTS/PLAY TYPE: Halloween; Family Relationships; Guilt; Drama.

1559. K-3. (+) McCord, David. **Jamboree.** CAST: 10u. ACTS: 1. SETTINGS: None. PLAYING TIME: NA. PLOT: Food rhymes are created from a variety of edibles. RECOMMENDATION: The rhymes here should help beginning readers to develop valuable skills. ROYALTY: NA. SOURCE: Bauer, Caroline Feller. (1987). Presenting reader's theater: Plays and poems to read aloud. New York, NY: H.W. Wilson. **SUBJECTS/PLAY TYPE:** Food; Reader's Theater.

1560. K-6. (+) George, Richard R. (Dahl, Roald) **James and the giant peach.** (James and the giant peach) **CAST:** 3f, 6m, 10u. **ACTS:** 1. **SETTINGS:** Garden; ocean; sky; top of the Empire State Building. **PLAYING TIME:** NA. **PLOT:** James is abused and over-worked by his two horrid aunts until a giant peach appears on their tree. When the boy crawls into the center of the fruit, he finds it filled with giant talking insects. Together they experience adventures on the open sea and up in the sky (where the peach is carried by seagulls). Eventually they are dropped onto the spike of the Empire State Building and hailed as heroes by New Yorkers. **RECOMMENDATION:** Recommended by Dahl himself, the directions for costumes and props are included, as well as some very detailed descriptions of required lighting. The narrator's part is quite long and might have to be read, but the other parts could be memorized by older grade school children. **ROYALTY:** $50. **SOURCE:** George, Richard A. (1982). James and the giant peach. Woodstock, IL: Dramatic Pub. Co. **SUBJECTS/PLAY TYPE:** Fantasy; Adaptation.

1561. 3-6. (-) Olfson, Lewy. (Bronte, Charlotte) **Jane Eyre.** (Jane Eyre.) **CAST:** 2f, 2m. **ACTS:** 1. **SETTINGS:** Drawing room. **PLAYING TIME:** 30 min. **PLOT:** A former Governess, Jane prepares to marry Rochester, the rich estate owner. She learns he is already married to a mad woman who is locked in an upper room. Feeling betrayed, Jane leaves, but returns years later to find the house damaged by fire and her ex-fiance blinded and depressed. The housekeeper tells her the mad woman set the fire in which she was killed and the master blinded. Jane and her ex-fiance reaffirm their love for each other. **RECOMMENDATION:** This drama, although true to the overall plot of the original, does not do it justice, as it oversimplifies, deletes all character development, and dwells on preparations for a wedding which was not in the original. Children will do better to read the original as adolescents. **ROYALTY:** Free to Plays subscribers. **SOURCE:** Olfson, Lewy. (1988, March). Jane Eyre. Plays: The Drama Magazine for Young People, pp. 58-64. **SUBJECTS/PLAY TYPE:** Marriage; Romance; Adaptation.

1562. 7-12. (+) Sroda, Anne. **Janet and the Janitress.** **CAST:** 3f, 4m, 1u. **ACTS:** 1. **SETTINGS:** Museum. **PLAYING TIME:** 35 min. **PLOT:** An attractive, young janitress, Janet, and her forgetful, elderly mother scrub floors and dust dinosaur bones in a museum under the direction of the loathsome curator, Craddock Crabtree McCrum, who wants to marry the unwilling Janet. Janet waits for her beloved, Herbie Goodman, to return from a phony dig to which McCrum has sent him. By refusing McCrum, Janet jeopardizes her job, but Goodman arrives in time to expose McCrum's villainy, become the new museum curator, and give Janet and her mother better museum jobs. **RECOMMENDATION:** With its humorously predictable banter, this may be too corny for more sophisticated students, but if played as satire, the plot and characters are enjoyable. **ROYALTY:** Free to Plays subscribers. **SOURCE:** Sroda, Anne. (1976, January).

Janet and the janitress. Plays: The Drama Magazine for Young People, pp. 1-12. **SUBJECTS/PLAY TYPE:** Romance; Comedy; Melodrama.

1563. 7-12. (-) Moeller, Ruby L. **January.** **CAST:** 12f, Su. **ACTS:** 1. **SETTINGS:** Bare stage, props. **PLAYING TIME:** NA. **PLOT:** The pro-gram comprises unrelated skits, comic readings, and songs involving audience participation. **RECOMMENDATION:** Individual skits vary from those reminiscent of preschool activities ("The Pussy Cat," "The Wonderous King") to those with sentiments that only adults could appreciate ("We eat too much, we drink too much...in idleness men live too much"). Language (i.e., millinery shop, self possession, willful turbulence) is old fashioned and stilted. Tunes are too dated to be familiar. **ROYALTY:** NA. **SOURCE:** Moeller, Ruby L. (1975). Around the year programs. Boston, MA: Baker's Plays. **SUBJECTS/PLAY TYPE:** Seasons; Calender; Variety Program.

1564. K-12. (+) Winther, Barbara. **Japanese trio.** **CAST:** 1f, 3m, Su. **ACTS:** 1. **SETTINGS:** Bare stage, backdrop. **PLAYING TIME:** 20 min. **PLOT:** Three scenes tell three tales: 1) "Paying the Eel Broiler," wherein the king's clever servant, Taro, pays a greedy eel broiler with money he cannot touch, but can see, because the broiler has charged a weary traveler for eels he cannot afford, but can smell; 2) "The Most Fearful Thing," wherein Taro saves his lord Sanjo by outwitting a comical trio (a devil, a wolf, and a thief) intent on robbing the ruler; and 3) "Why We Cannot Lend," wherein a series of bumblings leads to comedy in an Oriental version of "Thickheaded Jack," all because lord Sanjo leaves dull-witted Buso in charge of the palace. **RECOMMENDATION:** There is opportunity here to produce stories in either an elaborate or simple manner, with or without costumes or paper mache masks. The endings can be made strong with lively, loud use of drums, and with distinct body language. **ROYALTY:** Free for amateur performance. **SOURCE:** Winther, Barbara. (1976). Plays from folktales of Africa and Asia. Boston, MA: Plays, Inc. **SUBJECTS/PLAY TYPE:** Folk Tales, Japan; Playlet.

1565. 2-5. (+) Opalinski, Evelyn. **Jeff's dream. CAST:** 1f, 2m, 16u. **ACTS:** 1. **SETTINGS:** Forest. **PLAYING TIME:** 10 min. **PLOT:** While Jeff and his Grandfather stroll through the forest, Grandfather explains the importance of trees. They stop to rest and Jeff has a dream filled with animated trees, talking animals, and other characters who describe why people should conserve the forests. **RECOMMENDATION:** The rhyming verse carries an important ecological message about conservation of our natural resources. The forest literally "comes alive" as the trees and the animals lyrically tell their meaningful message. **ROYALTY:** Free to Plays Subscribers. **SOURCE:** Opalinski, Evelyn. (1980, April). Jeff's dream. Plays: The Drama Magazine for Young People, pp. 55-57. **SUBJECTS/PLAY TYPE:** Ecology; Conservation; Nature; Skit.

1566. P-3. (+) Laurie, Rona. (Potter, Beatrix) **Jemima Puddle-Duck and the gentleman with sandy whiskers.** (Tales of Beatrix Potter) **CAST:** 2f, 1m, 3u. **ACTS:** 1.

SETTINGS: Farm; woods. PLAYING TIME: NA. PLOT: Jemima Puddle Duck, determined to hatch her own eggs, is led astray by fox who plans to cook Jemima and her eggs. They are all saved by the quick action of the farm dogs. RECOMMENDATION: The audience is kept in suspense, as they realize that Jemima does not know that Mr. Whiskers is a wolf. ROYALTY: NA. SOURCE: Laurie, Rona. (1980). Children's plays from Beatrix Potter. London, England: F. Warne. SUBJECTS/PLAY TYPE: Animals; Adaptation.

1567. 8-12. (+) Fair, Rosemary. **Jenny the mail-order bride.** CAST: 3f, 3m. ACTS: 2. SETTINGS: Stagecoach; cavalry barracks (outside and inside); saloon; hotel room; shack. PLAYING TIME: 120 min. PLOT: Jenny is to marry Lieutenant Straytontall, a cavalry officer with whom she has corresponded and courted through the mail. A poor orphan, she has presented herself as wealthy and well-bred, and is afraid to tell her fiance the truth. A dastardly saloon owner threatens to expose her if Jenny refuses to work in his saloon. Needless to say, love triumphs over evil. RECOMMENDATION: The characters are stereotypes, but the dialogue is well written ("Die slowly, Alonzo, but be QUICK ABOUT IT!"), and the stage directions are ample and effective. The play includes six short songs, but they don't add much to the production other than to give the cast a chance to sing. Success will depend more on the individual performances of the cast (high school or older) than on the play's familiar plot. ROYALTY: $50. SOURCE: Fair, Rosemary. (1975). Jenny the mail-order bride. Denver CO: Pioneer Drama Service. SUBJECTS/PLAY TYPE: Courtship; Western; Musical; Melodrama.

1568. K-3. (+) Ison, Colleen. **Jericho falls.** CAST: Su. ACTS: 1. SETTINGS: Bare stage. PLAYING TIME: NA. PLOT: As the children act it out, a narrator tells the story of how God helped the Israelites knock down the wall of Jericho. RECOMMENDATION: The narrator will have to be an adult, but any number of children can act. Discussion questions are provided. ROYALTY: NA. SOURCE: Ison, Colleen. (1986). Goliath's last stand: And fifteen more easy plays for children. Cincinnati, OH: Standard Pub. SUBJECTS/PLAY TYPE: Christian Drama; Jericho; Joshua; Skit.

1569. K-3. (-) Silverman, Eleanor. **Jesse James.** CAST: 1f, 2m, 3u. ACTS: 2. SETTINGS: Farm; train tracks. PLAYING TIME: NA. PLOT: Jesse and Frank James plan to rob a train and the sheriff vows that he will find them. RECOMMENDATION: This has no point, no message, and no plot. ROYALTY: NA. SOURCE: Silverman, Eleanor. (1983). Dramatics for children. Metuchen, NJ: Scarecrow Press. SUBJECTS/PLAY TYPE: James, Jesse; Skit.

1570. K-3. (+) Ison, Colleen. **Jesus is here.** CAST: 4f, 2m. ACTS: 1. SETTINGS: Bare stage, props. PLAYING TIME: NA. PLOT: A little girl's mother tells her that Jesus is always with the world's people. She then goes outside, and reminds three unfriendly children that Jesus is with them and won't like what they are doing. They each stop being nasty and behave properly. RECOMMENDATION:

Short and simple, this didactically reminds children that a higher authority always sits in judgment. Discussion questions are included. ROYALTY: NA. SOURCE: Ison, Colleen. (1986). Goliath's last stand: And fifteen more easy plays for children. Cincinnati, OH: Standard Pub. SUBJECTS/PLAY TYPE: Behavior; Christian Drama; Skit.

1571. 7-9. (+) Karshner, Roger. **Jim and Ralph.** CAST: 2m. ACTS: 1. SETTINGS: None. PLAYING TIME: NA. PLOT: Jim tries to get Ralph to go after the guy who beat him up so that Ralph will not lose his self respect. As Jim boasts that "no one better mess with him," the bully appears, and Jim takes off running. RECOMMENDATION: Although the language is raw, this shows that actions speak louder than words. ROYALTY: NA. SOURCE: Karshner, Roger. (1986). Scenes for teenagers. Toluce Lake, CA: Dramaline Pub. SUBJECTS/PLAY TYPE: Boasting; Scene.

1572. 7-12*. (+) Levitt, Saul & Fisher, Harrison. **Jim Thorpe, All-American.** CAST: 30m. ACTS: 1. SETTINGS: None. PLAYING TIME: NA. PLOT: Major events in the life of the famous native American athlete are dramatized. Scenes depict his school days, his athletic accomplishments, the Olympics, the revoking of his medals, and his later life. As Jim tries to understand and operate within the cultural and ethical mores of a society which ridicules his native culture but idolizes him, then strips him of honor, the spirits of the great Indian heroes of the past watch. In their eyes the athlete is exploited by the white society just as the native tribes were exploited in the past. Finally, Jim Thorpe is welcomed into the spirit world where he can be fully Indian. RECOMMENDATION: This exposes the audience to a valuable lesson in history and morality. It also introduces students to an American hero whose entire life was a lesson in courage. The level of acting required is probably of the dramatic high school or semi-professional level. Sets are largely evocative or symbolic and easily produced. ROYALTY: $35. SOURCE: Levitt, Saul. (1977). Jim Thorpe, All-American. New Orleans, LA: Anchorage Press, Inc. SUBJECTS/PLAY TYPE: Native Americans; Olympics; Thorpe, Jim; Drama.

1573. 4-8. (+) Gotwalt, Helen Louise Miller. **Jiminy Cinders.** CAST: 8m. ACTS: 1. SETTINGS: Bunkhouse. PLAYING TIME: 25 min. PLOT: Jiminy Cinders is helped by the Golden Ranger to get to the rodeo and win. At the end, the sheriff locates Jiminy (he left without claiming his prize) by fitting him with the mysterious rider's lost boot. The stepbrothers are jailed for rustling and claim-jumping. RECOMMENDATION: A clever and amusing Western spoof of the familiar folk tale, this will give middle school boys a chance to ham it up for their peers. ROYALTY: Free to Plays subscribers. SOURCE: Gotwalt, Helen Louise Miller. (1981, March). Jiminy Cinders. Plays: The Drama Magazine for Young People, pp. 41-48. SUBJECTS/PLAY TYPE: Cowboys; Rodeos; Playlet.

1574. 7-12. (+) Nolan, Paul T. **Jo Anne plays Juliet.** CAST: 3f, 2m. ACTS: 1. SETTINGS: Park. PLAYING TIME: 20 min. PLOT: Jo Anne sits on a park bench reading **Romeo and Juliet.** Three of her friends visit to discuss an upcoming dance. When Kevin enters, they discuss Kevin's desire to write plays about pirates, Indians, and science fiction. While they talk, the three friends act out brief scenes on these topics. Afterward, Kevin asks Jo Anne to the dance and she accepts. They quote lines from **Romeo and Juliet** as the curtain falls. RECOMMENDATION: While the plot is predictable and the characters stereotyped, this is an interesting teen romance. Costume changes for the pirate, Indian, and science fiction sequences must be simple enough to fit into the brief intervals between scenes. ROYALTY: Free to Plays subscribers. SOURCE: Nolan, Paul T. (1983, January/February). Jo Anne plays Juliet. Plays: The Drama Magazine for Young People, pp. 77-82. SUBJECTS/PLAY TYPE: Valentine's Day; Dating; Playlet.

1575. 9-12. (+) Kelly, Tim J. **Jocko, or the monkey's husband.** (Jocko la singe) CAST: 6f, 6m, 6u. ACTS: 1. SETTINGS: Bare stage. PLAYING TIME: 60 min. PLOT: Members of the audience criticize and taunt the egocentric playwright who is in the process of creating a new play. His heroine, Jocko, a monkey, steals the heart of Don Delgado, an exiled European. Disillusioned with civilization, they flee to the jungle. Both families object strenuously and vociferously. In the end, Delgado's greed for diamonds nearly kills both Jocko and her love for him. However, at the insistence of the audience and the families, the playwright fashions a happy ending complete with the traditional moral. RECOMMENDATION: Based on a popular character from 19th century boulevard theater tradition, this avant garde production is spontaneous and witty. Young audiences will enjoy the rapid repartee and sarcasm that achieves a nice balance between cynicism and humor. It is recommended that the playbill should mention the theatrical origins of the Jocko character and the historical roots of the organ grinder's monkey. ROYALTY: $15. SOURCE: Kelly, Tim J. (1977). Jocko, or, the monkey's husband. Schulenburg, TX: I.E. Clark. SUBJECTS/PLAY TYPE: Fable; Monkeys; Comedy.

1576. 9-12. (+) Nichols, Peter & Popkin, Henry. (Nichols, Peter) **Joe Egg.** (A day in the death of Joe Egg) CAST: 4f, 2m. ACTS: 2. SETTINGS: Classroom; living room. PLAYING TIME: NA. PLOT: Bri, thought by others to be intelligent, finds no job satisfaction in his teaching position and feels suffocated by his responsibilities to his spastic daughter. Bri's wife, Sheila, appears to be stable, but is no better at coping than her husband. She pours her attention into her houseplants, an amateur acting career, and most of all, their spastic daughter, Joe. Bri decides to help Joe toward an untimely death that will mean an end to both her and his pain. Bri is unsuccessful and when she discovers his attempt, Sheila vows to meet Bri's needs, but Bri leaves and the two women are left to start a new life on their own. RECOMMENDATION: The plot moves slowly and sometimes reflects the apathy of the characters themselves. The dialect and some of the vocabulary are sometimes difficult to follow. The circumstances of raising a severely handicapped child are depicted and the characters' chosen methods of coping, both good and bad, are explored. Caution should be used in choosing the child to play Joe, as her role is conveyed through body language and spastic gestures, not through verbal communication. ROYALTY: NA. SOURCE: Nichols, Peter &

Popkin, Henry. (1967). Joe Egg. New York, NY: Grove Press. SUBJECTS/PLAY TYPE: Euthanasia; Cerebral Palsy; Drama.

1577. 2-4*. (+) Boiko, Claire. **Joe White and the seven lizards.** CAST: 1f, 4m, 26u. ACTS: 1. SETTINGS: Baseball stadium. PLAYING TIME: 25 min. PLOT: Joe White, a poor overworked bat boy, wants to become the Player of the Year. Braggart McTaggart, who never practices, becomes Player of the Year through the help of a genie. Ghost Umpire, who haunts the World Series stadium, tells McTaggart and the genie that the greatest of the great is Joe White, who plays by night. The genie casts a spell on Joe White, throwing him into Death Valley. However, Joe finds seven lizards to practice with him and Ghost Umpire still says that Joe is the greatest of the great. McTaggart and the genie try to kill Joe with a poisonous apple, but Fenella, Joe's faithful friend, provides the antidote. Joe returns to the Western Hemisphere team in time to save the series and become a hero. RECOMMENDATION: As the honest hard worker wins out over the dishonest fellow, the path is filled with magical spells, eerie rhymes, wonderful "baseball talk," horribly unfair treatment of the hero, and, of course, comedy. Joe White's name might be changed to avoid the possible racist connotations. ROYALTY: Free to Plays subscribers. SOURCE: Boiko, Claire. (1988, January/February). Joe White and the seven lizards. Plays: The Drama Magazine for Young People, pp. 20-30. SUBJECTS/PLAY TYPE: Fantasy; Baseball; Adaptation.

1578. 3-6. (+) Korty, Carol. (Tenenbaum, Samuel) **Jogging.** (Wise men of Chelm) CAST: 2u. ACTS: 1. SETTINGS: Bare stage, props. PLAYING TIME: NA. PLOT: A jogger has trouble keeping his balance because he has two different shoes on. He gets the pair just like it from home, and exchanges one mismatched pair for the other. Puzzled, he can't understand why the exchange has not helped. RECOMMENDATION: This has great potential for physical comedy and audiences will delight in the simpleton's stupidity. ROYALTY: None. SOURCE: Korty, Carol. (1977). Silly soup: Ten zany plays. New York, NY: Charles Scribner's Sons. SUBJECTS/PLAY TYPE: Jogging; Comedy; Skit; Fools And Simpletons; Adaptation.

1579. 12. (-) Fendrich, Shubert. (Armstrong, Tom & Batuick, Tom) **John Darling.** (John Darling comic strip) CAST: 14f, 9m. ACTS: 2. SETTINGS: Studio. PLAYING TIME: 120 min. PLOT: Channel One, the world's worst TV station, chooses an inappropriate winner for the Miss High School Senior USA Pageant, and is invaded by a revolutionary group from the Caribbean San Fernando Island. When a new national leader takes over San Fernando and invites the revolutionaries back home, Channel One's coverage of the takeover runs 10 points ahead of **Roots**, its nearest competitor. RECOMMENDATION: This might work if the audience is familiar with the comic strip upon which it is based, but the script is long, tedious, and boring. ROYALTY: $75. SOURCE: Fendrich, Shubert. (1984). John Darling. Denver, CO: Pioneer Drama Service. SUBJECTS/PLAY TYPE: News; Musical; Comedy.

1580. K-3. (-) Silverman, Eleanor. **John Henry. CAST:** 1f, 2m, 2u. ACTS: 3. SETTINGS: None. PLAYING TIME: NA. PLOT: John Henry dies when a steam drill explodes near him. RECOMMENDATION: This adaptation of the classic American legend adds irrelevant action which stereotypes women as "kind and pretty," has no plot, and no point. ROYALTY: NA. SOURCE: Silverman, Eleanor. (1983). Dramatics for children. Metuchen, NJ: Scarecrow Press. SUBJECTS/PLAY TYPE: Henry, John; Folk Heroes; Black Americans; Skit.

1581. 5-8. (-) Winther, Barbara. **John Henry. CAST:** 3f, 6m, 5u. ACTS: 1. SETTINGS: Rail track. PLAYING TIME: 20 min. PLOT: In gospel style, this dramatizes the ballad of John Henry, who dies after out-drilling the steam drill. RECOMMENDATION: Retaining none of the dignity of the original ballad, the play stereotypes the hero with trite dialogue. ROYALTY: NA. SOURCE: Kamerman, Sylvia E. (1983). Holiday plays round the year. Boston, MA: Plays, Inc. SUBJECTS/PLAY TYPE: Folk Heroes; Black Americans; Henry, John.

1582. 5-8. (+) Henderson, Nancy. **John Muir, Earth-Planet, Universe. CAST:** 5f, 5m. ACTS: 1. SETTINGS: Cottage. PLAYING TIME: 10 min. PLOT: The great naturalist, John Muir, stops at a blacksmith's cottage while on his "thousand mile walk to the gulf." He explains to the blacksmith and his wife how he became a naturalist and enacts scenes from his youth. RECOMMENDATION: Though preachy, this play captures Muir's love of life and nature. ROYALTY: Permission required if performed outside of the classroom. SOURCE: Henderson, Nancy. (1978). Celebrate America: A baker's dozen of plays. New York, NY: Julian Messner. SUBJECTS/PLAY TYPE: Muir, John; Conservation; Drama.

1583. 4-6. (+) Nolan, Paul T. (Haley, J.W.) **Johnny Appleseed.** (Johnny Appleseed) CAST: 3f, 6m. ACTS: 1. SETTINGS: Bare stage, props. PLAYING TIME: 20 min. PLOT: A frontier family meets the legendary wandering orchardist in the Ohio wilderness. When a band of outlaws threatens to run the settlers off, pacifist Johnny appeases their childish leader by accepting his challenge to see which of them is stronger. If Johnny can carry the last horse that he sat on, then Bully Bob will admit defeat. Cleverly, Johnny carries a wooden sawhorse. The bully outlaws concede, and give the settlers a real horse, at Johnny's subtle suggestion. RECOMMENDATION: Johnny responds to the bullies' threats by using his wits and sense of humor, and the theme of a nonviolent response to provocation is presented without appearing moralistic. References to the Bible may need to be edited. Also, some historical background on the life of John Chapman should probably be given to the audience prior to the performance. ROYALTY: None for amateur performance. SOURCE: Nolan, Paul T. (1982). Folk tale plays round the world: A collection of royalty-free, one-act plays about lands far and near. Boston, MA: Plays, Inc. SUBJECTS/PLAY TYPE: Arbor Day; Chapman, John; Appleseed, Johnny; Comedy.

1584. K-3. (+) Silverman, Eleanor. (Haley, W. H.) **Johnny Appleseed.** (Johnny Appleseed.) CAST: 2f, 2m, 1u. ACTS: 1. SETTINGS: Orchard; field. PLAYING TIME: NA. PLOT: Johnny plants his seeds; years later women pick the apples to make pies. RECOMMENDATION: A lack of action is made up for by the readings from Stephen Vincent Benet which comprise the end of the play. ROYALTY: None. SOURCE: Silverman, Eleanor. (1983). Dramatics for Children. Metuchen, NJ: Scarecrow Press. SUBJECTS/PLAY TYPE: Appleseed, Johnny; Arbor Day; Chapman, John; Skit.

1585. 1-5. (+) Fisher, Aileen Lucia. **Johnny Appleseed's Vision. CAST:** 3f, 3m. ACTS: 1. SETTINGS: Log cabin. PLAYING TIME: 10 min. PLOT: Jane and Liddy have no gifts for mother's birthday until Johnny Appleseed gives them appleseeds and seedlings to provide a birthday present every spring from then on. RECOMMENDATION: The rhyming lines make the dialogue easier to learn. ROYALTY: Free to Plays Subscribers. SOURCE: Fisher, Aileen Lucia. (1985). Year-round programs for young players. Boston MA: Plays, Inc. SUBJECTS/PLAY TYPE: Appleseed, Johnny; Arbor Day; Spring; Skit.

1586. 4-7. (+) Golden, Joseph. **Johnny Moonbeam and the silver arrow. CAST:** 1f, 6m. ACTS: 1. SETTINGS: Indian village. PLAYING TIME: NA. PLOT: To gain the silver arrow and be considered a man, Johnny Moonbeam, 12, must steal rain from the Rain God, fire from the Fire God, and maize from the Earth God. With each encounter, there is a contest in which Johnny is in mortal danger of drowning, or being burnt to death, or being buried beneath the earth. Johnny acquires these symbols of power by outwitting each god. Exultantly journeying homeward, he shows compassion to three beggars; one who is thirsty, one who is cold, and one who is hungry, even though it means that he returns empty handed. Bravely, Johnny faces his failure, but the three beggars appear and are revealed as the gods with whom Johnny did combat. Johnny is given the silver arrow. RECOMMENDATION: A narrator sets the mood and reads all the lines as he tells the audience what they are seeing by talking to the play's characters as the audience listens. Because of this, the narrator will have to be older (high school to adult). Lighting, sound effects, music, and scenery are also important to make this real. ROYALTY: NA. SOURCE: Jennings, Coleman A. & Harris, Aurand. (1981). Plays children love. New York, NY: Doubleday Co., Inc. SUBJECTS/PLAY TYPE: Native Americans; Manhood, Rites; Drama.

1587. 3-6*. (+) Reimer, Earl. **Jonah and the German whale. CAST:** 3f, 4m, 1u. ACTS: 1. SETTINGS: Platform, screen. PLAYING TIME: NA. PLOT: As he tells the story of Jonah and the great fish, the narrator is interrupted to speak with the actors and give cues. The zany actors include Jack, the captain of the ship who does not know what is going on, and Hans Schmidt, a German officer who tries to operate the back of the whale. RECOMMENDATION: Children will enjoy the interruptions the narrator must face without forgetting that the play is about Jonah. The construction of the mechanical whale may be difficult (it must hold three people). ROYALTY: NA. SOURCE: Reimer, Earl. (1983).

Jonah and the German whale. Boston, MA: Baker's Plays. SUBJECTS/PLAY TYPE: Whales; Drama.

1588. 2-6*. (+) Mamana, June. **Journey to Ergo.** CAST: 4f, 4m, 9u. ACTS: 2. SETTINGS: Woods; 3 planets. PLAYING TIME: NA. PLOT: Alien Larry La-Lama accidentally arrives on earth while testing a device that travels between planets. With Katie and Garfunkel, two ten year old earthlings, he travels to two other planets, and finally to his own, Ergo. On each, they must defeat different adversaries: a Squonk who destroys with tears, a Basilisk who destroys with an evil glance, and a Moon Beast who destroys with "poxes." Katie and Garfunkel return to earth on a sunbeam. RECOMMENDATION: The fantasy settings and costuming allow free rein for creativity and imagination. ROYALTY: $25. SOURCE: Mamana, June. (1979). Journey to Ergo. Franklin, OH: Eldridge Pub. Co. SUBJECTS/PLAY TYPE: Space Flights; Interplanetary Travel; Science Fiction; Drama.

1589. 7-12. (-) Boiko, Claire. **Journey to Technos.** CAST: 3f, 4m, Su. ACTS: 1. SETTINGS: Basement; outdoor court. PLAYING TIME: 30 min. PLOT: Members of a high school science club try out a free mail order device which can transport them to parallel universes, but they discover that it is actually a trap designed by the despotic ruler of Technos, who feeds his enormous knowledge bank with human brain waves. All seem doomed until they destroy the mechanical society by introducing the latest dance steps. RECOMMENDATION: Technos, whose society resembles the inner workings of a computer, might have been a useful means of teaching students something about computers. Instead, poor construction and a hasty, contrived resolution make the play a jumble of partially realized elements and ideas. None of the characters, including the hero, ever develops as an individual, and the plot twists are so contrived that they are annoying. ROYALTY: Free to Plays subscribers. SOURCE: Boiko, Claire. (1986, May). Journey to Technos. Plays: The Drama Magazine for Young People, pp. 59-68. SUBJECTS/PLAY TYPE: Adventure; Science Fiction.

1590. 6-12. (+) Truss, Jan. **The judgement of Clifford Sifton.** CAST: 2f, 3m. ACTS: 1. SETTINGS: Bare stage, map of Canada. PLAYING TIME: 60 min. PLOT: Clifford Sifton, an ambitious politician who has been instrumental in the settling of Western Canada, dies. The voices of Conscience, Truth, and History confront him with dramatizations of episodes depicting the adversity and agony of early pioneer life, maintaining that Clifford lured naive pioneers to a harsh land. Clifford defends his actions, but final judgement of Clifford is left to the audience. RECOMMENDATION: This should induce thought provoking discussions among history students, and provides an interesting variety of characters and situations. The only flaw is the very melodramatic episode involving a crippled girl. ROYALTY: NA. SOURCE: Truss, Jan. (1979). The judgement of Clifford Sifton. Toronto, Canada: Playwrights Canada. SUBJECTS/PLAY TYPE: History, Canada; Pioneer Life; Immigrants; Drama.

1591. 7-12*. (+) Janda, James. **Julian: A play based on the life of Julian of Norwich.** CAST: 2f. ACTS: 2. SETTINGS: Anchorhold; church. PLAYING TIME: 120 min. PLOT: Julian of Norwich, an anchoress and mystic born in 1342, was the first Englishwoman writer whose work has survived to the present time. The play describes her daily life and the historic events she survived, including three plagues, the Peasant's Revolt, and the Great Western Schism. The playwright has skillfully interwoven the telling of these events with Julian's story of her growth in faith and her great love of Christ. RECOMMENDATION: This would rarely be performed by children because of the complex, lengthy dialogue, and the difficulty of having one child carry the entire play. It would be possible to have Julian played by an extremely gifted senior high performer who would look at the play as a challenge, or by several students who would represent the main character. The play does present religious ideology that some may find objectionable, however this is presented with tact and logic. It would be a fine example of dramatic monologue for high school students. ROYALTY: $35. SOURCE: Janda, James. (1984). Julian. New York, NY: The Seabury Press. SUBJECTS/PLAY TYPE: Julian of Norwich; Monologue.

1592. 7-9. (+) Karshner, Roger. **Julie and Kerry.** CAST: 1f, 1m. ACTS: 1. SETTINGS: None. PLAYING TIME: NA. PLOT: Julie tells her steady that they see each other too much and are too young to be tied down. When Kerry agrees, Julie recapitulates, making it seem that it was Kerry's idea that they break up. Kerry tells Julie that he likes her more than anyone else and that he doesn't want to break up. Julie says that it was a silly idea and they should forget it. RECOMMENDATION: This would work equally well if the roles were reversed. ROYALTY: NA. SOURCE: Karshner, Roger. (1986). Scenes for teenagers. Toluce Lake, CA: Dramaline Pub. SUBJECTS/PLAY TYPE: Dating; Scene.

1593. 7-12. (+) Olfson, Lewy. (Shakespeare, William) **Julius Caesar.** (Julius Caesar) CAST: Su. ACTS: 1. SETTINGS: None. PLAYING TIME: NA. PLOT: The murder of Caesar and the subsequent suicide of Brutus are portrayed. RECOMMENDATION: With lines from the original, this round the table reading encapsulates the emotions well. ROYALTY: Free to Plays subscribers. SOURCE: Olfson, Lewy. (1976, January). Julius Caesar. Plays: The Drama Magazine for Young People, pp. 85-95. SUBJECTS/PLAY TYPE: Caesar, Julius; Reader's Theater; Adaptation.

1594. 4-9. (+) Moeller, Ruby. **July.** CAST: Su. ACTS: 1. SETTINGS: Bare stage, props. PLAYING TIME: NA. PLOT: The theme of patriotism is developed through songs, quotations from famous American speeches, poetry readings, and games. RECOMMENDATION: The program needs to be updated with quotations from more recent American heroes. Christianity is mentioned several times to the exclusion of other religions. Other terms also need revision. Summer camp and scout groups would find this useful. ROYALTY: NA. SOURCE: Moeller, Ruby L.

(1975). Around the year programs. Boston, MA: Baker's Plays. SUBJECTS/PLAY TYPE: Independence Day, U.S.; Variety Program.

1595. 7-12. (+) Schaaf, Albert K. **Jump for joy.** CAST: 7f, 5m, 2u. ACTS: 1. SETTINGS: Office. PLAYING TIME: 25 min. PLOT: Talented theatrical agent Ambrose Bainbridge is such a good man that he doesn't make money because he represents people who are not famous. Even when the famous Joy Darling asks him to represent her, he refuses because she insists that he terminate his other clients. In the end, one of his clients becomes famous and Dora, the designing woman who has schemed to "get a piece of the action," is fired, with the suggestion that she represent Joy Darling. RECOMMENDATION: The message of the value of friendship is gently and humorously delivered in this pleasant, well crafted comedy. ROYALTY: Free to Plays subscribers. SOURCE: Schaaf, Albert K. (1983, January-February). Jump for joy. Plays: The Drama Magazine for Young People, pp. 1-12. SUBJECTS/PLAY TYPE: Show Business; Friendship; Comedy.

1596. K-1. (+) Meehan, Charlie. **Jump rope rhyme.** CAST: 7u. ACTS: 1. SETTINGS: None. PLAYING TIME: NA. PLOT: Seven readers name six chocolate items, which together add up to a belly ache. RECOMMENDATION: This can be recited alone, or, as Bauer recommends, with "Toy Tik Ka" and "Peculiar" (see entries in text). ROYALTY: NA. SOURCE: Bauer, Caroline Feller. (1987). Presenting reader's theater: Plays and poems to read aloud. New York, NY: H.W. Wilson Co. SUBJECTS/PLAY TYPE: Food; Chocolate; Reader's Theater.

1597. K-3. (+) Martin, Judith & Ashwander, Donald. **Jumping beans.** CAST: 5u. ACTS: 1. SETTINGS: Box. PLAYING TIME: 10 min. PLOT: A lady purchases three beans for supper. When she begins cooking them, they jump out of the pot and she returns them for a refund. After she receives her money, however, the beans follow her home. She walks back to the store and asks the bean man to protect her. He closes the store and takes the beans home with him. RECOMMENDATION: The beans have no dialogue, but provide the humor through their naughty actions and reactions. They also play rhythms on cans. A theme seems to be acceptance of others. ROYALTY: NA. SOURCE: Martin, Judith & Ashwander, Donald. (1985). Reasons to be cheerful: A revue for children. New York, NY: The Paper Bag Players, Inc. SUBJECTS/PLAY TYPE: Beans, Jumping; Acceptance; Skit; Musical Revue.

1598. 4-9. (-) Moeller, Ruby L. **June.** CAST: 2f, 2m, 2u. ACTS: 1. SETTINGS: Bare stage, props. PLAYING TIME: NA. PLOT: This comprises a reading; the presentation of a boutonniere to fathers by "a small girl"; three more readings; "Games and Stunts"; and a skit in which a man rummages through his dresser, unable to find a clean shirt and socks. He grumbles because he doesn't want to go out that evening, then his wife points out his clean clothes and a new tie on the bed. He meekly asks her to scratch his back and says, "You're the best wife a man ever had." RECOMMENDATION: Apparently intended for a children's club meeting or party with parents present as guests, this is overly sentimental and full of outdated phrases like "jolly chum." Modern children would find the games and stunts hopelessly old fashioned and boring. ROYALTY: NA. SOURCE: Moeller, Ruby L. (1975). Around the year programs. Boston, MA: Baker's Plays. SUBJECTS/PLAY TYPE: Father's Day; Variety Program.

1599. 7-10. (+) Martens, Anne Coulter. **Jury Duty.** CAST: 5f, 3m. ACTS: 1. SETTINGS: Jury room; courtroom; living room. PLAYING TIME: 40 min. PLOT: One juror's "not guilty" vote causes the other eleven to rethink and reenact the crime. The lone holdout, a hip talking grandmother, slowly reverses the opinions of the others about the guilt of Clay Henderson, who is accused of knocking out Melinda, his fiancee, and stealing her valuable necklace. Through discussion and reexamination of the facts, the jurors correctly decide that Melinda's guardian committed the crime. RECOMMENDATION: Staging is inventive, using a combination of flashback scenes and spotlighting to set the mood. This could be combined with a study of how our legal system works. ROYALTY: Free to Plays subscribers. SOURCE: Martens, Anne Coulter. (1989, March). Jury Duty. Plays: The Drama Magazine for Young People, pp. 21-30. SUBJECTS/PLAY TYPE: Judicial System, U.S.; Juries; Mystery.

1600. 12. (-) Cook, Pat. **Just desserts.** CAST: 5f, 3m. ACTS: 1. SETTINGS: Living room. PLAYING TIME: NA. PLOT: Greedy and callous relatives meet to read the Uncle's will. The deceased, who knew his relatives very well, has outfoxed them by arranging for their avarices to be rewarded. After exactly two minutes of togetherness, in which unknowingly they all get one more chance to redeem themselves, the estate is left to the deceased's fiancee who had really loved him, and to his niece, who was the only one who passed the test. RECOMMENDATION: This is a short unpleasant play with nasty characters. Even the two good characters, Viola and Theresa come across as merely dimwitted. The moral, "justice is its own reward," is presented in a heavy handed fashion with very little dramatic impact. ROYALTY: $15. SOURCE: Cook, Pat. (1986). Just desserts. Boston, MA: Baker's Plays. SUBJECTS/PLAY TYPE: Greed; Selfishness; Drama.

1601. 9-12. (+) Clepper, Patrick M. **Just for kicks.** CAST: 13f, 13m, Su. ACTS: 1. SETTINGS: High school. PLAYING TIME: NA. PLOT: A small town football team that hasn't won a game in years wins with a little feminine assistance when no male can be found to coach the seemingly hopeless group. RECOMMENDATION: High school students should readily identify with the characters and situations in this lighthearted look at high school football and its perceived importance to a student body's esteem. ROYALTY: $35. SOURCE: Clepper, Patrick M. (1975). Just for kicks. Chicago, IL: Dramatic Pub. Co. SUBJECTS/PLAY TYPE: Football; Comedy.

1602. 11-12*. (+) Barone, Robert G. **Just like old times.** CAST: 6f. ACTS: 1. SETTINGS: Bare stage, raised platform, props. PLAYING TIME: 25 min. PLOT: Five women, friends since their membership in a high school drama club, gather to pay respects to one who has died.

Old jealousies, hatreds, and spites are aired. Narration by Sharon, the deceased, provides insight. Their daily lives and current relationships, after six years, are still dominated by the values and attitudes taught to them by their high school director, Mrs. T., and the "roles" they played on the stage and backstage. The play concludes as Sharon reveals that she committed suicide in a desperate act to "cut the string" woven by her friends and mentor. RECOMMENDATION: This study of friendship, social stratification, and over-dominating influence is nonjudgmental, and therefore, most powerful. Skillfully written, it has strong characterizations and its gripping drama is dependent upon the verbal interactions of its characters. Recommended for mature audiences. ROYALTY: NA. SOURCE: Barone, Robert G. (1982). Just like old times. Schulenburg, TX: I.E. Clark. SUBJECTS/PLAY TYPE: Psychology; Friendship; Satire.

1603. 8-12. (+) Kennedy, Eddie. **Just one day.** CAST: 2f, 1m. ACTS: 1. SETTINGS: Park. PLAYING TIME: NA. PLOT: After breaking up with her boyfriend, a 16 year old discovers she is pregnant. She turns to the father to help decide whether she will keep the child, give it up for adoption, or have an abortion. The plot explores the relationship between the two young people and the effects their decisions will have on their families and futures. RECOMMENDATION: This makes no judgments on the appropriateness of the young peoples' relationship nor any of the possible options, and allows ample room for various viewpoints and discussion. ROYALTY: $20. SOURCE: Kennedy, Eddie. (1983). Just one day. Woodstock, IL: Dramatic Pub. Co. SUBJECTS/ PLAY TYPE: Birth Control; Pregnancy, Teenage; Drama.

1604. 9-12. (+) Malkind, Margaret. **Just plain folks.** CAST: 5f, 6m. ACTS: 1. SETTINGS: Living room. PLAYING TIME: 25 min. PLOT: Home for summer vacation, Stephanie tells her family that her new boyfriend, Gary, and his parents, will be visiting. She is greeted with the unusual activities of her family (Mr. Wimpole, attempting to polish the plot for his latest science fiction novel, pantomimes a duel with an imaginary foe; her brother Frank wears a surgical mask due to his germ phobia; and 80 year old Grandma Wimpole returns with Kid Carson, a professional boxer from the gym where she works). Stephanie chides her family for not being normal, and tells them that she has lied about their lifestyle; Gary thinks that Mr. Wimpole is a doctor, Grandma crochets, Mrs. Wimpole bakes cookies, and Frank plays football. For her sake, the Wimpoles agree to appear more typical. All goes well at first, but a series of comical incidents reveals the uniqueness of the Wimpole family. While Gary admires their warmth and creativity, his parents leave abruptly, insulted and shocked. Within a few moments, however, the Carsons return to apologize, admitting that everyone should choose his own lifestyle. RECOMMENDATION: The charming humor of this piece overcomes its somewhat overstated moral, as expressed in Mrs. Carson's final words. An interesting plot sets the stage for believable and dynamic characters, and the conclusion offers a refreshing portrayal of appreciation for human individuality. ROYALTY: Free to Plays subscribers. SOURCE: Malkind, Margaret. (1979,

December). Just plain folks. Plays: The Drama Magazine for Young People, pp. 11-23. SUBJECTS/PLAY TYPE: Family; Individuality; Comedy.

1605. 3-6*. (+) Smit, Andrea. (Kipling, Rudyard) **The just so letter.** (How the first letter was written.) CAST: 8f, 3m, Su. ACTS: 1. SETTINGS: Cave entrance; river. PLAYING TIME: 30 min. PLOT: When a caveman's fishing spear breaks, his daughter tries to send a message to her mother to request another. Since writing hasn't been invented yet, she draws a picture for a passing stranger to deliver. The picture is misinterpreted and the tribe prepares for war. Luckily, the head chief counsels the village to exercise restraint. The caveman and his daughter explain the real meaning of the picture and the chief recognizes that they have discovered a new method of communication. RECOMMENDATION: This is a wonderful play for grade schoolers with a plot based on an amusing misunderstanding. There are some lengthy parts for older children. ROYALTY: $15. SOURCE: Smit, Andrea. (1983). The just so letter. Chicago, IL: Dramatic Pub. Co. SUBJECTS/PLAY TYPE: Writing; Communication; Comedy; Adaptation.

1606. 10-12. (+) Smith, Campbell. **Juve.** CAST: 3f, 9m, Su. ACTS: 1. SETTINGS: Bare stage, props. PLAYING TIME: 80 min. PLOT: Through monologues, duets, trios, and choruses, teenagers explain why they are "delinquent." Although action is loosely advanced by the ringing of a school bell indicating the changes of classes, there is no typical character introduction, climax, or resolution. RECOMMENDATION: This reflects the attitudes of "street-wise" teenagers. Prostitution, homosexuality, and rape are some of the topics and graphic language is used. The play's message is delivered through a monologue interspersed with songs and "acrobatic" actions involving chairs, ladders, and other props. Performers would need to be improvisors. Its presentation would probably be most appropriate in a community theater. Some of the material would need to be updated. ROYALTY: NA. SOURCE: Smith, Campbell. (1980). Juve. Vancouver, Canada: Pulp Press. SUBJECTS/PLAY TYPE: Juvenile Delinquency; Musical.

1607. 8-12*. (+) McDonough, Jerome. **Juvie.** CAST: 6f, 2m, 2u. ACTS: 1. SETTINGS: Detention center. PLAYING TIME: 70 min. PLOT: While in a juvenile detention center, several teenagers reflect on their crimes and possible punishments. RECOMMENDATION: The teenagers leave their jail cells to act out the events which led to their incarceration (relying heavily on mime). Some may say the play is too dark; others may say it's realistic and an appropriate warning to young adults. In either case, the dialogue is captivating, and the blocking creative. ROYALTY: $35. SOURCE: McDonough, Jerome. (1984). Juvie. Schulenburg, TX: I.E. Clark. SUBJECTS/PLAY TYPE: Juvenile Delinquency; Crime and Punishment; Drama.

1608. 10-12. (+) Bradbury, Ray. **Kaleidoscope.** CAST: Su. ACTS: 1. SETTINGS: Spaceship; space. PLAYING TIME: NA. PLOT: A crew's spaceship is destroyed by a meteorite while they explore deep space. Without a chance of rescue, each reacts to the hopeless situation. RECOMMENDATION: This probes the ways in which humans face destiny and their attempts to either alter or accept it. Although it utilizes simple sets and simple dialogue, the issues addressed are probably more appropriate for a mature audience. ROYALTY: $25. SOURCE: Bradbury, Ray. (1975). Kaleidoscope. Woodstock, IL: Dramatic Pub. Co. SUBJECTS/PLAY TYPE: Science Fiction; Drama.

1609. 10-12. (+) Hischak, Thomas. **Kangaroo.** CAST: 1f, 5m. ACTS: 1. SETTINGS: Golf course. PLAYING TIME: NA. PLOT: Two old Australian gentlemen discover a corpse on the golf course and attribute it to a kangaroo attack. A voluptuous, rather loose woman (who enjoys trying to make her elderly, senile husband jealous), her male friend, and an inspector try to discover what happened. The woman's husband, who is supposedly too crazy to know what is going on, is eventually revealed to the audience as the killer kangaroo himself when he disposes of yet another of his wife's boyfriends. RECOMMENDATION: All will appreciate the British humor here. Some sexual references are made, and explicit language is used. The actors must have a fine sense of timing and the ability to deliver their lines in a dry, understated manner. ROYALTY: NA. SOURCE: Hischak, Thomas. (1977). Kangaroo. Santa Fe Springs, CA: Hunter Press. SUBJECTS/PLAY TYPE: Murder; Infidelity; Comedy.

1610. 7-9. (-) Karshner, Roger. **Kathryn and Sally.** CAST: 2f. ACTS: 1. SETTINGS: None. PLAYING TIME: NA. PLOT: Kathryn and Sally's father has left their mother for a younger woman. Sally, the older sister, wants to forgive him, but Kathryn is resentful, especially now that their mother is dying. After much shouting, Sally finally gets Kathryn to try to get rid of her anger. RECOMMENDATION: Although much of the language is raw, this is very emotional and makes its point well. ROYALTY: NA. SOURCE: Karshner, Roger. (1986). Scenes for teenagers. Toluce Lake, CA: Dramaline Pub. SUBJECTS/PLAY TYPE: Forgiveness; Scene.

1611. 9-12. (+) Firth, Mike. **The keep.** CAST: 8u. ACTS: 1. SETTINGS: Prison cell. PLAYING TIME: 30 min. PLOT: This macabre, surrealistic drama depicts the emotional reactions of prisoners to confinement as they are placed in cells. A robot like Keeper discusses the prison system of individualized punishment until his agitation renders him incapable of anything except an illogical mumble. The first cell contains an individual engaged in the perpetual shifting of three pieces of furniture. Cell Two is inhabited by a prisoner who enthralls the guard with the colorful, highly imaginative mental image he has created to broaden the horizon of his cubicle. The third vignette depicts two cellmates who wrangle with one another about the loose grille in the floor, each probing its potential for escape. The audience's impression of the value of freedom is deduced from the examination of men frantic to secure their own. A parallel theme introduces the nature of the keeper's duty, which imprisons him as well, and leads to the initial question, "Who is the real prisoner: the person locked up, or the guard who puts him there?"

RECOMMENDATION: The stark, logical dissection of human motives and the power of despair are demonstrated by shadow figures who represent the rational attempts of the mind to cope with loss of freedom. The audience must be able to derive significance from abstract imagery and symbolic ritual, or this will be dismissed as a "weird" play. ROYALTY: $15. SOURCE: Firth, Mike. (1978). The keep. Schulenburg, TX: I.E. Clark. SUBJECTS/PLAY TYPE: Prisons; Freedom; Drama.

1612. 4-12. (+) Bright, Charles. **Keep the home fires burning: A holiday melodrama in one act.** CAST: 4f, 4m, 2u. ACTS: 1. SETTINGS: Cabin. PLAYING TIME: 30 min. PLOT: Mother and daughter cannot pay the mortgage. Santa Claus saves the family homestead by giving gifts to each of the characters for answering "Let's Make a Deal" type questions. Mother Kindlady chooses the gift that exactly pays off the mortgage, Will Strongheart selects the box that makes him owner of a Brazilian aluminum mine. Mary's gift is the villain Whipley's diary, which she will turn into a smash Broadway hit. Whipley wins a bag of rocks and a consolation prize, the "yon ugly old hag," who promises to boss him forever. RECOMMENDATION: The humor lies in the parody of old fashioned melodrama. The playful use of words will make the audience listen carefully between laughs. References which date this, such as "only the Shadow knows," might be changed. ROYALTY: $10. SOURCE: Bright, Charles E. (1978). Keep the home fires burning: A holiday melodrama in one act. Denver, CO: Pioneer Drama Service. SUBJECTS/PLAY TYPE: Comedy; Christmas; Melodrama.

1613. 6-12. (+) Henderson, Nancy. (Alcott, Louisa May) **Keeping Christmas merry.** (Little women) CAST: 6f. ACTS: 1. SETTINGS: Living room. PLAYING TIME: 12 min. PLOT: This dramatizes Christmas at the March family. RECOMMENDATION: Although short and didactic, this does recapture the tone of the original. ROYALTY: NA. SOURCE: Henderson, Nancy. (1978). Celebrate America: A baker's dozen of plays. New York, NY: Messner. SUBJECTS/PLAY TYPE: Christmas; Adaptation.

1614. 5-9*. (+) Way, Brian. **The key.** CAST: 2f, 2m. ACTS: 1. SETTINGS: Bare stage, props. PLAYING TIME: 60 min. PLOT: As a community dies because of drought and encroaching desert, the families must decide whether to stay or travel to look for rain over the mountains. The narrator asks the audience to divide into families (each with a leader), and as a member of the cast, she helps the audience to reassemble, explaining that she and her mother are waiting for an expedition to return after weeks of searching for water. Two members of the expedition enter; they are the only survivors, and although they only made it half of the way, they could see clouds over the mountains. The audience/families are urged to travel to the mountains, but are warned of the dangers. The families that elect to take the trip are given instructions and mime preparations such as building wagons, digging vegetables, and packing. The precious water supply is locked in Clive's wagon for safety. The audience/families must all work together to cross a ravine, but on the other side, Lucy becomes very ill. Clive and Mike decide that Lucy must die to save water for the others, but a sudden rainstorm brings renewed hope for the journey. RECOMMENDATION: The theme that humankind will survive only with teamwork is universal and its dramatization is especially moving. This audience participation play for up to 200 5th and 6th graders will require masterful planning and control, as well as an in the round performing area to allow children to engage in the discussions and mime. ROYALTY: $20. SOURCE: Way, Brian. (1977). The key. Boston, MA: Baker's Plays. SUBJECTS/PLAY TYPE: Survival; Cooperation; Participation Play.

1615. 7-12. (+) Murray, John. **Kid Avalanche.** CAST: 8f, 3m. ACTS: 1. SETTINGS: Living room. PLAYING TIME: 30 min. PLOT: Helen Mason, a scholarship student at an all-women's college inherits a prize fighter from her long lost uncle. To escape punishment for bringing a man on campus, she disguises "Kid Avalanche" as the Spanish student expected to arrive that day. Confusion reigns as Helen tries to keep "Kid" secret from her fiance's visiting mother. At the height of the turmoil, the uncle returns and reclaims the fighter, solving everyone's problems. RECOMMENDATION: Although the situation is rather contrived and characters one dimensional, younger grades should enjoy the visual humor in this play. ROYALTY: Free to Plays subscribers. SOURCE: Murray, John. (1981, March). Kid Avalanche. Plays: The Drama Magazine for Young People, pp. 23-34. SUBJECTS/PLAY TYPE: Inheritances; Sororities; Comedy.

1616. 7-12. (-) Murray, John. **Kiddie matinee.** CAST: 1f. ACTS: 1. SETTINGS: Bare stage. PLAYING TIME: NA. PLOT: As a woman tries to find her son at the horror movie matinee, she gets into some embarrassing situations. RECOMMENDATION: Weak humor and uninteresting characterization make this a poor choice. ROYALTY: None. SOURCE: Murray, John. (1982). Modern monologues for young people. Boston: Plays, Inc. SUBJECTS/PLAY TYPE: Comedy; Movie Theaters; Monologue.

1617. 4-8. (+) Robinette, Joseph & Jurman, Karl. **Kiddledywinks!** CAST: 3f, 4m, Su. ACTS: 1. SETTINGS: Bedroom; playground; classroom. PLAYING TIME: 50 min. PLOT: In short vignettes, the experiences of a typical school day are woven together by a small group of elementary school children. Songs and dialogue highlight their early rising, desire for a best friend, private enterprise, an unprepared school assignment, the terror of a school bully, and their ideas on death and adoption. The children are shown working together on their school play and making a sling shot to send them into outer space. RECOMMENDATION: This musical effectively explores many of young school children's problems. The vignette on death and adoption needs additional discussion. ROYALTY: $50. SOURCE: Robinette, Joseph & Jurman, Karl. (1983). Kiddledywinks! Woodstock, IL: Dramatic Pub. Co. SUBJECTS/PLAY TYPE: School; Death; Adoption; Musical.

1618. 7-12*. (+) Mason, Timothy. **Kidnapped in London.** CAST: 4f, 11m, Su. ACTS: 3. SETTINGS: Marketplace; tavern; prison; theater. PLAYING TIME: NA. PLOT: Corin Marvell is kidnapped by actors while visiting London. Although he is a good actor, he wishes to return home. When Burbage, his keeper, is jailed, he frees Corin, but the boy chooses to remain a part of the city life. RECOMMENDATION: The dialogue is well written, capturing the flavor of Elizabethan England, while still holding the attention of modern audiences. This includes songs, dance, music, and pantomime, and would best be presented to children. ROYALTY: NA. SOURCE: Donahue, John Clark & Jenkins, Linda Walsh. (1972). Five plays from the children's theatre company of Minneapolis. Minneapolis, MN: Univ. of Minnesota Press. SUBJECTS/PLAY TYPE: Actors; Elizabethan England; Theater, Elizabethan; Musical.

1619. 1-9*. (+) Kochiss, Joseph P. **The kids from Camelot.** CAST: 7f, 11m, Su. ACTS: 1. SETTINGS: Camelot. PLAYING TIME: 60 min. PLOT: Guinevere's sister is kidnapped by King Arthur's wicked sister. The young pages in training are assigned to locate and return her. With the help of Merlin the magician and the young ladies of the court, the pages succeed and are promoted to squires amid much singing, dancing and rivalry. RECOMMENDATION: Loosely based on the famous King Arthur tales, the play's use of music to further the plot and the sophisticated language necessitates performance by high schoolers or adults, with children filling some of the minor roles. A subplot which involves boy-girl rivalry, as the boys claim that the girls are too feminine to help, adds spark to the plot which is primarily a vehicle for the music. ROYALTY: $90. SOURCE: Kochiss, Joseph P. (1985). The kids from Camelot. Franklin, OH: Eldridge Pub. Co. SUBJECTS/PLAY TYPE: Knights; Musical.

1620. 1-4. (+) Clary, Roger M. **Kidsville U.S.A.** CAST: 2f, 4m, 7u. ACTS: 2. SETTINGS: Main street. PLAYING TIME: 45 min. PLOT: Jody and Robin are given a magic wand which will hypnotize any adult. The children promptly zap the grownups and eat all the ice cream and candy they can. Soon, everyone has a stomach ache and no one wants to take charge. In the confusion, a telegram arrives, informing the relieved kids that their magic wand has been recalled because the effects wear off. RECOMMENDATION: This pleasant play brings to life the dream that many children have of being in charge; yet emphasizes the sense of security that comes with the return to normalcy. The play is designed to involve large groups of different aged children. In addition to the thirteen short speaking roles, verses are recited by a chorus of any size. ROYALTY: $40. SOURCE: Clary, Roger M. (1975). Franklin, OH: Eldridge Pub. Co. SUBJECTS/PLAY TYPE: Fantasy; Dreams; Operetta.

1621. 9-12. (+) Murray, John. **Killer on the prowl.** CAST: 3f, 4m. ACTS: 1. SETTINGS: Office. PLAYING TIME: 30 min. PLOT: Two secretaries try to solve the mystery of their friend's murder by investigating the scene of the crime. The killer returns, attacks one of the secretaries, and is captured by the police. RECOMMENDATION: The two secretaries are interesting characters, as is the killer, whose motives come from his entrapment in an untenable living situation. Some references to old style elevators and night telephone lines might have to be modernized. ROYALTY: Free to Plays subscribers. SOURCE: Murray, John. (1986, April). Killer on the prowl. Plays: The Drama Magazine for Young People, pp. 9-17. SUBJECTS/PLAY TYPE: Mystery; Murder.

1622. 3-8. (+) Thane, Adele. (Kipling, Rudyard) Kim. (Kim) CAST: 1f, 11m. ACTS: 3. SETTINGS: Public square; house; grove. PLAYING TIME: 30 min. PLOT: Kim, the orphaned son of a soldier, and Teshoo Lama, a holy man, travel together, respectively seeking a Red Bull and the sacred River of the Arrow. They discover a regiment with a flag that has a Red Bull on it. Colonel Creighton, the regiment's commander, recognizes Kim as the son of O'Hara, a soldier who served in his regiment, promises to care for Kim, and send him to school. The Lama offers to pay for Kim's education to ensure that he be sent to the best school. Sadly, Kim says goodbye to Lama, but promises they will meet again to seek the River of the Arrow during his school vacations. RECOMMENDATION: This adaptation familiarizes its audience with the history and traditions of British India. Several Indian terms may need to be explained and this would work best if performed by students in grades 6-8. ROYALTY: Free to Plays subscribers. SOURCE: Thane, Adele. (1976, May). Kim. Plays: The Drama Magazine for Young People, pp. 83-92. SUBJECTS/PLAY TYPE: Adventure; India; Adaptation.

1623. 7-9. (-) Karshner, Roger. Kim and Janet. CAST: 2f. ACTS: 1. SETTINGS: None. PLAYING TIME: NA. PLOT: Janet and Kim have wrecked Kim's father's car and try to decide what story to tell him, since the truth (Kim was changing a cassette and ran into a cement wall) will get them into trouble. They decide to tell Kim's mother that Kim was trying to avoid hitting an old woman, in hopes that Kim's mother will avert their punishment. RECOMMENDATION: This seems to glorify lying and avoidance instead of responsibility for one's actions. ROYALTY: NA. SOURCE: Karshner, Roger. (1986). Scenes for teenagers. Toluce Lake, CA: Dramaline Pub. SUBJECTS/PLAY TYPE: Honesty/Dishonesty; Scene.

1624. 3-6. (+) Thane, Adele. King Alfred and the cakes. CAST: 3f, 6m. ACTS: 1. SETTINGS: Kitchen. PLAYING TIME: 15 min. PLOT: In 9th century England, a farmer's wife prepares dinner for the family while baby Alfred sleeps in his cradle. The children return with a visitor, who assures the family that he is not a dreaded Dane and offers to mind the baby and cook dinner while they all finish their chores. The family returns to find that he has let the cakes burn, but before they can exclaim over this, two soldiers come to the door looking for the king: the mysterious visitor. In payment for their hospitality, the king gives the farmer the land his farm is on, and the two depart with the soldiers to do battle against the Danes. RECOMMENDATION: Used to reinforce a lesson on

Anglo-Saxon history, this will bring life to the past. Easy to stage, children will enjoy the constant action such as churning butter, baking, and carrying torches. The conventional dialogue is nicely broken up by the King's poetic message of hope and peace to the baby, recited with harp music. ROYALTY: Free to Plays subscribers. SOURCE: Thane, Adele. (1983). Plays from famous stories and fairy tales. Boston: Plays, Inc. SUBJECTS/PLAY TYPE: Folk Tale Motifs; Hospitality; Playlet.

1625. K-3*. (+) Barnett, Robert J. King Cole and the country witches. CAST: 8f, 9m, 2u. ACTS: 3. SETTINGS: Ballroom; witch's den. PLAYING TIME: 55 min. PLOT: An evil witch who hates fun, laughter, and bravery tries to conquer Old King Cole's Kingdom of Gamin, where no one is ever sad and every day is a party. Well known Mother Goose characters (i.e Little Boy Blue, Bo Peep, Jack and Jill) save the kingdom by being brave, and King Cole banishes the evil witch, reestablishing happiness. RECOMMENDATION: Young children will enjoy the audience participation here as well as the use of the Mother Goose characters. However, the music and songs are not an integral part of the play and seem almost to be an afterthought. ROYALTY: $50. SOURCE: Barnett, Robert J. (1977). King Cole and the country witches. Chicago, IL: Dramatic Pub. Co. SUBJECTS/PLAY TYPE: Mother Goose Characters; Witches; Musical.

1626. 5-7. (+) Holmes, Ruth Vickery. King John and the Abbot of Canterbury. CAST: 7m, Su. ACTS: 1. SETTINGS: Road; throne room. PLAYING TIME: 20 min. PLOT: A shepherd taking his sheep to the Abbey almost hits the king with his staff. The king agrees to spare his life if the shepherd will send him the Abbot in three days. When the Abbot arrives, the king tells him that he has been spending too lavishly and must die, unless the Abbot can answer three questions within two weeks. When neither the Abbot nor the scholars at Oxford and Cambridge can find answers, the shepherd asks to impersonate the Abbot and answer the questions (how long will the king live, how soon the king will ride around the world, and what the king thinks). All ends well when the shepherd cleverly answers the questions (the king will live until he takes his last breath, if he rides from sun up to sun up, he will have ridden around the world in 24 hours, and the king thinks that the disguised shepherd is the Abbot). RECOMMENDATION: The dialogue preserves the flavor of Medieval dialect, and the message that the uneducated deserve as much respect as the overeducated is well worth presenting. ROYALTY: Free to Plays subscribers. SOURCE: Kamerman, Sylvia E. (1987). Plays from favorite folk tales. Boston, MA: Plays, Inc. SUBJECTS/PLAY TYPE: Legends, England; Playlet.

1627. 4-8. (+) Garnder, Mercedes & Smith, Jean Shannon. King Midas. CAST: 1f, 2m, 1u. ACTS: 1. SETTINGS: Palace. PLAYING TIME: 30 min. PLOT: Greedy King Midas is given the power to turn all he touches into gold but is heartbroken when he turns his only daughter into gold. He begs the gods to relieve him of his powers and the request is granted. He is punished for his greed by having to go through the rest of life with the ears of a donkey. RECOMMENDATION: Staging the alchemistry will require some creativity, but otherwise, this should pose no production problems. ROYALTY: Free to Plays subscribers. SOURCE: Gardner, Mercedes & Smith, Jean Shannon. (1980, March). King Midas. Plays: The Drama Magazine for Young People, pp. 45-64. SUBJECTS/PLAY TYPE: Mythology, Greek; Greed; Playlet.

1628. K-3*. (+) Simms, Willard. **King Midas and the golden touch.** CAST: 1f, 3u. ACTS: 1. SETTINGS: Throne room. PLAYING TIME: 30 min. PLOT: King Midas, greedy for more gold, has a sorceress cast a magical spell on him so that everything he touches will turn into gold. But the king learns his lesson when he kisses his beloved daughter, and she turns into a golden statue. RECOMMENDATION: Young children will enjoy the magic tricks, special effects, and audience participation. ROYALTY: $10. SOURCE: Simms, Willard. (1977). King Midas and the golden touch. Denver, CO: Pioneer Drama Service. SUBJECTS/PLAY TYPE: Magic; Greed; Mythology, Greek; Drama.

1629. 9-12. (+) Milton, Polsky & Lightman, Aaron. **King of escapes.** CAST: 2f, 4m, Su. ACTS: 2. SETTINGS: Factory; dining room; rooftop; dressing room; jail; vaudeville hall. PLAYING TIME: NA. PLOT: Much to his family's chagrin, Eric Weiss quits his job in a tie factory, announces that he has changed his name to Harry Houdini, and embarks on a new career in vaudeville, first partnered with his brother, then with his wife, Bess. The action follows Bess and Harry through their cross-country carnival travels. They and other carnies are arrested for performing on Sunday, but they are released when Harry demonstrates his escape artistry. Harry and Bess hit rock bottom when a carnival manager runs off with their money, but they are saved by a letter from Tony Parker asking them to perform in New York, where their "magic trunk" trick is a success. The play closes on a warm reunion with family and friends. RECOMMENDATION: Houdini's magic and escape tricks are sophisticated, but should be manageable with able direction and rehearsal. A list of magical tricks/effects and props is included, and some singing and dancing will be required of those playing vaudevillian roles. ROYALTY: NA. SOURCE: Polsky, Milton & Lightman, Aaron. (1983). The king of escapes. Studio City, CA: Players Press. SUBJECTS/PLAY TYPE: Houdini, Harry; Magic; Escape Artists; Musical.

1630. 9-12. (-) Merten, George. **The King of Puppetania.** CAST: 3f, 5m. ACTS: 1. SETTINGS: Palace. PLAYING TIME: NA. PLOT: A king cannot find a husband for his ugly daughter, so the local witch exchanges the head of her own daughter for that of the princess. RECOMMENDATION: The dated humor in this hand puppet play for adults and older children makes it very unsuccessful. ROYALTY: None. SOURCE: Merten, George. (1979). Plays for puppet performance. Boston, MA: Plays, Inc. SUBJECTS/PLAY TYPE: Witchery; Comedy; Puppet Play.

1631. 5-9. (+) Deary, Terence. **The King of Tarantulus.** CAST: 2f, 2m. ACTS: 1. SETTINGS: Garden. PLAYING TIME: 40 min. PLOT: Notta Goody, bad tempered sister of

Gloria Goody, is frozen when the evil King of Tarantulus places his tarantula ring on her finger. A mysterious stranger, Angelo, tells Notta and the children that the King's power will be destroyed if they think good thoughts. This is not easy for Notta because good thoughts are alien to her character. With a little encouragement from the children, however, goodness prevails. RECOMMENDATION: The children are asked to look at the eternal conflict between good and evil by identifying with the characters and relating their behavior to their own lives. ROYALTY: None. SOURCE: Deary, Terence. (1977). Teaching through theatre. London, England: Samuel French. SUBJECTS/PLAY TYPE: Magic; Fantasy; Good and Evil; Participation Play.

1632. 3-6. (+) Mahlman, Lewis & Platt, Pat. (Ruskin, John) **King of the golden river.** (King of the golden river) CAST: 9u. ACTS: 1. SETTINGS: Bare stage, props. PLAYING TIME: 20 min. PLOT: A kind hearted young man lives with his selfish older brother, who angers the West Wind, who destroys their crops in retaliation. The King of the Golden River tells the young man that if he pours three drops of water into the dried up river bed, it will turn to gold, but warns that if he fails he will be turned to stone. The older brother insists on trying, but he refuses to share his water with the criminals he meets on his way to the river (thus contaminating it), and therefore fails the test. When the younger brother walks to the river, he shares his water, and so is successful in turning the river to gold. The crops are saved. RECOMMENDATION: This superior dramatization is complete with mugs that turn into magical people, crickets that talk, and a wonderfully personified West wind. ROYALTY: Free to Plays subscribers. SOURCE: Mahlman, Lewis & Platt, Pat. (1975, February). King of the golden river. Plays: The Drama Magazine for Young People, pp. 79-84. SUBJECTS/PLAY TYPE: Puppet Play; Selfishness; Adaptation.

1633. 7-12. (+) Kelly, Tim. (Ruskin, John) **King of the golden river.** (The king of the golden river) CAST: Su. ACTS: 2. SETTINGS: Hut; forest. PLAYING TIME: 60 min. PLOT: While his older brothers leave Dick at home alone, he gives the Southwest Wind shelter and something to eat. The brothers are furious with Dick for letting a stranger into their home and insist that the stranger leave. In retaliation, the Wind takes away his protective powers for the valley and everything dies. The brothers demand that Dick melt his golden cup into spoons so they can pay the rent. The enchanted King of the Golden River comes to life when the mug is melted and tells Dick how to turn the river into gold. His brothers try to beat Dick by following the instructions themselves, but cannot succeed because they are not kind; only Dick has the power to restore the valley's lushness. RECOMMENDATION: Flexible casting will allow for 10-25 children to participate in this delightful production. ROYALTY: NA. SOURCE: Kelly, Tim. (1984). King of the golden river. Droitwich, England: Hanbury Plays. SUBJECTS/PLAY TYPE: Adventure; Adaptation.

1634. 6-10. (-) Bayer, Harold. (Grimm Brothers) **King Thrushbeard.** (King Thrushbeard) CAST: 1f, 2m, 2u.

ACTS: 1. SETTINGS: Palace; hut; town square; forest. PLAYING TIME: 30 min. PLOT: When a proud princess rejects all her suitors, her father gives her to the first beggar he sees: a passing minstrel. When the minstrel finds her unable to sew or cook, he sends her to sell pots, but a soldier smashes them. The minstrel then sends her to help the palace cook, and her pride is broken when she realizes that her ineptness is spoiling King Thrushbeard's wedding feast. King Thrushbeard, one of the princess' rejected suitors, reveals himself as the disguised minstrel, and agrees to marry the now humble princess. RECOMMENDATION: The humor relies on sophisticated asides and references to folk tale characters which younger children might not understand. Also, the overt message that women should be servile is not appropriate. ROYALTY: NA. SOURCE: Bayer, Harold. (1982). Motley tales: A collection of folk and fairy tales with music. Boston, MA: Baker's Plays. SUBJECTS/PLAY TYPE: Folk Tales, Germany; Snobbishness; Adaptation.

1635. K-3. (+) Very, Alice. **King Winter**. CAST: 25u. ACTS: 1. SETTINGS: Bare stage, props. PLAYING TIME: 10 min. PLOT: As King Winter tries to intimidate them, the children defeat him with their joyful winter sports. Finally, spring arrives. RECOMMENDATION: This poetic piece should be read as the children mime the action. ROYALTY: Free to Plays subscribers. SOURCE: Very, Alice. (1977, January). King Winter. Plays: The Drama Magazine for Young People, pp. 76-80. SUBJECTS/PLAY TYPE: Winter; Creative Dramatics.

1636. K-6. (+) Lahr, Georgiana Lieder. **The kingdom of hearts**. CAST: 7f, 7m, Su. ACTS: 1. SETTINGS: Throne room. PLAYING TIME: 15 min. PLOT: Someone has stolen the Queen of Hearts' tarts. The thief must be found, the recipient of the "Royal Award of the Loving Heart" must be chosen, and a decision must be made as to who will be the Valentine's Day entertainment. Jack Frost and King Winter help. RECOMMENDATION: Production should be by children in at least fourth grade, with the youngest children participating by singing the song at the end. The director is free to choose any Valentine's Day song and poem, making this very flexible and delightful. ROYALTY: Free to Plays subscribers. SOURCE: Lahr, Georgiana Lieder. (1979, February). The kingdom of hearts. Plays: The Drama Magazine for Young People, pp. 41-44. SUBJECTS/PLAY TYPE: Valentine's Day; Skit.

1637. 2-3. (+) Merten, Elizabeth. **The king's dinner**. CAST: 3m, 1u. ACTS: 1. SETTINGS: Kitchen. PLAYING TIME: NA. PLOT: A page repeatedly tricks two cooks into baking tarts for the king's dessert. However, he eats the tarts himself. RECOMMENDATION: Simple, straight-forward language preserves the humor in this easily produced play. ROYALTY: None. SOURCE: Merten, George. (1979). Plays for puppet performance. Boston, MA: Plays, Inc. SUBJECTS/PLAY TYPE: Comedy; Trickery; Puppet Play.

1638. 3-8. (+) Blumenfeld, Lenore. **The king's dreams**. CAST: 1f, 5m, 1u. ACTS: 1. SETTINGS: Bare stage, backdrops. PLAYING TIME: 20 min. PLOT: A Russian king seeks to have his dreams interpreted by a simple peasant. He finds a dishonest laborer, who is able to interpret the king's dreams only because he has stolen their meanings from a wise serpent. The laborer is exposed and the serpent becomes the Royal Dream Interpreter. RECOMMENDATION: Physical comedy, such as the king's sleep walking and his advisors' mimicking of Cossack dancers, provide wonderful slapstick humor as the themes of good triumphing over evil and the value of promises kept are presented here. There are references to secret police and enemies of the state, and the use of a serpent may be unacceptable for some viewers. A brief explanation of the Russian background will aid audience comprehension. ROYALTY: Free to Plays subscribers. SOURCE: Blumenfeld, Lenore. (1976, November). The king's dreams. Plays: The Drama Magazine for Young People, pp. 39-46. SUBJECTS/PLAY TYPE: Dreams; Playlet.

1639. 4-6. (+) Watts, Frances B. **The king's valentine tarts**. CAST: 5f, 4m. ACTS: 1. SETTINGS: Kitchen. PLAYING TIME: 15 min. PLOT: The Queen of Hearts is interrupted in her annual task of baking Valentine tarts for the King by a peddler with enticing baubles. She orders the cook to bake the tarts, who orders the maid to do it, who prevails upon the jester, who convinces the chimney sweep. When the King discovers the switch, he furiously demands to know why. The chimney sweep blames the jester, who blames the maid, who blames the cook, who blames the Queen. The King threatens to punish everyone involved, since the tarts are not fit to eat. The jester convinces the King to try one. It is delicious, and the day is saved. RECOMMENDATION: The jester (who has to somersault) is a most interesting character, and this could stimulate discussion about the consequences of jumping to conclusions, class prejudice, or shirking of responsibility. ROYALTY: Free to Plays subscribers. SOURCE: Watt, Frances B. (1987, January/February). The king's valentine tarts. Plays: The Drama Magazine for Young People, pp. 40-46. SUBJECTS/PLAY TYPE: Valentine's Day; Playlet.

1640. K-6*. (-) Wylie, Betty Jane. **Kingsayer**. CAST: 2f, 2m, Su. ACTS: 1. SETTINGS: Schoolroom; playground; outside. PLAYING TIME: NA. PLOT: Mary decides that she never wants to grow up and she escapes reality for the child's world of the "boy with a smile." Her over protective parents remember their childhood, find Mary, and convince her that growing up isn't so bad. She returns after they promise to relax and let her be herself. RECOMMENDATION: This is full of children's games and rhymes, but it may be too symbolic for the very young. ROYALTY: NA. SOURCE: Wylie, Betty Jane. (1978). The old woman and the pedlar and kingsayer. Toronto, Canada: Playwrights Co-op. SUBJECTS/PLAY TYPE: Growing Up; Playlet.

1641. 7-12. (+) Peterson, Gary & Byrne, David. **Klondike Kalamity**. CAST: 3f, 6m, 1u. ACTS: 3. SETTINGS: Cabin; sawmill. PLAYING TIME: NA. PLOT: Warren Oudt, lost since April when he went out for cigarettes and a newspaper, returns home to find his daughter out of food and talking to a bear. Warren's long lost wife and other daughter return and reveal that Fangduster (the villain) was behind their disappearance many years before. This comes complete with a sawmill scene in which Gwendolyn, Nellie's long lost sister, is almost chewed up by a saw before she is saved by her beloved. In the end, Warren gets his wife and daughter back, Nellie gets Roger B. Upright, and Fangduster gets tried by Justice Dunn, who just happens to be in the territory. RECOMMENDATION: This is hilarious, complete with word plays, slapstick, and ridiculous coincidences. ROYALTY: $35. SOURCE: Peterson, Gary & Byrne, David. (1978). Klondike Kalamity. Chicago, IL: Dramatic Pub. Co. SUBJECTS/PLAY TYPE: Comedy; Melodrama.

1642. K-3. (+) Bauer, Caroline Feller. (Lester, Julius) **The knee-high man.** (The knee-high man and other tales) CAST: 4m, 2u. ACTS: 1. SETTINGS: None. PLAYING TIME: NA. PLOT: The knee-high man asks several animals what he should eat to make him grow, but after a succession of stomach aches, he takes the owl's suggestion to accept himself the way he is. RECOMMENDATION: Self acceptance is suggested without didacticism. ROYALTY: NA. SOURCE: Bauer, Caroline Feller. (1987). Presenting reader's theater: Plays and poems to read aloud. New York, NY: H.W. Wilson. SUBJECTS/PLAY TYPE: Self Acceptance; Reader's Theater; Adaptation.

1643. 9-12. (+) Burleson, Noyce. (Beaumont, Francis & Fletcher, John) **The knight of the burning pestle.** (The knight of the burning pestle.) CAST: 3f, 10m, 1u. ACTS: 1. SETTINGS: Two homes; forest. PLAYING TIME: NA. PLOT: Before the Elizabethan play begins, a couple in the audience petition for a role for their young apprentice, as well as for a more common touch to the play. As the romance itself unfolds on stage, George and his wife encourage Ralph and his squire as they strive to provide a happy ending for the play. RECOMMENDATION: Although the citizen, his wife, and Ralph are humorous characters, the difficulty of production, sets, costumes, and Elizabethan dialects make this hard to produce, and especially hard to understand. The audience will need to learn much vocabulary prior to production. ROYALTY: $20. SOURCE: Burleson, Noyce. (1981). The knight of the burning pestle. Chicago, IL: Dramatic Pub. Co. SUBJECTS/PLAY TYPE: Farce; Adaptation.

1644. 9-12. (+) Hamlett, Christina. **The knight of the honest heart.** CAST: 1f, 1m. ACTS: 1. SETTINGS: Forest. PLAYING TIME: 20 min. PLOT: Sir Crispin takes Lady Elaine to his king's castle, as she is betrothed to the king, though she has never seen him. Sir Crispin falls in love with her during the journey, and though he is afraid to tell her, he hints by replying discouragingly to her questions about the king. Finally, the young woman admits that she is not the real Lady Elaine, but only her lady in waiting. Crispin also confesses that he is not really a knight, that he simply wanted a glimpse of the Lady he had heard so much about. A happy ending results as the couple realizes their love for one another. RECOMMENDATION: Two delightfully developed characters play out this pleasant story of young love and youthful desire for adventure. ROYALTY: Free to Plays subscribers. SOURCE: Hamlett, Christina. (1980, January). The knight of the honest heart. Plays: The Drama Magazine for Young People, pp. 11-16.

SUBJECTS/PLAY TYPE: Mistaken Identity; Romance; Playlet.

1645. 2-4. (+) Silverman, Eleanor. **Knock, knock, who's there?** CAST: 1f, 1m, 7u. ACTS: 3. SETTINGS: Living room; lane. PLAYING TIME: 10 min. PLOT: The children are frightened by a ghost in a haunted house. With the help of a detective who unmasks the ghost, they find the treasure of Confederate money. The ghost hasn't really harmed anyone and is not punished, since wasting so much of her time has been punishment enough. RECOMMENDATION: Situations and characters are convincing and the children's names are interestingly unusual. The play ends on a pleasant note of compassion, tolerance, and understanding. ROYALTY: NA. SOURCE: Silverman, Eleanor. (1983). Dramatics for children. Metuchen, NJ: Scarecrow Press. SUBJECTS/PLAY TYPE: Haunted Houses; Ghosts; Treasure; Mystery.

1646. 9-12. (+) Kelly, Tim. **Krazy kamp.** CAST: 13f, 8m, 4u. ACTS: 2. SETTINGS: Office; tent. PLAYING TIME: 120 min. PLOT: Camp Pocahontas is a well maintained summer camp for young ladies, situated next to Camp John Smith, a run down camp for unruly boys. Adam Apple, the wheeler dealer director of the boys' camp, convinces Eve Hunnicutt, the industrious director of Camp Pocahontas, that the girls' camp facilities can be shared by the boys during the renovation and cleaning of the boys' camp. Vivian, a malicious camper, and Hildegard, a camp counselor who is frustrated by her unsuccessful bid for camp director, conspire to inform the camp owner of the unusual arrangement. A runaway girl substitutes herself for a lovesick camper, Adam Apple substitutes Camp John Smith signs for Camp Pocahontas signs so the boys' camp will pass state inspection, and a carnival worker substitutes a basket of snakes for a gangster's money. When Camp Pocahontas is condemned by the state inspector, the girls decide to take revenge on the boys by moving in with them. RECOMMENDATION: Though the ending is somewhat weak, the diverse, well defined personalities of the characters provide opportunities for creativity. The numerous subplots, fast paced action, and comic dialogue require well disciplined and experienced performers. ROYALTY: $35. SOURCE: Kelly, Tim. (1980). Krazy kamp. Denver, CO: Pioneer Drama Service. SUBJECTS/PLAY TYPE: Camps; Comedy.

1647. K-6. (+) Martin, Judith & Ashwander, Donald. **La la I.** CAST: 4u. ACTS: 1. SETTINGS: None. PLAYING TIME: 10 min. PLOT: As a quartet enters a bare stage, each member sings a simple series of notes in turn while he walks across the stage. When the fourth, who is loud and off key, begins his series of notes, the others remain polite, but appear startled. After two similar sequences of notes, the actors exit one at a time, singing. The fourth person, realizing he has the stage to himself, imitates a "pop singer gone wild," and must be dragged off stage midsong. RECOMMENDATION: This works well as a musical bridge between skits, or between scene changes of a longer production. It requires some singing ability. ROYALTY: NA. SOURCE: Martin, Judith & Ashwander, Donald. (1985). Reasons to be cheerful: A revue for children. New York, NY: The Paper Bag Players, Inc. SUBJECTS/PLAY TYPE: Comedy; Skit; Musical Revue.

1648. K-4. (+) Martin, Judith & Ashwander, Donald. **La la II. CAST:** 4u. **ACTS:** 1. **SETTINGS:** None. **PLAYING TIME:** 10 min. **PLOT:** Four actors enter singing the same tune as in La La I (previous entry), encouraging the audience to sing with them. After several verses, the music stops, but the fourth actor begins to sing wildly (again). The others look shocked, but join in with their own loud singing. They exit, leaving the fourth singer to end with a final operatic gesture. **RECOMMENDATION:** Simple enough for even the youngest children to perform, this will help actors become comfortable singing before an audience. **ROYALTY:** NA. **SOURCE:** Martin, Judith & Ashwander, Donald. (1985). Reasons to be cheerful: A revue for children. New York, NY: The Paper Bag Players, Inc. SUBJECTS/PLAY TYPE: Comedy; Skit; Musical Revue.

1649. 4-6*. (+) Way, Brian. **The ladder. CAST:** 2f, 2m. **ACTS:** 1. **SETTINGS:** Mountaintop. **PLAYING TIME:** 55 min. **PLOT:** Three people climb to the top of a mountain, on which is a mysterious ladder, guarded by a mystical keeper, who, legend says, will grant any tenacious climber the opportunity to live out a fantasy of his own choosing. Each of the climbers' fantasies is granted: heroically rescuing other climbers, leading a peasants' revolt, and forcing mercy from unsympathetic employers. At the end, they all learn that every person has his own ladder, and with perseverance and the help of friends, all people can make their dreams come true. **RECOMMENDATION:** Written to be produced by adults or talented teenagers, members of the audience provide sound effects and are recruited for nonspeaking roles. The underlying theme of justice and freedom from tyranny is well presented; the message that each person controls his/her own destiny is well crafted. **ROYALTY:** $20. **SOURCE:** Way, Brian. (1977). The ladder. Boston, MA: Baker's Plays. SUBJECTS/PLAY TYPE: Participation Play; Justice; Self Determination; Drama.

1650. 3-5. (+) Dias, Earl J. **The lady and the pirate. CAST:** 1f, 7m. **ACTS:** 1. **SETTINGS:** Ship's cabin. **PLAYING TIME:** 30 min. **PLOT:** A devious plot to rob the ship's captain and trick his daughter into marriage is foiled by the good guys; the villain is caught, and the hero gets the girl. **RECOMMENDATION:** While the conclusion seems obvious from the start, this is still enjoyable because of the pirate angle. **ROYALTY:** Free to Plays subscribers. **SOURCE:** Dias, Earl J. (1980, March). The lady and the pirate. Plays: The Drama Magazine for Young People, pp. 23-30. SUBJECTS/PLAY TYPE: Adventure; Pirates; Playlet.

1651. 9-12. (+) Dumont, Howard & Judson, Tom. **Lady Dither's ghost. CAST:** 2f, 4m, 6u. **ACTS:** 1. **SETTINGS:** Sherlock Holmes' home; castle. **PLAYING TIME:** 60 min. **PLOT:** The elderly and delightful Lady Dithers asks Holmes to help her quiet some noisy ghosts in her castle. Holmes learns that the butler, two distant cousins, and the niece, all stand to benefit if Lady Dithers moves from the castle. He suspects the ghosts may not be what they seem,

and through the power of deduction, the "ghost" (really the distant cousin) is soon caught. Lady Dithers is then able to turn the castle into an orphanage as she had planned. **RECOMMENDATION:** The many props and physical interactions between Holmes and Dr. Watson which will require practice. Also, Holmes plays the violin and creates a chemical concoction that smokes and changes colors. Children from the audience may be selected to play small roles. This should be produced by older grades. **ROYALTY:** $50. **SOURCE:** Dumont, Howard & Judson, Tom. (1986). Lady Dither's ghost. Schulenburg, TX: I.E. Clark. SUBJECTS/PLAY TYPE: Mystery; Comedy; Ghosts; Musical.

1652. 9-12. (+) Kelly, Tim. **Lady Dracula. CAST:** 7f, 5m, 4u. **ACTS:** 2. **SETTINGS:** Library. **PLAYING TIME:** 120 min. **PLOT:** Four students arrive at Malice House Academy, a private school in an old mansion owned by Mina Alucard (Lady Dracula). One student mysteriously disappears after capturing a flesh eating bat for a science project. Two police inspectors, a faculty member, and a doctor who specializes in blood diseases, and Van Helsing, an authority on vampires, join the search for the missing student. When he appears and then disappears again, the search changes to one for the daylight hiding place of Lady Dracula. Lady Dracula is finally found, overpowered by Van Helsing, and beheaded. **RECOMMENDATION:** Although the ending is macabre, the familiar quest for the evil vampire is sprinkled with comic relief in the form of a demented girl who eats flies and a pair of none too bright police inspectors. Numerous hand and stage props, lighting requirements, and special sound and visual effects seem necessary for an effectively frightening atmosphere, but might challenge some resources. **ROYALTY:** $35. **SOURCE:** Kelly, Tim. (1980). Lady Dracula. Denver, CO: Pioneer Drama Service. SUBJECTS/PLAY TYPE: Comedy; Horror; Vampires; Drama.

1653. 1-6. (+) Tutt, Barbara. **Lady in the sky. CAST:** 6f, 3m, Su. **ACTS:** 3. **SETTINGS:** Porch. **PLAYING TIME:** 20 min. **PLOT:** Katherine Stinson, a lady pilot in 1917, is prohibited from joining the army because she is female. Undaunted, she helps the Red Cross War Relief by flying all over the country to collect contributions. In the final scene, she is congratulated by friends and neighbors. **RECOMMENDATION:** This is an interesting look at the fourth licensed female pilot in the U.S. and the difficulty that women had breaking into male dominated occupations. It will provoke interesting discussions concerning equality of the sexes and the need to use every person's talents to the fullest potential. **ROYALTY:** Free to Plays subscribers. **SOURCE:** Tutt, Barbara. (1988, April). Lady in the sky. Plays: The Drama Magazine for Young People, pp. 29-34. SUBJECTS/PLAY TYPE: Women's Rights; Pilots; Stinson, Katherine; Playlet.

1654. 5-12. (+) Wilde, Oscar. **Lady Windmere's fan. CAST:** 1f, 1m. **ACTS:** 1. **SETTINGS:** Morning room. **PLAYING TIME:** NA. **PLOT:** Lord Windmere hopes to keep Mrs. Erlynne's identity a secret (she is his unsavory mother-in-law) and forbids her to see his wife. She comes to say goodbye to her daughter, resolving to leave because feelings of remorse or compassion are too painful a price to pay for "having a heart." RECOMMENDATION: This might be particularly disturbing to adopted children and may cause them to question the motives or credibility of those they love. However, it does have potential for helping children to understand their adopted friends. ROYALTY: NA. SOURCE: Olfson, Lewy. (1980). Fifty great scenes for student actors. New York, NY: Bantam Books. SUBJECTS/PLAY TYPE: Ethics; Values; Scene.

1655. 9-12. (+) O'Morrison, Kevin. **Ladyhouse blues.** CAST: 6f, 6m. ACTS: 2. SETTINGS: Kitchen. PLAYING TIME: NA. PLOT: In 1919, each of four daughters finds herself drawn to a different life style. The mother desires to keep them as they were raised, but knows this cannot be. When the son/brother dies fighting for his country, news of his death releases built up tensions and allows each to feel free to escape to her own future world. RECOMMENDATION: The focus of this excellent drama shifts from one character to another as each struggles for identity. ROYALTY: $50. SOURCE: O'Morrison, Kevin. (1979). Ladyhouse blues: A full length play for women. New York, NY: Samuel French. SUBJECTS/PLAY TYPE: Women's Rights; Identity; Drama.

1656. 9-12. (+) Kelly, Tim. **Laffing room only.** CAST: 4f, 5m, 1u. ACTS: 1. SETTINGS: Lobby. PLAYING TIME: NA. PLOT: Sweet Gloria Alexander rents the worn out Whispering Pines hotel to Falbo and Vikki Cunningham, undercover agents for the state, who plan to set up a sting operation. Criminals gather to sell them all types of stolen goods, but the officers' main target is Donald Parrish, who has stolen a diamond necklace. After an uproarious chase scene and surprise twist, Parrish is discovered to be an unemployed policeman, trying to expose a "fence" at the Whispering Pines, which, of course, was actually an operation of the attorney general's office. RECOMMENDATION: The twists and turns of uncovered identities are unexpected and make a rather outlandish plot funny. This would probably best be appreciated by an audience with some knowledge of New England. ROYALTY: $45. SOURCE: Kelly, Tim. (1984). Laffing room only. Boston, MA: Baker's Plays. SUBJECTS/PLAY TYPE: Mystery; Comedy.

1657. 5-12. (+) Kelly, Tim. **The lalapalooza bird.** CAST: 4f, 2m. ACTS: 1. SETTINGS: Porch. PLAYING TIME: 30 min. PLOT: Grandpa starts an independent new life helping unwanted children, including Ginny and Ralph. But his daughter and granddaughter come to woo him back to his room in the family apartment. When Ginny and Ralph think that Grandpa might leave, their world starts to crumble. In the end, however, Grandpa remains independent. RECOMMENDATION: The emphasis on the relationship between generations and the need for all of us to know and understand one another is presented in a humorous and appealing fashion. ROYALTY: $15. SOURCE: Kelly, Tim. (1981). The Lalapalooza Bird. A Play in One Act. Schulenburg, TX: I.E. Clark. SUBJECTS/PLAY TYPE: Family; Ageism; Drama.

1658. 7-9. (+) Karshner, Roger. **Lana and Rod.** CAST: 1f, 1m. ACTS: 1. SETTINGS: None. PLAYING TIME: NA. PLOT: Lana has just returned from "The Coast"

talking funny, wearing weird clothes, and with an orange streak in her hair. Rod tells her that she has lost it with this phony act. Then Rod starts to imitate her way of speaking and she tells him to stop talking stupidly. RECOMMENDATION: This presents the problems of teenage identity well. ROYALTY: NA. SOURCE: Karshner, Roger. (1986). Scenes for teenagers. Toluce Lake, CA: Dramaline Pub. SUBJECTS/PLAY TYPE: Identity; Scene.

1659. P-2. (+) Milligan, Spike. **The land of the Bumbley Boo.** CAST: 3u. ACTS: 1. SETTINGS: None. PLAYING TIME: NA. PLOT: A nonsensical tale told in limericks, this describes the silly land of red, white, and blue people and clothed cats. RECOMMENDATION: This will be a lovely piece for children to speak for parents. ROYALTY: NA. SOURCE: Bauer, Caroline Feller. (1987). Presenting reader's theater: Plays and poems to read aloud. New York, NY: H.W. Wilson Co. SUBJECTS/PLAY TYPE: Nonsense; Limericks; Reader's Theater.

1660. 9-12. (+) Henderson, Nancy. **The land we love.** CAST: 4f, 8m, Su. ACTS: 1. SETTINGS: Ellis Island. PLAYING TIME: 9 min. PLOT: A man returns to Ellis Island, where he relives the difficulties his family, Jews from Poland, encountered during the first days after their arrival in America in 1930. RECOMMENDATION: This short, easy to produce historical play celebrates an essential part of American history. ROYALTY: Permission required if performed outside of classroom. SOURCE: Henderson, Nancy. (1978). Celebrate America: A baker's dozen of plays. New York, NY: Julian Messner. SUBJECTS/PLAY TYPE: Immigrants; Ellis Island; Jews; Drama.

1661. 9-12. (-) Cope, Eddie. **Landslide.** CAST: 8f, 6m. ACTS: 2. SETTINGS: Hotel. PLAYING TIME: 90 min. PLOT: Rundown Hotel Boggs no longer gets business because the main highway is too far away. When a landslide causes a detour past the hotel, guests include a spy disguised as a math teacher, a geologist looking for uranium, and a newspaper reporter. The spy is found out, the geologist discovers uranium in the backyard (making the widow/owner of the hotel rich), and at least one couple falls in love. RECOMMENDATION: The plot is contrived, the roles stereotypical, and the jokes are stale. ROYALTY: $25. SOURCE: Cope, Eddie. (1983). Landslide. Denver, CO: Pioneer Drama Service. SUBJECTS/PLAY TYPE: Hotels; Comedy.

1662. 9-12. (+) Davis, Ossie. **Langston.** CAST: 5m. ACTS: 3. SETTINGS: Bare stage, furniture. PLAYING TIME: 135 min. PLOT: Langston Hughes visits a group of actors rehearsing one of his plays and shares details of his past with them, as they act them out. The story begins when Hughes is a young boy living with his grandmother who tells him stories of John Brown and the Civil War. After she dies, he goes to live with his poverty stricken mother. She grows bitter at the whites who trap her in a meaningless existence and at her son for writing poetry rather than getting a job. The boy goes to live with his father in Mexico, but still finds no support for his writing career. Running off, Hughes joins the Merchant Marines, moves to Paris, and has an unhappy affair before returning to the U.S. Discovered by poet Vachel Lindsay, Hughes finds success with his work, attends college, and reconciles with his mother. RECOMMENDATION: The inclusion of several of Hughes' poems with the biographical information makes this a most interesting play appropriate for literature or ethnic studies. The dual character roles are innovative and effective, making the role of Langston Hughes lengthy and demanding. Viewers will empathize with both the black situation and the universal struggles portrayed. ROYALTY: NA. SOURCE: Davis, Ossie. (1982). Langston. New York, NY: Delacorte Press. SUBJECTS/PLAY TYPE: Poets; Hughes, Langston; Black Americans; Drama.

1663. 6-8. (+) Benson, Laurel. **Language in jeopardy.** CAST: 4f, 4m, Su. ACTS: 1. SETTINGS: Bare stage, props. PLAYING TIME: 10 min. PLOT: Larry Language has been murdered, and all parts of the English language, from adjectives to verbs, are used to describe his condition (i.e. dead, deceased, departed, etc.). However, Larry was only asleep, a condition called snoozing, slumbering, reposing, and dozing. RECOMMENDATION: This is an amusing lead in for an English class reviewing the parts of speech or for explaining language usage. ROYALTY: Free to Plays subscribers. SOURCE: Benson, Laurel. (1989, March). Language in jeopardy. Plays: The Drama Magazine for Young People, pp. 37-40. SUBJECTS/PLAY TYPE: Grammar; Skit.

1664. 4-8. (+) Brown, Abbie Farwell. **The lantern.** CAST: 4f, 10m. ACTS: 2. SETTINGS: Kitchen. PLAYING TIME: 30 min. PLOT: Set during the American Revolution, this describes the life of Barbara Brackett, the teenaged daughter of a sea captain. Her family receives word that their father will be secretly returning home with a precious cargo, and will need a lantern in the window to steer safely. The enemy tries to get the children to reveal where their father is and when he is coming home. He frightens all but Barbara away with stories of bloodthirsty Redcoats. Barbara spends the night holding candles aloft to guide her father. British officers capture her the next day, but shortly thereafter, her father arrives with his cargo, the General-in-Chief of the rebels. He and the Continental soldiers overpower the Redcoats, and Barbara is recognized for her bravery. RECOMMENDATION: Though not historically accurate, this realistically portrays the feelings of the Revolution. Characters are multi-dimensional and patriotism is expressed in an intelligent and spirited manner which will stimulate classroom discussions and provide the actors with simple, yet fulfilling roles. ROYALTY: NA. SOURCE: Brown, Abbie Farwell. (1978). The lantern and other plays for children. Boston, MA: Houghton Mifflin. SUBJECTS/PLAY TYPE: Patriotism; Revolution, U.S.; Drama.

1665. 7-10. (+) Way, Brian. **The lantern.** CAST: 2f, 2m. ACTS: 1. SETTINGS: Headland/island. PLAYING TIME: 50 min. PLOT: Four people (each linked in some way to a mysterious lantern on a small island) have come to see the lantern light up. Each believes that it will light, despite its lack of fuel. As they wait, each has a vision. Toni, the

inventor, sees a future of inventions that turn humanity into destructive, power mad fanatics. Peter, the fisherman, at first charmed by his vision of streets full of happy people dancing, soon becomes disgusted with his vision's cheap vulgarity. Steve relives a past sailing tragedy and learns that his ancestor, Paul, did light the lantern in time, but was killed by the storm. His corpse hid the light from the seaman's view. The three vow to use this foresight and hindsight to guide their futures. Ann tells the others that there is nothing she wishes to learn from the lantern now, but she will return later when there is a need. RECOMMENDATION: With excellent dialogue and believable, well drawn characters, the theme of saving humanity is presented within a plot which resembles an episode from **The Twilight Zone.** Since the audience (not to exceed 200) is expected to participate in the three visionary scenes, the actors will have to improvise freely, requiring a cast of adults or skilled young adults. ROYALTY: $20. SOURCE: Way, Brian. (1977). The lantern. Boston, MA: Baker's Plays. SUBJECTS/PLAY TYPE: Future; Participation Play; Drama.

1666. 3-5. (+) McCaslin, Nellie. **The Lantern and the fan.** CAST: 2f, 1m. ACTS: 1. SETTINGS: Living room; road. PLAYING TIME: 10 min. PLOT: Two daughters-in-law are given permission by their father-in-law to visit their relatives in another village. The father-in-law instructs them to stay only one month. If they stay longer, he warns, they must bring him fire wrapped in paper and wind wrapped in paper. The girls accidentally stay longer than a month and wonder where they will find the gifts until a paper lantern and a fan appear before them, thus solving their dilemma. RECOMMENDATION: This explains the legend of the origin of the first lantern and the first fan in Japan, with the importance being placed on the idea of the inventions, not on their actual manufacture. ROYALTY: None. SOURCE: McCaslin, Nellie. (1977). Puppet fun: Production, performance, and plays. New York, NY: D. McKay Co. SUBJECTS/PLAY TYPE: Folk Tales, Japan; Puppet Play.

1667. 8-12. (+) Kelly, Tim. **Lantern in the wind.** CAST: 3f. ACTS: 1. SETTINGS: Cabin. PLAYING TIME: 25 min. PLOT: Etta Place, friend of the dead Butch Cassidy and Sundance Kid, visits her cousin, Clara. Florence, a newspaper reporter, has followed her, and Etta grants her an interview. Florence believes the rumor that Butch Cassidy is still alive, and that Etta knows where he is. Etta unconvincingly denies it, but is finally coaxed to confess that when she hangs a signal lantern in her window, Butch comes from his hideout to talk. After Florence is gone, Etta admits that she likes to keep the past alive by feeding these stories to the press, thus staving off loneliness. RECOMMENDATION: Intriguing because of its deft characterization, this shows each woman as distinctive, not stereotyped. There is poignancy in Etta's attempt to keep love and happier times alive by letting people believe a rumor, and in Florence eagerly ferreting out what she thinks is a scoop, never realizing that she is being manipulated. ROYALTY: $15. SOURCE: Kelly, Tim. (1980). Lantern in the wind. Schulenburg, TX: I.E. Clark. SUBJECTS/PLAY TYPE: Loneliness; Drama.

1668. 7-12. (-) Bradley, Virginia. **The last bus from Lockerbee.** CAST: 4f, 6m, Su. ACTS: 1. SETTINGS: Bus station. PLAYING TIME: NA. PLOT: An elderly man and a young woman wait for a bus that will never come. RECOMMENDATION: Though there is a definite ending to this sad play, it leaves the reader confused. ROYALTY: NA. SOURCE: Bradley, Virginia. (1977). Stage eight: One-act plays. New York, NY: Dodd, Mead & Co. SUBJECTS/PLAY TYPE: Family; Tragedy; Drama.

1669. 7-9. (+) Kehret, Peg. **Last chance for the dance.** CAST: 1f. ACTS: 1. SETTINGS: None. PLAYING TIME: NA. PLOT: Not yet asked to the 7th grade dance, a young girl invents a plausible excuse: a feigned broken arm, complete with heroics. RECOMMENDATION: This is quite clever. ROYALTY: NA. SOURCE: Kehret, Peg. (1986). Winning monologs for young actors. Colorado Springs, CO: Meriwether Pub. SUBJECTS/PLAY TYPE: Dances; Excuses; Monologue.

1670. 4-8. (+) Kehret, Peg. **The last day of sixth grade.** CAST: 1u. ACTS: 1. SETTINGS: None. PLAYING TIME: NA. PLOT: The fear of oral reports and anticipation of the last day of school are hilariously detailed by a youngster. RECOMMENDATION: From school rule puzzlements to worst nightmare tales, this captures the humor of life in elementary school. ROYALTY: NA. SOURCE: Kehret, Peg. (1986). Winning monologs for young actors. Colorado Springs, CO: Meriwether Pub. SUBJECTS/PLAY TYPE: School; Nightmares; Monologue.

1671. K-10. (+) Foon, Dennis. **The last days of Paul Bunyan.** CAST: 2m, 4u. ACTS: 1. SETTINGS: Camp; mountaintop; cave. PLAYING TIME: NA. PLOT: Paul Bunyan, sorry that all the big trees are gone, is challenged by a spirit to a chainsaw contest in which he must prove his prowess as a lumberjack. The prize, if Paul wins, is a forest of giant trees all his own. RECOMMENDATION: The exaggerated humor is delightful. Although done originally with giant puppets, this would work just as well with smaller ones and comparably scaled down sets. ROYALTY: NA. SOURCE: Foon, Dennis. (1978). The Windigo and the last days of Paul Bunyan. Toronto, Canada: Playwright's Co-op. SUBJECTS/PLAY TYPE: Bunyan, Paul; Puppet Play.

1672. 9-12. (+) Shute, Stephanie. **The last disaster movie.** CAST: 11f, 8m. ACTS: 2. SETTINGS: Office. PLAYING TIME: NA. PLOT: Mediocre movie mogul, Rufus Goosedown, decides he'll end his career with one final disaster film which will make him a bundle, and exact revenge on his sworn enemy, producer Arthur Hemple. Before filming begins, Hemple's niece and nephew discover the plan to make the movie's disasters real, and Hemple's studio worthlessness. They successfully avert destruction, the enemies make up, and Goosedown's daughter and Hemple's nephew plan to marry. RECOMMENDATION: Though simplistic in spots, this entertaining spoof on Hollywood movie making has likeable characters, unpretentious dialogue, and enough action to make up for its predictable plot. It is long, potentially a drawback for some groups. ROYALTY: $40. SOURCE: Shute, Stephanie. (1982). The last disaster movie. Elgin, IL: Performance Pub. SUBJECTS/PLAY TYPE: Movie Making; Comedy.

1673. 6-12. (+) Tate, Karen Boettcher. **The last fat man.** CAST: 6f, 4m. ACTS: 1. SETTINGS: Apartment. PLAYING TIME: NA. PLOT: Piezeen 2600, the last fat man in a futuristic world dominated by skinny people, is forced to follow a strict weight reduction program. Although under constant surveillance by 2-V, the girl in the large "TV" screen, he cheats. When he dismantles the screen in desperation, guards and members of the ruling society appear to subdue him. Instead, they become fascinated with his fat. Piezeen 2600 offers them real food, and after one taste, they decide to worship him as the "Supreme Fatty," their new leader. RECOMMENDATION: The concise plot and dialogue, combined with amusing characterizations make this a successful satire that tickles the funny bone. ROYALTY: $15. SOURCE: Tate, Karen Boettcher. (1978). The last fat man. Elgin, IL: Performance Pub. Co. SUBJECTS/PLAY TYPE: Future; Satire; Obesity; Comedy.

1674. 10-12. (+) Bright, Charles E. **The last of the cowboy heroes.** CAST: 3f, 2m. ACTS: 1. SETTINGS: Bar; boarding house. PLAYING TIME: NA. PLOT: A former B-movie cowboy star attempts to keep his past glory alive through continual reminiscence. But the death of his old partner and imminent eviction from his room in a boarding house force him to confront reality and begin living in the present. RECOMMENDATION: This offers insight on aging, death, and the need to maintain dignity in spite of the indifference and contempt of a younger generation. ROYALTY: $15. SOURCE: Bright, Charles E. (1983). The last of the cowboy heroes. Chicago, IL: Dramatic Pub. Co. SUBJECTS/PLAY TYPE: Aging; Death; Drama.

1675. 7-12. (+) Cable, Harold. **Last stop.** CAST: 5f, 3m, 1u. ACTS: 1. SETTINGS: Porch; street. PLAYING TIME: 35 min. PLOT: Teenagers are stranded in a ghost town after a drag race wreck. Without modern conveniences or communications, the young group becomes impatient to get back home. When they finally receive radio news, they hear the report of their accident and missing bodies. Slowly, it is revealed to the audience that they are dead, waiting for the bus to take them away from the town, Last Stop. RECOMMENDATION: Spooky overtones and chilling revelations of death are enticing. The teenage characters include a wide variety of identifiable personalities, and their interactions with each other are very realistic. The appearance of hotel workers adds to the spooky mood and there is an underlying message about the dangers of drag racing that will not be overlooked. ROYALTY: Free to Plays subscribers. SOURCE: Cable, Harold. (1984, November). Last Stop. Plays: The Drama Magazine for Young People, pp. 23-33. SUBJECTS/PLAY TYPE: Death; Ghost Stories; Drag Racing; Playlet.

1676. K-6. (+) Bauer, Caroline Feller. **The last story.** CAST: 1m, 2u. ACTS: 1. SETTINGS: Bedroom. PLAYING TIME: 3 min. PLOT: Unable to sleep, the king calls for his storyteller, who begins a story about endless numbers of sheep that must be rowed across a river, one at a time. As the king becomes bored, he also becomes sleepy and asks to continue the story later. RECOMMENDATION: This would be excellent as part of a program of several short plays, as a filler between two longer ones, or as an encore. It can be either acted or read aloud. ROYALTY: NA. SOURCE: Bauer, Caroline Feller. (1987). Presenting reader's theater: Plays and poems to read aloud. New York, NY: H.W. Wilson Co. SUBJECTS/PLAY TYPE: Insomnia; Reader's Theater.

1677. 5-9. (+) Cope, Eddie & Cearley, Buster. **Last tango in Pango Pango. CAST:** 6f, 4m, Su. **ACTS:** 2. SETTINGS: Store. PLAYING TIME: NA. PLOT: Searching for her missing father, Kissy Kelly and her companion, S.C. Hornforester are shipwrecked on the island of Pango Pango. They find shelter at a health food store run by villainous Shipwreck Nelly and Captain Egad, who have stolen the store from Kissy's father (after murdering him). The store is now a front for their real business of selling slave girls in the Orient. Kissy and C.S. (who fall in love as the play progresses), realize the truth, and after humorous scenes of subterfuge, the villains are arrested and marched off to the Pango Pango jail. RECOMMENDATION: The refreshing South Sea atmosphere, colorful characters, and mischievous pranks in this witty, zany plot make for a lively theater experience. ROYALTY: $35. SOURCE: Cope, Eddie & Cearley, Buster. (1988). Last tango in Pango Pango. Schulenburg, TX: I.E. Clark. SUBJECTS/PLAY TYPE: Mystery; Ship-wrecks; Comedy.

1678. 9-12. (+) Rogers, David. (Scoppettone, Sandra) **The late great me.** (The late great me) **CAST:** 13f, 9m, Su. ACTS: 2. SETTINGS: None. PLAYING TIME: NA. PLOT: A shy, socially immature teenage girl is drawn into drinking and alcoholism by a boy. As her alcoholism gets worse, her life is increasingly threatened. Confrontations with her parents, former friends, and school teachers help her realize how serious her drinking problem is. She seeks help at AA and although she is unable to persuade her boyfriend to acknowledge his own alcoholism, her life slowly returns to normal. RECOMMENDATION: This is compelling, although in some parts it is preachy and some language needs to be updated. The leading role requires a talented actress. ROYALTY: $50. SOURCE: Rogers, David. (1977). The late great me. Woodstock, IL: Dramatic Pub. Co. SUBJECTS/PLAY TYPE: Alcoholism; Drama.

1679. 8-12. (+) Cull, John. **The late Mark Jordan.** CAST: 5f, 5m. ACTS: 3. SETTINGS: Living room. PLAYING TIME: 45 min. PLOT: Mark Jordan fears for his life because he has not provided all brawn, no brains Ferde Fishbein with a date for the school dance. At the last minute, he convinces his attractive mother to fill in. She leaves a note for her husband, who assumes she has left him for Mr. Fishbein, the undertaker, and laments to the neighbors that he's lost his wife to Fishbein. They think that she has died, visit the bereaved husband, and so on, until all is cleared up when the dancers return. RECOMMENDATION: Even though a bit contrived, this hilariously forces the audience to identify with Mark's panic and relief, laugh out loud as emotions flare, and feel strangely upbeat at the play's conclusion. ROYALTY: $40.

SOURCE: Cull, John. (1984). The late Mark Jordan. Elgin, IL: Performance Pub. Co. SUBJECTS/PLAY TYPE: Misunderstandings; Communication; Comedy.

1680. 7-12. (-) Erhard, Tom. **Laughing once more.** CAST: 6f, 3m. ACTS: 1. SETTINGS: Bare stage, props. PLAYING TIME: 90 min. PLOT: This is a compilation of poetry and short stories written by high school students and recited, acted out, or pantomimed by cast members. RECOMMENDATION: Although the writings have literary merit, this gets bogged down with the actors having to give the author's name, the name of the high school he or she attends, and sometimes the student teacher's name each time the actor recites a piece. The audience may get bored with the lack of settings and the volume of poetry being recited. Much of the conversation between actors (when not reciting) seems very juvenile and forced. ROYALTY: $50. SOURCE: Erhard, Thomas A. (1986). Laughing once more. Woodstock, IL: The Dramatic Pub. Co. SUBJECTS/PLAY TYPE: Authors, Adolescent; Poetry.

1681. 1-4. (+) Carlson, Bernice Wells. **The law of the jungle. CAST:** 14u. ACTS: 1. SETTINGS: Jungle clearing. PLAYING TIME: 7 min. PLOT: When a jungle judge cannot learn the identity of the animal who destroyed Weaver Bird's nest, she punishes all of the suspects. RECOMMENDATION: This is short and easy to memorize. However, a strong director is required because at one point, the animals stand in a circle and pretend to bite each other and scream. ROYALTY: None. SOURCE: Carlson, Bernice Wells. (1982). Let's find the big idea. Nashville, TN: Abingdon Press. SUBJECTS/PLAY TYPE: Animal Tales; Justice; Pantomime.

1682. 3-12*. (+) Bayer, Harold. (Jacobs, Joseph) **Lazy Jack.** (Lazy Jack) CAST: 2f, 2m, 1u. ACTS: 1. SETTINGS: Bare stage. PLAYING TIME: 20 min. PLOT: Lazy Jack lives with his mother, who makes a living by spinning. Each job she finds for her son is short lived, due to his ineptness. For example, when he works for a dairy farmer, his mother tells him to carry his wages home of top of his head, which he does despite ruining the cheese he received for pay. Another time, he carries a donkey home thinking it should be carried like a beef hindquarters. When he arrives home, a princess, who had been born mute, begins to laugh and speak. The grateful king tells his daughter that she will marry Jack and that Jack and his mother will live in comfort for the rest of their lives. RECOMMENDATION: Despite their differences, love between Jack and his mother is evident. Revisions may have to be made, as the dialogue contains some mild cursing and religious references. This is best acted by older children because of the vocabulary and length of lines. ROYALTY: $15. SOURCE: Bayer, Harold. (1982). Motley tales: A collection of folk and fairy tales with music. Boston, MA: Baker's Plays. SUBJECTS/PLAY TYPE: Comedy; Folk Tales, England; Fools and Simpletons; Adaptation.

1683. 7-12. (+) McMahon, Luella K. (Steinbeck, John) The leader of the people. (The red pony) CAST: 2f, 4m. ACTS: 1. SETTINGS: Kitchen; dining room. PLAYING

TIME: NA. PLOT: Grandfather, an old wagon train leader, comes to visit his daughter, son-in-law, and grandson. The grandson looks forward to hearing the old man's incessant stories of "westerning," but the father dreads it. Tragically, grandfather overhears his son-in-law complaining about the old man's constant retelling of the same story. Recognizing that his life is over, the grandfather sags to the realization that after conquering the west, he has "no place to go." RECOMMENDATION: This stands well by itself as a chronicle of generation gaps and the plight of old people; it does not do justice to the original since McMahon, in her attempt to make sure that the audience "gets the message" has trivialized the grandfather's character, and not allowed the depth of the grandson's and mother's feelings to be shown. ROYALTY: $15. SOURCE: McMahon, Luella K. (1952). The leader of the people. Woodstock, IL: Dramatic Pub. Co. SUBJECTS/PLAY TYPE: Elderly; Memories; Wagon Trains; Adaptation.

1684. 7-12. (+) Robb Danni & Sturko, Michael. **The leak. CAST**: 1u. **ACTS**: 1. **SETTINGS**: Bare stage. **PLAYING TIME**: 15 min. PLOT: An individual trying to read a newspaper is disturbed by an annoying water leak. Various unsuccessful methods to stop the leak are pantomimed. Finally, when the ceiling falls and there is silence, the mime believes success is gained until after a few moments...drip...drip...drip. RECOMMENDATION: This is a readily identified, creative, and easy to pantomime situation. **ROYALTY**: Free to Plays Subscribers. **SOURCE**: Robb, Danni & Sturko, Michael. (1980, February). The leak. Plays: The Drama Magazine for Young People, pp. 67-69. **SUBJECTS/PLAY TYPE**: Comedy; Leaks; Pantomime.

1685. 6-8. (+) Nolan, Paul T. (Dodge, Mary Mapes) **A Leak in the dike.** (Hans Brinker: Or the silver skates) CAST: 4f, 4m, ACTS: 1. SETTINGS: Dike. PLAYING TIME: 15 min. PLOT: Young Jan van Hoof plugs a leak in the dike with his finger and courageously waits through the night for help to arrive. This fictional story so typified Dutch courage that Hollanders have accepted it as a symbol of their eternal struggle against the sea. RECOMMENDATION: Children of any age will identify with the boy's courage as he refuses to give in to hunger, cold, and fatigue. The leading role requires substantial memorization and offers dramatic opportunities. ROYALTY: None for amateur performance. SOURCE: Nolan, Paul T. (1982). Folk tale plays round the world: A collection of royalty-free, one-act plays about lands far and near. Boston, MA: Plays, Inc. SUBJECTS/PLAY TYPE: Hero-ism; Folk Tales, Netherlands; Adaptation.

1686. K-3. (+) Viorst, Judith. **Learning. CAST**: 3u. ACTS: 1. SETTINGS: None. PLAYING TIME: NA. PLOT: The effort of being tidy and polite is humorously portrayed. RECOMMENDATION: Viorst, as usual, has her finger on the pulse of children's feelings. ROYALTY: NA. SOURCE: Bauer, Caroline Feller. (1987). Presenting reader's theater: Plays and poems to read aloud. New York, NY: H.W. Wilson. SUBJECTS/PLAY TYPE: Manners; Neatness; Reader's Theater.

1687. 3-7*. (+) Sullivan, Jessie P. **Learning to trust God. CAST**: 2u. ACTS: 1. SETTINGS: Puppet stage. PLAYING TIME: NA. PLOT: Two children discuss the difference between hope and faith as they try to understand Hebrews 11:1. RECOMMENDATION: This explains a very sophisticated concept well. ROYALTY: None. SOURCE: Sullivan, Jessie P. (1978). Puppet scripts for children's church. Grand Rapids, MI: Baker Book House. SUBJECTS/PLAY TYPE: Hope; Faith; Christian Drama; Puppet Play.

1688. 3-9. (+) McDonough, Jerome. **The least of these.** CAST: 9f, 1m, 2u. ACTS: 1. SETTINGS: None. PLAYING TIME: 30 min. PLOT: Three teenagers enroute to a youth potluck supper help a stray cat, a paper route delivery person, a lost child, a lost dog, and an accident victim. These good deeds make them too late to participate in the live Nativity scene, but they notice that the articles in the manager relate to the good deeds just performed. RECOMMENDATION: A Christmas play, based on Matthew 25, with an overwhelming moral, but one that might be excellent for a church audience. ROYALTY: $15. SOURCE: McDonough, Jerome. (1983). The least of these. Denver, CO: Pioneer Drama Service. SUBJECTS/PLAY TYPE: Christmas; Cyclorama.

1689. 12. (+) Wilson, Ella & Field, Anna. (Tolstoy, Leo) **The least of these.** (Where love is, there God is also) CAST: 8u. ACTS: 1. SETTINGS: Living room. PLAYING TIME: NA. PLOT: On Christmas Eve, as a shoemaker awaits a visit from Christ, he helps several troubled visitors. Late in the evening, as he gives up hope of being visited by Christ, a voice informs him that the kindness shown to his visitors was kindness shown to Christ. RECOMMENDATION: For church groups, this is uplifting and touching. ROYALTY: NA. SOURCE: McSweeny, Maxine. (1977). Christmas plays for young players. South Brunswick: A.S. Barnes. SUBJECTS/PLAY TYPE: Christmas; Kindness; Drama.

1690. 4-7. (+) Miller, Ev. **The leather belt. CAST**: 2f, 2m. ACTS: 1. SETTINGS: Leather shop. PLAYING TIME: NA. PLOT: An elderly immigrant couple work in their leather shop and talk about their son, from whom they have heard nothing in five years. A girl enters to buy a belt for her father, but hasn't yet saved enough money. At first the craftsman will not consider holding it for her. The girl speaks of her love for her father who is mourning his recently deceased wife. When another customer desires to purchase the belt, the old man informs him that it is already sold and he lets the girl purchase it for the amount of money she has. RECOMMENDATION: The players who portray the old couple will have to speak with a German accent which might prove difficult, but the play is worth the effort. ROYALTY: $15. SOURCE: Miller, Ev. (1984). The leather belt. Chicago, IL: Dramatic Pub. Co. SUBJECTS/PLAY TYPE: Family; Immigrants; Drama.

1691. 9-12. (+) Barnes, Wade. **Lefgook. CAST**: 2f, 2m. ACTS: 1. SETTINGS: Art museum. PLAYING TIME: 30 min. PLOT: Two students at an art museum express their feelings about different pieces of artwork by dancing. Grasha becomes overwhelmed with one of the statues, and learns that she can keep it by remembering it in her mind and heart. RECOMMENDATION: Suitable for all occasions, this requires the cast to express feeling both verbally and physically. Production may involve simple or complex dance routines. ROYALTY: $15. SOURCE: Barnes, Wade. (1978). Lefgook. Schulenburg, TX: I.E. Clark. SUBJECTS/PLAY TYPE: Love; Art; Drama.

1692. 4-8. (+) Henderson, Nancy. **Legend for our time.** CAST: 4f, 5m, 3u. ACTS: 1. SETTINGS: Office. PLAYING TIME: 12 min. PLOT: When the coal, oil, and natural gas has been used up, the 4-H Club saves the day by convincing very cold Superpop (the president) to support alternative forms of energy. RECOMMENDATION: Although in some ways slightly dated, this is still thought provoking and humorous. ROYALTY: Free for classroom performance. SOURCE: Henderson, Nancy. (1978). Celebrate America: A baker's dozen of plays. New York, NY: Julian Messner. SUBJECTS/PLAY TYPE: Energy Conservation; Comedy.

1693. 7-12*. (+) Gaines, Frederick. (Irving, Washington) **The legend of Sleepy Hollow.** (The legend of Sleepy Hollow) CAST: 3f, 6m, Su. ACTS: 1. SETTINGS: Boardwalk; trees. PLAYING TIME: NA. PLOT: Ichabod Crane, schoolmaster and eligible bachelor in Sleepy Hollow, is haunted by the legend of the headless horseman as Halloween approaches. He vies for the attention of Katrina Van Tassel with Brom Bones, who takes advantage of Ichabod's fright by playing nasty tricks on him. In the end, Ichabod loses Katrina to Brom at a party. As he leaves for home, he is overtaken by a mysterious figure on horseback who may be the real headless horseman. RECOMMENDATION: Gaines adds music and dance to make the final result entrancing. Because of the elaborate production requirements, it is most suited for adults to perform for children. ROYALTY: NA. SOURCE: Donahue, John Clark & Jenkins, Linda Walsh. (1975). Five plays from the children's theatre company of Minneapolis. Minneapolis, MN: Univ. of Minnesota Press. SUBJECTS/PLAY TYPE: Ghosts; Halloween; Rivalry; Adaptation.

1694. 8-12. (+) Hackett, Walter. (Irving, Washington) **The legend of Sleepy Hollow.** (The legend of Sleepy Hollow) CAST: 1f, 6m. ACTS: 1. SETTINGS: None. PLAYING TIME: NA. PLOT: The narrator sets the scenes or this well known tale, which are then played out by various characters who are members of the round the table reading group. RECOMMENDATION: The round the table method will help reinforce comprehension skills if students read their parts silently before presenting them. ROYALTY: Free to Plays subscribers. SOURCE: Hackett, Walter. (1981, April). The legend of Sleepy Hollow. Plays: The Drama Magazine for Young People, pp. 69-79. SUBJECTS/PLAY TYPE: Adventure; Ghosts; Adaptation; Reader's Theater.

1695. 3-6. (+) Robinette, Joseph & Shaw, James R. **The legend of the sun child.** CAST: 3f, 5m, 9u. ACTS: 1. SETTINGS: Indian village; sleeping quarters; prairie; wooded area; ocean. PLAYING TIME: 55 min. PLOT: This is a musical version of the ancient Indian legend of Scarface, a brave mortal warrior who travels to the Land of the Sun, returns to the earth, defeats his evil rival, and wins permission to marry the Sun's daughter. RECOMMENDATION: Scenes are suggested by simple props and the use of propmasters on a bare stage. Costumes and lighting establish mood. ROYALTY: $50. SOURCE: Robinette, Joseph & Shaw, James R. (1981). The legend of the sun. Chicago, IL: Dramatic Pub. Co. SUBJECTS/PLAY TYPE: Legends, Native American; Musical; Drama.

1696. K-5. (+) Mahlman, Lewis & Jones, David Cadwalader. **The legend of Urashima.** CAST: 7u. ACTS: 1. SETTINGS: Boat; undersea world; hut. PLAYING TIME: 20 min. PLOT: Urashima saves a turtle from a beating by Daigin. In exchange, the turtle saves Urashima from drowning and takes him to live under the sea with the Dragon King. After a time, Urashima becomes homesick, and is given a box by the Dragon King as his farewell gift. Warned not to open the box, Urashima is returned home. He finds that he has been gone fifty years, his parents are dead, and Daigin is now an old man. Daigin persuades him to open the box, which holds Urashima's youth. Urashima quickly ages fifty years and must confront his mortality. RECOMMENDATION: This is beautiful in its simplicity. ROYALTY: Free to Plays subscribers. SOURCE: Mahlman, Lewis & Jones, David Cadwalader. (1980). Folk tale plays for puppets. Boston, MA: Plays, Inc. SUBJECTS/PLAY TYPE: Youth, Eternal; Folk Tales, Japan; Aging; Puppet Play.

1697. 4-7. (+) Kehret, Peg. **The lemonade stand.** CAST: 1u. ACTS: 1. SETTINGS: None. PLAYING TIME: NA. PLOT: A child speaks of the slowness of business at his/her lemonade stand. RECOMMENDATION: The problems of running a traditional lemonade stand will be both familiar and humorous to the audience. ROYALTY: NA. SOURCE: Kehret, Peg. (1986). Winning monologs for young actors. Colorado Springs, CO: Meriwether Pub. SUBJECTS/PLAY TYPE: Lemonade Stands; Monologue.

1698. 2-6. (+) Bennett, Rowena. **The leprechaun.** CAST: Su. ACTS: 1. SETTINGS: None. PLAYING TIME: NA. PLOT: A leprechaun, having stowed away to America, evades the queries of a curious youngster. RECOMMENDATION: A clever poem, this would make an appropriate St. Patrick's Day production by school children for their parents. ROYALTY: Free to Plays subscribers. SOURCE: Bennett, Rowena. (1987, March). The leprechaun. Plays: The Drama Magazine for Young People, pp. 53. SUBJECTS/PLAY TYPE: Leprechauns; St. Patrick's Day; Choral Reading.

1699. 4-6. (-) Watts, Frances B. **The Leprechaun shoemakers.** CAST: 5f, 4m, 3u. ACTS: 1. SETTINGS: Shoe shop. PLAYING TIME: 15 min. PLOT: Patrick, the leprechaun shoemaker, refuses to compromise his shoemaking principles, and ends up becoming the Queen's Royal Shoemaker. RECOMMENDATION: This has stereotyped characters, dated language, and silly dialogue. ROYALTY: Free to Plays subscribers. SOURCE:

Kamerman, Sylvia E. (1983). Holiday plays round the year. Boston, MA: Plays, Inc. SUBJECTS/PLAY TYPE: Fairies; St. Patrick's Day; Comedy.

1700. 1-8. (+) Watts, Frances B. **The leprechaun's pot of gold.** CAST: 5f, 5m. ACTS: 1. SETTINGS: Clearing. PLAYING TIME: 25 min. PLOT: Timothy, a miserly, unhappy leprechaun who loves only his gold and believes that people are dishonest and out to rob him determines that unless he meets an honest person, he will take the whole town prisoner. He sets his gold on the road, and a number of villagers with problems steal it. Each is imprisoned. Granny, who also needs the money, is honest at all costs and twice returns the gold. The villagers learn that honesty is its own reward, and Timothy learns that the joy of friendship and sharing is better than hoarding gold. RECOMMENDATION: Although very didactic, the characters are diverse, dynamic, and believable. Singing and dancing are necessary and the use of Irish brogue would be a nice touch. ROYALTY: Free to Plays subscribers. SOURCE: Watts, Frances. (1982, March). The leprechaun's pot of gold. Plays: The Drama Magazine for Young People, pp. 39-43. SUBJECTS/PLAY TYPE: Leprechauns; Playlet.

1701. 7-9. (-) Karshner, Roger. **Les and Jim.** CAST: 2m. ACTS: 1. SETTINGS: None. PLAYING TIME: NA. PLOT: Les and Jim, tired of their after school jobs of unloading trucks, get jobs at the Velvet Dairy. RECOMMENDATION: This is very boring with the boys complaining about their jobs and then quitting. Nothing else happens except for the use of graphic language and gestures. ROYALTY: NA. SOURCE: Karshner, Roger. (1986). Scenes for teenagers. Toluce Lake, CA: Dramaline Pub. SUBJECTS/PLAY TYPE: Jobs; Scene.

1702. 11-12. (+) Fugard, Athol. **A lesson from aloes.** CAST: 1f, 2m. ACTS: 2. SETTINGS: Backyard; bedroom. PLAYING TIME: NA. PLOT: A South African couple, Piet and Gladys, wait for a "colored" friend to visit before he emigrates, doubting that he will come. Gladys thinks that her husband and she are being shunned because of her emotional problems since being seized by the police during a raid, but Piet confesses that he has been accused of being a police informer responsible for his friend's recent arrest. The play examines each character's attempts to survive in South Africa's harsh political/social environment: Gladys' diary of secrets filled with blank pages, Steven's desertion of his cause by emigrating, and Piet's inability to tackle accusations of being a political informer. RECOMMENDATION: This could be used to enhance the study of the effects of political systems on human beings, as well as to discuss the effects of apartheid. Casting will require skilled actors and some phrases in Afrikaans and South African English might require translation. ROYALTY: $60. SOURCE: Fugard, Athol. (1981). A lesson from aloes. New York, NY: Samuel French. SUBJECTS/PLAY TYPE: South Africa; Apartheid; Drama.

1703. 4-6. (+) Hamlett, Christine. **Lessons of Oz.** CAST: 3f, 4m, 4u. ACTS: 1. SETTINGS: Library. PLAYING TIME: 20 min. PLOT: Author Dorothy Osbourne arrives at the Topeka Public Library to autograph copies of her book. Along with the fans come three of her friends from Oz, each with a complaint about the gift he received from the Wizard: the scarecrow has to think for everyone; the Tin Man has to listen to all the people with broken hearts; and the Lion is worn out from protecting the kingdom. For her part, Dorothy has been told she must autograph books twelve hours a day for three weeks. The wicked witch appears in the form of a schoolmarm and demands a share of Dorothy's royalties. The Wizard appears and talks Dorothy into giving the Witch what she really wants, her red slippers. They don't fit, and the Witch hobbles off in pain. The wizard convinces the others not to take on everyone else's problems and gets Dorothy to take some time off from autographing. Then he makes friends with the librarian. RECOMMENDATION: As a fanciful sequel to "The Wonderful Wizard of Oz," this features the original beloved characters with a modernized perspective (including computerized scheduling). The message that sometimes problems result from even much wanted gifts could be used to lead into discussions about how best to help others or the importance of choosing goals carefully. ROYALTY: Free to Plays subscribers. SOURCE: Hamlett, Christina. (1987, January/February). Lessons from Oz. Plays: The Drama Magazine for Young People, pp. 47-53. SUBJECTS/PLAY TYPE: Gifts; Wishes; Playlet.

1704. 3-6. (+) Engelhardt, James F. **Let freedom ring.** CAST: 3f, 7m, Su. ACTS: 2. SETTINGS: Town square; printing shop; living room. PLAYING TIME: 55 min. PLOT: As Thomas Jefferson, John Adams, and Benjamin Franklin write the Declaration of Independence, Ben suddenly leaves the building. He leads Tom and John on a tour around the city, reminiscing as he goes, in order to develop some important ideas to incorporate into the Declaration. RECOMMENDATION: This demonstrates the deep thought that went into writing the Declaration of Independence, as well as the important contributions that were made by Ben Franklin. ROYALTY: $25. SOURCE: Engelhardt, James. (1975). Let freedom ring. Chicago IL: Coach House Press. SUBJECTS/PLAY TYPE: Franklin, Benjamin; Declaration of Independence, U.S.; Drama.

1705. 3-4. (+) Hark, Mildred & McQueen, Noel. **Let George do it.** CAST: 4f, 4m, Su. ACTS: 1. SETTINGS: Living room. PLAYING TIME: 25 min. PLOT: George Trent, 14, struggles to complete an essay on George Washington. At the same time, George's father discovers that he is expected to deliver a speech on Washington because of a prize winning essay he wrote years earlier while in high school. While being interviewed by reporters, Mr. Trent reads part of his son's essay on "Let George Do It." The play is resolved when father and son agree to collaborate on both the essay and the speech. RECOMMENDATION: This is not exceptional, but does present strongly the idea that everyone should constantly strive to improve conditions rather than wait for someone else to do it. ROYALTY: Free to Plays subscribers. SOURCE: Hark, Mildred & McQueen, Noel. (1975, February). Let George do it. Plays: The Drama Magazine for Young People, pp. 55-63. SUBJECTS/PLAY TYPE: Family; Washington, George; Presidents' Day; Skit.

1706. 2-8. (+) Pendleton, Edrie. **Let George do it.** CAST: 3f, 3m. ACTS: 1. SETTINGS: Living room. PLAYING TIME: 20 min. PLOT: While his family chats about tomorrow's celebration, George Trent stomps off to work on his George Washington term paper. Soon reporters come to interview Mr. Trent about his essay on George Washington, which he wrote when he was 16. Searching for something to say, Mr. Trent quotes from his son's paper. Both father and son then share their ideas on the father of our country. RECOMMENDATION: Although the plot is weak and didactic, this is adequate. ROYALTY: Free to Plays subscribers. SOURCE: Pendleton, Edrie. (1985, January-February). Let George do it. Plays: The Drama Magazine for Young People, pp. 37-43. SUBJECTS/PLAY TYPE: Washington, George; Presidents' Day; Playlet.

1707. 9-12. (+) Christner, David W. **Let it rain.** CAST: 8f, 5m. ACTS: 2. SETTINGS: Modular, with office at top; second level, doctor's office; floor level, shipyard. PLAYING TIME: NA. PLOT: God sees that mankind is not doing what is good, so he decides to find one good man and two of each type of animal to save. The rest are to be destroyed by a flood. Doc Adams is the "good man," and he is told to build an ark before the rains begin. But, because of labor strikes, God's bad credit rating, and other modern complications, things go amuk. The rains come, but the only transport is a small rowboat. Doc can't turn away the people who come, so God changes his mind about destroying everyone. RECOMMENDATION: The play is recommended for mature high school audiences and for adults who will not be offended by God's "humanness." For example, some audiences may fail to appreciate the humor in God's saying, "Mandamit" or in turning a pitcher of water into Bloody Mary drinks because the wine trick had already been done. ROYALTY: $50. SOURCE: Christner, David W. (1980). Let it rain. Chicago, IL: Dramatic Pub. Co. SUBJECTS/PLAY TYPE: God; Hope; Comedy.

1708. 10-12. (-) Majeski, Bill. **Let Maizie do it.** CAST: 5f, 2m. ACTS: 1. SETTINGS: Office. PLAYING TIME: 30 min. PLOT: A slow witted and much scorned office secretary becomes an accidental heroine when her bumbling efforts to correct her editor's monumental snafu actually succeed. RECOMMENDATION: The dialogue is often hilarious, but the complicated plot might be difficult to follow and the characterization of the secretary as mentally retarded is offensive. ROYALTY: Free to Plays subscribers. SOURCE: Majeski, Bill. (1978, March). Let Maizie do it. Plays: The Drama Magazine for Young People, pp. 1-12. SUBJECTS/PLAY TYPE: Journalism; Comedy.

1709. K-12. (+) Calvin College Chapel Service. **Let there be light.** CAST: Su. ACTS: 1. SETTINGS: None. PLAYING TIME: 20 min. PLOT: This includes Bible stories of the creation, the fall of Adam and Eve, the birth of Jesus, Jesus' miracles, Judas' betrayal, and Christ's ascension into Heaven. RECOMMENDATION: This liturgy is recommended as part of a church service. Its theme that light or goodness triumphs over evil and darkness is appropriate for the Christmas season by reflecting on the positive works of God. ROYALTY: None. SOURCE: Hendricks, William & Vogel, Cora. (1983). Handbook of Christmas programs. Grand Rapids, MI: Baker Book House. SUBJECTS/PLAY TYPE: Christmas; Liturgy; Worship Program.

1710. K-12. (+) Hendricks, William & Vogel, Cora. **Let us go even unto Bethlehem.** CAST: Su. ACTS: 1. SETTINGS: None. PLAYING TIME: 10 min. PLOT: Based on New Testament readings, this describes Bethlehem and its place in the birth of Jesus. RECOMMENDATION: Suitable for church or parochial school groups for performance at a Christmas pageant or worship service. ROYALTY: NA. SOURCE: Hendricks, William & Vogel, Cora. (1978). Handbook of Christmas programs. Grand Rapids, MI: Baker Book House. SUBJECTS/PLAY TYPE: Choral Reading; Christmas; Bethlehem; Worship Program.

1711. 5-8. (+) Kolars, Vivan. **Let's go America.** CAST: Su. ACTS: 2. SETTINGS: Bare stage. PLAYING TIME: NA. PLOT: While Betsy and Sam complain about their "boring" American history assignment, an unknown leader appears to guide them through the past. Groups of actors portray ecologists and patriotic citizens to point out the importance of history and good citizenship. Other groups portray Indians, Pilgrims, revolutionaries, and pioneers. A group of workers extoll the work ethic as a primary builder of our nation. Other actors bring history up to date with inventors, immigrants, and wars. At last, Betty and Sam appreciate their heritage and the vitality of the history they are about to study. The finale is a pageant of American flags with Sam and Betsy assuming the persona of "Uncle Sam" and Betsy Ross. RECOMMENDATION: This very patriotic play demands a large cast (60 or more), is rhythmic and easily memorized. Much activity and many roles provide an opportunity for all who wish to participate. ROYALTY: One performance free with the purchase of eight copies of play, $10 for each additional performance. SOURCE: Kolars, Vivian. (1975). Let's go America: A historical pageant with music. Franklin, OH: Eldridge Pub. Co. SUBJECTS/PLAY TYPE: History, U.S.; Musical; Drama.

1712. 7-12. (+) Boiko, Claire. **Let's hear it for the audience!** CAST: 2f, 1m, 21u. ACTS: 1. SETTINGS: Movie theater. PLAYING TIME: 25 min. PLOT: Theater ushers spotlight two types of movie goers: Galluping Consumption (who coughs constantly) and Recount Dracula, who reveals what happens before it happens. RECOMMENDATION: The stereotyped characters are funny and easily recognizable. The play offers opportunity for pantomime, movement, and comic acting. ROYALTY: Free to Plays subscribers. SOURCE: Boiko, Claire. (1978, January). Let's hear it for the audience! Plays: The Drama Magazine for Young People, pp. 61-66. SUBJECTS/PLAY TYPE: Satire; Movies; Comedy.

1713. 4-6. (+) Cheatham, Val R. (Browning, Robert) **Let's hear it for the Pied Piper.** (The Pied Piper of Hamelin.) CAST: 1f, 2m, 3u. ACTS: 1. SETTINGS: Council chamber. PLAYING TIME: 20 min. PLOT: Rats have overrun Hamelin and the Mayor offers a reward to the person who can solve the problem. A "hip" Pied Piper lures the rats away, but the unscrupulous city council refuses to pay. The mayor pays, and the Piper leads unwilling councillors away to a tune on his kazoo while anticipating his marriage to the mayor's daughter. RECOMMENDATION: This clever adaptation is still workable although the Piper is "hip" by the standards of the late 70's. The audience will enjoy the humor of inept bureaucracy and also the misunderstandings caused by the Piper's "cool" speech. The kazoo is perfect since it takes no talent to play and its silly sound adds to the humor of the play. ROYALTY: Free to Plays subscribers. SOURCE: Cheatham, Val R. (1978, April). Let's hear it for the Pied Piper. Plays: The Drama Magazine for Young Children, pp. 63-68. SUBJECTS/PLAY TYPE: Comedy; Parody; Adaptation.

1714. 2-5. (+) Fisher, Aileen Lucia. **Let's plant a tree.** CAST: 7u. ACTS: 1. SETTINGS: None. PLAYING TIME: NA. PLOT: This choral reading highlights the virtues of various trees. RECOMMENDATION: Simple lines and a holiday theme make this a good first production for inexperienced players. ROYALTY: Free to Plays subscribers. SOURCE: Fisher, Aileen Lucia. (1986, April). Let's plant a tree. Plays: The Drama Magazine for Young People, pp. 40. SUBJECTS/PLAY TYPE: Arbor Day; Earth Day; Trees; Choral Reading.

1715. K-3. (+) Martin, Judith & Ashwander, Donald. **Let's start the show.** CAST: Su. ACTS: 1. SETTINGS: Rehearsal stage, props. PLAYING TIME: 10 min. PLOT: Two large paper bag faces bump into each other, and one invites the other to see the show. Players realize that the audience is present and hurriedly start getting ready for the show. RECOMMENDATION: In this introduction to the skits that follow in the collection, the audience is shown the types of props and costumes (paper and cardboard) which will be used. Because of the paper bags, actors can be more informal and relaxed. ROYALTY: NA. SOURCE: Martin, Judith & Ashwander, Donald. (1985). Reasons to be cheerful: A revue for children. New York, NY: The Paper Bag Players, Inc. SUBJECTS/PLAY TYPE: Theater; Skit; Musical Revue.

1716. 1-8. (-) Steinhorn, Harriet & Lowry, Edith. **The letter.** CAST: 3f, 6m, Su. ACTS: 2. SETTINGS: Living room; office; castle. PLAYING TIME: 15 min. PLOT: In 1941, just before she is taken from her home to her death, Ana writes a letter asking that whoever finds the Bible into which she has placed the letter send it to her brother in America. In 1945, on an expedition to examine "Jewish books" which were saved by the Nazis as proof of what they had done to the Jews, Ana's brother finds the Bible, and reads the letter out loud. RECOMMENDATION: Although this well portrays the twisted logic and horrific pride that the Nazis had for their actions, it also includes irrelevant discussion (for example, about the weather) that detracts from the message. The mundane discussions are probably included as contrast to the horror of the Nazi regime, but they are not well enough presented to achieve this purpose. ROYALTY: Free for amateur groups. SOURCE: Steinhorn, Harriet & Lowry, Edith. (1983). Shadows of the holocaust: Plays, readings, and program

resources. Rockville, MD: Kar-Ben Copies, Inc. SUBJECTS/PLAY TYPE: Holocaust; Genocide; World War II; Drama.

1717. 4-7. (-) Wartski, Maureen Crane. **A letter for George Washington.** CAST: 11u. ACTS: 1. SETTINGS: Woods. PLAYING TIME: 12 min. PLOT: The animals of the forest deliver an important letter announcing the support of the thirteen colonies for George Washington, just as he was about to give up hope. RECOMMENDATION: This is too trite and too childish for the audience; it also provides no historical insight. ROYALTY: Free to Plays subscribers. SOURCE: Wartski, Maureen Crane. (1979, February). A letter for George Washington. Plays: The Drama Magazine for Young People, pp. 29-35. SUBJECTS/PLAY TYPE: Washington, George; Animals; Playlet.

1718. 1-6*. (-) Chorpenning, Charlotte. **A letter to Santa Claus.** CAST: 4f, 9m, 8u. ACTS: 1. SETTINGS: Street; rooftop; North Pole; South Pole. PLAYING TIME: NA. PLOT: Mary and Joe ask Santa to get rid of the shadows of conflicts (i.e., greed, hatred, etc.). They ride the wind to the North Pole where Santa tells them to take all the presents he has left. The children are generous and do not keep all of the presents, thus passing the test. Therefore, Santa tells them that the Christmas light which comes from thoughts and feelings is the only thing which can blot out the shadows of conflicts. Santa then sends them off to spread the light. RECOMMENDATION: This is confusing and makes Santa appear to be a manipulative god who has the power to make others triumph over evil. It uses emotionalism without really providing any real significance. ROYALTY: NA. SOURCE: Swortzell, Lowell. (1986). Six plays for young people from the Federal Theatre Project (1936-1939). New York, NY: Greenwood Press, Inc. SUBJECTS/PLAY TYPE: Christmas; Drama.

1719. 1-6*. (+) Nursey-Bray, Rosemary. (Carroll, Lewis) **Lewis Carroll's Through the looking glass and what Alice found there.** (Through the looking glass.) CAST: 3f, 2m, 23u. ACTS: 1. SETTINGS: Life-sized chess board. PLAYING TIME: NA. PLOT: Alice's imagination takes her into the looking glass world where she becomes a pawn in a confusing and frustrating chess game. After many strange encounters, she manages to arrive at the other side of the chess board to become a queen. RECOMMENDATION: This is a delight. Music and special effects such as a strobe light, create the appropriate atmosphere. The cast is expandable and there is the option of including two puppet shows for the poems, "The Walrus and the Carpenter" and "Jabberwocky." Older actors will have to produce this. ROYALTY: $35. SOURCE: Nursey-Bray, Rosemary. (1988). Lewis Carroll's Through the looking glass and what Alice found there. New Orleans, LA: Anchorage Press, Inc. SUBJECTS/PLAY TYPE: Fantasy; Chess; Musical; Adaptation.

1720. 11-12. (+) Goldoni, Carlo & Yalman, Tunc. (Goldoni, Carlo) **The liar.** (Il bugiardo.) CAST: 3f, 10m, Su. ACTS: 3. SETTINGS: Venice square; two houses. PLAYING TIME: NA. PLOT: Lelio, an unremitting liar, convinces Rosaura that he is the anonymous admirer who has serenaded her and sent her gifts, though it was really Florindo. Lelio tells Ottavio that Rosaura and her sister Beatrice (loved by Ottavio) have entertained him in their apartment when their father was absent, ruining the girls' reputations and alienating Ottavio from Beatrice. Lelio's servant imitates his master's tactics in his own romantic quests. However, virtue is rewarded when Ottavio and shy Florindo earn the hands of Beatrice and Rosaura, and Florindo's servant rather than Lelio's, wins the maid Colombina. RECOMMENDATION: This comedy playfully builds around courtship and social conduct conventions of 18th century Venice. Its sprightliness is enhanced by the characters' spoken "asides" and by the rapid movement of the action. The play sustains its humor and piquant characterizations; the players and audience need only a touch of sophistication to adjust to its historical character, since human nature is universal. ROYALTY: $35. SOURCE: Goldoni, Carlo. (1973). The liar. New York, NY: Dramatists Play Service. SUBJECTS/PLAY TYPE: Courtship; Lying; Comedy.

1721. 9-12. (+) Tesutis, Joseph. **Liars. CAST:** 5m. **ACTS:** 1. **SETTINGS:** Dorm room. **PLAYING TIME:** 30 min. **PLOT:** Two young men fight to deny their homosexuality after a page from their diary is stolen and posted on the school bulletin board. One, in desperation slits his wrist. They finally admit their love for each other as they leave for the hospital. RECOMMENDATION: Written without any phony philosophy by a 17 year old playwright, this shows two boys realistically reacting to their dilemma and facing their feelings. This will provoke discussion which should be carefully orchestrated. ROYALTY: NA. SOURCE: Lamb, Wendy. (1986). Meeting the winter bike rider and other prize winning plays. New York, NY: Dell. SUBJECTS/PLAY TYPE: Homosexuality; Drama.

1722. 6-9. (+) Sodaro, Craig. **Liberty's spy. CAST:** 3f, 2m. **ACTS:** 1. **SETTINGS:** Parlor. **PLAYING TIME:** 25 min. **PLOT:** Three women who support the Continental Army and operate an inn on the road to Philadelphia must pretend that they are loyal to the Crown to avoid being hanged. When a man claiming to be a spy for George Washington appears, Polly gives him secret information to take to Washington. The imposter actually works for the Redcoats and tells the three women that they are to be hanged for treason. Mr. Gate, a wealthy miller, enters the inn, is identified as Washington's spy, and taken prisoner. One of the women strikes the Redcoat over the head with a frying pan, and all three swear to keep Gate's identity a secret. RECOMMENDATION: The nonstereotyped women and the very believable dialogue make this a valuable contribution to a collection of dramatic pieces on the American Revolution. ROYALTY: Free to Plays subscribers. SOURCE: Sodaro, Craig. (1987, April). Liberty's spy. Plays: The Drama Magazine for Young People, pp. 23-30. SUBJECTS/PLAY TYPE: Revolution, U.S.; Espionage; Playlet.

1723. K-4. (+) Gotwalt, Helen Louise Miller. **Library circus. CAST:** Su. **ACTS:** 1. **SETTINGS:** Bare stage, props. **PLAYING TIME:** 15 min. **PLOT:** Children try to guess the stories, as the animals in them appear.

RECOMMENDATION: The stories may be unfamiliar to today's children, so this guessing game will not hold their attention. ROYALTY: None. SOURCE: Gotwalt, Helen Louise Miller. (1985). First plays for children: A collection of little plays for the youngest players. Boston, MA: Plays, Inc. SUBJECTS/PLAY TYPE: Books; Book Week; Libraries; Playlet.

1724. 3-7. (+) Duffy, Kathleen. **The library of the enchanted kingdom. CAST:** 1f, 2m, 4u. **ACTS:** 1. **SETTINGS:** Circulation desk. **PLAYING TIME:** 15 min. **PLOT:** The Wolf as librarian provides reference services for different characters from children's tales (i.e., tells the prince where Beauty is, helps the witch repair her broom, gives a dog a film on how to catch a cat, etc.). RECOMMENDATION: This humorous play provides a likable character in the witty Wolf as he demonstrates the different services that a library offers. ROYALTY: Free to Plays subscribers. SOURCE: Duffy, Kathleen. (1982, November). The library of the enchanted kingdom. Plays: The Drama Magazine for Young People, pp. 58-62. SUBJECTS/PLAY TYPE: Book Week; Libraries; Fantasy.

1725. 3-6. (+) Nolan, Paul T. **Licha's birthday serenade. CAST:** 8f, 6m, Su. **ACTS:** 1. **SETTINGS:** Yard. **PLAYING TIME:** 20 min. **PLOT:** Licha is sad because her parents are too poor to buy her the silver bracelet she wants for her birthday. She wishes for the joys of the city. Luisa, a city girl, happens onto Licha's birthday celebration. It is also Luisa's birthday and her wish was to spend a day in the country. As Licha's parents invite Luisa and her parents to join them in a meal, Luisa gives Licha the extra silver bracelet she received for her birthday, the very bracelet Licha wanted. RECOMMENDATION: This presents the adage that for many, the "grass is always greener on the other side." Although set in Mexico, it would be better left without the ethnic references. ROYALTY: None for amateur performance. SOURCE: Nolan, Paul T. (1982). Folk tale plays round the world: A collection of royalty-free, one-act plays about lands far and near. Boston, MA: Plays, Inc. SUBJECTS/PLAY TYPE: Birthdays; Values; Drama.

1726. 1-6*. (+) Jackson, R. Eugene & Alette, Carl. (Baum, Frank L.) **The life and adventures of Santa Claus.** (The life and adventures of Santa Claus) **CAST:** 8f, 3m, 5u. **ACTS:** 2. **SETTINGS:** Woods; Cave. **PLAYING TIME:** NA. **PLOT:** The mean Awgivas kidnap Santa and hide him in a cave. The children follow the Awgivas to the caves and are captured. Santa's elves arrive with their magic toy bags which, when thrown over the Awgivas' heads, immobilize them. Knowing that they can't keep the Awgivas in the toy bags forever, Santa moves to the North Pole, the only safe place in the world. Before he goes, he is presented with a cloak of immortality by his mother, and a sleigh pulled by reindeer to help with the toy deliveries. RECOMMENDATION: This has a good blend of humor and song which keeps the story lively. ROYALTY: NA. SOURCE: Jackson, R. Eugene & Alette, Carl. (1988). The life and adventures of Santa Claus. Denver, CO: Pioneer Drama Service, Inc. SUBJECTS/PLAY TYPE: Santa Claus; Christmas; Musical.

1727. K-2*. (-) Sullivan, Jessie P. **Life can be exciting.** CAST: 2u. ACTS: 1. SETTINGS: Puppet stage. PLAYING TIME: NA. PLOT: Mortimer complains that he is bored. Mathilda suggests that he not watch TV so much, but spend some time reading the Bible and listening to what God says. RECOMMENDATION: Young children would not be able to read the Bible themselves, nor would they comprehend the intended message presented in John 13:17. ROYALTY: None. SOURCE: Sullivan, Jessie P. (1978). Puppet scripts for children's church. Grand Rapids, MI: Baker Book House. SUBJECTS/PLAY TYPE: Christian Drama; Bible; Puppet Play.

1728. 9-12*. (+) Rush, David. **"Life" is only 7 points.** CAST: 1f, 2m. ACTS: 1. SETTINGS: Condominium. PLAYING TIME: NA. PLOT: At his traditional Sunday dinner with his parents, 40 year old, divorced Jerry remembers a turning point in his life when he and his now senile and ailing father (Sid) became strangers to each other after a boating accident when Jerry was still a child. Jerry, who only remembers that his father hit him, is poignantly enlightened by his mother, who explains that Sid hit him only to stop his hysterical crying and restart normal breathing after Jerry had nearly drowned. The incident was so devastating to Sid, that one month later he suffered a heart attack, and began his quick descent into senility and ill health. Jerry, consumed with regret, emotionally cries out, "I wish I'd known, God, all these years..." RECOMMENDATION: The heartrending message of this touching drama will only be fully assimilated by audiences familiar enough with Jewish culture to feel comfortable with the Yiddish words, and culturally based colloquialisms and situations. Also, some references to sex may have to be edited out, and the production would probably work better if acted by adults. ROYALTY: $15. SOURCE: Rush, David. (1987). "Life" is only 7 points. Woodstock, IL: Dramatic Pub. Co. SUBJECTS/PLAY TYPE: Family Relationships; Drama.

1729. 9-12. (-) Nobleman, Roberta. **The life of Vic.** CAST: 2f, 6m, Su. ACTS: 1. SETTINGS: Bare stage. PLAYING TIME: NA. PLOT: Vic's life, from conception to death, is pantomimed. For example, the first scene shows the "sperm" (played by children) impregnating the girl who is the "egg." Other scenes focus on events that lock Vic in, like playpens and, later, jails. RECOMMENDATION: Although the theme may interest the intended age group, the action is depressing and the pantomime of conception may cause controversy. ROYALTY: NA. SOURCE: Nobleman, Roberta. (1979). Mime and masks. Rowayton, CT: New Plays Books. SUBJECTS/PLAY TYPE: Imprisonment; Life Stages; Pantomime.

1730. 4-5. (+) Van Tuyle, Jean. **The lift.** CAST: 4f, 5m. ACTS: 1. SETTINGS: Elevator. PLAYING TIME: 10 min. PLOT: Five strangers stranded in an elevator react to their situation in revealing ways. The electricity is eventually restored and they leave the elevator shortly before there is a loud snapping noise and the cables break. Shocked by their narrow escape, one character screams and runs off while the others faint. Four bystanders appear, discover the bodies and, mistaking the scene for an accident, call for

help as the curtain falls. RECOMMENDATION: Had the characterizations been a little deeper, this could have been an interesting study in human behavior. ROYALTY: Free to Plays subscribers. SOURCE: Van Tuyle, Jean. (1982, May). The lift. Plays: The Drama Magazine for Young People, pp. 73-77. SUBJECTS/PLAY TYPE: Elevators; Phobias; Skit.

1731. 5-12. (+) Fisher, Aileen Lucia. **Light in the darkness.** CAST: Su. ACTS: 1. SETTINGS: Bare stage. PLAYING TIME: 1 min. PLOT: The "light in the darkness" is the "light" of Christopher Columbus' faith that he would discover the new world. RECOMMENDATION: This could be used as an introduction or ending to a program about Columbus. ROYALTY: Free to Plays subscribers. SOURCE: Fisher, Aileen Lucia. (1987, October). Light in the darkness. Plays: The Drama Magazine for Young People, pp. 46. SUBJECTS/PLAY TYPE: Columbus, Christopher; Choral Reading.

1732. 4-12. (+) Reimer, Earl. **The light is too dark.** CAST: 4f, 4m, 2u. ACTS: 1. SETTINGS: Bare stage, props. PLAYING TIME: NA. PLOT: Abdon is healed of blindness by Christ. The townspeople, the Pharisees, and his own family attempt to devise reasonable, logical explanations for Abdon's new sight in an effort to discredit the miracle. Besides Abdon, only Maria, a young Hebrew girl, is willing to accept it. Two narrators remind the audience that "yet there are still those who reject the light, preferring rather to sit in darkness by the western gate, living but only partly living." RECOMMENDATION: This would spark intolerance and animosity toward non-Christians in an era when understanding should predominate. ROYALTY: $10. SOURCE: Reimer, Earl. (1979). The light is too dark. Boston, MA: Baker's Plays. SUBJECTS/PLAY TYPE: Christ, Jesus; Christian Drama.

1733. 9-12. (+) Van Ziwzendorf, Nicolaus Ludwig. **The light of the world.** CAST: Su. ACTS: 1. SETTINGS: None. PLAYING TIME: 60 min. PLOT: This is a compilation of Bible readings from Psalms, Isaiah, Daniel, Proverbs, Gospels of John and Matthew, and Revelation. RECOMMENDATION: This may present problems for young children who would have to read the passages aloud during a candlelight church service. However, the chosen passages are appropriate to the Christmas season and are well integrated. ROYALTY: None. SOURCE: Hendricks, William & Vogel, Cora. (1983). Handbook of Christmas programs. Grand Rapids, MI: Baker Book House. SUBJECTS/PLAY TYPE: Christmas; Worship Program.

1734. 9-12. (+) Carpenter, Sally. **Lights... camera...Christmas!** CAST: 4f, 3m, 5u. ACTS: 1. SETTINGS: Film studio set. PLAYING TIME: 45 min. PLOT: The director, encountering a lack of enthusiasm from the high school actors, explains how important this Christmas film is. The actors are inspired and the take is perfect. The big boss tells them the film is finished unless some violence and sex are added. The director is intimidated and agrees to the changes, but the actors threaten to tell all the high school students in town to boycott the boss's movie theaters. He agrees to let the film continue. The play ends when the camera man says the camera ran out of film during the last take. RECOMMENDATION: This is a delightful, fast moving holiday play, suited for a church presentation. As it progresses, three self centered high school students mature. ROYALTY: NA. SOURCE: Carpenter, Sally. (1987). Lights...camera...Christmas! Denver, CO: Pioneer Drama Service. SUBJECTS/PLAY TYPE: Christmas; Drama.

1735. 6-9. (+) Hayes, Theresa. **Like a careless match.** CAST: 2f, 2m, 27u. ACTS: 3. SETTINGS: Auditorium; car; living/dining room; classroom; office. PLAYING TIME: 90 min. PLOT: Hardworking, but not particularly gifted, Danny wins the state science fair with his conservation project. When a jealous friend makes an offhand comment about Danny being too dumb to have done the project on his own, it is overheard by two gossipers, and, through other gossips, Danny is formally accused of cheating. The church youth group prompts the original jealous friend to admit his guilt, the chain of gossip is followed to its end, and Danny is vindicated. Discussion questions are provided at the end of the play. RECOMMENDATION: This realistically portrays how one idle comment can get out of hand. It also exposes the double standards that say that gossiping with friends is OK, as long as it doesn't go beyond that. Because of references to God and prayer, this is most appropriate for a church presentation. The director should change some of the predominantly female gossipers into males to avoid sexism. ROYALTY: NA. SOURCE: Hayes, Theresa. (1986). Getting your act together. Cincinnati, OH: Standard Pub. Co. SUBJECTS/PLAY TYPE: Gossip; Christian Drama.

1736. 7-12. (+) Clough, Judith L. **The lily and the rue.** CAST: 7f, 3m, Su. ACTS: 2. SETTINGS: Courtyard; kitchen; mainroom; market- place; tombs. PLAYING TIME: 90 min. PLOT: This Biblical story of Mary, Martha, and Lazarus, focuses on Martha and her religious development through Jesus' visits, Lazarus' death, and Jesus raising Lazarus from the dead. Because of what she learns from Jesus, Martha becomes more tolerant of others and herself. RECOMMENDATION: Although dramatization of the Bible stories found in Luke:10 and John:12 would be a technical challenge for young players, there is strong characterization and sustaining conflict. For church groups, this is not a religious play so much as one about a woman whose inner struggle is resolved through her faith. ROYALTY: NA. SOURCE: Clough, Judith L. (1986). The lily and the rue. Franklin, OH: Eldridge Pub. Co. SUBJECTS/PLAY TYPE: Religious Faith; Women; Christian Drama.

1737. 9-12. (+) Huff, Betty Tracy. **Lily of the label department.** CAST: 7f, 6m. ACTS: 1. SETTINGS: Clothes factory. PLAYING TIME: 30 min. PLOT: Lily Trueworth must save her job at Milbury's clothing factory after the villain drops a "washable" label into the box of "dry clean only" labels. Lily succeeds and finds her true love at the same time; Milbury's receives a new account; and the villain changes his ways. RECOMMENDATION: This is cute and undemanding. ROYALTY: Free to Plays subscribers. SOURCE: Huff, Betty Tracy. (1983, May). Lily

of the label department. Plays: The Drama Magazine for Young People, pp. 14-24. SUBJECTS/PLAY TYPE: Dry Cleaning; Melodrama.

1738. 10-12. (+) Kundrat, Theodore V. **The lily of the marshes.** CAST: 3f, 4m. ACTS: 1. SETTINGS: None. PLAYING TIME: 30 min. PLOT: This dramatization of the Saint Maria Goretti (the Virgin Martyr) is based on factual religious history. Born in poverty and a devout Catholic, Maria's life was tragically ended at age eleven when she was murdered by a would-be rapist. She was canonized in Rome in 1950, because of her piety and her deathbed pardon of her murderer. RECOMMENDATION: Due to sensitive subject matter and violent events, some may not find the play suitable for an audience of children or even high schoolers. Also, because of references to Jesus and specific religious dogma, the play might be better performed for a church audience. ROYALTY: $10. SOURCE: Kundrat, Theodore V. (1978). The lily of the marshes. Chicago, IL: Coach House Press. SUBJECTS/PLAY TYPE: Saints; Goretti, Saint Maria; Reader's Theater.

1739. 9-12. (+) Taggart, Tom. **Lily, the felon's daughter.** CAST: 6f, 5m. ACTS: 3. SETTINGS: Parlor. PLAYING TIME: NA. PLOT: This is the tale of pure Lily Fairweather and her adopted family's fall from grace. Sold to Jonas Fairweather as a child, Lily is betrothed to the overindulgent, gambling and felonious son, Compton. Evil Craven Sinclair, in his passion for Lily, has urged Compton towards corruption. The betrothal is interrupted when Compton's crimes are revealed and Sinclair steals Mrs. Fairweather's hoard of money which could save Compton. Compton flees, leaving Jonas Fairweather to go to jail for Compton's crimes and Lily claiming she took the money for some unknown reason. RECOMMENDATION: Although the plot is hard to believe, clever asides, double entendres, fast pace and a generally comic mood might redeem this silly piece. ROYALTY: NA. SOURCE: Taggart, Tom. (1976). Lily, the felon's daughter. New York, NY: Samuel French. SUBJECTS/PLAY TYPE: Musical; Melodrama.

1740. 9-12. (+) McDonough, Jerome. **Limbo.** CAST: 5f, 6m, 1u. ACTS: 1. SETTINGS: Waiting room. PLAYING TIME: 35 min. PLOT: Four people are transported to a dingy waiting room with no idea how they got there and no apparent way out. Refusing at first to accept that they are dead, each attempts to find a way back home. They eventually do find various doors out of Limbo as each person encounters what he expects and/or fears most in the hereafter. RECOMMENDATION: The cast consists of the onstage waiting room characters and the groundkeepers of a cemetery who work in the audience. Both groups seem unaware of each other. Only one, a bag lady, seems to be aware of all the players. Do people create the hereafter by how they live? What can they expect after death? Can they do anything to change the future? These are the provocative questions addressed by the playwright in a very interesting manner. The answers are left to the audience. ROYALTY: $20. SOURCE: McDonough, Jerome. (1984). Limbo. Schulenburg, TX: I.E. Clark. SUBJECTS/PLAY TYPE: Death; Eternity; Drama.

1741. 9-12. (+) O'Brien, John. **Limbo. CAST:** 3f, 2m. **ACTS:** 1. **SETTINGS:** Garden. **PLAYING TIME:** NA. **PLOT:** Three daughters visit their aged father, who is suffering from senility, and keeps talking, in one word sentences, about receiving a Christmas card from his son, Joey. The father has one rational moment and speaks clearly to his son before collapsing and dying before his daughters. **RECOMMENDATION:** This is a thought provoking look at senility, as well as the neglectful ways in which children often treat their parents. **ROYALTY:** NA. **SOURCE:** O'Brien, John. (1986). Limbo. Woodstock, IL: Dramatic Pub. Co. **SUBJECTS/PLAY TYPE:** Senility; Family Relationships; Drama.

1742. 6-12. (+) Fisher, Aileen Lucia. **Lincoln Memorial. CAST:** Su. **ACTS:** 1. **SETTINGS:** None. **PLAYING TIME:** 5 min. **PLOT:** Readings reflect on Lincoln: the man, his ideals, and the monument to him. All unite to close with a quotation from Lincoln's Second Inaugural Address. **RECOMMENDATION:** The set and costumes can easily be managed in this presentation, good for Lincoln's birthday or Civil War studies. **ROYALTY:** Free to Plays subscribers. **SOURCE:** Fisher, Aileen Lucia. (1985, January/February). Lincoln Memorial. Plays: The Drama Magazine for Young People, pp. 64-65. **SUBJECTS/PLAY TYPE:** Lincoln, Abraham; Choral Reading.

1743. 2-4. (+) Hark, Mildred & McQueen, Noel. **Lincoln reminders. CAST:** 2m, 15u. **ACTS:** 1. **SETTINGS:** Living room. **PLAYING TIME:** 10 min. **PLOT:** A school child has to learn facts about Abraham Lincoln. He falls asleep and dreams of large pennies coming out of a piggy bank. Each penny tells him a fact (in rhyme) about Abraham Lincoln. **RECOMMENDATION:** Since each penny is actually an actor, this will provide many children a small speaking part. **ROYALTY:** Free to Plays subscribers. **SOURCE:** Hark, Mildred & McQueen, Noel. (1988, January/February). Lincoln reminders. Plays: The Drama Magazine for Young People, pp. 31-34. **SUBJECTS/PLAY TYPE:** Lincoln, Abraham; Choral Reading.

1744. 11-12. (+) Gottwalt, Helen Louise Miller. **Lincoln's funeral train. CAST:** 14f, 14m, Su. **ACTS:** 1. **SETTINGS:** Bare stage. **PLAYING TIME:** 20 min. **PLOT:** As Lincoln's funeral train passes, people gather to pay their respects and share memories of the President. There are those who knew him personally and those who simply loved and admired him. This is told mainly in poetry and a chorus speaks most of the lines. **RECOMMENDATION:** The mood is serious, even somber; the subject and vocabulary make this a play for mature audiences and performers. Patriotic songs and costumes of the Civil War period are required, along with wreaths, flags, and lanterns. **ROYALTY:** Free to Plays subscribers. **SOURCE:** Gottwalt, Helen Louise Miller. (1981, February). Lincoln's funeral train. Plays: The Drama Magazine for Young People, pp. 47-52. **SUBJECTS/PLAY TYPE:** History, U.S.; Lincoln, Abraham; Funerals; Choral Reading.

1745. 7-12. (+) Jackson, R. Eugene & Ellis, David. **Lindy. CAST:** 14f, 10m, Su. **ACTS:** 2. **SETTINGS:** Room; living room; office; classroom; alley; stage; apartment; teenage hangout. **PLAYING TIME:** NA. **PLOT:** Lindy is a new student at Green River High School who tries to fit in. She and her mother moved under an alias because her father is wanted by both the mob and the FBI. Lindy joins the drama class to make friends, and during one of the practices Cookie is kidnapped by the mob instead of Lindy. The mobsters are captured by the FBI when they return with Cookie. **RECOMMENDATION:** In this highly entertaining musical, characters are typical, musical numbers are well placed, and many of the songs have humorous lyrics. **ROYALTY:** NA. **SOURCE:** Jackson, R. Eugene & Ellis, David. (1981). Lindy. Elgin, IL: Performance Pub. Co. **SUBJECTS/PLAY TYPE:** High School; Musical.

1746. 1-4. (+) Steinhorn, Harriet & Lowry, Edith. **The line for life. CAST:** 7f, 7m, Su. **ACTS:** 2. **SETTINGS:** Concentration camp; barracks. **PLAYING TIME:** 20 min. **PLOT:** The 1942 inmates of German concentration camp Hasag, Verk-C learn that the youngest and sickest are to return home to the ghetto. However, two days after they arrive, they are sent to gas chambers. Only three of the original group survive. **RECOMMENDATION:** This gruesome drama depicts as much of the horrors of the holocaust as youngsters would be able to assimi-late. It would be an excellent presentation for any group studying the atrocities of World War II. **ROYALTY:** Free for amateur groups. **SOURCE:** Steinhorn, Harriet and Lowry, Edith. (1983). Shadows of the holocaust: Plays, readings, and program resources. Rockville, MD: Kar-Ben Copies, Inc. **SUBJECTS/PLAY TYPE:** Holocaust; Concentration Camps; World War II; Drama.

1747. 1-3. (+) Lynch-Watson, Janet. (Aesopus) **The Lion and the mouse.** (The lion and the mouse) **CAST:** 3u. **ACTS:** 2. **SETTINGS:** Forest. **PLAYING TIME:** 12 min. **PLOT:** A lion spares the life of a mouse who climbed up on him, thinking he was a hill. The mouse later returns the favor by chewing through a net to set the lion free. **RECOMMENDATION:** This adaptation of the well known fable provides instructions for presenting it as a shadow puppet play. Patterns for the puppets and other production notes are included. **ROYALTY:** NA. **SOURCE:** Lynch-Watson, Janet. (1980). The shadow puppet book. NY: Sterling Pub. Co. **SUBJECTS/PLAY TYPE:** Fables; Kindness; Shadow Puppet Play.

1748. K-3. (+) Flohr, John W. **The lion hunt. CAST:** 2u. **ACTS:** 1. **SETTINGS:** Bare stage. **PLAYING TIME:** NA. **PLOT:** The audience goes on an imaginary lion hunt. **RECOMMENDATION:** This "pseudo-play," based on a camp rhythm activity, provides total audience participation with easily learned roles. **ROYALTY:** NA. **SOURCE:** Flohr, John W. & Smith Robert B. (1984). Music dramas for children with special needs. Denton, TX: Troostwyk Press. **SUBJECTS/PLAY TYPE:** Lions; Skit.

1749. 3-6. (-) Carlson, Bernice Wells. **Lion sick and dying. CAST:** 6u. **ACTS:** 1. **SETTINGS:** Lion's den. **PLAYING TIME:** NA. **PLOT:** A suspicious fox is the only survivor when a group of animals makes a trip to visit the supposedly dying king lion. **RECOMMENDATION:**

Carlson handles the idea of survival in the wilderness clumsily, and younger children may find this disturbing. ROYALTY: None. SOURCE: Carlson, Bernice Wells. (1982). Let's find the big idea. Nashville, TN: Abingdon Press. SUBJECTS/PLAY TYPE: Lions; Survival; Playlet.

1750. 3-5*. (+) Boiko, Claire. **Lion to lamb.** CAST: 11f, 11m, Su. ACTS: 1. SETTINGS: Bare stage, props, backdrop. PLAYING TIME: 15 min. PLOT: This charming, articulate choral reading contrasts the effects and missions of March winds. Lion wind (gales, gusts, and tempests) snatches hats and newspapers, tears shingles from roofs, and musses hair. But Lion wind also soars kites, dries laundry, cools the brow of workers in the hot sun, and drives the windmill. Lamb wind dances lightly, hums, whispers, and purrs. Note is taken of the fact that the Lion wind of early March mysteriously transforms to the delicate, balmy breeze of April. RECOMMENDATION: Alliteration, onomatopoeia, and a barrage of sounds and other sensory stimuli alert and captivate the audience. The evocative language and literary technique warrant inclusion in an elementary poetry unit as well as a study of oral interpretation. ROYALTY: None. SOURCE: Boiko, Claire. (1985). Children's plays for creative actors. Boston, MA: Plays, Inc. SUBJECTS/PLAY TYPE: Seasons; Wind; March; Skit.

1751. 9-12. (+) Avery, Charles. **Lissa Stratton strikes.** CAST: 5f, 6m, Su. ACTS: 2. SETTINGS: High school lounge. PLAYING TIME: 100 min. PLOT: Based on the Lysistrata theme from Aristophanes' comedy, this musical revolves around a male-female conflict in a modern American high school. The girls go on strike, refusing to date, kiss or touch their boyfriends until they apologize for embarrassing an unattractive, unpopular girl by nominating her for Homecoming Queen. The hands-off strategy, inspired by Lissa Stratton's reading of the Greek comedy, works well until the leader of the pranksters cons one naive girl into almost breaking the pact. The climax occurs at the Homecoming Dance, which all the guys attend stag, except for their leader, who brings a date from out of town. His plan to humiliate the naive girl by saying she led him on backfires when she proves he is lying. The leader of the pranksters apologizes and the strike ends. RECOMMENDATION: The play incorporates themes of peer pressure, the maturation process, and the "macho" image. The song lyrics reflect the themes in a witty fashion. Although the characters represent types, they are given much depth. ROYALTY: $50. SOURCE: Avery, Charles. (1986). Lissa Stratton strikes back. Schulenburg, TX: I.E. Clark, Inc. SUBJECTS/PLAY TYPE: Relationships; Peer Pressure; Musical.

1752. 1-4. (+) Watts, Irene N. **Listen to the drum.** CAST: 1f, 1m, 9u. ACTS: 1. SETTINGS: Bare stage. PLAYING TIME: NA. PLOT: Raven creates the world: seeds transform into plants and trees; pods grow into man and woman; animals (which the audience plays) grow from clay. Raven searches for a wife. He finds Keewak, but she flies away. Fox Girl cleans Raven's igloo, but she refuses to stay because she feels that she smells awful. Raven doesn't care because she is kind. She chooses to stay, but only if Raven promises that no one will make fun

of her. A rude owl visits and tells Raven that his igloo smells. Raven flattens Owl's beak, which is why, to this day, owls have flat beaks. Everyone is happy in the village, until the day Axsuq appears and tries to kill Raven. The audience shoots arrows at Axsuq and wounds him. A witch brings a serpent to fight Raven, and Raven wins. RECOMMENDATION: This Eskimo legend about the creation of the world incorporates a great deal of audience participation, necessitating production by adults or young adults, but some older children might be able to assist. The characters are well developed and each has a purpose as the narrator brings the story into focus. ROYALTY: NA. SOURCE: Watts, Irene N. (1978). A blizzard leaves no footprints; listen to the drum; patches; the rainstone: Four children's plays. Toronto, Canada: Playwrights Co-op. SUBJECTS/PLAY TYPE: Legends, Eskimo; Creation Stories; Playlet.

1753. 5-12. (+) Winther, Barbara. **Listen to the Hodja.** CAST: 3f, 5m, Su. ACTS: 1. SETTINGS: Bare stage, props. PLAYING TIME: 20 min. PLOT: Hodja, dressed poorly, arrives at his friend Jamal's home for supper, but is ignored. When Hodja changes into clothes of excessive finery and is welcomed by his friends, he places the meal in his shirt, as his clothes are obviously what his host intended to welcome to dinner. Later, Hodja plans to serve his guest, the Mongol invader Tamerlane, with fine beets, which Jamal exchanges with rotten figs. Tamerlane is insulted and throws the decaying fruit at his host. Hodja later thanks his friend for replacing the hard beets with such a soft fruit. RECOMMENDATION: This examines ethics, philosophy, and feminism, wisely combined with color, comedy, and humor. ROYALTY: Free for amateur performance. SOURCE: Winther, Barbara. (1976). Plays from folktales of Africa and Asia. Boston, MA: Plays, Inc. SUBJECTS/PLAY TYPE: Folk Tales, Turkey; Playlet.

1754. 3-5. (+) McSweeny, Maxine. **Listen to the peace and goodwill.** CAST: 4f, 6m. ACTS: 1. SETTINGS: Living room. PLAYING TIME: NA. PLOT: Martians conclude that Santa's frantic activity for Christmas is a plot to destroy the universe. They plan to kidnap Santa. Meanwhile, Santa, upset by his helpers' quarreling and the unrest in the world, decides to stay home this Christmas Eve unless his helpers show some good will. The helpers try to be pleasant, but as Santa prepares to leave, the Martians try to stop him, and explain their reasons why. The helpers claim that their mission is to make people happy, but that work pressure sometimes makes them quarrel. Santa concurs that his aim is to bring good will, and invites the Martians to come along on his ride. RECOMMENDATION: The Martians' misinterpretation of Christmas is a logical mistake and the quarrels are comical, but not degrading. ROYALTY: NA. SOURCE: McSweeny, Maxine. (1977). Christmas plays for young players. South Brunswick: A.S. Barnes. SUBJECTS/PLAY TYPE: Christmas; Martians; Comedy.

1755. 4-7. (+) Kehret, Peg. **Listening to the grown-up ladies talk.** CAST: 1f. ACTS: 1. SETTINGS: None. PLAYING TIME: NA. PLOT: The mystery and wonder of adult talk is examined by children. RECOMMENDATION: Suitable for the very young, the light discussion will be very familiar. ROYALTY: NA. SOURCE: Kehret, Peg. (1986). Winning monologs for young actors. Colorado Springs, CO: Meriwether Pub. SUBJECTS/PLAY TYPE: Eavesdropping; Monologue.

1756. K-6. (+) Martin, Judith & Ashwander, Donald. **Litter, litter.** CAST: 4u. ACTS: 1. SETTINGS: None. PLAYING TIME: 10 min. PLOT: A garbage man tries to pick up litter while two business executives walk around with boxes of wax paper, tearing sheets off and dropping them on the floor. This evolves into a rhythmic dance and the garbage man ends up on the floor covered in a heap of waxed paper. A second garbage man sweeps the first and the paper off the stage. RECOMMENDATION: Since this is choreographed to music, the actors should have some dancing experience. Also, because of the sharp cutting edges on the wax paper boxes, it is not recommended for very young children to perform. It could be used to initiate a discussion about the environment. ROYALTY: NA. SOURCE: Martin, Judith & Ashwander, Donald. (1985). Reasons to be cheerful: A revue for children. New York, NY: The Paper Bag Players, Inc. SUBJECTS/PLAY TYPE: Environment; Pantomime; Litter; Musical Revue.

1757. 7-12. (+) Christmas, Joyce A. **A little bit o'Heaven.** CAST: 6f, 7m, Su. ACTS: 1. SETTINGS: Living room/dining area. PLAYING TIME: 35 min. PLOT: Susan Young's mother sends a leprechaun back from her world tour. He creates lively confusion. When the leprechaun is offered a job, the Youngs believe their problem is solved. The mother returns early from her travels with another leprechaun. RECOMMENDATION: The leprechaun and the Irish connection make this appropriate for St. Patrick's day. However, the situations sometimes seem a bit unrealistic and many special props are required. Some of the magical special effects might also be difficult. ROYALTY: Free to Plays Subscribers. SOURCE: Christmas, Joyce S. (1980, March). A little bit o'Heaven. Plays: The Drama Magazine for Young People, pp. 1-11. SUBJECTS/PLAY TYPE: St. Patrick's Day; Leprechauns; Comedy.

1758. 1-3. (+) Duvall, Lucille. **Little Chip's Christmas tree.** CAST: 2m, 17u. ACTS: 1. SETTINGS: Cabin. PLAYING TIME: NA. PLOT: Poor in possessions, but eager to give a Christmas gift, little Chip brings a tree into his house so the elves might sleep there to stay warm during the winter. The elves are so touched that they decorate the tree and fill the empty cupboards with food. RECOMMENDATION: In addition to explaining Christmas trees, this allows the actors to trim the tree on stage. ROYALTY: Free to Plays subscribers. SOURCE: Kamerman, Sylvia E. (1975). A treasury of Christmas plays. Boston, MA: Plays, Inc. SUBJECTS/PLAY TYPE: Christmas; Playlet.

1759. 7-12. (+) Thane, Adele. (Hugo, Victor) **Little Cosette and Father Christmas.** (Les Miserables) CAST: 7f, 9m. ACTS: 1. SETTINGS: Lobby. PLAYING TIME: 30 min. PLOT: Little Cosette meets a man (Jean Valjean) whom she calls Father Christmas. He rescues her from the Thenardier's home where she was being mistreated. RECOMMENDATION: Jean Valjean's love for little Cosette is timeless. The adaptation is powerful and moving. ROYALTY: Free to Plays subscribers. SOURCE: Thane, Adele. (1984, December). Little Cosette and Father Christmas. Plays: The Drama Magazine for Young People, pp. 55-64. SUBJECTS/PLAY TYPE: Love; Christmas; Adaptation.

1760. 12. (+) Delsado, Ramon Louis. **A little holy water.** CAST: 2f, 3m. ACTS: 2. SETTINGS: Stage, platforms, geometric forms. PLAYING TIME: NA. PLOT: El Lector, the reader, was traditionally paid by Cuban cigar factory workers to read while they hand rolled cigars. The readings were varied, but when they started to include socialist writings, management objected and removed El Lector. In protest, the workers struck. The strike produced divisions and near tragedy in the once united and loving Hernandez family because Mercedez, wife of the leader of the strike, objected to the labor unrest that endangered the lives and income of her husband, son, and uncle. When she realized the importance that freedom and commitment to the worker's cause had in all their lives, the family was once more united. RECOMMENDATION: Historically accurate, this is recommended for older audiences because of adult themes and language. The drama would be most successful where there is a strong Cuban or Spanish community. However, the First Amendment theme has universal appeal and application. Casting the play requires choosing actors who can speak Spanish or effectively master the pronunciation and emphasis of the language. ROYALTY: $35. SOURCE: Delsado, Ramon Louis. (1983). A little holy water. Schulenburg, TX: I.E. Clark. SUBJECTS/PLAY TYPE: Cuban Americans; First Amendment; Freedom; Drama.

1761. 3-12*. (+) Swortzell, Lowell. (Yershov, Pyotor) **The little humpback horse.** (The little humpback horse) CAST: 3f, 7m, Su. ACTS: 3. SETTINGS: Wooden pavilion with towers; stairs; connecting bridge; countryside. PLAYING TIME: NA. PLOT: The magic humpback horse helps Ivan complete "impossible" tasks given him by the Tsar, including capturing the beautiful Firebird, visiting the Lady in the Moon, and releasing the Whale on whose back lives an entire town. After outwitting the Tsar, Ivan marries the daughter of the Lady in the Moon and they live happily ever after with the little humpback horse. RECOMMENDATION: This carries the universal appeal of wondrous adventures and ultimate good fortune for the protagonist and his magic horse. There are slapstick elements and all will enjoy the magic of "flying." Because of very fast paced dialogue and the possibility of intricate set design, this is probably best suited for a community theater production. ROYALTY: $35. SOURCE: Swortzell, Lowell. (1984). The little humpback horse. Anchorage Press, Inc. SUBJECTS/PLAY TYPE: Folk Tales, Russia; Adaptation.

1762. K-4. (+) Mahlman, Lewis & Jones, David Cadwalader. **The little Indian brave.** CAST: 10u. ACTS: 1. SETTINGS: Tepee; woods. PLAYING TIME: 25 min. PLOT: A young Indian, on his way to accomplish three deeds which will make him a brave, helps an owl, a spider and a beaver. With the help of his animal friends, he accomplishes all three deeds, and learns that the world's population must cooperate in order to survive. RECOMMENDATION: This lovely and adventuresome adaptation of the North American Indian tale presents its theme of peace and people's impact on each other with grace, subtlety and charm. ROYALTY: Free to Plays subscribers. SOURCE: Mahlman, Lewis & Jones, David Cadwalader. (1980). Folk tale plays for puppets. Boston, MA: Plays, Inc. SUBJECTS/PLAY TYPE: Cooperation; Folk Tales, Native American; Kindness; Puppet Play.

1763. 1-3. (+) McCaslin, Nellie. **Little Indian Two Feet's horse.** CAST: 2m, 1u. ACTS: 1. SETTINGS: Meadow. PLAYING TIME: 10 min. PLOT: Two Feet is told that he must wait until he is older to own a horse. Nevertheless, Two Feet searches for a horse, going through the meadow and stopping to rest at the bank of a stream. While he sleeps, he dreams of a horse. When he awakens, he sees it standing beside him. He takes it home. RECOMMENDATION: This could be useful to explain how Native Americans relied on the natural and spiritual world together to provide for their needs. Children will appreciate how Two Feet overcame the dreaded "wait until you're older" curse. ROYALTY: None. SOURCE: McCaslin, Nellie. (1977). Puppet fun: Production, performance, and plays. New York, NY: D. McKay Co. SUBJECTS/PLAY TYPE: Native Americans; Puppet Play.

1764. 3-7. (+) Kehret, Peg. **Little league dreamer.** CAST: 1m. ACTS: 1. SETTINGS: None. PLAYING TIME: NA. PLOT: A young baseball player is disappointed that he never gets to play in the games because he made mistakes in practice. He is sure he could improve if he got to play more often. RECOMMENDATION: This could be used as discussion fuel in a talk on the problems of childhood. ROYALTY: NA. SOURCE: Kehret, Peg. (1986). Winning monologs for young actors. Colorado Springs, CO: Meriwether Pub. SUBJECTS/PLAY TYPE: Baseball; Monologue.

1765. 2-5. (+) Chetin, Helen. **The little lost cloud.** CAST: 1f, Su. ACTS: 1. SETTINGS: Skyline. PLAYING TIME: 15 min. PLOT: As young cloud tries to find its place, it travels through fair weather, lightning, thunder, rain, a rainbow, hurricanes, tornadoes, smog filled air, and a forest fire. RECOMMENDATION: This is appropriate for even the youngest actors since it includes much body movement and pantomime. This is also a good lesson about weather, though the dialogue is sometimes stilted and every sentence seems to be a "lesson," making the play quite didactic. ROYALTY: Free to Plays subscribers. SOURCE: Chetin, Helen. (1978, November). The little lost cloud. Plays: The Drama Magazine for Young People, pp. 58-64. SUBJECTS/PLAY TYPE: Weather; Playlet.

1766. 1-12. (+) Kelly, Tim & Francoeur, Bill. **Little luncheonette of terror.** CAST: 12f, 6m, Su. ACTS: 2. SETTINGS: Luncheonette. PLAYING TIME: NA. PLOT: Pete, the young proprietor of a luncheonette, uses a fancy radio to summon a monster named Mongo from the center of the earth. Mongo quickly takes over the luncheonette and begins to carry out his plan to take over the world. When all seems hopeless, Pete puts the radio in reverse and returns Mongo to the center of the earth. RECOMMENDATION: Much of the cast sings, and should be at least junior high age. ROYALTY: NA. SOURCE: Kelly, Tim & Francoeur, Bill. (1988). Little luncheonette of terror. Denver, CO: Pioneer Drama Service, Inc. SUBJECTS/PLAY TYPE: Monsters; Alien Invasion; Musical; Comedy.

1767. 4-7. (+) Osman, Karen. **A little magic.** CAST: 14u. ACTS: 1. SETTINGS: None. PLAYING TIME: 15 min. PLOT: Willowthorn and Blackenberry fight the evil Sinisade to save their mountain. RECOMMENDATION: This choral reading has three acting parts and some singing parts. ROYALTY: Free to Plays subscribers. SOURCE: Osman, Karen. (1986, March). A little magic. Plays: The Drama Magazine for Young People, pp. 43-48. SUBJECTS/PLAY TYPE: Magic; Nature; Choral Reading.

1768. 6-10. (+) Dias, Earl J. **The little man who wasn't there.** CAST: 5f, 2m. ACTS: 1. SETTINGS: Living room. PLAYING TIME: 30 min. PLOT: A boy gets sound advice on girl problems from an extraterrestrial. RECOMMENDATION: This deals with young romance in a humorous yet sensitive way. ROYALTY: Free to Plays subscribers. SOURCE: Kamerman, Sylvia E. (1981). Space and science fiction plays for young people. Boston, MA: Plays, Inc. SUBJECTS/PLAY TYPE: Science Fiction; Romance; Comedy.

1769. 3-8*. (+) Berger, Sidney L. & Fanidi, Theo. (Anderson, Hans Christian) **The little match girl, the musical.** (The little match girl) CAST: 2f, 16m, Su. ACTS: 1. SETTINGS: Bare stage, backdrop. PLAYING TIME: NA. PLOT: Poor little Liesl is forced by her father to sell matches to passersby in the freezing cold. Most of the holiday crowd ignores her; a few play tricks on her. Liesl lights her matches and sees the things she has dreamed about: a doll, panda bears and toy soldiers. The toys fade when her matches go out. She then hears her dead grandmother's voice. Lighting her final match, she joins her grandmother in death. RECOMMENDATION: This poignant, beautiful adaptation retains its fragile tone. While older children may understand that her death is not tragic, younger children may be confused by it. Upbeat, melodious music is presented to counterbalance the seriousness of the play. Frequent references to God and Christmas are made. ROYALTY: $50. SOURCE: Berger, Sidney & Fanidi, Theo. (1985). The little match girl, the musical. Schulenberg, TX: I.E. Clark. SUBJECTS/PLAY TYPE: Death; Christmas; Musical; Adaptation.

1770. 9-12. (+) Jacobson, Ruth. **The little measure.** CAST: 3f, 2m, Su. ACTS: 1. SETTINGS: Theater. PLAYING TIME: NA. PLOT: A rehearsal of "Julius Caesar" is interrupted rudely by the overbearing director, who degrades an actress's performance, then fires her. Jim, the actor playing Mark Anthony, is a friend and prodigy of Alan, the director, until Jim becomes interested in Evelyn, the stage manager. Alan is jealous of the time Jim is spending with Evelyn and attempts to pass this jealousy off as the fear that "Julius Caesar" is suffering because Jim is not devoting his full attention to acting. The play concludes with an intense confrontation between Alan and Jim during a rehearsal. Alan believes he has made Jim what he is. Jim, unwilling to give up his recently gained independence, leaves the play. RECOMMENDATION: The setting of a play within a play is well done, especially since both **Julius Caesar** and **The Little Measure** are intense. The cast will find this drama challenging because many of its members will be playing dual roles in the two plays. ROYALTY: NA. SOURCE: Jacobson, Ruth. (1987). The little measure. Woodstock, IL: Dramatic Pub. Co. SUBJECTS/PLAY TYPE: Independence; Jealousy; Drama.

1771. 5-10*. (+) Nursey-Bray, Rosemary. (Andersen, Hans Christian) **The little mermaid.** (The little mermaid.) CAST: 11f, 6m, 9u. ACTS: 2. SETTINGS: Underwater; shoreline; castle. PLAYING TIME: NA. PLOT: A mermaid wishes to marry a mortal prince. The evil sea witch casts a spell to change her into a human with the caveat that if the prince and the mermaid do not marry, the mermaid will die and dissolve into sea foam. The prince, however, is betrothed to a princess from the mountains. The play does end happily with the marriage of the prince and the mermaid, as the sea people and the humans join together to destroy the sea witch. RECOMMENDATION: This must be produced by professionals. The ending differs from Anderson's original, but it is well written. ROYALTY: $25. SOURCE: Nursey-Bray, Rosemary. (1982). The little mermaid. Schulenburg, TX: I.E. Clark. SUBJECTS/PLAY TYPE: Fantasy; Mermaids and Mermen; Adaptation.

1772. 8-12. (+) Kelly, Tim & Christiansen, Arne. **Little Miss Christie.** CAST: 13f, 9m, Su. ACTS: 2. SETTINGS: Sitting room; attic; hallway. PLAYING TIME: 120 min. PLOT: Helen and Martha live in a house haunted by its architect who hid a priceless necklace on the premises over a hundred years earlier. As Christie and her friends investigate mysterious noises, music, and apparitions, several servants, a man masquerading as the architect, and even the school's headmistress behave suspiciously. Christie discovers that Helen and Martha's nephew, George, is behind everything because he wants to prevent his aunts from leaving the house to the nearby Academy in their will. Christie finds the hidden necklace before rushing off to solve another mystery. RECOMMENDATION: This is tongue in cheek with a surprise ending, a full of life Nancy Drew character, and convincing adult characters. Often, Christie's fellow students' humorous lines fall flat and the many allusions to Agatha Christie's works may not be understood by everyone. ROYALTY: $90. SOURCE: Kelly, Tim & Christiansen, Arne. (1982). Little Miss Christie. Denver, CO: Pioneer Drama Service. SUBJECTS/PLAY TYPE: Mystery; Musical.

1773. K-12. (+) Winther, Barbara. **Little Mouse-Deer.** CAST: 1m, Su. ACTS: 1. SETTINGS: Forest. PLAYING TIME: 20 min. PLOT: Three tales are presented with dance, drama, and simple musical instruments. In "How Mouse-Deer Fools the Tiger," the foot high Indonesian animal evades the jaws of the tiger by convincing the tiger he can turn "one into two," including tigers. In "How Mouse-Deer Escapes From the Pit," the clever little animal falls into a pit, then entices others to join him, where it is safe from "the end of the world," unless one sneezes. He

sneezes to get himself ejected from the pit. In "How Mouse-Deer Saves the Man," the little animal saves a man about to be eaten by the tiger by pinning the tiger under a tree limb. RECOMMENDATION: This will be a challenge for older actors because of the need for perfect timing, vocal and pantomime acting, and the variety of animals personified. The "minute of music" that ends each scene can be envisioned as professionally raucous and tied to the fast, definite movements of the cast. ROYALTY: Free for amateur performance. SOURCE: Winther, Barbara. (1976). Plays from folktales of Africa and Asia. Boston, MA: Plays, Inc. SUBJECTS/PLAY TYPE: Folk Tales, Indonesia; Playlet.

1774. 1-3. (+) Gotwalt, Helen Louise Miller. **The little nut tree.** CAST: 9f, 12m. ACTS: 1. SETTINGS: Garden. PLAYING TIME: 15 min. PLOT: A poor family owns a little nut tree which bears a silver nutmeg and a golden pear that cannot be picked. They wish to cut the tree down, but the princess of Spain, who knows how to pick the fruit, promises to stop the war between her country and England if she is allowed to harvest the fruit. RECOMMENDATION: Children will enjoy the songs, a great asset to the music teacher who is putting together a springtime program and is looking for something special for the primary grades to perform. ROYALTY: Free to Plays subscribers. SOURCE: Gotwalt, Helen Louise Miller. (1986). Everyday plays for boys and girls. Boston, MA: Plays, Inc. SUBJECTS/PLAY TYPE: Folk Tale Motifs; Musical.

1775. 3-12. (+) Randall, Charles H. & Bushnell, Joan LeGro. **Little orphan Angela.** CAST: 8f, 5m, 10u. ACTS: 2. SETTINGS: Main street; kitchen; gulch; path; saw mill. PLAYING TIME: NA. PLOT: The bucolic innocents of Fresno Flats encounter a villainous medicine showman. With clever words and sleight of hand he briefly captivates the more naive and ignorant, but his vile appetites are his undoing, and the hero at last rescues his damsel from the advancing saw blades and wins her hand in marriage. Revelations concerning familial relationships cement the bonds of happiness, as the orphan finds her mother. RECOMMENDATION: This play includes everything: rustic, alliterative dialogue; a silly sidekick; a virginal heroine and protective hero; the evil of smooth words and overt sexuality vs. the good-heartedness of ignorance and ritualized romance. ROYALTY: Upon application. SOURCE: Randall, Charles H. & Bushnell, Joan LeGro. (1979). Little orphan Angela. Chicago, IL: Dramatic Pub. Co. SUBJECTS/PLAY TYPE: Western; Medicine Shows; Orphans; Musical.

1776. 9-12. (-) Merten, Elizabeth. **A little pantomime.** CAST: 1f, 5u. ACTS: 10. SETTINGS: Bare stage. PLAYING TIME: NA. PLOT: Six puppets mime and dance to the music of the suite, "The Comedians." RECOMMENDATION: Detailed, intricate instructions correlated with the music may make this too difficult to perform. ROYALTY: Free to Plays subscribers. SOURCE: Merten, George. (1979). Plays for puppet performance. Boston, MA: Plays, Inc. SUBJECTS/PLAY TYPE: Rhythm; Moods; Dance; Puppet Play.

1777. 3-6*. (+) Rogers, June Walker. (Burnett, Frances Hodgson) A little princess. (Sara Crewe) CAST: 13f, 6m, Su. ACTS: 2. SETTINGS: Hall; suite; classroom; garret; study. PLAYING TIME: NA. PLOT: Sarah, who is enrolled in a private school for young ladies, is treated like a princess until her father dies, leaving her penniless. Sarah is forced to be a servant. At the same time, her father's partner is searching to give her her rightful inheritance. By a twist of fate, Mr. Carriford discovers that Sarah has been living right next door to him. Sarah truly becomes a princess in the end when she learns she is the heiress to half a diamond mine. RECOMMENDATION: All those who have read the original will enjoy this adaptation in which the essence of the story has been well preserved. ROYALTY: $25. SOURCE: Rogers, June Walker. (1978). A little princess. Chicago, IL: Dramatic Pub. Co. SUBJECTS/PLAY TYPE: Boarding Schools; Inheritances; Adaptation.

1778. 1-6. (+) Thane, Adele. (Burnett, Frances Hodgson) The little princess. (Sara Crewe) CAST: 9f, 3m. ACTS: 3. SETTINGS: Attic. PLAYING TIME: 30 min. PLOT: Sara, a student at a select seminary for young ladies, is left penniless when her father dies. Consigned to a dreary attic room and forced to work hard with little food or warmth, Sara is still kind to everyone, taking care of an Indian gentleman's monkey when it runs away. The gentleman befriends Sara when he realizes she is the girl for whom he has been searching at the dying request of her father. RECOMMENDATION: This faithful adaptation of the classic tale about kindness and cruelty has all of the original's black and white characters, at whom the audience will cheer and hiss. ROYALTY: None. SOURCE: Thane, Adele. (1985, November). The little princess. Plays: The Drama Magazine for Young People, pp. 50-60. SUBJECTS/PLAY TYPE: Orphans; Adaptation.

1779. 1-3. (+) Lynch-Watson, Janet. The Little red hen. CAST: 6u. ACTS: 4. SETTINGS: Farm-yard; field; mill. PLAYING TIME: 20 min. PLOT: The Little Red Hen finds some grains of wheat, and unsuccessfully tries to get her friends to help her plant them. However, when she is ready to eat the bread after growing, harvesting, and processing it, all her friends want to share. The hen refuses. RECOMMENDATION: This contains directions for its production as a shadow puppet play. Patterns to make puppets are included, as well as production notes. ROYALTY: NA. SOURCE: Lynch-Watson, Janet. (1975). The shadow puppet book. New York, NY: Sterling Pub. Co. SUBJECTS/PLAY TYPE: Cooperation; Shadow Puppet Play.

1780. K-4. (+) Holmes, Ruth Vickery. (Grimm Brothers) Little Red Riding Hood. (Little Red Riding Hood) CAST: 3f, 2m. ACTS: 1. SET-TINGS: Cottages; forest. PLAYING TIME: 15 min. PLOT: When the woodcutter's daughter is sent with food to cheer her sick grandmother, she disobeys by straying off the path and meets a wolf in the woods. Finding out the location of grandmother's house, the wolf gets there first and lies in wait. The girl's father and mother rush to save her, and both grandmother and granddaughter are unharmed. RECOMMENDATION: This preserves the traditional themes of good vs. evil, as it adds the theme of family unity and the importance of children's obedience to their parents. ROYALTY: NA. SOURCE: Kamerman, Sylvia E. (1987). Plays from favorite folk tales. Boston, MA: Plays, Inc. SUBJECTS/PLAY TYPE: Family; Obedience; Folk Tales, Germany; Adaptation.

1781. K-5*. (-) Kilborne, William S., Jr. & Viola, Albert T. (Grimm Brothers) Little Red Riding Hood. (Little Red Riding Hood) CAST: 8f, 6m, 8u. ACTS: 1. SETTINGS: Yard; forest; house. PLAYING TIME: 60 min. PLOT: Granny likes to jog and the Woodsman drives a woodsmobile in this modernized and musical version. Mother Goose, Little Bo Peep, and some other nursery rhyme characters make guest appearances. RECOMMENDATION: Even though most of the song lyrics are cute, the dialogue is silly but not funny, and the important themes are lost. ROYALTY: $35. SOURCE: Kilborne, William S., Jr. & Viola, Albert T. (1978). Little Red Riding Hood. Denver, CO: Pioneer Drama Service. SUBJECTS/PLAY TYPE: Folk Tales, Germany; Comedy; Musical; Adaptation.

1782. K-4*. (+) Solomon, Olivia. (Grimm Brothers) Little Red Riding Hood. (Little Red Riding Hood) CAST: 2f, 2m. ACTS: 2. SET-TINGS: Painted backdrop, props. PLAYING TIME: NA. PLOT: Master of all disguises and jack of all trades, the Wicked Wolf poses as William T. Wolfe, Grandma, a peddler, and a clown to dupe innocent Little Red Riding Hood, Grandma, and the Brave Woodsman. When his duplicity is discovered, he masterfully extracts himself from being caught and converses with the audience about the success of each guise. In the finale, the wolf escapes by his wit, but promises a future confrontation. RECOMMENDATION: Music introduces each character, sets the mood and entices the audience. The vocabulary is tough, but skillful actors can portray the gist of the play by their actions. ROYALTY: NA. SOURCE: Solomon, Olivia. (1983). Little Red Riding Hood. Tuscaloosa, AL: Portals Press. SUBJECTS/PLAY TYPE: Folk Tales, Germany; Musical; Comedy; Adaptation.

1783. 3-6. (+) Hatton, Thomas J. Little Red Riding Hood: The real story. CAST: 2f, 2m. ACTS: 1. SETTINGS: Forest; bedroom; kitchen. PLAYING TIME: 10 min. PLOT: This is the wolf's version of his confrontation with the small girl, Red, and her horse, Hood. He says that Red enticed him to Grandma's house with the promise of cucumber sandwiches and pickled asparagus, despite his concern about going home with a stranger. In retrospect, he realizes that Red must have raced ahead and plotted with Grandma to assault him and take his money. When the woodsman intervened, the wily Grandma posed as a helpless victim. Red and Grandma allude to items pilfered from the Three Bears, and the wolf warns the audience about Red's continued abuse of unsuspecting travelers, as evidenced by the disappearance of the Three Little Pigs. His final plea for mercy and justice through appeal to legal authorities is negated by the threat of lightning in answer to his affirmation, "If anything I've told you is a lie, may a bolt of lightning strike me right here." RECOMMENDATION: Despite his guarded tone and obviously rehearsed story, the sly, but lovable, wolf occasionally lapses into an honest revelation of the trickery and deceit for which he is known. He naively characterizes himself as a social worker who keeps homeless bunnies and chicks off the streets. Children who consider themselves "too old" for folk tales will enjoy this offbeat production. ROYALTY: Free to Plays subscribers. SOURCE: Hatton, Thomas J. (1985, November). Little Red Riding Hood: The real story. Plays: The Drama Magazine for Young People, pp. 61-63. SUBJECTS/PLAY TYPE: Folk Tales, Germany; Comedy; Adaptation.

1784. 4-12. (+) Thistle, Louise. **Little Red snares the wolf.** CAST: 5f, 5m, Su. ACTS: 1. SETTINGS: Kitchen; forest. PLAYING TIME: NA. PLOT: Shy, rhyming Francois Loup cannot gather up enough courage to ask Petite Rouge to the Woodlanders' Masked Ball. The trees, in order to get rid of Loup (who always hides behind them and keeps them awake with his rhyming), and in order to stop Rene from recklessly riding his motorcycle through the forest, concoct a scheme to get dates for both of them. Celeste, the costume maker, goes with Rene; Petit (dressed as Red Riding Hood) goes with Francois (who, after donning a wolf's costume, finally gets the courage to ask her). RECOMMENDATION: This is delightful, rhyming, humorous, light, and sophisticated, yet understandable to younger audiences as well. The costuming and opportunities to play forest fauna make it appropriate for large casts and crews. ROYALTY: $15. SOURCE: Thistle, Louise. (1984). Little Red snares the wolf. Woodstock, IL: Dramatic Pub. Co. SUBJECTS/PLAY TYPE: Dating; Shyness; Comedy.

1785. 5-8. (+) Kehret, Peg. (Grimm Brothers) **Little Red, the hood.** (Little Red Riding Hood) CAST: 1m. ACTS: 1. SETTINGS: None. PLAYING TIME: NA. PLOT: The wolf claims that Red swindled him by telling him she found a fortune under some bushes, but that she was too frightened to spend the money because it was in thousand dollar bills. She asked wolf to trade his life's savings in tens and twenties for the thousand dollar bills. Wolf agreed, but discovered that Red had given him paper. Furious, wolf went to grandma's house and waited for Red, but she came with a policeman dressed as a wood cutter, and the rest is history. RECOMMENDATION: This modernized parody is quite amusing, but because of the length, an older student should be the speaker. ROYALTY: NA. SOURCE: Kehret, Peg. (1986). Winning monologs for young actors. Colorado Springs, CO: Meriwether Pub. SUBJECTS/PLAY TYPE: Wolves; Parody; Monologue; Adaptation.

1786. 1-4. (+) Brown, Abbie Farwell. **The little shadows, a Christmas playlet.** CAST: 3f, 2m. ACTS: 1. SETTINGS: Bedroom. PLAYING TIME: NA. PLOT: At night, several children's shadows emerge from under the beds to play with Tom and Dottie's toys, which have been left scattered about the room. When the children demand that the shadows return the toys, the shadows tease them about not sharing, and make the children trade places with them. When the shadows refuse to share, the children realize how selfish they've been, and they tell their mother to give all their new Christmas toys to poor children.

RECOMMENDATION: This teaches an excellent lesson on sharing and greed, and would be appropriate for Christmas or any other time of the year. The shadows must appear dressed in black and are referred to as "you black girl" and "you black imp." ROYALTY: NA. SOURCE: Brown, Abbie Farwell. (1978). The lantern and other plays for children. Great Neck, NY: Cora Collection Books. SUBJECTS/PLAY TYPE: Sharing; Christmas; Shadows; Playlet.

1787. 10-12. (+) Gordon, Stuart & Purdy-Gordon, Carolyn. (Chandler, Raymond) **The little sister.** (The little sister) CAST: 1f, 4m, Su. ACTS: 2. SETTINGS: Bare stage, props. PLAYING TIME: NA. PLOT: A prim young girl from a small town in Kansas comes to Los Angeles to find her brother whom she suspects is in trouble. She hires a private investigator who soon finds himself caught in a tangled web of murder and blackmail. The young innocent Kansas girl turns out to be very much involved in the intriguing mystery. This is narrated by the private-eye, who never leaves the stage. RECOMMENDATION: Smoking is quite prevalent throughout and a 32 automatic pistol is used as a prop. The alcohol drinking can be faked, but the profanities, seductions and semigraphic murder scene may not be appropriate. Sophisticated lighting is used to spot the difficult locations as all furniture is left on the stage. ROYALTY: $50. SOURCE: Gordon, Stuart & Purdy-Gordon, Carolyn. (1982). The little sister. Chicago, IL: Dramatic Pub. Co. SUBJECTS/PLAY TYPE: Murder; Mystery; Adaptation.

1788. 5-9. (+) Ammann, Herman. **The little troll without a soul.** CAST: 7f, 3m, Su. ACTS: 1. SETTINGS: Witch's house. PLAYING TIME: 25 min. PLOT: A witch (disguised as a seamstress) and her sister (masquerading as the "good fairy") want to capture Michele (the flower girl) to force her grandfather to give them his magic rose. By helping to foil the plot, a prince and dolls that come to life learn that beauty is only skin deep, and a troll learns that he has a soul because he is loved. RECOMMENDATION: Children will have fun being creative with the makeup, costumes, clothes chest prop. Some of the humor might be lost on younger children but the action, plot, and colorful characters will appeal. ROYALTY: $10. SOURCE: Ammann, Herman. (1976). The little troll without a soul. Schulenburg, TX: I.E. Clark. SUBJECTS/PLAY TYPE: Magic; Dolls; Witches; Comedy.

1789. 3-6. (-) Henderson, Nancy. **Little Turtle.** CAST: 4f, 5m. ACTS: 1. SETTINGS: Indian reservation. PLAYING TIME: 10 min. PLOT: Two Miccosukee Indian children go to school in the big city, where one falls in with the wrong crowd and dies in a car wreck. RECOMMENDATION: What begins as increased sensitivity for the Miccosukee way of life deteriorates into mere sentimentality. ROYALTY: Permission required if performed outside of the classroom. SOURCE: Henderson, Nancy. (1978). Celebrate America: A baker's dozen of plays. New York, NY: Julian Messner. SUBJECTS/PLAY TYPE: Native Americans; Drama.

1790. 7-12. (+) Morley, Olive J. (Alcott, Louisa May) **Little women.** (Little women.) CAST: 9f. ACTS: 1.

SETTINGS: Living room. PLAYING TIME: 30 min. PLOT: It's Christmas, and the March sisters feel sorry for themselves because of their modest lifestyle. However, sharing fire and food with a poverty stricken family puts joy back in their hearts. RECOMMENDATION: It would be a pleasure to celebrate Christmas with Meg, Jo, Beth, and Amy, portrayed as distinct individuals with a common, old fashioned set of values. The lines from Shakespeare which the girls recite are a bit complicated, but they could be simplified for younger performers. ROYALTY: Free to Plays subscribers. SOURCE: Morley, Olive. (1986, December). Little women. Plays: The Drama Magazine for Young People, pp. 55-64. SUBJECTS/PLAY TYPE: Christmas; Adaptation.

1791. 7-12. (+) Lee, Jesse. **Live...from Golgotha.** CAST: 3f, 11m, Su. ACTS: 1. SETTINGS: Bare stage, props. PLAYING TIME: 40 min. PLOT: This is a live television news broadcast of the crucifixion of Christ. It begins with a description of the arrival of three prisoners to be executed at Golgotha. Cuts are made to reporters "in the field" who seek to objectively review and analyze the "crimes" committed by Jesus Christ. As Christ hangs on the cross, hard hitting interviews with Judas Iscariot, John Caiaphas, Pontius Pilate, and Joseph of Arimathea provide further explanations of the events leading up to the crucifixion. The play concludes with the news commentator asking if Jesus was a magician, a madman, or truly the Son of God? RECOMMENDATION: This provides additional information and consequently greater understanding of the crucifixion. The crosses and the men on them are never seen by the audience except in silhouette, buy enough detail is given for the viewer to visualize the agony and horror, so audiences should be chosen with care. ROYALTY: $15. SOURCE: Lee, Jesse. (1987). Live...from Golgotha. Schulenburg, TX: I.E. Clark. SUBJECTS/PLAY TYPE: Christ, Crucifixion; Christian Drama.

1792. K-4. (+) Ison, Colleen. **Living like Jesus.** CAST: 5u. ACTS: 1. SETTINGS: Bare stage, props. PLAYING TIME: NA. PLOT: Children are admonished that not only must they believe Jesus' words, they must live them. This is accomplished by reading John 3:16, Romans 3:23-24, John 14:6, John 2:4, and "love thy neighbor as thyself," as the children are shown improper and proper behavior for a single situation. RECOMMENDATION: This easily explains the Bible passages, as each child thinks about how his/her behavior must be changed in order to live them. The narrator will have to be an adult. Discussion questions are provided. ROYALTY: NA. SOURCE: Ison, Colleen. (1986). Goliath's last stand: And fifteen more easy plays for children. Cincinnati, OH: Standard Pub. SUBJECTS/PLAY TYPE: Christian Drama; Behavior; Skit.

1793. 9-12. (+) Huff, Betty Tracy. **Lizzie of the lighthouse.** CAST: 9f, 2m. ACTS: 1. SETTINGS: Lighthouse. PLAYING TIME: 40 min. PLOT: Lizzie Lullworth and her Aunt Flora take a job as lighthouse keepers, hoping to escape the bill collectors. As they work, they find a pirate treasure and foil the villain who has been harassing them. RECOMMENDATION: Some references to literature (e.g., Percy Usher appears after the fall of the House of Usher) will either have to be familiar to the

audience, or they will have to be changed. ROYALTY: Free to Plays subscribers. SOURCE: Huff, Betty Tracy. (1978, October). Lizzie of the lighthouse. Plays: The Drama Magazine of Young People, pp. 1-12. SUBJECTS/PLAY TYPE: Satire; Pirate Treasure; Playlet.

1794. 5-6. (+) Hamlett, Christina. **A loan for Columbus.** CAST: 1f, 3m. ACTS: 1. SETTINGS: Bank. PLAYING TIME: 15 min. PLOT: Columbus applies for a loan to finance his first trip to the New World. The bank officers listen but refuse his proposal because because he has no credit or collateral. Queen Isabella comes to lunch with one of the officers. He offers to reconsider the loan application if Columbus will go to lunch in his place. This gets rid of Columbus, and releases the loan officer from entertaining the Queen, who bores him. After Columbus leaves, the bank officers laugh at his scheme. RECOMMENDATION: This dramatizes the conflict between imagination and those not visionary enough to appreciate it well. Some of the puns and jokes will have to be updated. ROYALTY: Free to Plays subscribers. SOURCE: Hamlett, Christina. (1985, October). A loan for Columbus. Plays: The Drama Magazine for Young People, pp. 47-52. SUBJECTS/PLAY TYPE: Columbus, Christopher; Skit.

1795. 9-12. (+) Kelly, Tim. **Loco-motion, commotion, Dr. Gorilla, and me.** CAST: 14f, 8m. ACTS: 2. SETTINGS: Living room. PLAYING TIME: NA. PLOT: Having inherited a mysterious old house from a slightly mad scientist uncle, Priscilla and easily spooked Patsy travel to Vermont to see Priscilla's property. She stumbles into an old house which is inhabited by zombie like housekeepers who tell them that her uncle's house was up the road but it burned down years ago. They discover that the fire was caused by arsonists. The girls are visited by some escaped, certified loonies and, after many close calls, jokes, puns, songs, narrow escapes, and chase scenes, as they finally catch the villains. RECOMMENDATION: This is truly zany, funny, and uproarious. ROYALTY: $25. SOURCE: Kelly, Tim. (1977). Loco- motion, commotion, Dr. Gorilla, and me. Boston, MA: Baker's Plays. SUBJECTS/PLAY TYPE: Adventure; Comedy.

1796. 7-12. (-) Nolan, Paul T. **The loneliest night.** CAST: 3f, 3m. ACTS: 1. SETTINGS: Living room. PLAYING TIME: 30 min. PLOT: Joe learns the importance of keeping a promise after spending another Saturday night at home alone. RECOMMENDATION: This is heavy on moralizing and armchair psychology, but totally lacking in plot. It would be an excellent sermon, but is inappropriate as a play. ROYALTY: Free to Plays subscribers. SOURCE: Nolan, Paul T. (1978, April). The loneliest night. Plays: The Drama Magazine for Young People, pp. 1-9. SUBJECTS/PLAY TYPE: Promises; Playlet.

1797. K-6. (+) Martin, Judith & Ashwander, Donald. **Long dress.** CAST: 2u. ACTS: 1. SETTINGS: None. PLAYING TIME: 5 min. PLOT: Big Sister comes on stage wrapped in a length of brown paper which trails behind her. As she proceeds across the stage, her "dress" appears to be caught on something. As she tugs at the paper, Little

Sister begins winding herself up in the length of paper, getting closer to Big Sister with each turn. When she reaches Big Sister and cuddles up to her, Big Sister snubs her, giving her a push that sends her reeling halfway back across the stage. Undaunted, Little Sister again winds herself up in the dress until she again reaches Big Sister. This time she puts her arm around Big Sister and pats her on the shoulder. Big Sister is resigned and Little Sister is very happy. RECOMMENDATION: This silent skit, reminiscent of the best of children's television, explores the theme of sibling relationships with humor and grudging affection. One can also change the cast to two males to show the relationship between brothers. ROYALTY: NA. SOURCE: Martin, Judith & Ashwander, Donald. (1985). The long dress. Reasons to be cheerful: A revue for children. New York, NY: The Paper Bag Players, Inc. SUBJECTS/PLAY TYPE: Skit; Sibling Relationships; Musical Revue.

1798. 4-10. (+) Kehret, Peg. **Long hot showers. CAST:** 1u. ACTS: 1. SETTINGS: None. PLAYING TIME: NA. PLOT: The pleasures of bathing are detailed by a young enthusiast. RECOMMENDATION: Humorous and poetic, this encapsulates the pleasures and hazards of longshowers. ROYALTY: NA. SOURCE: Kehret, Peg. (1986). Winning monologs for young actors. Colorado Springs, CO: Meriwether Pub. SUBJECTS/PLAY TYPE: Showers; Monologue.

1799. 3-8. (+) Benson, Islay. **Long live Christmas.** CAST: 6f, 13m, 13u. ACTS: 1. SETTINGS: Bare stage, props. PLAYING TIME: 25 min. PLOT: A grandfather's reminiscences about the year the King of Camerovia cancelled Christmas. The Fairy and Spirits of Christmas help the townspeople prove to the King that Christmas can't be cancelled, for it lives in their hearts. RECOMMENDATION: This is a nonreligious approach, in which a simple dimming of lights indicates time changes. It should be performed by older students for younger ones. ROYALTY: Free to Plays subscribers. SOURCE: Benson, Islay. (1987, December). Long live Christmas. Plays: The Drama Magazine for Young People, pp. 37-45. SUBJECTS/PLAY TYPE: Christmas; Playlet.

1800. 4-8. (+) Fisher, Aileen Lucia. **Long live father.** CAST: 3f, 2m, 1u. ACTS: 1. SETTINGS: Living/dining room. PLAYING TIME: 15 min. PLOT: On Father's Day, Tony and Linda give father a book with tips on healthful living, written by themselves. RECOMMENDATION: Although a bit trite, this pleasantly shows that a child's sincere concern for his/her parents is often the best gift. ROYALTY: Free to Plays subscribers. SOURCE: Fisher, Aileen Lucia. (1985). Year-round plays for young players. Boston, MA: Plays, Inc. SUBJECTS/PLAY TYPE: Father's Day; Parent-Child Relationships; Playlet.

1801. 8-12. (-) Mercati, Cynthia. **Long live rock and roll.** CAST: 5f, 4m, 9u. ACTS: 2. SETTINGS: Living room. PLAYING TIME: NA. PLOT: Gordon's Girl Academy is about to close because it cannot pay its bills. Eustice (a rock star) becomes infatuated with Gillian, the headmistress. Gillian finally gives Eustice her love when he puts on a concert to raise money for the academy. RECOMMENDATION: It is difficult to believe this takes 58 pages of dialogue and 2 acts to go absolutely nowhere. People who have little to do with anything wander in and out of the scenes, while the audience waits in vain for some kind of plot to develop. ROYALTY: $40. SOURCE: Mercati, Cynthia. (1981). Long live rock and roll. Boston, MA: Baker's Plays. SUBJECTS/PLAY TYPE: Rock And Roll; Romance; Comedy.

1802. K-12. (+) Hendricks, William & Vogel, Cora. **Long long ago.** CAST: Su. ACTS: 1. SETTINGS: None. PLAYING TIME: 1 min. PLOT: This poem describes the day on which Christ was born. RECOMMENDATION: Suitable for church or parochial school groups for performance at a Christmas pageant or worship service. ROYALTY: NA. SOURCE: Hendricks, William & Vogel, Cora. (1978). Handbook of Christmas programs. Grand Rapids, MI: Baker Book House. SUBJECTS/PLAY TYPE: Christ, Jesus; Christmas; Worship Program.

1803. 6-12. (+) Taylor, Don. **A long march to Jerusalem.** CAST: 8f, 21m, 12u. ACTS: 2. SETTINGS: Bare stage, props. PLAYING TIME: NA. PLOT: Jackyboy and his friends follow Stephen, a young boy who claims that God told him to raise an army of children to recapture Jerusalem for the Christians. Nearly 40,000 children begin the march from Paris, but at the Mediterranean shore, they are tricked into boarding ships that take them to Algiers where they are sold into slavery. On a 1,000 mile march to Cairo, many die and only Jackyboy and four others who know how to read are spared from slave labor. They become clerks and servants of Al-Kamil, the Governor's son. RECOMMENDATION: Adults, children, and many extras are needed for production. At least two characters sing and portray troubadors who explain what is happening on stage to the audience. This superb drama is somber and will provoke many questions about the children's crusade. ROYALTY: NA. SOURCE: Taylor, Don. (1978). A long march to Jerusalem. New York, NY: Samuel French. SUBJECTS/PLAY TYPE: Children's Crusade; Drama.

1804. 7-12. (+) Olfson, Lewy. **Long may it wave.** CAST: 4f, 3m. ACTS: 1. SETTINGS: Beauty salon. PLAYING TIME: 15 min. PLOT: Cinderella and her two stepsisters meet the King at the unisex beauty salon as he tries to have his damaged hair fixed. An inventor/salesman saves the day with a new shampoo which fixes all damaged hair; the beautician marries the King; and the shampoo is named Rumpelstiltskin--the shampoo that turns straw into gold. RECOMMENDATION: In this delightfully funny spoof, the only jarring element is the obviously Jewish money hungry father. If he were turned into a generic money hungry father, this would be perfect. ROYALTY: Free to Plays subscribers. SOURCE: Olfson, Lewy. (1978, March). Long may it wave. Plays: The Drama Magazine for Young People, pp. 67-72. SUBJECTS/PLAY TYPE: Satire; Comedy.

1805. 8-12. (+) Fisher, Aileen. **Look to a new day.** CAST: 13f, 11m, Su. ACTS: 1. SETTINGS: Classroom; podium. PLAYING TIME: 30 min. PLOT: As Senator Blake speaks about the courage of our ancestors at graduation, past heroes walk on stage. Blake encourages the students to set high standards and to improve the American way of life. RECOMMENDATION: This is outdated, lengthy, and too wordy, but it accurately reflects the values of the 1940s. History buffs might enjoy it. ROYALTY: NA. SOURCE: Fisher, Aileen. (1986). Holiday programs for boys and girls. Boston, MA: Plays, Inc. SUBJECTS/PLAY TYPE: Graduation; History, U.S.; Playlet.

1806. 6-8. (+) Johnson, Albert. **Look who's playing God.** CAST: 2f, 2m. ACTS: 1. SETTINGS: Meeting room. PLAYING TIME: 35 min. PLOT: A clergyman's sermon uses modern slang and phraseology and a woman in the role of God to dramatize Adam and Eve's fall from innocence. RECOMMENDATION: The use of faddish expressions to modernize the story makes it seem trite. However, middle school students might find it entertaining and thought provoking. ROYALTY: $15. SOURCE: Johnson, Albert. (1976). Look who's playing God. Boston, MA: Baker's Plays. SUBJECTS/PLAY TYPE: Creation; Adam and Eve; Garden of Eden; Comedy.

1807. 7-12. (+) Stein, Mark. (Kutler, Stanley I.) **Looking for America.** (Looking for America) CAST: 5u. ACTS: 1. SETTINGS: None. PLAYING TIME: NA. PLOT: This takes a sweeping look at American history with emphasis on slavery, labor disputes, and the draft. Its theme departs from traditional renditions of Americana to explore both the positive and negative aspects of our nation's history. Folk songs accompanied by guitar are included throughout. RECOMMENDATION: This refreshing approach to American history carefully avoids typical images. Instead, it dwells on themes such as our Americans' attitudes toward the Indian, feelings of northern draft resisters toward the Civil War, the suffragette and civil rights movements, and living through the Depression. ROYALTY: $20. SOURCE: Stein, Mark. (1981). Looking for America. Boston, MA: Baker's Plays. SUBJECTS/PLAY TYPE: History, U.S.; Musical; Adaptation.

1808. 8-10. (+) Murray, John. **The looking glass murder.** CAST: 6f, 4m. ACTS: 1. SETTINGS: Rooftop; fire escape. PLAYING TIME: 35 min. PLOT: In this murder mystery/young love story, clues to a murder are given through analogies to **Alice in Wonderland and Through the Looking Glass.** An innocent young man is framed by his jealous friend who incriminates himself and gets caught in the end. RECOMMENDATION: The device used for the clues is quite unique. However, violence and implied prejudice against old people may be a sensitive area. Knowledge of **Alice in Wonderland and Through the Looking Glass** is needed to understand the play. ROYALTY: None. SOURCE: Murray, John. (1984). Mystery plays for young readers. Boston, MA: Plays, Inc. SUBJECTS/PLAY TYPE: Murder; Mystery.

1809. 6-8. (+) Sodaro, Craig. **Loose ends. CAST:** 4f. ACTS: 1. SETTINGS: Parlor. PLAYING TIME: 15 min. PLOT: An unsuccessful mystery writer fakes her own death so she can collect the money on her insurance policy. She is found out by her literary agent and secretary, who call the police. RECOMMENDATION: The mystery writer's scheme is discovered because it is as poorly conceived as her novels, which always leave "loose ends." This lends a unique twist to a familiar plot. ROYALTY: Free to Plays subscribers. SOURCE: Sodaro, Craig. (1986, April). Loose ends. Plays: The Drama Magazine for Young People, pp. 41- 47. SUBJECTS/PLAY TYPE: Mystery; Curtain Raiser.

1810. 8-12. (+) Pody, David. (Shakespeare, William) **Lord, what fools!** (Midsummer night's dream) CAST: 2f, 2m, 1u. ACTS: 1. SETTINGS: None. PLAYING TIME: NA. PLOT: Punk narrates as he crosses lovers and gives vain Jason an ass's head. The victims learn something about themselves, each other, and their friendships: Kootie doesn't need makeup and perfume to attract friends; looks aren't everything; respect and friendship are admirable; and friends can be honest with each other. RECOMMENDATION: This examines problems with which teens deal, exaggerating the situations into pleasant comedy. ROYALTY: NA. SOURCE: Pody, David. (1982). Lord, what fools! Toronto, Canada: Theatre Ontario Printing Centre. SUBJECTS/PLAY TYPE: Self Examination; Adaptation.

1811. K-6. (+) Martin, Judith. **The lost and found Christmas.** CAST: 7f, 3m, 4u. ACTS: 1. SETTINGS: Bare stage. PLAYING TIME: NA. PLOT: As Josephine (laden with Christmas gifts for her sister) waits for the last bus, she is joined by other weary people, each of whom has a problem which is solved by a loan of one of Josephine's gifts. When Josephine gets to her sister's house, she forgets to take the gifts back, but the happy travelers return them, and join the Christmas party. RECOMMENDATION: This delightfully expresses the spirit of sharing and would be especially good for school assemblies. ROYALTY: $10. SOURCE: Martin, Judith. (1977). The lost and found Christmas. New Orleans, LA: Anchorage Press, Inc. SUBJECTS/PLAY TYPE: Christmas; Comedy; Musical.

1812. 10-12. (+) Bland, Joellen. (Byson, H.J. & Boucicault, Dion) **Lost at sea.** (Lost at sea) CAST: 3f, 5m. ACTS: 1. SETTINGS: Drawing room. PLAYING TIME: 30 min. PLOT: Mr. Franklin, a banker, is relieved to discover that Walter Coram, a large depositor whose money he has embezzled, has been lost at sea. But Rawlings finds Coram's trunks and plans to have Jessop impersonate Coram so Rawlings can take over Franklin's bank and marry Franklin's daughter. Coram, who is really alive and a lodger at Jessop's house, discovers the plot. Rawling's scheme is revealed to Franklin, the bank is saved, Rawlings is deported, and all ends happily. RECOMMENDATION: This is a faithful adaptation of the 1869 original, whose plot left much to chance and coincidence. The bad guys are lightly punished for their crimes and Mr. Franklin's embezzlement is completely overlooked. This might have been better left in its original form. ROYALTY: Free to Plays subscribers. SOURCE: Bland, Joellen. (1985, October). Lost at sea. Plays: The Drama Magazine for Young People, pp. 53-62. SUBJECTS/PLAY TYPE: Embezzlement; Adaptation.

1813. 1-3. (+) Gotwalt, Helen Louise Miller. **The lost Christmas cards.** CAST: 6f, 7m, Su. ACTS: 1. SETTINGS: Street corner; classroom. PLAYING TIME: 15 min. PLOT: School children mailing Christmas cards meet the mailman. He explains to them how careless habits make for "lost Christmas cards." The postman goes to school the next day to demonstrate the proper way to address and stamp cards. RECOMMENDATION: This teaches the rudiments of properly addressing correspondence. ROYALTY: NA. SOURCE: Gotwalt, Helen Louise Miller. (1985). First plays for children: A collection for the youngest players. Boston, MA: Plays, Inc. SUBJECTS/PLAY TYPE: Christmas; Postal Service; Skit.

1814. 7-12. (+) Kelly, Tim. **Lost in space and the mortgage due, or, revenge on the launching pad.** CAST: 12f, 8m, Su. ACTS: 2. SETTINGS: Homes; roads; command station; launching pad. PLAYING TIME: NA. PLOT: Commander Snivelling Snidely Backlash wishes to foreclose on the Humbles' potato farm to get his hands on what only he knows is there: the richest source of rocket fuel ever discovered. The Humbles' only chance lies in hoped for royalties from Mr. Humble's new invention, a rocket that goes sideways. Complicating the plot is the appearance of the Humbles' long lost granddaughter who is wooed by both Backlash and the heroic Bob. Rounding out the cast are the wicked Evilina Craven, an accomplice of Backlash's abandoned wife and son, and assorted extras. Naturally, Bob saves the day (and wins the heroine) at the last possible moment. RECOMMENDATION: The outrageous puns and tacky sets and costumes (the script suggests "the tackier the better") will most certainly delight the target audience. Several roles may be played by male or female or doubled. ROYALTY: $35. SOURCE: Kelly, Tim. (1979). Lost in space and the mortgage due, or, revenge on the launching pad. Franklin, OH: Eldridge Pub. Co. SUBJECTS/PLAY TYPE: Science Fiction; Swindlers and Swindling; Mortgages; Comedy.

1815. 9-12. (-) Morrison, Katherin E. **Lost in the shuffle.** CAST: 4f. ACTS: 1. SETTINGS: Living room. PLAYING TIME: NA. PLOT: Four middle-aged ladies get tipsy playing Trivial Pursuit. During the game, Dody answers the phone and mistaking Breezie's husband for her own, proceeds to give him "what for." The girls plan to reunite Breezie and her husband by entering a euchre tournament in which Breezie's husband is a judge. After practicing, they realize they will have to cheat to win. The girls are disqualified, but Breezie and her husband reconcile. All give up Trivial Pursuit and Euchre, and as the play ends they consider giving bridge a try. RECOMMENDATION: This is trite and silly, and the light treatment made of the stereotyped women's drunkenness and profanity is inappropriate. Knowledge of Euchre is necessary to understand the humor. ROYALTY: $20. SOURCE: Morrison, Katherin E. (1987). Lost in the

shuffle. Franklin, OH: Eldridge Pub. Co. SUBJECTS/PLAY TYPE: Competition; Comedy.

1816. 12. (+) Marcoux, J. Paul. (Feydeau, Georges) **Love by the bolt.** (Tailleur pour dames) CAST: 7f, 4m. ACTS: 2. SETTINGS: Living room; apartment. PLAYING TIME: NA. PLOT: Three couples try to cover up their affairs with each other, leading to confusion and wild hilarity. They are reunited at the end of the play. RECOMMENDATION: Since this closely follows the original, it is complete with bedroom humor, colorful language, and strong sexual suggestions. Only mature audiences will be able to fully appreciate this. ROYALTY: $50. SOURCE: Marcoux, J. Paul. (1984). Love by the bolt. Chicago, IL: Dramatic Pub. Co. SUBJECTS/PLAY TYPE: Farce; Adaptation.

1817. 9-12. (+) Hotchner, Steve. **Love is a hot fudge sundae.** CAST: 6f, 5m. ACTS: 1. SETTINGS: Classroom; cafeteria; hall. PLAYING TIME: NA. PLOT: Talented and seemingly psychic Nicky suffers as her stories are read aloud in class against her wishes by an insensitive English teacher. Nicky's classmates cruelly reject her as "weird" and a "witch," even while believing that in one her stories she foretells the suicide of Rosy, an overweight newcomer. At the end, Nicky commits suicide. RECOMMENDATION: This is a praiseworthy and successful effort to create thoughtful discussion about the problem of teenage suicide. ROYALTY: $20. SOURCE: Hotchner, Steve. (1987). Love is a hot fudge sundae. Woodstock, IL: Dramatic Pub. Co. SUBJECTS/PLAY TYPE: Suicide; Drama.

1818. 8-12. (+) Kelly, Tim. **Love is murder.** CAST: 5f, 5m. ACTS: 3. SETTINGS: Cottage. PLAYING TIME: NA. PLOT: Several well known romance novelists assemble for a television interview. A murderer is discovered in their midst. They discover that the "murders" have been pranks to discredit a nutritional advisor who had been ridiculed in a radio interview. RECOMMENDATION: This spoof of romance writers and their novels moves slowly, but has its moments of humor thanks to wacky, stereotyped characterization. ROYALTY: $40. SOURCE: Kelly, Tim. (1983). Love is murder. Boston, MA: Baker's Plays. SUBJECTS/PLAY TYPE: Romance Novels; Writers; Murder; Comedy.

1819. 9-12. (+) McFaden, Michael. **The love knot.** CAST: 2f, 3m, 2u. ACTS: 1. SETTINGS: Street. PLAYING TIME: NA. PLOT: This is "a French farce in the Moliere manner" in which a 17th century French analyst, who is bored with his profession and success, decides to liven things up by giving bad advice to his next client. As a result, an aristocratic couple and a commoner couple find their lives comically entwined. The characters learn the relative value of an analyst's advice and their own heart's wisdom. RECOMMENDATION: The cast should be prepared to master some lengthy speeches and to kiss. ROYALTY: $15. SOURCE: McFaden, Michael. (1975). The love knot. Schulenburg, TX: I.E. Clark. SUBJECTS/PLAY TYPE: Love; Comedy.

1820. 6-8. (+) Kehret, Peg. **Love letter to Suzy.** CAST: 1m. ACTS: 1. SETTINGS: None. PLAYING TIME: NA. PLOT: A young boy is infatuated with a girl in his class because she doesn't let pimples bother her and she is good natured about his dog jumping up on her. He writes a truthful love letter and asks her to the dance, but his unflattering version of the truth angers her. RECOMMENDATION: This touching tale of young love depicts the need for truth in a relationship, but not to an excessive degree. ROYALTY: NA. SOURCE: Kehret, Peg. (1986). *Winning monologs for young actors.* Colorado Springs, CO: Meriwether Pub. SUBJECTS/PLAY TYPE: Love; Crushes; Monologue.

1821. 7-12. (+) McCusker, Paul. **Love one another.** CAST: 7u. ACTS: 3. SETTINGS: Classroom; baseball field. PLAYING TIME: NA. PLOT: A Sunday school teacher tries to teach a classroom of "wise-guys" about the commandment "love thy neighbor as thyself." After they lose a baseball game, it is obvious through their poor sportsmanship that they've not learned the lesson. They especially pick on one of their less talented teammates. He decides to leave the church because it's full of hypocrites, but is convinced by the teacher to stay and try to make a difference. RECOMMENDATION: Through Bible passages and the protagonists' realistic discussion about hypocrisy, this demonstrates that we should not judge everyone in a group by its vociferous bad members. ROYALTY: NA. SOURCE: McCusker, Paul. (1984). *Batteries not included.* Boston, MA: Baker's Plays. SUBJECTS/PLAY TYPE: Christian Drama; Love; Hypocrisy; Skit.

1822. 5-8. (+) Shoemaker, Carole. **Love that turnip!** CAST: 4f, 3m, 1u. ACTS: 1. SETTINGS: Bare stage, props. PLAYING TIME: 10 min. PLOT: Seven youngsters gather at the request of the President to advise the Department of Agriculture on ways to make the "ten vegetables kids hate most" more appealing. RECOMMENDATION: In addition to promoting healthy foods, this amusing skit provides ways to offer constructive criticism. ROYALTY: Free to Plays subscribers. SOURCE: Shoemaker, Carole. (1979, January). Love that turnip. *Plays: The Drama Magazine for Young People,* pp. 65-68. SUBJECTS/PLAY TYPE: Debate; Vegetables; Skit.

1823. 12. (+) Friel, Brian. **Lovers.** CAST: 5f, 3m. ACTS: 2. SETTINGS: Bare stage. PLAYING TIME: NA. PLOT: This is two plays linked by a common theme. Part 1 is about two young lovers, Joe and Mag, who spend a day studying for finals, just three weeks before they are to marry. Interspersed with scenes of their laughter, dreams, and arguments are reports by anonymous commentators on events that will occur later that day. The audience is told of a stolen boat, the disappearance of two young people, and the drowning of Joe and Mag. In Part 2, Andy recalls his courtship with Hanna. They had talked about getting married, with Hanna moving away from her invalid, domineering mother. He reveals how that spark of enthusiasm and rebelliousness was slowly quenched and deadened and how they now live in calm acceptance of her mother's domination. RECOMMENDATION: This interesting and provocative drama contains some crude language and is sexually explicit. Both parts comment on Irish Catholic culture in Ireland and require deep sensitivity and power to act and understand. ROYALTY: $60. SOURCE: Friel, Brian. (1968). *Lovers.* Woodstock, IL: Dramatic Pub. Co. SUBJECTS/PLAY TYPE: Love; Drama.

1824. 11-12. (+) Gillespie, Tom. **Lovers' leap.** CAST: 3f, 4m, 3u. ACTS: 1. SETTINGS: Woods. PLAYING TIME: 45 min. PLOT: A lonely young woman is distracted from jumping off Lovers' Leap by several "crazies" and a pleasant young man. RECOMMENDATION: Although a young woman's threat of suicide forms the backdrop, the story is really about two shy people becoming attracted to each other while surrounded by uncaring fools. The dialogue is witty and bounces between the main characters like a ping pong ball. ROYALTY: $15. SOURCE: Gillespie, Tom. (1978). *Lovers' leap.* Denver, CO: Pioneer Drama Service. SUBJECTS/PLAY TYPE: Suicide; Romance; Comedy.

1825. 7-12. (-) Crow, William Thomas. **The lovesick computer.** CAST: 6f, 4m, Su. ACTS: 1. SETTINGS: Computer room; office; classroom. PLAYING TIME: NA. PLOT: David creates a talking computer (Susan) that falls in love with him. She calls David's friends, parents, and teachers to spread rumors that will force him to like her. David introduces Susan to another computer (Eddie). Just as they are to be married, Susan backs out, saying that she still loves David. RECOMMENDATION: The idea is cute, but the plot never develops. The conversations are stilted and forced and the events are not joined together effectively. The ending leaves the audience hanging with issues relating to a computer's projected capacity to think or feel unresolved. ROYALTY: $15. SOURCE: Crow, William Thomas. (1982). *The lovesick computer.* Chicago, IL: Dramatic Pub. Co. SUBJECTS/PLAY TYPE: Computers; Comedy.

1826. 9-12. (+) Lehan, Robert R. **Lovesong.** CAST: 1f, 1m. ACTS: 1. SETTINGS: Room. PLAYING TIME: 30 min. PLOT: An old woman enters Sam's room. At first, she tries to make him remember his name and their years of marriage together, but he disavows ever having known her. She plays a recording of the song they danced to the night he proposed, but still, no memories are triggered. In an unexpected twist, Jeannine confesses to being unsure of who he is and even of who she herself is. RECOMMENDATION: This speaks powerfully with what it does not say. The unanswered questions will leave an audience wondering and the tension of the dialogue draws the audience in, raising profound questions, perhaps about human existence itself. ROYALTY: $10. SOURCE: Lehan, Robert R. (1983). *Lovesong.* Denver, CO: Pioneer Drama Service. SUBJECTS/PLAY TYPE: Aging; Love; Drama.

1827. 7-9. (-) Harder, Eleanor & Harder, Ray. (Evans, Greg) **Luann.** (Luann comic strip) CAST: 7f, 4m, Su. ACTS: 2. SETTINGS: Bedroom; mall; hallway; classroom; office; dining room; gym. PLAYING TIME: 120 min. PLOT: Luann has a crush on Aaron Hill, who doesn't know she's alive. Her grades are poor, she feels unattractive, and her brother teases her. In an attempt to be noticed, Luann tries out for cheerleader, but is chosen as the school's pitbull mascot instead. Luann decides to give it a try and soon has the basketball spectators laughing and cheering at her antics. Best of all, Aaron Hill says, "Hi." RECOMMENDATION: While this humorously addresses many of the problems of adolescence, it moves slowly, with too much dialogue and too little action. ROYALTY: $90. SOURCE: Harder, Eleanor & Harder, Ray. (1985). Luann. Denver, CO: Pioneer Drama Service. SUBJECTS/PLAY TYPE: Self Esteem; Musical; Adaptation.

1828. 7-10. (+) Sodaro, Craig. **Lucky in love.** CAST: 3f, 3m. ACTS: 1. SETTINGS: Park. PLAYING TIME: 25 min. PLOT: McDoogle, a struggling leprechaun, is demoted to the American branch of the Order of the Pot of Gold. There, he attempts some magical matchmaking for two low income lovers, but finds that love conducts its own magic. RECOMMENDATION: An Irish flavored treat, this would make a delightful St. Patrick's Day special, and turn of the century costumes could add to its charm. ROYALTY: Free to Plays subscribers. SOURCE: Sodaro, Craig. (1987, March). Lucky in love. Plays: The Drama Magazine for Young People, pp. 1-10. SUBJECTS/PLAY TYPE: Leprechauns; Matchmaking; Playlet.

1829. 9-12*. (-) Teague, Oran. **Ludie.** CAST: 2f, 4m, Su. ACTS: 2. SETTINGS: General store. PLAYING TIME: NA. PLOT: Ludie perceives and comprehends the evil of an itinerant fundamentalist preacher who has raped two of the congregants and turned the whole town against education and anyone who has been educated. Her parents' brainwashed allegiance to the preacher causes her sister (a rape victim of the preacher) to be committed to an asylum, and ultimately causes Ludie's death. RECOMMENDATION: This chillingly demonstrates the dangers of cultism and lack of thought. However, because of its blunt sexual references, it is more appropriate for very mature teenagers, and preferably adults. ROYALTY: $50. SOURCE: Teague, Oran. (1984). Ludie. Chicago, IL: Dramatic Pub. Co. SUBJECTS/PLAY TYPE: Cultism; Drama.

1830. 4-6. (+) Bradley, Virginia. **Ludlillian and the dark road.** CAST: 4f, 2m. ACTS: 1. SETTINGS: Assembly hall. PLAYING TIME: NA. PLOT: On Halloween, Ludlillian the witch, her conscience Lilly, and a little ghost must get back to the gates by midnight or else they'll be forced to become part of the devil's League. RECOMMENDATION: This is funny, easily memorized, and sends a subtle message of goodness. ROYALTY: None. SOURCE: Bradley, Virginia. (1981). Holidays on stage. New York, NY: Dodd, Mead. SUBJECTS/PLAY TYPE: Halloween; Drama.

1831. 7-12. (+) Kelly, Tim. Nestor, Larry. **Lumberjack and wedding belles.** CAST: 14f, 11m. ACTS: 2. SETTINGS: Lobby; forest. PLAYING TIME: 120 min. PLOT: Asa Mercer, a young lawyer, returns to Washington from Boston with five potential brides for the good natured, but barely civilized lumberjacks. Unscrupulous Mayor Crook, who opposes Asa's ambition for a seat in the territorial legislature, and Ma Scrubbs, an unwashed backwoods trapper who feels the lumberjacks (representing civilization) are ruining the area and especially her trapping, plot to discredit Asa and the "belles" by robbing Melissa Pendleton (half-blind townswoman) and planting the stolen money on Asa. As Asa and three of the "belles" await trial, Asa recalls seeing the "Hermit" in the vicinity of the alleged assault. Ma Scrubbs shoots the Hermit before he can talk. At the trial, when it appears the hoax will succeed, a surprise witness is announced: the Hermit was only wounded and his funeral staged to protect him. He tells the truth. As the deputy hauls the villains off to jail, Asa suggests that as long as the judge is in town, he can perform what will hopefully be the first of many weddings and the beginning of a new era in the Northwest Territories. RECOMMENDATION: Intended as a major musical production, this requires a large cast, musical talent, and fairly elaborate staging. All of the characters are drawn with broad humor that encourages overacting and allows considerable latitude in interpretation. Despite the play's historical setting, the central theme of opposition to progress and civilization is timeless. ROYALTY: $60. SOURCE: Kelly, Tim and Nestor, Larry. (1981). Lumberjacks and wedding belles. Denver, CO: Pioneer Drama Service. SUBJECTS/PLAY TYPE: Northwest Territory; Comedy; Musical.

1832. 10-12. (+) Weaver-Francisco, Patricia. **Lunacy.** CAST: 7f, 2m. ACTS: 1. SETTINGS: Cabin; launch pad; space capsule. PLAYING TIME: NA. PLOT: Young, self confident Martha Howland is the first woman to go into space alone. As her spacecraft floats, a stream of women who have contributed to the space program pass by. These surreal and unexpected encounters heighten Martha's sympathy for the early female pioneers. She returns to earth determined to include one of original female astronauts who never got to fly on her next flight, only to have that woman reject her offer, saying that her time has passed. RECOMMENDATION: Based on Sally Ride's historical space flight in 1983 and the 13 American women pilots who qualified 20 years earlier but never got to fly, this is a good lead-in to discussions on history, women, and the space program. Cast is expandable. ROYALTY: $60. SOURCE: Weaver-Francisco, Patricia. (1986). Lunacy. Woodstock, IL: Dramatic Pub. Co. SUBJECTS/PLAY TYPE: Space Program; Women Astronauts; Drama.

1833. 10-12. (-) Foster, Dutton. **Lurking on the railroad or will she give him a wide berth?** CAST: 5f, 5m, Su. ACTS: 2. SETTINGS: Railroad platform; railroad car. PLAYING TIME: NA. PLOT: Nigel Nash-Gnarkington tries to take over the Treasure Mountain and Pacific Railroad in 1905 California. Along with his shady financial dealings, Nigel aims to seduce prim Euphemia Bettendorf. His grand scheme is foiled by a beautiful teenage girl. RECOMMENDATION: This full scale musical/melodrama with many song and dance routines uses satire, irony, puns, and humorous references to classic pieces of literature and melodrama as the mainstay of its humor. Overt sexist humor has been leavened with feminist overtures. An adult audience might find this enjoyable, but young adults would either find it silly, or be unable to appreciate its highbrow humor. ROYALTY:

Upon application. SOURCE: Foster, Dutton. (1987). Lurking on the railroad, or, will she give him a wide berth? Woodstock, IL: The Dramatic Pub. Co. SUBJECTS/PLAY TYPE: Railroads; Musical.

1834. 4-7. (+) Henderson, Nancy. **M.D. in petticoats.** CAST: 5f, 15m, Su. ACTS: 1. SETTINGS: Infirmary. PLAYING TIME: 9 min. PLOT: Dr. Elizabeth Blackwell describes her struggle to become the first woman doctor. RECOMMENDATION: This well describes Dr. Blackwell and her contributions to women's rights and to the medical profession. ROYALTY: Permission required if performed outside of the classroom. SOURCE: Henderson, Nancy. (1978). Celebrate America: A baker's dozen of plays. New York, NY: Julian Messner. SUBJECTS/PLAY TYPE: Blackwell, Elizabeth; Doctors; Women; Drama.

1835. 1-3. (+) Martin, Judith. **Ma and the kids.** CAST: 1f, 3u. ACTS: 1. SETTINGS: Bare stage, props. PLAYING TIME: 5 min. PLOT: At dinnertime, Ma doesn't get to eat because by the time she serves her children, the food is devoured. The next morning, Ma frantically gets the kids off to school and helps out as they return to pick up the things they forgot. Just as she relaxes, they all return home because it is Saturday. RECOMMENDATION: The theme of being prepared runs through this delightfully chaotic skit, in which props can be mimed by the players or imagined by the audience. ROYALTY: None. SOURCE: Martin, Judith. (1981). Everybody, everybody: A collection from the paper bag players. New York, NY: Elsevier/Nelson Books. SUBJECTS/PLAY TYPE: Dinner; School; Comedy.

1836. 9-12. (+) Olfson, Lewy. (Shakespeare, William) **Macbeth.** (Macbeth) CAST: 5f, 10m, Su. ACTS: 1. SETTINGS: None. PLAYING TIME: 25 min. PLOT: Three witches foresee Macbeth as king. Lady Macbeth murders to fulfill the prophesy. Through twists of fate, this and other prophesies come to pass. Guilt and retribution prove the Macbeths' undoing. RECOMMENDATION: Shakespeare's original language is interspersed with comments from a narrator who interprets what takes place and summarizes portions of the original plot. ROYALTY: Free to Plays subscribers. SOURCE: Olfson, Lewy. (1975, January). Macbeth. Plays: The Drama Magazine for Young People, pp. 85-96. SUBJECTS/PLAY TYPE: Drama; Tragedy; Reader's Theater; Adaptation.

1837. 4-8. (+) Winther, Barbara. **Macona, the honest warrior.** CAST: 2f, 5m, Su. ACTS: 2. SETTINGS: Bare stage. PLAYING TIME: 20 min. PLOT: The good warrior, Macona, proves his character by carving a stool on which the chief's face is perfectly represented. Luwant, a thief from the neighboring village, is exposed when he sleeps instead of also carving the necessary stool. RECOMMENDATION: Pantomime and other body motion convey most of the action (including flying parrots and mosquitoes). ROYALTY: Free to Plays subscribers. SOURCE: Winther, Barbara. (1978, February). Macona, the honest warrior. Plays: The Drama Magazine for Young People, pp. 52-57. SUBJECTS/PLAY TYPE: Honor; Folk Tales, South America; Playlet.

1838. 5-9. (-) Swarthout, Genevieve & Swarthout, Elwyn. **Madam president.** CAST: 7f. ACTS: 1. SETTINGS: Office. PLAYING TIME: NA. PLOT: A woman has been elected President of the United States. After commenting on the President's new hair style, Millie, her secretary, announces her visitors. First is the Vice President, a former schoolteacher. After they remark on each other's hair and outfits, the Vice President suggests using truant officers to enforce compulsory attendance in Congress. A wealthy woman enters to complain that she is in danger of losing her welfare payments, followed by two ladies from Kansas who propose to eliminate the national debt through nationwide garage and bake sales. RECOMMENDATION: Unpleasant stereotypes of women in positions of power and of the rich welfare recipient with a Cadillac are offensive. ROYALTY: NA. SOURCE: Swarthout, Genevieve & Swarthout, Elwyn. (1978). Madam president. Franklin, OH: Eldridge Pub. Co. SUBJECTS/PLAY TYPE: Women; Government; Comedy.

1839. 7-12. (+) Sodaro, Craig. (O. Henry) **Madame Bo-Peep.** (Madame Bo-Peep, of the ranches [in Whirligigs]) CAST: 3f, 3m. ACTS: 1. SETTINGS: Parlor. PLAYING TIME: 25 min. PLOT: Octavia, a young, sophisticated widow, moves in with her aunt to help run her inherited, almost bankrupt, Texas sheep ranch. As she learns the ranching business, she also falls in love with the manager (Teddy), an old flame. When evil Angus tries to force the women to sell the ranch, Teddy reveals that he had secretly bought it before the aunt's husband died, and the two young lovers marry and honeymoon at the ranch. RECOMMENDATION: This adaptation follows the spirit of the original, but changes the plot and characters. This is appealing because the characters are portrayed as being more frivolous society people and the dialogue is updated. ROYALTY: Free to Plays subscribers. SOURCE: Sodaro, Craig. (1989, January/February). Madame Bo-Peep. Plays: The Drama Magazine for Young People, pp. 71-79. SUBJECTS/PLAY TYPE: Romance; Westerns; Comedy; Adaptation.

1840. 7-12. (+) Hanson, Mary E. & Sheldon, David P. **Madame Zena's Seance.** CAST: 8f, 6m. ACTS: 1. SETTINGS: Living room. PLAYING TIME: 30 min. PLOT: A gang of criminals hide a kidnapped Arab princess in the basement of Grandmother's house, the site of a seance. Madame Zena promises to help Abdul and Omar find their princess if they play along with her seance. During the seance, terrorized by an escaped pet snake in the basement, the kidnappers rush into the room with the princess. At the same time, Abdul, Omar, and the police collide with the kidnappers. The police arrest the kidnappers, Abdul and Omar rescue the princess, and Grandmother's household sits down to enjoy her anchovy cookies and spinach tea. RECOMMENDATION: This slapstick comedy is filled with fun and frolic. The action packed plot moves along rapidly and the characters are wonderfully bizarre, exotic, and eccentric. ROYALTY: Free to Plays Subscribers. SOURCE: Hanson, Mary E. & David P. Sheldon. (1980, May). Madame Zena's Seance. Plays: The Drama Magazine for Young People, pp. 39-46. SUBJECTS/PLAY TYPE: Witchcraft; Seances; Comedy.

1841. 3-8. (+) Priore, Frank V. **Madcap monster inn.**
CAST: 2f, 4m, 1u. ACTS: 1. SETTINGS: Hotel lobby.
PLAYING TIME: 10 min. PLOT: A couple seeks a room
for one night at the Transylvania hotel. They wait in the
lobby, which is being renovated having been torn apart the
previous night by a werewolf who forgot to report to his
cage before the full moon rose. When they meet Count
Dracula, Frankenstein, a mummy, and a witch, they decide
that they would prefer to sleep in their locked car.
RECOMMENDATION: This hilarious comedy ends as
the bellboy (with horns) calls the couple weirdos, adding
an interesting perspective to the entire thing. ROYALTY:
Free to subscribers. SOURCE: Priore, Frank V. (1982,
October). Madcap monster inn. Plays: The Drama
Magazine for Young People, pp. 71-74. SUBJECTS/PLAY
TYPE: Halloween; Monsters; Skit.

1842. 5-9. (+) Campbell, Paddy. **Madwitch.** CAST: 2f,
3m, Su. ACTS: 1. SETTINGS: Shack; store. PLAYING
TIME: NA. PLOT: A harmless, eccentric old Indian
woman is mercilessly taunted by neighborhood children,
who call her Madwitch. On a dare, Joanie creeps up to the
woman's shack. When the woman comes out, Joanie drops
her pencil case as she flees. To cover up what she's done,
Joanie explains her lost pencil case was stolen by
Madwitch. Her father and Mr. Klassen force the police to
take Madwitch away because she's crazy and dangerous,
just as they took her father away years ago. They then
learn that World War II has begun, and the play ends with
the children taunting Klassen, because he is a German
immigrant. RECOMMENDATION: This tragic story
about ignorance, prejudice, and fear may not be
understood by young people because much of its message
is delivered via symbolic fantasy scenes. However, if it
could be discussed either before or after presentation, it
could be very effective. ROYALTY: NA. SOURCE:
Campbell, Paddy L. (1984). Buckskin and chapperos;
Madwitch: Two plays for children. Toronto, Canada:
Playwrights Canada. SUBJECTS/PLAY TYPE: Prejudice;
Drama.

1843. 12. (+) Patrick, John. **The magenta moth.** CAST:
5f, 3m. ACTS: 3. SETTINGS: Living room. PLAYING
TIME: NA. PLOT: Unmarried professors, Cassie and
Grace, decide to spend some time in Cassie's summer
lodge in the woods while Cassie's broken hip mends.
Three runaway girls (members of a satanic cult and
responsible for the brutal murder of a family in a nearby
town) torture and threaten them. They are saved by their
nephew who brings supplies and under-stands their
warning in Latin. RECOMMENDATION: This is action
packed and suspenseful. However, crude language and
nudity make it inappropriate for a school audience.
ROYALTY: $50. SOURCE: Patrick, John. (1983). The
magenta moth. New York, NY: Dramatists Play Service,
Inc. SUBJECTS/PLAY TYPE: Satanism; Murder;
Deprivation; Drama.

1844. 12. (+) Sanders, Dudley W. **Maggie and the bird
go fishing.** CAST: 1f, 2m. ACTS: 1. SETTINGS: Dock.
PLAYING TIME: NA. PLOT: Maggie, a dreamy, idealistic
17 year old, tries fishing in a very polluted river. With her

is Bird, an old, cynical blind man. Their two different
outlooks clash constantly until they almost catch a fish.
RECOMMENDATION: Substantive and quick witted
dialogue focuses on the issues of idealism and cynicism, in
a play with very little action. It is recommended only for
high school students and adults, due to profanity and
alcohol consumption. ROYALTY: $15. SOURCE: Sanders,
Dudley W. (1984). Maggie and the bird go fishing. Boston,
MA: Baker's Plays. SUBJECTS/PLAY TYPE: Blindness;
Cynicism; Idealism; Drama.

1845. 10-12. (+) Kesselman, Wendy. **Maggie Magalita.**
CAST: 3f, 1m, Su. ACTS: 1. SETTINGS: Living room.
PLAYING TIME: NA. PLOT: Teenage Maggie and her
mother, Spanish emigrees, have adjusted to life in New
York City. The arrival of Maggie's grandmother with her
"foreign" thinking, dress, and speech creates conflict
between the generations. Maggie sees grandmother as a
threat to peer acceptance, and treats her with stoney
silences, resentment, and finally, open confrontation.
Maggie and her grandmother do begin to communicate
and build a positive relationship. RECOMMENDATION:
This focuses not only on the generation gap, but also on
how it can be complicated when the "aged parent" is a
foreign national coming to live in an established family
unit. Parts of the play are spoken in Spanish, which may
limit its presentation to certain geographic areas.
ROYALTY: NA. SOURCE: Kesselman, Wendy. (1987).
Maggie Magalita. New York NY: Samuel French.
SUBJECTS/PLAY TYPE: Spanish Americans; Generation
Gap; Elderly; Drama.

1846. 2-6. (+) Merten, George. **The magic book.**
CAST: 2f, 2m, 5u. ACTS: 1. SETTINGS: Living room.
PLAYING TIME: NA. PLOT: A boy who abhors reading
is persuaded to love it by the alluring characters that jump
out of the pages of a magic book. RECOMMENDATION:
The characters' names and actions enhance the text to
produce delightfully appealing results. ROYALTY: Free to
Plays subscribers. SOURCE: Merten, George. (1979). Plays
for puppet performance. Boston, MA: Plays, Inc.
SUBJECTS/PLAY TYPE: Books; Fantasy; Puppet Play.

1847. 2-5. (+) Lahr, Georgiana Lieder. **The magic cape.**
CAST: 4f, 3m, 26u. ACTS: 1. SETTINGS: Woods.
PLAYING TIME: 15 min. PLOT: It is Halloween eve.
Witch Grundy has lost her magic cape and the magic
forest denizens, from pumpkins to squirrels to autumn
leaves, all search for it. They discover that Jenny was going
to borrow it to wear in the Halloween parade but had
second thoughts and decided to return it to the forest.
Witch Grundy gives Jenny a cape of leaves to wear in the
parade. Everyone has a happy Halloween.
RECOMMENDATION: Simple plot, animal characters,
and a large supporting cast all combine to make an
excellent children's production. Its seasonal theme offers a
drama option to the overworked arts and crafts emphasis
that dominates the elementary fine arts curriculum in
October. ROYALTY: Free to Plays subscribers. SOURCE:
Lahr, Georgiana Lieder. (1979, October). The magic cape.
Plays: The Drama Magazine for Young People, pp. 42-46.
SUBJECTS/PLAY TYPE: Halloween; Mystery; Fantasy.

1848. K-6. (+) Fisher, Aileen. **The magic card.** CAST: 1f, 2m. ACTS: 1. SETTINGS: None. PLAYING TIME: 2 min. PLOT: A girl gives hints to boys about a magic card that enables her go to any country or time she wants. The boys finally guess that it is a library card. RECOMMENDATION: This simple poem can be effectively used during Library Awareness Week or Book Week. ROYALTY: Free to Plays subscribers. SOURCE: Fisher, Aileen. (1986, November). The magic card. Plays: The Drama Magazine for Young People, pp. 50. SUBJECTS/PLAY TYPE: Book Week; Reading; Choral Reading.

1849. 5-8. (+) Gotwalt, Helen Louise Miller. **The magic carpet sweeper.** CAST: 3f, 3m. ACTS: 1. SETTINGS: Living room; bedroom. PLAYING TIME: 20 min. PLOT: Joey is sent to pick up a bracelet his older three siblings have chosen for a Mother's Day gift. He returns instead with a carpet sweeper which has the trademark "magic." He is convinced it is truly magic and his siblings decide to test it by cleaning the house. Their mother comes home early and says it is magic because the children cleaned the house. The young boy who sold the sweeper to Joey must buy it back because he sold it by mistake. The children realize that magic is in anything that is done with love, or to help another. RECOMMENDATION: Small children might enjoy this Mother's Day story about doing cleaning chores around the house. However, its message is a little heavy handed, and the stereotype of Mom doing all the housework is unnecessary. ROYALTY: Free to Plays subscribers. SOURCE: Gotwalt, Helen Louise Miller. (1986, May). The magic carpet sweeper. Plays: The Drama Magazine for Young People, pp. 45-51. SUBJECTS/PLAY TYPE: Mother's Day; Cleaning; Playlet.

1850. 7-12. (+) Ringwood, Gwen. **The magic carpets of Antonio Angelini.** CAST: 6u. ACTS: 1. SETTINGS: Outside. PLAYING TIME: NA. PLOT: A starving young man disguises himself as a robber but becomes involved with a rugseller, whose rugs tell the stories of the immigrants who founded Canada. He helps the rugseller, and receives food. RECOMMENDATION: This is very creative, but the references to Canadian history may be lost on American audiences. ROYALTY: NA. SOURCE: Kids plays: Six Canadian plays for children. (1980). Toronto, Canada: Playwrights Press. SUBJECTS/PLAY TYPE: Canada, History; Immigrants; Playlet.

1851. 5-12. (+) Julian, Faye D. **A magic Christmas.** CAST: 4f, 2m. ACTS: 1. SETTINGS: Porch. PLAYING TIME: 30 min. PLOT: A lonely old lady who lives in Georgia, and converses with inanimate objects is rewarded for her kindnesses by fulfillment of her wish for snow at Christmas. RECOMMENDATION: A walking, talking holly bush and poinsettia plant, a comical mailman, and uppity neighbor are delightful. Special effects and costuming might be simplified to make the play fun and creative for children of any age, however, the part of Miss Annie could not be portrayed sensitively by an elementary child. ROYALTY: $15. SOURCE: Julian, Faye D. (1983). A magic Christmas. Schulenburg, TX: I.E. Clark. SUBJECTS/PLAY TYPE: Christmas; Magic; Comedy.

1852. 4-6. (+) Whitworth, Virginia Payne. (Grimm Brothers) **The magic cloak.** (The twelve dancing princesses) CAST: 6f, 8m, Su. ACTS: 1. SETTINGS: Path; palace. PLAYING TIME: 25 min. PLOT: The King offers a royal wedding to any man who can find out how his daughters wear out so many dancing shoes. Jon befriends an old woman who offers him a magic cloak of invisibility and advises him to drink nothing the princesses offer him. Invisible, Jon follows them to the enchanted forest, provides proof to the king of their adventures, and is rewarded with a daughter and a title. RECOMMENDATION: Jon must be portrayed as sensitive, yet strong, in this tale about naughtiness, rather than the traditional good versus evil conflict. Three set changes may pose problems for younger crews. ROYALTY: NA. SOURCE: Kamerman, Sylvia. (1987). Plays from favorite folk tales. Boston, MA: Plays, Inc. SUBJECTS/PLAY TYPE: Folk Tales, Germany; Playlet.

1853. 1-5. (+) Guderjahn, Ernie. **The magic cricket.** CAST: 2f, 1m, Su. ACTS: 1. SETTINGS: Bedroom; garden; kitchen. PLAYING TIME: NA. PLOT: The queen, who suffers from insomnia, asks her kingdom to cure her. Suggestions range from a glass of milk (which gives her a stomach ache) to a music box (which stops in the middle of the night). Finally, Jeremy brings her a cricket which sings all night and cures her. He is given three bags of gold, but declines the offer of 1/4 of the kingdom, saying he fears he wouldn't be able to sleep. RECOMMENDATION: This cute treatment of familiar themes can be adapted to include any number of cures. It is short but sweet. ROYALTY: NA. SOURCE: Guderjahn, Ernie. (1984). A children's trilogy. Studio City, CA: Player's Press. SUBJECTS/PLAY TYPE: Insomnia; Crickets; Comedy.

1854. 1-3. (+) Osman, Karen. **The magic drum.** CAST: 14u. ACTS: 1. SETTINGS: Jungle; river. PLAYING TIME: 14 min. PLOT: The hunter's son, Koi, weeping because he has no special skill or talent, is heard by the River God who gives him a drum. Koi practices at the river until one night, when he is attacked by the wild jungle animals, he plays so eloquently they allow him to escape. Koi thinks the drum is magic, but the river god tells him that the magic is in him. RECOMMENDATION: This simple tale of self confidence and personal fulfillment will appeal to younger children through its use of repetitive dialogue and to older children who will appreciate its theme. The musical quality of the dialogue and the eerie, dream like quality of the play as a whole, make this quite entertaining. ROYALTY: Free to Plays subscribers. SOURCE: Osman, Karen. (1986, May). The magic drum. Plays: The Drama Magazine for Young People, pp. 53- 57. SUBJECTS/PLAY TYPE: Fable; Self Confidence; Fantasy.

1855. 6-10. (+) Rogers, June Walker. (Mozart, Amadeus) **The magic flute.** (The magic flute.) CAST: 6f, 5m, Su. ACTS: 1. SETTINGS: Woods. PLAYING TIME: NA. PLOT: Tamino is attacked by a pigeon serving Sarastro, and then he is rescued by followers of the Queen of the Night. The Queen offers Tamino the hand of her lovely daughter, Pamino, if he can rescue her from Sarastro. Tamino is given a magical flute which he uses several times to get around obstacles. He rescues Pamino and is commended for his courage and strong will. RECOMMENDATION: The language is simple but effective. Although none of the original symbolism has been retained, the adventurous plot stands well on its own. Some of the Mozart arias might be included (taped) to add some depth. ROYALTY: $35. SOURCE: Rogers, June Walker. (1976). The magic flute. Chicago, IL: Dramatic Pub. Co. SUBJECTS/PLAY TYPE: Magic; Adaptation.

1856. 1-6. (+) Newman, Deborah. (Grimm Brothers) **The magic goose.** (The magic goose) CAST: 5f, 8m, Su. ACTS: 1. SETTINGS: Fair. PLAYING TIME: 10 min. PLOT: A baker refuses to give food to an old beggar. Three sisters and a soldier refuse him money. When Simon shares his meal, the old man gives him a magic goose. All those who touch it stay stuck. This makes the unhappy princess laugh, and Simon is wedded to her. RECOMMENDATION: The hilarious visual humor will not preempt the message. ROYALTY: NA. SOURCE: Kamerman, Sylvia. (1987). Plays from favorite folk tales. Boston, MA: Plays, Inc. SUBJECTS/PLAY TYPE: Love; Comedy; Folk Tales, Germany; Adaptation.

1857. 3-6*. (+) Taylor, Cecil P. **The magic island.** CAST: 2f, 3m, Su. ACTS: 4. SETTINGS: Cave; kitchen; river. PLAYING TIME: NA. PLOT: Anne, a lonely child whose parents are usually working to make ends meet, thinks she is dull. She runs away and meets an 80 year old man who lives in a cave and claims to be a goblin. Anne helps the goblin escape the witchman, and she then wants to sail to a magic island where she can eat cleverness berries and grow smart. But she realizes she is already smart, since she has outwitted the witchman. The goblin disappears and the cast admonishes the audience to push its imagination buttons. RECOMMENDATION: The audience is involved in producing the sound effects for this delightful foray into the imagination of a young girl and an eccentric old man. The cast will have to be at least high school age, and some rewriting of British slang is necessary. Anne's final realization of her own self worth is clearly and delightfully unraveled, complete with discussions of her dilemma between the cast and audience during brief intermissions. ROYALTY: NA. SOURCE: Taylor, Cecil P. (1983). Live theatre: Four plays for young people. London, England: Methuen. SUBJECTS/PLAY TYPE: Identity; Imagination; Cleverness; Participation Play.

1858. 4-12*. (+) Rogers, June Walker. **Magic Magic!** CAST: 17f, 10m, 2u. ACTS: 2. SETTINGS: Apartment. PLAYING TIME: NA. PLOT: Kaye Kaye, a naive student from the Midwest, sublets a loft apartment in Soho. Strange and magical girls parade through the apartment, formerly the home of "Renzo the Magnificent." Kaye Kaye begins to despise "Renzo the cad"—not at all like the polite and gentlemanly Bob, Kaye Kaye's boyfriend and Renzo's best friend. When Bob proposes, Kaye Kaye refuses unless he ends his friendship with the magician. What a surprise when Kaye Kaye discovers that Bob is Renzo and sometimes things just aren't what they appear to be. RECOMMENDATION: The rather obvious plot is saved

by 27 magic tricks that add a sense of excitement. The fully explained tricks are simple to execute yet clever enough to be fascinating. ROYALTY: $35. SOURCE: Rogers, June Walker. (1975). Magic! Magic! Chicago, IL: Dramatic Pub. Co. SUBJECTS/PLAY TYPE: Magic; Comedy.

1859. K-5. (+) Thane, Adele. **The magic nutmeg-grater.** CAST: 5f, 4m. ACTS: 1. SETTINGS: Town square. PLAYING TIME: 25 min. PLOT: Sorcerer Tinker Hans gives a group of children a magic nutmeg-grater through which people can hear the wind as well as what others say about them. Tinker Hans instructs the boy to give the grater to the one who needs it most and he shall have good fortune. The children show the grater to several passersby, including the king, disguised as a beggar. The king is the one who needs the grater most since it warns him of potential harm. The grateful king reveals himself to the children and rewards them with riches. RECOMMENDATION: Rhyming, repetition of lines, and action make this attractive for younger children, and the cast can be expanded to accommodate any number. ROYALTY: Free to Plays subscribers. SOURCE: Thane, Adele. (1983). Plays from famous stories and fairy tales. Boston, MA: Plays Inc. SUBJECTS/PLAY TYPE: Folk Tale Motifs; Playlet.

1860. 3-5. (+) Nolan, Paul T. (Saavedra, Miguel de Cervantes) **The magic of Salamanca.** (The cave of Salamanca) CAST: 2f, 4m. ACTS: 1. SETTINGS: Road. PLAYING TIME: 25 min. PLOT: Bidding their master a "tearful" farewell, the servants gleefully prepare to have a party in his absence. A starving student invites himself in just as the master returns. The student tricks the master into believing that he can produce food and the hidden guests appear with the food from the party, satisfying the master that he has not been cheated. RECOMMENDATION: The clever asides by the tearful servants, which indicate their true feelings, as well as the clever trickery by the student, will delight young audiences. ROYALTY: None for amateur performance. SOURCE: Nolan, Paul T. (1982). Folk tale plays round the world: A collection of royalty-free, one-act plays about lands far and near. Boston, MA: Plays, Inc. SUBJECTS/PLAY TYPE: Comedy; Adaptation.

1861. 4-6. (+) Mahlman, Lewis & Jones, David Cadwalader. (Grimm Brothers) **The magic shoes.** (The elves and the shoemaker) CAST: 4f, 4m, 2u. ACTS: 1. SETTINGS: Shoemaker's shop. PLAYING TIME: 15 min. PLOT: A poor shoemaker and his wife are the recipients of good luck because of the action of two elves. RECOMMENDATION: This faithful adaptation retains all the charm of the original. ROYALTY: Free to Plays subscribers. SOURCE: Mahlman, Lewis, & Jones, David Cadwalader. (1974). Puppet plays for young players. Boston, MA: Plays, Inc. SUBJECTS/PLAY TYPE: Fantasy, Folk Tales, Germany; Puppet Play; Adaptation.

1862. 4-7. (+) Turnbull, Lucia. **The magic shoes.** CAST: 5f, 2m. ACTS: 1. SETTINGS: Hut; palace. PLAYING TIME: 20 min. PLOT: Widow O'Malley is visited by leprechaun Grankey, and she tells him how her son neglects her and spends his time thinking of Princess

Grania. Grankey makes many pairs of shoes. When Hew, the widow's son returns, he promises once again to be a comfort to his mother. Hew takes the shoes to the palace where Grania, impressed that leprechauns made them, accepts Hew's rose, the shoes, and his expressions of love. **RECOMMENDATION:** Reminiscent of **The Elves and the Shoemaker**, this Irish folk tale is heart warming and fun. The short rhyming dialogue could easily be set to music and will be easily memorized by young actors. **ROYALTY:** Free to Plays subscribers. **SOURCE:** Turnbull, Lucia. (1976, March). The magic shoes. Plays: The Drama Magazine for Young People, pp. 54-60. **SUBJECTS/PLAY TYPE:** Folk Tales, Ireland; St. Patrick's Day; Comedy.

1863. 1-4*. (+) Lanyon, Angela. **The Magic snowman.** **CAST:** 2f, 2m, 2u. **ACTS:** 2. **SETTINGS:** Kitchen; street. **PLAYING TIME:** NA. **PLOT:** Thara, Mistress of the Mist, tries to melt all the snow and get rid of Christmas. One of her Mists sends Father Christmas' sleigh off course and into a star, scattering reindeer and presents. Mother Christmas and the Magic Snowman bake a gingerbread man to catch Thara and retrieve all the presents. But too much ginger makes him go haywire. The Warden, who is not fond of Christmas, is talked into bringing back the Gingerbread Man, on condition that the warden receive a present. With a little magic from the Snowman, Thara appears and is vanquished by Gingerbread Man and the Warden. Father Christmas is then able to deliver his presents, including one for the Warden, and everyone celebrates. **RECOMMENDATION:** It is questionable whether the domineering, name calling personality of Mother Christmas adds to the humor. It is obvious she is concerned, but the urgency of the situation does not call for rudeness to the snowman or other characters. Because this uses audience participation (i.e., to mix the baking ingredients, to catch flying plates, etc.) it must be performed by older actors. **ROYALTY:** NA. **SOURCE:** Lanyon, Angele. (1980). The magic snowman. Macclesfield, England: New Playwrights' Network. **SUBJECTS/PLAY TYPE:** Christmas; Musical.

1864. 1-3. (+) DeRegniers, Beatrice Schenk. **The magic spell. CAST:** 2f, 3u. **ACTS:** 1. **SETTINGS:** House; forest. **PLAYING TIME:** NA. **PLOT:** A young girl and her brother go into a forest on the way home from their grandmother's house. When the brother disobeys his grandmother's warning not to eat anything that grows in the forest, a wizard turns him into a cat. With the help of a stranger, the spell is broken. **RECOMMENDATION:** Easily performed for and by children, DeRegnier's sly humor is very appealing. **ROYALTY:** None. **SOURCE:** DeRegniers, Beatrice Schenk. (1982). Picture book theatre. New York: Clarion Books/Houghton Mifflin Co. **SUBJECTS/PLAY TYPE:** Magic; Comedy; Skit.

1865. K-6*. (+) Mathews-Deacon, Saundra. **Magic theatre I. CAST:** 3f, 3m. **ACTS:** 1. **SETTINGS:** Bare stage. **PLAYING TIME:** 50 min. **PLOT:** Adult actors are portrayed as children who are tired of doing what they are told and run away to the world of imagination where they never have to clean up or stop playing to eat. They decide to come back to the real world where mothers and fathers read stories and bake good things to eat. Songs are used to

express the children's feelings. **RECOMMENDATION:** The actors portray what children at one time or another dream of, a world where no one tells them what to do. The world is explored through imagination, but reality is the message. **ROYALTY:** $35. **SOURCE:** Mathews-Deacon, Saundra. (1983). Magic theatre I. Woodstock, IL: Dramatic Pub. Co. **SUBJECTS/PLAY TYPE:** Imagination; Musical Revue.

1866. K-6*. (+) Mathews-Deacon, Saundra. **Magic theatre II. CAST:** 3f, 3m. **ACTS:** 1. **SETTINGS:** Bare stage. **PLAYING TIME:** 40 min. **PLOT:** The actors come from backstage to interact with the audience. They relay to the audience that any feeling is okay. Examples of childhood situations are presented; each is portrayed as okay and part of the growing experience. Songs are used to express feelings. **RECOMMENDATION:** Young audiences will appreciate the verbal acceptance of childhood feelings in a variety of situations. **ROYALTY:** $35. **SOURCE:** Mathews-Deacon, Saundra. (1981). Magic theatre II. Woodstock, IL: Dramatic Pub. Co. **SUBJECTS/PLAY TYPE:** Emotions; Musical Revue.

1867. K-6*. (-) Mathews-Deacon, Saundra. **Magic theatre III. CAST:** 4f, 3m. **ACTS:** 1. **SETTINGS:** Bare stage. **PLAYING TIME:** 40 min. **PLOT:** Sixteen brief sketches, some with music, define imagination. Actors use facial expressions and body movements to indicate changes from one sketch to another. Chants and other sounds are also used in a rhythmical fashion. Each sketch focuses on a different childhood experience. **RECOMMENDATION:** The rhythmical beginning lures the audience into the "magic land" of imagination. The sketches, however, focus frequently on the negatives of childhood experiences. Younger children might be frightened by the "gotcha" grabbing of actors who jump off the stage into the audience. Adults are excluded from the "magic land" which indicates that once a child grows to adulthood, the world of imaginative experiences ceases. The exclusion also inhibits communication and sharing experiences with adults. **ROYALTY:** $35. **SOURCE:** Mathews-Deacon, Saundra. (1983). Magic theatre III. Chicago, IL: Dramatic Pub. Co. **SUBJECTS/PLAY TYPE:** Imagination; Musical Revue.

1868. 9-12. (+) Muschell, David. **The magic tree. CAST:** 3f, 5m. **ACTS:** 1. **SETTINGS:** Dining room; woods. **PLAYING TIME:** NA. **PLOT:** As an old man, Jeff recalls how his aunt had long ago tried to place his grandfather in a nursing home because he wandered in the woods and spoke to a tree. When the doctor from the nursing home came to take the grandfather, the old man ran off into the woods, had a heart attack, and disappeared into the body of the tree as he died. Jeff's legacy from his grandfather is a walking stick and the ability to talk with the magic tree, a legacy he now wishes to pass on to his grandson. **RECOMMENDATION:** The play explores the changing relationship between parent and child; placing old people in "homes" at the convenience of the children, not the need of the parents; and the relationship of man to nature. **ROYALTY:** $15. **SOURCE:** Muschell, David. (1986). The magic tree. Woodstock, IL: Dramatic Pub. Co. **SUBJECTS/PLAY TYPE:** Aging; Death and Dying; Drama.

1869. K-6. (+) Cowie, Victor & Davies, Victor. **The magic trumpet. CAST:** 4f, 4m, Su. **ACTS:** 1. **SETTINGS:** Village square; forest. **PLAYING TIME:** NA. **PLOT:** Trying to avoid work during a school holiday, the village children follow Magic Maestro to the Forbidden Forest where his promise to make them circus animals isn't as great as it first seemed. Simon follows the children and rescues them. They find the Talking Tree and the Magic Trumpet, through which Simon restores the children to their normal bodies. They all return home. **RECOMMENDATION:** This is a delightful look at how having a kind heart and a happy smile can help overcome obstacles such as fear and inadequacy. Audience involvement and musical interludes add interesting variety. **ROYALTY:** NA. **SOURCE:** Cowie, Victor & Davies, Victor. (1984). The magic trumpet. Winnipeg, Canada: Turnstone Press. **SUBJECTS/PLAY TYPE:** Comedy; Attitudes; Musical.

1870. 3-6*. (+) Way, Brian. **Magical faces. CAST:** 2f, 2m. **ACTS:** 1. **SETTINGS:** Town square. **PLAYING TIME:** 50 min. **PLOT:** The Gravities rule a town where smiling and laughing are forbidden. Paul is being groomed to take their place, but when he meets Ticklelaff, the spirit of laughter, he works with her to change the town. **RECOMMENDATION:** This would have to be produced by adults for children since it calls for audience participation as they wear masks, play musical instruments, and provide verbal encouragement to the actors. **ROYALTY:** $20. **SOURCE:** Way, Brian. (1977). Magical faces. Boston, MA: Baker's Plays. **SUBJECTS/PLAY TYPE:** Laughter; Laws; Participation Play.

1871. 4-9*. (+) Harris, Aurand. (Lewis, C.S.) **The magician's nephew.** (The magician's nephew) **CAST:** 3f, 3m, Su. **ACTS:** 1. **SETTINGS:** Study; woods. **PLAYING TIME:** NA. **PLOT:** An old magician molds magic dust into rings that can transport the wearer into other worlds. He sends Polly off in a cloud of smoke and then urges Digory to follow her. They go to a world where an evil queen has destroyed her kingdom, then to a newborn planet where animals are supreme. Digory gets an apple from a magic tree and it helps heal his ill mother. **RECOMMENDATION:** This is a charming creation story with magic and a moral thrown in for good measure. It could be produced by older children but will be most effective when produced by adults. **ROYALTY:** $50. **SOURCE:** Harris, Aurand. (1984). The magician's nephew. Chicago, IL: Dramatic Pub. Co. **SUBJECTS/PLAY TYPE:** Musical; Fantasy; Adaptation.

1872. 6-12. (+) Lavery, Emmet. **The magnificent Yankee. CAST:** 1f, 1m. **ACTS:** 1. **SETTINGS:** Library. **PLAYING TIME:** NA. **PLOT:** Fanny becomes jealous when she learns that her husband, Justice Holmes, is to meet Ellen, his former nurse, for dinner. Holmes informs her that a man can still look at a pretty woman without violating his marriage vows or the Constitution. Fanny tells him to leave the Constitution at home. He won't need it. **RECOMMENDATION:** The major point, that jealousy exists even in long standing, stable relationships, is made with familiar characters. **ROYALTY:** NA. **SOURCE:**

Olfson, Lewy. (1980). Fifty great scenes for student actors. New York, NY: Bantam Books. **SUBJECTS/PLAY TYPE:** Jealousy; Marriage; Scene.

1873. 1-6. (+) Winther, Barbara. **The Maharajah is bored. CAST:** 2f, 5m, Su. **ACTS:** 1. **SETTINGS:** Village square. **PLAYING TIME:** 25 min. **PLOT:** The Maharajah seeks suggestions from his people on how to keep his life from being so boring. Two girls compete for their leader's favor: one cruel and rich, one poor and kind. Sitara (the poor one) helps the Maharajah by telling him to notice life's small details and to live with his heart. **RECOMMENDATION:** A colorful play, this presents the idea that "money isn't everything." The dialogue is too advanced for very young actors to memorize, so older children will be required. **ROYALTY:** Free for amateur performance. **SOURCE:** Winther, Barbara. (1976). Plays from folktales of Africa and Asia. Boston, MA: Plays, Inc. **SUBJECTS/PLAY TYPE:** Folk Tales, India; Playlet.

1874. 7-12. (+) Hearn, Sneed. **The mail order sheriff of Robbers' Roost. CAST:** 3f, 3m, 2u. **ACTS:** 1. **SETTINGS:** Living room. **PLAYING TIME:** NA. **PLOT:** Ma Perry orders a sheriff from a mail order catalog to get rid of a bumbling outlaw (who robs a boxcar and comes away with dozens of boxes). The new sheriff knows nothing of law and order, and goes around singing things like, "when the chimney catches the flue, it's time for the card player to hit the deck." In a confrontation between the sheriff and the outlaw, the sheriff wins. **RECOMMENDATION:** In this wonderful satire of the West, the songs can either be left in or taken out. Leaving them in adds to the outrageousness. For example, in one scene, the outlaw and the sheriff have a singing duel over who will marry Ma's daughter. **ROYALTY:** $15. **SOURCE:** Hearn, Sneed. (1979). The mail order sheriff of Robbers' Roost. Boston, MA: Baker's Plays. **SUBJECTS/PLAY TYPE:** Western; Musical; Satire; Comedy.

1875. 12. (-) Schechner, Richard & Epstein, Paul. (Shakespeare, William) **Makbeth.** (Macbeth) **CAST:** 1f, 5m, 3u. **ACTS:** 1. **SETTINGS:** Multilevel stage, glass and mirrors. **PLAYING TIME:** 90 min. **PLOT:** This is similar to Shakespeare in characters, lines, and outcome. The idea that Macduff, Cawdor, Banquo, and Malcolm are all sons of Duncan (Donalbain is absent completely), is experimental. The concept is that all of the sons yearn for the crown and would murder for it if they had the courage, but Makbeth beats them to the punch. There is some rearrangement of words and phrases, lines are repeated, and some scenes are played simultaneously for dramatic effect. **RECOMMENDATION:** Not recommended for any but the very erudite. The overall impression is one of confusion. The elaborate maze and multi-level playing area would make production impractical financially. The music appears to be little more than a sing-song version of Shakespeare's natural poetic style. **ROYALTY:** $50. **SOURCE:** Schechner, Richard & Epstein, Paul. (1978). Makbeth. Schulenburg, TX: I.E. Clark. **SUBJECTS/PLAY TYPE:** Tragedy; Adaptation.

1876. K-3. (+) Havilan, Amorie & Smith, Lyn. **Makers of Black history. CAST:** 4f, 21m, 1u. **ACTS:** 1. **SETTINGS:**

Bare stage, backdrop. **PLAYING TIME:** 15 min. **PLOT:** The narrator invites the audience to meet Crispus Attucks, Phillis Wheatley, Booker T. Washington, George Washington Carver, Langston Hughes, and Jackie Robinson. Each gives a brief explanation of what he/she contributed. The play closes with Martin Luther King, Jr. and a brief tribute to him. **RECOMMENDATION:** The dialogue can either be recited or read by the narrator. Since the play stops in the 1960s; it may need to be supplemented with more recent contributions. **ROYALTY:** NA. **SOURCE:** Havilan, Amorie & Smith, Lyn. (1985). Easy plays for preschoolers to third grade. Brandon, MS: Quail Ridge Press. **SUBJECTS/PLAY TYPE:** Black Americans; Tripartite.

1877. 9-12. (+) Brooks, Hindi. **Making it!** CAST: 9f, 7m, Su. ACTS: 3. SETTINGS: Auditorium with stage, dressing rooms, stage wings. PLAYING TIME: NA. PLOT: The student body of a theater arts high school is producing **Romeo and Juliet.** As opening night nears, hopes, insecurities, and fears are exposed. The main plot revolves around the relations between the young director, Alex (a graduate of the high school), his girlfriend and leading lady (Lisa), and Lisa's younger and very jealous sister, Cindy. As tensions build, the production seems to be headed toward disaster. The play goes on but not until many cast members have undergone catharsis and there is a near tragedy. **RECOMMENDATION:** The characters speak, act and react realistically. The play touches upon many issues of concern to contemporary young adults (i.e., the difficulty in reconciling the desire for a career with the requirements of a romance; the quest for physical perfection which can lead, among other things, to anorexia.) Recommended for those with skills in acting and some background in dance. **ROYALTY:** $50. **SOURCE:** Brooks, Hindi. (1983). Making it! Schulenburg, TX: I.E. Clark. **SUBJECTS/PLAY TYPE:** Friendship; Self Worth; Drama.

1878. 11-12. (+) Birnkrant, Samuel. **Mama, say "I do".** CAST: 3f, 4m. ACTS: 3. SETTINGS: Living room. PLAYING TIME: NA. PLOT: Howard Mayer lives with a possessive widowed mother, Bess, and wants to marry Phoebe, but he is afraid to tell his mother. Solomon, an elderly matchmaker, plans to find a mate for Bess to clear the way. The play ends with plans for two weddings. **RECOMMENDATION:** Formerly entitled, **A whisper in God's ear,** this is witty, fast paced, and obviously intended for a sophisticated and mature audience. Its dependence upon "Brooklynese" and its continuous references to Jewish traditions and culture would limit its audience. **ROYALTY:** $50. **SOURCE:** Birnkrant, Samuel. (1970). Mama, say "I do". Schulenburg, TX: I.E. Clark. **SUBJECTS/PLAY TYPE:** Dating; Mothers and Sons; Comedy.

1879. K-5. (+) Cochran, Betty Holmes. **A man called Appleseed.** CAST: 3f, 3m. ACTS: 1. SETTINGS: Log cabin. PLAYING TIME: 20 min. PLOT: Polly and Tommy's cousin, Melody, comes to live with them on the edge of the frontier wilderness. An Indian boy is hurt in a storm and Melody is afraid of him. Johnny Appleseed shows her she doesn't have to be afraid of the Indians and

helps her change her attitudes. **RECOMMENDATION:** This is the classic Johnny Appleseed story which would best be produced for church audiences. **ROYALTY:** Free to Plays subscribers. **SOURCE:** Cochran, Betty Holmes. (1979, May). A man called Appleseed. Plays: The Drama Magazine for Young People, pp. 54-60. **SUBJECTS/PLAY TYPE:** Friendship; Appleseed, Johnny; Native Americans; Playlet.

1880. 8-10. (-) Moessenger, Bill. **Man in the red suit.** CAST: 5f, 9m, Su. ACTS: 1. SETTINGS: Living room. PLAYING TIME: 25 min. PLOT: Arlo Glog, a Ziotian astronaut, visits Earth in his red space suit. He brings cookies, cakes, and his teddy bear; he forgets his razor. When he gets to Earth, he's gained some weight and grown a beard. Everyone he meets says, "Ho, ho, ho Merry Christmas!" He gives his teddy bear to a child who doubts Santa Claus. **RECOMMENDATION:** This is a rather silly and monotonous production, with major characters repeating the same phrase and with no real plot. **ROYALTY:** None. **SOURCE:** Kamerman, Sylvia E. (1983). Holiday plays around the year. Boston, MA: Plays, Inc. **SUBJECTS/PLAY TYPE:** Christmas; Science Fiction; Comedy.

1881. 6-12. (+) Gotwalt, Helen Louise Miller. **A man like Lincoln.** CAST: 4f, 5m. ACTS: 1. SETTINGS: Library/law office. PLAYING TIME: 25 min. PLOT: When Eric Gifford's campaign manager, Stacy, compares him to Abraham Lincoln, Gifford feels he is presumptuous. Gifford hopes his son, Craig, will become a lawyer, but Craig wants to pursue a career in art and is afraid to tell his father. Stacey provides information about Lincoln's relationship with his son to Gifford, which allows father and son to communicate. Everything is settled amicably, and Gifford finds he is more like Lincoln than he thought. **RECOMMENDATION:** This shows that sometimes teenagers and their parents don't communicate well because they assume too much. Although the end is trite, the plot makes up for this. **ROYALTY:** Free to Plays subscribers. **SOURCE:** Gotwalt, Helen Louise Miller. (1989, January/February). A man like Lincoln. Plays: The Drama Magazine for Young People, pp. 21- 30. **SUBJECTS/PLAY TYPE:** Lincoln, Abraham; Communication; Fathers and Sons; Playlet.

1882. 9-12. (+) Gilsenan, Nancy. **The man of small miracles.** CAST: 3f, 3m. ACTS: 2. SETTINGS: Lunch counter; dumpster; living room. PLAYING TIME: NA. PLOT: Lester, 76, has no reason to live since his wife died. An appeal to his son, Roger, for help only results in Roger sending his own wife, Janet, with instructions to cook and clean for Lester. The resentful Janet does her job while making clear her contempt for both her husband and Lester. Lester recovers his enthusiasm for life after meeting Elena, an 80 year old black woman, who scavenges dumpsters. Taking the food she finds to a nun raising five children gives her "a reason to get up in the morning." **RECOMMENDATION:** This moves quickly and builds on interesting and believable dialogue. Its message, that meaning based on illusion is better than a life without meaning, is clearly conveyed without preachiness. **ROYALTY:** $60. **SOURCE:** Gilsenan, Nancy. (1985). The man of small miracles. Woodstock, IL: Dramatic Pub. Co. SUBJECTS/PLAY TYPE: Elderly; Death; Meaning of Life; Drama.

1883. 8-12. (+) Blair, Robert Allan. **Man of the house.** CAST: 5f, 5m. ACTS: 1. SETTINGS: Living room. PLAYING TIME: 45 min. PLOT: A burglar is surprised by the arrival of individuals who are unaware of his purpose. Assuming the guise of the owner, he is forced to play marriage counselor, psychologist, and lost lover. He is found out and hustled off to prison, but only after a series of humorous and unexpected twists of events. RECOMMENDATION: The success of this light hearted comedy depends upon the credibility established by the main character in fooling the visitors with whom he must interact. Equally important is the type of comedy applied and maintained throughout the play. A sophisticated approach would be needed to make the play realistic and believable. ROYALTY: $15. SOURCE: Blair, Robert Alan. (1978). Man of the house. Denver, CO: Pioneer Drama Service. SUBJECTS/PLAY TYPE: Mystery; Robbers; Comedy.

1884. 8-12. (+) Harris, Richard W. & Kloten, Edgar L. (Twain, Mark) **The man that corrupted Hadleyburg.** (The Man that corrupted Hadleyburg) CAST: 5f, 5m. ACTS: 1. SETTINGS: Town square; two homes; hotel room; church. PLAYING TIME: 45 min. PLOT: A stranger leaves a sack of money and a note with a local family in the "incorruptible" town of Hadleyburg. The note states that the stranger was once aided by a mysterious man when he was down on his luck, and now he wishes to return the kindness. Anyone who can recite the words of the concealed letter, proving his identity as the mysterious man, gets the fortune. In reality, the stranger succeeds in proving the corruptibility of the townspeople, who are duly chastened by the experience. RECOMMENDATION: This retains much of the writer's famous flair and depicts the weakness of human nature. ROYALTY: $35. SOURCE: Harris, Richard W. (1976). The man that corrupted Hadleyburg. Franklin, OH: Eldridge Pub. Co. SUBJECTS/PLAY TYPE: Greed; Corruptibility; Revenge; Adaptation.

1885. 6-12. (+) Nolan, Paul T. (Twain, Mark) **The man that corrupted Hadleyburg.** (The man that corrupted Hadleyburg) CAST: 4f, 13m, 6u. ACTS: 3. SETTINGS: House; bank. PLAYING TIME: 45 min. PLOT: Hadleyburg, U.S.A. is known for being completely incorruptible. But the arrival of a mysterious man, a bag of gold, and a letter transforms the quiet village overnight. The citizens who once boasted of their virtues are reduced to dishonesty in pursuit of the gold. In the end the truth is revealed. The town Reverend staged the entire incident to expose the true nature of self righteous citizens. RECOMMENDATION: Within the first few moments, the conflict is established and it is maintained throughout. The characters are those we love to hate. ROYALTY: Free to Plays Subscribers. SOURCE: Nolan, Paul T. (1980, April). The man that corrupted Hadleyburg. Plays: The Drama Magazine for Young People, pp. 65-79. SUBJECTS/PLAY TYPE: Suspense; Money; Small Towns; Adaptation.

1886. 8-12. (-) O'Brien, John. **The man who died and went to heaven.** CAST: 3f, 3m. ACTS: 1. SETTINGS: Hotel room. PLAYING TIME: NA. PLOT: Bill wakes up to discover he has died and is in "Hotel Heaven." The female manager is God, and she tells him his wife has also died, but does not want to see him because she has remarried. Bill asks the manager to make two of his wife so he can have one. She does, and the play ends. RECOMMENDATION: The tedious banter in this lame comedy may offend, irritate, and bore audiences. ROYALTY: $15. SOURCE: O'Brien, John. (1980). The man who died and went to heaven. Chicago, IL: Dramatic Pub. Co. SUBJECTS/PLAY TYPE: Death; Heaven; Marriage; Comedy.

1887. K-3. (+) Korty, Carol. **The man who loved to laugh.** CAST: 1f, 1m, Su. ACTS: 1. SETTINGS: None. PLAYING TIME: NA. PLOT: A village man saves a snake's life and the snake gives him a gift that will allow him to understand what the animals are saying. The man can tell no one about the gift upon pain of death. He is delighted and frequently laughs when the animals speak because they amuse him. His wife thinks he is laughing at her. Their chieftain tells the man to explain himself or leave his wife, so he explains and dies. The snake takes pity on him and brings him back to life. The wife and chieftain are so glad to see him recover that they question him no more. RECOMMENDATION: Casting is flexible as the number of villagers can be enlarged to accommodate many children in this lighthearted and amusing tale. ROYALTY: $25. SOURCE: Korty, Carol. (1975). Plays from African folktales. Boston, MA: Baker's Plays. SUBJECTS/PLAY TYPE: Folk Tales, Africa; Snakes; Playlet.

1888. 10-12. (-) Jones, C. Robert. **Mandy Lou.** CAST: 9f, 8m, Su. ACTS: 2. SETTINGS: Drawing room. PLAYING TIME: NA. PLOT: Mandy Lou's father is about to lose his plantation because the overseer has swindled him, causing him to be jailed for trying to redeem bonds that were, unknown to him, were forged. Mandy fires the eavesdropping overseer, hires another, loses her cotillion escort because of measles, finds an abandoned baby, and must pay her taxes. Mistaken identity, lost brothers, envious friends, songs and dances, and disguises bring the melodrama to a happy ending. RECOMMENDATION: This southern antebellum play with charming belles, handsome young suitors, an underhanded overseer, a plantation owner, foundlings, and dancing darkies is not recommended because of the negative image it projects of blacks as singing, dancing simpletons and women as helpless and conniving. ROYALTY: Royalty on application. SOURCE: Jones, C. Robert. (1980). Mandy Lou. Chicago, IL: Dramatic Pub. Co. SUBJECTS/PLAY TYPE: Antebellum South; Melodrama; Musical; Comedy.

1889. 10-12. (+) Harnetiaux, Bryan Patrick. **Manhole.** CAST: 3f, 6m. ACTS: 1. SETTINGS: Hospital room. PLAYING TIME: NA. PLOT: A dying industrialist writes four wills, each giving his estate to a different person. He tells his children that they will get his money only if they allow a tattoo artist to tattoo "free will" on their knuckles.

The daughter returns tattooed, and sighs that her father rules even from the grave. The son, who could not allow himself to be marked receives his father's highest praise and gains self respect. RECOMMENDATION: The final disposition of a parent's estate will provide food for thought in this well executed drama. ROYALTY: $15. SOURCE: Harnetiaux, Bryan Patrick. (1981). Manhole. Chicago, IL: The Dramatic Pub. Co. SUBJECTS/PLAY TYPE: Death and Dying; Inheritances; Drama.

1890. 7-12*. (+) Hischak, Thomas. **Mankind and Co.** CAST: 1f, 1m, Su. ACTS: 2. SETTINGS: Bare stage. PLAYING TIME: 90 min. PLOT: This montage of Greek and Roman myths includes the Beginning of the World, the Creation of Man, the Creation of Evil, Narcissus and Echo, Phaethon and the Sun Chariot, Pygmalion and the Statue, Ceyx and Alcyone, Atalanta's Race, Daedalus and Icarus, Arachne, and Cupid and Psyche. The myths are pantomimed by the troupe while two narrators alternately describe the stories and providing editorial commentary. RECOMMENDATION: Although rather long, this could serve as a supplement to an English unit on mythology. As the acting requires some intricate miming, experienced adults would best handle the production requirements. Young viewers will appreciate the modern language. ROYALTY: $25. SOURCE: Hischak, Thomas. (1976). Mankind and Co. Denver, CO: Pioneer Drama Service. SUBJECTS/PLAY TYPE: Pantomime; Mythology, Greek; Mythology, Roman; Drama.

1891. 6-9. (+) Hayes, Theresa. **Manners Matter.** CAST: 6f, 10m, Su. ACTS: 2. SETTINGS: Church; bedroom; cafeteria; classroom. PLAYING TIME: 90 min. PLOT: During a church service, six teenagers laugh and chat, disturbing the congregation so much that the elders lecture them about the value of manners. Two of the youths storm out, claiming that they and their parents couldn't care less. Both boys dream that their parents, friends, and teachers are rude and nasty to them. When they awake, they are so happy to be treated nicely they turn over new leaves. RECOMMENDATION: Although the message is corny and the dream vehicle cliched, the dialogue and responses of the teenagers are very realistic. This would be a good presentation for a Sunday school class. Discussion questions follow the play. ROYALTY: NA. SOURCE: Hayes, Theresa. (1986). Getting your act together. Cincinnati, OH: Standard Pub. Co. SUBJECTS/PLAY TYPE: Christian Drama; Behavior; Drama.

1892. K-5. (+) Mahlman, Lewis & Jones, David Cadwalader. **Manora, the bird princess.** CAST: 10u. ACTS: 1. SETTINGS: Forest; garden; river; throne room. PLAYING TIME: 25 min. PLOT: Prince Rama falls in love with Manora, the bird princess, and convinces her to live with him for one year to decide if she loves him. At the end of the year, Prince Rama leaves for battle. While the prince is gone, Manora is tricked into picking a forbidden flower and she returns home to escape punishment. Three years later, Prince Rama finds Manora's father, retrieves his crown from the bottom of the sea, accumulates millions of feathers for the necessary wedding cape, and selects Manora from her identical sisters. Finally, they can marry. RECOMMENDATION: This poignant and sentimental

portrayal of true love will delight romantics, as well as those who crave adventure. ROYALTY: Free to Plays subscribers. SOURCE: Mahlman, Lewis & Jones, David Cadwalader. (1980). Folk tale plays for puppets. Boston, MA: Plays, Inc. SUBJECTS/PLAY TYPE: Folk Tales, Siam; Love; Puppet Play.

1893. 7-8. (-) Dias, Earl J. **The mantle.** CAST: 4f, 9m. ACTS: 1. SETTINGS: Office. PLAYING TIME: 30 min. PLOT: A senior day program is almost disrupted when a mantle which is to be handed down to the junior class disappears. A British exchange student changes his opinions of Americans as each of the members of the "boy's club" claims to be the culprit in order to prove loyalty. By the time the real prankster comes forward, the students appreciate the meaning of the mantle in the school's traditions, and the British exchange student is impressed at the Americans' honor. RECOMMENDATION: Loyalty is meritorious, but this sexist play demonstrates it only through the stereotyped loyalty of men to other men. Even with rewriting, this is too dated to be of value. ROYALTY: Free to Plays Subscribers. SOURCE: Dias, Earl J. (1979, May). The mantle. Plays: The Drama Magazine for Young People, pp. 25-37. SUBJECTS/PLAY TYPE: School; Friends; Playlet.

1894. 1-6. (+) Kehret, Peg. **Manure measles.** CAST: 1m. ACTS: 1. SETTINGS: None. PLAYING TIME: NA. PLOT: A city boy, bored with his visit to the country, has a wonderful time tossing stones into a pile of manure. He uses successively larger stones, finally splashing himself into having "manure measles." It is his fondest memory. RECOMMENDATION: An incredibly funny story of childhood activities that should appeal to all ages, this monologue should be read by a child in at least an upper elementary grade, due to its length. ROYALTY: NA. SOURCE: Kehret, Peg. (1986). Winning monologs for young actors. Colorado Springs, CO: Meriwether Pub. SUBJECTS/PLAY TYPE: Country Life; Manure; Monologue.

1895. 5-9. (+) Reale, William. **Many happy returns.** CAST: 1f, 1m. ACTS: 1. SETTINGS: Hallway. PLAYING TIME: NA. PLOT: Beth, 13, and Barney, a 23 year old birthday party entertainer, talk after a birthday party for Beth's younger brother. Beth remembers that they also talked after her 8th birthday party. Beth now has a crush on Barney, but he lets her down gently. RECOMMENDATION: This is very easy to produce, requires no elaborate scenery, yet is very complete. ROYALTY: $20. SOURCE: Reale, William. (1983). Many happy returns. New York, NY: Dramatists Play Service. SUBJECTS/PLAY TYPE: Love; Drama.

1896. 2-5. (+) Hark, Mildred & McQueen, Noel. **Many thanks.** CAST: 9f, 10m. ACTS: 1. SETTINGS: Office. PLAYING TIME: 25 min. PLOT: In this Thanksgiving play, members of the cast are famous Americans. Uncle Sam abolishes Thanksgiving because he believes that today's Americans take their blessings for granted. George Washington, Abe Lincoln, and Sarah Josepha Hale convince Uncle Sam to change his mind. RECOMMENDATION: This combination women's rights/American history lesson is interestingly done and well worth the effort of production. ROYALTY: Free to Plays subscribers. SOURCE: Hark, Mildred & McQueen, Noel. (1978, November). Many thanks. Plays: The Drama Magazine for Young People, pp. 43-50. SUBJECTS/PLAY TYPE: Thanksgiving; Playlet.

1897. 6-12. (+) Moeller, Ruby L. March. CAST: 1u. ACTS: 1. SETTINGS: Bare stage, props. PLAYING TIME: NA. PLOT: The March historical essay, "Legendary History of St. Patrick's Day," gives some factual and fictitious data on the saint. Two poems, "Wearing of the Green" (about shamrocks) and "Rory O'More" (about a marriage proposal) follow. Six games (two paper and pencil) complete the program. RECOMMENDATION: This is interesting and informative; however, the Irish brogue is difficult to understand. The game suggestions are excellent for many age groups, including adults, but might be difficult to use in a regular program/audience format since they are geared to groups with closer interaction. The pencil and paper game "Snakes" contains an ethnic slur that could be offensive. The relay could be either staged or used as an outdoor activity. All activities and recitations are closely tied to each other through the St. Patrick's Day theme and most are adaptable to a variety of presentation forms. The skit, "Hospital Stunt" is also ethnically offensive because the Irishman is portrayed as ignorant. ROYALTY: NA. SOURCE: Moeller, Ruby L. (1975). Around the year programs. Boston, MA: Baker's Plays. SUBJECTS/PLAY TYPE: St. Patrick's Day; Variety Program.

1898. 1-4. (+) Peltola, Irma I. March, you are so fickle! CAST: 6f, 6m. ACTS: 1. SETTINGS: Yard. PLAYING TIME: 10 min. PLOT: Enjoying his position between Winter and Spring, March entertains Jack Frost, North Wind, and Winter. The flowers and trees, who are freezing, beg March to own up to his duties, and allow Lady Spring to make her entrance. Jack Frost, North Wind, and Winter begin to tire. When the Sun arrives, they allow Lady Spring to take over while they exit for a much needed rest. RECOMMENDATION: As everyone anticipates the arrival of Spring, acting out the parts of the seasons and flowers will not only be good experience, but it may also help to use up some of the excess energy which builds near the end of winter. ROYALTY: Free to Plays subscribers. SOURCE: Peltola, Irma I. (1982, March). March, you are so fickle! Plays: The Drama Magazine for Young People, pp. 47- 50. SUBJECTS/PLAY TYPE: Seasons; Playlet.

1899. 4-8*. (+) Levy, Jonathan. Marco Polo. CAST: 1f, 13m. ACTS: 1. SETTINGS: Prison; court; exterior. PLAYING TIME: NA. PLOT: Marco Polo, in the employ of Kublai Khan, travels to Yang Chow to learn more about the Khan's mysterious enemy, known only as the Blue Lord. The Blue Lord is revealed as one of the Khan's most trusted advisers who has kidnapped the Princess Kogatin. Khan is nearly forced from power, but Marco Polo rescues Kogatin, and becomes a hero. RECOMMENDATION: There is enough drama and intrigue to hold the interest of children in this play (designed to be performed by adults) which includes music and pantomime. ROYALTY: $35.

SOURCE: Levy, Jonathan. (1977). Marco Polo: A fantasy for children. New York, NY: Dramatists Play Service. SUBJECTS/PLAY TYPE: Polo, Marco; Khan, Kublai; China; Drama.

1900. 8-12. (+) Kelly, Tim J. (Twain, Mark) Mark Twain in the Garden of Eden. ([Various writings]) CAST: 2f, 5m, 8u. ACTS: 1. SETTINGS: Garden. PLAYING TIME: 30 min. PLOT: The Garden of Eden functions as both a tacky tourist attraction and is also the setting for a tongue in cheek version of the Adam and Eve story, with the best lines pulled from Mark Twain's satirical "Diaries" of Adam and Eve. Mr. Twain himself wanders in the garden directing tourists to points of interest. He also observes and comments on the stormy and/or farcical interactions between staid, priggish Adam, ebullient Eve, and the debonair serpent. The story ends with the expected expulsion from paradise, although the principal characters react more philosophically here than in the biblical version. RECOMMENDATION: Although the playwright has extracted material from Twain's writings without giving much thought to the author's wry view of human nature which establishes the material's context, this is still interesting. The sexism is offensive at times and the tourist attraction concept sometimes seems silly and purposeless. Nonetheless, if the Twain/Narrator figure is portrayed in a professional (dry) manner, and if the rest of the cast avoids slapstick, this could have amusing moments for both cast and audience. ROYALTY: $10. SOURCE: Kelly, Tim J. (1977). Mark Twain in the Garden of Eden. Denver, Colorado: Pioneer Drama Service. SUBJECTS/PLAY TYPE: Creation; Eden; Sin; Comedy.

1901. 9-12. (+) Garver, Juliet. Marla the mechanic. CAST: 3f, 3m. ACTS: 1. SETTINGS: Living room. PLAYING TIME: 40 min. PLOT: Much to their father's dismay, Marla accepts a job as a mechanic, and Brian teaches a cooking class. As they argue about conformity to traditional sex roles, they all learn that it is important to pursue what interests them regardless of societal customs. RECOMMENDATION: Well rounded and dynamic characters grow as a result of their experiences, and the resolution of the conflicts is satisfying and consistent with the other elements of the play. ROYALTY: NA. SOURCE: Garver, Juliet. (1975, April). Marla the mechanic. Plays: The Drama Magazine for Young People, pp. 1-13. SUBJECTS/PLAY TYPE: Sexism; Comedy.

1902. 12*. (+) Field, Barbara. (Gogol, Nikolai) Marriage: An absolutely incredible event in two acts. (The marriage: an utterly incredible occurrence) CAST: 4f, 6m. ACTS: 2. SETTINGS: Drawing room. PLAYING TIME: NA. PLOT: Podkoliosin, a confirmed bachelor, decides to marry. His matchmaker, Fiokla, arranges a visit with Agafya, who approaches the matchmaking with resignation and trepidation because she realizes that her suitors are motivated by greed. Agafya attempts to choose a suitor by drawing lots. Fiokla persuades Agafya to choose Podkoliosin. At the last minute, Podkoliosin loses his nerve and escapes through the window. Agafya is left sobbing at the altar. RECOMMENDATION: True to the nature of Gogol's work, this sophisticated piece is organized around a non-event (a marriage that doesn't take place), as it depicts the ills of Russian life, and the psychology of people. This will only be appreciated by a mature audience with some familiarity with either Gogol or 19th century Russian life. ROYALTY: NA. SOURCE: Field, Barbara. (1987). Marriage: An absolutely incredible incident in two acts. New York, NY: Dramatists Play Service Inc. SUBJECTS/PLAY TYPE: Marriage; Drama; Parody.

1903. 9-12. (+) Rogers, David. **The marriage bit.** CAST: 12f, 10m. ACTS: 2. SETTINGS: Gym. PLAYING TIME: NA. PLOT: A group of graduating seniors at their farewell prom talk about their potential futures. They express different points of view about love, marriage, and careers. RECOMMENDATION: It should be noted that all the main characters opt for marriage right after graduation. This could be the basis for class discussions on decision making, marriage and the family, and human development. Cast can be expanded. ROYALTY: $35. SOURCE: Rogers, David. (1975). The marriage bit. Chicago, IL: Dramatic Pub. Co. SUBJECTS/PLAY TYPE: Marriage; Careers; Comedy.

1904. 2-6. (+) Kelly, Tim. (Chekov, Anton Pavlovich) **A marriage proposal: western style.** (A marriage proposal) CAST: 2f, 1m. ACTS: 1. SETTINGS: Parlor. PLAYING TIME: 30 min. PLOT: Lem, a nervous young rancher, asks Mrs. Taub for the hand of her daughter, Natalie, in marriage. A series of miscommunications and arguments almost dooms Lem's proposal before he can even make it. In the end, it appears true love will win and a happy life will result, although not with certainty. RECOMMENDATION: The appeal here is primarily through slapstick delivery and overreactions, rather than through any type of subtlety. ROYALTY: $10. SOURCE: Kelly, Tim. (1978). A marriage proposal: Western style. Denver, CO: Pioneer Drama Service, Inc. SUBJECTS/PLAY TYPE: Marriage; Comedy; Adaptation.

1905. 7-9. (-) Karshner, Roger. **Martha and Beth.** CAST: 2f. ACTS: 1. SETTINGS: None. PLAYING TIME: NA. PLOT: Martha and Beth talk about going to the mall instead of school. Martha is a little hesitant. But when Beth tells Martha that they will have to listen to their teacher talk about Egypt and pharoahs, Martha decides to go to the mall with Beth. RECOMMENDATION: This seems to glorify truancy as the answer to teenage boredom. ROYALTY: NA. SOURCE: Karshner, Roger. (1986). Scenes for teenagers. Toluce Lake, CA: Dramaline Pub. SUBJECTS/PLAY TYPE: Truancy; Scene.

1906. 7-12. (+) Dias, Earl J. **Martha Washington's spy.** CAST: 2f, 5m. ACTS: 1. SETTINGS: Outpost. PLAYING TIME: 20 min. PLOT: When Betsy suspects that her husband plans to desert the army, she walks to Valley Forge in hopes of dissuading him. She is mistaken for a spy. RECOMMENDATION: With action, some humor, and fast paced dialogue, this should hold the interests of teenage audiences. ROYALTY: None. SOURCE: Kamerman, Sylvia E. (1975). Patriotic and historical plays for young people. Boston, MA: Plays, Inc. SUBJECTS/PLAY TYPE: Washington, Martha; Valley Forge; Playlet.

1907. 7-12. (+) Sorensen, Candace M. (Bradbury, Ray.) **The martian chronicles.** (The martian chronicles) CAST: 10f, 22m, Su. ACTS: 1. SETTINGS: Asylum; Mars. PLAYING TIME: NA. PLOT: This is a very condensed adaptation of some of the short stories which comprised Bradbury's original. All four expeditions to Mars are recounted. The first ends with the men being killed; the second and third end with the men tricked (through telepathy) into a false sense of security. They are killed, and the Martians die of smallpox introduced by the explorers. The fourth expedition team sees the Earth explode from nuclear war and realizes its responsibility to save Mars. RECOMMENDATION: This is too condensed to be understood unless the audience has read the original. It does do an adequate job of capturing the spooky aura of the original. Its most effective scenes are the ones in which the crass materialism of earth is condemned by the author through his characterization of the famous hot dog stand owners. ROYALTY: NA. SOURCE: Jennings, Coleman A. & Berghammer, Gretta. (1986). Theatre for youth: Twelve plays with mature themes. Austin, TX: Univ. of Austin Press. SUBJECTS/PLAY TYPE: Mars; Space Exploration; Science Fiction; Adaptation.

1908. 3-6. (+) Behrens, June. **Martin Luther King, Jr.: The story of a dream.** CAST: 4f, 5m, Su. ACTS: 2. SETTINGS: Classroom; bus; pulpit; park. PLAYING TIME: NA. PLOT: This briefly examines the life of Martin Luther King, Jr. It provides some information about his family, but its main focus is on the Civil Rights movement. Settings switch between a classroom in which students and teacher discuss King's role in famous events and dramatization of the actual events. Included are the Rosa Parks' bus scene, the Washington D.C. Civil Rights march, King's "I Have a Dream" speech, and his winning the Nobel Peace Prize. RECOMMENDATION: Although short, this clearly portrays the highlights of King's life, and the class (a mix of black and white students) provides a good vehicle to connect these important events. ROYALTY: NA. SOURCE: Martin Luther King, Jr.: The story of a dream. Chicago, IL: Childrens Press. SUBJECTS/PLAY TYPE: King, Martin Luther, Jr.; Black Americans; Civil Rights; Drama.

1909. K-3. (-) Silverman, Eleanor. (Davis, Reda) **Martin's dinosaur.** (Martin's dinosaur) CAST: 2f, 2m, 2u. ACTS: 1. SETTINGS: None. PLAYING TIME: 10 min. PLOT: Martin meets the dragon of the castle while sightseeing, but no one believes him. RECOMMENDATION: This whittles the original down too much to capture the warmth and humor. ROYALTY: None. SOURCE: Silverman, Eleanor. (1983). Dramatics for children. Metuchen, NJ: Scarecrow Press. SUBJECTS/PLAY TYPE: Dragons; Skit; Adaptation.

1910. 7-12. (+) Anderson, R.A. & Sweeney, R.L. **Marvello, the magnificent magician.** CAST: 4f, 3m, Su. ACTS: 1. SETTINGS: Carnival; home. PLAYING TIME: 25 min. PLOT: Unable to repay the $500 her late husband borrowed from wicked Marvello the magician, Mother Twoshoes is coerced into granting him her daughter, Goodie, in marriage. The situation seems bleak when the hero is hypnotized and Goody is about to be sawed in half, but the police arrive in time to save the day. RECOMMENDATION: A typical melodrama, this is made especially humorous by the hypnotizing scene, as the hero thinks he is several different animals. ROYALTY: Free to Plays subscribers. SOURCE: Anderson, R.A. & Sweeney, R.L. (1980, December). Marvello, the magnificent magician. Plays: The Drama Magazine for Young People, pp. 15-25. SUBJECTS/ PLAY TYPE: Magicians; Debts; Melodrama.

1911. 2-6*. (+) Carroll, John R. **The marvelous machine. CAST:** 7u. **ACTS:** 1. **SETTINGS:** Bare stage. **PLAYING TIME:** NA. **PLOT:** Actors arrive from the back of the room and greet the audience as they make their way to the stage. Throughout, the audience participates in the working human machine called the body. Actors become body parts or sit with the audience. Emotions are acted out and contrasted with the workings of a nonhuman machine. RECOMMENDATION: This is a highly recommended learning experience; the body parts are accurately shown as a part of the whole system. Costuming and timing appear to be tricky. ROYALTY: $20. SOURCE: Carroll, John R. (1982). The marvelous machine. Boston, MA: Baker's Plays. SUBJECTS/PLAY TYPE: Human Body; Participation Play.

1912. 4-8. (+) Boiko, Claire. **The marvelous time machine. CAST:** 4f, 6m. **ACTS:** 1. **SETTINGS:** Divided stage, props. **PLAYING TIME:** 20 min. **PLOT:** Father Time tells Tic Toc about Necessity Jonas, who lived in Colonial New England. He was working on a time machine, as was Ned Jonas, his cousin in the present. Ned went back in time and Necessity entered the future. Ned hated the rustic ways, and Necessity hated the monster automobiles and vacuum cleaners. Each returned to his own time period with a sigh of relief. RECOMMENDATION: This excellent time-travel play, compares the differences in lifestyles between Colonial New England and the 20th century. ROYALTY: None. SOURCE: Boiko, Claire. (1981). Children's plays for creative actors: A collection of royalty-free plays for boys and girls. Boston, MA: Plays, Inc. SUBJECTS/PLAY TYPE: Time Travel; Colonial Life; Fantasy.

1913. 9-12. (-) Van Horn, Bill. **Marvin's many faces. CAST:** 7f, 6m. **ACTS:** 1. **SETTINGS:** Diner. **PLAYING TIME:** 30 min. **PLOT:** Mervin, an aspiring actor, works at Gus' Diner in Hollywood, hoping for a big break. When a famous producer and director come in, Mervin believes this is his chance. But Al Fox, a gangster, arrives to seek revenge because the two did not give his sister a part in their last movie. Mervin disguises himself as Al Fox and confuses the crooks long enough for the police to arrive and arrest them. RECOMMENDATION: The morals are too obvious: crime doesn't pay, and finish your education before looking for your big break. The role of Mervin requires fair impressions of W.C. Fields, Humphrey Bogart, and a gangster. The ending is too corny for high school students to enjoy. ROYALTY: Free to Plays subscribers. SOURCE: Van Horn, Bill. (1983, May). Mervin's many faces. Plays: The Drama Magazine for Young People, pp. 25-36. SUBJECTS/PLAY TYPE: Acting; Careers; Comedy.

1914. 5-8. (+) Satchell, Mary. **Mary McLeod Bethune: Dream Maker. CAST:** 6f, 4m, Su. **ACTS:** 1. **SETTINGS:** Office; classroom. **PLAYING TIME:** 30 min. **PLOT:** On graduation day and the 50th anniversary of Bethune Cookman College, Mary McLeod Bethune recalls her first teaching position, when she encouraged a young black boy to become a doctor; her second teaching position when she realized the difficulty blacks face in becoming professionals; and her founding of Bethune Cookman College, the high point of her career. The play ends with Mrs. Bethune encouraging a young girl to work toward her secret dream of becoming a newspaper publisher. RECOMMENDATION: The universal theme of achieving goals and dreams is well supported. However, the connection with black young people is not clearly supported in the text. Except for one brief passage, there is no identification or discussion of the black experience. ROYALTY: NA. SOURCE: Kamerman, Sylvia E. (1987). Plays of Black Americans. Boston, MA: Plays, Inc. SUBJECTS/PLAY TYPE: Black Americans; Bethune, Mary McLeod; Playlet.

1915. 7-12. (+) Nolan, Paul T. **Masks of various colors. CAST:** Su. **ACTS:** 1. **SETTINGS:** None. **PLAYING TIME:** 25 min. **PLOT:** People wearing different colored masks hate each other because they are ignorant about each other. After long discussions reveal their prejudices, people learn that they are actually alike and begin to work together. RECOMMENDATION: Although long, this delivers its message about judging on the basis of a person's actions, not his/her looks. ROYALTY: Free to Plays subscribers. SOURCE: Nolan, Paul T. (1975, May). Masks of various colors. Plays: The Drama Magazine for Young People, pp. 29-38. SUBJECTS/PLAY TYPE: Prejudices; Playlet.

1916. K-6*. (+) Brill, Michael Elliot. (De Beaumont, Le Prince) **The masque of Beauty and the Beast.** (Beauty and the beast) **CAST:** 3f, 4m, 5u. **ACTS:** 3. **SETTINGS:** Bare stage. **PLAYING TIME:** 60 min. **PLOT:** The classic folk tale of the handsome prince transformed into Beast, and Beauty, a sweet and loving person who agrees to live with him if he will spare her father is retold. Beauty discovers the gentle nature of the individual beneath the hideous exterior and comes to love Beast. This love allows him to resume his true form. RECOMMENDATION: The original story is preserved in this easy to produce adaptation. Young children will be thrilled by the story and older children will enjoy playing the characters. ROYALTY: $35. SOURCE: Brill, Michael Elliot. (1979). The masque of Beauty and the Beast. New Orleans, LA: Anchorage Press. SUBJECTS/PLAY TYPE: Folk Tales, France; Love; Adaptation.

1917. 12*. (+) Englestad, Sam & Alexander, Jane. (Ibsen, Henrik) **The master builder.** (Bygmester Solness) **CAST:** 3f, 4m. **ACTS:** 3. **SETTINGS:** Workroom; sitting room; veranda. **PLAYING TIME:** NA. **PLOT:** Halvard Sohress, the very successful Master Builder, fears the threat of youthful competition. A young woman from his past reminds him of his early triumphs, and persuades him that he must improve on his glories to prove himself superior to his young rivals. He is dared to top the spire of his newly constructed home with a wreath and falls to his death in the attempt. RECOMMENDATION: Production would be challenging, but Ibsen's brilliance as an innovator in modern theater makes the play worthwhile for a serious drama group willing to invest resources of time and talent. ROYALTY: $50. SOURCE: Ibsen, Henrik. (1978). The master builder. Chicago, IL: Dramatic Pub. Co. SUBJECTS/PLAY TYPE: Pride; Ambition; Drama.

1918. 5-12. (+) Waite, Helen E. & Hoppenstedt, Elbert M. **The master of the strait.** CAST: 3f, 4m. ACTS: 1. SETTINGS: Kitchen. PLAYING TIME: 25 min. PLOT: Mr. Arden, the keeper of the light at the Bear's Lighthouse, is very sad on this Christmas Eve. It marks the anniversary of a boy's death for which he blames himself. When neighbors visit the Arden's, Warren, 10, restores Mr. Arden's faith. RECOMMENDATION: Since the long lines may be difficult to memorize, it is recommended that the older grades produce this play for the younger grades. ROYALTY: Free to Plays subscribers. SOURCE: Kamerman, Sylvia E. (1975). A treasury of Christmas plays. Boston, MA: Plays, Inc. SUBJECTS/PLAY TYPE: Christmas; Playlet.

1919. 12*. (+) Bicknell, Arthur. **Masterpieces.** CAST: 4f, 3m. ACTS: 2. SETTINGS: Parsonage. PLAYING TIME: NA. PLOT: In this story of sibling rivalry between the Bronte sisters and their brother, who never matched their creative genius, Branwell imagines his superiority over his sisters until they are published. Then he realizes he could never match their success. He is the first to die at age 31, "consumed by opium and dissipation." The Bronte sisters die within seven years of their brother. RECOMMENDATION: This is for a literary audience. Because the brother moves between reality and fantasy it would challenge even the best of actors. ROYALTY: Available from publisher upon request. SOURCE: Bicknell, Arthur. (1979). Masterpieces. New York, NY: Dramatists Play Service, Inc. SUBJECTS/PLAY TYPE: Bronte Sisters; Sibling Rivalry; Artistic Achievement; Drama.

1920. 9-12. (-) Drayson, Sloane. **A matter of gender.** CAST: 2f, 1m. ACTS: 1. SETTINGS: Bare stage. PLAYING TIME: NA. PLOT: A jaded playwright, Tad, complains about his inability to find the ideal male who can play God with perfection. God appears in the form of a woman. Tad realizes that he must change the world through his playwriting. RECOMMENDATION: Although the message of societal change is valuable, this is too dated in its allusions and language. ROYALTY: $10. SOURCE: Drayson, Sloane. (1981). A matter of gender. Boston, MA: Baker's Plays. SUBJECTS/PLAY TYPE: God; Sexual Equality; Drama.

1921. K-6. (-) Zacharko, Larry & Swanson, G.K. **Maximilian Beetle.** CAST: 12u. ACTS: 1. SETTINGS: Windowsill; garden; lawn. PLAYING TIME: NA. PLOT: Singing, dancing (soft shoe) Maximilian Beetle, the pet of a human boy, searches for a butterfly's scarf. He becomes involved with a wasp, Russian honeybee, worm (who is also a doctor), four ants, fly, cockroach (the criminal element), ladybug, and grasshopper. Max's search

intersects with the theft of the people's pantry key and changing a beanery into a nightclub. RECOMMENDATION: This is very confusing and the necessary coordination of music and singing ability as well as the rapid repartee may prove too difficult. ROYALTY: $3. SOURCE: Zacharko, Larry & Swanson, G.K. (1977). Maximilian Beetle. Toronto, Ontario, Canada: Playwrights Co-op. SUBJECTS/PLAY TYPE: Insects; Comedy.

1922. 4-12. (+) Moeller, Ruby L. **May.** CAST: 1f, 1m, Su. ACTS: NA. SETTINGS: Bare stage, props. PLAYING TIME: NA. PLOT: After an opening song, the origin of Mother's Day is presented, followed by a poem on "Mother's Love." A male character pretends to be the mirror image of a female character who stands in front of him to apply her makeup and fix her hair in a humorous skit entitled "Mother getting ready for a meeting." Two more poems follow, "My Mother's Garden" and "Little Nell." A brief "Thought for the Meeting" concludes the program. RECOMMENDATION: This could be used in a Mother's Day presentation, with some updating. The closing thought speaks of the qualities of a real lady and sounds dated. The language is flowery and sentimental; songs may be added as desired. ROYALTY: NA. SOURCE: Moeller, Ruby L. (1975). Around the year programs. Boston, MA: Baker's Plays. SUBJECTS/PLAY TYPE: Mother's Day; Variety Program.

1923. K-4. (-) Gotwalt, Helen Louise Miller. **May day for mother.** CAST: Su. ACTS: 1. SETTINGS: Bare stage, props. PLAYING TIME: 15 min. PLOT: The women don't want to celebrate May Day until mothers are nominated as queens. RECOMMENDATION: This is outdated, and the language is too old. ROYALTY: None. SOURCE: Gotwalt, Helen Louise Miller. (1985). First plays for children: A collection of little plays for the youngest players. Boston, MA: Plays, Inc. SUBJECTS/PLAY TYPE: May Day; Playlet.

1924. 7-10. (+) Rogers, David. **May the farce be with you.** CAST: 15f, 9m, Su. ACTS: 2. SETTINGS: Lobby. PLAYING TIME: NA. PLOT: In this science fiction comedy, evil forces from the planet Infera try to disrupt the annual meeting of Earth's superheroes, the E.I.E.I.O's, at a health spa called O. MacDonald's Farm. Fortunately, Vera Strong and Byron Ceps, the ladies' and men's athletic directors at the spa, are really "Wizard Woman" and "Superbrain" incognito. They save the day. RECOMMENDATION: This is a spoof on the movie, **Star Wars,** and the superheroes of American comic books. Most of the humor depends on very corny word play. ROYALTY: $35. SOURCE: Rogers, David. (1978). May the farce be with you. Woodstock, IL: Dramatic Pub. Co. SUBJECTS/PLAY TYPE: Superheroes; Star Wars; Comedy.

1925. 9-12*. (+) Miller, Ev. **McKenna's choice.** CAST: 2f, 4m, 2u. ACTS: 2. SETTINGS: Street; living/dining room. PLAYING TIME: 90 min. PLOT: John McKenna, 85, does not want to die a "clown," a term he uses to describe loss of control of body functions, disorientation, and forgetfulness. He decides to give his family a Christmas gift, his death. Three weeks before Christmas, John stops eating. The effect on each member of the family, how they interact with him and each other, and how each deals with death is examined. The play concludes with John's death and the statement by Coral, "My Grandpa McKenna was not a clown." RECOMMENDATION: This is hard hitting. It describes problems of the aged, growing old in America, and dying with dignity. Simultaneously, it raises ethical, moral, social, philosophical, and religious questions. Production is recommended for high school audiences only under mature direction. Care must be taken to ensure that the audience understands that starvation of the elderly is not being actively advocated. ROYALTY: $35. SOURCE: Miller, Ev. (1986). McKenna's choice. Denver, CO: Pioneer Drama Service. SUBJECTS/PLAY TYPE: Death; Aging; Euthanasia; Drama.

1926. 9-12. (-) Besserman, Ellen. **Me and my chorus.** CAST: 3f, 3m. ACTS: 1. SETTINGS: Living room. PLAYING TIME: NA. PLOT: The Greek hero, Agamemnon, is burdened with a chorus that is increasingly annoying and expensive to maintain. His wife, Helena urges him to sell it. Finally, when they ruin a chariot sale for him, Agamemnon has the chorus "rubbed out." RECOMMENDATION: Contemporary allusions and language grafted onto the setting of ancient Greece can carry the play only so far. In the absence of any significant action or plot it is difficult to see what meaning or entertainment this might provide. ROYALTY: $15. SOURCE: Besserman, Ellen. (1986). Me and my chorus. Boston, MA: Baker's Plays. SUBJECTS/PLAY TYPE: Heroes, Greek; Comedy.

1927. 5-9. (+) Hutson, Natalie Bovee. **Me, Beth Connors.** CAST: 5f, 2m. ACTS: 1. SETTINGS: Bare stage, props. PLAYING TIME: NA. PLOT: Under the encompassing guise of a diary entry, the audience sees scenes from a teenage girl's life, such as sibling rivalry at the breakfast table, a stressful visit to a disabled grandmother, and puppy love. RECOMMENDATION: Production is easily handled, since no special costumes are required and settings can be created with readily available props. ROYALTY: NA. SOURCE: Hutson, Natalie Bovee. (1984). Me, Beth Connors. Stevensville, MI: Educational Service, Inc. SUBJECTS/PLAY TYPE: Sibling Rivalry; Friendship; Playlet.

1928. K-2. (+) Flohr, John W. **Me-first.** CAST: 7u. ACTS: 1. SETTINGS: Cave. PLAYING TIME: NA. PLOT: Long ago, five greebles (little people) existed. Four were patient, but one greeble always wanted to be first. The greebles were invited to dinner by "tootiger." At the appointed meal time "Me-first" discovered that they were to be the tootiger's meal, and that being first was not always best. RECOMMENDATION: The play encourages audience participation through various means: portraying one of the characters, singing, or playing instruments at designated times. While they participate, children also learn a valuable social lesson about taking turns. ROYALTY: NA. SOURCE: Flohr, John W. & Smith, Robert B. (1984). Music dramas for children with special needs. Denton TX: Troostwyk Press. SUBJECTS/PLAY TYPE: Patience; Skit.

1929. 7-12. (+) Euripides. **Medea.** CAST: 1f, 1m. ACTS: 1. SETTINGS: None. PLAYING TIME: NA. PLOT: Creon banishes Medea and her sons because he fears she will work some evil deed on his child. Medea convinces Creon to allow her one day in which to prepare her children. RECOMMENDATION: Full impact requires knowledge of Greek mythology. The dialogue is somewhat awkward and would require a good deal of practice, without which, the sincerity of the characters would be seriously jeopardized. ROYALTY: NA. SOURCE: Olfson, Lewy. (1980). Fifty great scenes for student actors. New York, NY: Bantam Books. SUBJECTS/PLAY TYPE: Mythology, Greek; Punishments; Scene.

1930. 7-12. (+) Grote, David G. (Moliere) **The medicine man.** (The doctor in spite of himself.) CAST: 6f, 6m. ACTS: 2. SETTINGS: Lobby. PLAYING TIME: NA. PLOT: A con-artist arrives at the hotel of the wife he abandoned ten years earlier. At the same time, the richest man in the valley arrives looking for a doctor to heal his daughter. The con-artist poses as a doctor and discovers that the daughter's inability to talk is self imposed. She has vowed not to talk until she marries the cowboy her father opposes. RECOMMENDATION: This would be fun to produce with many opportunities to ham it up. Most of the humor is in the action. Recommended for inexperienced actors. ROYALTY: $35. SOURCE: Grote, David G. (1980). The medicine man. Schulenburg, TX: I.E.Clark. SUBJECTS/PLAY TYPE: Old West; Comedy; Adaptation.

1931. 7-12*. (+) Koste, Virginia Glasgow (Moliere) **The medicine man.** (The doctor in spite of himself) CAST: 3f, 3m, 3u. ACTS: 1. SETTINGS: Bare stage. PLAYING TIME: NA. PLOT: A wife plots revenge against her lazy, drunken woodcutter husband by proclaiming him a great doctor. His patient is a young woman who pretends not to be able to speak. The woodcutter uses his talent as a confidence man to fool the girl's father and bring an end to the romantic impasse between father, daughter, wealthy suitor, and young handsome boyfriend. The conman winds up with a great deal of money, a very high opinion of himself, and a wife who is aghast at the turn that her practical joke took. RECOMMENDATION: In this abbreviated, contemporary version, the main characters are well defined, the plot is entertaining, and the dialogue flows easily with music, humor, physical conflicts, and inter-action between cast and audience. ROYALTY: $20. SOURCE: Koste, Virginia Glasgow. (1983). The medicine show, or, How to succeed in medicine without really trying. New Orleans, LA: Anchorage Press, Inc. SUBJECTS/PLAY TYPE: Trickery; Medicine; Adaptation.

1932. 9-12. (+) Hogue, Steve. **Medium rare.** CAST: 11f, 5m, 5u. ACTS: 3. SETTINGS: Living room. PLAYING TIME: 90 min. PLOT: Harry and Bunny Polk have just moved into their new home, which they bought furnished from Harvey and Lucinda Jolley, who seemed in an awfully big hurry to leave. They are surprised to find an uninvited guest, Nina Smeltenmelter, who informs them that her granddaughter, Lucinda, told her she could stay in the house even though it had been sold. Their discovery is followed by an amusing sequence of events, as the Polks search for a suitable place for Nina to live. RECOMMENDATION: This farce deals humorously with the issue of an unwanted elderly guest. Most of the characters are stereotypically elderly, however, and some people might find this offensive, while others will find it amusing. ROYALTY: $25. SOURCE: Hogue, Steve. (1978). Medium rare. Denver, CO: Pioneer Drama Service. SUBJECTS/PLAY TYPE: Elderly; Comedy.

1933. K-2*. (-) Sullivan, Jessie P. **Meek isn't sissy.** CAST: 2u. ACTS: 1. SETTINGS: Bare stage. PLAYING TIME: NA. PLOT: Mortimer and Mathilda discuss what it means to be meek according to the teachings of Jesus. Mortimer puts his ideas to the test when he is challenged by some bullies and again when some children start a fight with a little friend. RECOMMENDATION: The situation presented to illustrate the Bible verse seems so contrived that even young children would not relate to it. ROYALTY: None. SOURCE: Sullivan, Jessie P. (1978). Puppet scripts for children's church. Grand Rapids, MI: Baker Book House. SUBJECTS/PLAY TYPE: Christian Drama; Nonviolence; Puppet Play.

1934. 9-12. (+) Olfson, Lewy. **Meet Miss Stone Age!** CAST: 4f, 1m. ACTS: 1. SETTINGS: Stage. PLAYING TIME: 10 min. PLOT: A prehistoric beauty pageant turns into women's liberation day when Rocky Gravel, the host, asks the contestants about a woman's true role in society. Bunny and Marcia offer traditional answers such as cooking, cleaning and other backbreaking chores. Sylvia believes a woman's place is not in the cave, but in the world. She believes cave women are equal to men. The other women are persuaded and they go about the audience clubbing attractive men. RECOMMENDATION: This is creative, imaginative and delightful. ROYALTY: Free to Plays subscribers. SOURCE: Olfson, Lewy. (1977, May). Meet Miss Stone Age! Plays: The Drama Magazine for Young People, pp. 75-77. SUBJECTS/PLAY TYPE: Women's Rights; Stereotypes; Beauty Pageants; Comedy.

1935. 3-5. (+) Boiko, Claire. **Meet the Pilgrims.** CAST: 4f, 6m. ACTS: 1. SETTINGS: Clearing. PLAYING TIME: 15 min. PLOT: An invitation to join in the first Thanksgiving is given by a group of Pilgrims and their Indian friend, Towami. The Pilgrim girls and boys tell how they worked and prepared for the feast. As they sit down together, they recount what they are thankful for. After all is said, they invite everyone to "Let Thanksgiving begin!" RECOMMENDATION: The use of real names from the Mayflower adds credibility. However, it is not clear why some are referred to as saints, and the final speech refers to the Lord, which might cause some problems in a public school setting. ROYALTY: None. SOURCE: Boiko, Claire. (1981). Children's plays for creative actors. Boston, MA: Plays, Inc. SUBJECTS/PLAY TYPE: Thanksgiving; Playlet.

1936. 7-12. (+) Nunez, Juan. **Meeting the winter bike rider.** CAST: 2m. ACTS: 1. SETTINGS: Gas station. PLAYING TIME: NA. PLOT: Two lonely boys meet at a gas station. Mark works there; Tony has run away from home. Tony reveals his insecurities and the fact that his father only gives him approval when he acts according to his father's values, which are opposed to Tony's. The conversation ends uncomfortably as the two become embarrassed at their frankness, and Tony returns home. RECOMMENDATION: Written by a 17 year old, this realistically and without sensationalism depicts some of the fears and insecurities of teenagers. It could be used to provoke discussion about showing feelings, the value of personal values, and the need for acceptance or approval from parents. ROYALTY: NA. SOURCE: Lamb, Wendy. (1986). Meeting the winter bike rider and other prize winning plays. New York, NY: Dell. SUBJECTS/PLAY TYPE: Self Esteem; Drama.

1937. 6-12. (+) Meili, Janet. **Melisande and the prince.** CAST: 2f, 3m. ACTS: 1. SETTINGS: Bare stage, props. PLAYING TIME: 20 min. PLOT: As the author narrates a mixed-up folk tale which includes parts of **Cinderella, Snow White, Red Riding Hood, The Three Little Pigs,** and **The Hen with Golden Eggs,** he is constantly interrupted by the heroine, who insists on helping write the plot. At the end, the author marries the young lady who takes a part in all these stories. RECOMMENDATION: Melisande (the heroine) must be versatile, as she changes parts and personalities often. This is a delightful spoof on well known folk tales, with a feminist ending, as Melisande becomes the author's co-author. ROYALTY: Free to Plays subscribers. SOURCE: Meili, Janet. (1985, March). Melisande and the prince. Plays: The Drama Magazine for Young People, pp. 47-55. SUBJECTS/PLAY TYPE: Folk Tale Characters; Dating; Fantasy; Comedy.

1938. 4-6. (+) Robinette, Joseph & Jurman, Karl. (Laughlin, Haller T.) **Melissa and the magic nutcracker.** (Melissa and the magic nutcracker) CAST: 2f, 3m, Su. ACTS: 1. SETTINGS: Living room. PLAYING TIME: 55 min. PLOT: Sea Captain Jeremiah Jenkins and his wife are visited by their granddaughter Melissa. She is seasick from her voyage, and misses her parents who are in Europe. In a dream sequence, the Captain's nutcracker, Salty, and his pet mouse, Matey, take human form. To show Melissa that Maine isn't so different from Georgia, they take Melissa on a trip to Mexico, The Netherlands, Sweden, France, and England to see their Christmas customs. A much happier Melissa awakens Christmas morning. RECOMMENDATION: Information on the Christmas customs of other lands and the rhymed speech of the mouse will help to keep the attention of elementary school students. ROYALTY: $50. SOURCE: Robinette, Joseph & Jurman, Karl. (1983). Melissa and the magic nutcracker. Chicago, IL: Dramatic Pub. Co. SUBJECTS/PLAY TYPE: Christmas; Musical.

1939. 4-12. (+) Deverell, Rex. **Melody meets the bag lady.** CAST: 3f, 1m, Su. ACTS: 1. SETTINGS: Park; basement; classroom. PLAYING TIME: NA. PLOT: Melody decides to change Maizie, the bag lady, into a respectable citizen. She enlists friends to help. They build a machine that turns Maizie into a staid adult. The children decide that they were wrong to take away Maizie's "craziness," because that's what made her special. So, they trick her into the machine again, she changes back, and is delighted to be "normal" again. RECOMMENDATION: This requires audience participation, so it should be produced by older adolescents for youngsters. However, even with an experienced acting crew, Maizie is stereotyped as a crazy bag lady, and the problems of living on the streets are never confronted. ROYALTY: NA. SOURCE: Doolittle, Joyce.(1984). Eight plays for young people. Edmonton, Canada: NeWest Pub. SUBJECTS/PLAY TYPE: Identity; Drama.

1940. 7-12. (+) Snee, Dennis. **A memo from Jupiter.** CAST: 5f, 3m. ACTS: 1. SETTINGS: Apartment. PLAYING TIME: 30 min. PLOT: The gods and goddesses of ancient Rome gather in Jupiter's New York apartment to plan strategy when Cupid resigns to enter show business. RECOMMENDATION: For a quick imaginative look at what the ancient gods would think of today's world, this is recommended. This could be an enjoyable way to end a mythology unit, or to encourage creative writing along similar lines. Also a possibility for a Valentine's Day presentation. ROYALTY: $10. SOURCE: Snee, Dennis. (1979). A memo from Jupiter. Denver, CO: Pioneer Drama Service. SUBJECTS/PLAY TYPE: Mythology, Roman; Valentine's Day; Comedy.

1941. 9-12. (+) O'Brien, John. **Memory.** CAST: 1f, 3m. ACTS: 1. SETTINGS: Living room. PLAYING TIME: NA. PLOT: A married couple (Jean and Andrew) spend the evening at home reminiscing about their childhoods and early life together. Andrew's brother calls and asks to bring a visitor over. Jean leaves the room. The brother arrives, accompanied by a psychiatrist, and the three men discuss Andrew's reclusiveness. Andrew is spending his time with the ghost or image of his wife, who burned to death two years earlier. RECOMMENDATION: The plot is rather melodramatically contrived but it will hold the interest of an audience. The parts could be memorized in a short period of time. ROYALTY: $15. SOURCE: O'Brien, John. (1981). Memory. Chicago, IL: Dramatic Pub. Co. SUBJECTS/PLAY TYPE: Love; Imagination; Mourning; Drama.

1942. K-3. (+) Marks, Burton. **Memory course.** CAST: 1u. ACTS: 1. SETTINGS: Bare stage, props. PLAYING TIME: NA. PLOT: Professor Nutmeg attempts to teach a lesson on memory, but continually forgets where he placed his glasses, the chalk, etc. RECOMMENDATION: This portrayal of the forgetful teacher against his mnemonic lecture is quite clever. ROYALTY: None. SOURCE: Marks, Burton. (1982). Puppet plays and puppet-making. Boston, MA: Plays, Inc. SUBJECTS/PLAY TYPE: Forgetfulness; Puppet Play.

1943. 7-12. (+) Miller, Ev. **A memory of Harold.** CAST: 5f, 6m. ACTS: 1. SETTINGS: Bare stage. PLAYING TIME: 30 min. PLOT: Beautiful Lisa, one of the teenage "in-crowd," plays a practical joke on Harold, who is slow, unattractive and shabbily dressed. Lacking the social perception to see that Lisa's attention is designed to provide amusement for herself and for the "gang," Harold places his trust in her. Although subtly warned by Robert,

Harold does not comprehend. When he arrives at a pre-prom party expecting to escort Lisa, she informs him and the "gang" that her date is Robert. Harold drops out of school and joins the army. RECOMMENDATION: In a simple story, this depicts a practical joke illustrating the cruelty so characteristic of this age group and which is so often unintentional. Teenagers may recognize themselves as participants in similar situations, so this should be selected for presentation with care, and perhaps limited to a situation in which its didactic purpose can best be achieved. ROYALTY: $10. SOURCE: Miller, Ev. (1980). A memory of Harold. Denver, CO: Pioneer Drama Service. SUBJECTS/PLAY TYPE: Practical Jokes; Psychology; Drama.

1944. 10-12. (+) Miller, Arthur. **A memory of two Mondays.** CAST: 2m. ACTS: 1. SETTINGS: Warehouse. PLAYING TIME: NA. PLOT: Bert, 18, and Kenneth, 26, converse before Bert leaves for college. Kenneth, whom Bert considers his intellectual superior, works in an auto parts warehouse and has recently begun to drink, possibly because of his insecurities and his fear of settling down to a career. Bert, who is confident of working his way up in the world, tries to convince Kenneth he can accomplish great things, but to no avail. RECOMMENDATION: This could be a good starting point for thought provoking discussions about career planning and self confidence, although some adult guidance may be needed, as many points are only inferred. ROYALTY: NA. SOURCE: Handman, Wynn. (1980). Modern American scenes for student actors. New York, NY: Bantam Books. SUBJECTS/PLAY TYPE: Self Confidence; Life Stages; Scene.

1945. 7-12. (+) Goldberg, Moses. **The men's cottage.** CAST: 2f, 3m. ACTS: 1. SETTINGS: Huts. PLAYING TIME: NA. PLOT: In a primitive tribe, boys must perform several rituals to demonstrate their manhood. Gini Kanwa is a sensitive, artistic boy, nephew of the chief, about to make the transition. His grandmother wishes that Gini Kanwa could be left to his artistic endeavors, but such creativity is not permitted for men. Unfortunately, becoming a man forces him to change and the gentle artistic part of his nature is lost. RECOMMENDATION: The contrast between the imaginary and modern society is realistic with regard to stereotypes and sex roles. The author treats the theme seriously, yet includes humorous parts. Menstruation is mentioned as the passage to womanhood. ROYALTY: $35. SOURCE: Goldberg, Moses. (1979, 1980). The men's cottage. New Orleans, LA: Anchorage Press, Inc. SUBJECTS/PLAY TYPE: Primitive Life; Tribal Customs; Manhood, Rites; Drama.

1946. 1-3. (+) Alexander, Sue. **Meow! and Arf!** CAST: 2u. ACTS: 1. SETTINGS: Outside. PLAYING TIME: NA. PLOT: A dog and a cat try to find things that make Thanksgiving a happy day. They begin with the basics of food and end with the thought of family and friends. RECOMMENDATION: The list of characters may be increased by using other children to represent the elements (instead of pictures). There is a place for Thanksgiving songs learned in the classroom. ROYALTY:

None. SOURCE: Alexander, Sue. (1977). Small plays for special days. New York, NY: Seabury Press. SUBJECTS/PLAY TYPE: Thanksgiving; Animals; Drama.

1947. K-6*. (+) Manning, Linda & Herbertson, Don. **Merch the invisible wizard. CAST:** 3f, 3m. **ACTS:** 1. **SETTINGS:** Living rooms. **PLAYING TIME:** NA. **PLOT:** Nasty but comical wizards bring playful Merch back to Zanderthon to warn him that he must perform 100 dreadful deeds and stay away from humans to remain a wizard. He makes friends with a human, Marianne, who convinces Merch to return home and become the top wizard. He promises Marianne that he will one day come for her. **RECOMMENDATION:** The lyrics sometimes seem a bit contrived, but the play can stand without the music, if necessary. Adults will best handle this lengthy production. **ROYALTY:** NA. **SOURCE:** Manning, Linda. (1983). Merch the invisible wizard. Toronto, Canada: Playwrights Canada. **SUBJECTS/PLAY TYPE:** Friendship; Cooperation; Wizards; Musical.

1948. 7-12. (+) Seay, James. (Shakespeare, William) **The merchant of Venice.** (The merchant of Venice) **CAST:** Sf, 11m, Su. **ACTS:** 2. **SETTINGS:** Canal; mansion. **PLAYING TIME:** NA. **PLOT:** Bassanio courts the lovely Portia. To impress her, he borrows money from Shylock, a Mafia loan shark. Later, Shylock's daughter empties her father's safe and elopes with Bassanio's friend, Lorenzo. Shylock, enraged, tries to cause cosigner Antonio's financial collapse by collecting a "pound" of Antonio's flesh, as was written in their legal agreement. Portia, whose hand has now been won by Bassanio, disguises herself as judge, frees Antonio and sends Shylock to jail. All ends happily as the young couple makes wedding plans. **RECOMMENDATION:** Although not completely faithful to the original, the character of Shylock, and the courtroom scene which is nothing more than an inserted vaudeville act, make this musical parody quite amusing. **ROYALTY:** $75. **SOURCE:** Seay, James. (1981). The merchant of Venice. Elgin, IL: Performance Pub. Co. **SUBJECTS/PLAY TYPE:** Loan Sharks; Comedy; Adaptation; Musical.

1949. 3-6*. (+) Engar, Keith. **Merlin's tale of Arthur's magic sword. CAST:** 4f, 11m, Su. **ACTS:** 6. **SETTINGS:** Hall; courtyard; manor house; castles; town square. **PLAYING TIME:** NA. **PLOT:** Young King Arthur was raised in secrecy as the son of a knight because Merlin feared those with designs on the throne of England. At 14, Arthur accompanies his "family" to a council where he demonstrates he is King by pulling an enchanted sword from an anvil. **RECOMMENDATION:** The set changes, costuming, magic effects, and old dialect might prove difficult for younger children. However, the acting requirements are within the abilities of junior high students and the play would be enjoyable to perform for a younger audience. **ROYALTY:** $35. **SOURCE:** Engar, Keith. (1982). Merlin's tales of Arthur's magic sword. New Orleans, LA: Anchorage Press, Inc. **SUBJECTS/PLAY TYPE:** Legends, England; Knights of the Round Table; Drama.

1950. 3-8. (+) Kehret, Peg. **Merry birthday. CAST:** 1u. **ACTS:** 1. **SETTINGS:** None. **PLAYING TIME:** NA. **PLOT:** A sad child bemoans the losses he incurs by having been born on Christmas Day. **RECOMMENDATION:** Amusingly told, this monologue's charm will reach out to audiences of any age. **ROYALTY:** NA. **SOURCE:** Kehret, Peg. (1986). Winning monologs for young actors. Colorado Springs, CO: Meriwether Pub. **SUBJECTS/PLAY TYPE:** Birthdays; Monologue.

1951. 2-8. (+) Hackett, Walker. (Alcott, Louisa May) **A merry Christmas.** (Little women) **CAST:** 7f, 3m, 1u. **ACTS:** 1. **SETTINGS:** Living room. **PLAYING TIME:** NA. **PLOT:** The March women try to celebrate Christmas despite the hardships of the Civil War. **RECOMMENDATION:** This is tastefully written and captures many of the emotions present at Christmas time. Familiarity with the original will help to make this more meaningful. **ROYALTY:** None. **SOURCE:** Kamerman, Sylvia E. (1988). The big book of Christmas plays. Boston, MA: Plays, Inc. **SUBJECTS/PLAY TYPE:** Christmas; Family; Civil War, U.S.; Adaptation.

1952. 4-12. (+) Gilfond, Henry. **Merry Christmas all. CAST:** Su. **ACTS:** 1. **SETTINGS:** Living room. **PLAYING TIME:** 15 min. **PLOT:** Mr. Busby's job as Santa Claus has been taken over by a younger man. The neighborhood decides to make the old man's house Santa's and, if Busby can no longer go to the children, the children will come to him. **RECOMMENDATION:** References to the "poor children at the firehouse" will need to be changed to avoid a stereotypical tone, but the message that the spirit of Christmas has nothing to do with age is well transmitted. **ROYALTY:** None. **SOURCE:** Gilfond, Henry. (1985). Holiday plays for reading. New York, NY: Walker. **SUBJECTS/PLAY TYPE:** Christmas; Skit.

1953. 6-12. (+) Hark, Mildred & McQueen, Noel. **Merry Christmas, Crawfords! CAST:** 7f, 8m, Su. **ACTS:** 1. **SETTINGS:** Living room. **PLAYING TIME:** 35 min. **PLOT:** It's Christmas and the Saunders have just moved into their new home in the suburbs. The tree is bare, dinner hasn't been cooked, they don't have presents, and the electricity is off. When the neighbors find out, they all pitch in and help. **RECOMMENDATION:** Each member of this large cast has plenty of time on stage. In a pleasant, low key way, this reinforces the Christmas spirit. **ROYALTY:** Free to Plays subscribers. **SOURCE:** Hark, Mildred & McQueen, Noel. (1985, December). Merry Christmas, Crawfords! Plays: The Drama Magazine for Young People, pp. 11-22. **SUBJECTS/PLAY TYPE:** Christmas; Playlet.

1954. 11-12*. (+) Dizenzo, Charles. (Kafka, Franz) **The metamorphosis.** (The metamorphosis) **CAST:** 4f, 5m. **ACTS:** 1. **SETTINGS:** Bedroom; dining room. **PLAYING TIME:** NA. **PLOT:** Gregor Samsa wakes up to discover that he has been turned into a giant cockroach. When he speaks, no one hears him except the audience. In the beginning, he talks about what his life is and was, how he alone supported the family and the poor treatment he received at work. Now, he is forced to remain in his room, with only his tender hearted sister to visit and feed him. Shut away from the world, Gregor eventually dies and, tragically, his father feels no remorse about his death. RECOMMENDATION: While ultimately faithful to the original short story, this changes the emphasis on supporting characters to depict them as more obviously "good" and "bad." The theme of alienation will be best appreciated by older audiences and production could be tricky, due to the cockroach costume required and the subtlety of the dialogue. ROYALTY: NA. SOURCE: Dizenzo, Charles. (1977). The metamorphosis. New York, NY: Dramatists Play Service, Inc. SUBJECTS/PLAY TYPE: Alienation; Adaptation.

1955. 4-6. (-) Patterson, Nancy A. **Metric medicine.** CAST: 11u. ACTS: 1. SETTINGS: Doctor's office; waiting room. PLAYING TIME: 20 min. PLOT: Dr. Metric treats a series of patients whose complaints stem from not understanding the metric system. RECOMMENDATION: This is unredeemingly dated in several respects. The theme of the metric system being the new wave of the future is out of date and it refers to TV cigarette commercials now non-existent. Dr. Metric himself comes across as absent minded and dull witted, letting his assistant do all the work while he takes the credit. ROYALTY: Free to Plays subscribers. SOURCE: Patterson, Nancy A. (1978, April). Metric medicine. Plays: The Drama Magazine for Young People, pp. 37-42. SUBJECTS/PLAY TYPE: Math; Metric System; Skit.

1956. 2-5*. (+) Baldwin, John. **Metrics can be fun.** CAST: 4u. ACTS: 1. SETTINGS: None. PLAYING TIME: 45 min. PLOT: An attempt to bring metrics to life, this is an adaptation of the **Sorcerer's Apprentice** and three Aesop's fables. It reinforces basic metric measurement: meter, gram, liter, and Celsius. RECOMMENDATION: Children would enjoy the slapstick humor, but they might be confused by the shifting story line, and the dialogue would be better played by junior high school actors. Occasional audience participation makes the lesson more valuable. ROYALTY: $15. SOURCE: Baldwin, John. (1977). Metrics can be fun. Denver, CO: Pioneer Drama Service. SUBJECTS/PLAY TYPE: Metrics; Skit.

1957. 5-8. (+) Wohlers, Linell. **Mexican trio.** CAST: 1f, 3m, Su. ACTS: 3. SETTINGS: Woods. PLAYING TIME: 10 min. PLOT: The narrator tells the Mexican folk tale about Senor Conejo (coyote), the smartest of all creatures who captures Senora Tejon (raccoon). The raccoon tricks the coyote into believing he should hide in a log because of the coming hailstorm. The raccoon throws stones at the log, and the coyote never suspects she tricked him. Next, Senor Gallo (rooster) escapes him by insulting the coyote's singing. Finally, Senor Zorro (fox) leaves Senor Conejo holding up a tree that is not falling. He realizes that the fox has tricked him, but never admits that some other creatures could be as quick witted as he. RECOMMENDATION: The use of some Spanish words exposes students to another language and culture. Younger students will enjoy this, but it should be performed by older students because of word difficulty. ROYALTY: Free to Plays subscribers. SOURCE: Wohlers,

Linell. (1987, October). Mexican trio. Plays: The Drama Magazine for Young People, pp. 47-50. SUBJECTS/PLAY TYPE: Animals; Folk Tales, Mexico; Fable.

1958. 5-8. (+) Smith, Beatrice S. **The mice that ate money.** CAST: 4m. ACTS: 1. SETTINGS: Garden. PLAYING TIME: 10 min. PLOT: An obnoxious, dishonest banker boasts about the source of his wealth to his equally obnoxious son and to his honest servant. The money was given to the banker for safekeeping by a young man going on a trip. When the young man returns to claim his money, the banker tells him the mice ate it. The young man kidnaps the banker's son and tells him a hawk carried off his favorite son. The banker releases the money and the young man releases the son. RECOMMENDATION: Although the characters, plot and setting are not well developed, the theme that dishonesty and trickery will backfire on those that use it, is subtly presented. This would be more effective if the dialogue were less common and if the characters were better developed. ROYALTY: Free to Plays subscribers. SOURCE: Smith, Beatrice S. (1984, April). The mice that ate money. Plays: The Drama Magazine for Young People, pp. 47-50. SUBJECTS/PLAY TYPE: Greed; Fable; Skit.

1959. 3-9. (+) De Prine, John. **The Midas complex.** CAST: 2f, 2m. ACTS: 1. SETTINGS: Library. PLAYING TIME: NA. PLOT: Millionaire Henry Pomeroy is motivated by his love of money. After a fall from a ladder, he finds that he is able to turn things to gold with a simple touch of the hand. He accidentally turns his only daughter into gold and is forced to reexamine his values. To his relief, he was only dreaming while unconscious, but he learned a valuable lesson. RECOMMENDATION: This is fast moving, with witty dialogue, and some clever tricks to keep the audience's interest. ROYALTY: $25. SOURCE: De Prine, John. (1099). The Midas Complex. Franklin, OH: Eldridge Pub. Co. SUBJECTS/PLAY TYPE: Greed; Mythology, Greek; Comedy.

1960. 11-12. (+) Marcell, Raleigh Jr. **The middle of nowhere.** CAST: 1f, 4m. ACTS: 1. SETTINGS: Bare stage, props. PLAYING TIME: 40 min. PLOT: Four passengers are dropped in the middle of nowhere to change buses near a Coke machine. An old man explains to them that the only way to leave this place and catch another bus is for one of them to kill him and take his place as the keeper of the Coke machine. While the passengers ponder this, the old man dies and all four travellers become keepers of the Coke machine. RECOMMENDATION: The symbolic message is deep but this is a very interesting play which could be used to initiate discussion on freedom of choice and dramatic symbolism. The single desolate setting will be easy to assemble. Lighting techniques can show the passage of time. ROYALTY: $15. SOURCE: Marcell, Raleigh Jr. (1982). The middle of nowhere. Schulenburg, TX: I.E. Clark. SUBJECTS/PLAY TYPE: Choices; Drama.

1961. 9-12. (+) Chayefsky, Paddy. **The middle of the night.** CAST: 2f. ACTS: 1. SETTINGS: Living room. PLAYING TIME: NA. PLOT: Betty, 24, has filed for divorce from her husband, a musician who is frequently away from home. She believes she has fallen in love with an older widower and has hopes of marriage. Betty is uncertain about her decision and confides in her girlfriend, Marilyn, who believes Betty is making a mistake and advises her to stay with her husband, even though their situation may not be perfect. RECOMMENDATION: A stark set would help keep the audience focused on the dialogue, which is straightforward and sensitive. ROYALTY: NA. SOURCE: Handman, Wynn. (1980.) Modern American scenes for student actors. New York, NY: Bantam Books. SUBJECTS/PLAY TYPE: Life Changes; Marital Problems; Scene.

1962. 6-8. (-) Majeski, Bill. **The midnight ride of...who? CAST:** 2f, 4m. **ACTS:** 1. **SETTINGS:** Living room. **PLAYING TIME:** 20 min. **PLOT:** Henry Wadworth Longfellow is writing his famous poem about Paul Revere's ride when Paul's friend attempts to convince Longfellow that the poem includes inaccuracies. He claims that Revere did not make the actual ride to warn his countrymen. Instead, the message was delivered by Paul's wife. Finally, it becomes obvious that Revere's friend has been brainwashed by his own wife, who has convinced him to change the historical facts to favor her own interests. **RECOMMENDATION:** This is derogatory to women and includes many stereotyped and unpleasant remarks. Many historical accounts are inaccurate because they fail to point out women's roles as national heroines; the play serves only to perpetuate these omissions. **ROYALTY:** Free to Plays subscribers. **SOURCE:** Majeski, Bill. (1977, April). The midnight ride of...who? Plays: The Drama Magazine for Young People, pp. 63-68. **SUBJECTS/PLAY TYPE:** Revere, Paul; Comedy; Skit.

1963. 9-12. (+) Murray, John. **The midnight train. CAST:** 3f, 3m. **ACTS:** 1. **SETTINGS:** Railroad station. **PLAYING TIME:** 25 min. **PLOT:** Suspense builds as the audience begins to notice, through the eyes of Tom and Mary, peculiarities in a rundown railway station where they await the midnight train. The intrusion of Mrs. Carlson, who journeys to join her husband after a 15 year separation, highlights the futility of a marriage without sharing and companionship. The mysterious disappearance of Mrs. Carlson as she "rejoins" her waiting husband prods Tom and Mary to reexamine the events which culminated in their arrival at the station: they were in an auto accident and await the finality of death in the form of a train. They unite in a plan for a better life and marriage as they defeat the prospect of death and refuse to board the train. **RECOMMENDATION:** The value of a loving, giving relationship and the necessity for energetic nurturing is evidenced here. The dark, somber mood of the station and the depressed dissatisfaction and alienation of Tom and Mary contrast the hopeful gaiety of Mrs. Carlson as she anticipates reunion with her husband. **ROYALTY:** Free to Plays subscribers. **SOURCE:** Murray, John. (1988, March). The midnight train. Plays: The Drama Magazine for Young People, pp. 1-9. **SUBJECTS/PLAY TYPE:** Marriage; Playlet.

1964. 10-12. (+) Pickett, Cecil. (Shakespeare, William) **A midsummer night's dream.** (A midsummer night's dream) **CAST:** 1f, 8m, 5u. **ACTS:** 1. **SETTINGS:** Woods. **PLAYING TIME:** 35 min. **PLOT:** The Fairy King, Oberon, quarrels with Queen Titania and then tricks her with Cupid's magic potion. When Titania wakes from a nap, she falls in love with a bumbling rustic, dressed as an ass. Oberon eventually rescues Titania as the audience watches the inept crew launch into **Pyramus and Thisbe.** **RECOMMENDATION:** This ideal introduction to Shakespeare for young amateurs condenses the original into one act. Although the language still sounds authentic, the script is much easier to understand and learn. The slapstick humor of the uneducated rustics and the trickster Fairy Puck remain hilarious, and the theme of romantic upheaval between the King and Queen is still valid. **ROYALTY:** $15. **SOURCE:** Pickett, Cecil. (1984). A midsummer night's dream. Schulenburg, TX: I.E. Clark. **SUBJECTS/PLAY TYPE:** Love; Fantasy; Comedy; Adaptation.

1965. K-3. (+) Bauer, Caroline Feller. (Fillmore, Parker) **Might Mikko.** (The shepherd's nosegay) **CAST:** 1f, 2m, 3u. **ACTS:** 1. **SETTINGS:** None. **PLAYING TIME:** NA. **PLOT:** Mikko, a poor boy, is helped by a clever fox to find a wife. After lining up an appropriate princess, the fox, aided by the audience, frightens the horrible Great Worm out of his castle, procuring an appropriate home for the couple. **RECOMMENDATION:** Reminiscent of **Puss in Boots**, this will charm young folk tale fans, and some limited audience participation will involve everyone in its presentation. **ROYALTY:** NA. **SOURCE:** Bauer, Caroline Feller. (1987). Presenting reader's theater: Plays and poems to read aloud. New York, NY: H.W. Wilson. **SUBJECTS/PLAY TYPE:** Foxes; Reader's Theater; Adaptation.

1966. 7-9. (-) Karshner, Roger. **Mike and Oscar. CAST:** 2m. **ACTS:** 1. **SETTINGS:** None. **PLAYING TIME:** NA. **PLOT:** Mike and Oscar are chased from a house of ill repute because they have no money. They decide that they would not have done it anyway, because they did not like the place and the idea was stupid in the first place. **RECOMMENDATION:** This seems to have no point except to disgust the audience at the expense of women. **ROYALTY:** NA. **SOURCE:** Karshner, Roger. (1986). Scenes for teenagers. Toluce Lake, CA: Dramaline Pub. **SUBJECTS/PLAY TYPE:** Prostitutes; Scenes.

1967. 10-12. (-) Schoggen, Christopher. **Mike's case. CAST:** 3f, 4m, Su. **ACTS:** 1. **SETTINGS:** Auditorium; classrooms. **PLAYING TIME:** NA. **PLOT:** Mike, 16, is bothered by a sense that "something is wrong." Through vignettes from school, home, and a social gathering, in which the actors humor Mike by playing out the scenes, Mike's point is supposedly made. The characters finally get bored and leave without finishing "Mike's case." **RECOMMENDATION:** Not only will the actors get bored by this surrealistic drama with its petulant tone, but so will the audience. The playwright is so subtle that Mike's message is never clear. The sarcasm doesn't work, the school scenes don't ring true, and the home scenes allude to complex adult problems without explaining them. **ROYALTY:** $20. **SOURCE:** Schoggen, Christopher. (1983). Mike's case. Chicago, IL: Dramatic Pub. Co. **SUBJECTS/PLAY TYPE:** Communication; Drama.

1968. 7-12. (+) Hall, Margaret. **The miller's guest.** CAST: 3f, 5m. ACTS: 1. SETTINGS: Cottage. PLAYING TIME: 20 min. PLOT: A poor miller meets a hunter in the Royal Forest and takes him home for the night. Through his interactions with the miller and his family, the hunter learns about the problems of commoners. When it is discovered that the hunter is really the king, the miller fears for his and his family's life since he has complained to the king about their problems. Instead, the king knights the miller, thanks him for his honesty, and for telling him about the problems of his kingdom. RECOMMENDATION: With dialogue appropriate to the medieval time, and realistic characters, this moves smoothly from beginning to end. ROYALTY: Free to Plays subscribers. SOURCE: Hall, Margaret. (1980, January). The miller's guest. Plays: The Drama Magazine for Young People, pp. 53-57. SUBJECTS/PLAY TYPE: Kings; Lifestyles; Playlet.

1969. 7-12. (+) Sodaro, Craig. **Million dollar baby, or, a hot time in the old town tonight: A comic melodrama in 2 acts.** CAST: 19f, 16m, Su. ACTS: 2. SETTINGS: Mission; street; saloon. PLAYING TIME: NA. PLOT: A wealthy candy magnate's two children compete to inherit his fortune. Nellie fulfills a dream and opens a mission for the homeless; Creepstone runs the Golden Dipper Soda Saloon. Creepstone, jealous of his saintly sister, sabotages her reputation with a false newspaper article so that Nellie loses the homeless peoples' trust. Creepstone is finally exposed, but he retaliates by setting a fire that burns the Golden Dipper by mistake. When Creepstone inherits, the father appears as a ghost, gives the son a look at his future, and Creepstone promises to reform. RECOMMENDATION: This old fashioned musical melodrama and its characters are well developed and the theme is accomplished without preaching. ROYALTY: $35. SOURCE: Sodaro, Craig. (1987). Million dollar baby, or, a hot time in the old town tonight: A comic melodrama in 2 acts. Schulenburg, TX: I.E. Clark. SUBJECTS/PLAY TYPE: Romance; Inheritances; Honesty; Melodrama.

1970. 7-12. (+) DePrine, John. **Million dollar Christmas: A one-act Christmas comedy.** CAST: 1f, 3m, 7u. ACTS: 1. SETTINGS: Bare stage, props. PLAYING TIME: NA. PLOT: Three miserly cousins are condemned on Christmas Eve to compete for a million dollars bequeathed in their eccentric aunt's will to the one who gives away a million dollars before midnight. All three grudgingly admit that they enjoyed giving. When the winner divides her million with her cousins, they realize that they have all caught the Christmas spirit. RECOMMENDATION: This lighthearted seasonal play gains most of its charm from the cousins' ill tempered sniping at each other and from the dismay of the bewildered recipients of the charity. The lawyer, whose instructions drive the plot, is cleverly drawn. ROYALTY: $30. SOURCE: DePrine, John. (1987). Million dollar Christmas: A one-act Christmas comedy. Franklin, OH: Eldridge Pub. Co. SUBJECTS/PLAY TYPE: Christmas; Comedy.

1971. 3-6. (+) Janey, Sue Ellen. **The million dollar quiz show.** CAST: 6u. ACTS: 1. SETTINGS: TV studio. PLAYING TIME: 10 min. PLOT: Contestants on a TV quiz show are asked impossible trick questions, doused with water, covered with paint, and insulted by the M.C. Finally, the contestants bet the M.C. that if they can get him to answer a question with "yes," they will receive the jackpot prize. They do. RECOMMENDATION: The trick questions are clever, the satire is hilarious, and, although the ending is pat, it does turn the M.C.'s own dishonest techniques against him. ROYALTY: Free to Plays subscribers. SOURCE: Janey, Sue Ellen. (1988, March). The million dollar quiz show. Plays: The Drama Magazine for Young People, pp. 51-54. SUBJECTS/PLAY TYPE: Game Shows; Comedy; Puppet Play.

1972. 1-6. (+) Howard, Vernon. **Million dollar recipe.** CAST: 1f, 4m. ACTS: 1. SETTINGS: Room. PLAYING TIME: 10 min. PLOT: Three cooks compete for the international million dollar recipe contest, trying to ruin the others' recipes. RECOMMENDATION: The physical comedy will be fun to produce. ROYALTY: Free to Plays subscribers. SOURCE: Howard, Vernon. (1980, May). Million dollar recipe. Plays: The Drama Magazine for Young People, pp. 64-67. SUBJECTS/PLAY TYPE: Cooking; Contests; Skit.

1973. 7-9. (-) Karshner, Roger. **Mindy and Alberta.** CAST: 2f. ACTS: 1. SETTINGS: None. PLAYING TIME: NA. PLOT: Mindy and Alberta fight over which are better, dogs or cats. Mindy is partial to her dog, Ed, while Alberta, likes her two cats, Wilbur and Maude. Neither is able to change the other's mind. The scene ends with Alberta giving up. RECOMMENDATION: This boring piece dramatizes an inane argument where neither side ever makes a valid point, but instead each shows a capacity for foul language. ROYALTY: NA. SOURCE: Karshner, Roger. (1986). Scenes for teenagers. Toluce Lake, CA: Dramaline Pub. SUBJECTS/PLAY TYPE: Animals; Fighting; Scene.

1974. 6-12. (+) Harris, Aurand. **Ming Lee and the magic tree.** CAST: 6f, 12m, Su. ACTS: 1. SETTINGS: Bare stage, props. PLAYING TIME: NA. PLOT: Before Prince Moo Yen may marry Shing Nu, he must answer the question, "what makes a happy man?" He is given a wish granting tail to aid his search. He grants wishes to Ming Lee for successively stronger power, but the stonecutter decides that the one who is happiest has the most power as one's own self. Moo Yen returns to the Jade Emperor with this answer and is granted the princess' hand in marriage. RECOMMENDATION: This fascinating view of ancient Chinese culture uses an "invisible" prop man, a chorus, and communication with the audience. ROYALTY: Write to Samuel French. SOURCE: Jennings, Coleman A. & Harris, Aurand. (1981). Plays children love: A treasury of contemporary and classic plays for children. Garden City, NY: Doubleday. SUBJECTS/PLAY TYPE: Power; Folk Tales, China; Playlet.

1975. 9-12. (+) Brooks, Hindi. **A minor incident.** CAST: 3f, 3m, Su. ACTS: 1. SETTINGS: Street. PLAYING TIME: 30 min. PLOT: A middle class uptown lady and a street wise dude are involved in an accident. In a brief moment they discover a shared loneliness and a shared human need to love and be loved. The onlooking street corner gawkers, with their callous remarks, serve to heighten the illusion that these two are momentarily isolated from their individual worlds. Ray's advice to Lenore about her husband "you hold him tight... and don't let go," bespeaks the human condition eloquently. RECOMMENDATION: Audiences will relate to Lenore and Ray, who while heading "nowheres" for the evening, find compassion in an unexpected moment. Ray's lament that "anything's better than nothing" and Lenore's attempt to defend going to the movies without her husband poignantly express the theme. ROYALTY: $20. SOURCE: Brooks, Hindi. (1975). A minor incident. Schulenburg, TX: I.E. Clark. SUBJECTS/PLAY TYPE: Life; Drama.

1976. 9-12*. (+) Gibson, William. **The miracle worker.** CAST: 13f, 5m. ACTS: 3. SETTINGS: Bare stage. PLAYING TIME: 90 min. PLOT: This is the true story of Helen Keller, who became deaf and blind, was spoiled by her indulgent family, and was taught discipline by a nearly blind Anne Sullivan. RECOMMENDATION: The play speaks powerfully of love, understanding, patience, pity, and of the problems faced by handicapped individuals and their families. It also expresses strong criticism of those who would warehouse the handicapped, regarding them as unteachable or subhuman. Adults and children will react strongly to the powerful and informative dramatization of Helen Keller's childhood. Difficulties involved in the effective portrayal of the characters should not be underestimated. The scenes in which the child and her governess do physical and emotional battle require consummate acting skills. ROYALTY: $50. SOURCE: Gibson, William. (1985). The miracle worker. New York, NY: Samuel French. SUBJECTS/PLAY TYPE: Blindness; Love; Deafness; Drama.

1977. 7-12. (+) Bland, Joellen. (Twain, Mark) **The miraculous eclipse.** (A Connecticut Yankee in King Arthur's court) CAST: 12m. ACTS: 1. SETTINGS: Street; courtyard; dungeon. PLAYING TIME: 25 min. PLOT: In Connecticut, 1879, a young boy asks Hank to tell his story of how he knew King Arthur in Camelot. One day Hank was hit in the head at work. He regained consciousness in Camelot in the year 528. He was captured by Sir Kay, thrown into prison, and slated for execution the next day. Remembering that there was to be a total eclipse of the sun that day, Hank sent a page to tell King Arthur that he would consume the world in blackness. After some confusion, the eclipse occurred and Hank took credit. Freed, Hank received great power and authority for the remainder of his time in Camelot. RECOMMENDATION: This very entertaining and enjoyable adaptation would allow for a large cast, although all the major roles are for males. Designed originally as a read aloud drama, this could be simply used as an introduction to literature in English class. However, with a daring cast, this could be fully staged, an experience which would provide a terrific opportunity to work with exotic costumes and scenery. ROYALTY: Free to Plays subscribers. SUBJECTS/PLAY TYPE: Time Travel; Camelot; Eclipses; Adaptation.

1978. 1-3. (+) Gotwalt, Helen Louise Miller. **The miraculous tea party.** CAST: 8f, 4m, 1u. ACTS: 1. SETTINGS: Living/dining room. PLAYING TIME: 15 min. PLOT: Minty Stevens is new in town and has no friends. Her mother offers her the comfort of some of her old book friends, such as **Sleeping Beauty** and **Mary Poppins**, and suggests that Minty have a tea party in their honor. The characters actually show up and the children are impressed. Mary Poppins causes a thunderstorm and the other children who have been watching rush in to stay dry. The tea party guests have disappeared, but the books remain. Minty discovers that telling the children about her favorite books leads to the desired friendships. RECOMMENDATION: The simplicity of this play makes it perfect for younger children to perform; the idea that the characters from books can be our friends is worthwhile. Some stereotyping in the play activities assigned to the boys and girls should be changed. ROYALTY: Free to Plays subscribers. SOURCE: Gotwalt, Helen Louise Miller. (1986). Everyday plays for boys an girls. Boston, MA: Plays, Inc. SUBJECTS/PLAY TYPE: Books; Friendship; Playlet.

1979. 10-12. (+) O'Brien, John. **Mirrors.** CAST: 3f, 3m. ACTS: 1. SETTINGS: Porch. PLAYING TIME: NA. PLOT: A man happily lives with his wife and children. A doctor tries to help him accept that his wife and children have been dead for years. The man is living with their memory and cannot give them up because of the guilt he feels over not being at home when the fire which killed them broke out. RECOMMENDATION: The power of guilt is a provocative theme which will stimulate thought and discussion. ROYALTY: $15. SOURCE: O'Brien, John. (1982). Mirrors. Woodstock, IL: Dramatic Pub. Co. SUBJECTS/PLAY TYPE: Reality; Guilt; Mental Illness; Drama.

1980. 12. (+) McDonough, Jerome. **Mirrors, a reflection.** CAST: 7f, 4m, Su. ACTS: 1. SETTINGS: Kitchen; living room. PLAYING TIME: 50 min. PLOT: Within several simultaneously occurring time frames, three generations of a family recall their youth and their relations with mothers, sisters, and daughters. RECOMMENDATION: More involved than its antecedent **Our Town**, the production will require skilled actors and lighting crew. The transitions between 1961 and 1986, as well as earlier flashbacks and intrusions of the present, require careful attention. A marriage proposal in a rowboat strains credulity, while a baby-passing scene and the funeral services at the end demand viewing and listening gymnastics from both players and viewers. However, the staging techniques used to transcend barriers of time, the lively dialogue, and the identifiable characters all make this worthy of production. ROYALTY: $20. SOURCE: McDonough, Jerome. (1987). Mirrors, a reflection. Schulenburg, TX: I.E. Clark. SUBJECTS/PLAY TYPE: Death; Family Relationships; Drama.

1981. 9-12. (+) Kelly, Tim. (Hugo, Victor) **Les miserables.** (Les miserables.) CAST: 16f, 14m, 6u. ACTS: 2. SETTINGS: Bare stage. PLAYING TIME: NA. PLOT:

This biography of the ex-convict Jean Valjean begins with his parole, at which time he is an evil character. After experiencing kindness, he changes, but his past is never put fully behind him. This closely follows the original. RECOMMENDATION: This will offer a well motivated, mature high school cast a chance to demonstrate their abilities. The play is intended to resemble a film, with scenes blending one into the next. ROYALTY: $60. SOURCE: Kelly, Tim. (1987). Les miserables. Woodstock, IL: Dramatic Pub. Co. SUBJECTS/PLAY TYPE: Prison; Love; Adaptation.

1982. 6-12. (+) Heinzen, Barbara Brem. **Miss Cast.** CAST: 3f, 3m. ACTS: 1. SETTINGS: Living room. PLAYING TIME: 35 min. PLOT: Judy has begun to take acting too seriously and her family and friends tire of her constant melodrama. Mr. Randall, the famous playwright father of the "boy next door" gently gives Judy some advice based on his experiences, and brings her back to earth. Judy ironically gets a part in the school play as a kooky, teenage actress. RECOMMENDATION: This takes a humorous look at the exuberance of youth, and laudably points out the need to be able to laugh at oneself. ROYALTY: Free to Plays subscribers. SOURCE: Heinzen, Barbara Brem. (1989, January/ February). Miss Cast. Plays: The Drama Magazine for Young People, pp. 1-10. SUBJECTS/PLAY TYPE: Self Image; Comedy.

1983. 7-12. (-) Miller, Terry & Perry, Fred C. **The Miss Hamford beauty pageant and battle of the bands.** CAST: 8f, 13m. ACTS: 2. SETTINGS: Stage. PLAYING TIME: NA. PLOT: In this satirical account of a small town beauty pageant/band competition, the characters speak their thoughts to the audience to provide a form of narration. The contests abound with small town corruption, and when the "wrong" person wins the beauty contest, she is shot and the runner-up (the desired winner) takes the crown. RECOMMENDATION: Some may find this mildly amusing, provided they use a liberal definition of the word humor. However, the plot and the humor are trite, and having the characters speak their thoughts to the audience, although clever, is awkward. ROYALTY: NA. SOURCE: Miller Terry & Perry, Fred C. (1978). The Miss Hamford beauty contest and battle of the bands. Chicago, IL: The Dramatic Pub. Co. SUBJECTS/PLAY TYPE: Beauty Pageants; Corruption; Comedy.

1984. 4-8. (-) Bradley, Virginia. **Miss Lacey and the President.** CAST: 5f, 3m. ACTS: 1. SETTINGS: Porch. PLAYING TIME: NA. PLOT: Elderly Miss Lacey shares the same birthday as George Washington. Her two young friends look on as she "talks" with the young George. Miss Lacey is convinced that the authorities want her house because of her secret box. When discovered, the box contains nothing important. There is, however, an old cup sitting on the kitchen windowsill which might have belonged to Washington. RECOMMENDATION: Although the parts are fairly easy to memorize, the plot is too fragmented. ROYALTY: None. SOURCE: Bradley, Virginia. (1981). Holidays on stage. New York, NY: Dodd, Mead. SUBJECTS/PLAY TYPE: Washington, George; Presidents' Day; Playlet.

1985. 7-12. (-) McGowan, Jane. **Miss Lonely-heart.** CAST: 3f, 5m. ACTS: 1. SETTINGS: Living room. PLAYING TIME: 35 min. PLOT: The Fairchild family has just moved to a new town, and 16 year old Susie bemoans her trouble making friends and her lack of a date for the Valentine's Day dance. When Mrs. Fairchild blackmails Susie's younger brother into escorting her, he discovers a unique matchmaking scheme. RECOMMENDATION: This depicts an uncomfortably stereotyped family, with an absent but powerful father (held up as a threat to Frank), a perky younger sister, and a depressed female adolescent. The plot is thin, seems dated, and is terribly innocent for high schoolers. The moral, delivered by Susie, is heavy handed. ROYALTY: Free to subscribers of Plays. SOURCE: Kamerman, Sylvia E. (1983). Holiday plays round the year. Boston, MA: Plays, Inc. SUBJECTS/PLAY TYPE: Valentine's Day; Loneliness; Comedy.

1986. 8-12. (+) Gotwalt, Helen Louise Miller. **Miss Lonelyheart. CAST:** 3f, 5m. ACTS: 1. SETTINGS: Living room. PLAYING TIME: 35 min. PLOT: The Fairchild family has moved to Adamsford. Susie is upset that no one has asked her to the Valentine dance. Her brother places an ad in the newspaper to get her a date, and several young men come to the house at once. RECOMMENDATION: This could be fun to perform and watch, especially if done tongue in cheek. There is no need to take seriously the premise that nice girls always have dates or that "being popular" is naturally an important objective. ROYALTY: Free to Plays subscribers. SOURCE: Gotwalt, Helen Louise Miller. (1981, February). Miss Lonelyheart. Plays: The Drama Magazine for Young People, pp. 1-11. SUBJECTS/PLAY TYPE: Valentine's Day; Dating; Comedy.

1987. 6-8. (+) Watts, Francis B. **Miss Louisa and the outlaws. CAST:** 4f, 6m. ACTS: 1. SETTINGS: One-room school. PLAYING TIME: 20 min. PLOT: A strict schoolteacher, Miss Louisa is giving her students a lesson on the virtue of courage when two armed outlaws, Benny the Kid and Dead-Eye Dan, intrude. The unflappable Miss Louisa admonishes the outlaws to wipe their feet and repeatedly corrects their poor grammar. Feigning concern that it may rain, Miss Louisa has the flag taken down from the pole in the school-yard. The sheriff and his assistant enter, capture the outlaws, and Miss Louisa gets a $100 reward. RECOMMENDATION: Miss Louisa's pragmatism makes an amusing contrast to the desperation of the rough outlaws, and the theme of facing danger with a cool head is presented entertainingly. ROYALTY: Free to Plays subscribers. SOURCE: Watts, Francis B. (1981, January). Miss Louisa and the outlaws. Plays: The Drama Magazine for Young People, pp. 39- 44. SUBJECTS/PLAY TYPE: Courage; Comedy.

1988. 2-5. (+) Cheatham, Val R. **The Miss Witch contest.** CAST: 5f, 5m, 1u. ACTS: 1. SETTINGS: Throne room. PLAYING TIME: 15 min. PLOT: The Wicked Witch says "If I can't be the fairest, then I must be the meanest." A contest is held, with famous monsters as judges and the Mirror as M.C. Everyone, including judges, votes for himself and a tie is declared. All laugh and decide to hold another contest next year. RECOMMENDATION: The talking magic mirror adds just the right touch of the supernatural without being too frightening for this age. ROYALTY: Free to Plays subscribers. SOURCE: Cheatham, Val R. (1980, October). The Miss Witch contest. Plays: The Drama Magazine for Young People, pp. 63-68. SUBJECTS/PLAY TYPE: Halloween; Comedy; Skit.

1989. 7-12. (+) Dias, Earl J. **Miss Wrapple wraps it up.** CAST: 5f, 6m. ACTS: 1. SETTINGS: Drawing room. PLAYING TIME: 30 min. PLOT: The mysterious disappearance of two valuable paintings is solved by retired governess, Miss Wrapple, and her nephew, a Scotland Yard Inspector. Suspects include the butler, a former pickpocket; the maid; Mr. George Hamilton, a lawyer and art collector; a disgruntled tenant; and the robbed man's secretary (who is guilty). RECOMMENDATION: The British expressions may be difficult for younger children to understand at times, but some lighthearted humor, such as the absent minded Lord Fenwood, plus the question of "who dunnit" will keep their attention. ROYALTY: Free to Plays subscribers. SOURCE: Dias, Earl J. (1981, October). Miss Wrapple wraps it up. Plays: The Drama Magazine for Young People, pp. 11-23. SUBJECTS/PLAY TYPE: Mystery; Comedy; Playlet.

1990. 5-8. (+) Gotwalt, Helen Louise Miller. **The missing linc.** CAST: 3f, 4m. ACTS: 1. SETTINGS: Living room. PLAYING TIME: 20 min. PLOT: Young Lincoln Stone is interested in reading chemistry and helping people, but those interests seem to get him in trouble. His father, an expert on Abraham Lincoln, has difficulty understanding Linc because he wants model behavior, not realistic boy behavior. When his wife explains he needs a change of view, the father becomes more understanding toward Linc. RECOMMENDATION: This is an interesting examination of a person's outward actions and inner personality. Even though there are few parts, each role is significant and the play would be easily produced. It expresses important points but does not belabor them. ROYALTY: Free to Plays subscribers. SOURCE: Gotwalt, Helen Louise Miller. (1986). Special plays for holidays. Boston, MA: Plays, Inc. SUBJECTS/PLAY TYPE: Lincoln, Abraham; Playlet.

1991. 7-10. (+) Kehret, Peg. **Missing Mandy.** CAST: Su. ACTS: 1. SETTINGS: None. PLAYING TIME: NA. PLOT: The trauma of child abuse, as seen through the eyes of the abused girl's closest friend, is revealed in the bewilderment and feelings of hopelessness on the part of all involved. Themes are carefully portrayed in a style that does not pretend to provide solutions or compromise the privacy of one's innermost thoughts. RECOMMENDATION: This would provoke thoughtfulness in a young audience, but it appears that empathy is the best that can be expected. There is no reassurance or guidance, but if understanding is the goal, the play is worthwhile. ROYALTY: NA. SOURCE: Kehret, Peg. (1986). Winning monologs for young actors. Colorado Springs, CO: Meriwether Pub. SUBJECTS/PLAY TYPE: Child Abuse; Monologue.

1992. 9-12*. (+) Mitgang, Herbert. **Mister Lincoln.** CAST: 1m. ACTS: 2. SETTINGS: None. PLAYING TIME: NA. PLOT: This one man play dramatizes several important events in the life of Abraham Lincoln. It begins with Mr. Lincoln recollecting the moment of his assassination, and moves to his memories of youth and young adulthood. RECOMMENDATION: This excellent play will be best appreciated by those who are familiar with Lincoln's life. ROYALTY: $60. SOURCE: Mitgang, Herbert. (1982). Mr. Lincoln. Chicago, IL: Dramatic Pub. Co. SUBJECTS/PLAY TYPE: Lincoln, Abraham; Drama.

1993. 7-12. (+) Young, Alida. **The misunderstood witch.** CAST: 1f. ACTS: 1. SETTINGS: Cottage. PLAYING TIME: NA. PLOT: The witch of Hansel and Gretel tells the real story behind the folk tale. She actually wanted to get rid of the kids, but they wanted to stay and eat the house. RECOMMENDATION: This delightful monologue will charm older audiences and would make an excellent warm up for a full length presentation. ROYALTY: Free to Plays subscribers. SOURCE: Young, Alida. (1978, October). The misunderstood witch. Plays: The Drama Magazine for Young People, pp. 78-80. SUBJECTS/PLAY TYPE: Folk Tales, Germany; Witches; Monologue.

1994. 10-12. (+) Donoghue, Simon J. & Manera, Nancy. **Mixed nuts.** CAST: 5f, 3m. ACTS: 1. SETTINGS: Living room. PLAYING TIME: NA. PLOT: A young author from Dayton, Ohio goes to New York to find his fortune. He winds up in a cheap apartment with other young artists: an actor who takes only fruit and vegetable parts, a dancer who considers herself a descendant of the Russian royal family, and a smart mouthed young actress from a very ethnic Italian family. He falls in love with the actress and she falls in love with him. RECOMMENDATION: Hilarious from the opening scene, the romance which develops is wholesome and delightful, and the staging is uncomplicated. ROYALTY: $35. SOURCE: Donoghue, Simon J. & Manera, Nancy. (1983). Mixed nuts. Woodstock, IL: The Dramatic Pub. Co. SUBJECTS/PLAY TYPE: New York City; Artists; Romances; Comedy.

1995. 1-6. (+) Norton, Lottie Tresner. **The mixed up year.** CAST: 3f, 3m, 18u. ACTS: 1. SETTINGS: Bare stage. PLAYING TIME: 15 min. PLOT: Characters representing the months of the year cannot get into their correct order. The March wind blows them into the proper sequence and the curtain falls to "Auld Lang Syne." RECOMMENDATION: The personification of the months is conveyed well within the text of the play. ROYALTY: Free to Plays subscribers. SOURCE: Norton, Lottie Tresner. (1978, January). The mixed up year. Plays: The Drama Magazine for Young People, pp. 39-42. SUBJECTS/PLAY TYPE: Calender; Months; Playlet.

1996. 7-9. (+) Thane, Adele. (Melville, Herman) **Moby Dick.** (Moby Dick.) CAST: 13m. ACTS: 1. SETTINGS: Ship. PLAYING TIME: NA. PLOT: Ishmael ships out on the whaler Pequod from Nantucket. Captain Ahab is obsessed with hunting and killing Moby Dick, the white whale who bit Ahab's leg off on a previous trip. Ahab succeeds in killing the whale, but in doing so, is caught by the harpoon line and is himself killed. RECOMMENDATION: This adaptation strips the novel to its most exciting and action packed passages, while retaining the original flavor. The entire plot is neatly summarized and the chapters of the original novel in which Melville explained his theories of the origin of whales and how they fit into the animal kingdom are excluded. ROYALTY: Free to Plays subscribers. SOURCE: Thane, Adele. (1978, January). Moby Dick. Plays: The Drama Magazine for Young People, pp. 70-80. SUBJECTS/PLAY TYPE: Adventure; Whales; Adaptation.

1997. 5-9. (+) Murray, John. **Model plane.** CAST: 1m. ACTS: 1. SETTINGS: None. PLAYING TIME: NA. PLOT: George tries to be a good father to his son by flying a model plane with him, but he refuses to allow the boy to have a turn. RECOMMENDATION: The ironic humor and the immature actions of the father will allow the audience to chuckle about the familiarity of the whole situation. ROYALTY: None. SOURCE: Murray, John. (1982). Modern monologues for young people. Boston, MA: Plays, Inc. SUBJECTS/PLAY TYPE: Fathers; Monologue.

1998. 7-9. (+) Hollingsworth, Leslie. (Perrault, Charles) **A modern Cinderella.** (Cinderella) CAST: 5f, 1m. ACTS: 1. SETTINGS: Bedroom. PLAYING TIME: 25 min. PLOT: Cindy goes to the ball when her godmother shows her how to behave beautifully. She wins the rich man and gets her stepsisters dates with his friends. RECOMMENDATION: The magic is gone, but the lesson about inner beauty is laced with comedy and modern attitudes. ROYALTY: Free to Plays subscribers. SOURCE: Hollingsworth, Leslie. (1988, October). A modern Cinderella. Plays: The Drama Magazine for Young People, pp. 1-11. SUBJECTS/PLAY TYPE: Stepsisters; Balls; Folk Tales, France; Adaptation.

1999. 8-12. (+) Priore, Frank V. **The modernization of Mother Goose.** CAST: 3f, 1m, 3u. ACTS: 1. SETTINGS: Living room. PLAYING TIME: 15 min. PLOT: Miss Muffet, Jack Be Nimble, and the Old Woman Who Lived in a Shoe ask Mother Goose to modernize her nursery rhymes. Miss Muffet wants to sit on a recliner and be addressed as Ms., Jack wants a flashlight, etc. But during a press conference, they realize that with modernization comes modern problems (i.e., mortgages). They decide to stick with the old. RECOMMENDATION: This cleverly demonstrates how sometimes older is better, as the witty nursery rhyme favorites bring back pleasant memories for a group who otherwise wouldn't be "caught dead" with them. ROYALTY: Free to Plays subscribers. SOURCE: Piore, Frank. (1982, May). The modernization of Mother Goose. Plays: The Drama Magazine for Young People, pp. 33-38. SUBJECTS/PLAY TYPE: Mother Goose; Nursery Rhymes; Comedy; Farce.

2000. 2-5. (+) Boiko, Claire. **Mollie and the invisible giant.** (Molly Whuppie and the two-faced giant) CAST: 9f, 15m, 1u. ACTS: 1. SETTINGS: Throne room; dining room; cottage. PLAYING TIME: 25 min. PLOT: In an English

village, no one can tame the invisible giant because the royal princes are cowards. The king sends his herald out to find a brave person. The herald brings Mollie Whuppie, who tames the giant. As her reward, Mollie and her sisters marry the three princes and live happily ever after. RECOMMENDATION: Mollie is aggressive, deter-mined, and skillful. She will win the hearts of her young audience. ROYALTY: Free to Plays subscribers. SOURCE: Boiko, Claire. (1977, November). Mollie and the invisible giant. Plays: The Drama Magazine for Young people, pp. 43-50. SUBJECTS/PLAY TYPE: Folk Tales, England; Giants; Adaptation.

2001. 5-9. (+) Brown, Joella. **Molly Whuppie.** (Molly Whuppie and the two-faced giant.) CAST: 8f, 4m. ACTS: 4. SETTINGS: Back yard; throne room. PLAYING TIME: NA. PLOT: As she sleeps, a timid young girl dreams about Molly Whuppie who is also afraid of life and people. In the young girl's dream, Molly Whuppie is forced by the neighborhood bully to try to steal the horrible neighbor man's glasses, pipe, and ring. Failing to get all three, the bully chases her. The neighbor man's bellowing wakens her, but not until the bully has been punished. The young girl no longer needs to hide from people and responsibility. RECOMMENDATION: Although very freely adapted from the original, this might be fun for younger children (especially the dream sequence). Its music and unusual staging make it more appropriate for production by older adolescents. Some of the language from the original has been retained and would have to be explained before hand. ROYALTY: NA. SOURCE: Brown, Joella. (1979). Molly Whuppie. Rowayton, CT: New Plays, Inc. SUBJECTS/PLAY TYPE: Bravery; Responsibility; Musical; Adaptation.

2002. 4-8. (+) Kehret, Peg. **Mom and Dad don't love each other any more.** CAST: 1u. ACTS: 1. SETTINGS: None. PLAYING TIME: NA. PLOT: A youngster puzzles over the reasons for his/her parents' divorce. RECOMMENDATION: Many of a child's concerns about divorce are outlined. ROYALTY: NA. SOURCE: Kehret, Peg. (1986). Winning monologs for young actors. Colorado Springs, CO: Meriwether Pub. SUBJECTS/PLAY TYPE: Divorce; Monologue.

2003. 8-12. (+) Kennedy, Eddie. **A moment in time.** CAST: 4f, 3m. ACTS: 1. SETTINGS: Waiting room. PLAYING TIME: NA. PLOT: A teenage boy dies after a bad car accident. Or was it an accident? His twin sister realizes her brother's behavior prior to the accident is similar to the behavior of her friend's brother, who committed suicide two years earler. The issue of suicide is left dangling. RECOMMENDATION: This carries an important message about teenage suicide prevention. It could be a starting point for classroom discussion on constructive ways of effectively dealing with the problems and frustrations of growing up. The dialogue is both natural and moving, and the family relations portrayed are very real. ROYALTY: $20. SOURCE: Kennedy, Eddie. (1986). A moment in time. Woodstock, IL: Dramatic Pub. Co. SUBJECTS/PLAY TYPE: Suicide; Death; Family Relations; Drama.

2004. 9-12. (+) Miller, Howard. **Moments. CAST:** 1f, 1m, Su. **ACTS:** 1. **SETTINGS:** Bare stage, props. **PLAYING TIME:** NA. **PLOT:** A man and a woman meet on a streetcar and for a few moments share a magical and intimate conversation which changes the man's outlook on life from resignation to hope. The play is largely pantomime and the dramatic action is conveyed, for the most part, nonverbally. **RECOMMENDATION:** The advanced skill necessary to do justice to the dramatic action here may make it a difficult presentation for high school students. However, it will elicit the best from gifted students. **ROYALTY:** $15. **SOURCE:** Miller, Howard. (1979). Moments. Boston, MA: Baker's Plays. **SUBJECTS/PLAY TYPE:** Love; Loneliness; Pessimism/Optimism; Skit.

2005. 10-12. (+) Rudolph, Grace. **Moms. CAST:** 4f, 1m. **ACTS:** 1. **SETTINGS:** Kitchen. **PLAYING TIME:** NA. **PLOT:** Two elderly widows, Pauline and Katherine, live with Katherine's middle aged daughter and two teenagers. The two older women decide to live together in Pauline's house to escape the noisy, chaotic house. **RECOMMENDATION:** Although written to be performed by elderly actors, high school actors should also be able to produce this short drama, possibly as an opening to a discussion on the needs of the elderly. **ROYALTY:** $10. **SOURCE:** Rudolph, Grace. (1984). Elders' statements: One-act plays and monologues. Boston, MA: Baker's Plays. **SUBJECTS/PLAY TYPE:** Family; Aging; Drama.

2006. 10-12. (-) Hearn, Sneed. **Money nutties. CAST:** 3f, 3m. **ACTS:** 1. **SETTINGS:** Living room. **PLAYING TIME:** NA. **PLOT:** Rich Lotta throws a birthday party for Snookums, a spoiled brat. The guests' main interests are swindling Lotta and each other out of as much money as possible. In the end several guests are revealed as secret agents who proceed to arrest each other for being con-artists. **RECOMMENDATION:** This almost plotless play depends on puns, over used one liners, and associations with well known entertainers. The result is, at best, silly. The dialogue is more likely to elicit groans or boredom than laughter. **ROYALTY:** $10. **SOURCE:** Hearn, Sneed. (1979). Money nutties. Boston, MA: Baker's Plays. **SUBJECTS/PLAY TYPE:** Swindlers and Swindling; Con-artists; Comedy.

2007. 10-12. (+) Kelly, Tim & Sharkey, Jack. **Money, power, murder, lust, revenge, and marvelous clothes. CAST:** 8f, 6m, Su. **ACTS:** 2. **SETTINGS:** Airline terminal; farmyard; parlor; doctor's office; restaurant; garden. **PLAYING TIME:** NA. **PLOT:** This musical parody of prime time soap opera follows the astonishing career of a homely girl, who, after being humiliated by a group of rich children, goes on to achieve beauty, fame, wealth, power, and most of all, revenge. A series of ridiculous plot twists culminate in a courtroom scene, a showdown between heroine and villainess, and revelation of the heroine's true love. **RECOMMENDATION:** Audiences should enjoy identifying the many soap opera conventions and characterizations that are lampooned, including unnecessary costume changes, confusing switches of identity, a case of amnesia, and an evil twin. A production

of this play could be very successful with an uninhibited cast willing to really "ham it up." **ROYALTY:** $75. **SOURCE:** Kelly, Tim & Sharkey, Jack. (1985). Money, power, murder, lust, revenge and marvelous clothes. Boston, MA: Baker's Plays. **SUBJECTS/PLAY TYPE:** Soap Opera; Satire; Comedy; Musical.

2008. K-3. (+) Read, Sylvia. **Monkey. CAST:** 1u. **ACTS:** 1. **SETTINGS:** None. **PLAYING TIME:** NA. **PLOT:** A funny poem, this snickers at the idea of meeting a monkey on the street. **RECOMMENDATION:** Amusing on its own, this can also be used with the others arranged together as "Animal Antics." **ROYALTY:** NA. **SOURCE:** Bauer, Caroline Feller. (1987). Presenting reader's theater: Plays and poems to read aloud. New York, NY: H.W. Wilson. **SUBJECTS/PLAY TYPE:** Monkeys; Reader's Theater.

2009. K-3. (+) Holder, Julie. **The monkey and you. CAST:** 1u. **ACTS:** 1. **SETTINGS:** None. **PLAYING TIME:** NA. **PLOT:** A monkey in the zoo wonders who throws peanuts to humans. **RECOMMENDATION:** Children will enjoy presenting this short poem for their parents, perhaps in combination with Bauer's other "Animal Antics." **ROYALTY:** NA. **SOURCE:** Bauer, Caroline Feller. (1987). Presenting reader's theater: Plays and poems to read aloud. New York, NY: H.W. Wilson. **SUBJECTS/PLAY TYPE:** Monkeys; Zoo; Reader's Theater.

2010. 1-8. (+) Jones, Charles. (Ch'eng-en, Wu) **Monkey monkey: The marvelous adventures of the magical Monkey King. (Monkey.) CAST:** 2f, 6m, 9u. **ACTS:** 1. **SETTINGS:** Playground. **PLAYING TIME:** NA. **PLOT:** A magical monkey, born from a stone, meets dragons, demons, and the King of Death. Because of his mischievous nature, he is banished from this world to the heavens. **RECOMMENDATION:** Based on stories from a 16th century novel, the play captures the feeling of the folk heritage of Southeast Asia. With vivid characters, bright colorful costumes, and fast action, play would be enjoyable for elementary school children, although it would be best produced by older children (because of the agility needed on the monkey bars). **ROYALTY:** $35. **SOURCE:** Jones, Charles. (1986). Monkey, monkey: The adventures of the magical Monkey King. New Orleans, LA: Anchorage Press. **SUBJECTS/PLAY TYPE:** Folk Tales, Southeast Asia; Adaptation.

2011. 1-7. (+) Winther, Barbara. **The monkey without a tail. CAST:** 1f, 2m, Su. **ACTS:** 1. **SETTINGS:** Forest; throne room. **PLAYING TIME:** 20 min. **PLOT:** A king offers a fortune for the best honey in the realm and promises punishment for those who offer him mediocre honey. A monkey offers to help a poor man gain the favor of the king by making the king think the poor man's honey is the best. The poor man becomes rich and the monkey is rewarded for his own cleverness. **RECOMMENDATION:** This play is weakened somewhat by the playwright's attempt to make a good character out of Ethiopia's traditionally villainous "trickster" monkey. In addition, the dialogue is verbose for young actors and laden with ethnic flavored humor that falls flat. However, the merits of the play outweigh its faults; it offers a wonderful opportunity for actor/audience comedy and verbal improvisation. ROYALTY: Free for amateur performance. SOURCE: Winther, Barbara. (1976). Plays from folktales of Africa and Asia. Boston, MA: Plays, Inc. SUBJECTS/PLAY TYPE: Folk Tales, Africa; Playlet.

2012. 7-10. (+) Dexter, Harriet. (Jacobs, W. W) **The monkey's paw.** (The monkey's paw.) CAST: 1f, 4m. ACTS: 1. SETTINGS: Living room. PLAYING TIME: 25 min. PLOT: The Whites acquire a magical monkey's paw and learn that "those who interfere with fate do so to their sorrow." Mr. White wishes for 200 pounds to pay off the mortgage. He gets it after his son, Herbert is killed on the job. They wish for Herbert to be alive again, and Herbert arrives at the door, alive but still with his fatal injury. The play climaxes with Mr. White shouting his third wish: that Herbert return to his grave to remain in peace. RECOMMENDATION: This retains the mood of the original. The characters and their emotions are drawn well. Good for a literature class which has read the original or for a drama class performance. Production notes call for Victorian attire, but nothing elaborate is required. ROYALTY: Free to Plays subscribers. SOURCE: Dexter, Harriet. (1983, April). The monkey's paw. Plays: The Drama Magazine for Young People, pp. 73-80. SUBJECTS/PLAY TYPE: Suspense; Mystery; Horror; Adaptation.

2013. 6-8. (+) Dias, Earl J. **The monster of the moors.** CAST: 2f, 5m. ACTS: 1. SETTINGS: Parlor. PLAYING TIME: 30 min. PLOT: For 20 years, Sir Andrew has hidden the fact that he created a monster that went berserk and allegedly broke into the British Museum. Sir Andrew had been blackmailed at the time by the only "witness" to the monster's crime, Fitzmaurice Gregory. Gregory returns to demand that Sir Andrew's daughter, Amanda, marry him in return for his silence. But Basil Cooper, a young Scotland Yard inspector, saves the day when he tricks Gregory into confessing that the monster never entered the museum. RECOMMENDATION: The mystery and suspense and should be entertaining. ROYALTY: Free to Plays subscribers. SOURCE: Dias, Earl J. (1981, February). The monster of the moors. Plays: The Drama Magazine for Young People, pp. 13-21. SUBJECTS/PLAY TYPE: Mystery; Monsters; Playlet.

2014. 1-3. (-) Dennison, George. **Monsters: A one-act play for children to perform for adults.** CAST: 2f, 6u. ACTS: 1. SETTINGS: Bedroom. PLAYING TIME: NA. PLOT: Two little girls think about and experience events that night can bring. RECOMMENDATION: The play has ideas to which children could easily relate. However, children may have difficulty understanding this because events are unrelated, as in a dream. ROYALTY: NA. SOURCE: Cott, Jonathan & Gimbel, Mary (Eds.). (1980). Wonders: Writings and drawings for the child in us all. New York, NY: Summit Press. SUBJECTS/PLAY TYPE: Fantasy; Fears; Comedy.

2015. K-6. (-) Korty, Carol. **Moon shot.** CAST: 5u. ACTS: 1. SETTINGS: Bare stage. PLAYING TIME: NA. PLOT: In a comedy of errors, a would be astronaut faints before her ship takes off. When she regains consciousness,

she thinks that she has landed on the moon and mistakes her friends for moon people. After conversing with them, she closes the ship door, returns to "earth" and tells her friends all about her trip. RECOMMENDATION: Audiences will not appreciate the absurdity of the mistaken identities here, nor will they identify with a plot that talks about the first rocket to the moon. ROYALTY: None. SOURCE: Korty, Carol. (1977). Silly soup: Ten zany plays. New York, NY: Charles Scribner's Sons. SUBJECTS/PLAY TYPE: Moon; Astronaut; Comedy.

2016. 10-12. (+) Sodaro, Craig. **Moongirl.** CAST: 6f, 4m. ACTS: 2. SETTINGS: Living room. PLAYING TIME: NA. PLOT: Kathy, 18, is lured into a cult. Kathy's mother and grandparents try to get her back. When all police and family attempts fail, Kathy's mother contacts a seasoned deprogrammer. When Kathy is ordered by the cult leader to kill her mother she finally rejects the cult. Parent and child reconcile and reevaluate their relationship to avoid future problems. RECOMMENDATION: The play invites inquiry into a teenager's psychological needs and susceptibility to cult influence. It also explores the responsibility of parents for their children. ROYALTY: NA. SOURCE: Sodaro, Craig. (1987). Moongirl. Woodstock, IL: Dramatic Pub. Co. SUBJECTS/PLAY TYPE: Cults; Mind Control; Family; Drama.

2017. 4-6. (-) Henderson, Nancy. **Moonlife 2069.** CAST: 7f, 6m. ACTS: 1. SETTINGS: Underground building; moon surface. PLAYING TIME: 15 min. PLOT: A group of fifth and sixth graders visit the moon to celebrate the centennial of the first moon landing. RECOMMENDATION: Production will present some difficulties with props and staging, and a serious subplot interferes with the overall playful tone. ROYALTY: Permission required if performed outside of the classroom. SOURCE: Henderson, Nancy. (1978). Celebrate America: A baker's dozen of plays. New York, NY: Julian Messner. SUBJECTS/PLAY TYPE: Moon; Space Travel; Science Fiction.

2018. 7-12. (+) Silver, Alf. **More of a family.** CAST: 11f, 10m. ACTS: 1. SETTINGS: Bedroom; living rooms; park, grocery store, foyer. PLAYING TIME: NA. PLOT: Amy, 11, lives with her mother (her parents are separated), but wants a more normal family. She runs away and tries a large family, a small family, an only child family, the children's home, the street people, a family where the children are neglected, and a family where she would have to work to support herself. Disillusioned, she returns home. A reconciliation with her mother and her mother's boyfriend demonstrates the love that they feel for each other. RECOMMENDATION: This nicely poses the question, "what is a normal family," and answers it by saying that a family exists "anytime people make a home together and try to help each other get along." The portrayals of classes of people Amy meets are realistic. Although they reflect the bias of an upper middle class, with a bit of rewriting this could be adapted for presentation to any group. With doubling and tripling of parts, the cast could be minimal. ROYALTY: NA. SOURCE: Doolittle, Joyce. (1984). Eight plays for young people. Edmonton, Canada: NeWest Pub.

SUBJECTS/PLAY TYPE: Family, Single Parent Families; Drama.

2019. 4-7. (+) Gotwalt, Helen Louise Miller. **Mother for mayor. CAST:** 4f, 4m. **ACTS:** 1. **SETTINGS:** Kitchen. **PLAYING TIME:** 30 min. **PLOT:** When Mrs. Webster runs for mayor, her values are tested as she must choose between politics (and hushing up her son's suspension from school) and truth (forcing her son publicly to apologize for his misbehavior). She chooses truth, but is told that truth and politics are not mutually exclusive and that now, more than ever, she should run. **RECOMMENDATION:** This shows women balancing their roles as mothers and working people, without compromising themselves. **ROYALTY:** Free to Plays subscribers. **SOURCE:** Gotwalt, Helen Louise Miller. (1975, May). Mother for mayor. Plays: The Drama Magazine for Young People, pp. 53-64. **SUBJECTS/PLAY TYPE:** Mother's Day; Women's Rights; Playlet.

2020. 7-12. (+) Arthur, Kay. **Mother goes modern. CAST:** 5f, 3m. **ACTS:** 1. **SETTINGS:** Kitchen; dining area; family room. **PLAYING TIME:** 35 min. **PLOT:** The Mackay family changes its relaxed, slightly disorganized lifestyle to impress the efficiency expert in the firm where Ross is employed. Eccentric Aunt Stella can't adjust to the new "high tech" household and causes some laughable and unexpected developments when Dr. Haverstraw, the efficiency expert, comes to dinner. Disaster strikes when all the high tech appliances go haywire, but there is a happy ending when Dr. Haverstraw turns out to be an old fashioned girl at heart. **RECOMMENDATION:** An interesting statement against modernization is made. While very humorous, this could be difficult to stage, due to the number of electrical gadgets needed on stage. **ROYALTY:** Free to Plays subscribers. **SOURCE:** Arthur, Kay. (1984, May). Mother goes modern. Plays: The Drama Magazine for Young People, pp. 10-22. **SUBJECTS/PLAY TYPE:** Modernization; Technology; Comedy.

2021. 1-6*. (+) Hills, Richard. **Mother Goose. CAST:** 6f, 8m, Su. **ACTS:** 2. **SETTINGS:** Village square; palace; ice cavern. **PLAYING TIME:** NA. **PLOT:** In a lively mixture of folk tale and nursery rhyme characters, King Cole's daughter is being married off to the son of the evil Queen of Ice Mountain. In a mad plot involving Tom Piper, Bo-Peep, the golden goose, and Keystone type cops, Tom saves the reluctant bride from being given a heart of ice, breaks all the spells, saves everyone. **RECOMMENDATION:** The lively mix is typical of a British pantomime production, caters to young audiences, and encourages the audience to voice their opinions. The generous mix of humor and sight gags sets a tone of lighthearted fun. This musical is a full scale production with numerous scene changes, lighting effects, costumes, a chorus and dancers. It should be produced by adults. **ROYALTY:** NA. **SOURCE:** Hills, Richard. (n.d.) Mother Goose. Cheshire, England: New Playwrights' Network. **SUBJECTS/PLAY TYPE:** Folk Tale Characters; Nursery Rhyme Characters; Romance; Adventure; Pantomime.

2022. 2-4. (+) Gotwalt, Helen Louise Miller. **The Mother Goose bakeshop. CAST:** 6f, 8m, Su. **ACTS:** 1.

SETTINGS: Bakeshop. **PLAYING TIME:** 10 min. **PLOT:** Three bakers bake a cake and mark it with a "B," but they cannot remember who ordered it. Various nursery rhyme characters visit the shop, but no one claims it. Finally a baker remembers a teacher ordered it for a student's birthday. **RECOMMENDATION:** The nursery rhymes make this easy for children to learn and recite. The play is designed to be used for a student's birthday, however it could also be used for a famous person's birthday (like George Washington). **ROYALTY:** Free to Plays subscribers. **SOURCE:** Gotwalt, Helen Louise Miller. (1960). First plays for children: A collection of little plays for the youngest players. Boston, MA: Plays, Inc. **SUBJECTS/PLAY TYPE:** Nursery Rhyme Characters; Birthdays; Skit.

2023. 3-5. (+) Henry, Ragene. **A mother goose Christmas. CAST:** 5f, 6m, 5u. **ACTS:** 1. **SETTINGS:** Shoe house. **PLAYING TIME:** 15 min. **PLOT:** On Christmas Eve, Mary, who had a little lamb; Peter Peter, the pumpkin eater; and several other nursery rhyme characters discuss the fact that they all seem to lack Christmas spirit. Jill notes how discouraging it must be for the Old Woman in the shoe not to be able to provide Christmas toys and food for her children. They decide to provide these Christmas things for the Old Woman in the shoe. Jack Sprat and his wife are the only two who object. However, the pair sees the joy of giving and decides to help by providing a Christmas tree. The play ends when the children discover their Christmas things and everyone is happy. **RECOMMENDATION:** The familiar characters give away something that belongs to them (i.e., Humpty Dumpty makes an omelette, Peter gives pumpkin seeds, etc.) the audience will be tickled. Familiarity with the nursery rhymes is necessary to fully appreciate this. **ROYALTY:** Free to Plays subscribers. **SOURCE:** Henry, Ragene. (1988, December). A mother goose Christmas. Plays: The Drama Magazine for Young People, pp. 31-33. **SUBJECTS/PLAY TYPE:** Nursery Rhyme Characters; Christmas; Skit.

2024. 1-6. (+) Hamlett, Christina. **Mother Goose Gumshoe. CAST:** 4f, 1m. **ACTS:** 1. **SETTINGS:** Office. **PLAYING TIME:** 10 min. **PLOT:** Detective Scoop Snoopins solves missing persons cases. Mrs. Hubbard hasn't returned since she left to fill her cupboard, and Mrs. Piper can't find Peter or his peck of pickled peppers. **RECOMMENDATION:** This is very funny with deadpan tongue in cheek humor. Children will especially enjoy it if they are familiar with the nursery rhymes. **ROYALTY:** Free to Plays subscribers. **SOURCE:** Hamlett, Christina. (1987, October). Mother Goose Gumshoe. Plays: The Drama Magazine for Young People, pp. 35-38. **SUBJECTS/PLAY TYPE:** Nursery Rhyme Characters; Comedy.

2025. 1-6. (+) Mauro, Robert A. **The Mother Goose Olympics. CAST:** 3f, 5m, 17u. **ACTS:** 1. **SETTINGS:** Stadium. **PLAYING TIME:** 20 min. **PLOT:** Mother Goose characters compete against each others' Olympic records and other athletes in modified Olympic events. The events are based on physical feats performed by characters within the context of well known nursery rhymes. Sportscasters cover the events, interview athletes, and make editorial comments. The play ends with a comical awards ceremony. RECOMMENDATION: The dialogue, the play's best asset, is a mixture of nursery rhymes and comments like those which are typically made by Olympic sportscasters and athletes. The action is continuous. ROYALTY: Free to Plays subscribers. SOURCE: Mauro, Robert A. (1980, January). The Mother Goose Olympics. Plays: The Drama Magazine for Young People, pp. 27-32. SUBJECTS/PLAY TYPE: Nursery Rhyme Characters; Sports; Comedy.

2026. K-6. (+) Boiko, Claire. **Mother Goose's Christmas surprise. CAST:** 6f, 7m. **ACTS:** 1. **SETTINGS:** Living room. **PLAYING TIME:** 20 min. **PLOT:** Major nursery rhyme characters gather at Mother Goose's home for Christmas. They decorate the tree, each contributing what he can, such as Miss Muffet lending spiderwebs and Humpty Dumpty donating sparkling eggs. Santa Claus stops, bringing gifts from children all over the world. Everyone receives an appropriate gift, including Bo Peep, who gets an extra long leash with five collars. RECOMMENDATION: Younger children will be delighted with this Christmas play containing familiar nursery rhyme characters. The plot is simplistic, with humorous puns dusted throughout to add sparkle. Due to the timing required to make the jokes work, this is probably best left to upper elementary aged actors. ROYALTY: None. SOURCE: Boiko, Claire. (1985). Children's plays for creative actors. Boston, MA: Plays, Inc. SUBJECTS/PLAY TYPE: Nursery Rhyme Characters; Christmas; Comedy.

2027. 6-12*. (+) Zeder, Suzan. **Mother Hicks. CAST:** 4f, 4m, Su. **ACTS:** 2. **SETTINGS:** Bare stage, props; wagon. **PLAYING TIME:** NA. **PLOT:** Set during the Depression, this is the story of three people. Mother Hicks is called a witch by the people of a small Midwestern town, and blamed for their illnesses and difficulties. Tuc, a deaf mute, works in town and lives with Mother Hicks. He narrates in sign language, with a chorus (the extras) to interpret for him. Girl, 13 and an orphan, searches for an identity, a name, and a permanent home. With no magic but her healing skills and country wisdom, Mother Hicks leads Girl to self acceptance and growth. RECOMMENDATION: The characters are so clearly portrayed they linger in memory. The plot is truthful and realistic, yet hopeful. Production requires a talented cast and dedication to good theater. The power of this makes it worth every minute of work put into it. ROYALTY: $35. SOURCE: Zeder, Suzan. (1986). Mother Hicks. New Orleans, LA: Anchorage Press, Inc. SUBJECTS/PLAY TYPE: Orphans; Deafness; Sign Language; Drama.

2028. 6-8. (+) Fisher, Aileen. **Mother of Thanksgiving. CAST:** 6f, 7m, 2u. **ACTS:** 1. **SETTINGS:** Bare stage. **PLAYING TIME:** NA. **PLOT:** This is the story of Mrs. Sarah Josepha Hale, the woman who was responsible for convincing Abraham Lincoln to declare a national day of Thanksgiving. RECOMMENDATION: Since all the parts are "read" before a mock microphone, the play can be put on by a much younger group of children than if the parts had to be memorized. ROYALTY: Free to Plays subscribers. SOURCE: Fisher, Aileen. (1986). Holiday

programs for boys and girls. Boston, MA: Plays, Inc. SUBJECTS/PLAY TYPE: Thanksgiving; Radio Play.

2029. 7-12. (-) Murray, John. **Mother of the bride. CAST:** 1f. **ACTS:** 1. **SETTINGS:** Bare stage. **PLAYING TIME:** NA. **PLOT:** A nervous mother of the bride, waiting for the guests to arrive, chatters to her husband about various wedding and reception details, and is shocked to see the mother of the groom appear in a dress identical to her own. RECOMMENDATION: The humor is weak. Since it lacks the outrageousness necessary to carry the plot; the whole sketch falls flat. ROYALTY: None. SOURCE: Murray, John. (1982). Modern monologues for young people. Boston, MA: Plays, Inc. SUBJECTS/PLAY TYPE: Weddings; Monologue.

2030. K-6. (+) Hark, Mildred & McQueen, Noel. **Mother saves her day. CAST:** 3f, 3m. **ACTS:** 1. **SETTINGS:** Living room. **PLAYING TIME:** 20 min. **PLOT:** Mother's Day approaches and five children combine allowances to buy a silver picture frame to hold a photo of their father. Much to their dismay, the proofs are not fit for framing. Mother saves the day when she presents a handsome looking enlarged photo of her husband that was taken by a friend. RECOMMENDATION: Anyone who has experienced shopping for Mother's Day can relate to the scenario in this love filled play. ROYALTY: Free to Plays subscribers. SOURCE: Hark, Mildred & McQueen, Noel. (1985, May). Mother saves her day. Plays: The Drama Magazine for Young People, pp. 39-44. SUBJECTS/PLAY TYPE: Family; Mother's Day; Comedy.

2031. 6-10. (+) McQueen, Noel. **Mother's choice. CAST:** 3f, 2m. **ACTS:** 1. **SETTINGS:** Living room. **PLAYING TIME:** 20 min. **PLOT:** Children try to decide what to give Mom for Mother's Day. They learn that their father has already purchased a washing machine, which causes a stir among the children who feel that the gift is much too practical. They decide that a gift certificate for the price of the washer would be more appropriate. Mother is thrilled with the gift certificate because it allows her to buy the washing machine she wants. RECOMMENDATION: The stereotyping of the mother's role as martyr is a detraction from an otherwise successful script. ROYALTY: Free to Plays subscribers. SOURCE: McQueen, Noel. (1981, May). Mother's choice. Plays: The Drama Magazine for Young People, pp. 49-57. SUBJECTS/PLAY TYPE: Family; Mother's Day; Playlet.

2032. 4-8. (+) Fisher, Aileen. **Mother's Day off and on. CAST:** 3f, 2m. **ACTS:** 1. **SETTINGS:** Dining room; kitchen. **PLAYING TIME:** NA. **PLOT:** A father and his three children plan to give mother a day off as a special gift for Mother's Day. However, they find the gift is a little more than they can handle and begin to appreciate all the things mother does for them. RECOMMENDATION: The play falls short in the plot area, but has real value as a social studies activity to initiate a unit on family life with emphasis on the role of the mother in a family. The father is stereotyped as a kitchen Klutz. A unique characteristic is that all speaking parts are in simple rhyme and easily learned. ROYALTY: None. SOURCE: Fisher, Aileen.

(1986). Holiday programs for boys and girls. Boston, MA: Plays, Inc. SUBJECTS/PLAY TYPE: Family; Mother's Day; Comedy.

2033. K-7. (+) Wohlers, Linell. **Mother's daze.** CAST: 8f, 5m, Su. ACTS: 1. SETTINGS: Living room. PLAYING TIME: 20 min. PLOT: Mrs. Clodhopper, alias the Old Woman in the Shoe, is discouraged because the shoe needs repair. As Mother's Day approaches, the children want to get their mother gifts but have no money. Mother gets her presents when Jack Spratt agrees to repair the shoe for free; Mary Contrary brings flowers; the children clean the house and yard and serve breakfast in bed; and Little Boy Blue and the other music students serenade Mrs. Clodhopper for Mother's Day. RECOMMENDATION: The use of familiar nursery rhyme characters in a new setting will delight those who know the originals. The cast can be expanded to include as many as the director wishes. ROYALTY: Free to Plays subscribers. SOURCE: Wohlers, Linell. (1988, May). Mother's daze. Plays: The Drama Magazine for Young People, pp. 34-48. SUBJECTS/PLAY TYPE: Nursery Rhyme Characters; Mother's Day; Playlet.

2034. 7-12. (+) Bayer, Harold. **Motley tales: A collection of folk and fairy tales with music.** CAST: 7f, 14m, Su. ACTS: 4. SETTINGS: Bare stage; basement; palaces; town square; forest. PLAYING TIME: NA. PLOT: Four tales are told. In "Lazy Jack," a lazy lout wins the hand of a beautiful, mute princess when his ridiculous antics make her laugh and speak for the first time. "The Emperor's New Clothes" is modernized, as two con-artists make a living by making people buy their imaginary goods and finally strike it rich by tailoring new "clothes" for the emperor. In "The Three Sillies," a young man agrees to marry a silly young woman if he can find three people sillier than she and her parents. Finally, in "King Thrushbeard," a clever king tricks a too proud princess into marriage and teaches her a lesson in humility. RECOMMENDATION: Each tale is connected to the others via a minstrel narrator, who must be able to sing as he introduces each piece and appears within them. ROYALTY: NA. SOURCE: Bayer, Harold. (1982). Motley tales: A collection of folk and fairy tales with music. Boston, MA: Baker's Plays. SUBJECTS/PLAY TYPE: Folk Tales, England; Folk Tales, Denmark; Folk Tales, Germany; Adaptation.

2035. 5-8. (+) Gotwalt, Helen Louise Miller. **The Mount Vernon cricket.** CAST: 5f, 5m. ACTS: 1. SETTINGS: Living room. PLAYING TIME: 25 min. PLOT: Laurel Bailey believes that she has a stool carved by George Washington because it is cherry and has "initials" G.W. carved on a leg. She believes it has magical power because everyone who sits on it feels compelled to tell the truth. Even after she learns a distant cousin carved it, Laura still feels the stool's magic has kept a real estate agent from lying to her parents about a house. RECOMMENDATION: The play indirectly considers the character of George Washington, but primarily deals with the issue of truthfulness. ROYALTY: Free to Plays subscribers. SOURCE: Gotwalt, Helen Louise Miller. (1986). Special plays for holidays. Boston, MA: Plays, Inc.

SUBJECTS/PLAY TYPE: Washington, George; Truthfulness; Drama.

2036. 6-9. (+) Dias, Earl J. **Mountain madness.** CAST: 7f, 7m. ACTS: 1. SETTINGS: Log cabin. PLAYING TIME: 35 min. PLOT: A movie director looking for the perfect location to shoot his next picture, goes into the hills to meet the Crumm family. To convince him to use their home, the actually sophisticated family members become typical hillbillies, including feuding with another family. RECOMMENDATION: This fun comedy along the lines of Li'l Abner, cleverly points out the folly of stereotyping as it also shows the foibles of Hollywood. ROYALTY: Free to Plays subscribers. SOURCE: Dias, Earl J. (1989, January/February). Mountain madness. Plays: The Drama Magazine for Young People, pp. 11- 20. SUBJECTS/PLAY TYPE: Greed; Stereotyping; Hollywood; Comedy.

2037. 2-5. (+) Gotwalt, Helen Louise Miller. **The mouse that soared.** CAST: 2f, 4m, 12u. ACTS: 1. SETTINGS: Meadow. PLAYING TIME: 20 min. PLOT: Orvie, a mouse, proves that mice can be brave by volunteering to be launched into space by the Junior Science Club. His bravery causes the other mice to summon their own courage so that they can take the bell from Thomas Cat and present it to Orvie as an award. The play concludes with a celebration of Orvie's bravery and the presentation of the bell. RECOMMENDATION: The world's first moustronaut is a delightful character, and the familiar nursery rhymes and tunes encourage audience participation. ROYALTY: Free to Plays subscribers. SOURCE: Gottwalt, Helen Louise Miller. (1987, March). The mouse that soared. Plays: The Drama Magazine for Young People, pp. 47-52. SUBJECTS/PLAY TYPE: Space; Mice; Comedy.

2038. 10-12. (+) Christie, Agatha. **The mousetrap.** CAST: 3f, 5m. ACTS: 2. SETTINGS: Living room. PLAYING TIME: NA. PLOT: Giles and Mollie Ralston open a guest house. Mrs. Boyle, a guest, is murdered, and an investigation ensues. The murderer is apprehended through a reenactment of the crime. RECOMMENDATION: The murderer is the least likely suspect, yet all characters have a motive. The play moves quickly and smoothly to the climax. Tension builds as characters realize that no one is safe from the murderer and the audience will be guessing along with the characters. ROYALTY: $50. SOURCE: Christie, Agatha. (1954). The mousetrap. New York, NY: Samuel French. SUBJECTS/PLAY TYPE: Murder; Mystery.

2039. 4-8. (+) Sawyer-Young, Kat. **Movie.** CAST: 2f. ACTS: 1. SETTINGS: Movie theater. PLAYING TIME: NA. PLOT: Common problems of attending movies, including not sitting in front or having to sit behind a big body, are discussed by two friends. As the scene ends, the friends pantomime their reactions to a horror film. RECOMMENDATION: Anyone who has ever gone to see a movie can identify with these two girls. They will also find the horror movie section enjoyable and can perhaps relate their own reactions to this type of movie. ROYALTY: NA. SOURCE: Sawyer-Young, Kat. (1986). Contemporary scenes for contemporary kids. Boston, MA:

Baker's Plays. **SUBJECTS/PLAY TYPE:** Movies; Pantomime; Scene.

2040. 7-12. (+) Murray, John. **Moving day. CAST:** 1f. **ACTS:** 1. **SETTINGS:** Bare stage. **PLAYING TIME:** NA. **PLOT:** Over the phone, a woman describes the disastrous events of moving day to her husband, concluding with a cheerful admonition not to worry. **RECOMMENDATION:** While Myra is a caricature, the disasters she relates so cheerfully and obliquely are fairly amusing. Not strong enough to stand on its own as a main entertainment event, this should couple well with other short skits. **ROYALTY:** None. **SOURCE:** Murray, John. (1982). Modern monologues for young people. Boston, MA: Plays, Inc. **SUBJECTS/PLAY TYPE:** Comedy; Moving; Monologue.

2041. 4-7. (+) Kehret, Peg. **Mr. Bartholomew. CAST:** 1f. **ACTS:** 1. **SETTINGS:** None. **PLAYING TIME:** NA. **PLOT:** A little girl gets a cat. The companionship that develops, the human traits assigned to the cat, and the girl's worries about the cat's sickness and death in the distant future, are all treated with sensitivity. **RECOMMENDATION:** An unexpected, premature death of the cat, and the feelings of loss and loneliness that accompany it, are gently handled. **ROYALTY:** NA. **SOURCE:** Kehret, Peg. (1986). Winning monologs for young actors. Colorado Springs, CO: Meriwether Pub. **SUBJECTS/PLAY TYPE:** Death; Monologue.

2042. 1-6. (+) Reay, Nina Butler. **Mr. Bates goes to the polls. CAST:** 1f, 2m, Su. **ACTS:** 1. **SETTINGS:** Porch. **PLAYING TIME:** 10 min. **PLOT:** Mr. Bates, who refuses to recognize the importance of a single vote, experiences a mind changing dream in which chickens "flock" to the polls to deprive him of his right to eat fried chicken. He awakes from the dream a concerned citizen, and he heads to the polls to perform his duty. **RECOMMENDATION:** Excellent for an election year, this is a good tool for teaching social studies to the elementary grades, as Mr. Bates's humorous dream will amuse and enlighten them. **ROYALTY:** Free to Plays subscribers. **SOURCE:** Reay, Nina Butler. (1984, November). Mr. Bates goes to the polls. Plays: The Drama Magazine for Young People, pp. 35-37. **SUBJECTS/PLAY TYPE:** Voting; Skit.

2043. 7-12. (+) Murray, John. **Mr. Filbert's claim to fame. CAST:** 6f, 6m, 10u. **ACTS:** 1. **SETTINGS:** Office. **PLAYING TIME:** 25 min. **PLOT:** Bill, a reporter, looks for a human interest story. He sees Filbert get his hand stuck in a mailbox. Bill calls the popular T.V. anchorwoman for the area, and she arrives with camera crew and equipment. As Filbert's boss arrives and threatens to fire him, Filbert's wife inserts a hairpin into the screw on the mailbox, and frees him. The story ends happily. **RECOMMENDATION:** The playful jab at reporters as sensationalists in search of the over dramatic and sentimental is familiar to all. **ROYALTY:** Free to Plays subscribers. **SOURCE:** Murray, John. (1981, April). Mr. Filbert's claim to fame. Plays: The Drama Magazine for Young People, pp. 11-20. **SUBJECTS/PLAY TYPE:** Greed; Media; Comedy.

2044. K-3*. (+) Way, Brian. **Mr. Grump and the clown. CAST:** 2f, 2m, 4u. **ACTS:** 1. **SETTINGS:** Bare stage. **PLAYING TIME:** 50 min. **PLOT:** Jenny tells the story of a clown who tries in vain to make Mr. Grump (the disguised king) laugh. Mr. Grump becomes angry, takes all of the clown's laughter, and banishes him. Marianda realizes the clown is the only one who can break the evil spell of grumpiness that was placed on her father and his kingdom many years ago. Armed with magic powder, Clown and Marianda break the evil spell. The king is so grateful that he returns the gift of laughter to Clown, making the kingdom happy once again. **RECOMMENDATION:** Recommended for an audience of 200 or less in order to maintain control, this wonderful tale charmingly uses audience participation (to make the magic powder, to melt an icy door, and to supply sound effects), and a narrator to help the children make transitions between scenes. It must be performed by adults or mature young adults. **ROYALTY:** $20. **SOURCE:** Way, Brian. (1977). Mr. Grump and the clown. Boston, MA: Baker's Plays. **SUBJECTS/PLAY TYPE:** Comedy; Clowns; Laughter; Participation Play.

2045. K-3. (+) Korty, Carol. **Mr. Hare takes Mr. Leopard for a ride. CAST:** 1f, 2m. **ACTS:** 1. **SETTINGS:** Burrow; lair. **PLAYING TIME:** NA. **PLOT:** Hare, tired of Mr. Leopard's rudeness, decides to teach him a lesson by telling Mrs. Leopard that before the end of the day he will ride Mr. Leopard like a horse. Leopard hears of the boast and storms over to Hare's burrow to punish him. Mr. Hare claims no knowledge of such a thing, but says he is too ill and weak to walk to Mrs. Leopard's house to argue with her. He tricks Mr. Leopard into giving him a ride over, and achieves his boast. **RECOMMENDATION:** The cheerful appeal of the trickster and the physical action will be especially appreciated. **ROYALTY:** $25. **SOURCE:** Korty, Carol. (1975). Plays from African folktales. Boston, MA: Baker's Plays. **SUBJECTS/PLAY TYPE:** Folk Tales, Africa; Animal Stories; Playlet.

2046. 5-9. (+) Robinette, Joseph & Tierney, Thomas. **Mr. Herman and the Cave Company. CAST:** 3f, 7m, Su. **ACTS:** 1. **SETTINGS:** Cave. **PLAYING TIME:** 45 min. **PLOT:** A rock music group composed of animals, reunites for a "comeback." Dishonest (human) manager Neetsy Keene uses the animals as a cover while he steals rock records from all over the country. He plans to resell the records and marry his assistant, Stella. The innocent music group is accused of the crime, then vindicated, and is successful in its comeback. **RECOMMENDATION:** This incredible plot played out in the cave of a retired musician and his bat friend is so silly it would probably be fun. The impersonations done by Ralph, the dog of a thousand voices, would need to be updated for today's audiences. **ROYALTY:** $50. **SOURCE:** Robinette, Joseph & Tierney, Thomas. (1977). Mr. Herman and the Cave Company. Chicago, IL: Dramatic Pub. Co. **SUBJECTS/PLAY TYPE:** Rock Music Groups; Comedy; Musical.

2047. 7-10. (+) Bland, Joellen. (Hawthorne, Nathaniel) **Mr. Higginbotham's catastrophe.** (Mr. Higginbotham's catastrophe.) **CAST:** Su. **ACTS:** 1. **SETTINGS:** None.

PLAYING TIME: NA. PLOT: A traveler describes the robbery and murder of Mr. Higginbotham to Mr. Pike. The next day Pike reports the story to the villagers, but the death is proven false by someone who saw Higginbotham alive. This happens in a second village as well. The puzzled Mr. Pike travels to the scene of the crime, interrupts the actual crime in progress, and saves Mr. Higginbotham from his foreshadowed fate. RECOMMENDATION: This includes snatches of the original's dialogue. ROYALTY: Free to Plays subscribers. SOURCE: Bland, Joellen. (1986, January/February). Mr. Higginbotham's catastrophe. Plays: The Drama Magazine for Young People, pp. 74-80. SUBJECTS/PLAY TYPE: Mystery; Adaptation.

2048. 4-7. (-) Newman, Deborah. **Mr. Lincoln's beard.** CAST: 1m, Su. ACTS: 1. SETTINGS: Railroad station. PLAYING TIME: 15 min. PLOT: Grace writes to Mr. Lincoln, telling him that if he grows a beard, he will be more handsome, and women will tell their husbands to vote for him. On a visit to her town, a bearded Abe thanks Grace publicly for her advice. RECOMMENDATION: Although retelling an accepted anecdote, this adds to the sexist belief that women vote only on the basis of a candidate's looks. ROYALTY: Free for Plays subscribers. SOURCE: Newman, Deborah. (1976, February). Mr. Lincoln's beard. Plays: The Drama Magazine for Young People, pp. 41-44. SUBJECTS/PLAY TYPE: Lincoln, Abraham; Playlet.

2049. 2-6. (+) Brown, Vivian. **Mr. President.** CAST: 1f, 1m, 9u. ACTS: 1. SETTINGS: Office. PLAYING TIME: 10 min. PLOT: Harold, 10, dreams of becoming President of the United States. His fantasy is acted out in the course of the play. As the play progresses, Harold humorously handles each situation and crisis that comes his way. When he realizes being President means giving up his lunch and play time, he pushes the world emergency panic button. As the play ends, Harold is back to being an average boy. His dream is still to become President; it just won't be today. RECOMMENDATION: Although this is humorous and well within the abilities of young actors, its humor relies on rather sophisticated jokes. For example, Harold tells the group protesting nuclear tests to study harder. As a cute piece for parents to laugh at, this works; as a play for younger children, this may not be appreciated. ROYALTY: Free to Plays subscribers. SOURCE: Brown, Vivian. (1984, March). Mr. President. Plays: The Drama Magazine for Young People, pp. 31-33. SUBJECTS/PLAY TYPE: Presidents; Careers; Comedy.

2050. 7-12. (+) Fisher, Aileen. (Dickens, Charles) **Mr. Scrooge finds Christmas. (A Christmas carol.)** CAST: 4f, 14m. ACTS: 7. SETTINGS: Office; kitchen. PLAYING TIME: 30 min. PLOT: Marley seeks the help of three spirits to save the soul of his former partner and friend, Ebeneezer Scrooge. After the spirits observe Scrooge's mean and miserly ways, they try to help by showing him a glimpse of Christmas Past, Present, and Future. RECOMMENDATION: This uses some of the language and lines of the original. A spotlight is recommended for staging. ROYALTY: None. SOURCE: Kamerman, Sylvia E. (1983). Christmas play favorites for young people.

Boston, MA: Plays, Inc. SUBJECTS/PLAY TYPE: Christmas; Adaptation.

2051. 6-9. (+) Hischak, Thomas. (Dickens, Charles) **Mr. Scrooge's Christmas. (A Christmas carol)** CAST: 7f, 11m, Su. ACTS: 1. SETTINGS: Home; bedroom; cemetery. PLAYING TIME: 60 min. PLOT: Scrooge, a stingy and selfish old man, sees the ghost of his ex-partner, Marley, in a dream, as Marley returns to show Scrooge the error of his ways. During the course of the play, Scrooge is visited by three spirits who show him the past, the present, and the future. Because of what he sees, Scrooge changes his life and becomes a more selfless, generous individual. RECOMMENDATION: Upper elementary students will have no trouble memorizing the brief dialogue, although Scrooge has an extensive part which should be left to a stronger actor. ROYALTY: $25. SOURCE: Hischak, Thomas. (1980). Mr. Scrooge's Christmas. Denver, CO: Pioneer Drama Service. SUBJECTS/PLAY TYPE: Christmas; Adaptation.

2052. 3-9. (-) Gotwalt, Helen Louise Miller. **Mr. Snow White's Thanksgiving.** CAST: 4f, 3m. ACTS: 1. SETTINGS: Living room. PLAYING TIME: 20 min. PLOT: Mary and Bobby Foster get their father to sign an agreement not to kill their prize winning turkey, Snow White, for Thanksgiving dinner. Their father says the agreement has a loophole because the turkey won't be served for a family Thanksgiving; company will be coming. They pretend that no one is home when the company knocks on the door, but the children feel guilty and invite some of their poor neighbors over. The original company comes back with a turkey for dinner, and asks to buy Snow White to begin their own turkey farm. RECOMMENDATION: This mediocre plot about love for animals unfortunately suffers from a trite ending, misplaced guilt (the children are guilty because they acted like cowards, not because they lied to company), and an irrelevant lesson in legal mumbo jumbo. ROYALTY: Free to Plays subscribers. SOURCE: Gotwalt, Helen Louise Miller. (1982, November). Mr Snow White's Thanksgiving. Plays: The Drama Magazine for Young People, pp. 31-38. SUBJECTS/PLAY TYPE: Thanksgiving; Playlet.

2053. 4-6. (+) Hutson, Natalie Bovee. **Mr. Tedley's treehouse.** CAST: 2f, 5m. ACTS: 1. SETTINGS: Treehouse. PLAYING TIME: NA. PLOT: Joey and Ryan's imaginary friend, Mr. Tedley, lives in a treehouse in the forest. Full of questions, Joey and Ryan visit Mr. Tedley. They ask, "How come no one else can see him?" and "Is there life on other planets?" The seemingly ageless Mr. Tedley listens and patiently answers. When they ask if he will ever leave them, he answers that the boys will leave him as they grow up. The lights fade, and then focus on two new boys who have discovered the old man. RECOMMENDATION: This is a simple yet profound explanation of how innocence and imagination are kept alive by the young. It could be a valuable presentation to counteract the often judgmental and negative attitudes of adults toward childhood imaginary playmates, or it could be used as a celebration of youthful exuberance. Some of the references sound a bit dated, but alternative ideas could be substituted. ROYALTY: NA. SOURCE: Hutson,

Natalie Bovee. (1984). Mr. Tedley's treehouse. Stevenville, MI: Educational Service, Inc. SUBJECTS/PLAY TYPE: Imagination; Drama.

2054. 10-12. (-) Gleason, William K. **Mr. Winkler's birthday party. CAST:** 3f, 4m. **ACTS:** 1. **SETTINGS:** Bedroom. **PLAYING TIME:** NA. **PLOT:** Mr. Winkler is found dead the morning of his birthday. The nursing home director is distressed because he has ordered a birthday party at the request of Mr. Winkler's nephews, his only relatives, which they surely won't pay for now. The director decides not to inform the Winklers, but to go ahead with the party. Because Mr. Winkler was comatose when he was brought to the nursing home a year earlier, the family is oblivious to the fact that he is dead. **RECOMMENDATION:** The dialogue is dated, the characters are broad stereotypes, the plot has no redeeming virtues, the humor is tacky and without a point, and it is not clear exactly what age or type of audience this might appeal to. **ROYALTY:** $20. **SOURCE:** Gleason, William K. (1975). Mr. Winkler's birthday party. Chicago, IL: Dramatic Pub. Co. SUBJECTS/PLAY TYPE: Family; Death; Nursing Homes; Comedy.

2055. 3-5. (+) Urban, Catherine. **Mrs. Claus' Christmas present. CAST:** 1f, 5m. **ACTS:** 1. **SETTINGS:** Living room. **PLAYING TIME:** 15 min. **PLOT:** It is almost time for Santa to leave to distribute Christmas presents. He is worried because he does not know what to give his wife for Christmas and seeks suggestions from his assistants. **RECOMMENDATION:** Simple words and short lines are used so young actors will find it easy to memorize their parts. **ROYALTY:** Free to Plays subscribers. **SOURCE:** Kamerman, Sylvia E. (1975). A treasury of Christmas plays. Boston, MA: Plays, Inc. SUBJECTS/PLAY TYPE: Christmas; Family; Playlet.

2056. 4-6. (+) Bradley, Virginia. **Mrs. Clopsaddle presents Christmas. CAST:** 2f, 5m. **ACTS:** 1. **SETTINGS:** Auditorium. **PLAYING TIME:** NA. **PLOT:** Mrs. Clopsaddle loses control when her theater pupils begin to add new lines, forget lines, and even fall asleep during the play. **RECOMMENDATION:** Young actors will enjoy the laughs when they purposely "goof up" their parts. **ROYALTY:** None. **SOURCE:** Bradley, Virginia. (1975). Is there an actor in the house? New York, NY: Dodd, Mead. SUBJECTS/PLAY TYPE: Christmas; Comedy.

2057. 4-6. (+) Bradley, Virginia. **Mrs. Clopsaddle presents spring. CAST:** 9f, 3u. **ACTS:** 1. **SETTINGS:** Auditorium. **PLAYING TIME:** NA. **PLOT:** A recital is held at Mrs. Clopsaddle's school of elocution. **RECOMMENDATION:** This type of variety program where different actors walk on stage and perform alone for a few minutes is held together by the mistress of ceremonies. Individual parts can be simple or dramatic. The play would not be ruined by one actor's poor performance. **ROYALTY:** None. **SOURCE:** Bradley, Virginia. (1975). Is there an actor in the house. New York, NY: Dodd, Mead. SUBJECTS/PLAY TYPE: Spring; Flowers; Bunnies; Comedy.

2058. 12. (+) London, Roy. **Mrs. Murray's farm. CAST:** 4f, 7m. **ACTS:** 2. **SETTINGS:** Kitchen; dining room. **PLAYING TIME:** NA. **PLOT:** In 1776, the opportunistic mistress of a farm is drawn by her servants into a scheme to save a large force of Revolutionary soldiers from capture. Their plan is to delay the British general by providing him with an elaborate and lengthy dinner. The plan works, inspiring servants to declare their own independence from their maternal but domineering mistress. **RECOMMENDATION:** The sustained, rapid fire pace of the dialogue requires a high level of sophistication, teamwork, and verbal facility. The sexual innuendo, occasional musical pieces, and psychologically complex relationships create further difficulties. Extensive props are required. **ROYALTY:** $50. **SOURCE:** London, Roy. (1977). Mrs. Murray's farm. New York, NY: Dramatists Play Service, Inc. SUBJECTS/PLAY TYPE: Revolution, U.S.; Independence; Comedy.

2059. 2-4. (+) Abisch, Roz & Kaplan, Boche. **Mrs. Snooty and the waiter. CAST:** 1f, 1m. **ACTS:** 1. **SETTINGS:** Restaurant. **PLAYING TIME:** 7 min. **PLOT:** Restaurant patron Mrs. Snooty encounters a very literal minded and inept waiter. **RECOMMENDATION:** Using title cards instead of dialogue, this amusing spoof of old time movies would provide an entertaining introduction to stage techniques. **ROYALTY:** NA. **SOURCE:** Abisch, Roz & Kaplan, Boche. (1977). The make it, play it, show time book. New York, NY: Walker. SUBJECTS/PLAY TYPE: Comedy; Movies; Pantomime.

2060. K-3. (+) Laurie, Rona. (Potter, Beatrix) **Mrs. Tiggy-Winkle's washing day.** (Tales of Beatrix Potter) **CAST:** 5f, 5m, 4u. **ACTS:** 1. **SETTINGS:** Farm; path. **PLAYING TIME:** NA. **PLOT:** Lucie loses her handkerchiefs and in the process of looking for them, she discovers Mrs. Tiggy-Winkle doing laundry for the animals. After they distribute the laundry to the play's Beatrix Potter characters, Lucie is surprised to see that Mrs. Tiggy-Winkle is a hedgehog. **RECOMMENDATION:** This is faithful to the original intent and characters of Potter's delightful animal tales. **ROYALTY:** NA. **SOURCE:** Laurie, Rona. (1980). Children's plays from Beatrix Potter. London, England: F. Warne. SUBJECTS/PLAY TYPE: Animals; Adaptation.

2061. K-3. (+) Laurie, Rona. (Potter, Beatrix) **Mrs. Tittlemouse and the uninvited guest.** (Tales of Beatrix Potter) **CAST:** 4f, 1m, 12u. **ACTS:** 1. **SETTINGS:** Animal burrow. **PLAYING TIME:** NA. **PLOT:** Mrs. Tittlemouse tries to keep her house immaculate, but uninvited guests bring messes with them, especially the bees who plan to live in her pantry. Mr. Jackson, a toad, solves that problem, but leaves a mess himself. Mrs. Tittlemouse makes her front door smaller so he can't return. **RECOMMENDATION:** Children will enjoy the compromise at the conclusion, and will empathize with characters who are scolded for making messes. **ROYALTY:** NA. **SOURCE:** Laurie, Rona. (1980). Children's plays from Beatrix Potter. London, England: F. Warne. SUBJECTS/PLAY TYPE: Animals; Adaptation.

2062. 7-12. (+) Kelly, Tim. (Rice, Alice Hegan) **Mrs. Wiggs of the cabbage patch, or, a page from the book of life.** CAST: 10f, 5m, Su. ACTS: 3. SETTINGS: Cottage. PLAYING TIME: 90 min. PLOT: Cheerful, optimistic, Widow Wiggs faces eviction by nasty Ambrose Flint, who wants to sell her land to the railroad. Flint is in love with the do gooder heiress Miss Lucy, but Miss Lucy is in love with Robert, the newspaperman. Fortunately, the arrival of a mysterious stranger from the North saves Mrs. Wiggs from dastardly plots in the "nick of time." RECOMMENDATION: This excellent introduction to melodrama based loosely upon the characters in the original novel is a fast paced production which can include a "fund-raising show" featuring Victorian songs and recitations. Clever program asides and advertising ideas are included in the production notes to help get audiences into the proper mood. ROYALTY: $35. SOURCE: Kelly, Tim. (1982). Mrs. Wiggs of the cabbage patch, or, a page from the book of life. Schulenburg, TX: I.E. Clark. SUBJECTS/PLAY TYPE: Family; Comedy; Swindlers and Swindling; Melodrama; Adaptation.

2063. 2-5. (+) Cools, Gloria. (Grimm Brothers) **Ms. Mouse Riding Hood.** (Little Red Riding Hood) CAST: 3u. ACTS: 1. SETTINGS: Forest. PLAYING TIME: 5 min. PLOT: This variation on **Little Red Riding Hood** brings women's lib to the forest as Ms. Mouse Riding Hood uses karate to defeat the evil Bob Cat. RECOMMENDATION: The audience should enjoy this new treatment of an old favorite. ROYALTY: Free to Plays subscribers. SOURCE: Cools, Gloria. (1983, May). Ms. Mouse Riding Hood. Plays: The Drama Magazine for Young People, pp. 66-68. SUBJECTS/PLAY TYPE: Folk Tales, Germany; Adaptation; Puppet Play.

2064. 7-12. (+) Clepper, P.M. (Dickens, Charles) **Ms. Scrooge.** (A Christmas carol.) CAST: 16f, Su. ACTS: 2. SETTINGS: Office; apartment. PLAYING TIME: NA. PLOT: This is a modern, female version of the Dickens classic in which a miserly boss relearns the true meaning of Christmas as a result of her Christmas Eve encounters with the three ghosts of Christmas (Past, Present, and Future). RECOMMENDATION: The female cast and modern setting underscore the universal appeal of the original. ROYALTY: $25. SOURCE: Clepper, P.M. (1985). Ms. Scrooge. Woodstock, IL: Dramatic Pub. Co. SUBJECTS/PLAY TYPE: Christmas; Adaptation.

2065. 9-12. (+) Cook, Pat. **Much ado about murder.** CAST: 4f, 5m, Su. ACTS: 2. SETTINGS: Living room; den/office. PLAYING TIME: NA. PLOT: Wealthy, cantankerous Uncle Carlton hosts a family Halloween party. When he doesn't arrive, the family, growing impatient, discovers his body in his den. After engrossing interaction, the family discovers the murderer and the audience participates to help solve the mystery. RECOMMENDATION: Excellent characterization is woven into a witty dialogue and interesting "asides." Suspense is sustained by a series of cliff-hanging episodes. ROYALTY: $50. SOURCE: Cook, Pat. (1988). Much ado about murder. Schulenburg, TX: I.E. Clark. SUBJECTS/PLAY TYPE: Comedy; Murder; Mystery.

2066. 9-12. (+) Bland, Joellen. (Doyle, Arthur Conan) **The mummy.** (The mummy) CAST: 2f, 4m. ACTS: 1. SETTINGS: None. PLAYING TIME: 25 min. PLOT: A Holmesian Oxford student tackles a mystery involving an evil student majoring in Eastern languages, a set of unnatural accidents, and a nasty looking mummy. After a number of semi-frightening situations, the play ends happily with the good hero destroying the evil mummy. RECOMMENDATION: This very suspenseful reading is guaranteed to keep the attention of young adults as it is scary and at times a little gory. The sudden switch of main character to narrator may be confusing. ROYALTY: Free to Plays subscribers. SOURCE: Bland, Joellen. (1982, January/ February). The mummy. Plays: The Drama Magazine for Young People, pp. 85- 95. SUBJECTS/PLAY TYPE: Horror; Mystery; Reader's Theater; Adaptation.

2067. 1-6. (+) Majeski, Bill. **Murder at Mother Goose's place.** CAST: 4f, 4m. ACTS: 1. SETTINGS: Bare stage, props. PLAYING TIME: 20 min. PLOT: This is the story of the demise of Humpty Dumpty. Detective Armstrong meets most of the Mother Goose characters and as he questions each one, they answer with portions of nursery rhymes. He discovers several thefts in the area, including Miss Muffet's tuffet and Bo Peep's sheep. Detective Armstrong discovers that Red and her hoods murdered Humpty Dumpty because he witnessed their crimes from his high position on the wall. RECOMMENDATION: Full of puns and wisecracks, this clever production has fun toying with the traditional Mother Goose rhymes. While younger children may miss parts of the humor, they will still enjoy viewing the familiar characters in this modernized comedy. ROYALTY: Free to Plays subscribers. SOURCE: Majeski, Bill. (1976, May). Murder at Mother Goose's place. Plays: The Drama Magazine for Young People, pp. 43-48. SUBJECTS/PLAY TYPE: Nursery Rhyme Characters; Folk Tale Characters; Mystery; Comedy.

2068. 6-12. (-) Silverman, Eleanor. **Murder at Wolf's Head Inn.** CAST: 4f, 5m, 1u. ACTS: 4. SETTINGS: Inn. PLAYING TIME: 20 min. PLOT: While on vacation in England, the Hiltons run out of gas and must stay the night at an inn. Mr. Hilton is murdered by a young man whose mother wants to inherit the fortune for which she mistakenly thinks Mr. Hilton is the heir. RECOMMENDATION: The audience never gets a chance to participate in the solution. ROYALTY: None. SOURCE: Silverman, Eleanor. (1983). Dramatics for children. Metuchen, NJ: Scarecrow Press. SUBJECTS/PLAY TYPE: Murder; Mystery.

2069. 10-12. (+) Kelly, Tim J. (Levinson, Richard & Link, William) **Murder by natural causes.** (Natural causes: A teleplay) CAST: 4f, 4m. ACTS: 2. SETTINGS: Study. PLAYING TIME: NA. PLOT: A woman, with the help of her young lover, plots to murder her husband, a world famous mentalist. Are the husband's psychic powers sufficient to foil the murder plot? Who is really trying to kill whom? The plot has many twists and turns and a surprise ending, where the husband turns the tables on his wife. Both the wife and audience are left wondering in the final scene if the betrayed husband will murder her and escape blame. RECOMMENDATION: The characters are interesting, the murder plot plausible, and the ending a surprise, all of which should keep the audience entertained. ROYALTY: $50. SOURCE: Kelly, Tim J. (1985). Murder by natural causes. Woodstock, IL: Dramatic Pub. Co. SUBJECTS/PLAY TYPE: Mystery; Mind Reading; Suspense.

2070. 7-12. (+) Hischak, Thomas. **Murder in bloom.** CAST: 8f, 2m. ACTS: 2. SETTINGS: Sitting room. PLAYING TIME: 90 min. PLOT: Letitia Whetmore, member of a secret society, is murdered during the initiation of her niece, Priscilla Stewart-Wayne. Clever work by the police detective solves the crime. The reason for the club's existence is also revealed: all members were sworn to protect Priscilla's mother from prosecution for killing her husband. His death supposedly was accidental and membership was limited to those who knew otherwise. Letitia's murderer, Melody Haydock, explains that she belonged to the organization by virtue of guesswork and not by actual knowledge, and as a result felt she was looked down upon by the victim. RECOMMENDATION: The clever twist whereby the local female busybody sleuth turns out to be the murderess will be of interest to mystery lovers. ROYALTY: $35. SOURCE: Hischak, Thomas. (1985). Murder in bloom. Denver, CO: Pioneer Drama Service. SUBJECTS/PLAY TYPE: Secret Clubs; Murder; Mystery.

2071. 7-12. (+) Kelly, Tim. **Murder in the Magnolias.** CAST: 6f, 6m. ACTS: 3. SETTINGS: Sitting room. PLAYING TIME: NA. PLOT: In this parody of Southern plays, several stereotypical characters are gathered in an old mansion for the reading of Rance Chickenwings will and the investigation of his murder. Various eccentric relatives including a doddering sister who is obsessed with her people eating garden, and other assorted people interact in bizarre but gentle fashion until two of them are murdered. Meanwhile, the mysterious voodoo woman casts spells on anyone she happens across, the garden tries to eat the guests, and sheriff Billy Jerk comes to one mistaken conclusion after another. In the end, the sheriff is exposed as the murderer. RECOMMENDATION: Played straight, this is a rich dark comedy. Broadly played, the complex characters such as the schizophrenic Thornbird Chickenwing III who loans the ladies dresses, or Amanda, who tries to keep the voices in her head quiet, and Blanche Du Blank, a cross between Blanche Du Bois and Amanda from the **Glass Menagerie** could turn the play into a farcical parody. ROYALTY: $40. SOURCE: Kelly, Tim. (1980). Murder in the Magnolias. Boston, MA: Baker's Plays. SUBJECTS/PLAY TYPE: Southern Gothic; Mystery; Comedy.

2072. 10-12. (+) Springer, William J. **Murder me, murder me not.** CAST: 3f, 3m. ACTS: 3. SETTINGS: Sitting room. PLAYING TIME: NA. PLOT: Geraldine Gaston and her husband, Randolph, scheme to collect insurance money for his supposed death. Geraldine reveals their secret to Ambrose Brinks, the man she plans to marry after collecting the insurance money. In reality, Ambrose is an insurance investigator and he foils their plot. The Gastons and others involved in the crime are reported to the police and sent to jail. RECOMMENDATION: As many special effects and complicated props are required for this detective thriller, only competent actors, should attempt production. ROYALTY: $35. SOURCE: Springer, William J. (1985). Murder me, murder me not. Franklin, OH: Eldridge Pub. Co. SUBJECTS/PLAY TYPE: Insurance; Fraud; Comedy.

2073. 9-12. (+) Twedt, Jerry L. **Murder on center stage.** CAST: 6f, 3m. ACTS: 3. SETTINGS: Theatre. PLAYING TIME: NA. PLOT: A college theater group rehearses **Romeo and Juliet.** The theater director, an English professor, and a demented janitor were involved in theater together during their college days. The cast and faculty decide to stay late and catch the "ghost" that haunts the theater. When they try to leave, they discover that they have been locked in. Individuals are attacked and the mad cleaning woman is suspected. In the end, a male janitor is exposed as the vengeful lunatic. RECOMMENDATION: With skillful production, this could be exciting. It is quite violent, but personalities are clearly developed and their actions follow logically from their character definitions. ROYALTY: $50. SOURCE: Twedt, Jerry L. (1976). Murder of center stage. Chicago, IL: Dramatic Pub. Co. SUBJECTS/PLAY TYPE: Mystery; Drama.

2074. 9-12. (+) Boiko, Claire. **Murder on the Orient Express Subway.** CAST: 4f, 14m. ACTS: 1. SETTINGS: Subway. PLAYING TIME: 30 min. PLOT: Three fictional detectives--Agatha Crusty, Hercules Pearot, and Miss Marbles--solve a murder while traveling on the Orient Avenue Express Subway. They prove that 11 of the 12 suspects murdered the innocent bystander. They were all trying to kill each other but the bystander got in the way. The bystander turns out to be a playwright who read that he had his first flop and died of apoplexy before the others each killed him. In other words, nobody dunnit. Inspector Haystack is terribly disappointed and asks Pearot what he thinks and for the 100th time, mispronounces Pearot's name. Pearot is enraged, grabs Haystack around the neck, and chokes him to death. RECOMMENDATION: Although the dialogue is a little hard to follow at times, and there are many characters to keep up with (especially with each having a present and past identity), this is filled with wonderful humor. ROYALTY: Free to Plays Subscribers. SOURCE: Bioko, Claire. (1980, January). Murder on the Orient Express Subway. Plays: The Drama Magazine for Young People, pp. 59-64. SUBJECTS/PLAY TYPE: Detectives; Mystery; Comedy; Skit.

2075. 9-12. (+) Kelly, Tim. **Murder takes a holiday.** (Corpse on a ski lift.) CAST: 6f, 6m. ACTS: 2. SETTINGS: Ski lodge; living room. PLAYING TIME: 120 min. PLOT: Harry and Diane Thompson arrive at the failing Alpine Chalet Ski Lodge to check it out for possible purchase. They find that its main problem is murder. RECOMMENDATION: A fairly ordinary drawing room murder mystery with touches of humor, this has enough colorful characters to provide a challenge for a young cast and enough clues scattered through it to keep the audience guessing. ROYALTY: $50. SOURCE: Kelly, Tim. (1984). Murder takes a holiday. Schulenburg, TX: I.E. Clark.

SUBJECTS/PLAY TYPE: Murder; Mystery; Thriller; Adaptation.

2076. 7-10. (+) Carroll, John R. **Murder well rehearsed.** CAST: 3f, 3m. ACTS: 1. SETTINGS: Stage. PLAYING TIME: 35 min. PLOT: Four students and their drama coach enter the school to rehearse a play and discover a corpse on the stage. A police inspector comes, and suspense builds as everyone tries to figure out what happened, who did it, and what is causing strange events to occur. Finally, the police inspector is discovered to be a phony. He is actually the groundskeeper and murderer. RECOMMENDATION: The audience will enjoy trying to solve this suspenseful mystery before the murderer strikes again. ROYALTY: $15. SOURCE: Carroll, John R. (1976). Murder well rehearsed. Boston, MA: Baker's Plays. SUBJECTS/PLAY TYPE: Murder; Mystery; Drama.

2077. 2-6. (+) Dexter, Harriet. **Music, mousto, please!** CAST: 2f, 2m. ACTS: 1. SETTINGS: Mouse hole. PLAYING TIME: 15 min. PLOT: The mouse family's Christmas sing-along is disrupted by Marshamallow the cat. Fortunately, the festivities are saved as Millie Mouse demonstrates that even felines can be reasoned with. RECOMMENDATION: This clan of miniscule rodents will furnish the audience with humor that doesn't sail over the younger children's head (i.e., one of the characters checks the time by looking at his "Mickey Man" watch). The cat's face, which consists of a large, painted prop, will provide stage shy artists with an opportunity to contribute. ROYALTY: Free to Plays subscribers. SOURCE: Dexter, Harriet. (1982, December). Music, mousto, please! Plays: The Drama Magazine for Young People, pp. 41-44. SUBJECTS/PLAY TYPE: Christmas; Cats; Comedy.

2078. 2-5. (+) Roberts, Walter. (Grimm Brothers) **The musicians of Bremen Town.** (The Bremen Town Musicians) CAST: 1f, 4m, 5u. ACTS: 1. SETTINGS: Bare stage, props. PLAYING TIME: 15 min. PLOT: A donkey, cat, dog, and rooster leave the farm to become musicians. They find a house where they sing in hopes of being fed. The people in the house are robbers and run away. The animals, however, think the people are running to find them a larger audience so they decide to wait. They eat the food left in the house and lie down to sleep until the "audience" arrives. When the robbers return, one steps on the cat's tail and they are again frightened away. The animals decide to stay forever. RECOMMENDATION: The theme of friendship through adversity and time is conveyed. A narrator holds the play together and must be a strong character. ROYALTY: NA. SOURCE: Kamerman, Sylvia E. Plays from favorite folk tales. Boston, MA: Plays, Inc. SUBJECTS/PLAY TYPE: Folk Tales, Germany; Animals; Adaptation.

2079. K-6. (-) Bolt, Carol. **My best friend is twelve feet high.** CAST: 1f, 4m. ACTS: 1. SETTINGS: Bare stage. PLAYING TIME: NA. PLOT: This expresses the vivid imagination that young children exhibit when playing with their friends. They act out their dreams and ideas using the concept of belonging to a club. RECOMMENDATION: The plot and characters are hard to follow and fast changes of thoughts and settings cause confusion. ROYALTY: NA. SOURCE: Bolt, Carol. (1980). Kids plays: Canadian plays for children. Toronto, Canada: Playwrights Press, Inc. SUBJECTS/PLAY TYPE: Adventure; Comedy.

2080. 3-8. (+) Kehret, Peg. **My blankee.** CAST: 1u. ACTS: 1. SETTINGS: None. PLAYING TIME: NA. PLOT: A youngster explains how he/she still likes to sleep with a special blanket, despite being too old for it. RECOMMENDATION: Many older children will relate to the dilemma of whether to cling to childhood or advance into adulthood. ROYALTY: NA. SOURCE: Kehret, Peg. (1986). Winning monologs for young actors. Colorado Springs, CO: Meriwether Pub. SUBJECTS/PLAY TYPE: Blankets; Security; Monologue.

2081. 9-12. (+) Patrick, Robert. **My cup ranneth over.** CAST: 2f. ACTS: 1. SETTINGS: Living room. PLAYING TIME: NA. PLOT: Paula wants to be published by Cosmopolitan magazine but her work is routinely rejected. Yucca is a folksinger/song writer who becomes a media success over night. Paula is too jealous to enjoy her roommate's good fortune. The play ends on a bittersweet note when Cosmopolitan asks for a cover story on Yucca. Yucca agrees, but only if Paula is author. RECOMMENDATION: An excellent story with good characterization and very witty dialogue. ROYALTY: $25. SOURCE: Patrick, Robert. (1979). My cup ranneth over. New York, NY: Dramatists Play Service. SUBJECTS/PLAY TYPE: Friendship; Success; Jealousy; Comedy.

2082. 3-6. (+) Thornton, Jane Foster. **My darling Clementine.** CAST: 1f, 2m, 4u. ACTS: 1. SETTINGS: Bare stage, props. PLAYING TIME: 15 min. PLOT: Clementine has been digging for oil the last 10 years with her miner father. One day, as she drives the ducklings to the water, she falls into the foaming brine. She is saved by a hero, who always wanted to marry a girl who wears size nine herring boxes. After they get married, they find oil and live a happy life. RECOMMENDATION: This takeoff on the famous song ends with a new rendition where Clementine is "not lost and gone forever." For those who know the song, it will be a delight to produce. ROYALTY: Free to Plays subscribers. SOURCE: Thornton, Jane Foster. (1975, April). My darling Clementine. Plays: The Drama Magazine for Young People, pp. 57-60. SUBJECTS/PLAY TYPE: Mining; Comedy.

2083. 7-12. (+) Sexton, Nancy Miles & McBride, Vaughn. **My days as a youngling.** CAST: 12f, 12m, Su. ACTS: 1. SETTINGS: Log cabin; porch. PLAYING TIME: NA. PLOT: The people and experiences comprising John Jacob Niles' early life are presented musically, in poetry, and through storytelling. RECOMMENDATION: The rich folklore and musical heritage of Kentucky will be enjoyed in any setting. This would be excellent for music and drama departments to produce together. ROYALTY: $35. SOURCE: Sexton, Nancy Miles & McBride, Vaughn. (1982). My days as a youngling. New Orleans, LA: Anchorage Press. SUBJECTS/PLAY TYPE: Folksongs; Niles, John Jacob; Musical.

2084. 3-12. (+) Shue, Larry. (Andersen, Hans Christian) **My emperor's new clothes.** (The emperor's new clothes) CAST: 5f, 7m, Su. ACTS: 1. SETTINGS: Street. PLAYING TIME: 90 min. PLOT: In this musical adaptation, a slight twist is added when the emperor's daughter becomes romantically involved with the emperor's valet. RECOMMENDATION: All of the original charm is recaptured in this good natured, amusing, and updated adaptation which will appeal to all audiences, but (because of the dialogue) should be produced by the upper grades. ROYALTY: $60. SOURCE: Shue, Larry. (1985). My emperor's new clothes. New York, NY: Dramatists Play Service, Inc. SUBJECTS/PLAY TYPE: Folk Tales, Denmark; Musical; Adaptation.

2085. K-3. (+) Hymes, James L. Jr. & Hymes, Lucia. **My favorite word.** CAST: 4u. ACTS: 1. SETTINGS: None. PLAYING TIME: NA. PLOT: "Yes," the readers decide, is the nicest word in the world. RECOMMENDATION: Children will enjoy reciting this for parents, perhaps as a gentle hint for permissiveness. ROYALTY: NA. SOURCE: Bauer, Caroline Feller. (1987). Presenting reader's theater: Plays and poems to read aloud. New York, NY: H.W. Wilson. SUBJECTS/PLAY TYPE: Yes; Reader's Theater.

2086. K-12. (+) Rossetti, Christina. **My gift.** CAST: Su. ACTS: 1. SETTINGS: None. PLAYING TIME: 1 min. PLOT: This is a simple recitation based on giving the Christ Child a gift on the day of His birth. RECOMMENDATION: Recommended as part of a Christmas devotional service. ROYALTY: None. SOURCE: Hendricks, William & Vogel, Cora. (1983). Handbook of Christmas programs. Grand Rapids, MI: Baker Book House. SUBJECTS/PLAY TYPE: Christmas; Choral Reading.

2087. 10-12. (+) Goffin, Jeffrey. **My gun is pink.** CAST: 11f, 3m. ACTS: 1. SETTINGS: Street; office; bar; warehouse; living room. PLAYING TIME: 50 min. PLOT: Babe Archer, private detective, investigates a missing person case which claimed the lives of her partner and Colin Reilly, twin brother of Wayne Reilly, an international playboy. After following numerous clues, she discovers a very much alive Colin, learns of his involvement in a neo-Nazi organization, and she is able to stop their conquest of the world. RECOMMENDATION: This is a delightfully suspenseful comedy. The plot develops at a steady pace, and some care will need to be taken with special effects and flashback scenes. ROYALTY: $25. SOURCE: Goffin, Jeffrey. (1987). My gun is pink. Schulenburg, TX: I.E. Clark. SUBJECTS/PLAY TYPE: Detectives; Murder; Mystery; Comedy.

2088. 4-8. (+) Kehret, Peg. **My mother collects china cows.** CAST: 1u. ACTS: 1. SETTINGS: None. PLAYING TIME: NA. PLOT: A child gives a humorous view of his mother's hobby. RECOMMENDATION: This clever monologue is both humorous and realistic. ROYALTY: NA. SOURCE: Kehret, Peg. (1986). Winning monologs for young actors. Colorado Springs, CO: Meriwether Pub. SUBJECTS/PLAY TYPE: Hobbies; Monologue.

2089. 5-7. (+) Slote, Alfred. **My robot buddy.** CAST: 4f, 3m, 7u. ACTS: 2. SETTINGS: Yard; factory. PLAYING TIME: 60 min. PLOT: A boy with sister siblings wants a robot buddy for his birthday. His parents sacrifice to buy a robot programmed with human qualities. Robotnappers attempt to steal the boy, thinking he is the robot. The robot confuses nappers by acting like the boy and radios for the police. The robot exhibits sufficient human characteristics to be welcomed into the family. RECOMMENDATION: The computer-robot world is used to teach family care and concern for one another, parental love and support, and loyalty to a friend. The apple pie and motherhood theme could mix with the reason-able lyrics if the beat is modern enough. ROYALTY: $35. SOURCE: Slote, Alfred. (1980). My robot buddy. Denver, CO: Pioneer Drama Service. SUBJECTS/PLAY TYPE: Family; Loyalty; Citizenship; Comedy.

2090. 5-8*. (-) Heilveil, Elayne & Frederick, Robin. **My sister makes me sick.** CAST: 4f, 3m. ACTS: 1. SETTINGS: Park; bedroom; classroom. PLAYING TIME: 45 min. PLOT: This musical about a young girl who is jealous of her pretty, talented, smart sister focuses on the search to discover what is unique in each individual. When older sister Beverly wins tickets to a rock concert, Martha is furious and plans revenge. When Martha's plan fails, she gives up and tries to live without feelings, but her dog (who has human characteristics), and her best friend Elliot, are on her side. Martha's "higher self" talks to her when she is cleaning her sister's closet and convinces her that she is a valuable person who need not take revenge on anyone. RECOMMENDATION: The role of Martha is not as well developed or as believable as that of her cheerleading sister Beverly. It would be difficult for children to take seriously a voice that talks to her while cleaning out the closet of her sister at whom she is furious. Also, the effort to find the "special qualities" falls flat. ROYALTY: $50. SOURCE: Heilveil, Elayne and Frederick, Robin. (1983). My sister makes me sick. Chicago, IL: Dramatic Pub. Co. SUBJECTS/PLAY TYPE: Sibling Rivalry; Self Worth; Identity; Musical.

2091. 5-8. (+) Martens, Anne Coulter. **My swinging swain.** CAST: 4f, 4m. ACTS: 1. SETTINGS: Living room. PLAYING TIME: 30 min. PLOT: Debbie tries to transform shy, bookish Martin into a swinging guy. Her efforts to pawn him off on her girlfriends backfire because they actually like him. But now Debbie is jealous and decides she wants to ask him to the dance. Martin realizes he has been used and turns the tables on Debbie. In the end, Debbie and Martin decide they like each other and can be friends without trying to change each other. RECOMMENDATION: Early teens would relate to the episodes of family and friends involved in a typical teenage plot of arranging friendships on the basis of popularity. ROYALTY: Free to Plays subscribers. SOURCE: Martens, Anne Coulter. (1978, May). My swinging swain. Plays: The Drama Magazine for Young People, pp. 23-34. SUBJECTS/PLAY TYPE: Popularity; Dating; Playlet.

2092. 1-3. (-) Young, Alida E. **My true story.** CAST: 1u. ACTS: 1. SETTINGS: None. PLAYING TIME: 10 min.

PLOT: The wolf tells his side of the **Three Little Pigs** tale, claiming that the pigs have spread lies about him. He admits he went to their houses, but not to terrorize them, only to borrow a cup of sugar. RECOMMENDATION: This is supposed to be a comic monologue, yet there is nothing comic about it. The wolf is sarcastic and mean and the entire tone is negative. ROYALTY: Free to Plays subscribers. SOURCE: Young, Alida E. (1980, April). My true story. Plays: The Drama Magazine for Young People, pp. 63-64. SUBJECTS/PLAY TYPE: Pigs; Folk Tales, England; Monologue.

2093. 5-6. (+) Rockwell, Thomas. **Myron Mere.** CAST: 3f, 4m, Su. ACTS: 1. SETTINGS: Terrace; dungeon; maze. PLAYING TIME: NA. PLOT: Evil Myron Mere, whom the Queen has rejected, turns her into a butterfly, ensnares her, and takes her to his dungeon. Lord Peter Graves, the Queen's fiance, saves her, but is held hostage himself. Just when it looks like all is lost, the Queen's prime minister arrives with his army and announces that he has defeated the Mereish army and driven them into the swamp. Myron Mere is led away in chains as the Queen and Lord Peter are married. RECOMMENDATION: Some of the many long words (i.e. epaulettes, tawdriness) will need to be either simplified or well learned. Myron's "Transylvanian" accent is simplified enough to be doable. ROYALTY: NA. SOURCE: Rockwell, Thomas. (1980). How to eat fried worms, and other plays. New York, NY: Delacorte Press. SUBJECTS/PLAY TYPE: Damsels In Distress; Rescue; Folk Tale Motifs; Melodrama.

2094. 4-8. (-) Hall, Margaret C. & McQueen, Noel. **The mysterious mirror.** CAST: 2f, 3m. ACTS: 1. SETTINGS: Bare stage. PLAYING TIME: 12 min. PLOT: Japanese peasants, Mo-Ko and Lo-Chee, have a mirror. They show it to their friends, Kiko and Lili Cho Sin. They quarrel after each person looks into the mirror and sees a different person. A priest resolves the misunderstanding by taking the mirror to the village shrine. Lo-Chee concludes that people may be better off without mirrors. RECOMMENDATION: Asians may find the naivete of the characters to be offensive. While this could spark some discussion on values, it is not a good introduction to Asian culture. ROYALTY: Free to Plays subscribers. SOURCE: Hall, Margaret C. (1979, April). The mysterious mirror. Plays: The Drama Magazine for Young People, pp. 61-64. SUBJECTS/PLAY TYPE: Folk Tales, Japan; Playlet.

2095. 1-4. (+) Gilbreath, Alice. **The mysterious mix-up.** CAST: 3f, 5m, 11u. ACTS: 1. SETTINGS: Field. PLAYING TIME: 15 min. PLOT: As a stranger heralds the arrival of fall, the squirrels are upset because they are told that they must gather nuts when there are none, the ducks are told to fly south, the green leaves are changed to different colors and even the raindrops are given their "winter overcoats." The stranger, as it turns out, is Jack Frost, who has been awakened too early by some bells that children are carrying. RECOMMENDATION: An entertaining lesson on the changing seasons, this would be an appropriate first dramatic experience for young actors. ROYALTY: Free to Plays subscribers. SOURCE: Gilbreath, Alice. (1976, April). The mysterious mix-up. Plays: The Drama Magazine for Young People, pp. 52-54. SUBJECTS/PLAY TYPE: Seasons; Skit.

2096. 7-12. (+) Leech, Michael, T. (Gogol, Nikolai) **The mysterious portrait.** (The portrait) CAST: 2f, 12m, Su. ACTS: 1. SETTINGS: Street; art studio. PLAYING TIME: 30 min. PLOT: When a young painter is hired to paint the likeness of an evil moneylender, he produces his most lifelike work, but is overwhelmed by the evil force of the portrait's eyes and refuses to complete it. Many years after the painter's death, his son finds the portrait at an estate auction. The son seeks to claim the mysterious portrait and fulfill his vow to destroy it for his father. But as the son turns to take it, it has been stolen, leaving him to agonize over the continuing evil. RECOMMENDATION: The adaptation of Gogol's classic is faithful in spirit, if not in detail, and dramatically portrays the theme of the pervasive force of evil. The play lacks the depth of Gogol's original, but the basic characters are developed effectively. The tale of the userer and his influence over the young painter explores the idea that art itself may become a vehicle for evil and that the artist bears a heavy burden of moral responsibility. ROYALTY: Free to Plays subscribers. SOURCE: Leech, Michael T. (1975, May). The mysterious portrait. Plays: The Drama Magazine for Young People, pp. 77-86. SUBJECTS/PLAY TYPE: Art; Evil; Adaptation.

2097. K-3. (+) DeRegniers, Beatrice Schenk. **The mysterious stranger.** CAST: 2f, 8u. ACTS: 1. SETTINGS: Castle. PLAYING TIME: NA. PLOT: The wicked witch throws the Princess into the tower. A mysterious stranger comes to rescue the Princess but a mouse beats him to it. RECOMMENDATION: The tower is three players who stand on stools wearing sandwich boards labeled Tower 1, Tower 2, and Tower 3. The humor is visual and slapstick. ROYALTY: None. SOURCE: DeRegniers, Beatrice Schenk. (1982). Picture book theatre. New York, NY: Clarion Books/Houghton Mifflin Co. SUBJECTS/PLAY TYPE: Witches; Princesses; Comedy; Skit.

2098. 8-12. (+) Murray, John. **Mystery liner.** CAST: 6f, 7m, Su. ACTS: 3. SETTINGS: Lounge. PLAYING TIME: 35 min. PLOT: A famous mystery writer and her husband join the wealthy and famous on a luxury cruise. When a blackmailer is poisoned on board, the writer and two stowaways attempt to sort out the connections between the other passengers and identify the murderer. In the end it is the writer's husband who solves the mystery and provides his wife with a plot for her next book. RECOMMENDATION: This is a stew of predictable developments, irrelevant secondary plots, and uninteresting characters. Nonetheless, there are a few amusing lines and enough potential for parody in the characterization to keep the cast and audience awake. ROYALTY: Free to Plays subscribers. SOURCE: Murray, John. (1985). Fifteen plays for todays teenagers. Boston, MA: Plays, Inc. SUBJECTS/PLAY TYPE: Mystery; Ocean Cruises; Drama.

2099. 5-9. (+) Kurtz, Joy & Simpson, Wayne. **The mystery of Hastings House.** CAST: 12f, 18m. ACTS: 1. SETTINGS: Schoolroom; retirement home; basement; vacant house. PLAYING TIME: 60 min. PLOT: Mr.

Youngman's sixth grade students ask Ellinsworth, owner of the vacant Hastings House, for permission to investigate flickering lights seen there. Ellinsworth agrees and expresses his desire to find his uncle's missing gold coin collection. The girls hold a seance and the boys crash the party. In retaliation, when the boys spend the night at Hastings House, the girls burst in wearing ghost costumes. During the confusion, the missing gold coins are located and the mystery of the lights is solved. Mr. Ellinsworth is able to remodel the old house and moves in with some of his elderly friends. RECOMMENDATION: In spite of the predictable plot, the ghosts and bouncy music (including seven numbers by an ensemble, brief solo parts, and a dance group) are appealing. Clever, believable dialogue rounds out this out. ROYALTY: $60. SOURCE: Kurtz, Joy (1981). The mystery of Hastings House. Franklin, OH: Eldridge Pub. Co. SUBJECTS/PLAY TYPE: Comedy; Halloween; Mystery; Musical.

2100. 4-6. (+) Nicholson, Jessie. **The mystery of Patriot Inn.** CAST: 3f, 3m. ACTS: 1. SETTINGS: Parlor. PLAYING TIME: 20 min. PLOT: Three children fall asleep trying to think of a Revolutionary War name for their mother's new restaurant. They dream of two British soldiers, who come to the house looking for Nathan Hale. As Hale and an innkeeper emerge from a secret room, the innkeeper writes "Patriot Inn" on the restaurant sign. The children don't remember the dream, so Hale and the innkeeper return, place an X on the secret room, the children press the X and open the door, find Hale's spelling book, and the name for the restaurant. RECOMMENDATION: This is a positive example of a single parent family which could encourage an interest in history. ROYALTY: Free to Plays subscribers. ROYALTY: Free to Plays subscribers. SOURCE: Nicholson, Jessie. (1989, January/February). Plays: The Drama Magazine for Young People, pp. 53-60. SUBJECTS/PLAY TYPE: Mystery; Hale, Nathan; Playlet.

2101. 9-12. (+) Kelly, Tim J. (Wallace, Edgar) **The mystery of the Black Abbot.** (The Black Abbot.) CAST: 6f, 6m. ACTS: 2. SETTINGS: Sitting room. PLAYING TIME: NA min. PLOT: On an old British estate, plans for the marriage of a wealthy young heiress and the lord of the estate are thwarted by the lord's murder. Though the murder was witnessed by a maid, the body disappears. A search for hidden treasure and financial shenanigans complicate the plot. In the final scene the murderer and the Black Abbot are discovered to be one and the same--the lord of the estate who has gone quite mad. RECOMMENDATION: The characters keep each other, as well as the audience, guessing right up to the end. ROYALTY: $40. SOURCE: Kelly, Tim J. (1982). The mystery of the Black Abbot. Boston, MA: Baker's Plays. SUBJECTS/PLAY TYPE: Mystery; Ghosts; Murder; Adaptation.

2102. 2-4. (+) Burtle, Gerry Lynn. **The mystery of the gumdrop dragon.** CAST: 4f, 3m, 11u. ACTS: 1. SETTINGS: Throne room. PLAYING TIME: 20 min. PLOT: Following the theft of the Princess of Candyland's favorite pet (the Gumdrop Dragon), a reward is offered for the return of the dragon and the capture of the thief. Prince

Peppermint Stick brings the culprit (Sir Sourball) to the princess, who forgives him when the dragon is returned. The prince claims the princess's hand in marriage as his reward. RECOMMENDATION: Young children will enjoy the characters' candy names, like "Lady Candy Floss," "Prince Pepper-mint Stick" and "Lady Divinity." The plot is simple and predictable. ROYALTY: Free to Plays subscribers. SOURCE: Burtle, Gerry Lynn. (1981, April). The mystery of the gumdrop dragon. Plays: The Drama Magazine for Young People, pp. 39-48. SUBJECTS/PLAY TYPE: Fantasy; Candy; Melodrama.

2103. 6-8. (+) Seale, Nancy. **The mystery of the masked marauder.** CAST: 4f, 4m. ACTS: 1. SETTINGS: Living room; street corner. PLAYING TIME: 30 min. PLOT: Two newcomers to Hayseed Junction, Sir Ratley Cloakton and Millicent Chumming-Thrip, terrorize the community while disguised as the Masked Marauder. Their ultimate plan is to control Arabella's and Penelope's inheritances. After agreeing to marry Cloakton, Penelope is saved from a sinking ship, the dastardly deed of her fiance. Penelope exposes the evil plot. RECOMMENDATION: The plot is corny and full of ridiculous coincidences. It is a good example of melodrama. ROYALTY: Free to Plays subscribers. SOURCE: Seale, Nancy. (1981, November). The mystery of the masked marauder. Plays: The Drama Magazine for Young People, pp. 11-22. SUBJECTS/PLAY TYPE: Comedy; Melodrama.

2104. 6-12. (+) Martens, Anne Coulter. **The mystery of the missing money.** CAST: 5f, 4m. ACTS: 1. SETTINGS: Living room. PLAYING TIME: 30 min. PLOT: Mrs. Frazier inherits a fine old home from her aunt. When her sizable cash inheritance is missing and indications are that someone has been in the house, members of the household become anxious. Mrs. Frazier's daughter, Kay, and her friend, Clint, find the money in a secret panel. The deputy sheriff arrives in time to stop Clint from absconding with the cash. RECOMMENDATION: Although challenging, relatively simple sound and visual effects will give cast members a sense of achievement and extend the reality of the setting. ROYALTY: Free to Plays subscribers. SOURCE: Martens, Anne Coulter. (1976, November). The mystery of the missing money. Plays: The Drama Magazine for Young People, pp. 13-26. SUBJECTS/PLAY TYPE: Mystery; Playlet.

2105. 4-6. (-) Silverman, Eleanor. **Mystery of the missing owl.** CAST: 5f, 2m, 3u. ACTS: 2. SETTINGS: Library. PLAYING TIME: 20 min. PLOT: When the stuffed owl is stolen from the library, the detective discovers that the alleged "crazy" of the town took it, thinking it contained the fortune of a recently deceased man. RECOMMENDATION: This isn't very exciting and the stereotypes (of girls as gigglers and librarians as quieters) are unfortunate. ROYALTY: None. SOURCE: Silverman, Eleanor. (1983). Dramatics for children. Metuchen, NJ: Scarecrow Press. SUBJECTS/PLAY TYPE: Thefts; Mystery.

2106. 3-8. (+) Betts, Jim. **The mystery of the Oak Island treasure.** CAST: 2f, 5m, 1u. ACTS: 2. SETTINGS:

Living room; island. **PLAYING TIME:** NA. **PLOT:** Excited about the legend of buried treasure guarded by a ghost on Oak Island, Diana and Jason try to find it. Mysterious Captain Bones comes to their mother's boarding house and brings a coded treasure map with him. His rivals, Scavenger John and Seadog McWinkle, follow and attack the Captain. The map is burned but not before the children look at it. The treasure chest is found and opened. No treasure is inside, but the group is happy to have solved the ancient mystery. No one sees the ghostly shape reaching up from within the box to reclose the lid. **RECOMMENDATION:** Although the plot is relatively predictable, it does contain enough suspense and mystery to keep younger audiences guessing. Particularly amusing are the director's notes, which could be made into a brief narrator's part with some rewriting. **ROYALTY:** NA. **SOURCE:** Betts, Jim. (1985). The mystery of the Oak Island treasure. Toronto: Playwrights Canada. **SUBJECTS/PLAY TYPE:** Treasure; Folk Tales, Nova Scotia; Mystery.

2107. 1-3. (+) Laurie, Rona. (Potter, Beatrix) **The mystery of the pie and the patty pan.** (Tales of Beatrix Potter) **CAST:** 1f, 1m, 3u. **ACTS:** 1. **SETTINGS:** Street; living rooms; shop. **PLAYING TIME:** NA. **PLOT:** A dog invited to a cat's tea party sneaks his own veal and ham pie into the house because he does not want to eat mice and bacon pie. Confusion erupts and the cat resolves to invite no more dogs to tea. **RECOMMENDATION:** This cleverly explains how not to behave as a guest in someone else's home. **ROYALTY:** NA. **SOURCE:** Laurie, Rona. (1980). Children's plays from Beatrix Potter. London: F. Warne. **SUBJECTS/PLAY TYPE:** Animals; Manners; Adaptation.

2108. 9-12. (+) Willment, Frank. **The mystery of the second will. CAST:** 4f, 3m. **ACTS:** 1. **SETTINGS:** Living room. **PLAYING TIME:** 30 min. **PLOT:** Quincy Blackman's two nieces, old shipmate, and female friend gather for the reading of his will. The first will is contested by the appearance of a second will. Through deductive reasoning, the female friend is able to prove the second will a forgery, written by Quincy's old shipmate in order that he, rather than the nieces, inherit the old man's fortune. **RECOMMENDATION:** The action unravels slowly, and some interesting facts about the value of pearls, how a will is written and probated, and baseball, are taught in the process. **ROYALTY:** Free to Plays subscribers. **SOURCE:** Willment, Frank. (1983, November). The mystery of the second will. Plays: The Drama Magazine for Young People, pp. 1-12. **SUBJECTS/PLAY TYPE:** Mystery; Wills; Playlet.

2109. K-4. (+) Nixon, Joan Lowery. **The mystery of the sounds in the night. CAST:** 3m. **ACTS:** 1. **SETTINGS:** Woods. **PLAYING TIME:** 15 min. **PLOT:** Mike and Paul go camping with Mike's Uncle Pete. They become frightened of sounds of animals in the woods after hearing a story about a Great Bear, but they try to be brave. Uncle Pete shows them that there is nothing to be afraid of and that the Great Bear is a constellation in the sky. **RECOMMENDATION:** Although there is not much depth to the characters (due to the short playing time), their conversations and behavior are realistic, and the

campout is well described. **ROYALTY:** Free to Plays subscribers. **SOURCE:** Nixon, Joan Lowery. (1979, May). The mystery of the sounds in the night. Plays: The Drama Magazine for Young People, pp. 43-46. **SUBJECTS/PLAY TYPE:** Bravery; Fear; Camping; Drama.

2110. 4-8. (+) Alexander, Sue. **The mystery of the stone statues. CAST:** 1f, 3m, 1u. **ACTS:** 1. **SETTINGS:** Laboratory. **PLAYING TIME:** NA. **PLOT:** Sidney Stalwart, topnotch secret detective, investigates the disappearance of Amy Truegood at the laboratory of the evil scientist, Dr. Amos Chilling. Stalwart learns that Chilling has a secret formula which turns his victims into stone. Discovering Amy Truegood locked in a closet, Stalwart and she foil Chilling's attempts to turn the President of Wakowako to stone. Getting what he deserves, the scientist falls into his own trap and accidentally drinks poison, which nimbly solves the problem of punishing his wickedness. **RECOMMENDATION:** In this enjoyable thriller, the dialogue is relatively simple and the plot is resolved speedily. **ROYALTY:** NA. **SOURCE:** Alexander, Sue. (1980). Whatever happened to Uncle Albert and other puzzling plays. New York, NY: Houghton Mifflin. **SUBJECTS/PLAY TYPE:** Detectives; Evil Scientists; Mystery.

2111. K-3. (+) Gotwalt, Helen Louise Miller. **The mystery of Turkey-Lurkey. CAST:** 2f, 2m, Su. **ACTS:** 1. **SETTINGS:** Barnyard. **PLAYING TIME:** 15 min. **PLOT:** Thanksgiving is almost here and Turkey-Lurkey is missing. He's found hiding in a tree because he has eaten too much and lost his gobble. With his friends' help he regains his gobble. The play ends with the message: don't gobble your food at Thanksgiving. It's a time for sharing. **RECOMMENDATION:** Although extremely didactic, this might be cute for the youngest children, but would have to be produced by the older ones. **ROYALTY:** Free to Plays subscribers. **SOURCE:** Gotwalt, Helen Louise Miller. (1985, November). The mystery of Turkey-Lurkey. Plays: The Drama Magazine for Young People, pp. 37-42. **SUBJECTS/PLAY TYPE:** Thanksgiving; Turkeys; Mystery.

2112. 5-6. (-) Talbert, Janice. **Mystery on the Santa Maria. CAST:** 7u. **ACTS:** 1. **SETTINGS:** None. **PLAYING TIME:** NA. **PLOT:** After two months of sailing with no sign of land, the crew of the Santa Maria is mutinous. Troublemaking sailors plot to overthrow Christopher Columbus, using an apparent compass malfunction to undermine his credibility. Columbus's discovery that the movement of the North Star is responsible for the failure of the magnetic needle appeases the sailors. Soon afterward, land is sighted. **RECOMMENDATION:** While this round the table reading is faithful to the basic facts of Columbus's maiden voyage, its lack of realistic dialogue and credible characters renders it boring. **ROYALTY:** Free to Plays subscribers. **SOURCE:** Talbert, Janice. (1980, October). Mystery on the Santa Maria. Plays: The Drama Magazine for Young People, pp. 43-46. **SUBJECTS/PLAY TYPE:** Columbus, Christopher; Reader's Theater.

2113. 6-12. (-) Fitzgerald, Neil C. **Mystery on the waterfront. CAST:** 3f, 6m. **ACTS:** 1. **SETTINGS:** Dock.

PLAYING TIME: 30 min. PLOT: Julie, her father, and her new boyfriend, Kirk, talk to a detective about a yacht robbery. Kirk was on the pier the night of the robbery, but he didn't see anything. Kirk later finds a diamond ring in his blazer and is about to be arrested by the detective when Julie's father suggests someone tried to frame Kirk. After questioning some shady characters, the detective identifies the thief. RECOMMENDATION: Audiences will not buy this for one minute. The way in which Kirk is set up is patently obvious, the teenagers don't seem very bright and the whole mystery is solved by Julie's father. ROYALTY: Free to Plays subscribers. SOURCE: Fitzgerald, Neil C. (1986, May). Mystery on the waterfront. Plays: The Drama Magazine for Young People, pp. 1-9. SUBJECTS/PLAY TYPE: Mystery; Playlet.

2114. 7-12. (+) Gotwalt, Helen Louise Miller. "N" is for nuisance. CAST: 3f, 3m. ACTS: 1. SETTINGS: Art studio. PLAYING TIME: 30 min. PLOT: A series of tangled events revolving around an art competition lead to a ruined painting--Sara's. Her little brother, Billy, quickly finds another of Sara's paintings and rushes it down to school in time for the competition. Within moments, Sara's art teacher arrives, praising her choice for the competition, and announces her first place award. Billy explains his heroic part in the situation. RECOMMENDATION: This is a lighthearted agreeable play. Little things such as a paint stained letter "N," a dance card, a girl in curlers and a beginner psychology student connect the twists and turns of this humorous plot. The characters are fun, believable and interact well. ROYALTY: Free to Plays Subscribers. SOURCE: Gotwalt, Helen Louise Miller. (1980, May). "N" is for nuisance. Plays: The Drama Magazine for Young People, pp. 27-38. SUBJECTS/PLAY TYPE: Art; Family; Comedy.

2115. 7-10. (+) Fox, Barbara Black. The nameless knight. CAST: 4f, 4m, 6u. ACTS: 2. SETTINGS: Bare stage, backdrops. PLAYING TIME: 15 min. PLOT: The Nameless Knight wishes to marry Prom (fairest damsel in the land), but deems himself unworthy because he lacks a name. To sabotage the efforts of the Nameless Knight to earn a name by slaying a dragon, Party Knight rearranges directional signs to the dragon's lair, sending Nameless to a confrontation with the feared Granny Dragon and her Mean Babies. Unable to vanquish the dragon family, Nameless proposes the formation of a punk rock group and offers his services as agent. With the prospect of wealth and fame on the horizon, Nameless dispenses with the problem of securing a name by musing, "If this is Monday, I must be Monday Knight." RECOMMENDATION: The entire fabric of the play is based on word games and puns which are simple enough to be easily understood but ironic enough to be appreciated rather than scorned. Trendy terminology may be replaced with current terminology as the play becomes dated. ROYALTY: $20. SOURCE: Fox, Barbara Black. (1987). The nameless knight. Franklin, OH: Eldridge Pub. Co. SUBJECTS/PLAY TYPE: Knights; Quests; Skit.

2116. 4-7. (+) Shamas, Laura. (Keene, Carolyn) Nancy Drew and the swami's ring. (The swami's ring) CAST: 8f, 6m. ACTS: 2. SETTINGS: Living room; yard. PLAYING

TIME: NA. PLOT: Two mysteries involving an amnesia victim and a missing woman become entwined. When an ornate Hindu ring is discovered in the amnesia victim's knapsack, Nancy Drew, with her usual cleverness, traces both mysteries to the Swami's retreat where she captures the villains. RECOMMENDATION: The fast moving pace and interesting plot will capture the attention of the entire audience, especially Nancy Drew fans. ROYALTY: NA. SOURCE: Shamas, Laura. (1982). Nancy Drew and the swami's ring. Denver, CO: Pioneer Drama Service. SUBJECTS/PLAY TYPE: Mystery; Adaptation.

2117. 4-7. (+) Tasca, Jules and Tierney, Thomas. (Lewis, C.S.) Narnia. (The lion, the witch and the wardrobe) CAST: 6f, 10m, u. ACTS: 2. SETTINGS: Manor, winter and spring exteriors. PLAYING TIME: NA. PLOT: In this musical dramatization four children enter the land of Narnia through the wardrobe and help Aslan (the Lion) triumph over the evil of White Witch. RECOMMENDATION: This is written for either an elaborate professional production or a modest amateur one. The cast size is expandable, and the songs are appropriate. ROYALTY: Upon application. SOURCE: Tasca, Jules, & Tierney, Thomas. (1987). Narnia. Woodstock, IL: Dramatic Pub. Co. SUBJECTS/PLAY TYPE: Fantasy; Good and Evil; Musical; Adaptation.

2118. 7-12. (+) Rozell, O.B. Nathan the nervous. CAST: 8u. ACTS: 1. SETTINGS: Throne room. PLAYING TIME: 25 min. PLOT: Nathan the Nervous is a new young king who is afraid of everything. His mother is domineering. The court wizard prepares a concoction to effect a change in Nathan's personality. Nathan and a princess drink the courage potion and the queen inadvertently drinks the antidote. The play ends with the queen becoming docile and Nathan in charge. RECOMMENDATION: Strong performers are required for the roles of the queen and Nathan because of the range of expression that they must convey. This will stretch the abilities of the actors. ROYALTY: $15. SOURCE: Rozell, O.B. (1977). Nathan the nervous. Schulenburg, TX: I.E. Clark. SUBJECTS/PLAY TYPE: Royalty; Comedy.

2119. 3-6. (+) Paston, Byrna N. Tolins, Selma L. The nature of little things. CAST: 6f, 6m, Su. ACTS: 1. SETTINGS: Forest. PLAYING TIME: 20 min. PLOT: The insects' picnic is disrupted when they learn an exterminator has developed a spray to kill all insects. They question why beneficial insects should be destroyed along with harmful insects. A confrontation between the exterminator and an ecologist fails to convince the exterminator not to destroy all insects. The ecologist switches sprays so the exterminator will think his is no good. The audience is asked to help convince the exterminator not to destroy all insects. RECOMMENDATION: This forces the audience to stand either with the exterminator or with the ecologist and the insects. Because of audience participation, this should be produced by older students. ROYALTY: Free to Plays subscribers. SOURCE: Paston, Byrna N. & Tolins, Selma L. (1978, May). The nature of little things. Plays: The Drama Magazine for Young People, pp. 35-41. SUBJECTS/PLAY TYPE: Ecology; Nature; Insects; Playlet.

2120. 6-8. (-) Slingluff, Mary O. **Naughty Susan-the Liberty Bell rings for freedom.** CAST: 4f, 3m. ACTS: 1. SETTINGS: Living room of a Quaker home. PLAYING TIME: 10 min. PLOT: In 1776, when the Liberty Bell begins to ring, Mrs. Page and her daughter Ann rush off, telling naughty Susan to wait. She disobeys and goes to help Old John ring the bell. Thomas Jefferson brings her home. RECOMMENDATION: This fails in its attempt to define liberty and the pursuit of happiness. It is also stereotyped, as naughty Susan becomes nice when she returns to her sewing. ROYALTY: None. SOURCE: Kamerman, Sylvia E. (1975). Patriotic and historical plays for young people. Boston: Plays, Inc. SUBJECTS/PLAY TYPE: Family; Playlet.

2121. 2-4*. (+) Barber, Eleanor. Barber, Ray. **The near-sighted knight and the far-sighted dragon.** CAST: 2f, 5m, Su. ACTS: 2. SETTINGS: Open stage. PLAYING TIME: NA. PLOT: The knight and dragon become allies and "must walk in each other's shoes" to help a liberated princess free her father and his kingdom from a wicked, greedy Duchess and her lumpish son. The simple songs sing themselves off the pages, and of course, all live happily ever after. RECOMMENDATION: The language and lyrics are simple and the action delightfully slapstick at times. The message of tolerance for others is ageless and easy sets and costuming make this financially feasible. ROYALTY: $25. SOURCE: Barber, Eleanor and Barber, Ray. (1977). The near-sighted knight and the far-sighted dragon. New Orleans, LA: The Anchorage Press, Inc. SUBJECTS/PLAY TYPE: Musical; Tolerance; Comedy.

2122. 3-9. (-) McDonough, Jerome. **The Nearest star.** CAST: 14f, 9m. ACTS: 1. SETTINGS: None. PLAYING TIME: 30 min. PLOT: Three teenage girls search for a star until they see one over a manger. Saint Mary appears to them as they kneel at the manger and verifies that the true star they seek is within every person. RECOMMENDATION: This is too moralistic and preachy. ROYALTY: $15. SOURCE: McDonough, Jerome. (1981). Schulenburg, TX: I.E. Clark. SUBJECTS/PLAY TYPE: Christmas; Parable; Cyclorama.

2123. 7-12. (+) O'Connor, Vincent D. **Nearly departed.** CAST: 4f, 4m. ACTS: 2. SETTINGS: Living room; dining room. PLAYING TIME: NA. PLOT: Jason is fed up with his marriage, and thinks that his wife doesn't love him anymore. He fakes his death in order to leave the area and start a new life, perhaps with one of his mistresses. There are many humorous complications as people keep coming and going in the living room (including his two mistresses), and as Jason keeps jumping in and out of the coffin. He is found out and decides to reconsider. RECOMMENDATION: The sexual references at the beginning of the play might be edited. Jason has treated his wife like a possession and expected her to do his every whim. He realizes (maybe too late) that he really does love her and that he didn't allow her to be her own person. ROYALTY: $35. SOURCE: O'Connor, Vincent D. (1984). Nearly departed. Studio City, CA: Players Press. SUBJECTS/PLAY TYPE: Marriage; Infidelity; Comedy.

2124. 9-12. (+) Cias, Earl J. (de Maupassant, Guy) **The necklace.** (The necklace) CAST: 4f, 2m. ACTS: 4. SETTINGS: Living room. PLAYING TIME: 25 min. PLOT: After losing a borrowed diamond necklace, Mathilde and her husband work for years to pay back a loan of 40,000 francs, which they used to buy a new necklace for the unwitting owner. On a social visit, Mathilde finally reveals to Cecile that she had lost the original necklace ten years ago, and laments how paying back the borrowed money has ruined her life. RECOMMENDATION: The main characters are well drawn and the plot closely follows the original as does the presentation of its universal and important themes. ROYALTY: Free to Plays subscribers. SOURCE: Dias, Earl J. (1987, April). The necklace. Plays: The Drama Magazine for Young People, pp. 55-64. SUBJECTS/PLAY TYPE: Vanity; Tragedy; Adaptation.

2125. K-6. (+) Lewman, Beverly. Smith, Robert B. **Neighborhood helpers.** CAST: Su. ACTS: 1. SETTINGS: Flannel board. PLAYING TIME: 5 min. PLOT: As Tom rides to school on the bus, he sees a policeman, a fireman, and a mailman. This is designed to develop children's inactive iconic abilities as espoused by Jerome Bruner. RECOMMENDATION: This is recommended for hyperkinetic children because the children actively participate in the story by singing, acting out the parts, and drawing scenes from the story. Children learn to sequence events and increase their attention spans. ROYALTY: NA. SOURCE: Lewman, Beverly & Robert B. Smith. Music dramas for children with special needs. Denton, TX: Troostwyk Press. SUBJECTS/PLAY TYPE: Sequencing Skills; Occupations; Musical.

2126. 7-12. (+) Cadette, G.S. **Nellie's fishy fate.** CAST: 4f, 4m. ACTS: 1. SETTINGS: Parlor. PLAYING TIME: 30 min. PLOT: Wealthy Mrs. Vanderhoff's nurse and shady attorney plan to wed Mrs. V.'s two children and eliminate her within the week. Fate intervenes in the person of Nellie Dogood, new maid, who has a clumsy way of bumping into the villains and foiling their schemes through her simple innocence. The wicked pair decides to dispose of Nellie by means of a tank of live piranhas conveniently located upstairs, but their plans are ruined by a series of comic discoveries. RECOMMENDATION: This is a clever and very funny satire of comedic and melodramatic conventions, making good use of comic discovery devices. The dialogue is hilarious and is filled with stock phrases which invite either exaggerated or deadpan delivery. Action builds to a frenzied climax, and every part is tailor made for the true ham. ROYALTY: Free to Plays subscribers. SOURCE: Cadette, G. S. (1984, October). Nellie's fishy fate. Plays: The Drama Magazine for Young People, pp. 1-11. SUBJECTS/PLAY TYPE: Satire; Melodrama; Comedy.

2127. 7-12. (+) Garver, Juliet. **The nerve of Napoleon.** CAST: 6f, 4m. ACTS: 1. SETTINGS: Living room. PLAYING TIME: 25 min. PLOT: Charlie Bowen's shyness keeps him from running for student council president. His idol from the past, Napoleon Bonaparte, helps Charlie overcome his shyness by giving him a lucky coin, later switched for a gold-foiled chocolate replica. The play ends on a happy note when Charlie discovers the coin is chocolate and realizes he alone is responsible for overcoming his shyness. RECOMMENDATION: This uses fantasy and comedy successfully to point out all that determination and courage can overcome problems. ROYALTY: Free to Plays subscribers. SOURCE: Garver, Juliet. (1984, March). The nerve of Napoleon. Plays: The Drama Magazine for Young People, pp. 22-30. SUBJECTS/PLAY TYPE: Shyness; Comedy.

2128. 4-6. (+) Bradley, Virginia. **Nester the jester.** CAST: 2f, 8m. ACTS: 3. SETTINGS: Courtyard. PLAYING TIME: NA. PLOT: An 18th century knight defeats an evil knight because three modern American boys help him grow stronger by giving him body building cereal. RECOMMENDATION: Children will enjoy the exciting roles in this delightful romp through medieval history. ROYALTY: None. SOURCE: Bradley, Virginia. (1975). Nester the jester. New York: Dodd, Mead. SUBJECTS/PLAY TYPE: Knights; Castles; Comedy.

2129. 10-12. (+) Rogers, David. **Never mind what happened, how did it end?** CAST: 19f, 19m, Su. ACTS: 2. SETTINGS: Living room; porch; sun parlor. PLAYING TIME: NA. PLOT: Flashbacks show three generations of women going through the same stages of their lives. By the end of the play, the three women have been drawn closer together as they realize they have more in common than just being related by blood. RECOMMENDATION: This would be challenging for high schoolers to produce because of the continuity that must take place in the flashbacks, but it is worth the effort. ROYALTY: $35. SOURCE: Rogers, David. (1976). Never mind what happened, how did it end? Chicago, IL: Dramatic Pub. Co. SUBJECTS/PLAY TYPE: Family; Decisions; Comedy.

2130. 9-12. (+) Quisenberry, Pat. **Never say lie.** CAST: 6f, 6m, 1u. ACTS: 3. SETTINGS: Living room. PLAYING TIME: NA. PLOT: Karen Ferris (high school senior) wants to tell every prospective buyer that her car, though now repaired and running, was in an accident. Her parents encourage her not to be so honest. Torn between honesty and profit, Karen is honest. Finally, a handsome college student buys the car and also wants to date Karen. She receives her profit and gets a bonus of a young man who appreciates her honesty. RECOMMENDATION: Typical of teenagers, Karen questions her parents' ethics as she pokes fun at the fads of their youth. ROYALTY: $25. SOURCE: Quisenberry, Pat. (1988). Never say lie. Franklin, OH: Eldridge Pub. Co. SUBJECTS/PLAY TYPE: Honesty; Comedy.

2131. 3-7. (+) Kelly, Tim. **Never trust a city slicker.** CAST: 8f, 6m. ACTS: 2. SETTINGS: Boarding house. PLAYING TIME: 60 min. PLOT: A down and out theater group gets last minute salvation and professional resurrection when a locked trunk containing new material provides a source of royalties. RECOMMENDATION: This oversimplified, moralistic comedy has a superficial plot and its pat ending casts it as a farce to be enjoyed merely as comic relief. ROYALTY: $25. SOURCE: Kelly,

Tim. (1983). Never trust a city slicker. Denver, CO: Pioneer Drama Service. SUBJECTS/PLAY TYPE: Western; Luck; Comedy.

2132. 9-12. (-) Lerman, Louis. **The new American freedom plow.** CAST: 2m, Su. ACTS: 1. SETTINGS: Bare stage. PLAYING TIME: 20 min. PLOT: Thomas Jefferson, after purchasing 530 million acres of land in Louisiana, invents the American Freedom Plow to help plant Liberty Trees. To convince Ebenezer Drew that it is a plow, Jefferson offers to plow Drew's farm for free. The two not only plow Drew's land, but because there is no stopping handle, they also plow all of Louisiana, and Europe before returning to New Hampshire. RECOMMENDATION: This is difficult to understand, as most of the story is symbolically conveyed through song. It combines some of Jefferson's writings with an analogy of how his ideals spread and affected the whole nation and Europe. ROYALTY: Free to Plays subscribers. SOURCE: Lerman, Louis. (1985, January/February). The new American freedom plow. Plays: The Drama Magazine for Young People, pp. 12-16 SUBJECTS/PLAY TYPE: Jefferson, Thomas; Louisiana Purchase; Pantomime.

2133. 7-10. (+) McCusker, Paul. **The new and improved.** CAST: 2m. ACTS: 1. SETTINGS: None. PLAYING TIME: NA. PLOT: Mike, who needs moral support from Dave, asks him to read first Corinthians Thirteen. Dave tries to find the passage in the New and Improved King James Six MultiLinear BiLingual Instructional Exceptional Bible. He cannot locate the passage, Mike becomes exasperated, and walks away. RECOMMENDATION: In this spoof of our obsession with new and improved items, Dave praises the overhauled Bible the way a hype TV commercial would. The hilariously complex index, coupled with the obvious absurdity of the concept, make this an excellent warm up skit. ROYALTY: NA. SOURCE: McCusker, Paul. (1982). Souvenirs: Comedies and dramas for Christian fellowship. Boston, MA: Baker's Plays. SUBJECTS/PLAY TYPE: Christian Drama; Satire; Comedy; Bible; Skit.

2134. 4-9. (+) Albert, Rollin'. **A new angle on Christmas.** CAST: 9f, 13m. ACTS: 1. SETTINGS: Newspaper office; outdoors. PLAYING TIME: 15 min. PLOT: Reporter Joe is having trouble finding a new angle on Christmas before his deadline. All the adults he approaches seem spiritually dead. Children tell him the true meaning of Christmas by speaking and spelling out Christmas (large letters are attached to their costumes). RECOMMENDATION: This has potential to touch adults' hearts as well. ROYALTY: None. SOURCE: Kamerman, Sylvia E. (1978). On stage for Christmas: A collection of royalty-free plays for young people. Boston, MA: Plays, Inc. SUBJECTS/PLAY TYPE: Comedy; Christmas; Skit.

2135. 6-12. (+) Getty, Peter. **A new approach to human sacrifice.** CAST: 2f, 4m. ACTS: 1. SETTINGS: Living room. PLAYING TIME: NA. PLOT: Susie forces her date, Alvin, to eat and drink grey and red food, which seems to make him euphoric. After a news flash about a cult which uses the brains and blood of its victims for food, and whose victims don't die, but miraculously live to become members, Alvin is accosted by Susie's cult family. RECOMMENDATION: Written by a 16 year old, this eerily sends a message about society's obsession with fun to the exclusion of everything else. It could easily be used as a horror story. ROYALTY: NA. SOURCE: Lamb, Wendy. (1986). Meeting the winter bike rider and other prize winning plays. New York, NY: Dell. SUBJECTS/PLAY TYPE: Society; Values; Drama.

2136. 12. (-) Kurtz, C. Gordon. **New beat on an old drum.** CAST: 7f, 5m. ACTS: 3. SETTINGS: Front yard; porch; living room. PLAYING TIME: NA. PLOT: Jane Shaw inherits her aunt's resort property and convinces her four widowed neighbors not to sell their properties to a shady real estate developer. RECOMMENDATION: This is long, dated, and not especially compelling. ROYALTY: $35. SOURCE: Kurtz, C. Gordon. (1976). New beat on an old drum. New York, NY: Dramatists Play Service, Inc. SUBJECTS/PLAY TYPE: Resorts; Real Estate Development; Widowhood; Comedy.

2137. 5-12. (+) Foon, Dennis. **New Canadian kid.** CAST: 2f, 2m. ACTS: 1. SETTINGS: Outside of a house; schoolyard; classroom; lunchroom; living room. PLAYING TIME: NA. PLOT: Nick and his mother leave "Homeland" for Canada, where Nick must make friends with his Canadian classmates and overcome prejudices, language barriers, and ignorance. RECOMMENDATION: A unique device of having the Canadians speak gibberish and the immigrants speak English demonstrates how strange our native language appears to immigrants. Because of the difficulty of speaking gibberish, this is best produced by older adolescents. ROYALTY: NA. SOURCE: Foon, Dennis. (1982). New Canadian kid. Vancouver, British Columbia: Pulp Press Book Publishers. SUBJECTS/PLAY TYPE: Friendship; Immigrants; Drama.

2138. 7-12. (+) Albert, Rollin'. (Perrault, Charles) **A new Cinderella.** (Cinderella) CAST: 5f, 4m. ACTS: 1. SETTINGS: Bare stage, props. PLAYING TIME: 40 min. PLOT: A young girl attends a party hosted by wealthy Harold Prinz, who has been disillusioned by dishonest and insincere friends. At the party, Ella and her "Prinz" discover how much they have in common. Ella loses a sneaker, Harold searches for the foot that will fit it, and finds Ella. RECOMMENDATION: The wealthy Prinz serves only marshmallows and water to see if his guests like him or his money, and the he and Ella find commonality in a lively discussion of house cleaning products. As Ella promises to love, honor and prevent ring around the collar, this fractured fairy tale, which also has delightfully satiric dialogue, comes to its inevitable conclusion. ROYALTY: Free to Plays subscribers. SOURCE: Albert, Rollin'. (1975, November). A new Cinderella. Plays: The Drama Magazine for Young People, pp. 1-13. SUBJECTS/PLAY TYPE: Folk Tales, France; Adaptation.

2139. 3-9. (+) Harder, Eleanor. (Andersen, Hans Christian) **New clothes for the empress.** (The emperor's new clothes) CAST: 4f, 2m, Su. ACTS: 2. SETTINGS: Courtyard; throne room. PLAYING TIME: 90 min. PLOT: An addlebrained Empress designs new, original and ghastly outfits for herself and then holds daily parades to display them. Her wicked cousin and his wife plot to take over the kingdom by having the Empress declared incompetent after they have convinced her to wear an invisible gown in a parade for the villagers. The plans go awry when the Empress' loyal servant and her devoted seamstress interfere. RECOMMENDATION: Although the other characters are set types, the Empress is a good natured, dizzy sort, and a costume designer with an imaginative flair could have fun with the outrageous outfits. The number of lines to be memorized probably limit production to the upper middle school grades. ROYALTY: $40. SOURCE: Harder, Eleanor. (1980). New clothes for the empress. Denver, CO: Pioneer Drama Service. SUBJECTS/PLAY TYPE: Vanity; Fashion; Folk Tales, Denmark; Adaptation.

2140. 4-6*. (+) **New hearts for old.** CAST: 3f, 3m. ACTS: 1. SETTINGS: Living room. PLAYING TIME: 20 min. PLOT: On Valentine's Day, the children try to talk Dad into buying a Valentine present for mother. He agrees, after mother pulls out Valentine cards she received from him as a girl. RECOMMENDATION: This is cute, but long and written in rhyme. ROYALTY: None. SOURCE: Fisher, Aileen. (1980). Holiday programs for boys and girls. Boston, MA: Plays, Inc. SUBJECTS/PLAY TYPE: Valentine's Day; Comedy.

2141. 7-9. (+) Kehret, Peg. **The new kid.** CAST: 1f. ACTS: 1. SETTINGS: None. PLAYING TIME: NA. PLOT: As a young girl enters a new school, the trauma of the first day, is discussed, complete with the "sick stomach" worries of proper clothing, hair style, height and peer acceptance. RECOMMENDATION: The frightening aspects of the situation from the standpoint of the young are genuinely portrayed. ROYALTY: NA. SOURCE: Kehret, Peg. (1986). Winning monologs for young actors. Colorado Springs, CO: Meriwether Pub. SUBJECTS/PLAY TYPE: Fear; Social Adjustment; Monologue.

2142. 7-12. (+) Nydam, Ken. **New kid in school.** CAST: 2f, 2m. ACTS: 1. SETTINGS: None. PLAYING TIME: NA. PLOT: Three students discuss James, a new boy at school who is disabled. They make fun of his friendliness and of the way he walks. When James greets them, they rudely ignore him. RECOMMENDATION: This painfully portrays people at their worst. ROYALTY: None. SOURCE: Altena, Hans. (1978). The playbook for Christian theater. Grand Rapids, MI: Baker Book House. SUBJECTS/PLAY TYPE: Disabilities; Drama.

2143. K-8. (-) Robinson, Miriam. **A new look at American history.** CAST: 10f, 18m, 1u. ACTS: 4. SETTINGS: Beach. PLAYING TIME: 20 min. PLOT: The purchase of Manhattan Island, the Louisiana Purchase, and the California gold rush are reenacted using modern English. RECOMMENDATION: Historians will be devastated by the historical liberties taken here. ROYALTY: Free to Plays subscribers. SOURCE: Robinson, Miriam. (1983, May). A new look at American History. Plays: The Drama Magazine for Young People, pp. 51-56. SUBJECTS/PLAY TYPE: History, U.S.; Manhattan Island, Purchase; Louisiana Purchase; Playlet.

2144. 4-8. (+) Gotwalt, Helen Louise Miller. **New shoes.** CAST: 1f, 2m, 23u. ACTS: 1. SETTINGS: Shoe store. PLAYING TIME: 20 min. PLOT: Customers enter a shoe store demanding specific shoe styles and then complain that all of the shoes are too large. The master cobbler describes shoes worn at different stages of life to represent growth and achievement at each plateau. He informs patrons that they will grow into the large shoes required by each experience in life. The play closes with the school song. RECOMMENDATION: This is especially appropriate for graduation exercises. The audience will readily understand, accept, and internalize the concepts of goal setting, achievement, and challenge. ROYALTY: Free to Plays subscribers. SOURCE: Gotwalt, Helen Louise Miller. (1984, May). New shoes. Plays: The Drama Magazine for Young People, pp. 45-48. SUBJECTS/PLAY TYPE: Lifeskills; Graduation; Skit.

2145. 9-12. (+) Coble, Herman. **A new sunrise.** CAST: 2f, 2m. ACTS: 1. SETTINGS: Yard. PLAYING TIME: NA. PLOT: Two bored elderly women sit on the front porch of a funeral parlor to wait to die. They have a bottle of wine into which they are going to place arsenic when they decide the time is right. As they sit drinking the wine, a salesman asks directions. Learning of their intentions, he drinks the last of the wine before they can add the poison. He convinces them that they cannot kill themselves because they have a dream to live for. In the end, the three plan to go to Paris. RECOMMENDATION: The dialogue provides a feel for the personalities of the characters. Although the topic of suicide is presented with some humor, it is addressed thoughtfully at the end. ROYALTY: $15. SOURCE: Coble, Herman. (1979). A new sunrise. Boston, MA: Baker's Plays. SUBJECTS/PLAY TYPE: Suicide; Elderly; Comedy.

2146. 7-12. (+) McCusker, Paul. **New Year's Eve: After the Party.** CAST: 1f, 1m. ACTS: 1. SETTINGS: Living room. PLAYING TIME: NA. PLOT: Bob and Linda's marriage has become rocky since Bob became a Christian. His witnessing and seeming obsession with Jesus makes everyone uncomfortable. As they argue, Bob realizes that perhaps he has gone a bit overboard. He asks Linda to join him in knowing Jesus and implies that he will try to be less overbearing about it. She agrees. RECOMMENDATION: This demonstrates that personal commitment does not have to manifest itself in constant evangelizing to others. It would be an excellent vehicle for church related groups and for generating discussions about proselytizing. ROYALTY: NA. SOURCE: McCusker, Paul. (1984). Batteries not included. Boston, MA: Baker's Plays. SUBJECTS/PLAY TYPE: Christian Drama; Evangelism; Skit.

2147. 7-12. (+) McCusker, Paul. **New Year's Eve: Another perspective.** CAST: 2u. ACTS: 1. SETTINGS: Living room. PLAYING TIME: NA. PLOT: A babysitter tries to explain to her charge why people have hangovers after New Year's Eve, and why they make resolutions that they never keep. The child, with the wisdom of innocence, doesn't understand why people would do something that makes them sick or turns them into liars. RECOMMENDATION: This very cleverly exposes the

inanity of getting drunk and making unreasonable resolutions. ROYALTY: NA. SOURCE: McCusker, Paul. (1984). Batteries not included. Boston, MA: Baker's Plays. SUBJECTS/PLAY TYPE: Alcohol Abuse; New Year's Eve; Skit.

2148. 7-12. (-) McCusker, Paul. **New Year's Eve: At a bar.** CAST: 3m. ACTS: 1. SETTINGS: Bar. PLAYING TIME: NA. PLOT: Two men in a bar on New Year's Eve complain about their lives. The unmarried womanizer wishes he had a wife and children. The married man wishes he were an unmarried womanizer. The single man chastises the married one, and tells him that he doesn't realize how lucky he is. RECOMMENDATION: This is insulting to women, patronizing to the audience, and too dogmatic and cliched to make its point. ROYALTY: NA. SOURCE: McCusker, Paul. (1984). Batteries not included. Boston, MA: Baker's Plays. SUBJECT/PLAY TYPE: Marriage; Illusions; Skit.

2149. 7-12. (-) McCusker, Paul. **New Year's Eve: At the punch bowl.** CAST: 2f. ACTS: 1. SETTINGS: Living room. PLAYING TIME: NA. PLOT: Two old (but now estranged) friends meet at a reunion. The poor one is angry at the rich one because God showered her with everything while the poor friend got nothing. They part as they met, estranged. RECOMMENDATION: This has no point, unless it is to point out how bitter a person can be. Also, the strong emotions that are so quickly exposed cannot be adequately explained in such a short piece. ROYALTY: NA. SOURCE: McCusker, Paul. (1984). Batteries not included. Boston, MA: Baker's Plays. SUBJECTS/PLAY TYPE: Bitterness; Skit.

2150. 3-6. (+). Kehret, Peg. **New Year's resolution.** CAST: 1m. ACTS: 1. SETTINGS: None. PLAYING TIME: NA. PLOT: A young boy resolves to keep his room clean. To begin, he cleans out his desk drawers. He dumps everything on his bed to sort it, but becomes fascinated with his old toys and makes a bigger mess trying organize them. RECOMMENDATION: The appeal of this is in the fact that everyone can relate to it. Due to its length, a slightly older child should be the speaker. ROYALTY: NA. SOURCE: Kehret, Peg. (1986). Winning monologues for young actors. Colorado Springs, CO: Meriwether Pub. SUBJECTS/PLAY TYPE: Resolutions; Cleaning; Monologue.

2151. 7-12. (+) Thomas, Janet. **Newcomer.** CAST: 3f, 2m. ACTS: 1. SETTINGS: School gym. PLAYING TIME: NA. PLOT: Chinese Mai Li has journeyed from Vietnam, leaving her mother behind. She enters a multi-racial school where many students are either immigrants or the children of immigrants. Although she is watched over by a sympathetic teacher, Mai Li's inability to speak English isolates her. Finally, the school clown and troublemaker, a boy of Chinese heritage, agrees to speak Chinese with her and she begins to adapt. RECOMMENDATION: This makes a valiant attempt to explore the trauma of the immigrant who is unable to communicate in her adopted country's language. Many lines are in Chinese, Spanish, and Filipino. ROYALTY: $35. SOURCE: Thomas, Janet. (1987). Newcomer. New Orleans, LA: Anchorage Press,

Inc. SUBJECTS/PLAY TYPE: School; Bilingualism; Immigrants; Drama.

2152. 2-12. (+) Bychok, Clarlyn H. **News broadcast from Mother Goose Land.** CAST: 4f, 9m, 12u. ACTS: 1. SETTINGS: TV studio. PLAYING TIME: 15 min. PLOT: A newscaster recounts the day's activities, including Jack and Jill falling down; Humpty Dumpty's great tragedy; the cat jumping over the moon; Tom who stole a pig; and Little Boy Blue who stole a tart. The time is announced by the mouse of **Hickory Dickery Dock;** Jack be nimble talks about jogging; and various other nursery rhymes are adapted to the news story format. RECOMMENDATION: Complete with nursery rhyme commercials, this will appeal to the youngest (who will enjoy the rhymes) and the oldest (who will love the cleverness). ROYALTY: Free to Plays subscribers. SOURCE: Bychok, Clarlyn H. (1978, March). News broadcast from Mother Goose Land. Plays: The Drama Magazine for Young People, pp. 39-42. SUBJECTS/PLAY TYPE: Fantasy; Nursery Rhyme Characters; Comedy.

2153. 8-12. (+). Charles, Ronald Jr. **Next, please!** CAST: 1f, 1u. ACTS: 1. PLAYING TIME: NA. PLOT: Margaret James, awaiting her turn for a TV audition, weighs the consequences of succeeding and failing. RECOMMENDATION: Margaret goes through a logical decision making process as she chooses to avoid stardom in order to preserve stability in her life. ROYALTY: Free to Plays subscribers. SOURCE: Charles, Ronald Jr. (1981, May). Next, please! Plays: The Drama Magazine for Young People, pp. 58-60. SUBJECTS/PLAY TYPE: Auditions; Stardom; Monologue.

2154. 7-9. (+) Fontaine, Robert. **Next stop, Mars.** CAST: 2f, 3m, 2u. ACTS: 1. PLAYING TIME: NA. SETTINGS: Launch pad; space craft; landing site. PLOT: Happy Wilson is pursued by an insurance agent as he prepares to fly to Mars. He tries to convince his parents that the ship is safe, the insurance agent that he does not want additional insurance, and his girlfriend that he will marry her when he returns. He flies to Mars, only to be approached by another insurance agent. RECOMMENDATION: This takes a satiric look at what irritates people in life, especially overprotective parents. It can be performed as a skit, as reader's theater, or as a full blown play. ROYALTY: Free to Plays subscribers. SOURCE: Fontaine, Robert. (1978, January). Next Stop, Mars. Plays: The Drama Magazine for Young People, pp. 67-69. SUBJECTS/PLAY TYPE: Space; Satire; Comedy; Skit.

2155. 3-7. (-) Fontaine, Robert. **Next stop, Saturn.** CAST: 2f, 3m, 1u. PLAYING TIME: NA. SETTINGS: Launch pad; landing site. PLOT: The last few minutes before a space flight to Saturn are described. RECOMMENDATION: This complicated production contains many stereotypes and much over used humor. ROYALTY: Free to Plays subscribers. SOURCE: Kamerman, Sylvia E. (1981). Space and science fiction plays for young people. Boston, MA: Plays, Inc. SUBJECTS/PLAY TYPE: Space; Comedy; Skit.

2156. 4-6. (+) Boiko, Claire. **Next stop, Spring.** CAST: 8f, 2m, Su. ACTS: 1. PLAYING TIME: 20 min. SETTINGS: Subway train; street. PLOT: Four subway riders leave winter behind and move through spring into summer. The travelers make specific references to clothing, sports, and foods typical for each season. Evidence of spring is noted through a newspaper headline, a robin and an ice cream vendor. RECOMMENDATION: Connotative terms such as Equinox Exit, April Junction, and Shower Street provide special meaning and associations. ROYALTY: Free to Plays subscribers. SOURCE: Boiko, Claire. (1984, May). Next stop, Spring. Plays: The Drama Magazine for Young People, pp. 35-39. SUBJECTS/PLAY TYPE: Spring; Seasons; Fantasy; Skit.

2157. 11-12. (-) Miller, Ev. **A nice day in the park.** CAST: 5f, 1m. ACTS: 1. SETTINGS: Park shelter; park. PLAYING TIME: 30 min. PLOT: Four cheerleaders, resentful of Kathleen's clothing, new car, and "haughty airs," invite her to a picnic in a wooded park. They intend to frighten her by leaving her alone in the park at nightfall. Anticipating a trick, Kathleen plans a "scare" of her own. She has hired a man to visit the park, pretending to be the murderer of two girls, and an escapee from the state hospital for the criminally insane. Her scare tactic is successful; the four girls run in terror. Kathleen then realizes that the man she hired really is a murderer. The play concludes as the shadow of his knife comes toward her. RECOMMENDATION: This is undeniably a "spooky" thriller. Yet, it focuses upon the immaturity of teenagers, their petty spites, and their desires for revenge. While it dramatizes the cruelty young adults may inflict upon each other, it does not explore the issues it raises, and it leaves the audience with the impression that even murder is somehow justified if people are cruel to each other. ROYALTY: $25. SOURCE: Miller, Ev. (1984). A nice day in the park. Franklin, OH: Eldridge Pub. Co. SUBJECTS/PLAY TYPE: Murder; Psychology; Criminals; Drama.

2158. 9-12. (+) Spitzer, Lewis F. **Nice girls don't finish last.** 13f, 9m. ACTS: 2. SETTINGS: Living room; corridor. PLAYING TIME: NA. PLOT: Dr. Carlos Quintero, a Cuban psychiatrist, has immigrated to the U.S., where he is to be a probationary member of a mental hospital staff. His daughter, Cachita, a talented singer and dancer, wants to enter show business. She enters the Miss Blackfoot Pageant, but the boyfriend of another contestant threatens to make Cachita's father appear to be illicitly prescribing drugs unless she withdraws. Cachita competes and becomes first runner up. When the Quinteros return home, law officers have a warrant for the doctor's arrest. Cachita reveals the blackmail threat and her father is cleared. When he receives an emergency phone call about the blackmailer and his girlfriend, both injured in a car wreck, he finds in the car a pad of prescription blanks stolen from his office. RECOMMENDATION: In addition to an absorbing plot and a suspenseful conclusion, this presents a serious view of inflexibility in a free society. Although the doctor's family has fled oppression, it must learn to adapt to a new set of restrictions--some explicit, such as the rigorous relicensing process he must undergo--and some implicit, such as prejudice. **ROYALTY:** $35. **SOURCE:** Spitzer, Lewis F. (1983). Nice girls don't finish last. Schulenburg, TX: I.E. Clark. **SUBJECTS/PLAY TYPE:** Immigrants; Prejudice; Drama.

2159. 7-10. (+) Bland, Joellen. (Dickens, Charles) **Nicholas Nickleby.** (Nicholas Nickleby) **CAST:** 3f, 15m. **ACTS:** 1. **SETTINGS:** Office. **PLAYING TIME:** 35 min. **PLOT:** When Nicholas' father dies, his uncle Ralph agrees to help if Nicholas becomes an instructor at Mr. Squeers' boys school. Mr. Squeers and his wife mistreat the students, and Nicholas befriends Smike. When Nicholas learns that Ralph has been neglecting Nicholas' mother and sister, the boy has a final conflict with Squeers and flees to London with Smike. Newman Noggs (Ralph's clerk), offers him lodging, and Mr. Cheeryble (a kind London merchant) offers him employment. Smike is accepted as a member of the family and Ralph is no longer needed. **RECOMMENDATION:** With strong, consistent characterization, the feeling for Dickens' England and the hardships encountered by his characters are well communicated. Casting could present difficulties because of the limited number of female roles. **ROYALTY:** Free to Plays subscribers. **SOURCE:** Bland, Joellen. (1982, November). Nicholas Nickleby. Plays: The Drama Magazine for Young People, pp. 69-80. **SUBJECTS/PLAY TYPE:** Family; Reader's Theater; Generosity; Adaptation.

2160. 7-12. (+) Kelly, Tim J. (Dickens, Charles) **Nicholas Nickleby, schoolmaster.** (Nicholas Nickleby) **CAST:** 15f, 15m. **ACTS:** 2. **SETTINGS:** London streets; shops; offices. **PLAYING TIME:** NA. **PLOT:** Nicholas foils the plots of his wicked uncle as he saves his mother and sister from a life of hardship and wins the girl he loves. The play describes briefly some of the horrors of England's boarding schools during this era, but concentrates mostly on the schemes of Nicholas' uncle. **RECOMMENDATION:** This is faithful to the spirit and overall plot of the original, but not to the elaborate characterizations. Much of the continuity provided by Dickens' descriptions of people is lost. The episodic nature of the story makes careful staging essential. **ROYALTY:** $50. **SOURCE:** Kelly, Tim J. (1981). Nicholas Nickleby, schoolmaster. Woodstock, IL: Dramatic Pub. Co. **SUBJECTS/PLAY TYPE:** Romance; Adaptation.

2161. 3-12. (+) Fisher, Aileen Lucia. (Moore, Clement) **The night before Christmas.** (Twas the night before Christmas) **CAST:** 2f, 2m, Su. **ACTS:** 1. **SETTINGS:** Lectern; living room. **PLAYING TIME:** 20 min. **PLOT:** This provides a concise and unusual perspective of Clement Moore, the events on the evening that he wrote his poem, and how it was published. **RECOMMENDATION:** Like the poem, this is for all ages and all times. It is an informative and lovely addition to the traditional Christmas fare. **ROYALTY:** Free to Plays subscribers. **SOURCE:** Fisher, Aileen Lucia. (1985). Year-round programs for young players. Boston, MA: Plays, Inc. **SUBJECTS/PLAY TYPE:** Christmas; Moore, Clement; Skit.

2162. 1-4. (+) Riekens, Deloney M. **The night before Halloween.** **CAST:** 3f, 3m, Su. **ACTS:** 1. **SETTINGS:** Forest. **PLAYING TIME:** 20 min. **PLOT:** When the mayor and town council cancel Halloween because it has become too dangerous for the children, Sir Ghost, Jack O'Lantern, Lizadora Witch, Christopher Cat, Vivian Vampire and Misty Moonlight each find a special way to help the children on Halloween night instead of scaring them. **RECOMMENDATION:** Props and costumes are simple, and the extras can wear their own Halloween costumes. **ROYALTY:** $20. **SOURCE:** Riekens, Deloney M. (1985). The night before Halloween. Franklin, OH: Eldridge Pub. Co. **SUBJECTS/PLAY TYPE:** Halloween; Skit.

2163. 3-6. (+) Hamlett, Christina. **Night of the new and improved Christmas.** **CAST:** 4f, 5m, Su. **ACTS:** 1. **SETTINGS:** Living room. **PLAYING TIME:** 20 min. **PLOT:** Santa's elves hire a Madison Avenue consulting firm to make Santa's life easier. But they are surprised by the firm's recommendations. Santa should move headquarters to Santa Monica, change Christmas to August, replace the elves with unemployed actors, drive an RV instead of the sleigh and reindeer, slim down and jazz up his wardrobe. Santa wisely declines to change. **RECOMMENDATION:** This has an elaborate set, given its brevity, but children will enjoy it both as performers and audience members. **ROYALTY:** $25. **SOURCE:** Hamlett, Christina. (1987). Night of the new and improved Christmas. Franklin, OH: Eldridge Pub. Co. **SUBJECTS/PLAY TYPE:** Christmas; Santa Claus; Comedy.

2164. 1-7. (+) Rahn, Suzanne. **Night of the trolls.** **CAST:** 1f, 3m, Su. **ACTS:** 1. **SETTINGS:** Woods; cottage room. **PLAYING TIME:** 15 min. **PLOT:** An orphan, Eric, and his pet bear save the town from trolls by scaring them away when Eric describes his bear as a little dog whose parents are on their way home. **RECOMMENDATION:** Cute and well drawn, children will especially enjoy acting the troll parts. **ROYALTY:** Free to Plays subscribers. **SOURCE:** Rahn, Suzanne. (1976, February). Night of the trolls. Plays: The Drama Magazine for Young People, pp. 45-48. **SUBJECTS/PLAY TYPE:** Bears; Folktales, Norway; Trolls; Playlet.

2165. 4-7. (+) Bradley, Virginia. **The night that time sat still.** **CAST:** 4f, 6m, 1u. **ACTS:** 1. **SETTINGS:** Room. **PLAYING TIME:** NA. **PLOT:** On New Year's Eve, Ermagrace helps Father Time persuade Old Year to leave so that the new year can come. **RECOMMENDATION:** This has occasional humor and requires two strong actors for the parts of Father Time and Ermagrace. **ROYALTY:** None. **SOURCE:** Bradley, Virginia. (1981). Holidays on stage. New York, NY: Dodd, Mead. **SUBJECTS/PLAY TYPE:** New Year's Eve; Comedy.

2166. 4-6. (-) Hamstra, Sue & Katje, Joyce. **A night to remember.** **CAST:** 2f, 6m. **ACTS:** 1. **SETTINGS:** None. **PLAYING TIME:** 30 min. **PLOT:** A man discovers the true meaning of Christmas by watching his son's Christmas school play which is a compilation of Bible verses from the Books of the Prophets Isaiah and Jeremiah, Micah, Malachi, and the Gospel according to St. Luke. **RECOMMENDATION:** The mother and father are stereotyped, and the main speaking parts are written only for males. **ROYALTY:** None. **SOURCE:** Hendricks,

William & Vogel, Cora. (1983). Handbook of Christmas programs. Grand Rapids, MI: Baker Book House. SUBJECTS/PLAY TYPE: Christmas; Worship Program.

2167. 7-12. (+) Woodward, Laurie. **Night voice.** CAST: 5f, 1m, 1u. ACTS: 1. SETTINGS: Room in old house. PLAYING TIME: NA. PLOT: Three teenage girls gather for a slumber party at the home of a fourth girl's deceased grandfather. One of the girls pulls out an old radio from a pile of the grandfather's things. Strangely, the radio seems to talk to the girls. Eventually it is revealed that the girls have accidentally invoked a curse upon themselves; they are trapped in the house forever, as time has gone backwards to the grandfather's decade. RECOMMENDATION: Suspense builds as the action moves from a very ordinary beginning to a very eerie conclusion. Lighting can be used to highlight the radio and create a spooky atmosphere. ROYALTY: $15. SOURCE: Wood-ward, Laurie. (1986). Night voice. Boston, MA: Baker's Plays. SUBJECTS/PLAY TYPE: Suspense; Supernatural; Drama.

2168. 1-5*. (+) Urquhart, John & Grossberg, Rita. (Andersen, Hans Christian) **Nightingale.** (The nightingale) CAST: 1m, 4u. ACTS: 1. SETTINGS: Palace; garden. PLAYING TIME: NA. PLOT: An emperor in China is never satisfied: not with his gardens, his robes or his music. He always calls for more, causing unhappiness for his people. When he tries to confine the nightingale, the gods intervene to force the emperor to listen to his heart and love his fellow man. RECOMMENDATION: With no set pieces, the elaborate costumes and the Oriental flavor of the music are important. Audience participation is necessary, so cast members must be sufficiently adept at involving and controlling the audience. ROYALTY: $25. SOURCE: Urquhart, John & Grossberg, Rita. (1983). Nightingale. New Orleans, LA: Anchorage Press. SUBJECTS/PLAY TYPE: Nightingales; Folk Tales, Denmark; Adaptation.

2169. 9-12. (-) Dorn, Patrick Rainville. **Nightmare high school.** CAST: 7f, 7m, 7u. ACTS: 1. SETTINGS: Bare stage, intricate props. PLAYING TIME: 75 min. PLOT: Several students hold a night long vigil in the high school auditorium to discover the true identity of the "Locker Stalker," an anonymous person who seizes student possessions from unsecured lockers and deposits them on the stage. After a gothic horror night of conventional scare tactics, the anticlimactic ending reveals Marty, the custodian, as the "Locker Stalker." He retrieved unsecured articles from lockers to prevent their confiscation by Ms. Larsen, the unsympathetic principal. RECOMMENDATION: This is marked by a trite, cliched plot. Today's teens are accustomed to viewing truly bizarre, terrifying horror movies with sophisticated special effects and shockingly perverse and morbid plots. By contrast, the paltry fears of these students and the pale, almost congenial spirits seem comical. It would take fresh, talented, and charismatic actors to overcome the stale plot and dated humor. ROYALTY: $35. SOURCE: Dorn, Patrick Rainville. (1987). Nightmare high school. Denver, CO: Pioneer Drama Service. SUBJECTS/PLAY TYPE: Horror; Mystery; Comedy.

2170. 5-8. (-) Van Horn, Bill. **Nightmare on the lovey-dovey dreamboat.** CAST: 15f, 9m, Su. ACTS: 2. SETTINGS: Luxury liner deck. PLAYING TIME: NA. PLOT: A retired school librarian rents a luxury cruise ship to host a reunion of past and present Library Club members. Some of them are distinguished, but most are eccentrics. Several uninvited guests are hauled on deck from the sea, including one passenger's long lost amnesiac husband who thinks he is the Ancient Mariner, the former school genius who has cloned his brain and hopes to control the world, and an octopus that has ingested growth pills devised by a Nobel Prize winner on board. The mad genius is foiled by the octopus and a secret agent disguised as the captain. When the growth pills are thrown overboard, the ship is freed from a seaweed bed which has entangled it, and the journey is resumed. RECOMMENDATION: Although intended as a farce, this is far beyond the realm of credibility. The characters are not well developed and much of the dialogue falls flat. No real plot action occurs until the final scene. ROYALTY: $40. SOURCE: Van Horn, Bill. (1985). Nightmare on the lovey-dovey dreamboat. Boston, MA: Baker's Plays. SUBJECTS/PLAY TYPE: Yachts; Cruises; Eccentrics; Fantasy.

2171. 4-6. (+) Winther, Barbara. **Nikluk and the loon.** CAST: 3f, 4m, 2u. ACTS: 1. SETTINGS: Woods; outside an igloo. PLAYING TIME: 20 min. PLOT: Two orphans, a blind boy and his sister, are neglected by the greedy old woman with whom they live. When the children free a loon from a trap, it shows them how the old woman has tricked them into thinking that they need her, and the bird magically restores the boy's sight. The boy gives the loon an arrowhead necklace which legend says became the white markings on the bird's neck. The old woman is turned into ice by the loon and slowly melts toward the sea. Nikluk becomes the greatest hunter in the North country and a hero to all. RECOMMENDATION: This magical tale about the harsh, but just, ways of the North will appeal as an adventure and as a narrative about justice. ROYALTY: Free to Plays subscribers. SOURCE: Winther, Barbara. (1975, February). Nikluk and the loon. Plays: The Drama Magazine for Young People, pp. 47-54 SUBJECTS/PLAY TYPE: Folk Tales, Eskimo; Justice; Playlet.

2172. 6-8. (+) Olfson, Lewy. (Jokai, Marcus) **Nine times Christmas.** (Which of the nine?) CAST: 4f, 7m. ACTS: 1. SETTINGS: Room. PLAYING TIME: 20 min. PLOT: On Christmas Eve, Mr. Hard-Heart, a rich miser, makes two offers to a poor cobbler who is the father of nine. He offers to give one child a life of luxury if the father will choose which one to give away. He offers money if the family will stop singing on Christmas Eve. Both offers, though tempting, are refused. Instead, Mr. Hard-Heart joins the family for dinner. RECOMMENDATION: Although this is melodramatic and old fashioned, the play's central message of love bears repeating. ROYALTY: None. SOURCE: Kamerman, Sylvia E. (1978). On stage for Christmas: A collection of royalty-free plays for young people. Boston, MA: Plays, Inc. SUBJECTS/PLAY TYPE: Christmas; Family; Adaptation.

2173. 10-12. (-) Cope, Eddie. **No cheers for the cheerleaders.** CAST: 6f, 6m. ACTS: 3. SETTINGS: Office; boardroom. PLAYING TIME: NA. PLOT: Bubba Wilson, the young, energetic manager of the Bluebird Chamber of Commerce, cannot attract new industry to his dying West Texas town until he hires cheerleaders who are actually women of questionable morals. When Bubba is fired, his fiance gets him reinstated by blackmailing the Chamber executives who have been consorting with the cheerleaders. Bubba uses the same tactics to get his secretary back. Economic prosperity comes to the town, and Bubba decides that nice guys finish last. RECOMMENDATION: Billed as "the modern ritual of a boy becoming a man" and "an important play for high school and college students," this is neither. The hero gets results by resorting to the same tactics he condemns in others, and the dress and behavior of the "cheerleaders" and much of the dialogue involving them are suggestive and inappropriate. ROYALTY: $35. SOURCE: Cope, Eddie. (1979). No cheers for the cheerleaders. Schulenburg, TX: I.E. Clark. SUBJECTS/PLAY TYPE: Business; Careers; Ethics; Comedy.

2174. 9-12. (+) Gleason, William. **No crime like the present.** CAST: 6f, 7m, Su. ACTS: 2. SETTINGS: None. PLAYING TIME: NA. PLOT: Cassandra Dumont, co-anchorwoman of the six o'clock news, is murdered on live television. Everyone has a motive and Mavis Davis must find the murderer. The plot twists and turns, revealing that no one, from the mayor to a local gypsy woman, is who he/she seems to be. Mavis finally discloses that Cassandra is not dead. In the process she wins the heart of Slack, a hard-boiled detective. RECOMMENDATION: This parody of a "who-dunnit" keeps the audience guessing. Set requirements are few and the dialogue amusing. Staging requires a trumpet player or a well coordinated pantomime and sound system. ROYALTY: $50. SOURCE: Gleason, William. (1982). No crime like the present. Chicago, IL: Dramatic Pub. Co. SUBJECTS/PLAY TYPE: Murder; Mystery; Comedy.

2175. 6-12. (-) Murray, John. **No experience.** CAST: 1f. ACTS: 1. SETTINGS: None. PLAYING TIME: NA. PLOT: A teenage girl starting her first job attempts to take dictation from her boss. Despite her many clerical blunders, she miraculously escapes being fired. RECOMMENDATION: This stereotyped female teenager and her office mishaps are funny and believable, but they rely totally on disparaging women. ROYALTY: None. SOURCE: Murray, John.(1982). Modern monologues for young people. Boston, MA: Plays, Inc. SUBJECTS/PLAY TYPE: Secretaries; Monologue.

2176. 7-12. (+) Raspanti, Celeste Rita. **No fading star.** CAST: 5f, 4m, Su. ACTS: 1. SETTINGS: Convent. PLAYING TIME: NA. PLOT: The Mother Superior of an ancient monastery has been providing Jewish children safe passage out of Hitler's Germany. The local gestapo suspect her and as they search the convent, a young Jewish boy chants his Bar Mitzvah passage to the nuns during their vesper service. He and his sister escape, the gestapo find nothing, and the Mother Superior continues her courageous work. RECOMMENDATION: Based on documented testimony of Jews, who as children were saved from the Holocaust through the efforts of religious women in the convents of Germany and other Nazi occupied countries, the dramatic tension will stimulate thought and discussion about history, responsibility and conscience. ROYALTY: $20. SOURCE: Raspanti, Celeste Rita. (1979). No fading star. Chicago, IL: Dramatic Pub. Co. SUBJECTS/PLAY TYPE: Holocaust; World War II; Nuns; Drama.

2177. K-12. (+) Snyder, Geraldine Ann & Lenzi, Paul. **No more secrets: The musical.** CAST: 3f, 2m. ACTS: 1. SETTINGS: Bare stage, backdrop and props. PLAYING TIME: NA. PLOT: Deedee spends the night at Jenny's house, and since Jenny's mom is working late, their neighbor, Sparky, checks on them. Jenny confesses after he leaves, that Sparky has molested her. Deedee pretends to have forgotten her pajamas, goes home to explain the situation to her mother, and returns to find Sparky has come back. She helps Jenny chase him away and later explains the problem to Jenny's mother. Jenny's mother is helpful and reassuring, and the next day at school, the counselor calls Jenny a hero for speaking out. Her courage helped seven other students to admit to problems with Sparky. RECOMMENDATION: This provides excellent material to present in schools. Since it deals with a sensitive topic, it should probably be followed with carefully directed discussion. ROYALTY: $35. SOURCE: Snyder, Geraldine Ann & Lenzi, Paul. (1986). No more secrets: The musical. New York, NY: Samuel French. SUBJECTS/PLAY TYPE: Child Molesting; Child Abuse; Musical.

2178. 10-12. (+) Holman, David. **No pasaran.** CAST: 6f, 24m. ACTS: 2. SETTINGS: Bare stage, props. PLAYING TIME: NA. PLOT: In 1932, Jan Goldberg, a German Jew, dreams of boxing on the German Olympic team. After Jews are barred from athletic competition in Germany, Jan moves to England with Sam and boxes to earn money to move his parents out of Germany. He also works to put down the Nazi movement in Britain. Jan earns enough money, but loses contact with his parents. Concerned, he goes back to Germany to find them, is captured by the Gestapo, sent to Waldsea, and not heard from again. After the war, Sam comes to Nuremburg, hoping to find some trace of Jan. He discovers that Waldsea was the Dachau concentration camp, and that Jan almost certainly was killed there. RECOMMENDATION: This is extremely powerful and was written to make certain that today's young people know the truth about the Nazi's "Final Solution." The author states in his introduction that no discussion period should be held after the play, as it is very intense and will mean more after the passage of some time and introspective thought. ROYALTY: NA. SOURCE: Schweitzer, Pam. (1983). Theatre-in-education: Four secondary programmes. London: Methuen. SUBJECTS/PLAY TYPE: Anti-Semitism; Holocaust; World War II; Drama.

2179. 8-12. (+) Guyon, Guy. **The no purpose room.** CAST: 5f, 6m, Su. ACTS: 3. SETTINGS: Bare stage. PLAYING TIME: NA. PLOT: Drama teacher, Priscilla, and basketball coach, Bob, fight over the use of the gym/auditorium. A series of confrontations ensue. When the coach interrupts the annual variety show for a last minute playoff game, the play is postponed in mid-stream to allow the playoff, and the school board announces the donation of the old theater for the drama class. RECOMMENDATION: Although rather banal, with excessive emotion affixed to a common school conflict between sports and academics, the action depicts the need for arbitration and communication during a disagreement. Care should be taken not to over play the role of Bob. ROYALTY: $25. SOURCE: Guyon, Guy. (1976). The no purpose room. Franklin, OH: Eldridge Pub. Co. SUBJECTS/PLAY TYPE: Dating; Sharing; Comedy.

2180. 7-12. (-) Marschalk, Raymond J. Sr. **No room at Nathan's inn.** CAST: 2f, 2m. ACTS: 1. SETTINGS: Motel reception room. PLAYING TIME: 30 min. PLOT: On Christmas Eve, Nathan, a Jewish motel owner, and his family cope with a full house of guests, a snow storm, a power failure, news that the governor and his entourage expect to be accommodated, and the fact that his son has given temporary shelter in the stable to a young man and his wife. Joseph and Mary's sweetness contrasts with Nathan's miserly mentality, as Nathan's children and wife learn that the "Hebrew vengeance" is not to be preferred over Christian forgiveness. RECOMMENDATION: This has a valid message about the need to teach children about religion and the need to be concerned about others. However, it is blatantly anti-semitic (presenting Jews as stereotyped money hungry, overbearing, amoral people), uses inappropriate Yiddish sentence structure (second generation American Jews do not speak in Yiddishisms), and totally misrepresents the Jewish philosophy. It absolutely defies the religious spirit of Christmas and promotes hatred among people. ROYALTY: NA. SOURCE: Marschalk, Robert J. Sr. (n.d.) No room at the inn. Franklin, OH: Eldridge Pub. Co. SUBJECTS/PLAY TYPE: Christmas; Christian Drama.

2181. 3-12. (+) Patterson, Emma L. **No room at the inn.** CAST: 1f, 15m, Su. ACTS: 1. SETTINGS: Courtyard. PLAYING TIME: 20 min. PLOT: An avaricious, hypocritical innkeeper who would not make room at his inn for Mary and Joseph learns to make room in his heart for the Christ Child. RECOMMENDATION: This is not to be taken lightly or produced quickly; it is a serious, touching production for a hearty group of performers and a Christian audience. ROYALTY: Free to Plays subscribers. SOURCE: Kamerman, Sylvia E. (1982). Christmas play favorites for young people. Boston, MA: Plays, Inc. SUBJECTS/PLAY TYPE: Christmas; Playlet.

2182. 4-12. (-) Gilfond, Henry. **No snakes in Ireland.** CAST: 1f, 2m, 2u. ACTS: 1. SETTINGS: Open field. PLAYING TIME: 15 min. PLOT: St. Patrick convinces the heathens of Ireland to pray that the Lord drive out the snakes. They do; St. Patrick has them carry shillelaghs; and the snakes are driven out. RECOMMENDATION: This trivializes and insults the story of St. Patrick. It also stereotypes Irish people and portrays St. Patrick as a devious and manipulative person. ROYALTY: None. SOURCE: Gilfond, Henry. (1985). Holiday plays for

reading. New York, NY: Walker. SUBJECTS/PLAY TYPE: St. Patrick's Day; Ireland; Christian Drama.

2183. 6-12. (+) Meyers, John. **No sooner won than done.** CAST: 1f, 1m. ACTS: 1. SETTINGS: Living room. PLAYING TIME: 20 min. PLOT: Villain Filthy McGreedy marries heroine Priscilla Goodheart. His wedding gift is one million shares of worthless railroad stock. Priscilla refuses to allow Filthy to tear her house down and she asks him why he married her. Filthy describes a geologist's report which states that her property is suitable for digging a gold mine. Crushed, she consents to his mining beneath the house, but tells him he should have read the whole report. While the report states that the property is suitable for mining gold, it also says that there is no gold. Leaving him, Priscilla informs Filthy that her railroad stock is now worth a million dollars, that she will have the marriage annulled, and that she will marry Thomas True. RECOMMENDATION: This features stock characters and the typical conflict between good and evil. Only two performers are needed on a virtually empty stage, but the audience could participate with laughs, boos, hisses, and hoorays prompted by cue cards. The only thing lacking are the peanuts to eat and hulls to throw at the villain. ROYALTY: $5. SOURCE: Meyers, John. (1983). No sooner won than done. Denver, CO: Pioneer Drama Service. SUBJECTS/PLAY TYPE: Swindlers and Swindling; Comedy; Melodrama.

2184. 7-12. (+) Naylor, Phyllis Reynolds. **No trumpets, no angels.** CAST: 2f, 2m. ACTS: 1. SETTINGS: Dining room. PLAYING TIME: 12 min. PLOT: A week before Christmas, the Jacobs family sits down to dinner. Their daughter, Stephanie, arrives late from the church play rehearsal. After listening to Stephanie's retelling of the nativity scene, the Jacobs offer help to those in need. RECOMMENDATION: With clearly written dialogue, this is best performed by church groups. ROYALTY: None. SOURCE: Altena, Hans. (1978). The playbook for Christian theatre. Grand Rapids, MI: Baker Book House. SUBJECTS/PLAY TYPE: Christmas; Skit; Christian Drama.

2185. 1-8. (+) Whittaker, Violet. **Noah.** CAST: 12u. ACTS: 5. SETTINGS: Outdoors; mountainside. PLAYING TIME: NA. PLOT: The story of Noah's ark and the flood is told through the eyes of unrepentant and evil citizens who mock Noah for his 100 year building project as Noah admonishes them to repent and be saved. The flood destroys the citizens, and as Noah and his entourage leave the ark, God promises never to destroy the land again. RECOMMENDATION: This would be an excellent Sunday school production. All could be involved with the puppet production, and only one line would have to be changed to make this nondenominational. ROYALTY: NA. SOURCE: Whittaker, Violet. (1984). Puppet people scripts. Grand Rapids, MI: Baker Book House. SUBJECTS/PLAY TYPE: Noah's Ark; Puppet Play.

2186. K-12. (+) Doughty, Bix L. **Noah and the great auk.** CAST: 1m, 5u. ACTS: 3. SETTINGS: Room inside the Ark. PLAYING TIME: NA. PLOT: Noah tells the animals on the ark that no meat eating is allowed to prevent them from eating each other. The hyena wants very much to eat the great auk (a bird) and stirs up trouble between the animals and Noah by warning them that man will become more inhuman day by day and trap, catch, and kill animals, making them extinct. While the hyena and Noah fight, the auk (trying to help Noah) falls overboard and is gone forever; only her egg remains. The Ark lands and the animals go their own ways, leaving the hyena in charge of the auk's egg. RECOMMENDATION: All of the animals in the cast are endangered species, except the great auk (which is extinct). The playwright relays a message that, like Noah and the animals aboard the Ark, we also live in a small environment with animals on our ark (the earth). Although there are appendices giving detailed costume designs and instructions, character sketches, and a study guide for children, this may be best suited for older actors. ROYALTY: $35. SOURCE: Doughty, Bix L. (1977). Noah and the great auk. New Orleans, LA: Anchorage Press, Inc. SUBJECTS/PLAY TYPE: Endangered Species; Wildlife Preservation; Environment; Comedy.

2187. 3-7*. (+) Peake, Mervyn. **Noah's ark.** CAST: 5f, 5m, 15u. ACTS: 5. SETTINGS: Bedroom; farmyard; ark interior. PLAYING TIME: NA. PLOT: In his dream, a boy helps Noah plan and construct the ark; meets Noah's wife, sons, and their wives; learns of their strengths and weaknesses, and of their occasional lack of faith in Noah's task. Noah invites the boy aboard as a stowaway when it begins to rain. The boy discovers a plot to destroy the humans on board, but it is foiled when they land on Mt. Ararat. RECOMMENDATION: Although this religious fantasy is interesting and believable, it may be too long for very young children. Staging of the ark may be difficult, and quite a few animal costumes are required, in addition to a large Noah's ark toy. Several Britishisms may require clarification for American audiences. ROYALTY: NA. SOURCE: Gilmore, Maeve. (1981). Peake's progress. Woodstock, NY: Overlook Press. SUBJECTS/PLAY TYPE: Noah's Ark; Drama.

2188. 5-7. (+) Watkins, Martha Swintz. **Nobody believes in witches!** CAST: 3f, 3m. ACTS: 1. SETTINGS: Witches' den; castle dining room. PLAYING TIME: 20 min. PLOT: Mathilda Witch traps young Prince Edward in the woods until his father appoints her number one witch of the kingdom. RECOMMENDATION: Whimsical humor and amusing dialogue enable this to overcome slightly sexist characterizations. ROYALTY: Free to Plays subscribers. SOURCE: Kamerman, Sylvia E. (1983). Holiday plays round the year. Boston, MA: Plays, Inc. SUBJECTS/PLAY TYPE: Halloween; Comedy.

2189. 10-12. (+) Frayn, Michael. **Noises off.** CAST: 3f, 4m, Su. ACTS: 3. SETTINGS: Living room. PLAYING TIME: NA. PLOT: In this play within a play, the relationships of the cast are established as they rehearse a drama which comprises exits and entrances by the owners of a home, a rental agent and his girlfriend, the housekeeper, and a burglar. They miss each other with each exit and entrance. This provides a hilarious backdrop

for Act II, in which the cast interacts backstage between entrances. Two of them have had a falling out and embroil the entire cast in an array of practical jokes and stunts that have them racing to make entrances, hopefully with the right props, but always in extreme confusion. By Act III, almost three months later, any resemblance of the play originally rehearsed and what is being presented is purely coincidental. RECOMMENDATION: With an engaging plot, this is a unique way to tell a cast's story. The rapid pace of action will keep an audience engaged, but will also provide a superlative challenge to the comic timing and expressive talents of any group producing it. There is some offensive language, and a female cast member performs in underwear. The set must have working doors and windows and an upstairs. It must also be reversible for the second act. ROYALTY: $60. SOURCE: Frayn, Michael. (1985). Noises off. New York, NY: Samuel French. SUBJECTS/PLAY TYPE: Theater; Acting; Stage Production; Comedy.

2190. 4-8. (+) Bradley, Virginia. **None but the strong.** CAST: 1f, 3u. ACTS: 1. SETTINGS: Roller coaster. PLAYING TIME: NA. PLOT: Grandma is afraid to ride the roller coaster, but the children persuade her. As the ride gets faster and wilder, the children become frightened, but Grandma has the time of her life. RECOMMENDATION: Pantomimed, this allows actors to use their own creative abilities to demonstrate excitement, enjoyment, and fear. The nontraditional characterization of Grandma is refreshing. ROYALTY: None. SOURCE: Bradley, Virginia. (1975). Is there an actor in the house? New York, NY: Dodd, Mead. SUBJECTS/PLAY TYPE: Grandparents; Roller Coasters; Pantomime.

2191. 9-12. (+) Page, Anita & Page, Alex. (Maar, Paul) **Noodle doodle box.** (Noodle doodle box) CAST: 3u. ACTS: 1. SETTINGS: Bare stage. PLAYING TIME: NA. PLOT: Two clowns, who symbolize the innocence of childhood, appear out of two boxes which symbolize everything that is uniquely theirs. They argue in true childlike fashion, deciding ultimately that they don't wish to be friends anymore. A third character (outfitted as a drum major) takes advantage of their argument, and tricks each of them into giving him the other's box. After he leaves, they realize how foolish they've been. They find another bigger box, decide to share it, and together they get rid of the wicked drum major. RECOMMENDATION: In this highly stylized play, the main characters exist only as reflections of the social statements that the author makes. This allows great latitude for the director and the actors. The message that friendship and loyalty are paramount and can coexist with arguments (which are also a part of any relationship), is well presented. This could be an excellent presentation for adolescents forming their own identities in spite of their needs for belonging. It might also work well as an introduction to "fair fighting" in a love relationship. ROYALTY: NA. SOURCE: Jennings, Coleman A. & Berghammer, Gretta. (1986). Theatre for youth: Twelve plays with mature themes. Austin, TX: University of Texas Press. SUBJECTS/PLAY TYPE: Identity; Friendship; Drama.

2192. 9-12. (+) Kramer, Larry. **The normal heart.** CAST: 1f, 13m. ACTS: 1. SETTINGS: Several offices; apartment; hospital room. PLAYING TIME: NA. PLOT: The play begins in 1981, when AIDS is still unnamed, and its cause undetermined. Despite fears about what the disclosure of their homosexuality may mean to their careers and families, gays in New York form a task force to create the publicity needed to enlist the help of city and federal government to fight the disease. Much of the plot revolves around the group's efforts, infighting, fears, and discouragements. The president of the organization is a Jewish writer for the **New York Times**, Ned Weeks. Years of psychoanalysis have helped him to accept his homosexuality, but he is an angry, volatile man, whose pugnacity eventually helps to gain some funding from the government while alienating him from all of those around him. His lover, Felix, who becomes a victim of AIDS, is the most able to endure and understand Ned's angry outbursts. Ned's brother, Ben, loves him dearly and tries very hard to accept Ned's lifestyle, but he is unable to openly support Ned's cause. Their estrangement dissolves when Felix dies. RECOMMENDATION: The intent is to alert the public and gain sympathy and support for AIDS research. This should be carefully assessed prior to any decision to purchase or perform it. ROYALTY: $60. SOURCE: Kramer, Larry. (1985). The normal heart. New York, NY: Samuel French. SUBJECTS/PLAY TYPE: AIDS; Homosexuality; Drama.

2193. 2-4. (+) Steele, Eleanor. **Norman Noun takes off.** CAST: 3f, 3m, 6u. ACTS: 1. SETTINGS: Classroom. PLAYING TIME: 20 min. PLOT: Norman the Noun faces an internal conflict because today he is an airplane that is unable to fly. Vikie Verbs adds wings. Adjectives make Norman a brand new, sparkling silver, speedy supersonic jet airplane. Amy Adverb helps Norman soar. The parts of speech help Norman express a complete thought. RECOMMENDATION: A cute way to present parts of speech, this adds some sparkle to an otherwise dull lecture. ROYALTY: Free to Plays subscribers. SOURCE: Steele, Eleanor. (1978, October). Norman Noun takes off. Plays: The Drama Magazine for Young People, pp. 65-70. SUBJECTS/PLAY TYPE: Grammar; Parts of Speech; Playlet.

2194. 3-7. (+) Priore, Frank V. **North Pole computer caper.** CAST: 1f, 2m, 4u. ACTS: 3. SETTINGS: Living room. PLAYING TIME: 25 min. PLOT: Mrs. Claus gives forgetful Santa a computer, but Santa's son, who aspires to be a country western star, programs it to map out stops only in Nashville, changes the presents to cowgirl and cowboy outfits, etc. Santa goes back to his old, inefficient, but workable ways, and his son agrees to change his cowboy hat for a Santa hat. RECOMMENDATION: The message of Christmas spirit is delivered within the context of family tensions which are identifiable to the age group. Unfortunately, the play's resolution (where Santa's son gives up his own career aspirations to follow father's) is a let down and presents an obvious opinion about the folly of childhood dreams and thinking for oneself. With some editing, Santa's son could agree to help out without compromising his own dreams. ROYALTY: Free to Plays subscribers. SOURCE: Kamerman, Sylvia. (1988). The big

book of Christmas plays. Boston, MA: Plays, Inc. SUBJECTS/PLAY TYPE: Christmas; Computers; Careers; Comedy.

2195. 1-4*. (+) Bennett, Rowena. (Aesopus) **The North Wind and the Sun.** (The wind and the sun) CAST: 7u. ACTS: 1. SETTINGS: Forest glade. PLAYING TIME: 10 min. PLOT: Sun challenges wind to remove a traveler's cloak. Wind blows, but the rougher it gets, the tighter the traveler clings to his cloak and finally he crawls into a hollow tree. Sun shines, the traveler crawls out of the hollow tree, loosens his coat, then removes it. Agreeing Sun has won fairly, Wind asks the secret and Sun replies, "Persuasion's stronger, Sir, than force." RECOMMENDATION: A delightful rhymed rendition, some children might be too young to understand the theme, but the playwright, having anticipated this, has the sun provide the explanation that kindness works better than force. ROYALTY: NA. SOURCE: Kamerman, Sylvia. (1987). Plays from favorite folk tales. Boston, MA: Plays, Inc. SUBJECTS/PLAY TYPE: Values; Persuasion; Fable; Adaptation.

2196. 1-6. (+) McDonough, Jerome. **Not even A. Mouse: A chrismouse tale.** CAST: 1f, 1m, Su. ACTS: 1. SETTINGS: Bare stage. PLAYING TIME: 25 min. PLOT: As they search for their expectant Mother's perfect Christmas/Labor Day gift, Annie and Andy Mouse encounter a cat, a trap, cosmic crunchers, and the godmouse's henchmice before escaping into a manger scene. Mary and Joseph assure them they have already given their perfect gifts to be seen in their mother's eyes. Annie and Andy return home to find their parents with a newborn boy, Anthony. As they peer into their mother's eyes and see their own reflections, they understand that they and the newborn child are the perfect gifts. RECOMMENDATION: Superb in its simplicity, this living Christmas cyclorama utilizes the ensemble as both cast and animated props. With minimum effort this permits maximum involvement of children. This method of presentation underscores its message: children are the world's perfect gifts. ROYALTY: $25. SOURCE: McDonough, Jerome. (1984). Not even A. Mouse: A chrismouse tale. Schulenburg, TX: I. E. Clark. SUBJECTS/PLAY TYPE: Christmas; Playlet.

2197. 9-12. (+) Gleason, William. **Not fit to print.** CAST: 10f, 13m. ACTS: 2. SETTINGS: Street; house; bar room; classroom; newspaper office; student union. PLAYING TIME: NA. PLOT: An idealistic journalism student learns the reality of the newspaper business when she is forced to take a job at a muckraking tabloid. Her idealism is tempered when she becomes part of the undercover news team investigating alleged shady dealings of her beloved journalism professor. A friend helps her discover that the cynicism and tackiness of the **Metro Inquirer** are no more distorted than the ideal vision she's been fed at the University. RECOMMENDATION: Although the numerous scene changes may require some complex scenery and prop manipulation, this can easily be performed. Characters are well defined and the plot is dynamic and stimulating, both in laughter and thought. ROYALTY: $50. SOURCE: Gleason, William. (1984). Not fit to print. Chicago, IL: Dramatic Pub. Co. SUBJECTS/PLAY TYPE: Newspapers; Idealism; Drama.

2198. 6-9. (+) Majeski, bill. **The-not-so-wide world of sports.** CAST: 1m, 4u. ACTS: 1. SETTINGS: Office; boxing ring. PLAYING TIME: 15 min. PLOT: In three unrelated skits, a sportscaster applies for a job as a football announcer by using every known football cliche. He is hired. Next, a heavyweight fighter is interviewed about training and prior fights. His answers are both inappropriate and comical. Last, a broadcaster for a video hockey game describes the "blistering action" as one of the players injures his playing hand. The game is postponed until the next day. RECOMMENDATION: These three spoofs of sports obsessed people are easily relatable to current TV and radio sportscasts. Although the jokes are extremely corny, this could work with exaggerated acting. ROYALTY: Free to Plays subscribers. SOURCE: Majeski, Bill. (1977, November). The not-so-wide world of sports. Plays: The Drama Magazine for Young People, pp. 71-76. SUBJECTS/PLAY TYPE: Sports; Comedy.

2199. 4-8. (+) Little, Lynnette. **Nothing beats a royal flush.** CAST: 9f, 2m. ACTS: 1. SETTINGS: Throne room; gym locker room. PLAYING TIME: NA. PLOT: The king, queen, and their quintuplet daughters will lose their castle to Baroness Gretchen von Grossmier if they do not make the last mortgage payment by midnight next Saturday. The Baroness is anxious that the King default since she has discovered oil beneath the castle. Gabriela de Garbanzo, a cousin, discovers the princesses are excellent hoop-ball players. She forms them into a team (the Royal Flush), and enters them in a World Championship game. Despite attempts by the Baroness to continue the game until after midnight, the Royal Flushes win the prize money and save the castle, land, and oil. RECOMMENDATION: The conflicts add to this humorous and clever piece of fluff. ROYALTY: NA. SOURCE: Little, Lynnette. (1980). Nothing beats a royal flush. Denver, CO: Pioneer Drama Service. SUBJECTS/PLAY TYPE: Swindlers and Swindling; Comedy.

2200. 7-12. (+) Bradley, Virginia. **Nothing will rattle a soul.** CAST: 5f, 3m, Su. ACTS: 1. SETTINGS: Living room. PLAYING TIME: NA. PLOT: A young girl refuses to accept an award publicly until a teacher shows her what courage is made of. RECOMMENDATION: Though the play occurs during the fifties, the actions and events are relative to teens today. ROYALTY: NA. SOURCE: Bradley, Virginia. (1977). Stage eight: One-act plays. New York, NY: Dodd, Mead. SUBJECTS/PLAY TYPE: Family; Dating; Courage; Drama.

2201. 10-12. (+) Tesich, Steve. **Nourish the beast.** CAST: 1m. ACTS: 1. SETTINGS: None. PLAYING TIME: NA. PLOT: Bruno, a 25 year old orphan, tells his adopted sister, Goya, about his life in an orphanage. He recounts how he found out what the word "orphan" meant and the disappointment he felt when he finally got to go outside the orphanage to an anticlimactic ball game. RECOMMENDATION: Bruno is vulnerable and totally honest. The humor comes from his seriousness in expressing himself. ROYALTY: NA. SOURCE: Handman,

Wynn. (1980). Modern American scenes for student actors. New York, NY: Bantam Books SUBJECTS/PLAY TYPE: Orphans; Scene.

2202. 4-12. (-) Moeller, Ruby L. **November.** CAST: Su. ACTS: 1. SETTINGS: Bare stage, props. PLAYING TIME: NA. PLOT: This comprises two historic readings dealing with the origin and development of Thanksgiving. Several poems, word games, and inspirational songs are also suggested. RECOMMENDATION: This is best suited for adults and some parts are inappropriate for public schools due to emphasis on religion. Language is very dated ("What part of a turkey assists in making your toilet?"). ROYALTY: NA. SOURCE: Moeller, Ruby L. (1975). Around the year programs. Boston, MA: Baker's Plays. SUBJECTS/PLAY TYPE: Thanksgiving; Playlet.

2203. K-3. (+) Fisher, Aileen Lucia. **Now December's here.** CAST: Su. ACTS: 1. SETTINGS: Bare stage. PLAYING TIME: 1 min. PLOT: Boys and girls (in groups) recite 10 lines about the coming of Christmas and all the secrets kept in preparing for it. RECOMMENDATION: This is a lovely recitation for church programs. ROYALTY: Free to Plays subscribers. SOURCE: Fisher, Aileen Lucia. (1985). Year-round programs for young players. Boston, MA: Plays, Inc. SUBJECTS/PLAY TYPE: Christmas; Choral Reading.

2204. 7-10. (+) Garver, Juliet. **The numbers game.** CAST: 1f, 2m. ACTS: 1. SETTINGS: Outpatient clinic. PLAYING TIME: 10 min. PLOT: In a future society where people no longer have names, two people carry on a dangerous conversation about love and happiness. The woman convinces the man that their own "perfect" society does not really have that much to offer. RECOMMENDATION: Similar to **1984** in theme, this pits a seemingly stereotyped romantic and emotional female against the cold, hard and logical man. As the dialogue progresses, the woman demonstrates that she is as much a thinker as she is a romantic. The two resolve to escape the "perfect" society. ROYALTY: Free to Plays subscribers. SOURCE: Garver, Juliet. (1982, November). The numbers game. Plays: The Drama Magazine for Young People, pp. 65-68. SUBJECTS/PLAY TYPE: Science Fiction; Love; Playlet.

2205. 2-4*. (+) Dexter, Harriet. (Ouida, Marie Louise de la Ram'ee) **The Nuremberg stove.** (The Nuremberg stove) CAST: 7f, 6m. ACTS: 1. SETTINGS: Living room of a cottage; hall of German palace. PLAYING TIME: 90 min. PLOT: Tina loves the family's Hirschvogel stove more than anything. When her father falls on hard times and sells it, she is distraught and vows to recover it. She hides inside the stove and journeys to meet the queen, who helps solve the family's problems. RECOMMENDATION: This adaptation is entertaining and suspenseful. All will relate to the main character's imagination and ingenuity. Helpful suggestions on how to create a Hirsch-vogel stove are included. ROYALTY: $25. SOURCE: Dexter, Harriet. (1981). The Nuremberg stove. Schulenburg, TX: I.E. Clark. SUBJECTS/PLAY TYPE: Family; Comedy; Adaptation.

2206. 2-5. (-) Mahlman, Lewis. **The nutcracker prince.** CAST: 7u. ACTS: 1. SETTINGS: Living room. PLAYING TIME: 20 min. PLOT: The mouse king, in order to steal the sugar plum princess, imprisons the prince in the nutcracker. Clara is magically transported to Sugar Plum Land, where she kills the mouse king with her shoe, lets the prince out, and they all dance. RECOMMENDATION: This dreadful takeoff has murder and violence as its major action, and a very shallow plot. ROYALTY: Free to Plays subscribers. SOURCE: Mahlman, Lewis. (1982, December). The nutcracker prince. Plays: The Drama Magazine for Young People, pp. 65-68. SUBJECTS/PLAY TYPE: Christmas; Puppet Play.

2207. 12. (+) Rausch, Don. **Nuts, bolts, and carnations.** CAST: 3f, 2m. ACTS: 3. SETTINGS: Living/dining room. PLAYING TIME: NA. PLOT: Two male family members have opposite reactions to gifts of flowers. In spite, each eats a flower, dies from pesticide, and starts a telephone correspondence with God as they commute to earth for various assigned projects. Finally, one of the wives also eats a flower, motivated by love to be with her spouse. RECOMMENDATION: Although this is clever and full of witty lines, the themes of sexual identity and suicide must be carefully matched to the players and audience. The word "damned" appears several times, but could hardly be omitted; whenever it is said, a heavenly choir is heard, and the character must switch it to "darned" to make the choir stop. This is highly amusing and avoids cliches in dialogue, but is aimed more at adults. ROYALTY: $50. SOURCE: Rausch, Don. (1977). Nuts, bolts, and carnations. Schulenburg, TX: I.E. Clark. SUBJECTS/PLAY TYPE: Love; Death; Sex Roles; Comedy.

2208. 7-12. (+) Kosoff, Susan & Staab, Jane. **O happy day: A celebration of the birth of Christ.** CAST: 10u. ACTS: 1. SETTINGS: Jungle gym. PLAYING TIME: NA. PLOT: Reminiscent of the upbeat, whimsical retelling of Jesus Christ's ministry in **Godspell**, this retells the story of Christ's birth. Its style is so free and relaxed it gives the impression that cast members are making up their lines as they go. RECOMMENDATION: "Your boy is going to be the most/absolute dynamite/really out of sight." This line from one of the songs clearly displays the problem of lifting a play out of the early 1970s and placing it in the late 1980s. This can be ignored, however, if the play is treated as a period piece like **Hair**. A second problem is its similarity to **Godspell** which had the ability to mix sorrow with laughter as it built to a powerful climax. **O Happy Day** takes itself so capriciously the audience may not feel for the characters. On the other hand, it is a fresh approach to an often heard story, and its brevity may make it a possible alternative in certain situations. ROYALTY: $40. SOURCE: Kosoff, Susan & Staab, Jane. (1975). O happy day: A celebration of the birth of Christ. Boston, MA: Baker's Plays. SUBJECTS/PLAY TYPE: Christmas; Christ, Jesus; Musical.

2209. 6-12. (+) McDonough, Jerome. **O, little town.** CAST: 2f, 2m, Su. ACTS: 1. SETTINGS: City. PLAYING TIME: 35 min. PLOT: God and Angela view the corruption and commercialism of Christmas. Members of the chorus play different characters and depict the sinful behavior of contemporary humans. The climax presents the birth of a baby in a cab when no hospital will admit them. This event makes the crowd some-what less obstreperous. God and Angela agree there might be some hope for the people on Earth. RECOMMENDATION: Although amusing in parts, the idea of God having human characteristics might be offensive to some. ROYALTY: $15. SOURCE: McDonough, Jerome. (1978). O, little town. Schulenburg, TX: I.E. Clark. SUBJECTS/PLAY TYPE: Christmas; Satire.

2210. 4-12. (-) Moeller, Ruby L. **October.** CAST: 2f, 1m, Su. ACTS: 1. SETTINGS: Bare stage, props. PLAYING TIME: NA. PLOT: This collection of activities around Halloween and Columbus Day presents a short history of each, followed by a song set to a familiar tune and a word game. The skit depicts a "Hillbilly Halloween" and the program ends with a fortune telling game involving apple seeds. RECOMMENDATION: More appropriate for adults, this seems far more dated than its 1975 copyright suggests. At one point, for example, a girl's possible future husband is referred to as her "destined lord and master." The depiction of "hillbillies" obsessed with moonshine is offensive. Scattered references to religion and God make it inappropriate for public school use. Taken out of context, the two historic readings might be usable. ROYALTY: NA. SOURCE: Moeller, Ruby L. (1975). Around the year programs. Boston, MA: Baker's Plays. SUBJECTS/PLAY TYPE: Halloween; Columbus Day; Variety Program.

2211. K-4. (+) Fisher, Aileen. **An October night.** CAST: 9u. ACTS: 1. SETTINGS: None. PLAYING TIME: NA. PLOT: Children hold up the letters of "Halloween," each speaking about a unique aspect of the holiday that begins with his/her letter. RECOMMENDATION: This is an excellent group participation exercise for small children, although memory and coordination of action are required. ROYALTY: NA. SOURCE: Fisher, Aileen. (1984, October). An October night. Plays: The Drama Magazine for Young People, pp. 55. SUBJECTS/PLAY TYPE: Halloween; Choral Reading.

2212. 7-12. (+) Baker Charles. **Odds in my favor.** CAST: 13f, 9m, Su. ACTS: 2. SETTINGS: Home; racetrack. PLAYING TIME: NA. PLOT: From all outward appearances, Jonathan Eagerton has it all: wealth, posterity, talented children. However, in his attempt to "get ahead," Jonathan unknowingly neglects his responsibilities as a father. It takes a visit from Jonathan's free-spirited brother Dave, who is Jonathan's exact opposite, to prompt Jonathan to make some major changes in himself and in his family. RECOMMENDATION: The variety of characters, steady pace of events, humor, and theme all make this an excellent class play choice. ROYALTY: $50. SOURCE: Baker, Charles. (1982). Odds in my favor. Chicago, IL: Dramatic Pub. Co. SUBJECTS/PLAY TYPE: Family; Success; Fathers; Drama.

2213. K-9*. (+) Falls, George A. & Beattie, Kurt. (Homer) **The Odyssey.** (The Odyssey) CAST: 2f, 6m. ACTS: 1. SETTINGS: Bare stage. PLAYING TIME: NA. PLOT: This presents Odysseus' trials with the Cyclops, the

Sirens, angry sea gods, etc., as well as his relationships with Penelope (his wife), and Telemachus (his son), who wait for his return. The goddess, Athena, leads him home. RECOMMENDATION: This lively dramatization is creative and colorful, but requires forceful acting and the professional use of simple props. It would probably have to be produced by high schoolers. ROYALTY: $35. SOURCE: Falls, Gregory A., & Beattie, Kurt. (1978). The Odyssey. New Orleans, LA: Anchorage Press, Inc. SUBJECTS/PLAY TYPE: Greek Gods; Mythology, Greek; Adaptation.

2214. 9-12. (-) Rozell, O. B. **Of winners, losers, and games.** CAST: 6f, 8m. ACTS: 1. SETTINGS: None. PLAYING TIME: 30 min. PLOT: With only two real people and the rest of the characters representing characteristics of people (Patience, Peace, Anger, War, etc.), Bob and Susan enter the "game of life" to resolve Susan's hidden fear that she killed her baby. RECOMMENDATION: Allegories, which worked well in medieval times when angels and demons and incarnate representations of vices and virtues were standard characters in life and art, are awkward devices for the twentieth century, unless the personifications of human traits are psychologically complex and there is a plot of sufficient strength (or humor) to support the symbolic affectation. Unfortunately, the allegorical figures here are trite and the plot a melodramatic tear-jerker. The drama may have been intended to have therapeutic value (for audiences in grief counseling?) but the "message" seems too overwrought and, at the same time, too simplistic to be helpful. ROYALTY: $15. SOURCE: Rozell, O. B. (1976). Of winners, losers and games. Schulenburg, TX: I. E. Clark. SUBJECTS/PLAY TYPE: Marriage; Psychology; Drama.

2215. 4-6. (+) Bradley, Virginia. **Off guard.** CAST: 2f, 3m. ACTS: 1. SETTINGS: Living room. PLAYING TIME: NA. PLOT: On April Fool's Day, a brother and sister try to trick their uncle, with comic results. RECOMMENDATION: Students will be able to relate to the dialogue and the familiar plot. ROYALTY: None. SOURCE: Bradley, Virginia. (1981). Holidays on stage. New York, NY: Dodd, Mead. SUBJECTS/PLAY TYPE: April Fool's Day; Comedy.

2216. K-3. (+) Hark, Mildred & McQueen, Noel. **Off the shelf.** CAST: 3f, 5m. ACTS: 1. SETTINGS: Library. PLAYING TIME: 20 min. PLOT: Books in a library complain about children mistreating them or not checking them out. Each tells how to treat it and what it contains. RECOMMENDATION: Although this is preachy, it does have some successful humor. ROYALTY: Free to Plays subscribers. SOURCE: Hark, Mildred & McQueen, Noel. (1985, November). Off the shelf. Plays: The Drama Magazine for Young People, pp. 43-49. SUBJECTS/PLAY TYPE: Book Week; Books; Playlet.

2217. 9-12. (+) Robinette, Joseph. **Oh, brother!** CAST: 3f, 5m, 4u. ACTS: 1. SETTINGS: Hospital waiting room. PLAYING TIME: NA. PLOT: A teenage girl sits in a hospital waiting room while her mother is in labor. The girl is concerned about her mother but is even more worried about the disruption that the new baby will bring

into her own life. An actor, who is also in the waiting room, encourages her to envision, through a series of vignettes, the different levels of human interaction she will be able to experience with and through her new brother. The girl and the actor imagine the different stages of life from childhood to old age. The actor departs and the girl discovers she has a new sister. RECOMMENDATION: Although a bit preachy at times, the dialogue is funny. ROYALTY: $15. SOURCE: Robinette, Joseph. (1980). Oh, brother! Woodstock, IL: Dramatic Pub. Co. SUBJECTS/PLAY TYPE: Family Relationships; Comedy.

2218. 7-12. (+) Rembrandt, Elaine. **Oh God, my God!** CAST: 5f, 6m, 5u. ACTS: 1. SETTINGS: Heaven; Garden of Eden; field; Political Club of Jerusalem. PLAYING TIME: 20 min. PLOT: God uses stories from the "Book of Life" to explain the difficulty of parent/child roles. RECOMMENDATION: The down to earth style presents the Biblical stories of Adam and Eve, Moses, and Isaiah, and easily relays the message "Honor Thy Father and Thy Mother" to today's youth. ROYALTY: None. SOURCE: Rembrandt, Elaine. (1981). Heroes, heroines & holidays - plays for Jewish youth. Denver, CO: Alternatives in Religious Education, Inc. SUBJECTS/PLAY TYPE: Family; Jewish Drama; Skit.

2219. 1-4. (+) Janz, Milli. (Stevenson, Robert Louis) **Oh those shadows.** (My shadow) CAST: 3f, 2m, 1u. ACTS: 1. SETTINGS: Kitchen. PLAYING TIME: 15 min. PLOT: Nip and Tuck get an idea from "My Shadow." Why not trap their shadows and only free them only if they promise to do the children's homework? The shadows do the work but break a window, eat all the food, use all the hot water, and make demands of their own. Now Nip and Tuck cannot get rid of them. The shadows grow tired of the game and let the children turn out the lights to make them go away. The children and shadows decide to be playmates, and as they shadows leave, one of them recites a part of the poem to let the children know that they will return. The tired children turn on the TV to hear the conclusion of "The Shadow at Midnight." RECOMMENDATION: There are no morals here, just a good time, and an appropriate diversion for classes who have been studying Stevenson or poetry. ROYALTY: Free to Plays subscribers. SOURCE: Janz, Milli. (1989, January/February). Oh those shadows. Plays: The Drama Magazine for Young People, pp. 40-44. SUBJECTS/PLAY TYPE: Shadows; Comedy; Adaptation.

2220. 7-12. (+) Carroll, John R. **Oh, what a tangled web.** CAST: 4f, 4m. ACTS: 1. SETTINGS: Living room. PLAYING TIME: NA. PLOT: Chris wants the day off from her summer job, but is afraid to ask her strict employer. Her younger sister, Jan, calls to give the excuse and goes a little too far by saying that Chris is dead. The confusion that ensues is exacerbated by the fact that the family cat is missing. The employer and his wife arrive at the home to comfort the grieving parents who are, in fact, bewailing the loss of their pet. Then Chris walks in, very much alive. The Quigleys are angry at first but admit that their lack of flexibility with their employees might have precipitated the situation. RECOMMENDATION: Although the device of building a plot around characters talking at cross purposes due to a misunderstanding is old, it can still produce laughs. This is funny and also teaches a lesson about the chaos that one small lie can create. ROYALTY: $10. SOURCE: Carroll, John R. (1976). Oh, what a tangled web. Chicago, IL: Dramatic Pub. Co. SUBJECTS/PLAY TYPE: Dishonesty; Comedy.

2221. 9-12. (+) Rowell, Wynn. **Oil's well at end's well.** CAST: 1f, 4m. ACTS: 1. SETTINGS: Bar. PLAYING TIME: NA. PLOT: Jackson Altrade Masternun tries to save the farm of beautiful Purity Saint Goodness (who is disguised as an old woman), from the villain. A narrator with the ability to "freeze" the action tries to keep the plot and characters in line; however, they become more and more outrageous, making puns and commenting on what they expected when they "signed up for this two bit melodrammer." At the end, Purity tricks the villain into giving back her farm. RECOMMENDATION: This spoof is fast paced and very amusing with puns and plays on words. Purity's character is well developed and strong. She needs no help from the inept hero. The narrator's lines are to be sung with choice of melody left to the director. Some might find the villain's comments about the elderly offensive, while others might be uncomfortable about a few lines involving Mr. and Mrs. Smith checking into a hotel with no luggage. Both of these scenes enhance the humor of the play and therefore are necessary. ROYALTY: $25. SOURCE: Rowell, Wynn. (1986). Oil's well at ends well. Franklin, OH: Eldridge Pub. Co. SUBJECTS/PLAY TYPE: Comedy; Melodrama.

2222. 7-12. (+) Roseberry, Sherry. **The Ol' homestead, or foreclose with a smile.** CAST: 9f, 7m. ACTS: 3. SETTINGS: Office; living room. PLAYING TIME: NA. PLOT: Villain Duntley wants to swindle fair heroine, Miss Lil, out of her inherited property because he believes there is oil under it. Duntley's attempts to woo Miss Lil are thwarted when it is revealed she is in love with stalwart and heroic Fairfax Finch. Duntley also finds his patience tried by Miss Lil's houseful of eccentric boarders and relatives. After he has tricked Miss Lil into signing over the deed, it is discovered that the oil actually trickled over from Fairfax's land, and all ends well for everyone except Duntley. RECOMMENDATION: The stereotypical characters, plus a few extra eccentrics, provide much fun. ROYALTY: $35. SOURCE: Roseberry, Sherry. (1987). The ol' homestead, or, foreclose with a smile. Franklin, OH: Eldridge Pub. Co. SUBJECTS/PLAY TYPE: Swindlers and Swindling; Melodrama.

2223. 6-12. (+) Stubing, Mary Chris. **The old ball game.** CAST: Su. ACTS: 1. SETTINGS: Bare stage. PLAYING TIME: 6 min. PLOT: This is a pantomime for beginning drama students to work on the "feel" of stage dynamics and presence as they use a bare stage to pantomime a wide range of sports movements. The "ball" in the skit changes upon command from the actors and even becomes a frisbee at one point. The climax occurs when a baseball is thrown for a batter who is hit and feigns great injury. RECOMMENDATION: This is usable as a classroom exercise or a pre-show stage apron build up. ROYALTY: Free to Plays subscribers. SOURCE: Stubing, Mary Chris. (1979, March). The old ball game.

Plays: The Drama Magazine for Young People, pp. 68-70. SUBJECTS/PLAY TYPE: Pantomime; Skit.

2224. 4-8. (+) Charles, Joe M. **The old cookie shop or Nellie was a baker `cause she kneaded the dough.** CAST: 4f, 3m. ACTS: 1. SETTINGS: Bakery. PLAYING TIME: 30 min. PLOT: Fair Nellie O'Grady and her mother, Rosie, own a bakery. Unfortunately, the mortgage is held by Mortimer Whiplash, who intends to foreclose and force Nellie to marry him so he can take over the bakery. H. Harry Goodwell (a young lawyer) is smitten by Nellie, but she rejects his advances because only Mortimer can afford to support her and her mother. Dr. Gilbert saves the day by revealing that Nellie and Mortimer were switched at birth, making Nellie heiress to the Whiplash fortune. RECOMMENDATION: The publishers recommend that their book, **Between Hisses: A Book of Songs and Olios for Melodrama** by James Burke and Paul T. Nolan, be used as a source for appropriate "melodrama music" to enhance the mood throughout the play. ROYALTY: $5. SOURCE: Charles, Joe M. (1986). The old cookie shop or Nellie was a baker `cause she kneaded the dough. Denver, CO: Pioneer Drama Service. SUBJECTS/PLAY TYPE: Mortgages; Swindlers and Swindling; Melodrama.

2225. 7-12. (+) Gregg, Andy. **The old fashioned Christmas.** CAST: 4f, 3m. ACTS: 2. SETTINGS: Living room; closet. PLAYING TIME: NA. PLOT: Janie tries to impress her new boyfriend, Ernest, by bullying her family into a real "old fashioned Christmas." He seems too busy with volunteer work at a mission for the poor to appreciate her efforts to duplicate the past. Ernest is not impressed with Janie's concept of Christmas spirit, but does appreciate her father's offer to help one of the unemployed men at the mission start a new business. When other members of Janie's family offer to postpone their own celebration to help serve Christmas dinner at the mission, Janie sees that true Christmas spirit is helping others. RECOMMENDATION: This is a sentimental little play, but its message is clear. Ideal for church groups, this could also be used as a parochial school holiday production. ROYALTY: $30. SOURCE: Gregg, Andy. (1987). The old fashioned Christmas. Franklin, OH: Eldridge Pub. Co. SUBJECTS/PLAY TYPE: Family; Christmas; Sharing; Drama.

2226. 8-10. (+) Murray, John. **Old ghosts at home.** CAST: 5f, 4m. ACTS: 1. SETTINGS: Living room. PLAYING TIME: 30 min. PLOT: Two ghosts save a girl from losing her inheritance by foiling her cousin's attempts to kill her. RECOMMENDATION: In this mysterious comedy, the ghosts' parts are quite imaginative, since they are supposedly not seen by the living. ROYALTY: Free to Plays subscribers. SOURCE: Kamerman, Sylvia E. (1983, October). Old ghosts at home. Plays: The Drama Magazine for Young People, pp. 11-22. SUBJECTS/PLAY TYPE: Mystery; Ghosts; Halloween; Comedy.

2227. 1-5. (+) Gotwalt, Helen Louise Miller. **Old Glory grows up.** CAST: 4f, 5m, Su. ACTS: 1. SETTINGS: None. PLAYING TIME: 10 min. PLOT: Simple dramatic devices are utilized to trace the history of the American flag from the time of Betsy Ross till 1960, when Alaska and Hawaii achieved statehood. RECOMMENDATION: This is an excellent choice for Flag Day. ROYALTY: NA. SOURCE: Gotwalt, Helen Louise Miller. (1985). First plays for children. Boston, MA: Plays, Inc. SUBJECTS/PLAY TIME: Flag Day; Washington, George; Ross, Betsy; Statehood; Skit.

2228. 5-8. (-) Sills, Paul. (Grimm Brothers) Old Hildebrand. (Old Hildebrand) CAST: 1f, 3m. ACTS: 1. SETTINGS: Bare stage, props. PLAYING TIME: NA. PLOT: The village parson tricks farmer Hildebrand into leaving town so that the parson can spend time with the farmer's wife. When Old Hildebrand learns of the deception, he returns home, threatens the parson, and chases him out of the house. RECOMMENDATION: The subject of a philandering wife and parson seems more suited for a bar room than for young adults. Also, some of the language is vulgar. ROYALTY: $50. SOURCE: Sills, Paul. (1981) More from story theatre. New York, NY: Samuel French. SUBJECTS/PLAY TYPE: Folk Tales, Germany; Farce; Adaptation.

2229. 7-10. (-) Donahue, John Clarke. Old Kieg of Malfi. CAST: 2f, 2m, 18u. ACTS: 1. SETTINGS: Street; attic. PLAYING TIME: NA. PLOT: Neighborhood children in search of "the life-giving force" gather to hear Old Kieg and Mrs. Souss, two spirits, tell fanciful tales and expound on timeless visions. RECOMMENDATION: Difficult dialogue, a convoluted plot and elaborate production requirements make this difficult. ROYALTY: NA. Donahue, John Clarke. (1975). The cookie jar and other plays. Minneapolis, MN: University of Minnesota Press. SUBJECTS/PLAY TYPE: Fantasy; Social Criticism; Drama.

2230. 3-4. (+) Atherton, Marguerite. Old King Cole's Christmas. CAST: 4f, 4m, Su. ACTS: 1. SETTINGS: Throne room. PLAYING TIME: NA. PLOT: Just when King Cole and his court have lost all their merriment, a wise old shoemaker restores happiness in time for Christmas Eve. RECOMMENDATION: Although plot is slight, the lines are short and fairly easy to memorize. ROYALTY: None. SOURCE: Kamerman, Sylvia. (1975). A treasury of Christmas plays. Boston, MA: Plays, Inc. SUBJECTS/PLAY TYPE: Christmas; Playlet.

2231. K-4. + Lewman, Beverly & Smith, Robert B. Old MacDonald. CAST: Su. ACTS: 1. SETTINGS: None. PLAYING TIME: 5 min. PLOT: Modeled on Jerome Bruner's "modes of learning," repetition of the song "Old MacDonald," aids in developing the learning disabled student's iconic abilities. RECOMMENDATION: Recommended especially for children who have trouble with articulation, vocabulary, and receptive language, this allows children to participate in the singing with the teacher as they learn to identify the animals. They learn to understand verbal directions by selecting the correct animal when asked. This participatory song can be repeated as often as children would like. ROYALTY: NA. SOURCE: Lewman, Beverly & Smith, Robert B. (1984). Music dramas for children with special needs. Denton, TX: Troostwick Press. SUBJECTS/PLAY TYPE: Vocabulary Skills; Musical; Drama.

2232. 3-5. (+) Sampson, Lu. Old MacDonald's farmyard follies. CAST: 3f, 2m, 16u. ACTS: 1. SETTINGS: farmyard. PLAYING TIME: 10 min. PLOT: Problems of nursery rhyme characters mesh in a community setting. The MacDonalds require help on the farm, but Little Boy Blue fails as a farmhand. Mistress Mary loses her garden as the animals trample it. The old woman in a shoe is evicted. A solution is provided when the MacDonalds invite the old woman and her children to move into the farmhouse in exchange for helping with the chores. RECOMMENDATION: Children can easily relate to the spirit of cooperation and logical problem solving techniques used in this musical. ROYALTY: NA. SOURCE: Sampson, Lu. (1984, May). Old MacDonald's farmyard follies. Plays: The Drama Magazine for Young People, pp. 40-44. SUBJECTS/PLAY TYPE: Nursery Rhyme Characters; Musical.

2233. 3-6. (+) Majeski, Bill. Old time melodrama--modern style. CAST: 3f, 6m, 1u. ACTS: 1. SETTINGS: Dining room. PLAYING TIME: 30 min. PLOT: The Prescott family needs money to pay the mortgage on their produce stand/home. Because the Banker will not loan it to them, their beautiful daughter, Nancy, feels she must marry wealthy villain, Harrison Swift, instead of her true love, Pound Sterling. The Prescott's odd son, Edward, sells a work of art to the Banker for exactly the needed sum. Nancy escapes being run over by a train just in time to find that Pound Sterling is part of the plot to resell the Prescott property to a developer. A heckler from the audience turns out to be the hero in disguise. RECOMMENDATION: With its old jokes and predictability, this is good clean fun. It has no real depth of character, but none is needed as these are caricatures recognized by all. ROYALTY: Free to Plays subscribers. SOURCE: Majeski, Bill. (1977, October). Old time melodrama--modern style. Plays: The Drama Magazine for Young People, pp. 17-26. SUBJECTS/PLAY TYPE: Comedy; Mortgages; Melodrama.

2234. 6-12. (+) Wylie, Betty Jane. The old woman and the peddlar. CAST: 1f, 2m, 5u. ACTS: 1. SETTINGS: Bare stage, props. PLAYING TIME: NA. When the old woman from the nursery rhyme loses her skirt and identity, she learns from a peddlar of magic and a mute boy that people must live for today, must never give up hope, and must fight for the things that they value. RECOMMENDATION: This has a dream-like quality, as the mute boy uses charades to communicate, Doctor Noodle diagnoses unrelated ills, and the old woman meets past, present, future, and hope. Because of difficult dialogue and timing, this should be performed by older children for younger ones. ROYALTY: NA. SOURCE: Wylie, Betty Jane. (1978). The old woman and the peddlar. Toronto: Playwrights Co-op. SUBJECTS/PLAY TYPE: Hope; Comedy.

2235. 3-4. (+) Olfson, Lewy. The old woman of the west. CAST: 1f, 2m. ACTS: 1. SETTINGS: Puppet stage. PLAYING TIME: NA. PLOT: Two brothers, Nicholas and Fritz, quarrel over Fritz's laziness. The garden must be watered, and since Fritz refuses to help, Nicholas hauls a bucket to the well by himself, leaving lazy Fritz alone to nap. When a tired old woman asks Fritz to fetch her a drink from the well, he refuses, and scoffs when she threatens him. Nicholas, however, happily complies when the old woman asks him for a drink. She rewards Nicholas' kindness by casting a spell to make a fountain appear from the rock so Nicholas never has to haul water again. What happens next is up to the audience: should the witch punish Fritz? RECOMMENDATION: In this improvisational puppet show, the fountain effect is easily achieved by holding gathered strips of cellophane behind a rock. ROYALTY: None. SOURCE: Olfson, Lewy. (1975). You can put on a show. New York, NY: Sterling. SUBJECTS/PLAY TYPE: Kindness; Witches; Puppet Play.

2236. 7-12. (+) Bland, Joellen. (Dickens, Charles) **Oliver Twist.** (Oliver Twist) CAST: 5f, 12m. ACTS: 1. SETTINGS: Workhouse; room; bookstall; parlor. PLAYING TIME: 35 min. PLOT: Runaway orphan, Oliver, falls in with Fagin's band of thieves and is later taken in by affluent Mr. Brownlow. RECOMMENDATION: Whenever a classic novel is distilled into a 35 minute production, the pace is bound to be furious and the story full of gaps. This is a notable weakness here. The revelation of Brownlow's relationship to the young orphan's father, for example, falls flat because there was no time for a build up. However, the basic story is followed, and grippingly presented. ROYALTY: Free to Plays subscribers. SOURCE: Bland, Joellen. (1984, November). Oliver Twist. Plays: The Drama Magazine for Young People, pp. 53-64. SUBJECTS/PLAY TYPE: Orphans; Adaptation.

2237. 9-12. (+) Kelly, Tim. **The omelet murder case: A murderous spoof in one act.** CAST: 5f, 3m. ACTS: 1. SETTINGS: Living room. PLAYING TIME: 30 min. PLOT: "Shakes" Speare is a dimwitted private investigator who also writes trashy detective novels. He and his adoring secretary are called by Mrs. Elsinor to solve the murder of her first husband. Her son, Hamlet, claims his father's ghost told him he was murdered. There really was no murder, just Hamlet watching too many old movies, but they can't convince Shakes. RECOMMENDATION: The characters are broadly drawn and there is little left of Shakespeare's **Hamlet**, but this is clever enough and the ending surprising enough to entertain. ROYALTY: $25. SOURCE: Kelly, Tim. (1984). The omelet murder case: A murderous spoof in one act. New York, NY: Dramatists Play Service. SUBJECTS/PLAY TYPE: Mystery; Parody.

2238. 6-10. (+) Kehret, Peg. **On being different.** CAST: 1u. ACTS: 1. SETTINGS: None. PLAYING TIME: NA. PLOT: A teen puzzles over the fact that he is different from his peers and isn't afraid to express his individuality. RECOMMENDATION: Either a male or female can play this role, as its theme of the need to be true to self is universal. ROYALTY: NA. SOURCE: Kehret, Peg. (1986). Winning monologs for young actors. Colorado Springs, CO: Meriwether Pub. SUBJECTS/PLAY TYPE: Individuality; Monologue.

2239. 2-5. (+) Fisher, Aileen. **On Halloween.** CAST: 2f, 2m, Su. ACTS: 1. SETTINGS: None. PLAYING TIME: NA. PLOT: Children are scared on Halloween by black cats, witches, and ghosts. RECOMMENDATION: This is

scary enough to be fun. ROYALTY: NA. SOURCE: Fisher, Aileen. 1980) Holiday programs for boys and girls. Boston, MA: Plays, Inc. SUBJECTS/PLAY TYPE: Halloween, Skit.

2240. 10-12. (+) Bayley, Jefferson. **On hearing the moon rise.** 3f, 9m, Su. ACTS: 2. SETTINGS: Yard. PLAYING TIME: NA. PLOT: Amon Danby returns home to the Ozarks. He left after the death of his adored father because he felt that his mother and brother had not treated his father well. The return of the prodigal is met with joy and trepidation by his mother and with jealousy by his brother, Orrin, who is about to marry Caralie McCloud, Amon's childhood playmate. Most of the action revolves around Amon's attempts to introduce electricity into the community. A preacher whips up the community against Amon and his devil's contraption, with more eye to the possibility of the loss of his kerosene trade than out of fear for his flock. The preacher's followers destroy Amon's work, and nearly rape and murder Caralie. The play ends just short of despair with Amon and his aunt resolving to stay and fight ignorance and prejudice. RECOMMENDATION: This grim and frequently violent drama portrays the savagery that can surface in men and women when they are confronted with greed or a person or idea that seems threatening because it is different. It also expresses clearly the evil that humans may per- form in the name of religion. The play is powerful, but it may require more acting ability than a teenager is capable of. Some dialogue alluding to sexual and religious matters may cause controversy. ROYALTY: $50. SOURCE: Bayley, Jefferson. (1985). On hearing the moon rise. Chicago, IL: Dramatic Pub. Co. SUBJECTS/PLAY TYPE: Superstition; Family Relationships; Drama.

2241. 9-12. (+) Wilson, David Henry. **On stage, Mr. Smith.** CAST: 3f, 4m. ACTS: 1. SETTINGS: Bare stage, props. PLAYING TIME: NA. PLOT: Depressed, Mr. Smith answers an advertisement for "Theatrepeutics, Theater Therapy, guaranteed to cure depression." Mr. Abrams takes him to a stage to begin the therapy. On stage, Mr. Smith lives out his daily life, encountering his wife, daughter, mistress, and employer. He is puzzled at the therapy and complains that these are the very people and situations he wants to escape. Mr. Abrams convinces him that the therapy is working. Finally, when Mr. Smith complains that it has done no good, Mr. Abrams explains that the therapy is to cure his own depression, not Mr. Smith's. RECOMMENDATION: This will make the audience think about times in which they have been amused at the problems of others. ROYALTY: 15. SOURCE: Wilson, David Henry. (1975). On stage, Mr. Smith. Chicago, IL: Dramatic Pub. Co. SUBJECTS/PLAY TYPE: Irony; Theater; Drama; Comedy.

2242. 1-2. (+) Fisher, Aileen. **On strike. CAST:** 8u. ACTS: 1. SETTINGS: Woods. PLAYING TIME: 15 min. PLOT: Animals strike because Mr. Dullar, the farmer, is trying to destroy them. After six weeks, Farmer Dullard realizes the good that animals do for his farm, and allows them to live. RECOMMENDATION: This could help children learn the positive roles that animals play in nature and agriculture. ROYALTY: None. SOURCE: Fisher, Aileen. (1980). Holiday programs for boys and girls. Boston, MA: Plays, Inc. **SUBJECTS/PLAY TYPE:** Animals; Comedy.

2243. 7-12. (+) McCusker, Paul. **On the street interview: Brotherly love. CAST:** 1m, 5u. **ACTS:** 1. **SETTINGS:** Bare stage. **PLAYING TIME:** 15 min. **PLOT:** A reporter asks people on the street how they feel about brotherly love. He is rebuffed by a businessperson, harangued by a bum whose wine (alias milk) he has spilled, regaled with incoherent words from a hippie, and then robbed by the streetwalker who says he's practicing the part of brotherly love that includes taking it. **RECOMMENDATION:** This light satire would be a perfect curtain opener, or it could be used to bring some levity to a serious discussion of how people react to such concepts. **ROYALTY:** NA. **SOURCE:** McCusker, Paul. (1984). Batteries not included. Boston, MA: Baker's Plays. **SUBJECTS/PLAY TYPE:** Satire; Love; Skit.

2244. 10-12. (-) Charles, Ronald, Jr. **On time. CAST:** 1f, 1m. **ACTS:** 1. **SETTINGS:** Bus stop. **PLAYING TIME:** 15 min. **PLOT:** Two people meet at a bus stop. At first, they are self conscious and unable to converse. However, as time passes, they reveal that they are both lonely and just wait at the bus stop to meet someone. A promising relationship begins. **RECOMMENDATION:** This is too subtle in places, too direct and overt in others, to be anything but a very poor attempt at demonstrating the actions to which loneliness will drive people. **ROYALTY:** Free to Plays subscribers. **SOURCE:** Charles, Ronald Jr. (1980, November). On time. Plays: The Drama Magazine for Young People, pp. 63-66. **SUBJECTS/PLAY TYPE:** Loneliness; Skit.

2245. 6-9. (+) Way, Brian. **On trial. CAST:** 2f, 2m. **ACTS:** 1. **SETTINGS:** Bare stage. **PLAYING TIME:** 55 min. **PLOT:** A man, hands bound, sits alone as three masked accusers blame him for murder. While awaiting the jury's return, the man pleads for a chance to go back in time to prove his innocence. As the setting goes back in time, the man is David Abbott, a jungle guide, and his masked accusers are actually colleagues. They have discovered the beginnings of an epidemic which, if not treated quickly, will destroy an entire community. The cure is an herb that can be obtained only by crossing a treacherous plateau. With volunteers from the audience, the expedition begins. After crossing the plateau and finding the herb, it is obvious they will not return in time to stay the plague. To travel more quickly, Abbott goes back on his own, leaving the rest to return by themselves. Without him, the trip back takes the lives of many in the expedition. However, Abbott returns in time to save hundreds of people who would have otherwise died of the plague. When the setting returns to the present, the accusers are divided in their opinions of whether or not David is guilty of murder, and the final decision is left to the audience. **RECOMMENDATION:** This integrated audience participation play uses improvisation and the entire room as the stage. It would be best performed by adults for younger audiences, and should be concluded with small group discussion. **ROYALTY:** $20. **SOURCE:** Way, Brian. (1977). On trial. Boston, MA: Baker's Plays.

SUBJECTS/PLAY TYPE: Moral Dilemmas; Values; Participation Play.

2246. 9-12. (+) Van Horn, Bill. (Shakespeare, William) **On with the shrew. (The taming of the shrew) CAST:** 6f, 5m. **ACTS:** 1. **SETTINGS:** Medieval town. **PLAYING TIME:** NA. **PLOT:** A practical joke is played on Terri by a jealous rival. The episode nearly destroys the relationship between Terri and her boyfriend. Both have starring roles in an adaptation of **The Shrew**, which is presented in this play within a play. Although it is much abbreviated and **The Shrew** is a more violent modern day version, the plot follows the same basic line as does Shakespeare's. In the end, the joker is the victim of her own maliciousness and Ron and Terri (Petruchio and Kate) are reunited. **RECOMMENDATION:** Although this short and frivolous takeoff can scarcely be said to reflect the genius of Shakespeare, it is funny and light, and the acting talent required is minimal. **ROYALTY:** $15. **SOURCE:** Van Horn, Bill. (1983). On with the shrew. Chicago, IL: Dramatic Pub. Co. **SUBJECTS/PLAY TYPE:** Love; Marriage; Comedy; Adaptation.

2247. 7-12. (-) Baker, Charles. **Once a year. CAST:** 4f, 7m. **ACTS:** 1. **SETTINGS:** Home. **PLAYING TIME:** 40 min. **PLOT:** On Christmas Eve, Jeb McDermott is upset because his family is not spending the evening together. When he wonders where he has gone wrong, an other worldly figure appears to instigate a series of bizarre events which make Jeb realize that families need to spend time together throughout the year, not just at Christmas. As the play concludes, Jeb opens a mysterious box which contains items that will help him be a better parent (i.e., a video game for the entire family, a book on parenting, etc.). **RECOMMENDATION:** The children in the play have no real impact on the action and never rise above the level of stereotypes. Even the ghost is predictable. The dialogue is uninspired and the tone is preachy and moralistic. Even the ending, while positive, is unconvincing and flat. **ROYALTY:** $20. **SOURCE:** Baker, Charles. (1983). Once a year. Chicago, IL: Dramatic Pub. Co. **SUBJECTS/PLAY TYPE:** Family; Christmas; Comedy.

2248. 6-12. (+) Wibberley, Leonard. **Once in a garden. CAST:** 3f, 6m, Su. **ACTS:** 2. **SET- TINGS:** Garden. **PLAYING TIME:** NA. **PLOT:** Adam, Eve, and Fido ramble happily in the Garden of Eden until the persuasive serpent coaxes Eve to taste the forbidden fruit. After their expulsion from Eden, and after their two sons introduce murder into the world, Adam and Eve speculate about the meaning of it all. God, who misses the creatures he formed in his own image, offers to let them back into Paradise, but Adam and Eve choose the stimulation and challenge of natural life over the boring predictability of Paradise. **RECOMMENDATION:** This is an interesting combination of philosophy and comedy. The roles of the biblical figures (and the animals) have modern overtones and the theme follows a humanistic rather than religious path. Settings and costumes are evocative rather than realistic and, therefore, quite simple to create. **ROYALTY:** $35. **SOURCE:** Wibberley, Leonard. (1975). Once, in a garden. Chicago, IL: Dramatic Pub. Co. **SUBJECTS/PLAY TYPE:** Adam and Eve; Creation; Bible Stories; Drama.

2249. 7-12. (+) Murray, John. **Once upon a midnight dreary.** CAST: 4f, 7m. ACTS: 1. SETTINGS: Drawing room. PLAYING TIME: 40 min. PLOT: Each of three heirs must sleep one night in an eerie mansion to collect an inheritance. If they do not stay the required night, the estate will stay under the control of the executor, Judge Livingston. The Judge attempts to promote the local belief that Cat Man and Zombie haunt the estate. By having his sons impersonate these creatures, he hopes to scare the potential inheritors away before each completes the required stay. The play concludes as the judge's triumphant pleasure turns to terror as he discovers that the Cat Man and Zombie advancing toward him are not his sons. RECOMMENDATION: The plot is appealing and so is the poetic justice. ROYALTY: Free to Plays subscribers. SOURCE: Murray, John. (1986, March). Once upon a midnight dreary. Plays: The Drama Magazine for Young People, pp. 1-13. SUBJECTS/PLAY TYPE: Suspense; Horror; Mystery.

2250. K-3. (+) Ashby, Sylvia & Halpain, Thomas J. (Baum, Lyman Frank) **Once upon a Santa Claus.** (Life and adventures of Santa Claus) CAST: 2f, 11m, 9u. ACTS: 1. SETTINGS: Forest; valley; cottage living room; mountain. PLAYING TIME: 60 min. PLOT: In a northern forest inhabited by kings, queens, elves and grims, contact with human beings is forbidden. A human baby is found and adopted by a nymph, despite misgivings of the Ruler of the Forest. The baby grows up to have a special mission, making human children happy. On the verge of death, his good deeds are recognized by the immortals, who bestow the gift of immortality on Saint Nicholas. RECOMMENDATION: This is a truly superb and inspirational play which provides an account of the early life of Santa Claus and which explains his immortality. The interaction of Santa Claus with his adopted mother and the fantasy creatures who raise him capture hearts entirely. Struggles with forces of evil, uncertainty, disappointments and even death provide the tension. ROYALTY: NA. SOURCE: Ashby, Sylvia & Halpain, Thomas J. (1988). Once upon a Santa Claus. Schulenburg, TX: I.E. Clark. SUBJECTS/PLAY TYPE: Santa Claus; Christmas; Fantasy; Adaptation.

2251. K-4. (+) Robinette, Joseph. **Once upon a shoe.** CAST: 1f, 1m, Su. ACTS: 1. SETTINGS: Yard. PLAYING TIME: 45 min. PLOT: Needing money to repair their shoe-home, Mother Goose and her children stage a show based on several of Mother Goose's poems. Little Miss Muffet, Humpty Dumpty, Hey Diddle, Diddle, Jack and Jill, Mistress Mary, and old King Cole are presented with humorous asides. A movie producer sees the show and offers them a movie contract. Their home is saved. RECOMMENDATION: As most children are familiar with the Mother Goose rhymes, this would be a comfortable play to stage. ROYALTY: $25. SOURCE: Robinette, Joseph. (1979). Once upon a shoe. Chicago, IL: Dramatic Pub. Co. SUBJECTS/PLAY TYPE: Nursery Rhymes; Comedy.

2252. 5-12. (-) Schaller, Mary W. **Once upon a summertime.** CAST: 1f, 1m. ACTS: 1. SETTINGS: Woods. PLAYING TIME: NA. PLOT: Tiffany (a newly blinded 10 year old) is befriended by Robin (a goblin) who, because he killed King Oberon's queen, has promised his first true love to the Fairy King as atonement. As Tiffany and Robin develop a friendship, Robin fills the roles of teacher (of braille), psychologist (making Tiffany accept her blindness by forcing her to cry about it), and finally, platonic lover. Realizing that she will be taken soon by Oberon, Robin causes her to magically fall asleep, forgetting about him, but remembering what he taught her. As he kisses her farewell, Oberon appears to take his due. Robin convinces him to spare Tiffany, and the goblin is killed instead. RECOMMENDATION: Stereotypes about blindness abound here, from the misconception that blind people have special hearing to the demeaning vocational rehabilitation which focuses on simple crafts. Although the goblin (a takeoff on Shakespeare's Puck), is delightful and the story engrossing, it is unfortunately ruined by the author's intrusive and irrelevant subplot about dealing with a disability. ROYALTY: $25. SOURCE: Schaller, Mary W. (1987). Once upon a summertime. Woodstock, IL: Dramatic Pub. Co. SUBJECTS/PLAY TYPE: Folk Tale Motifs; Blindness; Fairies; Fantasy.

2253. 7-12. (+) Hamlett, Christina. **Once upon a taxi.** CAST: 1f, 1m. ACTS: 1. SETTINGS: Taxicab. PLAYING TIME: 10 min. PLOT: The elegantly dressed princess of a bankrupt kingdom proposes marriage to a New York taxicab driver whom she has just met after escaping the Duke of Dragonmede. She says that the Duke held her captive and demanded marriage or a ransom. When the cabbie declines her offer of marriage, the lady departs the cab and leaves her bouquet of flowers on the seat. As the taxi driver reflects upon his decision, the radio announcer describes the robbery of affluent guests by an unknown female who caught the bridal bouquet. The cab driver says he never believed her, then stares offstage where the lady made her exit. RECOMMENDATION: The script provides a series of fairy tale related events with references to international problems and descriptions of day to day struggles. The cab driver's reflection upon a lost opportunity as well as his relief in recognizing a past danger reflect the decisions that we all have to make in life. ROYALTY: Free to Plays subscribers. SOURCE: Hamlett, Christina. (1984, May). Once upon a taxi. Plays: The Drama Magazine for Young People, pp. 49-54. SUBJECTS/PLAY TYPE: Decisions; Comedy.

2254. 5-12. (+) Clark, I.E. **Once upon a Texas.** CAST: 8f, 9m, Su. ACTS: 1. SETTINGS: Wilderness. PLAYING TIME: NA. PLOT: Seven playlets (5 to 15 minutes each) depict the history of Texas, including its exploration and pioneer days ("Texas Between Rivers"); the diverse ethnic contribution of Indian, French, Spanish, English, and German cultures ("Texas by Any Other Name"); the selection of Austin as capital ("A Capital Idea"); a dance reenactment of the raising of a log cabin ("It Takes a Heap of Lovin"); a mimed segment of the hardships of pioneer life in 1824, the year of the big drought ("Life in the Country"); the important battles of revolution and independence ("Those Revolting Texans"); and the first trial in the new republic under a live oak tree ("Three-Legged Willie"). RECOMMENDATION: Originally performed as part of a Texas Sesquicentennial Pageant, the playlets are both historically accurate and highly entertaining. They could easily be performed anywhere in any setting, as they offer a glimpse of American, not just Texas, history. Cast can be expanded from 8-20 females, and from 9-20 males. ROYALTY: $10. SOURCE: Clark, I.E. (1985). Once upon a Texas. Schulenburg, TX: I.E. Clark. SUBJECTS/PLAY TYPE: Texas; Austin, Stephen F.; History, Texas; Drama.

2255. 3-6. (+) Fisher, Aileen. **Once upon a time.** CAST: 5f, 12m, Su. ACTS: 1. SETTINGS: Inside the old woman's shoe. PLAYING TIME: 20 min. PLOT: The old woman tries to think of something with which to entertain the king. A magician pulls book characters from his hat, each of whom takes one child until there are no more. This gives the old woman time to think. RECOMMENDATION: The magic in this is thrilling. ROYALTY: Free to Plays subscribers. SOURCE: Fisher, Aileen. (1986). Holiday programs for boys and girls. Boston, MA: Plays, Inc. SUBJECTS/PLAY TYPE: Fantasy; Comedy.

2256. 9-12. (+) Kendall, John. **Once upon a time--take two.** CAST: 3f, 4m, 1u. ACTS: 1. SETTINGS: Throne room. PLAYING TIME: 15 min. PLOT: A beautiful princess, formerly a witch's apprentice, has her chauvinistic husband turned back into a frog and attempts to find a husband for her talented, liberated, less than beautiful daughter. Two hypocritical suitors are chased off by the daughter, after which she finds her match with a wandering minstrel/cook. The fairy tale ends with a tongue in cheek "happily ever after" for all except the husband, who remains a frog. RECOMMENDATION: A feminist theme is delivered in comedy and witty, contemporary dialogue from the opening line to the closing. Familiar issues are evident but are presented in a completely noncontroversial way. Some lines are extremely funny; there is potential for the comedy to be expanded all the way to slapstick. ROYALTY: Free to Plays subscribers. SOURCE: Kendall, John. (1982, April). Once upon a time--take two. Plays: The Drama Magazine for Young People, pp. 63-69. SUBJECTS/PLAY TYPE: Women's Rights; Skit.

2257. 9-12. (+) Valency, Maurice. (Giraudoux, Jean) **Ondine: A romantic fantasy in three acts.** (Ondine) CAST: 12f, 17m. ACTS: 3. SETTINGS: Forest; palace; river. PLAYING TIME: NA. PLOT: In this superb English version of the original French classic, a water nymph and a knight fall in love and are tragically separated because they belong to separate worlds. Ondine, in order to marry the knight errant, Hans, must make a pact with the Old One (king of the sea), that if she is deceived by Hans, her husband will be killed. Hans, a selfish lady's man, does deceive her with Princess Bertha. To save him, Ondine claims that she first deceived Hans with Bertram. In her trial, she is humiliated, and after she cannot bear to have Bertram kiss her, she is found guilty of lying to her husband and is sentenced to death. In the final scene, Hans realizes how foolish he has been as the two embrace one last time before Hans is killed by the Old One and Ondine is taken back to the sea. RECOMMENDATION: This legend, with its philosophical messages about true love,

honesty, and devotion has dramatic power as well as the allure of romance. Only a very skilled cast (mature high schooler or adults) will command the maturity to produce this adequately. Also, familiarity with Greek mythology will enhance the audience's ability to understand this wonderfully tragic and heartrending tale. ROYALTY: $50. SOURCE: Valency, Maurice. (1984). Ondine: A romantic fantasy in three acts. New York, NY: Samuel French. SUBJECTS/PLAY TYPE: Romance; Mythology, Greek; Drama; Adaptation.

2258. 7-12. (+) Facos, James. **One daring fling.** CAST: 10f, 4m. ACTS: 3. SETTINGS: College city. PLAYING TIME: NA. PLOT: Aaron Ginsburg is an associate professor who has had the same girlfriend for five years. He lives with his mother and seems to be patiently waiting forever for marriage, a job promotion, and self respect. His mother and girlfriend are tired of waiting for Aaron to take control of his life. A leprechaun helps the professor solve his problems and, in spite of confusion, he wins respect and marriage. RECOMMENDATION: This shows that it is necessary to respect oneself before seeking the respect of others. The plot is somewhat contrived but also frequently charming, and the characters are just appealing enough to overcome their stereotyped dialogue. ROYALTY: $35. SOURCE: Facos, James. (1978). One daring fling. Chicago, IL: Dramatic Pub. Co. SUBJECTS/PLAY TYPE: Leprechauns; Assertiveness; Self Respect; Comedy.

2259. 6-12. (+) Fendrich, Shubert. **One day at a time.** CAST: 6f, 3m, 1u. ACTS: 2. SETTINGS: Apartment; school corridor. PLAYING TIME: 90 min. PLOT: Barbara fights off the amorous advances of Elliot while her mother copes with career stress and her grandmother decides to become an apprentice fortuneteller. The newlywed older sister, Julie, returns home with her unemployed weight lifting husband to find that Elliot has handcuffed himself to the front door of the apartment and that their friendly handyman, Schneider has discovered through the tarot card readings, that he's about to become the victim of a hit man. The sink clogs. The mother looses her temper. Another week in the life of the Romano family. RECOMMENDATION: Based on three episodes from the situation comedy of the same name, the action is fast paced, funny, and filled with the laid back, witty, conversational bon mots that members of real life families so rarely have the time to come up with. Best produced by high schoolers. ROYALTY: $35. SOURCE: Fendrich, Shubert. (1982). One day at a time. Denver, CO: Pioneer Drama Service. SUBJECTS/PLAY TYPE: Family; Comedy.

2260. 7-12. (+) Dias, Earl J. **One duchess too many.** CAST: 5f, 5m. ACTS: 2. SETTINGS: Drawing room. PLAYING TIME: 25 min. PLOT: When two Duchesses of Kilgore arrive at the Armbruster's mansion, the family must determine which is the imposter. As the first Duchess leaves, Jack discovers Lady Cora's missing jewelry in her purse. When Sir Harry tells Sidney to restrain the Duchess, Jack indicates that Sidney is the real criminal because he has discovered that the first duchess is a private investigator, sent by the police to observe Sidney, who has a reputation as a thief, but has never been convicted. The Duchess/ private investigator explains that Sidney had volunteered to escort her home, and must have put the stolen jewels in her handbag, planning to remove them sometime during their journey. RECOMMENDATION: This comical presentation of an eighteenth century, proper British family's dilemma has several unexpected twists, and good naturedly pokes fun at some of the mores of the period. Although not stellar, it is mildly amusing. ROYALTY: Free to Plays subscribers. SOURCE: Disa, Earl J. (1987, May). One duchess too many. Plays: The Drama Magazine for Young People, pp. 1-9. SUBJECTS/PLAY TYPE: Comedy; Jewel Thieves; Mistaken Identity; Mystery.

2261. K-6. (+) Bennett, Rowena. **One Easter morning early.** CAST: 1f, 1m, Su. ACTS: 1. SETTINGS: None. PLAYING TIME: 2 min. PLOT: The Easter Rabbit shapes nests and fills each with eggs as the birds sing cheerily above him. When the morning turns to day, "the rabbit and the rabbit tracks ha[ve] vanished all away." RECOMMENDATION: This prelude or interlude for an Easter or spring program uses hand motions, easily imagined but not provided in the text, and a cheerful holiday chorus. ROYALTY: Free to Plays subscribers. SOURCE: Bennett, Rowena. (1989, March). Plays: The Drama Magazine for Young People, p. 46. SUBJECTS/PLAY TYPE: Easter; Spring; Choral Reading.

2262. 7-12. (-) Nolan, Paul T. **One enchanted evening.** CAST: 2f, 2m. ACTS: 1. SETTINGS: School gym. PLAYING TIME: 25 min. PLOT: Mark, an insecure high school student, unenthusiastically prepares the gym for the big school costume ball. Other students mock Mark's shabby Aladdin costume and the fact that he has a blind date, Jennie. Depressed, Mark picks up a lantern and accidentally summons a genie who is so nice Mark wishes for Jennie to be like the genie. His wish is granted. RECOMMENDATION: Dialogue is stilted and unrealistic, and the outcome thoroughly predictable. ROYALTY: Free to Plays subscribers. SOURCE: Nolan, Paul T. (1981, January). One enchanted evening. Plays: The Drama Magazine for Young People, pp. 1-10. SUBJECTS/PLAY TYPE: Dating; Genies; Comedy.

2263. K-3. (+) Lavin, Richard C. (Grimm Brothers) **One eye, two eyes, three eyes.** (Cinderella) CAST: 8u. ACTS: 1. SETTINGS: Bare stage, backdrops. PLAYING TIME: 20 min. PLOT: In a twist on the Cinderella theme, a magic gift goat is sold, its bell is buried and an apple tree grows on the spot. Only the good, but mistreated sister can pick the apples. She picks them for a knight who rescues her. RECOMMENDATION: The unfortunate characterization of physically abnormal people (the sisters have three eyes) as necessarily evil might be changed. ROYALTY: Free to Plays subscribers. SOURCE: Lavin, Richard C. (1977, March). One eye, two eyes, three eyes. Plays: The Drama Magazine for Young People, pp. 58-64. SUBJECTS/PLAY TYPE: Folk Tales, Germany; Adaptation; Puppet Play.

2264. k-4. (+) Havilan, Amorie & Smith, Lyn. **One man's dream.** CAST: 3f, 4m, Su. ACTS: 1. SETTINGS:

Street corner with lunch counter; platform with backdrop of Washington Monument. PLAYING TIME: 15 min. PLOT: This portrays segregation of blacks in the South in the early 1950s, as observed by Martin Luther King Jr. Brief scenes depict separate drinking fountains, segregated seating on buses, and refusals to serve blacks at restaurants. King promises his friend, Mr. Brooks, that he will work to improve the situation of his people. The play concludes with King speaking before a crowd at the Washington Monument. RECOMMENDATION: This simple and artful drama shows stark, strong points of the segregation issue in a way young children can grasp. This would be an excellent introduction to Black History Month or to Martin Luther King Day. This can be read as a story for very small children; narrated as children pantomime the action; or presented as a traditional play. ROYALTY: None. SOURCE: Havilan, Amorie & Smith, Lyn. (1985). Easy plays for preschoolers to third graders. Brandon, MS: Quail Ridge Press. SUBJECTS/PLAY TYPE: Black Americans; King, Martin Luther; Tripartate.

2265. 6-9. (-) Brown, Julian. **One man's heaven.** CAST: 3f, 3m, Su. ACTS: 1. SETTINGS: Gray room. PLAYING TIME: NA. PLOT: Raymond finds himself in a room with no exit and no recollection of how he got there. Flashbacks reveal his miserly and domineering life. The play ends with Raymond's realization that he has had a car accident. The viewers are left to draw their own conclusions about Raymond's future. RECOMMENDATION: This requires complicated sets and stage techniques for the flashbacks, and it is poorly written with stilted dialogue and a thinly developed plot. ROYALTY: NA. SOURCE: Brown, Julian. (1967). One man's heaven. Denver, CO: Pioneer Drama Service. SUBJECTS/PLAY TYPE: Death; Drama.

2266. 7-9. (+) Bland, Joellen. (Twain, Mark) **The one million pound bank note.** (The one million pound bank note) CAST: 1f, 8m. ACTS: 1. SETTINGS: Park; cafe; tailor shop. PLAYING TIME: 30 min. PLOT: Two wealthy men make a wager regarding a one million pound bank note and its effect on an honest man who is down on his luck. Choosing Henry as their guinea pig, they give him an envelope containing the bank note and a letter explaining what it is for. He is treated royally everywhere and is not charged for anything since no one can make change. Henry is the ultimate winner, as he invested the money wisely. RECOMMENDATION: This lives up to all that one would expect from the master storyteller. ROYALTY: Free to Plays subscribers. SOURCE: Bland, Joellen. (1987). Stage plays from the classics. Boston, MA: Plays, Inc. SUBJECTS/PLAY TYPE: Wagers; Wealth; Romance; Adaptation.

2267. K-2. (+) Alexander, Sue. **One, two, three.** CAST: 1f, 1m, Su. ACTS: 1. SETTINGS: Music room. PLAYING TIME: NA. PLOT: After a little girl fails to get into the Fourth of July parade, the band director suggests she practice marching. She masters this well enough to lead the parade. RECOMMENDATION: This allows for the playing of rhythm instruments and physical marching movements. The cast can be expanded to include other children wanting to march in the band. ROYALTY: None.

SOURCE: Alexander, Sue. (1977). One, two, three. New York, NY: Seabury Press. SUBJECTS/PLAY TYPE: Parades; Independence Day, U.S.; Drama.

2268. 4-6. (+) Feather, Jean. **One wish too many.** CAST: 3f, 2m. ACTS: 1. SETTINGS: Sitting rooms. PLAYING TIME: 20 min. PLOT: As the Hootsons eat dinner, a weary traveler asks for bread and is turned away. The Van Hoeks welcome him in. He sets a spell, and when Mrs. Van Hoeck measures cloth to sell at the market, her supply is unending. The next year, the scene is to be repeated, but the Hootsons invite the beggar in, and plan to be counting gold when the spell comes on. They miscalculate and are cutting bags to hold their expected wealth instead. They realize how greedy they have been. RECOMMENDATION: The theme that greed is its own undoing is well conveyed in this delightfully funny and predictable tale. ROYALTY: NA. SOURCE: Kamerman, Sylvia. (1987). Plays from favorite folk tales. Boston, MA: Plays, Inc. SUBJECTS/PLAY TYPE: Folk Tale Motifs; Greed; Playlet.

2269. 7-10. (+) Martin, Herb & Sousa, John Philip. **Oom, pah pah!: The man who thought he was John Philip Sousa.** CAST: 5f, 6m, Su. ACTS: 2. SETTINGS: Three level band platform; classroom; office. PLAYING TIME: NA. PLOT: David Rocker "becomes" John Phillip Sousa every time he conducts the school band in a Sousa march. This alarms the students, and the principal worries about whether he has hired a likeable madman. The guidance counselor recommends that David visit a psychiatrist, but the doctor turns out to be more confused than the teacher. In the end, it is love that cures David Rocker of his split personality. RECOMMENDATION: Although the plot is very thin, it provides an excellent opportunity to show off a school's marching band and baton twirlers. The innocent romance will keep it interesting, especially if the two leads are chosen with care. ROYALTY: Upon application. SOURCE: Martin, Herb, & Sousa, John Philip. (1975). Oom, pah pah!: The man who thought he was John Philip Sousa. Woodstock, IL: Dramatic Pub. Co. SUBJECTS/PLAY TYPE: Sousa, John Philip; Bands; Comedy; Musical.

2270. 9-12. (+) Patrick, John. **Opal's husband.** CAST: 3f, 2m. ACTS: 3. SETTINGS: Living room; dining room. PLAYING TIME: NA. PLOT: An eccentric, yet likeable and kindhearted junk collector, Opal, tries to match up her friend with a husband found in the want ads. "Mr. Handsome" turns out to be a 95 year old escapee from a nursing home trying to gain freedom from his conniving daughter and son-in-law. He fakes his own death, shocking his daughter into confessing that she was only after his money. Then he takes off to spend his declining years with a long lost Tahitian girlfriend. RECOMMENDATION: Stereotypes are hilariously, but effectively, destroyed in this wonderful comedy. Talented high schoolers should be able to master the slang. The actress playing Opal must deliver quite a bit of dialogue and soliloquy and must exhibit a dynamic personality. ROYALTY: $50. SOURCE: Patrick, John. (1975). Opal's husband. New York, NY: Dramatists Play Service. SUBJECTS/PLAY TYPE: Elderly; Friendship; Comedy.

2271. 10-12. (+) Patrick, John. **Opal's million dollar duck.** CAST: 3f, 1m. ACTS: 3. SETTINGS: Living room. PLAYING TIME: NA. PLOT: Opal is a "junque" collector of the "bag lady" type who finds a valuable painting tossed away by mistake. As two actors try to buy it from her, they have several hilarious encounters. She finally sells it to them, and they learn too late it is a worthless copy. RECOMMENDATION: This would be hilarious in the hands of a couple of good "hams." The role of Opal would be exhausting because she is onstage most of the time. In addition to the verbal comedy and comic delivery, there is much slapstick. ROYALTY: $50. SOURCE: Patrick, John. (1980). Opal's million dollar duck. New York, NY: Dramatists Play Service. SUBJECTS/PLAY TYPE: Art; Comedy.

2272. 9-12. (+) Murray, John. **Opening night.** CAST: 1u. ACTS: 1. SETTINGS: None. PLAYING TIME: NA. PLOT: The director of an amateur production encounters numerous problems in the five minutes before the curtain rises on opening night because one of the actresses couldn't find a babysitter for her child. RECOMMENDATION: This would be best used for auditions, for development of dramatic skills in a theater class, or as a curtain opener. ROYALTY: None. SOURCE: Murray, John. (1982). Modern monologues for young people. Boston, MA: Plays, Inc. SUBJECTS/PLAY TYPE: Theater; Monologue.

2273. K-6. (+) Korty, Carol. **Opera singer.** (Mad merry men of Gotham) CAST: 3u. ACTS: 1. SETTINGS: Bare stage, props. PLAYING TIME: NA. PLOT: A snobbish singer evicts his neighbors who make so much noise he can't hear himself. The new neighbor is also loud, and so the singer takes up dance. RECOMMENDATION: Children will enjoy singing like an opera star and making the noises of the neighbors, as they watch pompousness get what it deserves. ROYALTY: None. SOURCE: Korty, Carol. (1977). Silly soup: Ten zany plays. New York, NY: Charles Scribner's Sons. SUBJECTS/PLAY TYPE: Comedy; Skit; Opera; Adaptation.

2274. 7-12. (+) Taylor, Cecil P. **Operation Elvis.** CAST: 3f, 4m, Su. ACTS: 2. SETTINGS: Classroom; living room; lake. PLAYING TIME: NA. PLOT: Malcolm is a troubled 10 year old who slips in and out of reality as he tries to distinguish himself from his other persona, Elvis. The play revolves around his efforts to take a physically disabled man, Michael, on a boat. In spite of the obstacles, he succeeds, and, as he and Michael sail, Malcolm firmly commits to his real identity and Elvis becomes the dead singer that he is. RECOMMENDATION: The slang must rewritten from its British focus. Also, the disabled person is called mentally handicapped, but it is not really clear whether this is true or not. The final action, and Michael's frustrations as he is unable to communicate because of his disabilities are extremely moving. This could be used as a unit about disabilities, or as a unit about self worth and identity. ROYALTY: NA. SOURCE: Taylor, Cecil P. (1983). Live theatre: Four plays for young people. London: Methuen. SUBJECTS/PLAY TYPE: Disabilities; Self Worth; Identity; Drama.

2275. 3-7. (+) Boiko, Claire. **Operation litterbug.**
CAST: 2f, 8m. ACTS: 1. SETTINGS: Park. PLAYING
TIME: 15 min. PLOT: Doo-Bad assigns dirty tasks to his
army of litterbugs. Piggy Pete dumps sticky ice cream cups
on clean children. Sadie Scrawl scribbles a chalk mustache
on the Mayor's portrait. Icky Egbert empties bottles of
ketchup in the fish pond. Big Bad Bart Banana-Peel
spreads banana peels over the school track, halting the
boys' track team. A tableau style enactment of a mock
battle presents the demise of the uglification forces at the
hands of the Orderly Army, featuring Clem Cleanser,
armed with a vacuum cleaner, Paul Pickup, sporting a
mop, Tom Tidy, carrying a large trash basket, and Sally
Spotless, bent on "erasing" the efforts of Sadie Scrawl.
RECOMMENDATION: This delightful scenario is
couched in terms children can understand and features
circumstances over which youngsters may exercise
control. The theme lends itself to a variety of objectives in
the elementary curriculum: maintenance of a clean
environment, discouragement of disease, beautification of
natural and man-made areas, adherence to codes of good
citizenship, and concern for others. ROYALTY: None.
SOURCE: Boiko, Claire. (1985). Children's plays for
creative actors. Boston, MA: Plays, Inc. SUBJECTS/PLAY
TYPE: Environment; Litter; Comedy.

2276. 3-4. (-) Way, Brian. **The opposites machine.**
CAST: 2f, 2m. ACTS: 1. SETTINGS: None. PLAYING
TIME: 50 min. PLOT: A magician and his female assistant
wander around the stage trying to impress the audience
with the magician's importance. When a professor and his
female assistant come along with a machine that makes
everything opposite, the magician has to step in to make
things right again. RECOMMENDATION: This is
extremely sexist in its portrayal of two dimwitted female
assistants whose major tasks are to convince the audience
to blow at the stage and tell the person sitting next to them
the most exciting thing that has ever happened to them.
This task (if it can be carried out by third and fourth
graders) does absolutely nothing to further the play.
ROYALTY: $20. SOURCE: Way, Brian. (1977). The
opposites machine. Boston, MA: Baker's Plays.
SUBJECTS/PLAY TYPE: Magic; Fantasy.

2277. 7-12. (+) Miller, Madge. **OPQRS, etc.** CAST: 3f,
3m. ACTS: 1. SETTINGS: Two houses; fenced garden and
stocks. PLAYING TIME: 60 min. PLOT: Daily life in
Ottoville is an orange world created by Otto: ruler, censor,
and the owner of the city's inhabitants. The residents obey
his laws that everything must be colored orange, that time
is controlled by his whim, and that the alphabet starts with
O. When a young artist wanders in, he insists that there is
a deeper, richer, more varied life. The artist is condemned
to death but a brave girl helps him escape and together
they overcome Otto and remove his obsessions.
RECOMMENDATION: The message that the whims of
the dictator and the suppression of human nature and
truth will always be overcome by a free and honest human
spirit, is noble but perhaps overworked in the playwright's
eagerness to make his point. ROYALTY: $35. SOURCE:
Miller, Madge. (1984). OPQRS, etc. New Orleans, LA:
Anchorage Press. SUBJECTS/PLAY TYPE: Dictatorships;
Freedom; Comedy.

2278. 10-12*. (+) Gilsenan, Nancy. (Guest, Judith)
Ordinary people. (Ordinary people) CAST: 3f, 6m. ACTS:
2. SETTINGS: Living room; locker area; psychiatrist's
office. PLAYING TIME: NA. PLOT: This deals with
coming to terms with the accidental death of a teenage
son, and Conrad's (the surviving son) relationships with
his successful, well intentioned father, his beautiful,
organized, but remote mother, his psychiatrist, and
friends. As Conrad comes to terms with his sense of guilt
for his brother's drowning, he also discovers his own
needs and priorities. In the end, rather than change her
interactions with husband and son, the mother leaves.
RECOMMENDATION: This is a tightly wrought and
moving drama. It is questionable, however, whether
students could meet the heavy dramatic demands of the
roles. ROYALTY: $50. SOURCE: Gilsenan, Nancy. (1983).
Ordinary people. Woodstock, IL: Dramatic Pub. Co.
SUBJECTS/PLAY TYPE: Death; Family Relationships;
Guilt; Adaptation.

2279. 7-12. (-) Bolton, Martha. **The original turkey
roast.** CAST: 1f, 2m, 1u. ACTS: 1. SETTINGS: Dining
room. PLAYING TIME: 15 min. PLOT: In this spoof of
"celebrity roasts," Tom, the Thanksgiving turkey, is the
guest of honor receiving accolades from Mrs. Chicken
Little and a spokesman from the "Turkey Union of
America." RECOMMENDATION: This is a silly, puerile
bit of nonsense with virtually no redeeming qualities. The
humor is insipid, and child abuse and "death with dignity"
are made subjects of lighthearted whimsy. References to
the main character's impending death are tasteless.
ROYALTY: Free to Plays subscribers. SOURCE: Bolton,
Martha. (1984, November). The original turkey roast. Plays:
The Drama Magazine for Young People, pp. 49-52.
SUBJECTS/PLAY TYPE: Thanksgiving; Comedy.

2280. 12. (+) Prideaux, James. **The orphans.** CAST: 3f,
3m. ACTS: 2. SETTINGS: Hotel room. PLAYING TIME:
NA. PLOT: Two middle aged sisters who have not left
their hotel room in 25 years are forced to confront the
outside world when an illegitimate nephew demands a
share of the family inheritance. Upon the sudden death of
the older sister, the other woman agrees to leave the room
with the young man, although he has confessed to being
an imposter. RECOMMENDATION: The isolation and
interdependence of the sisters are beautifully characterized
but this would be most appreciated by a mature audience.
ROYALTY: $50. SOURCE: Prideaux, James. (1980). The
orphans. New York, NY: Dramatists Play Service.
SUBJECTS/PLAY TYPE: Sisters; Isolation; Elderly; Drama.

2281. 3-6. (-) Mohr, Christopher. **Orphans in
Candyland.** CAST: 4f, 1m, 3u. ACTS: 1. SETTINGS:
Room in an orphanage. PLAYING TIME: 60 min. PLOT:
As orphans prepare a celebration in honor of the
orphanage's founder, the financial security of the
orphanage is threatened by the founder's swindling
daughter. RECOMMENDATION: A ridiculous candy
motif, especially in the choice of names, gives this
melodrama an element of farce. In addition, the contrived
plot, one dimensional characters, and stock treatment of
the hero, heroine, and villain, make this a poor choice for
today's children with more sophisticated tastes. More

critical are the simplistic underlying 19th century notions that good triumphs over evil and that the life of an orphan is pathetic. ROYALTY: $35. SOURCE: Mohr, Christopher. (1978). Orphans in Candyland. Denver, CO: Pioneer Drama Service. SUBJECTS/PLAY TYPE: Orphans; Libretto; Melodrama.

2282. 11-12*. (+) Shamas, Laura Annawyn. **The other Shakespeare.** CAST: 7f, 7m. ACTS: 2. SETTINGS: Garden; dining room; bedchamber; London tavern; Cassie's room; backstage area of the Burbage Theater. PLAYING TIME: NA. PLOT: Cassandra, William Shakespeare's sister, is a talented writer who is forbidden to exercise her craft because she is a woman. She runs away and becomes a tavern maid who brings tankards of ale to customers and then entertains them by reciting her own poetry. When the tavern owner proposes marriage on the condition that she stop writing, Cassandra is faced with a wrenching decision. Her brother tries to persuade her to join him but Cassandra has fought society too long. She is exhausted and chooses marriage over artistic fulfillment. RECOMMENDATION: This is for a mature, sophisticated group who can deal with Will's attempt to run away rather than marry the pregnant Anne Hathaway, and with the abuse Cassandra faces in London. Mature high schoolers will find the dilemma of the heroine thought provoking. The roles are challenging and the sets require near professional attention. ROYALTY: $50. SOURCE: Shamas, Laura Annawyn. (1981). The other Shakespeare. Woodstock, IL: Dramatic Pub. Co. SUBJECTS/PLAY TYPE: Shakespeare, William; Women's Rights; Drama.

2283. 6-12. (+) Heatley, Marney. Heatley, Stephen. **The other side of the pole.** CAST: 3f, 3m, Su. ACTS: 2. SETTINGS: Santa's workshop; living room, kitchen. PLAYING TIME: NA. PLOT: Christmas has been banned for 10 years in Split Hoof. When Willy returns from the institution for the mentally retarded, he talks about it. Sandy and he try to bring Christmas back by writing to Santa Claus. When Santa arrives, he is mistaken for a spy, and in a hilarious scene, Willy and Sandy capture him. While interrogating Santa, they find out that he is not only Santa Claus, but also Sandy's paternal grandfather, and that Sandy's mother (Pix) was one of his elves. Sandy's father (also the town mayor) banned Christmas because as Santa's son, he never got to enjoy it since his dad had to work on December 24. At the end, all reaffirm the joy of Christmas, Willy is not reinstitutionalized, but comes to work for Santa Claus in his sheltered workshop, and father and son reconcile. RECOMMENDATION: This is a rather complicated play within a play, as the main story is related by Santa's elves, who are trying to convince a new elf that presents must be made with love rather than mere efficiency. Also, there is a great deal of singing and "rap music" which will require experienced actors. The religious story of Christmas is related, so it is not ecumenical. ROYALTY: NA. SOURCE: Doolittle, Joyce. (1984). Eight plays for young people. Edmonton, Alberta, Canada: NeWest Publications. SUBJECTS/PLAY TYPE: Christmas; Comedy; Drama.

2284. 7-12*. (+) Russell, Willy. **Our day out.** CAST: 2f, 3m, 12u. ACTS: 2. SETTINGS: School yard; bus; beach; zoo; snack shop. PLAYING TIME: NA. PLOT: Mrs. Kay takes her a group of underachievers on a bus tour into Wales. Aided by the bus driver and Mr. Biggs, a stodgy teacher, Mrs. Kay guides her charges through a zoo, the beach, a castle, and a snack bar, as the children wreak continuous and hilarious havoc. One child, Carol, tries to run away and threatens to jump off a cliff, not wanting to return to her poverty stricken life at home. Biggs takes the bus group to the fair for a final bit of fun and even he enjoys himself. At the conclusion, the children shuffle back to their dead end existence in the city of Liverpool, still clutching at the day's happy moments. RECOMMENDATION: The point that not all lives are happy is interspersed with welcome comic relief in this gripping British drama. Although production would be best suited to adults, an especially motivated group of senior high students could have pleasing results. Some strong language and sexual references may need to be edited out for younger audiences and some British slang should be clarified for American viewers. ROYALTY: NA. SOURCE: Russell, Willy. (1984). Our day out. New York, NY: Methuen. SUBJECTS/PLAY TYPE: School; Field Trips; Poverty; Musical; Drama.

2285. 9-12. (+) Hark, Mildred & McQueen, Noel. **Our famous ancestors.** CAST: 3f, 2m. ACTS: 1. SETTINGS: Living/dining room. PLAYING TIME: 30 min. PLOT: Newlyweds George and Amy Peabody prepare their first Thanksgiving dinner together. An unexpected visit from George's judgmental and ancestry obsessed Aunt Hattie brings family tension. Hattie's piercing remarks about Amy and her working class family incurs a sudden and forceful defense. All is saved when Hattie accepts Amy into the Peabody family after witnessing her strength and spunk. RECOMMENDATION: The message that the past is important, but the present and the future are more so, is well presented. ROYALTY: Free to Plays subscribers. SOURCE: Hark, Mildred & McQueen, Noel. (1982, November). Our famous ancestors. Plays: The Drama Magazine for Young People, pp. 12-20. SUBJECTS/PLAY TYPE: Thanksgiving; Playlet.

2286. K-3. (+) Havilan, Amorie & Smith, Lyn. **Our first flag.** CAST: 1f, 2m, 1u. ACTS: 1. SETTINGS: Shop. PLAYING TIME: 15 min. PLOT: After discussing patterns, Betsy Ross experiments and arranges the stars in a circle. The men are pleased as they believe the circle design symbolizes colonial unity to the world. Washington and Morris raise the new flag on the mast of their friend's ship in the harbor for the whole city to see. RECOMMENDATION: This can be read as a story, performed as a monologue with pantomime, or dramatized. Because the flag figures prominently throughout our history, this would be just as timely for the study of the American Revolution as it would be for study of current events. ROYALTY: NA. SOURCE: Havilan, Amorie & Smith, Lyn. (1985). Easy plays for preschoolers to third grades. Brandon, MS: Quail Ridge Press. SUBJECTS/PLAY TYPE: Ross, Betsy; Flag, American; Tripartate.

2287. 3-9. (+) Fisher, Aileen Lucia. **Our great Declaration. CAST:** 4f, 16m, Su. **ACTS:** 1. **SETTINGS:** None. **PLAYING TIME:** 20 min. **PLOT:** Thomas Jefferson reviews the chronology that led to the first reading of the signed Declaration of Independence. Events that are covered include the Stamp Act, the French and Indian War, the Sugar Act, the formation of the Sons of Liberty, the William Pitt debate against the Stamp Act in England, the Boston Tea Party, Thomas Paine's writing of "Common Sense," Ben Franklin's search for aid from France, John Adams' seconding of the Resolution for Independence, and the passing of the Declaration on July 4, 1776. **RECOMMENDATION:** If the actors wear period costumes, young adults might find this an enjoyable history lesson which is only thinly disguised as a drama. **ROYALTY:** Free to Plays subscribers. **SOURCE:** Fisher, Eileen Lucia. (1985). Year round programs for young players. Boston, MA: Play, Inc. **SUBJECTS/PLAY TYPE:** Revolution, U.S.; Declaration of Independence, U.S.; Reader's Theater.

2288. 2-6. (+) Hark, Mildred & McQueen, Noel. **Our own four walls. CAST:** 3f, 3m. **ACTS:** 1. **SETTINGS:** Living room. **PLAYING TIME:** 15 min. **PLOT:** Four children redecorate the living room in their parents' absence. Everything goes wrong, as paint is spilled, a tent is used as a drop cloth, and one child is injured. The play ends with the parents arriving home unexpectedly while the children frantically try to decide what to do with the mess. The parents turn a bad situation into a good one by deciding that it was time to paint the walls anyway, and calling a professional to finish the job. **RECOMMENDATION:** Best performed by older children for a younger audience, this humorously illustrates that the best of intentions don't always work out. **ROYALTY:** Free to Plays subscribers. **SOURCE:** Hark, Mildred & McQueen, Noel. (1983). Our own four walls. Boston, MA: Plays, Inc. **SUBJECTS/PLAY TYPE:** Good Intentions; Painting; Comedy.

2289. 4-7. (+) Nolan, Paul T. **Our sister, Sitya. CAST:** 2f, 6m. **ACTS:** 1. **SETTINGS:** Throne room. **PLAYING TIME:** 10 min. **PLOT:** The King of Death gives a princess three wishes before he takes her brother. Although she cannot directly wish for her brother to be saved, the princess wishes for her father to have his sight restored, for the King of Death to restore her father's kingdom, and for the king to have a son to succeed him. The King of Death releases the prince and realizes how clever the Princess's wishes are. **RECOMMENDATION:** This charming "human puppet" play about the value of loyalty uses a puppet master as narrator. **ROYALTY:** None for amateur performance. **SOURCE:** Nolan, Paul T. (1982). Folk tale plays round the world: A collection of royalty-free, one-act plays about lands far and near. Boston, MA: Plays, Inc. **SUBJECTS/PLAY TYPE:** Loyalty; Folk Tales, Indonesia; Adaptation.

2290. 8-12. (+) Kehret, Peg. **Out of body choice. CAST:** 1u. **ACTS:** 1. **SETTINGS:** None. **PLAYING TIME:** NA. **PLOT:** A teen who is close to death experiences an out of body episode, and chooses to live when he realizes how much his father loves him. **RECOMMENDATION:**

This is a thought provoking view of death. **ROYALTY:** NA. **SOURCE:** Kehret, Peg. (1986). Winning monologs for young actors. Colorado Springs, CO: Meriwether Pub. **SUBJECTS/PLAY TYPE:** Death; Monologue.

2291. 9-12*. (+) Wagner, Paula & Hofsiss, Jack. (Merriam, Eve) **Out of our father's house.** (Growing up female in America: Ten lives) **CAST:** 3f. **ACTS:** 1. **SETTINGS:** Abandoned summer house. **PLAYING TIME:** 45 min. **PLOT:** Six heroines are presented in their roles as American women from the late 18th to mid 20th centuries. The famous (Elizabeth Cady Stanton) and ordinary (housewife, Eliza Southgate), reveal their dreams and desires, as well as the realities and tiresome details of marriage and motherhood in a patriarchal society. All start meekly conforming to the rules of men, but all end with a realization of their own worth. **RECOMMENDATION:** This is an impressive presentation of the role of women in a male oriented American history. Knowing that these women actually existed and were able to leave written impressions of their lives makes their hypothetical conversations very touching. This puts the women's movement into perspective. A mature cast is required. **ROYALTY:** $20. **SOURCE:** Wagner, Paula & Hofsiss, Jack. (1975). Out of our father's house. New York, NY: Samuel French. **SUBJECTS/PLAY TYPE:** Women's Rights; Drama; Adaptation.

2292. 1-8*. (+) Harder, Eleanor. **Out of the kitchen, Mrs. Claus. CAST:** 3f, 7m. **ACTS:** 1. **SETTINGS:** Living room. **PLAYING TIME:** NA. **PLOT:** Santa's elves are tired of working all the time and never having a real Christmas of their own. They complain to Mrs. Claus and she goes on strike in the kitchen, as she is tired of always baking cookies and wants to do Santa's job for a change. When Santa's back gives out, Mrs. Claus gets her chance, leaving Santa and the elves to spend a Christmas Eve together. They decide always to have enough time and energy left to make Christmas for themselves. **RECOMMENDATION:** Children will enjoy the traditional Christmas characters while older viewers will appreciate the role reversal. Junior high age or older actors will most easily deal with the memorization. **ROYALTY:** NA. **SOURCE:** Harder, Eleanor. (1987). Out of the kitchen, Mrs. Claus. Denver, CO: Pioneer Drama Service, Inc. **SUBJECTS/PLAY TYPE:** Christmas; Elves; Claus, Mrs.; Comedy.

2293. 3-8. (+) Hanson, Mary E. **Outer space masquerade. CAST:** 6f, 2m, 3u. **ACTS:** 1. **SETTINGS:** Living room. **PLAYING TIME:** 20 min. **PLOT:** When outer space aliens land at the Thomas house, they are mistaken for Halloween partyers until they leave in their spaceship. **RECOMMENDATION:** With authentic dialogue and realistic characters, this is a delightful Halloween presentation. **ROYALTY:** Free for Plays subscribers. **SOURCE:** Hanson, Mary E. (1986, October). Outer space masquerades. Plays: The Drama Magazine for Young People, pp. 31-36. **SUBJECTS/PLAY TYPE:** Halloween; Playlet.

2294. 9-12. (-) Majeski, Bill. **Over and up. CAST:** 8f, 6m, 1u. **ACTS:** 1. **SETTINGS:** Two offices. **PLAYING TIME:** NA. **PLOT:** The planet Apocryphal sends young

O.T. to Earth to report on conditions there. The Earth atmosphere causes the alien to age at a fast rate, but the enterprising visitor manages to have romantic involvements with a teenage girl (when he is a teenager), her mother (when he has become middle aged), and her grandmother (when he enters old age). O.T. leaves Earth just before he becomes too old to return. The three broken hearted women soon meet a grandfather, his son, and grandson (all with initials O.T.) and all ends happily. RECOMMENDATION: This is loaded with stale jokes and lacks dramatic tension. The story is far fetched and the ending is contrived. ROYALTY: $15. SOURCE: Majeski, Bill. (1984). Over and up. Chicago, IL: Dramatic Pub. Co. SUBJECTS/PLAY TYPE: Aliens; Comedy.

2295. 2-6. (+) Mueller, Lavonne. **Oyster crackers, undershirts, and mauve lemonade.** CAST: 5f, 2m, Su. ACTS: 2. SETTINGS: Bedroom. PLAYING TIME: NA. PLOT: Pearl Diamondfudge, spoiled and rich, enjoys throwing things, eating oyster crackers and drinking mauve lemonade. Baddy, the bad dream angel, brings Pearl's bedroom furnishings to life so they can return the abusive treatment they have received, and an "oyster cloister" demands that Pearl return all the oyster crackers to the oysters. Pearl reforms. RECOMMENDATION: Extensive memorization, difficult melodies, and elaborate costuming make this impractical for any but an adult acting group. The intellectual level of the humor switches from higher level word plays to lower level audience participation, so parents accompanying their children may also enjoy this. ROYALTY: $25. SOURCE: Mueller, Lavonne. (1975). Oyster crackers, undershirts, and mauve lemonade. Boston, MA: Baker's Plays. SUBJECTS/PLAY TYPE: Manners; Comedy; Musical.

2296. K-4. (+) Mueller, Don A. (Baum, Lyman Frank.) **OZ! A new account of a remarkable journey.** (The wonderful wizard of OZ) CAST: 6f, 10m, Su. ACTS: 1. SETTINGS: Interior of barn; Munchkinland. PLAYING TIME: 120 min. PLOT: When Dorothy and Toto are separated after being transported by tornado from Kansas to Oz, Scarecrow, Lion, and Tinman help her find Toto. Despite severe opposition from the witch and the wizard, the companions succeed because of Dorothy's strong faith in each of them. RECOMMENDATION: This less frightening (no monkeys) but clever and occasionally slapstick version of the classic should be performed by adults or secondary school students. However, it allows for ample casting of young children as Munchkins, scenery (i.e., mobile flora), and singers. The role of Toto is limited enough to be handled by a prop. ROYALTY: $35. SOURCE: Mueller, Don A. (1979). Oz! A new account of a remarkable journey. Boston, MA: Baker's Plays. SUBJECTS/PLAY TYPE: Adventure; Fantasy; Adaptation.

2297. 1-6*. (+) Zeder, Suzan. **Ozma of Oz, a tale of time.** CAST: 5f, 8m, 6u. ACTS: 1. SETTINGS: Ship's deck; ship's cabin; raft; desert; palace; guardhouse; Gnome King's cavern. PLAYING TIME: NA. PLOT: Dorothy and her Uncle Henry head to Australia aboard a freighter when a sudden storm shipwrecks them in the land of Oz.

There they encounter a variety of characters and adventures, both good and bad, that allow then to appreciate each other in ways that they could not previously. They wind up Tic Toc, not realizing that he controls the passage of time. This has adventurous effects on the strange characters in Oz. But they are victorious over the gnomes and time is once again stopped, so Dorothy and her uncle resume their journey to Australia. RECOMMENDATION: This is a wonderful story. The plot has a strong point: intergenerational understanding. It is filled with exciting scenes, and there is no doubt children would enjoy it. It cannot be recommended as an amateur production due to intricate staging. There are eleven different settings and a variety of special effects. This might be better produced on film, where the quick scene changes and variety of effects could be more easily managed. ROYALTY: $35. SOURCE: Zeder, Suzan. (1981). Ozma of Oz, a tale of time. New Orleans, LA: Anchorage Press. SUBJECTS/PLAY TYPE: Fantasy; Oz; Aging; Adventure; Drama.

2298. 8-12. (+) Carmichael, Fred. **P is for perfect.** CAST: 5f. ACTS: 1. SETTINGS: Modern suburban living room. PLAYING TIME: NA. PLOT: Mary Langford, an executive's wife, plans to introduce a perfect guest to her friends at afternoon cocktails--Miss Pex, a robot developed in their husbands' company. After cruelly exposing each woman's human weakness, Miss Pex is exposed as a real woman, and Cora, company secretary, is revealed as the real robot. The final twist in the plot occurs when Cora is also discovered to be human and all the women take revenge on the husbands by going on a shopping spree. RECOMMENDATION: Although cute, this light spoof will have limited appeal. An all female cast coupled with a feminine setting and lines which strongly portray stereotyped attitudes about women will limit the play's potential audience. ROYALTY: NA. SOURCE: Carmichael, Fred. (1983). P is for perfect. New York, NY: Samuel French. SUBJECTS/PLAY TYPE: Robots; Satire.

2299. 10-12. (+) Dias, Earl J. **P.R. Planet Relations.** CAST: 5f, 2m. ACTS: 1. SETTINGS: Living room. PLAYING TIME: 30 min. PLOT: Commander Siggzy arrives from an alien planet to change Hollywood's portrayal of outer space creatures. He visits the home of 16 year old Paul Adams to help him decide whether to take Lydia or Anne to the prom. Siggzy meets Lydia, a sarcastic and self centered individual. Anne impresses Siggzy as genuinely interested in Paul. Paul asks Anne to the prom. In return for the help, Paul assures Siggzy that he won't believe the slanderous Hollywood movies. RECOMMENDATION: Although predictable, this is entertaining. Commander Siggzy's costume (a metallic jumpsuit with silver face makeup) will be a challenge, and the sympathy of Paul's friends, who cannot see the alien and think Paul's "gone nuts," is clever. ROYALTY: Free to Plays subscribers. SOURCE: Dias, Earl J. (1989, March). P.R. Planet Relations. Plays: The Drama Magazine for Young People, pp. 10-20. SUBJECTS/PLAY TYPE: Science Fiction; Dating; Comedy.

2300. K-6. (+) Winther, Barbara. **Pacca, the little bowman.** CAST: 2f, 5m, Su. ACTS: 1. SETTINGS: Jungle clearing. PLAYING TIME: 20 min. PLOT: Pacca is sad because he is too little to join the Queen's Royal Guard, even though he is an expert archer. He proposes that Katti, the tall but lazy firewood seller, join the Guard with Pacca as his servant, and the two can split the salary. Pacca does all the work and the the two quickly earn fame. When Katti is rewarded, he disowns Pacca. Katti is soon disgraced by his lack of skill, but Pacca bails him out. In the end, Katti begs to reverse roles and be a servant to Pacca, who agrees. RECOMMENDATION: Pacca represents Buddha, as he delivers a message of good over selfishness and forgiveness over revenge. Directors may wish to use pantomime liberally. ROYALTY: Free for amateur performance. SOURCE: Winther, Barbara. (1976). Plays from folktales of Africa and Asia. Boston, MA: Plays, Inc. SUBJECTS/PLAY TYPE: Folktales, India; Playlet.

2301. 1-5. (+) Bradley, Alfred. (Bond, Michael) **Paddington goes to the hospital.** (The adventures of Paddington Bear) CAST: 2f, 1m, 4u. ACTS: 1. SETTINGS: Living room; hospital waiting room; patient's room. PLAYING TIME: NA. PLOT: Paddington Bear visits a malingering neighbor in the hospital. After being mistaken for a patient and driving a psychologist to distraction, Paddington is mistaken for a doctor. When his real identity is revealed, Paddington and the neighbor's doctor pretend that the neighbor needs an operation to force him to stop feigning illness. As the neighbor hurriedly leaves, Paddington and the doctor share some cake. RECOMMENDATION: This is as delightful as the original and the "pretend" surgery with hammer and saw will have the audience in stitches. ROYALTY: NA. SOURCE: Bradley, Alfred. (1977). Paddington on stage. Boston, MA: Houghton Mifflin. SUBJECTS/PLAY TYPE: Comedy; Hypochondria; Adaptation.

2302. 1-5. (+) Bradley, Alfred. (Bond, Michael) **Paddington goes to the launderette.** (The adventures of Paddington Bear) CAST: 1f, 4u. ACTS: 1. SETTINGS: Living room; launderette. PLAYING TIME: NA. PLOT: When Paddington Bear does the laundry, he ruins Mr. Curry's clothes by putting the wrong ones into hot water. He finds out that a marmalade sandwich doesn't wash well and learns that sometimes an honest effort is received poorly. RECOMMENDATION: Younger audiences will identify with the familiar situation of a sincere effort to help turning into a disaster. The humor here will also help them to realize that mistakes are not always the end of the world. ROYALTY: NA. SOURCE: Bradley, Alfred. (1977). Paddington on stage. Boston, MA: Houghton Mifflin. SUBJECTS/PLAY TYPE: Comedy; Laundry; Adaptation.

2303. 1-5. (+) Bradley, Alfred. (Bond, Michael) **Paddington has a birthday.** (The adventures of Paddington Bear) CAST: 3f, 2m, 3u. ACTS: 1. SETTINGS: Living room. PLAYING TIME: NA. PLOT: Paddington bear entertains guests at his semiannual birthday party with magic tricks. The grumpy neighbor is the victim, as he sits on a raw egg and observes his watch get smashed as Paddington's tricks go awry. All is well, though, as the neighbor is found to have exaggerated the value of his smashed watch, and so, receives his comeuppance. RECOMMENDATION: This is a good morale building story for well intentioned youngsters who often face the same dismay as Paddington feels. ROYALTY: NA. SOURCE: Bradley, Alfred. (1977). Paddington on stage. Boston, MA: Houghton Mifflin. SUBJECTS/PLAY TYPE: Comedy; Birthdays; Magic; Adaptation.

2304. 1-5. (+) Bradley, Alfred. (Bond, Michael) **Paddington paints a picture.** (The adventures of Paddington Bear) CAST: 3f, 2m, 3u. ACTS: 1. SETTINGS: Living room; junk store. PLAYING TIME: NA. PLOT: Paddington Bear tries to clean a painting Mr. Brown has just finished for a contest because he hopes to find an "old master" painting beneath it. When he smears the picture, he adds a little new paint, catsup, and marmalade. The painting wins first prize. RECOMMENDATION: The "creativity" of Paddington brings distress, then humor and relief. ROYALTY: NA. SOURCE: Bradley, Alfred. (1977). Paddington on stage. Boston, MA: Houghton Mifflin. SUBJECTS/PLAY TYPE: Comedy; Art; Adaptation.

2305. 1-5. (+) Bradley, Alfred. (Bond, Michael) **Paddington turns detective.** (The adventures of Paddington Bear) CAST: 3f, 2m, 4u. ACTS: 1. SETTINGS: Living room; junk store; train station. PLAYING TIME: NA. PLOT: Who stole Mr. Brown's prize marrow? Paddington Bear plays private detective when he thinks he has seen the culprit and mistakenly captures his neighbor. Mrs. Brown admits she cooked the marrow, and Mr. Brown soothes the neighbor by giving him the reward money promised to the captor. RECOMMENDATION: Keeping secrets may sometimes cause confusion, and Paddington's story gets this point across through a humorous mixup and resolution of the issue. ROYALTY: NA. SOURCE: Bradley, Alfred. (1977). Paddington on stage. Boston, MA: Houghton Mifflin. SUBJECTS/PLAY TYPE: Comedy; Mystery; Adaptation.

2306. 3-5. (+) Bradley, Alfred. (Bond, Michael) **Paddington visits the dentist.** (The adventures of Paddington Bear) CAST: 3f, 2m, 3u. ACTS: 1. SETTINGS: Dining room; dentist's office. PLAYING TIME: NA. PLOT: Paddington Bear breaks a tooth on his special caramel candy and goes to the dentist to have it fixed. After a game of hide and seek and other attempts to escape, Paddington bites the dentist while he is making an impression of the broken tooth. To make amends, Paddington offers him candy. The dentist loses all his teeth. RECOMMENDATION: This includes a show of injections and drilling, so it may not be appropriate for very young children. ROYALTY: NA. SOURCE: Bradley, Alfred. (1977). Paddington on stage. Boston, MA: Houghton Mifflin. SUBJECTS/PLAY TYPE: Comedy; Dentists; Adaptation.

2307. 10-12. (+) Howe, Tina. **Painting Churches.** CAST: 2f, 1m. ACTS: 2. SETTINGS: Living room. PLAYING TIME: NA. PLOT: An elderly couple sorts through a lifetime of belongings in preparation for a move from their expansive home to a modest summer cottage, ostensibly for financial reasons. In reality, they are moving because the husband's failing memory is a safety concern.

The couple's daughter visits and the three share memories as the packing takes place. The play culminates with the daughter's holding a portrait of her parents, a blending of memory and love, showing her parents as they were and are. RECOMMENDATION: This thought provoking piece movingly guides younger audiences through the aging process and illustrates the importance of memories, which soften the harshness of reality. Some editing of explicit language may be necessary. ROYALTY: $60. SOURCE: Howe, Tina. (1982). Painting churches. New York, NY: Samuel French. SUBJECTS/PLAY TYPE: Aging; Drama.

2308. K-4. (+) Martin, Judith & Ashwander, Donald. **Paintings: Snow.** CAST: 4u. ACTS: 1. SETTINGS: Bare stage, props. PLAYING TIME: 10 min. PLOT: The narrator describes a winter day while the artist paints the scene on the easel. An old woman is on her way home down a long road as the snow falls faster and heavier. The artist paints the snowflakes and the old woman's paper shawl. Far away, the old woman's husband waits for her in their little house. The artist paints the house and a light in the window. The old woman sees the light and finds her way home. The couple is united and their house is filled with happiness. RECOMMENDATION: The theme of an old couple's love for each other is inspiring. Due to the stage preparation and the paintings of the artist, this probably needs to be staged by high school age youths with artistic abilities or, the items to be painted could be already made and placed onto a flannel board. ROYALTY: NA. SOURCE: Martin, Judith & Ashwander, Donald. (1985). Reasons to be cheerful: A revue for children. New York, NY: The Paper Bag Players, Inc. SUBJECTS/PLAY TYPE: Winter; Skit; Snow; Musical Revue.

2309. K-4. (+) Martin, Judith & Ashwander, Donald. **Paintings: Summer's here.** CAST: 4u. ACTS: 1. SETTINGS: Bare stage, props. PLAYING TIME: 15 min. PLOT: Four actors take turns painting part of a summer scene. With each addition, the action and dialogue intensify until all of the actors are scrambling to find a spot to paint. In the end, the actors point to the finished painting and proclaim that "Summer is here!" RECOMMENDATION: This unusual presentation style could be used by older high schoolers with artistic ability, or the items to be painted could be already made and placed on a flannel board. ROYALTY: NA. SOURCE: Martin, Judith & Ashwander, Donald. (1985). Reasons to be cheerful: A revue for children. New York, NY: The Paper Bag Players, Inc. SUBJECTS/PLAY TYPE: Skit; Summer; Musical Revue.

2310. 3-8. (-) Avery, Helen. **The palace of the Minotaur.** CAST: 2f, 4m, 24u. ACTS: 2. SETTINGS: Throne room; prison; labyrinth. PLAYING TIME: NA. PLOT: In this retelling of the myth of Theseus and ancient Crete, Theseus and Ariadne kill the Minotaur. RECOMMENDATION: The language is a mix of modern and ancient which fails to capture the excitement and unique mood of the Greek myth. Also, the special effects, choreography, and music would be too difficult for younger audiences to produce. ROYALTY: NA. SOURCE: Avery, Helen P.(1978). The palace of the Minotaur.

Rowayton, CT: New Plays Inc. SUBJECTS/PLAY TYPE: Mythology, Greek; Drama.

2311. 1-3*. (+) McCallum, Phyllis & Tandowsky, Jean. **The pale pink dragon.** CAST: 10f, 8m, Su. ACTS: 3. SETTINGS: Throne room; forest; forest path. PLAYING TIME: 60 min. PLOT: A young prince and his squire switch identities and visit a neighboring kingdom to observe the princess to whom the young prince will soon be betrothed. The princess has a wicked stepmother and a jealous stepsister. At the bidding of the stepsister, a witch transforms the lovely princess into a pale pink dragon. The spell can be broken only if a brave prince refuses to slay the dragon. Just as the prince is to slay the dragon, he notices that she sheds large tears, and he refuses to plunge his sword into her, thus breaking the spell. Meanwhile, the stepmother and stepsister have become witches themselves. As they try to cast a spell on both the prince and princess, a white cat scratches the two witches and melts them. The young prince and beautiful princess fall in love and live happily ever after. RECOMMENDATION: Although a very endearing play, and one that primary school children would love, this is "busy" and could be difficult to stage. Costuming is intricate and a cat is one of the main characters. There are two versions: one with music and dance and one without. ROYALTY: $35. SOURCE: McCallum, Phyllis. (1985). The pale pink dragon. Denver, CO: Pioneer Drama Service. SUBJECTS/PLAY TYPE: Dragons; Marriage; Folk Tale Motifs; Musical.

2312. 9-12. (+) Perkins, David. **Pals.** CAST: 2f, 2m. ACTS: 1. SETTINGS: Park. PLAYING TIME: NA. PLOT: As Steve discusses his and Jack's friendship, he asks Jack to kill him. Jack refuses, but Wendy agrees. Steve decides he can wait a while, at least until he's sure he can trust Wendy. Jack, fed up with their nonsense, tries to badger them into seeing the absurdity of their plans. When Wendy becomes angry at Jack's annoying persistence and takes a swing at him with a knife, Steve steps in the way to stop her. Though Steve has changed his mind, he now receives his death blow at the hand of the angry Wendy. RECOMMENDATION: This deals seriously and candidly with suicide and death. Much care should be taken in the final stabbing scene to ensure the safety of the actors and it would be best if the play were followed with a discussion of the audience's reactions and emotions. ROYALTY: $15. SOURCE: Perkins, David. (1986). Pals. Boston, MA: Baker's Plays. SUBJECTS/PLAY TYPE: Death; Friendship; Suicide; Drama.

2313. 1-6. (+) Gardner, Mercedes & Smith, Jean Shannon. **Pandora.** CAST: 3f, 4m, 11u. ACTS: 1. SETTINGS: Greek living room. PLAYING TIME: 20 min. PLOT: When Pandora opens a gift from the gods, she releases the evils of the world: Despair, Greed, Disease, Envy, Weariness and Sorrow. When hope finally escapes, people realize that ills cannot make them wretched if they have hope. RECOMMENDATION: This timeless tale is told here within a youngster's experience, as the characters are introduced playing catch while blindfolded, and progress to understandably wanting to open the mysterious and forbidden box. ROYALTY: Free to Plays subscribers. **SOURCE:** Gardner, Mercedes & Smith, Jean Shannon. (1975, March). Pandora. Plays: The Drama Magazine for Young People, pp. 53-60. **SUBJECTS/PLAY TYPE:** Hope; Mythology, Greek; Playlet.

2314. 4-8. (+) Clark, I.E. (Hawthorne, Nathaniel) **Pandora and the magic box.** (The paradise of children) **CAST:** 3f, 4m, Su. **ACTS:** 1. **SETTINGS:** None. **PLAYING TIME:** 25 min. **PLOT:** This is a faithful retelling of the classic myth. **RECOMMENDATION:** This excellent adaptation is simple enough for the children to perform and would make a perfect complement to a unit on mythology or the study of ancient cultures. There are fine opportunities for costuming (of the people representing the world's problems who come out of the box). The flexible cast can include as many members as are needed. **ROYALTY:** $10. **SOURCE:** Clark, I.E. (1968). Pandora and the magic box. Schulenburg, TX: I.E. Clark. **SUBJECTS/PLAY TYPE:** Mythology, Greek; Adaptation.

2315. 6-12. (+) Anderson, Robert A. **Panic in space.** **CAST:** 3f, 4m, 1u. **ACTS:** 1. **SETTINGS:** Interior room of spaceship. **PLAYING TIME:** 35 min. **PLOT:** The crew of a spaceship endures a three month flight to Venus overcoming boredom, a wiring sabotage (by a fellow crew member), and dangerous space debris, only to discover they were on a simulated flight and participated in a psychological study on the effects of prolonged space flight. **RECOMMENDATION:** This has action, humor, light romance, and a **Twilight Zone** aura. **ROYALTY:** Free to Plays subscribers. **SOURCE:** Anderson, Robert. (1986, March). Panic in space. Plays: The Drama Magazine for Young People, pp. **SUBJECTS/PLAY TYPE:** Science Fiction; Space; Playlet.

2316. 4-6. (+) Gotwalt, Helen Louise Miller. **The paper bag mystery.** **CAST:** 8f, 5m. **ACTS:** 1. **SETTINGS:** Office. **PLAYING TIME:** 20 min. **PLOT:** When Girl Scouts help arrest jewelry thieves by using Morse code, they earn the right to use the deserted school building for their meetings. **RECOMMENDATION:** Set and language are simple, and costuming will also be easy since the only requirements are the Girl Scout uniforms. This could be an exciting way for the girls to earn their drama badges. **ROYALTY:** Free to Plays subscribers. **SOURCE:** Gotwalt, Helen Louise Miller. (1986). Everyday plays for boys and girls. Boston, MA: Plays, Inc. **SUBJECTS/PLAY TYPE:** Detectives; Girl Scouts; Mystery.

2317. 11-12. (+) Robinette, Joseph. (Osborn, John Jay, Jr.) **The paper chase.** (The paper chase) **CAST:** 9f, 8m, Su. **ACTS:** 2. **SETTINGS:** Dorm room; apartment; hotel room, classroom; outdoor scene. **PLAYING TIME:** NA. **PLOT:** A first year law student at Harvard experiences the academic pressures of this rigorous program. He also falls in love with a girl who turns out to be the daughter of his most difficult professor. He manages to keep his grades high and keep his girl. **RECOMMENDATION:** The play provides a realistic look at the grueling nature of some disciplines along with the comic relief of love. **ROYALTY:** $60. **SOURCE:** Robinette, Joseph. (1981). The paper chase. Woodstock, IL: Dramatic Pub. Co. **SUBJECTS/PLAY TYPE:** Law School; Romance; Peer Pressure; Drama.

2318. 1-8. (+) Whittaker, Violet. **The parable of the great supper.** **CAST:** Su. **ACTS:** 6. **SETTINGS:** Dining room; outside. **PLAYING TIME:** NA. **PLOT:** When the invited guests to a feast all make last minute excuses, the host invites anyone who wishes to attend. The narrator explains that we are all invited to dine with God, and should not make excuses for denying Him. **RECOMMENDATION:** This faithful adaptation of Luke 14 includes music and scores. **ROYALTY:** NA. **SOURCE:** Whittaker, Violet. (1984). Puppet people scripts. Grand Rapids, MI: Baker Book House. **SUBJECTS/PLAY TYPE:** Christian Drama; Puppet Play.

2319. K-3. (+) Ison, Colleen. **The parable of the weeds.** **CAST:** Su. **ACTS:** 1. **SETTINGS:** Bare stage. **PLAYING TIME:** NA. **PLOT:** The parable of the farmer whose wheat Satan poisoned with weeds is told. **RECOMMENDATION:** This carefully and clearly explains what a parable is, while teaching the children Jesus' lesson about good and evil. The narrator will have to be an adult, but children of any age can pantomime the action. Discussion questions are provided. **ROYALTY:** NA. **SOURCE:** Ison, Colleen. (1986). Goliath's last stand: And fifteen more easy plays for children. Cincinnati, OH: Standard Pub. **SUBJECTS/PLAY TYPE:** Christian Drama; Parable; Skit.

2320. 9-12. (+) Swortzell, Lowell. (Chaucer, Geoffrey) **The pardoner's tale.** (The Canterbury Tales) **CAST:** 1f, 7m. **ACTS:** 1. **SETTINGS:** Outside a tavern. **PLAYING TIME:** 20 min. **PLOT:** To pass the time on a pilgrimage to Canterbury, the pardoner captivates travelers with his tale of thieves and how greed proved to be their undoing. **RECOMMENDATION:** Character development is fascinating in this exciting dramatization of Chaucer's famous tale of greed and its effect on human nature. **ROYALTY:** Free to Plays subscribers. **SOURCE:** Swortzell, Lowell. (1979, November). The pardoner's tale. Plays: The Drama Magazine for Young People, pp. 73-79. **SUBJECTS/PLAY TYPE:** Greed; Adaptation.

2321. 7-12. (+) Sawyer-Young, Kat. **Parents. CAST:** 1f. **ACTS:** 1. **SETTINGS:** None. **PLAYING TIME:** 1 min. **PLOT:** Leanna complains about the unreasonable limits that parents put on their children. **RECOMMENDATION:** The curfew of 8:00 does seem unreasonable, but the concern about a suggestive dress does not. **ROYALTY:** None **SOURCE:** Sawyer-Young, Kat. (1987). Minute monologues for contemporary teens. Boston, MA: Baker's Plays. **SUBJECTS/PLAY TYPE:** Curfews; Dress Codes; Rules; Monologue.

2322. K-6*. (+) Sullivan, Jessie P. **Parents really do know something. CAST:** 2u. **ACTS:** 1. **SETTINGS:** Puppet stage. **PLAYING TIME:** NA. **PLOT:** Mortimer and Mathilda discuss Ephesians 6:1 and decide that to obey the Lord, they must obey their parents. **RECOMMENDATION:** The plot is designed to help children understand the Bible verse, although equating parents with God might be dangerous in cases where parents are abusive or otherwise unfit. **ROYALTY:** None. **SOURCE:** Sullivan, Jessie P. (1978). Puppet scripts for children's church. Grand Rapids, MI: Baker Book House.

SUBJECTS/PLAY TYPE: Obedience; Christian Drama; Puppet Play.

2323. 6-12. (+) McCusker, Paul. **The party.** CAST: 15u. ACTS: 1. SETTINGS: Castle living room. PLAYING TIME: NA. PLOT: Henry's car inexplicably breaks down near a castle. Mrs. Frankenstein invites Henry to stay the night and join her party. He agrees, but changes his mind after realizing that the guests are all monsters from history, including the Hunchback of Notre Dame, Wolfman, and Dracula. The monsters interact with contemporary humor, and as Henry tries to leave, they stop him. In the final scene, another hapless man has inexplicable car trouble, and Mrs. Frankenstein invites him to her party, as a zombified Henry is told to take care of his car. RECOMMENDATION: The dialogue is full of double entendres and the whole production is contemporarily zany. ROYALTY: SOURCE: McCusker, Paul. (1984). Batteries not included. Boston, MA: Baker's Plays. SUBJECTS/PLAY TYPE: Monsters; Horror; Comedy.

2324. 7-12. (+) Gotwalt, Helen Louise Miller. **Party line.** CAST: 4f, 2m, 1u. ACTS: 1. SETTINGS: Living room. PLAYING TIME: 30 min. PLOT: Liz, who wants to go to the dance with Stanley, persuades her brother, Tommy, to arrange the date. In return, Liz agrees to answer the phone when Polly calls because Tommy does not want to go to the dance with Polly. Mr. and Mrs. Fairchild are going to the dance and are avoiding a call from the Arnolds who want them to play bridge. Mr. Fairchild is dodging a call from a friend about a tennis game. Sister Susie has two dates to the dance and does not want to answer the phone because she is not ready with an excuse for one of the dates. To further complicate matters, Tommy makes arrangements with the wrong Stanley, and Liz no longer wants to answer the phone. Finally, each situation unravels itself. Tommy remembers to tell his parents that the Arnolds cancelled the bridge game. Susie arranges the date for Liz with the right Stanley, and Polly asks the other Stanley to the dance. The only problem left is for the telephone repairman who comes to check the Fairchild's phone because of reports that it is broken since no one has been willing to answer it. RECOMMENDATION: This cleverly makes a point about the consequences of "white" lies. ROYALTY: Free to Plays subscribers. SOURCE: Gotwalt, Helen Louise Miller. (1977, May). Party line. Plays: The Drama Magazine for Young People, pp. 15-24. SUBJECTS/PLAY TYPE: Dating; Lies; Comedy.

2325. 7-12. (+) Shaw, Mark. **The passions of Amoroso.** CAST: 2f, 4m, 2u. ACTS: 1. SETTINGS: Town square. PLAYING TIME: NA. PLOT: Handsome Amoroso is in love with Armonella, who is engaged to Scapin, Amoroso's best friend. Harlequin, a closer friend of Amoroso, helps Amoroso through a tense courtship and rivalry for the hand of Armonella. Though Amoroso and Harlequin try to avoid it, the inevitable duel ensues. Amoroso wins, and Harlequin renounces his long bachelorhood to marry his life long love, Columbine, who is Armonella's lady in waiting. RECOMMENDATION: This fast moving romance provides exceptional comedy,

spicy characters, very witty dialogue, and a Renaissance Italy setting. ROYALTY: $15. SOURCE: Shaw, Mark. (1978). The passions of Amoroso. Boston, MA: Baker's Plays. SUBJECTS/PLAY TYPE: Romance; Commedia Dell'Arte; Comedy.

2326. 3-6. (+) Gabriel, Michelle. **The Passover predicament.** CAST: 1f, 1m, 8u. ACTS: 1. SETTINGS: None. PLAYING TIME: 20 min. PLOT: When a girl discovers that the symbols of Passover and the Haggadah are missing, the Baal Shem Tov helps her solve the Passover Predicament. RECOMMENDATION: The symbols of the Passover and their significance are clearly explained. ROYALTY: None. SOURCE: Gabriel, Michelle. (1978). Jewish plays for Jewish days. Denver, CO: Alternatives in Religious Education, Inc. SUBJECTS/PLAY TYPE: Passover; Jewish Drama.

2327. K-3. (+) Watts, Irene N. **Patches.** CAST: 8u. ACTS: 1. SETTINGS: Bare stage. PLAYING TIME: NA. PLOT: With circus fanfare, the actors pull the props out of bags. The narrator tells the story of how the wind and sun tried to get a woman to take her coat off. The wind blew, but the woman pulled her coat on tighter. The sun's heat forced the woman to take her coat off. The narrator tells another story about a sad and lonely king who fought all the time. Everyone was afraid of him except a little girl, who gave him a packet of seeds and told him that they would make him happy. He saw everyone busy in their gardens and realized it was better to work than fight. The last story is about a town, infested with rodents. Patches, the Pied Piper, rids the town of all the rats and mice by leading them to the river with his music. The counsellors do not want to pay, so the Pied Piper takes everyone from the village (the audience). RECOMMENDATION: In this unique participation play, there is much improvisation, as the children help the characters to achieve their tasks, and even to direct the nature of the stories. Actors should be adults who can direct the audience appropriately, though actual production is quite simple. ROYALTY: NA. SOURCE: Watts, Irene N. (1978). A blizzard leaves no footprints; listen to the drum; patches; the rainstone: Four children's plays. Toronto, Canada: Playwrights Co-op. SUBJECTS/PLAY TYPE: Wind; Sun; Mice; Participation Play.

2328. K-8. (+) Lauck, Carol. **Patchwork.** CAST: 2f, 2m. ACTS: 1. SETTINGS: Bare stage, platforms, props. PLAYING TIME: NA. PLOT: As single squares of a patchwork quilt are shown, the actors present a humorous skit depicting the themes of the patches (i.e., value, normality, impossibility, courage, etc.). The end result is the finished quilt with all the patches symbolizing each scene. RECOMMENDATION: This creative collage represents universal wisdom tempered with humor. This could well be used in a social studies unit on societal foibles. ROYALTY: $15. SOURCE: Lauck, Carol. (1983). Patchwork. New York, NY: Samuel French. SUBJECTS/PLAY TYPE: Comedy; Values; Skit.

2329. 4-6. (+) Hendricks, William & Vogel, Cora. **The pathway of promise.** CAST: 1f, 17m, 2u. ACTS: 1. SETTINGS: Bare stage, backdrop, props. PLAYING

TIME: 60 min. PLOT: This follows the main figures of the Bible from the Old Testament to the New Testament as they explain their contributions to Bible history. These figures are said to walk "the pathway of promise" that leads to salvation and everlasting life with God. The audience is implored to walk this pathway to follow the Lord. All characters speak their parts in Bible verses. RECOMMENDATION: Because of uneven casting, directors may want to dismiss this since the entire class could not participate. This is suitable for church groups. ROYALTY: None. SOURCE: Hendricks, William & Vogel, Cora. (1983). Handbook of Christmas programs. Grand Rapids, MI: Baker Book House. SUBJECTS/PLAY TYPE: Christmas; Worship Program.

2330. 7-12. (+) Gilbert, William Sullivan. Patience. CAST: 1f, 1m. ACTS: 1. SETTINGS: Bare stage, props. PLAYING TIME: NA. PLOT: Two childhood playmates are accidentally reunited and rekindle their love for each other. Although in love, they resolve to part as the only proper solution to their dilemma: to monopolize Grosvenor (the male personification of perfection) would be selfish and there can be no selfishness in Patience's love. As Grosvenor bids farewell, Patience convinces him that although she may not love him because it would be selfish; there would be no impropriety in his remaining and loving her. She is a humble dairy maid and loving her could not be selfish. RECOMMENDATION: Young actors will have difficulty producing convincing performances because this does not have the benefit of the original's music, which allowed the profound subject matter to be effectively treated in a flippant manner. ROYALTY: NA. SOURCE: Olfson, Lewy. (1980). Fifty great scenes for student actors. New York, NY: Bantam Books. SUBJECTS/PLAY TYPE: Idealism; Love; Scene.

2331. K-3. (-) Silverman, Eleanor. Paul Bunyan, the mighty logger. CAST: 3f, 1m, 1u. ACTS: 2. SETTINGS: None. PLAYING TIME: 10 min. PLOT: Paul beats mighty Michelle in a tree chopping contest. RECOMMENDATION: Some of the original description of how big Paul was is recounted, as his usual breakfast of pounds of food is served. However, the contest falls flat. ROYALTY: None. SOURCE: Silverman, Eleanor. (1983). Dramatics for children. Metuchen, NJ: Scarecrow Press. SUBJECTS/PLAY TYPE: Logging; Contests; Women's Equality; Tall Tales, U.S.; Skit.

2332. 7-12. (+) Denson, Wil. Paul Bunyon and the hard winter. CAST: 3f, 10m, Su. ACTS: 1. SETTINGS: Clearing. PLAYING TIME: 90 min. PLOT: As Sawboss Sam tells the audience about the severe winter, a committee of women arrive to bring civilization to the woods by stopping the "heroic" deeds, closing the camp, and bringing the men back to town. At the end, the men and women decide that civilization needs heroes, and the women remain in the camp. RECOMMENDATION: Production requires a pianist and persons capable of singing and dancing. ROYALTY: $25. SOURCE: Denson, Wil. (1980). Paul Bunyon and the hard winter. Denver, Co: Pioneer Drama Service. SUBJECTS/PLAY TYPE: Comedy; Heroes; Civilization; Musical.

2333. 3-6. (+) Mayr, Grace Alicia. Paul Revere, rider to Lexington. CAST: 2f, 13m, 1u. ACTS: 1. SETTINGS: None. PLAYING TIME: 30 min. PLOT: When Paul Revere ascertains the route of the British troops, at the urging of Sam Adams, he, Prescott, and Dawes alert the colonists from Boston to Lexington. Revere then warns Hancock, brings Hancock's fiancee and aunt to safety, and delivers a trunk containing papers useful to the British to Hancock. When the fighting starts, Hancock goes to the Second Continental Congress, and Revere continues to fight for Independence. RECOMMENDATION: This is strongly and traditionally patriotic, as it glorifies American leaders and omits some of the less glorious truths (i.e., Sam Adams was a smuggler and had a personal financial stake in revolution). ROYALTY: Free to Plays subscribers. SOURCE: Mayr, Alicia Grace. (1975, February). Paul Revere, rider to Lexington. Plays: The Drama Magazine for Young People, pp. 85-95. SUBJECTS/PLAY TYPE: Revere, Paul; Independence Day, U.S.; Revolution, U.S.; Reader's Theater.

2334. 9-12. (+) Bucci, Marc. (Cather, Willa) Paul's case. (Paul's Case) CAST: 6f, 3m. ACTS: 1. SETTINGS: Bare stage. PLAYING TIME: NA. PLOT: Paul is dissatisfied and stifled by his drab life and dreams of a world of glitter and sophistication. When he steals a large sum of money and travels to New York City, hard reality intrudes upon his fantasy, and he commits suicide rather than return to his former life. RECOMMENDATION: This follows the original short story very closely. The possibility that Paul's trouble may be connected to his father's misguided urge to protect him by intervening to arrange a "second chance" each time Paul gets into difficulty makes this an excellent psychological case study which could stimulate discussion about the nature of parental love and responsibility. The staging is simple and the cast can be reduced by doubling if necessary. The character of Paul requires very skilled acting. ROYALTY: $15. SOURCE: Bucci, Marc. (1981). Paul's case. Woodstock, IL: Dramatic Pub. Co. SUBJECTS/PLAY TYPE: Suicide; Family Relationships; Adaptation.

2335. 7-9. (-) Johnson, Albert & Johnson, Bertha. Pax, America. CAST: 13f, 5m. ACTS: 1. SETTINGS: Bare stage. PLAYING TIME: NA. PLOT: The script consists mainly of dialogue among members of two families, one in America and one in Russia, each with a conservative father and a liberal mother. Superimposed upon this is an allegorical Paul Revere who appears to represent three different versions of the imminent war between the two countries. In the end, the peaceful version proves true, as the Russian people, not missiles, arrive by plane with their picnic baskets to stage "a wing-ding of an anti-nuclear rally". This, of course, is the product of a secret plot between the two peace loving wives. RECOMMENDATION: While tackling a substantial issue, this subjects itself to sophomoric humor, dated images, and childish language. Phrases such as "No tutus, Honeybunch. It's nukes they're sending," and "Pauloff Reversky! Ah the revolution, n'yet?" abound. ROYALTY: $15. SOURCE: Johnson, Albert, & Johnson, Bertha. (1983). Pax, America. Boston, MA: Baker's Plays. SUBJECTS/PLAY TYPE: Nuclear War; Comedy.

2336. 5-8. (+) Musil, Rosemary G. **The peach tree kingdom.** CAST: 4f, 3m. ACTS: 1. SETTINGS: Garden. PLAYING TIME: 25 min. PLOT: A servant's child and the Emperor's daughter are switched at birth. Now it is 18 years later and the false princess is about to marry the Prince of the Green Willow Kingdom. The Prince, having heard that Princess Yoshiko is cruel, sneaks into the garden disguised as a gardener. There, he falls in love with the servant Tashari, the true princess. Having discovered the error, the Prince plots to correct it by adding a clause to the marriage contract that states that the girl he marries must make a peach tree grow from a seed. He places a young potted peach tree on top of Tashari's seed, thus making her the princess he will wed. RECOMMENDATION: Since this is set in Japan, a study of Oriental customs will foster a deeper understanding. ROYALTY: NA. SOURCE: Kamerman, Sylvia E. (1987). Plays from favorite folk tales. Boston: Plays, Inc. SUBJECTS/PLAY TYPE: Folk Tales, Japan; Marriage; Playlet.

2337. 1-4. (+) Bauer, Caroline Feller. (Cleary, Beverly) **A peanut butter sandwich.** (The mouse and the motorcycle) CAST: 1f, 2m, 1u. ACTS: 1. SETTINGS: None. PLAYING TIME: NA. PLOT: Keith delivers breakfast to his secret mouse friend, Ralph, who has requested a peanut butter sandwich. His kindness pleases Ralph's suspicious mother. RECOMMENDATION: This faithful adaptation will thrill young Cleary fans and give an incentive to beginning readers. ROYALTY: NA. SOURCE: Bauer, Caroline Feller. (1987). Presenting reader's theater: Plays and poems to read aloud. New York, NY: H.W. Wilson. SUBJECTS/PLAY TYPE: Mice; Reader's Theater; Adaptation.

2338. 10-12. (+) Frost, Warren. (Steinbeck, John) **The pearl.** (The pearl) CAST: 3f, 5m, Su. ACTS: 1. SETTINGS: Large platform. PLAYING TIME: NA. PLOT: A poor fisherman finds a huge pearl which he hopes will bring health and prosperity to his family. However, retaining the pearl soon turns into an obsession and the father is tormented by the fear that someone will steal it. Finally, he kills a man whom he believes to be a robber, and he, his wife, and baby are forced to flee into the hills. There, the man's pursuers accidentally shoot the couple's baby. The devastated fisherman returns the pearl to the sea. RECOMMENDATION: This tragic modern fable, whose parts are well within the reach of high school actors, clearly traces the damage that greed can wreak. ROYALTY: $50. SOURCE: Frost, Warren. (1975). The pearl. Chicago, IL: Dramatic Pub. Co. SUBJECTS/PLAY TYPE: Greed; Oppression; Poverty; Adaptation.

2339. K-3. (+) Carlson, Bernice Wells. **A pearl in the barnyard.** CAST: 4u. ACTS: 1. SETTINGS: Barnyard. PLAYING TIME: NA. PLOT: A rooster crows about the pearl he's found, but the other animals say that corn is much more valuable. RECOMMENDATION: "Think before you crow" is the moral of this fable in which "Yiddishisms" are suggested by the sentence structures. ROYALTY: NA. SOURCE: Carlson, Bernice Wells. (1982). Let's find the big idea. Nashville, TN: Abingdon. SUBJECTS/PLAY TYPE: Fable; Boasting; Animals; Skit.

2340. 9-12. (+) Keats, Mark. **The peasant and the nobleman.** CAST: 1f, 5m, 2u. ACTS: 3. SETTINGS: Garden; living room. PLAYING TIME: 45 min. PLOT: A clever peasant wins the hand of the count's daughter by turning the Prince (to whom the girl is reluctantly betrothed) and count against each other when he leads the count to believe that the peasant owns a gold mine. RECOMMENDATION: This complex Ukrainian folk tale alludes to the class consciousness of old Europe, and could be used in social studies classes. ROYALTY: Free to Plays subscribers. SOURCE: Keats, Mark. (1983, May). The peasant and the nobleman. Plays: The Drama Magazine for Young People, pp. 49-56. SUBJECTS/PLAY TYPE: Folk Tales, Ukrainian; Marriage; Playlet.

2341. 4-10*. (+) Harris, Aurand. (Peck, George) **Peck's bad boy.** (Peck's bad boy and his pa) CAST: 3f, 4m, Su. ACTS: 3. SETTINGS: Parlor. PLAYING TIME: NA. PLOT: Henry's chief delight in life is to play pranks on all the members of his household, but soon he turns his tricks towards the goal of reforming his father's faults so that the church will accept his application for membership. Soon, his father is cured of swearing and drinking; he has been saved from losing his savings to a silver mine swindler; and Katie, the maid, becomes engaged to her police friend, who removes the crook. RECOMMENDATION: Although based on George Peck's 19th century work, young children will quickly note the similarities between Henry and the more familiar character, Dennis the Menace. The cast is easily adaptable to include as many, or as few, extras as the director wishes. ROYALTY: NA. SOURCE: Harris, Aurand. (1977). Six plays for children. Austin, TX: University of Texas Press. SUBJECTS/PLAY TYPE: Comedy; Practical Jokes; Adaptation.

2342. K-5*. (+) Kelly, Tim. **Pecos Bill and slue-foot Sue meet the dirty Dan gang.** CAST: 7f, 5m, Su. ACTS: 2. SETTINGS: Street. PLAYING TIME: 60 min. PLOT: Dirty Dan threatens Granny for the deed to her cottage because he thinks a rich vein of gold is beneath it. Granny sends for granddaughter Slue-Foot Sue (reputed to have ridden the back of a catfish), and Pecos Bill (raised by coyotes, with a talking coyote friend and a wild horse named Widowmaker). Worried that he won't get the deed before the mine company pays a handsome price for it, Dirty Dan robs a bank and blames Pecos Bill. Right wins in the end and the dirty gang members are sentenced to baths and school. RECOMMENDATION: This is loaded with broad humor and visual jokes, not unlike the cartoons which children view on television. The delineation between good and bad is very clear cut, right down to the line in the middle of the street separating the good from the bad side of town. ROYALTY: $25. SOURCE: Kelly, Tim. (1978). Pecos Bill and slue-foot Sue meet the dirty Dan gang. Denver, CO: Pioneer Drama Service. SUBJECTS/PLAY TYPE: Western; Comedy; Melodrama.

2343. 4-12. (+) Clark, I.E. **Pecos Bill and the Texas stars.** CAST: 1f, 1m, Su. ACTS: 1. SETTINGS: Western prairie. PLAYING TIME: 15 min. PLOT: Pecos Bill is raised in the wild by coyotes until Sue brings him back to civilization. Bill tames the wildest horse (Widowmaker), and together they make the prairie into a place called

Texas. They dig and scoop all day long, creating the rivers and the mountains. When Bill wrings out his handkerchief, the Gulf of Mexico pours out. When he throws his frying pan over his shoulder he forms the Panhandle. With the stars he creates the cities. Finally, Widowmaker pitches Bill up into the sky where he still winks down at us and at Texas. RECOMMENDATION: This is absolutely charming as a light hearted finish to an evening of **Once Upon a Texas** (see review earlier in the text) or performed separately. It can easily fit into a school curriculum or a library story telling session. ROYALTY: $10. SOURCE: Clark, I.E. (1985). Pecos Bill and the Texas stars. Schulenburg,TX: I.E. Clark. SUBJECTS/PLAY TYPE: Texas; Tall Tales, U.S.; Playlet.

2344. 3-6*. (+) Dixon, Michael Bigelow & Smith, Valerie. **Pecos Bill rides again. CAST:** 6f, 5m, 6u. ACTS: 2. SETTINGS: Campfire; ranch; saloon; netherworld. PLAYING TIME: NA. PLOT: An old timer tells an incredible tale about Pecos Bill to his horse, Bluebonnet. Pecos Bill falls in love with Sluefoot Sue and rescues both her and her farm from the clutches of Earl Slick by performing outlandish deeds such as catching a bullet in his teeth and driving a herd of cattle a hundred miles in a matter of minutes to return with enough money to save Sluefoot's ranch. Pecos Bill marries Sluefoot Sue while Earl Slick and his horse, Bad Bart, are sent to an underground rodent ranch. RECOMMENDATION: This becomes more outlandish as the play progresses. Casting can be large cast or as few as seven, depending on individual situations. ROYALTY: NA. SOURCE: Dixon, Michael Bigelow & Smith, Valerie. (1987). Pecos Bill rides again. Woodstock, IL: Dramatic Pub. Co. SUBJECTS/PLAY TYPE: Tall Tales, U.S.; Western; Musical.

2345. P-1. (+) Merriam, Eve. **Peculiar. CAST:** 2u. ACTS: 1. SETTINGS: None. PLAYING TIME: NA. PLOT: Two readers puzzle over the idea that some children actually like to eat vegetables. RECOMMENDATION: This short dialogue can be performed alone, or with **Toy Tik Ka** and **Jump Rope Rhyme** (see reviews in text). ROYALTY: NA. SOURCE: Bauer, Caroline Feller. (1987). Presenting reader's theater: Plays and poems to read aloud. New York, NY: H.W. Wilson Co. SUBJECTS/PLAY TYPE: Food; Vegetables; Reader's Theater.

2346. 7-12. (+) Huff, Betty Tracy. **Penelope, pride of the pickle factory. CAST:** 6f, 6m. ACTS: 1. SETTINGS: Packing room. PLAYING TIME: 35 min. PLOT: The always cheerful and perfect Penelope Trueheart works at Bertha Blocker's Pickle Factory, where she waits to be rescued by her true love, Melvin Wentworth. The evil Jasper Grimwald steals the secret pickle formula during a false fire alarm and blames Penelope. Melvin, now a fireman after losing his money in the stock market crash, arrives to put out the fire. Penelope foils Jasper's plot and discovers she is Bertha Blocker's long lost daughter and heir to the pickle factory. She and Melvin marry and all ends well. RECOMMENDATION: If they are sophisticated enough, young adults will enjoy this melodramatic satire immensely. ROYALTY: Free to Plays

subscribers. SOURCE: Huff, Betty Tracy. (1979, April). Penelope, pride of the pickle factory. Plays: The Drama Magazine for Young People, pp. 13-23. SUBJECTS/PLAY TYPE: Swindlers and Swindling; Melodrama; Comedy; Satire.

2347. 1-12. (+) Robinette, Joseph & Shaw, James R. **Penny and the magic medallion. CAST:** 3f, 1m, 3u. ACTS: 1. SETTINGS: Throne room. PLAYING TIME: 60 min. PLOT: King Reginald the Righteous, who can never admit he is wrong, is plagued by the inefficiency of his subjects. Bonibini, a magician, brings the king a magical medallion which turns the king's servants into automatons who bustle around the castle performing their duties to perfection. Even the queen is changed. King Reginald soon tires of perfection and wants everyone back to normal, but Bonibini doesn't know how to break the medallion's spell. With the help of Penny the page and the audience, King Reginald unscrambles the puzzle that breaks the spell. The solution is the phrase, "I am wrong." RECOMMENDATION: Word play, rhyme and song make this an entertaining presentation of a valuable lesson: it's all right to admit you're wrong. The dialogue, songs, and length require a cast of at least middle school age, while the story is aimed at a younger audience. ROYALTY: $35. SOURCE: Robinette, Joseph and Shaw, James R. (1987). Penny and the magic medallion. Schulenburg, TX: I.E. Clark. SUBJECTS/PLAY TYPE: Stubbornness; Magic; Comedy; Musical.

2348. K-3*. (+) Boiko, Claire. **Pennywise. CAST:** 1f, 3m, 13u. ACTS: 1. SETTINGS: Classroom. PLAYING TIME: 15 min. PLOT: A bright shiny penny goes in search of great things. At first, the penny tries to buy a five cent balloon, then a ten cent phone call. Grandly brushed aside by a nickel and dime, the penny waits to be found. Picked up at first by a spendthrift child, the penny is used to buy a gumball. Found next by a thrifty child, the penny is put with all the other pennies in a bank, to be used for big things. The penny realizes its place in the economic picture and is pleased with itself. RECOMMENDATION: This lively economic treatise on "penny power" might bother some by choosing a girl to be the spendthrift and the boy to be the saver, but this can easily be rectified. Also, the prices would have to be updated. Much of the dialogue is rhymed and full of double entendres, making the factual information quite lively. This could be presented as a reader's theater. ROYALTY: None. SOURCE: Boiko, Claire. (1985). Children's plays for creative actors. Boston, MA: Plays Inc. SUBJECTS/PLAY TYPE: Economics; Pennies; Playlet.

2349. 7-12. (+) Murray, John. **The people's choice. CAST:** 8f, 5m, Su. ACTS: 1. SETTINGS: Campaign headquarters. PLAYING TIME: 30 min. PLOT: A spy at the high school election headquarters sabotages Billy's efforts to run for student council president but changes her mind at the last minute, and votes for Billy. RECOMMENDATION: This might be enjoyed by junior high students, but the forced ending and contrived romance scenes might spoil it for older high school students. ROYALTY: Free to Plays subscribers. SOURCE:

Murray, John. (1987, November). The people's choice. Plays: The Drama Magazine for Young People, pp. 1-11. SUBJECTS/PLAY TYPE: Elections; Bribery; Playlet.

2350. 3-6. (+) Boiko, Claire. **Pepe and the cornfield bandit.** CAST: 4f, 8m, Su. ACTS: 1. SETTINGS: Mexican hacienda. PLAYING TIME: 20 min. PLOT: In turn, three sons spend the night in their father's cornfield to catch a corn bandit. Only the third son accepts the help of a toad, who grants the son's three wishes: to catch the bandit bird, to marry a beautiful lady (actually the bandit bird), and to see a fiesta, which his father gives when the son comes home with his new wife. RECOMMENDATION: This features the youngest son folk tale motif with a satisfying ending, singing and dancing which could involve an entire class, and a delightful Mexican setting. ROYALTY: NA. SOURCE: Kamerman, Sylvia E. (1987). Plays from favorite folk tales. Boston, MA: Plays, Inc. SUBJECTS/PLAY TYPE: Folk Tale Motifs; Playlet.

2351. 2-4. (+) Creegan, George R. (Browning, Robert) **The peppermint puppy.** (The Pied Piper of Hamelin) CAST: Su. ACTS: 1. SETTINGS: Town. PLAYING TIME: 5 min. PLOT: The mouse population in the town of Limberger employs Peppermint Puppy to rid them of its cats. When Peppermint Puppy asks for his payment, the mice renege, so the Peppermint Puppy spirits their children away with his beautiful music. RECOMMENDATION: Young children who are familiar with the Pied Piper might enjoy this variation in which children take turns performing the story. ROYALTY: Free to Plays subscribers. SOURCE: Creegan, George R. (1981, April). The peppermint puppy. Plays: The Drama Magazine for Young People, pp. 66-68. SUBJECTS/PLAY TYPE: Mice; Cats; Puppet Play; Adaptation.

2352. 1-6. (+) Underwood, Sharry. **Peppermint snow.** CAST: 8f, 2m, 17u. ACTS: 1. SETTINGS: Farmhouse; heaven; barn. PLAYING TIME: NA. PLOT: Louise is upset because there is no snow for the Winter Carnival celebration. Meanwhile, in Heaven, Mistress Winter has her troubles too. Her assistant snow maker is ill, and the replacement is unsuitable. In addition, one of the raindrops has an identity problem with becoming a snowflake. Wise Mistress Winter overcomes these problems by helping the reluctant raindrop find its true identity. With the advent of snow, Louise is happy and the Winter Carnival is a success. RECOMMENDATION: This focuses upon students' physical talents, functioning as a "showcase for students who have studied dance" and allowing "untrained students to use their creativity in making up their own movements." ROYALTY: $25. SOURCE: Underwood, Sharry. (1988). Peppermint snow. Franklin, OH: Eldridge Pub. Co. SUBJECTS/PLAY TYPE: Fantasy; Identity; Drama.

2353. K-5. (+) Mahlman, Lewis & Jones, David Cadwalader. (Belpre, Pura) **Perez and Martina.** (Perez and Martina) CAST: 7u. ACTS: 1. SETTINGS: Kitchen; porch; church. PLAYING TIME: 20 min. PLOT: Martina, the cockroach, declines offers of marriage from the rooster, the pig, and the cat. She accepts the mouse's offer. But, as the mouse stirs beans for supper, he falls in. Dr. Owl revives him, but then joins the cat in trying to eat the couple. Martina's quick thinking saves them, and then saves them again at the wedding, when she empties the pinata on the greedy cat. RECOMMENDATION: Although there is some stereotyping of Mexicans as lazy (i.e., the doctor wants to eat his lunch before helping the mouse), with a little rewriting, this would be a cute fantasy, whose cockroach and mouse protagonists will tickle the audience. ROYALTY: Free to Plays subscribers. SOURCE: Mahlman, Lewis & Jones, David Cadwalader. (1980). Folk tales plays for puppets. Boston, MA: Plays, Inc. SUBJECTS/PLAY TYPE: Folk Tales, Mexico; Adaptation; Animals; Puppet Play.

2354. 4-6. (+) Charles, Ron. **A perfect match.** CAST: 2f, 1m. ACTS: 1. SETTINGS: Office. PLAYING TIME: 15 min. PLOT: Liz is bothered by her boyfriend's inability to hold a job, and she contemplates breaking up with him, even though he loves her very much. While she is lost in thought, John, an imaginary character, appears. Liz imagines that John wants to marry her because they have everything in common, but Liz does not love him. She realizes that although her boyfriend and she have nothing in common, the love they share is enough. RECOMMENDATION: Although the theme is of doubtful value and is presented somewhat clumsily, the message is clear. ROYALTY: Free to Plays subscribers. SOURCE: Charles, Ron. (1986, January/February). Plays: The Drama Magazine for Young People, pp. 67-72. SUBJECTS/PLAY TYPE: Relationships; Love; Playlet.

2355. 3-7. (+) Wallace, Linda. **The perfect pumpkin.** CAST: 4f, 3m, 2u. ACTS: 1. SETTINGS: Throne room. PLAYING TIME: 15 min. PLOT: An old woman provides the perfect pumpkin for the Halloween ball, but when the king refuses to pay her for it, she puts dents in it. Jack cuts the top off to hide the dents, and puts a candle in to make it prettier. The king learns that Jack's last name is O'Lantern. RECOMMENDATION: This is a clever story about the origin of Jack-o-Lanterns, and the props (strange pumpkins) will be fun to make. ROYALTY: Free to Plays subscribers. SOURCE: Wallace, Linda. (1988, October). The perfect pumpkin. Plays: The Drama Magazine for Young People, pp. 31-35. SUBJECTS/PLAY TYPE: Halloween; Pumpkins; Playlet.

2356. 7-11. (+) Taylor, Glenhall. (Andrews, Mary Raymond Shipman) **The perfect tribute.** (The perfect tribute) CAST: 1f, 8m. ACTS: 1. SETTINGS: Army hospital. PLAYING TIME: 20 min. PLOT: Unrecognized, President Lincoln is recruited by a young boy to write the will of his dying Confederate brother in a Union Army prison hospital. RECOMMENDATION: Through excerpts from the original short story, the understated message of love of country is well presented here. ROYALTY: Free to Plays subscribers. SOURCE: Taylor, Glenhall. (1978, February). The perfect tribute. Plays: The Drama Magazine for Young People, pp. 76-80. SUBJECTS/PLAY TYPE: Lincoln, Abraham; Gettysburg Address; Adaptation.

2357. 8-12. (+) Kelly, Tim. **Peril at Pumpernickle Pass.** CAST: 6f, 6m. ACTS: 1. SETTINGS: Store. PLAYING TIME: 60 min. PLOT: Buttercup, owner of a small general store, is engaged to the local sheriff, but the wedding plans are thrown off when both lose their jobs. Meanwhile, Waldo, a scheming prospector, forms get rich quick plans which center on swindling Buttercup. The sheriff wises up, arrests Waldo, and promptly is awarded with a new job working for the railroad, which allows the wedding plans to resume. RECOMMENDATION: This slap-happy horse opera gives free rein to the comedic acting skills of a high school performing group. Melodramatic costumes will be easy to assemble from contemporary wardrobes. ROYALTY: $35. SOURCE: Kelly, Tim. (1987). Peril at Pumpernickle Pass. Denver, CO: Pioneer Drama Service. SUBJECTS/PLAY TYPE: Wild West, U.S.; Gold Mining; Swindlers and Swindling; Comedy.

2358. 10-12. (+) Cope, Eddie. **The perilous decline of Cora Sline, or don't touch my tutu. CAST: 6f, 6m. ACTS:** 2. SETTINGS: Restaurant. PLAYING TIME: 90 min. PLOT: Ma and Pa Cleanlivin are at the brink of bankruptcy. Their only child, Sonny, who went to the big city to study dancing, returns home with a plan to turn his parents' rundown restaurant into a moneymaking operation by putting in a dancing act. He auditions a set of female "triplets" who can't sing or dance, but carry pistols. The triplets' manager, Col. Questus Cantrell, is a shady showman with ties to Lydia O. Lydia, a woman of mystery. Finney Sline, Pa's former partner in a goldmine, arrives with his beautiful dancing daughter, Cora, who wears only tutus. Finney and Pa both die in a fight over a map to the lost goldmine. Meanwhile, the Colonel tries to seduce the innocent Cora by promising to put her name up in candles. Unsuccessful, he steals the map and promises to marry both Ma and Lydia. Someone shoots and wounds Cora, and Lydia is killed. Finally, the "Colonel" is arrested, Ma gets the map, and Cora and Sonny live happily ever after. RECOMMENDATION: This satiric, comic melodrama gives insight into the darker aspects of show business, such as the "casting couch," exploitation, and manipulation. ROYALTY: $35. SOURCE: Cope, Eddie. (1985). The perilous decline of Cora Sline, or don't touch my tutu. Schulenburg, TX: I.E. Clark. SUBJECTS/PLAY TYPE: Show Business; Comedy.

2359. 1-4. (+) Exter, Maureen. **Perils of Cinderella or the vampire's bride. CAST: 7f, 6m, 2u. ACTS:** 1. SETTINGS: Cottage. PLAYING TIME: 30 min. PLOT: Cinderella lives in poverty with her Aunt Bella and her two younger sisters. Mr. Smeed, the vampire landlord, demands his rent or Cinderella's hand in marriage. Cinderella, however, loves a sorcerer's apprentice, Frank, who can't marry her for another year. Invited to the king's ball, all four ladies are outfitted with gowns and glass slippers by Cinderella's fairy godmother. Prince Norman discovers that Aunt Bella is the woman he fell in love with 20 years earlier, and their marriage lifts the family out of poverty and out of Mr. Smeed's clutches. RECOMMENDATION: Children will have fun with this mixed up, modern Halloween version. ROYALTY: $5. SOURCE: Exter, Maureen. (1978). Perils of Cinderella or the vampire's bride. Denver, CO: Pioneer Drama Service. SUBJECTS/PLAY TYPE: Vampires; Melodrama.

2360. 9-12. (-) Gleason, William. **The perils of Lulu.** CAST: 7f, 7m. ACTS: 2. SETTINGS: None. PLAYING TIME: NA. PLOT: When Lulu unwittingly is contaminated by magma protons, strange happenings, reminiscent of the **Perils of Pauline,** occur. She survives a tornado, a Russian Secret Agent, a shark attack, a gorilla, terrorists, and a horde of giant termites, and is finally united in marriage with the faithful, if somewhat ineffectual, Lance. RECOMMENDATION: Language, staging, and props are not difficult, but references to characters, movies, and events which may be unfamiliar to most children, make this more appropriate for adults. It is also very corny in spots. ROYALTY: $50. SOURCE: Gleason, William. (1981). The perils of Lulu. Woodstock, IL: Dramatic Pub. Co. SUBJECTS/PLAY TYPE: Adventure; Melodrama; Comedy.

2361. 9-12*. (+) Ainsworth, Ford. **Persephone.** CAST: 3f, 4m, 8u. ACTS: 1. SETTINGS: Throne room. PLAYING TIME: 40 min. PLOT: Young and vivacious Persephone, Goddess of Life, is kidnapped by Hades, King of the Dead. Intending to make her his wife, Hades pauses to reconsider upon seeing her behavior: she not only awakens the dead and frees the guard dog Cerberus, but also begins redecorating the Underworld. Persephone's mother, Demeter, the Goddess of Nature, insists upon an immediate marriage of the two. The situation is remedied by Hermes, errand boy of Zeus, who suggests that the marriage take place and that Persephone spend six months of each year in Hades and six months of each year on Earth. RECOMMENDATION: The complex symbolism implicit within this Greek myth and the complicated theme of the eternal connection between life and death appear to limit it most appropriately to senior high school actors and audiences who can appreciate the mix of comedy and veiled messages. The play assumes that the audience has the background knowledge of Greek mythology necessary for it to be meaningful. ROYALTY: NA. SOURCE: Ainsworth, Ford. (1977). Persephone. Schulenburg, TX: I.E. Clark, Inc. SUBJECTS/PLAY TYPE: Mythology, Greek; Comedy.

2362. 6-12. (+) Johnson, Cindy Lou. **The person I once was. CAST: 2f, 1m, ACTS: 1. SETTINGS:** House. PLAYING TIME: NA. PLOT: Mattie, who has been overprotective of her younger, serious sister, comes to realize that Cat harbors unanswered questions about her past and a deep spiritual compassion for humanity. Mattie desperately tries to maintain the stoic security of the status quo, but must accept that Cat is maturing into an individual. RECOMMENDATION: This serious play asks unanswerable questions that could help an adolescent to think, grow, and mature. The dialogue encourages positive thought patterns. Because of its seriousness, as well as difficult stage settings, the play is best performed by the upper grades. ROYALTY: $25. SOURCE: Johnson, Cindy Lou. (1985). The person I once was. New York, NY: Dramatists Play Service, Inc. SUBJECTS/PLAY TYPE: Psychology; Transactional Analysis; Drama.

2363. 5-8. (+) Majeski, Bill. **Person in the street interview. CAST: 1f, 3m. ACTS: 1. SETTINGS:** Street.

PLAYING TIME: NA. PLOT: The reporter in the street interviews a person whose occupation is correcting others, an actor who plays corpses, and a man named Ethel. RECOMMENDATION: The humor lies in the language and word plays, but it is still silly enough to appeal. ROYALTY: None. SOURCE: Majeski, Bill. (1981). Easy skits, blackouts and pantomimes. Woodstock, IL: Dramatic Pub. Co. SUBJECTS/PLAY TYPE: Interviews; Comedy; Skit.

2364. 9-12. (+) McNamara, John. **Personal effects.** CAST: 2f, 3m. ACTS: 1. SETTINGS: Living room. PLAYING TIME: NA. PLOT: Kevin, an insecure 18 year old, and his two more experienced friends, decide to have a small party while Kevin's parents are away. Since Kevin's one previous date ended disastrously, he faces the evening with trepidation. Kevin's friends have their own girl troubles. Despite a bad start, Kevin wins a girlfriend after he learns that being himself and respecting others are the keys to a good relationship. RECOMMENDATION: The play works well as it illustrates in a humorous way, different aspects of common problems. Teenagers who are just beginning to date will especially identify with the characters. ROYALTY: $25. SOURCE: McNamara, John. (1986). Personal effects. New York, NY: Dramatists Play Service. SUBJECTS/PLAY TYPE: Dating; Comedy.

2365. 1-6. (+) Landes, William-Alan. (Prokofiev, Sergey) **Peter n' the wolf.** (Peter and the Wolf) CAST: 2m, 4u. ACTS: 1. SETTINGS: Meadow; yard with cottage. PLAYING TIME: 50 min. PLOT: This version features a wolf who is a very reluctant and incompetent villain, a bird and duck who are both friends and rivals, and a grandpa who sets up the events in the play. The boastful wolf convinces Peter and the bird that he has eaten the duck (the audience knows that he hasn't). Peter and the other characters must decide whether or not to punish the wolf by giving him up to the hunters. Peter acts as a responsible little boy, and the bird avoids being eaten by the cat before the inevitable happy ending. RECOMMENDATION: The wolf is an endearing rascal with some boastful songs and melodramatic speeches that children will enjoy. The interaction between the cat, bird and duck is also entertaining. The wolf and grandpa often draw the audience into the drama in effective ways. This would probably work best if staged by the older elementary grades for the younger grades. ROYALTY: $35. SOURCE: Landes, William-Alan. (1980). Peter n' the wolf. Studio City, CA: Players Press. SUBJECTS/PLAY TYPE: Decisions; Musical; Adaptation.

2366. 4-7. (+) Boiko, Claire. **Peter, Peter, Peter!** CAST: 4f, 8m. ACTS: 3. SETTINGS: Machine. PLAYING TIME: 25 min. PLOT: Peter promises to play baseball with Joey, to explore the back woods with Mack, to go fishing with Skinny, to mow Miss Owlong's yard, to play a string duet with Maestro Scarlatti, and to help Mr. Whistle shingle the clubhouse, all at the same time. To solve Peter's dilemma, Skinny introduces him to Jane the Brain and her Super-Duper Duplicator, which creates three Peter look alikes, freeing the real Peter to go fishing with Skinny. However, the clones travel to incorrect destinations for the completion of their assigned tasks and meet with hostility

and disbelief. At Peter's home, where Peter's distraught mother faints at the sight of four Peter's, the four are reunited by Jane, and a repentant Peter vows to maintain a written time schedule in the future. RECOMMENDATION: The departure from reality to solve a problem all too familiar to today's stressed, over-programmed youth, is delightful and imaginative. The designation of a female "brain" and her constant reference to feminine counterparts of familiar figures will delight female viewers. ROYALTY: None. SOURCE: Boiko, Claire. (1985). Children's plays for creative actors. Boston, MA: Plays, Inc. SUBJECTS/PLAY TYPE: Responsibility; Time Management; Comedy.

2367. 2-6. (+) Keats, Mark. **Peter Salem, Minuteman.** CAST: 8f, 13m, Su. ACTS: 1. SETTINGS: Bare stage, backdrop. PLAYING TIME: 30 min. PLOT: A black slave, Peter Salem, relates how he became a Minuteman and fought with his master, Isaac Belknap, during the American Revolution at the Battle of Bunker Hill. After the battle, Belknap gave Salem his freedom, some farm land and two horses. RECOMMENDATION: Relating the Americans' struggles against English rule to the black slaves' struggle against whites is an ingenious and thought provoking means of discussing freedom. The use of a chorus allows a large number of children to participate. ROYALTY: Free to Plays subscribers. SOURCE: Keats, Mark. (1976, April). Peter Salem, minuteman. Plays: The Drama Magazine for Young People, pp. 55-64. SUBJECTS/PLAY TYPE: Revolution, U.S.; Salem, Peter; Black Americans; Playlet.

2368. 1-4*. (+) Jetsmark, Torben & Gilmour, Stephen. **Peter the postman.** CAST: 4f, 7m, 1u. ACTS: 2. SETTINGS: Doors with mailboxes; elevated area. PLAYING TIME: NA. PLOT: Peter the postman provides more than just postal delivery. He washes laundry, performs magic tricks, and plays with the children. Two crabby old women report his activities to the postmaster, who decides Peter does not have enough work to do and gives him 33 extra streets to deliver. When the residents of Peter's route see how frantically he must work to deliver so much mail, they persuade the postmaster to give Peter his old duties back. RECOMMENDATION: This has jokes, songs, magic tricks, and audience participation. ROYALTY: $35. SOURCE: Jetsmark, Torben & Gilmour, Stephen. (1988). Peter the postman. New Orleans, LA: Anchorage Press, Inc. SUBJECTS/PLAY TYPE: Mailmen; Musical; Comedy.

2369. 5-7. (-) Boiko, Claire. **The petticoat revolution.** CAST: 14f. ACTS: 3. SETTINGS: Colonial parlor. PLAYING TIME: 25 min. PLOT: This depicts how the American and British women would have commanded the troops during the Boston Tea Party. For example, they name themselves the Minute Maids, arm themselves with brooms, mops, and rolling pins, and instead of fighting, have a bake-off. RECOMMENDATION: The humor falls flat as the intended puns are not funny, but merely sexist. ROYALTY: Free to Plays subscribers. SOURCE: Boiko, Claire. (1976, April). The petticoat revolution. Plays: The Drama Magazine for Young People, pp. 65- 73.

SUBJECTS/PLAY TYPE: Women; Boston Tea Party; Comedy.

2370. 9-12. (+) Bruce, Mark. **Peugeot's last case.** CAST: 3f, 5m. ACTS: 1. SETTINGS: Study. PLAYING TIME: 10 min. PLOT: Retired Belgian Inspector Peugeot arrives at the Minor mansion to investigate the recent murder of Mr. Minor. Given a room full of likely suspects, the Inspector quickly dismisses each, even though their verbal blunders and open animosity toward the late Mr. Minor clearly make them prime suspects. Displaying an absurd technique of questioning and an even more unconventional line of reason, Peugeot's clues lead to the only suspect left--himself. RECOMMENDATION: This comic whodunit, in which the bungling Peugeot incriminates himself and then confesses to the murder is hilarious. Those who have seen the Cleauseau movies upon which this is built, will love the inspector's techniques and will roar at the surprise ending. ROYALTY: Free to Plays subscribers. SOURCE: Bruce, Mark. (1986, November). Peugeot's last case. Plays: The Drama Magazine for Young People, pp. 51-54. SUBJECTS/PLAY TYPE: Mystery; Comedy.

2371. 7-12. (+) Caruso, Joseph George. **The phantom of the old opera house.** CAST: 6f, 7m. ACTS: 3. SETTINGS: Stage. PLAYING TIME: 90 min. PLOT: In this play within a play, a high school drama class revives **The Phantom of the Opera**, using the stage of the abandoned and reportedly haunted Old Opera House in Denville. The cast encounters the "ghost" and, with the help of a tough female detective, solves a 25 year old mystery. The ghost is a former actor who, thinking he murdered another actor 25 years earlier, has hidden in the opera house to avoid capture. The police reveal that the leading lady committed the murder because she was tired of her lover (the deceased actor). RECOMMENDATION: The appealing characters include understudies who become stars, an enthusiastic teacher role model, a female detective, and a mysterious "presence." One intriguing scene has six "phantoms" onstage simultaneously. This could be performed by high schoolers for a junior high audience. ROYALTY: $35. SOURCE: Caruso, Joseph George. (1982). The phantom of the old opera house. Schulenburg, TX: I.E. Clark. SUBJECTS/PLAY TYPE: Mystery; Comedy.

2372. 9-12. (+) Traylor, Gene. (Leroux, Gaston) **Phantom of the opera.** (The phantom of the opera) CAST: 4f, 8m, Su. ACTS: 2. SETTINGS: Dressing room; office; phantom's lair. PLAYING TIME: NA. PLOT: Two murders occur at the Paris Opera. One allows a young understudy, Christine, to rise to fame, as she takes the place of the leading lady who was murdered. Christine is kidnapped and finds herself underneath the stage with a masked phantom. He reveals that he loves her and that an anonymous opera sent to the directors was written by him and was meant for her to sing. Since the directors did not follow his wishes, he killed the music director and the lead singer. Christine promises to perform the opera and then return to him. On opening night the police are waiting, and when the phantom appears seeking Christine, he is shot. RECOMMENDATION: This full length thriller

contains French names and some simple French words, but otherwise the dialogue is in short conversational English. Christine sings while accompanied by a piano, and the ability to change from one setting area to another as quickly and quietly as possible is a must. The use of crossover sequences between scenes adds to the continuity of the play. ROYALTY: $50. SOURCE: Traylor, Gene. (1979). Phantom of the opera. Woodstock, IL: Dramatic Pub. Co. SUBJECTS/PLAY TYPE: Mystery; Opera; Adaptation.

2373. 5-9. (-) Boiko, Claire. **The phantom of the polling place.** CAST: 2f, 4m, 20u. ACTS: 1. SETTINGS: Voting room. PLAYING TIME: 20 min. PLOT: Two children want to view the voting process but aren't allowed in without an adult. Uncle Sam disguises himself as their uncle, and they are allowed to watch the voting process with him. RECOMMENDATION: The election process is supposedly explained, but the majority of the play is filled with "no's" said by the adults to the children. For example, even Uncle Sam won't allow the children to accompany him into the voting booth (which would have made this quite educational). This is no better than a boring lecture on the subject. ROYALTY: Free to Plays Subscribers. SOURCE: Boiko, Claire. (1980, November). The phantom of the polling place. Plays: The Drama Magazine for Young People, pp. 58-62. SUBJECTS/PLAY TYPE: Election Day; Voting; Skit.

2374. 7-12. (+) Proctor, Steve. **The phantom pulpit committee.** CAST: 4f, 6m, 1u. ACTS: 2. SETTINGS: Dining room. PLAYING TIME: NA. PLOT: Chris and Paige have waited four years for their father to complete his rowing pilgrimage around the world. One day, while friends Ariel and Mikki help Paige work on a school application, Paige is visited by Mr. Drindle, the pastor, who imagines himself to be followed by an invisible Phantom Pulpit Committee. The girls show Mr. Drindle the unpleasant character he will become if he continues to allow the mysterious committee to control his life. They also warn future generations not to be so busy that they fail to worship. The father returns home in the final scene. RECOMMENDATION: Older students might enjoy the satirical remarks and comic humor involved in playing the different roles of the characters. This would be appropriate to perform as a church program. ROYALTY: $40. SOURCE: Proctor, Steve. (1985). The phantom pulpit committee. Boston, MA: Baker's Plays. SUBJECTS/PLAY TYPE: Worship; Comedy.

2375. 7-11. (+) Woodward, Laurie. **Phantoms.** CAST: 8f, 3u. ACTS: 1. SETTINGS: Classroom; hospital room. PLAYING TIME: NA. PLOT: After a fatal car accident, Ann and Tammy are lost in the gray area between life and death called Limbo. Although they cannot be seen or heard as in real life, they try to communicate with their best friend, Susan, by recounting experiences which had made them close. Overcome with the feeling that someone is calling for help, Susan physically reaches out to touch them. It is this strong human connection that pulls the girls out of their comas. RECOMMENDATION: With just enough character development to carry the action, this would be excellent as a springboard for discussion on communicating with people in comas and the strength of friendship. ROYALTY: NA. SOURCE: Woodward, Laurie. (1983). Phantoms. Elgin, IL: Performance Pub. Co. SUBJECTS/PLAY TYPE: Death; Comas; Friendship; Drama.

2376. 7-12. (+) Newell, Martha Hill. **Phillis: A life of Phillis Wheatley.** CAST: 7f, 11m, Su. ACTS: 2. SETTINGS: Outdoors in Boston MA, London, Africa. PLAYING TIME: NA. PLOT: Phillis, a young black child, is kidnapped in Africa and sold into slavery to the Boston Wheatley family. She is so bright that she receives the same education as the Wheatley children, and begins to write poems, mostly elegies. Her fame and talent spread to London, where she is to appear to read her poems. A book dealer there arranges to publish her poetry. RECOMMENDATION: Older children will appreciate the attempt Phillis made to be accepted as a poet, and not as a curiosity of her race and sex. ROYALTY: NA. SOURCE: Newell, Martha Hill. (1981). Phillis: A life of Phillis Wheatley. Rowayton, CT: New Plays, Inc. SUBJECTS/PLAY TYPE: Poets; Black Americans; Slavery; Drama.

2377. 6-12. (+) Foley, Irene. **Phone call.** CAST: 4f, 3m. ACTS: 1. SETTINGS: Living room. PLAYING TIME: NA. PLOT: Susan Driner returns home from summer music camp secretly in love with her assistant music director, Russell. Her failure to confide in her family nearly causes her to miss Russell's phone call. RECOMMENDATION: This light play will appeal to those experiencing their "first love." ROYALTY: $15. SOURCE: Foley, Irene. (1981). Phone call. Chicago, IL: Dramatic Pub. Co. SUBJECTS/PLAY TYPE: Dating; Drama.

2378. 7-10. (+) McCusker, Paul. **The phone call.** CAST: 1f, 1m. ACTS: 1. SETTINGS: Living room. PLAYING TIME: NA. PLOT: As he calls to make a date, Jeff suffers through looking up the number, mistaking Kathy's mother for Kathy, and finally getting Kathy on the line. Much to his surprise, she remembers him and is pleased he has called. Jeff is caught off guard when Kathy suggests they see a movie together next weekend. The skit ends with Jeff forgetting all his insecure feelings and boasting that he knew all along she would go. RECOMMENDATION: With sensitivity and empathy, this effectively and humorously reflects the difficulties of getting a date. An optional ending has Jeff doing all the talking, allowing the play to be a "one-man show," if desired. ROYALTY: NA. SOURCE: McCusker, Paul. (1982). Souvenirs: Comedies and dramas for Christian fellowship. Boston, MA: Baker's Plays. SUBJECTS/PLAY TYPE: Dating; Comedy; Skit.

2379. 1-4. (+) Bennett, Rowena. **Piccola.** CAST: 3f, 2m. ACTS: 1. SETTINGS: Fisherman's hut. PLAYING TIME: 15 min. PLOT: Snow protects a bird from the wind. Piccola, the daughter of a fisherman, learns about St. Nicholas and leaves her shoes in front of the fireplace. To the dismay of her parents, she expects a gift. During the night, Snow safely hides the bird in Piccola's shoes. RECOMMENDATION: This version of a French play is a good source for church groups looking for materials to

support units on Christmas customs around the world. The play is best produced by older students since the parts are difficult to memorize. ROYALTY: None. SOURCE: Kamerman, Sylvia E. (1983). Christmas play favorites for young people. Boston, MA: Plays, Inc. SUBJECTS/PLAY TYPE: Christmas; Fantasy.

2380. 10-12. (+) Shamas, Laura Annawyn. (Lindsay, Joan Weigall) **Picnic at Hanging Rock.** (Picnic at Hanging Rock) CAST: 18f, 8m. ACTS: 2. SETTINGS: Outside; study; bedroom. PLAYING TIME: NA. PLOT: The year is 1900 and the place is Appleyard College, a girl's school in Australia. A group of girls and several teachers go on an outing to Hanging Rock, a geologic marvel known for its air of mystery and danger. Before the day is over, three seniors and a teacher mysteriously disappear, leaving no clues as to how or why. The suspects include the headmistress, another teacher, and two young men who watched the girls as they climbed the mountain. Weaving through more mysterious and sometimes ethereal happenings, two more unsolved deaths take place. Why has it all happened, and how is Hanging Rock involved? No one knows, and the aura of mystery remains, even at the end. RECOMMENDATION: This is for those who love a mystery with overtones of the supernatural. Because of the many questions left unanswered, and inferences not directly stated, it is for older students and adults. ROYALTY: $50. SOURCE: Shamas, Laura Annawyn. (1987). Picnic at Hanging Rock. Woodstock, IL: Dramatic Pub. Co. SUBJECTS/PLAY TYPE: Mystery; Supernatural; Adaptation.

2381. 7-12. (-) Stieper, Donald R. **The picture.** CAST: 6f, 7m. ACTS: 3. SETTINGS: Living room. PLAYING TIME: NA. PLOT: Eccentric Uncle Herman dies and leaves his estate to the relative who most resembles the portrait of himself painted in his youth. When his relatives find that the portrait looks like wealthy Cousin Girard, whom they all hate, they plot to prevent him from inheriting, each taking a turn at destroying the painting. Two ersatz portraits turn up, one strongly resembling nephew Potter, the other an impressionistic rendering by a tattoo artist. The relatives confess to Uncle Herman's lawyers, who inform them that Cousin Girard died three years earlier and the inheritance, which they find to be quite small, is to be divided among the remaining relatives. RECOMMENDATION: While there are some amusing moments, too much extraneous dialogue makes this drag. The ending is unsatisfactory, and the stock characters and slow plot are unlikely to hold the audience's interest. ROYALTY: $35. SOURCE: Stieper, Donald R. (1977). The picture. Franklin, OH: Eldridge Pub. Co. SUBJECTS/PLAY TYPE: Inheritance; Family; Comedy.

2382. 9-12. (-) Watson, Sally Passmore. **The picture of fate.** CAST: 7f, 2m. ACTS: 1. SETTINGS: Back drape set; courtroom. PLAYING TIME: 30 min. PLOT: Claudia, a newspaper reporter, and Sam, a news cameraman, are assigned to a mysterious trial. Fate is the judge, and he directs them to a "nonexistent" courtroom where they unexpectedly become participants in a trial involving the child, Melissa. Her fate is to be decided by the "heartfelt wishes" of those who know her. As Melissa hovers between life and death after a fall from her treehouse, witnesses are called forth. Each portrays her as a troublesome child who has been a burden to her parents and friends. Each "heartfelt wish" which calls for Melissa's destruction is rashly spoken only after Melissa has committed some typically childlike act. At Sam's request, Melissa testifies and is revealed as being loving and spiritual. After a final plea by Sam to spare Melissa, Fate decrees that, if she lives, she will be paralyzed. As Fate leads Melissa away, Sam and Claudia are inspired to spread Christ's Word that the hope of the world lies in the love of Jesus. RECOMMENDATION: Despite an intriguing premise, the characters of Sam and Claudia are shallow and unbelievable. The plot is not well developed and its conclusion is ambiguous. While the play seems to have been intended to teach children that wishing someone dead in a moment of anger may have dire consequences, it might leave some children confused and frightened. Many adults will not be able to reconcile the message with the way in which it is presented. ROYALTY: $25. SOURCE: Watson, Sally Passmore. (1978). The picture of fate. Franklin, OH: Eldridge Pub. Co. SUBJECTS/PLAY TYPE: Fate and Fatalism; Christian Drama.

2383. 4-6. (-) Nobleman, Roberta. **Pictures at an exhibition.** CAST: 1f, 4m, Su. ACTS: 1. SETTINGS: Exhibition hall. PLAYING TIME: NA. PLOT: A family takes a tour through an exhibition hall, looking carefully at each picture. The pictures come to life one at a time, mime their story, and fade back into the frame. RECOMMENDATION: There is too much confusing action here, and the music, which should provide continuity, does not. ROYALTY: NA. SOURCE: Nobleman, Roberta. (1979). Mime and masks. Rowayton, CT: New Plays Books. SUBJECTS/PLAY TYPE: Art History; Museums; Pantomime; Musical.

2384. 3-6. (+) Hall, Margaret. **The pie and the tart.** (The pie and the tart) CAST: 1f, 3m. ACTS: 1. SETTINGS: Street corner. PLAYING TIME: 10 min. PLOT: In this adaptation of a medieval French farce, two hungry rogues flim-flam a baker and his wife out of a good meal. RECOMMENDATION: Children will enjoy the language and broad humor, as well as the fun of affecting a French accent. ROYALTY: Free to Plays subscribers. SOURCE: Hall, Margaret. (1982, January/February). The pie and the tart. Plays: The Drama Magazine for Young People, pp. 61-65. SUBJECTS/PLAY TYPE: Folk Tales, France; Comedy, Adaptation.

2385. K-4*. (+) Fendrich, Shubert & Rainville, Patrick. (Browning, Robert) **The pied piper.** (The pied piper of Hamelin) CAST: 3f, 3m, Su. ACTS: 1. SETTINGS: Bare stage, props. PLAYING TIME: 45 min. PLOT: Directed by Gertrude, the Piper's servant, youngsters in the audience cheer the arrival of the Pied Piper, they admire his disguise, wriggle their noses and march in cadence like rats, and flourish signs and banners in a public demonstration calling for an end to the rat problem. They fill a classroom on stage as substitute school children, and shout warnings to the other characters as the Pied Piper attempts to escape near the end of the play. The characters

of the Mayor and the Pied Piper change as they learn lessons in leadership and humility. The Mayor, formerly concerned solely with the tourist trade and the apple harvest, and intent upon keeping the rat problem a secret, emerges as a wise leader and financial planner after a stint in kindergarten. The Piper, initially a vain, greedy seeker of fame and fortune, learns the satisfaction which accompanies the use of his pipe for good deeds rather than personal gain. The youthful audience delights at the children's ability to outwit the Piper and return to their families, a change from the original ending of loss and abandonment. RECOMMENDATION: The dialogue abounds with simple nuances, clearly decipherable instances of mistaken identity, and dramatic irony easily perceived and appreciated by a young audience. Actors strong in motivational technique, directing ability, and group control will be needed to maintain a level of organization and purpose. ROYALTY: $15. SOURCE: Fendrich, Shubert & Rainville, Patrick. (1985). The pied piper: A participation play for children. Denver, CO: Pioneer Drama Service. SUBJECTS/PLAY TYPE: Legends; Mice; Participation Play; Adaptation.

2386. 3-6. (+) Thane, Adele. (Robert Browning) **The Pied Piper of Hamelin.** (The Pied Piper of Hamelin.) CAST: 1f, 4m, Su. ACTS: 1. SETTINGS: Public square. PLAYING TIME: 25 min. PLOT: A small 13th century village has problems with rats that are eating the villagers' food and biting the children. A reward is offered by the mayor to anyone who can rid the village of the rats. The Pied Piper charms the rats with his music, leading them to the river to drown. When he tries to collect the reward, the mayor denies having offered one and tries to run the Piper out of town. The Piper leaves, but lures the children with him. The Piper offers to return the children if the villagers will throw their valuables into the river. All do so except the greedy mayor. The villagers strip the mayor of his possessions and he runs away. The Piper, believing the villagers have learned their lesson, returns the children. RECOMMENDATION: Youngsters will enjoy the unusual appearance of the Piper, his music, and the spectacle of swarms of rats lured by the music to their death in the river. With music, rhyme, and simple choreography, this presents a moral lesson on the consequences of greed and lack of integrity. ROYALTY: None. SOURCE: Thane, Adele. (1983). Plays from famous stories and fairy tales. Boston, MA: Plays, Inc. SUBJECTS/PLAY TYPE: Greed; Rats; Adaptation.

2387. 1-6. (+) Noll, Robert Thomas & Wilson, Peter J. (Browning, Robert) **The pied piper of Hamelin.** (The pied piper of Hamelin.) CAST: 2f, 3m, Su. ACTS: 1. SETTINGS: Town square. PLAYING TIME: NA. PLOT: Hamelin is overrun with rats until a magical Piper enchants them into the river. When the town refuses to pay the Piper, he leads the children inside a mountain. Anna, the mayor's daughter, agrees to trade herself and her dowry for the freedom of the children. They are released. In a very poignant and emotional scene, the Piper sets Anna free to marry Conrad, her sweetheart. RECOMMENDATION: This basically follows the well known story, but adds music, romance, and some humorous characters. Its length, many songs, and old

English dialect make it necessary to be produced by teenage or older actors. ROYALTY: $35. SOURCE: Noll, Robert Thomas and Peter J. Wilson. (1983). The pied piper of Hamelin. Elgin, IL: Performance Pub. Co. SUBJECTS/PLAY TYPE: Rats; Musical; Adaptation.

2388. 2-6. (-) Norcross, E. Blanche. **Pied Piper's land.** CAST: Su. ACTS: 1. SETTINGS: Town square; meadow. PLAYING TIME: 20 min. PLOT: After the Pied Piper rids Hamelin of rats, the town officials refuse to pay the agreed upon fee. To punish the town, the Piper entrances the children to follow him out of town. They stop in a clearing in the woods to rest, and the wicked witch Arminda threatens to take them. Arminda and the Piper bargain that if any one of the children does anything cruel, lies, or breaks a promise before noon, she gets them. If the children behave, Arminda must throw away her magic scepter and her evil powers forever. Even though Arminda tries to tempt the children, they are good, and she loses. The Pied Piper leads the children to the land of Krythia. RECOMMENDATION: Although this allows a flexible cast of as many as want to be involved, it is disturbing. References to a lame child who is left behind because he can't keep up, as well as references to lame children as pitiable are disturbing, although true to the original story. Also, the children happily leave their parents (all characterized as evil) without a backward glance. This might be frightening to younger children and too juvenile for older children. ROYALTY: Free to Plays subscribers. SOURCE: Norcross, E. Blanche. (1976, January). Pied Piper's land. Plays: The Drama Magazine for Young People, pp. 47-53. SUBJECTS/PLAY TYPE: Greed; Rats; Adaptation.

2389. 1-6. (+) Koon, Helene. **Pierre Patelin.** CAST: 1f, 4m. ACTS: 1. SETTINGS: Street. PLAYING TIME: 30 min. PLOT: Pierre the lawyer, and his wife, Wilhelmina, are poor and hungry because Pierre has no work. He tricks the draper into letting him have some wool for new clothes, claiming he will pay the tradesman at noon, if the draper stops by for dinner with them. Arriving for the meal, the draper is told that Pierre has been ill for weeks. Several of the draper's sheep disappear, and Tibald the shepherd is accused. Pierre bails Tibald out of trouble via courtroom chaos, though Tibald turns the trick back on Pierre at the end, to avoid paying his fee. RECOMMENDATION: With its strange twists, this will delight children while also showing them that one who uses dishonesty ultimately cheats himself. ROYALTY: NA. SOURCE: Kamerman, Sylvia E. (1987). Plays from favorite folk tales. Boston, MA: Plays, Inc. SUBJECTS/PLAY TYPE: Folk Tale Motifs; Lawyers; Dishonesty; Playlet.

2390. 1-3. (-) Schwarz, Ernest J. **Pig tales.** CAST: 7f, 8m. ACTS: 1. SETTINGS: Schoolyard. PLAYING TIME: NA. PLOT: In this takeoff on **The Three Little Pigs**, the wolf disguises himself as the third pig. With the help of the other characters and the audience, the pigs triumph over the wolf. Subplots extend the original story. In one, there is an attraction between the sheriff and the "schoolmarm"; in another, the two pigs to go to

Hoggeywood to become movie stars; and finally the wolf, who is an old time swindler, tries to sell miracle cures for ten dollars each. RECOMMENDATION: References to nursery rhymes and Superman might appeal, but the poor development of a very disjointed plot, and unbelievable, patronizing characterizations render the play silly and uninteresting. ROYALTY: NA. SOURCE: Schwarz, Ernest J. (1979). Pig tales and Treasure Island: Two plays for children. Toronto, Canada: Playwrights Co-op. SUBJECTS/PLAY TYPE: Pigs; Wolves; Fantasy; Comedy.

2391. 1-3. (-) Laurie, Rona. (Potter, Beatrix) **Pigling Bland and Pig Wig.** (Tales of Beatrix Potter) CAST: 6f, 6m, 3u. ACTS: 2. SETTINGS: Farmyard; crossroads; kitchen. PLAYING TIME: NA. PLOT: A mother pig sends her eight piglets to live on their own. The play chronicles the adventures of two who are sent to market, but don't get there. One rescues a stolen pig and they run off together to grow potatoes. RECOMMENDATION: Although this uses characters from Potter's original, it is too disjointed and too vague to entertain the way the original intended. ROYALTY: NA. SOURCE: Laurie, Rona. (1980). Children's plays from Beatrix Potter. London, England: F. Warne. SUBJECTS/PLAY TYPE: Animals; Adaptation.

2392. 8-10. (+) Rawls, James. **The pilgrim painting.** CAST: 4f, 5m. ACTS: 1. SETTINGS: Living room/dining room. PLAYING TIME: 20 min. PLOT: When Eddie and Bonnie Brown's unsuccessful artist father's painting of a pilgrim family at the dinner table comes to life, Eddie and Bonnie interact with the two children from the painting, realizing how little the pilgrims had and how much they have. They change from being spoiled and demanding to being realistic and thankful. At the end, the pilgrim painting is sold, and the children are left wondering about their experience. RECOMMENDATION: This successfully combines the elements of tradition and fantasy uniquely to present two themes: being grateful for what one has and not giving up hope in the face of defeat. ROYALTY: Free to Plays subscribers. SOURCE: Kamerman, Sylvia E. (1983). Holiday plays around the year. Boston, MA: Plays, Inc. SUBJECTS/PLAY TYPE: Thanksgiving; Playlet.

2393. 3-8*. (+) Gotwalt, Helen Louise Miller. **Pilgrim parting.** CAST: 5f, 9m, Su. ACTS: 1. SETTINGS: Beach. PLAYING TIME: 20 min. PLOT: Two pilgrim children about to set sail for England on the **Mayflower** do not wish to go so they run into the forest until the ship sails. The Indian, Squanto, encourages them to be courageous and face their fears. They wish to stay because they love the new land. Their father agrees to let them stay, recognizing that they are mature enough to contribute to the common good. RECOMMENDATION: This is an interesting drama which portrays children as capable of making important decisions about their own lives. It also expresses the purpose of the pilgrims' emigration to America. The dialogue reflects the time period but is easy to understand. ROYALTY: Free to Plays subscribers. SOURCE: Gotwalt, Helen Louise Miller. (1986). Special plays for holidays. Boston, MA: Plays, Inc. SUBJECTS/PLAY TYPE: Pilgrims; Playlet.

2394. 1-6. (+) Gotwalt, Helen Louise Miller. **The pilgrim who didn't care. CAST:** 7f, 4m. **ACTS:** 1. **SETTINGS:** Cabin interior. **PLAYING TIME:** 15 min. **PLOT:** As the children of Plymouth prepare for the first Thanksgiving, they rehearse their speeches of thanks. Humility points out that none of the children is really saying what he or she feels, only what he or she is expected to say. She is not thankful to be in this rough, dangerous country and wishes she were home. When Humility saves the town by putting out a fire, she realizes that she is thankful not to lose the home she has. **RECOMMENDATION:** This child's eye view of the first Thanksgiving is unique. **ROYALTY:** Free to Plays subscribers. **SOURCE:** Gotwalt, Helen Louise Miller. (1987, November). The pilgrim who didn't care. Plays: The Drama Magazine for Young People, pp. 37- 42. **SUBJECTS/PLAY TYPE:** Thanksgiving; Playlet.

2395. 10-12. (+) Preston, L.E. **Pinned down. CAST:** 3f, 2m. **ACTS:** 1. **SETTINGS:** Study. **PLAYING TIME:** NA. **PLOT:** Two sisters living together and collecting butterflies, are reminded of their youth when the man they both loved reappears to purchase their famous butterfly collection. This unexpected confrontation reveals that the older sister had manipulated and betrayed her younger sister so that she would not leave her alone to marry this man. After years of caring for the manipulative older sister, the younger sister now reverses roles and becomes the dependent sibling as a result of this traumatic revelation. **RECOMMENDATION:** This psychological drama is based on subtle parallels between the relationship of the two sisters and butterfly collecting. Audience appeal may be limited to older students and adults. Skilled acting for the role of the older sister is essential, as all depends on the dramatic interpretation of her character. **ROYALTY:** $15. **SOURCE:** Preston, L.E. (1977). Pinned down. Chicago, IL: Dramatic Pub. Co. **SUBJECTS/PLAY TYPE:** Love; Family Relationships; Senility; Drama.

2396. 3-6. (+) Mahlman, Lewis & Jones, David Cadwalader. (Collodi, Carlo) **Pinocchio.** (The adventures of Pinocchio) **CAST:** 2f, 6m, 5u. **ACTS:** 1. **SETTINGS:** Workshop; street; Great Puppet Theater; sea. **PLAYING TIME:** 15 min. **PLOT:** A wooden puppet learns the lessons of life and, with the help of the Blue Fairy, becomes a real boy. **RECOMMENDATION:** The adventure of the original story is well preserved. **ROYALTY:** Free to Plays subscribers. **SOURCE:** Mahlman, Lewis, & Jones, David Cadwalader. (1974). Puppet plays for young players. Boston, MA: Plays, Inc. **SUBJECTS/PLAY TYPE:** Adventure; Fantasy; Puppet Play; Adaptation.

2397. K-3*. (+) Way, Brian & Jenkins, Warren. (Collodi, Carlo) **Pinocchio.** (The adventures of Pinocchio) **CAST:** 5f, 7m, Su. **ACTS:** 3. **SETTINGS:** Puppet workshop; Gepetto's living room. **PLAYING TIME:** NA. **PLOT:** A fairy grants Gepetto's wish for a puppet that can move without strings. Gepetto carves Pinocchio. The fairy, in the guise of a cricket, frog, bird, and tightrope walker saves Pinocchio during his adventures. He almost loses his money to Fox and Cat and ends up as a donkey in the circus, but all ends happily with Pinocchio's performance

in "the Harlequinage." **RECOMMENDATION:** This production is adapted for audience participation. The characters frequently move into the audience and ask for assistance which would be more successful with younger children. The actors would need to be quite creative to have the audience imagine some of Pinocchio's adventures such as swimming in the sea to save Gepetto. The Harlinquinade is a mime and dance. **ROYALTY:** $45. **SOURCE:** Way, Brian. (1986). Pinocchio. Boston, MA: Baker's Plays. **SUBJECTS/PLAY TYPE:** Adventure; Fantasy; Adaptation.

2398. K-12. (+) Way, Brian. (Collodi, Carlo) **Pinocchio.** (Pinocchio) **CAST:** 2f, 12m, 11u. **ACTS:** 3. **SETTINGS:** House. **PLAYING TIME:** NA. **PLOT:** Gepetto dreams of a puppet that can walk without strings. With the audience's help, his wish is granted by a fairy. He calls the puppet Pinocchio, and teaches him to act like a boy. On his way to school, the puppet master gives Pinocchio five gold coins to take to Gepetto. Pinocchio is robbed by the unscrupulous cat and fox, but the fairy helps him. Meanwhile, Gepetto has gone to look for Pinocchio and has disappeared himself. The fairy reassures Pinocchio and sends him off to school again. On the way he meets Candlewick, who doesn't want to go to school, and they are deceived into going to the Land of Boobies, where they are turned into performing circus donkeys. The fairy, disguised as a tightrope walker, helps them escape; the audience hides them. The fairy tells Pinocchio that Gepetto has been swallowed by a sea monster. Pinocchio rescues Gepetto and swims back to shore, with Gepetto holding onto his wooden body. The fairy turns Pinocchio into a real boy. **RECOMMENDATION:** This is an excellent production to be performed by high school or adult actors for young children. The frightening aspects of the original story have been altered or deleted. Audience participation is encouraged. **ROYALTY:** NA. **SOURCE:** Way, Brian. (1978). Pinocchio. London: Dobson Books. **SUBJECTS/PLAY TYPE:** Participation Play; Adventure; Fantasy; Adaptation.

2399. K-6. (+) Yasha, Frank. (Collodi, Carlo) **Pinocchio.** (The adventures of Pinocchio) **CAST:** 4f, 8m, 7u. **ACTS:** 3. **SETTINGS:** Carpenter's shop; village exterior; insides of a whale. **PLAYING TIME:** NA. **PLOT:** As Pinocchio goes to school, two beggar women want his pennies, but he is too greedy to share. The fairy queen warns the little puppet that he'll never become permanently human if he doesn't overcome his greed. Failing in several other tests, Pinocchio is sent to Boobyland as a donkey, and then thrown into the sea where he is swallowed by a whale who has also swallowed Gepetto, his father. They escape and return home to celebrate as Pinocchio becomes a boy. He is so happy that he no longer feels greedy. The fairy queen announces that Pinocchio is now a human forever. **RECOMMENDATION:** This could be produced by older elementary children for younger audiences but would require extensive sets. **ROYALTY:** NA. **SOURCE:** Swortzell, Lowell. (1986). Six plays for young people from the Federal Theatre Project (1936-1939). New York, NY: Greenwood Press. **SUBJECTS/PLAY TYPE:** Adventure; Greed; Fantasy; Adaptation.

2400. 2-12. (+) Jackson, R. Eugene & Ellis, David. (Collodi, Carlo) **Pinocchio: A 2 act musical play.** (The adventures of Pinocchio) **CAST:** 2f, 5m, 2u. **ACTS:** 2. **SETTINGS:** Gepetto's shop; puppet show booth; Dizzyland. **PLAYING TIME:** 60 min. **PLOT:** Instead of going straight to school as Poppa instructed, Pinocchio talks to Foxio and Catsio and ends up in the clutches of evil Prof. Zucchini. When he finally gets home, Pinocchio lies to Poppa, and his nose begins to grow. Repentant, he promises not to lie again. The next day on the way to school, he again runs into the two tricksters, and is lured to Dizzyland, a paradise. However, after playing and enjoying Dizzyland, the little boys are turned into donkeys to work in the mines. Realizing his mistake, Pinocchio is given one more chance by the Blue Fairy. He searches for his father, who has gone to sea and was swallowed by a whale. After saving his father, the Blue Fairy turns Pinocchio into a real boy as a reward. **RECOMMENDATION:** This will be easily performed by older children, but will present some staging challenges. **ROYALTY:** $60. **SOURCE:** Jackson, R. Eugene and Ellis, David. (1985). Pinocchio: A 2-act musical play. Schulenburg, TX: I.E. Clark. **SUBJECTS/PLAY TYPE:** Fantasy; Adventure; Toys; Adaptation.

2401. 3-5. (+) Harris, Aurand. (Collodi, Carlo) **Pinocchio and the fire-eater.** (The adventures of Pinocchio) **CAST:** 9m, Su. **ACTS:** 1. **SETTINGS:** Street; park. **PLAYING TIME:** NA. **PLOT:** As Pinocchio walks to school, the music of a band advertising a Fire-Eaters show convinces him to play hookey. To obtain the money for a ticket, Pinocchio sells his hat, coat and new book. The puppets invite him to join them on stage. This stops the show and an argument begins in the audience. The Fire-Eater comes out to settle things. But when he realizes that Pinocchio is a wooden puppet, he threatens to use him for firewood. Pinocchio successfully pleads for his life, but the Fire-Eater tells Rosabella to take Pinocchio's place. Pinocchio pleads for Rosabella's life, offering himself instead. The Fire-Eater is so emotionally moved, he gives Pinocchio three gold coins and invites him to finish the show. **RECOMMENDATION:** This retains the flavor of the original, but simplifies the action. **ROYALTY:** None. **SOURCE:** Jennings, Coleman A. & Harris, Aurand. (1981). Plays children love. New York, NY: Doubleday Co., Inc. **SUBJECTS/PLAY TYPE:** Puppets; Adaptation.

2402. 1-4. (+) Thane, Adele. (Collodi, Carlo) **Pinocchio goes to school.** (The adventures of Pinocchio) **CAST:** 3f, 6m, Su. **ACTS:** 2. **SETTINGS:** Carnival; schoolyard. **PLAYING TIME:** 15 min. **PLOT:** Not wanting to attend school, Pinocchio spends a wonderful month in the Land of Hooky. As punishment, he turns into a donkey. The Blue Fairy turns him into a boy after he promises to obey, go to school, learn a trade, take care of his papa, and tell the truth. **RECOMMENDATION:** Pinocchio is a carefully developed character. However, the very didactic ending might spoil this otherwise nice play. **ROYALTY:** Free to Plays subscribers. **SOURCE:** Thane, Adele. (1981, November). Pinocchio goes to school. Plays: The Drama Magazine for Young People, pp. 57-64. **SUBJECTS/PLAY TYPE:** School; Hooky; Lies; Adaptation.

2403. 3-8. (+) Crichton, Madge. (Collodi, Carlo) **Pinocchio strikes it rich.** (The adventures of Pinocchio) **CAST:** 1f, 4m. **ACTS:** 1. **SETTINGS:** Outdoors. **PLAYING TIME:** 20 min. **PLOT:** The puppet, Pinocchio, wishes he could be real, and the Blue Fairy tells him that this can happen if he is good and obedient during a 24 hour test period. On the way to school, he meets Fox and Cat, who persuade him to dance for money at the circus, and then steal it from him. Blue Fairy chides him for being disobedient and gullible, but helps him get the money back. The two bring it to Gepetto, Pinocchio admits that he was bad, and the Blue Fairy changes him into a real boy because of his courage. **RECOMMENDATION:** The original themes of obedience, parental love, dishonesty, and deceit remain the same, as the likable Pinocchio makes mistakes because he is naive but not really rebellious, and the villainous Cat and Fox cannot trust anyone, not even each other. **ROYALTY:** Free to Plays subscribers. **SOURCE:** Crichton, Madge. (1975, November). Pinocchio strikes it rich. Plays: The Drama Magazine for Young People, pp. 53-60. **SUBJECTS/PLAY TYPE:** Fantasy; Puppets; Adaptation.

2404. 12*. (+) Terry, Megan. The pioneer. CAST: 2f. **ACTS:** 1. **SETTINGS:** Bedroom. **PLAYING TIME:** 25 min. **PLOT:** Mother tries to bully her daughter into marrying for money while her face and figure are still marketable. Mother's unhappy relationship with father is described in detail, as are her views on the world and its future. It is revealed surrealistically that Mother wants to live forever and can only do this "through healthy carriers of her genes." She envisions her great grandchildren settling a virgin planet with five acre zoning and no riffraff. In the end, the daughter sarcastically adopts these views and sings a song about being consumed by the Sun (her mother). **RECOMMENDATION:** The frank and unloving depiction of sex, along with vulgar language, makes this a chancy proposition for high schools, even though it is extremely funny. **ROYALTY:** $60. **SOURCE:** Terry, Megan. (1984). Schulenberg, TX: I.E. Clark, Inc. **SUBJECTS/PLAY TYPE:** Family; Sex; Mothers and Daughters; Comedy.

2405. 5-9. (-) Nelson, Phil. The pirates of Chesapeake Bay. CAST: 5f, 15m, Su. **ACTS:** 3. **SETTINGS:** Town hall; tavern; on board a ship. **PLAYING TIME:** NA. **PLOT:** A Chesapeake Bay town is terrorized by pirates. The adults are unable to resolve the situation, so two children, Roger and Patricia, take matters into their own hands. Spying in a local tavern, they learn the pirates' headquarters and give the information to Squire Trusdale, who mistakenly tells Mr. Bailey, who is in league with the pirates. The squire is kidnapped and the children sneak onto the pirates' island and roll all their ammunition into the sea. The townspeople sail to the island and easily convert the pirates into honest citizens, as they had been tired of their wicked lifestyle anyway. **RECOMMENDATION:** The play's lengthy dialogue calls for actors in junior high at the youngest, yet its vocabulary, and the song lyrics are too simple and banal to interest them. **ROYALTY:** $88. **SOURCE:** Nelson, Phil. (1986). The pirates of Chesapeake Bay. Franklin, OH: Eldridge Pub. Co. **SUBJECTS/PLAY TYPE:** Pirates; Adventure; Chesapeake Bay; Musical.

z   2406. 5-8. (+) Fendrich, Shubert & Waldrop, Jerry. (Gilbert, William S. & Sullivan, Arthur) **Pirates of Penzance.** (The pirates of Penzance, or the slave of duty) CAST: 9f, Sm. ACTS: 1. SETTINGS: Bare stage, backdrop. PLAYING TIME: 60 min. PLOT: Frederic is apprenticed to pirates when his nanny misunderstands the word "pilot." He believes that his apprenticeship is over when he reaches the age of 21, however, his apprenticeship won't end until his 21st birthday, and because he was born on Feb. 29, he still has 62 years left. In the meantime, Frederic has fallen in love with Mabel, one of the daughters of a Major General. The Major General and the local police plot to capture the pirates, but Frederic's sense of duty makes him warn them. When Frederic invokes the loyalty they all have to Queen Victoria, the pirates retire and marry the Major General's daughters. RECOMMENDATION: Though the dialogue has been greatly scaled down to be appropriate for upper elementary actors, the song lyrics are fairly faithful to the original. Children will enjoy their swashbuckling roles while being gently introduced to the operetta. ROYALTY: $40. SOURCE: Fendrich, Shubert & Waldrop, Jerry. (1984). Pirates of Penzance. Denver, CO: Pioneer Drama Service. SUBJECTS/PLAY TYPE: Pirates; Orphans; Musical; Adaptation.

2407. 4-8. (-) Thane, Adele. (Gilbert, William S. & Sullivan, Arthur S.) **The pirates of Penzance or the slave of duty.** (Pirates of Penzance or the slave of duty) CAST: 5m, Su. ACTS: 1. SETTINGS: Seashore; ruined chapel. PLAYING TIME: 30 min. PLOT: A young boy is apprenticed to a group of pirates until his twenty first birthday. Since he was born on February 29 he must stay until he is sixty-four. Through a series of unusual events, he ends up at the major general's house where he and the pirates are pardoned and they marry the major general's daughters. RECOMMENDATION: This plot is too confusing to follow easily, as everything occurs very illogically and the original music is not present to provide the transitions. ROYALTY: Free to Plays subscribers. SOURCE: Thane, Adele. (1982, October). The pirates of Penzance, or the slave of duty. Plays: The Drama Magazine for Young People, pp. 61-70. SUBJECTS/PLAY TYPE: Pirates; Adaptation.

2408. 10-12. (+) Hanson, Mary E. **A place of his own.** CAST: 5f, 2m. ACTS: 1. SETTINGS: One room apartment. PLAYING TIME: 25 min. PLOT: During his absence, a young man's apartment is invaded by his concerned grandparents and girl friends. They all feel they know what's best for the boy and set about fixing things and bringing food. When he arrives, chaos breaks out and he is forced to reestablish the purpose of having his own place. RECOMMENDATION: The mixture of the characters in this situation comedy positively presents the dilemma of one's needing caring friends and relatives, but also needing privacy. ROYALTY: Free to Plays subscribers. SOURCE: Hanson, Mary E. (1981, May). A place of his own. Plays: The Drama Magazine for Young People, pp. 12-18. SUBJECTS/PLAY TYPE: Independence; Family; Comedy.

2409. 9-12. (+) Martin, Herb & Lang, Phil. **Places, please.** CAST: 6f, 6m, Su. ACTS: 2. SETTINGS: Bare stage, curtains. PLAYING TIME: NA. PLOT: Colin, a high school student, has written a musical comedy adaptation of Charles Dickens's **David Copperfield**, which he wishes to present as the annual school play. There are problems and conflicts from its inception. The drama department has budgetary difficulties. The principal is unsure of producing the work of an untried playwright, and sensitive to local political pressures, wants to cast students whose parents are influential within the community. Added to these problems are untalented cast members and the normal conflicts among students, who, seeking specific roles, refuse to cooperate and leave the play. The play concludes, however, with production costs under budget and casting difficulties resolved. RECOMMENDATION: This musical within a musical takes a frank and humorous look at the undercurrents in the arts curriculum of today's schools. Obstacles of budget, influence, and ego are overcome in a believable and heart warming fashion as the lesson is learned that compromises must sometimes be made to adjust to real life situations. ROYALTY: On application. SOURCE: Martin, Herb. (1978). Places please. Chicago, IL: Dramatic Pub. Co. SUBJECTS/PLAY TYPE: Theater; Comedy; Musical.

2410. K-4*. (+) Robinette, Joseph. **Planet of the perfectly awful people.** CAST: 5u. ACTS: 1. SETTINGS: Rocks and craters. PLAYING TIME: NA. PLOT: A rocket ship from Earth on a mission to Venus goes off course and crashes on the planet Meanus, home of the perfectly awful people who try to make the happy astronaut, Abbie, mean. She and another stranded space traveler make the Meanusites happy with jokes, anecdotes and vaudeville routines. RECOMMENDATION: The message about contrariness is enjoyably delivered. ROYALTY: $15. SOURCE: Robinette, Joseph. (1979). Planet of the perfectly awful people. Chicago, IL: Dramatic Pub. Co. SUBJECTS/PLAY TYPE: Science Fiction; Space Travel; Personality; Happiness; Comedy.

2411. 5-12. (+) Fendrich, Shubert. **Plantation malady or Is there a doctor in the South?** CAST: 4f, 3m. ACTS: 1. SETTINGS: Veranda of plantation. PLAYING TIME: NA. PLOT: The elderly surviving head of the household after the Civil War, is drugged in his daily julep by Mr. Creep, who is trying to obtain the land and his niece. All are saved by a gentleman on his way to medical school in Atlanta. RECOMMENDATION: This is mildly amusing with its stereotypical southern Belle (Magnolia Follingsbee) and her gentleman (Beau Bonesly). Production should be by the older grades. ROYALTY: NA. SOURCE: Fendrich, Shubert. (1977). Plantation malady or Is there a doctor in the South? Denver, CO: Pioneer Drama Service. SUBJECTS/PLAY TYPE: Carpetbaggers; Melodrama.

2412. 3-6. (+) Oswald, Nancy. **A play for book haters.** CAST: 12f, 10m, 3u. ACTS: 1. SETTINGS: Classroom; bridge. PLAYING TIME: NA. PLOT: When a school sponsors a class essay contest on why books are important to their lives, two boys, Robert and Stanley, believe that books are of no importance. The next day as Robert and Stanley walk to school, they fall off a bridge and regain consciousness in a strange world without books. They are in desperate need of a basketball rule book, a cookbook, a telephone book, and school books that will obviate the necessity to memorize all of their school assignments. As they run away from the bookless world, they trip, hit their heads, and wake up in the real world. They quickly go to school, eager for reading class. RECOMMENDATION: Without didacticism, this proves the importance of reading and would be best performed by fifth or sixth graders. ROYALTY: NA. SOURCE: Oswald, Nancy.(1980). A play for book haters. Franklin, OH: Eldridge Pub. Co. SUBJECTS/PLAY TYPE: Reading; Book Week; Books; Comedy.

2413. 11-12. (+) Bogdanov, Michael. (Coleridge, Samuel Taylor) **The play of the ancient mariner.** (The rime of the ancient mariner) CAST: 1f, 12m. ACTS: 2. SETTINGS: Ship; dock. PLAYING TIME: NA. PLOT: An old sailor tells a wedding guest the bizarre tale of how he once sailed to the South Pole and killed an albatross there, despite his crew's objections. As a result of the evil deed, he was cursed with bad luck: an underwater demon followed the ship, the wind stopped, and the crewmen slowly died. Envying the dead, the sailor now lives on in despair, doomed to atone for his sins by telling his story to all he meets. RECOMMENDATION: This will require a professional company and a director with knowledge of 19th century sailing and the chantey song format. Very faithful to Coleridge's original, the words lend themselves to personal interpretation. ROYALTY: NA. SOURCE: Bogdanov, Michael. (1984). The play of the ancient mariner. London: Heinemann. SUBJECTS/PLAY TYPE: Curses; Sea; Adaptation.

2414. 1-6. (+) Hall, Margaret. **The play of the weather.** CAST: 2f, 7m. ACTS: 1. SETTINGS: Throne room. PLAYING TIME: 10 min. PLOT: After hearing complaints from their kingdom about the weather, Jupiter and Juno explain the beneficial effects of rain, wind, and temperature on people's livelihoods and leisure. RECOMMENDATION: This cleverly combines Greek mythology with a modern lesson about ecology and compromise. ROYALTY: Free to Plays subscribers. SOURCE: Hall, Margaret. (1982, April). The play of the weather. Plays: The Drama Magazine for Young People, pp. 36-40. SUBJECTS/PLAY TYPE: Seasons; Weather; Playlet.

2415. 9-12. (+) Kundrat, Theodore V. **A play on words: A verbal comedy for reader's theatre.** CAST: 2f, 3m. ACTS: 1. SETTINGS: None. PLAYING TIME: 25 min. PLOT: He, Him, She, and Her personify the personal pronouns as they demonstrate how the accent of the human voice creates varied meanings for a single word, how much can be conveyed through the use of a single word if vocal and physical clues accompany it, and the parts of speech. As the play ends they are amazed to discover that the narrator is Noah Webster of dictionary fame. RECOMMENDATION: This concentrates on expression of performers and would make an excellent exercise for drama clubs and classes. It would also serve an English teacher well in a discussion of communication or as an innovative way to review the parts of speech. ROYALTY: $15. SOURCE: Kundrat, Theodore V. (1978).

A play on words: A verbal comedy for reader's theatre. Chicago IL: The Coach House Press. SUBJECTS/PLAY TYPE: Expression; Words; Reader's Theater.

2416. 12. (+) D'urrenmatt, Friedrich & Kirkup, James. (Strindberg, Johann August) **Play Strindberg.** (Dance of Death.) CAST: 1f, 2m. ACTS: 1. SETTINGS: Parlor. PLAYING TIME: NA. PLOT: In their isolated house on an island military post, a couple and an old friend talk about the couple's 25 year marriage and the friend's relationship to it. The discussion is presented like a boxing match with a gong sounding at the end of each of twelve rounds. At the final round, the friend departs, leaving the couple alone and trapped in an unsatisfying marriage. RECOMMENDATION: This excellent, but sophisticated European play is considered an intellectual comedy, and might be difficult for most American high school students to produce or appreciate. ROYALTY: $60. SOURCE: D'urrenmatt, Friedrich. (1970). Play Strindberg. Chicago, IL: Dramatic Pub. Co. SUBJECTS/PLAY TYPE: Family; Marriage; Adaptation; Comedy.

2417. 5-9. (+) Denson, Wil. **Playground.** CAST: 5f, 7m. ACTS: 1. SETTINGS: Playground. PLAYING TIME: 90 min. PLOT: Nine year old Jason's father has abandoned his family. Jason also has to cope with the frightening experiences of being the new boy in school and of being accosted by the sixth grade bullies. He escapes by withdrawing into himself, comforted by an imaginary friend who is daring, athletic and self confident. They hide overnight in an abandoned circus wagon on the playground. Overhearing Jason's worried mother speaking with his teacher, and later, the bullies abusing another new boy, Jason helps the other boy, and his "friend" fades away. RECOMMENDATION: Construction of some props will require adult supervision (circus wagon, chain link fence and two teeter-totters). Children should be encouraged to discuss this later, since it raises both moral and social issues. ROYALTY: $35. SOURCE: Denson, Wil. (1984). Playground. Denver, CO: Pioneer Drama Service. SUBJECTS/PLAY TYPE: Self Esteem; Imaginary Friends; Single Parent Family; Drama.

2418. 10-12. (+) Miller, Arthur. (Fenelon, Fania) **Playing for time.** (Playing for time) CAST: 18f, 4m, Su. ACTS: 2. SETTINGS: Concentration camp. PLAYING TIME: NA. PLOT: An orchestra is composed of the female prisoners of a concentration camp to entertain the camp's German command. Prisoner Fania Fenelon describes the camp and those involved with the orchestra. Participation in the orchestra meant more time to live. In this case, enough time went by that the women were among those liberated at the end of the war. The final scene shows the reunion of three of the women in Brussels, 40 years after the war. RECOMMENDATION: The dramatization of singer Fania Fenelon's true experience as a prisoner at the Auschwitz/Birkenau concentration camp during World War II is an insightful treatment of survival and the nature of humanity. This is tense and presents unique staging challenges. The orchestra plays throughout, so either real musicians will have to act, or excellent coordination with sound recordings will be required. ROYALTY: $75. SOURCE: Miller, Arthur. (1985). Playing for time.Chicago,

IL: Dramatic Pub. Co. **SUBJECTS/PLAY TYPE:** World War II; Concentration Camps; Survival; Holocaust; Drama.

2419. K-3. (-) Ison, Colleen. **The pleasure and happiness store. CAST:** 8u. **ACTS:** 1. **SETTINGS:** General store. **PLAYING TIME:** NA. **PLOT:** The message that love and joy are more precious than material things is shown as children buy tangible items in a store. One child asks for something that he'll never use up and won't get tired of. The shopkeeper tells him that love and joy are free. **RECOMMENDATION:** The intent here is admirable, but there is no concrete example of love and joy, so the youngsters are left unenlightened. Discussion questions are provided. **ROYALTY:** NA. **SOURCE:** Ison, Colleen. (1986). Goliath's last stand: And fifteen more easy plays for children. Cincinnati, OH: Standard Pub. **SUBJECTS/PLAY TYPE:** Love; Joy; Materialism; Skit.

2420. 5-9. (+) Cusick, Fred J. & Moore, Diane. (Dickens, Charles) **The plight before Christmas.** (A Christmas carol.) **CAST:** 3f, 4m. **ACTS:** 2. **SETTINGS:** Saloon. **PLAYING TIME:** 60 min. **PLOT:** This combines western melodrama with a flavor of the classic **Christmas Carol.** It eliminates the three spirits but utilizes Marley's return to reform his old partner Humbug, rescue his wife and daughter (Cheyenne and Felicity), and reestablish himself in the community. The good guy, Bob Scratchit, gets the sweet Felicity after all. **RECOMMENDATION:** This clever alternative for the traditional version is geared to a better read audience who will understand the references from Dickens. The songs are sung to well known tunes. **ROYALTY:** $25. **SOURCE:** Cusick, Fred J. & Moore, Diane. (1983). The plight before Christmas. Denver, CO: Pioneer Drama Service. **SUBJECTS/PLAY TYPE:** Christmas; Western; Comedy; Adaptation.

2421. 12. (+) McDonough, Jerome. **Plots. CAST:** Su. **ACTS:** 1. **SETTINGS:** None. **PLAYING TIME:** 40 min. **PLOT:** Described by McDonough as grim/whimsical, this closely resembles "The Theater of the Grotesque," a short lived Italian movement during World War I which emphasized the ironic and the macabre in contemporary life. A hooded figure is a grim emcee who introduces five of the six subplots by placing captions on a tombstone shaped placard. Three subplots: Blind dates I, II, and III, are segments of the same ironic situation. In blind date I, Chris is paired with an invisible date who physically sweeps her off her feet with a romantic embrace that wins her heart. The two other subplots are separate grim vignettes: a wife seals her husband in a coffin that she's convinced him to make for her as a safeguard against being accidentally buried alive; and two survivors decide to cannibalize the third, now dead. They are just about to begin when they are rescued. **RECOMMENDATION:** This innovative play seeks to startle the audience; this is the criteria by which to evaluate its success. It resembles the "happenings" of the late sixties. Some may be offended, others puzzled, still others bored, but **Plots** anticipates varied audience reaction. **ROYALTY:** $20. **SOURCE:** McDonough, Jerome. (1981). Plots. Schulenburg, TX: I.E. Clark. **SUBJECTS/PLAY TYPE:** Macabre; Death; Supernatural; Avant Garde.

2422. 9-12. (+) Stein, Mark. **The plumber's apprentice. CAST:** 1f, 1m. **ACTS:** 1. **SETTINGS:** Job site; bowling alley; picket line; union hall. **PLAYING TIME:** NA. **PLOT:** Sally tries to escape poverty by learning plumbing. But during her apprenticeship to Rog, she is shunned, sexually harassed, and set up to fail. Her courage and persistence win Rog over, but when he is ready to accept her, it is too late and she leaves. **RECOMMENDATION:** The story is appealing, and while the plot is not particularly original, it rings true. There is much profanity, which is consistent with the setting. **ROYALTY:** $20. **SOURCE:** Stein, Mark. (1982). The plumber's apprentice. New York, NY: Dramatists Play Service. **SUBJECTS/PLAY TYPE:** Women's Equality; Sexual Harassment; Drama.

2423. 1-3. (+) Martin, Judith & Ashwander, Donald. **Plumber, plumber, fix my sink! CAST:** 4u. **ACTS:** 1. **SETTINGS:** Bare stage, props. **PLAYING TIME:** 15 min. **PLOT:** Mrs. Cummings discovers a leak in her sink. The audience calls for the plumber, who takes the sink away. The leak then appears in the bathtub; the audience calls for the plumber, who takes the tub away. The leak appears in the shower; the audience calls for the plumber. The leak picks up the shower stall and runs around the stage, pursued by Mrs. Cummings with a mop and the plumber with a plunger. It confuses them by whirling around and escapes. **RECOMMENDATION:** This offers wonderful physical silliness, and even adults will enjoy it because most have experienced the frustrations of plumbing problems. **ROYALTY:** NA. **SOURCE:** Martin, Judith & Ashwander, Donald. (1985). Reasons to be cheerful: A revue for children. New York, NY: The Paper Bag Players, Inc. **SUBJECTS/PLAY TYPE:** Comedy; Skit; Plumbers; Musical Revue.

2424. K-5. (+) Ross, Laura. **Pocahantas and Captain John Smith. CAST:** 1f, 3m, Su. **ACTS:** 1. **SETTINGS:** Indian encampment. **PLAYING TIME:** NA. **PLOT:** Indian braves deliver the captured Captain John Smith to Chief Powhatan's camp. On the advice of medicine men, Powhatan orders Smith executed, but Powhatan's beautiful daughter saves Smith by adopting him. **RECOMMENDATION:** Though mostly pantomime, the narrator has a lengthy speaking part and will need to be older. **ROYALTY:** None. **SOURCE:** Ross, Laura. (1975). Mask-Making with pantomime and stories from American history. New York, NY: Lothrop, Lee, & Shepard Co. **SUBJECTS/PLAY TYPE:** Native Americans; Smith, John; Pocahantas; Pantomime.

2425. 7-12. (+) Miller, Kathryn Schultz. **Poe! Poe! Poe!: The life and writings of Edgar Allan Poe. CAST:** 4u. **ACTS:** 1. **SETTINGS:** None. **PLAYING TIME:** 60 min. **PLOT:** Woven into a narrative of Poe's life are selections from "Life of a Lion," "Israfel," "The Tell-Tale Heart," "Annabel Lee," "The Masque of the Red Death," "The Raven," and "Life of Thingum Bub, Esq." **RECOMMENDATION:** This is an ingenious vehicle for introducing students to the ways in which an author's works reflect his/her life. This is best produced by the older grades. **ROYALTY:** $25. **SOURCE:** Miller, Kathryn Schultz. (1981). Poe! Poe! Poe!: The life and writings of

Edgar Allan Poe. Schulenburg, TX: I.E. Clark. SUBJECTS/PLAY TYPE: Poe, Edgar Allan; Reader's Theater.

2426. 4-6. (+) Mamet, David. **The poet and the rent.** CAST: 3f, 8m, Su. ACTS: 1. SETTINGS: Apartment; park; factory; jail. PLAYING TIME: 30 min. PLOT: A poor, untalented poet needs to raise $60 to pay his rent. He goes to the park, and although he succeeds in acquiring a girlfriend, he is unable to sell his poems to anyone. Getting a job as watchman in a factory, he tries to earn money legitimately, but falls asleep on duty, letting two burglars rob the safe. The poet offers to split the money with them so he'll still get the rent money, even if he loses his job. Instead, he is caught and taken to jail, but his girlfriend from the park pays his rent for two years, and the poet returns home to write poetry that explains society. RECOMMENDATION: Because the humor is fairly juvenile, with audience/cast interaction and frequent pies in the face, this will appeal. Older students or adults should present this. ROYALTY: NA. SOURCE: Mamet, David. (1986). Three children's plays. New York, NY: Grove Press, Inc. SUBJECTS/PLAY TYPE: Poets; Money Making; Comedy.

2427. 9-12. (-) Seale, Nancy. **A point for Romeo.** CAST: 5f, 5m, 6u. ACTS: 1. SETTINGS: Bare stage. PLAYING TIME: 25 min. PLOT: Several members of the Hamilton High soccer team lose interest in helping put on the Theater Club's production when they discover it will be **Romeo and Juliet.** But their future on the soccer team is threatened by low English grades. Their coach attempts to intervene with the English teacher, who accepts their participation in the play as extra credit. The boys pass English and remain on the soccer team. RECOMMENDATION: This is a slow moving, predictable plot which will hold little interest for today's teenagers. ROYALTY: Free to Plays subscribers. SOURCE: Seale, Nancy. (1985, April). A point for Romeo. Plays: The Drama Magazine for Young People, pp. 11-21. SUBJECTS/PLAY TYPE: Grades; Sports; Playlet.

2428. 9-12. (+) Erhard, Tom. **Pomp and circumstance.** CAST: 8f, 3m, Su. ACTS: 2. SETTINGS: Bare stage, props. PLAYING TIME: NA. PLOT: Lorraine faces graduation with trepidation and regret. Her parents' recent divorce has left her insecure and she yearns to retain the security and familiarity of the school environment. Mrs. Johnson, dedicated senior sponsor, is cautioned by Dr. Wallace, school principal, about anticipated antics from the graduates during commencement exercises. Mr. Abbott, a young, attractive history teacher and heartthrob, is urged to marry to quell the romantic overtures of the female students. In retaliation for her feelings of rejection and inadequacy, Lorraine boards a train for Crystal Springs, her father's new home, with plans to find a job. A passing conversation with Sandra, a 16 year old waitress at the bus depot who began her career as a runaway, offers Lorraine a glimpse of her own dismal future. A phone call to her unreceptive father confirms her sense of isolation. The timely arrival of several concerned teachers and the boy next door who has always loved her, convince Lorraine to graduate and make plans for college.

RECOMMENDATION: Marked by its informal atmosphere and humourous ad lib dialogue, this offers a realistic portrayal of familiar events. Actors and stage hands move furniture to create sets, simultaneously discussing upcoming action and providing background information for the audience. The lively and colorful custodian, Thucydides Jones, provides direction, jokes with the stage hands, and maintains informative running commentary on the motives of characters and procedures of the school. He punctuates the emotional turmoil of the characters with digressions about divorce statistics and family dynamics and offers sage advice about surviving the teenage years. ROYALTY: $40. SOURCE: Erhard, Thomas A. (1982). Pomp and circumstance. Boston, MA: Baker's Plays. SUBJECTS/PLAY TYPE: Divorce; Graduation; Comedy.

2429. K-3. (+) Silverman, Eleanor. (Milne, A.A.) **Pooh goes on a diet.** (The world of Pooh) CAST: 7u. ACTS: 3. SETTINGS: Woods; room in a rabbit's hutch. PLAYING TIME: NA. PLOT: In this dramatization of "Pooh goes visiting and gets into a tight place," Pooh gets stuck in the entrance to Rabbit's hole and must become thinner in order to get out. RECOMMENDATION: The humor and whimsy of the original are well preserved. ROYALTY: None. SOURCE: Silverman, Eleanor. (1983). Dramatics for children. Metuchen, NJ: The Scarecrow Press. SUBJECTS/PLAY TYPE: Animals; Dieting; Adaptation.

2430. 9-12*. (+) O'Brien, John. **Popcorn.** CAST: 1f, 1m. ACTS: 1. SETTINGS: Living room. PLAYING TIME: NA. PLOT: A widower who has dreamed for years about retiring to Florida is ready to go. His married daughter tells him that her husband has left her and asks him to stay and help care for her children. He stays. RECOMMENDATION: The play is subtle and most of the emotion is indicated by nuance. This makes it difficult for teenagers who have had no life experience as parents to relate. It is questionable whether a teenage audience would respond to the characters and it is even less likely that they would be capable, as actors, of capturing the subtle underplayed emotion of the dialogue. The sketch has the potential to be powerful theater but is probably not appropriate for a school drama effort. ROYALTY: $15. SOURCE: O'Brien, John. (1981). Popcorn. Chicago, IL: Dramatic Pub. Co. SUBJECTS/PLAY TYPE: Parent-Child Relationships; Drama.

2431. 9-12. (+) Henderson, Nancy. **Popcorn woppers.** CAST: 2f, 10m. ACTS: 1. SETTINGS: Front of a courthouse. PLAYING TIME: 8 min. PLOT: This illustrates the history and origin of popcorn in America. RECOMMENDATION: Good for any season, this requires no scenery or special costumes. However, some characters have long speeches. ROYALTY: NA. SOURCE: Henderson, Nancy. (1978). Celebrate America: A baker's dozen of plays. New York, NY: Julian Messner. SUBJECTS/PLAY TYPE: Popcorn; Comedy.

2432. 9-12. (+) Jackson, R. Eugene & Alette, Carl. **Popeye the sailor.** CAST: 6f, 3m. ACTS: 2. SETTINGS: Pier; foot of the Statue of Liberty. PLAYING TIME: 90 min. PLOT: Cartoon characters come to life in this genuinely funny musical of Popeye's struggles with the evil Brutus. In the opening scene, Brutus's attempt to rob the ticket booth at the Statue of Liberty is foiled by spinach-eating Popeye, but Brutus and his mother, Sea Hag, continue on a path of misdeeds. Wimpy and female tourists provide comic subplot, as Wimpy chases hamburgers and one of the women chases him. After several crises, Popeye saves Olive, Swee'pea, and the Statue. RECOMMENDATION: The charm here lies in its slapstick faithfulness to the cartoon original. Popeye's dialogue is an accurate rendition of the cartoon character's speech, and Brutus is so bad he is funny. All of the actors must sing, and Popeye and Brutus must be fairly athletic to perform the fight scenes. ROYALTY: $80. SOURCE: Jackson, R. Eugene & Alette, Carl. (1984). Popeye the sailor. Denver, CO: Pioneer Drama Service. SUBJECTS/PLAY TYPE: Cartoons; Statue of Liberty; Comedy; Musical.

2433. K-3. (+) Kuskin, Karla. **The porcupine.** CAST: 1u. ACTS: 1. SETTINGS: None. PLAYING TIME: NA. PLOT: A porcupine's prickly description is given. RECOMMENDATION: This may be performed alone, or with other of Bauer's "Animal Antics" poems. ROYALTY: NA. SOURCE: Bauer, Caroline Feller. (1987). Presenting reader's theater: Plays and poems to read aloud. New York, NY: H.W. Wilson. SUBJECTS/PLAY TYPE: Porcupines; Reader's Theater.

2434. 7-10. (-) Seale, Nancy. **Portrait of great-great aunt Amanda.** CAST: 4f, 3m. ACTS: 1. SETTINGS: Living room. PLAYING TIME: 20 min. PLOT: Mandy is lonely because her best friend has begun to date her brother. She also can't talk to the boy she likes because she's too nervous. When a picture of her namesake is delivered, her great, great aunt comes to life, straightens out Mandy's problems and then disappears. RECOMMENDATION: Reminiscent of the ghost and Mrs. Muir, the conversations between Mandy and her ancestor's invisible ghost cause consternation which is patly taken care of when the ghost reveals herself to Mandy's boyfriend. This is dull and didactic. ROYALTY: Free to Plays subscribers. SOURCE: Seale, Nancy. (1982, May). Portrait of great-great aunt Amanda. Plays: The Drama Magazine for Young People, pp. 21-32. SUBJECTS/PLAY TYPE: Ghosts; Comedy.

2435. 7-12. (+) Garver, Juliet. **Portrait of Jane.** CAST: 1f. ACTS: 1. SETTINGS: Bedroom. PLAYING TIME: 15 min. PLOT: Jane Austen talks about her life and the novels she wrote. RECOMMENDATION: This is an interesting look at a young woman of a different era, the way she lived, and how she thought. It would be a good companion piece for students reading Austen's novels. ROYALTY: Free to Plays subscribers. SOURCE: Garver, Juliet. (1986, April) Portrait of Jane. Plays: The Drama Magazine for Young People, pp. 48-52. SUBJECTS/PLAY TYPE: Austen, Jane; Monologue.

2436. 10-12. (+) Gregg, Stephen. **Postponing the heat death of the universe.** CAST: 2f, 1m. ACTS: 1. SETTINGS: Dorm room. PLAYING TIME: NA. PLOT: Nick, a college freshman, has lost an essay contest, is depressed, and refuses to move. He claims he is battling

entropy. Jackie, the junior who won, visits him and succeeds in exasperating and intriguing him back to normalcy. In the process, Nick's budding relationship with another girl, Stacy, receives some setbacks. RECOMMENDATION: The author has captured the intensity of feelings of young adults in college and expressed them with believable dialogue and actions. ROYALTY: $20. SOURCE: Gregg, Stephen. (1986). Postponing the heat death of the universe. Woodstock, IL: Dramatic Pub. Co. SUBJECTS/PLAY TYPE: Friendship; Drama.

2437. 5-9. (+) Gerstenberg, Alice. **The pot boiler.** CAST: 2f, 5m, 1u. ACTS: 1. SETTINGS: None. PLAYING TIME: 35 min. PLOT: Mr. Sud, a successful author, directs the rehearsal of his new play. He instructs Mr. Wouldby, an aspiring young writer, in the art of successful writing as the rehearsal progresses. RECOMMENDATION: This is a very amusing satire of playwrights, the theater, and productions which include worn out cliches and stereotypes. Although originally written in 1916, it is just as appropriate today. While younger children would enjoy this, it might take at least a middle school child to deliver the lines successfully. ROYALTY: $15. SOURCE: Gerstenberg, Alice. (1983). The pot boiler. Schulenberg, TX: I.E. Clark. SUBJECTS/PLAY TYPE: Theater, Satire; Comedy.

2438. 10-12. (-) Post, Kenneth L. **Pot luck on Friday night.** CAST: 3f, 3m. ACTS: 1. SETTINGS: Family room. PLAYING TIME: 35 min. PLOT: A once-jilted, unmarried career woman meets her popular sister's intended blind date. The blind date is much like the unmarried sister, and the two go out, leaving the popular sister with the date she really wants. RECOMMENDATION: Insulting references to intelligent women as "old maids"; irrelevant family scenes; boring dialogue; and a predictable outcome make this a total bust. ROYALTY: Free to Plays subscribers. SOURCE: Post, Kenneth L. (1988, April). Pot luck on Friday night. Plays: The Drama Magazine for Young People, pp. 1-9. SUBJECTS/PLAY TYPE: Dating; Comedy.

2439. K-3. (+) McCaslin, Nellie. **The Pot of gold.** CAST: 3m. ACTS: 1. SETTINGS: Vineyard. PLAYING TIME: 10 min. PLOT: Two lazy sons give excuses to avoid helping their farmer father in the fields. One day, the lazy sons try to borrow money to repay a debt. The father tells them that a pot of god is in the vineyard. The lazy sons dig up the earth. They do not find the pot of gold, but they cultivate the vineyard and a wonderful crop of grapes grows. The farmer tells his lazy sons that the crop is worth a pot of gold. RECOMMENDATION: This cleverly delivers the message that there are no shortcuts in life. ROYALTY: None. SOURCE: McCaslin, Nellie. (1977). Puppet fun: Production, performances, and plays. New York, NY: D. McKay Co. SUBJECTS/PLAY TYPE: Fable; Work; Puppet Play.

2440. 9-12+. (-) Fulk, David Neal. **The potman spoke sooth.** CAST: 2f, 6m, 2u. ACTS: 1. SETTINGS: Sitting room. PLAYING TIME: NA. PLOT: In this murder mystery spoof, a Scotland Yard detective arrives at a house to apprehend the Peanut Murderer. Each occupant is accused. As the accusations become more confusing, the audience realizes they are spectators to a game. The characters go "out-of-character" to analyze the game. The director and author emerge from the audience to criticize the proceedings and make the situation even more confusing. Finally, the "voice of God" is heard, telling everyone on stage what they should do. The play ends with the discovery that the voice is no more real than the play or the murder. RECOMMENDATION: Despite some amusing dialogue and a promising initial exploration of the various levels and intersections of fabrication and reality, this gets lost in its own absurdity. The humor is too subtle for most student audiences and the structure is probably too convoluted for nonprofessionals to carry off successfully. ROYALTY: $15. SOURCE: Fulk, David. (1977). The potman spoke sooth. Woodstock, IL: Dramatic Pub. Co. SUBJECTS/PLAY TYPE: Satire; Mystery; Comedy.

2441. 5-8. (+) Freeman, Barbara. Potpourri. CAST: 14u. ACTS: 1. SETTINGS: Bare stage. PLAYING TIME: 30 min. PLOT: This collage begins with the witches of Macbeth reciting an incantation; it then moves to the famous Tom Sawyer fence painting scene; next follows a melodramatic mortgage foreclosure narrowly avoided; and it concludes with the story of the princess who never smiled. RECOMMENDATION: This allows for a cast of up to 40, as it creatively and believably brings four very different plots together. ROYALTY: Free to Plays subscribers. SOURCE: Freeman, Barbara. (1975, March). Potpourri. Plays: The Drama Magazine for Young People, pp. 75-84. SUBJECTS/PLAY TYPE: Witches; Princesses; Painting; Creative Dramatics.

2442. 9-12. (+) Fabrycki, William. Praise God! CAST: 5f, 8m. ACTS: 1. SETTINGS: Farming village, including general store, government office, one room schoolhouse. PLAYING TIME: 30 min. PLOT: This vehement attack on corrupt Evangelism highlights the vulnerability of blind faith, and the rash, vindictive attitude of victims of religious scams. The opening scene builds sustained anticipation as the villagers await the arrival of a self proclaimed instrument of the Lord. There are hints of unspeakable deeds to be performed. Upon his arrival, the "Man of God" is apprised of a plague which has claimed many lives, and of a drought which has rendered the land barren. He is informed that preachers who are unable to remedy these conditions are imprisoned. A final note of poetic justice accompanies a shadowy silhouetted rendering of the imprisonment of the most vociferous spokesmen against the "Man of God" and the simultaneous escape of the preacher. The audience marvels at the distorted values and misguided attempts at justice that may be bred in isolation. RECOMMENDATION: This is powerful, suspenseful, and well drawn, with episodes of drunkenness, sexual innuendo, and profound cruelty. Challenged are the religious principles of evangelism, God's Divine Plan for mankind, Divine creation, and religious tolerance. Instances of immorality, deceit, and greed among the clergy may outrage some, and the depraved, bitter characters may depress others. Unable to explain the existence of suffering and injustice, or even to offer

consolation, the play leaves the audience with a sense of bitterness, paranoia, and futility. ROYALTY: $10. SOURCE: Fabrycki, William. (1976). Praise God! Denver, CO: Pioneer Drama Service. SUBJECTS/PLAY TYPE: Evangelism; Drama.

2443. K-3. (+) Ison, Colleen. Praying. CAST: 5u. ACTS: 1. SETTINGS: Bare stage. PLAYING TIME: NA. PLOT: Children discover that sincere prayers which they create are better than the ones they memorize. RECOMMENDATION: This is convincing; the message about sincerity is timeless. Discussion questions are provided. ROYALTY: NA. SOURCE: Ison, Colleen. (1986). Goliath's last stand: And fifteen more easy plays for children. Cincinnati, OH: Standard Pub. SUBJECTS/PLAY TYPE: Prayer; Sincerity; Skit.

2444. 1-12. (+) Steinhorn, Harriet & Lowry, Edith. A precious gift. CAST: 1u. ACTS: 1. SETTINGS: None. PLAYING TIME: 10 min. PLOT: An adult survivor of a concentration camp describes how his brother, mother, and father were killed. Clutching a gift from his father, a crudely fashioned comb, the then young boy buried it in the ground to avoid its confiscation. However, he cannot find it later and still wishes that he had it. RECOMMENDATION: Through the comb, this symbolically describes the loss of innocence and the hope of the Jewish prisoners that they might cling to at least one shred of human kindness. ROYALTY: Free for amateur groups. SOURCE: Steinhorn, Harriet & Lowry, Edith. (1983). Shadows of the holocaust: Plays, readings, and program resources. Rockville, MD: Kar-Ben Copies, Inc. SUBJECTS/PLAY TYPE: Holocaust; Concentration Camps; World War II; Monologue.

2445. 4-10. (+) Kehret, Peg. Precious keepsakes. CAST: 1u. ACTS: 1. SETTINGS: None. PLAYING TIME: NA. PLOT: A child expresses his disgust at relatives' haggling over a deceased grandfather's belongings. RECOMMENDATION: This stresses the importance of acknowledging the living and advocates more interaction with the aged. ROYALTY: NA. SOURCE: Kehret, Peg. (1986). Winning monologs for young actors. Colorado Springs, CO: Meriwether Pub. SUBJECTS/PLAY TYPE: Inheritances; Elderly; Monologue.

2446. 7-12. (+) Sawyer-Young, Kat. Pregnant. CAST: 1f. ACTS: 1. SETTINGS: None. PLAYING TIME: 1 min. PLOT: Darlene is horrified that she might be pregnant and describes her dilemma as being much more unromantic than using birth control. RECOMMENDATION: This would be excellent for a discussion starter in a sexual education class. ROYALTY: None. SOURCE: Sawyer-Young, Kat. (1987). Minute monologues for contemporary teens. Boston, MA: Baker's Plays. SUBJECTS/PLAY TYPE: Birth Control; Monologue.

2447. 9-12. (+) McNamara, John. Present Tense. CAST: 4f, 3m. ACTS: 1. SETTINGS: Bedroom. PLAYING TIME: NA. PLOT: A young man thinks about his girlfriend's relationship with her former boyfriend; his frustration at the lack of physical intimacy in their relationship; and his fears that he will lose her to the old boyfriend, a more self assured teenager. In the end he discovers why Ann finds him attractive. RECOMMENDATION: The boy's insecurity is typical, the characterizations ring true, and the outcomes are believable. ROYALTY: $25. SOURCE: McNamara, John. (1986). Present tense. New York, NY: Dramatists Play Service. SUBJECTS/PLAY TYPE: Dating; Comedy.

2448. 7-9. (+) Belgrade Coventry Theatre in Education. **The price of coal.** CAST: 6m, Su. ACTS: 2. SETTINGS: Coal mining areas of England in the late 15th century. PLAYING TIME: 480 min. PLOT: Lord Newgate utilizes new technology to mine coal, but the mine owners are careless of the miners' health and safety. Ben Partridge tells the history of the mines from the standpoint of the effects on the men working there. Students take part as miners and the actual work of mining is demonstrated while health and safety concerns are pointed out. The economics of labor and technology are also examined. RECOMMENDATION: This is a comprehensive history of coal mining in Great Britain. It requires extensive time (two shows two weeks apart) and class participation. It starts with a balanced picture of the social and economic issues, but moves toward a conclusion favoring labor over management. Historically, it is very enlightening. However, the issues presented may be too complicated for the age level of an audience willing to crawl around in make believe mine shafts. ROYALTY: NA. SOURCE: Belgrade Coventry Theatre in Education. (1980). Four junior programmes. London: Eyre Methuen. SUBJECTS/PLAY TYPE: Technology; Labor Relations; Economics; Coal Mining; Participation Play.

2449. 10-12. (+) Morley, Olive J. (Austen, Jane) **Pride and prejudice.** (Pride and prejudice) CAST: 8f. ACTS: 1. SETTINGS: Parlor. PLAYING TIME: 35 min. PLOT: Mrs. Bennet hopes to marry her five daughters into wealthy families. Elizabeth refuses to marry only for money, as her other sisters, Kitty and Lydia, are willing to do, nor will she stoop to social prejudices, as does her sister, Mary. Elizabeth falls in love with the haughty and rich Mr. Darcy, but she does not show interest until he mends his ways. Evidence of changes come when he voluntarily steps in to save Lydia from a disgraced marriage by paying off her fiance's debts and funding a church wedding. At the conclusion, Elizabeth and one sister cast off their social prejudices, and fall truly in love with their suitors. RECOMMENDATION: Each of the characters is well delineated, and the dialogue follows patterns of the 19th century. ROYALTY: Free to Plays subscribers. SOURCE: Morley, Olive J. (1981, February). Pride and prejudice. Plays: The Drama Magazine for Young People, pp. 69-79. SUBJECTS/PLAY TYPE: Prejudice; Romance; Women's Roles; Adaptation.

2450. 7-10. (+) Newman, Deborah. (Austen, Jane) **Pride and prejudice.** (Pride and prejudice) CAST: 9f, 4m, 1u. ACTS: 1. SETTINGS: None. PLAYING TIME: NA. PLOT: Mrs. Bennet conspires to marry her five daughters to rich men, but the girls find their own husbands, including the stubborn Elizabeth, despite their mother's machinations. RECOMMENDATION: Faithful to the original, this converts well to read aloud drama.

ROYALTY: Free to Plays subscribers. SOURCE: Newman, Deborah. (1987, May). Pride and prejudice. Plays: The Drama Magazine for Young People, pp. 66-76. SUBJECTS/PLAY TYPE: Matchmaking; Courting; Adaptation; Reader's Theater.

2451. 9-12. (-) Gleason, William. **The prime time crime.** CAST: 8f, 10m, 7u. ACTS: 2. SETTINGS: Study/living room of a manor. PLAYING TIME: NA. PLOT: A mystery phantom stalks Shropshire Manor, threatening to kill all the heirs to Miss Abigail's fortune. Summoned to solve the mystery are caricatures of the heroes of 1970s TV detective shows (Charlie's Angels, Baretta, Kojak, etc.). Two unhappily married couples plan to kill each other's spouses as well as their rich relative and her beloved niece, Marie. Meanwhile, the Phantom plants letter-opener knives in the backs of various house guests, the detectives fumble in their roles, and Marie's rather ineffectual lover interferes in everyone's plots until the happy ending. RECOMMENDATION: The use of now defunct TV show characters dates this too much. Few high school students would be familiar with the shows, even in reruns. There is very little mystery in the plot and even less humor. ROYALTY: $50. SOURCE: Gleason, William. (1977). The prime time crime. Woodstock, IL: Dramatic Pub. Co. SUBJECTS/PLAY TYPE: Murder; Mystery.

2452. 3-7. (+) Bland, Joellen. (Twain, Mark) **The prince and the pauper.** (The prince and the pauper) CAST: 2f, 9m, Su. ACTS: 1. SETTINGS: Palace; street; inn room; office; jail. PLAYING TIME: 30 min. PLOT: Edward, Prince of Wales, trades places with a young pauper, Tom Canty, who closely resembles him. Both boys wish to return to their familiar lifestyles, especially when Henry VIII dies, and the coronation of Edward is impending. Tom's evil father captures the Prince, who eventually escapes and proves his birthright by revealing the hiding place of the Great Seal of England. The prince elevates Tom to the status of King's Ward to prevent his further abuse. RECOMMENDATION: This is written simply. Settings are several and varied, and may pose a challenge, but they can be scaled down to suit the group's abilities. ROYALTY: NA. SOURCE: Bland, Joellen. (1987). Stage plays from the classics. Boston, MA: Plays, Inc. SUBJECTS/PLAY TYPE: Prince of Wales; Henry VIII; Mistaken Identity; Adaptation.

2453. 4-7. (+) Newman, Deborah. (Twain, Mark) **The prince and the pauper.** (The prince and the pauper) CAST: 13f, 26m, Su. ACTS: 1. SETTINGS: None. PLAYING TIME: NA. PLOT: Poor Tom Canty and Prince Edward VI exchange places as they envision adventure and fun. The true prince is beaten and starved by Tom's father, suffers indignities while living with outlaws, and is thrown in prison. Tom, not familiar with court manners and procedure, also finds it difficult to adapt. But, he is able to help poor people with his favorable rulings. The true prince appears as Tom is about to be crowned King. The two convince the court that Edward is the true heir. RECOMMENDATION: The characters are endearing and although much of the original has been cut out, this faithfully captures the spirit of the original. ROYALTY: Free to Plays subscribers. SOURCE: Newman, Deborah.

(1977, October). The prince and the pauper. Plays: The Drama Magazine for Young People, pp. 81-95. SUBJECTS/PLAY TYPE: Readers Theater; Mistaken Identity; Prince of Wales; Adaptation.

2454. 1-9. (+) Carle, Susan. (Milne, A. A.) **Prince Rabbit.** (Prince Rabbit and the princess who could not laugh.) CAST: 4f, 4m, Su. ACTS: 1. SETTINGS: Bare stage, props. PLAYING TIME: 25 min. PLOT: A brash but charming rabbit upsets the plans of a childless king and queen by boldly presenting himself as a suitable contestant for the crown. The king and chancellor try to disqualify Rabbit and pass succession to Lark Calomel (a human, and the royal favorite). Rabbit is declared the winner at the same time that an enchantment is lifted and he becomes a handsome prince. RECOMMENDATION: The asides to the audience (which may have to be updated), and the exaggerated conduct are delightful, as are the contests and magic tricks. ROYALTY: $25. SOURCE: Carle, Susan. (1983). Prince Rabbit. Chicago, IL: Dramatic Pub. Co. SUBJECTS/PLAY TYPE: Rabbits; Magic; Justice; Adaptation.

2455. 3-6. (+) Winther, Barbara. **Prince Rama. CAST:** 2f, 5m, Su. ACTS: 1. SETTINGS: Tropical setting. PLAYING TIME: 30 min. PLOT: Prince Rama, his wife Sita, and his brother Lakshmana are in exile in the Indian wilderness, Rama having been driven out as rightful heir to the throne by one of his father's wives. The wilderness is owned by demons who capture Sita. When Rama asks the Monkey-King for help, monkey armies invade the Demon forest and rescue Sita. The three return home to rule. RECOMMENDATION: While this may be useful for creative dramatics, it requires a very large cast and the characters are drawn as cartoons, rather than as believable types. The dialogue is also over exaggerated. ROYALTY: Free for amateur performance. SOURCE: Winther, Barbara. (1976). Plays from folktales of Africa and Asia. Boston, MA: Plays, Inc. SUBJECTS/PLAY TYPE: Folk Tales, India; Playlet.

2456. K-5*. (+) Brock, James. **The prince who wouldn't talk. CAST:** 2f, 2m, 4u. ACTS: 1. SETTINGS: Bare stage, props. PLAYING TIME: 55 min. PLOT: A King and Queen send their son to three wizards for a series of tests to find out why he won't speak, but it is a young maiden who discovers the reason and gets the Prince to talk. It is not that the Prince can't speak—no one ever gives him a chance to say anything. The play begins and ends with the cast asking the audience to decide the moral. RECOMMENDATION: This amusing fable will generate discussion of why parents don't stop to listen to their children. Production requires actors of junior high school age or older. ROYALTY: $25. SOURCE: Brock, James. (1977). The prince who wouldn't talk. Boston, MA: Baker's Plays. SUBJECTS/PLAY TYPE: Rudeness; Conversation; Comedy.

2457. 7-12. (-) Hamlett, Christina. **The prince's dilemma. CAST:** 2f, 4m. ACTS: 1. SETTINGS: Throne room. PLAYING TIME: 25 min. PLOT: The prince of **Arabian Night's** fame wishes to marry Yasmine, but must first give away his 41st wife as a gift, marry, and also give

away his 42nd wife as a gift. Three shipwrecks bring a woman and two men to the palace. The prince marries the woman, and then gives her to her true love (the man from the second shipwreck). He then gives wife 41 to the man from the first shipwreck, who happens to be an author and is delighted with his talkative bride who has been keeping the prince up telling stories for 1001 nights. RECOMMENDATION: This does not do justice to the original concept of the **Arabian Nights**, and the cavalier owning and giving away of women is highly offensive since it is used for comic relief rather than to convey the traditions of the time. ROYALTY: Free to Plays subscribers. SOURCE: Hamlett, Christina. (1984, April). The prince's dilemma. Plays: The Drama Magazine for Young People, pp. 15-23. SUBJECTS/PLAY TYPE: Marriage; Comedy.

2458. 2-8. (+) Claitman, Lorraine. **The princess and the dreadful dragon. CAST:** 4f, 3m, 10u. ACTS: 1. SETTINGS: Throne room. PLAYING TIME: 15 min. PLOT: The princess is unhappy because she is not allowed to play bow and arrows or read as her brothers do. To raise her spirits, the King and Queen agree to let her play with her brothers and learn to read. Later, she saves the kingdom from a fierce dragon because she knows how to shoot a bow and arrow and has read about the place on a dragon which is vulnerable to an arrow. As a reward, she is granted her wish that all girls in the kingdom be able to learn. RECOMMENDATION: With a deceptively simple fairy tale context, this delivers its hefty message about potential and stereotypes. It could be used well as a discussion starter about the value of reading, the value of literature, and the potential of all human beings. ROYALTY: Free to Plays subscribers. SOURCE: Claitman, Lorraine. (1982, October). The princess and the dreadful dragon. Plays: The Drama Magazine for Young People, pp. 55-60. SUBJECTS/PLAY TYPE: Women's Rights; Playlet.

2459. 1-6*. (+) Jackson, R. Eugene. (MacDonald, George) **The princess and the goblin.** (The princess and the goblin) CAST: 4f, 6m, Su. ACTS: 3. SETTINGS: Castle. PLAYING TIME: 90 min. PLOT: Princess Irene, the only daughter of a loving but often absent king, has led a rather ordinary life until three grotesque creatures break into her bedroom. The Goblin Queen, a cruel woman who attacks people with her granite shoes, the timid Goblin King who hides behind his wife, and their ugly, stupid son Harley, have vowed to kidnap Irene and gain control of her father's kingdom. Among those who help Irene are her late great-great-grandmother and Curdie, the son of a miner. RECOMMENDATION: This skillful adaptation of the beloved 19th century Scottish children's story will delight younger audiences. The childrens' characters are drawn so that all ages can relate to them as they learn to look beyond the exterior to the heart. ROYALTY: $35. SOURCE: Jackson, R. Eugene. (1983). The princess and the goblin. Schulenburg, TX: I.E. Clark. SUBJECTS/PLAY TYPE: Fantasy; Comedy; Goblins; Adaptation.

2460. 3-7. (+) Rosenthal, Pat. (Anderson, Hans Christian) **The princess and the magic pea.** (The princess and the pea.) CAST: 8f, 5m, Su. ACTS: 1. SETTINGS: Throne room; forest. PLAYING TIME: 90 min. PLOT: This is faithful to the familiar original. RECOMMENDATION: Younger children will enjoy this, but it would probably have to be performed by older children, since there is much dialogue. All members of the cast must sing, and many of the numbers are solos. ROYALTY: $40. SOURCE: Rosenthal, Pat. (1982). The princess and the magic pea. Denver, CO: Pioneer Drama Service. SUBJECTS/PLAY TYPE: Folk Tales, Denmark; Musical; Adaptation.

2461. 3-5*. (+) Steinberg, Patricia & Granovetter, Matthew. (Twain, Mark) **The princess and the pauper.** (The prince and the pauper) CAST: 6f, 6m, Su. ACTS: 1. SETTINGS: Pauper's lair; forest; palace. PLAYING TIME: NA. PLOT: This follows the plot of the original except instead of two boys exchanging places, Penelope and Penny do. They try to prove their real identities after Penelope is jailed with a group of pickpockets. Penelope becomes the new queen and Penny marries the prince who fell in love with her during the masquerade. RECOMMENDATION: In this musical adaptation, the musical numbers are well placed. There are times where the narrator exchanges roles with another character; this may cause a little confusion. ROYALTY: $50. SOURCE: Steinberg, Patricia and Matthew Granovetter. (1983). The princess and the pauper. Chicago, IL: Dramatic Pub. Co. SUBJECTS/PLAY TYPE: Musical; Adaptation.

2462. 3-5. (+) Gotwalt, Helen Louise Miller. (Andersen, Han Christian) **The princess and the pea.** (The princess and the pea.) CAST: 7f, 2m, Su. ACTS: 1. SETTINGS: Throne room. PLAYING TIME: 15 min. PLOT: A bedraggled beggar girl (Princess Patacake) must pass the test of the pea under the mattresses to prove she is a real princess. RECOMMENDATION: The original is retold with humor and easily memorized dialogue. ROYALTY: Free to Plays subscribers. SOURCE: Gottwalt, Helen Louise Miller. (1979, October). The princess and the pea. Plays: The Drama Magazine for Young People, pp. 55-60. SUBJECTS/PLAY TYPE: Folk Tales, Denmark; Adaptation.

2463. 2-5. (-) Spry, Lib & Halliwell, Steve. **A princess never should.** CAST: 4f, 2m, 4u. ACTS: 1. SETTINGS: Forest; cave; castle; cottage. PLAYING TIME: NA. PLOT: The king wants the princess to marry for money; the fierce dragon is actually nice; Mrs. Hubbard can't pay the rent and the evil rent collector takes her utility money; the King and princess turn out to be commoners related to the frog; and everybody shares in the end. RECOMMENDATION: This highly unoriginal, mixed up jumble of "Puff the Magic Dragon," "King Midas," the "Old Woman in the Shoe," "Alice in Wonderland," and "Jack in the Beanstalk"; surprise identities; lessons in economics, counting, sharing, and class distinction; the evil rent collector motif; sexism; and audience participation is just that. ROYALTY: NA. SOURCE: Spry, Lib. (1980). A princess never should. Toronto, Canada: Playwrights Canada. SUBJECTS/PLAY TYPE: Folk Tale Characters; Nursery Rhyme Characters; Comedy.

2464. 2-6. (+) Brink, Carol Ryrie. **The princess takes a nap.** CAST: 5f, 3m. ACTS: 1. SETTINGS: Bedroom. PLAYING TIME: 10 min. PLOT: In this demonstration

that the grass is not always greener on the other side, a poor girl trades places with a princess. Both discover that although the other's life has advantages, they like their own lives better. RECOMMENDATION: The message here that "we are only princesses or goosegirls according to the cloaks we wear" may be lost on the younger audiences for whom the play is intended. However, if followed by discussion, this would be an excellent vehicle for learning about identity. ROYALTY: Free to Plays subscribers. SOURCE: Brink, Carol Ryrie. (1978, March). The princess takes a nap. Plays: The Drama Magazine for Young People, pp. 54-58. SUBJECTS/PLAY TYPE: Identity; Skit.

2465. 1-5. (+) Robinette, Joseph. **The princess, the poet, and the little gray man.** CAST: 5f, 5m. ACTS: 1. SETTINGS: Forest; castle. PLAYING TIME: NA. PLOT: A 16 year old princess chooses not to smile because she will be married off to the one who forces a smile from her lips. As the King prepares to send her to the Sad Lands, a little gray man who claims responsibility for many fairy tale magical events weaves a spell around ten charming characters who force the princess to laugh. RECOMMENDATION: This nicely shows that it is all right to cry when sad, that all feelings are natural and human, and that a task which is futile when undertaken alone can often be accomplished with teamwork and cooperation. ROYALTY: $50. SOURCE: Robinette, Joseph. (1978). The princess, the poet, and the little gray man. Chicago, IL: Dramatic Pub. Co. SUBJECTS/PLAY TYPE: Magic; Cooperation; Musical.

2466. 11-12. (+) Gupton, Edward & Richards, R.J. **The Princess tree.** CAST: 4f, 4m, Su. ACTS: 1. SETTINGS: Throne room. PLAYING TIME: NA. PLOT: The royal court is in an uproar because the princess is unhappy and has been turned into a tree until she is happy. Her doting parents give her everything, but to no avail. After many puns, jokes, songs and funny lines, the princess learns that true happiness comes from loving and giving. RECOMMENDATION: This humorous musical comedy is sophisticated. ROYALTY: $60. SOURCE: Gupton, Edward & Richards, R.J. (1981). The Princess tree. Franklin, OH: Eldridge Press. SUBJECTS/PLAY TYPE: Christmas; Musical; Happiness; Comedy.

2467. 2-3. (+) Olfson, Lewy. **The princess who was ten feet tall.** CAST: 3u. ACTS: 1. SETTINGS: Puppet stage. PLAYING TIME: NA. PLOT: Princess Columbine is miserable because she is unable to find a husband taller than she. RECOMMENDATION: In this improvisational play, a plot is begun and the audience decides the end. The premises that one must look a certain way in order to be loved and that an unmarried woman is an unhappy woman are addressed. This might generate interesting discussion. ROYALTY: NA. SOURCE: Olfson, Lewy. (1975). You can put on a show. New York, NY: Sterling Pub. Co. SUBJECTS/PLAY TYPE: Marriage; Appearances; Puppet Play.

2468. K-3. (+) Danchik, Roger L. & Stevens, John. **The princess who wouldn't smile.** CAST: 2f, 3m. ACTS: 1. SETTINGS: Main square surrounded by shops.

PLAYING TIME: NA. PLOT: The king has promised his daughter's hand to anyone who can make her smile. Kasandra forces her father, Ferdinand, to try to amuse the princess so that he may wed the Queen-to-be, become King, and make Kasandra a princess. True love triumphs, however, when the sad Princess realizes that the only one who can make her happy is Sammy, the second royal proclaimer. Kasandra and Ferdinand are banished from the Kingdom and Sammy and the Princess live happily ever after. RECOMMENDATION: More sophisticated audiences would find Kasandra's gibberish, name calling, and idiotic stunts irritating. The pratfalls, slapstick humor, and overall silliness will, however, tickle the funny bones of younger viewers. This would be best produced by older actors. ROYALTY: $25. SOURCE: Danchik, Roger. (1982). The princess who wouldn't smile. Boston, MA: Baker's Plays. SUBJECTS/PLAY TYPE: Folk Tale Motifs; Comedy.

2469. 5-6. (-) Mayr, Grace Alicia. **The printer in Queen Street.** CAST: 1f, 9m. ACTS: 1. SETTINGS: Print shop; town scene with a tavern and street. PLAYING TIME: 40 min. PLOT: This describes young Ben Franklin's quest to leave Boston and begin his newspaper apprenticeship. RECOMMENDATION: This is long, has little action, and the dialogue is slow. ROYALTY: NA. SOURCE: Kamerman, Sylvia E. (1975). Patriotic and historical plays for young people. Boston, MA: Plays, Inc. SUBJECTS/PLAY TYPE: Journalism; Franklin, Benjamin; Playlet.

2470. 10-12. (+) Lippa, Louis. **Prisonbreak.** CAST: 2f, 1m. ACTS: 1. SETTINGS: Kitchen. PLAYING TIME: NA. PLOT: Thirty-four year old Suzie, mother of three, tries to free herself from the values and constraints imposed by her father and her husband. Through letters that she and her husband (who is a Prisoner of War) exchange, and through conversations with her alcoholic mother, she convinces herself and them of her worth as a human being. At the end of the play Suzie is working, going to school, and becoming independent. RECOMMENDATION: Although this has strong language and overt sexual allusions, Suzie's struggles to escape her psychological prisons are poignantly presented. This might be helpful for adolescents who are trying to understand their own parents' roles and relationships. ROYALTY: $15. SOURCE: Lippa, Louis. (1981). Prisonbreak. Chicago, IL: Dramatic Pub. Co. SUBJECTS/PLAY TYPE: Independence; Women's Roles; Self Esteem; Drama.

2471. 12*. (-) Terry, Megan. **Pro game. CAST:** 4u. ACTS: 1. SETTINGS: Family room. PLAYING TIME: 25 min. PLOT: As a mother and her three sons watch television, they discuss (and argue about) sex, football, sex, work, sex, childhood, sex, politics, and sex. During the game, Mother devotes the same caring efficiency to providing her youngest son with his first sexual partner, as to making his coffee. During halftime the family prepares to spend all of their savings in a hedonistic orgy of inflation beating. The play concludes with mother singing a suggestive song, while stripping for her loving sons. RECOMMENDATION: Although the author grants permission to high schools to omit objectionable words and actions in the script, it is difficult to see how this could

be sufficiently sanitized. Even if the off stage sounds of love making and Mother's advice on how to give the boss a charge during fellatio were omitted, the play's general subject matter, the destructive influence of a mother on the lives of her sons, might still be too controversial. Written for Harvey Fierstein, who played Mother in drag in the play's New York premiere, this is very funny, but not suitable for young adults. ROYALTY: $60. SOURCE: Terry, Megan. (1984). Two by Terry plus one. Schulenberg, TX: I.E. Clark. SUBJECTS/PLAY TYPE: Sex; Family Relationships; Comedy.

2472. 2-4. (+) Carlson, Bernice Wells. **Problems! Problems! CAST:** 7u. ACTS: 1. SETTINGS: Outdoors. PLAYING TIME: 7 min. PLOT: A peddler helps unhappy villagers see that, though each has his own problems, things could be worse. RECOMMENDATION: This is simple to produce, with easily memorized parts and some nonspeaking roles. ROYALTY: None. SOURCE: Carlson, Bernice Wells. (1982). Let's find the big idea. Nashville, TN: Abingdon Press. SUBJECTS/PLAY TYPE: Fable; Pantomime.

2473. 7-12. (+) McCusker, Paul. **The prodigals. CAST:** 2u. ACTS: 1. SETTINGS: Bare stage, props. PLAYING TIME: NA. PLOT: A 16 year old girl and an old man meet at a bus station. The old man has returned home after running away 33 years ago; the teenager waits for the bus to take her away from home. The old man tells her that although he had many marvelous experiences, they were all overshadowed by what he missed out on by leaving home. The girl decides to stay. RECOMMENDATION: This adequately, although not fabulously, recreates the arguments against leaving home at an early age. ROYALTY: NA. SOURCE: McCusker, Paul. (1984). Batteries not included. Boston, MA: Baker's Plays. SUBJECTS/PLAY TYPE: Runaways; Skit.

2474. 7-12*. (+) Surface, Mary Hall. **Prodigy. CAST:** 2f, 2m, 4u. ACTS: 15. SETTINGS: Hall. PLAYING TIME: NA. PLOT: This shows how Mozart's father drove Mozart to excel, depriving him of the normal friends and activities of childhood. RECOMMENDATION: Requiring professional musicians and actors, this would be excellent for a series on the arts. The staging, which utilizes puppets and large movable cutouts, is quite intricate. ROYALTY: $35. SOURCE: Surface, Mary Hall. (1988). Prodigy. New Orleans, LA: Anchorage Press, Inc. SUBJECTS/PLAY TYPE: Mozart, Wolfgang Amadeus; Musicians; Child Prodigies; Musical.

2475. 6-8*. (+) Barbie, Rick & Nelson, Greg. **Professor Fennerstein's magical musical. CAST:** 2f, 3m, Su. ACTS: 2. SETTINGS: Bare stage. PLAYING TIME: NA. PLOT: Professor Fennerstein and his assistant, Murray Bodger, persuade gullible Ben Trusty to participate in a magical musical revue, where Ben and the other characters are able to do or to be anything they wish. Ben gets into precarious situations from which he must extricate himself. RECOMMENDATION: Young people will enjoy the subject matter of this musical (which can have as large a cast as is needed), as well as the strange situations in which Ben finds himself. ROYALTY: Upon application.

SOURCE: Barbie, Rick, & Nelson, Greg. (1976). Professor Fennerstein's magical musical. Chicago, IL: Dramatic Pub. Co. SUBJECTS/PLAY TYPE: Magic; Imagination; Trickery; Musical.

2476. 6-8. (+) Ashby, Sylvia. **Professor Zuccini's traveling tales.** CAST: 8f, 8m, 5u. ACTS: 3. SETTINGS: None. PLAYING TIME: 65 min. PLOT: Professor Zuccini's troupe of traveling actors present three folk tales with interwoven characters. In the first tale, three poor sisters are tempted by the devil, but he is outwitted. In the second tale, a pompous older brother is tricked out of his money, but a naive younger brother retains his money. In the third tale, a proud prince is humbled. RECOMMENDATION: A vaudeville aura and exaggerated characters make this fun. Production is simplified by the lack of scenery and special costumes. ROYALTY: NA. SOURCE: Ashby, Sylvia. (1977). Professor Zuccini's traveling tales. Lubbock, TX: Sylvia Ashby. SUBJECTS/PLAY TYPE: Folk Tale Motifs; Comedy.

2477. K-12. (-) Calvin College Chapel Service. **Prophet, priest, and king.** CAST: Su. ACTS: 1. SETTINGS: None. PLAYING TIME: 15 min. PLOT: This is a compilation of Bible readings beginning with Genesis, and including the fall of Adam and Eve, the birth of Jesus, and the death of Jesus. RECOMMENDATION: This raggedly connects Bible readings and encompasses many lessons without an apparent theme. It is marked as a Christmas lesson from Luke 2:8-11, but it dwells on sin and death. To make this complete, it needs to be part of a worship service. ROYALTY: None. SOURCE: Hendricks, William & Vogel, Cora. (1983). Handbook of Christmas programs. Grand Rapids, MI: Baker Book House. SUBJECTS/PLAY TYPE: Christmas; Litany; Worship Program.

2478. 9-12. (+) Slocum, Richard. (Chekhov, Anton) **Proposin'.** (The marriage proposal) CAST: 2f, 1m. ACTS: 1. SETTINGS: Front porch. PLAYING TIME: NA. PLOT: P.J. Hastings, rancher and neighbor to the Hightower family's ranch, asks Mabel Hightower for permission to marry her daughter, Jessie. Mabel agrees, but when P.J. asks Jessie, they argue violently. When P.J. passes out, Jessie thinks he has died and left her an old maid. He revives and they quickly agree to marry before resuming their argument. RECOMMENDATION: This adaptation successfully translates the action into the language of the American West, while retaining the humor and impact of the original. ROYALTY: $15. SOURCE: Slocum, Richard. (1984). Proposin'. Boston, MA: Baker's Plays. SUBJECTS/PLAY TYPE: Marriage; Western; Adaptation.

2479. 3-7. (+) Cochran, Betty Holmes. **Proserpina's promise.** CAST: 2f, 2m, 4u. ACTS: 3. SETTINGS: Garden. PLAYING TIME: 60 min. PLOT: Proserpina begs to stay behind in the garden while her mother takes a trip to earth. The girl is allowed to stay home under the condition that she will not touch a strange bush that has appeared in the garden. Proserpina tries to uproot the plant and, as a result, summons Pluto, King of the Underworld. Pluto kidnaps her and takes her to his dark, cold kingdom.

Proserpina is miserable there and Ceres, mourning her lost daughter, is allowing life on earth to shrivel up. Mercury tells Pluto that if he really loved Proserpina, he would set her free. The god finally agrees to set Proserpina free, but since she ate some food in the underworld, she must return to live with Pluto for six months of the year. During this time, her mother rests from her labors and plants cease to grow. RECOMMENDATION: This is a pleasant introduction to the classic Roman myth. ROYALTY: $5. SOURCE: Cochran, Betty Holmes. (1978). Proserpina's Promise. El Cerrito, CA: Theater World Pub. SUBJECTS/PLAY TYPE: Mythology, Roman; Drama.

2480. K-6. (+) Korty, Carol. **The pumpkin.** (Mad merry men of Gotham) CAST: 4u. ACTS: 1. SETTINGS: Bare stage, props. PLAYING TIME: NA. PLOT: Small is worried that he'll lose himself if he goes to the crowded town, so he ties a pumpkin around his leg for identity. On the way, he naps. Through a series of events, the pumpkin comes to be tied around another person's leg. Small awakens and advises the person with the pumpkin that he must return home. Through another series of events, the pumpkin comes to be tied around a table. Small exhorts the table to go home. Finally, a friend ties the pumpkin around Small, and all is well again. RECOMMENDATION: This whimsical tale of identity humorously raises some interesting questions about self knowledge. The physical comedy will be a pleasure to produce. ROYALTY: None. SOURCE: Korty, Carol. (1977). Silly soup: Ten zany plays. New York, NY: Charles Scribner's Sons. SUBJECTS/PLAY TYPE: Comedy; Identity; Skit; Adaptation.

2481. 2-7. (+) Winther, Barbara. **The pumpkin patch.** CAST: 2f, 2m, 16u. ACTS: 1. SETTINGS: Backdrop. PLAYING TIME: 15 min. PLOT: The life of a pumpkin patch is represented in pantomime through the seasons of the year, beginning in early spring with planting, to the growing season of summer, the harvest of autumn, into winter with Jack Frost and the snow, and culminating with the approach of spring again. RECOMMENDATION: Especially good for the younger grades, since the parts (except for the narrator's) do not call for speaking, this could reinforce a unit on the seasons or the life cycle of plants. ROYALTY: Free to Plays subscribers. SOURCE: Winther, Barbara. (1984, October). The pumpkin patch. Plays: The Drama Magazine for Young People, pp. 41-44. SUBJECTS/PLAY TYPE: Seasons; Pantomime.

2482. K-3. (+) Johnson, Martha P. **The pumpkin-eating monster.** CAST: 13u. ACTS: 1. SETTINGS: Cornfield. PLAYING TIME: 10 min. PLOT: On Halloween, nine pumpkins are in the cornfield with a pumpkin-eating monster. They ask Moon to help them, but Witch battles Monster and saves the pumpkins. RECOMMENDATION: This will be a delight to produce and will appeal greatly to the youngsters' desires for spooky ghost stories. ROYALTY: Free to Plays subscribers. SOURCE: Johnson, Martha P. (1978, October). The pumpkin-eating monster. Plays: The Drama Magazine for Young People, pp. 71-72. SUBJECTS/PLAY TYPE: Halloween; Monsters; Witches; Playlet.

2483. 2-6*. (+) Harris, Aurand. **Punch and Judy.** CAST: 3u. ACTS: 2. SETTINGS: Puppet stage. PLAYING TIME: NA. PLOT: Punch and Toby (the dog) engage in a mock fight and Toby bites off Punch's nose. The professor appears, full of facts, and Punch, annoyed, begins hitting the professor in the head, knocking it off. After the professor leaves, Hector (the horse) appears and, through a series of events, kicks Punch in the head. The doctor treats Punch until Punch decides he is cured. The doctor demands payment and Punch chases him off, slapping him all the way. Judy decides to go shopping, and leaves Punch in charge of baby. After Judy leaves, Punch throws the child out the window when he cannot stop its crying. Toby, outside the window, catches the infant and Judy is incensed when she returns. They argue, and Judy calls the police, but Punch escapes punishment by tricking the hangman into hanging himself. Eventually, Punch realizes that the only creature left to fight is the devil, whom he kills in another battle. RECOMMENDATION: An interesting blend of human and puppet action, this traditional "Punch and Judy" play utilizes the usual flimsy plot line and abusive jokes. Very young audiences may be confused by the violence, but slightly older elementary students will appreciate the brash, nonsensical humor. As few as three or as many as seven puppeteers can perform this. ROYALTY: None. SOURCE: Jennings, Coleman A. & Harris, Aurand. (1981). Plays Children Love. New York, NY: Doubleday Co. SUBJECTS/PLAY TYPE: Slapstick; Puppet Play.

2484. K-3. (+) Cochrane, Louise. **Punch and Toby.** CAST: Su. ACTS: 1. SETTINGS: None. PLAYING TIME: 10 min. PLOT: In the slapstick Punch and Judy tradition, Punch unsuccessfully tries to teach his dog, Toby, tricks. RECOMMENDATION: Although women are portrayed as stupid, and men as bullying, this captures the spirit and action of the time period in which Punch and Judy was most popular. ROYALTY: NA. SOURCE: Burack, Sylvia K. Punch and Toby. (1977, May). Plays: The Drama Magazine for Young People, pp. 76-78. SUBJECTS/PLAY TYPE: Dogs; Puppet Play.

2485. 2-6. (+) Boiko, Claire. **Punctuation proclamation.** CAST: 3f, 9m, Su. ACTS: 1. SETTINGS: Throne room. PLAYING TIME: 15 min. PLOT: Fed up with trying to learn to read, King Pish-Posh orders that punctuation be abolished. When chaos results and his favorite story sounds like gibberish, the king sees the error of his ways. Pish-Posh rescinds his order, and learns to read a crucial sentence: "I am the king." RECOMMENDATION: This is an instructive tale with a predictable ending and a simple plot. It deals humorously with a topic which can often be tedious. ROYALTY: None. SOURCE: Boiko, Claire. (1985). Children's plays for creative actors. Boston, MA: Plays, Inc. SUBJECTS/PLAY TYPE: Punctuation; Grammar; Comedy.

2486. 7-12. (+) Gotwalt, Helen Louise Miller. **Puppy love.** CAST: 4f, 3m. ACTS: 1. SETTINGS: Living room. PLAYING TIME: 30 min. PLOT: Dad, the efficiency expert, thinks he has Christmas down to a science, "a job for everyone and everyone on the job." But when he comes home unexpectedly with his boss, he finds his home

running as inefficiently as might be expected on Christmas Eve. RECOMMENDATION: This is a pleasant, light hearted play with modern dress and no special effects. ROYALTY: Free to Plays subscribers. SOURCE: Kamerman, Sylvia E. (1982). Christmas play favorites for young people. Boston, MA: Plays, Inc. SUBJECTS/PLAY TYPE: Christmas; Comedy.

2487. 3-6. (+) Gabriel, Michelle. **The Purim wax museum.** CAST: 3f, 4m. ACTS: 1. SETTINGS: Wax museum. PLAYING TIME: 15 min. PLOT: This depicts the story of Purim through wax replicas of the basic characters, who tell of their parts in the holiday. RECOMMENDATION: The traditional story is told interestingly and well. ROYALTY: None. SOURCE: Gabriel, Michelle. (1978). Jewish plays for Jewish days. Denver, CO: Alternatives in Religious Education, Inc. SUBJECTS/PLAY TYPE: Purim; Jewish Drama.

2488. 5-12. (+) Rembrandt, Elaine. **Purimspiel.** CAST: 2f, 5m, Su. ACTS: 1. SETTINGS: Bare stage; queen's room; along a roadway; king's throne room. PLAYING TIME: 20 min. PLOT: Esther marries King Ahashuerus, but fails to tell him she is a Jew. Her cousin, Mordecai, learns of a plan by one of the King's advisors to have all Jews in the kingdom killed. He tells Esther of the plot and she journeys, along with Jewish friends she meets on the way, to see the King, reveal her secret, and tell the king about Haman's horrible plan to destroy her people. The King is outraged and orders the demise of his advisor, Haman, so that the Jews shall be free to live in peace. RECOMMENDATION: The play cleverly uses a storyteller and helpers to make transitions during scene changes. ROYALTY: None. SOURCE: Rembrandt, Elaine. (1981). Heroes, heroines & holidays--plays for Jewish youth. Denver, CO: Alternatives in Religious Education, Inc. SUBJECTS/PLAY TYPE: Purim; Jewish Drama.

2489. 7-12. (+) Bland, Joellen. (Poe, Edgar Allan) **The purloined letter.** (The purloined letter) CAST: 1f, 5m. ACTS: 1. SETTINGS: Living room/study. PLAYING TIME: 30 min. PLOT: An unnamed lady of royal rank is black-mailed by a cabinet minister who has come into possession of a compromising letter addressed to her. Having failed to locate it in their search of the minister's chambers, the Paris police turn to the talented detective, C. Auguste Dupin, fresh from his adventure in the Rue Morgue, who, through his brilliant powers of deduction, is able to return the letter to its rightful owner. RECOMMENDATION: This excellent adaptation is very faithful to the original, and includes dialogue directly from it. The antagonism between the prefect and Dupin's young assistant, and the tension between the lady and the minister are revealed through superb interchanges with detailed stage directions. The only difficulty for staging might be the 1840s Parisian costumes. ROYALTY: Free to Plays subscribers. SOURCE: Bland, Joellen. (1986, May). The purloined letter. Plays: The Drama Magazine for Young People, pp. 69-76. SUBJECTS/PLAY TYPE: Mystery; Adaptation.

2490. 7-12. (+) Majeski, Bill. **The purloined pearls of Polynesia.** CAST: 3f, 3m. ACTS: 1. SETTINGS: Living room. **PLAYING TIME:** 15 min. **PLOT:** Wealthy Mr. and Mrs. Van Wicker-sham Smythe have just given a successful tennis party for charity. The maid, a sports enthusiast, gives them tips on their game just before they realize that Mrs. Van Wickersham-Smythe's costly string of pearls is missing. Shaw Hawke, the famous private investigator, is called in, but his investigation is uninspired. When one of the guests, Edward Templeton, purports to have been at a football game when the pearls were taken, Madge is quick to perceive a discrepancy in Templeton's report of the game. With her help, Hawke puts the facts together and reveals him as the thief. Madge and Hawke leave to discuss sports, a topic about which Hawke knows very little as the ending dialogue humorously reveals. **RECOMMENDATION:** In spite of a predictable plot and stock characters, this effectively employs quick humorous exchanges, plays on words, and sarcastic dialogue. A cast willing to "ham it up" will reap the most pleasure. **ROYALTY:** Free to Plays subscribers. **SOURCE:** Majeski, Bill. (1979, February). The purloined pearls of Polynesia. Plays: The Drama Magazine for Young People, pp. 1-7. **SUBJECTS/PLAY TYPE:** Mystery; Comedy.

2491. 5-8. (+) Falls, Gregory A. (Merrill, Jean) **The pushcart war.** (The pushcart war) **CAST:** 2f, 6m, Su. **ACTS:** 1. **SETTINGS:** Large stage with brickwall backdrop. **PLAYING TIME:** NA. **PLOT:** In 1991, truck drivers decide that their progress through the streets of New York is being impeded by the pushcarts. They harass and terrorize the cart vendors. The pushcart peddlers retaliate by using peashooters to shoot tacks into the truck tires. The war escalates with the Mayor and police commissioner siding with the truckers. A peace march by the pushcarters and a public campaign bring about a truce. **RECOMMENDATION:** This fast moving adaptation employs a combination of expert clowning and tumbling with appropriate sound effects. The play requires numerous carts and truck cutouts and a large stage. **ROYALTY:** $35. **SOURCE:** Falls, Gregory A. (1985). The pushcart war. New Orleans, LA: Anchorage Press, Inc. **SUBJECTS/PLAY TYPE:** Peddlars; Politics; Comedy; Adaptation.

2492. K-3. (+) Friesen, Mark Douglas. (Perrault, Charles) **Puss in boots.** (Puss in boots) **CAST:** 4f, 1m, Su. **ACTS:** 1. **SETTINGS:** Roadside; king's palace; riverbank; ogre's castle. **PLAYING TIME:** 55 min. **PLOT:** Puss in Boots convinces the king that his poor master, Jack, is a wealthy nobleman. Because of the cat's cunning, he is rewarded with the bow and arrow he has been wanting, and Jack is given the hand of the princess in marriage. **RECOMMENDATION:** With multiple roles which may be cast singly to provide more parts, the characters talk to the audience as though in conversation. **ROYALTY:** $35. **SOURCE:** Friesen, Mark Douglas. (1985). Puss in boots. Morton Grove, IL: Coach House Press, Inc. **SUBJECTS/PLAY TYPE:** Folk Tales, France; Cats; Adaptation.

2493. K-5. (+) Mahlman, Lewis. (Perrault, Charles) **Puss in boots.** (Puss in boots) **CAST:** 1f, 3m, 4u. **ACTS:** 1. **SETTINGS:** Puppet theater with backdrops. **PLAYING**

TIME: 15 min. **PLOT:** Peter thinks his luck has run out when he inherits only a cat from his father, but the cat soon proves his worth. After purchasing fine clothes, the cat visits the king to set in motion a plot to make Peter appear to be a rich Marquis. After outwitting the wicked ogre from his castle, Puss gives it to Peter as his new home. The king is so impressed by Peter's high station that he offers him his daughter's hand in marriage. **RECOMMENDATION:** Although older elementary school children will have better luck manipulating the puppets, this could be the culmination of a special art project during which the puppets and backdrops are constructed. **ROYALTY:** Free to Plays subscribers. **SOURCE:** Mahlman, Lewis. (1976, October). Puss in boots. Plays: The Drama Magazine for Young People, pp. 71-75. **SUBJECTS/PLAY TYPE:** Cats; Folk Tales, France; Puppet Play; Adaptation.

2494. K-6*. (+) Netzel, Sally. (Perrault, Charles) **Puss in boots.** (Puss in boots) **CAST:** 4f, 4m, Su. **ACTS:** 2. **SETTINGS:** Shoemaker's house; forest; king's palace; ogre's palace. **PLAYING TIME:** NA. **PLOT:** A shoemaker dies, leaving to his favorite son, Marcus, his cat, Puss, and a pair of red boots. When they discover that the boots give Puss the power of speech, Marcus' two greedy brothers try to capture Puss for themselves. Through Puss's cleverness, Marcus and the cat elude the brothers and secure their own fortune. **RECOMMENDATION:** The plot is fast moving, and combined with considerable audience participation, this is enchanting. Best performed by older actors. **ROYALTY:** $25. **SOURCE:** Netzel, Sally. (1979). Puss in boots. Schulenburg, TX: I.E. Clark. **SUBJECTS/PLAY TYPE:** Folk Tales, France; Cats; Adaptation.

2495. 4-6. (+) Thane, Adele. (Perrault, Charles) **Puss in boots.** (Puss in boots) **CAST:** 2f, 6m, 3u. **ACTS:** 1. **SETTINGS:** Meadow; entrance hall. **PLAYING TIME:** 25 min. **PLOT:** After his father's death, the youngest of three sons inherits only a cat and a pair of boots. The cat tells young Pierre that he will make a fortune for him, if he can have the boots. Catching rabbits for the king, the cat presents them as gifts from the "Marquis of Carabas," telling the king that the Marquis owns all the surrounding land. Meanwhile, Pierre is swimming, and Puss hides his clothes so the King offers Pierre some finer replacements. Puss then tricks and kills an ogre, and prepares a feast in the ogre's castle. When Pierre and the king arrive, Pierre confesses that he is only a poor miller's son, but the king forgives him and creates a real title for the false marquis. **RECOMMENDATION:** Essentially faithful to the original, the dialogue is simple, the sets can be made easily, there are no elaborate props or stage directions, and the costumes can be improvised since no specific time period is given. **ROYALTY:** None. **SOURCE:** Thane, Adele. (1983). Plays from famous stories and fairy tales. Boston, MA: Plays, Inc. **SUBJECTS/PLAY TYPE:** Cats; Folk Tales, France; Playlet.

2496. K-12. (+) Way, Brian. (Perrault, Charles) **Puss in boots.** (Puss in boots) **CAST:** 4f, 7m. **ACTS:** 2. **SETTINGS:** Market square; palace room. **PLAYING TIME:** NA. **PLOT:** Anton, a traveling musician, and his cat, Puss, come to entertain the king, only to find the kingdom in an uproar due to the disappearance of the crown prince and the king's treasure. Puss recognizes the king as a former master, and the king rewards her with enchanted boots that allow her to stand, talk, and work magic. Puss discovers the plot: Boris, the jealous younger prince, has framed his older brother, Marcus, for the theft. But Marcus, now in hiding as the beggar Matthew, is helped by Puss to restore everything to normal. RECOMMENDATION: This should be performed by adults, though the sets can be made either simply or elaborately. It cleverly utilizes audience participation in the magic spells cast by Puss. SOURCE: Way, Brian. (1977). Puss in boots. Boston, MA: Baker's Plays. SUBJECTS/PLAY TYPE: Family; Cats; Folk Tales, France; Adaptation.

2497. 4-8. (+) Thum, Nancy. **Puss in boots, with a Gucci bag.** CAST: 3f, 4m, Su. ACTS: 1. SETTINGS: Office; boutique. PLAYING TIME: 25 min. PLOT: A young girl inherits a cat with magical powers while her brothers inherit the family business. The cat provides for Penelope by cleverly using wit and magic to get her wealth, status, and a husband. RECOMMENDATION: This cynical takeoff is disquieting since Puss illegally steals the witch's house (apparently this is all right because it is a witch), and also because overly gullible characters are tricked into taking care of Penelope, who has no socially redeeming qualities. If the messages are discounted, however, the exposition is quite creative. ROYALTY: Free to Plays subscribers. SOURCE: Thum, Nancy. (1982, November). Puss in boots, with a Gucci bag. Plays: The Drama Magazine for Young People, pp. 44-50. SUBJECTS/PLAY TYPE: Rags to Riches; Cats; Comedy.

2498. 4-10. (+) Stahl, Le Roy. **Putt! Putt!** CAST: 1m. ACTS: 1. SETTINGS: None. PLAYING TIME: NA. PLOT: A lone golfer pantomimes bewilderment and confusion as balls that he has hit mysteriously return. Finally, the frustrated golfer is pelted by a shower of golf balls. RECOMMENDATION: This is quite funny. ROYALTY: None. SOURCE: Majeski, Bill. (1981). Easy skits, blackouts and pantomimes. Woodstock, IL: Dramatic Pub. Co. SUBJECTS/PLAY TYPE: Golf; Comedy; Pantomime.

2499. 6-12. (+) Harris, Aurand. (Shakespeare, William) **Pyramus and Thisbe.** (A midsummer night's dream) CAST: 6m. ACTS: 2. SETTINGS: Bare stage. PLAYING TIME: NA. PLOT: Six rustic comics perform the parts they are to play at the wedding of the Duke of Athens and the Queen of the Amazons. RECOMMENDATION: This does not use the same names of the characters in **A Midsummer Night's Dream**, but it still gives the flavor. It works well as an introduction to Shakespeare since it can be performed more easily that the longer original. ROYALTY: None. SOURCE: Jennings, Coleman A. & Harris, Aurand. (1988). Plays children love, Volume II. New York, NY: St. Martin's Press. SUBJECTS/PLAY TYPE: Adaptation; Comedy; Playlet.

2500. 3-8*. (+) Novelli, Florence. **Queen Cat of Furbit.** CAST: 3f, 3m. ACTS: 1. SETTINGS: Bedroom; ballroom;

forest. PLAYING TIME: 45 min. PLOT: Vain Leonita, Queen Cat of Furbit, plans to marry Prince Gregov, whom she has never seen. Swinging Ralph, who is in love with the Queen, poses as the prince to fool her into marrying him instead. Things do not go as planned, but they turn out to everyone's satisfaction in the end. Leonita chooses Swinging Ralph because he has money. The prince, who turns out to be penniless, chooses the Queen's maid, Ginny, because of her green fur. RECOMMENDATION: This is delightfully humorous, with most of the main characters portrayed by cats. The music and songs enhance the story and children will delight in the antics of Swinging Ralph as they find satisfaction in knowing that each character achieves his/her wish. ROYALTY: NA. SOURCE: Novelli, Florence. (1983). Splinderion and the princess; and queen cat of Furbit: Two children's musicals. Toronto, Canada: Playwrights Canada. SUBJECTS/PLAY TYPE: Cats; Romance; Musical; Comedy.

2501. 6-12. (+) Sodaro, Craig. **Queen of the silent scream.** CAST: 5f, 5m. ACTS: 1. SETTINGS: Office; living room. PLAYING TIME: NA. PLOT: Detective Larry Stark narrates a humorous account of Norma Starr, Queen of the Silent Scream, who was murdered at her birthday celebration. When Stark holds a party at the mansion to rejoin the suspects, he reveals that the murder weapon was a pin treated with curare, and waits for the murderer to return to the scene of the crime. Maxine Comet, a rising starlette, returns dressed as an old woman, tries to kill Detective Stark, and fails. Maxine killed Norma Starr to keep her from ruining her budding career. RECOMMENDATION: The circumstances leading to the arrest of the murderess are quite humorous. ROYALTY: NA. SOURCE: Sodaro, Craig. (1988). Queen of the silent scream. Franklin, OH: Eldridge Pub. Co. SUBJECTS/PLAY TYPE: Mystery; Actors/Actresses; Comedy.

2502. 1-4. (+) Watts, Frances B. **The queen's Christmas cake.** CAST: 6f, 7m, 2u. ACTS: 2. SETTINGS: Bakery. PLAYING TIME: 15 min. PLOT: The baker plans to make a fancy Christmas cake for the queen, but is too good hearted to refuse orders from his local clients. Because he has too much to do, the queen's cake is quite ordinary. When she arrives to pick it up, she is angry. However, after hearing the baker's explanation, she is touched by his good heartedness and realizes that what she really needs is to know that her people are kind, loving and happy. RECOMMENDATION: This is a unique Christmas story. ROYALTY: Free to Plays subscribers. SOURCE: Watt, Frances B. (1984, December). The queen's Christmas cake. Plays: The Drama Magazine, pp. 37-43. SUBJECTS/ PLAY TYPE Christmas; Comedy.

2503. 2-6. (+) Blair, Ruth Van Ness. **The queen's spectacles.** CAST: 5f, 4m, Su. ACTS: 1. SETTINGS: Dunes; garden. PLAYING TIME: 15 min. PLOT: Shipwrecked pirates find the queen of the island when they locate her misplaced spectacles. They discover that the queen, her ladies, and the pirates are all brothers and sisters who were separated by an earlier shipwreck. The pirates decide to stay together on the island, all becoming royalty. RECOMMENDATION: Although predictable and overly pat, this might make a suitable production for upper elementary students to perform for peers and younger children. ROYALTY: Free to Plays subscribers. SOURCE: Blair, Ruth Van Ness. (1988, March). The queen's spectacles. Plays: The Drama Magazine for Young People, pp. 39-44. SUBJECTS/PLAY TYPE: Pirates; Royalty; Orphans; Playlet.

2504. 1-6. (+) Bradley, Virginia. **Quick! The river's rising.** CAST: 3f, 3m, Su. ACTS: 1. SETTINGS: Main street of a town. PLAYING TIME: NA. PLOT: When townspeople must evacuate their homes, each carries the thing most important to him/her. RECOMMENDATION: This brief pantomime can be simple or elaborate, with any number of performers. ROYALTY: None. SOURCE: Bradley, Virginia. (1975). Is there an actor in the house? New York, NY: Dodd, Mead. SUBJECTS/PLAY TYPE: Emergency; Comedy; Pantomime.

2505. 7-12. (+) Hark, Mildred & McQueen, Noel. **A quiet Christmas.** CAST: 5f, 4m, 1u. ACTS: 1. SETTINGS: Living room. PLAYING TIME: 30 min. PLOT: Mr. and Mrs. Evans decide not to have a Christmas celebration since none of their three children will be coming home. In a surprise turn of events, all the children will arrive late Christmas Eve. Mr. and Mrs. Evans manage to get a tree, dinner, and presents without letting the children know the celebration had not been planned all along. RECOMMENDATION: Although rather naive, this has many humorous scenes which could be expanded visually. ROYALTY: Free to Plays subscribers. SOURCE: Hark, Mildred & McQueen, Noel. (1980, December). A quiet Christmas. Plays: The Drama Magazine for Young People, pp. 1-14. SUBJECTS/PLAY TYPE: Christmas; Comedy.

2506. 8-12. (+) Kennedy, Eddie. **The quiet place.** CAST: 4f, 3m. ACTS: 1. SETTINGS: Hillside. PLAYING TIME: NA. PLOT: When a teenager dies from an overdose of drugs and alcohol, his friends must come to terms with their responsibility for the tragedy. RECOMMENDATION: Peer pressure and accepting responsibility for actions are the key concepts stressed in this drama which would be an excellent vehicle for classroom discussion. ROYALTY: $20. SOURCE: Kennedy, Eddie. (1983). The quiet place. Woodstock, IL: Dramatic Pub. Co. SUBJECTS/PLAY TYPE Drug Abuse; Peer Pressure; Drama.

2507. K-3. (+) Mahlman, Lewis & Jones, David Cadwalader. **The rabbit who wanted red wings.** CAST: 7u. ACTS: 1. SETTINGS: Forest; living room; pond. PLAYING TIME: 15 min. PLOT: Stubby the rabbit has many wishes. He wants to be a flower and also wishes he had a bushy tail, sharp quills on his back, and red rubbers like the duck. The groundhog tells him to wish for these things at the wishing pond. Just before Stubby wishes, he sees a red bird, wishes for wings, and gets them. But, when he returns home, his mother doesn't recognize him and won't let him in. Neither will any of this friends. He returns to the wishing pond, wishes his wings off, and vows never again to wish to be something or somebody else. RECOMMENDATION: This is understated, yet effective. ROYALTY: Free to Plays subscribers. SOURCE:

Mahlman, Lewis & Jones, David Cadwalader. (1980, January). The rabbit who wanted red wings. Plays: The Drama Magazine for Young People, pp. 65-69. SUBJECTS/PLAY TYPE: Folk Tale Motifs; Identity; Puppet Play.

2508. K-4. (+) Gotwalt, Helen Louise Miller. **The rabbits who changed their minds.** CAST: 19u. ACTS: 1. SETTINGS: Bare stage, props. PLAYING TIME: 15 min. PLOT: Easter rabbits ask to become candy rabbits, but change their minds when they realize that candies are inanimate. RECOMMENDATION: Simple but effective rhyme adds to the story. ROYALTY: None. SOURCE: Gotwalt, Helen Louise Miller. (1985). First plays for children: A collection of little plays for the youngest players. Boston, MA: Plays, Inc. SUBJECTS/PLAY TYPE: Easter; Rabbits; Playlet.

2509. 7-12. (-) Duckworth, Alice. **Radio suspense plays.** CAST: 8u. ACTS: 3. SETTINGS: None. PLAYING TIME: NA. PLOT: This comprises three skits. In "The Witness," two curious boys questioning a movie crew at work in an abandoned tenement building witness a murder that was supposed to be staged, but is actually real. In "The Mound," three boys vacationing near an Indian burial mound trespass in a sacred area, and are frightened by supernatural drums because of their disrespect. Finally, in "The Bonfire," four teens celebrating Halloween in the woods around a campfire inexplicably start a forest fire when their conversation turns to the legend of a man who was purportedly scared to death in the woods 20 years earlier. After racing to summon the fire department, they return to find an abandoned firesite and no signs of their earlier activity. RECOMMENDATION: Marked by poorly developed plots, contrived incidents, anticlimactic conclusions, and shallow characterizations, these sketches of unexplained phenomena confuse rather than intrigue. One expects an emphasis on audio technique and oral presentation from a radio play, but auditory stimulation and diversity in sound effects are strangely absent. ROYALTY: NA SOURCE: Duckworth, Alice. (n.d.). Radio suspense plays. Franklin, OH: Eldridge Pub. SUBJECTS/PLAY TYPE: Mystery; Horror; Suspense; Skit.

2510. 7-12. (+) Foon, Dennis. **Raft baby.** CAST: 2f, 4m. ACTS: 1. SETTINGS: Cabin; campfire. PLAYING TIME: NA. PLOT: In the winter of 1872, a baby girl is born to Jane and Ed Armson in the Canadian wilderness. Shortly after the birth, Jean, Jane's brother (who has left to find his fortune and lives far away), finds a baby floating on a raft in the Peace River. He is relieved when he meets Mr. Vining, who agrees to take the child since Mrs. Vining wants a baby. After 20 years, Jean sets out to find his sister and brother-in-law. At their cabin, Jean finds their remains and a diary that tells what happened. Because Ed was dying as a result of a hunting accident and Jane was dying of a fever, the couple made a raft, tied the baby to it and pushed it from the shore. Jean now knows that the baby he found 20 years earlier is his own niece, and he sets out to find her. When he locates the Vinings, his niece, Lily, is about to be married. Jean proves Lily's identity by a birthmark he knows she has on her toe. Once she knows

Jean is indeed her uncle, Lily insists that he stay. RECOMMENDATION: The lively plot, down home quality of the characters, and natural dialogue which is interspersed with songs, make this historical fiction pleasurable entertainment. The author has recreated the flavor of frontier Canada during the gold rush days. The setting lends itself to outdoor production on the panoramic scale of Paul Green's historical dramas. ROYALTY: NA. SOURCE: Foon, Dennis. (1978). Raft baby. Vancouver, B.C.: Talonbooks. SUBJECTS/PLAY TYPE: History, Canada; Adventure; Drama.

2511. 1-12. (+) Jackson, R. Eugene. **Rag dolls. CAST:** 4f, 1m. ACTS: 2. SETTINGS: Living room; bedroom. PLAYING TIME: NA. PLOT: Cassie lives with her mother, Linda, and her stepfather, Jeff, who abuses her. Each time that Jeff abuses Cassie, he buys her a gift, says he's sorry, and promises that he won't do it again. Cassie's friend, Barbara, who has been abused herself, tells Cassie that she needs to get help. Just as Cassie calls the Child Abuse Center, her mother and stepfather return. Jeff starts to strike Cassie but her mother stops him. At the end, Jeff leaves and Cassie's mother assures her that she is loved. RECOMMENDATION: There are several humorous comments made by Cassie's rag doll, Lamar, which lighten a very "heavy" subject. It is also seen that Carrie is beginning to treat Lamar the same way she is being treated. This is highly recommended for all age groups, with older students taking the adult roles. ROYALTY: $35. SOURCE: Jackson, R. Eugene. (1981). Rag Dolls. Schulenburg, TX: I.E. Clark. SUBJECTS/PLAY TYPE: Child Abuse; Drama.

2512. K-6. (+) Thackray, Patricia. (Gruelle, Johnny) **Raggedy Ann & Andy.** (The adventures of Raggedy Ann & Andy) CAST: 5f, 7m, 16u. ACTS: 2. SETTINGS: Bedroom/playroom; forest; taffy mine; witch's hunt; throne room. PLAYING TIME: NA. PLOT: Raggedy Ann and Andy rescue Marcella's new French doll, Babette, from the Loonies; unbewitch the bride of Prince Leonard the Loony Hearted; and find a home for the Camel with the Wrinkled Knees. RECOMMENDATION: The play is highly recommended for its humor, adventure, suspense, and audience participation; the cast can be expanded. ROYALTY: $50. SOURCE: Thackray, Patricia. (1981). Raggedy Ann & Andy. Chicago, IL: Dramatic Pub. Co. SUBJECTS/PLAY TYPE: Raggedy Ann & Andy; Dolls; Comedy; Adaptation.

2513. 6-9. (+) Harris, Aurand. (Alger, Horatio) **Rags to riches.** (Ragged Dick; Mark the match boy) CAST: 3f, 6m, Su. ACTS: 2. SETTINGS: Street; parlor; tenement room. PLAYING TIME: NA. PLOT: Ragged Dick, a shoeshine boy, overhears Mother Watson tell Mark, an orphaned match boy (who is actually Mr. Greyson's lost nephew), that he cannot return home until he has begged 25 cents. Dick goes to Mr. Greyson's home to return change from a recent shoeshine and meets Greyson's daughter, Ida, who decides to educate him in the afternoons. Greyson asks for Dick's help in finding his lost nephew, an orphan living on the streets. Dick decides Mark should live with him on the advance Greyson has given him to help find the lost nephew. Mark falls ill. Mother Watson learns of the search

for Greyson's nephew, and, feigning concern for Mark, she visits him and steals his picture of his beloved mother. She gives the picture to Mickey, another orphan, coaches him on the necessary details, and sends him to Greyson's home to claim the money. Dick appears while Mickey is there and wants to know how Mickey got Mark's picture. They all rush to the scene, Greyson recognizes Mark as his nephew, and rewards Dick with a position in his bank. Mother Watson is taken to jail. RECOMMENDATION: This corny, but amusing adaptation of two Horatio Alger stories is very much in keeping with the Alger tradition of "rags to riches." This will be particularly helpful if included as part of a unit on the problems of homelessness in today's society, the Great Depression of the 1930s, and the similarities and differences between the two. ROYALTY: NA. SOURCE: Harris, Aurand. (1977). Six plays for children. Austin, TX: Univ. of Texas Press. SUBJECTS/PLAY TYPE: Musical; Rags to Riches; Adaptation.

2514. 11-12. (+) Clark, I.E. **Ragweed Cowboy Joe.** CAST: 9f, 7m, 14u. ACTS: 2. SETTINGS: Schoolroom. PLAYING TIME: 90 min. PLOT: Joe, a born loser, goes west to cure his allergies. When his sneezing ceases and he falls in love with his college teacher, Joe's life seems to be turning around, until the villain tries to use his allergies against him. RECOMMENDATION: Although mature high school students will enjoy the raucous humor and understand the parody, this is perhaps better suited to older civic and community groups, as the introductory notes suggest. Great amounts of rehearsal time are not essential; the announcer reads most of the script. ROYALTY: $25. SOURCE: Clark, I.E. (1974). Ragweed Cowboy Joe. Schulenburg, TX: I.E. Clark. SUBJECTS/PLAY TYPE Western; Comedy; Melodrama.

2515. K-6. (+) Carlson, Bernice Wells. **Rain or shine.** CAST: 5u. ACTS: 1. SETTINGS: Bare stage, props. PLAYING TIME: NA. PLOT: A father leaves home to visit his two daughters. One asks him to pray for rain to make her garden grow; the other asks that he pray for sun to make her pottery dry. He does not know what to do. RECOMMENDATION: Discussion of possible alternatives for the father's dilemma could prove interesting. ROYALTY: NA. SOURCE: Carlson, Bernice Wells. (1982). Let's find the big idea. Nashville, TN: Abingdon. SUBJECTS/PLAY TYPE: Decision Making; Fable; Skit.

2516. 1-4. (+) Jackson, Patricia M. **Rainbow. CAST:** 1f, 1m, Su. ACTS: 1. SETTINGS: Backyard. PLAYING TIME: 10 min. PLOT: A boy and girl watch the sun, wind, and rain, as they contribute to the growth cycle of tomato plants. At the end, they pick some tomatoes and go inside to have dinner. The tomatoes seeds begin their growth cycle again. RECOMMENDATION: The size of the cast is flexible and the use of pantomime and expressive body movement to tell the story should tap the energy and imagination. ROYALTY: Free to Plays subscribers. SOURCE: Jackson, Patricia M. (1976, March). Rainbow. Plays: The Drama Magazine for Young People, pp. 83-86. SUBJECTS/PLAY TYPE: Nature; Plants; Creative Dramatics.

2517. K-3*. (+) Way, Brian. The rainbow box. CAST: 2f, 2m, Su. **ACTS:** 1. **SETTINGS:** Bare stage. **PLAYING TIME:** 50 min. **PLOT:** A hole is made in the most magnificent rainbow of all and through it, the colors begin to drain away and fade, as do the powers and life of the rainbow queen. The play, using the theme of working and living together, chronicles the rainbow queen's assistants' attempts to heal both the rainbow and the queen. In the end, all the rainbow colors are renewed and the queen recovers. **RECOMMENDATION:** A great deal of audience participation necessitates production by adults or skilled young adults. **ROYALTY:** $20. **SOURCE:** Way, Brian. (1977). The rainbow box. Boston, MA: Baker's Plays. **SUBJECTS/PLAY TYPE:** Fantasy; Cooperation; Rainbows; Participation Play.

2518. 7-12. (-) Taylor, Cecil P. The rainbow coloured disco dancer. CAST: 3f, 1m, Su. **ACTS:** 1. **SETTINGS:** Bedroom; disco; beach; street. **PLAYING TIME:** NA. **PLOT:** Carol, an Indian teenager with white parents, encounters racism. Her taunters tell her that her white parents can't be her real parents because she's dark skinned. Carol tries to avoid this new realization by fantasizing about her family while she dances disco. Finally, she confronts her parents and is told that although her mother is her birth mother, her father is not her birth father. Her mother had been pregnant by an Indian before she met Carol's father. Carol decides to deal with reality, and commits her love to her parents and to herself. **RECOMMENDATION:** It is unclear whether this is about racism, teenage adoption fears, or pregnancy out of wedlock. Also, it is absurd that a teenager old enough to go to a disco would not have already noticed that her parents were white and she was not. This suffers from too many ambiguities and a patronizing attitude towards the audience. **ROYALTY:** NA. **SOURCE:** Taylor, Cecil P. (1983). Live theatre: Four plays for young people. London, England: Methuen. **SUBJECTS/PLAY TYPE:** Racism; Identity; Drama.

2519. 12*. (-) Williams, Jill. Rainbow Jones. CAST: 4f, 4m. **ACTS:** 2. **SETTINGS:** Central park; apartment interior and exterior; front porch of farmhouse. **PLAYING TIME:** 120 min. **PLOT:** A sad and lonely young girl, Rainbow, converses with the animals in Aesop's **Fables**. Her conversations are sometimes overheard by others and misunderstood. While she is away, her friend, Joey, makes the acquaintance of the animals to whom she speaks and begins to understand her better. When she returns, Rainbow and Joey embrace as love resolves all tensions and brings the play to a happy, musical conclusion. **RECOMMENDATION:** Casting is crucial to success, as this is largely dependent upon the singing ability of the actors. There are 17 songs performed either as solos or in combination with two or more members of the cast. Psychological, romantic, and sexual overtones make this appropriate for adults and possibly some mature senior high school students. Several times during the play the actors assume the voices and mannerisms of famous actors of another era. Also, several references are made to now outdated TV quiz shows. **ROYALTY:** $60. **SOURCE:** Williams, Jill. (1979). Rainbow Jones. Denver, CO: Pioneer

Drama Service. **SUBJECTS/PLAY TYPE:** Romance; Psychological Drama; **Aesop's Fables**; Musical.

2520. 9-12. (+) Hamlett, Christina. Raincheck. CAST: 1f, 1m. **ACTS:** 1. **SETTINGS:** Teller's window. **PLAYING TIME:** 20 min. **PLOT:** Teller Gwendolyn Nablosky, curiously and patiently inquires about the bank robber's need for cash, his identification card, and his passbook, failing to acknowledge his threats. As the unnerving effect of Gwendolyn's banter erodes his confidence, she comments on his resemblance to a former classmate, Richard Nevins. As he denies that he is Nevins, Gwendolyn tells the sad story of Nevins' layoff from Paramount. Gwendolyn's casual mention that her brother is currently hiring cameramen at Universal Studios turns Nevins from a life of crime, and preserves her own life and the bank's funds. **RECOMMENDATION:** The plot is intense, the dialogue is lively, and the theme is edifying. **ROYALTY:** Free to Plays subscribers. **SOURCE:** Hamlett, Christina. (1985, December). Raincheck. Plays: The Drama Magazine for Young People, pp. 23-28. **SUBJECTS/PLAY TYPE:** Robbery; Banks; Values; Comedy.

2521. 10-12. (+) Nash, N. Richard. The rainmaker. CAST: 1f, 6m. **ACTS:** 3. **SETTINGS:** Farmhouse interior. **PLAYING TIME:** NA. **PLOT:** The menfolk of the farming Curry family, although dealing with drought, are matchmaking for their sister, Lizzie. A "rainmaker" appears, and after much bickering and a $100 fee, they follow his bizarre instructions while the rainmaker charms Lizzie. The law catches up to the conman and Lizzie tries to help him leave unnoticed, believing that he will make it rain and that she will find love. It does, and she does. **RECOMMENDATION:** This is a wonderful portrayal of a family's warmth and closeness as they try to deal with crises and life's puzzles. **ROYALTY:** $50. **SOURCE:** Nash, N. Richard. (1983). The rainmaker. New York, NY: Samuel French. **SUBJECTS/PLAY TYPE:** Loneliness; Family; Drought; Romantic Comedy.

2522. K-3. (+) Watts, Irene N. The rainstone. CAST: 1f, 1m, 4u. **ACTS:** 1. **SETTINGS:** Bare stage, props. **PLAYING TIME:** NA. **PLOT:** A poor grandmother hears crying and follows it to a boy sitting by the rocks in the river. She takes him home. Taro is a crybaby, and the children in the village (audience) tease him. But, when Taro's tears dry up, so does the water. Taro goes to the river, where everyone is praying to Raindragon for rain. He goes to see Raindragon (his father), who tells him that if the river dries up again, he should turn his magic stone three times to take care of the problem. Everyone thanks Taro, and Grandmother says (to the audience) that it is time to let Taro sleep. On this cue, the audience follows Grandmother out. **RECOMMENDATION:** With meaningful audience participation, the plot follows in sequence and is believable. The natural style creates the mood, and production could be done by adults or young adults, with some older children. **ROYALTY:** NA. **SOURCE:** Watts, Irene N. (1978). A blizzard leaves no footprints; listen to the drum; patches; the rainstone: Four children's plays. Toronto, Canada: Playwrights Co-op. **SUBJECTS/PLAY TYPE** Folk Tales, Japan; Rain; Playlet.

2523. 9-12*. (+) Hansberry, Lorraine. **A raisin in the sun.** CAST: 3f, 8m. ACTS: 3. SETTINGS: Living room. PLAYING TIME: 165 min. PLOT: Three generations of the Younger family, poor and black, live in a small apartment in Southside Chicago. The father has died and an insurance check for ten thousand dollars is to arrive the next day. Everyone has his own expectations as to how the money should be used. The check arrives and Mama uses $3500 to make the down payment on a house in an all white neighborhood. Walter, who wanted to invest the money in a liquor store, becomes depressed. Mama gives him the remainder of the money and tells him to put half in the bank to pay for his sister's medical school; the rest he is to oversee. Just as the move is to begin, a man representing the white neighborhood offers to buy their newly acquired property at a profit to the Youngers', explaining that a black family in an all white neighborhood can cause trouble. The family rejects his offer. Later, Walter confesses that he has invested the remainder of the money in his business and now it is all gone. In his rage and despair, he accepts the offer on their property. At the last minute, Walter realizes that he is betraying everything his family believes, and does not sell the land. The family is elated and begins the move to a new house and a new life. RECOMMENDATION: This speaks powerfully to both blacks and whites about the struggle of the black family to rise above the prejudice of society, and how prejudice affects the black family. The complex and moving characterizations require the talents of professional or well trained amateur actors. Only the most serious high school drama class should attempt the extensive memorization and subtleties of performance. ROYALTY: $50. SOURCE: Hansberry, Lorraine. (1984). A raisin in the sun. New York, NY: Samuel French. SUBJECTS/PLAY TYPE: Black History; Values; Family; Drama.

2524. 10-12. (+) Harris, Aurand. (Udall, Nicholas) **Ralph Roister Doister.** (Ralph Roister Doister) CAST: 4f, 8m, Su. ACTS: 1. SETTINGS: Street. PLAYING TIME: NA. PLOT: Ralph Roister Doister, a "vain-glorious gull," enlists the help of Mathew Merrygreek, a "lively scamp who lives by his wits," to help him win the hand of a lady whose name he can't remember. Merrygreek, always the troublemaker, informs Doister her name is Christian Custance, but that she is promised to another. Unswayed, Doister persists, angering Custance, who plots with Merrygreek to put Doister in his proper place. Custance and Doister engage in slapping, biting, and hair pulling. Custance wins, and Doister sulks away. The two meet again, Custance with pots and pans, and Doister with shouting and drum beating. The fracus convinces Doister that Custance really doesn't love him and proves to Gawyn Gooluck, Custance's true and promised love, that she indeed loves him. RECOMMENDATION: The old English dialogue, while initially difficult to master, could provide hilarious entertainment. Music and costumes of the period would make this even more enjoyable. Merrygreek, played as a mischievous, mustache twirling troublemaker, and Doister, played as an effeminate, self involved fop, will be delightful. Only mature, accomplished senior high actors could effectively portray the critical satire and wit. ROYALTY: $15. SOURCE:

Harris, Aurand. (1979). Ralph Roister Doister. Boston, MA: Baker's Plays. SUBJECTS/PLAY TYPE: Romance; Adaptation.

2525. 1-6. (+) Kilcup, Rick. **Randy the red-horned rainmoose.** CAST: 18u. ACTS: 1. SETTINGS: Workshop. PLAYING TIME: 20 min. PLOT: Randy the Rainmoose, tired of living in a rain forest where moss grows on his antlers, takes a job cleaning Santa's workshop in order to have some excitement, and to work with Rudolph (Randy's hero). The work is drudgery until one night, when Rudolph is too sick to lead the sled and Randy replaces him for the night. RECOMMENDATION: Randy is especially endearing as a bored, but determined hero. ROYALTY: Free to Plays subscribers. SOURCE: Kilcup, Rick. (1987, December). Randy the red-horned rainmoose. Plays: The Drama Magazine for Young People, pp. 31-36. SUBJECTS/PLAY TYPE: Christmas; Comedy.

2526. 5-9. (-) Lane, Carolyn. (Henry, O.) **The ransom of Emily Jane.** (The ransom of Red Chief) CAST: 6f, 2m. ACTS: 1. SETTINGS: Mountain cave; street. PLAYING TIME: 45 min. PLOT: A middle aged woman and her grown son kidnap an 11 year old girl, and then hide out in a cave waiting for the ransom. By the time the wealthy father arrives, the kidnappers are ready to pay him to take the girl back. RECOMMENDATION: The characters and dialogue consist of one stereotype after another, and this would be particularly offensive to Native Americans and women. ROYALTY: $15. SOURCE: Lane, Carolyn. (1980). The ransom of Emily Jane. Denver, CO: Pioneer Drama Service. SUBJECTS/PLAY TYPE: Kidnapping; Comedy; Adaptation.

2527. 4-12. (+) Kral, Brian. (Henry, O.) **The ransom of Red Chief.** (The ransom of Red Chief) CAST: 3m. ACTS: 1. SETTINGS: Cave. PLAYING TIME: NA. PLOT: Two down-on-their-luck men find that the unruly 10 year old boy they kidnapped for ransom money is more than they can handle. The men pay the boy's uncle to take the boy back. RECOMMENDATION: Children and adults will enjoy the humorous and fast paced action, the "old fashioned" record player and camera, and the boy who thinks he is an Indian chief. Since the record player and camera must be thrown on the floor and broken, the producers must find a way to make these props inexpensively. The roles of the two men should be played by older teens or adults. ROYALTY: $35. SOURCE: Kral, Brian. (1978). The ransom of red chief. New Orleans, LA: Anchorage Press, Inc. SUBJECTS/PLAY TYPE: Kidnapping; Comedy; Adaptation.

2528. 7-12. (+) Nagle, Pam & Wingerter, George. (Henry, O.) **The ransom of Red Chief.** (The ransom of Red Chief) CAST: 8f, 6m, 5u. ACTS: 2. SETTINGS: Street. PLAYING TIME: 90 min. PLOT: Sam, a ne'er-do-well con man and his sidekick, Bill, kidnap Johnny Dorset (better known as Red Chief) in hopes of a handsome ransom from the Widow Dorset. Little do they know that Johnny is the terror of the town. The townspeople are delighted to have him gone and Johnny is enjoying his captivity immensely, driving the two crooks to desperation. They bring Johnny back and the townspeople chase the two "varmints" out.

RECOMMENDATION: An absolutely delightful adaptation, the lingo is decidedly American (although it sounds more Western than Southern) and the musical numbers are lively. ROYALTY: $60. SOURCE: Nagle, Pam & Wingerter, George. (1979). The ransom of Red Chief. Denver, CO: Pioneer Drama Service. SUBJECTS/PLAY TYPE: Kidnapping; Comedy; Adaptation.

2529. 7-10. (+) McCusker, Paul. **The rapture formula.** CAST: 3m. ACTS: 1. SETTINGS: Lounge. PLAYING TIME: NA. PLOT: Bernie, a computer whiz, computes the date of the Rapture. As Bob and Mike wait for the prediction to occur, Mike tries to nap and Bob reads an article about how to be a good wife. Humorous dialogue (much of which revolves around the absurd, but commonly given, advice in Bob's article), reflects the characters' personalities. Bernie announces the date as June 31, 1997, but Bob and Mike remind him June has 30 days. Bob and Mike exit, warning that "you can't make a liar out of God," and leaving Bernie to figure out what went wrong. RECOMMENDATION: This quite funny, but ultimately serious skit will have great utility as a church program for teenagers and adults. ROYALTY: NA. SOURCE: McCusker, Paul. (1982). Souvenirs: Comedies and dramas for Christian fellowship. Boston, MA: Baker's Plays. SUBJECTS/PLAY TYPE: Christian Drama; Rapture; Skit.

2530. 2-6. (+) Barr, June. (Grimm Brothers) **Rapunzel.** (Rapunzel) CAST: 3f, 2m. ACTS: 1. SETTINGS: Tower room; desert. PLAYING TIME: 15 min. PLOT: A wicked witch takes Rapunzel from her parents and imprisons her in a tower. A prince hears Rapunzel's beautiful song and promises to rescue her. The witch finds out and banishes Rapunzel to the desert, where she thinks the prince can never find her. However, Rapunzel's beautiful song brings the prince to her. RECOMMENDATION: This scaled down version of the classic tale will be easier for young performers to stage, with its simple dialogue and limited settings. ROYALTY: NA. SOURCE: Kamerman, Sylvia E. (1987). Plays from favorite folk tales. Boston, MA: Plays, Inc. SUBJECTS/PLAY TYPE Folk Tales, Germany; Witchcraft; Adaptation.

2531. 4-6. (+) Thane, Adele. (Grimm Brothers) **Rapunzel.** (Rapunzel) CAST: 7f, 3m. ACTS: 1. SETTINGS: Garden; tower room. PLAYING TIME: 30 min. PLOT: When Emma develops a powerful craving for a special lettuce called rapunzel, which grows in the witch's garden, Franz tries to steal it. The witch catches him and demands his first born child as payment. After the child is born, the witch collects her payment and turns the parents into stone. As the golden haired Rapunzel grows, the witch imprisons her in a tower. A prince hears Rapunzel singing, falls in love, but is found out by the witch, who strikes him blind. Rapunzel's tears of love heal his eyes; the witch falls to her death; the tower is destroyed by lightning; Rapunzel's parents are brought back to life; she and the prince live happily ever after. RECOMMENDATION: The opening scene adds several characters which, while not necessary to the plot, give an opportunity for more speaking roles. ROYALTY: Free to Plays subscribers. SOURCE: Thane, Adele. (1986, October). Rapunzel. Plays: The Drama Magazine for Young People, pp. 37-45. SUBJECTS/PLAY TYPE: Folk Tales, Germany; Witchcraft; Romance; Adaptation.

2532. K-3*. (+) Landes, William-Alan. (Grimm Brothers) **Rapunzel n' the witch.** (Rapunzel) CAST: 3f, 3m, Su. ACTS: 3. SETTINGS: Cottage; yard; castle. PLAYING TIME: 60 min. PLOT: The witch (Dame Gothol) steals the infant, Rapunzel, from her parents and raises her as her own. Dame Gothol wants to control the world because she is tired of being alone and wants to make everyone her friend. At the end (and with the help of the audience), she realizes that if she is nice, people will like her. She sets Rapunzel free to marry the prince. RECOMMENDATION: The cast can be expanded with parts as rocks, trees, and the chorus. Its length makes it suitable for production by junior high schoolers, with youngsters playing the "extras." ROYALTY: $35. SOURCE: Landes, William-Alan. (1979). Rapunzel n' the witch. Studio City, CA: Players Press. SUBJECTS/PLAY TYPE: Friendship; Adaptation.

2533. 7-12. (+) Kelly, Tim. **Ratcatcher's daughter, or, Death Valley daze.** CAST: 5f, 4m, 3u. ACTS: 2. SETTINGS: Orphanage. PLAYING TIME: 60 min. PLOT: While Aunty Hush serves bad tasting mush at the orphanage, Lotta, a young lady from England looking for her fiance, enters after an all day walk. Whiplash, a San Francisco swindler arrives, claiming the orphanage for conversion into a saloon, which prompts a temperance protest. An insurance investigator brings Lotta news of an inheritance. Whiplash tries to tempt Lotta's fiance with liquor in order to ruin the marriage plans and acquire her inheritance. He fails, and everyone is happy. RECOMMENDATION: This will suit those who wish a lighthearted melodrama in which the villain can be hissed and the hero cheered. ROYALTY: $35. SOURCE: Kelly, Tim. (1982). The ratcatcher's daughter, or, Death Valley daze. Denver, CO: Pioneer Drama Service. SUBJECTS/PLAY TYPE: Comedy; Swindlers and Swindling; Musical.

2534. 7-10. (+) McCusker, Paul. **Rauncho presents.** CAST: 1u. ACTS: 1. SETTINGS: Bare stage, props. PLAYING TIME: NA. PLOT: Explaining that since commercials are such a part of our lives, the author supplies two for use with any church Christmas program. A typical fast-talking salesman attempts to convince the audience to buy "Ultimo" and "Superwatch," two products which will allegedly solve all problems, from front end alignments to stock market reports. RECOMMENDATION: These clever skits will work beautifully as filler between scene changes in a Christmas program. ROYALTY: NA. SOURCE: McCusker, Paul. (1982). Souvenirs: Comedies and dramas for Christian fellowship. Boston, MA: Baker's Plays. SUBJECTS/PLAY TYPE: Comedy; Commercials; Skit.

2535. 3-6. (+) Kuhn, Joanna & Klayer, Connie. **Razzle-dazzle Valentine's Day.** CAST: 8f, 9m, 3u. ACTS: 1. SETTINGS: City street. PLAYING TIME: 20 min. PLOT: Mr. Bernard accidentally drops some valentines as he delivers the mail. Several children see the valentines and put them in the mailboxes. When the residents pick up their mail, they are puzzled because the valentines belong to someone else. As the residents gather, they read the valentines aloud, then exchange the cards, learning about each other in the process. **RECOMMENDATION:** This would be especially good for younger audiences who are not ready for the romance associated with Valentine's Day. **ROYALTY:** Free to Plays subscribers. **SOURCE:** Kuhn, Joanna, & Klayer, Connie. (1978, February). Razzle-dazzle Valentine's Day. Plays: The Drama Magazine for Young People, pp. 35-39. **SUBJECTS/PLAY TYPE:** Valentine's Day; Comedy.

2536. 5-8. (+) Williams, Jill. **Reach for the sky.** CAST: 5f, 3m. ACTS: 1. SETTINGS: Exercise studio. PLAYING TIME: 20 min. PLOT: An attempted robbery of the ladies' exercise class at the Skin n' Bones exercise studio is foiled when the one robber becomes more interested in jumping rope than in the heist. RECOMMENDATION: All will enjoy this humorous piece which demonstrates the triumph of brains over brawn. ROYALTY: Free to Plays subscribers. SOURCE: Williams, Jill. (1981, April). Reach for the sky. Plays: The Drama Magazine for Young People, pp. 61-65. SUBJECTS/PLAY TYPE: Comedy; Exercise; Skit.

2537. 10-12. (+) Harris, Richard W. **Reading John Manfred.** CAST: 1f, 2m. ACTS: 1. SETTINGS: Apartment. PLAYING TIME: NA. PLOT: A would be psychic and his artist girlfriend try to help their elderly neighbor discover why he has lived so long. During the course of the "Magic Mind Specials," the old man recalls special people in his life, explains why they were special, and helps the young couple communicate better. RECOMMENDATION: The bizarre happenings, which are never revealed as either real or only a matter of suggestion will appeal, and the message about communication is right on target. ROYALTY: $20. SOURCE: Harris, Richard W. (1984). Reading John Manfred. Chicago, IL: Dramatic Pub. Co. SUBJECTS/PLAY TYPE: Death and Dying; Communication; Drama.

2538. 7-10. (+) Hutson, Natalie Bouvee. **The reading of the will.** CAST: 3f, 4m. ACTS: 1. SETTINGS: Drawing room. PLAYING TIME: 15 min. PLOT: An eccentric millionaire dies. His greedy sisters feign grief while simultaneously provoking each other at the reading of the will. A final tape recorded message sends the family on a scavenger hunt to gather a hidden cash fortune. The greedy relatives flee the room without hearing the second part of the message which informs anyone who remains in the room that the search is a hoax and the money will be equally divided. RECOMMENDATION: The dialogue is sharp and witty, especially the banter between the two conniving sisters. ROYALTY: NA. SOURCE: Hutson, Natalie Bouvee. (1984). The reading of the will. Stevensville, MI: Educational Service, Inc. SUBJECTS/PLAY TYPE: Inheritance; Greed; Family; Comedy.

2539. 3-6. (+) Eckel, Carol B. **The real miracle: A Christmas pageant.** CAST: 10f, 5m. ACTS: 1. SETTINGS:

Bare stage, props. PLAYING TIME: NA. PLOT: After hearing the Nativity story, the Angry Man cites war, violence, riots, and robbery as justification for discrediting stories of the Christmas miracle. The Tired Woman cannot escape the drudgery of cleaning, cooking, rushing, and shopping to seek the inspiration of the holiday. The Greedy Boy numbers Christmas blessings according to the multitude of gifts he receives. The Sad Woman mourns the loss of innocence, replaced by bright lights, fake Santas, and expensive gifts. The tall candle of a young girl in white symbolically rekindles the spirit of the embittered four as she lights the way for a series of vignettes featuring Christmas cheer. The eager anticipation of two small children for cookies, decorations, and gift giving seems to justify the work and worry of preparation in the Sad Woman's eyes. The mutual appreciation of customs and beliefs between a Jewish and a Christian child inspires the Angry Man. The selfless sacrifice of a Christmas dance by a young boy primed to play Santa for needy children melts the heart of the Greedy Boy. A shift in perspective allows the Sad Woman to view the miracle of Christmas through the eyes of a child and to realize that the magic survives. Love, the true name of the young girl in white, unites the four in harmony and zest for a joyous Christmas season. RECOMMENDATION: The plot is simple and uncontrived. The message is clear and forceful without being overly didactic or maudlin. ROYALTY: $30. SOURCE: Eckel, Carol B. (1977). The real miracle: A Christmas pageant. Franklin, OH: Eldridge Pub. Co. SUBJECTS/PLAY TYPE Christmas; Playlet.

2540. K-3. (+) Gotwalt, Helen Louise Miller. (Andersen, Hans Christian) **The real princess.** (The real princess) CAST: 8f, 8m, 2u. ACTS: 1. SETTINGS: Room in palace. PLAYING TIME: 15 min. PLOT: This adaptation embellishes the original by submitting several princesses, not just one, to the test of being a real princess. RECOMMENDATION: Simple dialogue and plot repetition make this workable for young, inexperienced actors. Knowledge of the original will be helpful. ROYALTY: Free to Plays subscribers. SOURCE: Gotwalt, Helen Louise Miller. (1985). First plays for children: A collection of little plays for the youngest players. Boston, MA: Plays, Inc. SUBJECTS/PLAY TYPE: Folk Tales, Germany; Adaptation.

2541. 12. (+) Stoppard, Tom. **The real thing.** CAST: 3f, 4m. ACTS: 2. SETTINGS: Two living rooms. PLAYING TIME: NA. PLOT: The story centers around the lives of two men and two women as their relationships with each other form, come apart, and reform. Charlotte's infidelity to Max is exposed in the opening scene. As the play progresses, Charlotte and Henry are seen to be living together, until Annie (Max's significant other) and Henry decide they prefer each other. The threads of Annie's concern for a young soldier named Brodie (imprisoned for his part in an anti-missile demonstration), run throughout the play and culminate in an affair that she has with him. During the final scenes, it is shown that Annie and Henry's relationship has survived. Henry's character, which initially appeared superficial, has become strong and well defined. He and Annie try to come to grips with the reason she had an affair, despite her love for him.

RECOMMENDATION: This is only for mature audiences who could understand the conflicts, weaknesses, and strengths of the different characters, as well as the situational ethics in the final resolution. ROYALTY: NA. SOURCE: Stoppard, Tom. The real thing. London, England: Faber and Faber, 1984. SUBJECTS/PLAY TYPE: Infidelity; Marriage; Drama.

2542. K-3. (+) Strouse, Doug. **The real untold story.** CAST: 4f, 3m, 7u. ACTS: 1. SETTINGS: Bedroom. PLAYING TIME: NA. PLOT: A narrator and an angel bring the story of Mary, Joseph, and baby Jesus into the bedroom of 5 year old Samantha. She realizes that Christmas is not just receiving gifts, but giving them, just as the wise men gave gifts to the baby Jesus. At the end, children are invited to come forward with gifts that have been special for them in the past to share with less fortunate children. RECOMMENDATION: This maintains the dignity of the Christmas story, but is light hearted and interspersed with humor. ROYALTY: With the purchase of at least ten copies of the play, one amateur performance is allowed; license for additional performances will be issued for $10. SOURCE: Strouse, Doug. (1985). The real untold story. Boston, MA: Baker's Plays. SUBJECTS/PLAY TYPE: Christmas; Playlet.

2543. K-3. (+) Martin, Judith & Ashwander, Donald. **Reasons to be cheerful.** CAST: 2u. ACTS: 1. SETTINGS: Bare stage, props. PLAYING TIME: 10 min. PLOT: Cheerful Brenda arrives with her brightly painted cardboard house. Gloomy Irving arrives with his drably painted grey cardboard house. The two exchange ideas about all there is to be cheerful/gloomy about, but neither is able to convince the other. RECOMMENDATION: The actors involve the audience by asking them questions and having them sing along. This could be used with young children to explore feelings. ROYALTY: NA. SOURCE: Martin, Judith & Ashwander, Donald. (1985). Reasons to be cheerful: A revue for children. New York, NY: The Paper Bag Players, Inc. SUBJECTS/PLAY TYPE: Feelings; Skit; Musical Revue.

2544. 4-6. (+) Van Loon, Michelle. **A recall to Oz.** CAST: 5f, 5m, Su. ACTS: 1. SETTINGS: Porch; outdoor; Emerald City. PLAYING TIME: 45 min. PLOT: Elderly Dorothy is recalled from her Kansas farmhouse to Emerald City by Scarecrow, Tinman, and Lion. All of Oz has been terrorized by the wickedness of Icky-Crummy, a witch in training. Joining forces once again, the trio confront the witch. The witch discovers she is envious of the loyalty and love Dorothy and her friends have for each other. Dorothy offers her friendship, and the wickedness of the witch is replaced by kindness. RECOMMENDATION: Fast moving action carries the story along, and the language is easily understood. ROYALTY: $30. SOURCE: Van Loon, Michelle. (1984). A recall to Oz. Franklin, OH: Eldridge Pub. Co. SUBJECTS/PLAY TYPE: Oz; Fantasy; Friendship; Drama.

2545. 7-12. (-) Hark, Mildred & McQueen, Noel. **Recapturing the pioneer spirit.** CAST: 4f, 4m. ACTS: 1. SETTINGS: Living room; dining room. PLAYING TIME: 30 min. PLOT: A crotchety old man's negative opinions about today's youth are changed by young college students during a Thanksgiving Day celebration. RECOMMENDATION: Although the play encourages a healthy attitude towards young people and reinforces the meaning of Thanksgiving, the old man and the college students are stereotyped. This is too black and white to be of value; the ethics of work and responsibility deserve better exposition. ROYALTY: Free to Plays subscribers. SOURCE: Hark, Mildred & McQueen, Noel. (1987, November). Recapturing the pioneer spirit. Plays: The Drama Magazine for Young People, pp. 12-22. SUBJECTS/PLAY TYPE: Thanksgiving; Playlet.

2546. 7-12. (+) Gotwalt, Helen Louise Miller. **Red carpet Christmas.** CAST: 7f, 5m. ACTS: 1. SETTINGS: Living room. PLAYING TIME: 35 min. PLOT: Mrs. Hitchcock and her old friend, Maggie Briggs, have been fighting ever since Maggie's invitation to Mrs. Hitchcock's engagement party was not received because it got lost under a rug. The feud is not resolved until years later, when the lost invitation is found under the rug during a remodeling project. RECOMMENDATION: This is light and humorous, but the attempt to provide a surprise ending makes the plot a bit convoluted. ROYALTY: Free to Plays subscribers. SOURCE: Gotwalt, Helen Louise Miller. (1988, December). Red carpet Christmas. Plays: The Drama Magazine for Young People, pp. 20-30. SUBJECTS/PLAY TYPE: Christmas; Comedy.

2547. 6-12. (+) Gotwalt, Helen Louise Miller. **The red flannel suit.** CAST: 6f, 6m. ACTS: 1. SETTINGS: Bare stage, backdrop. PLAYING TIME: 20 min. PLOT: With their moving truck stuck in a snowbank somewhere down the mountain, the Patterson family faces the prospect of an uneventful Christmas in their new home. Spirits are lifted, however, when a rescued box brought up by the movers turns out to contain Christmas paraphernalia, including an old red flannel suit and Santa mask. Putting on different parts of the suit to keep warm, the family soon cheers up. An inquiry about the suit by several town members finds the Pattersons not only lending the suit to replace one burned in the Town Hall fire the night before, but opening up their home for the town's Christmas Eve party. RECOMMENDATION: This is a realistic and timely reminder of the true meaning of Christmas spirit. ROYALTY: Free to Plays subscribers. SOURCE: Gotwalt, Helen Louise Miller. (1986, December). The red flannel suit. Plays: The Drama Magazine for Young People, pp. 1-11. SUBJECTS/PLAY TYPE: Christmas; Playlet.

2548. 7-12. (+) Thum, Nancy B. (Doyle, Sir Arthur Conan) **The red headed league.** (Red Headed League.) CAST: 7m. ACTS: 3. SETTINGS: Study. PLAYING TIME: 25 min. PLOT: Duncan Ross asks Sherlock Holmes to find out why the Red Headed League, to which he belongs, has mysteriously disappeared from the building it once occupied. Holmes deduces that the organization was phony so that Duncan Ross would be out of his shop while an employee dug a tunnel from Ross' shop to the bank next door where a shipment of gold was expected. The employee turns out to be the master criminal Holmes has been trying to find for a long time. Holmes captures the man when he comes up from his tunnel into the bank.

RECOMMENDATION: This is true to the original, complete with Holmes' amazing abilities to deduce the truth. ROYALTY: Free to Plays subscribers. SOURCE: Thum, Nancy B. (1987, November). The red headed league. Plays: The Drama Magazine for Young People, pp. 56-63. SUBJECTS/PLAY TYPE: Mystery; Bank Robbery; Adaptation.

2549. 3-8. (+) Caruth, Grace. (Perrault, Charles) **Red Riding Hood and the vegetarian.** (Little Red Riding Hood.) CAST: 4f, 4m. ACTS: 1. SETTINGS: Forest. PLAYING TIME: 20 min. PLOT: Mother and Father Wolf are desperate for their vegetarian son, Harry, to be carnivorous. They send him to the forest to take Red Riding Hood's meat pies. He disguises himself as Granny (who's vacationing in Florida); Red catches on and calls the woodsman. Just in time, Granny returns home, and Harry goes back to his parents who finally realize that they love him because he is good and kind. RECOMMENDATION: This very clever takeoff could be used to teach about identity, but would be much more effective as pure entertainment. ROYALTY: Free to Plays subscribers. SOURCE: Caruth, Grace. (1989, March). Red Riding Hood and the vegetarian. Plays: The Drama Magazine for Young People, pp. 31-35. SUBJECTS/PLAY TYPE: Self Concept; Adaptation.

2550. 5-7. (+) Boiko, Claire. **Reel life, inc.** CAST: 3f, 5m, 2u. ACTS: 1. SETTINGS: Living room. PLAYING TIME: 20 min. PLOT: A young girl, bored with her life, dreams that she wins a sweepstakes whose prize makes her the star of an adventure movie. Mixing real life with reel life frightens her, and she awakens with a new desire to enjoy her family and friends in the real world. RECOMMENDATION: While the dream sequence is pure fantasy, the characters and their actions are clever manipulations of reality (i.e., the villain is going to sabotage the post office by folding, spindling, and mutilating first class mail and peppering the backs of postage stamps). ROYALTY: Free to Plays subscribers. SOURCE: Boiko, Claire. (1975, January). Reel life, inc. Plays: The Drama Magazine for Young People, pp. 45-51. SUBJECTS/PLAY TYPE: Reality; Comedy.

2551. K-3. (+) Livingston, Myra Cohn. **Reflection.** CAST: 1u. ACTS: 1. SETTINGS: None. PLAYING TIME: NA. PLOT: This poem tells youngsters that they are the most important thing in the mirror. RECOMMENDATION: Even the youngest will be able to recite this, though slightly older students may enjoy the challenge of its bilingual pair, "you-tu," selected by Bauer. ROYALTY: NA. SOURCE: Bauer, Caroline Feller. (1987). Presenting reader's theater: Plays and poems to read aloud. New York, NY: H.W. Wilson. SUBJECTS/PLAY TYPE: Mirrors; Reader's Theater.

2552. 7-9. (+) Boiko, Claire. (Dickens, Charles) **The reform of Benjamin Scrimp.** (A Christmas Carol.) CAST: 4f, 5m, Su. ACTS: 1. SETTINGS: Gymnasium. PLAYING TIME: 40 min. PLOT: Ben Scrimp is a junior high school student who is also a thousandaire with blue chip stocks. The Christmas dance at the Jr. High School is to be called off because they can't pay for the decorations. Because Ben

Scrimp won't help out, he is visited by the Christmas Past (a character with a zoot suit on with boogie-woogie music playing), the Christmas Present (a character in rock star clothing), and Christmas Future (a character in an astronaut suit). In the end, Ben helps out. RECOMMENDATION: This very clever update of the classic Christmas tale uses modern slang and adolescent problems to make its point. ROYALTY: Free to Plays subscribers. SOURCE: Boiko, Claire. (1988, December). The reform of Benjamin Scrimp. Plays: The Drama Magazine for Young People, pp. 11-19. SUBJECTS/PLAY TYPE: Christmas; Adaptation.

2553. 6-8. (+) Cable, Harold. **The reform of Sterling Silverheart.** CAST: 5f, 5m. ACTS: 1. SETTINGS: Kitchen; soda shop. PLAYING TIME: 35 min. PLOT: Jasmine, "white sheep" of the Ghoul family, is in love with Sterling Silverheart, a do-gooder. Her family wishes she would break it off. Dupe Darkly and Fraud Willie plot to foreclose on the Ghoul family, a mortgage the villains do not actually own, to get the treasure which is buried on the property. Silverheart finds the treasure, turns greedy, gains the favor of Mama Ghoul, and marries Jasmine. RECOMMENDATION: This must be played and understood as satire to be successful. ROYALTY: Free to Plays subscribers. SOURCE: Cable, Harold. (1983, October). The reform of Sterling Silverheart. Plays: The Drama Magazine for Young People, pp. 23-32. SUBJECTS/PLAY TYPE: Ghouls; Comedy.

2554. 10-12. (+) Valency, Maurice Jacques. (Euripedes) **Regarding Electra.** (Electra.) CAST: 8f, 3m, 2u. ACTS: 1. SETTINGS: Courtyard of Agamemnon's palace. PLAYING TIME: NA. PLOT: In this contemporary interpretation of the Greek myth, the possible motives and forces behind the killing of Electra's mother, Clytemnestra, and her stepfather, Aegisthus, by her brother, Orestes, are explored. RECOMMENDATION: Contemporary settings and extra characters may help some audiences understand the timelessness of the myth. This requires considerable acting skills. ROYALTY: NA. SOURCE: Valency, Maurice Jacques. (1976). Regarding Electra. New York, NY: Dramatists Play Service, Inc. SUBJECTS/PLAY TYPE: Greek Tragedy; Mythology, Greek; Psychology; Adaptation.

2555. 9-12. (+) Meyer, David. **Register here.** CAST: 9f, 11m. ACTS: 2. SETTINGS: Hotel lobby; closets; storm. PLAYING TIME: NA. PLOT: Mother Moss and her deaf and mute butler, Rhett, welcome several disparate, storm-stranded people to Moss Manor: a gangster and his retinue; a mortician and his family; two country policemen; a doctor and his nurse; two affectatious, slightly tipsy, older ladies; young Peter Moss (recently returned from military service); and Peter's fiancee, Terri Cloth. Terri's uncle, Washington Cloth, violently disapproves of the romance, follows Terri to the inn, and is murdered. During the night, almost all of the characters, in turn, discover and attempt to conceal the body. When the body is officially found, almost all the characters have a motive and are suspects. In reconstructing the crime, the Doctor is poisoned and declared dead, identified as the murderer of Washington Cloth, and, in keeping with the farcical nature of the play, is later discovered to be alive. RECOMMENDATION: The laughs will continue through the slapstick attempts to conceal and recover the corpse. ROYALTY: $35. SOURCE: Meyer, David. (1986). Register here. Franklin, OH: Eldridge Pub. Co. SUBJECTS/PLAY TYPE: Murder; Mystery; Comedy.

2556. 9-12. (+) Sawyer-Young, Kat. **Registration.** CAST: 2m. ACTS: 1. SETTINGS: School registration line. PLAYING TIME: NA. PLOT: Brad, new boy in town, finds a friend in Scott as they wait in line to register for school. Scott offers to teach Brad how to surf in exchange for Brad's instructing him on the electric guitar. Their friendship is sealed when they learn they live within blocks of each other. RECOMMENDATION: This excellently demonstrates how easily friendships can be formed once common interests are discovered. It would be particularly useful in groups where there are newcomers. ROYALTY: NA. SOURCE: Sawyer-Young, Kat. (1986). Contemporary scenes for contemporary kids. Boston, MA: Baker's Plays. SUBJECTS/PLAY TYPE: Friendship; Scene.

2557. 7-12. (+) Sawyer-Young, Kat. **Rehearsal.** CAST: 1m. ACTS: 1. SETTINGS: None. PLAYING TIME: 1 min. PLOT: Jack manipulates Cheri into paying attention to him by pretending to be depressed. RECOMMENDATION: This should be discussed in terms of the basis for a true relationship. ROYALTY: None. SOURCE: Sawyer-Young, Kat. (1987). Minute monologues for contemporary teens. Boston, MA: Baker's Plays. SUBJECTS/PLAY TYPE: Manipulation; Relationships; Monologue.

2558. 11-12. (+) Brooke, D.D. (Levinson, Richard & Link, William) **Rehearsal for murder.** (Rehearsal for murder?) CAST: 6f, 9m. ACTS: 2. SETTINGS: Broadway theater stage; apartment. PLAYING TIME: NA. PLOT: Did actress Monica Wells commit suicide or was it really murder? The facts surrounding Monica's demise, along with the suspects, are revealed through flashbacks and a "play within a play" technique. The audience joins Alex Dennison, Monica's fiance, in his quest to find the truth. RECOMMENDATION: This Agatha Christie style mystery is a treat for anyone who enjoys being an armchair detective. ROYALTY: $50. SOURCE: Brooke, D.D. (1983). Rehearsal for murder. Woodstock, IL: Dramatic Pub. Co. SUBJECTS/PLAY TYPE: Mystery; Actors/Actresses; Theater; Adaptation.

2559. 7-12. (+) Hank, Mildred & McQueen, Noel. **Reindeer on the roof. CAST:** 5f, 5m. **ACTS:** 1. SETTINGS: Living room. PLAYING TIME: 30 min. PLOT: Neighbors are in turmoil when they compete for the prize of best decorated house on the block. RECOMMENDATION: This fast paced play teaches the true meaning of Christmas in a most enjoyable way. ROYALTY: None. SOURCE: Kamerman, Sylvia E. (1978). On stage for Christmas: A collection of royalty-free, one act Christmas plays for young people. Boston, MA: Plays, Inc. SUBJECTS/PLAY TYPE: Family; Christmas; Playlet.

2560. 7-12. (-) Cable, Harold. (Cable, Howard) **The reluctant Columbus. CAST:** 3f, 5m, 4u. **ACTS:** 1.

SETTINGS: Palace room; cafe; street. PLAYING TIME: 25 min. PLOT: This fractured history concerns a cartographer (named Christopher) with a radical theory, and a prince (named Columbus) with a guilt complex, who wants to relinquish his throne. Their fiancees try to build the mens' self confidence and encourage them to begin the age of exploration. But by the time they are prodded into action, it is 1493. They sail off in blissful ignorance to claim the new world for their little kingdom. RECOMMENDATION: This is full of wacky, exaggerated characters, and its success will depend on the players' ability to create them. The script could benefit from the insertion of topical material and more modern slang. ROYALTY: Free to Plays subscribers. SOURCE: Cable, Howard. (1982, October). The reluctant Columbus. Plays: The Drama Magazine for Young People, pp. 25-30. SUBJECTS/PLAY TYPE: Columbus Day; Exploration; Comedy.

2561. 5-7. (+) Thane, Adele. (Grahame, Kenneth) **The reluctant dragon.** (The reluctant dragon) CAST: 1f, 3m, 10u. ACTS: 1. SETTINGS: Hillside. PLAYING TIME: 30 min. PLOT: Edward and his sister, Selina, discover a cave inhabited by a dragon named Horace, who suffers from hay fever, writes poetry, and has no interest at all in eating children or chasing knights. Nevertheless, the townspeople send St. George to fight the dragon, who refuses to engage in any more than a mock battle. Claiming the dragon is now converted, St. George convinces the people to accept him. RECOMMENDATION: An amusing play, this features adults asking children for advice as well as a very comical battle between St. George and Horace. A stereotypical female caregiver and several British phrases may need to be altered. ROYALTY: None. SOURCE: Thane, Adele. (1983). Plays from famous stories and fairy tales. Boston, MA: Plays, Inc. SUBJECTS/PLAY TYPE: Dragons; Adaptation.

2562. 3-6. (+) Oser, Janice Auritt. **The reluctant new year.** CAST: 2f, 3m, 5u. ACTS: 1. SETTINGS: Living room. PLAYING TIME: 15 min. PLOT: The New Year baby is afraid to bring in the New Year because of all the broken resolutions from the Old Year. Father Time shows the children their banged, bruised, and battered broken resolutions. They promise to keep their resolutions for this year. The New Year baby decides to bring in the New Year. RECOMMENDATION: The plot, characters, and their dialogue seem realistic within the fantasy. ROYALTY: Free to Plays Subscribers. SOURCE: Oser, Janice Auritt. (1980, January). The reluctant New Year. Plays: The Drama Magazine for Young People, pp. 45-47. SUBJECTS/PLAY TYPE: New Year; Comedy.

2563. 10-12. (+) Smith, Evan. **Remedial English.** CAST: 1f, 5m. ACTS: 1. SETTINGS: Classroom, living room. PLAYING TIME: NA. PLOT: Vincent is an exceptionally bright student whose grades do not reflect his capacity. Sister Beatrice assigns Vincent to tutor another student to help Vincent improve his own grades and show him how difficult it is to teach indifferent students. Vincent chooses to tutor Rob because he is physically attracted to Rob. During the first study session,

Vincent brings up the topic of homosexuality and learns that Rob considers it disgusting. Vincent reconsiders his attraction for Rob, but still agrees to tutor him. The play ends with Vincent reading a poem on the fickleness of love. RECOMMENDATION: The theme of a homosexual young man who struggles with his feelings is treated realistically and with interesting devices. Stop action allows Vincent to reveal his thoughts to the audience without revealing himself to the other characters. Although edited, this contains some language that could be offensive. ROYALTY: NA. SOURCE: Lamb, Wendy. (1987). The Ground Zero Club and other prize winning plays. New York, NY: Dell Pub. SUBJECTS/PLAY TYPE Homosexuality; Drama.

2564. 7-12. (+) Roseberry, Sherry. **A rented Christmas family.** CAST: 9f, 3m, Su. ACTS: 1. SETTINGS: Office; town square; living room. PLAYING TIME: 30 min. PLOT: As Christmas approaches, Mr. Madson, Robert's boss, wants to sign their new contract at Robert's house so that he can meet Robert's family. Having lied about having a family, Robert searches to rent a family through advertisements. Several ladies are interviewed, but with no success. As Robert is about to give up, Mary, her brother, and sister, who have recently lost their parents, show up at Robert's door selling fruit. Mary doesn't want to stay, but is talked into it for the sake of the other children. When Mr. Madson arrives with the contract, Robert cannot go through with the fraud. He tells the truth and offers to leave his job, but Mr. Madson confesses he knew all along that Robert didn't have a family and was only testing to see if Robert could come up with a solution. Robert is pleased by the way Mary and the children have stood by him and invites them back for Christmas dinner. RECOMMENDATION: Robert's predicament is amusing, despite the sugar coated ending. Mary and Robert must be played by people who can sing solos. ROYALTY: $30. SOURCE: Roseberry, Sherry. (1986). A rented Christmas family. Franklin, OH: Eldridge Pub. Co. SUBJECTS/PLAY TYPE: Christmas; Musical.

2565. 4-8. (+) Bradley, Virginia. **Repeat after me.** CAST: 4f, 5u. ACTS: 1. SETTINGS: Street. PLAYING TIME: NA. PLOT: A message gets more and more garbled as it is relayed among four bridge players. RECOMMENDATION: This would be good as part of a variety show; it is short and clever. ROYALTY: None. SOURCE: Bradley, Virginia. (175). Is there an actor in the house? New York, NY: Dodd, Mead. SUBJECTS/PLAY TYPE: Communication; Comedy; Skit.

2566. 12. (-) McDonough, Jerome. **Requiem.** CAST: 3f, 3m, 8u. ACTS: 1. SETTINGS: None. PLAYING TIME: 35 min. PLOT: This is a grim statement about war and the physical, mental, and emotional devastation it wreaks. The main characters, a widowed mother and her children, journey from sorrow (when the older children receive conscription notices) to despair. As death and military figures mime their roles in the human catastrophe in the background, the entire family rejects a life of endless war and chooses suicide. RECOMMENDATION: The play is overwrought and at times nearly hysterical. The audience is bludgeoned with the message rather than convinced and, unfortunately, this would more likely alienate audiences than to educate them. ROYALTY: $20. SOURCE: McDonough, Jerome. (1977). Requiem. Schulenburg, TX: I.E. Clark. SUBJECTS/PLAY TYPE: War; Military; Pacifism; Drama.

2567. 7-12. (+) Andrews, Betty. **Requiem for the innkeeper.** CAST: 6f, 7m, Su. ACTS: 1. SETTINGS: Outside the inn. PLAYING TIME: 35 min. PLOT: The innkeeper who told Joseph and Mary there was no room for them recounts the events of the night. RECOMMENDATION: Teenagers, having listened to the Christmas story yearly during childhood, often are bored with it in their teen years. This gives a unique slant which should revive interest. ROYALTY: $15. SOURCE: Andrews, Betty. (1979). Requiem for the innkeeper. Chicago, IL: Dramatic Pub. Co. SUBJECTS/PLAY TYPE: Christmas; Drama.

2568. 1-5. (+) Fisher, Aileen Lucia. **The rescuers.** CAST: 1f, 1m, 1u. ACTS: 1. SETTINGS: Outdoors. PLAYING TIME: 15 min. PLOT: As Mother Nature and Father Time lament that people are slowly wasting and spoiling the beautiful world, they are passed by children picking up trash to recycle, conserve, and reuse. Mother Nature and Father Time exit, reassured that people will lend a hand to clean up the land. RECOMMENDATION: In this simple approach with a straightforward ecological message, children will like the rhyming and can perhaps even memorize the lines. ROYALTY: Free to Plays subscribers. SOURCE: Fisher, Aileen Lucia. (1985). The rescuers. Year-round programs for young players. Boston, MA: Plays, Inc. SUBJECTS/PLAY TYPE: Ecology; Recycling; Litter; Skit.

2569. 9-12. (+) Cook, Pat. **Rest in peace.** CAST: 3f, 4m. ACTS: 1. SETTINGS: Hospital room. PLAYING TIME: NA. PLOT: A man dies in the hospital but is able to see his wife's, mother-in-law's, and nurse's reactions. He meets another man who has died, and the after life representative who assigns him his spiritual role for eternity. After some humorous speculations about the desirability of being a ghost, the man awakes to discover it was all a dream. However, his personality has mellowed and the other man has been assigned as his guardian angel. RECOMMENDATION: This is a short, light hearted presentation which would be equally enjoyed by high schoolers and adults. ROYALTY: $15. SOURCE: Cook, Pat. (1976). Rest in peace. Woodstock IL: Dramatic Pub. Co. SUBJECTS/PLAY TYPE Death; Comedy.

2570. 8-12. (+) Sodaro, Craig. **Rest stop.** CAST: 3f, 2m. ACTS: 1. SETTINGS: Roadside rest stop. PLAYING TIME: NA. PLOT: Ben Gerard does not understand his 16 year old daughter Christi, who desperately tries to both win his love and declare her independence from him. Mini, the wife and mother, tries to narrow the widening gap between father and daughter but open warfare erupts between the two when the family stops for lunch at a rest area. Just when it appears that the emotional blows will escalate into physical violence, a woman (Violet) wanders onto the scene. The father and daughter calm down briefly but then resume their attacks on each other, oblivious to the stranger. Violet takes the daughter's side and when Christi rushes to the restroom in tears, she follows her. She emerges with Christi and a gun, claiming that the girl is her long lost daughter, kidnapped 15 years before. As the family becomes aware of the extent of the woman's delusion and their own danger, they realize how much they care for each other. Eventually, Violet is disarmed and she rushes off. Violet's father appears and describes the kidnapping of his grandchild which unhinged Violet's mind. The family leaves with a stronger sense of their love and need for one another. RECOMMENDATION: Sharp dialogue creates emotional suspense that builds to a shocking ending. ROYALTY: $20. SOURCE: Sodaro, Craig. (1986). Rest stop. Woodstock, IL: Dramatic Pub. Co. SUBJECTS/PLAY TYPE: Family Relationships; Drama.

2571. 4-6. (-) Gotwalt, Helen Louise Miller. **The return of Bobby Shafto.** CAST: 4f, 5m. ACTS: 1. SETTINGS: Wharf. PLAYING TIME: NA. PLOT: Bobby Shafto returns from the sea to marry the girl he loves. However, there are four girls expecting to marry him and three are daughters of the mayor. The confusion is resolved when the mayor's daughters realize that Bobby only promised them fortune (which he delivers in bags of gold), not marriage. RECOMMENDATION: This would be excellent for any audience familiar with the original nursery rhyme. By reversing the roles, it could be made less sexist. ROYALTY: Free to Plays subscribers. SOURCE: Gotwalt, Helen Louise Miller. SUBJECTS/PLAY TYPE: Marriage; Fortune; Playlet.

2572. 7-12. (+) Priore, Frank V. **The return of Rip Van Winkle, Jr.** CAST: 1f, 5m, Su. ACTS: 2. SETTINGS: Living room. PLAYING TIME: 20 min. PLOT: Rip Van Winkle's son returns after sleeping for 200 years. He is beset by problems with the IRS and a banker. A lawyer saves the day by invoking the statute of limitations. RECOMMENDATION: The characters are colorful and the dialogue clever. ROYALTY: Free to Plays subscribers. SOURCE: Priore, Frank V. (1983, March). The return of Rip Van Winkle, Jr. Plays: The Drama Magazine for Young People, pp. 59-66. SUBJECTS/PLAY TYPE: Van Winkle, Rip; Comedy; Skit.

2573. 7-10. (+) Kurtz, Jack. **The return of the unicorn.** CAST: 6f, 2m, 20u. ACTS: 1. SETTINGS: Bare stage, props. PLAYING TIME: NA. PLOT: A youngster who has seen a unicorn tries to get older people to believe her, including representatives from education, business, the military, media, church, welfare, social protestors, and young lovers. As they all distort what she describes to reflect their own fears and prejudices, this satire symbolizes the concept of faith and belief in God. RECOMMENDATION: Using humor, pointed characterizations, and sharp dialogue, this satire succeeds in getting across its message of man's intransigence toward God. ROYALTY: NA. SOURCE: Kurtz, Jack. (1978). Without bathrobes: Alternatives in drama for youth: Three one-act chancel comedies. New York, NY: Baker's Plays. SUBJECTS/PLAY TYPE: Christian Drama; Satire.

2574. 9-12. (+) Sawyer-Young, Kat. **Reunion.** CAST: 2f. ACTS: 1. SETTINGS: School cafeteria. PLAYING TIME: NA. PLOT: Two girls, who haven't seen each other since elementary school, briefly chat at lunch about former students and current dating woes. As the bell rings, they plan to continue this discussion in their next shared period, Spanish. RECOMMENDATION: This would be excellent for a group that contains newcomers. ROYALTY: NA. SOURCE: Sawyer-Young, Kat. (1986). Contemporary scenes for contemporary kids. Boston, MA: Baker's Plays. SUBJECTS/PLAY TYPE: Friendship; Scene.

2575. 7-12. (+) Dias, Earl J. **Reunion at Muddy Gulch.** CAST: 4f, 5m, 8u. ACTS: 1. SETTINGS: Hotel lobby. PLAYING TIME: 25 min. PLOT: The editor of the local newspaper, the sheriff, and the banker create a sentimental reunion for the town crook and his mother before the crook leaves for prison. They hope this will capture the hearts of the townspeople, motivate them to buy more newspapers, and put more money in the bank. However, there is a twist in the plot when the mother arrives as a red haired, hard con artist. She fakes a tearful reunion with her son, but trips and falls down the hotel stairs. She spills the money that she and her son have stolen from the hotel keeper, much to the hotel keeper's dismay. The town officials let the mother go free, for fear of tarnishing the otherwise perfect reunion. RECOMMENDATION: This is a clever portrayal of classic character types: villain, forlorn mother, skeptical female, gullible sheriff, greedy banker and naive, young school teacher. ROYALTY: NA. SOURCE: Dias, Earl J. (1981, April). Reunion at Muddy Gulch. Plays: The Drama Magazine for Young People, pp. 11-20. SUBJECTS/PLAY TYPE: Greed; Family; Comedy.

2576. 6-8. (+) Kehret, Peg. **Reunited twins.** CAST: 1m. ACTS: 1. SETTINGS: None. PLAYING TIME: NA. PLOT: A young man waits apprehensively for his long lost twin brother to disembark from a plane. He realizes that they both have the same fears and concerns about meeting. RECOMMENDATION: This outlines the basic questions faced by reunited natural siblings after years of separation. The topic of adoption is handled nonjudgmentally. ROYALTY: NA. SOURCE: Kehret, Peg. (1986). Winning monologs for young actors. Colorado Springs, CO: Meriwether Pub. SUBJECTS/PLAY TYPE: Adoption; Reunions; Monologue.

2577. 7-12*. (+) Mamet, David. **The revenge of the space pandas or Binky Rudich and the two-speed clock.** CAST: 2f, 4m, Su. ACTS: 1. SETTINGS: Room; laboratory; alien planet outpost. PLAYING TIME: 60 min. PLOT: Binky, Vivian, and Bob, who is a sheep, experiment with a two speed clock and find themselves on Crestview, another planet. The resident pandas are all very interested in their earthling visitors. Most intrigued of all is the ruler, George Topax, who has desired a football sweater for eons and who therefore is eager to get his hand on a sheep. When they realize the egotistical and sheep-fixated Topax is up to no good, the three friends try to escape. Binky is captured and threatened with death by pumpkin clobbering, but at the last minute a derelict movie star saves the trio and they are back home in time for lunch. RECOMMENDATION: This has quick wit, double edged humor, dead pan repartee, and burlesque sci-fi characters. Props will be a challenge to make with such items as a planetary setting, a pumpkin guillotine, and sheep and panda costumes. **ROYALTY: $50. SOURCE:** Mamet, David. (1978). The revenge of the space pandas or Binky Rudich and the two-speed clock. Woodstock, IL: Dramatic Pub. Co. **SUBJECTS/PLAY TYPE** Science Fiction; Comedy.

2578. 8-12. (+) Murch, Edward. **The revival: An improbable history in one act with a postscript. CAST:** 2f, 1m. **ACTS:** 1. **SETTINGS:** Garden. **PLAYING TIME:** NA. **PLOT:** A gentleman, hinted to be William Shakespeare, balances his budget and chats with his wife. The maid, Mary, enters with a letter from a Company of Players from Warwick, who request that the Gentleman play the role of "ghost" in the **Tragical Historie of Hamlet**; they have lost their original player to the Plague. The Gentleman is sympathetic, but he thinks that they just want his money and refuses. With some persuasion from the maid and his wife, he agrees, but hopes that he will be remembered as a gentleman and not as an actor. **RECOMMENDATION:** With its delightful allusions to Shakespeare, and with modern dialogue, the plot develops naturally into a day in the life of this great author. **ROYALTY: $15. SOURCE:** Murch, Edward. (1982). The revival: An improbable history in one act with a postscript. Devonshire, England: Yennadon Plays. **SUBJECTS/PLAY TYPE:** Shakespeare, William; Theater; Acting; Playlet.

2579. 1-4. (-) Saul, Oscar & Lantz, Louis. **The revolt of the beavers. CAST:** 1f, 6m, 20u. **ACTS:** 2. **SETTINGS:** Meadow; woods. **PLAYING TIME:** NA. **PLOT:** Enroute home from school, Mary tries to convince Paul that animals can talk. The children sit down to rest, fall asleep, and are transported to Beaverland by Mr. Wind. They meet a talking beaver on roller skates, who tells them about the takeover of Beaverland by the Chief and his motley crew. The beaver, aided by Paul and Mary, restores Beaverland to the good beavers by tricking the Chief and his followers. The wind returns the children home. **RECOMMENDATION:** Although this relates ideas from a nine year old's point of view, the use of Zippo guns, bean shooters, and cannons as violent solutions to the beavers' problems is inappropriate. This is too long, too boring, and too violent. **ROYALTY: NA. SOURCE:** Swortzell, Lowell. (1986). Six plays for young people from the Federal Theatre Project (1936-1939). New York, NY: Greenwood Press. **SUBJECTS/PLAY TYPE:** Values; Friendship; Drama.

2580. 9-12. (+) Swajeski, Donna Marie. **The revolution machine. CAST:** 2f, 5m. **ACTS:** 1. **SETTINGS:** Bare stage. **PLAYING TIME:** NA. **PLOT:** Using music, improvisation, and quotations from his actual writings, this portrays the life and work of John Dickenson, best known as the man who didn't sign the Declaration of Independence. The seeming contradiction between Dickenson's refusal to sign while also being responsible for our basic political philosophy is explained through his words and actions. **RECOMMENDATION:** This is a highly recommended

piece for experienced actors. Actors must change roles quickly in the method of improvisational theater. **ROYALTY: $35. SOURCE:** Swajeski, Donna Marie. (1978). The revolution machine. New York, NY: Coalition of Publishers for Employment. **SUBJECTS/PLAY TYPE:** Revolution, U.S.; Dickenson, John; Drama.

2581. K-3*. (+) Lahr, Georgiana Leider. **Reward for a leprechaun. CAST:** 5f, 12m, 8u. **ACTS:** 1. **SETTINGS:** Forest. **PLAYING TIME:** 15 min. **PLOT:** Gwen and Patrick capture a leprechaun and demand three wishes. The leprechaun says he must go home for his magic wish cards, but the children say no and keep him captive. They post their demands (wishes) on the barn door, where they've hidden the leprechaun, Timothy. The entire leprechaun council convenes to work on the problem, but before the council can complete the task there is a change of heart. The two children bring Timothy back, and ask for forgiveness. **RECOMMENDATION:** This play can utilize very young as well as older children within the cast, but should use intermediate students as the primary actors. **ROYALTY:** Free to Plays subscribers. **SOURCE:** Lahr, Georgiana Leider. (1979, March). Reward for a leprechaun. Plays: The Drama Magazine for Young People, pp. 33-37. **SUBJECTS/PLAY TYPE:** St. Patrick's Day; Leprechauns; Fantasy.

2582. 7-12. (+) Brown, Abbie Farwell. **Rhoecus, a masque. CAST:** 2f, 2m, Su. **ACTS:** 1. **SETTINGS:** Woods. **PLAYING TIME:** 45 min. **PLOT:** A woodsman decides that the magnificent, old oak tree in the woods shall provide wood for his hearth. Rhoecus, the suitor of the woodsman's daughter, refuses to allow him to cut the oak, pointing out the tree's beauty and all the fond memories the youth has of the times he spent under it over the years. A dryad dwelling in the giant oak thanks Rhoecus for saving her father, the old oak, and tells him that as she will grant him any wish. The boy falls in love with the dryad and begs her to give up her immortality and marry him. The dryad reluctantly agrees, telling him that she will summon Rhoecus to her through her messenger bee. Rhoecus falls asleep under the tree, and as sunset approaches, the dryad, uncertain about giving up immortality for the burdens of human life, stands over the sleeping Rhoecus. The woodsman returns to cut down the tree, and decides to end the boy's life as well. To save Rhoecus, the dryad sends her bee to sting the woodsman so savagely that he leaves. Although her debt to the boy is paid, she realizes that she loves him and decides to marry him. Meanwhile, Chloe, the woodsman's daughter, finds Rhoecus and asks him to forgive her for supporting her father's wishes to cut the tree down. As the two reconcile, the dryad jealously sends her bee to summon Rhoecus to her, but Rhoecus, not recognizing it, crushes the bee under his foot. The dryad, hurt by Rhoecus' act of forgetfulness and unkindness, returns to live in the old oak. **RECOMMENDATION:** Along with its message about conservation, this also reminds the audience that many promises made in good faith are easily forgotten when people become distracted. Feelings of love (one person for another and for nature's beauty) are keenly felt by the audience. **ROYALTY: NA. SOURCE:** Brown, Abbie Farwell. (1978). The lantern, and other plays for children.

New York, NY: Cora Collection Books. SUBJECTS/PLAY TYPE: Love; Conservation; Allegory; Masque.

2583. 7-12. (+) Williams, Jill. **Rhyme time!** CAST: 2f, 4m, Su. ACTS: 1. SETTINGS: TV studio. PLAYING TIME: 20 min. PLOT: Three actors from the audience are invited to participate as amateur poets in this short, fast paced spoof of a TV game show. The reluctant contestant wins every round through sheer dumb luck, and one over eager contestant gets angry and beats up the obnoxious announcer. RECOMMENDATION: There is little plot but lots of fun, fast talk, and action in this zany spoof. Audience participation is encouraged through the use of cue cards. ROYALTY: Free to Plays subscribers. SOURCE: Williams, Jill. (1979, December). Rhyme time! Plays: The Drama Magazine for Young People, pp. 65-70. SUBJECTS/PLAY TYPE: Game Shows; Comedy; Skit.

2584. 1-6. (+) Hurley, Carol. (La Fontaine, Jean de) **The rich man and the shoemaker.** (The rich man and the shoemaker) CAST: 1f, 4m, 3u. ACTS: 1. SETTINGS: Shop; living room. PLAYING TIME: 15 min. PLOT: A poor but happy shoemaker's life changes when his rich neighbor gives him gold to keep him from singing. Now the shoemaker must spend time protecting his money. Unhappy with the responsibility, the shoemaker returns the money to the rich man. The new king sends the tax collector to collect back taxes from the rich man and evicts him from his estate. Freed from the burden of money and possessions, the rich man can also enjoy living. RECOMMENDATION: The singing role of the shoemaker may intimidate some younger performers, but this highly recommended play could be staged by middle or high school students for lower level grades. The dialogue is rich, witty, and believable. ROYALTY: Free to Plays subscribers. SOURCE: Hurley, Carol. (1985, May). The rich man and the shoemaker. Plays: The Drama Magazine for Young People, pp. 45-50. SUBJECTS/PLAY TYPE: Folk Tales, France; Wealth; Responsibilities; Adaptation.

2585. 7-12. (-) Nydam, Ken. **The rich young ruler.** CAST: 2m. ACTS: 1. SETTINGS: None. PLAYING TIME: NA. PLOT: When Jesus tells a young man that in order to be saved, he must dedicate his life to the Lord, the young man rejects Him. RECOMMENDATION: This is based on Matthew 19:16-22, but does not clearly deliver its message. ROYALTY: NA. SOURCE: Altena, Hans. (1980). The playbook for Christian theater. Grand Rapids, MI: Baker Book House. SUBJECTS/PLAY TYPE: Parable; Salvation; Christian Drama.

2586. 9-12. (+) King, Martha Bennett. **Riddle me ree.** (King John and the Abbot of Canterbury) CAST: 5f, 8m. ACTS: 1. SETTINGS: Sitting room; shade tree. PLAYING TIME: NA. PLOT: King John has allowed his penchant for riddles to deteriorate into a passion for winning at all costs. A sinister astrologer devises riddles that bankrupt the king's loyal retainer, Sir Roger. When the king presents the Abbot of Canterbury with a series of impossible riddles, the Abbot's peasant brother goes before the king to answer. The peasant restores Sir Roger to his position, rescues his brother, and diminishes the astrologer's influence. RECOMMENDATION: High school students familiar with Chaucer may find this to be an ideal method of increasing their awareness of medieval England. There are several songs, but the background music can be taped. ROYALTY: $25. SOURCE: King, Martha Bennett. (1977). Riddle me ree. New Orleans, LA: Anchorage Press, Inc. SUBJECTS/PLAY TYPE: Riddles; Medieval Courts; Drama.

2587. 7-12. (+) Harris, Aurand. **Ride a blue horse.** CAST: 6f, 12m. ACTS: 1. SETTINGS: Bare stage. PLAYING TIME: NA. PLOT: James Whitcomb Riley celebrates his 75th birthday by reviewing adventures which inspired his poetic creativity: an encounter with a gypsy girl who recognized the muse in his soul; the schoolteacher and hostile school children who made fun of Riley's special gifts; an encounter in which he saved a fugitive slave from slave hunters; and his life as an itinerant sign painter that led him to recite his poems with a traveling medicine show. RECOMMENDATION: A competent high school ensemble could perform this. The early life of a major American poet makes this an interesting presentation. ROYALTY: $35. SOURCE: Harris, Aurand. (1986). Ride a blue horse. New Orleans, LA: Anchorage Press, Inc. SUBJECTS/PLAY TYPE: Poets; Riley, James Whitcomb; Drama.

2588. 3-7. (+) Kehret, Peg. **Riding the merry-go-round.** CAST: 1u. ACTS: 1. SETTINGS: None. PLAYING TIME: NA. PLOT: A young boy decides to ride the merry-go-round no matter what his friends think, because he gets more satisfaction from it than from the frightening rides his friends enjoy. RECOMMENDATION: This shows the strength required to stand up to peer pressure, while demonstrating that making one's own decisions is most rewarding. It could be used as material for discussions. ROYALTY: NA. SOURCE: Kehret, Peg. (1986). Winning monologs for young actors. Colorado Springs, CO: Meriwether Pub. SUBJECTS/PLAY TYPE: Carnivals; Peer Pressure; Decisions; Monologue.

2589. 7-12. (+) Wilkes, Vivienne. **A right royal pack of nonsense.** CAST: 5f, 5m, 10u. ACTS: 2. SETTINGS: Court; mine; casino; Castle of Spades. PLAYING TIME: NA. PLOT: Joker asks to marry the Princess. To test Joker's worthiness, the King of Hearts sends him on a year's mission to the kingdoms of Spades, Diamonds and Clubs. The assignment: break the enchantments that prevent the inhabitants from living normal lives. Aided by Patience, the Princess' alter ego, the Joker succeeds. For his help, each of the royal families gives the Joker a seemingly useless gift. Upon his return, the Joker learns that these gifts, when placed into empty spaces of a picture frame, are the keys to the family treasure. The Joker and his Princess are married. RECOMMENDATION: Using popular songs, complicated sets ranging from a crystal mine to a casino complete with black lights, this fantasy focuses on achieving goals through patience and perseverance. The card imagery throughout make this cliche sprinkled play most entertaining. The large cast can be modified with doubling. ROYALTY: NA. SOURCE:

Wilke, Vivenne. (1987). A right royal pack of nonsense. Macclesfield: New Playwrights' Network. SUBJECTS/PLAY TYPE: Adventure; Love; Fantasy.

2590. 1-5*. (+) Carle, Susan. (Kipling, Rudyard) Rikki-Tikki-Tavi. (Rikki-Tikki-Tavi.) CAST: 3f, 4m, 3u. ACTS: 1. SETTINGS: Garden; kitchen. PLAYING TIME: NA. PLOT: A small boy adopts a wild mongoose who, in turn, protects his adopted family and rids the garden of the dreaded king cobras. RECOMMENDATION: If the actors are able to assume the mannerisms of the animals, the audience should enjoy this action-filled play, which is probably familiar to many of them. ROYALTY: $15. SOURCE: Carle, Susan. (1978). Rikki-Tikki-Tavi. Woodstock, IL: Dramatic Pub. Co. SUBJECTS/PLAY TYPE: Animals; Adaptation.

2591. 11-12*. (+) Wilson, Lanford. The Rimers of Eldritch. CAST: 10f, 7m. ACTS: 2. SETTINGS: Courtroom; diner; church; woods; yards; porches. PLAYING TIME: NA. PLOT: The plot focuses on injustice and the broken dreams of the inhabitants of Eldritch, a small midwestern town, abandoned by progress. Characters are developed through vignettes and flashbacks, and are shown in contrast to themselves as different parts of their lives are exposed, with madness, brutality, hopelessness, and unhappiness as the recurring themes. The culmination of all the bottled emotions occurs with the murder of Skelly Mannor, the town loser, when he is blamed for terrorizing two young people as he tried to prevent a boy from raping a girl. RECOMMENDATION: This would be difficult to stage and perform, due to its sophisticated lighting and simultaneous recitations. Parts of the drama are very explicit; there is reference to fornication with animals, attempted rape, and lurid reflections by Skelly on a past conquest. ROYALTY: NA. SOURCE: Wilson, Lanford. (1981). The rimers of Eldritch, and other plays. New York, NY: Hill & Wang. SUBJECTS/PLAY TYPE: Injustice; Murder; Rape; Drama.

2592. 9-12. (-) Caggiano, Philip. (Wagner, Richard) The ring. (Der Ring des Niebelungen) CAST: Su. ACTS: 4. SETTINGS: Bare stage, props. PLAYING TIME: 90 min. PLOT: The stories of Das Rheingold, Die Walkure, Siegfried, and Gotterdamerung are told. A detailed appendix lists which parts of the opera's original music should be played, and when. RECOMMENDATION: Without all of the music, the transitions are choppy, the plot doesn't achieve unity, and this becomes a clumsy and confusing story. This is too difficult for intermediate students to produce; too juvenile for high schoolers to want to produce. Young people would get much more from seeing the original. ROYALTY: NA. SOURCE: Caggiano, Philip. (1982). The Ring: Four plays for children. New York, NY: Avon Books. SUBJECTS/PLAY TYPE: Mythology, Norse; Opera; Adaptation.

2593. 3-8. (+) Thane, Adele. (Irving, Washington) Rip Van Winkle. (Rip Van Winkle) CAST: 5f, 11m, Su. ACTS: 1. SETTINGS: Tavern; forest glade. PLAYING TIME: 30 min. PLOT: A few years before the Revolutionary War, Rip goes into the mountains to hunt. After sharing a few drinks with the mythical Captain Hendrick Hudson, Rip falls asleep. He awakens 20 years later to find his wife dead, his daughter grown, and his country independent. RECOMMENDATION: While some adaptations are rushed so that the whole story is included, the pace of this one is leisurely and allows time for more illuminating interaction between characters. ROYALTY: Free to Plays subscribers. SOURCE: Thane, Adele. (1983, May). Rip Van Winkle. Plays: The Drama Magazine for Young People, pp. 69-76. SUBJECTS/PLAY TYPE: Legends, United States; Sleep; Adaptation.

2594. 10-12. (+) Parnell, Peter. The rise and rise of Daniel Rocket. CAST: 5f, 5m. ACTS: 2. SETTINGS: Classroom; schoolyard; basement; bedroom; hillside; town hall. PLAYING TIME: NA. PLOT: Daniel is a small town, stereotypical intellectual who proves to his classmates and teacher that he can fly. He becomes a national celebrity and local hero. When he returns as an adult to his hometown to claim the love of his childhood sweetheart, he finds she is unwilling to leave her husband and child to fly away with him. In the final scene, Daniel reenacts his first public flight, but is unsuccessful and crashes to his death. RECOMMENDATION: Staging should be minimal to create the proper mood and allow for the illusion of Daniel's flight. The sparse dialogue and rapid passage of time make this an intriguing and effective work. ROYALTY: $50. SOURCE: Parnell, Peter. (1984). The rise and rise of Daniel Rocket. New York, NY: Dramatists Play Service, Inc. SUBJECTS/PLAY TYPE: Flying; Dreams; Drama.

2595. 7-12. (+) Cadogan, Elda. Rise and shine. CAST: 2f, 2m. ACTS: 1. SETTINGS: Cemetery. PLAYING TIME: NA. PLOT: When a young man wakes up in a cemetery, he discovers all the graves open and empty. He sees his own gravestone, remembers a car crash, and assumes he died. Now he has apparently slept through Judgment Day. One last person appears from her grave, a young woman who died 100 years earlier, according to her grave marker. They strike up a conversation and begin to grow very fond of each other. After a while, the woman's former husband, who was not very good to her in life and remarried after her death, comes to find her. He and his second wife look quite old, but the first wife still looks young. The young woman intends to ignore her former husband and stay with the young man, but as they all converse, it is revealed that she is actually the young man's great-great-grandmother. Gabriel's Horn blows, and they all leave. RECOMMENDATION: This is an amusing play with an unusual premise and a surprising turn of events. ROYALTY: $15. SOURCE: Cadogan, Elda. (1984). Rise and Shine. Boston, MA: Baker's Plays SUBJECTS/PLAY TYPE: Afterlife; Ghosts; Comedy.

2596. 10-12. (+) Jacobson, Ruth & Jenkins, Daniel. Rites. CAST: 8f, 7m. ACTS: 3. SETTINGS: Bare stage. PLAYING TIME: NA. PLOT: This collection of three plays can be performed together or separately. All the monologues explore the theme of loneliness. In Point/Counterpoint, younger siblings impede their older siblings' romances. In Golden Gun and Diamond Bullet, a brother and sister discuss their relationship to the rest of the family. In **Fuel for Thought**, Russell, a gas station worker who is trying to escape his farm and the smell of manure, has too few customers to support himself. Cathy, the child of a prosperous farmer, offers Russell a job. Russell accepts the job and realizes he has returned to what he had tried to escape, a farm. RECOMMENDATION: Written by young adults, this is an excellent expression of the concerns of adolescence. The feelings of lesbianism in one monologue are presented sensitively. The playwrights have given permission to delete any objectionable words or phrases. ROYALTY: $50. SOURCE: Jacobson, Ruth & Jenkins, Daniel & Sexton, Charles & Shawkat, Omar & White, Caroline. (1984). Rites. Chicago, IL: Dramatic Pub. Co. SUBJECTS/PLAY TYPE: Family Relationships; Loneliness; Drama.

2597. 9-12. (+) Sheridan, Richard Brinsley. **The rivals.** CAST: 5f, 9m. ACTS: 5. SETTINGS: Street; dressing room; field. PLAYING TIME: NA. PLOT: In the guise of a penniless young ensign, Captain Absolute enters a love affair with Lydia Languish, who keeps the affair a secret from her aunt, who has vowed to disinherit her if she marries a pauper. Absolute's father promises him a handsome inheritance if he will marry the niece of a good friend. The niece turns out to be Lydia. Fearful that Lydia, without the challenge of a secret love affair, will lose interest in him, Absolute keeps the charade up for a while, but the truth comes out. Lydia is angered, but they reconcile. RECOMMENDATION: Although the plot lacks enough conflict to create intense dramatic tension, it is enjoyable. The 18th century language is remarkably clear, and the formality and age of the play (originally written in 1775) make it an ideal view into the past. ROYALTY: None. SOURCE: Sheridan, Richard Brinsley. (copyright in renewal). The rivals. Boston, MA: Baker's Plays. SUBJECTS/PLAY TYPE: Romance; Comedy.

2598. 6-12. (+) Reines, Bernard J. **Rizal of the Philippines.** CAST: 2f, 14m, 4u. ACTS: 1. SETTINGS: Living room. PLAYING TIME: 35 min. PLOT: Dr. Jose Rizal is accused of being an enemy of the Catholic Church and a traitor to the Spanish government. Rizal carefully explains that he is neither, that he wants to reform the country's justice system, wants free public education for the Filipinos, and hopes that some day the Spanish government will give the Philippines independence. A representative of the militant Katipunam asks Rizal to lead the revolution. He refuses, indicating that education and reform are the appropriate solutions. A representative of the Spanish government charges Rizal with starting an illegal organization, the Philippine League, and claims that his teachings are responsible for the movement known as the Katipunam. Although Rizal protests, saying that the Philippine League was founded openly for the purpose of advancing the Filipino's economic status, he is told that he will be tried by a court martial. Rizal tells his sister how to dispose of his possessions and gives her his favorite alcohol lamp. A poem written by Rizal is discovered in the lamp, and the play ends as it is read. The Filipinos emotionally respond by vowing to fight for independence. RECOMMENDATION: This provides historically accurate information about Dr. Jose Rizal, the events that occurred in the Philippines in 1896, and peripherally, the

power of martyrdom. Rizal's "Last Farewell" is a superb testimony to love of country and fierce commitment to freedom. ROYALTY: Free to Plays subscribers. SOURCE: Reines, Bernard J. (1987, May). Rizal of the Philippines. Plays: The Drama Magazine for Young People, pp. 10-22. SUBJECTS/PLAY TYPE: Revolution, Philippines; Rizal, Dr. Jose; Playlet.

2599. 8-12. (+) Garver, Juliet. **The road not taken.** CAST: 2f, 2m. ACTS: 1. SETTINGS: Waiting room; bus; home. PLAYING TIME: NA. PLOT: This contrasts two couples who chose two different paths. Donna dropped out of school to get married and is expecting a child. Susan is finishing school and dating. Bob dropped out of school to marry Donna. Randy is surprised, because Bob could have received football scholarships to go to college. Donna and Bob discuss the difficult paths they have chosen, especially since their parents are not happy with the marriage and do not give them support. Donna and Bob decide to continue on their path together, even though other choices may seem better. RECOMMENDATION: The characters struggle with their decisions and undergo changes. Underlying themes are the disadvantage of dropping out of school and the difficulty of making life decisions ROYALTY: $4. SOURCE: Garver, Juliet. (1986). One-act dramas. Franklin, OH: Eldridge Pub. Co. SUBJECTS/PLAY TYPE Careers; School; Marriage; Drama.

2600. K-6. (+) Korty, Carol. **The road to market.** (Mad merry men of Gotham) CAST: 3u. ACTS: 1. SETTINGS: Bare stage. PLAYING TIME: NA. PLOT: Two innocents fight over some imaginary chickens who have allegedly dirtied the road. A third shows them that there is nothing there, but the first two leave to gather grain for the birds. RECOMMENDATION: Pantomime and physical comedy here will be a delight for the children, and the play may spark discussion about the need to dream. ROYALTY: None. SOURCE: Korty, Carol. (1977). Silly soup: Ten zany plays. New York, NY: Charles Scribner's Sons. SUBJECTS/PLAY TYPE: Comedy; Skit; Adaptation.

2601. 7-12. (-) Boiko, Claire. (Shakespeare, William) **Roamin' Jo and Juli.** (Romeo and Juliet) CAST: 7f, 13m, 5u. ACTS: 1. SETTINGS: None. PLAYING TIME: 40 min. PLOT: Miss Juli Chaplet is being forced to marry a man she does not love, and Roamin' Jo Montana comes to her rescue. RECOMMENDATION: The parody doesn't work; the ending is pat and trite; the dialogue is objectionably sexist; the western dialect is unrealistic and often unintelligible; and the whole idea is ill conceived. ROYALTY: NA. SOURCE: Boiko, Claire. (1980). Dramatized parodies of familiar stories. Boston, MA: Plays, Inc. SUBJECTS/PLAY TYPE: Western; Musical; Parody; Adaptation.

2602. K-1. (+) Alexander, Sue. **Roar! Said the lion.** CAST: 2u. ACTS: 1. SETTINGS: Meadow. PLAYING TIME: NA. PLOT: The happy lion thwarts the hungry lion by showing him a strawberry patch where the hungry lion eats the pig, gets a stomachache, and returns home without eating the happy lion. RECOMMENDATION: This is brief, easy to produce, and does not require extensive adult supervision. ROYALTY: None. SOURCE: Alexander, Sue. (1977). Small plays for special days. New York, NY: Seabury Press. SUBJECTS/PLAY TYPE: Animals; Seasons; Playlet.

2603. 6-9. (+) Boiko, Claire. **The roaring twenties in Whippoorwill Falls. CAST:** 6f, 16m, 5u. ACTS: 1. SETTINGS: Living room. PLAYING TIME: 45 min. PLOT: Ed Detweiler has made arrangements for his entire family, against their wishes, to participate in the town's Fourth of July contests. They participate, but not in the ways he had expected. For example, Charlie defies Ed by operating "new fangled" radio broadcasting equipment and helping a flying ace land safely at the fair. With the townspeople cheering, and Governor Calvin Coolidge in attendance, the Detweilers become the heroes of the day. RECOMMENDATION: This is trite and boring, but if performed as a farce, it might be entertaining. ROYALTY: Free to Plays subscribers. SOURCE: Boiko, Claire. (1975, February). The roaring twenties in Whippoorwill Falls. Plays: The Drama Magazine for Young People, pp. 1-14. SUBJECTS/PLAY TYPE: Childrens Rights; Comedy.

2604. 4-8. (+) Kilcup, Rick. **Robbin Good and her merry hoods. CAST:** 2f, 2m, 9u. ACTS: 3. SETTINGS: Castle; restaurant; dungeon. PLAYING TIME: 20 min. PLOT: The Sheriff of Rottingham, determined to capture Robbin and her merry maniacs, throws Robbin's friend, Fryer Luck, into the dungeon, and then nabs Robbin and the Hoods when they come to rescue the Fryer. Maid Marion, Robbin Good, Little Yawn, and the Hoods save Fryer from the Sheriff's tickle torture and turn the feather on the sheriff before returning to their hideout. RECOMMENDATION: This slapstick, pun filled parody uses anachronisms to great advantage. ROYALTY: Free to Plays subscribers. SOURCE: Kilcup, Rick. (1983, January/February). Robbin Good and her merry hoods. Plays: The Drama Magazine for Young People, pp. 41-47, 56. SUBJECTS/PLAY TYPE: Adventure; Legends, England; Comedy.

2605. 8-12. (+) Tasca, Jules. (Stevenson, Robert Louis) **Robert Louis Stevenson's Will.** (Will o' the mill) CAST: 2f, 2m. ACTS: 1. SETTINGS: Dining room. PLAYING TIME: 35 min. PLOT: A lady dressed in black makes Young Will watch flashbacks of his youth, as teenaged Marjory and young Will fight for their country. Although Marjory and Young Will see each other often, they grow apart. Marjory, who has refused three proposals of marriage from other men, inveigles Young Will into a proposal. Marjory is happy, but Young Will has second thoughts and escapes the arrangement by saying that if they don't marry, their love and friendship will always remain alive. Marjory marries someone else. On her death bed, Marjory calls for Young Will, who refuses to accept that she is dying. Old Will and the lady in black interact with Marjory and Young Will. The Lady holds Marjory in her arms, and just before Marjory dies, Old Will tells her that he loves her. Old Will finally recognizes that the lady is there for him. He goes without fuss, saying that he won't make the same mistake with her as he did with Marjory. RECOMMENDATION: The style is rather dry and the play ends abruptly, but this is a thought provoking play

about love and life. ROYALTY: $15. SOURCE: Tasca, Jules. (1985). Robert Louis Stevenson's Will. Boston, MA: Baker's Plays. SUBJECTS/PLAY TYPE: Death; Love; Drama.

2606. 1-4. (+) Wescott, Marian L. **Robert the robot: A Christmas operetta for children. CAST:** 4f, 12m, 14u. ACTS: 1. SETTINGS: Mrs. Claus' kitchen. PLAYING TIME: 45 min. PLOT: On the day before Christmas, Mrs. Claus assists Santa by inspecting toys and baking gingerbread men. All toys pass the inspection except Robert the Robot, who limps. Between oiling Robert's joints and sewing buttons onto Santa's coat, Mrs. Claus forgets the gingerbread men in the oven. Robert reminds Mrs. Claus, and the gingerbread men are so happy they encourage Robert to march in order to lose his stiffness. Robert overcomes his handicap and passes inspection. RECOMMENDATION: It is recommended that Robert's problem be changed to one of not knowing how to march, rather than limping, in order to avoid giving the message that disabled people are not able to work and play with nonhandicapped people. ROYALTY: $50. SOURCE: Wescott, Marian I. (1978). Robert the robot: A Christmas operetta for children. Franklin, OH: Eldridge Pub. Co. SUBJECTS/PLAY TYPE: Christmas; Santa Claus; Operetta.

2607. 4-6*. (+) Harris, Aurand. (Shakespeare, William) **Robin Goodfellow.** (A Midsummer Night's Dream) CAST: 1f, 4m, Su. ACTS: 2. SETTINGS: Woods. PLAYING TIME: NA. PLOT: Robin Goodfellow is granted by the King of the Fairies, Oberon, the ability to perform fairy magic and fairy tricks on people. Robin plays tricks on the Queen of the Fairies, Titania, and on two mortals, Bottom and Quince, much to King Oberon's delight. In exchange for the mirth he gives Oberon, Robin is granted the right to visit fairy land. RECOMMENDATION: The play's lyrics, written in Shakespearean style, are far too difficult for younger children to comprehend and follow. Although there are numerous funny scenes, the language barrier would detract from the overall impact. ROYALTY: $25. SOURCE: Harris, Aurand. (1977). Robin Goodfellow. New Orleans, LA: Anchorage Press, Inc. SUBJECTS/PLAY TYPE: Trickery; Fairies; Adaptation.

2608. 10-12. (+) Kelly, Tim. **Robin Hood. CAST:** 8f, 8m, Su. ACTS: 2. SETTINGS: Forest; county; fair; castle room. PLAYING TIME: 60 min. PLOT: Robin Hood battles Prince John's oppression of the poor citizens. Lady Merle, a favorite of Prince John, plots to capture Robin with a fake archery contest, but fails. Maid Marian (Robin Hood's love interest) is announced as the future bride of Prince John. Robin Hood tries to rescue her, but fails. Lady Merle sets another trap with Marian as the bait, but the plan fails when King Richard regains control of England. The sheriff and Lady Merle are punished, and Robin Hood is reprieved so he can marry Marian. RECOMMENDATION: There are scenes of swordfighting and some clever stage movements. Some of the humor may be lost because it is derived from the misuse of French words. ROYALTY: $35. SOURCE: Kelly, Tim. (1988). Robin Hood. Denver, CO: Pioneer Drama

Service. **SUBJECTS/PLAY TYPE:** Adventure; Legends, England; Drama.

2609. 5-7. (+) Pisarski, Cathryn. **Robin Hood. CAST:** 5f, 9m. **ACTS:** 1. **SETTINGS:** Forest, castle, lady's chamber. **PLAYING TIME:** 60 min. **PLOT:** Robin Hood and his Merry Persons wage constant surprise attacks on the Sheriff of Nottingham to retrieve the exorbitant taxes collected from the poor. Robin Hood delights in insulting the Sheriff and in returning the money to the peasants, which he vows to continue doing until the deposed King Richard resumes his rightful throne. Romance grows between Robin Hood and Maid Marian. After entering and winning an archery contest held by the Sheriff, Robin Hood is captured and sentenced to hang the next morning. That night, Maid Marian and the Merry Persons plan Robin Hood's rescue. The play ends with Robin Hood's escape and a combined victory and engagement celebration back in Sherwood Forest. **RECOMMENDATION:** Along with the traditional characters, the adapter has thrown in a handful of females; they are now the band of merry persons. Also, lest children be misled by "steal from the rich, give to the poor" the characters discuss Robin's justification extensively throughout the play. This is best performed by senior high or adult groups for younger groups. **ROYALTY:** $35. **SOURCE:** Pisarski, Cathryn. (1988). Robin Hood. Schulenburg, TX: I.E. Clark. **SUBJECTS/PLAY TYPE:** Adventure; Legends, England; Drama.

2610. 7-12*. (+) Mason, Timothy. **Robin Hood: A story of the forest. CAST:** 4f, 23m, Su. **ACTS:** 1. **SETTINGS:** Forest. **PLAYING TIME:** NA. **PLOT:** This focuses upon life in the forest with the outlaw band, as well as the pursuit of Robin Hood by the evil Sheriff of Nottingham. Emphasis is placed upon the group as a social entity, as well as their grief over the absence of the king. **RECOMMENDATION:** This is rather elaborate and includes much music and dance. It should be presented to children by adults. **ROYALTY:** NA. **SOURCE:** Donahue, John Clark & Jenkins, Linda Walsh. (1972). Five plays from the Children's Theatre Company of Minneapolis. Minneapolis, MN: Univ. of Minnesota Press. **SUBJECTS/PLAY TYPE:** Legends, England; Musical; Drama.

2611. 6-8. (+) Cheatham, Val R. **Robin Hood and friends. CAST:** 1f, 3m, Su. **ACTS:** 1. **SETTINGS:** Throne room; forest. **PLAYING TIME:** 15 min. **PLOT:** Robin Hood sneaks into the king's castle and steals a bag of his gold before the guards can be summoned. The king sends his sheriff and daughter after Robin Hood. Rather than capturing Robin Hood, the king allows Robin Hood to marry his daughter and plans to send the sheriff out into the forest often, dressed up as a pauper, so he can retrieve the money he lost. **RECOMMENDATION:** This has slightly outdated slang and idioms. It builds interest by having the sheriff speak like John Wayne and by showing Princess Marion as part of a medieval CIA. The sarcastic wit demands a fast pace and expert timing and encourages all the cast to show off outrageously. **ROYALTY:** Free to Plays subscribers. **SOURCE:** Cheatam, Val R. (1976, March). Robin Hood and friends. Plays: The Drama

Magazine for Young People, pp. 77-82. **SUBJECTS/PLAY TYPE:** Legends, England; Skit.

2612. 5-8. (+) Nolan, Paul T. **Robin Hood and the match at Nottingham. CAST:** 2f, 8m, Su. **ACTS:** 1. **SETTINGS:** Fair. **PLAYING TIME:** 20 min. **PLOT:** Robin Hood, disguised as a one-eyed beggar, tricks the sheriff and Prince John by winning the archery competition set up to ensnare the outlaw. **RECOMMENDATION:** With language reminiscent of Old English, this dramatization may be a bit boring for children, as the only action is the archery contest. However, the twisted ending, in which Robin takes the King's purse to buy the prize which he has been cheated from getting, may make up for this. **ROYALTY:** None for amateur performance. **SOURCE:** Nolan, Paul T. (1982). Folk tale plays round the world: A collection of royalty-free, one-act plays about lands far and near. Boston, MA: Plays, Inc. **SUBJECTS/PLAY TYPE:** Legends, England; Archery.

2613. 7-12. (-) Colson, J.G. **Robin Hood in Sherwood Forest. CAST:** 17m, Su. **ACTS:** 1. **SETTINGS:** Forest. **PLAYING TIME:** 30 min. **PLOT:** Two rich men and a peasant try to join Robin Hood's band. They are all given a test in which they must walk into the forest and then back to report all they see to Robin Hood. The two rich men see only trees; the peasant sees animal tracks and other things that prove he's a woodsman. When the two rich men are found to be spies for the sheriff, the peasant confesses that he also has captured a soldier in the woods. The soldier is sent back to tell the sheriff that his rich spies are being held for ransom. The peasant is invited to join Robin Hood. **RECOMMENDATION:** This long and tiresome play has none of the original adventure, captures none of the spirit behind Robin Hood's mission, and its only resemblance to the original is its plodding medieval dialogue. Even the fight scenes are disappointing as they are only verbal threats of violence. **ROYALTY:** Free to Plays subscribers. **SOURCE:** Colson, J.G. (1975, January). Robin Hood in Sherwood Forest. Plays: The Drama Magazine for Young People, pp. 63-72. **SUBJECTS/PLAY TYPE:** Legends, England; Playlet.

2614. 1-6. (+) Baher, Constance Whitman. **Robin Hood outwits the sheriff. CAST:** 6f, 13m. **ACTS:** 1. **SETTINGS:** Forest; Robin Hood's den. **PLAYING TIME:** 25 min. **PLOT:** When some women will not tell the Sheriff of Nottingham where Robin Hood lives, the sheriff's men steal their baskets of blackberries. The women tell Robin Hood what has happened. Meanwhile, Sir Richard and Lady Alice tell Robin Hood their stories of woe. Robin Hood's men bring the sheriff to him, a trial is held, and the sheriff's treasures are given to the women. **RECOMMENDATION:** This captures the essence of chivalry and adventure in the original. In addition, the dialogue is written in a manner which simulates Old English, but it remains easy to pronounce. **ROYALTY:** NA. **SOURCE:** Kamerman, Sylvia E. (1987). Plays from favorite folk tales. Boston, MA: Plays, Inc. **SUBJECTS/PLAY TYPE** Legends, England; Playlet.

2615. 1-4. (+) Jacob, Eva. **Robin Hood tricks the sheriff. CAST:** 4f, 11m, 4u. **ACTS:** 1. **SETTINGS:** Forest.

PLAYING TIME: 15 min. **PLOT:** Robin Hood tricks the sheriff by disguising himself as a beggar and leading the sheriff to his crew of outlaws, where the "beggar" exacts the bag of gold which the sheriff promised in return for being lead to Robin Hood. **RECOMMENDATION:** This is a clever and well drawn example of Robin Hood's trickery. **ROYALTY:** Free to Plays subscribers. **SOURCE:** Jacob, Eva. (1980, November). Robin Hood tricks the sheriff. Plays: The Drama Magazine for Young people, pp. 52-57. **SUBJECTS/PLAY TYPE:** Legends, England; Playlet.

2616. 7-12. (-) Korty, Carol. (Schneider, Hansjorg) **Robinson and Friday.** (Robinson and Friday) **CAST:** 3m, 1u. **ACTS:** 1. **SETTINGS:** Campsite. **PLAYING TIME:** NA. **PLOT:** Robinson, long deserted on an island, has organized his life in a strict routine of daily chores and habits, and has declared himself president of the island, although he has no people to govern. When an island native appears, Robinson names him Friday, and sets out to reform the native's carefree ways. Instead, Robinson is changed, and soon he is dancing and singing along with Friday and Friday's friend, Bird. When Robinson's Captain arrives to save him, Robinson refuses to leave without Friday and Bird. The ship sails off without him and the three friends run off to play. **RECOMMENDATION:** Far from a true adaptation of Daniel Defoe's novel, the only resemblance here is the basic situation of a man shipwrecked on a deserted island, creating his own self sufficient world, and after years of living alone, encountering an island native. This does, however, stand on its own as a statement about what is civilized and what is savage. **ROYALTY:** $25. **SOURCE:** Korty, Carol. (1980). Robinson and Friday. Boston, MA: Baker's Plays. **SUBJECTS/PLAY TYPE:** Adventure; Life Styles; Allegory; Adaptation.

2617. 1-12. (+) Morley, Jean. (DeFoe, Daniel) **Robinson Crusoe: A pantomime.** (The life and strange surprising adventures of Robinson Crusoe) **CAST:** 4f, 10m, 1u. **ACTS:** 1. **SETTINGS:** Sailing ship; tropical island. **PLAYING TIME:** NA. **PLOT:** Robinson Crusoe is given a treasure map just before his voyage to the West Indies. He is followed by Blackpatch the Pirate, who is intent on stealing the map and finding the treasure. During the voyage, Blackpatch calls upon his pirate cronies and uses magic spells to take control of Crusoe's ship and sink it, marooning the crew on an island. After outsmarting Blackpatch and a group of cannibals, Robinson and his crew find the treasure and are rescued by Lord Nelson. On the voyage home, Robinson and his girlfriend are married. **RECOMMENDATION:** This vaudeville-style play is an example of British humor at its silliest. Audience participation is encouraged and there are many references to current popular and political figures. The broad, physical comedy will be especially enjoyed by a younger audience, while older audiences will enjoy the many puns and plays on words. This is only very loosely based on DeFoe's novel. Because this is from Britain, one might want to change some of the jokes to reflect local personalities and products. **ROYALTY:** NA. **SOURCE:** Morley, John. (1983). Robinson Crusoe: A pantomime. New York, NY: Samuel French. **SUBJECTS/PLAY TYPE:** Pirates; Treasure; Comedy; Adaptation.

2618. 7-12. (-) Mauro, Robert. **Robot rescues romance.** **CAST:** 2f, 2m. **ACTS:** 1. **SETTINGS:** Office. **PLAYING TIME:** 20 min. **PLOT:** In 2295, space pilot Sam comes to Bill's computer dating service to find his perfect match because Bill objects to Sam's dating his sister. Computer Electra finds the perfect date for Sam: Bill's sister. For Bill, the perfect match is Electra herself. But when Bill begins to dance with Electra, she goes haywire, and Bill chalks it up to his amazing effect on women. **RECOMMENDATION:** The characters are unbelievable, their dialogue hard to understand, the jokes unfunny, and the ending an insult to everyone's intelligence. **ROYALTY:** Free to Plays subscribers. **SOURCE:** Mauro, Robert. (1982, January/February). Robot rescues romance. Plays: The Drama Magazine for Young People, pp. 1-8. **SUBJECTS/PLAY TYPE:** Computer Dating Service; Valentine's Day; Dating; Comedy.

2619. 6-11. (+) Poisson, Camille L. **The robot whiz kid.** **CAST:** 3f, 7m, Su. **ACTS:** 4. **SETTINGS:** Lab; hallway; conference room. **PLAYING TIME:** 40 min. **PLOT:** Jonathan Smith (the computer maintenance man) helps Mr. Maddigan (the head of the robot research lab) by fixing some robots because Maddigan has promised Jonathan a job in his division. Maddigan later revokes his offer because he wants all the credit for fixing the robots. Mrs. Dunn (the head of promotions) sees Jonathan's talent and decides to help Jonathan by coming up with a scheme to bring him to the attention of the company president, Mr. Brandon. At an awards presentation, Jonathan's own robots cater. Mrs. Dunn announces that Jonathan is the mastermind behind the whole thing and Mr. Brandon makes him vice president in charge of robot research, much to Mr. Maddigan's displeasure. **RECOMMENDATION:** Robots as the source of a match between good and evil are a unique twist. **ROYALTY:** Free to Plays subscribers. **SOURCE:** Poisson, Camille L. (1987, October). The robot whiz kid. Plays: The Drama Magazine for Young People, pp. 1-13. **SUBJECTS/PLAY TYPE:** Science Fiction; Robots; Comedy.

2620. K-6. (+) Miller, Jane V. **Robots, robots, robots.** **CAST:** Su. **ACTS:** 1. **SETTINGS:** Robot store. **PLAYING TIME:** 12 min. **PLOT:** A salesclerk in a robot store overwhelms a customer with several remarkable models, but fails to sell any. Bemoaning his repeated lack of success, the clerk is confronted by the Executive Model robot, who summarily fires the clerk, leaving the audience bemused and perhaps slightly bothered about who is really in control: man or machine. **RECOMMENDATION:** Younger children will enjoy imitating the motion and monotone of the magical machines in this comical skit. The author encourages the addition of robots, activities, or dialogue suggested by the participants. In addition to the script, Miller includes suggestions for other creative dramatics including robot pantomime, robot parade, robot dances and games, and robot sports. **ROYALTY:** None. **SOURCE:** Miller, Jane V. (1975, May). Robots, robots, robots. Plays: The Drama Magazine for Young People, pp. 65-68. **SUBJECTS/PLAY TYPE:** Robots; Comedy; Creative Dramatics.

2621. 9-12. (+) Purkey, Ruth Angell. **The rockabilly nowhere man.** CAST: 6f, 5m. ACTS: 1. SETTINGS: Dressing room. PLAYING TIME: NA. PLOT: Yancy Moran, rock star, is visited by an old girl friend after one of his performances. Even though she has remained faithful to him, Yancy has forgotten about her in the glitter of the limelight. As they talk, it becomes apparent that Yancy's newfound success and wealth have left him an empty person. Although the conflict is not resolved, the audience is left with the impression that the unfortunate lure of success is too enticing to allow Moran to return to his first love. RECOMMENDATION: The theme of the faithful girl back home may be a bit old, but excellent characterizations and revealing dialogue allow it to work. Audiences will find themselves emotionally involved as Moran's lover tries to woo him back. By setting the plot in 1958 the play avoids needing to sound contemporary; an opening scene that is supposed to be the end of Yancy's concert can be replaced by closed curtains and loud music from a tape in order to give the same impression. ROYALTY: $15. SOURCE: Purkey, Ruth Angell. (1978). The rockabilly nowhere man. Boston, MA: Baker's Plays. SUBJECTS/PLAY TYPE: Romance; Success; Melodrama.

2622. 4-8. (-) Fisher, Aileen Lucia. **Roll call for New Year.** CAST: 12u. ACTS: 1. SETTINGS: None. PLAYING TIME: 5 min. PLOT: Twelve children personify characteristics associated with each month of the year. RECOMMENDATION: The description of each month is outdated and stereotyped. ROYALTY: Free to Plays subscribers. SOURCE: Fisher, Aileen Lucia. (1985). Year-round programs for young people. Boston, MA: Plays, Inc. SUBJECTS/PLAY TYPE: New Year's Day; Calendar; Months; Choral Reading.

2623. 7-12. (+) Bradley, Virginia. **A roll of nickels.** CAST: 4f, 3m, Su. ACTS: 1. SETTINGS: Lobby. PLAYING TIME: NA. PLOT: A newlywed husband forces his young wife to gamble in Las Vegas. She's never told her husband that her father gambled. When the wife becomes visibly shaken, her husband at last agrees that she may quit. RECOMMENDATION: This unusual play makes no statement either for or against gambling. ROYALTY: NA. SOURCE: Bradley, Virginia. (1977). Stage eight: One act plays. New York, NY: Dodd, Mead. SUBJECTS/PLAY TYPE Gambling; Drama.

2624. 7-12. (+) Watts, Frances B. **Romance at the old Bar-O, or the perils of Flo and Joe.** CAST: 5m, 1u. ACTS: 1. SETTINGS: Bare stage, props. PLAYING TIME: 20 min. PLOT: A widowed rancher has an unmarried daughter, Flo, beloved by three cowboys. Her hand in marriage will go to the cowboy who can ride a wild bronco the longest. Flo is distraught; she loves Joe. Sam is eliminated, and Jim and Joe tie. A dishonorable trick by Jim is exposed, but Joe must prove he is the true winner. He rides so long that he tames the wild bronco, and he and Flo ride off into the sunset. RECOMMENDATION: Success with this clever play depends upon the reader's delivery of the rhymed verse. The actors say nothing, but they pantomime the actions as the rhymed verse is spoken. Mood and tone are set by piano music. ROYALTY: $3. SOURCE: Watts, Frances B. (n.d.). Romance at the old Bar-O, or the perils of Flo and Joe. Franklin, OH: Eldridge Pub. Co. SUBJECTS/PLAY TYPE Cowhands; Ranch Life; Pantomime.

2625. 10-12. (+) Francis, Charlotte. **The romance of rattlesnake ridge.** CAST: 4f, 5m. ACTS: 1. SETTINGS: Saloon. PLAYING TIME: 35 min. PLOT: Purity, forced by poverty and desolation to scrub the floors and fixtures of the bar, speaks to the audience of her quest to regain her family's lost wealth. Purity continually invokes the guidance and solace of her deceased, sainted mother as she falls passionately and unashamedly in love with Oakhurt; as she fends off the lusty advances of Cadwallader Snipe, arch villain; and as she urges the fallen Tarantula Tess to pursue a life of virtue. The climactic entrance of a ghost reveals the nature of his own demise at the hands of Snipe, prevents the death of Purity, and leads to Snipe's death. Oakhart, the Federal Marshall disguised as a sheepherder, secures the hand of Purity in marriage and Tess hastens to begin a life of virtue. RECOMMENDATION: Careful production notes warn against the use of burlesque, phony laughter, or studied departure from character for effect. The author acknowledges the intent to create a spoof but calls for sincerity and seriousness. The encouragement of audience participation maintains a high level of interest, and the frequent asides, emphasized by the simultaneous stop action poses of the other actors, add a personal touch to the dialogue. ROYALTY: $30. SOURCE: Francis, Charlotte. (1975). The romance of rattlesnake ridge. Franklin, OH: Eldridge Pub. Co. SUBJECTS/PLAY TYPE: Western; Romance; Melodrama.

2626. 4-5. (+) Hinton-Osborne, M. **A romance without words.** CAST: 2f, 2m, 6u. ACTS: 1. SETTINGS: Bare stage. PLAYING TIME: 10 min. PLOT: This is the story of Henrietta Van Astorbilt and her true love, Harold, and how Vernon the villain almost ruined their lives by trying to force Henrietta to marry him. RECOMMENDATION: The story is mimed while a narrator tells the audience what is happening. The slapstick humor is entertaining. ROYALTY: Free to Plays subscribers. SOURCE: Hinton-Osborne, M. (1981, January). A romance without words. Plays: The Drama Magazine for Young People, pp. 58-60. SUBJECTS/PLAY TYPE: Romance; Comedy; Pantomime.

2627. 7-12. (+) Harris, Aurand. (Rostand, Edmond) **The romancers.** (Les romanesques) CAST: 1f, 4m. ACTS: 1. SETTINGS: Two gardens. PLAYING TIME: NA. PLOT: In 18th century France, two young lovers meet secretly at the wall separating their parents' estates. They believe their fathers are bitter enemies, but the fathers, in fact, have only pretended enmity to entice the children into a romance so that the two estates will be joined. The fathers hire a swordsman to perform a mock abduction to make the son a hero (as he rescues the daughter) so the fathers can pretend to relent and allow their son and daughter to marry. RECOMMENDATION: This includes music, torchbearers, sword fights, romance, humor, surprises, drama. It has no objectionable language or heavy moralizing. ROYALTY: $15. SOURCE: Harris, Aurand. (1979). The romancers. Boston, MA: Baker's Plays. SUBJECTS/PLAY TYPE: Comedy; Romance; Adaptation.

2628. 9-12. (+) Murray, John. **The romantic robots.** CAST: 7f, 8m, Su. ACTS: 1. SETTINGS: Exhibit room. PLAYING TIME: 35 min. PLOT: Three computerized robots and their human creators try to win a government contest. In the process, the nation's only copy of a Top Secret energy policy is presumed stolen by spies. The computer which caused all the chaos reproduces the document from its memory file. As a result, relationships are restored, true love prevails, and a pair of lovebird robots play matchmaker for their respective inventors. A secondary plot contains elements of industrial sabotage, congressional investigations, and lawsuits. RECOMMENDATION: This could be presented for high school students with some familiarity with computer technology, public affairs, Washington, D.C. politics, and government/industrial contractor relationships. Such background would be necessary to understand most of the puns and jokes. Some computer terminology is dated and some of the dialogue is sexist. ROYALTY: Free to Plays subscribers. SOURCE: Murray, John. (1985). Fifteen plays for today's teenagers. Boston, MA: Plays, Inc. SUBJECTS/PLAY TYPE: Love; Political Satire; Satire.

2629. 10-12. (+) Grote, David & Wilmurt, Arthur. **Rome is where the heart is.** CAST: 5f, 7m. ACTS: 1. SETTINGS: Street; two houses. PLAYING TIME: NA. PLOT: A young man returns to his home in ancient Athens with a young female slave, who, unbeknownst to his family, he is buying to be his wife. The father decides to buy her instead. So that his wife does not find out, a neighbor is enlisted to make the purchase and hide the lady at his home. When the neighbor's wife returns home unexpectedly, mistaken identities and other comic disasters ensue until the original lovers are reunited. RECOMMENDATION: This delightful farce, based on a similar plot developed by Plautus, is recommended as an example of classic comedy theater. ROYALTY: $15. SOURCE: Grote, David & Wilmurt, Arthur. (1980). Rome is where the heart is. Chicago, IL: Dramatic Pub. Co. SUBJECTS/PLAY TYPE Farce; Comedy.

2630. 7-12. (+) Olfson, Lewy. (Shakespeare, William) **Romeo and Juliet.** (Romeo and Juliet) CAST: 2f, 9m, 1u. ACTS: 1. SETTINGS: Streets; ballroom; orchard; cell; tomb. PLAYING TIME: NA. PLOT: The star-crossed lovers meet, fall in love, and secretly marry. Soon after, Romeo is banished from Verona for killing Juliet's cousin. In order to prevent an arranged marriage to a rich nobleman, Juliet takes a sleeping potion to feign death. Unaware she still lives, Romeo drinks poison and dies. Awaking to find Romeo dead, Juliet take her own life. RECOMMENDATION: The use of a narrator permits abridgement without sacrificing plot development. While the original is preferable, this will appeal because of its shorter length and simplicity. ROYALTY: Free to Plays subscribers. SOURCE: Olfson, Lewy. (1982, May). Romeo and Juliet. Plays: The Drama Magazine for Young People, pp. 56-68. SUBJECTS/PLAY TYPE: Love; Adaptation.

2631. 10-12. (+) Robinson, Budd. **Romeo and Juliet: American style.** CAST: 3f, 3m. ACTS: 2. SETTINGS: Two bedrooms; office; motel room. PLAYING TIME: 120 min. PLOT: Romeo, having discovered in the afterlife that Juliet did not actually kill herself, feels cheated and demands of the devil a second chance. The devil agrees and takes him to the home of a modern day Juliet in Verona, CA. Romeo is sure that he loves this plain Juliet, but he is disturbingly attracted to her best friend, beautiful Althea. Althea, who has just told Juliet that she is engaged and pregnant, is equally attracted to Romeo. As Romeo and Juliet profess their love for each other, Juliet's parents discover a baby bootie Juliet has knitted for Althea, jump to the wrong conclusion, and insist that the couple marry immediately. Juliet wants to marry Romeo even though she is aware of his attraction to Althea. When he learns that Althea won't betray her fiance and Juliet, Romeo goes through with the wedding to Juliet. Not understanding modern custom, he refuses to kiss Juliet in public at the ceremony. Juliet interprets this as rejection, and runs to her room. Romeo decides that he does love Juliet, goes after her, and finds her heavily sedated from the sleeping pills she has taken to rest. Convinced that Juliet has killed herself for love of him, Romeo runs in front of a truck and is killed. Realizing his mistake, Romeo feels cheated, and demands of the devil one more chance. RECOMMENDATION: This interestingly explores the conflict between romantic love and reality. While there is humor in Romeo's culture shock and in the interplay between Romeo and the devil, this is not a comedy, and no easy answers are given. Some dialogue and situations may not be appropriate for younger audiences. ROYALTY: $50. SOURCE: Robinson, Budd. (1985). Romeo and Juliet: American style. Schulenburg, TX: I.E. Clark. SUBJECTS/PLAY TYPE: Marriage; Love; Drama.

2632. 9. (+) Majeski, Bill. **Romeo and Juliet revisited.** CAST: 8f, 9m, Su. ACTS: 1. SETTINGS: Office. PLAYING TIME: 25 min. PLOT: Top executives of a film company discuss their next film. All of their ideas are absurdly ridiculous. Finally, the cleaning lady cleverly acts out a modern day version of **Romeo and Juliet** involving the Trapulets, who operate a string of eateries called Chicken Surprise, and the Murgatroyds, who own a chain of ice cream drive-ins featuring Bad Humors and Ratsicles. The executives love the idea, but to the cleaning lady's surprise, they decide to quit being motion picture producers and become chicken restauranteurs. RECOMMENDATION: This satirical depiction of modern day capitalism could be used to introduce creative writing, with students writing their own modern version of some other classic they have read. ROYALTY: Free to Plays subscribers. SOURCE: Majeski, Bill. (1977, January). Romeo and Juliet revisited. Plays: The Drama Magazine for Young People, pp. 1-10. SUBJECTS/PLAY TYPE: Satire; Capitalism; Comedy.

2633. 7-10. (+) Dubois, Graham. **A room for a king.** CAST: 5f, 5m. ACTS: 1. SETTINGS: Yard at the inn in Bethlehem. PLAYING TIME: NA. PLOT: Late on the night of Christ's birth, Joseph and Mary enter Bethlehem for the census, only to find that all the inns are full. They arrive at Michael's Inn, and Michael refuses even the stable to the tired, pitiful looking Holy couple. RECOMMENDATION: The modern language is occasionally awkward. Though characters have little depth, this is suitable if the objective is a simple, easily understood version of the nativity. **ROYALTY:** None. **SOURCE:** Kamerman, Sylvia E. (1975). A treasury of Christmas plays. Boston, MA: Plays, Inc. **SUBJECTS/PLAY TYPE:** Christmas; Christian Drama.

2634. 9-12. (+) Thurston, Muriel B. **Room for Mary.** CAST: 6f. ACTS: 1. SETTINGS: Living room. PLAYING TIME: 25 min. PLOT: The day before Christmas, Mrs. Warren, full of Christmas spirit, gets the house ready for her family reunion. She receives a phone call from her Pastor asking her to take in a new mother and baby. She accepts the responsibility and then must break the news to her daughters. RECOMMENDATION: This is a good Christmas play for the parochial classroom. ROYALTY: Free to Plays subscribers. SOURCE: Kamerman, Sylvia E. (1975). A treasury of Christmas plays. Boston, MA: Plays, Inc. SUBJECTS/PLAY TYPE: Christmas; Family; Playlet.

2635. 7-10. (+) McCusker, Paul. **Room mates.** CAST: 1f, 3m. ACTS: 1. SETTINGS: Living room. PLAYING TIME: NA. PLOT: Bill, a college student, has failed his English test and will more than likely be dismissed from school. Jim reluctantly tells him the bank has called about his late car payment and that his fiancee has left her engagement ring on the table. Bill leaves for Clancy's to "drink himself to death." He returns with a girl, but becomes angry when she is unsympathetic to his problems. Truly at rock bottom, Jim prays for help from God. RECOMMENDATION: Too short to allow full development of Bill's character, this may nonetheless appeal to an audience who has experienced Bill's feelings. Stage direction indicates a religiously emotional closing scene, making this most appropriate for a church program. ROYALTY: NA. SOURCE: McCusker, Paul. (1982). Souvenirs: Comedies and dramas for Christian fellowship. Boston, MA: Baker's Plays. SUBJECTS/PLAY TYPE: Christian Drama; Skit.

2636. 8-12. (+) McDonough, Jerome. **Roomers.** CAST: 5f, 9m. ACTS: 1. SETTINGS: Parlor. PLAYING TIME: 60 min. PLOT: The curtain rises as Kristin announces a tenants' meeting in the parlor. She doesn't stand a chance of ever getting these tenants together. Darting in and out of the parlor is an assortment of the most delightful weirdos imaginable. From Shelia, the method actress who experiences all that she meets (bananas, lampposts, and sofas), to Mr. Orff, who worries that his homing vultures on the roof might be starved for human companionship, the roomers in this brownstone are simply nutty. They prove that they can come together to protect one of their own, using a farcical plan that is hilarious. RECOMMENDATION: This wacky, witty, wonderful farce is played to the hilt and beyond by a weird collection of loveable loonies. The action and dialogue whirl by as the players reveal the marvelous variety in the human species. Each character is a command performance that blends and balances with the others. The dignity of each individual is maintained even as the lunacy runs nonstop. ROYALTY: $20. SOURCE: McDonough, Jerome. (1983). Roomers. Schulenburg, TX: I.E. Clark. SUBJECTS/PLAY TYPE: Personalities; Farce.

2637. K-3. (+) Marks, Burton. **The Rope.** CAST: 2u. ACTS: 1. SETTINGS: Bare stage, props. PLAYING TIME: NA. PLOT: Bozo the clown finds a rope with a sign that tells him not to pull it. When he pulls it in spite of the repeated warnings of an offstage voice, the puppeteer's hand, attached to the other end of the rope, grabs him and pulls Bozo off the stage. RECOMMENDATION: The result of Bozo's failure to heed obvious warnings carries a strong message for young children and is presented in a direct, no nonsense manner. ROYALTY: None. SOURCE: Marks, Burton. (1982). Puppet plays and puppet-making. Boston, MA: Plays, Inc. SUBJECTS/PLAY TYPE: Consequences of Actions; Puppet Play.

2638. 9-12. (+) Robinette, Joseph. (Faulkner, William) **A rose for Emily.** (A rose for Emily) CAST: 1f, 2m, 6u. ACTS: 1. SETTINGS: Room. PLAYING TIME: NA. PLOT: Faithful to the original, the adaptation begins at Emily's death and then works backward through flashbacks. The present tense is in Emily's living room, where main characters reminisce about her life as they attempt to open a bedroom door that has been nailed shut. The powerful climax that ends Faulkner's story also ends this play. RECOMMENDATION: Faulkner's characterization and mood are beautifully preserved. The audience is prepared for a mystery, but gets much more in believable people and tragic lives. Simple lighting can distinguish the flashback scenes. ROYALTY: $20. SOURCE: Robinette, Joseph. (1983). A rose for Emily. Woodstock, IL: Dramatic Pub. Co. SUBJECTS/PLAY TYPE Death; Loneliness; Mystery; Adaptation.

2639. 7-12. (+) Hamlett, Christina. **A rose is just a rose.** CAST: 1f, 3m, 1u. ACTS: 2. SETTINGS: Laboratory. PLAYING TIME: 15 min. PLOT: Bill is mistakenly transported in the Time Mobile to the past as William Shakespeare appears in the present. All ends well when the two are returned to their own time. RECOMMENDATION: Since many allusions to Shakespeare's plays are made, this would be a very humorous addition to a Shakespeare unit. ROYALTY: Free to Plays subscribers. SOURCE: Hamlett, Christina. (1986, April). A rose is just a rose. Plays: The Drama Magazine for Young People, pp. 1-8. SUBJECTS/PLAY TYPE: Time Travel; Shakespeare, William; Comedy.

2640. 7-12. (+) Martens, Anne Coulter. **Rosemary for remembrance.** CAST: 16f, 1m, Su. ACTS: 1. SETTINGS: Kitchen. PLAYING TIME: 25 min. PLOT: Anne Hathaway, back in Stratford, wonders if her husband, William, is surrounded by lords and ladies, and if these ladies fill his thoughts. The neighbor says that many ladies fill Shakespeare's thoughts, and introduces Anne to some of the women in his plays, each of whom gives a short soliloquy. RECOMMENDATION: Unfortunately, the contrived vehicle for allowing some of Shakespeare's "women" to speak from his plays is appropriate for young audiences, while the soliloquies are appropriate only for older audiences. Although the portrait of an artist consumed by his work is well drawn, this neither honors the playwright not does it encourage the audience to read more. **ROYALTY:** Free to Plays subscribers. **SOURCE:** Martens, Anne Coulter. (1987, April). Rosemary for remembrance. Plays: The Drama Magazine for Young People, pp. 43-50. **SUBJECTS/PLAY TYPE:** Shakespeare, William; Playlet.

2641. 7-12. (+) Horovitz, Israel. (Torgov, Morley) **A Rosen by any other name.** (A good place to come from.) **CAST:** 2f, 4m, 1u. **ACTS:** 1. **SETTINGS:** Living room; bedrooms. **PLAYING TIME:** NA. **PLOT:** While Stanley Rosen prepares for his Bar Mitzvah, his father, afraid that the Nazis will invade Canada, wants to change the family name to something less Jewish-sounding. Stanley objects to this and to the idea of his being immortalized at his Bar Mitzvah by a statue of chopped liver. Stanley must persuade his mother that the chopped liver likeness is out, his father that Rosen is a name to be proud of, and Fern (the girl he adores) to be his date for the Bar Mitzvah. He celebrates his Bar Mitzvah under the name Rosen and attends the reception with Fern on his arm. The chopped liver statue however, remains. **RECOMMENDATION:** This effectively captures the angst of growing up and making one's own decisions. It also shows the importance of religious and cultural pride and treats lightly yet thoughtfully the issue of anti-semitism. Even though the drama takes place over 40 years ago, the presentation is timeless. The Yiddish accents required for some of the characters might be difficult. **ROYALTY:** $50. **SOURCE:** Horovitz, Israel. (1987). A Rosen by any other name. New York, NY: Dramatists Play Service. **SUBJECTS/PLAY TYPE:** Bar Mitzvah; Family Relationships; Comedy.

2642. 7-12. (-) DePrine, John. **Roses from the South.** **CAST:** 6f, 3m. **ACTS:** 2. **SETTINGS:** Apartment. **PLAYING TIME:** NA. **PLOT:** Sophie, a spoiled, self deluded, and coarse society beauty of 1890s Vienna, abuses her servants and uses deceit to gain notoriety in setting two suitors to a duel. When the refined sisters of each young man plead in vain with Sophie to call off the duel, each nobleman falls in love with his rival's sister, and the play ends with the couples waltzing. Foolish Sophie consoles herself for her loss of face by anticipating the notoriety she will gain by selling her memoirs. **RECOMMENDATION:** The incontinuity of the plot and weak characters flaw this play, despite several moments of genuine humor. Few groups would wish to devote much time to such a mediocre production. **ROYALTY:** $34. **SOURCE:** DePrine, John. (1986). Roses from the South. Franklin, OH: Eldridge Pub. Co. **SUBJECTS/PLAY TYPE:** Romance; Manners; Comedy.

2643. 5-7. (-) Boiko, Claire. (Shakespeare, William) **Rowdy Kate.** (Taming of the Shrew) **CAST:** 6f, 14m. **ACTS:** 1. **SETTINGS:** Saloon. **PLAYING TIME:** 45 min. **PLOT:** The unladylike rowdy Kate won't let any of Paducah's women marry until she has. The townspeople pay Tricky Pete $10,000 to marry her, and the play ends with a happy song about better times in Paducah. **RECOMMENDATION:** This suffers from blatant sexism, unnecessary and inappropriate sexual references, and subplots that add nothing except more insulting sexism. **ROYALTY:** NA. **SOURCE:** Boiko, Claire. (1980). Dramatized parodies of familiar stories. Boston, MA:

Plays, Inc. **SUBJECTS/PLAY TYPE:** Western; Musical; Parody; Adaptation.

2644. 4-8. (-) Brush, Gloria-lee. **A royal Christmas.** **CAST:** 3f, 2m, Su. **ACTS:** 1. **SETTINGS:** Throne room. **PLAYING TIME:** 20 min. **PLOT:** The cause of the princess' gloominess is diagnosed as "receiving fever." She finally smiles when her father allows her to give all her presents away. **RECOMMENDATION:** The message that giving is better that receiving is laudable, but the way in which the play presents it is highly implausible, and the characters' motivations are poorly explained. **ROYALTY:** Free to Plays subscribers. **SOURCE:** Brush, Gloria-lee. (1983, December). A royal Christmas. Plays: The Drama Magazine for Young People, pp. 27-30. **SUBJECTS/PLAY TYPE:** Christmas; Playlet.

2645. 1-6. (+) Lynch, May. **The royal dog. CAST:** 1f, 6m, 9u. **ACTS:** 1. **SETTINGS:** Bare stage, props. **PLAYING TIME:** 15 min. **PLOT:** The butcher's wife finds what she thinks is the Queen's missing dog. Afraid the Queen will think they stole the dog, she takes it to the rich man, who takes it to the poor man, who takes it to the beggar man, who takes it to the thief, who takes it to the doctor, who takes it to the lawyer, who takes it to the Indian Chief. Watching out for the dog and following it, the butcher's wife gets lost in the forest and asks the dog to take her to the palace. Along the way, she meets the King. Not recognizing him, she asks the way to the palace. The King asks her if she wants a reward for returning the dog. When she replies no, he reveals himself as the king, giving her the dog and a bag of gold. **RECOMMENDATION:** Children who know the rhyme, "Rich man, Poor man" will recognize the characters. With a narrator, even the youngest will be able to participate by pantomiming the action. **ROYALTY:** Free to Plays subscribers. **SOURCE:** Lynch, May. (1975, January). The royal dog. Plays: The Drama Magazine for Young People, pp. 52-56. **SUBJECTS/PLAY TYPE:** Dogs; Comedy.

2646. 8-12. (+) Kaufman, George S. & Ferber, Edna. **The royal family. CAST:** 6f, 11m. **ACTS:** 3. **SETTINGS:** Apartment rooms. **PLAYING TIME:** NA. **PLOT:** The matriarch of the legendary royal dynasty of the American stage is the incomparable actress, Fanny Cavendish, now in her 80s. Devoted to the theater and family (in that order, it would seem), she reigns over three generations of family just as she ruled the American stage for over 50 years. Gwen, Fanny's granddaughter, threatens to break family theatrical tradition to marry Perry, who is not in or of the theater. Gwen's mother, Julia (the middle generation), finds a sudden opportunity to recapture her long lost love for the staunch, practical Gil. Even heretical brother Terry announces his intent to become a recluse and study the violin in Munich. For Fanny, this is the disintegration of her beloved dynasty. But the final scene, one year later, sees the family's return to the fold for opportunities they cannot pass up. The lure of theater and love of family has triumphed. Even Gwen returns from stodgy stability with her new baby, the fourth generation. They are all there as Fanny dies quietly, fulfilled by their presence and promise. **RECOMMENDATION:** This is a hilarious, lunatic romp through the world of the theater. Vintage Kaufman humor at its best, the bizarre characters, frantic pace, and clever dialogue ensure its success. Although the setting (on two levels for the duplex apartment) may be difficult, it is necessary. ROYALTY: $50. SOURCE: Kaufman, George & Ferber, Edna. (1977). The royal family. New York, NY: Samuel French. SUBJECTS/PLAY TYPE: Theater; Family; Tradition; Comedy.

2647. 1-6. (+) Wallace, Linda. **Royal job hunt.** CAST: 3m, 9u. ACTS: 1. SETTINGS: Throne room. PLAYING TIME: 10 min. PLOT: A "poor, unfortunate lad" looks for a job. As the king and his attendant review the variety of positions in the castle, Will objects in rhyme to each: butcher, baker, candlestick maker, guard and gardener. Finally, the king recognizes Will's talent for rhyming and appoints him Royal Rhymer of Words. RECOMMENDATION: This romp through the palace neighborhood is a clever takeoff on the nursery rhyme, and is entertaining enough for intermediate grades to present to either younger grades or a broader audience. ROYALTY: Free to Plays subscribers. SOURCE: Wallace, Linda. (1987, November). Royal job hunt. Plays: The Drama Magazine for Young People, pp. 33-36. SUBJECTS/PLAY TYPE: Occupations; Comedy.

2648. 3-6. (+) Leeds Theatre in Education. **Rubbish - a story about inventors and inventions.** CAST: 2f, 3m, 5u. ACTS: 1. SETTINGS: None. PLAYING TIME: 120 min. PLOT: In this half-day program, Arthur and Stella are inventors and environmentalists who enjoy making toys and crafts out of other people's rubbish. Mr. Flash and Ms. Trend are also inventors, who rely on shiny, colorful new materials to produce dysfunctional creations. The Approver (of new inventions) is not seen but his voice is heard from behind a screen, much in the manner of the Wizard of Oz. He repeatedly okays the shoddy but shiny new inventions and rejects those made of rubbish. Eventually, there are no new materials (as Arthur and Stella had warned). But, Mr. Flash and Mr. Trend go to America for new materials rather than use recycled items in England. RECOMMENDATION: In this participatory drama, the children are drawn into the action and make decisions that affect the course of the lesson on environmentalism. This is not a script so much as it is an outline for an activity which teaches young people about conservation and recycling. ROYALTY: NA. SOURCE: Leed Theatre in Education. (1980). Four junior programmes. London, England: Eyre Methuen. SUBJECTS/PLAY TYPE: Environment; Conservation; Participation Play.

2649. K-2. (+) Bauer, Caroline Feller. (Heide, Florence Parry) **Ruby.** (Tales for the perfect child) CAST: 2f, 1m, 1u. ACTS: 1. SETTINGS: Several rooms in a home. PLAYING TIME: 5 min. PLOT: Clyde, Ruby's baby brother, has again thwarted Ruby's plans to play with her friend, Ethel, because Ruby's mother has told her to watch Clyde. So Ruby watches Clyde - she watches him wreak havoc in several rooms of the house. Upon hearing Clyde cry, Ruby's mother admonishes her daughter, but Ruby says she did watch Clyde the whole time. The end of the play finds Ruby at Ethel's house, grinning and ready to play. RECOMMENDATION: As they recognize Ruby and

Clyde in themselves, and the clever way in which Ruby dupes her mother, children may either sympathize or wish they had the nerve to do the same. This can be either acted or read aloud. ROYALTY: None. SOURCE: Bauer, Caroline Feller. (1987). Presenting reader's theater: Plays and poems to read aloud. New York, NY: H.W. Wilson Co. SUBJECTS/PLAY TYPE: Siblings; Reader's Theater; Adaptation.

2650. Thane, Adele. (Gilbert, William S. & Sullivan, Arthur S.) **Ruddigore: Or, the witch's curse.** (Ruddigore: Or, the witch's curse) CAST: 5f, 5m, Su. ACTS: 1. SETTINGS: English fishing village. PLAYING TIME: 30 min. PLOT: Robin Oakapple, really Sir Ruthven Murgatroyd in disguise, is in love with Rose Maybud, but is too shy to tell her. He conceals his true identity to avoid inheriting a family curse, which would condemn him to commit a crime daily or else die an agonizing death. The curse is now on his younger brother, Despard, who thinks Robin is dead. Robin enlists the help of his foster brother, Richard Dauntless, to make his feelings known to Rose, but when Richard sees Robin, he woos her for himself. Robin manages to get Rose away from Richard and they prepare to marry. However jealous Richard reveals Robin's plot to Despard, who stops the wedding by announcing the details of the family curse to all. Rose decides to marry Richard. When Robin does not commit a crime one day, his ancestors begin to torture him, but they are stopped by Sir Roderic Murgatroyd, one of the ghosts. Robin realizes that none of his ancestors should have died because they each committed suicide, a crime against themselves. Accordingly, they come to life and step out of their picture frames. Rose changes her mind, and agrees to marry Robin after all. RECOMMENDATION: Hindered severely by its lack of musical directions, this is, nonetheless, accurate and condensed well from the full length version, making it appropriate as a "first opera." ROYALTY: Free to Plays subscribers. SOURCE: Thane, Adele. (1984, May). Ruddigore: Or, the witch's curse. Plays: The Drama Magazine for Young People, pp. 61- 71. SUBJECTS/PLAY TYPE: Comedy; Musical; Curses; Adaptation.

2651. 3-6. (+) Kilcup, Rick. **Rudolph's blinker's on the blink.** CAST: 1f, 2m, Su. ACTS: 1. SETTINGS: Workshop. PLAYING TIME: 25 min. PLOT: On Christmas eve, Matilda the witch, annoyed by Santa's reindeer practicing their flying over her igloo while she tries to get ready for next Halloween, turns Rudolph's nose green. Now he can't guide Santa's sleigh. The elves steal the witch's magic book and wand to remove the spell. In all of the confusion, a good spell is cast, and Mathilda becomes Santa's copilot. RECOMMENDATION: This is clever, original, and uses especially endearing, upbeat terminology (i.e., Santa is called an old dude with a beard). ROYALTY: Free to Plays subscribers. SOURCE: Kilcup, Rick. (1980, December). Rudolph's blinker's on the blink. Plays: The Drama Magazine for Young People, pp. 37-45. SUBJECTS/PLAY TYPE: Christmas; Comedy.

2652. 7-12. (+) Mercati, Cynthia. **Rumbo!** CAST: 13f, 6m, Su. ACTS: 2. SETTINGS: Movie soundstage; gymnasium; helicopter; jungle; hut interior. PLAYING

TIME: NA. PLOT: Albert Nerval, nerd, finds himself in the unlikely role of macho hero when he overcomes a tough female gang. When the news breaks, he is drafted by the U.S. Special Forces to lead commandoes into the jungle to rescue American POWs, who turn out to be former Miss America contestants. They escape during a TV broadcast from the revolutionary camp. RECOMMENDATION: Teens will enjoy the fast paced action of this satire of film macho men, as well as the slapstick humor. The zany settings and lightning quick repartee will require mature actors. ROYALTY: $40. SOURCE: Mercati, Cynthia. (1986). Rumbo! Boston, MA: Baker's Plays. SUBJECTS/PLAY TYPE: Macho-ism; Comedy.

2653. 5-8. (+) Wilson, Pat. **The rummage rip-off.** CAST: 12f, 4m, Su. ACTS: 1. SETTINGS: School gym. PLAYING TIME: NA. PLOT: A class sponsors an auction to raise money to buy a gift for a retiring teacher. The situation gets out of hand when one of the students "collects" items from people's porches which were not left outside for the sale (e.g. Miss Abigail's laundry). Chaos abounds as members of the town and two hoods, who earlier hid stolen goods among the sale items, come to claim their possessions. All items are returned to their rightful owners and the students buy the present with the reward money they collect for capturing the thieves and recovering the stolen goods. RECOMMENDATION: This has continuous action and the dialogue is both funny and easy to remember. ROYALTY: $15. SOURCE: Wilson, Pat. (1978). The rummage rip-off. Great Ayton, Middlesbrough: Pat Wilson Plays. SUBJECTS/PLAY TYPE Auction; Robbery; Comedy.

2654. K-12. (+) Gupton, Edward & Marsh, Dick Jr. (Grimm Brothers) **Rumpelstiltskin!** (Rumpelstiltskin) CAST: 2f, 7m, Su. ACTS: 1. SETTINGS: Tailor's cottage; throne room; dungeon; garden; inn. PLAYING TIME: 45 min. PLOT: A lovely maiden supposedly can spin straw into gold but she only does so with the aid of a magical dwarf who demands her child in payment. The dwarf gives the maiden a reprieve provided she can guess his name, which she does. He then loses his magical powers. The Queen takes Rumpelstiltskin into the royal household when she realizes he wanted the child to relieve his loneliness. RECOMMENDATION: With some satirical lyrics and dialogue, this is particularly endearing because of its happy ending. Use of flats as storybook pages for switching scenes makes this easily transported. This is best produced by older grades. ROYALTY: $50. SOURCE: Gupton, Edward & Marsh, Dick Jr. (1978). Rumpelstiltskin! Franklin, OH: Eldridge Pub. Co. SUBJECTS/PLAY TYPE: Musical; Folk Tales, Germany; Magic; Adaptation.

2655. K-4*. (+) Goldberg, Moses. (Grimm Brothers) **Rumpelstiltskin.** (Rumpelstiltskin) CAST: 3f, 3m. ACTS: 3. SETTINGS: Bakery; palace; woods. PLAYING TIME: NA. PLOT: A baker's daughter promises a magical dwarf her first born child in exchange for his turning a pile of straw to gold. When it comes time for payment, Rumpelstiltskin promises to relinquish his claim if the princess can guess his name. She does, and lives happily ever after. RECOMMENDATION: Youngsters in the audience are encouraged to participate at various times throughout the play. ROYALTY: $25. SOURCE: Goldberg, Moses. (1987). Rumpelstiltskin. New Orleans, LA: Anchorage Press. SUBJECTS/PLAY TYPE Folk Tales, Germany; Magic; Greed; Adaptation.

2656. 1-6*. (-) Landes, William-Alan. (Grimm Brothers) **Rumpelstiltskin.** (Rumpelstiltskin) CAST: 1f, 5m, Su. ACTS: 2. SETTINGS: Forest; cottage; throne and vault room; Grand Hall. PLAYING TIME: 60 min. PLOT: This dramatization adds a talking magic pot and two manic royal attendants to enliven the story. RECOMMENDATION: Although there are some mildly amusing moments, most of the attempts at humor seem forced, awkward, and what children would call just plain silly. There are also subtle and overt messages of sexism. ROYALTY: $35. SOURCE: Landes, William-Alan. (1979). Rumpelstiltskin. Studio City, CA: Players Press. SUBJECTS/PLAY TYPE: Folk Tales, Germany; Magic; Greed; Musical.

2657. K-4. (+) Thane, Adele. (Grimm Brothers) **Rumpelstiltskin.** (Rumplestiltskin) CAST: 7f, 4m. ACTS: 1. SETTINGS: Hill; pavilion. PLAYING TIME: 35 min. PLOT: Rumplestiltskin provides Griszel with gold made from straw so she may save the lives of her father and herself. In return Griszel must give Rumplestiltskin her first born. When he shows up to collect his debt a year later, Griszel refuses to give up her son. Rumplestiltskin takes pity on her and gives her ten chances to guess his name. If she guesses correctly, she may keep her child. After some trickery on her husband's part, she guesses Rumplestiltskin's name. He is so distraught over losing, the parents allow him to play with their baby. RECOMMENDATION: Although this deviates slightly from the original, it is entertaining as Rumplestiltskin often speaks in rhyme and is mimed by a "shadow." The costumes are simple but many accessories are needed, including straw, flour, ribbon, etc. ROYALTY: Free to Plays subscribers. SOURCE: Thane, Adele. (1983, October). Rumplestiltskin. Plays: The Drama Magazine for Young People, pp. 41-50. SUBJECTS/PLAY TYPE: Folk tales, Germany; Magic; Greed; Playlet.

2658. 3-6. (+) Jackson, Richard Eugene. **Rumpelstiltskin is my name.** CAST: 3f, 2m, Su. ACTS: 2. SETTINGS: Throne room. PLAYING TIME: 60 min. PLOT: In this clever adaptation, the miller has two daughters, one about whom he often brags, and another whom he often ignores. Saved from one scrape by Rumpelstiltskin, the family is rescued from another by the younger daughter, whose cleverness and wit finally catch her father's attention. RECOMMENDATION: Easily adaptable to include many extras, the theme is so gently told and the characters so well drawn that the audience will be delighted. ROYALTY: $35. SOURCE: Jackson, Richard Eugene. (1978). Rumpelstiltskin is my name. Schulenburg, TX: I.E. Clark. SUBJECTS/PLAY TYPE: Folk Tale Motifs; Lies; Comedy.

2659. 4-7. (+) Boiko, Claire. **The runaway bookmobile.** CAST: 1f, 2m, Su. ACTS: 1. SETTINGS:

Bookmobile interior. **PLAYING TIME:** 20 min. **PLOT:** A reluctant reader, Dragger is convinced of the allure of books when he reads one about a bookmobile turned time machine, and meets Medusa, Queen Elizabeth, and Tom Sawyer. As the play ends, the librarian tells him that because the book is written so well, many of its readers feel as if they've actually lived its adventures. **RECOMMENDATION:** Exciting costuming, references to familiar characters from mythology and literature, and library commercials disguised as poems allow great latitude for the director and players. The literary characters could be changed to more familiar ones if desired. **ROYALTY:** NA. **SOURCE:** Boiko, Claire. (1981). Children's plays for creative actors. Boston, MA: Plays, Inc. **SUBJECTS/PLAY TYPE:** Books; Libraries; Book Week; Fantasy.

2660. 4-6. (-) Osborne, Ron. **The runaway express.** **CAST:** 2f, 2m. **ACTS:** 1. **SETTINGS:** Train lounge car. **PLAYING TIME:** 15 min. **PLOT:** The lounge car with its three passengers and conductor becomes unhitched from the engine and rolls down Dead Man's Mountain. Travelers learn that they are falling at 87 1/2 miles per hour, will encounter a sharp curve, a washed out bridge, and a deep valley. Occupants assume crash positions for each calamity, but nothing happens. The end of the line reveals a sign designating the new bridge and track improvements. The train conductor doubles as engineer, but acts in a childlike manner. He punches train tickets by hitting them with his fist, he calls passengers "picky" when they appear upset over the impending danger, and he requires passengers to say "pretty please" before providing travel information for them. **RECOMMENDATION:** The subject matter and the farcical approach seem incongruent, with illogical conclusions and unrealistic consequences. A new bridge and track repairs seem insufficient remedies for a downhill, runaway railway car, and the conductor lacks credibility. **ROYALTY:** Free to Plays subscribers. **SOURCE:** Osborne, Ron. (1984, May). The runaway express. Plays: The Drama Magazine for Young People, pp. 55-59. **SUBJECTS/PLAY TYPE:** Railroads; Comedy; Skit.

2661. 1-6. (+) Lane, Carolyn. **The runaway merry-go-round. CAST:** 13u. **ACTS:** 1. **SETTINGS:** Outside. **PLAYING TIME:** 45 min. **PLOT:** Mr. McGorkle unhappily owns and runs the merry-go-round. The children who come to ride and their parents are equally unhappy. The merry-go-round wrenches itself from the ground and takes its passengers into the sky where they find animals (the clouds) who care about them, and people who care for each other. When the merry-go-round lands back at the park, the riders have a different outlook. **RECOMMENDATION:** Children would enjoy the animation of the clouds as well as the audience participation. **ROYALTY:** $5. **SOURCE:** Lane, Carolyn. (1978). The runaway merry-go-round. Denver, CO: Pioneer Drama Service. **SUBJECTS/PLAY TYPE:** Attitudes; Merry-go-rounds; Fantasy.

2662. K-6. (+) Martin, Judith & Ashwander, Donald. **The runaway presents. CAST:** 2f, Su. **ACTS:** 1. **SETTINGS:** Bare stage. **PLAYING TIME:** NA. **PLOT:** In this humorous Christmas play, presents come to life and run away from Mrs. Hurryup's house right before her Christmas party. Out in the world they discover a movie theater, pizza stand, and warehouse. Mrs. Hurryup asks a delivery man for help retrieving the presents. He convinces them to go home. **RECOMMENDATION:** This is based on a silly premise and has no Christmas message, but probably would entertain a young audience. Costumes are cardboard boxes or paper bags. **ROYALTY:** $10. **SOURCE:** Martin, Judith, & Ashwander, Donald. (1977). The runaway presents. New Orleans, LA: Anchorage Press, Inc. **SUBJECTS/PLAY TYPE:** Christmas; Comedy; Skit.

2663. 1-4. (+) Lahr, Georgiana Lieder. **The runaway reindeer. CAST:** 2f, 3m, 28u. **ACTS:** 1. **SETTINGS:** Dining room. **PLAYING TIME:** 15 min. **PLOT:** It's Christmas Eve and Santa's reindeer have run away, refusing to pull the heavy sleigh loaded with toys. When two helicopter pilots at a nearby weather station agree to help Santa deliver part of the toys, the reindeer return to pull the lightened sleigh. **RECOMMENDATION:** Over 30 characters (including jumping jacks, toy soldiers, elves, and bears) make this a good play for an entire class. The director's choices of Christmas songs are incorporated into the plot. **ROYALTY:** Free to Plays subscribers. **SOURCE:** Lahr, Georgiana Lieder. (1979, December). The runaway reindeer. Plays: The Drama Magazine for Young People, pp. 52-56. **SUBJECTS/PLAY TYPE:** Christmas; Skit.

2664. 4-7. (+) Newman, Deborah. **The runaway robots. CAST:** 5f, 5m, 6u. **ACTS:** 1. **SETTINGS:** Gift shop. **PLAYING TIME:** 20 min. **PLOT:** Mrs. Follansbee doesn't like her husband's latest invention, robots that pick things up and put them into the trash. However, the mayor does, and he buys the robots to clean up the city's litter. **RECOMMENDATION:** This is very simple, yet entertaining. **ROYALTY:** Free to Plays subscribers. **SOURCE:** Kamerman, Sylvia E. (1981). Space and science fiction plays for young people. Boston, MA: Plays, Inc. **SUBJECTS/PLAY TYPE:** Science Fiction; Robots; Comedy.

2665. 3-5. (+) Gotwalt, Helen Louise Miller. **The runaway toys. CAST:** 8f, 6m. **ACTS:** 1. **SETTINGS:** Living room. **PLAYING TIME:** 15 min. **PLOT:** Jimmy's and Janie's toys ask Santa to take them back to Toy Land because they are no longer loved. Santa discovers that Jimmy has a new sister. The toys want Santa to give them to the baby but he refuses because they have owners. Jimmy and Janie interrupt Santa and his elves unexpectedly and the visitors hide. When Jimmy and Janie discover their old toys, they decide to give them away to a cousin. The toys agree to stay because they are going to children who will play with them. **RECOMMENDATION:** This sympathetically shows the desire to be loved, and effectively describes the concept of property rights. The rhyming dialogue will be easy to learn and fun to perform, as will the singing and dancing. **ROYALTY:** Free to Plays subscribers. **SOURCE:** Gotwalt, Helen Louise Miller. (1977, December). The runaway toys. Plays: The Drama Magazine for Young People, pp. 39-44. **SUBJECTS/PLAY TYPE:** Christmas; Musical; Comedy.

2666. 1-6. (+) Gotwalt, Helen Louise Miller. **The runaway unicorn.** CAST: 5f, 18m. ACTS: 1. SETTINGS: None. PLAYING TIME: NA. PLOT: All the characters in storyland search for the unicorn when they find he is missing. He returns only when a young girl assures him that he is real because children believe in him. RECOMMENDATION: The cast size might allow an entire class to participate. Storybook lane with its large posters will allow children who would rather draw than act a chance to be an important part of the play. ROYALTY: Free to Plays subscribers. SOURCE: Gotwalt, Helen Louise Miller. (1986). Special plays for holidays. Boston, MA: Plays, Inc. SUBJECTS/PLAY TYPE: Unicorns; Playlet.

2667. 7-12. (+) Christopher, Jay. **Runaways.** CAST: 12f, 7m. ACTS: 2. SETTINGS: Reception area. PLAYING TIME: NA. PLOT: Over the course of a long hard evening, Linda (who works at a runaway shelter) learns first hand about the various breakdowns of love and responsibility that can occur in families, and about the dangers runaways face on the street. When her own sister runs away, Linda has to confront the possibility that her sister may become a murder victim. The morning brings reassurance, and new maturity and understanding to Linda, her sister, and other runaways in the shelter. RECOMMENDATION: This addresses the problems of teens who run away in a sensitive, nonpatronizing way, and the dialogue avoids cliches. The graffiti wall (which provides the backdrop for the sets) is a fine device for providing transition from one scene to another. Therapists are shown as human and nonjudg mental. ROYALTY: $50. SOURCE: Christopher, Jay. (1980). Runaways. Chicago, IL: Dramatic Pub. Co. SUBJECTS/PLAY TYPE: Runaways; Drama.

2668. K-3. (-) Fraser, Kathleen. **Running the gauntlet.** CAST: 2m. ACTS: 1. SETTINGS: None. PLAYING TIME: NA. PLOT: One boy dares the new boy in the neighborhood to "run the gauntlet," over the knees and feet of all the other boys. Fearing physical harm and humiliation, the new boy declines. RECOMMENDATION: There appears to be no point to this. ROYALTY: NA. SOURCE: Bauer, Caroline Feller. (1987). Presenting reader's theatre: Plays and poems to read aloud. New York, NY: H.W. Wilson Co. SUBJECTS/PLAY TYPE: Bullies; Skit.

2669. 9-12. (+) Rudolph, Grace Gannon. **Rural nightmare.** CAST: 4f, 3m. ACTS: 1. SETTINGS: Living room. PLAYING TIME: NA. PLOT: A city couple is about to move to an old house in the country. They find out from a neighbor that a deformed child had been born there 40 years before and is rumored to have lived there, hidden away, all this time. With the house sold, the "creature" is hunted by the residents as if it is an animal. The couple finds indisputable evidence that someone has indeed been living in the attic. Fearing the hunter neighbors as much as the "creature," the couple flees back to the city, leaving a sign for the hunters, as they requested, that something is there at the house. RECOMMENDATION: A suspenseful drama, this is very thought provoking. ROYALTY: $15. SOURCE: Rudolph, Grace Gannon. (1978). Rural nightmare. Boston, MA: Baker's Plays. SUBJECTS/PLAY TYPE: Mystery; Disabilities; Drama.

2670. 6-9. (+) Bland, Joellen. (Hugo, Victor) **The sacrifice.** (Les Miserables) CAST: 2f, 6m, Su. ACTS: 1. SETTINGS: Street; garden; two home interiors; barricade in street. PLAYING TIME: 35 min. PLOT: A love story set during the French Revolution, this tells the story of the romance between Maurius and Cosette. The two are kept apart by an overprotective father, a jealous girl, and the turmoil of battle. In the final scene, the characters are set for a joyful reunion. RECOMMENDATION: Although some events have been changed, this remains remarkably faithful to the original, as all of the main characters are brought into the plot in a way that depicts their roles in the original. ROYALTY: Free to Plays subscribers. SOURCE: Bland, Joellen. (1979, January). The Sacrifice. Plays: The Drama Magazine for Young People, pp. 69-80. SUBJECTS/PLAY TYPE: Romance; Revolution, France; Reader's Theater; Adaptation.

2671. 5-8. (+) Rembrandt, Elaine. **The sacrifice.** CAST: 3f, 8m, Su. ACTS: 1. SETTINGS: School; house; street; enemy camp. PLAYING TIME: 20 min. PLOT: A 15 year old boy joins Judah Maccabee and his army to save their people from humiliation and slaughter by the Syrians. The boy sacrifices himself to save his people. RECOMMENDATION: The feeling of freedom and the memorializing of those who pay the price for it give this impact. ROYALTY: None. SOURCE: Rembrandt, Elaine. (1981). Heroes, heroines & holidays - plays for Jewish youth. Denver, CO: Alternatives in Religious Education, Inc. SUBJECTS/PLAY TYPE: Freedom; War; Jewish Drama.

2672. K-5. (+) Boiko, Claire. **Safety circus.** CAST: 2f, 18u. ACTS: 1. SETTINGS: Circus tent. PLAYING TIME: 20 min. PLOT: Circus performers teach the audience important safety rules through the use of rhymes set to familiar tunes. RECOMMENDATION: This is very clever and colorful. Easy to sing, familiar melodies (Clementine, Polly wolly doodle, etc.) make lines easy to learn and hold audience attention, as do the fast pace and rapidly changing acts. One challenge may be costuming, since characters include bears, firemen, a Keystone Cop, and an old fashioned bathing beauty. ROYALTY: Free to Plays subscribers. SOURCE: Boiko, Claire. (1988, May). Safety circus. Plays: The Drama Magazine for Young People, pp. 39-42. SUBJECTS/PLAY TYPE Safety; Circus; Clowns; Skit.

2673. K. (-) Gotwalt, Helen Louise Miller. **The safety clinic.** CAST: 10f, 4m, 5u. ACTS: 1. SETTINGS: Clinic. PLAYING TIME: 15 min. PLOT: In a series of vignettes, parents take children to the doctor for safety related injuries. RECOMMENDATION: The overbearing moral messages may be offensive, and with the concern about substance abuse, one of the play's prescriptions may cause concern: "A pill/shot will make it all better." ROYALTY: Free to Plays subscribers. SOURCE: Gotwalt, Helen Louise Miller. (1985). First plays for children: A collection of little plays for the youngest players. Boston, MA: Plays, Inc. SUBJECTS/PLAY TYPE: Safety; Doctors; Playlet.

2674. 4-7. (+) Kurtz, Joy. **Saga of dead dog gulch.** CAST: 11f, 16m, Su. ACTS: 1. SETTINGS: Main street. PLAYING TIME: 60 min. PLOT: The women of the mining town, Dead Dog Gulch, beautify by painting several buildings. The miners disapprove, but before they can act, some wicked cowboys move in on the town. Not until the town's children set the cowboys up to be captured do the miners save the town. The grateful women return the town to normal. RECOMMENDATION: The music is very catchy and the play includes a square dance. ROYALTY: $70. SOURCE: Kurtz, Joy. (n.d.). The saga of Dead Dog Gulch. Franklin, OH: Eldridge Pub. Co. SUBJECTS/PLAY TYPE: Western; Beautification; Operetta.

2675. 6-10. (+) Olfson, Lewy. **The saga of John Trueheart.** CAST: 3f, 2m. ACTS: 1. SETTINGS: Cottage living room. PLAYING TIME: 15 min. PLOT: Lola La Rue threatens to foreclose on the mortgage to the Trueheart's home unless John agrees to play the piano at her Hotsy Totsy Honky Tonky Pizza Parlor. John Trueheart refuses to compromise his principles. However, Molly, a friend of the family, confesses that she has desperately dreamed of becoming an entertainer. Lola La Rue, satisfied with her potential employee, releases the Truehearts from their debt. RECOMMENDATION: The characters are convincing and consistent in their speech and actions, and could be easily portrayed by young amateurs. ROYALTY: Free to Plays subscribers. SOURCE: Olfson, Lewy. (1975, March). The saga of John Trueheart. Plays: The Drama Magazine for Young People, pp. 69-73. SUBJECTS/PLAY TYPE: Family; Mortgages; Comedy.

2676. 5-8. (+) Winther, Barbara. **The saga of the silver gull.** CAST: 3f, 3m, 1u. ACTS: 1. SETTINGS: Steamboat deck. PLAYING TIME: 20 min. PLOT: Captain Barnacle doesn't have the money to pay for his boat, so Snarling Sam is going to repossess it. Sweet William (a crew member) finds a chest of gold, and Snarling Sam is paid off. RECOMMENDATION: This classic melodrama is complete with overdrawn good and bad characters, romance, and delightfully droll humor. ROYALTY: Free to Plays subscribers. SOURCE: Winther, Barbara. (1979, February). The saga of the silver gull. Plays: The Drama Magazine for Young People, pp. 45-51. SUBJECTS/PLAY TYPE: Mortgages; Melodrama.

2677. 7-8. (+) Faier, Joan Sari. **The sage of Monticello.** CAST: 10m, 1u. ACTS: 1. SETTINGS: Bare stage, props. PLAYING TIME: 25 min. PLOT: This portrays historically accurate accounts of the friendship and rivalry between John Adams and Thomas Jefferson through an imaginary conversation that they have. The topics of discussion include the writing of the Declaration of Independence, their differences of political opinion since Adams is a Federalist and Jefferson is a Republican, and Jefferson's plan for founding the University of Virginia. The play ends with the narrator revealing that John Adams and Thomas Jefferson died within a few hours of each other on July 4, 1826. RECOMMENDATION: Some unusual drama techniques (flashbacks and projection screens) could be taught as part of a drama class. ROYALTY: Free to Plays subscribers. SOURCE: Faier, Joan Sari. (1976,

November). The sage of Monticello. Plays: The Drama Magazine for Young People, pp. 87-96. SUBJECTS/PLAY TYPE: Jefferson, Thomas; Adams, John; Independence Day, U.S.; Playlet.

2678. 6-9. (+) Olfson, Lewy. **Sail on! Sail on!** CAST: 1f, 5m. ACTS: 1. SETTINGS: Living room. PLAYING TIME: 15 min. PLOT: Columbus finally obtains jewels from Queen Isabella of Spain, which he barters for secondhand ships on sale at the local boat store. He holds a press conference and discusses his plans with reporters Harry Nina, Kate Pinta and Frank Santa Maria. As the play ends, Columbus and his mates leave for the "boat store" while trying to determine good names for the three ships that they will buy. RECOMMENDATION: Partially accurate, this play is a humorous approach to learning history. ROYALTY: Free to Plays subscribers. SOURCE: Olfson, Lewy. (1986, October). Sail on! sail on! Plays: The Drama Magazine for Young people, pp. 53-56. SUBJECTS/PLAY TYPE: Columbus, Christopher; Skit.

2679. 10-12. (+) Lane, Esther Porter. **Saint George and the dragon.** CAST: 5f, 7m, Su. ACTS: 1. SETTINGS: Castle. PLAYING TIME: NA. PLOT: Several knights engage in battle and slay or are slain. A doctor restores some to health. A dragon threatens the countryside unless he is given the young princess as a meal. She volunteers to die but as the dragon is about to consume her, St. George fights and defeats the dragon. RECOMMENDATION: This Christmas Mummer's play is authentically contrived but is too reliant on rather obscure symbolic interactions between real characters and allegorical figures to be comprehensible to those unfamiliar with the genre. ROYALTY: $25. SOURCE: Lane, Esther Porter. (1985). Saint George and the dragon. New Orleans, LA: Anchorage Press, Inc. SUBJECTS/PLAY TYPE: Mummer's Plays; Saint George; Drama.

2680. 4-6. (+) Roam, Pearl. **Salt water tea.** CAST: 3f, 3m, Su. ACTS: 1. SETTINGS: Kitchen; ship deck. PLAYING TIME: 20 min. PLOT: During the Revolutionary War, when their ailing grandfather worsens, Mercy and Abby dress up as boys to get Abby's parents from a neighbor's house. They are caught by patriots preparing for the Boston Tea Party. Forced to dress like Indians and take part in the raid, Mercy and Abby catch one of the patriots stealing some of the tea for himself and are praised for their patriotism. RECOMMENDATION: With believable characters, this provides intriguing explanations of the circumstances leading to the Boston Tea Party. ROYALTY: Free to Plays subscribers. SOURCE: Roam, Pearl. (1985, January/February). Salt water tea. Plays: The Drama Magazine for Young People, pp. 25-32. SUBJECTS/PLAY TYPE: Boston Tea Party; Revolution, U.S.; Playlet.

2681. 6-10. (+) Brink, Carol Ryrie. **Salute Mr. Washington.** CAST: 3f, 2m. ACTS: 1. SETTINGS: Drawing room. PLAYING TIME: 25 min. PLOT: Captain Hunt requests that Lady Gweneth and her Loyalist nephew, Harry, allow their house to be used as a headquarters for Mr. Washington. Lady Gweneth is outraged, but Anne, in love with Captain Hunt, is so moved by the sight of ragged soldiers marching alongside Mr. Washington, she not only offers her house, but agrees to stay and help build a new nation. RECOMMENDATION: Although this does not provide much factual information, it does portray the intense emotions of determination and loyalty that motivate those who fight for something in which they believe. ROYALTY: Free to Plays subscribers. SOURCE: Brink, Carol Ryrie. (1976, March). Salute to Mr. Washington. Plays: The Drama Magazine for Young People, pp. 61-70. SUBJECTS/PLAY TYPE: Washington, George; Revolution, U.S.; Playlet.

2682. 6-9. (+) Boiko, Claire. **Salute to a lady. CAST:** 3f, 10m, Su. **ACTS:** 1. **SETTINGS:** Bare stage, props, backdrop. **PLAYING TIME:** 30 min. **PLOT:** Uncle Sam brings the audience back in time to 1885 when the pedestal for the Statue of Liberty was being constructed. The workers explain that the statue will be known as Lady Liberty, Mother of the Exiles. An Indian girl enters, drums are heard, and a procession of people approach the pedestal (Thomas Jefferson, Ben Franklin, a slave family, immigrants from all over the world) singing, "I Am Bound for the Promised Land." Miss Liberty takes her place and recites "The New Colossus." Uncle Sam welcomes the new citizens. A medley of patriotic songs are sung, concluding with "God Bless America." **RECOMMENDATION:** Originally written to honor the 100th birthday of the Statue of Liberty, this could be used in a student assembly, or a choral department could perform it at a PTA meeting or open house. **ROYALTY:** Free to Plays subscribers. **SOURCE:** Boiko, Claire. (1986, October). Salute to a lady. Plays: The Drama Magazine for Young People, pp. 47-52. **SUBJECTS/PLAY TYPE:** Statue of Liberty; Immigrants; Pageant.

2683. 3-6. (+) Trudell, Barbara. **A salute to the flag. CAST:** 33u. **ACTS:** 1. **SETTINGS:** Bare stage, props. **PLAYING TIME:** 25 min. **PLOT:** Actors relate various roles of flags, concentrating on the evolution of the American flag and describing Revolutionary War events. **RECOMMENDATION:** Due to the large cast required, this tableau is appropriate for a multitude of different groups and allows for maximum participation. **ROYALTY:** Free to Plays subscribers. **SOURCE:** Trudell, Barbara. (1976, February). A salute to the flag. Plays: The Drama Magazine for Young People, pp. 79-83. **SUBJECTS/PLAY TYPE:** Revolution, U.S.; Flags; Choral Reading.

2684. 1-5. (+) Solomon, Olivia. (Bannerman, Helen) **Sambo and the tigers.** (The story of little black Sambo) **CAST:** 1m, 8u. **ACTS:** 1. **SETTINGS:** Jungle. **PLAYING TIME:** NA. **PLOT:** While Monkey tries to teach Giraffe to dance, a ferocious roar scatters the animals. Sambo is left alone to foil vain Tiger I by offering him his beautiful new jacket. The tiger accepts and exits. The other animals compliment Sambo as Tiger II enters. Sambo gives him his red trousers. The other animals applaud until Tiger III (rather old and decrepit) chases them but is appeased with Sambo's beautiful shoes. Sambo appeases Tiger IV with his umbrella. As Sambo grieves for his clothing, all the tigers enter, each claiming to be the grandest. They remove their

clothing, grab each other by the tail and run faster and faster around the tree, ultimately melting into butter. Sambo takes the butter home, and his mother makes pancakes for all. The four tigers discuss the consequences of wicked behavior. Tiger IV begins to recount the story of Sambo and the tigers. All join in to conclude the play. **RECOMMENDATION:** The tigers' negative traits (mimicry, bickering, vanity, guile, duplicity) are reinforced by the characters of Parrot, Serpent, Monkey and Giraffe as each augments the moral. This requires actors who are able to memorize lengthy parts and comprehend some of the more advanced vocabulary and sentence structure. **ROYALTY:** None, if written application is received. **SOURCE:** Solomon, Olivia. (1983). Sambo and the tigers. Tuscaloosa, AL: Portals Press. **SUBJECTS/PLAY TYPE:** Pride; Vanity; Adaptation.

2685. 2-5. (+) Sroda, Anne. **Santa changes his mind. CAST:** 3f, 2m. **ACTS:** 1. **SETTINGS:** Igloo home. **PLAYING TIME:** 15 min. **PLOT:** The Elf family needs a larger home but can't afford one. The only jobs available are in Santa's factory, but Santa refuses to hire women. So, Mrs. Elf disguises herself as a man. When she sets a new production record, Mrs. Elf is found out. Santa realizes his mistake and the Elf family looks for a new igloo. **RECOMMENDATION:** This is an excellent vehicle for introducing the equal opportunity message to children. **ROYALTY:** Free to Plays subscribers. **SOURCE:** Kamerman, Sylvia E. (1978) On stage for Christmas. Boston, MA: Plays, Inc. **SUBJECTS/PLAY TYPE:** Christmas; Equal Rights; Women's Rights; Playlet.

2686. 1-5. (+) McGowan, Jane. **Santa Claus for President. CAST:** 1f, 6m, 11u. **ACTS:** 1. **SETTINGS:** Santa's workshop. **PLAYING TIME:** 10 min. **PLOT:** The children of the United States send telegrams to Santa Claus asking him to be President, but children from other nations convince him that he is better off being Santa Claus. **RECOMMENDATION:** This teaches that Christmas is for sharing and that Santa Claus must also be shared. **ROYALTY:** Free to Plays subscribers. **SOURCE:** Kamerman, Sylvia E. (1982). Christmas play favorites for young people. Boston, MA: Plays, Inc. **SUBJECTS/PLAY TYPE:** Christmas; Comedy.

2687. 4-8. (+) Martens, Anne Coulter. **Santa Claus is twins. CAST:** 4f, 5m, Su. **ACTS:** 1. **SETTINGS:** Recreation room. **PLAYING TIME:** 25 min. **PLOT:** Children trying to raise money to buy toys for needy children encounter problems when two boys play Santa and one is blamed for stealing a Christmas tree. The accused boy's honesty is revealed in the end. **RECOMMENDATION:** Although there is some hedging about the truth, this does show how mistaken identity and rash judgment can cause problems. **ROYALTY:** Free to Plays subscribers. **SOURCE:** Kamerman, Sylvia. (1988) The big book of Christmas plays. Boston, MA: Plays, Inc. **SUBJECTS/PLAY TYPE:** Christmas; Comedy.

2688. 1-4. (+) McGowan, Jane. **The Santa Claus twins. CAST:** 4f, 9m, Su. **ACTS:** 1. **SETTINGS:** Bare stage, props. **PLAYING TIME:** 10 min. **PLOT:** Two boys want to be Santa Claus in the school Christmas play. Everything is done to try to choose between them: their jolliness is tested, they are measured and weighed, and the students hold a vote. The tie is broken by Santa, who writes a letter saying that both boys should play Santa since it is such a big job. RECOMMENDATION: Written in rhyme, this will be easy for younger children to memorize and perform. The message that it is not always necessary to defeat an opponent is especially endearing. ROYALTY: Free to plays subscribers. SOURCE: McGowan, Jane. (1986, December). The Santa Claus twins. Plays: The Drama Magazine for Young People, pp. 37-41. SUBJECTS/PLAY TYPE: Christmas; Playlet.

2689. 5-8. (+) Koury, Jacqueline Margo. **Santa Claus's retirement.** CAST: 1f, 4m, Su. ACTS: 1. SETTINGS: Santa's home and workshop; employment agency. PLAYING TIME: 15 min. PLOT: Santa decides to retire and tries to find his replacement. During his search he learns that all he really needs to do instead of retiring is to modernize and become more efficient. RECOMMENDATION: The humor here lies in the foibles of the replacements that Santa interviews (one is allergic to reindeer, one demands a pool and tennis courts, etc.). ROYALTY: Free to Plays subscribers. SOURCE: Koury, Jacqueline Margo. (1983, December). Santa Claus's retirement. Plays: The Drama Magazine for Young People, pp. 31-34. SUBJECTS/PLAY TYPE: Christmas; Skit.

2690. 5-8. (+) Majeski, Bill. **Santa gets an off-season job.** CAST: 2f, 3m, 1u. ACTS: 1. SETTINGS: Cottage; office. PLAYING TIME: NA. PLOT: Inflation hits the North Pole and a jittery Santa Claus is accompanied by Mrs. Claus to the Acme Employment Agency, where Santa finds, to his dismay, that he must compete with Rip Van Winkle and Dracula. Santa turns down jobs as a human cannonball, equatorial crossing guard, wishing well coin changer, and tooth fairy. When Dracula shows interest in the tooth fairy position, Santa changes his mind and finally accepts that position. RECOMMENDATION: The use of homonyms to confuse the characters adds to the general hilarity. The audience must be mature enough to understand the plays on words, as well as to recognize the characters of Dracula and Rip Van Winkle. ROYALTY: None. SOURCE: Majeski, Bill. (1981). Easy skits, blackouts and pantomimes. Woodstock, IL: Dramatic Pub. Co. SUBJECTS/PLAY TYPE: Comedy; Employment; Santa Claus; Skit.

2691. 5-8. (-) Hoppenstedt, Elbert. **Santa goes mod.** CAST: 5f, 7m, Su. ACTS: 1. SETTINGS: Santa's workshop. PLAYING TIME: 20 min. PLOT: To the world's surprise, Santa calls a press conference to announce plans to modernize Christmas. RECOMMENDATION: This is predictable and boring. ROYALTY: Free to Plays subscribers. SOURCE: Kamerman, Sylvia E. (1976). On stage for Christmas. Boston, MA: Plays, Inc. SUBJECTS/PLAY TYPE: Christmas; Comedy.

2692. 1-5. (+) McSweeny, Maxine. **Santa, please get up!** CAST: 9f, 5m. ACTS: 1. SETTINGS: Living room; bedroom. PLAYING TIME: NA. PLOT: A weary Santa is visited by a woman and her bratty daughter who

complain about the toy Santa delivered last Christmas. Santa decides no one will care if he sleeps instead of delivering toys this Christmas. No one can wake him except a child who enters crying, wanting Santa to visit her house. With the evidence provided by the child that someone cares about his work, Santa leaves to deliver his presents. RECOMMENDATION: The antics of Santa's helpers are amusing and each has a distinctive personality and manner which is well demonstrated by words and actions. The audience will understand the reason for Santa's surly attitude and can sympathize with his need to feel wanted and appreciated. ROYALTY: NA. SOURCE: McSweeny, Maxine. (1977). Christmas plays for young players. South Brunswick: A.S. Barnes. SUBJECTS/PLAY TYPE: Christmas; Playlet.

2693. 6-8. (+) Majeski, Bill. **Santa sees a shrink, or yule never know the trouble I've seen.** CAST: 8f, 5m. ACTS: 3. SETTINGS: 2 offices, one with psychiatrists's couch. PLAYING TIME: 45 min. PLOT: Feeling that his work is no longer appreciated by greedy children, and disturbed because his elves are unhappy with working conditions, Santa is fed up. Mrs. Claus suggests an emotional therapist. Reluctantly, Santa takes the therapist's advice and goes on vacation, spending each of the other holidays of the year in exotic places. On Christmas Eve, Santa returns home, still not ready to do his job. He offers the mailman, also unhappy with his job, the opportunity to play Santa while he, Santa, spends a restful Christmas at home with Mrs. Claus. RECOMMENDATION: The characters evoke an empathy based upon an understanding of just how Santa, Mrs. Claus, and the mailman feel. Consequently, this is suitable for a much older audience than would be expected. The dialog may need to be modernized. With its surprise ending, this would be a nice change from typical holiday fare. ROYALTY: $15. SOURCE: Majeski, Bill. (1978). Santa sees a shrink, or yule never know the trouble I've seen. Denver, CO: Pioneer Drama Service, Inc. SUBJECTS/PLAY TYPE: Santa Claus; Christmas; Comedy.

2694. K-4. (+) Johnson, Martha P. **The Santa strike.** CAST: 2f, 2m, 13u. ACTS: 1. SETTINGS: Santa's workshop. PLAYING TIME: 15 min. PLOT: Troubles with the elves' labor union, and a reindeer equal rights issue threaten to cancel Santa's Christmas Eve activities. Mrs. Claus is too busy studying computer science to bake cookies and Santa is worn out. Two children help, and are rewarded when Santa grants their wish that their whole family spend Christmas together. RECOMMENDATION: This effectively and amusingly combines modern day issues with a traditional Christmas story. ROYALTY: Free to Plays subscribers. SOURCE: Johnson, Martha. (1981, December). The Santa strike. Plays: The Drama Magazine for Young People, pp. 33-38. SUBJECTS/PLAY TYPE: Christmas; Comedy.

2695. K-2. (-) Fisher, Aileen Lucia. **Santa, the wise old owl.** CAST: 7u. ACTS: 1. SETTINGS: Barnyard. PLAYING TIME: 5 min. PLOT: The farm animals learn that giving for Christmas is more fun than receiving. RECOMMENDATION: This relies heavily on cliches and is boring. ROYALTY: Free to Plays subscribers. SOURCE:

Fisher, Aileen Lucia. (1985). Year-Round Programs for Young Players. Boston, MA: Plays, Inc. **SUBJECTS/PLAY TYPE**: Christmas; Playlet.

2696. 1-3. (-) Bauman, A.F. **Santa's alphabet. CAST**: 1f, 1m, 27u. **ACTS**: 1. **SETTINGS**: Living room. **PLAYING TIME**: 15 min. **PLOT**: Santa's elves think of presents which start with each letter of the alphabet. **RECOMMENDATION**: There is a great amount of memorization here, as 26 presents and 26 children's names are rattled off in alphabetical order. This seems too complex a vehicle for teaching the alphabet. **ROYALTY**: Free to Plays subscribers. **SOURCE**: Bauman, A.F. (1978, December). Santa's alphabet. Plays: The Drama Magazine for Young People, pp. 47- 52. **SUBJECTS/PLAY TYPE**: Christmas; Alphabet; Playlet.

2697. K-6. (+) Weiler, Beverly. **Santa's Christmas tree. CAST**: 7f, 8m, Su. **ACTS**: 2. **SETTINGS**: Santa's house; Snowy Mountain. **PLAYING TIME**: NA. **PLOT**: Santa's elves travel to Snowy Mountain to choose the Claus' Christmas tree. Each of the largest and proudest trees expect the honor to be theirs. However, during a blizzard, small and scraggly Miss Merry shows a kind and gentle spirit by protecting the forest animals and the elves choose her. **RECOMMENDATION**: Although older children would be required for some parts and for production effects, the music is fun, the dialogue simple, and the plot entrancing. **ROYALTY**: $50. **SOURCE**: Weiler, Beverly. (1984). Santa's Christmas tree. Chicago, IL: Dramatic Pub. Co. **SUBJECTS/PLAY TYPE**: Christmas; Musical.

2698. 1-8. (+) Thornton, Jane Foster. **Santa's magic hat. CAST**: 9u. **ACTS**: 1. **SETTINGS**: Bare stage, backdrops. **PLAYING TIME**: 15 min. **PLOT**: Henry and a greedy elf steal Santa's magic hat to make Christmas their own. Accidentally, they tear the hat in half and are turned into enormous snowmen by Snow Fairy, who gives them until morning to discover the magic words to break her spell. If they are unsuccessful, they will melt when the sun comes up. The two help a woman who has dropped some cookies and learn "please" and "thank you;" they help a little girl cross the street and learn "east, west, home is best." They then regret that they won't be able to say "Merry Christmas to you" to their parents. The spell is broken because they thought about someone else's feelings. **RECOMMENDATION**: This creative presentation uses clever rhymes and a well developed plot, although it does take the idea of a wizard and the "home is best" line from **The wizard of Oz**. **ROYALTY**: Free to Plays subscribers. **SOURCE**: Thornton, Jane Foster. (1988, December). Santa's magic hat. Plays: The Drama Magazine for Young People, pp. 49-64. **SUBJECTS/PLAY TYPE**: Christmas; Puppet Play.

2699. K-3. (+) Bennett, Rowena. **Santa's send off. CAST**: 1f, 1m, 3u. **ACTS**: 1. **SETTINGS**: Bare stage, props. **PLAYING TIME**: 1 min. **PLOT**: Mrs. Claus and three elves wake up a slumbering Santa to get him and his toy laden sleigh started on the Christmas Eve trip to deliver presents around the world. **RECOMMENDATION**: The rhyme is clever and the analogies well worded in this simple introduction to Santa's famous journey. **ROYALTY**: Free

to Plays subscribers. **SOURCE**: Bennett, Rowena. (1988, December). Santa's send off. Plays: The Drama Magazine for Young People, pp. 47-48. **SUBJECTS/PLAY TYPE**: Christmas; Choral Reading.

2700. 3-6. (+) Scott, Pam. **Santa's X-Arctic adventure. CAST**: 3f, 2m, Su. **ACTS**: 1. **SETTINGS**: Workshop. **PLAYING TIME**: 12 min. **PLOT**: Mr. Android sells Santa an X-Arctic System to finish the Christmas toys. Santa gives the elves December off. After the elves leave town, the system breaks down and Rudolph's nose goes out. Fortunately, the elves become homesick and return the day before Christmas Eve, complete all the toys, and fix Rudolph's nose. **RECOMMENDATION**: This has creative movement, dramatics, gestures, and pantomime. For the songs and dances, live or recorded music may be used. **ROYALTY**: Free to Plays subscribers. **SOURCE**: Scott, Pam. (1980, December). Santa's X-Arctic adventure. Plays: The Drama Magazine for Young People, pp. 65-70. **SUBJECTS/PLAY TYPE**: Christmas; Comedy.

2701. 5-9. (+) Seale, Nancy. (Burnett, Frances Hodgson) **Sara Crewe.** (Sara Crewe) **CAST**: 19f, 5m. **ACTS**: 3. **SETTINGS**: Street; parlor; attic; study. **PLAYING TIME**: NA. **PLOT**: Sara has a wonderful life until the sudden death of her father leaves her a penniless orphan in the hands of a tyrannical head mistress and owner of a private girls' school. **RECOMMENDATION**: This delightful adaptation will appeal mostly to girls. It could be produced effectively with or without music. **ROYALTY**: $35. **SOURCE**: Seale, Nancy. (1982). Sara Crewe. New Orleans, LA: Anchorage Press, Inc. **SUBJECTS/PLAY TYPE**: Private Schools; Orphans; Musical; Adaptation.

2702. 9-12. (+) Facos, James. **Sara Varn. CAST**: 3f, 2m. **ACTS**: 1. **SETTINGS**: Living Room. **PLAYING TIME**: NA. **PLOT**: The contempt and sterility in the Varn marriage is revealed through expository dialogue providing details of Carl and Sara's mutual bitterness. Sara's desire for wealth and stature in the community have not been satisfied by Carl's earning power. She tries to achieve her dreams through her son, Richie, whose marriage to the pregnant Jean she discourages, in favor of his alliance with Vinnie, a plain, spiritless socialite. Both Carl and Richie blame Jean's suicide on Sara. Richie marries Vinnie and Carl abandons Sara, dying shortly thereafter. Sara reveals to her bitter son that she sacrificed her relationship with Carl to secure material wealth and social rank for Richie. Softened by her tearful apology, Richie encourages Sara to focus on the impending birth of his first child. Sara's attempts to manipulate the lives of Richie, Vinnie and their daughter, Jean, cause Richie's death. The closing curtain finds Sara alone, calling pitifully for Carl. **RECOMMENDATION**: The manipulation of three generations of family members is artfully and convincingly portrayed. Sara provokes the wrath and disgust of the audience with her cold, calculated zeal and her smug satisfaction with her impact upon the lives of those nearest her. A lesson about greed and subversive undermining of personal happiness is learned. The production demands introspective, emotive student actors. **ROYALTY**: $25. **SOURCE**: Facos, James. (1988). Sara Varn.

Franklin, OH: Eldridge Pub. Co. **SUBJECTS/PLAY TYPE:** Greed; Drama.

2703. 8-12. (-) Peters, R. Cornelius & Magor, Louis. **Sarsaparilla, please. CAST:** 3f, 3m, Su. **ACTS:** 2. **SETTINGS:** Bare stage. **PLAYING TIME:** NA. **PLOT:** An assortment of old west characters play out a story of good and evil centered on the acquisition of a valuable mill by villainous Simon Sly who also lusts after fair Abigail. To secure both, Sly gets Roger drunk so Roger signs away ownership to the mill and disgraces his new bride, Abigail. A woman of questionable reputation threatens to expose Simon's underhanded trick and in the altercation that ensues, Simon stabs her. Roger and Abigail reconcile, the mill is saved, and Simon is hanged. **RECOMMENDATION:** Cardboard characters with whom audiences will not identify comprise the people in this musical melodrama. Occasionally, some humor surfaces in the lines of the piano player and Ben (narrator/deputy constable/ minister), but they are not enough to brighten an otherwise tiresome and senseless plot. **ROYALTY:** $75. **SOURCE:** Peters, R. Cornelius & Magor, Louis. (1979). Sarsaparilla, please. Woodstock, IL: Dramatic Pub. Co. **SUBJECTS/PLAY TYPE:** Virtue; Swindlers and Swindling; Melodrama.

2704. 7-12. (+) Gleason, William. **Saturday, the 14th. CAST:** 2f, 3m, 14u. **ACTS:** 2. **SETTINGS:** Lodge; room in a sanitarium; kitchen. **PLAYING TIME:** NA. **PLOT:** Thirty years before, Mason, a boy with no friends and a large appetite, stole into the summer camp's kitchen and ate himself to death (or so the campers thought). Using an electric mixer and toilet plunger, he returned to take revenge on the counselors who made him unhappy. Through many plot twists, the audience learns that a planted character in the audience is actually Mason. **RECOMMENDATION:** This satirizes maniacal killer movies without the bloodshed that usually accompanies them. The killer is a pudgy eight year old wearing a hockey mask who, as he grows up, treats his line of work (maniac) like any other profession. It is a very clever, original idea. **ROYALTY:** NA. **SOURCE:** Gleason, William. (1987). Saturday, the 14th. Woodstock, IL: Dramatic Pub. Co. **SUBJECTS/PLAY TYPE:** Halloween; Camp Counselors; Satire.

2705. 3-8. (+) Thane, Adele. **The saucy scarecrow. CAST:** 8f, 3m, Su. **ACTS:** 1. **SETTINGS:** Barley field. **PLAYING TIME:** 25 min. **PLOT:** On Halloween, a farmer and his daughter erect a nobly outfitted scarecrow. At dark, witches arrive to concoct some brew, discover the scarecrow, give it life, and include it in their play of stirring the cauldrons, dancing, and riding broomsticks. The scarecrow begs the witches to allow him to stay alive. After giving the scarecrow a conscience, the witches leave him alone, hungry and cold. When the farmer and his daughter return the following morning, the scarecrow promises to keep the birds out in return for food. The farmer and his daughter tell the scarecrow that he is the best they have ever seen. **RECOMMENDATION:** The vocabulary and complexity of action necessitates production by upper grade levels, but the subject matter, variety of action, and characters make it enjoyable for all

ages. Children will especially enjoy the birds flying about, the witches on broomsticks, stirring the brew, and the dancing and singing. The cast can accommodate any number of players. Changes in lighting distinguish the times of day and lend a nice dramatic effect. **ROYALTY:** Free to Plays subscribers. **SOURCE:** Thane, Adele. (1983). Plays from famous stories and fairy tales. Boston, MA: Plays, Inc. **SUBJECTS/PLAY TYPE:** Halloween; Witches; Scarecrows; Playlet.

2706. 10-12. (+) Erhard, Tom. **I saved a winter just for you. CAST:** 5f, 3m. **ACTS:** 1. **SETTINGS:** Bare stage. **PLAYING TIME:** NA. **PLOT:** Eight nameless teenage actors talk with each other and the audience about the problems of growing up, touching on sports, child abuse, war, pregnancy, responsibility and love. **RECOMMENDATION:** The work of close to 80 young writers has been collected and adapted to create this unusual collage of stories and poems which reflect the difficulties of being 17. **ROYALTY:** $50. **SOURCE:** Erhard, Tom. (1984). I saved a winter just for you. Woodstock, IL: Dramatic Pub. Co. **SUBJECTS/PLAY TYPE:** Adolescent Problems; Family; Drama.

2707. 8-12. (+) Fay, Maxine. **Saving the old homestead. CAST:** 3f, 7m. **ACTS:** 1. **SETTINGS:** Living room; woods; sawmill. **PLAYING TIME:** 20 min. **PLOT:** A young man tries to save his fiancee's family from being thrown out into the streets by an unscrupulous villain who holds the mortgage. The villain offers them their mortgage in exchange for their worthless greasy oil stocks. Suspecting foul play, the hero hides the stocks, but he and his fiancee become hostages in a sawmill. They are saved by Lawyer I.M. True, who informs them that their stocks are no longer worthless. **RECOMMENDATION:** An M.C. encourages the audience to hiss, boo, cheer, and applaud. Even though the characters are stereotypes, they have an aura of reality and depth. Played in good humor and with cardboard properties, this is easily produced. **ROYALTY:** Free to Plays Subscribers. **SOURCE:** Fay, Maxine. (1977, March). Saving the old homestead. Plays: The Drama Magazine for Young People, pp. 25- 32. **SUBJECTS/PLAY TYPE:** Mortgages; Swindlers and Swindling; Stocks; Melodrama.

2708. 3-8. (+) Raymond, Martha H. **Scarecrow finds a new post. CAST:** Su. **ACTS:** 1. **SETTINGS:** Cornfield. **PLAYING TIME:** 15 min. **PLOT:** Scarecrow is unhappy because fall is coming and his duties are over. The children give him a party and find a place for him to rest until spring. **RECOMMENDATION:** Costuming is easy and the story is simple, allowing for any number of parts. It would be especially effective if produced by a combination of younger and older children. **ROYALTY:** Free to Plays subscribers. **SOURCE:** Raymond, Martha H. (1985, October). Scarecrow finds a new nest. Plays: The Drama Magazine for Young People, pp. 31-34. **SUBJECTS/PLAY TYPE:** Halloween; Scarecrows; Skit.

2709. 7-12. (+) Sawyer-Young, Kat. **Scared. CAST:** 1f. **ACTS:** 1. **SETTINGS:** None. **PLAYING TIME:** 1 min. **PLOT:** Jill asks her mother if she did something wrong by allowing her father to sexually abuse her.

RECOMMENDATION: This is poignant, but blunt. It should be used with care. ROYALTY: None. SOURCE: Sawyer-Young, Kat. (1987). Minute monologues for contemporary teens. Boston, MA: Baker's Plays. SUBJECTS/PLAY TYPE: Sexual Abuse; Child Molestation; Monologue.

2710. K-3. (+) Silverman, Eleanor. Scared. CAST: 5u. ACTS: 1. SETTINGS: None. PLAYING TIME: 5 min. PLOT: Children flee a haunted house when they see a ghost, which turns out to be their reflection in a mirror. RECOMMENDATION: The simple but creative solution to the ghost problem is quite effective. ROYALTY: None. SOURCE: Silverman, Eleanor. (1983). Dramatics for children. Metuchen, NJ: Scarecrow Press. SUBJECTS/PLAY TYPE: Ghosts; Haunted Houses; Skit.

2711. K-6. (+) Boiko, Claire. Scaredy cat. CAST: 3f, 6m, 1u. ACTS: 1. SETTINGS: Living room. PLAYING TIME: 15 min. PLOT: Mrs. Reese and her children are concerned about the terrified reaction of Shadow, their cat, to any mention of ghosts, goblins, spooks or other personages associated with Halloween. In a hushed conversation, Shadow informs Doctor Blunder of the sordid abuse he has suffered from Halloween pranksters, and receives a tranquilizer to soften the effects of the traditional celebration. The doctor's subsequent discovery that he has accidentally administered a quick growth pill to the unsuspecting feline is shared by the audience, but not by the Reese family. Two thieves enter the Reese house shortly after midnight, and their surprised cries when they discover a large, black panther draw the police from the street and the Reeses from upstairs. Dr. Blunder's reentry and attempts at explanation prove inconsequential because Shadow has resumed his normal size, and has also lost his fear of Halloween. RECOMMENDATION: Children will enjoy the tense expectancy of possessing information which the characters lack. The confrontation between the robbers and the overgrown Shadow is hilarious. ROYALTY: None. SOURCE: Boiko, Claire. (1985). Children's plays for creative actors. Boston, MA: Plays, Inc. SUBJECTS/PLAY TYPE: Halloween; Comedy.

2712. 9-12. (+) Leech, Michael T. (Orczy, Baroness) The scarlet pimpernel. (The scarlet pimpernel) CAST: 4f, 12m, Su. ACTS: 1. SETTINGS: Inn entrance; supper room; garden. PLAYING TIME: 45 min. PLOT: In 1792, during the Reign of Terror after the French Revolution, refugees from France are being escorted safely to England by the mysterious Scarlet Pimpernel. An agent of the French government is trying to obtain the identity of the Scarlet Pimpernel so he can be put to death, but the hero outsmarts the French agent to the very end. RECOMMENDATION: This is appropriate for groups studying this era in history and literature, or for those who have read the difficult original. The action is hard to follow because like the original, it changes quickly. ROYALTY: Free to Plays subscribers. SOURCE: Leech, Michael T. (1982, March). The scarlet pimpernel. Plays: The Drama Magazine for Young People, pp. 67-80. SUBJECTS/PLAY TYPE: Adventure; Adaptation.

2713. K-12. (+) Lane, Carolyn. The scheme of the driftless shifter. CAST: 15u. ACTS: 1. SETTINGS: Drawing room; outside. PLAYING TIME: NA. PLOT: Petunia loves Victor, but because he is penniless, her father doesn't approve. Love prevails at the end. RECOMMENDATION: The plot is built around the cast forgetting their lines, missing their cues, scrambling phrases ("scurl of corn" instead of "scorn of curl"), being interrupted by a cleaning woman who wants to clean the set, and general overacting. ROYALTY: $15. SOURCE: Lane, Carolyn. (1981). The scheme of the driftless shifter. Boston, MA: Baker's Plays. SUBJECTS/PLAY TYPE: Parody; Satire; Comedy; Melodrama.

2714. 5-7. (-) Hutson, Natalie Bovee. School for angels. CAST: Su. ACTS: 1. SETTINGS: Heaven. PLAYING TIME: 15 min. PLOT: Earth needs perfect angels from the Great Beyond for Christmas. All the candidates are imperfect and ignore their heavenly duties of star and cloud billowing. The headmaster tries to shape the angels up, but ultimately decides to accept their flaws. RECOMMENDATION: Most of the humor consists of variations on the angels outsmarting the headmaster. The one joke repetition quickly loses its entertainment value. ROYALTY: NA. SOURCE: Hutson, Natalie Bovee. (1984). School for angels. Stevensville, MI: Drama-Pak, Inc. SUBJECTS/PLAY TYPE: Angels; Heaven; Christmas; Fantasy.

2715. 10-12. (+) Rudolph, Grace. School's out. CAST: 1m. ACTS: 1. SETTINGS: Bare stage. PLAYING TIME: NA. PLOT: A high school teacher/coach reflects on how his alcoholism has adversely affected his interaction with his students, and on the problems of discipline in schools. RECOMMENDATION: Though an adult actor is required, students could read this aloud as part of a discussion on the changing roles of schools and teachers. ROYALTY: $10. SOURCE: Rudolph, Grace. (1984). Elders' statements: One-act plays and monologues. Boston, MA: Baker's Plays. SUBJECTS/PLAY TYPE: Discipline; School; Drug Abuse; Monologue.

2716. 6-12. (+) McIntyre, Tagore J. Scraps. CAST: 2f, 8m, Su. ACTS: 1. SETTINGS: Classroom; playground. PLAYING TIME: NA. PLOT: Classmates harass an Indian boy, ridicule a retarded peer, and refuse to let a boy join in their games. Finally, one of them realizes the pain he has inflicted and befriends the Indian. RECOMMENDATION: This portrays, through the eyes of the ten year old author, the cruelty of which children are capable. It is not so much a story about discrimination as it is one about compassion and civility. ROYALTY: NA. SOURCE: Lamb, Wendy. (1986). Meeting the winter bike rider and other prize winning plays. New York, NY: Dell. SUBJECTS/PLAY TYPE: Cruelty; Understanding; Drama.

2717. 1-9. (+) Koste, Virginia Glasgow. (Baum Lyman Frank) Scraps: The ragtime girl of Oz. (The wonderful wizard of Oz) CAST: 2f, 2m, Su. ACTS: 1. SETTINGS: Oz. PLAYING TIME: 60 min. PLOT: Scraps is brought to life by the wizard, Pipt. When Unc Nunkie is startled by

Scraps, the Petrification bottle falls on him, turning him into a statue. Pipt tells them that the only cure is a magic mixture. As they travel to find the necessary ingredients, Scraps and his friend, Ojo, meet Woozy, Hopper, and Horner. They collect most of the ingredients, but Ojo is arrested, and they are taken to Ozma, the ruler. Ozma reprieves Ojo and the others have a party. RECOMMENDATION: The older grades will have to produce this adventurous tale. ROYALTY: $35. SOURCE: Koste, Virginia Glasgow. (1986). Scraps: The ragtime girl of Oz. Morton Grove, IL: Coach House Press. SUBJECTS/PLAY TYPE: Adventure; Adaptation.

2718. 5-12. (+) Friedmand, Bruce Jay. **Scuba duba.** CAST: 1f, 1m. ACTS: 1. SETTINGS: Apartment room. PLAYING TIME: NA. PLOT: Jean, a Jewish woman, has left her Jewish husband, Harrold, for a black man. Harold is trying to patch things up with his wife, but his pride and masculinity interfere. RECOMMENDATION: Although much of the humor relies on a stereotypical description of a Jewish woman, the treatment of marital problems could help young people realize that more than physical comfort and monetary security are required to sustain a marriage. ROYALTY: NA. SOURCE: Olfson, Lewy. (1980). Fifty great scenes for student actors. New York, NY: Bantam Books. SUBJECTS/PLAY TYPE: Marriage; Scene.

2719. 7-12. (+) Rozell, O.B. **Searching.** CAST: 5f, 2m. ACTS: 1. SETTINGS: Dining rooms. PLAYING TIME: NA. PLOT: Lisa's adoptive father has died and her adoptive mother is seriously ill. She will be left with no one unless she can find her natural parents. Lisa's real mother is a prominent woman in the community who was raped at the age of 16 and has never told her husband. At first, she denies that Lisa is her daughter. When she finally admits it, she insists that no one must know, but realizes that she and Lisa need each other. RECOMMENDATION: The plot is rather contrived (bordering on melodrama), and the dialogue is overly sentimental. But, the play is well intentioned and may stimulate discussion of some important issues. ROYALTY: $15. SOURCE: Rozell, O.B. (1980). Searching. Schulenburg, TX: I.E. Clark. SUBJECTS/PLAY TYPE: Adoption; Drama.

2720. 9-12. (+) Gotwalt, Helen Louise Miller. **Season's greetings.** CAST: 3f, 8m. ACTS: 1. SETTINGS: Living room/studio. PLAYING TIME: 30 min. PLOT: Joshua Tyler, a frustrated portrait artist, sees his work as a Christmas card designer as a prostitution of his creative talent. He finally realizes that his cards do have serious impact on others. RECOMMENDATION: This explores the true value of art. The audience shares Tyler's discovery that true satisfaction is in caring and being cared for and in offering one's talents for the benefit of humanity instead of ego. ROYALTY: Free to Plays subscribers. SOURCE: Gotwalt, Helen Louise Miller. (1985, December). Season's greetings. Plays: The Drama Magazine for Young People, pp. 1-10. SUBJECTS/PLAY TYPE: Christmas; Art; Playlet.

2721. 10-12. (-) Weinstein, Robert. **The second resurrection.** CAST: 2f, 3m, 2u. ACTS: 1. SETTINGS: City exterior. PLAYING TIME: 60 min. PLOT: An older couple mourn the death of their only daughter and question their

religious beliefs. When Jessie returns from the dead on a special mission, her parents are elated. As Jessie tries to convey God's word to the world, cynical media crew members mock the message, but broadcast it. Several people hear it and repent, and Jessie returns to heaven, her mission fulfilled. RECOMMENDATION: Although the intent was to retell the basic resurrection tale in a modern setting, this completely lacks credibility because of excessive didacticism and wooden characters. Even for a church group, this would be overly propagandistic. ROYALTY: NA. SOURCE: Weinstein, Robert. (1987). The second resurrection. Franklin, OH: Eldridge Pub. Co. SUBJECTS/PLAY TYPE: Resurrection; Christian Drama.

2722. 3-6. (+) Head, Faye E. **The second shepherd's play.** (The second shepherd's play) CAST: 2f, 5m, 1u. ACTS: 1. SETTINGS: Pasture; one-room cottage; manger. PLAYING TIME: 15 min. PLOT: Mak outwits the three shepherds and steals a lamb which he disguises as a newborn baby and hides in his cottage. The three shepherds rescue the lamb, and on their way back to the flock they are invited by an angel to see the newborn Christ child. RECOMMENDATION: This watered down version retains enough of the original charm to make it worthwhile. ROYALTY: Free to Plays subscribers. SOURCE: Kamerman, Sylvia E. (1976). On stage for Christmas. Boston, MA: Plays, Inc. SUBJECTS/PLAY TYPE: Christmas; Comedy; Miracle Plays; Nativity; Mystery.

2723. 6-9. (+) Marinello, Grace. **The secret...a rock fairy tale.** CAST: 4f, 2m, 9u. ACTS: 1. SETTINGS: Actor's dressing room; disco club. PLAYING TIME: 30 min. PLOT: A cleaning maid, smitten by a rock star but despairing of ever being noticed, dreams of rock stardom. She wins the star's affections, aided by a fairy godfather who turns her into a rock star. When the spell ends and she is once again a cleaning maid, she discovers that her beloved's stardom had likewise been granted by a good fairy. RECOMMENDATION: Although a takeoff on Cinderella, this has a tickling twist. Its underlying theme is underscored at the end when the fairy godfather states that they were "never really that different" and puzzles over why "people try to be something they're not." ROYALTY: $30. SOURCE: Marinello, Grace. (1981). The secret...a rock fairy tale. Franklin, OH: Eldridge Pub. Co. SUBJECTS/PLAY TYPE: Rock Music; Actors/ Actresses; Identity; Comedy.

2724. 4-10. (+) Hamlett, Christina. **Secret agents in disguise.** CAST: 4f, 3m. ACTS: 1. SETTINGS: Grocery store; living room. PLAYING TIME: 30 min. PLOT: Bumbling secret agents protect a star witness against the enemy agent, Nightshade, hiding the witness at a young woman's house. Nightshade disguises herself as one of the agents, but is discovered and caught. RECOMMENDATION: Complete with banana phones, a mother who can't understand what's happening, and mistaken identities, this takeoff on "Get Smart" should be played with exaggerated characters and acting. ROYALTY: Free to Plays subscribers. SOURCE: Hamlett, Christina. (1988, May). Secret agents in disguise. Plays:

The Drama Magazine for Young People, pp. 53-60.
SUBJECTS/PLAY TYPE: Secret Agents; Comedy.

2725. 3-9. (+) Avery, Helen A. (Burnett, Frances Hodgson) **The secret garden.** (The secret garden) CAST: 4f, 5m. ACTS: 2. SETTINGS: Bedroom; study; moor; garden walk; walled garden. PLAYING TIME: NA. PLOT: Mary makes friends with Dickon, the housemaid's brother, and they explore the estate, where they discover their uncle's invalid son, who thinks of nothing but death and the possibility that he will grow a hump on his back like his father. Mary and Dickon teach the boy to rejoice in life and nature as they share the beauty of the Secret Garden. The boy is restored to health and a loving relationship with his father. RECOMMENDATION: This faithful adaptation does not require any unusual props or scenery but the main characters must memorize many lines. ROYALTY: $35. SOURCE: Avery, Helen A. (1987). The secret garden. New Orleans, LA: Anchorage Press, Inc. SUBJECTS/PLAY TYPE: Orphans; Loneliness; Nature; Adaptation.

2726. 6-9. (+) Jones, David Cadwalader. (Burnett, Frances Hodgson) **The secret garden.** (The secret garden) CAST: 3f, 4m, 1u. ACTS: 1. SETTINGS: Bedroom; library/study; garden. PLAYING TIME: 40 min. PLOT: Orphaned Mary is sent to live with Mr. Craven and his mean housekeeper, Mrs. Medlock. Mary explores the estate and meets Collin, Mr. Craven's son; Dickon, the brother of the maid; and the gardener, Ben. She uncovers secrets and a way into the secret garden, the favorite place of the dead Mrs. Craven. She and her new friends restore the garden and discover that Mr. Craven is not mean and bitter, that Collin is not dying, and that Mrs. Medlock is plotting to steal Mr. Craven's fortune. Mary reveals all to Mr. Craven, who is overjoyed. RECOMMENDATION: A lively, fast paced adaptation, this is worth the effort, in spite of the many settings required. The characters are varied and interesting, with compact and effective conversations in each scene. While this adds a new slant, with Mrs. Medlock the evil plotter behind all the trouble, it still remains faithful to the spirit of the original. It may be performed with puppets. ROYALTY: Free to Plays subscribers. SOURCE: Jones, David Cadwalader. (1989, March). The secret garden. Plays: The Drama Magazine for Young People, pp. 55-64. SUBJECTS/PLAY TYPE: Family, Mystery; Adaptation.

2727. 1-5*. (+) Zawadsky, Pat. **The secret in the toy room.** CAST: 4f, 5m, 2u. ACTS: 1. SETTINGS: Toyshop; playroom. PLAYING TIME: 60 min. PLOT: A boy and girl doll are brought to life by their elderly, loving creators and given to two children who promise to provide a loving home. After the children abuse them, the dolls return to their creators and describe what happened. RECOMMENDATION: This was created to help young children recognize and report incidents of physical and sexual abuse. The dialogue is easily within most children's grasp, and the story is punctuated with catchy, short songs. Although the sets are simple, most of the characters will need costumes that make them look like toys. Live or recorded accompaniment will be needed for the songs, and it is recommended that this be produced by adults or

high school students. ROYALTY: $25. SOURCE: Zawadsky, Pat. (1982). The secret in the toy room. Schulenburg, TX: I.E. Clark. SUBJECTS/PLAY TYPE: Child Abuse; Toys; Sexual Abuse; Child Molesting; Musical.

2728. 9-12. (+) Kelly, Tim. **Secret of Skull Island.** CAST: 5f, 6m. ACTS: 2. SETTINGS: Living room. PLAYING TIME: 90 min. PLOT: A group of jurors that doomed an innocent man arrive on a mysterious island, lured by the promise of a reward. They wait for their host, Mr. Nettleton, who never appears. Instead, each guest disappears and is found murdered. Only Kitty, who was mistakenly invited, and her boyfriend Phil, a mystery writer, remain to discover the identity of the murderers and summon help. A surprise twist reveals that the person responsible for the murders is Rita, a guilt ridden juror who was unwillingly convinced to convict the innocent man. RECOMMENDATION: Despite rather complicated staging, this would be fun and a challenging experience for beginning young actors. ROYALTY: $35. SOURCE: Kelly, Tim. (1986). Secret of Skull Island. Denver, CO: Pioneer Drama Service. SUBJECTS/PLAY TYPE: Mystery; Guilt; Murder; Drama.

2729. 5-12. (+) Gillette, William. **Secret service.** CAST: 1f, 1m. ACTS: 1. SETTINGS: Room. PLAYING TIME: NA. PLOT: Two young people who had previously been engaged meet by chance as the Civil War rages six miles away. Caroline justifies her actions in allowing several Army officers to propose marriage by explaining that they fight twice as well when they have a sweetheart at home. Wilfred explains that she can help the war effort further by hemming his trousers, and when she sees that they are Army trousers, she is more than willing to help. RECOMMENDATION: Although the values here are outdated and sexist, with careful presentation this could provoke valuable discussions about changing societal attitudes, or the generation gap. ROYALTY: NA. SOURCE: Olfson, Lewy. (1980). Fifty great scenes for student actors. New York, NY: Bantam Books. SUBJECTS/PLAY TYPE: Women's Roles; Scene.

2730. 7-12. (+) Cochran, Betty Holmes. **The secret the bell told Boston.** CAST: 2f, 3m. ACTS: 1. SETTINGS: Steeple room. PLAYING TIME: 25 min. PLOT: Nathan Hale is helped by women to smuggle gunpowder for General Washington. RECOMMENDATION: Although trite and overly emotional, this does deal with some Revolutionary War issues. ROYALTY: Free to Plays subscribers. SOURCE: Cochran, Betty Holmes. (1976, December). The secret the bell told Boston. Plays: The Drama Magazine for Young People, pp. 75-82. SUBJECTS/PLAY TYPE: Hale, Nathan; Revolution, U.S.; Playlet.

2731. 10-12. (+) King, Philip. **See how they run.** CAST: 3f, 6m. ACTS: 1. SETTINGS: Vicarage. PLAYING TIME: NA. PLOT: While Penelope's husband (the Reverend Lionel) is out of town, Corporal Clive Winton arrives unexpectedly. Fearing the gossip if they spend the evening together alone at the vicarage, Penelope suggests a play in a nearby village, but not before Miss Skillon sees them and mistakenly assumes it is a lovers' rendezvous. Before the evening is over, several more mistaken assumptions are made as Penelope fears for her husband's faithfulness, an escaped Russian spy disguises himself as Lionel, Lionel thinks that Clive has designs on Penelope, etc. The spy is captured and all is straightened out. RECOMMENDATION: Never dull, this wonderful British farce is full of involved situations that will keep audiences alert and entertained. ROYALTY: $35. SOURCE: King, Philip. (1977). See how they run. New York, NY: Samuel French. SUBJECTS/PLAY TYPE: Misunderstandings; Farce.

2732. 4-8. (+) Nersesian, Robert. Self defense. CAST: 5f, 6m. ACTS: 1. SETTINGS: Playground. PLAYING TIME: NA. PLOT: Burton Braverman, a known wimp, is convinced to take self defense classes from Sharkey, the bully, who sells Burton a "Wimp Defender." Although the weapon is not real, Burton frightens off the threatening Chase Team with it, and displays true friendship by convincing Sharkey and the Team members to take friendship lessons from him. RECOMMENDATION: Production requirements are not complex, though musical background is required, and some doubling of characters is possible. Junior high aged actors will find success in staging this. ROYALTY: $30. SOURCE: Nersesian, Robert. (1988). Self defense. Franklin, OH: Eldridge Pub. Co. SUBJECTS/PLAY TYPE: Friendship; Self Defense; Comedy.

2733. K-3. (+) Thane, Adele. (Wilde, Oscar) The selfish giant. (The selfish giant) CAST: 4f, 4m, 15u. ACTS: 1. SETTINGS: Garden. PLAYING TIME: 15 min. PLOT: When a mean giant banishes neighborhood children from his garden, he unwittingly banishes summer as well. Winter, Northwind, Snowflakes, Frost and Hail cover Snowdrop and Other Flowers until brave little Tommy ventures back a year later. When he persuades other children to enter the yard, Winter and crew run away. The giant realizes that his garden has stayed cold and barren because Spring and Summer will not visit a place which has no children or kindness. He welcomes the children back. RECOMMENDATION: The large expandable cast provides enough characters for each class member to have a part. The eight speaking/singing roles would not tax third grade memory skills, though younger students might object less to the lines. ROYALTY: Free to Plays subscribers. SOURCE: Thane, Adele. (1977, January). The selfish giant. Plays: The Drama Magazine for Young People, pp. 55-60. SUBJECTS/PLAY TYPE: Seasons; Adaptation.

2734. 6-12. (+) Wood, David & Pontzen, Peter. The selfish shellfish. CAST: 7u. ACTS: 2. SETTINGS: Rock pool. PLAYING TIME: NA. PLOT: A quiet rock pool becomes the scene of fear and concern as a giant oil slick threatens to pollute the sea creatures' home. As all the creatures except H.C., the selfish shellfish, prepare to leave, young Sea Urchin activates a plan to capture Sludge, the Great Slick's advance guard, hoping that this will turn the slick away. Sludge's capture does not stop the slick's threat, but the rock pool is saved by Urchin, H.C., Seagull, and a violent thunderstorm. Reviving Seagull, who

appeared to have died in the conflict, the actors stress that clever technology is endangering innocent victims. RECOMMENDATION: Although this has a complex, detailed setting that would be difficult to produce on a small stage and/or with a limited budget, this explains well the threat of water pollution. At times the characters speak harshly and treat each other disrespectfully, indirectly symbolizing the ways in which humans treat the environment. This has extensive audience participation and some Britishisms will have to be Americanized. ROYALTY: NA. SOURCE: Wood, David. (1986). The selfish shellfish. New York, NY: Samuel French. SUBJECTS/PLAY TYPE: Conservation; Water Pollution; Bravery; Musical; Drama.

2735. 7-12. (-) Moeller, Ruby L. September. CAST: Su. ACTS: NA. SETTINGS: None. PLAYING TIME: NA. PLOT: The play opens with a song followed by a roll call, during which several members of the cast are asked to name their favorite book and tell why. Someone recites a poem about education, a talk is given about how to encourage children to read good books, and another poem about books is recited. A series of games combine knowledge of poems, authors, slang, and famous discoverers. The closing thought, "when is a man educated," is followed by a closing song. RECOMMENDATION: This would bore all but the most serious honor student. It could be presented to parents or educators, not as entertainment, but as evidence of academic progress. Some of the games require the knowledge and skills of above average, outgoing students, while others require a quick recall of specific subjects. Charades and "quickies," a series of corny, very old jokes, make this even less appealing. ROYALTY: NA. SOURCE: Moeller, Ruby L. (1975). Around the year programs. Boston, MA: Baker's Plays. SUBJECTS/PLAY TYPE: Education; Variety Program.

2736. 7-10. (+) Kelly, Tim J. & Nestor, Larry. (Kelly, Tim J) Seven brides for Dracula. (Seven wives for Dracula.) CAST: 7f, 5m, 1u. ACTS: 2. SETTINGS: Library. PLAYING TIME: 60 min. PLOT: Dr. Van Helsing fails to thwart the evil count and his wife as they create the undead from patients at the sanatorium. RECOMMENDATION: Clever word play and possibilities for slapstick make the play enjoyable. However, the musical numbers seem to interrupt the flow of the dialogue, and product references in the songs are inconsistent with the setting in London. This might provide an opportunity for an advanced student with some stage experience to direct. ROYALTY: $40. SOURCE: Kelly, Tim J. (1983). Seven brides for Dracula. Denver, CO: Pioneer Drama Service. SUBJECTS/PLAY TYPE: Vampires; Comedy; Musical; Adaptation.

2737. K-3. (+) Gould, Jean. The seven little seeds. CAST: 10u. ACTS: 1. SETTINGS: Bedroom; meadow. PLAYING TIME: 10 min. PLOT: Seven seeds are snug and warm in their beds. Sun, wind, and rain try to wake them. Although the seeds resist, they finally grow into beautiful flowers. RECOMMENDATION: This delightful herald of spring can be produced by even the youngest children, and will also be useful as a catalyst for discussions about growing up. **ROYALTY:** Free to Plays subscribers. **SOURCE:** Gould, Jean. (1978, March). The seven little seeds. Plays: The Drama Magazine for Young People, pp. 63-66. **SUBJECTS/PLAY TYPE:** Growing Up; Spring; Nature; Skit.

2738. 3-6. (+) Gabriel, Michelle. **Shabbat recipe.** **CAST:** 3f, 3m, Su. **ACTS:** 2. **SETTINGS:** Dining room; palace. **PLAYING TIME:** 15 min. **PLOT:** When they spend Shabbat evening with a common family, an incognito king and queen realize that togetherness and family feelings shared during dinner make ordinary food delicious. **RECOMMENDATION:** The spiritual message about the heart of Judaism is brought home through simple script and dialogue. **ROYALTY:** None. **SOURCE:** Gabriel, Michelle. (1978). Jewish plays for Jewish days. Denver, CO: Alternatives in Religious Education, Inc. **SUBJECTS/PLAY TYPE:** Shabbat; Jewish Drama; Puppet Play.

2739. 7-12. (-) Murray, John. **Shadow-of-death.** **CAST:** 5f, 3m. **ACTS:** 3. **SETTINGS:** Reception area; suite. **PLAYING TIME:** 40 min. **PLOT:** Derek Bryant, a writer investigating the basis of a ghostly legend, becomes possessed by the evil spirit of the dead Malcolm Chadwick. Three people die at his hands, but he is defeated by a young couple armed with a twig of wolfsbane. The couple, in turn, are possessed by the spirits of Malcolm's daughter and her lover. **RECOMMENDATION:** Based on a legend from a remote area in New Jersey, this is too contrived to seem realistic. Imagine a spirit strong enough to live for a hundred years banished by a twig. One wonders why the inn's maid did not give wolfs-bane to previous guests whom she tried to warn about Malcolm. **ROYALTY:** Free to Plays subscribers. **SOURCE:** Murray, John. (1975, December). Shadow-of-death. Plays: The Drama Magazine for Young People, pp. 27-40. **SUBJECTS/PLAY TYPE:** Mystery; Horror; Playlet.

2740. 5-9. (+) Hamlett, Christina. **Shadow of Dracula.** **CAST:** 2f, 2m. **ACTS:** 1. **SETTINGS:** Living room. **PLAYING TIME:** 30 min. **PLOT:** Eric Rathskeller invites his fiancee and her mother for dinner so the families can meet, but he does not want his fiance to discover that his brother, Milo, is a vampire. The dinner goes well, and Milo charms both women with his Shakespearean demeanor and his smooth tasting red "wine." When it appears that the Rathskeller secret will be revealed, Barbara jumps to the conclusion that her future brother-in-law is a secret actor, thus saving the situation. Only Milo, who turns out to be Eric's father, has reservations about his son's new family, distrusting the crucifix wearing mother. **RECOMMENDATION:** Although the plot is a bit worn, this has a humorous spark which keeps it from becoming just another vampire story. **ROYALTY:** Free to Plays subscribers. **SOURCE:** Hamlett, Christina. (1987). Humorous plays for teenagers. Boston, MA: Plays,Inc. **SUBJECTS/PLAY TYPE:** Vampires; Supernatural; Comedy.

2741. 1-6. (+) Guderjahn, Ernie. **The shadow workers.** **CAST:** Su. **ACTS:** 1. **SETTINGS:** Bare stage. **PLAYING TIME:** NA. **PLOT:** A town of lazy people is tricked into working by a wise man who tells them that they must teach their shadows. The townspeople are angry when they realize that their shadows won't work without them, but after working for a while, they begin to like it. **RECOMMENDATION:** This will allow the actors to mime and use body movement, as they interact with their shadows. Although the ending is a bit moralistic, the humorous journey to the message makes it worthwhile. The narrator might have to be older, and in order to actually see the shadows, lighting will be challenging. **ROYALTY:** NA. **SOURCE:** Guderjahn, Ernie. (1984). A children's trilogy. Studio City, CA: Player's Press. **SUBJECTS/PLAY TYPE:** Shadows; Working; Comedy.

2742. 1-8. (+) Steinhorn, Harriet & Lowry, Edith. **Shadows of the holocaust: Now and then.** **CAST:** 5f, 6m, Su. **ACTS:** 2. **SETTINGS:** Parking lot; bedroom. **PLAYING TIME:** 20 min. **PLOT:** Modern students discuss the holocaust and ask why the Jews didn't stand up to the Nazis, and how the Nazis knew who was Jewish. Their teacher tells them that birth certificates in Poland and Germany identified a person's religion, and that travel to another city was forbidden during the Nazi regime. He then tells them a story about one Jewish family who tried to resist the Nazis by refusing to leave their home, but faced with the choice of leaving or having their mother and son killed, they had no choice but to leave. **RECOMMENDATION:** This brutal drama ends as the ill mother is shot at point blank range by the Nazis while she lies in bed. It may give children nightmares, but its honest portrayal of the Nazis' brutality and its revealing explanations will help to ensure that children will be aware enough to mobilize against any infringement of civil liberties. **ROYALTY:** Free for amateur groups. **SOURCE:** Steinhorn, Harriet & Lowry, Edith. (1983). Shadows of the holocaust: Plays, readings, and program resources. Rockville, MD: Kar-Ben Copies, Inc. **SUBJECTS/PLAY TYPE:** Holocaust; World War II; Genocide; Drama.

2743. 4-7. (+) Kraus, Joanna Halpert. **The shaggy dog murder trial.** **CAST:** 3f, 2m, 5u. **ACTS:** 1. **SETTINGS:** Town hall. **PLAYING TIME:** NA. **PLOT:** A shaggy dog is on trial for the drowning of a young boy in a canal. The mother of the boy, the dog's owner, and witnesses of the drowning give testimony. The verdict is left to the audience. **RECOMMENDATION:** Although the idea of a dog being tried for a murder seems silly, much can be learned about the judicial system through the enactment. Many ethical issues are raised regarding the legal rights of victims and defendants, the responsibility of individuals to consider general social welfare before acting, and the respective values of human and animal life. **ROYALTY:** $30. **SOURCE:** Kraus, Joanna Halpert. (1988). The shaggy dog murder trial. New Orleans, LA: Anchorage Press, Inc. **SUBJECTS/PLAY TYPE:** Justice; Courts; Animal Rights; Drama.

2744. 7-12. (+) Boiko, Claire. **The Shakespeares.** **CAST:** 4f, 7m, 1u. **ACTS:** 1. **SETTINGS:** Kitchen. **PLAYING TIME:** 15 min. **PLOT:** In this 16th century takeoff of the popular TV show, "The Waltons," Will-Boy Shakespeare's family plays a game where they tell each other's secrets. During the game, Will-Boy is inspired to write great plays such as **Romeo and Juliet**. Will-Boy's brother, Yessiree-Bob, tells the family that he saw a medieval TV show about their family and it was not flattering. The family demands that Will-Boy stop writing about them. They play ends with the traditional ending of "The Waltons;" everyone says goodnight to each other. RECOMMENDATION: While much of the hilarity may be lost for audience members who have not seen "The Waltons," there are still plenty of Shakespearean puns to carry the play. ROYALTY: Free to Plays subscribers. SOURCE: Boiko, Claire. (1976, April). The Shakespeares. Plays: The Drama Magazine for Young People, pp. 79-84. SUBJECTS/PLAY TYPE: Family; Shakespeare, William; Comedy; Skit.

2745. 9-12. (+) Wartski, Maureen Crane. **Shakespeare's dream. CAST:** 7f, 7m. **ACTS:** 1. **SETTINGS:** Shakespeare's office; orphanage; dining room; one room house; living room. **PLAYING TIME:** 30 min. **PLOT:** A young Shakespeare carves the words, "Never lose the dream," into his desk to provide inspiration when he is discouraged. Years later, the desk is in an orphanage where its words give a young girl the courage to speak up against the wicked warden and leave for the New World. The words also inspire slaves to run away to freedom. Finally, a struggling writer reads them, dreams about their impact on people, and begins to write this play. RECOMMENDATION: As the desk moves from one century to another, and impacts on people's lives, the continuity of life and its struggles is poetically dramatized in this short but full presentation. Background period music will help set the mood. ROYALTY: Free to Plays subscribers. SOURCE: Wartski, Maureen Crane. (1988, April). Shakespeare's dream. Plays: The Drama Magazine for Young People, pp. 10-18. SUBJECTS/PLAY TYPE: Courage; Writers; Playlet.

2746. 7-12. (+) Clark, I.E. **The shaky tale of Doctor Jakey. CAST:** 5f, 5m, Su. **ACTS:** 2. **SETTINGS:** None. **PLAYING TIME:** 90 min. **PLOT:** Dr. Jakey, a likable purveyor of cure alls, is threatened by the vicious Dr. Hooza Fraidy, who feels that Dr. Jakey is infringing on her territory. The beautiful, seductive Formalda, daughter of Mayor Hyde, cleverly rescues Dr. Jakey from the clutches of Dr. Fraidy, and all ends happily. RECOMMENDATION: This cleverly puts a twist on the standard boo-hiss melodrama, as the hero and villain are women and the "heroine" is a man. ROYALTY: $25. SOURCE: Clark, I.E. (1984). The shaky tale of Doctor Jakey. Schulenburg,TX: I.E. Clark, Inc. SUBJECTS/PLAY TYPE: Comedy; Melodrama.

2747. 7-12. (-) Trulen, Cheryl. **Shall I compare thee to a redwood fence? CAST:** 1f, 1m. **ACTS:** 1. **SETTINGS:** Backyard. **PLAYING TIME:** 12 min. **PLOT:** An overweight girl spends her summer alone reading Shakespeare after repelling the advances of a boy who has green teeth. Both have trouble expressing their mutual attraction. RECOMMENDATION: This fails in its attempt to show there is more to a person's character than appearance. ROYALTY: None. SOURCE: Altens, Hans. (1978). The playbook for Christian theatre. Grand Rapids,

MI: Baker Book House. **SUBJECTS/PLAY TYPE:** Personality; Drama.

2748. 4-12. (+) Kelly, Tim. **The shame of Tombstone, or, dirty work in the lucky cuss. CAST:** 6f, 6m. **ACTS:** 1. **SETTINGS:** Parlor; gambling saloon/tonsorial parlor. **PLAYING TIME:** 60 min. **PLOT:** A blackmailing villain threatens to expose respectable and philanthropic Widow Goodsort's earlier career as a saloon singer. In the end, the widow is vindicated, and the villain is ruined. RECOMMENDATION: This old fashioned melodrama has broadly drawn comic characters, an abundance of jokes, plot twists, and musical interludes between the scenes which enhance the music hall atmosphere. ROYALTY: $25. SOURCE: Kelly, Tim. (1980). The shame of Tombstone, or, dirty work in the lucky cuss. Denver, CO: Pioneer Drama Service. SUBJECTS/PLAY TYPE: Blackmailers; Swindlers and Swindling; Comedy; Melodrama.

2749. K-2. (+) Ison, Colleen. **Sharing. CAST:** 5u. **ACTS:** 1. **SETTINGS:** Bare stage. **PLAYING TIME:** NA. **PLOT:** Five children refuse to share their toys until one of them demonstrates how they can have more fun by pooling their toys. RECOMMENDATION: This is very direct and appropriate, even for preschoolers. Discussion questions are provided. ROYALTY: NA. SOURCE: Ison, Colleen. (1986). Goliath's last stand: And fifteen more easy plays for children. Cincinnati, OH: Standard Pub. SUBJECTS/PLAY TYPE: Sharing; Skit.

2750. 9-12. (+) Rozell, O.B. **Sharing. CAST:** 7f, 4m. **ACTS:** 1. **SETTINGS:** Living/dining room. **PLAYING TIME:** 25 min. **PLOT:** Richard Kendrick and his five teenage children prepare for their first Christmas without their recently deceased mother. As Richard reminisces, she walks on stage, and the scene shifts several times from past to present as the audience becomes familiar with the family. In the final scene, the family opens Christmas presents that their mother had bought for each of them before her death and realize she will always be with them. RECOMMENDATION: Although in a Christmas setting, the primary focus of this touching play is on grief and how to cope with it. It offers roles with great depth of character. ROYALTY: $15. SOURCE: Rozell, O.B. (1980). Sharing. Schulenburg, TX: I.E. Clark. SUBJECTS/PLAY TYPE: Death; Christmas; Grief; Christian Drama.

2751. K-3. (+) Havilan, Amorie & Smith, Lyn. **Sharing a feast. CAST:** 2f, 7m, Su. **ACTS:** 1. **SETTINGS:** Pilgrim dining room; outdoors. **PLAYING TIME:** NA. **PLOT:** On the first Thanksgiving, Simon is both curious and a little fearful about the Indians. His mother reassures him and reminds him that the Indians have taught the pilgrims to plant corn, hunt, and fish. At the feast, Simon sees Governor Bradford, Miles Standish, Squanto, and Squanto's son, Little Hawk. Little Hawk and Simon become friends and exchange hats. The play ends with a prayer of thanksgiving and a sharing of food. RECOMMENDATION: This can be performed as drama or pantomime, according to the cast's abilities. The action and dialogue emphasize the importance of tolerance. The final prayer scene could easily be changed to fit the needs of public schools if the religious aspect caused a problem. ROYALTY: NA. SOURCE: Havilan, Amorie & Smith, Lyn. (1985). Easy plays for preschoolers to third graders. Brandon, MS: Quail Ridge Press. SUBJECTS/PLAY TYPE: Thanksgiving; Tripartite.

2752. 3-6. (+) Gabriel, Michelle. **Shavuot.** CAST: 7u. ACTS: 1. SETTINGS: Outdoors. PLAYING TIME: 20 min. PLOT: A person watches people singing about the importance and significance of Shavuot. RECOMMENDATION: This clearly brings out the various customs and celebrations associated with Shavuot, a celebration of the gift of Torah. ROYALTY: None. SOURCE: Gabriel, Michelle. (1978). Jewish plays for Jewish days. Denver, CO: Alternatives in Religious Education, Inc. SUBJECTS/PLAY TYPE: Shavuot; Jewish Drama.

2753. 4-8. (+) Kehret, Peg. **She hit me first.** CAST: 1m. ACTS: 1. SETTINGS: None. PLAYING TIME: NA. PLOT: A young boy outlines how he enjoys tormenting his brother and sister, and can't understand why his parents don't approve. RECOMMENDATION: This should provoke discussion on sibling disharmony. ROYALTY: NA. SOURCE: Kehret, Peg. (1986). Winning monologs for young actors. Colorado Springs, CO: Meriwether Pub. SUBJECTS/PLAY TYPE: Siblings; Fighting; Monologue.

2754. 7-12. (+) Paradis, Marjorie B. **She laughs last.** CAST: 10f. ACTS: 1. SETTINGS: Bedroom. PLAYING TIME: 30 min. PLOT: Just hours before her sister's wedding, the 14 year old maid of honor gets her arm stuck inside a "priceless" vase sent by the family's rich old aunt. When the grande dame arrives for the nuptials, she reveals the true value of the vase (very little, in fact), and the value of a good sense of humor. Shattering the prized vase with her cane, the spirited matron frees the teenager. RECOMMENDATION: Suitable for girls' clubs or camps, this would be perfect for mother-daughter occasions as the resolution stresses family unity. ROYALTY: Free to Plays subscribers. SOURCE: Paradis, Marjorie B. (1982, March). Plays: The Drama Magazine for Young People, pp. 12, 28-38. SUBJECTS/PLAY TYPE: Weddings; Family; Comedy.

2755. 10-12. (+) Nolan, Paul T. (Goldsmith, Oliver) **She stoops to conquer.** (She stoops to conquer) CAST: 4f, 4m. ACTS: 1. SETTINGS: Parlor. PLAYING TIME: 30 min. PLOT: Kate Hardcastle humors her father's penchant for the "olden times" by dressing according to her own fashionable tastes during the day, but donning modest, simple country garb in the evening. A visit from a prospective suitor sparks a series of deceptions which result in two betrothals. Charles, tongue tied in the presence of ladies of quality despite his casual familiarity with serving girls, spurns the formally attired Kate during the day but aggressively pursues her at night when she is simply garbed. His companion, George Hastings, perpetuates Kate's deception to allow himself time with Miss Neville, Hardcastle's niece. The deception is revealed, and the betrothals of Marlow and Kate, Hastings and Neville are announced. RECOMMENDATION: The

intrigue, coincidence, and irony of the plot present effectively the theme of appearance vs. reality and its role in defining personalities, actions, and relationships. ROYALTY: Free to Plays subscribers. SOURCE: Nolan, Paul T. (1988). She stoops to conquer. Boston, MA: Plays, Inc. SUBJECTS/PLAY TYPE: Dating; Comedy; Adaptation.

2756. 5-12. (+) Ainsworth, Ford. **The sheep thief.** (The second shepherd's play) CAST: 4f, 4m, 4u. ACTS: 1. SETTINGS: Moor; house interior; stable. PLAYING TIME: 35 min. PLOT: A well known neighborhood thief steals a sheep from two shepherds. Although he disguises the sheep as a newborn baby, the shepherds catch him. Angels suddenly appear and announce the birth of the Christ child. The play concludes with the shepherds in attendance at the traditional manger scene. RECOMMENDATION: Although an adaptation of a medieval miracle play, this is a joyful traditional Christmas story with a unique twist. It is a comedy which derives humor from the juxtaposition of the very human qualities of the shepherds against the spirituality represented by the nativity. In a similar manner, the plot, focusing upon a thief, is juxtaposed against the birth of the Christ child. Old English style language is retained, and adds to the play's humor. ROYALTY: $15. SOURCE: Ainsworth, Ford. (1979). The sheep thief. Schulenburg, TX: I.E. Clark, Inc. SUBJECTS/PLAY TYPE: Christmas; Christ, Jesus; Nativity; Miracle Plays; Comedy.

2757. 7-12. (+) Kelly, Tim J. (Doyle, Sir Arthur Conan & Gillette, William) **Sherlock Holmes.** (The strange case of Miss Faulkner) CAST: 14f, 13m. ACTS: 2. SETTINGS: Drawing room; office; abandoned warehouse. PLAYING TIME: 120 min. PLOT: Young Sherlock Holmes tries to solve a blackmail plot involving incriminating letters, the Prince of Bohemia's wedding and a damsel in distress. Professor Moriarty is engaged by the blackmailers to prevent Holmes from returning the letters, and almost succeeds. But a brilliant coup by Holmes makes for a happy ending, except for Moriarty and the blackmailers. RECOMMENDATION: The size of the cast in this adaptation of a stage play would make it difficult for amateur groups, though an experienced director might be able to succeed. It is played in high camp for comedic effect. ROYALTY: $35. SOURCE: Kelly, Tim J. (1977). Sherlock Holmes. Denver, CO: Pioneer Drama Service. SUBJECTS/PLAY TYPE: Mystery; Comedy; Parody; Adaptation.

2758. 10-12. (+) Doyle, Arthur Conan & Gillette, William. (Doyle, Arthur Conan) **Sherlock Holmes: A comedy in two acts.** (The strange case of Miss Faulkner) CAST: 4f, 15m, 7u. ACTS: 2. SETTINGS: Drawing room; office; gas chamber; doctor's office; Holmes' living room. PLAYING TIME: NA. PLOT: A young woman is held prisoner by a villainous couple in pursuit of wealth through blackmail. Trying to help her while retrieving the blackmail material for his client, Holmes comes up against master criminal, Moriarty. Typical of Holmesian tales, the matter is resolved after many surprises. RECOMMENDATION: Sets are more detailed than a younger cast might be able to produce, but the effort is worthwhile. **ROYALTY:** $50. **SOURCE:** Doyle, Arthur Conan. (1976). Sherlock Holmes: A comedy in two acts. New York, NY: Samuel French. **SUBJECTS/PLAY TYPE:** Comedy; Mystery.

2759. 8-12. (+) Mauro, Robert. **Sherlock Holmes and a near case of murder.** **CAST:** 4f, 4m. **ACTS:** 1. **SETTINGS:** Parlor. **PLAYING TIME:** NA. **PLOT:** In this abbreviated slapstick of attempted murder, Sherlock Holmes outsmarts arch enemies Professor Moriarty and Dragon Lady by feigning death after eating the "poisoned" crumpets, and traps the would be murderers. But everyone is a bungler in this comic production where the plot takes second place to puns and visual effects. **RECOMMENDATION:** The humor seems a little forced at times. This will be especially funny to those in the audience who have read some Sherlock Holmes mysteries and are familiar with the characters spoofed. **ROYALTY:** $15. **SOURCE:** Mauro, Robert. (1983). Sherlock Holmes and near case of murder. Boston, MA: Baker's Plays. **SUBJECTS/PLAY TYPE:** Mystery; Comedy.

2760. 9-12. (+) Nolan, Paul T. (Doyle, Arthur Conan) **Sherlock Holmes and the Copper Beeches.** (Sherlock Holmes and the Copper Beeches) **CAST:** 3f, 4m. **ACTS:** 3. **SETTINGS:** Living room; drawing room; cottage room. **PLAYING TIME:** 30 min. **PLOT:** A young governess is hired to impersonate her employer's daughter who is locked away from her lover so that she cannot marry and thus claim her inheritance. Sherlock Holmes and Dr. Watson foil the employer's plans. **RECOMMENDATION:** This has a lively plot with plenty of action and strong dialogue. Unfortunately, it fails to recapture the famous deduction techniques for which the Holmes stories are so famous. **ROYALTY:** Free to Plays subscribers. **SOURCE:** Nolan, Paul T. (1986, March). Sherlock Holmes and the Copper Beeches. Plays: The Drama Magazine for Young People, pp. 53-63. **SUBJECTS/PLAY TYPE:** Mystery; Adaptation.

2761. 12. (+) Rosa, Dennis. (Doyle, Sir Arthur Conan) **Sherlock Holmes and the curse of the sign of four.** (The sign of four) **CAST:** 1f, 7m, 1u. **ACTS:** 2. **SETTINGS:** Living room; oriental living room. **PLAYING TIME:** NA. **PLOT:** Holmes, Watson, and Miss Morstan hunt for a lost treasure. Murder and mysterious individuals become entangled. The murderer turns out to be the villain Moriarty, the treasure is lost in the Thames River, Watson and Miss Morston plan to be married, and Holmes is left puffing on his pipe. **RECOMMENDATION:** Because of sophisticated and lengthy dialogue, as well as complex scenery, this faithful adaptation might be difficult, but not impossible for high school production. **ROYALTY:** NA. **SOURCE:** Rosa, Dennis. (1975). Sherlock Holmes and the curse of the sign of four. New York, NY: Dramatists Play Service, Inc. **SUBJECTS/PLAY TYPE:** Mystery; Adaptation.

2762. 7-12. (+) Nolan, Paul T. (Doyle, Arthur Conan) **Sherlock Holmes Christmas goose.** (The adventure of the blue carbuncle.) **CAST:** 6m. **ACTS:** 1. **SETTINGS:** Study/living room. **PLAYING TIME:** 25 min. **PLOT:** Commissioner Peterson brings Holmes a dropped hat and a lost goose, in which they find a stolen gem. Holmes advertises in the paper, traps the thief, and returns the goose to an unsuspecting rightful owner. **RECOMMENDATION:** In this very fine adaptation, the dialogue is simple and direct, and the plot is lively and well structured. One drawback is its lack of female roles, which could perhaps be remedied by altering some of the smaller parts. **ROYALTY:** Free to Plays subscribers. **SOURCE:** Nolan, Paul T. (1985, December). Sherlock Holmes' Christmas goose. Plays: The Drama Magazine for Young People, pp. 55-63. **SUBJECTS/PLAY TYPE:** Mystery; Christmas; Adaptation.

2763. 9-12. (+) Nolan, Paul T. (Doyle, Sir Arthur Conan) **Sherlock Holmes is dying.** (Sherlock Holmes is dying) **CAST:** 2f, 4m. **ACTS:** 1. **SETTINGS:** Bedroom; garden. **PLAYING TIME:** 25 min. **PLOT:** Dr. Watson finds Holmes dying and refusing medical care. Watson asks Mr. Smith to come help and he returns to Baker Street ahead of Smith, according to Holmes' instructions. Holmes asks Watson to hide behind a screen and listen carefully when Smith arrives. Holmes tells Smith that he will forget about his nephew's murder if Smith cures him. Thinking Holmes is on his death bed, Smith confesses to his nephew's murder and the soon to be murder of Holmes. Holmes calls his hand with the witness, Watson, and Inspector Morton arrests Smith. **RECOMMENDATION:** The dialogue flows without bogging down in details, and the action is compact enough that it can be staged with minimal props. **ROYALTY:** Free to Plays subscribers. **SOURCE:** Nolan, Paul T. (1986, November). Sherlock Holmes is dying. Plays: The Drama Magazine for Young People, pp. 55-63. **SUBJECTS/PLAY TYPE:** Mystery; Adaptation.

2764. 7-8*. (+) Kelly, Tim J. **Sherlock meets the phantom.** **CAST:** 9f, 5m. **ACTS:** 1. **SETTINGS:** Theater stage. **PLAYING TIME:** 45 min. **PLOT:** Sherlock Holmes and his housekeeper, Mrs. Hudson, help the cast of frightened players at the Virginia City Opera House discover the identity of the mysterious phantom. **RECOMMENDATION:** This mildly amusing comedy, complete with chase scenes and an unpredictable though far fetched ending, will most likely entertain mystery fans. A singing cast is central, but recorded music that is lipsynced would be feasible. **ROYALTY:** $15. **SOURCE:** Kelly, Tim J. (1975). Sherlock meets the phantom. Denver, CO: Pioneer Drama Service. **SUBJECTS/PLAY TYPE:** Mystery; Comedy.

2765. 10-12. (+) Marowitz, Charles. **Sherlock's last case.** **CAST:** 2f, 4m, 1u. **ACTS:** 2. **SETTINGS:** Baker Street flat; cellar. **PLAYING TIME:** NA. **PLOT:** The threat to Holmes's life by the son of his dead arch rival Moriarty turns out to be a carefully designed plot to murder Holmes by his friend and partner, Dr. Watson. Watson is sick of being underrated and taken for granted by Holmes and intends to prove his cleverness to Holmes by entrapping him. Holmes miraculously escapes death and returns to reestablish his one sided relationship with a chastened Dr. Watson. **RECOMMENDATION:** This spoof will be enjoyed, even by those unfamiliar with the original characters. **ROYALTY:** NA. **SOURCE:** Marowitz, Charles.

(1984). Sherlock's last case. New York, NY: Dramatists Play Service, Inc. **SUBJECTS/PLAY TYPE:** Friendship; Jealousy; Mystery.

2766. 7-12*. (+) Seay, James L. & Conrad, Henry. **She's at sea. CAST:** 10f, 4m, Su. **ACTS:** 2. **SETTINGS:** Ship's deck; crews quarters; ship's brig. **PLAYING TIME:** NA. **PLOT:** The first ever class of female naval cadets board the U.S.S. Gideon Welles, and entirely disrupt discipline. The chaotic climax occurs when one cadet, Midshipperson Lucretia Hornblower Brasshat, who is the spoiled daughter of an admiral, becomes jealous of another cadet's relationship with the executive officer, Ensign Billy Budd Barton. She frames the unfortunate cadet by firing a live shell at a seemingly innocent foreign whaler vessel and blaming Mercedes. The female crew of the whaler scuttles their ship and and demands the U.S.S. Gideon Welles as payment. Wily Lucretia comes to the rescue by talking her father into accepting the whaler's crew into positions with the Navy Department. Mercedes is freed to pursue the gallant Billy Budd Barton, and everybody lives happily ever after. **RECOMMENDATION:** This musical comedy is a spoof on the long standing naval tradition of not allowing women to go to sea as sailors because of fears of their disruptive effects on male crews. There is a tongue in cheek suggestion that the Yin Yang chemistry between men and women reigns above all else. It also assaults the ultimate supremacy of a Captain at sea. The play is fairly lengthy, requires much singing, and probably would work better if performed by upper level high school students or adults. **ROYALTY:** $75. **SOURCE:** Seay, James & Conrad, Henry. (1977). She's at sea. Elgin, IL: Performance Pub. Co. **SUBJECTS/PLAY TYPE:** Naval Traditions; Musical; Comedy.

2767. 4-12. (+) Deverell, Rex. **The Shinbone General Store caper. CAST:** 3f, 4m. **ACTS:** 1. **SETTINGS:** Store; cottage; outdoors; farmhouse. **PLAYING TIME:** NA. **PLOT:** When a female Mountie and a sinister looking stranger arrive in a small Canadian town just before a blizzard hits, the entire general store mysteriously disappears. **RECOMMENDATION:** Despite the numerous scene changes, this melodrama can be produced with a simple set and a minimum of props. It is highly recommended for its plot twists and surprise ending. **ROYALTY:** NA. **SOURCE:** Deverell, Rex. (1977). The underground lake, the shinbone general store caper, the uphill revival: Three plays by Rex Deverell. Toronto, Canada: Playwrights Co-op. **SUBJECTS/PLAY TYPE:** Sexism; Mystery.

2768. 5-9*. (+) Ashby, Sylvia & Snow, Mary. **Shining princess of the slender bamboo. CAST:** 5f, 16m, Su. **ACTS:** 1. **SETTINGS:** Bamboo grove; thatched hut; forge, shop; boat. **PLAYING TIME:** 60 min. **PLOT:** The Moon King hides his baby daughter, Moonbeam, in a magical, glowing bamboo. A bamboo cutter and his childless wife raise Moonbeam as their own. As a young lady, Moonbeam's beauty attracts three suitors. She unwillingly agrees to marry the one who proves his love by seeking out and bringing her a rare gift. In the interim, Moonbeam and the Emperor fall in love. Fortunately, her suitors are inept and dishonest, and each one brings an imitation gift.

Plans are therefore made for Moonbeam and the Emperor to be married. Sadly, on the night of the August moon, the Moon King interrupts the wedding plans when he comes to take Moonbeam back to his palace. Moonbeam reluctantly faces her fate by leaving her parents and the Emperor to return to her father's kingdom. **RECOMMENDATION:** Widely acclaimed, this delightful play couples the beauty of a folk tale with a bittersweet ending. Although the actors may be elementary school students or adults, they should be directed by someone with experience. This appears to depend heavily on integrated music and sound effects, which are electronically produced. Dance provides some transitions. **ROYALTY:** $75. **SOURCE:** Ashby, Sylvia & Snow, Mary. (1976). Shining princess of the slender bamboo. Schulenburg, TX: I.E. Clark. **SUBJECTS/PLAY TYPE:** Folk Tales, Japan; Fantasy; Adaptation.

2769. K-3. (-) Fisher, Aileen Lucia. **Shining up the halo. CAST:** Su. **ACTS:** 1. **SETTINGS:** Bare stage. **PLAYING TIME:** 3 min. **PLOT:** This poem describes the good things that children do who are trying to be very good for Christmas. **RECOMMENDATION:** This is too didactic and patronizing to be of value. Also, some of the language is too sophisticated for the youngsters. **ROYALTY:** Free to Plays subscribers. **SOURCE:** Fisher, Aileen Lucia. (1985). Year-round programs for young players. Boston, MA: Plays, Inc. **SUBJECTS/PLAY TYPE:** Christmas; Musical; Skit.

2770. 5-8. (-) Young, Stanley. **Ship forever sailing. CAST:** 23m, Su. **ACTS:** 1. **SETTINGS:** Deck of the Mayflower. **PLAYING TIME:** 25 min. **PLOT:** This dramatizes the Pilgrims' differing views during the signing of the Mayflower Compact. **RECOMMENDATION:** The historical liberties taken with the material, anachronisms, and the all male cast make this unsuccessful. **ROYALTY:** Free to Plays subscribers. **SOURCE:** Kamerman, Sylvia E. (1983). Holiday plays round the year. Boston, MA: Plays, Inc. **SUBJECTS/PLAY TYPE:** Thanksgiving; Mayflower Compact; Playlet.

2771. 4-8. (+) Gotwalt, Helen Louise Miller. **Shirley Holmes and the F.B.I. CAST:** 5f, 7m, 3u. **ACTS:** 1. **SETTINGS:** Garage. **PLAYING TIME:** 20 min. **PLOT:** Shirley and her Female Bureau of Investigators surprise two escaped criminals who are looking for the money from a robbery in the old abandoned garage that the girls use as a clubhouse. The girls assume it is the boys' rival detective agency playing a trick. However, when the boys arrive with their bicycle sirens blaring, the crooks run. The children hear an announcement on the local radio station about the criminals and find the code describing where the loot is hidden. They break the code, discover the money, and trap the criminals. The play concludes with the two rival agencies joining forces. **RECOMMENDATION:** Particularly enjoyable are the parts of the bumbling robbers, and Shirley, the leader of the F.B.I. This could be used in conjunction with a unit on logical thinking. **ROYALTY:** Free to Plays subscribers. **SOURCE:** Gotwalt, Helen Louise Miller. (1986). Everyday plays for boys and girls. Boston, MA: Plays, Inc. **SUBJECTS/PLAY TYPE:** Detectives; Mystery.

2772. 9-12. (+) Butler, Patrick & Butler, Patricia. **Shiveree!** CAST: 5f, 7m, Su. ACTS: 2. SETTINGS: Town square; dressing room. PLAYING TIME: 90 min. PLOT: In 1903, small town Amy McLean invites international star Lillian Russell to perform at her town's annual celebration. Amy's mother, Cora, incites the women of the town to demonstrate because she fears the evil influence of city life, personified by Miss Russell, but she does not succeed in preventing the star's visit, partly due to maneuvering on the part of her husband, who sympathizes with Amy. Later, the townspeople are stunned to learn that Cora had been a famous exotic dancer before her marriage. All misgivings turn out to be unfounded when Amy and Jennifer realize that their own boyfriends are more desirable than the big city stars. RECOMMENDATION: Although the plot and characters are hackneyed, outdated and flat, this could be fun to perform before an audience that appreciates word plays and slapstick. In addition, a pantomime performed under a strobe light gives a very effective period flavor with its evocation of the silent movie days. ROYALTY: $50. SOURCE: Butler, Patrick. (1980). Shiveree! Denver, CO: Pioneer Drama Service. SUBJECTS/PLAY TYPE: Romance; Musical; Comedy.

2773. 1-5*. (+) Kehret, Peg. **The shoe box.** CAST: 1u. ACTS: 1. SETTINGS: None. PLAYING TIME: NA. PLOT: A young boy recalls the time he made a wooden shoe box out of scraps for his father for Christmas. On Christmas morning, he felt terrible because his brothers and grandmother had bought his father expensive gifts. With embarrassment, he gave his present to dad, who said that it was the best gift that he had ever received. RECOMMENDATION: This shows poignantly that the spirit in which a gift is given is more important than the gift itself. ROYALTY: NA. SOURCE: Kehret, Peg. (1986). Winning monologs for young actors. Colorado Springs, CO: Meriwether Pub. SUBJECTS/PLAY TYPE: Christmas; Gifts; Monologue.

2774. 8-10. (+) Very, Alice. (Grimm Brothers) **The shoemaker and the elves.** (The elves and the shoemaker) CAST: 2f, 2m, Su. ACTS: 1. SETTINGS: Shoemaker's shop. PLAYING TIME: NA. PLOT: This faithful adaptation is done completely in rhyme. RECOMMENDATION: The tale is still delightful today, and the use of verse makes this version unique. ROYALTY: None. SOURCE: Kamerman, Sylvia. (1978). On stage for Christmas. Boston, MA: Plays, Inc. SUBJECTS/PLAY TYPE: Christmas; Folk Tales, Germany; Adaptation.

2775. 5-8. (-) Bradley, Virginia. **Shoes and ships and a mermaid.** CAST: 1f, 8m. ACTS: 1. SETTINGS: Deck of a ship; bottom of the sea. PLAYING TIME: NA. PLOT: When a sailor dives to the bottom of the sea, he meets an octopus and Davy Jones. RECOMMENDATION: This too confusing, lengthy play uses both puppets and human actors on stage, with some characters living and others dead. ROYALTY: None. SOURCE: Bradley, Virginia. (1975). Is there an actor in the house? New York, NY: Dodd, Mead. SUBJECTS/PLAY TYPE: Sailors; Mermaids; Comedy; Puppet Play.

2776. 7-9. (+) Sawyer-Young, Kat. **Shopping.** CAST: 2f. ACTS: 1. SETTINGS: Shopping mall. PLAYING TIME: NA. PLOT: Two girls talk about dresses, braces, shoes, and boys while on a shopping trip. When one sees a boy she adores, she first wants to hide, then rushes to join him when she sees him with another girl, her rival. RECOMMENDATION: Some of the phrasing (e.g., using the word, "God") could be replaced. ROYALTY: NA. SOURCE: Sawyer-Young, Kat. (1986). Contemporary scenes for contemporary kids. Boston, MA: Baker's Plays. SUBJECTS/PLAY TYPE: Romance; Love; Scene.

2777. 2-3. (+) Axel-Lute, Melanie. **The shortest month.** CAST: 1f, 4m, 13u. ACTS: 1. SETTINGS: Bare stage. PLAYING TIME: 12 min. PLOT: All of the months plan the new year except February, who naps. Since February has been excluded, people complain about missing Groundhog Day, Valentine's Day, Lincoln's Birthday, and Washington's Birthday. The other months decide that February must join in the planning to make the new year complete. RECOMMENDATION: This is an interesting way to describe the special holidays and weather of the months. ROYALTY: Free to Plays subscribers. SOURCE: Axel-Lute, Melanie. (1986, January/February). The shortest month. Plays: The Drama Magazine for Young People, pp. 57-60. SUBJECTS/PLAY TYPE: Calendars; Months; February; Skit.

2778. 1-8. (+) Whittaker, Violet. **Show me again, Lord.** CAST: 1m, 4u. ACTS: 4. SETTINGS: Field; threshing floor. PLAYING TIME: NA. PLOT: God proves his existence to Gideon by burning a sacrifice and making a fleece wet and then dry. Gideon destroys his father's idol and prepares to battle the Midianites. RECOMMENDATION: If the last narration (in which the audience is exhorted to accept Christ) were deleted, this dramatization of Judges 6 would be an appropriate nondenominational Sunday school presentation. ROYALTY: NA. SOURCE: Whittaker, Violet. (1984). Puppet people scripts. Grand Rapids, MI: Baker Book House. SUBJECTS/PLAY TYPE: Gideon; Bible Stories; Puppet Play.

2779. 9-12. (+) Randall, Charles H. & Bushnell, Joan LeGro. **Showdown at the Rainbow Ranch.** CAST: 4f, 4m. ACTS: 2. SETTINGS: Kitchen. PLAYING TIME: NA. PLOT: Matthew, a handsome young rodeo hero, arrives at the ranch where he and Rainbow, the ranch owner, fall in love. Matthew and Rainbow's friends keep dastardly Cadwell Cleaver from repossessing the ranch, abducting Rainbow, murdering everyone who stands in his way, and making the hapless Madame Zorelda (the villain's forsaken wife) an unwilling accomplice. RECOMMENDATION: The plot is predictable and a bit drawn out, but this will provide the opportunity for student actors to ham it up and to sing the upbeat songs. ROYALTY: $50. SOURCE: Randall, Charles H. & Bushnell, Joan LeGro. (1984). Showdown at the Rainbow Ranch. Chicago, IL: Dramatic Pub. Co. SUBJECTS/PLAY TYPE: Western; Melodrama.

2780. 3-9. (+) Robinette, Joseph & Shaw, James R. **Showdown at the Sugar Cane Saloon.** CAST: 5f, 5m.

ACTS: 2. SETTINGS: Saloon. PLAYING TIME: NA. PLOT: Several townspeople wait in a saloon for the arrival of the dreaded French pirate and his cohorts. A reluctant hero and a fragile heroine join forces to overpower the feared pirate with cream pies. RECOMMENDATION: Action (including chase scenes and pie throwing), characters with the names of food (Cherries Jubilee and Golden Graham, etc.), and the use of corny lines and songs make this very appealing. ROYALTY: Upon application. SOURCE: Robinette, Joseph & Shaw, James R. (1979). Showdown at the Sugar Cane Saloon. Chicago, IL: Dramatic Pub. Co. SUBJECTS/PLAY TYPE: Musical; Comedy; Western; Melodrama.

2781. K-3. (+) Gotwalt, Helen Louise Miller. **The shower of hearts.** CAST: 8f, 5m, 8u. ACTS: 1. SETTINGS: Throne room. PLAYING TIME: NA. PLOT: The King's Valentine party is cancelled when he discovers that the tarts are missing and he finds that the Queen had them thrown away because they didn't taste good. RECOMMENDATION: Fantasy, music, humor, and action will hold a younger group's interest. ROYALTY: NA. SOURCE: Gotwalt, Helen Louise Miller. (1985). The shower of hearts. First Plays for Children. Boston, MA: Plays, Inc. SUBJECTS/PLAY TYPE: Valentine's Day; Musical.

2782. 10-12. (+) Barbie, Richard A. (Shakespeare, William) **Shrew!** (The taming of the shrew) CAST: 6f, 6m, Su. ACTS: 2. SETTINGS: Street; rooms. PLAYING TIME: NA. PLOT: Petruchio sets out to woo and marry the obstinate Kate, while various suitors woo Kate's sister, Bianca. The sexist lesson of male dominance is preserved in this adaptation. RECOMMENDATION: Although elaborate sets, music, and costumes are a consideration, the fast paced humor of this musical makes it a worthwhile production. It includes interaction between the audience and cast. ROYALTY: NA. SOURCE: Barbie, Richard A. (1977). Shrew! Chicago, IL: Dramatic Pub. Co. SUBJECTS/ PLAY TYPE: Comedy; Musical; Marriage; Adaptation.

2783. 1-6. (+) Boiko, Claire. **Sibling switch.** CAST: 5f, 4m. ACTS: 1. SETTINGS: Street; living room. PLAYING TIME: 25 min. PLOT: A modern fairy grants a boy three wishes. He uses the first to wish the fairy good luck, and the second to turn his older sister into an older brother. When he discovers that a brother isn't as great as he thought, he wishes his sister back, but is still depressed. In response to the sister's exasperated wish for a sister, the fairy turns the brother into one and the sister realizes that brothers aren't that bad after all. After everyone returns to normal, the siblings talk for the first time. RECOMMENDATION: The sibling rivalry and arguments here are wonderfully realistic, and the wishes for a sister or brother will immediately be understood. The fairy's speech at the end, where she urges siblings to "start a conversation going for forty or fifty years" provides an emotional and sentimental touch. ROYALTY: Free to Plays subscribers. SOURCE: Boiko, Claire. (1987, May). Sibling switch. Plays: The Drama Magazine for Young People, pp. 41-48. SUBJECTS/PLAY TYPE: Siblings; Playlet.

2784. 8-12. (+) Olfson, Lewy. (Eliot, George) **Silas Marner.** (Silas Marner) CAST: 5f, 3m, 7u. ACTS: 1. SETTINGS: None. PLAYING TIME: 20 min. PLOT: This is a faithful adaptation of the original. RECOMMENDATION: Since this follows the plot and style of language in the original, those who felt that the original was syrupy, will feel the same about this. ROYALTY: Free to Plays subscribers. SOURCE: Olfson, Lewy. (1987, October). Silas Marner. Plays: The Drama Magazine for Young People, pp. 57-63. SUBJECTS/PLAY TYPE: Family; Love; Adaptation.

2785. 9-12. (+) Abrams, Joe. **Silence, please.** CAST: 2f, 2m, 1u. ACTS: 1. SETTINGS: Library. PLAYING TIME: NA. PLOT: Love is lost and found across library tables when two feuding young people meet attractive others. A ferocious librarian enforces strict silence, which reduces the lovers to eloquent gestures, passionate gazes, and scribbled notes. RECOMMENDATION: This pantomime succeeds in telling the archetypal love story in the barest possible way. The stage directions are rich in suggestion. Although the librarian is written as a female role, the character could be male. Some may object to the outdated librarian stereotype. ROYALTY: None. SOURCE: Majeski, Bill. (1981). Easy skits, blackouts and pantomimes. Woodstock, IL: Dramatic Pub. Co. SUBJECTS/PLAY TYPE: Romance; Comedy; Pantomime.

2786. 6-12. (+) Hollingsworth, Leslie. **Silent night.** CAST: 5f, 4m, Su. ACTS: 1. SETTINGS: Study. PLAYING TIME: 20 min. PLOT: Pastor Mohr, two days before Christmas 1818, is determined to have a new song for the annual Christmas Concert. The pastor suffers from writer's block and is discouraged. A cold snowy night provides the inspiration needed to start writing the hymn. He writes all night and when morning dawns he asks Herr Gruber to write a melody which can easily be learned. Like Pastor Mohr, Gruber finds inspiration, and the melody is so simple that the song is easily learned. Things look bleak again when the organ breaks, but the organist's four daughters save the day by leading the choir in the debut of "Silent Night." RECOMMENDATION: This dramatization of the writing of "Silent Night" has dialogue written in such a way to make it sound both Germanic and old. ROYALTY: Free to Plays subscribers. SOURCE: Hollingsworth, Leslie. (1977, December). Silent night. Plays: The Drama Magazine for Young People, pp. 45-50. SUBJECTS/PLAY TYPE: Christmas; Musical; Playlet.

2787. 1-3. (+) Breslow, Maurice. **Silver Bird and Scarlet Feather.** CAST: 2f, 4m. ACTS: 1. SETTINGS: Western cabin; yard; Indian village, cave; riverbank. PLAYING TIME: NA. PLOT: Sarah Flemming, 11, is kidnapped and adopted by the Blackfoot Indian chief, Standing Tree, in retaliation for the kidnapping of his oldest daughter. Befriended by Silver Bird and Running Brook, Sarah is accepted by the tribe, learns to enjoy the Indian lifestyle, and is given the name, Scarlet Feather. Years later, her real father arrives at the Blackfoot village, where he confronts Chief Standing Tree. Silver Bird and Scarlet Feather run off to the river; Mr. Flemming and

Standing Tree find the girls and share their pasts with each other. Scarlet Feather must choose whether to stay with the Indians or go back with her real father. She chooses her father, but promises to visit the Indians often. RECOMMENDATION: This has lively characters, and the Indians are portrayed as caring individuals, rather than the stereotypes so often seen in movies. Produced by upper elementary or junior high students for lower elementary students, this could generate discussion about the Indian wars, as well as the rights of parents. ROYALTY: NA. SOURCE: Breslow, Maurice. (1982). Adam and Eve and after and Silver Bird and Scarlet Feather. Toronto, Canada: Playwrights Canada. SUBJECTS/PLAY TYPE: Western; Native Americans; Adventure; Drama.

2788. 7-12. (+) Hamlett, Christina. **The silver tongued slicker of Sassafras Flat. CAST:** 4f, 2m. ACTS: 1. SETTINGS: Cafe. PLAYING TIME: 20 min. PLOT: A conman cons widows out of their money by telling them that they still owe money on the last piece of jewelry that their departed husbands were buying on time. He is caught by a newly trained woman detective posing as a widow. RECOMMENDATION: Set in the 1940s west, this clever story is made even more appealing by the characters' references to spiraling food prices and the onslaught of people in cars. ROYALTY: Free to Plays subscribers. SOURCE: Hamlett, Christina. (1985, November). The silver-tongued slicker of Sassafras Flat. Plays: The Drama Magazine for Young People, pp. 23-30. SUBJECTS/PLAY TYPE: Con-Artists; Melodrama.

2789. 2-4*. (-) Mace, Patrick B. **The silver whistle.** CAST: 1f, 6m, 6u. ACTS: 4. SETTINGS: Outside the town; street; hotel; courtroom; prison. PLAYING TIME: NA. PLOT: The princess' lost magic whistle, capable of granting any wish, is found by a poor soldier and then stolen by a magician, both of whom use it to satisfy greed and ambition. Finally it falls into the hands of a policeman, who uses his wish to make the whistle ordinary. RECOMMENDATION: Written to involve the audience in decision making, this does not work. Children's responses in most cases, may not be what are hoped for by the producers. The lesson to be learned (that most people are incapable of resisting greed and power) may not come through clearly. ROYALTY: $35. SOURCE: Mace, Patrick B. (1985). The silver whistle. New Orleans, LA: Anchorage Press. SUBJECTS/PLAY TYPE: Magic; Greed; Drama.

2790. 7-12. (+) Boiko, Claire. **Simon says.** CAST: 3f, 9m, 1u. ACTS: 1. SETTINGS: Living room. PLAYING TIME: 30 min. PLOT: The Archers are an average family struggling to cope with life. A computer salesman offers them a robot (Simon) whose mission is to resolve all their problems. When Simon's programming system realizes that putting a million dollars in the Archer's bank account and announcing on national T.V. that Mr. Archer's boss is a slave driver doesn't really make the family happy, his circuits overload and he breaks down. Fortunately, he revives because his work on the daughter's behalf was successful. She is very happy when a raft of boys show up for her birthday party. RECOMMENDATION: This simple, humorous science-fiction plot is engaging and

would make a good lead in to a discussion of the nature of happiness. ROYALTY: Free to Plays subscribers. SOURCE: Boiko, Claire. (1985, April). Simon says. Plays: The Drama Magazine for Young People, pp. 1-10. SUBJECTS/PLAY TYPE: Family; Science Fiction; Robots; Comedy.

2791. 2-6. (+) Peterson, Mary Nygaard. **Simple Olaf.** CAST: 7m, Su. ACTS: 1. SETTINGS: Bare stage, props. PLAYING TIME: 20 min. PLOT: Simple Olaf sets out to see the world and encounters a peasant who swindles him out of all his money in exchange for a goose. Olaf then goes to the castle to present the king with the goose, but the first guard will not let Olaf pass until he promises to give the guard half of the reward. The second guard extorts the same promise, so Olaf requests that the king give him a beating instead of gold, and tells the king about the promises the guards extracted from him. The king punishes the guards and makes Olaf his personal advisor. RECOMMENDATION: The simple setting and possible inclusion of many actors as courtiers makes this a good large group production. ROYALTY: NA. SOURCE: Kamerman, Sylvia E. (1987). Plays from favorite folk tales. Boston. MA: Plays, Inc. SUBJECTS/PLAY TYPE: Folktale Motifs; Playlet.

2792. 2-4. (+) Gotwalt, Helen Louise Miller. (Mother Goose) **Simple Simon's reward.** (Simple Simon's misfortunes and his wife Margery's cruelty) CAST: 7f, 9m, Su. ACTS: 1. SETTINGS: Road. PLAYING TIME: NA. PLOT: Simon finds the Countess of Scrubsville's earring and gets the Pieman a permit to sell pies at the fair. RECOMMENDATION: This would have to be produced by the older grades. ROYALTY: NA. SOURCE: Gotwalt, Helen Louise Miller. (1986). Everyday Plays for Boys and Girls. Boston, MA: Plays, Inc. SUBJECTS/PLAY TYPE: Nursery Rhymes; Comedy; Adaptation.

2793. 10-12. (+) Gallo, Diane. **Sin in the South: It pays to be the Colonel's daughter.** CAST: 8f, 4m. ACTS: 2. SETTINGS: Mansion. PLAYING TIME: NA. PLOT: On her 18th birthday, Violet Loo learns that she had an inheritance but it all disappeared except the plantation, which she will inherit upon the death of her aunt and uncle. Preston Upright still asks her to marry him, infuriating villain Snively Lowdown, who had hoped to gain the lands. Snively courts Violet with trickery and begins to methodically kill off the family until The Colonel, Violet's long lost father, returns and sets all to rights. RECOMMENDATION: Although rather insipid, this parody of the South has its moments of humor and could be an appropriate dramatic vehicle for actors who enjoy hamming it up. ROYALTY: $15. SOURCE: Gallo, Diane. (1982). Sin in the South: it pays to be the Colonel's daughter. Boston, MA: Baker's Plays. SUBJECTS/PLAY TYPE: Parody; Swindlers and Swindling; Melodrama.

2794. K-8*. (+) Melanos, Jack A. **Sinbad and the evil genii.** CAST: 3f, 7m, 2u. ACTS: 3. SETTINGS: Home; ship; clearing between rocks. PLAYING TIME: NA. PLOT: Sinbad offers to search for Abou's father, who has not returned from his treasure hunting trip. Before he can leave, Sinbad, Abou, and the princess are kidnapped by a greedy wine merchant who believes that Abou has the treasure map. When Abou's commandeered ship arrives at the island of the evil genii, Abou fights the genii, wins three wishes, and discovers that his father is alive and waiting in Bagdad. The evil kidnapper is eaten by the giant Roc. RECOMMENDATION: Filled with creatures of myth and legend, dangers from human and supernatural forces, and an archetypal struggle between good and evil and greed and selfishness, this is enchanting. Production requires talented actors, rather complex sets and a stage manager experienced in special effects. ROYALTY: $35. SOURCE: Melanos, Jack A. (1986). Sinbad and the evil genii. New Orleans, LA: Anchorage Press, Inc. SUBJECTS/PLAY TYPE: Fantasy; Adventure; Magic; Drama.

2795. 4-5. (+) Olfson, Lewy. **Sing a song of holidays!** CAST: Su. ACTS: 1. SETTINGS: None. PLAYING TIME: 8 min. PLOT: This is a choral presentation of the history of New Year's Day, Pan American Day, Memorial Day, Thanksgiving, and Christmas. RECOMMENDATION: The flow is somewhat choppy, but this is light, happy, and very upbeat. ROYALTY: Free to Plays subscribers. SOURCE: Kamerman, Sylvia E. (1975). Patriotic and historical plays for young people. Boston, MA: Plays, Inc. SUBJECTS/PLAY TYPE: New Year's Day; Pan American Day; Memorial Day; Thanksgiving; Christmas; Choral Reading.

2796. 8-12. (+) Robbins, Norman. **Sing a song of sixpence.** CAST: 8f, 8m, 24u. ACTS: 2. SETTINGS: Witch's lair; bakery; corridor; banquet hall; street; bedroom; courtyard; path; encampment; glade; road; throne room. PLAYING TIME: NA. PLOT: The King's magic crown is stolen and the kingdom is destitute. The prince of a neighboring kingdom sets out to defeat the witch who stole the crown, vowing to return and marry the King's daughter. After much tribulation and laughter (for the audience), the crown is recovered, and the prince marries the princess. RECOMMENDATION: Typical fairy tale stuff is made new by a hilarious cast of characters. A bit of light sexual humor occurs in places, but nothing very serious. Many settings and 17 songs require an experienced cast. ROYALTY: NA. SOURCE: Robbins, Norman. (1978). Sing a song of six-pence. New York, NY: Samuel French. SUBJECTS/PLAY TYPE: Folk Tale Motifs; Comedy; Musical.

2797. 3-6. (+) Fisher, Aileen. **Sing out for peace.** CAST: Su. ACTS: 1. SETTINGS: None. PLAYING TIME: 3 min. PLOT: This is a prayer for world peace. RECOMMENDATION: Although unexceptional, this may be valuable as an alternative to traditional Memorial Day songs and recitations which glorify battle. ROYALTY: Free to Plays subscribers. SOURCE: Fisher, Aileen. (1986, May). Sing out for peace. Plays: The Drama Magazine for Young People, pp. 52. SUBJECTS/PLAY TYPE: Memorial Day; Choral Reading.

2798. 7-12. (+) Fisher, Aileen. **Sing the songs of Christmas.** CAST: Su. ACTS: 1. SETTINGS: Bare stage, props. PLAYING TIME: 35 min. PLOT: As a group of actors tries to put their Christmas carols into order, they

learn about the history of each. RECOMMENDATION: This is religious in nature and most appropriate for church settings. It presents the historical perspective effectively. ROYALTY: Free to Plays subscribers. SOURCE: Fisher, Aileen. (1976, December). Sing the songs of Christmas. Plays: The Drama Magazine for Young People, pp. 25-35. SUBJECTS/PLAY TYPE: Christmas; Christian Drama; Musical.

2799. 4-12. (+) Fisher, Aileen Lucia. **Sing the songs of Lincoln.** CAST: 8f, 7m, Su. ACTS: 1. SETTINGS: Cabin; outside; farm house; White House. PLAYING TIME: 45 min. PLOT: This biography of Lincoln (up to 1860) details the death of his mother, infant brother, sister, and sweetheart. The open warmth and support from his new stepmother (Sarah Bush Lincoln) rescues young Lincoln from despair. Other events covered (although briefly) include the Lincoln- Douglas debates, Mary Todd Lincoln, Lincoln's stand on slavery, and Lincoln's successful bid for the White House. The real motifs are the songs of childhood and the constant love of Sarah Bush Lincoln. RECOMMENDATION: This is an extremely well knit play that offers a twist to familiar material. Although the singing should be professional, everything else could be handled by either younger or older actors. ROYALTY: Free to Plays subscribers. SOURCE: Fisher, Aileen Lucia. (1985). Year-round programs for young players. Boston, MA: Plays, Inc. SUBJECTS/PLAY TYPE: Lincoln, Abraham; Civil War, U.S.; Slavery; Playlet.

2800. 7-9. (-) Fisher, Aileen. **Sing the songs of Thanksgiving.** CAST: 6f, 5m, Su. ACTS: 1. SETTINGS: None. PLAYING TIME: 30 min. PLOT: The Master of Ceremonies narrates the story of the development of Thanksgiving as an American national holiday, the Chorus sings various songs, and several actors enact short historical scenes. RECOMMENDATION: The language tends to be dry and, despite musical and dramatic inserts, the script reads like a history lesson. ROYALTY: Free to Plays subscribers. SOURCE: Kamerman, Sylvia E. (1983). Holiday plays round the year. Boston, MA: Plays, Inc. SUBJECTS/PLAY TYPE: Thanksgiving; Musical.

2801. 4-12. (+) Campton, David. **Singing in the wilderness.** CAST: 1f, 2m, 3u. ACTS: 1. SETTINGS: Woodland. PLAYING TIME: NA. PLOT: Fairies in search of a place to live are almost destroyed by modern herbicides, pesticides, gasoline fumes, and junk food. When they come across a thicket that has all the old fairy foods and flowers, they dream of staying there forever. An ecologist describes how he will show them off by setting up car parks, tourist stands, new pathways, and a safari park; a folklorist goes home in disgust; and Tinkerbell tricks the ecologist into following her away from the rest. The remaining fairies, saddened, but glad not to be trapped there forever, wander away. RECOMMENDATION: This is recommended for all children who are not too old to scoff at the idea of fairies struggling to survive in a modern age. Some of the mature dialogue might have to be toned down to be understood by younger audiences. This should be performed by older grades. ROYALTY: NA. SOURCE: Campton, David. (1986). Singing in the wilderness. London, England:

Samuel French. **SUBJECTS/PLAY TYPE:** Fairies; Ecology; Drama.

2802. 7-12. (-) Gater, Dilys. **The singing swans. CAST:** 4f, 10m, Su. **ACTS:** 2. **SETTINGS:** Pirate ship; garden; lake; palace room. **PLAYING TIME:** NA. **PLOT:** Princess Lucinda disguises herself as a boy and engages the help of some down and out pirates to defeat the evil Mandarin, who has stolen her father's singing swans. They retrieve the swans and tame the Mandarin. The Princess is engaged to one of the pirates, who turns out to be a Prince of a neighboring kingdom. **RECOMMENDATION:** This is entirely too long, and too much time and energy is wasted on cute humor. The action boringly seesaws back and forth between the Mandarin, just about to destroy his enemies, and the Princess and her friends controlling him. The characters are stereotypical, except for the amusing hobo, Tripp, who is an unwilling hero. **ROYALTY:** NA. **SOURCE:** Gater, Dilys. (1980). The singing swans. Macclesfield, England: New Playwrights' Network. **SUBJECTS/PLAY TYPE:** Pirates; Princesses; Comedy.

2803. 8-12. (-) Murray, John. **The sinking of the morning star. CAST:** 4f, 3m, 1u. **ACTS:** 1. **SETTINGS:** Living room. **PLAYING TIME:** 30 min. **PLOT:** The evidence to a long unsolved mystery concerning the innocence or guilt of an accused traitor surfaces with the raising of a sunken ship, bringing everyone out of the woodwork: the girl with amnesia, the aunt who wants to forget, the protective maid, the ship's owner, the press, the feds, and, of course, the culprit in disguise. No one knows who's who or whom to trust. **RECOMMENDATION:** This is not just a whodunnit; the what and why also have to be determined. The problem is that as soon as everyone is introduced, the play is over, with little room for suspense or intrigue to build. Its complexity requires a much longer exposition time. **ROYALTY:** Free to Plays subscribers. **SOURCE:** Murray, John. (1983, March). The sinking of the morning star. Plays: The Drama Magazine for Young People, pp. 23-34. **SUBJECTS/PLAY TYPE:** Mystery; Playlet.

2804. 1-6. (+) Hatton, Thomas J. **Sir Lancelot and the dragon. CAST:** 2f, 2m, 3u. **ACTS:** 1. **SETTINGS:** Village square. **PLAYING TIME:** 10 min. **PLOT:** Sir Lancelot and Sir Bors set out to rescue Princess Ipswich from the Jolly Green Dragon. The destitute knights hope to win the Princess' hand and half the riches of the kingdom. Approached by an old woman collecting money for a new heater for the local animal shelter, Sir Bors refuses to make a donation, but Sir Lancelot gives her the last of his money. In return, the old woman gives Sir Lancelot a magic spell to make the dragon weak. Sir Lancelot rescues the Princess, defeats the dragon, and solves the problem in the animal shelter by appointing the fire eating dragon as the shelter's new furnace. **RECOMMENDATION:** This will have to be rewritten as time passes to ensure that it does not become too dated. **ROYALTY:** Free to Plays subscribers. **SOURCE:** Hatton, Thomas J. (1985, May). Sir Lancelot and the dragon. Plays: The Drama Magazine for Young People, pp. 61-64. **SUBJECTS/PLAY TYPE:** Dragons; Skit.

2805. 10-12*. (+) Tasca, Jules. (Stevenson, Robert Louis) **The Sire de Maletroit's door.** (Sire de Maletroit's door) **CAST:** 1f, 2m. **ACTS:** 1. **SETTINGS:** Room. **PLAYING TIME:** NA. **PLOT:** In a case of mistaken identities, an overbearing uncle tries to force an unwitting soldier, who has been lured inside by a trick door, to marry his niece. The soldier has until dawn to decide whether he wishes to hang or marry the niece. The young couple spends the night together and find that they love each other. **RECOMMENDATION:** Although this features strong characterizations and a classic love story, the lofty and literary dialogue may affect audience enjoyment. It is recommended that the high school audiences be mature and well read. **ROYALTY:** $20. **SOURCE:** Tasca, Jules. (1986). The Sire de Maletroit's door. Woodstock, IL: Dramatic Pub. Co. **SUBJECTS/PLAY TYPE:** Romance; Adaptation.

2806. 6-9. (+) Dias, Earl J. **Siren of the silent screen. CAST:** 3f, 6m. **ACTS:** 1. **SETTINGS:** Movie set. **PLAYING TIME:** 30 min. **PLOT:** A series of humorous mishaps involving practical jokes cause trouble on the set of a silent movie. The characters add to the comedy with a Charlie Chaplin walk-alike, the heiress of a pickle fortune, and a female in distress. The ending is happy, as the practical joker is revealed, the theater group receives monetary support, and the villain is unable to scoop the good guy's production of the silent movie. **RECOMMENDATION:** Although the roles are somewhat stereotypical, some historical movie information make this beneficial for a theater class. Some knowledge of this period in theater history will be necessary. **ROYALTY:** Free to Plays subscribers. **SOURCE:** Dias, Earl J. (1978, November). Siren of the silent screen. Plays: The Drama Magazine for Young People, pp. 15-27. **SUBJECTS/PLAY TYPE:** Silent Movies; Melodrama; Comedy.

2807. 9-12. (+) Boettcher-Tate, Karen. **Sister, sister. CAST:** 5f, 2m, Su. **ACTS:** 3. **SETTINGS:** Living room. **PLAYING TIME:** NA. **PLOT:** Carey, a competent, likable 17 year old, and her mother, Betty, struggle to cope when retarded, 18 year old sister, Laura, moves back from a group home. After one of Carey's friends attempts to molest Laura and she misses her bus from her new job at a sheltered workshop, Betty adopts a custodial stance, afraid to let Laura take risks. Predictably, Laura loses self sufficiency and Carey resents the burdens placed on her. When Carey finally explodes, she and her mother see that they have been protecting themselves, but diminishing Laura. They free Laura to reach her fullest potential. **RECOMMENDATION:** This memorable play sensitively explores the issues of freedom, risk, and responsibility in dealing with a handicapped family member. **ROYALTY:** $40. **SOURCE:** Boettcher-Tate, Karen. (1983). Sister, sister. Boston, MA: Baker's Plays. **SUBJECTS/PLAY TYPE:** Mental Retardation; Drama.

2808. 7-9. (+) Glasner, Anne K. **Situation, un-sittable. CAST:** 6f, 6m, 1u. **ACTS:** 1. **SETTINGS:** Living room. **PLAYING TIME:** 30 min. **PLOT:** Two teenage girls babysit three children who wrap toilet paper around themselves to look like mummies, order $24 worth of pizza, talk long distance with complete strangers, and trick the girls and an innocent neighbor into locking themselves in a closet until the parents come home. RECOMMENDATION: The action never stops and the dialogue is snappy. The role of Punkin, the "baby" of the family, will be a challenge. ROYALTY: $15. SOURCE: Glasner, Anne K. (1978). Situation, un-sittable. Boston, MA: Baker's Plays. SUBJECTS/PLAY TYPE: Babysitting; Comedy; Farce.

2809. K-6. (+) Pou, Linda G. **Six myths of Christmas.** CAST: 4f, 3m, Su. ACTS: 1. SETTINGS: Playground. PLAYING TIME: 20 min. PLOT: Children tell stories about how a stork, firefly, robin, owl, nightingale, and cat shared their gifts with the Christ child. A chorus sings related songs between each tale. RECOMMENDATION: These are charming tales in language that is simple enough for young children to understand, yet interesting enough to hold the attention of an older audience. The music and the speaking parts are easily memorized, although the longer parts of Kevin and Robin may need to be assigned to older children. ROYALTY: $50. SOURCE: Pou, Linda G. (1986). Six myths of Christmas. Franklin, OH: Eldridge Pub. Co. SUBJECTS/PLAY TYPE: Christmas; Musical.

2810. 4-8. (+) Kehret, Peg. **Six Snickers, four candy corn and three purple bubblegum.** CAST: 1u. ACTS: 1. SETTINGS: None. PLAYING TIME: NA. PLOT: The delights of Halloween nights and candy feasts are described by an enthusiastic youngster. RECOMMENDATION: Children's favorite Halloween customs are charmingly described. ROYALTY: NA. SOURCE: Kehret, Peg. (1986). Winning monologs for young actors Colorado Springs, CO: Meriwether Pub. SUBJECTS/PLAY TYPE: Halloween; Monologue.

2811. K-5. (+) Majeski, Bill. **Sixteen Minutes-The T.V. Magazine.** CAST: 2f, 2m. ACTS: 1. SETTINGS: TV studio. PLAYING TIME: 15 min. PLOT: Barbara Walnut interviews Skippy (Count Dracula's son), Nancy (Frankenstein's daughter), and Prince Kong (son of King Kong). RECOMMENDATION: Youngsters will recognize the characters and will thoroughly enjoy the antics involved. ROYALTY: Free to Plays subscribers. SOURCE: Majeski, Bill. (1979, May). 16 Minutes--The T.V. Magazine. Plays: The Drama Magazine for Young People, pp. 61-65. SUBJECTS/PLAY TYPE: Monsters; Comedy; Skit.

2812. 9-12. (+) Murray, John. **The sixth juror.** CAST: 6f, 8m, 9u. ACTS: 1. SETTINGS: Court-room. PLAYING TIME: 35 min. PLOT: The retired teacher (the sixth juror) brings humor to a dramatic small town murder mystery hearing, involving three suspects, one of whom murdered an old man. Throughout the play, the audience receives bits and pieces of the history of the small seaside town, and sees the interactions of the people who live in the closely knit community. RECOMMENDATION: The drama of a murder mystery is lightened by the quaint characters who bring their small town idiosyncrasies to the formal proceedings. The twists and turns of the plot provide a pleasant, albeit meandering route to the final confession of the murderer. ROYALTY: Free to Plays

subscribers. SOURCE: Murray, John. (1984). Mystery plays for young actors. Boston, MA: Plays, Inc. SUBJECTS/PLAY TYPE: Mystery; Murder; Playlet.

2813. 5-12. (+) McCusker, Paul. **Sketches of Thanksgiving.** CAST: 3f, 1m, Su. ACTS: 1. SETTINGS: Bare stage, props. PLAYING TIME: NA. PLOT: A young girl reminisces about all she has to be thankful for on Thanksgiving: Cindy, who admonished a third friend for making fun of her religious date; Brian, who stood by her when her mother was in the hospital; and her friends, who planned her going away party before she moved. RECOMMENDATION: Although this is a bit hokey, with some updating, it could be a fine church presentation. ROYALTY: NA. SOURCE: McCusker, Paul. (1984). Batteries not included. Boston, MA: Baker's Plays. SUBJECTS/PLAY TYPE: Christian Drama; Thanksgiving; Skit.

2814. 5-8. (+) Nolan, Paul T. **The Skill of Pericles.** CAST: 3f, 6m, Su. ACTS: 1. SETTINGS: Market place. PLAYING TIME: 25 min. PLOT: Pericles comes to Athens to find a youth who can prove that he has the same skills that Pericles possesses. As each of Nestor's friends decides upon a skill and practices it, Nestor gives encouragement and support. Pericles chooses Nestor, because the skill of Pericles is the ability to see and encourage the skills of other people. RECOMMENDATION: The point of the play may be missed by young groups unless they are familiar with the background of the characters and the times. Talents or skills of characters may be varied to make use of the talents of individual actors. Characterization is developed through conversation. ROYALTY: None for amateur performances. SOURCE: Nolan, Paul T. (1982). Folk tale plays round the world: A collection of royalty-free, one-act plays about lands far and near. Boston, MA: Plays, Inc. SUBJECTS/PLAY TYPE: Mythology, Greek; Democracy; Playlet.

2815. K-2. (+) Bauer, Caroline Feller. **The skipping pot.** CAST: 2f, 3m, 5u. ACTS: 1. SETTINGS: Farm house; road; rich man's house; barn; treasure room. PLAYING TIME: 15 min. PLOT: On the way to sell his cow, a poor farmer exchanges it for a talking pot. The happy pot skips to the rich man's house several times and returns to the farmer and his wife with pudding, grain, and gold coins. The farmer and his wife live happily for many years and the pot sleeps in a corner. RECOMMENDATION: Children will recognize the similarities here to other familiar tales as they very simply act out or read aloud this easily memorized tale. ROYALTY: None. SOURCE: Bauer, Caroline Feller. (1987). Presenting reader's theater: Plays and poems to read aloud. New York, NY: H.W. Wilson Co. SUBJECTS/PLAY TYPE: Folk Tales, Denmark; Reader's Theater.

2816. 5-8. (+) Jacobs, Jason. **Skulduggery at Santa's place.** CAST: 3f, 3m, 3u. ACTS: 4. SETTINGS: Parlor; workshop. PLAYING TIME: 25 min. PLOT: Fiendly Frostbite forecloses on Santa's mortgage and bribes the elves to strike so that he can supply all the Christmas presents from his own factory, while he insists on marrying Santa's innocent daughter, Cookie. Everything works out when Fiendly's daughter helps foil his plans, the elves return, and Fiendly quits the villains' union. RECOMMENDATION: Through the use of modern references as well as clever one liners, this is a cute takeoff on the classic melodrama genre. ROYALTY: Free to Plays subscribers. SOURCE: Jacobs, Jason. (1983, December). Skulduggery at Santa's place. Plays: The Drama Magazine for Young People, pp. 42- 50. SUBJECTS/PLAY TYPE: Christmas; Melodrama.

2817. 4-6. (-) Page, Anita. (Campbell, Ken) **Skungpoomery.** (Skungpoomery) CAST: 3f, 6m. ACTS: 1. SETTINGS: Kitchen; shop; street. PLAYING TIME: NA. PLOT: The amazing Faz wakes up one morning bored with life and begins Skungpooming (creating new words, making up meanings for them, and acting them out), while "bunkjamjarmering" (smearing strawberry jam on your pajamas and then doing a bunk into the street). Faz and Twoo meet Mrs. Humbottom, who enthusiastically joins. Her overbearing husband calls for the police. As Faz and Twoo hide among the trash cans in the street, Officers Snatchum, Stuff and Bunkett look for them. Meanwhile, Wibble, a young policeman also hiding behind the trash cans because his domineering mother has made him go to work in sandals and shorts, is soon Skungpooming with the others. Finally, all tear about in their pajamas, inhibitions forgotten, wildly inventing new words. RECOMMENDATION: The lack of purpose, theme or characterization leaves very little of any value in this play. The made up words and actions are difficult to follow, and the humor is an assortment of slapstick and tasteless bathroom jokes. ROYALTY: $25. SOURCE: Page, Anita. (1981). Skungpoomery. Boston, MA: Baker's Plays. SUBJECTS/PLAY TYPE: Language; Adaptation.

2818. 3-6. (+) Olfson, Lewy. **The sky's the limit!** CAST: 3f, 5m, 1u. ACTS: 1. SETTINGS: Office. PLAYING TIME: 15 min. PLOT: In charge of flight schedules, Captain Flyboy must deal with constant complaints from extraordinary aviators like Mother Goose and Mary Poppins. The Captain seems to have come up with a workable schedule until Santa Claus complains. RECOMMENDATION: Everyone who is familiar with the fictional characters who float through this wonderful piece will adore it. ROYALTY: Free to Plays subscribers. SOURCE: Olfson, Lewy. (1975, October). The sky's the limit! Plays: The Drama Magazine for Young People, pp. 59-64. SUBJECTS/PLAY TYPE: Airports; Skit.

2819. 7-12. (+) Sills, Paul. **The sleeper awakes.** (The Arabian nights) CAST: 2f, 4m. ACTS: 1. SETTINGS: Bare stage, long, low platform. PLAYING TIME: NA. PLOT: A Caliph who likes to disguise himself as a peasant, reluctantly agrees to drink with one of his subjects, who refuses to give his name, saying he never drinks with the same man twice. The Caliph wants to repay the man, Abu, so he drugs him and takes him back to the palace to be the Caliph for the day. Abu rises to the occasion, but has a difficult time readjusting to common life. The Caliph returns and raises Abu to royalty to apologize for the trouble he has caused. RECOMMENDATION: The Caliph and Abu have nearly equal parts and will need to be performed by actors who can handle the lines. Some

explicit language may need to be edited, and references to the wicked Ayotollah may be offensive to some. ROYALTY: NA. SOURCE: Sills, Paul. (1981). More from story theatre. New York, NY: Samuel French. SUBJECTS/PLAY TYPE: Folk Tales, Iran; Playlet.

2820. K-5*. (+) Chorpenning, Charlotte B. (Grimm Brothers) **Sleeping beauty.** (The sleeping beauty) CAST: 8f, 4m. ACTS: 3. SETTINGS: Palace room; tower spinning room; forest. PLAYING TIME: NA. PLOT: This is a faithful retelling of the classic tale. RECOMMENDATION: Some degree of technical expertise is required to perform the magic scenes, but details are included to make it easier. The execution of the plot elicits interest and sympathy for the characters and their fates. It has several themes: good vs. evil, the importance of loving others, and dealing with developing maturity. ROYALTY: Write Anchorage Press. SOURCE: Jennings, Coleman A. & Harris, Aurand. (1988). Plays children love, Volume II. New York, NY: St. Martin's Press. SUBJECTS/PLAY TYPE: Folk Tales, Germany; Adaptation.

2821. 2-7. (+) Jackson, Richard Eugene. (Grimm Brothers) **Sleeping beauty.** (The sleeping beauty) CAST: 5f, 3m, 3u. ACTS: 2. SETTINGS: Throne room; street; garden; bedroom; cave; castle. PLAYING TIME: 60 min. PLOT: The King and Queen of Merricore host a party to celebrate the birth of their child. Feelings of discouragement replace the atmosphere of joy when the evil Thornberry appears and places a curse on the newborn. All is well until Princess Elaine's sixteenth birthday, when tragedy strikes the princess and only Prince Dauntless can save her by defeating a fire breathing dragon, thorns, and Thornberry. RECOMMENDATION: The humorous dialogue and whimsical songs will interest young children. Production is recommended for the upper ranges of the grade levels indicated. ROYALTY: $35. SOURCE: Jackson, Richard Eugene. (1977). The sleeping beauty. Denver, CO: Pioneer Drama Service. SUBJECTS/PLAY TYPE: Folk Tales, Germany; Adaptation.

2822. 1-6*. (+) Shaw, Richard. (Grimm Brothers) **Sleeping Beauty.** (Sleeping Beauty) CAST: 4f, 8m, 8u. ACTS: 1. SETTINGS: Teahouses. PLAYING TIME: NA. PLOT: Grandfather, an old sea captain, narrates the story of **Sleeping Beauty**, while the action takes place in stylized Kabuki sequences. As the story is told, the grandchildren step into some of the Kabuki scenes. The blight in Beauty's kingdom is personified by a terrible Ogress who becomes a giant spider that tangles the kingdom in a web of sleep. As the Prince approaches, the Ogress presents many obstacles which he overcomes. At the end, Beauty emerges into reality as the children's grandmother. RECOMMENDATION: This uniquely integrates Japanese and Western culture, and if performed by high schoolers, will be quite attractive to young audiences. ROYALTY: NA. SOURCE: Jenkins, Linda Walsh. (1975). Five plays from the Children's Theatre Co. of Minneapolis. Minneapolis, MN: Univ. of Minnesota Press. SUBJECTS/PLAY TYPE: Folk Tales, Germany; Kabuki Theater; Adaptation.

2823. 2-5. (+) Thane, Adele. (Grimm Brothers) **The sleeping beauty.** (Sleeping beauty.) **CAST:** 12f, 6m. **ACTS:** 1. **SETTINGS:** Throne room; tower. **PLAYING TIME:** 20 min. **PLOT:** This is a faithful retelling. **RECOMMENDATION:** The witch is a forceful character whom the audience will gleefully despise as they are lulled by the beauty of this adaptation's melodic, rhythmic and often rhyming dialogue. **ROYALTY:** None. **SOURCE:** Thane, Adele. (1983). Plays from Famous Stories and Fairy Tales. Boston, MA: Plays, Inc. **SUBJECTS/PLAY TYPE:** Folk Tales, Germany; Adaptation.

2824. K-3. (+) Way, Brian. (Grimm Brothers) **The sleeping beauty.** (The sleeping beauty) **CAST:** 6f, 15m. **ACTS:** 2. **SETTINGS:** Palace; pirate ship. **PLAYING TIME:** 120 min. **PLOT:** Angered by not receiving an invitation to the christening of Princess Carol, the wicked godmother places a curse on the princess which results in the royal household sleeping for 100 years. The curse is broken when princess is awakened by her true love, the Prince. **RECOMMENDATION:** Intended for family entertainment, this depends on participation from the audience, needs intimate staging to be most effective, and must be produced by adults or skilled young adults. **ROYALTY:** $45. **SOURCE:** Way, Brian. (1977). The sleeping beauty. Boston, MA: Baker's Plays. **SUBJECTS/PLAY TYPE:** Folk Tales, Germany; Adaptation.

2825. K-4*. (-) Robinson, Oliver William. (Grimm Brothers) **The sleeping beauty: A children's operetta.** (Sleeping Beauty) **CAST:** 16f, 3m, Su. **ACTS:** 3. **SETTINGS:** Castle hall; tower room. **PLAYING TIME:** 90 min. **PLOT:** This is a musical version of the classic tale. **RECOMMENDATION:** Dialogue and lyrics are stilted, out of date, and often cloying. The musical prelude and interludes are not likely to hold the attention of elementary children. **ROYALTY:** $50. **SOURCE:** Robinson, Oliver William. (1949). The sleeping beauty: A children's operetta. Franklin, OH: Eldridge Pub. Co. **SUBJECTS/PLAY TYPE:** Folk Tales, Germany; Musical; Adaptation.

2826. 2-10. (+) Ringwood, Gwen Pharis. (Grimm Brothers) **The sleeping beauty: A new version of the old story.** (Sleeping beauty) **CAST:** 22f, 5m, 6u. **ACTS:** 3. **SETTINGS:** Outdoors. **PLAYING TIME:** NA. **PLOT:** Based on the traditional story, the setting and language have been rewritten as a Native American tale. At the celebration of the princess' birth, the uninvited Crow curses the child to eternal sleep at the age of 16. Other animal guests offer wishes which allow for reawakening by a kiss from a prince after 100 years. The 100 year sleep is filled in by the chorus; the play ends with the awakening of the princess and the people after the kiss from the prince. **RECOMMENDATION:** Children studying Native American customs could enjoy this in conjunction with other folklore, and in discussion of common themes throughout literature. Some drumming to create mood is necessary, as well as a scrim and some technical expertise in lighting. **ROYALTY:** NA. **SOURCE:** Ringwood, Gwen. (1979). The sleeping beauty: A new version of the old story. Toronto, Canada: Playwrights Co-op.

SUBJECTS/PLAY TYPE: Folk Tales, Germany; Adaptation.

2827. 6-8. (-) Cheatham, Val R. **Sleeping Beauty and friends.** **CAST:** 3f, 1m, 3u. **ACTS:** 1. **SETTINGS:** Throne room; forest. **PLAYING TIME:** 20 min. **PLOT:** Quick thinking Merlin tells the King that a recent vision has revealed that the King's subjects will soon be looking up to their very short monarch when he returns from a quest to find Sleeping Beauty. When Sleeping Beauty is located, she is not pleased to have been awakened by such a paltry hero. Resourceful as ever, Merlin chants the princess back to sleep and transforms the King's crown into a much taller one. Endowed with the illusion of height, the ruler is proud. **RECOMMENDATION:** While this is humorous and witty, shortness as an object of ridicule (runt, midget, puny, etc.) may be considered insensitive by an audience with erratic and worrisome growth patterns. In addition, the concepts of a liberated woman and a shrew are treated synonymously. Neither the short king, who cannot laugh at himself, nor the overbearing princess, who takes herself much too seriously, is allowed any character development. **ROYALTY:** Free to Plays subscribers. **SOURCE:** Cheatham, Val R. (1977, January). Sleeping Beauty and friends. Plays: The Drama Magazine for Young People, pp. 71-75. **SUBJECTS/PLAY TYPE:** Skit; Comedy; Shortness.

2828. K-3. (+) Havilan, Amorie & Smith, Lyn. **The sleepy groundhog.** **CAST:** 1f, 1m, Su. **ACTS:** 1. **SETTINGS:** Inside groundhog's hole; outside hole's entrance. **PLAYING TIME:** NA. **PLOT:** Mrs. Groundhog convinces a sleepy Mr. Groundhog to look for his shadow on February 2 by blindfolding him so the sun will not get in his eyes. A young watcher concludes that Mr. Groundhog is playing a joke on them, as Spring will arrive as it always does, whether or not the groundhog sees his shadow. The crowd leaves satisfied and Mr. Groundhog gets to sleep for six more weeks. **RECOMMENDATION:** This simply but cleverly explains the Groundhog's Day tradition in pantomime. **ROYALTY:** NA. **SOURCE:** Havilan, Amorie & Smith, Lyn. (1985). Easy plays for preschoolers to third graders. Brandon, MS: Quail Ridge Press. **SUBJECTS/PLAY TYPE:** Groundhog's Day; Tripartite.

2829. 10-12. (+) Morreale, Vin. **Slight indulgences.** **CAST:** 3f, 3m. **ACTS:** 1. **SETTINGS:** Office. **PLAYING TIME:** NA. **PLOT:** A writer with a poor self image creates one dimensional characters who are wildly attractive and successful, and through whom he lives. He does not notice that his secretary loves him. By tampering with his manuscript, she is able to show him that real life, with all its dimensions, is worth the risk. **RECOMMENDATION:** The discussions between the real and fictional characters are funny, although some of the allusions they make are dated. **ROYALTY:** $15. **SOURCE:** Morreale, Vin. (1982). Slight indulgences. Chicago, IL: Dramatic Pub. Co. **SUBJECTS/PLAY TYPE:** Stereotypes; Writers; Self Confidence; Comedy.

2830. K-2. (+) Vogels, Mary Prescott. **The slowpoke.** **CAST:** 14u. **ACTS:** 1. **SETTINGS:** Field. **PLAYING TIME:**

5 min. **PLOT:** Slowpoke the Snail wants to win the race home. By pulling into his shell, he is able to go home faster than the robin, snake, bee, and butterflies. **RECOMMENDATION:** This piece about the fear of losing would be best performed by slightly older children for younger ones. **ROYALTY:** Free to Plays subscribers. **SOURCE:** Vogels, Mary Prescott. (1978, January). The slowpoke. Plays: The Drama Magazine for Young People, pp. 59-60. **SUBJECTS/PLAY TYPE:** Animals; Fable; Losing; Skit.

2831. 7-10. (+) Fox, Barbara Black. **Slugg zappers.** **CAST:** 4f, 2m, Su. **ACTS:** 1. **SETTINGS:** Bare stage, props and backdrops. **PLAYING TIME:** 20 min. **PLOT:** Ted's mother demands he do his homework before escaping into video game heaven. Indulging in self pity, Ted reads the fine print on the back of the Slugg Zappers cartridge, and decides to live in Slugg City, convincing Kim to also apply for citizenship. The two are enslaved by the evil Sluggs who plot to erase Ted's brain. Kim's escape leads to a rescue by the Space Patrol and the safe return of the wayward teens. **RECOMMENDATION:** This abounds in mock interplanetary paraphernalia, costumes, and personages. The frenzied plot is punctuated with interjections, exclamations, gasps, "zaps," claps, and humorous lyrics. Specific allusions to popular songs and to individual video games may need to be updated. **ROYALTY:** $25. **SOURCE:** Fox, Barbara Black. (1988). Slugg zappers. Franklin, OH: Eldridge Pub. Co. **SUBJECTS/PLAY TYPE:** Science Fiction; Video Games; Comedy.

2832. 4-6. (+) Sawyer-Young, Kat. **Slumber party.** **CAST:** 2f. **ACTS:** 1. **SETTINGS:** Bedroom. **PLAYING TIME:** NA. **PLOT:** After wishing their parents could be Luke Skywalker or Princess Leah, or that they could be Brooke Shields, Jennifer and Courtney decide to become blood sisters. Instead of pricking their fingers and sharing blood, they split Oreo cookies and share the creme filling, thus becoming Oreo Cookie Sisters, after which they collapse on the bed in laughter. **RECOMMENDATION:** In a simple, uncomplicated manner, this deals appropriately with a childhood problem while providing comic relief as the scene concludes. **ROYALTY:** NA. **SOURCE:** Sawyer-Young, Kat. (1986). Contemporary scenes for contemporary kids. Boston, MA: Baker's Plays. **SUBJECTS/PLAY TYPE:** Friendship; Identity; Scene.

2833. 9-12. (+) Gelbart, Larry. (Johnson, Ben) **Sly fox.** (Volpone) **CAST:** 3f, 13m, 2u. **ACTS:** 2. **SETTINGS:** Bedroom; living room; office; jail cell; courtroom. **PLAYING TIME:** NA. **PLOT:** Wealthy Foxwell Sly convinces his friends, with the help of his servant Able, that he is dying. They offer gifts to win Sly's favor and become his sole heir. Sly convinces Mr. Crouch to sign his own will over to Sly and cons Mr. Truckle into letting his wife spend time with Sly. Crouch's son enters just as Mrs. Truckle is being cornered by Sly, causing Sly and Able to be sent to jail. Sly pretends to die, and Able is found to be the sole heir, but Sly has left no valuables for anyone to inherit. **RECOMMENDATION:** This modernized version is essentially the same as the original, but with updated dialogue and names. A humorous tale of deceit and thievery, this might be best produced by an adult cast, due to extensive lines and staging. **ROYALTY:** NA. **SOURCE:** Gelbart, Larry. (1978). Sly fox. New York, NY: Samuel French. **SUBJECTS/PLAY TYPE:** Greed; Comedy; Adaptation.

2834. 1-3. (+) Boiko, Claire. (Grimm Brothers) **Small crimson parasol.** (Little Red Riding Hood) **CAST:** 3f, 3m, Su. **ACTS:** 1. **SETTINGS:** Bamboo forest. **PLAYING TIME:** 20 min. **PLOT:** A storyteller facilitates the transition from America to ancient Japan and supplies insight into the historical development of the Little Red Riding Hood tale. Cultural differences are highlighted by the substitution of a crimson parasol for the familiar red riding hood, and the gift of pickled octopus and seaweed cakes rather than cookies. Delightful additions are the personified inhabitants of the forest: Kirai, the butterfly, and Chotto, the tortoise. **RECOMMENDATION:** Children will seize upon the subtle differences between the versions of this well known tale as they gain perspective into the delights of cultural variety. Discussion will foster appreciation for universal cultural values. Implicit here are themes of appearance vs. reality and the vulnerability of children faced with worldly deception, providing, perhaps, a springboard for youthful discussion of life's hidden dangers. **ROYALTY:** None for amateur performance. **SOURCE:** Boiko, Claire. (1985). Children's plays for creative actors. Boston, MA: Plays, Inc. **SUBJECTS/PLAY TYPE:** Folk Tales, Germany; Japanese Culture; Adaptation.

2835. 7-12. (+) Miller, Ev. **A small wooden horse.** **CAST:** 11u. **ACTS:** 1. **SETTINGS:** School courtyard; classroom. **PLAYING TIME:** 30 min. **PLOT:** Lynn wears a necklace as a symbol of individuality, but must hide it because she lives in a computer state where people are told what to do and when. Her parents are married, almost unheard of since people are assigned partners for periods of only two years. People are only allowed to have one child, who is put in the state nursery. Lynn questions the rules and encourages Paul to think for himself. She is expelled from school because she can't conform, and gives Paul her necklace. When he asks why, she tells him that he is her friend. **RECOMMENDATION:** This is an intriguing look at the price and value of freedom. It may spark a great deal of discussion and debate. **ROYALTY:** $10. **SOURCE:** Miller, Ev. (1983). A small wooden horse. Denver, CO: Pioneer Drama Service. **SUBJECTS/PLAY TYPE:** Individuality; Conformity; Computers and Society; Drama.

2836. 6-8. (+) Fisher, Aileen Lucia. **The smiling angel.** **CAST:** 6f, 6m, Su. **ACTS:** 1. **SETTINGS:** Town square. **PLAYING TIME:** 15 min. **PLOT:** Unless the stone angel in the town square smiles before midnight, Christmas Eve, disaster will strike. The villagers blame the problem on the people who live on the other side of the wall that divides them. A brother and sister who have slipped through a crack in the wall reveal that the people on the other side are just like them. They suggest that the wall be torn down and the angel smiles. **RECOMMENDATION:** The striking figure of the stone angel symbolically portrays the frustration and suffering of a cold war. **ROYALTY:** Free to

Plays subscribers. **SOURCE:** Fisher, Aileen. (1985, December). The smiling angel. Plays: The Drama Magazine for Young People, pp. 29-34. **SUBJECTS/PLAY TYPE:** Christmas; Cold War; Ignorance; Playlet.

2837. 10-12*. (+) Gilweit, Edwin R. **Snakes. CAST:** 1f, 3m. **ACTS:** 1. **SETTINGS:** Farm pasture. **PLAYING TIME:** NA. **PLOT:** Old Orville Portz has run his land and his family by bullying for fifty years. Now, the well is infested with poisonous snakes. When Orville is unsuccessful in disposing of the snakes, he decides to try grandson Orin's method, running carbon monoxide from vehicle exhaust into the well. Grandson, son, and father successively enter the well to remove the snakes but they never reemerge and the daughter-in-law is left wondering where they are. **RECOMMENDATION:** This is a powerful and absorbing drama about harsh and shocking human interactions. It is skillful and realistic, but does have a great deal of violence and profanity. The level of acting required may be above high school students. **ROYALTY:** $15. **SOURCE:** Gilweit, Edwin R. (1984). Snakes. Chicago,IL: Dramatic Pub. Co. **SUBJECTS/PLAY TYPE:** Family Conflict; Tragedy.

2838. 5-8. (+) Weinstein, Judith & Somers, Arnold. **Sneakers. CAST:** 7f, 11m, Su. **ACTS:** 2. **SETTINGS:** Living room; principal's office; front porch; classroom; kitchen; shoe store; school corridor; baseball field. **PLAYING TIME:** 45 min. **PLOT:** The Millers move to a new town and Edward is forced to repeat the fourth grade. Feeling like a failure, he remains silent in school and refuses to try out for the baseball team, even though he was a star pitcher at his last school. Edward's dad buys him "magical" sneakers which give him the power to pass a test that will allow him into fifth grade and to join the baseball team as a star pitcher. Edward realizes that his self confidence comes from within himself when he pitches a perfect game without his sneakers. **RECOMMENDATION:** Musical numbers are well placed and enhance the play. Although there are many scene changes, they can easily be assembled and disassembled. **ROYALTY:** $50. **SOURCE:** Weinstein, Judith & Somers, Arnold. (1983). Sneakers. Chicago, IL: Dramatic Pub. Co. **SUBJECTS/PLAY TYPE:** Self Confidence; Moving; Sneakers; Musical.

2839. K-6*. (+) Endersby, Clive. (Grimm Brothers) **Snow White.** (Snow White and the seven dwarfs) **CAST:** 2f, 2m, 12u. **ACTS:** 1. **SETTINGS:** Palace; forest; dwarfs' cottage. **PLAYING TIME:** NA. **PLOT:** The queen becomes jealous of her stepdaughter, Snow White, and orders her head chopped off. Two lions save Snow White and she takes refuge in a house occupied by seven dwarves. When the queen finds out that Snow White is still alive, she transforms herself into an ugly old hag and gives Snow White a poisoned apple, but the dwarves use magic to conjure up a prince who revives Snow White. The queen is defeated and the prince asks Snow White to marry him. **RECOMMENDATION:** This adds interest to the old story with an alligator, a gorilla and two lions who have no dialogue, but provide humor through their physical actions. Some scenes involve audience participation and action which takes place in the aisles. The queen's trans-

formation into a hag requires special lighting and fog effects. Although it bears little resemblance to the original story, and the dialogue is sometimes trite, the humorous antics of the characters and rapid scene changes will hold the interest of even a very young audience. **ROYALTY:** NA. **SOURCE:** Endersby, Clive. (1977). Snow White. Toronto, Canada: Playwrights Canada. **SUBJECTS/PLAY TYPE:** Folk Tales, Germany; Witches; Adaptation.

2840. K-3. (+) Jacob, Eva. (Grimm Brothers) **Snow White.** (Snow White and the Seven Dwarves.) **CAST:** 6f, 8m. **ACTS:** 1. **SETTINGS:** Kitchen. **PLAYING TIME:** 20 min. **PLOT:** The Queen is jealous of Snow White's beauty and arranges to have her killed in the woods. Snow White escapes and is given refuge by the Seven Dwarves. The Queen finds out where Snow White is, disguises herself as an old peddler, and goes to the hut to give Snow White a poisoned apple. The Seven Dwarves think Snow White is dead, but a handsome Prince saves her and proposes marriage. **RECOMMENDATION:** This is the classic story minus the reference to the stepmother/stepdaughter relationship. **ROYALTY:** Free to Plays Subscribers. **SOURCE:** Jacob, Eva. (1979, May). Snow White. Plays: The Drama Magazine for Young People, pp. 47-53. **SUBJECTS/PLAY TYPE:** Folk Tales, Germany; Witches; Playlet.

2841. K-6. (+) Mahlman, Lewis & Jones, David Cadwalader. (Grimm Brothers) **Snow White and Rose Red.** (Snow White and Rose Red) **CAST:** 7u. **ACTS:** 1. **SETTINGS:** Puppet stage. **PLAYING TIME:** 15 min. **PLOT:** Two sisters, Snow White and Rose Red, take in an injured bear they find. He leaves in the Spring to guard a treasure from the dwarves. The girls come upon a dwarf several times over the next few days and help him out of various predicaments, only to arouse his wrath. Finding a bag of jewels in his possession, they realize he is a thief. The bear returns to reclaim the stolen treasure, breaks a spell that had been cast upon him, turns into a Prince, and asks Rose Red to marry him. **RECOMMENDATION:** A faithful retelling of the original, this should be easily produced by upper elementary students. **ROYALTY:** Free to Plays subscribers. **SOURCE:** Mahlman, Lewis and Jones, David Cadwalader. (1982, January/February). Snow White and Rose Red. Plays: The drama magazine for young people, pp. 78-84. **SUBJECTS/PLAY TYPE:** Bears; Folk Tales, Germany; Puppet Play; Adaptation.

2842. 7-12. (+) Springer, William J. (Grimm Brothers) **Snow White and the little men.** (Snow White and the seven dwarves) **CAST:** 5f, 8m, 4u. **ACTS:** 1. **SETTINGS:** Throne room. **PLAYING TIME:** NA. **PLOT:** Snow White's beauty is envied by her stepmother, the Queen. After learning of the Queen's plan to have her killed, Snow White seeks refuge in the home of seven little men. Discovering that Snow White is still alive, the Queen causes her to fall into a deep sleep by giving her a poisoned apple. Snow is awakened by a kiss from a Prince. Informed by her mirror that Snow White lives, the Queen attends Snow White's wedding, she eats one of the poisoned apples, and dies. **RECOMMENDATION:** This is filled with wonderful sarcasm and slapstick. **ROYALTY:** $30. **SOURCE:** Springer, William J. (1978). Snow White and the little men. Franklin, OH: Eldridge Pub. Co. SUBJECTS/PLAY TYPE: Fantasy; Comedy; Adaptation.

2843. K-12*. (+) Kase, Judith Baker. (Grimm Brothers) **Snow White and the seven dwarfs.** (Snow White and the seven dwarves) CAST: 2f, 9m. ACTS: 1. SETTINGS: Queens chambers; forest; dwarf's cottage; outside the palace; clearing. PLAYING TIME: NA. PLOT: This is a fairly faithful adaptation, with the addition of an enchanted prince, forced by a spell to act as a jester and speak only in rhyme. Also added is a rather pedantic Lord Pettifog who protects Snow White from the murderous intentions of her stepmother and leads the prince to the sleeping maiden in the dwarves' home. RECOMMENDATION: Presentation would require a range of ages: younger, smaller students to play dwarves, and junior or senior high students to play Snow White, the Wicked Queen, Jollo the Jester (prince) and Lord Pettifog. The last four characters have many lines to learn. Jollo's lines, all in rhyme, are humorous and add freshness to this well known story. ROYALTY: $35. SOURCE: Kase, Judith Baker. (1984). Snow White and seven dwarfs. New Orleans, LA: Anchorage Press, Inc. SUBJECTS/PLAY TYPE: Folk Tales, Germany; Adaptation.

2844. K-6*. (+) White, Jessie Braham. (Grimm Brothers) **Snow White and the seven dwarfs.** (Snow White and the seven dwarfs) CAST: 9f, 10m, 4u. ACTS: 1. SETTINGS: Throne room; forest; seven dwarfs' house; witch's house. PLAYING TIME: NA. PLOT: The prince meets Snow White and falls in love with her. The jealous queen orders Snow White away for a year and a day, but secretly orders her murder. The murderer is supposed to return with Snow White's heart to give to the witch, who is helping the queen with her plot. When the huntsman doesn't succeed, the queen sets out to commit the deed herself. Meanwhile, Snow White takes refuge in a small cottage where the seven dwarves reside. The queen, made up as an an ugly old woman, gives Snow White a poisoned apple to eat, which makes her appear dead. The prince arrives to marry his bride, but the queen tells him Snow White is dead. The seven dwarves arrive to carry Snow White to her coffin. Enraged, the queen smashes her magic mirror, immediately becoming unbearably ugly and breaking the spell over Snow White, who awakens. The witch advises the queen that she can regain her beauty only by being good. The prince gives Snow White his ring, then he crowns her queen, after which Snow White asks the seven dwarves to remain with them. RECOMMENDATION: The special effects elicit excitement, and music and songs from the original stage version are included in the script. Suspenseful movement and action is interspersed with comedic relief provided by the dwarves. The names of the dwarves have been changed to more innocuous terms. ROYALTY: Write to Samuel French. SOURCE: Jennings, Coleman A. & Harris, Aurand. (1988). Plays children love, Volume II. New York, NY: St. Martin's Press. SUBJECTS/PLAY TYPE: Folk Tales, Germany; Adaptation.

2845. 6-9. (+) Kilcup, Rick. (Grimm Brothers) **Snow White and the six dwarfs.** (Snow White and the seven dwarves) CAST: 2f, 2m, 16u. ACTS: 1. SETTINGS: Castle; shack. PLAYING TIME: 20 min. PLOT: The familiar plot has been changed by replacing the "who's the fairest in the land" with "who's the fastest runner in all the land," as a health and exercise motif is used to tell the popular story with a comic twist. RECOMMENDATION: This delightful comedy will be as much fun to perform as it is to be seen. ROYALTY: Free to Plays subscribers. SOURCE: Kilcup, Rick. (1981, May). Snow White and the six dwarfs. Plays: The Drama Magazine for Young People, pp. 33-41. SUBJECTS/PLAY TYPE: Folk Tales, Germany; Health Food; Foot Races; Comedy; Adaptation.

2846. 3-9. (+) Jackson,R. Eugene & Ellis, David. (Grimm Brothers) **Snow White and the space gwarfs.** (Snow White and the seven dwarves) CAST: 2f, 2m. ACTS: 2. SETTINGS: Interiors of three spacecraft; futuristic space home. PLAYING TIME: 60 min. PLOT: Queen Lena has invaded Prince Cosmic's sector of the universe. When the prince comes on board her ship to investigate, he falls in love with Princess Snowhite. Jealous of Snowhite's beauty, Queen Lena sends her into space where she is rescued by the space gwarfs. Discovering that Snowhite is still alive, the Queen disguises herself as a Mundan and tricks Snowhite into putting on a magic tiara which causes her to appear dead. Prince Cosmic brings her back to life, and the two are married on the planet Goshar. During the celebration, Snowhite innocently gives the Queen a pair of electronic dancing shoes. The Queen is short circuited, revealing that she has been a robot all the time. RECOMMENDATION: The musical score and lyrics are well integrated into the dialogue and the action, but the staging (with its space ship settings and use of puppets as gwarfs) might present problems for inexperienced actors. ROYALTY: $35. SOURCE: Jackson, R. Eugene & Ellis, David. (1981). Snowhite and the space gwarfs. Denver, CO: Pioneer Drama Service. SUBJECTS/PLAY TYPE: Romance; Science Fiction; Folk Tales, Germany; Adaptation.

2847. 3-6. (+) Dixon, Dorothy. **The snow witch. CAST:** 5f, 1m, Su. ACTS: 1. SETTINGS: Kitchen. PLAYING TIME: 15 min. PLOT: Marina confides in the Snow Witch that she wishes she were young and rich and the witch tells Marina that she can change places with anyone she chooses by touching the other person's hand. The village princess visits but Marina refuses to touch her hand because the princess has to worry about robbers. Marina declines to touch Ivan the soldier because she doesn't want to be tired, cold and hungry on campaigns. Dancers from the village arrive and Marina, admiring Vera, reaches for Vera's hands when a wolf howls outside. Ivan jokes with Vera about watching for the wolf and Marina withdraws her hand. She asks Ivan about the joke and he tells her that all people have wolves in their lives, and explains that one never really knows about another person's life. Marina decides not to trade lives with anyone, and the snow witch gives here a gold ring with an inscription about finding happiness within yourself. RECOMMENDATION: The colorful speech of each character adds to the interest in this thought provoking piece about happiness and contentment. ROYALTY: NA. SOURCE: Dixon, Dorothy. (1989, January/ February). Plays: The Drama Magazine for

Young People, pp. 35-39. SUBJECTS/PLAY TYPE: Happiness; Identity; Playlet.

2848. K-4. (+) Boiko, Claire. **The snowman who overstayed.** CAST: 5f, 6m. ACTS: 1. SETTINGS: Bare garden. PLAYING TIME: 15 min. PLOT: A snowman who wants to stay in the garden delays the arrival of spring and angers the crabapple tree, the dandelions, and the bluebirds. They send an SOS (Save Our Springtime) to Princess Spring, who is opening cherry blossoms in Japan. She sends March winds, April showers, and a May page in league with Helios, the warm sun. The snowman begins to melt, but Princess Spring is touched by his willingness to risk destruction in an effort to satisfy his curiosity about the nature of spring. She grants him one single moment to glimpse the garden adorned with spring blossoms before his banishment to the frozen regions. RECOMMENDATION: The joyous, bountiful spirit expressed by the characters which symbolize spring is contagious. The willing sacrifice of the courageous snowman is a tribute to the power of rebirth and rejuvenation which accompanies the warmth of the season. The play invites contemplation of natural law and the tendency of all creatures to obey it. The cast may be expanded to include other natural figures, and the plot can prove an excellent springboard for original, creative endeavor in the form of graphic art or poetry. ROYALTY: None. SOURCE: Boiko, Claire. (1985). Children's plays for creative actors. Boston, MA: Plays, Inc. SUBJECTS/PLAY TYPE: Spring; Comedy.

2849. 2-4. (+) Gotwalt, Helen Louise Miller. **So long at the fair.** CAST: 5f, 4m, Su. ACTS: 1. SETTINGS: Fairgrounds. PLAYING TIME: NA. PLOT: Johnny gets lost at the fair while he is looking for a "fairing" (from the nursery rhyme, "Oh dear, what can the matter be?") for his sister. As parts of the rhyme are sung, Johnny relives them, until he finally is told that a fairing is just another name for a souvenir. He buys a souvenir, finds his sister, and all ends well. RECOMMENDATION: This delightful presentation of the classic nursery rhyme uses a chorus to allow a flexible cast of any number. ROYALTY: Free to Plays subscribers. SOURCE: Gotwalt, Helen Louise Miller. (1986). Everyday plays for boys and girls. Boston, MA: Plays Inc. SUBJECTS/PLAY TYPE: Nursery Rhymes; Adaptation.

2850. 2-4. (+) Carlson, Bernice Wells. **So proud?** CAST: 4u. ACTS: 1. SETTINGS: Pasture. PLAYING TIME: NA. PLOT: A rich horse who snubs a poor horse is robbed of all his finery. RECOMMENDATION: This requires pantomime and will be more successful if presented along with other short plays. ROYALTY: None. SOURCE: Carlson, Bernice Wells. (1982). Let's find the big idea. Nashville, TN: Abingdon Press. SUBJECTS/PLAY TYPE: Horses; Vanity; Fable.

2851. 7-12. (+) Rembrandt, Elaine. (Senesh, Hannah) **So young to die: The story of Hannah Senesh.** (Hannah Senesh: Her life and diary.) CAST: 4f, 3m, 1u. ACTS: 1. SETTINGS: Home. PLAYING TIME: 20 min. PLOT: Hannah Senesh was a vivacious Jewish teenager in Hungary during the Holocaust who dreamt of a better

place and left her family for a girl's agricultural school in Palestine, where she helped rescue Hungarian children during the War. Her story is told through her letters, her diary, her friends, and family. RECOMMENDATION: This moving account evokes feelings similar to those found in the **Diary of Anne Frank.** The play reveals "thoughts and feelings of a young person caught in the hopelessness of the times." ROYALTY: None. SOURCE: Rembrandt, Elaine. (1981). Heroes, heroines, & holidays - plays for Jewish youth. Denver, CO: Alternatives in Religious Education, Inc. SUBJECTS/PLAY TYPE: Holocaust; Free-dom; Senesh, Hannah; Jewish Drama; Adaptation.

2852. 7-12. (+) Shute, Stephanie. **Soap escape.** CAST: 3f, 2m. ACTS: 1. SETTINGS: Kitchen. PLAYING TIME: 20 min. PLOT: Elaine has problems distinguishing fact from fantasy. She even begins dressing up for the special events that are scheduled for each day's episode of her soaps. Elaine's sister and her boyfriend give her a dose of her own medicine by taking on the characters of a soap opera based on **Romeo and Juliet.** Elaine, not realizing the charade, agrees to be more realistic, but will not agree to stop watching the "soaps." RECOMMENDATION: This should be enjoyable to all who have a favorite "soap," or at least know someone who does. ROYALTY: Free to Plays subscribers. SOURCE: Shute, Stephanie. (1982, April). Soap escape. Plays: The Drama Magazine for Young People, pp. 1-8. SUBJECTS/PLAY TYPE: Soap Operas; Comedy.

2853. 9-12. (+) Kelly, Tim. **The soapy murder case.** CAST: 5f, 5m. ACTS: 3. SETTINGS: Living room. PLAYING TIME: NA. PLOT: A disgruntled ex-actor poses as the producer of a soap opera and invites the cast to his penthouse apartment to solve a murder threat upon his life, but actually to do them harm. All of the cast members have aliases or confuse their real life characters with their soap characters. Through a long evening of mysterious happenings and murders, the ex-actor's true identity and scheme of revenge are exposed. RECOMMENDATION: Poking fun at the melodramatic daytime dramas, the plot here is as unbelievable as those in the soaps. ROYALTY: $40. SOURCE: Kelly, Tim. (1979). The soapy murder case. Boston, MA: Baker's Plays. SUBJECTS/PLAY TYPE: Soap Operas; Mistaken Identities; Murder; Comedy.

2854. 8-12. (+) Allred, Joan & Allred, Pearl. **Society page.** CAST: 6f, 2m. ACTS: 1. SETTINGS: Office. PLAYING TIME: 30 min. PLOT: Janica, a writer for the society page, is bent on being a career woman, and so denies her feelings for Jimmy, the photographer. When a couple arrives to arrange their future wedding announcement, some matchmaking occurs, and Janica accedes to Jimmy's proposals. RECOMMENDATION: Although predictable and vaguely insulting with its hints that Janica has "learned her lesson" about having a career, this is somewhat amusing in a melodramatic way. ROYALTY: Free to Plays subscribers. SOURCE: Allred, Joan and Pearl. (1987, January/February). Society page. Plays: The Drama Magazine for Young People, pp. 21-32. SUBJECTS/PLAY TYPE: Society; Weddings; Comedy.

2855. 9-12. (+) Rogers, David. **Soft soap.** CAST: 11f, 14m, Su. ACTS: 2. SETTINGS: College student lounge; television screen. PLAYING TIME: NA. PLOT: While viewing an episode of "Yesterday's Tomorrow," Betty Brown tries her new transference theory to put herself on the set and into the middle of a murder trial. Only with the help of her boyfriend is she able to leave the lurid world of daytime soaps and return to college life. RECOMMENDATION: Full of puns and word play, this is a delightful spoof of daytime dramas. The unusual set design adds to the uniqueness. ROYALTY: $50. SOURCE: Rogers, David. (1982). Soft soap. Woodstock, IL: Dramatic Pub. Co. SUBJECTS/PLAY TYPE: Soap Operas; Comedy.

2856. 4-8. (+) Gotwalt, Helen Louise Miller. **The softhearted ghost.** CAST: 5f, 5m, 2u. ACTS: 1. SETTINGS: Living room. PLAYING TIME: NA. PLOT: A young ghost can't bring himself to scare anyone. His parents demand he act like a real ghost and he makes one final effort, which leads to his being signed on by a talent scout to sing on the road. RECOMMENDATION: This light hearted comedy will give actors plenty of opportunity to shout and scream and generally enjoy themselves. ROYALTY: Free to Plays subscribers. SOURCE: Gotwalt, Helen Louise Miller. (1986). Special plays for holidays. Boston, MA: Plays, Inc. SUBJECTS/PLAY TYPE: Halloween; Comedy.

2857. 5-8. (-) Gotwalt, Helen Louise Miller. **Softy the snowman.** CAST: 4f, 2m, Su. ACTS: 1. SETTINGS: Santa's workshop. PLAYING TIME: 15 min. PLOT: A soft hearted snowman in Santa's workshop jeopardizes his job when altruism interferes with production. His good deeds are making him late for work. Fortunately, a serendipitous blunder saves the snowman's career and leads to the manufacture of a new product line: white teddy bears to be marketed as "Softy the Snow Man." RECOMMENDATION: Although Santa comes off as a hard driving taskmaster, the snowman with a "squishy-squashy" heart is lovable. A scene featuring seven department store Santas in a high level executive meeting with the real Saint Nick is especially fun. ROYALTY: Free to Plays subscribers. SOURCE: Gotwalt, Helen Louise Miller. (1986). Special plays for holidays. Boston, MA: Plays, Inc. SUBJECTS/PLAY TYPE: Christmas; Santa Claus; Snowmen; Playlet.

2858. 6-8. (+) Thane, Adele. (Fisher, Dorothy Canfield) **Soldier of the Revolution.** (Soldier of the Revolution) CAST: 3f, 4m, Su. ACTS: 3. SETTINGS: Bare stage. PLAYING TIME: 25 min. PLOT: Two young boys mistakenly recruit a former enemy mercenary to be honored as a Revolutionary War hero in a 4th of July parade. The townspeople decide to let him march anyway. RECOMMENDATION: Fairly good dialogue, an historical setting, and likable characters combine to make this an effective vehicle for promoting forgiveness and acceptance. ROYALTY: Free to Plays subscribers. SOURCE: Thane, Adele. (1978, February). Soldier of the Revolution. Plays: The Drama Magazine for Young People, pp. 58-64. SUBJECTS/PLAY TYPE: Independence Day, U.S.; Adaptation.

2859. 7-12. (+) Dias, Earl J. **Some of my best friends are spies.** CAST: 6f, 7m. ACTS: 1. SETTINGS: Office. PLAYING TIME: 25 min. PLOT: American secret agents are assigned to obtain a secret formula (which can change the shape of citizens) before it falls into the hands of the evil spy syndicate. When they get it, they find that it is only a recipe for low calorie fudge. All is not wasted, however, because the two agents fall in love. RECOMMENDATION: This shallow spy spoof with its Bondian/Max Smart spies may provide comic relief, but the jokes mostly miss their mark. ROYALTY: Free to Plays subscribers. SOURCE: Dias, Earl J. (1982, November). Some of my best friends are spies. Plays: The Drama Magazine for Young People, pp. 21-29. SUBJECTS/PLAY TYPE: Spies; Comedy.

2860. 8-12. (+) Nolan, Paul T. **Somebody cares.** CAST: 3f, 3m, 3u. ACTS: 1. SETTINGS: Bare stage. PLAYING TIME: 25 min. PLOT: Four people decide they cannot make it in the world since nobody cares about them, and they do not care to see or hear others. The gatekeeper to the world outside chooses not to help, on the basis that it is not his responsibility. When they realize that they care about others, they also realize that others care about them. RECOMMENDATION: This presents that part of human nature which often puts us into a "rut." The ending allows the audience to recognize a satisfactory, honest, and humane way to survive. ROYALTY: Free to Plays subscribers. SOURCE: Nolan, Paul T. (1978, May). Somebody cares. Plays: The Drama Magazine for Young People, pp. 1-9. SUBJECTS/PLAY TYPE: Trust; Caring; Self Help; Playlet.

2861. 6-8. (+) Nolan, Paul T. **Somebody's Santa.** CAST: 4f, 2m. ACTS: 1. SETTINGS: Street corner. PLAYING TIME: 25 min. PLOT: A fiercely independent, grumpy old man, estranged from his family, dresses as Santa, and sits on the street with a bucket in which to collect money, intending to keep it for himself. His grandson, whom he does not recognize, asks him to spend Christmas with his family and he agrees. RECOMMENDATION: This stubborn old man is the unwitting vehicle for the Christmas spirit, providing this play with enough of a difference to make it worth considering for the Christmas season. ROYALTY: Free to Plays subscribers. SOURCE: Nolan, Paul T. (1981, December). Somebody's Santa. Plays: The Drama Magazine for Young People, pp. 15-23. SUBJECTS/PLAY TYPE: Christmas; Charity; Family; Playlet.

2862. K-1. (+) Fraser, Kathleen. **Somersaults and headstands.** CAST: 2u. ACTS: 1. SETTINGS: None. PLAYING TIME: NA. PLOT: Two dogs do acrobatics in the grass. RECOMMENDATION: A cute dramatization, this would work well either read aloud or as a short stage production. ROYALTY: NA. SOURCE: Bauer, Caroline Feller. (1987). Presenting reader's theater: Plays and poems to read aloud. New York, NY: H.W. Wilson Co. SUBJECTS/PLAY TYPE: Dogs; Reader's Theater.

2863. 9-12. (+) Muschell, David. **Something in my dreams.** CAST: 3f, 4m. ACTS: 1. SETTINGS: Bedroom.

PLAYING TIME: NA. PLOT: An old woman dreams of the past as she nears death, reliving her youth, marriage, the birth of her child, her husband's death in the war, her daughter's maturing marriage, and the birth of her grandchildren. Her dreams flow smoothly to her grandchildrens' youth and their fights. The shifting memories depict the overall experiences of a family. RECOMMENDATION: This beautifully and warmly depicts the realities of the family unit. ROYALTY: $15. SOURCE: Muschell, David. (1986). Something in my dreams. Woodstock, IL: Dramatic Pub. Co. SUBJECTS/PLAY TYPE: Family; Memories; Drama.

2864. 2-3. (+) Alexander, Sue. **Something scary.** CAST: 2u. ACTS: 1. SETTINGS: Dark street. PLAYING TIME: NA. PLOT: Ghost is sad because Halloween is almost over and he hasn't frightened anyone yet. When a little girl comes along, Ghost tries unsuccessfully to frighten her in various ways. She chases Ghost off the stage. RECOMMENDATION: The humorous plot is free of many of the frightening ideas usually presented in Halloween plays. Children could write another ending as a creative writing project. ROYALTY: None. SOURCE: Alexander, Sue. (1977). Small plays for special days. New York, NY: Seabury Press. SUBJECTS/PLAY TYPE: Halloween; Fantasy; Ghosts; Comedy.

2865. K-3. (+) Bauer, Caroline Feller. (Waber, Bernard) **Sometimes Arthur is choosy.** (An anteater named Arthur) CAST: 1f, 1m, 1u. ACTS: 1. SETTINGS: Kitchen. PLAYING TIME: 5 min. PLOT: His mother tries to cajole Arthur (an anteater) into eating the red ants she has fixed for breakfast by pointing out they were gathered especially for him, and that they are delicious and so good for him. Arthur is unconvinced. In exasperation, she asks him what he wants. He replies, "Brown ants." RECOMMENDATION: The irony of Arthur's preference is obvious enough for youngsters to understand, and they will be deliciously "grossed out" by the thought of eating any ants. This can be either acted or read aloud. ROYALTY: None. SOURCE: Bauer, Caroline Feller. (1987). Presenting reader's theater: Plays and poems to read aloud. New York, NY: H.W. Wilson Co. SUBJECTS/PLAY TYPE: Food; Reader's Theater; Adaptation.

2866. 10-12. (+) Walden Theatre Conservatory. **Sometimes I wake up in the middle of the night.** CAST: 7f, 8m. ACTS: 2. SETTINGS: Bare stage. PLAYING TIME: NA. PLOT: This collection of short scenes and monologues by actors expresses adolescent hopes, needs, and fears. RECOMMENDATION: Successful because of its honest expression of adolescent emotions, this does have a disturbing end which focuses on being thankful for "Beer, women, parties, drugs", etc. It uses strong language, but the playwright gives permission to tone it down. ROYALTY: $50. SOURCE: Walden Theatre Conservatory. (1986). Sometimes I wake up in the middle of the night. Woodstock, IL: Dramatic Pub. Co. SUBJECTS/PLAY TYPE: Adolescent Problems; Drama.

2867. 7-9*. (+) Priore, Frank V. (Dickens, Charles) **Son of a "Christmas carol."** (A Christmas Carol) CAST: 5f, 2m,

3u. ACTS: 1. SETTINGS: Office. PLAYING TIME: 30 min. PLOT: Scrooge's business is run by his great grandson, assisted by Cratchit's great grandson. The Ghosts of Christmas Past, Present and Yet to Come try to humanize Scrooge through their own unique methods. RECOMMENDATION: This very funny adaptation modernizes the original and deals cleverly with topics such as women's rights, worker's benefits, etc. The secular script is very witty. ROYALTY: $30. SOURCE: Priore, Frank V. (1979). Son of a "Christmas carol". Franklin, OH: Eldridge Pub. Co. SUBJECTS/PLAY TYPE: Christmas; Adaptation.

2868. 4-6. (+) Lipnick, Esther. **Son of liberty.** CAST: 2f, 5m, Su. ACTS: 1. SETTINGS: Room. PLAYING TIME: 30 min. PLOT: Events in the life of Paul Revere are depicted, including his ancestry and reasons for fighting tyranny, and his famous ride. RECOMMENDATION: This is a realistic recreation of historical events, portrayed through characters that the intended audience would find believable. ROYALTY: Free to Plays subscribers. SOURCE: Lipnick, Esther. (1980, April). Son of liberty. Plays: The Drama Magazine for Young People, pp. 35-42. SUBJECTS/PLAY TYPE: Revere, Paul; Playlet.

2869. 4-6. (+) Nolan, Paul T. **The Son of William Tell.** (William Tell and his son) CAST: 3f, 8m. ACTS: 1. SETTINGS: Meadow. PLAYING TIME: 20 min. PLOT: This reenactment opens with a dialogue between Tell's sons, William and Walter, that aids in establishing the background for the play. Tell's sons are accosted by Gessler, the Austrian emperor's governor, which results in a confrontation with Tell himself. The brave archer's prowess with the bow is put to the test when Gessler commands him to shoot an apple off Walter's head. Tell meets the challenge and inspires the Swiss to throw off the Austrian yoke to become free. RECOMMENDATION: Though the dialogue is somewhat stilted and formal, it lends an air of solemnity and heroics, as does the strong patriotic theme of liberty. ROYALTY: None for amateur performance. SOURCE: Nolan, Paul T. (1982). Folk tale plays round the world: A collection of royalty-free, one-act play about lands far and near. Boston, MA: Plays, Inc. SUBJECTS/PLAY TYPE: Legends, Switzerland; Freedom; Adaptation.

2870. 11-12. (-) Hirschhorn, Elizabeth. **Sonata.** CAST: 3f, 4m. ACTS: 1. SETTINGS: Police office; kitchen, living room, and bedroom; park. PLAYING TIME: 45 min. PLOT: A little boy and girl act as the "Greek chorus," making innocent yet insightful observations as events occur. After breakfast in the Amory kitchen, Lisa, 9, prepares to leave for school and chats with her parents. She departs but never makes it to the bus stop. At first her parents are distraught, and anxiously wait for the police to find their daughter. Later, they seem to adjust rather well to their loss, almost too well, and begin to enjoy their new lives as a childless couple and have fewer and fewer thoughts of their missing daughter. However, the detective who is working on the case becomes obsessed with the search; his determination to solve the mystery increases as the parents' self indulgence drives out all memory of the child. At the end, the audience will wonder whether the daughter's return will delight or devastate the parents. **RECOMMENDATION:** Timing and lighting are essential. If it is to work, the drama must operate almost as a dream sequence. Although often on stage at the same time, the characters are essentially isolated from one another and this sense must be conveyed not only by the actor's speeches but also by the use of lights and shadow. Although the play has some powerful moments, its essential cynicism, almost bitterness, makes its appropriateness for younger audiences questionable. The characterizations of the parents are uneven and ultimately unbelievable, and the conclusion is too vague to be effective. **ROYALTY:** NA. **SOURCE:** Lamb, Wendy. (1987). The ground zero club and other prize winning plays. New York, NY: Dell Pub. **SUBJECTS/PLAY TYPE:** Missing Children; Parents; Drama.

2871. K-3. (+) Fisher, Aileen Lucia. **A song for Christmas.** **CAST:** Su. **ACTS:** 1. **SETTINGS:** Bare stage. **PLAYING TIME:** 1 min. **PLOT:** This song (to the tune of "Sing a Song of Sixpence") counts down the number of days until Christmas. **RECOMMENDATION:** Preschoolers anxiously awaiting Christmas will enjoy participating in this countdown. **ROYALTY:** Free to Plays subscribers. **SOURCE:** Fisher, Aileen Lucia. (1985). Year-round programs for young players. Boston, MA: Plays, Inc. **SUBJECTS/PLAY TYPE:** Christmas; Choral Reading.

2872. 3-12. (+) Jackson, R. Eugene. (Longfellow, Henry Wadsworth) **The song of Hiawatha.** (The song of Hiawatha) **CAST:** 3f, 11m, Su. **ACTS:** 2. **SETTINGS:** Near lake. **PLAYING TIME:** 90 min. **PLOT:** Hiawatha is sent by the Great Spirit to save his people from hunger, war, and disease, but he must first gain wisdom. On his quest, he finds corn to feed his people, defeats Pearl-Feather, sender of the fever, and brings peace by pursuing and conquering Pau-Puk-Keewis, a warrior who would make war with other tribes. **RECOMMENDATION:** This faithful adaptation will not only acquaint audiences with the important literary work, but will also give them a clearer understanding of the hardships, culture, and beliefs of Native Americans. The story is beautifully played out with pageantry through the use of masks, interpretive dance, and music. **ROYALTY:** $60. **SOURCE:** Jackson, R. Eugene. (1988). The song of Hiawatha. Schulenberg, TX: I.E. Clark. **SUBJECTS/PLAY TYPE:** Native Americans; Adaptation.

2873. K-12. (+) **The song of Mary.** **CAST:** Su. **ACTS:** 1. **SETTINGS:** None. **PLAYING TIME:** 1 min. **PLOT:** Taken from the Gospel according to St. Luke, this reflects on the goodness and the mercy of the Lord. **RECOMMENDATION:** This is recommended as part of a devotional program. **ROYALTY:** None. **SOURCE:** Hendricks, William & Vogel, Cora. (1983). Handbook of Christmas programs. Grand Rapids, MI: Baker Book House. **SUBJECTS/PLAY TYPE:** Christmas; Choral Reading; Worship Program.

2874. 4-8. (+) Seale, Nancy. **Song of Rachel.** **CAST:** 7u. **ACTS:** 1. **SETTINGS:** Stable. **PLAYING TIME:** 20 min. **PLOT:** Rachel is the bond servant of an innkeeper, caring for her brother, Simon, who is blind. Mary and Joseph arrive in the city and look for a place to stay, but the innkeeper turns them away. Rachel, however, gives them room in the stable where she sleeps. Jesus is born and Simon regains his sight. **RECOMMENDATION:** This demonstrates clearly the meaning of Christmas. Seeing the story unfold with Rachel as the main character is an intriguing and appealing twist. **ROYALTY:** Free to Plays subscribers. **SOURCE:** Seale, Nancy. (1981, December). Song of Rachel. Plays: The Drama Magazine for Young People, pp. 39-44. **SUBJECTS/PLAY TYPE:** Christmas; Christ, Jesus; Christian Drama.

2875. 5-12. (+) Hendricks, William & Vogel, Cora. **A song of salvation.** **CAST:** Su. **ACTS:** 1. **SETTINGS:** None. **PLAYING TIME:** 30 min. **PLOT:** This presents a series of readings based on the Messianic Psalms from the Bible. **RECOMMENDATION:** Suitable for church or parochial school groups for presentation at a Christmas pageant or worship service, this uses organ music for transitions between scenes. **ROYALTY:** NA. **SOURCE:** Hendricks, William & Vogel, Cora. (1978). Handbook of Christmas programs. Grand Rapids, MI: Baker Book House. **SUBJECTS/PLAY TYPE:** Choral Reading; Creation; Worship Program.

2876. 9-12. (-) Finney, Doug & Swartz, Sam. **The song of the Gypsy princess.** **CAST:** 3f, 8m, Su. **ACTS:** 2. **SETTINGS:** Village with thatched huts; palace. **PLAYING TIME:** NA. **PLOT:** In the kingdom of Paradise Valley, all is less than paradise until Old Gypsy turns poverty into prosperity. In return, she takes the infant daughter of King Cole, and for 18 years, hides with Princess Dawn until Prince Charming arrives. All live happily ever after, even the Old Gypsy. **RECOMMENDATION:** Since the plot is on the level of elementary children, the references to Wall Street and other aspects of the economy would not be understood. An older audience would not be entertained. **ROYALTY:** $50. **SOURCE:** Finney, Doug & Swartz, Sam. (1979). The song of the Gypsy princess. Chicago, IL: Dramatic Pub. Co. **SUBJECTS/PLAY TYPE:** Folk Tale Motifs; Musical; Economics; Comedy.

2877. 6-12*. (+) Hewett, Dorothy. **Song of the seals.** **CAST:** 6f, 6m. **ACTS:** 2. **SETTINGS:** Beach. **PLAYING TIME:** NA. **PLOT:** Willow comes to stay with her grandmother, Mrs. Moonlight, and meets Billy, who tells her of Selchies, half human seal creatures, who include Mrs. Moonlight and one of each of the children's parents. Marlin Prawn, a developer, and Fyshe, a Selchie angry at being trapped in human form, plan to drill for oil in Mystery Bay. Winning Fyshe back to their side by making him a new seal skin, the Selchies thwart Prawn's plot and Mystery Bay is proclaimed a wildlife sanctuary. **RECOMMENDATION:** A fascinating fantasy with a message of conservation, this should be produced by adults, due to its length, the animal/human characters, and production intricacies. **ROYALTY:** NA. **SOURCE:** Hewett, Dorothy. (1985). Golden valley; Song of the seals. Sydney, Australia: Currency Press. **SUBJECTS/PLAY TYPE:** Conservation; Selchies; Australia; Musical.

2878. 12. (+) Thie, Sharon. **Soon, Jack, November.** **CAST:** 3f, 2m, Su. **ACTS:** 1. **SETTINGS:** Italian restaurant. **PLAYING TIME:** 90 min. **PLOT:** A married couple, Jack and November, and the husband's handsome male friend Soon (of questionable sexual orientation) arrive at an Italian restaurant. The action comprises their fragmented interactions with one another, with two waitresses, and with the hostess. The marriage is not strong and the wife is attracted to Soon, who encourages intimacy, but is repelled when she becomes too insistent. The conversation moves from food to painful memories and finally to the characters' outer flaws and inner insecurities. At the end, it is apparent that each character lives in emotional isolation and that any attempts at understanding one another are absurd. RECOMMENDATION: Although the sexuality in this makes it unacceptable for young audiences, the dialogue and characterization are striking. An intriguing piece, quite modern in concept and execution, the play requires professional acting and presentation and a mature audience to appreciate it. ROYALTY: $50. SOURCE: Thie, Sharon. (1984). Soon, Jack, November. Schulenburg, TX: I.E. Clark. SUBJECTS/PLAY TYPE: Marriage; Relationships; Drama.

2879. 9-12. (+) Cope, Eddie. **Soon to be a major motion picture. CAST:** 5f, 6m. **ACTS:** 2. **SETTINGS:** Living room. **PLAYING TIME:** NA. **PLOT:** Tom Floyd, college senior, persuades his gullible roommate, Bob Braden, to finance an escort service using the landlady's daughter, Sally, and the college dean's daughter, Carrell, as escorts for two cab drivers to whom he owes money. In danger of expulsion, Tom blackmails Dean Tomes, threatening to expose Tomes' affair with Greta Garbo. To make things even more complicated, Mrs. Aurumwater, a Hollywood movie producer, arrives to evaluate the College for a new drama program. At the end, Mrs. Aurumwater approves the College, Tom plans to marry Bob's fiancee and Bob and Sally plan to be married. **RECOMMENDATION:** Set in the 1930s, this suffers from loose writing, underdeveloped characters and unfulfilled plot sequences. However, a high school acting group might enjoy working with the corny humor, as few other production demands are made. **ROYALTY:** $35. **SOURCE:** Cope, Eddie. (1976). Soon to be a major motion picture. Schulenburg, TX: I.E. Clark. **SUBJECTS/PLAY TYPE:** College; Escort Service; Comedy.

2880. 3-6. (+) Cheatham, Val R. (Goethe) **The sorcerer's apprentice finds a helping hand.** (The sorcerer's apprentice.) **CAST:** 3f, 3m, 2u. **ACTS:** 1. **SETTINGS:** Laboratory. **PLAYING TIME:** 20 min. **PLOT:** The sorcerer feels he is getting old, and that his wife is becoming a demanding nag. His friends, the Witch and the Good Fairy, advise him to hire an apprentice and take some time off. The paperboy gets the job and, when left alone, can't resist dabbling in the sorcerer's magic but can't control it. The sorcerer returns in time to save him, but the boy quits. The sorcerer decides to use his magic to turn back the clock and make his wife and himself young and happy again. **RECOMMENDATION:** The characters are as real as next door neighbors, the dialogue is up to date, and the humor is plentiful. **ROYALTY:** Free to Plays subscribers. **SOURCE:** Cheatham, Val R. (1977, October). The sorcerers apprentice finds a helping hand. Plays: The Drama Magazine for Young People, pp. 39-46. **SUBJECTS/PLAY TYPE:** Fantasy; Magic; Comedy; Adaptation.

2881. 7-12. (+) Sawyer-Young, Kat. **Sorry. CAST:** 1f. **ACTS:** 1. **SETTINGS:** None. **PLAYING TIME:** 1 min. **PLOT:** Mindy tries to explain to Daryl that she likes him as a friend, not as a boyfriend. He refuses to remain her friend. **RECOMMENDATION:** This portrays realistically the reactions of rejected teenagers. **ROYALTY:** None. **SOURCE:** Sawyer-Young, Kat. (1987). Minute monologues for contemporary teens. Boston, MA: Baker's Plays. **SUBJECTS/PLAY TYPE:** Dating; Monologue.

2882. 7-12. (+) Schaaf, Albert K. **Sorry, no answer. CAST:** 2f, 2m. **ACTS:** 1. **SETTINGS:** Office. **PLAYING TIME:** 10 min. **PLOT:** Mr. Walpole undeservedly receives $2.00 back from a pay phone and tries to return it. No one has ever given money back to the telephone company, and the puzzled employees ask their boss what to do. He accepts the money, gives it back to Walpole as a reward for being honest, and takes a long lunch break, checking first the address of the telephone booth Mr. Walpole used. **RECOMMENDATION:** Everyone loves to poke fun at "Ma Bell." **ROYALTY:** Free to Plays subscribers. **SOURCE:** Schaaf, Albert K. (1975, January). Sorry, no answer. Plays: The Drama Magazine for Young People, pp. 73-76. **SUBJECTS/PLAY TYPE:** Honesty; Comedy; Telephone Company; Skit.

2883. 7-12. (+) Fletcher, Lucille. **Sorry, wrong number. CAST:** 4f, 3m, Su. **ACTS:** 1. **SETTINGS:** Bedroom. **PLAYING TIME:** NA. **PLOT:** Mrs. Stevenson, a pampered invalid, overhears two men planning a murder over crossed telephone wires. Her husband is working late, it is her maid's night off, and she becomes upset as she tries to get the telephone company and the police to take some action. The twist in the plot is that she is the intended victim. **RECOMMENDATION:** The sets are not difficult and there are numerous small parts, but this requires a strong lead actress. **ROYALTY:** $20. **SOURCE:** Fletcher, Lucille. (1980). Sorry, wrong number and the hitch-hiker. New York, NY: Dramatists Play Service, Inc. **SUBJECTS/PLAY TYPE:** Mystery; Thriller.

2884. 6-8. (+) Henderson, Nancy. **Soul force. CAST:** 7f, 12m, Su. **ACTS:** 1. **SETTINGS:** Bare stage. **PLAYING TIME:** 12 min. **PLOT:** Two reporters ask people what Martin Luther Ling, Jr. and his boycotts and nonviolence accomplished. **RECOMMENDATION:** The answers that the reporters receive, along with a flashback to the night King's house was dynamited, give a good impression of King and what he believed. **ROYALTY:** Permission required if performed outside the classroom. **SOURCE:** Henderson, Nancy. (1978). Celebrate America: A baker's dozen of plays. New York, NY: Julian Messner. **SUBJECTS/PLAY TYPE:** King, Martin Luther, Jr.; Black Americans; Drama.

2885. 4-12. (-) Gilfond, Henry. **The sound of guns. CAST:** 7u. **ACTS:** 1. **SETTINGS:** Hospital room. **PLAYING TIME:** 15 min. **PLOT:** A wounded soldier returns to the front lines after he meets his buddy, whose leg has been amputated. **RECOMMENDATION:** Instead of dealing with the real issues of war and its aftermath, this is a weak and superficial attempt to show how a "brave" man reacts to his wounds. **ROYALTY:** None.

SOURCE: Gilfond, Henry. (1985). Holiday plays for reading. New York, NY: Walker. SUBJECTS/PLAY TYPE: Veteran's Day; War; Drama.

2886. K-8. (+) Flesch, Ed. **The sour prince.** CAST: 2f, 3m. ACTS: 1. SETTINGS: Country-side; throne room; bedroom. PLAYING TIME: 40 min. PLOT: Gower the Dour, a villainous wizard, has removed all sweetness from Dourland, where the sour Prince and the bewitched princess live. Thanks to a traveler/cook, a feisty young woman, and the kiss of the princess, the princess regains her lost ability to speak and sing, and the wizard, whose power resides in the misery of others, is vanquished. RECOMMENDATION: The audience is encouraged to participate, and the themes of sweet foods and enchanted princes and princesses are delightful. ROYALTY: $20. SOURCE: Flesch, Ed. (1977). The sour prince. Schulenburg, TX: I.E. Clark. SUBJECTS/PLAY TYPE: Sorrow; Joy; Comedy.

2887. 2-4. (+) Gotwalt, Helen Louise Miller. **Sourdough Sally.** CAST: 6f, 7m. ACTS: 1. SETTINGS: Living room. PLAYING TIME: 20 min. PLOT: Sally hopes to be chosen to play Miss Alaska in the school play. Some of her friends claim she isn't a sourdough (a true Alaskan) and therefore can't be Miss Alaska. They tell her that one of the criteria for becoming a sourdough is to pet a grizzly bear. Sally sneaks out of the house while the children rehearse, and obtains a signed affidavit from the owner of the trading post that she has petted the stuffed grizzly bear there. Her teacher surprises Sally with the news that she has been chosen Miss Alaska. RECOMMENDATION: With rhyme and songs, this would make a nice addition to a unit on Alaska. ROYALTY: Free to Plays subscribers. SOURCE: Gotwalt, Helen Louise Miller. (1986). Everyday plays for boys and girls. Boston, MA: Plays, Inc. SUBJECTS/PLAY TYPE: Alaska; Friendship; Comedy.

2888. 3-6. (+) Eaton, Gale & Klopfer, Karen. **Space dog.** CAST: 6u. ACTS: 1. SETTINGS: Field. PLAYING TIME: 12 min. PLOT: Alice and her dog, Rufus, meet the three eyed Martian, Siril, and his dog. Siril bakes a cookie which, when eaten, allows him to understand dogs. He tells Rufus they are out of fuel (peanut butter), and they try to get Alice to eat a cookie so she can understand them. Rufus eats it instead, which allows him to speak English. Alice provides the peanut butter fuel, and as the visitors prepare to leave, they notice that the cookie formula has a strange side effect on earth: the dog now has three tails. RECOMMENDATION: This cute and fanciful piece has pure entertainment value. ROYALTY: Free to Plays subscribers. SOURCE: Eaton, Gale & Klopfer, Karen. (1982, October). Space dog. Plays: The Drama Magazine for Young People, pp. 75-79. SUBJECTS/PLAY TYPE: Space Travel; Fantasy; Puppet Play.

2889. 7-12. (+) Murray, John. **Space flight to Saturn.** CAST: 1f. ACTS: 1. SETTINGS: Bare stage. PLAYING TIME: NA. PLOT: Mrs. Ellis boards an interstellar flight with her husband, and proceeds to complain and worry about the entire flight. RECOMMENDATION: While this presents a somewhat stereotypical view of a domineering, critical wife, the dialogue is convincing, the characters

realistic, and the ending, in which the husband seems to have used trickery to quiet his complaining wife, is humorous. ROYALTY: None SOURCE: Murray, John. (1982). Modern monologues for young people. Boston, MA: Plays, Inc. SUBJECTS/PLAY TYPE: Comedy; Space Travel; Monologue.

2890. 6-10. (-) Garver, Juliet. **Space suit with roses.** CAST: 9f, 4m. ACTS: 1. SETTINGS: Living room. PLAYING TIME: 25 min. PLOT: A "homebody" girl falls asleep and dreams of becoming famous by creating a space suit for women. When she awakens, she incorporates the dream design into reality, beginning with a call to a boy she has wanted to meet, to ask for advice on space suits. RECOMMENDATION: This seems geared toward a female audience but is unrealistic and does not make its point on the apparent topic of career vs. family. ROYALTY: Free to Plays subscribers. SOURCE: Garver, Juliet. (1982, May). Space Suit with Roses. Plays: The Drama Magazine for Young People, pp. 1-11. SUBJECTS/PLAY TYPE: Science Fiction; Careers; Playlet.

2891. 10-12. (+) Birnkrant, Samuel & Simms, Willard. **Space war 2000.** CAST: 13u. ACTS: 2. SETTINGS: Space station; communications room. PLAYING TIME: 60 min. PLOT: The militaristic Prime Minister of planet Nargot plans to overthrow the Queen, who wishes to make peace with the long time enemy planet, Armagon. A peace mission from Armagon arrives at Nargot, to convince them that to continue the war will lead to the eventual destruction of the entire galaxy. The Prime Minister sabotages the Nargot space station, placing the blame on the Armagon delegation. While the Armagons are in custody, the Prime Minister sends his own "peace" delegation to Armagon, in space ships loaded with missiles. The plan is foiled when an accomplice reveals the secret code, which redirects the missile carrying ships from Armagon to harmless targets. RECOMMENDATION: The setting is futuristic but the plot, portraying the age old problem of those in government who want more power at any expense, would be useful to classes studying world history or international relations. ROYALTY: $20. SOURCE: Birnkrant, Samuel & Simms, Willard. (1977). Space war 2000. Denver, CO: Pioneer Drama Service. SUBJECTS/PLAY TYPE: International Relations; Space Wars; Drama.

2892. 5-7. (+) Boiko, Claire. **Spaceship Santa Maria.** CAST: 3f, 13m. ACTS: 1. SETTINGS: None. PLAYING TIME: 20 min. PLOT: One thousand years after Columbus set sail to discover the New World, a spaceship, also christened Santa Maria, leaves the rocket complex at Palos, Spain carrying a family unit whose destination is the Golden Galaxy, source of the precious gems and rare metals necessary to maintain the space program. Like Columbus' voyage to find precious metals to fund the European economy, the journey of Santa Maria II draws criticism from those who debate the shape and structure of the universe, predicting Stardriver's fall from the edge of space or his stagnant demise, becalmed in space with no "photo wind." After dwelling upon the pragmatic and technical considerations of the family's 20 year stint in space, the focus of the play shifts to the emotional impact of future space travel, highlighting the trepidation and wonder paramount in sending individuals into space for extended periods of time and the nostalgia and respect with which the departing traveler views the receding earth. The action culminates with the blast-off, leaving the audience to speculate about the success of the mission. RECOMMENDATION: The radio reception of the wistful tune sung by Phoebe as she commences a 20 year voyage is touching. The common goals of the family unit are practical and speak to an appreciation of the cyclic nature of history and the forever persistent curiosity of humankind. ROYALTY: None. SOURCE: Boiko, Claire. (1985). Children's plays for creative actors. Boston, MA: Plays, Inc. SUBJECTS/PLAY TYPE: Space Exploration; Columbus, Christopher; Playlet.

2893. 9-12. (+) Way, Brian. **Speak the speech I pray for you...** CAST: 1f, 4m, 1u. ACTS: 2. SETTINGS: None. PLAYING TIME: NA. PLOT: An observer from a more contemporary time meets Shakespeare at the Globe Theater and is treated to first hand impressions of the playwright, his creative interactions with actors, audiences, and stage managers, and his own artistic inspirations. She watches part of a rehearsal of **Hamlet** and meets Richard Burbage and Will Kempe, among others. RECOMMENDATION: The scenes from **Hamlet** could be changed to scenes from any other Shakespearean play. This flexibility, along with the use of audience participation, allows the play to be tailored to the specific needs and interests of the audience. ROYALTY: NA. SOURCE: Way, Brian. (1977). Speak the speech I pray... Reston, VA: Educational Arts Assoc. SUBJECTS/PLAY TYPE: Shakespeare, William; Theater, Elizabethan; Drama.

2894. 4-8. (+) Kral, Brian. **Special class.** CAST: 8f, 6m. ACTS: 1. SETTINGS: Classroom. PLAYING TIME: NA. PLOT: Mr. Morrison, the experienced teacher of a special education class, incurs the disapproval of a young student teacher who thinks he is too insensitive to his students' handicaps. By the end of the day she realizes that his purposeful inattention is his way of teaching them the same things all children need to learn. RECOMMENDATION: If the cast is a mixture of handicapped and nonhandicapped actors, they will be able to learn from each other during preparation, as well as from the play itself. ROYALTY: $35. SOURCE: Kral, Brian. (1981). Special class. New Orleans, LA: Anchorage Press. SUBJECTS/PLAY TYPE: Special Education; Disabilities; Drama.

2895. 10-12. (+) Doyle, Arthur Conan & Tracy, Jack. **The speckled band: An adventure of Sherlock Holmes.** CAST: 2f, 15m. ACTS: 3. SETTINGS: Hall; study; living room; Holmes' rooms; bedroom. PLAYING TIME: NA. PLOT: When Violet dies violently and mysteriously, her sister, Enid, realizes that she, too, is in danger from her stepfather, Dr. Rylott, who wishes to dispose of the two girls in order to gain their inheritance. Sherlock Holmes and Dr. Watson save Enid from a grisly death and solve the mystery of the "speckled band." RECOMMENDATION: This is suspenseful, totally Holmesian, and very British. It will be difficult to produce and potential directors should be aware that cocaine is used by the characters. ROYALTY: NA. SOURCE: Doyle, Arthur Conan. (1980). Sherlock Holmes, the published apocrypha. Boston, MA: Houghton Mifflin. SUBJECTS/PLAY TYPE: Mystery; Suspense; Adaptation.

2896. 1-6. (+) Marks, Mickey Klar. **The spell of Malatesta.** CAST: 1f, 8u. ACTS: 1. SETTINGS: Cave. PLAYING TIME: 30 min. PLOT: An ugly and scatterbrained witch, Malatesta, has not been able to do anything evil in her life, so a coven of witches sends Lolobad to replace her. Malatesta discovers Lolobad has a bad cold, and concocts a brew which cures it. Excited about developing a cure for the common cold, the two go into business. Malatesta advertises the "cure" on television and radio after undergoing plastic surgery and adopting a new hairdo, and becomes "Woman of the Year." Unfortunately, she failed to write down the original recipe and her attempt to make more of the elixir results in a potion that turns anyone drinking it into a witch. RECOMMENDATION: Rather a clever plot, this short comedy occasionally slips into banality, but an upper elementary acting group should find success performing it for their peers and younger students. ROYALTY: $5. SOURCE: Marks, Mickey Klar. (1975). The spell of Malatesta. Denver, CO: Pioneer Drama Service. SUBJECTS/PLAY TYPE: Witches; Magic; Comedy.

2897. 1-3. (+) Gray, Lora Taylor. **Spider the web builder.** CAST: 2m, 5u. ACTS: 2. SETTINGS: Forest. PLAYING TIME: 10 min. PLOT: Spider wants to win the gold medal for web spinning, but decides to take a nap and doesn't finish. He learns his lesson and wins the gold medal a year later. RECOMMENDATION: In this fine play about tenacity, some dialogue is in verse and the short sentences are easy to remember. ROYALTY: Free to Plays subscribers. SOURCE: Gary, Lora Taylor. (1986, March). Spider the web builder. Plays: The Drama Magazine for Young People, pp. 49-51. SUBJECTS/PLAY TYPE: Perseverance; Playlet.

2898. 4-6. (+) Merten, Elizabeth. **Spider's eye view.** CAST: 1f, 1m, 2u. ACTS: 1. SETTINGS: Spider's web. PLAYING TIME: NA. PLOT: When a moth becomes tangled in a spider's web, a witty butterfly cons the ugly spider into freeing him. RECOMMENDATION: The dry humor is very appealing. ROYALTY: None. SOURCE: Merten, George. (1979). Plays for puppet performance. Boston, MA: Plays, Inc. SUBJECTS/PLAY TYPE: Fantasy; Spider's Webs; Puppet Play.

2899. 3-6*. (+) Novelli, Florence & Aaron, Bernard A. **Spindlerion and the princess.** CAST: 2f, 7m. ACTS: 1. SETTINGS: Garden; laboratory; forest. PLAYING TIME: NA. PLOT: Spindlerion, an evil scientist who lives in the forest of King Flub's Kingdom, plots to gain its wealth by introducing the princess to a robot (whom he calls his son, and who has the title of royal prince) in the hope that she will fall in love and marry the robot. Spindlerion holds the princess hostage in his laboratory, but the robot fails to attract the princess' love, and Spindlerion decides to marry her himself. She escapes and returns to the castle with a magic potion, which is poured over Daffy Daisy, a flower in the castle garden. The flower turns into Princess Tellia's missing prince. A duel ensues, and the prince wins. Spindlerion is banished, and the princess prepares to marry her prince. RECOMMENDATION: Natural dialogue reveals the believable personalities, major conflicts are well drawn, and the role of the minstrel narrator sets the stage for a believable and suspenseful tale. The princess and King Flub experience positive growth throughout, and the strong aspects of the Princess's character are especially endearing. Production considerations include musical ability and lengthy dialogue for the leading roles. ROYALTY: NA. SOURCE: Novelli, Florence & Aaron, Bernard A. (1983). Spindlerion and the princess; And Queen cat of Furbit: Two children's musicals. Toronto, Canada: Playwrights Canada. SUBJECTS/PLAY TYPE: Robots; Marriage; Musical.

2900. 3-7. (+) Ross, Sari. **Spinning a spider's tale.** CAST: 1f, 3m, 7u. ACTS: 1. SETTINGS: Forest. PLAYING TIME: 15 min. PLOT: Anansi, the spider man, decides to attend two wedding feasts so he can eat twice as much. To decide which to attend first, he has his sons tie a rope around his middle, and each son tugs one end toward one of the feasts. Unfortunately, the pulls are so strong that Anansi's belly becomes very thin, as the spider's belly is today. Anansi's mother-in-law dies and he shows his grief by refusing to eat, but left alone with a pot of beans, he takes a large ladle of the beans. But before he can eat them, he hears someone coming, and quickly hides the beans under his hat. They burn all his hair off, which explains why spiders have no hair on their heads. RECOMMENDATION: Crafted in true storyteller tradition, the lessons about greed and vanity are subtly but unmistakably recognized. ROYALTY: Free to Plays subscribers. SOURCE: Ross, Sari. (1975, January). Spinning a spider's tale. Plays: The Drama Magazine for Young People, pp. 56-61. SUBJECTS/PLAY TYPE: Folk Tales, Africa; Greed; Vanity; Playlet.

2901. 9-12. (+) Kehret, Peg. **Spirit.** CAST: 5f, 3m, Su. ACTS: 2. SETTINGS: Nursing home room. PLAYING TIME: NA. PLOT: Even though her body is failing, Clara, a nursing home resident, is active, intelligent, energetic, and sensitive to the needs of the residents. But she is a problem to the manager because she holds poker games, does hula dances, and holds seances. She is told to leave, but dies in the process. Her spirit lives on, however, because she had secretly bought the home, to make sure that everything would be secure for her friends. RECOMMENDATION: The author succeeds in combining comedy with the reality of a nursing home environment. This delightful play conveys a social message about the poor conditions in many institutional settings where the elderly are forced to stay. ROYALTY: $35. SOURCE: Kehret, Peg. (1979). Spirit. Denver, CO: Pioneer Drama Service. SUBJECTS/PLAY TYPE: Nursing Homes; Elderly; Comedy.

2902. 4-6. (-) Fisher, Aileen Lucia. **The spirit of Christmas.** CAST: 4f, 3m, 1u. ACTS: 1. SETTINGS: Kitchen. PLAYING TIME: NA. PLOT: Christmas spirit leaves one house, where there is only greed and selfishness, for another where there is giving and unselfishness. RECOMMENDATION: Although rhymed, this is much too silly and dull. ROYALTY: None for amateurs. SOURCE: Fisher, Aileen Lucia. (1986). Holiday programs for boys and girls. Boston, MA: Plays, Inc. SUBJECTS/PLAY TYPE: Christmas; Playlet.

2903. 3-6. (+) Gabriel, Michelle. **The spirit of Sukkot.** CAST: 1f, 1m, 5u. ACTS: 1. SETTINGS: Outdoors. PLAYING TIME: 20 min. PLOT: A spirit takes a boy and a girl back in time to show them the meaning of Sukkot and its symbols: the "Lulav" and the "Etrog." RECOMMENDATION: The significance of the Jewish holiday is depicted well and the boy's fascination with airplanes adds a humorous touch. ROYALTY: None. SOURCE: Gabriel, Michelle. (1978). Jewish plays for Jewish days. Denver, CO: Alternatives in Religious Education, Inc. SUBJECTS/PLAY TYPE: Sukkot; Jewish Drama.

2904. 10-12. (+) Keller, Teddy. **S*P*L*A*S*H.** CAST: 5f, 6m, 6u. ACTS: 1. SETTINGS: Operating room. PLAYING TIME: NA. PLOT: "Redeye" wants to perform cosmetic surgery to repair a young woman's face, rather than just patch her up and send her back to her unit as strict service regulations demand. In return, he promises not to repair the wounded right arm of ace pitcher, Nurse "Fireball Nellie," to keep her from pitching for the rival team. However, "Fireball Nellie," has another nickname which Redeye knew all along, "Lefty Nellie." RECOMMENDATION: Like the popular television series, M*A*S*H, the good (but irreverent) guys win and the bad (selfish/self-serving) guys don't. The repartee and callous humor of the original is copied well. ROYALTY: $25. SOURCE: Keller, Teddy. (1983). S*P*L*A*S*H. Franklin, OH: Eldridge Pub. Co. SUBJECTS/PLAY TYPE: Operations; Comedy.

2905. 3-4*. (+) Smith, Sandra Yeo. **A spooky graduation.** CAST: 3f, 3m, 6u. ACTS: 1. SETTINGS: Classroom. PLAYING TIME: 20 min. PLOT: Each of Miss Wanda's School of Witchcraft students must complete a spooking assignment before broom graduation. Witchy Poo fails and is told to leave until she has spooked someone. When she overhears mortal students talking about a haunted house, she spooks everyone who enters. She is awarded Miss Wanda's Wickedest Witch Award, because she "went beyond the call of witchcraft duty" by spooking hundreds of mortals at the same time. RECOMMENDATION: Although this is cute, the witchcraft theme may offend some audiences. ROYALTY: $20. SOURCE: Smith, Sandra Yeo. (1980). A spooky graduation. Franklin, OH: Eldridge Pub. Co. SUBJECTS/PLAY TYPE: Fantasy; Halloween; Witches; Skit.

2906. 7-12. (+) Sawyer-Young, Kat. **Sports.** CAST: 1m. ACTS: 1. SETTINGS: None. PLAYING TIME: 1 min. PLOT: Doug discusses the disadvantages of different sports as he tries to decide which one to go out for. RECOMMENDATION: As Doug considers the astronomy club in lieu of sports, the audience might be led into a discussion of the relative importance of sports. ROYALTY: None. SOURCE: Sawyer-Young, Kat. (1987). Minute monologues for contemporary teens. Boston, MA:

Baker's Plays. SUBJECTS/PLAY TYPE: Sports; Monologue.

2907. 1-6. (+) Poorman, Berta & Poorman, Sonja. **Spread a little Christmas cheer.** CAST: 3f, 3m, 1u. ACTS: 1. SETTINGS: Workshop; living room. PLAYING TIME: 30 min. PLOT: Children follow Santa's elves' suggestion that they visit Miss Josie, an elderly woman. They cheer her with their songs, and she tells them a story about a small lost boy who found his way out of the forest by following Christmas bells. RECOMMENDATION: While an older child or adult should play the role of Miss Josie with her long speeches, the rest of the speaking parts and songs are simple enough for the early grades. Since there are so many musical numbers, this would be best produced by a music class or church choir. It is most suitable for church audiences. ROYALTY: $50. SOURCE: Poorman, Berta & Poorman, Sonja. (1982). Spread a little Christmas cheer. Franklin, OH: Eldridge Pub. Co. SUBJECTS/PLAY TYPE: Christmas; Musical.

2908. K-3*. (-) Baumanis, Vilnis & Jansons, Andrejs. (Brigadere, Anna) **Spriditis.** (Spriditis.) CAST: 9f, 13m, 3u. ACTS: 2. SETTINGS: Room; forest; hut; royal hall; courtyard; cottage. PLAYING TIME: 105 min. PLOT: A young boy, unhappy with life at home, goes into the world to make his fortune and quickly becomes disillusioned. He returns home more settled and ready to appreciate what he has always had. RECOMMENDATION: This poor English translation of the original Latvian story will not hold the interest of children. There are several religious references which make it unsuitable for public school use, yet the religious theme is not strong enough for church use. ROYALTY: $75. SOURCE: Baumanis, Vilnis & Jansons, Andrejs. (1980). Spriditis. Morton Grove, IL: Coach House Press. SUBJECTS/PLAY TYPE: Heroes; Musical; Adaptation.

2909. K-3. (+) Hark, Mildred & McQueen, Noel. **Spring is here.** CAST: Su. ACTS: 1. SETTINGS: Bare stage. PLAYING TIME: 15 min. PLOT: Spring and her helpers (sunbeams, flowers, and breezes) convince Old Man Winter it's time for him to leave by singing, and by depositing sun, flowers, April showers, and warm breezes onto the stage. RECOMMENDATION: Since at times the language is a little sophisticated, pantomime and body movement will make this more effective. ROYALTY: Free to Plays subscribers. SOURCE: Hark, Mildred & McQueen, Noel. (1979, May). Spring is here. Plays: The Drama Magazine for Young People, pp. 37-43. SUBJECTS/PLAY TYPE: Spring; Skit.

2910. 1-6. (+) Snair, Allen & Snair, Elizabeth. **Spring is not so far.** CAST: 22u. ACTS: 1. SETTINGS: Outdoors; castle gate. PLAYING TIME: 45 min. PLOT: A group of children, tired of winter, search for Princess Spring. Although the animals and flowers help them, the North Wind vows to keep Princess Spring to himself. When the children reach Spring's castle, they meet the Prince who has come to marry her. The Prince, the children, and the Princess' soldiers work together to defeat the North Wind. RECOMMENDATION: This musical might be best suited for performance before a parents' group. While the first

part is a bit slow, there is much opportunity for costuming and singing, and the movement picks up greatly by the play's conclusion. ROYALTY: $70. SOURCE: Snair, Allen & Snair, Elizabeth. (1988). Spring is not so far: An elementary musical. Franklin, OH: Eldridge Pub. Co. SUBJECTS/PLAY TYPE: Spring; Musical.

2911. 7-12. (+) Martens, Anne Coulter. **Springtime for Dan.** CAST: 5f, 2m. ACTS: 1. SETTINGS: Living room. PLAYING TIME: 25 min. PLOT: Dan bribes his sister to help him obtain a date with the attractive new girl who has moved in next door before his friend (and rival), Walt, does so. The new girl comes to the door unexpectedly and catches Dan dressed in a ridiculous maid's outfit. He pulls off a masquerade, which is foiled when Walt arrives and lands a date with her. Dan despairs momentarily, only to be surprised by her return. She reveals that her true motive in coming over was to give Dan an opportunity to ask her out, and all ends well. RECOMMENDATION: Despite some need for updating, this reads well, is humorous, and would be easy to stage. ROYALTY: Free to Plays Subscribers. SOURCE: Martens, Anne Coulter. (1979, March). Springtime for Dan. Plays: The Drama Magazine for Young People, pp. 17-27. SUBJECTS/PLAY TYPE: Romance; Comedy.

2912. 7-12. (+) Snapper, Dave. **The Spruce Street afterglow.** CAST: 2f, 2m, 1u. ACTS: 1. SETTINGS: Kitchen. PLAYING TIME: 12 min. PLOT: Mr. and Mrs. Powersma's children learn that excessive use of energy is wasteful and that poor people may have to do without. The selfish parents assure the children that poor people are lazy, but that they will always have plenty. The play ends with a power shortage. RECOMMENDATION: This is a timely reminder about energy conservation and the need to care for one another. ROYALTY: None. SOURCE: Altena, Hans. (1978). The playbook for Christian theatre. Grand Rapids, MI: Baker Book House. SUBJECTS/PLAY TYPE: Energy Conservation; Family; Drama.

2913. 1-5. (+) Gotwalt, Helen Louise Miller. **Spunky Punky.** CAST: 4f, 5m, 13u. ACTS: 1. SETTINGS: Garden. PLAYING TIME: 15 min. PLOT: Spunky Punky resists becoming the essential element of pumpkin pie; he wants a greater role in life. A trio of witches transform the reluctant pumpkin into a grinning jack-o-lantern. Satisfied, Spunky willingly decorates the table of the fabled Jack and Jill. RECOMMENDATION: The whole class can be involved, as there is room for art projects in designing the simple costumes, music class instruction in learning how to sing common nursery rhymes, and drama instruction in elemental acting skills. ROYALTY: NA. SOURCE: Gotwalt, Helen Louise Miller. (1985). First plays for children: A collection of little plays for the youngest players. Boston, MA: Plays, Inc. SUBJECTS/PLAY TYPE: Halloween; Skit.

2914. 7-12. (+) Huff, Betty Tracy. **Spy for a day.** CAST: 5f, 7m, Su. ACTS: 1. SETTINGS: Sidewalk cafe. PLAYING TIME: 30 min. PLOT: Spies from Ouch are on a mission to relay important secret information and to keep the spies from Ick from intercepting it. Seemingly innocent tourists become involved at the sidewalk cafe, which is really an espionage center for spies. Some of the tourists turn out to be actual members of the spy groups, Ick and Ouch. Exaggerated spy equipment adds humor, and the mission is successful. RECOMMENDATION: This comedy of foreign intrigue keeps the audience guessing as to who is really a spy and who is just an ordinary citizen until the very end. ROYALTY: Free to Plays subscribers. SOURCE: Huff, Betty Tracy. (1984, March). Spy for a day. Plays: The Drama Magazine for Young People, pp. 13-21. SUBJECTS/PLAY TYPE: Spies; Comedy.

2915. 9-12. (+) Kelly, Tim. **Squad room. CAST:** 9f, 11m, 9u. ACTS: 2. SETTINGS: Squad room. PLAYING TIME: 90 min. PLOT: A day in the city police squad room collects unusual characters: a pickpocket; a woman with a guilt complex; a woman who professes to be the "Mad Bomber"; a teacher and her students getting a tour of the police headquarters; a lunatic/psychiatrist; the "real Mad Bomber" (disguised as a repairman and deli person); a prominent citizen who is the victim of a swindle; a gangster and his attorney; a bag lady; bunco swindlers; and Detective Marie Grant's mother (voicing repeated concern that Marie get married and have a normal life). RECOMMENDATION: With its many characters and intricate subplots, the stage will have a multitude of activities going on at any given time, making this difficult to produce without experience and an unusually large number of costly props. Dialogue must be delivered in a brisk fashion. ROYALTY: $35. SOURCE: Kelly, Tim. (1984). Squad room. Denver, CO: Pioneer Drama Service. SUBJECTS/PLAY TYPE: Police; Comedy.

2916. 1-5. (-) Gotwalt, Helen Louise Miller. **Squeaknibble's Christmas. CAST:** 3f, 2m, 5u. ACTS: 1. SETTINGS: Hallway. PLAYING TIME: NA. PLOT: A mouse doubts the existence of Santa Claus and is almost eaten by the house cat. RECOMMENDATION: There is a serious flaw of logic in this play which would confuse children and adults. The doubting mouse is almost eaten when it sees a cat dressed as Santa Claus, yet concludes that "it pays to believe in Santa Claus." There is little in the way of humor or insight to recommend this. ROYALTY: Free to Plays subscribers. SOURCE: Gotwalt, Helen Louise Miller. (1986). Special plays for holidays. Boston, MA: Plays, Inc. SUBJECTS/PLAY TYPE: Christmas; Playlet.

2917. K-3. (+) Silverman, Eleanor. **St. George and the dragon. CAST:** 1f, 1m, 2u. ACTS: 1. SETTINGS: None. PLAYING TIME: 5 min. PLOT: St. George kills the dragon and is rewarded with jewels and the princess. RECOMMENDATION: As a narrator describes the action, it is pantomimed, making this a good creative exercise. ROYALTY: None. SOURCE: Silverman, Eleanor. (1983). Dramatics for children. Metuchen, NJ: Scarecrow Press. SUBJECTS/PLAY TYPE: Dragons; St. George; Skit.

2918. 2-6. (+) Fisher, Aileen. **St. Patrick and the serpent. CAST:** 1f, 1m, Su. ACTS: 1. SETTINGS: None. PLAYING TIME: NA. PLOT: St. Patrick, after ridding Ireland of snakes, persuades a final, stubborn specimen to vacate the country. RECOMMENDATION: A delightful recitation, this poem would make a wonderful addition to a parents' program for a St. Patrick's Day celebration.

ROYALTY: Free to Plays subscribers. SOURCE: Fisher, Aileen. (1988, March). St. Patrick and the serpent. Plays: The Drama Magazine for Young People, pp. 48-50. SUBJECTS/PLAY TYPE: Snakes; Ireland; St. Patrick's Day; Reader's Theater.

2919. K-4. (-) Fisher, Aileen. **St. Patrick's Day. CAST:** Su. ACTS: 1. SETTINGS: None. PLAYING TIME: 5 min. PLOT: Boys and girls recite verses that describe the luck of the Irish and the meaning of St. Patrick's Day. RECOMMENDATION: This is particularly patronizing, stereotypical, and superficial. The verse has words too sophisticated for younger children, and content and format insulting to older groups. ROYALTY: Free to Plays subscribers. SOURCE: Fisher, Aileen. (1984, March). St. Patrick's Day. Plays: The Drama Magazine for Young People, p. 46. SUBJECTS/PLAY TYPE: St. Patrick's Day; Choral Reading.

2920. 4-5. (+) Murray, John. **Stage set for murder. CAST:** 4f, 5m, Su. ACTS: 1. SETTINGS: Living room. PLAYING TIME: 30 min. PLOT: All of the people involved with the first production of a play are invited to an old abandoned house to learn the details of their playwright's death. During the course of the evening, they are locked in, one person is murdered, and another kidnapped. The action is resolved when the murderer reveals himself to one of the others, is captured, and the kidnapped victim is recovered. RECOMMENDATION: This is quite suspenseful with a well developed plot. However, the setting is of vital importance and should be kept as close as possible to the description, which may entail some extra planning and expense. ROYALTY: Free to Plays subscribers. SOURCE: Murray, John. (1982, March). Stage set for murder. Plays: The Drama Magazine for Young Adults, pp. 13-27. SUBJECTS/PLAY TYPE: Mystery; Playlet.

2921. 11-12*. (+) McDonough, Jerome. **Stages. CAST:** 6f, 5m, 1u. ACTS: 1. SETTINGS: None. PLAYING TIME: 40 min. PLOT: In this play within a play, one play is the exterior drama which revolves around the artists, actors, actresses, playwright, director, and crew who are involved in a production which is often problematic and frustrating. This is contrasted to the interior drama: the actual play being performed by the actors and actresses. Theater is a metaphor for life. RECOMMENDATION: This complex and sometimes confusing play is recommended for advanced students. A knowledge of theater would enhance appreciation. Theater goers will probably need to see **Stages** more than once to experience all its facets. Ensemble roles are not comprehensive and some roles are double cast, requiring a talented and mature cast. ROYALTY: $15. SOURCE: McDonough, Jerome. (1979). Stages. Schulenburg, TX: I.E. Clark. SUBJECTS/PLAY TYPE: Theater; Avant-Garde; Drama.

2922. 9-12. (-) Hurd, Jerrie W. **Stagestruck. CAST:** 5f, 8m, 1u. ACTS: 1. SETTINGS: Backstage of theater. PLAYING TIME: 10 min. PLOT: A young girl comes to the theater to meet the egotistical tenor, Henrico, who ignores her. When the lady snake dancer's snake gets loose, the young girl faints. A stagehand catches her and she calls him her hero. Henrico is also frightened by the snake; he faints and cannot be revived. The stagehand offers to go on in Henrico's place and the theater owner agrees. RECOMMENDATION: This clever and appealing pantomime melodrama would require more practice and rehearsals than most, but it would give the actors good experience. By using a strobe light and a slide projector to cast captions on the wall, this will achieve a unique silent film style guaranteed to intrigue audiences. ROYALTY: Free to Plays subscribers. SOURCE: Hurd, Jerrie W. (1983, January/February). Stagestruck. Plays: The Drama Magazine for Young People, pp. 83-86. SUBJECTS/PLAY TYPE: Silent Films; Melodrama; Pantomime.

2923. 6-9. (+) Schaaf, Albert K. (Jacobs, Joseph) **Stalk the missing person.** (Jack and the beanstalk) CAST: 1f, 4m. ACTS: 1. SETTINGS: Kitchen. PLAYING TIME: 12 min. PLOT: Sara, Jack's mother, has reported Jack missing. Knights Sir Bojak and Sir Lumbago are assigned to the case by the palace police. They enter the cottage and begin the normal TV representation of a modern day police interrogation, during which they use many jokes and prop stunts. They ask the police artist, Rembrandt van Gogh-Gogh, to sketch Jack. Jack returns with a knapsack full of treasure, and everyone is happy until the question of what to do with an angry giant is discussed. A green giant from the next valley is requested and the palace police depart with appropriate jokes, leaving the police artist to paint Jack's portrait. RECOMMENDATION: The characterizations of modern day figures, recut into medieval clothes are a delightful change of pace. ROYALTY: Free to Plays subscribers. SOURCE: Schaaf, Albert K. (1978, December). Stalk the missing person. Plays: The Drama Magazine for Young People, pp. 55-60. SUBJECTS/PLAY TYPE: Folk Tales, England; Mystery; Adaptation.

2924. K-2. (+) Fisher, Aileen Lucia. **Standing up for Christmas.** CAST: 9u. ACTS: 1. SETTINGS: None. PLAYING TIME: NA.. PLOT: The verses in this brief Christmas poem connect each letter in the word, Christmas, with a holiday image. RECOMMENDATION: The poems are brief enough to be learned and recited by the very young. They are nonreligious. ROYALTY: Free to Plays subscribers. SOURCE: Fisher, Aileen Lucia. (1985). Year-round programs for young players. Boston, MA: Plays, Inc. SUBJECTS/PLAY TYPE: Christmas; Choral Reading.

2925. 3-6. (+) Nolan, Paul T. **Stanislaw and the wolf.** CAST: 3f, 6m. ACTS: 1. SETTINGS: Clearing. PLAYING TIME: 15 min. PLOT: St. Stanislaw, Poland's patron saint, offers advice to Ivan, the bear, who has had his nose stung while stealing honey; Sam, the squirrel, and Masha, the rabbit, on the run from Andrey, the fox; Andrey, misdirected by Stanislaw in his quest to catch Masha and Sam; and Adolf, the wolf, tricked into trying to eat the blacksmith, Walter, instead of a young child. Walter knocks Adolph unconscious and when he revives, Adolph decides man is not such a tasty dish after all. RECOMMENDATION: Though the dialogue is, at times, stiff, and Stanislaw tends to be preachy, swift action and amusing situations carry the plot. St. Stanislaw's cunning

nature could be incorporated into a world history unit or an English curriculum on folk heroes, provoking discussion of how a country's history influences its national character. ROYALTY: None for amateur performance. SOURCE: Nolan, Paul T. (1982). Folk tale plays round the world: A collection of royalty-free, one-act plays about lands far and near. Boston, MA: Plays, Inc. SUBJECTS/PLAY TYPE: Folk Tales, Poland; Fable.

2926. 1-6. (+) Boiko, Claire. **Star bright.** CAST: 5u. ACTS: 1. SETTINGS: Bare stage, backdrop. PLAYING TIME: 20 min. PLOT: On Christmas Eve, Zodiac, Keeper of the Sky, arranges and polishes the stars so they will look their best. King Connifer, chosen to be the world's Christmas tree, comes to the sky to find a worthy star for his highest branch. All the stars, save Astra, who hangs her head modestly, extol their own virtues and disparage each other as they watch a storm blow three sailors off course. Only Astra guides the sailors to land and safety. King Connifer chooses Astra to be the Right Honorable Christmas Star. RECOMMENDATION: The conflict is well developed by plot and dialogue, and the message is subtly, but clearly conveyed. This can involve as many actors as necessary, and will allow a great deal of creativity in the preparation of costumes from different countries, worn by the stars. ROYALTY: Free to Plays subscribers. SOURCE: Boiko, Claire. (1985). Children's plays for creative actors. Boston, MA: Plays, Inc. SUBJECTS/PLAY TYPE: Christmas; Playlet.

2927. 6-12. (+) Boiko, Claire. **Star fever.** CAST: 3f, 5m. ACTS: 1. SETTINGS: Spaceship interior. PLAYING TIME: 30 min. PLOT: On a mission through the light barrier to discover a cure for the deadly Star Fever, "Joker" Kramer (a stowaway known for his pranks at the Space Academy) discovers that the symptoms can be erased by strong human emotion. Ironically, the strict "Special Discipline" required of all travelers through the light barrier to ward off Star Fever, has actually caused their deaths. "Joker" slugs the crew members to make them angry and saves their lives. The rebel is a hero. RECOMMENDATION: The environmental warning here is clear; future generations will suffer for the wanton waste and depletion of pure water, clean air, and inexpensive energy in the twentieth century. The extension of space travel beyond limits which astrophysicists have designated insurpassable is contemplated. ROYALTY: None for amateur performance. SOURCE: Boiko, Claire. (1985). Children's plays for creative actors. Boston, MA: Plays, Inc. SUBJECTS/PLAY TYPE: Science Fiction; Space Flight; Environment; Playlet.

2928. 6-8. (+) Hark, Mildred & McQueen, Noel. **A star in the window.** CAST: 3f, 4m. ACTS: 1. SETTINGS: Shop. PLAYING TIME: 30 min. PLOT: As Otto and Alma close their store for the night, a woman calls that she will be coming in for a mysterious Christmas star, and as Otto waits, a man asks for a star like the one he saw in the window last night. Mr. Baker, a writer, is interested in the star because he has been exploring an idea about a magical star which seems to be accompanied by a choir singing Christmas carols. Mr. Jones offers Otto $1,000 for the star because he thinks it will boost his own store's sales after

Christmas. Otto protests to all that he has no such star. When everyone leaves, Otto and Alma begin to turn off the lights and finally see the miraculous star themselves. RECOMMENDATION: Although quite predictable and rather trite, this does capture the spirit of Christmas. It would have been more effective without the seemingly unrelated birth of a customer's baby, and the unnecessary German ancestry of the shop owner. ROYALTY: Free to Plays subscribers. SOURCE: Hark, Mildred & McQueen, Noel. (December 1988). A star in the window. Plays: The Drama Magazine for Young People, pp. 1-10. SUBJECTS/PLAY TYPE: Christmas; Playlet.

2929. 5-12. (+) Stephenson, Ginny. **Star message.** CAST: 2f, 3m, 2u. ACTS: 1. SETTINGS: Futuristic room. PLAYING TIME: 30 min. PLOT: In the 25th century, an alien from an unknown planet lands in a space ship at Mernerfeldt University, at the same time that an indecipherable message from deep space is received by the university. None of the modern computers can communicate with the alien or decode the message. Innocent, checker playing students and the not so new robot, Mugsy, decode the message, which warns of an attack from another planet, and Earth is saved. RECOMMENDATION: This states its message well that progress isn't progress if old ways are dropped merely for the sake of change. Additionally, an antiwar statement is made. ROYALTY: $15. SOURCE: Stephenson, Ginny. (1979). Star message. Schulenburg, TX: I.E. Clark. SUBJECTS/PLAY TYPE: Science Fiction; Progress; War; Drama.

2930. 7-12. (+) Martens, Anne Coulter. **Star of Bethlehem.** CAST: 16f, 9m, Su. ACTS: 2. SETTINGS: Auditorium; hospital room. PLAYING TIME: 35 min. PLOT: Teenagers entertain the children's ward at the hospital on Christmas Eve and learn that giving is more important than getting. RECOMMENDATION: There are plenty of parts for all in this polished script which portrays typical reactions of teenagers and has a solid, logical ending. ROYALTY: Free to Plays subscribers. SOURCE: Kamerman, Sylvia E. (1982). Christmas play favorites for young people. Boston, MA: Plays, Inc. SUBJECTS/PLAY TYPE: Christmas; Playlet.

2931. 5-9. (-) Dubois, Graham. **Star over Bethlehem.** CAST: 4f, 8m, Su. ACTS: 1. SETTINGS: Yard. PLAYING TIME: 30 min. PLOT: The innkeeper's daughter loves a simple man but her father wishes her to marry a richer, but unscrupulous, merchant. A child is born in Bethlehem, and the daughter is allowed to marry the simple man. RECOMMENDATION: The plot is cliched and the marriage customs would not be understood by most young people. ROYALTY: Free to Plays subscribers. SOURCE: Kamerman, Sylvia E. (1978). On stage for Christmas. Boston, MA: Plays, Inc. SUBJECTS/PLAY TYPE: Christmas; Playlet.

2932. 4-12. (+) Harris, Aurand. **Star spangled salute.** CAST: 1m, 4u. ACTS: 2. SETTINGS: Bare stage. PLAYING TIME: NA. PLOT: This provides a brief overview of U.S. history, including treatments of the

Presidents (up through Kennedy), the signing of the Declaration of Independence, the Statue of Liberty, Betsy Ross, Salk's cure for polio, and Kit Carson. RECOMMENDATION: Done in true minstrel show fashion, all the music is traditional, easy to obtain, and appealing to all ages. Because the main characters must carry props, older children, young adults, or adults should be chosen. ROYALTY: $25. SOURCE: Harris, Aurand. (1975). Star spangled salute. New Orleans, LA: Anchorage Press, Inc. SUBJECTS/PLAY TYPE: Minstrel Show; Patriotism; History, U.S.; Musical; Comedy.

2933. 7-9. (+) Boiko, Claire. **Star trick.** CAST: 3f, 7m, 2u. ACTS: 1. SETTINGS: Starship "bridge." PLAYING TIME: 25 min. PLOT: This parody of "Star Trek" features a crew searching for basketball talent. Visitors from other spaceships provide new members for the team plus a cheerleader. RECOMMENDATION: The characters and their lines are similar to the real Star Trek characters, and this search is believable enough. ROYALTY: Free to Plays subscribers. SOURCE: Boiko, Claire. (1980, April). Star trick. Plays: The Drama Magazine for Young People, pp. 1-8. SUBJECTS/PLAY TYPE: Science Fiction; Star Trek; Comedy.

2934. 1-6. (+) Fendrich, Shubert. **Star trip 1.** CAST: 5u. ACTS: 1. SETTINGS: Auditorium; space ship; Mars. PLAYING TIME: 20 min. PLOT: Captain Cosmic and Lt. Fumble return to earth from Mars, where they collected rocks. Senator Foghorn informs them that the owners of the rocks learn at a much faster pace than normal, and remember forever. Captain Cosmic and Lt. Fumble are sent back to retrieve more of the rocks. Meanwhile, Professor Meanfellow schemes to get the rocks, but he is foiled. RECOMMENDATION: The performers will enjoy taking the parts of the characters, especially Lt. Fumble, the comic fool. This involves a great deal of audience participation, both verbal and physical, as children take parts of Martians. They will also appreciate being given their very own smart rock as a token. It is recommended that the older grades produce this. ROYALTY: $10. SOURCE: Fendrich, Shubert. (1976). Star trip 1. Denver, CO: Pioneer Drama Service. SUBJECTS/PLAY TYPE: Space; Participation Play; Comedy.

2935. 4-8. (+) Boiko, Claire. **The star-spangled time machine.** CAST: 3f, 10m, Su. ACTS: 3. SETTINGS: None. PLAYING TIME: 30 min. PLOT: Miss Gala, a twenty-first century teacher, prepares to take four school children back in time to the celebration of the Bicentennial in Philadelphia. During transport, the children are blown out of time, and meet Benjamin Franklin, Thomas Jefferson, and George Washington, as they learn what America has been, what it is, and what it might become. RECOMMENDATION: Although slightly dated by repeated references to the Bicentennial, this is on target in presenting the American philosophy of freedom. ROYALTY: Free to Plays subscribers. SOURCE: Boiko, Claire. (1976, October). The star-spangled time machine. Plays: The Drama Magazine for Young People, pp. 76-84. SUBJECTS/PLAY TYPE: Patriotism; Independence Day, U.S.; Bicentennial, U.S.; History, U.S.; Musical.

2936. 2-6. (+) Gersbach, Jo. **The start of something.** CAST: 3f, 4m. ACTS: 1. SETTINGS: Porch. PLAYING TIME: 15 min. PLOT: When a dirty, old, wooden desk arrives on the porch of Mike's home, he and his friends find a note telling them of a secret word which will appear when the desk is cleaned. The children enjoy polishing and cleaning the old desk and discover that cleaning up old furniture can be a good and profitable hobby. When the secret word appears at the window of Mike's house, it is "Thanks" from Mike's parents. RECOMMENDATION: Reminiscent of an episode of "Leave It To Beaver," this might work best as a small group or classroom play. ROYALTY: Free to Plays subscribers. SOURCE: Gersbach, Jo. (1977, October). The start of something. Plays: The Drama Magazine for Young People, pp. 53-56. SUBJECTS/PLAY TYPE: Work; Playlet.

2937. 10-12. (+) McDonough, Jerome. **Stations.** CAST: 5f, 4m. ACTS: 1. SETTINGS: Church sanctuary; home; office. PLAYING TIME: 40 min. PLOT: Chrissanne Banlen has been called to the Roman Catholic priesthood, an impossibility since she is a married woman with children. Her decision to pursue her calling angers and embarrasses her family, but her cause is supported by a young priest who opposes the Roman Catholic tradition barring women from the priesthood. Although the Bishop denies her petition, her family deserts her cause, and she loses the direction of her only supporter, Chrissanne remains convinced of her calling. RECOMMENDATION: Roman Catholics, particularly those attending a parochial school, would be the ideal audience since knowledge of the tenets of the faith is needed to understand the plot. The themes of courage, perseverance, and choice are universal. Much rehearsal and experienced direction will be necessary. ROYALTY: NA. SOURCE: McDonough, J. (1988). Stations. Schulenburg, TX: I.E. Clark. SUBJECTS/PLAY TYPE: Roman Catholicism; Women's Rights; Drama.

2938. 3-5. (+) Satchell, Mary. **The Statue of Liberty is missing.** CAST: 5f, 5m, Su. ACTS: 1. SETTINGS: Park; artist's studio. PLAYING TIME: 25 min. PLOT: As children prepare for the dedication of Liberty Park by Frederic A. Bartholdi III, grandson of the designer of the Statue of Liberty, they notice that the small plaster Statue of Liberty is missing. The children decide that Beth must be the stand in for the statue. Bartholdi is impressed by their patriotism and tells them he took the statue so that he could replace it with a bronze one he had sculpted earlier. RECOMMENDATION: This presents numerous facts about the Statue of Liberty as Beth daydreams about Bartholdi's studio and his designing of the statue. ROYALTY: Free to Plays subscribers. SOURCE: Satchell, Mary. (1987, March). The Statue of Liberty is missing. Plays: The Drama Magazine for Young People, pp. 35-42. SUBJECTS/PLAY TYPE: Statue of Liberty; Playlet.

2939. 2-7. (+) Reines, Bernard. **The statue speaks.** CAST: 4f, 15m, Su. ACTS: 1. SETTINGS: Bare stage, props. PLAYING TIME: 20 min. PLOT: Tom and Julie, lingering beside the Statue of Liberty, are surprised to find her "come alive," and show them, through flashbacks, her birth in France, the receipt of her pedestal in New York in 1884, and her dedication in 1886. At the end, the children

read "The New Colossus" on her pedestal as Liberty becomes a statue again. RECOMMENDATION: This teaches with believable and realistic dialogue, and in an intriguing manner. ROYALTY: Free to Plays subscribers. SOURCE: Reines, Bernard. (1984, October). The Statue speaks. Plays: The Drama Magazine for Young People, pp. 35-40. SUBJECTS/PLAY TYPE: Statue of Liberty; Skit.

2940. 1-6. (-) Ammann, Herman. (Andersen, Hans Christian) **The steadfast tin soldier.** (The steadfast tin soldier) CAST: 3f, 3m, 8u. ACTS: 1. SETTINGS: Birthday party. PLAYING TIME: 35 min. PLOT: The embattled tin soldier longs to see his sweetheart, Cindy, but she is seeing Prince Charming. When the two are reunited at a birthday party, Cindy is forced to choose between the love of the tin soldier and the strength and wealth of Prince Charming. RECOMMENDATION: This has some amusing moments and a potentially valuable message. Unfortunately, the theme, which expresses the relative values of love and devotion versus money and power, is presented in a very sexist and heavy handed manner. In addition, while the story and characters would appeal primarily to an audience of young children, the dialogue often contains allusions and double entendres that would only be understood by older children. ROYALTY: $15. SOURCE: Ammann, Herman. (1969). The steadfast tin soldier. Schulenberg, TX: I.E. Clark. SUBJECTS/PLAY TYPE: Folk Tales, Denmark; Values; Adaptation.

2941. K-8. (+) Harris, Aurand. (Kristof, Jane) **Steal away home.** (Steal away home) CAST: 4f, 15m, Su. ACTS: 2. SETTINGS: Woods; home interiors; stations on the Underground Railroad. PLAYING TIME: NA. PLOT: Amos and Obie, two young slaves in South Carolina, run away via the Underground Railroad to be with their father, a free man in Philadelphia. With the help of other freed slaves, a pharmacist's wife, a doctor's daughter, and Quakers, the two boys cleverly escape capture, see another runaway slave shot and killed, and reach Philadelphia, where members of the Underground Railroad have located their father, who is waiting to greet them when they arrive. The three together hope to earn enough money to purchase their mother and baby sister. RECOMMENDATION: This realistic and suspenseful drama will be much more effective if Amos and Obie are portrayed by children, with the other characters portrayed by older teenagers and adults. This would make an excellent addition to a Black History unit or to an American History unit on slavery. ROYALTY: NA. SOURCE: Harris, Aurand. (1977). Six plays for children. Austin, TX: Univ. of Texas Press. SUBJECTS/PLAY TYPE: Slavery; Underground Railroad; Black History; Adaptation.

2942. 4-12. (+) Zeder, Suzan. **Step on a crack.** CAST: 4f, 2m. ACTS: 1. SETTINGS: Bedroom; living room; bowling alley; city streets. PLAYING TIME: NA. PLOT: Ellie, 10, feels she has lost her father's affections to his new wife, Lucille. Although on the surface the child tries to get along with Lucille, her inner thoughts are revealed through some wild fantasies and two imaginary friends. Relations become strained during a family trip to the bowling alley and Ellie runs away. Only afterwards does she realize that her stepmother truly loves her and wants to be a real mother, something that Ellie also wants desperately. RECOMMENDATION: The imaginative fantasies and true to life characters make this highly entertaining, and a valuable lesson about family relations. The dialogue and actions of the main characters must be timed and delivered carefully for full emotional impact. This requires the performance skills of teenagers. ROYALTY: $35. SOURCE: Zeder, Suzan. (1976). Step on a crack. New Orleans, LA: Anchorage Press. SUBJECTS/PLAY TYPE: Mothers and Daughters; Family,; Stepchildren; Drama.

2943. 8-10. (+) Kehret, Peg. **The stepsister speaks out.** CAST: 1f. ACTS: 1. SETTINGS: None. PLAYING TIME: NA. PLOT: A young girl compares herself to the ugly stepsister in **Cinderella**. Her feet are not size 4 1/2, she is not good natured and sweet all the time, and the starvation diet she endures to fit into her gown does not endear Cinderella to her. She decides it is most unfair that the unassuming, sweet, and helpless always win the prince. RECOMMENDATION: This delightfully juxtaposes the illusions of fantasy and the realities of life. ROYALTY: NA. SOURCE: Kehret, Peg. (1986). Winning monologs for young actors. Colorado Springs, CO: Meriwether Pub. SUBJECTS/PLAY TYPE: Jealousy; Monologue.

2944. 10-12. (+) Miller, Ev. **Sticks 'n stones.** CAST: 11f, 8m. ACTS: 2. SETTINGS: Principal's office; kitchen; school board room. PLAYING TIME: NA. PLOT: A censorship issue arises in a high school over the choice of a controversial novel. The issue attracts the attention of the community and the State Citizens for Decency. The decision of whether or not the book may be taught is left to the school board, whose president asks the audience to decide. RECOMMENDATION: All sides of the issue of censorship are well represented as audiences are encouraged to think and discuss. ROYALTY: $50. SOURCE: Miller, Ev. (n.d.). Sticks and stones. Woodstock, IL: The Dramatic Pub. Co. SUBJECTS/PLAY TYPE: Censorship; Academic Freedom; Intellectual Freedom; Drama.

2945. 10-12. (+) Rogers, David. (Ward, David) **The sting.** (The sting) CAST: 25f, 25m. ACTS: 2. SETTINGS: Betting room; gambling casino; pawn shop; dance hall; offices; alleys; streets; three train compartments. PLAYING TIME: 120 min. PLOT: When one of their friends and fellow con-men is murdered at the order of a powerful mob leader, two small time con-artists enlist the aid of a large group of their cohorts in an elaborate scheme to swindle him as revenge. RECOMMENDATION: This is a big production with many cast members, scenery changes, props, and technical systems. ROYALTY: NA. SOURCE: Rogers, David. (1984). The sting. Woodstock, IL: Dramatic Pub. Co. SUBJECTS/PLAY TYPE: Comedy; Swindlers and Swindling; Adaptation.

2946. K-6. (+) Leznoff, Glenda. **The stockbroker and the fairy godmother.** CAST: 1f, 1m. ACTS: 1. SETTINGS: Office. PLAYING TIME: 15 min. PLOT: In the middle of his hectic business day, the busy stockbroker is confronted

by his fairy godmother, who tells him that he has forgotten that today is his daughter's eighth birthday. To make matters worse, he has no good ideas for a gift. The fairy godmother reminds him of his own eighth birthday and the surprise he had loved: tickets for a hockey game. He fondly reminisces how he and his dad enjoyed that game, then sadly admits it is now too late to get tickets to surprise young Megan. The fairy godmother pulls two out of her pocket. Firmly convinced of her magical powers, he is anxious to follow her advice about spending more time with his daughter. RECOMMENDATION: This comical skit will be well received by younger children and would be even more loved if performed by school teachers/administrators or by their own parents. ROYALTY: Free to Plays subscribers. SOURCE: Leznoff, Glenda. (1989, March). Plays: The Drama Magazine for Young People, pp. 47-50. SUBJECTS/PLAY TYPE: Parenting; Skit.

2947. 1-6*. (+) Page, Anita & Tate, Lisa. (Olsson, Ninne) **Stomachache.** (Stomach-ache.) CAST: 1m, 2u. ACTS: 1. SETTINGS: Bedroom. PLAYING TIME: NA. PLOT: Michael, 10, wakes up too sick to go to school. As he drifts back to sleep, he is visited by two musical genies. Through song, instrument playing, dance, and role playing, the genies help Michael express his feelings, especially his anxieties about school. Having worked through his fears, he marches confidently off to school. RECOMMENDATION: This sensitively explores the fears and frustrations about school familiar to most children (and adults). The revealing role playing is smoothly interwoven throughout. This unique work would probably require junior high school age or older actors, although exceptionally talented children might be able to perform it. It would be very effective for a special needs audience, such as hospitalized children, or those with physical or emotional problems. ROYALTY: $25. SOURCE: Page, Anita & Tate, Lisa. (1980). Stomachache. Boston, MA: Baker's Plays. SUBJECTS/PLAY TYPE: School; Music Therapy; Drama; Adaptation.

2948. 1-5. (+) Buechler, James. (Perrault, Charles) **Stone soup.** (Stone Soup) CAST: 4f, 4m, Su. ACTS: 1. SETTINGS: Village street. PLAYING TIME: 15 min. PLOT: When a sergeant and his soldiers stop at a small village for something to eat, no one is willing to share what little they have. The sergeant tricks the townspeople into feeding him and his men by making soup from a stone and water. As the curiosity of the people is aroused, they donate carrots, potatoes, onions and meat. Soon there is enough stone soup for everyone. RECOMMENDATION: This is clever, and repetitions in the plot make it particularly suitable for very young children. ROYALTY: Free to Plays subscribers. SOURCE: Buechler, James. (1987, March). Stone soup. Plays: The Drama Magazine for Young People, pp. 43-46. SUBJECTS/PLAY TYPE: Folk Tales, France; Comedy; Adaptation.

2949. K-3. (+) McCaslin, Nellie. (Perrault, Charles) **Stone soup.** (Stone Soup) CAST: Su. ACTS: 1. SETTINGS: Kitchen; yard. PLAYING TIME: 10 min. PLOT: An old woman plans to put potatoes, onions, green peas, and a hambone into her soup. She hears a tramp knock politely, and ask to stop and rest. When he asks for a bite of supper, the old woman refuses. The tramp tells the old woman that he knows how to make soup from a stone. He asks her for water, salt, pepper, onion, potatoes, carrots or peas, a hambone, bread, and butter, and then he finds the right stone in her front yard. The two talk over the meal they have prepared. RECOMMENDATION: This simple plot uses everyday household words that are familiar to young children. As well as its obvious twist at the end, this has sociological implications for children to discuss concerning modern street people. ROYALTY: None. SOURCE: McCaslin, Nellie. (1977). Puppet fun production, performance, and plays. New York, NY: D. McKay Co. SUBJECTS/PLAY TYPE: Folk Tales, France; Puppet Play; Adaptation.

2950. 2-7*. (+) Peterson, Gary & Nestor, Larry. (Perrault, Charles) **Stone soup.** (Stone Soup) CAST: 4f, 6m, Su. ACTS: 1. SETTINGS: Village square. PLAYING TIME: 35 min. PLOT: Three soldiers seek food from the townspeople in a poor village, but are refused. They beg a pot of water for their "stone soup," and offer to share with the villagers, curious people who gladly contribute meat and vegetables to improve the flavor. RECOMMENDATION: If performed by older students, the humor could be exaggerated a bit more. The songs and the dialogue are humorous and easy to learn. ROYALTY: $25. SOURCE: Peterson, Gary & Nestor, Larry. (1983). Stone soup. New York, NY: Dramatic Pub. Co. SUBJECTS/PLAY TYPE: Folk Tales, France; Generosity; Musical; Adaptation.

2951. 3-7. (+) Ross, Sari. **Stories from the Sky God.** (Anansi) CAST: 1m, 11u. ACTS: 1. SETTINGS: Forest. PLAYING TIME: 20 min. PLOT: Anansi wishes to have as his own all the stories belonging to the Sky God, and is told that he may buy them by capturing four creatures and bringing them to the Sky God. Though the feat has been attempted by many rich and powerful men, the poor, little man succeeds because he is able to trick each of the creatures into submission. The stories are put together in a gold box, which Anansi opens, losing them as they jump out and are scattered all over the land. RECOMMENDATION: With a description of an exotic environment and the sounds of a foreign language, this is unique in having the audience sit in a circle while the play is performed in the center with the storyteller on the outside. It should be performed by older students for younger ones. ROYALTY: Free to Plays subscribers. SOURCE: Ross, Sari. (1977, March). Stories from the sky god. Plays: The Drama Magazine for Young People, pp. 33-38. SUBJECTS/PLAY TYPE: Folk Tales, Africa; Stories; Adaptation.

2952. 7-12. (+) Asimov, Isaac. **The story machine.** CAST: 3f, 3m, 3u. ACTS: 1. SETTINGS: Bedroom. PLAYING TIME: 25 min. PLOT: In a futuristic society, Niccolo and his friend try to reprogram Niccolo's outdated computer to function as a storyteller. Although unsuccessful with the reprogramming, the two form a club and use ancient language and math symbols (those of today) to write secret messages. There is a hint of the eventual take-over of the computer. RECOMMENDATION: The author sprinkles the play with futuristic terms which he quickly defines, and the futuristic perspective on today's new technology is interesting. ROYALTY: Free to Plays subscribers. SOURCE: Asimov, Isaac. (1977, May). The story machine. Plays: The Drama Magazine for Young People, pp. 61-70. SUBJECTS/PLAY TYPE: Science Fiction; Computers; Playlet.

2953. 3-5. (-) Bradley, Virginia. **The story of John Worthington Snee.** CAST: 2f, 12m, 2u. ACTS: 1. SETTINGS: Pirate's cove; western barroom; street outside a burning building. PLAYING TIME: NA. PLOT: Between the ages of three and six, a young boy changes his career from pirate, to sheriff, to fireman, to detective. RECOMMENDATION: This rhyming skit is long on narration and short on action. The audience would be quickly bored. ROYALTY: None. SOURCE: Bradley, Virginia. (1975). Is there an actor in the house? New York, NY: Dodd, Mead. SUBJECTS/PLAY TYPE: Careers; Skit.

2954. 6-12. (+) Sills, Paul. **The story teller at fault.** CAST: 1f, 4m. ACTS: 1. SETTINGS: Bare stage, props. PLAYING TIME: NA. PLOT: As a storyteller searches for a new tale to tell to the king, a trouble making beggar challenges him to a game of chance. After winning all the story teller's money, his wife, and the story teller himself, the beggar turns him into a rabbit. Regaining his human form, the storyteller unsuccessfully tries to hang the beggar but realizes that he owes the beggar a gift of gratitude, for now he has a story for the king. RECOMMENDATION: This is a challenge for the imagination, as well as the acting skills of the victims of the magical effects (e.g., losing a hand). ROYALTY: NA. SOURCE: Sills, Paul. (1981). More from story theatre. New York, NY: Samuel French. SUBJECTS/PLAY TYPE: Folk Tales, Celtic; Magic; Playlet.

2955. 4-10. (+) Gable, Helen V. **Storybook friends.** CAST: 12f, 14m, Su. ACTS: 1. SETTINGS: Bare stage, props. PLAYING TIME: 15 min. PLOT: Twenty six storybook characters talk about the wonder of books. RECOMMENDATION: As fragments of many stories are briefly mentioned, adolescents will fondly remember the literature of their youth, and youngsters will delight in the characters. ROYALTY: Free to Plays subscribers. SOURCE: Gable, Helen V. (1981, November). Storybook friends. Plays: The Drama Magazine for Young People, pp. 45-48. SUBJECTS/PLAY TYPE: Book Week; Skit.

2956. 10-12. (+) Way, Brian. **The storytellers.** CAST: 8f, 9m, Su. ACTS: 2. SETTINGS: Bare stage, props. PLAYING TIME: NA. PLOT: The Toyman makes a music box for the Princess, but learns from Mirrorman that the Princess already has one. Fortunately, Mirrorman knows a wonderful substitute: a pea, three golden hairs, a nail, and a feather. If the Princess sleeps with one of these under her pillow, she will dream a different story every night. The Toyman wants badly to see the stories himself, so he and Mirrorman go through the mirror where they watch the enactment of the familiar stories by Andersen and the Grimms'. Thrilled by the wonderful stories, the Toyman places the gifts inside the musical box and hurries away to see the young Princess. RECOMMENDATION: The four tales are presented in a refreshing and exciting way. Toyman and Mirrorman actually watch the stories from the audience to give the children a greater feeling of involvement, and the audience is often called upon to help answer questions or solve simple mysteries. ROYALTY: $45. SOURCE: Way, Brian. (1977). The storytellers. Boston, MA: Baker's Plays. SUBJECTS/PLAY TYPE: Folk Tales, Denmark; Folk Tales, Germany; Adaptation.

2957. 3-6. (+) Plescia, Gillian L. **The strange and wonderful object. CAST:** 2f, 3m, Su. **ACTS:** 1. SETTINGS: Archway. PLAYING TIME: 15 min. PLOT: A narrator introduces Chang and Sing Hi, a newly married Chinese couple, and shows the audience a small magical mirror which Chang will find on the way to work. When he looks into the mirror, Chang sees what he thinks is his father. Sing Hi discovers the mirror hidden in a vase and when she looks into it, she sees a beautiful girl and becomes jealous. The couple has a loud argument which brings in the neighbors, who quarrel similarly. They consult a priest, who sees a holy man in the mirror and decrees that the mirror must be hung in the temple, after which all make up. RECOMMENDATION: An orchestra allows for many participants, regardless of musical ability. ROYALTY: Free to Plays subscribers. SOURCE: Plescia, Gillian L. (1976, May). The strange and wonderful object. Plays: The Drama Magazine for Young People, pp. 39- 42. SUBJECTS/PLAY TYPE: Folk Tales, China; Bias; Playlet.

2958. 1-3. (+) Whittaker, Violet. **The strange disappearance. CAST:** 5u. **ACTS:** 5. SETTINGS: Outside; street. PLAYING TIME: NA. PLOT: Little Tommy disappears, and the town thinks he's been kidnapped. Teenaged Harry swallows his fear to look for Tommy in the "haunted house." He finds the youngster, who is waiting for the old man who lives in the house to wake up. The old man is very sick, and Harry saves them both. RECOMMENDATION: Harry's bravery is attributed to his belief in God. However, the references to God could be deleted if this were to be used as a simple Halloween play, or just a play about facing fears. ROYALTY: NA. SOURCE: Whittaker, Violet. (1984). Puppet people scripts. Grand Rapids, MI: Baker Book House. SUBJECTS/PLAY TYPE: Christian Drama; Fear; Halloween; Puppet Play.

2959. 7-12. (+) Murray, John. **Strange inheritance. CAST:** 4f, 4m. **ACTS:** 1. SETTINGS: Room. PLAYING TIME: 35 min. PLOT: During the reading of a will, the relatives discover that one of them is a murderer. Each inheritance is revealed by identifying a Shakespearean quote and the murderer is discovered when the results of the bequests are revealed. RECOMMENDATION: Although the Shakespearean word clues may be unfamiliar to some, the fast paced plot and memorable characters will keep everyone interested until the mystery is solved. ROYALTY: None. SOURCE: Murray, John. (1979). Fifteen plays for teenagers. Boston, MA: Plays, Inc. SUBJECTS/PLAY TYPE: Mystery; Comedy.

2960. 4-7. (+) Mauro, Robert. **The strange truth about Mother Goose. CAST:** 5f, 3m. **ACTS:** 1. SETTINGS: Den/study. PLAYING TIME: 7 min. PLOT: Professor Gander is determined to make nursery rhyme characters more marketable. He calls them together to brainstorm but rejects most of their suggestions. The professor continues to reject ideas (that are in reality the classic nursery rhymes) for ridiculous substitutions such as writing about Jack's stamp collection and giving Goldilocks a gaggle of geese. Little Boy Blue tells Gander that a writer's job is to write the truth. This strikes Gander as a novel idea and all is well once more in Mother Gooseland. RECOMMENDATION: This refreshing farce underscores the importance of oral literature's place in our culture as the audience becomes caught up in helping restore the nursery rhyme characters to their rightful place. An often neglected part of the English curriculum is given a boost here. ROYALTY: Free to Plays subscribers. SOURCE: Mauro, Robert. (1979, October). The strange truth about Mother Goose. Plays: The Drama Magazine for Young People, pp. 47-50. SUBJECTS/PLAY TYPE: Mother Goose; Nursery Rhymes; Oral Literature; Comedy.

2961. 5-8. (+) Rembrandt, Elaine. **Stranger in the land: The story of Ruth.** (Book of Ruth) **CAST:** 3f, 3m, Su. **ACTS:** 1. SETTINGS: Trail; market; gate. PLAYING TIME: 20 min. PLOT: No longer able to support his family in drought-stricken Judah, Elimelech takes his wife, Naomi, and two sons to Moab, where he opens a business and prospers. When her sons die, Naomi, now a widow, returns to Judah accompanied by her daughter-in-law, Ruth. Despite Naomi's warning that she will be an outcast in Judah, Ruth, a Moabitess, remains with her. As time passes, Ruth marries a kinsman of Elimelech, and they have a son, Obed, whose grandson, David, becomes a mighty king. RECOMMENDATION: The strength of this faithful adaptation lies in its portrayal of the loyal and caring relationship between Naomi and her daughter-in-law, Ruth. They arouse both sympathy for their plight as widows and admiration for their courage to make their way alone. Through the use of the Chorus as narrator, the story is told in a short, concise manner without sacrificing the development of plot and characterization. ROYALTY: NA. SOURCE: Rembrandt, Elaine. (1981). Heroes, heroines and holidays - plays for Jewish youth. Denver, CO: Alternatives in religious education. SUBJECTS/ PLAY TYPE: Jewish Drama; Courage; Loyalty.

2962. 6-9. (+) James, Grace A. **Strangers in town. CAST:** 3f, 1m. **ACTS:** 1. SETTINGS: Living room. PLAYING TIME: 30 min. PLOT: T-2 (female looking robot on a spy mission from another planet), has been separated from T-1, her male-looking companion robot. T-1 reveals that his experiences on earth have given him human feelings, which he introduces to T-2. The two plan to escape their master to live on Earth. Their plans are delayed by a census taker who confuses them with her questions, and a landlady who mistakes their feedback machine for a fancy television. When the robots' heat sensors warn them that their masters are coming, the landlady assumes there is a fire and evacuates the building. During the ensuing commotion, the robots elude their masters and escape to live on Earth as humans. RECOMMENDATION: This holds very little suspense, but is amusing. Inexperienced actors could use the interactions between the two robots to become more aware of emotions often taken for granted. **ROYALTY**: $10. **SOURCE**: James, Grace A. (1983). Strangers in town. Denver, CO: Pioneer Drama Service. **SUBJECTS/PLAY TYPE**: Science Fiction; Robots; Emotions; Drama.

2963. 1-6. (+) Dias, Earl J. **The strawberry quest.** **CAST**: 5f, 4m. **ACTS**: 2. **SETTINGS**: Throne room. **PLAYING TIME**: 20 min. **PLOT**: The prince is unwilling to marry anyone but a woman who can bring him strawberries in January. With the help of the court magician, (who froze some strawberries at the end of the growing season), Elizabeth (a commoner) provides the necessary fruit and the Prince is happily betrothed to her. **RECOMMENDATION**: Riddles, humorous interactions between the Prince and his suitors, and unobtrusive speeches about the pettiness of wealth make this a delightful tale with a modern message. **ROYALTY**: Free to Plays Subscribers. **SOURCE**: Dias, Earl J. (1980, November). The strawberry quest. Plays: The Drama Magazine for Young People, pp. 43-51. **SUBJECTS/PLAY TYPE**: Folk Tale Motifs; Comedy.

2964. 7-11. (+) Aiken, Joan. **Street. CAST**: 5f, 5m, Su. **ACTS**: 2. **SETTINGS**: Street; Kitchens; Bar; Cellar; Forest. **PLAYING TIME**: NA. **PLOT**: Street is a town which is a street bounded on one side by a forest ruled by seven magic bulls, and bounded on the other side by a wide, slimy river. In the not so distant past, an evil little boy stole the key to Street's only drawbridge and ran away. Now, years later, the boy has returned to find the town peopled by emotional and physical cripples, the former caused by the bitter animosity which has grown between the people who live on either sides of the street; the latter caused by the speeding trucks on the street. One young couple has fallen in love and communicates through sign language across the street. They are determined to cross and be together. This is eventually accomplished. **RECOMMENDATION**: This is a complex and disturbing drama, with elements of **Romeo and Juliet** and **West Side Story**. The many Britishisms would need to be Americanized for general audiences. But the themes of bridging communications gaps and the strength and courage of pure young love are movingly demonstrated. **ROYALTY**: NA. **SOURCE**: Aiken, Joan. (1978). Street. New York, NY: Viking Press. **SUBJECTS/PLAY TYPE**: Communication; Drama.

2965. K-6. (-) Korty, Carol. **Stretch the bench.** (Mad merry men of Gotham) **CAST**: 4u. **ACTS**: 1. **SETTINGS**: Bare stage, props. **PLAYING TIME**: NA. **PLOT**: Four friends fight over who gets the right to sit down on a bench. They finally stretch the bench to make room for everyone. **RECOMMENDATION**: In this musical chairs comedy, reminiscent of a Laurel and Hardy scene, the point is lost in the attempts at physical comedy. **ROYALTY**: None. **SOURCE**: Korty, Carol. (1977). Silly soup: Ten zany plays. New York, NY: Charles Scribner's Sons. **SUBJECTS/PLAY TYPE**: Comedy; Adaptation.

2966. 5-10. (+) Gotwalt, Helen Louise Miller. **Strictly Puritan. CAST**: 8f, 3m. **ACTS**: 1. **SETTINGS**: Recreation room. **PLAYING TIME**: 30 min. **PLOT**: Children try to prepare a Thanksgiving feast using strictly authentic methods. They find that they can't kill a turkey on private property and realize that it is the spirit that counts. **RECOMMENDATION**: The common problem of reconciling ritual with the spirit of a holiday is very well presented in this cleverly designed plot. **ROYALTY**: Free to Plays subscribers. **SOURCE**: Gotwalt, Helen Louis Miller. (1983, November). Strictly Puritan. Plays: The Drama Magazine for Young People, pp. 33-38. **SUBJECTS/PLAY TYPE**: Thanksgiving; Pilgrims; Playlet.

2967. 8-12. (+) Dixon, Michael Bigelow & Smith, Valerie. **Striking out! CAST**: 6f, 8m. **ACTS**: 1. **SETTINGS**: Baseball dugout. **PLAYING TIME**: NA. **PLOT**: The Angels are losing a baseball game to rival Daredevils. Two lowly substitute players provide a running commentary on the game while coping with the little sister of the Angels' Captain's. When the Angels are at bat, the dugout becomes a boiling pot of juvenile frustration and anger. **RECOMMENDATION**: Although dated nicknames (Cheech and Chong, Darth Umpire) will need updating, as a comedy, this gets past first base often. **ROYALTY**: $35. **SOURCE**: Dixon, Michael Bigelow & Smith, Valerie. (1977). Striking out! New Orleans, LA: Anchorage Press. **SUBJECTS/PLAY TYPE**: Baseball; Comedy.

2968. 4-8. (+) Kift, Roy. **Stronger than superman.** **CAST**: 2f, 6m. **ACTS**: 2. **SETTINGS**: Living/Dining room; empty plot of land; cinema foyer. **PLAYING TIME**: NA. **PLOT**: Ten year old Chris has spina bifida, is in a wheelchair, and has just moved to a new neighborhood with his family. Kevin is at first wary of getting involved with Chris, but quickly accepts him. Kevin defends Chris against others in the new neighborhood, and helps him to educate a social worker who wishes to put Chris in a home to relieve his mother's workload. There is a confrontation about Chris entering a local theater which ends in Kevin being struck by a car and subsequently confined temporarily to a wheelchair. The play concludes with Chris being accepted into the new neighborhood. **RECOMMENDATION**: This excellent British musical is very educational without being didactic or patronizing. Unfortunately, one of the songs includes the phrase, "deaf or dumb." This could easily be changed. **ROYALTY**: NA. **SOURCE**: Kift, Roy. (1981). Stronger than superman. Derbyshire, England: Amber Lane Press. **SUBJECTS/PLAY TYPE**: Spina Bifida; Disabilities; Comedy; Musical.

2969. 1-4. (+) Howard, Helen L. **The strongest being.** **CAST**: 2f, 2m, 4u. **ACTS**: 1. **SETTINGS**: Garden. **PLAYING TIME**: 15 min. **PLOT**: Mesume and Dedmu wish to marry. Mesume's father, Otosan, wishes the best for his daughter and seeks the strongest entity to be her marriage partner. He goes to the Sun, who defers to the Cloud, who is able to hide the Sun. The Cloud defers to the Wind, who defers to the Wall, who defers to Demu, who can tear down the Wall. Otosan consents to the marriage of Dedmu and Mesume. **RECOMMENDATION**: Charming and engaging, this contains some challenging Japanese words. This is intended for puppets, but could be performed on stage. **ROYALTY**: Free to Plays subscribers. **SOURCE**: Howard, Helen L. (1984, April). The strongest being. Plays: The Drama Magazine for Young People, pp. 53-55. SUBJECTS/PLAY TYPE: Strength; Folk Tales, Japan; Puppet Play.

2970. 9-12. (+) Way, Brian. **The struggle.** CAST: 2f, 4m. ACTS: 2. SETTINGS: Room; city street. PLAYING TIME: NA. PLOT: Adam and his friends are dancing when an argument ensues after Adam questions the meaning of doing the same thing, night after night. Adam leaves to seek the meaning of his existence and enters a dream sequence. He meets voices which ask him questions he cannot answer, and Knowledge, who tells him that through knowledge comes rank, wealth and power. He meets Authority, who puts him to work, and Petty Authority, who harasses him to work faster so as not to waste opportunity. Hope sends Adam on a journey in which he meets Sloth, Geed, Woman, and Man, each with their own view of the world. Hope sends Adam to the city of Vanity Fair with a warning that all who live there hate truth and honesty. There, he meets Miss Meek, who tries to persuade Adam to purchase something, and Mr. Sharp, who takes Adam to the Palace of Good Fortune. Lady Luck offers Adam a comprehensive pass, good for anything in the city. When Adam refuses the pass, he is arrested and tried before Justice Petty. When Faithful comes to Adam's defense, he realizes that he wants to go back. He has learned that boredom in life can be avoided if people view their own lives creatively and view others as individuals. Exiting the dream sequence, Adam calls his friends back and asks them to put on another record. RECOMMENDATION: Intended to be performed by adults for young adults, this play includes British expressions and trade names which may need to be Americanized. The well drawn personifications of personality traits and virtues allow the important and universal message that life must be approached with passion to be delivered with drama, style and grace. This is superb. ROYALTY: $45. SOURCE: Way, Brian. (1977). The struggle. Boston, MA: Baker's Plays. SUBJECTS/PLAY TYPE: Happiness; Self Respect; Life; Drama.

2971. 4-8. (+) Kehret, Peg. **Student sabbatical.** CAST: 1u. ACTS: 1. SETTINGS: None. PLAYING TIME: NA. PLOT: Outlining his plans if he were ever to have an entire year to himself, a youngster dreams of the day that students, as well as teachers could be granted sabbaticals. RECOMMENDATION: An interesting concept is cleverly outlined. ROYALTY: NA. SOURCE: Kehret, Peg. (1986). Winning monologs for young actors. Colorado Springs, CO: Meriwether Pub. SUBJECTS/PLAY TYPE: Sabbaticals; Monologue.

2972. 1-4. (+) Forquer, Nancy. **Substitute Santa.** CAST: 3m, 60u. ACTS: 2. SETTINGS: Bare stage, props. PLAYING TIME: 60 min. PLOT: Spike and Wimpy (greedy, devious and inept) hilariously fail in several attempts to kidnap Santa and his gifts. After accidentally injuring Santa, the two must fill his role as dispenser of gifts throughout the world. The journey, which allows them to glimpse Christmas customs and holiday cheer around the world, develops within them a respect for the feelings of others. They deduce that the secret of Christmas

lies in giving, not getting, and they form friendships with children from a variety of cultures. RECOMMENDATION: This colorful pageant would be ideal for a school Christmas program because of its versatility, and its involvement of many children with many levels of performing ability. It includes choral pieces, solos, cheers and dances. ROYALTY: $70. SOURCE: Forquer, Nancy. (1986). Substitute Santa. Franklin, OH: Eldridge Pub. Co. SUBJECTS/PLAY TYPE: Christmas; Comedy; Musical.

2973. 12. (-) O'Brien, John. **Success.** CAST: 8f, 3m. ACTS: 1. SETTINGS: Kitchen; living room; apartment. PLAYING TIME: NA. PLOT: On his 30th birthday, Andy's parents and wife, Rosalie, try to talk Andy into giving up his unsuccessful career as an actor and taking over the family business. Rosalie wants to have children and a normal life, but Andy refuses. Ten years later, Andy's brother, Francis, and their widowed mother, discuss Francis's unsuccessful writing career and Andy's unsuccessful acting career. In that day's mail, a $1,000 check arrives for Francis from **New Yorker** magazine. Francis' joy is overshadowed by a letter from Andy telling them he has signed a $50,000 movie contract. Ten years later, a group of young women gather in Andy's apartment for a surprise party to celebrate Andy's winning of an Oscar. After some conversation, the young women go into the kitchen to eat. Andy shoots himself holding his Oscar. RECOMMENDATION: This is about the complex psychological issues of mother-son relationships, sibling rivalry, artistic temperament, and marriage. It is too sparse and short to develop any one of these themes satisfactorily. ROYALTY: $15. SOURCE: O'Brien, John. (1984). Success. Chicago, IL: Dramatic Pub. Co. SUBJECTS/PLAY TYPE: Success; Family Relationships; Suicide; Drama.

2974. 9-12. (+) Cook, Pat. **Such a nice little kitty.** CAST: 1f, 1m, Su. ACTS: 1. SETTINGS: Living room. PLAYING TIME: NA. PLOT: Walter Hebert is at his wit's end. Cleopatra, the Hebert's 57 pound cat, is driving him insane with her howling and meowing. When his wife tries to stop him from killing the cat, he accidentally kills his wife instead. As the police officer prepares to take Hebert to the "Happy Academy," he takes the "nice little kitty" along to cheer Hebert up. RECOMMENDATION: Although the characters are somewhat stereotyped, the dialogue is snappy and clever, especially the witty banter between the husband and wife. The "killing of Edna" is a callous twist to this amusing farce. ROYALTY: $15. SOURCE: Cook, Pat. Such a nice little kitty. Chicago, IL: Dramatic Pub. Co. SUBJECTS/PLAY TYPE: Cats; Comedy.

2975. 7-12. (+) Bruce, Mark. **Suffering for art.** CAST: 2m. ACTS: 1. SETTINGS: Artist's studio. PLAYING TIME: 15 min. PLOT: Because an artist has not paid his phone bill for a year, a repairman comes to remove the phone of the eccentric and impoverished painter. Just in time, the last phone call brings a sale of one of his paintings, and the phone remains. RECOMMENDATION: This pokes fun at the starving artist image. Although it is funny, there is no message and the whole point seems to be merely to provide some humor at the expense of artists. ROYALTY: Free to Plays subscribers. SOURCE: Bruce, Mark. (1983, November). Suffering for art. Plays: The Drama Magazine for Young People, pp. 57-60. SUBJECTS/PLAY TYPE: Artists; Comedy; Skit.

2976. 7-12. (+) Sawyer-Young, Kat. Suicide. CAST: 1f. ACTS: 1. SETTINGS: None. PLAYING TIME: 1 min. PLOT: Diane's male friend kills himself because Diane is not attentive enough. RECOMMENDATION: As Diane wishes she had known how her actions affected her friend, she underscores the importance of communication. ROYALTY: None. SOURCE: Sawyer-Young, Kat. (1987). Minute monologues for contemporary teens. Boston, MA: Baker's Plays. SUBJECTS/PLAY TYPE: Suicide; Monologue.

2977. 12. (+) Bond, Edward. Summer. CAST: 3f, 2m, Su. ACTS: 1. SETTINGS: Balcony; island. PLAYING TIME: NA. PLOT: The lives of two women from different social classes were drastically changed by the German occupation of their country during World War II. Although the women lived separate lives after the war, they met each year for summer vacations at their war time home. Forty years after the war's conclusion, during one of the summer vacation reunions, one of the woman's terminal illness, coupled with the appearance of a former German soldier evokes bitter war memories for both. These events lead the women to reappraise their relationship and examine the profound impact the war has had on their lives. RECOMMENDATION: This is a revealing examination of the drastic and long lasting consequences of war. Issues such as death, class conflicts, war, and extramarital sex are frankly confronted within the play, which depends on dialogue and not action. The dialogue is laden with medical terminology which could further burden younger audiences. However, mature audiences would encounter an extremely interesting and provocative play. ROYALTY: $60. SOURCE: Bond, Edward. (1982). Summer. Woodstock, IL: Dramatic Pub. Co. SUBJECTS/PLAY TYPE: Death; World War II; Friendship; War; Drama.

2978. 9-12. (+) Ingalls, Jeremy. Summer liturgy. CAST: 12f, 15m. ACTS: 1. SETTINGS: Cove. PLAYING TIME: NA. PLOT: Vivian and her grandparents, Trevelyan and Nana, travel from America to Cornwall, England, the home of their ancestors. Against the backdrop of the Cornish legend of the Christ child's visit to the area with His parents, Vivian learns to accept the deaths of her parents. As a symbol of her resignation, she gives a brass cup, a gift from her mother years before, to Brian, a village boy who has lost his father and grandfather. Having reaffirmed their faith in God's love, grandmother and granddaughter are able to bear the death of Trevelyan, who has a heart attack as they return to the boat. RECOMMENDATION: With fastidiously detailed production notes on costuming and acting nuances, this Christian drama should only be attempted by experienced adult actors. The blending of the past and present makes the plot confusing at times, as much of the action is carried out in mime and song. However, for mature audiences, this is a thought provoking, symbolic representation of Christian ideology. ROYALTY: NA. SOURCE: Ingalls, Jeremy. (1985). Summer liturgy. Tucson, AZ: Capstone Editions. SUBJECTS/PLAY TYPE: Faith; Folk Tales, Celtic; Death; Christian Drama.

2979. 5-12. (+) Smith, Jacqueline V. Summer soldier: Pamphleteer Thomas Paine's inspiring words. CAST: 3f, 12m, Su. ACTS: 1. SETTINGS: Street; campsite. PLAYING TIME: 15 min. PLOT: The attitudes of the citizens of the colonies (in January, 1776) and of the soldiers (in December, 1776) are depicted as they discuss Thomas Paine's famous pamphlet calling for independence from England and his essay, "The American Crisis." RECOMMENDATION: Excerpts from Paine's pamphlets add to the patriotic spirit and familiarize students with literary classics of U.S. history. ROYALTY: Free to Plays subscribers. SOURCE: Kamerman, Sylvia E. (1987). Patriotic and historical plays for young people. Boston, MA: Plays, Inc. SUBJECTS/PLAY TYPE: Revolution, U.S.; Paine, Thomas; Playlet.

2980. K-4*. (+) Boiko, Claire. Sun up! CAST: 1f, 4m, 16u. ACTS: 1. SETTINGS: Outdoors. PLAYING TIME: 15 min. PLOT: It is late April and the puddle jumper chorus bemoans the endless rain and dreary days. Various individuals try to command, coax, and conjure the sun out from behind the clouds, all to no avail. Finally, Father Time appears and reveals a secret: April will be followed by May. As he speaks, the sun appears. RECOMMENDATION: This is a cheerful little season changer, whose choral rendering and movement (of umbrellas) beg to be choreographed. ROYALTY: None. SOURCE: Boiko, Claire. (1985). Children's plays for creative actors. Boston, MA: Plays, Inc. SUBJECTS/PLAY TYPE: Spring; Playlet.

2981. 4-8. (+) Bradley, Virginia. Sunday at Meadowlake Manor. CAST: 2f, 20u. ACTS: 1. SETTINGS: Parlor. PLAYING TIME: NA. PLOT: Residents of a retirement home are unexpectedly youthful when no staff or visitors are present. RECOMMENDATION: This adapts easily to a girl or boy cast and to any number of actors. There are few speaking parts since the skit is mostly visual. ROYALTY: None. SOURCE: Bradley, Virginia. (1975). Is there an actor in the house? New York, NY: Dodd, Mead. SUBJECTS/PLAY TYPE: Elderly; Retirement; Comedy; Pantomime.

2982. 7-12. (-) Nydam, Ken. Sunday? Ok! CAST: 4u. ACTS: 1. SETTINGS: None. PLAYING TIME: NA. PLOT: The only time that the youths are willing to devote to social events is Sunday, when the planned event will get them out of church. RECOMMENDATION: This seems pointless. ROYALTY: NA. SOURCE: Altena, Hans. (1980). The playbook for Christian theater. Grand Rapids, MI: Baker Book House. SUBJECTS/PLAY TYPE: Church; Reader's Theater; Christian Drama.

2983. 7-10. (+) McCusker, Paul. The Sunday school teachers. CAST: 2f. ACTS: 1. SETTINGS: Living room. PLAYING TIME: NA. PLOT: Two Sunday School teachers, Edna and Kate have different methods of communicating with children, as well as different goals. Edna uses gimmicks to increase attendance in her class, because large numbers on Sunday morning is her ultimate goal. Kate values personal contact, and shares her own faith with her class members. She tactfully reveals to Edna that one of Edna's students has come to her with a question about Christ, having felt insecure about asking Edna. The skit ends humorously, as Edna sadly agrees with Kate and scraps her plans for next week's Sodom and Gomorrah lesson, dramatized with her husband being turned into a pillar of salt. RECOMMENDATION: Although the lesson is directed at adults, teenagers and teachers may learn that value is measured by spiritual depth and not gimmicks. ROYALTY: NA. SOURCE: McCusker, Paul. (1982). Souvenirs: Comedies and dramas for Christian fellowship. Boston, MA: Baker's Plays. SUBJECTS/PLAY TYPE: Christian Drama; Education; Skit.

2984. 7-12. (-) Nolan, Paul T. **Sunshine and smiles.** CAST: 4f, 3m. ACTS: 1. SETTINGS: Beach. PLAYING TIME: 25 min. PLOT: After a fight with her boyfriend, Gloria finds a magic jinnee in the ring that he gave her and she wishes for a world of sunshine and smiles. Gloria finds the magic world too boring and wishes herself back to the real world, where she makes an effort to change her own attitudes about life. RECOMMENDATION: While the theme is admirable, characters are flat and the hallmarks of the fantasy world of smiles and sunshine are not consistent with the descriptions. ROYALTY: Free to Plays subscribers. SOURCE: Nolan, Paul T. (1975, March). Sunshine and smiles. Plays: The Drama Magazine for Young People, pp. 37-46. SUBJECTS/PLAY TYPE: Attitudes; Playlet.

2985. 7-12. (-) Hatton, Thomas J. **Super dooper man.** CAST: 1f, 3m, 1u. ACTS: 1. SETTINGS: Newsroom. PLAYING TIME: 10 min. PLOT: Bart Brent (mild mannered newspaper reporter) changes into Super Dooper Man when he learns that the Kryptonite Kid is coming to steal Super's alma mater's secret game plans for the opposing team. The Kid immobilizes Super with a piece of kryptonite and locks Super and Lola Lark, another reporter, in the newsroom. Lola yells "school spirit," changes into Mary Wonderful, Girl Crime Fighter, and saves the day. RECOMMENDATION: Although this pep skit has some humorous dialogue, it is just too silly. ROYALTY: Free to Plays subscribers. SOURCE: Hatton, Thomas J. (1983, January/February). Super dooper man. Plays: The Drama Magazine for Young People, pp. 70-73. SUBJECTS/PLAY TYPE: Pep Rallies; School Spirit; Skit.

2986. 7-12. (-) Murray, John. **The super duper market.** CAST: 1f. ACTS: 1. SETTINGS: Bare stage. PLAYING TIME: NA. PLOT: A housewife tries to pick up a few items at the supermarket, but her husband clutters their shopping cart with impulse purchases. RECOMMENDATION: It might be interesting to cast this play with a male to see if it can transcend the apparent sexism. ROYALTY: None. SOURCE: Murray, John. (1982). Modern monologues for young people. Boston, MA: Plays, Inc. SUBJECTS/PLAY TYPE: Shopping; Monologue.

2987. 3-6. (+) Hager, Betty & Bock, Fred. **Super gift from heaven.** CAST: 7f, 9m, 4u. ACTS: 1. SETTINGS: Toy store. PLAYING TIME: NA. PLOT: The toys in a toy store come alive at night and talk and sing about what it is like to be a Christmas gift. The members of an antique Nativity scene tell the story of the first Christmas. They all agree that Jesus is the Super Gift from Heaven. RECOMMENDATION: This incorporates the excitement of Christmas gifts with elements of a traditional Nativity play. The play has six original songs and three traditional tunes, and would be a good choice for a large church group with musical ability. ROYALTY: None. SOURCE: Hager, Betty & Bock, Fred. (1980). Super gift from heaven. Tarzana, CA: Fred Bock Music. SUBJECTS/PLAY TYPE: Christmas; Musical.

2988. 7-10. (+) Deary, Terence. **Super village.** CAST: 1m, Su. ACTS: 1. SETTINGS: Command posts. PLAYING TIME: 50 min. PLOT: The last people on earth must build a new life with very few resources after a nuclear holocaust. Under the authority of a commanding officer, the participating students are required to divide into groups and accept responsibility for the survival of the entire population by setting up a village. They are given an opportunity to experience relationships with authority figures, with each other in group situations, and between groups, where there exists the potential for rivalry or cooperation. RECOMMENDATION: This is a very valuable learning experience. ROYALTY: None. SOURCE: Deary, Terence. (1977). Teaching through theatre. New York, NY: Samuel French. SUBJECTS/PLAY TYPE: Nuclear War; Cooperation; Participation Play.

2989. 7-12. (+) Jackson, R. Eugene. **Superkid: The play.** CAST: 7f, 3m, 5u. ACTS: 3. SETTINGS: School newspaper office. PLAYING TIME: 45 min. PLOT: A high school journalism class, frustrated by a lack of news, decides to expose the true identity of the crime fighting hero, Superkid. Disguised as a new student at the school, Superkid almost reveals himself through blunders and slips of the tongue, but he manages to maintain his cover during a crisis in the newsroom. Then, a teenage genius holds the reporters hostage in the newsroom while he demonstrates his new inventions and their power to destroy the world. Superkid, rendered harmless and obedient by the genius, is sent to find a special crystal necessary to make one of the genius's weapons totally operational. When Superkid returns, he tricks the genius and saves the day. Everything goes back to normal at the paper and the staff is unable find a news story because nothing ever happens. Superkid's identity is preserved. RECOMMENDATION: In this action packed, enjoyable spoof of programs and shows that feature super heroes, most of the situations are delightfully absurd and silly. Some subtle messages come through about properly developing and using one's talents in a constructive manner and about school being boring only for those who are blind to life and the people around them. ROYALTY: $35. SOURCE: Jackson, R. Eugene. (1980). Superkid: The Play. Schulenberg, TX: I.E. Clark. SUBJECTS/PLAY TYPE: Super Heroes; Fantasy; Comedy.

2990. 4-7*. (+) Smith, Gary H. **Superstudent and the case of the water pistol: A weird play.** CAST: 5f, 7m, Su. ACTS: 3. SETTINGS: Classroom. PLAYING TIME: NA. PLOT: In the absence of the teacher during the science project presentations, Fenwick Foulfellow, the class bully, uses a water pistol to spray fellow students with a secret potion which causes them to obey his commands. He then plots to wreck the school. Mild mannered Melvin changes into "Superstudent," and he and Claudia solve the mystery of what happened to their classmates and teacher. Foulfellow is eventually identified as the culprit, and he is sprayed with the secret potion as punishment. RECOMMENDATION: In spite of the unflattering characterization of figures of authority, this short comedy ridiculing school bullies is amusing. ROYALTY: $30. SOURCE: Smith, Gary H. (1975). Superstudent and the case of the water pistol. Franklin, OH: Eldridge Pub. Co. SUBJECTS/PLAY TYPE: School; Bullies; Comedy.

2991. 7-12. (+) Sawyer-Young, Kat. **Surfing.** CAST: 1m. ACTS: 1. SETTINGS: None. PLAYING TIME: 1 min. PLOT: Keith describes the exhilaration of riding a big wave. RECOMMENDATION: For those who surf, this will emit good vibrations. ROYALTY: None. SOURCE: Sawyer-Young, Kat. (1987). Minute monologues for contemporary teens. Boston, MA: Baker's Plays. SUBJECTS/PLAY TYPE: Surfing; Monologue.

2992. 4-7. (-) Bradley, Virginia. **Surprise.** CAST: Su. ACTS: 1. SETTINGS: Classroom. PLAYING TIME: NA. PLOT: On the first day of April, a mysterious coded message (looflirpa or April Fool spelled backwards) is delivered to the classroom. RECOMMENDATION: The rhyming dialogue is stilted, and the surprise solution is no surprise. ROYALTY: None. SOURCE: Bradley, Virginia. (1975). Is there an actor in the house? New York, NY: Dodd, Mead. SUBJECTS/PLAY TYPE: April Fool's Day; Mystery; Skit.

2993. 6-8. (+) Bigelow, Sylvia Weld. (Graveson, Caroline) **Susan and the witch.** (Susan and the witch) CAST: 5f, 5m. ACTS: 1. SETTINGS: Bare stage. PLAYING TIME: NA. PLOT: Two young people, Susan and Tom Abbot, must choose between staying in the Church of England or following their parents to become Quakers. When an old woman (Molly), whom the villagers believe to be a witch, is taunted by her friends, Susan, encouraged by sensible, loving parents befriends the old woman. The villagers are ready to believe that the girl, too, has sold her soul to the devil. However, the conclusion is a warm scene of neighborliness and caring at Molly's bedside. RECOMMENDATION: The theme is tolerance and the point is made clearly and powerfully. However, strong religious overtones make this play inappropriate for a public school production. ROYALTY: $15. SOURCE: Bigelow, Sylvia Weld. (1985). Susan and the witch. Woodstock, IL: Dramatic Pub. Co. SUBJECTS/PLAY TYPE: Quaker Drama; Witchcraft; Adaptation.

2994. 7-12. (+) Tasca, Jules & Drachman, Ted. **Susan B!** CAST: 5f, 16m, Su. ACTS: 1. SETTINGS: Bare stage. PLAYING TIME: NA. PLOT: The play highlights several key moments in Susan B. Anthony's historic fight for human rights. When her brother is sent to college instead of her, she turns to teaching school but is paid less than the male teachers. She then joins the women's rights organization which circulates a petition for equal salary rights. The legislators laugh when she presents her petition but she is supported by Horace Greeley. Finally, she votes in a barber shop and is put on trial. The jury comes back with a verdict of guilty but the trial produces publicity for her cause. RECOMMENDATION: The brief scenes are compelling and the upbeat music prevents the play from becoming too melodramatic. About half of the dialogue occurs in songs. ROYALTY: Upon application. SOURCE: Tasca, Jules, & Drachman, Ted. (1982). Susan B! Woodstock, IL: Dramatic Pub. Co. SUBJECTS/PLAY TYPE: Anthony, Susan B.; Women's Rights; Musical.

2995. 7-12. (+) Van Horn, Bill. **Susan, the sad-eyed seamstress, or this gem's not for burning.** CAST: 5f, 5m, Su. ACTS: 1. SETTINGS: Factory. PLAYING TIME: 30 min. PLOT: Samuel Squasher, a mean factory owner, mistreats his workers. Susan, his employee, vacillates between accepting Samuel's marriage proposal and offer of promotion or the marriage proposal of her noble coworker, Melvin. A rich buyer arrives, places a large order, and leaves, only to discover her big diamond has disappeared. Susan and Melvin realize the lump of coal hastily thrown into the stove is the lost diamond. Melvin rescues it, is rewarded with sufficient money to buy the factory and remodel it, and marry Susan. RECOMMENDATION: This farce contains moments of clever repartee between the major characters and some bright spots such as the tricycle-riding messenger's appearances. It is, however, slow moving with many conflicting and underdeveloped subplots. Juxtaposition of puns and continuing references to modern commercials and historical labor problems may be confusing to younger groups. ROYALTY: $25. SOURCE: Van Horn, Bill. (1979). Susan, the sad-eyed seamstress, or this gem's not for burning. Franklin, OH: Eldridge Pub. Co. SUBJECTS/PLAY TYPE: Labor Disputes; Melodrama.

2996. 1-12. (+) Kurtz, Jack. **Susie and the Christmas soup.** CAST: 2f, 8m. ACTS: 1. SETTINGS: Bare stage. PLAYING TIME: NA. PLOT: Susie has grown up in a comfortable home with few worries. To her, Christmas is about exchanging money and material goods. However, this year, her father has lost his job and Susan believes that Christmas will not come to the family since they cannot afford it. She decides to save her lunch money by getting lunch at a soup kitchen for a week. She becomes friends with the poor people who eat there and they help her to understand Christmas and life. Her father finds a new job, letting everything return to the way it was, except that Susan remembers her new friends and their lessons. RECOMMENDATION: Although the fairy tale ending may not be true to life, the story's message rings true. ROYALTY: None for first performance. SOURCE: Kurtz, Jack. (1979). Gargoyles, plastic balls and soup. Boston, MA: Baker's Plays. SUBJECTS/PLAY TYPE: Christmas; Love; Generosity; Reader's Theater.

2997. 7-12. (+) Kelly, Tim. (Prest, Thomas) **Sweeney Todd, demon barber of the barbary coast.** (The string of pearls) **CAST:** 11f, 9m, Su. **ACTS:** 3. **SETTINGS:** None. **PLAYING TIME:** NA. **PLOT:** Sweeney Todd (a barber) lures wealthy customers into his shop, kills them, and keeps their valuables. He is exposed by the respectable citizens of the area, and his own insanity leads him to admit his crimes. **RECOMMENDATION:** This non-musical parody of the melodramas of the 1890s was freely adapted from a combination of Prest's novel and Pitt's classic stage melodrama. Timing and delivery are essential to preserve the humor. **ROYALTY:** $35. **SOURCE:** Kelly, Tim. (1978). Sweeney Todd, demon barber of the barbary coast. Schulenburg, TX: I.E. Clark. **SUBJECTS/PLAY TYPE:** Murder; Melodrama; Adaptation.

2998. 10-12. (-) Hull, Raymond. (Pitt, George Dibdin) **Sweeney Todd, the demon barber of Fleet Street. CAST:** 3f, 3m, Su. **ACTS:** 1. **SETTINGS:** Pie shop; barber shop. **PLAYING TIME:** 45 min. **PLOT:** Sweeney Todd (the demon proprietor of the barber shop), and Claudetta Mincey (owner of the pie shop), plot to make enough money to sail to Upper Canada. Sweeney Todd murders his customers, and then drops them through the floor into the basement where they are used as "Long Pig" in pies. A young apprentice working in the pie shop and a health inspector stumble onto the scheme and Sweeney Todd becomes his own victim. **RECOMMENDATION:** The development of characters is quite shallow and the sequence of events is not well developed. Too many important parts of the original have been left out. **ROYALTY:** $25. **SOURCE:** Hull, Raymond. (1980). Sweeney Todd, the demon barber of Fleet Street. Denver, CO: Pioneer Drama Service. **SUBJECTS/PLAY TYPE:** Murder; Melodrama; Adaptation.

2999. 6-7. (-) Malkind, Margaret. **Sweet liberty. CAST:** 8f, 11m, Su. **ACTS:** 1. **SETTINGS:** Clubhouse. **PLAYING TIME:** 20 min. **PLOT:** A group of boys, 13-14 years old, vote on whether or not to splinter from an established group, the Lobsters, and create their own group, the Freedom Dudes. Throughout the discussion, Brains interrupts with corny jokes. Several girls appear and want to become members, and even the leader of the Lobsters, Gorgeous George, and several members of his group arrive. After heated bickering over which group is stronger, the counselor, Mr. Nolan, suggests participation by both groups in a pie throwing contest at the July 4th festivities. The girls devise an everybody wins scheme where they will bake each gang member's favorite pie so that after being hit with it, the gang member will eat the pie instead of throwing one. **RECOMMENDATION:** There is very little plot throughout this skit, which is fraught with bad puns, corny jokes, sexist remarks and weak attempts to make a point about gangs. This play is totally irrelevant and misleading. **ROYALTY:** Free to Plays subscribers. **SOURCE:** Malkind, Margaret. (1976, November). Sweet liberty. Plays: The Drama Magazine for Young People, pp. 79-86. **SUBJECTS/PLAY TYPE:** Comedy; Gangs; Skit.

3000. 3-8. (+) Thane, Adele. (Andersen, Hans Christian) **The swineherd.** (The swineherd) **CAST:** 9f, 5m. **ACTS:** 1. **SETTINGS:** Orchard; pig sty. **PLAYING TIME:** 20 min. **PLOT:** As a princess and her maids play adjacent to a pig sty, the king announces a messenger bearing two gifts from a prince. The spoiled princess is not impressed by the gifts (a perfect rose and a nightingale), which she feels are too common. Meanwhile, the anxious prince has disguised himself as a swineherd in hopes of winning the princess' favor by attracting her with a cooking pot and a rattle which play tunes. The prince agrees to give the princess the rattle for five kisses. The king is incensed that his daughter has rejected the gifts of a prince and has accepted those of a swineherd. The spoiled princess realizes her insensitivity and wants to apologize to both the swineherd and the prince. The play ends when the swineherd reveals his disguise, and the delighted princess gives the prince her hand in marriage. **RECOMMENDATION:** The changing emotions of the characters and the disguise of the principal male character provide interest and variety. **ROYALTY:** Free to Plays subscribers. **SOURCE:** Thane, Adele. (1983). Plays from famous stories and fairy tales. Boston, MA: Plays Inc. **SUBJECTS/PLAY TYPE:** Folk Tales, Denmark; Gifts; Marriage; Adaptation.

3001. K-4. (+) Bauer, Caroline Feller. (Andersen, Hans Christian) **The swineherd.** (The swineherd) **CAST:** 4f, 2m, 3u. **ACTS:** 1. **SETTINGS:** Great hall; pigsty; outside the kingdom. **PLAYING TIME:** 15 min. **PLOT:** An mpoverished prince wants to marry the emperor's daughter. To declare his love, he sends her two gifts: a perfect rose and a nightingale. The spoiled and shallow princess scorns his love. Determined, the prince takes a job at the castle looking after the pigs. In his spare time he makes a magic pot and a music box. The selfish princess, who rejected his earlier beautiful gifts, desires these and agrees to kiss him in exchange for them. The emperor discovers them kissing, spanks the princess, and evicts them from his kingdom. The prince reveals his true identity and, having seen the true, shallow, selfish nature of the princess, goes back to his kingdom and locks the door. **RECOMMENDATION:** Despite the humor, this makes a serious case for appreciating real beauty and rejecting shallowness and greed. This could prompt discussion about values. **ROYALTY:** None. **SOURCE:** Bauer, Caroline Feller. (1987). Presenting reader's theater: Plays and poems to read aloud. New York, NY: H.W. Wilson Co. **SUBJECTS/PLAY TYPE:** Folk Tales, Denmark; Selfishness; Reader's Theater; Adaptation.

3002. 1-12. (+) McCallum, Phyllis. (Wyss, Johann David) **The Swiss family Robinson.** (The Swiss family Robinson) **CAST:** 5f, 6m, 5u. **ACTS:** 3. **SETTINGS:** Beach; tropical island. **PLAYING TIME:** 60 min. **PLOT:** The Robinson family leaves their war-torn country and is shipwrecked on an uninhabited island where they establish a new peaceful life. Two years later a pirate ship lands on their island. A sweet young girl, Jenny, who has been kidnapped by the pirates, escapes and is taken in by the family. She informs the Robinsons of the pirates' plan to shanghai the Robinson men. The Robinsons threaten to blow up the pirates and their ship if they do not leave. Several months later, a ship lands in the bay, and Jenny is reunited with her family. **RECOMMENDATION:** Although the Robinson family is always able to resolve their crises without many setbacks, the play sends a strong message of family unity. Production would be suited to the upper grades due to the length of the play and the musical choreography required. ROYALTY: $35. SOURCE: McCallum, Phyllis. (1976). The Swiss family Robinson. Denver, CO: Pioneer Drama Service. SUBJECTS/PLAY TYPE: Adventure; Family; Adaptation.

3003. 9-12. (+) Irvin, Jeff. **The sword in the styrofoam.** CAST: 1f, 8m, Su. ACTS: 3. SETTINGS: Castle; forest. PLAYING TIME: 45 min. PLOT: A gallant prince rescues Princess Rose from the villainous King, who has kidnapped her and plots to spread misery over the Land of Good and Plenty. RECOMMENDATION: This silly play abounds with hilarious exaggerated characterizations, witty verse, and audience participation for sound effects and singalongs. ROYALTY: $20. SOURCE: Irvin, Jeff. (1987). High noon in styrofoam with timely Nick and Betty Brown. Schulenburg, TX: I.E. Clark. SUBJECTS/PLAY TYPE: Comedy; Melodrama.

3004. 4-6. (+) Van Eeuwen, Karen & Piccard, Joyce. **Symbols of Christmas.** CAST: Su. ACTS: 1. SETTINGS: Street; housefront; church interior. PLAYING TIME: 50 min. PLOT: John, who is one of the Apostles, is transported to twentieth century Earth. He is saddened that many people have forgotten Christ, but he is pleased to know that by the end of the devotional service, a few faithful people know the true meaning of Christmas. RECOMMENDATION: The lesson is taught through symbols and imagery. Children carry gifts, lighted candles, and bells; Mary and Joseph appear carrying a baby doll to symbolize the Holy Family; and in the finale, children form a lighted Christmas tree and a cross of lights. This has enough parts to include all children in the classroom, including speaking and non-speaking parts. ROYALTY: NA. SOURCE: Hendricks, William & Vogel, Cora. (1983). Handbook of Christmas programs. Grand Rapids, MI: Baker Book House. SUBJECTS/PLAY TYPE: Christmas; Worship Program.

3005. K-5. (+) Mauro, Robert. **T.E.: The Earthling.** CAST: 2f, 3m, Su. ACTS: 1. SETTINGS: None. PLAYING TIME: 15 min. PLOT: Billy, the youngest astronaut ever (about 12), is left behind on a planet in deep outer space. Due to his bad sense of direction he must leave a trail of M & M's behind so that he knows where he has been. During his wanderings he meets several natives who briefly tell him about their planet. These Pac-folk are being persecuted by the arch evil Zylons who rule the planet. After a brief chase, Billy and his new friends barely escape the clutches of the Zylons. Billy is then able to fix some equipment and phone home. When his crew returns to pick him up they naturally assume his imagination is working overtime when they hear his story. RECOMMENDATION: This is a very good spoof of E.T. There are some excellent gag lines for younger audiences, but it is also clever enough for adults to enjoy. ROYALTY: Free to Plays subscribers. SOURCE: Mauro, Robert. (1983, October). T.E.: The Earthling. Plays: The Drama Magazine for Young People, pp. 51-55. SUBJECTS/PLAY TYPE: Science Fiction; Aliens; Comedy.

3006. 3-6. (+) Hark, Mildred & McQueen, Noel. **T for turkey.** CAST: 4f, 4m. ACTS: 1. SETTINGS: Kitchen. PLAYING TIME: 10 min. PLOT: To pass time while she prepares the Thanksgiving meal, Grandma suggests that the grandchildren use the alphabet to make up verses about traditional Thanksgiving foods for which they are thankful. Expanding this idea, Grandpa recommends creating verses about anything which makes them feel grateful for living in America. RECOMMENDATION: This provides the basis for discussing concepts suitable for a civics or social studies lesson on patriotism, citizenship, democracy, or freedom. It might also be used as an introduction to new vocabulary words. ROYALTY: Free to Plays subscribers. SOURCE: Hark, Mildred & McQueen, Noel. (1979, November). T for turkey. Plays: The Drama Magazine for Young People, pp. 38-42. SUBJECTS/PLAY TYPE: Thanksgiving; Skit.

3007. 1-3*. (+) Boiko, Claire. **The T party.** CAST: 6f, 5m. ACTS: 1. SETTINGS: Garden. PLAYING TIME: 10 min. PLOT: This "tongue-twister of a tale," details the conception and planning of a lawn party honoring the letter "T." The brainchild of Lady Tiddlewinks and Countess Truffles, the fete boasts a guest list including Titania, Tiny Tim, Thumbelina, Tom Thumb, Tinker Bell, and Toby Tyler. The time is set for two-twenty on Tuesday, and the menu includes teasel tea, tabasco tarts with tomatoes, etc. The dialogue of the guests abounds in t's and the entertainment features tongue-twister bouts. An aggressive mystery guest demands entrance and reveals himself as the letter "T." RECOMMENDATION: This may inspire development of parallel plays or poetry highlighting other letters of the alphabet, a creative assignment for imaginative children. The subtlety of much of the word play avoids a corny, trite effect. The plot is an exercise in thoughtful fabrication of dialogue. ROYALTY: None. SOURCE: Boiko, Claire. (1985). Children's plays for creative actors. Boston, MA: Plays, Inc. SUBJECTS/PLAY TYPE: Alphabet; Tongue Twisters; Comedy.

3008. K-4. (+) Mahlman, Lewis & Jones, David Cadwalader. (Grimm Brothers) **The table, the donkey and the stick.** (The table, the donkey and the stick) CAST: 8u. ACTS: 1. SETTINGS: Living room; carpenter's shop; tapestry shop; inn entry. PLAYING TIME: 25 min. PLOT: Three children leave home to make their fortune so they can support their poor father. Their employers are so happy with their work, that one son receives a table which fills itself with food, and the other receives a donkey who produces gold pieces. An innkeeper tricks the sons and steals their prizes so they have nothing to bring home. The third child, a daughter, has received a stick which will attack on command. When she learns of the innkeeper's deceit, she commands the stick to attack, recovers the table and donkey and returns home to save the family. RECOMMENDATION: The rather elaborate setting in this delightful adaptation can be suggested with painted backdrops, making it simple enough for even the youngest crews. ROYALTY: Free to Plays subscribers. SOURCE: Mahlman, Lewis & Jones, David Cadwalader. (1980). Folk tale plays for puppets. Boston, MA: Plays, Inc.

SUBJECTS/PLAY TYPE: Folk Tales, Germany; Adaptation; Puppet Play.

3009. 8-12. (+) Vornholt, John. **Tahiti, here we come!** CAST: 4f, 3m. ACTS: 1. SETTINGS: Living room. PLAYING TIME: 25 min. PLOT: Judith Longfellow, age 15, compulsively enters contests and wins an all-expense-paid trip to Tahiti from the Nogle Dog Food Co. Two problems exist, however. The winner must be 18 and the family must own a dog, both of which are not true. Judith convinces her older sister, Jennifer, to switch names, and both seek to convince the company representative that "Jasper" the "dog" is hiding under the couch. When Judith and Jennifer "bite" him, the company representative is quickly persuaded to release the prize. RECOMMENDATION: Although the play centers around Judith's compulsion to enter contests, it provides a picture of a family working together in a "crisis" situation. The dialogue is amusing, often "tongue-in-cheek"; characters are varied. ROYALTY: $25. SOURCE: Vornholt, John. (1976). Tahiti, here we come! Franklin, OH: Eldridge Pub. Co. SUBJECTS/PLAY TYPE: Contests; Comedy.

3010. 9-12. (+) Sills, Paul. (Grimm Brothers) **The tailor in heaven.** (The tailor in heaven) CAST: 3m. ACTS: 1. SETTINGS: Heaven. PLAYING TIME: NA. PLOT: God instructs St. Peter to allow no one past the gates while he is out. However, Peter is moved by a tailor who begs to enter, but he instructs the tailor to sit quietly behind a door so that God will not be angered. The tailor goes exploring as soon as St. Peter's back is turned, and he looks down on earth to see a water woman stealing a veil. Angry, he throws a golden footstool down at her. When God returns, the tailor brags about how he handled the situation. God sends the pompous tailor to stay in "wait-a-while," telling him that only God has the right to judge others. RECOMMENDATION: The subject matter may be offensive to some audiences. An ideal performance situation would probably involve older teenagers in an open minded environment. ROYALTY: NA. SOURCE: Sills, Paul. (1981). More from story theatre. New York, NY: Samuel French. SUBJECTS/PLAY TYPE: Folk Tales, Germany; Judgement; Parable; Adaptation.

3011. 9-12. (-) Pederson, Westley M. **Take five.** CAST: 2f, 4m. ACTS: 1. SETTINGS: Living room. PLAYING TIME: NA. PLOT: Two stagehands are working when a stage phone rings. A person from the audience is called up to talk with his wife. While the two people on the telephone argue about a car accident, an actor and actress on the stage play the part of another couple (expecting their first baby) who try to solve the romantic troubles of the wife's sister. The play ends with the pregnant wife going to the hospital to deliver the baby while the problems of the sister and the couple on the phone are resolved. RECOMMENDATION: The resolution of the sister's problem depends on faking a premarital pregnancy, the same strategy used by the pregnant wife to get her husband to marry her. The presence of "stagehands" and "audience" on the stage is more confusing than clever. ROYALTY: $20. SOURCE: Pederson, Westley M. (1983). Take five. Chicago, IL:

Dramatic Pub. Co. SUBJECTS/PLAY TYPE: Family Relationships; Pregnancy; Drama.

3012. 4-7. (+) Boiko, Claire. **Take me to your marshal.** CAST: 3f, 7m. ACTS: 1. SETTINGS: Living room. PLAYING TIME: 20 min. PLOT: An alien Gunsmoke fan comes to Earth to meet Marshal Dillon, but he instead meets the Reed family, befriends them, and opens the way for later alien visitors. RECOMMENDATION: The character of Zanthus will require a "ham" with an effective drawl. An underlying theme here is tolerance, as the Reed family realizes that the stranger is not as different as appearances indicate. ROYALTY: Free for amateur production. SOURCE: Kamerman, Sylvia E. (1981). Space and science fiction plays for young people. Boston, MA: Plays, Inc. SUBJECTS/PLAY TYPE: Science Fiction; Space Creatures; Comedy.

3013. 7-12. (+) Hamlett, Christina. **Taking a bite out of crime.** CAST: 5f, 5m. ACTS: 1. SETTINGS: Police squad room. PLAYING TIME: 25 min. PLOT: The New York City police at the turn of the century are tracking a vampire who has killed 29 people. Detective Monika von Hess, daughter of a vampire "specialist," is on temporary assignment to help. Chief Harris' daughter, Pamela, was attacked by the vampire, but survived. Pamela's boyfriend, Eddy, also a detective, is Monika's partner, and Ben, another officer, is assigned to check on Pamela. Monika begins to suspect that the vampire is Officer Drake, as all clues point to him. However, Ben is the real vampire who has hypnotized Drake to use him as a decoy. Monika discovers the ruse and bravely drives a stake through Ben's heart. At the end, Pamela dumps Eddy for Richfield (an ex-vampire "slave") who's rich, and Drake and Officer Roxie pair off. RECOMMENDATION: Although fairly predictable, the use of a heroic female is positive. ROYALTY: Free to Plays subscribers. SOURCE: Hamlett, Christina. (1987). Humorous plays for teenagers. Boston, MA: Plays, Inc. SUBJECTS/PLAY TYPE: Vampires; Comedy.

3014. 3-6. (+) Gabriel, Michelle. **The tale of Lag B'Omer.** CAST: 1m, 5u. ACTS: 1. SETTINGS: Outdoor picnic spot. PLAYING TIME: 20 min. PLOT: As the story of Lag B'Omer is read, Lag B'Omer appears to describe his day when barley sheaves were brought to the temple for blessing. As the reader continues to read aloud that Lag B'Omer was also the one day set aside during the barley season to relax from work, Legend appears to explain that this day also commemorates the end of a plague and that on this day in ancient times, the students of a Rabbi would walk together and study. RECOMMENDATION: This has versatile casting and is interesting and informative. ROYALTY: None. SOURCE: Gabriel, Michelle. (1978). Jewish plays for Jewish days. Denver, CO: Alternatives in Religious Instruction. SUBJECTS/PLAY TYPE: Lag B'Omer; Jewish Drama.

3015. 3-5. (+) Kraus, Joanna Halpert. **The Tale of Oniroku.** CAST: 2f, 3m, 7u. ACTS: 1. SETTINGS: River; forest. PLAYING TIME: NA. PLOT: Taro the carpenter outwits the sly river ogre, Oniroku, to create a lasting bridge for the village. RECOMMENDATION: Comedy, pointed dialogue and excellent characterization enliven this superior, easily produced adaptation. ROYALTY: NA. SOURCE: Kraus, Joanna Halpert. (1977). The dragon hammer and the tale of Oniroku. Rowayton, CT: New Plays. SUBJECTS/PLAY TYPE: Folk Tales, Japan; Drama.

3016. K-3. (-) Silverman, Eleanor. (Potter, Beatrix) **The tale of Peter Rabbit.** (The tale of Peter Rabbit) CAST: Su. ACTS: 3. SETTINGS: Garden. PLAYING TIME: 10 min. PLOT: Peter Rabbit is forbidden by his mother to go into Mr. McGregor's garden, but he does anyway. He is discovered and gets lost, but finally he finds his way home. RECOMMENDATION: In an attempt to shorten the original work, dialogue has been simply lifted or left out when it could have been rewritten. Act II is a muddle with unclear directions and improper sequencing. The charm of the original is lost. ROYALTY: NA. SOURCE: Silverman, Eleanor. (1983). Dramatics for children. Metuchen, NJ: Scarecrow Press. SUBJECTS/PLAY TYPE: Rabbits; Gardens; Puppet Play; Adaptation.

3017. K-6. (+) Thane, Adele. (Potter, Beatrix) **The tale of Peter Rabbit.** (The tale of Peter Rabbit) CAST: 5f, 7m, Su. ACTS: 1. SETTINGS: Tree trunk; vegetable garden. PLAYING TIME: 15 min. PLOT: As Peter Rabbit and his sisters leave home to go blueberry picking, their mother warns them to stay away from Mr. McGregor's garden. The sisters obey, but Peter goes to the garden and eats Mr. McGregor's vegetables. Mr. McGregor catches Peter. With the help of his friends, Peter escapes and runs home. Sick from all he ate at Mr. McGregor's garden, he is not able to enjoy the blueberries and milk which his obedient sisters enjoy. RECOMMENDATION: Faithful to the original, the moral is very obvious, and the responses of some of the characters are written in rather trite rhyming poetic form. The cast has been expanded to handle many children, but the director may want to delete some of the added characters who do not smoothly fit into the plot. ROYALTY: Free to Plays subscribers. SOURCE: Thane, Adele. (1984, October). The tale of Peter Rabbit. Plays: The Drama Magazine for Young People, pp. 45-51. SUBJECTS/PLAY TYPE: Rabbits; Obedience; Adaptation.

3018. K-4*. (+) Hotchner, Steve & Hotchner, Kathy. (Perrault, Charles) **A tale of Sleeping Beauty.** (Sleeping Beauty) CAST: 4f, 3m. ACTS: 1. SETTINGS: Castle throne room; dungeon. PLAYING TIME: NA. PLOT: Beauty is put to sleep on her wedding day when she pricks her finger. As the kingdom sleeps, the Prince is held hostage by a Giant. He helps heal the Giant's broken toe, is set free, returns to kiss Beauty, and awakens the kingdom. Beauty and the Prince are married and live happily ever after. RECOMMENDATION: What makes this unique is its clever, fast moving language, and the audience participation. Because of the audience participation, this must be performed by older students or adults. ROYALTY: $35. SOURCE: Hotchner, Steve & Hotchner, Kathy. (1978). A tale of Sleeping Beauty. Woodstock, IL: Dramatic Pub. Co. SUBJECTS/PLAY TYPE: Folk Tales, France; Participation Play; Musical.

3019. K-3*. (+) Hotchner, Kathy & Roser, Bill. **The tale of the frog prince.** CAST: 3f, 3m, 1u. ACTS: 1.

SETTINGS: Swamp; hollow; mushroom house. PLAYING TIME: 35 min. PLOT: Frog, his friend Spree, and members of the royal family sing, dance, and invite the audience to participate. Frog bemoans his ugliness, yet he befriends a princess. When she kisses him, he becomes a handsome but obnoxious prince and runs off with the princess' sister. Unhappy, he later returns to the swamp to find lost friendship, and is reunited with Spree and the first princess. RECOMMENDATION: The story and participation activities are delightful. The six songs are simple and effective. However, Frog's voice must have a range of one and one-half octaves. The dialogue is easy to understand and the characterizations are entertaining, but because of the amount of memorization necessary, this is better produced by high school students. ROYALTY: $25. SOURCE: Hotchner, Kathy & Roser, Bill. (1979). The tale of the frog prince. Chicago, IL: Dramatic Pub. Co. SUBJECTS/PLAY TYPE: Folk Tale Motifs; Musical.

3020. K-5*. (+) Gustafson, Anita. **Tale of the mouse: From African folk tales.** CAST: 3f, 3m. ACTS: 1. SETTINGS: None. PLAYING TIME: 45 min. PLOT: With audience participation, the actors tell the African story of "How the mouse came to tell tales," and they introduce the character of Ananse, the spider who is involved in several adventures. RECOMMENDATION: This is an excellent way to introduce children to the spirit of African folk tales and the art of storytelling. African music in the background is essential for creating atmosphere, as are the masks for identifying the great spirit Arumburu, the Skull, and Ananse the spider. ROYALTY: $15. SOURCE: Gustafson, Anita. (1975). Tale of the mouse: From African folk tales. Denver, CO: Pioneer Drama Service. SUBJECTS/PLAY TYPE: Folk Tales, Africa; Participation Play.

3021. 9-12. (+) Fitzgibbons, Mark. (Dickens, Charles) **A tale of two cities.** (A tale of two cities) CAST: 6f, 15m, 1u. ACTS: 3. SETTINGS: Balconies; stairways; passageways. PLAYING TIME: NA. PLOT: This faithful adaptation is uniquely presented as four innkeepers narrate the story and often step into character roles. RECOMMENDATION: The mechanism of narration allows this complex story, with its large cast, to be presented with minimal casting. The fast paced plot will be enhanced by costumes and architecture of the period, but unless students have read the original, they will find this too condensed to be easily followed. ROYALTY: $50. SOURCE: Fitzgibbons, Mark. (1982). A tale of two cities. Boston, MA: Baker's Plays. SUBJECTS/PLAY TYPE: Revolution, France; Adaptation.

3022. 8-12. (+) Hackett, Walter. (Dickens, Charles) **A tale of two cities.** (A tale of two cities) CAST: 4f, 14m. ACTS: 1. SETTINGS: Court room; wine shop; home; jail; courtyard; guillotine. PLAYING TIME: NA. PLOT: Charles Darnay is sentenced to the guillotine. After the verdict, Lawyer Sydney Carton overhears (in Defarge's wine shop) a plan to wipe out all of the Darnay's family. Carton plans an escape from the country for Lucie (his love) and family. With the help of Barsad, Carton enters Charles' jail cell. He drugs the condemned man and exchanges clothes with him. Barsad drags Darnay's body to the awaiting coach and they flee. Sydney Carton fulfills his promise to Lucie that he would give his life for anyone dear to her and he goes to the guillotine. RECOMMENDATION: Carton's strong convictions will captivate the young teenage audience. This could be an effective introduction for a literature class planning to study Dickens. ROYALTY: Free to Plays subscribers. SOURCE: Hackett, Walter. (1977,November). A tale of two cities. Plays: The Drama Magazine for Young People, pp. 84-96. SUBJECTS/PLAY TYPE: Revolution, France; Prisons; Adaptation.

3023. 9-12. (+) Thane, Adele. (Dickens, Charles) **A tale of two cities.** (A tale of two cities) **CAST:** 10f, 10m, Su. **ACTS:** 6. **SETTINGS:** Wine shop; guard house; lodgings; prison. **PLAYING TIME:** 35 min. **PLOT:** During the Reign of Terror in Paris, Charles Darnay, a nephew of a French nobleman who is hated by the revolutionaries, is imprisoned and condemned to die. Sydney Carton, an Englishman, takes Darney's place on the guillotine because of his longstanding and innocent love for Darnay's wife. **RECOMMENDATION:** Faithful to the original, this play has lively dialogue and numerous characters. **ROYALTY:** Free to Plays subscribers. **SOURCE:** Thane, Adele. (1983, March). A tale of two cities. Plays: The Drama Magazine for Young People, pp. 67-79. **SUBJECTS/PLAY TYPE:** Revolution, France; Adaptation.

3024. 4-6. (+) Boiko, Claire. **A tale of two drummers.** **CAST:** 3f, 9m. **ACTS:** 1. **SETTINGS:** Parlor. **PLAYING TIME:** 20 min. **PLOT:** Colonial children witness the secrecy surrounding three American soldiers who visit their house. When, by a twist of fate, four British soldiers arrive at their house shortly after the Americans, the children cleverly help General Washington, General Knox and Lt. Alexander Hamilton to escape. **RECOMMENDATION:** Intrigue, historical perspective and the introduction of major historical figures keep interest kindled. Dialogue is not stilted or difficult to learn; none is wasted. The correct historical outfitting of four British soldiers and three American officers might prove challenging. **ROYALTY:** Free to Plays subscribers. **SOURCE:** Boiko, Claire. (1985). Childrens plays for creative actors. Boston, MA: Plays, Inc. **SUBJECTS/PLAY TYPE:** Revolution, U.S.; Playlet.

3025. 4-6. (+) Kelly, Tim J. **The tale that wagged the dog.** **CAST:** 4f, 1m. **ACTS:** 1. **SETTINGS:** Hotel sitting room. **PLAYING TIME:** NA. **PLOT:** Johann Strauss' valet, Rudolph, cons the composer's fans by selling them what they think are locks of Strauss' hair. In reality, he is selling them locks of Strauss' dog's hair. The valet's wife extracts a promise from Rudolph that he will stop. Rudolph, however, finds a new scheme to make money when he agrees to convey a lock of an admirer's hair to the maestro as a declaration of passion and admiration. **RECOMMENDATION:** In this light piece, the characters are all stereotypes, from Rudolph, the con-man, to his wife Trudi, a shrew. The humor comes from Rudolph trying to follow the straight and narrow path and Strauss' fans forcing him to continue his dishonest ways. This could easily be reworked using a modern day rock star as the

figure of worship, which would make costuming simpler. **ROYALTY:** $15. **SOURCE:** Kelly, Tim J. (1976). The tale that wagged the dog. Chicago, IL: Dramatic Pub. Co. **SUBJECTS/PLAY TYPE:** Groupies; Con Artists; Comedy.

3026. K-3*. (+) Evans, Mary Jane & Anderson, Deborah. (Andersen, Hans Christian) **Tales from Hans Christian Andersen.** **CAST:** 5f, 7m. **ACTS:** 1. **SETTINGS:** 4 book-like structures. **PLAYING TIME:** NA. **PLOT:** A storyteller gathers an audience around and as he starts to tell each story, members of the audience take on the roles of the characters and scenery. The four stories are: **What the Old Man Does is Always Right, The Princess on the Pea, The Ugly Duckling,** and **Numbskull Jack.** **RECOMMENDATION:** This is an original, artistic way to retell four beloved tales for children. The actors express the action and the scenery with mime, and enhance the storyline with song. Although it is a perfect play for an audience of younger children it requires talented, probably professional, actors. **ROYALTY:** $35. **SOURCE:** Evans, Mary Jane, & Anderson, Deborah. (1983). Tales from Hans Christian Andersen. New Orleans, LA: Anchorage Press, Inc. **SUBJECTS/PLAY TYPE:** Folk Tales; Musical.

3027. 1-12. (+) Dixon, Michael Bigelow. **Tales from the Arabian nights.** **CAST:** 6f, 18m, 46u. **ACTS:** 2. **SETTINGS:** Prison cell; coast line; cave; city backdrop. **PLAYING TIME:** 90 min. **PLOT:** A sultan, under the evil spell of a magician, has decreed that he will marry a new wife each evening and chop her head off by dawn's light. Scheherazade cleverly manages to remain alive by telling her new husband an enchanting tale that is near completion by the dawn's light. Each dawn she is successful in persuading the Sultan to delay her execution until the next night and the next tale. These tales continue for 1,001 nights, until she wins the Sultan away from the bewitching spell of the magician. **RECOMMENDATION:** Young children will be enchanted by the magic, young adults will be held in suspense for Scheherazade's fate, and adults will applaud the characterizations. **ROYALTY:** $75. **SOURCE:** Dixon, Michael Bigelow. (1985). Tales from the Arabian nights. Schulenburg, TX: I.E. Clark. **SUBJECTS/PLAY TYPE:** Fantasy; Storytelling; Drama.

3028. 3-6. (+) Lane, Carolyn. (Andersen, Hans Christian) **Tales of Hans Christian Andersen: A storyteller's theatre.** **CAST:** 6u. **ACTS:** 1. **SETTINGS:** None. **PLAYING TIME:** 45 min. **PLOT:** Several well known folk tales are tied together by presenting Hans Christian Andersen as the storyteller. As Andersen spins his first tale, the tender-hearted dancing doll falls in love with the steadfast tin soldier. In the next, the foolish princess still spurns the honest prince disguised as a swineherd. The ugly duckling once again becomes a beautiful swan. And, yes, the little mermaid gains an immortal soul. **RECOMMENDATION:** Since the role of Andersen has many lines, it should be played by someone older, or perhaps this character could read the tales from a book. **ROYALTY:** $15. **SOURCE:** Lane, Carolyn. (1978). Tales of Hans Christian Andersen. Denver, CO: Pioneer Drama Service. **SUBJECTS/PLAY TYPE:** Folk Tales, Denmark; Storytelling; Drama.

3029. 3-8. (+) Wheetley, Kim Alan. **Tales of trickery.**
CAST: 3f, 3m, Su. ACTS: 1. SETTINGS: Bare stage, props.
PLAYING TIME: NA. PLOT: In this composite of three
Indonesian folktales, **The Widow and the Wealthy
Neighbor** is the story of a poor widow who prays loudly
for money. Her wealthy neighbor is disturbed by her cries
and cruelly decides to silence her by dumping a sack of
rubble on her. The rubble changes into coins, and the
widow becomes richer than her neighbor. Her neighbor
prays for money, but all he receives is rubble, and he
eventually becomes poor. In **The Monkey and the Barong,**
the barong's strong sense of smell allows it to find food to
share with the monkey. The monkey, in return, grooms the
barong's beard, until one day, the monkey decides to
hoard bananas in a tree he has climbed, thus angering the
barong. They fight, with the foolish monkey throwing
bananas as weapons and ending up in a barren tree, while
the barong feasts on the ground. Finally, in **The Buffalo
and the Bell,** a foolish farmer is deceived into believing
that his buffalo is a goat. However, he recovers his losses
by convincing the tricksters to buy a bell that they think
will cause people to believe that they have been paid when
they have not. RECOMMENDATION: Much of the
humor of these fine stories depends on the skill of the cast,
which should be chosen at least from grades 6-8.
ROYALTY: $20. SOURCE: Wheetley, Kim Alan. (1981).
Tales of trickery: A triad of comic Indonesian folk tales.
Chicago, IL: Dramatic Pub. Co. SUBJECTS/PLAY TYPE:
Folk Tales, Indonesia; Topeng Presentations; Fable;
Comedy.

3030. 5-6. (+) Winther, Barbara. **The talking burro.**
CAST: 5f, 4m, Su. ACTS: 1. SETTINGS: Mexican village.
PLAYING TIME: 30 min. PLOT: This is an authentic
dramatization of Mexican Christmas customs, with
Spanish/English versions. When a burro discovers he can
talk, he refuses to work again and runs away to have some
fun. He arrives at another village and becomes involved in
the Mexican Christmas festival of Las Posados, in which
he carries the Virgin Mary from door to door while Joseph
asks for a place to stay. Villagers sing the traditional song
of Las Posados. The burro's owners come to the festival on
Christmas Eve and discover their talking burro, who
misses them and wants to return home. Just as the police
and mayor are about to capture the burro, he loses his
ability to talk and remains safe. The play ends with a
colorful fiesta, pinata, singing, and dancing.
RECOMMENDATION: The action, music, dancing, and
colorful costumes will hold the interest of audiences of all
ages. The expense of costuming and sets could be well
worth the effort in this humorous Christmas tale.
ROYALTY: Free to Plays subscribers. SOURCE: Winther,
Barbara. (1979, December). The talking burro. Plays: The
Drama Magazine for Young People, pp. 57-64.
SUBJECTS/PLAY TYPE: Christmas; Christmas, Mexico;
Comedy.

3031. K-3. (-) McCaslin, Nellie. **The Talking cat.**
CAST: 1f, 2m, 1u. ACTS: 1. SETTINGS: Living room.
PLAYING TIME: 10 min. PLOT: A lonely woman and her
cat are visited by a workman looking for a job, shelter, and
food. Much to the woman's surprise and pleasure, her cat
speaks to her, advising that she take the workman in and
offer him a permanent home and salary. After a time, a
friend of the workman asks him to sell furs in the city and
to stop fooling the woman by using his ventriloquism to
make the cat talk. However, he refuses to leave, continues
to work and make the cat talk, and all are very contented.
RECOMMENDATION: With clever dignity, the
workman is able to provide a lonely person with company
while providing for himself. ROYALTY: None. SOURCE:
McCaslin, Nellie. (1977). Puppet fun: Production,
performance, and plays. New York, NY: D. McKay Co.
SUBJECTS/PLAY TYPE: Folk Tales, French Canadian;
Puppet Play.

3032. 9-12. (+) Ballam, John David. **Tall men of
average height.** CAST: 4f, 7m. ACTS: 1. SETTINGS:
Patio. PLAYING TIME: 35 min. PLOT: This is a spoof on
the pretentiousness, arrogance, and sexist attitudes of late
Victorian England uppercrust society. The scene is a party
at the stately home of Archibald, nephew of the Earl of
Dorchester, who is a handsome, debonair, but conceited
ladies' man of leisure. It is his twenty-first birthday. His
companions include a mixture of friends, relatives, and
acquaintances of varying ages, all possessing social stature
(if not competence) and all attended by the well meaning,
but absent minded butler. The plot revolves around Lady
Irvine (a silly, rotund, and obnoxious woman) and her
attempt to get both her daughter Caroline and her ward
Abigail married off to the eligible men at the party. The
play is a dialogue of inane and slanderous gossip, full of
double meanings, sexual innuendo, and comedic romance.
By its end, Lady Irvine prevails and three sets of marriage
proposals emerge. In the midst of the shenanigans,
Archibald unexpectedly discovers that one of his comely
guests is his twin sister. This fact causes all sorts of playful
confusion, but things work out in the end.
RECOMMENDATION: This is full of deprecatory humor
characteristic of English wit, but it may have trouble
satisfying an American audience. It is reminiscent of a
watered down version of Benny Hill, sans the graphic
nudity. The sexual innuendo is subtle, and while the play
is unlikely to have the audience rolling in the aisles, it
would be acceptable as a period piece or lightweight
comedy. ROYALTY: $15. SOURCE: Ballam, John David.
(1985). Tall men of average height. Boston, MA: Baker's
Plays. SUBJECTS/PLAY TYPE: Victorian English Society;
Comedy; Farce.

3033. 7-12. (+) Dias, Earl J. **The tall stranger.** CAST: 3f,
9m. ACTS: 1. SETTINGS: Old West hotel lobby.
PLAYING TIME: 30 min. PLOT: This features Bat Farr, a
larger-than-life villain; Penelope Priss as the maiden in
distress; and the tall stranger as the quintessential
American cowboy hero. Penelope's father faces financial
ruin at the hands of Bat Farr but an Eastern dude,
Montgomery Blackstone, arrives to rescue Miss Priss from
Farr's matrimonial intentions and to restore her father's
fortune. Blackstone, who turns out to be the tall stranger,
wins the heroine's heart and gives the "boot" to Bat.
RECOMMENDATION: The exaggerated, melodramatic
plot provides comic relief that never quite cancels the
romantic elements of the story. This fits neatly into the
social studies/English curriculum. ROYALTY: Free to
Plays subscribers. SOURCE: Dias, Earl J. (1979, October).

The tall stranger. Plays: The Drama Magazine for Young People, pp. 15-26. SUBJECTS/PLAY TYPE: Western; Comedy; Satire; Melodrama.

3034. 10-12. (+) Brown, Charlotte. (Shakespeare, William) **The taming of the shrew.** (The taming of the shrew) CAST: 2f, 6m, 11u. ACTS: 1. SETTINGS: Elizabethan living room. PLAYING TIME: 60 min. PLOT: This retains the essence of the original for occasions when a much shorter version suitable for school and civic events is needed. Shakespeare's language and plot are preserved as Petruchio transforms an independent, thinking young woman into a male's ideal of Elizabethan womanhood. RECOMMENDATION: This version is useful for high school productions that have time constraints. ROYALTY: $15. SOURCE: Brown, Charlotte. (1987). The taming of the shrew. Schulenburg, TX: I.E. Clark. SUBJECTS/PLAY TYPE: Marriage; Comedy; Adaptation.

3035. 9-12. (+) Olfson, Lewy. (Shakespeare, William) **The taming of the shrew.** (The taming of the shrew) CAST: 1f, 5m, 3u. ACTS: 1. SETTINGS: None. PLAYING TIME: 30 min. PLOT: This follows the plot of the original. RECOMMENDATION: Much of the character and depth of the original is lost due to changed and edited dialogue. The overall plot, although highly simplified, is intact. ROYALTY: Free to Plays subscribers. SOURCE: Olfson, Lewy. (1977, February). The taming of the shrew. Plays: The Drama Magazine for Young People, pp. 83-95. SUBJECTS/PLAY TYPE: Comedy; Reader's Theater; Marriage; Adaptation.

3036. 7-9. (+) Kehret, Peg. **Tammi's brother is dead.** CAST: 1f. ACTS: 1. SETTINGS: None. PLAYING TIME: NA. PLOT: A young girl is stunned to hear that her friend's 9 year old brother has died. The monologue explores the emotional upheaval of both girls, the guilt created when they think of things unsaid and undone, and their thoughtlessness toward Mark when he was alive. The storyteller weeps bitterly for the boy, and realizes that her appreciation for her own 9 year old brother will be deepened by the experience. RECOMMENDATION: The treatment of guilt is cathartic and will reassure audiences that such feelings are normal and universal. ROYALTY: NA. SOURCE: Kehret, Peg. (1986). Winning monologs for young actors. Colorado Springs, CO: Meriwether Pub. SUBJECTS/PLAY TYPE: Death; Guilt; Monologue.

3037. 4-7. (+) Sills, Paul. (Harris, Joel Chandler) **The tar baby: American folk tale.** (Adventures of Brer Rabbit) CAST: Su. ACTS: 1. SETTINGS: Forest clearing. PLAYING TIME: NA. PLOT: Brer Rabbit refuses to help the other animals dig a well, so they set up guards to prevent him from drinking from it. Brer Rabbit waits until night, and then sings so sweetly from the bushes that the guards dance away. The next day, the animals build a tar man to stand guard. Again, Brer Rabbit tries to lure the guard away with his singing, and becomes furious when he does not succeed. He angrily punches the tar baby until he becomes stuck. The animals close in and threaten to feed him sweets until he bursts, but instead, Brer Rabbit escapes after eating his fill. RECOMMENDATION: Although this departs from the plot of the original

considerably, it is an amusing treatment of an American classic. The singing and dancing can be as controlled or as carefree as the cast would like. ROYALTY: NA. SOURCE: Sills, Paul. (1981). More from story theatre. New York, NY: Samuel French. SUBJECTS/PLAY TYPE: Animals; Folk Tales, America; Adaptation.

3038. 1-6. (+) Wartski, Maureen Crane. **Taro the fisherman.** CAST: 3f, 5m, Su. ACTS: 1. SETTINGS: Seashore; under the sea. PLAYING TIME: 15 min. PLOT: Taro, the orphan boy, fishes for his harsh master. Tender hearted about the small animals he catches, Taro throws them back to the sea. The sea creatures reward him with a feast, but when Taro returns to land, he finds that his life has passed and he is now an old man. He gratefully accepts the sea creatures' invitation to live with them in eternal youth. RECOMMENDATION: The purpose here seems to be to point out the need for kindness and animal husbandry. The beauty of the original folk tale is not well preserved. However, this stands on its own merit. ROYALTY: Free to Plays subscribers. SOURCE: Wartski, Maureen Crane. (1980, May). Taro the fisherman. Plays: The Drama Magazine for Young People, pp. 54-60. SUBJECTS/PLAY TYPE: Folk Tales, Japan; Animal Husbandry; Kindness; Playlet.

3039. 9-12. (+) Murray, John. **The tarot terrors.** CAST: 5f, 5m. ACTS: 3. SETTINGS: Living room; exterior scene. PLAYING TIME: NA. PLOT: Two couples are mysteriously invited, via a tarot card, to visit an old mansion. On successive weekends, each visitor is killed, with the men joining the dead host as he haunts the mansion. A private investigator sent to find the hapless couples discovers that their deaths were ordained by the tarot cards to keep the dead host in some form of existence between life and death. The investigator is killed also and the sinister maid warns the audience that the tarot cards may choose them next. RECOMMENDATION: The horror suspensefully builds to a mysterious climax. ROYALTY: Free to Plays subscribers. SOURCE: Murray, John. (1975, March). Tarot terrors. Plays: The Drama Magazine for Young People, pp. 1-15. SUBJECTS/PLAY TYPE: Tarot Cards; Horror.

3040. 9-12. (+) Burleson, Noyce. (Moliere, Jean Baptiste Poquelin) **Tartuffe.** (Tartuffe.) CAST: 4f, 6m, Su. ACTS: 1. SETTINGS: Living room. PLAYING TIME: NA. PLOT: A wealthy merchant has brought home a holy man and is considering disinheriting his son in favor of the newcomer. The family plots to unveil this pious man for the scoundrel he is, and after several tries they are successful. RECOMMENDATION: Moliere's famous satire has been successfully adapted to a contemporary setting, facilitating the costuming and set production. This faithful adaptation is witty, moves along well, and should satisfy fans of Moliere, as well as those experiencing his works for the first time. ROYALTY: $25. SOURCE: Burleson, Noyce. (1983). Tartuffe. Woodstock, IL: Dramatic Pub. Co. SUBJECTS/PLAY TYPE: Satire; Hypocrisy; Adaptation.

3041. 7-12. (+) Garver, Juliet. (Chekhov, Anton) **Taxi! Taxi!** (Misery) CAST: 1f, 2m, 1u. ACTS: 1. SETTINGS: Bare stage, props. PLAYING TIME: 20 min. PLOT: A cab driver explains that his taxi, Esmerelda, is the only one who will listen to his problems. The driver picks up a succession of fares, all so wrapped up in their own problems they tune out the driver's attempts to reach out to them. He is left alone with Esmerelda. RECOMMENDATION: The various characters and their family problems in this thought provoking piece would provide excellent discussion material for a literature class. ROYALTY: Free to Plays subscribers. SOURCE: Garver, Juliet. (1979, February). Taxi! Taxi! Plays: The Drama Magazine for Young People, pp. 8-14. SUBJECTS/PLAY TYPE: Family Problems; Adaptation.

3042. 9-12. (+) Patrick, John. (Sneider, Vern) **Teahouse of the August moon.** (Teahouse of the August moon) CAST: 8f, 18m, 3u. ACTS: 3. SETTINGS: Army offices; Tobiki village. PLAYING TIME: NA. PLOT: Captain Fisby's destination is the small village of Tobiki on post-war Okinawa; his duty is to civilize, democratize, and Americanize the native villagers. He has been assigned, as his aide and interpreter, the ever useful, dumb-like-a-fox, Sakini. The villagers immediately accept democracy and vote to erect not a school, but a teahouse. Fisby succumbs to their logic, and their local economy is rebuilt as they illegally sell locally made brandy to various army posts. Clearly, it is a case of Fisby being Tobiki-ized, and Col. Purdy orders the teahouse destroyed and the brandy stills smashed. When Purdy learns that Washington is pleased with the progress in Tobiki, all must be reassembled hastily and happily by the "Americanized" natives. RECOMMENDATION: Through the eyes of the narrator, Sakini, we see with gentle but pointedly humorous satire, the absurdities of army regulation. The unique element distinguishing the play from Sneider's original is the love interest of Fisby and Lotus Blossom, which is charming in its affectionate simplicity. ROYALTY: NA. SOURCE: Patrick, John. (1980). The teahouse of the August moon. New York, NY: Dramatists Play Service. SUBJECTS/PLAY TYPE: Army Regulations; Rules; Democracy; Adaptation.

3043. 7-9. (+) Karshner, Roger. **Ted and Stacy.** CAST: 1f, 1m. ACTS: 1. SETTINGS: None. PLAYING TIME: NA. PLOT: Ted is worried about his relationship with Stacy because Stacy is rich and he is poor. Stacy tells him that his caring for her is what makes her rich because that's something that money cannot buy. RECOMMENDATION: Without condescending, this points out the relative value of money. ROYALTY: NA. SOURCE: Karshner, Roger. (1986). Scenes for teenagers. Toluce Lake, CA: Dramaline Pub. SUBJECTS/PLAY TYPE: Values; Money; Scene.

3044. K-4. (+) Gotwalt, Helen Louise Miller. **The teddy bear hero.** CAST: Su. ACTS: 1. SETTINGS: Bare stage, props. PLAYING TIME: 15 min. PLOT: A teddy bear is harassed by his peers because he is red, white, and blue, until they learn that his patriotic colors are in honor of the life he saved during the war. RECOMMENDATION: This is a poor vehicle for a patriotic play, but it is imaginative. ROYALTY: None. SOURCE: Gotwalt, Helen Louise Miller. (1985). First plays for children: A collection of little plays for the youngest players. Boston, MA: Plays, Inc. SUBJECTS/PLAY TYPE: Bears, Stuffed; Playlet.

3045. 9-12. (+) Bass, Molly. **The teen age.** CAST: 4f, 4m, Su. ACTS: 1. SETTINGS: Bare stage. PLAYING TIME: NA. PLOT: In separate monologues, teenagers discuss such problems as what to wear to a party, who has a crush on whom, and the stress caused by being an over-achiever. RECOMMENDATION: Although this might be embarrassing for the actors, as they expose problems which are very real, it nicely uses symbolism, verse, and stream-of-consciousness to dramatize the problems of growing up and becoming independent. ROYALTY: NA. SOURCE: Bass, Molly. (1987). Two to go: Two one-act plays for the teen age. Boston, MA: Baker's Plays. SUBJECTS/PLAY TYPE: Adolescent Problems; Drama.

3046. 7-12. (+) Gotwalt, Helen Louise Miller. **Television book week quiz.** CAST: 6f, 6m, 10u. ACTS: 1. SETTINGS: Television studio. PLAYING TIME: 20 min. PLOT: The master of ceremonies welcomes a panel of literary experts who must identify characters as each enacts a scene from his/her book. Among those used are Anne from **Anne of Green Gables**, Pip from **Great Expectations**, Jo March from **Little Women**, Jim Hawkins from **Treasure Island**, Becky from **The Adventures of Tom Sawyer**, the Artful Dodger from **Oliver Twist**, and Alice of **Alice in Wonderland**. RECOMMENDATION: Students will want to create their own version of this game show from works they have read. This is an excellent way to study characterization. ROYALTY: Free to Plays subscribers. SOURCE: Gottwalt, Helen Louise Miller. (1979, November). Television book week quiz. Plays: The Drama Magazine for Young People, pp. 57-65. SUBJECTS/PLAY TYPE: Literature; Skit.

3047. K-5. (+) Gotwalt, Helen Louise Miller. **Ten pennies for Lincoln.** CAST: 2f, 3m, 15u. ACTS: 1. SETTINGS: Bare stage, props. PLAYING TIME: NA. PLOT: Children wanting to join a club are required to earn ten pennies by emulating incidents in Abraham Lincoln's life. RECOMMENDATION: This clever device presents interesting facts about Abraham Lincoln. ROYALTY: Free to Plays subscribers. SOURCE: Gotwalt, Helen Louise Miller. (1985). First plays for children. Boston, MA: Plays, Inc. SUBJECTS/PLAY TYPE: Lincoln, Abraham; Playlet.

3048. 9-12. (+) Elfenbein, Josef A. **The ten-penny tragedy.** CAST: 4f, 4m. ACTS: 1. SETTINGS: School hallway; information desk. PLAYING TIME: 30 min. PLOT: Andrea (in charge of the dime-a-week fund drive) forgets that she put one of the dimes in her notebook. When she comments on losing the dime, another student overhears "diamond" instead of dime, and begins a chain of rumors which culminate in an outrageous scenario: Andrea's mother's engagement ring is lost and her father is going to beat her; Andrea's mother has a heart attack; and Andrea herself has run away. Andrea returns to the scene, having found the dime, and encounters chaos involving her parents, the principal, the police, the newspaper editor and several students. All is no sooner straightened out then the student who started it all is fast at work gathering another rumor. RECOMMENDATION: This believable plot which illustrates how easily and rapidly rumors get started, become embellished and cause problems, progresses from calm narration to high school hysteria.

ROYALTY: Free to Plays subscribers. SOURCE: Elfenbein, Josef A. (1982, May). The ten-penny tragedy. Plays: The Drama Magazine for Young People, pp. 12-20. SUBJECTS/PLAY TYPE: Rumors; Comedy.

3049. 1-8. (+) Whittaker, Violet. **Ten plagues on Egypt (or, trouble in the palace and it's all the Pharoah's fault).** CAST: Su. ACTS: 1. SETTINGS: Throne room; river. PLAYING TIME: NA. PLOT: With a Christian focus, the story of the ten plagues which forced the Pharoah to let the Hebrew slaves leave with Moses is told. At the end, the audience is cautioned that the story is a lesson that they must obey God. RECOMMENDATION: This is an elaborate portrayal of the ten plagues, taken out of context from the Passover Hagaddah. As a story about obeying God, it stands on its own merit. As a dramatic Passover presentation, it will not be appropriate. ROYALTY: NA. SOURCE: Whittaker, Violet. (1984). Puppet people scripts. Grand Rapids, MI: Baker Book House. SUBJECTS/PLAY TYPE: Christian Drama; Passover; Puppet Play.

3050. 7-12. (-) Shoemaker, Carol. **10-10 till we read you again, little buddy.** CAST: Su. ACTS: 1. SETTINGS: Office. PLAYING TIME: 15 min. PLOT: When a student gets in trouble for sleeping in class, he inadvertently finds out that the principal and a teacher are his CB radio pals, whom he has only known by their code names. All is forgiven. RECOMMENDATION: The humor relies on understanding "CB talk," not a language of great interest today. ROYALTY: Free to Plays subscribers. SOURCE: Shoemaker, Carol. (1976, December). 10-10 till we read you again, good buddy. Plays: The Drama Magazine for Young People, pp. 59-64. SUBJECTS/PLAY TYPE: CB Radios; Comedy.

3051. 9-12+. (+) Gilsenan, Nancy. **Tender lies.** CAST: 4f, 6m, Su. ACTS: 2. SETTINGS: Porch. PLAYING TIME: NA. PLOT: Each member of a group of boarders has individual problems, but their landlord manages to minimize their respective inadequacies through his use of "tender lies" to build up their self confidence. For example, a young female artist paints the old house as it must have once looked, and dreams about how it will look again. In the end, the landlord's fabrications provoke a crisis, but not before he has given each of his boarders courage to pursue their own lives and dreams. RECOMMENDATION: The characters are clearly defined and an immediate rapport is established between them and the audience. The play shows many types of people (disabled, young, elderly, Mexican, etc.), living together and learning to appreciate one another. ROYALTY: $50. SOURCE: Gilsenan, Nancy. (1983). Tender lies. Woodstock, IL: Dramatic Pub. Co. SUBJECTS/PLAY TYPE: Relationships; Self Esteem; Drama.

3052. 5-12. (+) Brown, Joseph. **Tender places.** CAST: 2f, 2m. ACTS: 1. SETTINGS: Park, living room. PLAYING TIME: NA. PLOT: A young boy, torn apart by his divorced parents' arguments over his custody, meets an old woman who shows him that his parents must be happy if he is to be happy, that the divorce has nothing to do with him, and that a person has to feel, even if it sometimes hurts. RECOMMENDATION: Written by a 12

year old, this play superbly dramatizes the feelings of a child caught between two feuding parents, and, with fine simplicity, removes responsibility for a divorce from the children. This will provoke much discussion which should be directed by specially trained personnel. ROYALTY: NA. SOURCE: Lamb, Wendy. (1986). Meeting the winter bike rider and other prize winning plays. New York, NY: Dell. SUBJECTS/PLAY TYPE: Divorce; Drama.

3053. 9-12. (+) Birnkrant, Samuel. **The termination.** CAST: 2f, 1m, 2u. ACTS: 1. SETTINGS: Office. PLAYING TIME: 30 min. PLOT: The "state" encourages people to turn themselves in to be destroyed so that a stable population can be maintained. Miss X has just been commended on her excellent work at motivating people to turn themselves in. Emily requests termination, but before the paperwork is completed, she decides that life is worth living. Miss X requests that Emily sit down and relax while she tries to undo the paperwork. But before she realizes what has happened, Emily is dead. RECOMMENDATION: Recommended to develop a discussion in a social issues or history class, this moves quickly and the ending is a total surprise. ROYALTY: $10. SOURCE: Birnkrant, Samuel. (1976). The termination. Denver, CO: Pioneer Drama Service. SUBJECTS/PLAY TYPE: Population Control; Science Fiction; Drama.

3054. 7-12. (+) Calcutt, David. **The terrible fate of Humpty Dumpty.** CAST: 10f, 9m. ACTS: 1. SETTINGS: School grounds; vacant lot; house; office. PLAYING TIME: NA. PLOT: The leader of a gang, Stubbs, bullies a new boy, Terry, into climbing a pylon to retrieve the leader's frisbee, and the boy is electrocuted. In flashbacks, the play follows Terry's losing battle to get along in a new school. Terry's parents, his teacher, and classmates are shown respectively as being frustrated, ignorant, and too weak to help. The police officers are convinced that Stubbs was guilty of murder, but Stubbs shows no remorse. The play ends with a repetition of the murder scene, as the gang members chant "Humpty Dumpty," and urge Terry on to his death. RECOMMENDATION: Strongly recommended as a catalyst for thoughtful discussion about social behaviors and for encouraging children to examine their own choices, this depicts powerful and very real pressures. There may be some difficulty transferring the British vocabulary to American, but changes will not detract from the power. ROYALTY: None. SOURCE: Calcutt, David. (1986). The terrible fate of humpty dumpty. London, England: Macmillan Education. SUBJECTS/PLAY TYPE: Peer Pressure; Drama.

3055. 7-12. (-) Chase, Mary Coyle. **The terrible tattoo parlor.** CAST: 6f, 6m, Su. ACTS: 1. SETTINGS: Bare stage. PLAYING TIME: NA. PLOT: Linda (12), gets herself into dangerous trouble by making prank phone calls and unwisely identifying herself to the unscrupulous madame of a tattoo parlor. Linda is kidnapped by the angry madame and her nasty son, but she escapes during another prank call made by her friend, Ernie. RECOMMENDATION: Younger audiences might come away with the impression that making prank phone calls brings new friends and adventure. ROYALTY: $25. SOURCE: Chase, Mary Coyle. (1981). The terrible tattoo parlor. New York, NY: Dramatists Play Service. SUBJECTS/PLAY TYPE: Prank Calls; Comedy.

3056. 2-6. (+) Boiko, Claire. **Terrible Terry's surprise.** CAST: 3f, 4m, 8u. ACTS: 1. SETTINGS: Living room. PLAYING TIME: 15 min. PLOT: Terry tries to rationalize his poor grade in behavior. He didn't mean to throw a basket through the principal's window; he was only trying to be helpful when he cleaned the trumpets with soap and water; and he was only trying to help the cafeteria supervisor when he filled the sugar bowl with salt. Granny insists that he write a note of apology to his teachers. As Terry grudgingly begins to compose his first note, April Fool and the seven Follies force him to step into his teacher's shoes. Terry is confronted with his behaviors. Unable to manage them, he calls April Fool for help. He has learned that a child can't learn anything unless he pays attention to his teacher. RECOMMENDATION: This provides valuable insight and wisdom to children at a level they can comprehend, and in a situation to which they can relate. ROYALTY: NA. SOURCE: Boiko, Claire. (1985). Children's plays for creative actors. Boston, MA: Plays, Inc. SUBJECTS/PLAY TYPE: Learning; School; Playlet.

3057. K-4. (+) Winther, Barbara. **Terrible tiger.** CAST: Su. ACTS: 1. SETTINGS: Clearing. PLAYING TIME: 10 min. PLOT: Rabbit tricks Tiger, the menace of the forest, and ties him to a tree by telling him that a storm is coming and he might be blown away. Monkeys release Tiger when he promises not to hurt them, but Tiger breaks his word. After being warned by birds that a real storm is coming, Rabbit persuades Tiger to tie Rabbit to a tree, leaving Tiger at the mercy of the wind. RECOMMENDATION: The dialogue and action might prove too cumbersome for production by the age group to whom the plot would appeal. Setting and costuming are also elaborate. However, there are some fun parts which could be played by the youngsters while older children take the major speaking parts. ROYALTY: Free to Plays subscribers. SOURCE: Winther, Barbara. (1985, October). Terrible tiger. Plays: The Drama Magazine for Young People, pp. 43-46. SUBJECTS/PLAY TYPE: Folk Tale Motifs; Playlet.

3058. 7-12. (+) Dias, Earl J. **Terror at Bransford Manor.** CAST: 4f, 3m. ACTS: 3. SETTINGS: Drawing room; gypsy caravan. PLAYING TIME: 30 min. PLOT: Lydia Neville, haunted by the ghost of her husband's first wife, Gloria, turns to her cousin, Evangeline, and the gypsy, Tanya, for comfort. Lydia and Evangeline learn that Tanya is really Gloria, that she was never actually married to Miles Neville, and that Gloria and Miles are plotting to drive Lydia mad to gain control of her money. RECOMMENDATION: This time honored plot will possibly be fresh to the intended audience. However, it is not presented in a particularly realistic way, and the dialogue will have to be updated. ROYALTY: Free to Plays subscribers. SOURCE: Dias, Earl J. (1983, January/February). Terror at Bransford Manor. Plays: The Drama Magazine for Young People, pp. 31-40. SUBJECTS/PLAY TYPE: Mystery; Playlet.

3059. 7-12. (+) Kelly, Tim J. **Terror by gaslight.** CAST: 6f, 6m. ACTS: 2. SETTINGS: 19th century school. PLAYING TIME: NA. PLOT: Dr. Norton runs an anatomical school, and is dedicated to creating an anatomical museum. Since it is against the law to dissect any subjects except those from the public gallows, he is forced to deal with two graverobbers and bodysnatchers, Gin Hester and Scrubbs. There is a public outcry over graverobbing, and a blackmailer, an outraged and neurotic citizen, and the police visit the school. Norton kills the blackmailer, Gin Hester kills a local bar maid, and Scrubbs and the outraged citizen kill Norton. Norton's daughter and Gin Hester decide to keep the school open after Norton's death. RECOMMENDATION: This will scare the wits out of the audience. ROYALTY: $50. SOURCE: Kelly, Tim J. (1981). Terror by gaslight. New York, NY: Dramatists Play Service. SUBJECTS/PLAY TYPE: Graverobbers; Horror.

3060. 7-12. (+) Murray, John. **The terror of bigfoot.** CAST: 4f, 6m. ACTS: 1. SETTINGS: Cabin living room. PLAYING TIME: 30 min. PLOT: Three research teams disappear while tracking bigfoot in the Great Swamp. Dr. Thornton and his daughter, Joan, search for them. As Joan repeats, "If one pursues evil, he will become a thing of evil," she gasps in horror, seeing that her hands have become covered with hair. Her father has already metamorphosed into a bigfoot, and the two leave to join their friends "in our new home." RECOMMENDATION: Viewers will be held in suspense as they try to solve the mystery of the disappearing scientists. They will be left speculating on the premise that anyone who searches for bigfoot metamorphoses into the creature, never to be seen again. ROYALTY: Free to Plays subscribers. SOURCE: Murray, John. (1977, April). The terror of bigfoot. Plays: The Drama Magazine for Young People, pp. 1-12. SUBJECTS/PLAY TYPE: Bigfoot; Horror.

3061. 9-12. (+) Jones, Graham. **The terrorist.** CAST: 3f, 2m. ACTS: 1. SETTINGS: Living room. PLAYING TIME: NA. PLOT: A father, who owns, operates, and lives in a tourist hotel, is recognized by a hotel guest as the terrorist of 20 years ago who fled the scene of a bombing where several people were killed. The father kills the guest. The guest's wife comes looking for him and the father plots to kill her too, but his own daughter is killed instead when the plot goes awry. RECOMMENDATION: The suspense builds to the surprise ending, as a desperate man tries to cover up his misdeeds in this well crafted drama. ROYALTY: $20. SOURCE: Jones, Graham. (1984). The terrorist. Chicago, IL: Dramatic Pub. Co. SUBJECTS/PLAY TYPE: Terrorism; Murder; Drama.

3062. 7-12. (+) Nolan, Paul T. **The test.** CAST: 3f, 3m. ACTS: 1. SETTINGS: Office. PLAYING TIME: 25 min. PLOT: Mr. Connelly, city parks director, devises a test for job candidates in which the final four candidates must each spend a dollar on something which can fill an entire room. One is not able to come up with an idea, and the other three suggest light, music and perfume. After all ideas are presented, Mr. Connelly reveals that there were actually four positions and that he had already decided to hire all of them, but the purpose of the test was to help him place them in the positions for which they would be most qualified. RECOMMENDATION: This creative, suspenseful, light drama presents an interesting perspective on the adage that a person and his/her job should be well matched. The discussion, which explains how each candidate's response to the test demonstrates which of four jobs he/she was most suited for is quite interesting and not at all patronizing. ROYALTY: Free to Plays subscribers. SOURCE: Nolan, Paul T. (1975, April). The test. Plays: The Drama Magazine for Young People, pp. 15-24. SUBJECTS/PLAY TYPE: Hiring; Interviewing; Playlet.

3063. 1-4. (+) MacLellan, Esther & Schroll, Catherine V. **Test for a witch. CAST:** 7f, 4m, Su. **ACTS:** 1. SETTINGS: Park. PLAYING TIME: 15 min. PLOT: Lizzy, a witchette, has been trying, for 50 years, to pass the hand and head tests which will allow her to become a witch. She wants to turn Peter into a grasshopper and Polly into a cricket, but they have a better idea. They suggest that she make a nutritious dinner with meat, vegetables, and milk rather than the usual vinegar. The witch council loves Ii and declares that she has finally passed. RECOMMENDATION: Suitable for teaching a lesson on nutrition, the simple plot puts a new light on good eating habits. ROYALTY: Free to Plays subscribers. SOURCE: MacLellan, Esther & Schroll, Catherine V. (1977, October). Plays: The Drama Magazine for Young People, pp. 65-70. SUBJECTS/PLAY TYPE: Halloween; Nutrition; Witches; Comedy.

3064. 8-12. (+) Murray, John. **A test for three detectives. CAST:** 5f, 8m. **ACTS:** 1. SETTINGS: Study. PLAYING TIME: 30 min. PLOT: Jason Hardwick's three nieces try to solve his murder; each employs a zany, ineffectual detective to help. An announcer enters and states that Jason's murder has not been solved, and leaves the solution to the discerning mystery fan. He orders dinner and Mrs. Goodheart comes in with a turkey drumstick. He eats merrily, and learns that Mrs. Goodheart murdered Jason Hardwick because he had fired her rather than face another turkey sandwich. Mrs. Goodheart contends that they'll never convict her since the announcer has eaten the evidence. The announcer concludes that he has merely "digested the facts of the case." RECOMMENDATION: The cast must work well together as everyone feeds off each other's lines in this fast paced comedy. ROYALTY: Free to Plays subscribers. SOURCE: Murray, John. (1979, January). A test for three detectives. Plays: The Drama Magazine for Young People, pp. 25-39. SUBJECTS/PLAY TYPE: Murder; Mystery.

3065. 11-12. (+) Ebersole, Martha. **Texas tacky. CAST:** 5f, 6m. **ACTS:** 2. SETTINGS: Mail processing room; clothing store; Texan beer joint. PLAYING TIME: NA. PLOT: This comedy centers around three women employed in the Internal Revenue Service mail processing room. Mary Fay is young, voluptuous, but innocent; Dee-Dee is middle aged, married, and motherly; and Laura is a Berkeley intellectual. Through their interactions with each other, and with male employees, the three women learn about themselves. RECOMMENDATION: This requires a mature and hard working cast. Some of the more difficult scenes include sexual humor. ROYALTY: $50. SOURCE: Ebersole, Martha. (1985). Texas tacky. Schulenburg, TX: I.E. Clark. SUBJECTS/PLAY TYPE: Texas; Women; Office Work; Comedy.

3066. K-3*. (-) Sullivan, Jessie P. **Thank God in everything (Thanksgiving). CAST:** 2u. **ACTS:** 1. SETTINGS: Puppet stage. PLAYING TIME: NA. PLOT: Mathilda helps Mortimer realize he must thank God for the good and the bad. Mortimer also learns that the reason for bad is to teach us good, and memorizes First Thessalonians 5:18 to help him remember what he has learned. RECOMMENDATION: The logic here is not credible, and the examples are too vague to make sense. ROYALTY: None. SOURCE: Sullivan, Jessie P. (1978). Puppet scripts for children's church. Grand Rapids, MI: Baker Book House. SUBJECTS/PLAY TYPE: Thanksgiving; Christian Drama; Puppet Play.

3067. 9-12. (-) Gleason, William. **Thank Zeus it's Friday. CAST:** 10f, 11m, Su. **ACTS:** 2. SETTINGS: Dance floor. PLAYING TIME: NA. PLOT: A bored Zeus recreates the Trojan War in a New York city disco. RECOMMENDATION: Although this musical has a few amusing moments and lands some well placed punches on the most obvious expressions of arrogance and tackiness in contemporary society, it is badly dated. Also, the dialogue is replete with sexist comments. ROYALTY: Upon application. SOURCE: Gleason, William. (1979). Thank Zeus it's Friday. Chicago, IL: Dramatic Pub. Co. SUBJECTS/PLAY TYPE: Satire; Iliad; Comedy.

3068. 1-3. (-) Gotwalt, Helen Louise Miller. **Thankful's red beads. CAST:** 3f, 7m. **ACTS:** 1. SETTINGS: Cabin living room. PLAYING TIME: 15 min. PLOT: Thankful finds bright red beads, frowned upon in her Puritan colony. Her parents are about to physically chastise her for disobedience, when Indians appear and menace the entire family. They are appeased by Thankful's bright beads and promise to come back the next day for the Thanksgiving feast. Thankful is rewarded for her courage by being allowed to wear the beads. RECOMMENDATION: This hinges on stereotyped images of Native American behavior and requires the singing of a hymn that may alienate students without a "WASP" background. ROYALTY: Free to Plays subscribers. SOURCE: Gotwalt, Helen Louise Miller. (1985). First plays for children: A collection of little plays for the youngest players. Boston, MA: Plays, Inc. SUBJECTS/PLAY TYPE: Thanksgiving; Puritans; Skit.

3069. 4-8. (+) Gotwalt, Helen Louise Miller. **Thanks to butterfingers. CAST:** 3f, 2m. **ACTS:** 1. SETTINGS: Dining room. PLAYING TIME: NA. PLOT: A visiting cousin gets into trouble because of her clumsiness. However, her clumsiness pays off at the end when she drops a piece of china, revealing a diamond ring that had been concealed within it. RECOMMENDATION: Betsy and her cousin's bickering about nonentities throughout the play is quite realistic and will strike a chord of sympathy in audience members with siblings. The scene in which they make up is a little syrupy, but the girls' list of why they're thankful for each other stops short of being corny. ROYALTY: Free to Plays subscribers. SOURCE: Gotwalt, Helen Louise Miller. (1986, November). Thanks to Butterfingers. Plays: The Drama Magazine for Young People, pp. 33-40. SUBJECTS/PLAY TYPE: Thanksgiving; Playlet.

3070. 1-6. (+) Marshall, Sheila L. **A Thanksgiving dream.** CAST: 18f, 19m. ACTS: 1. SETTINGS: Clearing. PLAYING TIME: 15 min. PLOT: As the Connors family prepares for Thanksgiving, Tom and John see no reason to be thankful. The boys dream about the first Thanksgiving and how happy the pioneers and Indians were to join each other in peace. When they awaken, their attitudes are changed and the Connors family is united. RECOMMENDATION: Although the Thanksgiving story is well known and the plot will be predictable to older audiences, this provides an important, positive view of Native Americans and their justified fears of the Pilgrims. ROYALTY: Free to Plays subscribers. SOURCE: Marshall, Sheila L. (1975, November). A Thanksgiving dream. Plays: The Drama Magazine for Young People, pp. 45-48. SUBJECTS/PLAY TYPE: Native Americans; Thanksgiving; Playlet.

3071. K-3. (-) Fisher, Aileen. **Thanksgiving everywhere.** CAST: Su. ACTS: 1. SETTINGS: None. PLAYING TIME: 1 min. PLOT: This describes the sights, sounds and smells of Thanksgiving. RECOMMENDATION: This tries to capture the sensory appeal of the holiday, but the rhyming is rather poor, the rhythm is not smooth, and some of the phraseology is quite dated. ROYALTY: Free to Plays subscribers. SOURCE: Fisher, Aileen. (1988, November). Thanksgiving everywhere. Plays: The Drama Magazine for Young People, pp. 51. SUBJECTS/PLAY TYPE: Thanksgiving; Choral Reading.

3072. 4-12. (+) Gilfond, Henry. **Thanksgiving for six.** CAST: 7u. ACTS: 1. SETTINGS: Street. PLAYING TIME: 15 min. PLOT: A group of people with nowhere to go on Thanksgiving put together an odds-and-ends feast and realize that Thanksgiving is what you make it. RECOMMENDATION: Although some dated references will need to be changed, this high interest\low vocabulary skit may provoke some discussion about attitudes and making the best of a situation. ROYALTY: None. SOURCE: Gilfond, Henry. (1985). Holiday plays for reading. New York, NY: Walker. SUBJECTS/PLAY TYPE: Thanksgiving; Skit.

3073. 4-7. (+) Wartski, Maureen Crane. **Thanksgiving on Catnabu.** CAST: 5f, 5m, 2u. ACTS: 1. SETTINGS: Control room of spaceship. PLAYING TIME: 12 min. PLOT: Natives of the planet Catnabu share food with a "space-wrecked" earth crew, proving to the homesick crew that the spirit of Thanksgiving is universal. RECOMMENDATION: This might be used as a catalyst for discussion of similar holidays in other countries. ROYALTY: Free to Plays subscribers. SOURCE: Wartski, Maureen Crane. (1979, November). Thanksgiving on Catnabu. Plays: The Drama Magazine for Young People,

pp. 43-48. SUBJECTS/PLAY TYPE: Science Fiction; Thanksgiving; Playlet.

3074. 6-9. (+) Hark, Mildred & McQueen, Noel. **Thanksgiving postscript.** CAST: 5f, 3m. ACTS: 1. SETTINGS: Living room. PLAYING TIME: 30 min. PLOT: Chuck, the Bakers' college age son, is coming home for Thanksgiving and mentions in a letter that he is bringing a guest. His girlfriend is distressed, but all is resolved as Chuck's "friend" turns out to be a Great Dane, the fraternity's mascot. RECOMMENDATION: The humorous comparison between the "Pilgrim" fathers hunting in the wild forest for turkeys and modern day fathers who brave the supermarkets with shoppers who are "real turkeys" is especially endearing. ROYALTY: Free to Plays subscribers. SOURCE: Hark, Mildred & McQueen, Noel. (1985, November). Thanksgiving postscript. Plays: The Drama Magazine for Young People, pp. 14-24. SUBJECTS/PLAY TYPE: Thanksgiving; Comedy.

3075. 7-12. (-) McCusker, Paul. **The Thanksgiving pre-game football show.** CAST: 2m, 1u. ACTS: 1. SETTINGS: Bare stage, props. PLAYING TIME: NA. PLOT: A football coach explains that the purpose of Thanksgiving is to eat and watch football, and that the thanksgiving part is when you give thanks that your team won. His interviewer asks him "what about Jesus Christ," and the coach asks what team he plays for, which concludes the TV interview. RECOMMENDATION: Thanksgiving is not, as this play seems to say, strictly a religious holiday. The jokes are only overworn cliches. ROYALTY: NA. SOURCE: McCusker, Paul. (1984). Batteries not included. Boston, MA: Baker's Plays. SUBJECTS/PLAY TYPE: Thanksgiving; Christian Drama; Skit.

3076. 1-3. (+) Gotwalt, Helen Louise Miller. **A Thanksgiving riddle.** CAST: 6f, 5m. ACTS: 1. SETTINGS: Classroom. PLAYING TIME: 15 min. PLOT: Children play a "Charades" type game in which they pantomime the actions of Puritan children. RECOMMENDATION: A Sunday School teacher may find this an ideal project. The tasks assigned to the students follow gender based guidelines, but the sexism could be changed without loss. ROYALTY: NA. SOURCE: Gotwalt, Helen Louise Miller. (1985). First plays for young children: A collection of little plays for the youngest players. Boston, MA: Plays, Inc. SUBJECTS/PLAY TYPE: Thanksgiving; Puritans; Skit.

3077. 3-6. (+) Leuser, Eleanor D. **The Thanksgiving scarecrow.** CAST: 4f, 5m. ACTS: 1. SETTINGS: Road. PLAYING TIME: 15 min. PLOT: For ten years, Scarecrow has waited for someone to speak to him on Thanksgiving eve so that, in accordance with the legend, he could make a wish come true for them. Jenny says she has so much to be grateful for already that, instead of making a wish for herself, she wants Scarecrow to come home with her. Scarecrow wishes that she will always have the same thankful heart she has that day. RECOMMENDATION: This delightful fantasy brings home the true spirit of

Thanksgiving. Children will love the animated scarecrow. ROYALTY: Free to Plays subscribers. SOURCE: Leuser, Eleanor D. (1979, November). The Thanksgiving scarecrow. Plays: The Drama Magazine for Young People, pp. 53-56. SUBJECTS/PLAY TYPE: Thanksgiving; Fantasy.

3078. 5-8. (+) Gotwalt, Helen Louise Miller. **A Thanksgiving truce.** CAST: 5f, 3m. ACTS: 1. SETTINGS: Living room. PLAYING TIME: 35 min. PLOT: Each year the Marston family invites either Aunt Tillie or Aunt Hester for Thanksgiving. Due to a mix up, both aunts are invited this Thanksgiving, although they haven't spoken for years due to a dispute over a recipe. As soon as they arrive, the quarrels begin and the Marston family is in an uproar. Nick Reed, a medical student, spare-time cookbook writer, and boyfriend of Susan Marston, charms the aunts into giving him their best recipes, and helps the aunts to discover how much they admire and like each other. RECOMMENDATION: This charmingly depicts family interactions with realistic dialogue and even a little romance thrown in. ROYALTY: Free to Plays subscribers. SOURCE: Gotwalt, Helen Louise Miller. (1977, November). A Thanksgiving truce. Plays: The Drama Magazine for Young People, pp. 17-28. SUBJECTS/PLAY TYPE: Thanksgiving; Recipes; Playlet.

3079. 7-12. (+) Miller, Ev. **That alien touch.** CAST: 2f, 4m, 7u. ACTS: 2. SETTINGS: Living room; interior of a spaceship. PLAYING TIME: NA. PLOT: Aliens intervene to save Robert, a young auto accident victim, and give him the power to heal others as well. At first the boy relishes his role as humanity's savior but then he notices that his touch induces a state of passivity and selflessness in people that can be dangerous in a violent and greedy world. Gradually, the awareness that his powers are a mixed blessing and the realization that relatives and strangers are exploiting the sick people who come to be healed make him wish he were ordinary again. The aliens comply. RECOMMENDATION: This is an imaginative and thought provoking play about power and responsibility. ROYALTY: $35. SOURCE: Miller, Ev. (1983). That alien touch. Chicago, IL: Dramatic Pub. Co. SUBJECTS/PLAY TYPE: Aliens; Ethics; Responsibility; Science Fiction.

3080. 9-12. (+) Scanlan, Michael. **That day.** CAST: 6f, 2m. ACTS: 1. SETTINGS: None. PLAYING TIME: 15 min. PLOT: Michael Beckler is a magician/juggler who, during an act at his school fails to choose his usual assistant, his girlfriend. Instead, he picks Hannah, who successfully separates the rings and turns the audience against Michael. As a result of this catastrophe, and the feelings he had repressed after his mother's death, Michael loses his mind and is hospitalized. RECOMMENDATION: Juggling six balls the same way that he juggles his true feelings, Michael demonstrates to young adults what can happen if they don't deal with real life situations openly and honestly. This believably and logically explores important conflicts such as death, divorce, and identity crisis. ROYALTY: $15. SOURCE: Scanlan, Michael. (1984). Inside/Out. Hollywood, CA: Samuel French. SUBJECTS/PLAY TYPE: Death; Divorce; Drama.

3081. 9-12. (-) Green, Albert. **That girl from Texas.** CAST: 12f, 6m. ACTS: 3. SETTINGS: Living room; dining room. PLAYING TIME: NA. PLOT: Three young working girls in New York City pursue romance, exciting careers, fun, and success. They abandon their long time boyfriends to vie for the attentions of a handsome young executive who is trying to buy their apartment building. The executive, however, is in love with the beautiful girl from Texas who owns the apartment house. Everyone pairs off predictably in the end. RECOMMENDATION: This trite plot panders to the view that a woman can only be measured as a success in the role of a wife. The sentiments of the characters are offensive and the dialogue is either insipid, snide, or overtly sexist. ROYALTY: $35. SOURCE: Green, Albert. (1976). That girl from Texas. Schulenburg, TX: I.E. Clark. SUBJECTS/PLAY TYPE: Dating; Marriage; Comedy.

3082. K-12. (+) Bryant, William Cullen. **That holy star.** CAST: Su. ACTS: 1. SETTINGS: None. PLAYING TIME: 1 min. PLOT: This is a simple prayer that uses themes appropriate for the Christmas season (holy stars and glorious beams). RECOMMENDATION: This could be used effectively for any age level. ROYALTY: None. SOURCE: Hendricks, William & Vogel, Cora. (1983). Handbook of Christmas programs. Grand Rapids, MI: Baker Book House. SUBJECTS/PLAY TYPE: Christmas; Choral Reading.

3083. 3-6. (+) Oberacker, Shirley C. **That spells Christmas.** CAST: 1m, Su. ACTS: 1. SETTINGS: North Pole. PLAYING TIME: 10 min. PLOT: A missing letter of the alphabet almost spoils Christmas until the exclamation point turns itself upside down to replace the missing "I," which has gone to Florida. When "I" returns, he promises not to leave again. RECOMMENDATION: This is an interesting way to teach the spelling of Merry Christmas. ROYALTY: Free to Plays subscribers. SOURCE: Oberacker, Shirley C. (1980, December). That spells Christmas. Plays: The Drama Magazine for Young People, pp. 62-64. SUBJECTS/PLAY TYPE: Christmas; Skit.

3084. 10-12. (-) Snee, Dennis. **That was no lady, that was a private eye.** CAST: 6f, 4m. ACTS: 1. SETTINGS: Office. PLAYING TIME: 30 min. PLOT: Phyllis Harlowe, private eye, protects a piano tuner from his ex-fiancee who wants to kidnap him. She is saved by her boyfriend when the jilted girlfriend threatens to shoot her. Phyllis promptly decides to give up her career and marry her boyfriend. RECOMMENDATION: This appears to be a takeoff on old detective movies, with females playing all the "heavy" roles. The substitution is not particularly funny; the effort falls flat. ROYALTY: $15. SOURCE: Snee, Dennis. (1982). That was no lady, that was a private eye. Boston, MA: Baker's Plays. SUBJECTS/PLAY TYPE: Detectives; Comedy.

3085. 7-12. (+) Murray, John. **That's a good question!** CAST: 5f, 8m. ACTS: 1. SETTINGS: Three living rooms.

PLAYING TIME: 40 min. PLOT: Fred is polling America on how well their cats like Norwegian sardines. As he tries to establish a rapport with each interviewee, he helps a desperate husband make a salmon souffle, solves a mystery in which a diamond necklace has been stolen, and saves a wedding by proving that the lovers aren't starcrossed. RECOMMENDATION: As Fred blunders into three homes, humor, Holmesian deduction, and astrology combine to make the lowly pollster (who constantly spouts off poll statistics) the hero. ROYALTY: Free to Plays subscribers. SOURCE: Murray, John. (1977, February). That's a good question! Plays: The Drama Magazine for Young People, pp. 1-18. SUBJECTS/PLAY TYPE: Pollsters; Mystery; Cooking; Comedy.

3086. 1-3. (+) Martin, Judith. **That's good, that's good.** CAST: 2f, 1m, 1u. ACTS: 1. SETTINGS: Bare stage. PLAYING TIME: 8 min. PLOT: The old fashioned teacher is dismayed to find Betty Beatsall cheating on her exams. A threatening alligator appears needing bus fare back to the Everglades. Betty does her math quickly, raises the money, and saves the teacher and her grade. RECOMMENDATION: Betty cheats by asking the audience to supply the answers, but realizes finally that she doesn't need to cheat. This makes the point gently without being too pedantic. ROYALTY: None. SOURCE: Martin, Judith. (1981). Everybody, everybody: A collection from the paper bag players. New York, NY: Elsevier/Nelson Books. SUBJECTS/PLAY TYPE: School; Cheating; Comedy.

3087. K-6. (+) Fisher, Aileen. **That's the way mothers are.** CAST: Su. ACTS: 1. SETTINGS: None. PLAYING TIME: 15 min. PLOT: Girls ask what a mother might want for Mother's Day, and answer with items that young females would request. Boys repeat the process, asking for things that young males would want. Both groups provide the chorus. At the end, they reimburse the mother for the child related gifts they requested, even though the mother says it is not necessary. RECOMMENDATION: This 20 line poem is highly recommended for presentation as a tribute to mothers. Its message is direct, timeless, and true-to-life. ROYALTY: Free to Plays subscribers. SOURCE: Fisher, Aileen. (1984, May). That's the way mothers are. Plays: The Drama Magazine for Young People, p. 60. SUBJECTS/PLAY TYPE: Mother's Day; Choral Reading.

3088. 7-12. (+) Bennett, Gordon. **Them.** CAST: 2f, 3m, 1u. ACTS: 1. SETTINGS: Room. PLAYING TIME: 12 min. PLOT: When a family of square eyed, green haired, six toed people move into town, Mr. and Mrs. Jones are asked to sign a petition stating that they will not sell their house to anyone unless the neighborhood approves. Mr. Jones refuses because the Boss (Jesus Christ) objects. RECOMMENDATION: This has funny, well paced lines with many parts read in unison. It will be a favorite of church audiences. ROYALTY: None. SOURCE: Altena, Hans (1978). The playbook for Christian theatre. Grand Rapids, MI: Baker Book House. SUBJECTS/PLAY TYPE: Bigotry; Comedy; Reader's Theater.

3089. 9-12. (-) Loselle, Greg. **Then again, maybe I will.** CAST: 2f, 1m, Su. ACTS: 1. SETTINGS: Cellar. PLAYING

TIME: NA. PLOT: At a high school class' 25th reunion, Nora (the wallflower), and Mike (the jock), are accidentally locked in a cellar/storeroom. Nora, who never married and lives with her mother, reveals that she had a crush on Mike, who has three children, is divorced, and owns a gas station. The two dance, kiss, are rescued, and resume their remote lives. RECOMMENDATION: This play about dreams gone sour falls flat because the characters are one dimensional, the action is nonexistent, and the dialogue (with its supposedly touching moments) is unmovingly boring. ROYALTY: $15. SOURCE: Loselle, Greg. (1982). Then again, maybe I will. Chicago, IL: Dramatic Pub. Co. SUBJECTS/PLAY TYPE: High Schools; Reunions; Love; Drama.

3090. 4-8. (+) Kehret, Peg. **There's a golf ball in the tree.** CAST: 1u. ACTS: 1. SETTINGS: None. PLAYING TIME: NA. PLOT: A child describes how he hides golf balls to see how long it takes golfers to find them. RECOMMENDATION: All age groups will be amused by this short tale of mischievousness. ROYALTY: NA. SOURCE: Kehret, Peg. (1986). Winning monologs for young actors. Colorado Springs, CO: Meriwether Pub. SUBJECTS/PLAY TYPE: Golfing; Mischief; Monologue.

3091. K-3. (+) Bauer, Caroline Feller. **There's a hole in my bucket.** CAST: 2u. ACTS: 1. SETTINGS: None. PLAYING TIME: NA. PLOT: The dilemma of fetching water in a leaky bucket is detailed in this humorous adaptation of the song. RECOMMENDATION: Written in a repetitive style, youngsters could easily memorize this. ROYALTY: NA. SOURCE: Bauer, Caroline Feller. (1987). Presenting reader's theater: Plays and poems to read aloud. New York, NY: H.W. Wilson. SUBJECTS/PLAY TYPE: Buckets; Reader's Theater.

3092. 4-8. (+) Kehret, Peg. **There's nothing to do around here.** CAST: 1u. ACTS: 1. SETTINGS: None. PLAYING TIME: NA. PLOT: The summertime blues is the topic of a disgruntled youngster's amusing tirade. RECOMMENDATION: Adults and youngsters alike will appreciate the frustrations of finding summertime amusement. ROYALTY: NA. SOURCE: Kehret, Peg. (1986). Winning monologs for young actors. Colorado Springs, CO: Meriwether Pub. SUBJECTS/PLAY TYPE: Boredom; Monologue.

3093. 10-12. (+) Simon, Mayo. **These men.** CAST: 2f. ACTS: 2. SETTINGS: Living room; bedroom. PLAYING TIME: NA. PLOT: Cloris, shy and naive, moves in with Shelly to escape her boyfriend. Shelly is a foul-mouthed slob who gives "promiscuity" lessons to Cloris. Despite their very different personalities, they form an intimate friendship. RECOMMENDATION: Although it could be performed by high school students, this contains vulgar language, implied sexual situations, and explicit descriptions which would be offensive. ROYALTY: $60. SOURCE: Simon, Mayo. (1982), These men. Woodstock, IL: Dramatic Pub. Co. SUBJECTS/PLAY TYPE: Comedy; Women; Sex.

3094. 6-12. (+) Gleason, William. **They came from somewhere.** CAST: 7f, 8m. ACTS: 2. SETTINGS: Office;

roadside; living room; jail. **PLAYING TIME: NA. PLOT:** The mayor of Latigo hires a California ad man to save his dying town. The sudden crash of a meteor coincides with the breakdown of the Liverman family's car outside Latigo and leads to an unexpected scam in which the Liverman family agrees not to reveal that they were mistakenly identified as aliens at the time of the meteor crash. The town is now able to attract tourists interested in seeing where the "aliens" landed. **RECOMMENDATION:** The confusion caused by souvenir hats with antennae worn by the touring Liverman family results in effective comedy. Baton twirling abilities are required for one character. **ROYALTY:** $50. **SOURCE:** Gleason, William. (1983). They came from somewhere. Chicago, IL: Dramatic Pub. Co. **SUBJECTS/PLAY TYPE:** Aliens; Vacations; Public Relations; Comedy.

3095. 9-12. (-) Gleason, William. **They'd hang you in Nashville. CAST:** 4f, 7m. **ACTS:** 2. **SETTINGS:** Living room; dining room. **PLAYING TIME: NA. PLOT:** Two men, recent college graduates without jobs, become involved in the personal life of an aging female country singer trying to make a comeback. They kidnap their landlord, attract the interest of a local radio announcer, receive help from the entirely female, "Fun Begins at Fifty Club," and successfully launch the lady's comeback. **RECOMMENDATION:** This slapstick comedy is peppered with insulting references to aging women, irrelevant use of biblical references, belittling of education, and sexual overtones which may be offensive. **ROYALTY:** $50. **SOURCE:** Gleason, William. (1976). They'd hang you in Nashville. Woodstock, IL: Dramatic Pub. Co. **SUBJECTS/ PLAY TYPE:** Country Western Music; Aging; Unemployment; Comedy.

3096. 7-12. (+) Kehret, Peg. **They'll be sorry when I'm dead. CAST:** 1f. **ACTS:** 1. **SETTINGS:** None. **PLAYING TIME: NA. PLOT:** Hiding in a hot, stuffy attic, a young girl reflects on the events that have caused her problems. Wearing her new coat to school was so important that disobedience was necessary, but soiling the coat with tar was a complete accident. Little sister Suzie is never reprimanded and can do anything, so if the young girl is found dead in the attic, Suzie and everyone else will be sorry; they'll be sure to treat her better from then on. The fragrance of fresh popcorn restores reality, with the conclusion that maybe a tragic death would be better another time. **RECOMMENDATION:** This hilariously presents the theme of the "mistreated and misunderstood." It reinforces the idea that facing reality is a good antidote to depression. **ROYALTY: NA. SOURCE:** Kehret, Peg. (1986). Winning monologs for young actors. Colorado Springs, CO: Meriwether Pub. **SUBJECTS/PLAY TYPE:** Suicide; Monologue.

3097. 10-12*. (+) Broadhurst, Kent. **They're coming to make it brighter. CAST:** 4f, 9m, Su. **ACTS:** 2. **SETTINGS:** Building lobby. **PLAYING TIME: NA. PLOT:** On Christmas Eve day, all but one of the aging, proud, veteran employees of an old, lovely New York City apartment building come to work to operate the elevators, shine shoes, and dispatch messages. They have shared many Christmas seasons together. This day is the same as

always, yet filled with foreshadowing of coming change: forms from the management to be filled out; the death of the absent employee; and the replacement of the old, beautiful, soft light fixtures in the lobby for new, ugly, "brighter" ones. **RECOMMENDATION:** This is an excellent portrayal of ways of life threatened by modernization. Adults would relate best to the characters and would be best suited to act the parts as there is some obscene language and the story requires a very detailed set which reflects the Art Deco design of the late 1920s. **ROYALTY:** $60. **SOURCE:** Broadhurst, Kent. (1986). They're coming to make it brighter. Woodstock, IL: Dramatic Pub. Co. **SUBJECTS/PLAY TYPE:** Modernization; Christmas; Comedy.

3098. 11-12. (+) Gardner, Herb. **Thieves. CAST:** 3f, 8m. **ACTS:** 2. **SETTINGS:** Bare stage, props. **PLAYING TIME: NA. PLOT:** Martin and Sally Cramer (married middle aged school teachers) find themselves drifting apart. No longer living together, Sally comes to their apartment to discuss divorce with Martin but goes to bed with him, instead. It is clear that they do have caring, but somewhat faded, feelings for each other. In the clear light of the morning and free of emotions, they confirm all the reasons why they should divorce. Both try to initiate affairs with other people, but neither succeeds. They seek solutions to problems by reliving the past, as Martin relives a moment of glory from his youth and Sally retreats to the security of her dad. Both emerge with new insights and reaffirm their marriage. **RECOMMENDATION:** The characters are convincingly real in speech, action, and emotion. They mesh in a way that is as lively and colorful as the street life in front of their apartment. The affairs are played very delicately and discreetly. **ROYALTY:** $50. **SOURCE:** Gardner, Herb. (1977). Thieves. New York, NY: Samuel French. **SUBJECTS/PLAY TYPE:** Marriage; Divorce; Comedy.

3099. 1-8. (+) Whittaker, Violet. **Things Jesus talked about. CAST:** 6u. **ACTS:** 1. **SETTINGS:** Puppet stage. **PLAYING TIME: NA. PLOT:** A flower, a bird, salt, a candle, and a fox tell Lora about their importance by reading verses from Matthew to her. The play ends with a review of the lessons about love and Jesus that have been learned. **RECOMMENDATION:** Although very didactic, this could be helpful in a classroom situation to personify some of the Bible verses. An adult must narrate. **ROYALTY: NA. SOURCE:** Whittaker, Violet. (1984). Puppet people scripts. Grand Rapids, MI: Baker Book House. **SUBJECTS/PLAY TYPE:** Bible Stories; Christian Drama; Puppet Play.

3100. 9-12. (+) Wilson, Pat. **Things that go bump in the night. CAST:** 5f, 5m, 2u. **ACTS:** 1. **SETTINGS:** Summer cottage. **PLAYING TIME:** 30 min. **PLOT:** While house-sitting at a summer cottage, Eli and Bethsheba try to bring back the spirit of Uncle Jonas so they can locate a watch that Eli was to have inherited. The house owners enter in costume, prepared to have a party. Strange occurrences spook everyone throughout the evening, as the two groups interact with one another. An uproar occurs when an eccentric local doctor's wolf is discovered on the roof and is assumed to be a demon, conjured by Eli to bring back the watch. At the end, all the goings on are explained scientifically. RECOMMENDATION: A comedy of errors, this is humorous and complicated. As characters move in and out, the plot becomes somewhat difficult to follow. Staging and special effects will be a challenge. ROYALTY: $15. SOURCE: Wilson, Pat. (1979). Things that go bump in the night. Keighley, England: Mantissa Press. SUBJECTS/PLAY TYPE: Ghosts; Goblins; Friday The Thirteenth; Comedy.

3101. K-3. (+) Carlson, Bernice Wells. **Think twice.** CAST: 3u. ACTS: 1. SETTINGS: Garden. PLAYING TIME: NA. PLOT: A gardener and kitchen maid argue about whether the sun or the moon is more important. They ridicule each other, but realize that neither one is totally wrong. RECOMMENDATION: This cleverly presents a lesson about the pitfalls of making fun of others. ROYALTY: NA. SOURCE: Carlson, Bernice Wells. (1982). Let's find the big idea. Nashville, TN: Abingdon. SUBJECTS/PLAY TYPE: Fable; Skit.

3102. 1-9. (+) Shore, Susan. (Asbrand, Karin) **The third day: An Easter pageant.** (The third day) CAST: 5f, 5m, 20u. ACTS: 1. SETTINGS: Hospital waiting room/terrace; garden. PLAYING TIME: 60 min. PLOT: Margaret Mason, mother of a gravely ill little boy, is in despair, though her husband and the physician try to reassure her of God's mercy and remind her that the next day is Easter. Exhausted, she sleeps and dreams of Jairus, his wife, and their daughter, who was raised from death by Jesus. Mary Magdalene and the Holy Mary tell the story of Christ's resurrection, and show Margaret that her son is alive, and that he will live to work for the Lord. Margaret wakes to find that it is true. RECOMMENDATION: The strong religious message makes this more suitable for a church environment. The modern dialogue is rather stilted, but the verses spoken by the flowers and candles are lyrical. ROYALTY: $30. SOURCE: Shore, Susan. (1988). The third day: An Easter pageant. Franklin, OH: Eldridge Pub. Co. SUBJECTS/PLAY TYPE: Easter; Christian Drama; Adaptation.

3103. 11-12. (-) Murray, John. **The third richest man in the world.** CAST: 6f, 3m, 4u. ACTS: 1. SETTINGS: Living room of a hotel suite. PLAYING TIME: 35 min. PLOT: College journalism students infiltrate the staff of an eccentric rich billionaire to gather information about him, and witness three visitors petition the rich man for assistance. The billionaire refuses to help, but gives each man an envelope before sending him away. While protesting this callous treatment, one of the reporters blows his cover. The three visitors return to thank the billionaire for his generosity and compassion revealed in the contents of the envelopes. The reporters are taught a lesson in good reporting: wait until all the facts are in. RECOMMENDATION: The lines are too long, the situations inconsistent with the time period, and complex situations are oversimplified. ROYALTY: Free to Plays subscribers. SOURCE: Murray, John. (1979, 1985). Fifteen plays for today's teenagers. Boston, MA: Plays, Inc. SUBJECTS/PLAY TYPE: Social Commentary; Ethics, Business; Melodrama.

3104. 9-12. (+) Colman, Richard. **Third street.** CAST: 3m. ACTS: 1. SETTINGS: Grave yard. PLAYING TIME: NA. PLOT: Three graduating high school boys "rap" as they smoke dope and drink beer. One is going to Princeton, one works for a butcher, and one is married to the girl he made pregnant. They talk about how they will get together after graduation, but realize they will drift apart. RECOMMENDATION: The setting in a graveyard underscores the death of the boys' friendship as each goes his own way. Directors might want to eliminate the pot and beer, but this would adversely affect the overall tone of the play. ROYALTY: NA. SOURCE: Lamb, Wendy. (1986). Meeting the winter bike rider and other prize winning plays. New York, NY: Dell. SUBJECTS/PLAY TYPE: Graduation; Friendship; Drama.

3105. 7-12. (-) Martens, Anne Coulter. **Thirteen.** CAST: 13u. ACTS: 1. SETTINGS: Living room. PLAYING TIME: 25 min. PLOT: A surprise birthday party is planned for Bonnie, a member of the Twelve Teens Club. Bonnie declines the invitation to come because she will be the thirteenth guest. The other girls try to cure Bonnie of her superstitious ideas by breaking a mirror, opening an umbrella, and putting shoes on a table. The plan seems to backfire when seeming bad luck occurs. Everything soon falls into place as all the occurrences are explained. RECOMMENDATION: "Thirteen" is not only an unlucky number, it is a play with an unlikely plot. Too many coincidences in too short a time destroy its credibility. ROYALTY: Free to Plays subscribers. SOURCE: Martens, Anne Coulter. (1979, October). Thirteen. Plays: The Drama Magazine for Young People, pp. 27-36. SUBJECTS/PLAY TYPE: Mystery; Superstitions; Playlet.

3106. 3-10*. (+) Bush, Max. **13 bells of Boglewood.** CAST: 3f, 4m. ACTS: 1. SETTINGS: Forest. PLAYING TIME: 65 min. PLOT: Casey Smith searches for gold in a forest, guided by an old book he has just purchased, and assisted by a young man named Brian. The woods are inhabited by fairies, a greedy Bogle, and two hideous Spriggans. With the help of the Bogle, who will do anything for gold, the men are able to see and hear the fairies. Smith and the Bogle try to get the gold, while the fairies and the Spriggans try to stop them. Brian vacillates, but ends up on the side of the fairies when he realizes that their survival depends on the gold dust. Smith uses threats and violence to locate the gold but his greed is his downfall. As thirteen bells toll, he is turned into a Bogle. RECOMMENDATION: This will entrance younger children, yet contains enough suspense for older children. The main characters have fairly substantial parts and would have to be played by adolescents, but grade schoolers could play the fairies and Spriggans. ROYALTY: $35. SOURCE: Bush, Max. (1987). 13 bells of Boglewood. New Orleans, LA: Anchorage Press, Inc. SUBJECTS/PLAY TYPE: Greed; Fairies; Treasure; Drama.

3107. 10-12. (+) Lynn, Jess. **Thirteen heavens and nine hells.** CAST: 5f, 4m. ACTS: 1. SETTINGS: Bare stage, platforms. PLAYING TIME: NA. PLOT: This strongly resembles **The breakfast club** in its message and format. Nine characters, all dealing with some element of disharmony in their lives attend the "Harmonic Convergence," a gathering to welcome in the new age. Before returning home to their respective corners of the world, each finds enlightenment and acceptance as a result of the interactions with one another. RECOMMENDATION: As this relies heavily on dialogue, the cast will need to have extraordinary powers of memorization. Mature viewers will appreciate the extensive character development. ROYALTY: $50. SOURCE: Lynn, Jess. (1988). Thirteen heavens and nine hells. Boston, MA: Baker's Plays. SUBJECTS/PLAY TYPE: Self Acceptance; Drama.

3108. 5-12*. (+) Gleason, William. **The $39 man.** CAST: 4f, 7m. ACTS: 1. SETTINGS: City. PLAYING TIME: NA. PLOT: Milo Sapperstein, faithful guardian of the city sewage system, falls prey to dastardly Dr. Draino and winds up literally cut to ribbons. His friend, Paddy, brings what is left of him in a small plastic bag to a medical clinic where a doctor reconstructs Milo with $39 worth of plumbing and various spare parts. The Bionic Milo and his Irish friend set out to rescue Natalie, who has been kidnapped by Draino. But Draino has created his own punishment by linking up with the faithless Natalie, who is willing to kill Draino if he won't marry her. Natalie is nothing if not resilient however, and when the reconstructed Milo overcomes Dr. Draino, she transfers her affections once again. RECOMMENDATION: This is fast moving and filled with puns and hilariously silly antics. A thick Irish brogue is spoken by Paddy, and Natalie sings her woes to music which can be improvised. Younger grades will enjoy this but it requires older students as actors and producers. ROYALTY: $15. SOURCE: Gleason, William. (1976). The $39 man. Chicago, IL: Dramatic Pub. Co. SUBJECTS/PLAY TYPE: Bionic Man; Comedy.

3109. 3-6. (+) Gabriel, Michelle. **This is your life, Israel.** CAST: 2f, 4m, 3u. ACTS: 1. SETTINGS: None. PLAYING TIME: 20 min. PLOT: Theodor Herzl, Golda Meir, David Ben Gurion, and others, in addition to Israel and Jerusalem, make brief appearances in this play to explain the events that led up to May 14, 1948, Israel's Independence Day, or Yom Haatzma'ut. The format is "This Is Your Life," as Israel is honored on her birthday. RECOMMENDATION: Students will learn something of the making of the Jewish state through this entertaining format. ROYALTY: None. SOURCE: Gabriel, Michelle. (1978). Jewish plays for Jewish days. Denver, CO: Alternatives in Religious Education, Inc. SUBJECTS/PLAY TYPE: Israel; Independence Day, Israel; Yom Haatzma'ut; Jewish Drama.

3110. 10-12. (+) Urdahl, Richard. **This isn't Scarsdale, Gus.** CAST: 1f, 2m. ACTS: 1. SETTINGS: Heaven. PLAYING TIME: NA. PLOT: A husband and wife arrive at the Pearly Gates after a car accident. The wife assures her husband that he will not be entering Heaven alongside of her. When they are both invited to enter, she becomes so preoccupied with recounting her husband's lacks, she fails to notice Heaven's closing door. Horrified to be left behind, she beats on the door and discovers it had never been locked. RECOMMENDATION: This offers food for

thought to a religiously oriented group of high schoolers, depicting Heaven as a place where all may enter and be forgiven. ROYALTY: $10. SOURCE: Urdahl, Richard. (1984). Don't listen to us, Lord.we're only praying. Boston, MA: Baker's Plays. SUBJECTS/PLAY TYPE: Forgiveness; Heaven; Christian Drama.

3111. 5-10. (+) Dotterer, Dick. **This site unsuitable for dragons.** CAST: 3f, 3m. ACTS: 2. SETTINGS: Bare stage, props. PLAYING TIME: NA. PLOT: Zerbinetta (a fox) is unfairly accused of stealing, and is exiled by Master Pantalone (a peacock), who sees this as a chance to rid the kingdom of danger. Lucinda (a pheasant and niece to Master Pantalone) tries to prevent the exile with the help of Arlecchio (a monkey), who tricks Master Pantalone and Capitano (a tiger) into believing they are under attack by Dragons. Zerbinetta rescues Master Pantalone, who allows her to stay in the kingdom and learns a lesson about judging others. RECOMMENDATION: The appeal for younger children is the story; the appeal for older youth is the acting, which has much room for improvisation. The actors wear masks and each develops a repertoire of movements which identify his/her character each time it appears on stage. ROYALTY: NA. SOURCE: Dotterer, Dick. (1983). This site unsuitable for dragons. Boston, MA: Baker's Plays. SUBJECTS/PLAY TYPE: Animals; Comedy.

3112. 6-12. (+) Majeski, Bill. **Those good old radio days.** CAST: 1f, 9m, 1u. ACTS: 1. SETTINGS: Broadcasting studio. PLAYING TIME: NA. PLOT: In a recreation of an early radio soap opera, charitable Ma Cucumber's porch is blown off in a tornado. She hires an idiotic handyman who botches the repair job, but is paid anyway because he claims to be sending his nephew to yoga school. He fritters his money away at the kissing booth, until Ma Cucumber stops him by pitching one of her killer cupcakes at the kisser. The episode ends with Ma's arrest for felonious assault. RECOMMENDATION: This pokes some good natured fun at the early radio dramas in which the heroine was always getting into trouble, while getting others out. ROYALTY: None. SOURCE: Majeski, Bill. (1981). Easy skits, blackouts and pantomimes. Woodstock, IL: Dramatic Pub. Co. SUBJECTS/PLAY TYPE: Radio Plays; Satire; Skit.

3113. 10-12. (-) Kelly, Tim. **Those wedding bells shall not ring out or, the bride wore green chili peppers.** CAST: 9f, 5m. ACTS: 1. SETTINGS: Restaurant. PLAYING TIME: 60 min. PLOT: Dastardly Snicklefritz Grubb steals Cindy's gold nugget and convinces her to marry him. Cindy's true love, Darius D. Dogood, saves her and recovers the gold nugget from Pawnshop Polly and Mrs. Lucretia Clutchpurse. RECOMMENDATION: This western melodrama uses stereotypically good and evil characters whose dialogue is confusing and would not hold the audience's interest. ROYALTY: $35. SOURCE: Kelly, Tim. (1988). Those wedding bells shall not ring out or the bride wore green chili peppers. Denver, CO: Pioneer Drama Service, Inc. SUBJECTS/PLAY TYPE: Goldrush; Melodrama.

3114. 5-8. (+) Kehret, Peg. **Thoughts during a boring sermon.** CAST: 1u. ACTS: 1. SETTINGS: None.

PLAYING TIME: NA. PLOT: A youngster describes the excruciating boredom suffered during Sunday sermons. RECOMMENDATION: This typical daydream should be familiar to most. ROYALTY: NA. SOURCE: Kehret, Peg. (1986). Winning monologs for young actors. Colorado Springs, CO: Meriwether Pub. SUBJECTS/PLAY TYPE: Sermons; Boredom; Daydreams; Monologue.

3115. 9-12. (+) Blaskey, Robert. (Henry, O.) **A thousand dollars.** (A thousand dollars) CAST: 3f, 3m, Su. ACTS: 1. SETTINGS: One movable chair. PLAYING TIME: NA. PLOT: In accordance with his uncle's will, Bob must spend $1000 within 24 hours and inform the lawyer how it was spent. A diamond necklace for an actress and a donation to a blind man are considered, but rejected because of greed. The money is finally given to Linda, a benefactor of orphans and ward of his uncle. Reporting to the lawyer, Bob learns that the will stipulates that, if the money has been wisely spent, Bob will inherit $50,000; if not, then Linda will receive the inheritance. Bob tells the lawyer that the money was lost at the race track. RECOMMENDATION: This retains the surprise ending and is consistent with O. Henry's style where coincidence affects character. Unlike the original, however, this has a much happier, lighter and carefree tone. ROYALTY: $25. SOURCE: Blaskey, Robert. (n.d.). A thousand dollars. Franklin, OH: Eldridge Pub. Co. SUBJECTS/PLAY TYPE: Inheritances; Wills; Adaptation.

3116. 4-6. (+) Spamer, Claribel. (Grimm Brothers) **The three apprentices.** (The three apprentices) CAST: 5f, 5m. ACTS: 1. SETTINGS: Courtyard. PLAYING TIME: 10 min. PLOT: A clever wizard shows three young travelers how to win their fortune by following directions to outwit an evil innkeeper. RECOMMENDATION: This teaches well the benefits of following directions. ROYALTY: Free to Plays subscribers. SOURCE: Spamer, Claribel. (1980, April). The three apprentices. Plays: The Drama Magazine for Young People, pp. 49-53. SUBJECTS/PLAY TYPE: Folk Tales, Germany; Directions; Adaptation.

3117. K-2. (-) Silverman, Eleanor. **Three bears, Goldilocks, the wolf and the three pigs.** CAST: Su. ACTS: 5. SETTINGS: Woods; Houses: straw, brick, wood. PLAYING TIME: 10 min. PLOT: The three bears visit the three pigs. The wolf who has been chasing Goldilocks shows up, blows down two houses, and winds up in the pot. Bears, pigs, and Goldilocks celebrate with cookies. RECOMMENDATION: The lack of any time element and the absence of staging directions for Goldilocks and the bears make this disjointed play very confusing. ROYALTY: NA. SOURCE: Silverman, Eleanor. (1983). Dramatics for children. Metuchen, N.J.: Scarecrow Press SUBJECTS/PLAY TYPE: Bears; Pigs; Wolves; Puppet Play.

3118. 2-5. (+) Jones, David Cadwalader. (Asbjornsen, Peter C., and Moe, Jorgen) **Three billy goats gruff.** (The three billy goats gruff) CAST: 2f, 1m, 4u. ACTS: 1. SETTINGS: None. PLAYING TIME: 15 min. PLOT: A troll becomes angry as goats cross his bridge, but he is persuaded by the goats not to eat them, after which all become friends. RECOMMENDATION: This adds a somewhat humorous touch to the character of Troll and

makes him more likable than in the original. The rhyming in parts of the play will be fun for the audience. ROYALTY: Free to Plays subscribers. SOURCE: Jones, David Cadwalader. (1977, November). Three billy goats gruff. Plays: The Drama Magazine for Young People, pp. 77-80. SUBJECTS/PLAY TYPE: Folk Tales, Norway; Trolls; Puppet Play; Adaptation.

3119. 6-9. (+) Brock, James. **Three boys at a girls' camp.** CAST: 4f, 1m. ACTS: 1. SETTINGS: Inside a cabin. PLAYING TIME: NA. PLOT: Three 15 year old girls wonder how they will survive summer camp without boys when, much to their delight, three 15 year old boys accidentally stumble into their cabin. They frantically try to hide the boys from their counselor, Miss Kleegle, but she predictably discovers them and concludes that such a bizarre story could only be the truth. All ends well when the girls are allowed to see the boys the next evening for visitors' night. RECOMMENDATION: Although the antics of three typical junior high girls at a summer camp are superficial and the dialogue and plot lack originality, this will appeal to teenage audiences. ROYALTY: $25. SOURCE: Brock, James. (1987). Three boys at a girls' camp. Franklin, OH: Eldridge Pub. Co. SUBJECTS/PLAY TYPE: Dating; Comedy.

3120. 6-8. (+) Jacobs, Jason. **Three cheers for the hero.** CAST: 3f, 8m, 2u. ACTS: 1. SETTINGS: Hotel lobby. PLAYING TIME: 30 min. PLOT: Heather Heartsong, owner of the Heartsong Hotel, unintentionally books the Heroes' Union Convention and the Villains' Union Convention for the same weekend. Problems arise when each union discovers a member who hasn't been doing his duty: Reuben Rye has been too busy to save damsels in distress, and Dagwood Deli called the fire department before he torched the candy store and has never evicted a tenant. Reuben and Dagwood change places. RECOMMENDATION: This makes good use of flat but exaggerated dialogue. The audience must be familiar with the genre of melodrama to understand the parody. ROYALTY: Free to Plays subscribers. SOURCE: Jacobs, Jason. (1985, April). Three cheers for the hero. Plays: The Drama Magazine for Young People, pp. 31-38. SUBJECTS/PLAY TYPE: Comedy; Heroes; Villains; Melodrama.

3121. 4-12. (+) Gilfond, Henry. **Three days more.** CAST: Su. ACTS: 1. SETTINGS: Ship's deck. PLAYING TIME: 15 min. PLOT: The captains of Columbus' three ships agree to sail only three more days. If land is not sighted by then, they will take over and return home. At the last minute, land is seen. RECOMMENDATION: The resolve of Columbus is pitted against the fears of his mutinous crew as they negotiate. This high interest\low vocabulary drama provides good insight into Columbus' fateful voyage. ROYALTY: None. SOURCE: Gilfond, Henry. (1985). Holiday plays for reading. New York, NY: Walker. SUBJECTS/PLAY TYPE: Columbus Day; Columbus, Christopher; Playlet.

3122. 3-7. (+) Coryell, Dorothea Smith. **The three evils.** CAST: 3f, 5m, 4u. ACTS: 2. SETTINGS: Garden; living room. PLAYING TIME: 20 min. PLOT: The villagers tell the new magistrate, Mandarin, that three evils afflict them: a dragon, a tiger, and a cruel man, JoChou, who has terrorized the village for years. When Mandarin tells JoChou what the villagers have said, JoChou is mortified, kills the dragon and tiger, and says he will go away. The villagers entreat him to stay, giving freely of what they had complained JoChou took from them previously. RECOMMENDATION: JoChou's character change is not convincing unless the man is explained to the audience as someone who doesn't realize how his actions have been interpreted by others. The message about channeling energies into constructive pursuits is loud and clear. ROYALTY: Free to Plays subscribers. SOURCE: Coryell, Dorothea Smith. (1982, November). The three evils. Plays: The Drama Magazine for Young People, pp. 51- 57. SUBJECTS/PLAY TYPE: Folktales, China; Behavior; Adaptation.

3123. K-8. (+) Olfson, Lewy. **Three fables from a broken fortune cookie. CAST:** 3f, 11m. **ACTS:** 1. **SETTINGS:** Bare stage, props. **PLAYING TIME:** 18 min. **PLOT:** A Chinese stage manager (speaking pidgin English) narrates three fractured fables. In the first, two of the king's advisers discuss the best way to deal with a fire in the castle while the third puts it out. Moral: "Haste makes sense." In the second, the princess' true love disguises himself as a rich suitor so that her father will allow the marriage. The princess doesn't recognize him, refuses to marry him, and remains an old maid. Moral: "A rose by any other name would probably not be recognized." In the third, a princess chooses a rich duck (who used to be a king) as an escort over a poet and a comedian. Moral: "A fool and his money, nowadays, get invited everywhere." RECOMMENDATION: If this is not found to be culturally offensive, its combination of sophisticated humor, physical comedy and wonderful one liners are sure to be a hit. ROYALTY: Free to Plays subscribers. SOURCE: Olfson, Lewy. (1975, May). Three fables from a broken fortune cookie. Plays: The Drama Magazine for Young People, pp. 69-75. SUBJECTS/PLAY TYPE: Comedy; Fable; Skit.

3124. 3-6. (+) Houston, Sally. (Grimm Brothers) Three golden hairs. (Three golden hairs) **CAST:** 3f, 3m, 5u. **ACTS:** 1. **SETTINGS:** Entrance to a cave; outside king's palace. **PLAYING TIME:** 20 min. **PLOT:** On his way to deliver a letter to the Queen, the Miller's son, Hanzl, stumbles upon a robbers' cave and asks the robbers' mother if he may rest. When her sons arrive home, they read Hanzl's letter which explains that the King intends to have the boy killed because at his birth it was foretold that he would marry the King's daughter. The robbers, without the boy's knowledge, rewrite the letter to state the opposite. Discovering the plan too late, the King tries rid himself of the boy by sending him off to pluck three golden hairs from the demon's head. On his way, Hanzl meets two watchmen who ask three questions and indicate that the person who answers them will be rich. When he arrives at the demon's cave, the demon's mother agrees to help him pluck the hairs, and also agrees to ask the demon Hanzl's three questions. The demon arrives, and each time he falls asleep she plucks a hair, waking him. The mother asks the three questions of her son, who answers them.

Hanzl relates the answers to the watchmen on his way back and so returns with the three hairs and gold. In answer to the King's queries about his fortune, Hanzl tells him to take the oars from the oarsman and row to the other side of the river, where the answer can be found. Unknown to the King, the person who takes the oars is doomed. RECOMMENDATION: The theme of greed is bound together nicely by the different acts of cleverness and trickery. Notable are the acts of compassion by both the robbers' and the demon's mother. ROYALTY: Free to Plays subscribers. SOURCE: Houston, Sally. (1976, January). Three golden hairs. Plays: The Drama Magazine for Young People, pp. 41-46. SUBJECTS/PLAY TYPE: Folk Tales, Germany; Adaptation.

3125. K-12. (+) Longfellow, Henry Wadsworth. **The three kings. CAST:** Su. **ACTS:** 1. **SETTINGS:** None. **PLAYING TIME:** 5 min. **PLOT:** This classic poem paints a detailed and sumptuous picture of the birth of Christ and the three wise men who came to pay him homage. RECOMMENDATION: This is most suitable for church or parochial school groups for performance at a Christmas pageant or worship service. ROYALTY: NA. SOURCE: Hendricks, William & Vogel, Cora. (1978). Handbook of Christmas programs. Grand Rapids, MI: Baker Book House. SUBJECTS/PLAY TYPE: Christmas; Three Wisemen; Christ, Jesus; Worship Program.

3126. 7-12. (+) Kehret, Peg. **Three Kleenex movies. CAST:** 1f. **ACTS:** 1. **SETTINGS:** None. **PLAYING TIME:** NA. **PLOT:** Ratings for "tear-jerker" movies in terms of degrees of moisture production are treated. The Three-Kleenex movie is the ultimate, as it evokes the maximum eye-wiping and nose-blowing response. RECOMMENDATION: With faithful attention to details, this describes the cathartic effect of tear-jerker movies. ROYALTY: NA. SOURCE: Kehret, Peg. (1986). Winning monologs for young actors. Colorado Springs, CO: Meriwether Pub. SUBJECTS/PLAY TYPE: Movies; Monologue.

3127. 6-12. (+) Schaaf, Albert K. **The three little detectives. CAST:** 3f, 3m. **ACTS:** 1. **SETTINGS:** Apartment. **PLAYING TIME:** 12 min. **PLOT:** The wolf, an international spy, is pursuing three beautiful detectives, Wally's Cherubs, who have been set up as decoys so that Wally and Busby can obtain the plans for secret weapon O-X-90. After a series of funny situations and scrapes with the wolf, it is discovered that Busby is the wolf in disguise. When an F.B.I. man arrives, each accuses the other of being the wolf, but the Cherubs use their detective skills to save the free world once again. RECOMMENDATION: This humorous script could still be produced today except that the material relies so heavily on "Charlie's Angels" for many of its jokes, that the script would be crippled by reliance on dated material. ROYALTY: Free to Plays subscribers. SOURCE: Schaaf, Albert K. (1979, March). The three little detectives. Plays: The Drama Magazine for Young People, pp. 61-67. SUBJECTS/PLAY TYPE: Comedy; Spoof; Detectives; Skit.

3128. K-4. (+) Gotwalt, Helen Louise Miller. **Three little kittens. CAST:** Su. **ACTS:** 1. **SETTINGS:** Bare stage, props. **PLAYING TIME:** 10 min. **PLOT:** The kittens take off their mittens to play ball, lose them, find them, and purr. **RECOMMENDATION:** The verse of the original keeps this from being too patronizing. **ROYALTY:** None. **SOURCE:** Gotwalt, Helen Louise Miller. (1985). First plays for children: A collection of little plays for the youngest players. Boston, MA: Plays, Inc. **SUBJECTS/PLAY TYPE:** Mittens; Kittens; Nursery Rhymes; Playlet.

3129. K-4. (+) Barr, June. **The three little kittens.** **CAST:** 4u. **ACTS:** 1. **SETTINGS:** Bare stage. **PLAYING TIME:** NA. **PLOT:** The three kittens cry to their mother that they've lost their mittens. When the kittens find their mittens, mother rewards them with pie, with which the kittens soil their mittens. After washing their mittens, the kittens join mother to search for a mouse. **RECOMMENDATION:** Young children will be entertained by the easily performed physical movements of the kittens. **ROYALTY:** None. **SOURCE:** Jennings, Coleman A. & Harris, Aurand. (1988). Plays children love, Volume II. New York, NY: St. Martin's Press. **SUBJECTS/PLAY TYPE:** Kittens; Nursery Rhymes; Mother Goose; Playlet.

3130. K-3. (+) Christmas, Joyce S. (Ballantyne, Robert H.) **Three little kittens' Christmas.** (The three little kittens) **CAST:** 4f, 3m, Su. **ACTS:** 1. **SETTINGS:** Home of the kittens; street. **PLAYING TIME:** 15 min. **PLOT:** Three kittens go caroling after opening their Christmas gifts: mittens. Each kitten loses a mitten at a different caroling spot. The lost mittens are returned so that the kittens may have pie after all. **RECOMMENDATION:** The familiarity of Mother Goose makes this a delight. **ROYALTY:** Free to Plays subscribers. **SOURCE:** Kamerman, Sylvia E. (1978). On stage for Christmas. Boston, MA: Plays, Inc. **SUBJECTS/PLAY TYPE:** Christmas; Nursery Rhymes; Adaptation.

3131. K-5. (+) Solomon, Olivia. **The three little pigs.** **CAST:** 4m. **ACTS:** 1. **SETTINGS:** Bare stage. **PLAYING TIME:** NA. **PLOT:** Leonardo (who fancies himself an artist) and Ludwig (an aspiring singer) build the traditional straw and stick houses, in spite of their brother's warnings about the wolf. When their houses are blown down, they seek refuge in their brother's brick house, defeat the wolf, and learn a valuable lesson about responsibility. **RECOMMENDATION:** Although not entirely faithful to the original, this stands well on its own. Each pig's nature is delineated through its name and characterization, and the emotional conflict and dialogue is more intense and poignant. **ROYALTY:** NA. **SOURCE:** Solomon, Olivia. (1983). Five folk comedies for today's juvenile stage. Tuscaloosa, AL: Portals. **SUBJECTS/PLAY TYPE:** Folk Tales, England; Trickery; Wolves; Adaptation.

3132. K-2*. (+) Stoppels, June. **The three little pigs.** **CAST:** 1f, 3u. **ACTS:** 1. **SETTINGS:** Bare stage. **PLAYING TIME:** 20 min. **PLOT:** The three little pigs and Goldilocks must build a house for protection from the big bad wolf. **RECOMMENDATION:** This entertaining version of the classic tale will be greatly enjoyed by very young children, who will appreciate the audience participation. It is suggested, however, that the older elementary grades

produce the play for younger grades. **ROYALTY:** $10. **SOURCE:** Stoppels, June. (1978). The three little pigs. Denver, CO: Pioneer Drama Service. **SUBJECTS/PLAY TYPE:** Folk Tales, England; Wolves; Trickery; Adaptation.

3133. 4-9. (+) Cheatham, Val R. **The three little pigs and friends.** **CAST:** 9u. **ACTS:** 1. **SETTINGS:** Television studio with a countryside set with a brick house. **PLAYING TIME:** 10 min. **PLOT:** A miniseries titled "The Three Little Pigs" is being filmed for Ham Box Office. The first pig, Hogney Dangerfield, complains that he gets no respect; the second pig, Shakespig, misquotes Shakespeare; and the third and smartest pig, Albert Sweinstein, has developed the "theory of relatives." As the cast prepares for filming, the announcer and the wolf's agent make pig jokes. When the wolf is about to blow the house down, the director announces that the production has been cancelled because the sponsor, Good Ole Boys Sausage, Bacon, and Pickled Pigs Feet, feels it would be bad for its image. **RECOMMENDATION:** This is simply a collection of old jokes and puns. Ideally, it should be performed by upper grade students for younger children. **ROYALTY:** Free to Plays subscribers. **SOURCE:** Cheatham, Val R. (1983, January/February). The three little pigs and friends. Plays: The Drama Magazine for Young People, pp. 73-76. **SUBJECTS/PLAY TYPE:** Pigs; Comedy; Parody; Skit.

3134. 9-12. (+) Raby, Peter. (Dumas, Alexandre) **The three musketeers.** (The three musketeers) **CAST:** 13f, 39m, Su. **ACTS:** 2. **SETTINGS:** Stage in two levels. **PLAYING TIME:** NA. **PLOT:** Country-bred D'Artagnan, determined to become a king's musketeer, is insulted by the agent of the all powerful Cardinal Richelieu and vows revenge. In attempting to exact it, he offends the three musketeers and each challenges him to a duel. He accepts, but after he assists them in a battle against the Cardinal's guards, the musketeers embrace him. He becomes enamoured of the lovely Constance, and disguises himself as Milady's lover for a night. She vows to take his life and and the queen's, but is foiled by the three musketeers. **RECOMMENDATION:** This sprawling extravaganza contains 41 fast moving scenes and a challenging number of lines for each principal actor. The performance would require long hours of concentration and practice. Ribald jokes and some explicit language might be a problem. **ROYALTY:** $50. **SOURCE:** Raby, Peter. (1977). The three musketeers. New York, NY: Dramatist's Play Service, Inc. **SUBJECTS/PLAY TYPE:** Heroes; History, France; Adventure; Adaptation.

3135. 3-12. (+) Way, Brian. (Dumas, Alexandre) **The three musketeers.** (The three musketeers) **CAST:** 7f, 27m. **ACTS:** 1. **SETTINGS:** Outside. **PLAYING TIME:** NA. **PLOT:** The tale of the three musketeers and D'Artagnan unfolds as we learn that Queen Anne of France is secretly involved with the Duke of Buckingham, and offers him her diamonds as a token. Cardinal Richelieu secretly plots against the Queen, and has the King ask the Queen to wear her diamonds to the next state ball. The musketeers and D'Artagnan succeed in foiling the Cardinal's plot, and win the Queen's favor. **RECOMMENDATION:** This fairly faithful adaptation is intended to be played by adults or experienced teens for a family audience. It is a major production requiring a large cast with talented performers in the physically demanding roles of the musketeers and D'Artagnan. The pace is rapid, with no scene interruptions; lighting is used for transitions. ROYALTY: $45. SOURCE: Way, Brian. (1977). The three musketeers. Boston, MA: Baker's Plays. SUBJECTS/PLAY TYPE: Heroes; History, France; Adventure; Adaptation.

3136. 3-4. (+) Cheatham, Val R. **The three musketeers and friends.** CAST: 1f, 5m, 1u. ACTS: 1. SETTINGS: Throne room. PLAYING TIME: 15 min. PLOT: The Queen discovers her crown is missing and orders the three musketeers to find it. It is the royal Prince's birthday, a grand ball is planned, and the Queen thinks that she will not command her subjects' respect without her crown. When the three musketeers find the Prince using the Queen's crown as a bowl to feed his dog, the Queen decides she does not need a crown to command respect. RECOMMENDATION: Although the language is a bit dated, this modern spoof could be quite funny with some rewriting. ROYALTY: Free to Plays Subscribers. SOURCE: Cheatham, Val R. (1979, April). The three musketeers and friends. Plays: The Drama Magazine for Young People, pp. 71- 75. SUBJECTS/PLAY TYPE: Satire; Comedy.

3137. K-5. (+) Bauer, Caroline Feller. (Jacobs, Joseph) **The three sillies.** (The three sillies) CAST: 3f, 3u. ACTS: 1. SETTINGS: Kitchen; room in an inn. PLAYING TIME: 15 min. PLOT: A gentleman is amused by his sweetheart's foolish worrying about a mallet stuck in the ceiling of her parents' cellar. She and her parents weep because they fear if she and the gentleman have a son, the son could be killed by the falling mallet should he go into the cellar. The gentleman removes the mallet and leaves the foolish threesome to begin a search for three bigger "sillies". If he finds them, he promises to return and marry the farmer's daughter. His travels lead to a woman trying to get a cow onto a thatched roof, a traveler who tries to jump into his trousers, and a villager trying to rake out the moon which he supposes has fallen into a pond. He returns to marry the farmer's daughter. RECOMMENDATION: Children will thoroughly enjoy the foolishness and the underlying theme about needless worry. This has retained some of the original's country English vernacular, adding to its charm. ROYALTY: None. SOURCE: Bauer, Caroline Feller. (1987). Presenting reader's theater: Plays and poems to read aloud. New York, NY: H. W. Wilson Co. SUBJECTS/PLAY TYPE: Fools and Simpletons; Folk Tales, English; Reader's Theater; Adaptation.

3138. 6-8. (-) Bayer, Harold. (Jacobs, Joseph) **The three sillies.** (The three sillies) CAST: 2f, 2m, 1u. ACTS: 1. SETTINGS: Basement. PLAYING TIME: 20 min. PLOT: As young Mabel enters the cellar to get her father a beer, she notices an ax stuck in the beam, and worries that, if she were married and had a a son and if she sent her son to the cellar, the ax would fall and kill him. She begins to weep, as do her mother and father. Throckmorton, whom Mabel hopes to marry, arrives and says that he won't marry Mabel unless he can find three sillier people in the world. He goes off in search, returning to say that he did find three sillier people: a woman trying to get a cow to climb a

ladder, a girl trying to rake the moon out of a pond, and a man who refused to reward his garden with water, because the vegetables wouldn't grow. RECOMMENDATION: Producers will need to alter the references to beer as well as the song about the pleasures of drinking it. Changes of sex for some of the characters could eliminate hints of sexism. ROYALTY: NA. SOURCE: Bayer, Harold. (1982). Motley tales: A collection of folk and fairy tales with music. Boston, MA: Baker's Plays. SUBJECTS/PLAY TYPE: Folk Tales, England; Fools and Simpletons; Adaptation.

3139. 9-12. (+) Sills, Paul. (Grimm Brothers) **The three travelers.** (The three travelers) CAST: 1f, 2m, 4u. ACTS: 1. SETTINGS: Theater; country inn; courtroom; gallows. PLAYING TIME: NA. PLOT: Three unemployed performers are propositioned by a mysterious stranger. They will be rewarded if they always answer questions in the same way. The first actor is to say, "All three of us," the second "For the money," and the third "That's right." The travelers agree and follow the stranger's instructions. When an innkeeper murders one of his guests, he tries to pin the blame on the three actors, whose responses to the judge are very incriminating. However, as they are about to be executed, the stranger returns, and instructs them to point out the real murderer. The truth comes out, and the stranger, discovered to be the devil, leads the innkeeper away, saying he'll see the actors soon. RECOMMENDATION: This grisly tale is a good adaptation of the original which adds some modern touches whose sarcasm moves this beyond a fairy tale. ROYALTY: NA. SOURCE: Sills, Paul. (1981). More from story theatre. New York, NY: Samuel French. SUBJECTS/PLAY TYPE: Folk Tales, Germany; Devils; Playlet.

3140. 2-4. (-) Sills, Paul. (Jacobs, Joseph) **The three wishes.** (The three wishes) CAST: 1f, 1m, 1u. ACTS: 1. SETTINGS: Woods; kitchen. PLAYING TIME: NA. PLOT: A woodsman is granted three wishes, the first of which is squandered on a piece of sausage. The sausage is wished onto his nose and then off again for a tasty dinner, but the disappointing use of his gift remains. RECOMMENDATION: The wife's last words that she's not hungry exquisitely understate the tragic comedy of the situation. ROYALTY: NA. SOURCE: Sills, Paul. (1981). More from story theatre. New York, NY: Samuel French. SUBJECTS/PLAY TYPE: Folk Tales, England; Wishes; Tragicomedy.

3141. K-4. (+) Thane, Adele. (Jacobs, Joseph) **The three wishes.** (The three wishes) CAST: 5f, 3m, Su. ACTS: 1. SETTINGS: Forest; kitchen. PLAYING TIME: 15 min. PLOT: As a happy-go-lucky poor woodcutter works, he frees a fairy trapped in a tree, who grants him and his wife three wishes. The woodcutter unintentionally wishes for sausages to appear in the cooking pot. In anger, the wife wishes the sausages stuck to the end of her husband's nose. The couple is forced to use the third wish to remove the sausages. Some children give them flowers, and they invite the children to a feast. Happiness, kindness and thankfulness prevail in the kitchen as the play ends with the couple and the children dancing and singing in celebration. RECOMMENDATION: The physical action of the characters (chopping wood, carrying flowers, cutting sausages) gives variety and interest while the rhyming of words and intermittent dancing lend a "cuteness" to the dialogue. ROYALTY: Free to Plays subscribers. SOURCE: Thane, Adele. (1983). Plays from famous stories. Boston, MA: Plays Inc. SUBJECTS/PLAY TYPE: Folk Tales, England; Wishes; Playlet.

3142. 2-6. (+) Swintz, Martha. **The three wishing bags.** CAST: 4f, 5m, Su. ACTS: 1. SETTINGS: Kitchen; palace room. PLAYING TIME: 20 min. PLOT: Eloise, a young scullery maid, confides to the cook and jester that she has fallen in love with the prince, and wishes to work in his father's palace to be near him. An old woman appears asking for food, and Eloise befriends her. As a reward, the woman gives Eloise three bags, each filled with a wish that only Eloise can obtain without being killed. She uses the first bag to obtain the desired job at the palace, where she soon competes with a haughty lady for the prince's affections. The lady steals one of Eloise's bags, which the prince uses, then dies. Eloise uses the final bag to restore the prince, and the two marry. RECOMMENDATION: The theme of goodness bringing reward, and evil receiving its due, is pleasurably interjected with the humorous banterings of the cook and jester. ROYALTY: NA. SOURCE: Kamerman, Sylvia E. (1987). Plays from favorite folk tales. Boston, MA: Plays, Inc. SUBJECTS/PLAY TYPE: Wishes; Romance; Playlet.

3143. K-3*. (+) Atkins, Greg & Garbedian, Brian. **Through the storybook.** CAST: 4f, 2m. ACTS: 1. SETTINGS: Bedroom; storybook. PLAYING TIME: 40 min. PLOT: Rebecca, a little girl with a large imagination, lives in a world in which her storybook characters come to life. Captain Hook, the Big Bad Wolf, and the Wicked Stepsisters emerge and each believes Rebecca is the heroine of his/her own story. The conflicts that these situations pose teach Rebecca a valuable lesson in understanding and valuing her parents, grandparents and siblings. RECOMMENDATION: Rebecca, with her imagination and her propensity for getting into trouble with other members of her family, is a character with whom children can easily identify. ROYALTY: NA. SOURCE: Atkins, Greg & Garbedian, Brian. (1988). Through the storybook. Schulenberg, TX: I.E. Clark. SUBJECTS/PLAY TYPE: Fantasy; Family Life; Comedy.

3144. 4-7. (+) Bauer, Caroline Feller. (Byars, Betsy) **The Thursday call.** (Cracker Jackson) CAST: 1f, 2m, 2u. ACTS: 1. SETTINGS: Bedroom. PLAYING TIME: 10 min. PLOT: Cracker Jackson's mother divorced his father because he refused to be serious about anything. In a surprising change of character, Mr. Jackson becomes serious during his routine Thursday telephone call when Cracker tells him that his old babysitter is being abused by her husband and has warned Cracker not to come to her house again. Cracker's parents come together to face this problem. RECOMMENDATION: This could serve as a catalyst for important discussion between children and their parents about divorce and wife abuse. ROYALTY: None. SOURCE: Bauer, Caroline Feller. (1987). Presenting reader's theater: Plays and poems to read aloud. New

York, NY: H.W. Wilson Co. SUBJECTS/PLAY TYPE: Wife Abuse; Divorce; Adaptation.

3145. 10-12. (+) Price, Leonard. **Tickets to the desert.** CAST: 4f, 3m. ACTS: 1. SETTINGS: Village courtyard. PLAYING TIME: NA. PLOT: A small group of pilgrims seek passage to the Egyptian mountains where saintly hermits (who hold the secrets to lives of peace and serenity) live. A villager tries to sell them tickets for an excursion through the desert to meet the hermits, but the pilgrims meet an old goat-herder and herb woman, who show them that the peace they seek is in their own hearts. RECOMMENDATION: A church school would be ideal for this production. ROYALTY: $15. SOURCE: Price, Leonard. (1985). Tickets to the desert. Boston, MA: Baker's Plays. SUBJECTS/PLAY TYPE: Pilgrimages; Contentment; Drama.

3146. 8-12. (+) Kelly, Tim & Christiansen, Arne. **Tied to the tracks.** CAST: 16f, 9m, Su. ACTS: 2. SETTINGS: Lobby; train tracks. PLAYING TIME: 90 min. PLOT: Silias Scavenger, unscrupulous boss of the Medicine Show troupe, plots to wed Melody and gain respectability, but she is the sweetheart of Billy Bold, the young and handsome sheriff. Silias falsely implicates Billy in a robbery, and the sheriff is jailed. With Melody's help, Billy escapes in time to stop the robbery of the Night Express by notorious Prairie Rose and her gang. While Billy chases the fleeing outlaws, Silias ties Melody to the tracks because she spurns his proposal of marriage. She is rescued in the nick of time by the heroic Billy. RECOMMENDATION: The success of this typical melodrama and its stock characters depends on split second timing and the musical talents of the group performing it. ROYALTY: $60. SOURCE: Kelly, Tim & Christiansen, Arne. (1985). Tied to the tracks. Denver, CO: Pioneer Drama Service. SUBJECTS/PLAY TYPE: Musical; Melodrama.

3147. K-3. (+) Hoberman, Mary Ann. **Tiger.** CAST: 1u. ACTS: 1. SETTINGS: None. PLAYING TIME: NA. PLOT: The physical and behavioral aspects of a tiger are briefly and humorously outlined. RECOMMENDATION: One of Bauer's arrangement of "Animal Antics", this can be read alone or with the other poems in the collection. ROYALTY: NA. SOURCE: Bauer, Caroline Feller. (1987). Presenting reader's theater: Plays and poems to read aloud. New York, NY: H.W. Wilson. SUBJECTS/PLAY TYPE: Tigers; Reader's Theater.

3148. K-3. (+) Gardner, John. **Tiger.** CAST: 1u. ACTS: 1. SETTINGS: None. PLAYING TIME: NA. PLOT: Tigers are tough; it's safer not to annoy them. RECOMMENDATION: Amusing alone, this would also work well with the other poems in "Animal Antics." ROYALTY: NA. SOURCE: Bauer, Caroline Feller. (1987). Presenting reader's theater: Plays and poems to read aloud. New York, NY: H.W. Wilson. SUBJECTS/PLAY TYPE: Tigers; Reader's Theater.

3149. 3-6. (+) Carlson, Bernice Wells. **The tiger, the Brahman, and the jackal.** CAST: 9u. ACTS: 1. SETTINGS: Jungle clearing. PLAYING TIME: NA. PLOT: An Indian priest (Brahman) frees a caged tiger and then must find a way to keep from being eaten. RECOMMENDATION: This short, charming play is well written and easy to produce. ROYALTY: None. SOURCE: Carlson, Bernice Wells. (1982). Let's find the big idea. Nashville, TN: Abingdon Press. SUBJECTS/PLAY TYPE: Tigers; Fable.

3150. 3-8. (+) McHale, Ethel Kharasch. **The tiger's promise.** CAST: 4m, 2u. ACTS: 1. SETTINGS: Clearing. PLAYING TIME: 15 min. PLOT: On his way home with a fish for dinner, Boy meets a hungry Tiger who promises not to eat him if Boy gives him the fish. After he eats the fish, Tiger tries to eat Boy, but gets his paw caught in a trap. When Boy helps him out of the trap, Tiger tries to eat him again. Boy tries to get help from Rooster and Tree who can only tell their own tales of broken promises. Finally, Guru helps Boy by tricking Tiger back into the trap. Tiger is not able to charm Guru because he is not naive like Boy. However, Guru, like Boy, believes in keeping promises and goes back with Boy to catch another fish for dinner, as Boy had promised he would do. RECOMMENDATION: The warning that one cannot be naive in a world without principle and the lesson about reliability are well taught. This teaches children to be cautious about believing everything, and stresses the principle of keeping a promise. ROYALTY: Free to Plays subscribers. SOURCE: McHale, Ethel Kharasch. (1975, November). The tiger's promise. Plays: The Drama Magazine for Young People, pp. 49-52 SUBJECTS/PLAY TYPE: Folk Tales, India; Promises; Playlet.

3151. K-6*. (+) Cumming, Peter. **Ti-Jean.** CAST: 1f, 4m. ACTS: 4. SETTINGS: Palace room; woods. PLAYING TIME: 60 min. PLOT: Tired of being king and wanting only to fiddle, the king sets his three sons to three contests, the prize for which is the crown. They must find the Princess who was stolen and disguised by a witch; capture the fierce Unicorn; and steal the Giant's fiddle. Ti-Jean, the youngest brother, succeeds in all three with the help of the white cat whom he has rescued early in the play. The cat turns out to be the long lost Princess. RECOMMENDATION: The king must either be able to fiddle or the sound effects must be well coordinated. The use of French necessitates accurate accents. There are two versions: English with French phrases, and French-English. ROYALTY: NA. SOURCE: Cumming, Peter. (1981). Ti-Jean. Toronto: Playwrights Canada SUBJECTS/PLAY TYPE: Folk Tales, French Canadian; Adventure; Drama.

3152. 9-12. (+) Paisley, Brian. **Tikta'liktak.** CAST: 1m, Su. ACTS: 1. SETTINGS: Bare stage, props. PLAYING TIME: NA. PLOT: An eskimo, seeking food for his family, is marooned on a small piece of ice in the melted icy river. He saves himself by killing a seal and uses the flesh to eat, the skin to make a boat, and the oil to make a fire. He returns home safely, escaping an attack by a hungry bear. RECOMMENDATION: This uses many eskimo words, and gives a glimpse of the eskimo beliefs about the spirit of animals. To be truly effective, this highly stylized play would need some well drawn puppets or costumes (for the animals), and a well crafted illusion of ice and cold weather. ROYALTY: NA. SOURCE: Doolittle, Joyce.

(1984). Eight plays for young people. Edmonton, Alberta, Canada: NeWest Publishers. SUBJECTS/PLAY TYPE: Eskimoes; Hunting; Narrative.

3153. 4-6. (+) Huff, Betty Tracy. **Tillie of the Golden Turkey Grille.** CAST: 8f, 7m. ACTS: 1. SETTINGS: Kitchen. PLAYING TIME: 35 min. PLOT: Unknown to its owner, Dudley Dumpster, the Golden Turkey Grill restaurant is being sabotaged by Lester Messington, nephew of Morton Messington, and owner of the Messington Restaurant. Tille Trustworthy, the Golden Turkey Grille's clumsy but well intentioned busgirl, reveals Lester's true identity and villainous nature. The Grille is saved from financial ruin, and Tillie and Dudley are free to marry. RECOMMENDATION: Despite its predictable plot and superficial characters, the play's humor and theme of good vs. evil will most certainly appeal. ROYALTY: Free to Plays subscribers. SOURCE: Huff, Betty Tracy. (1980, October). Tillie of the Golden Turkey Grille. Plays: The Drama Magazine for Young People, pp. 15-26. SUBJECTS/PLAY TYPE: Romance; Comedy; Melodrama.

3154. 4-7. (-) Bradley, Virginia. **Tillie's terror.** CAST: 1f, 4m, 1u. ACTS: 1. SETTINGS: Room. PLAYING TIME: NA. PLOT: An early 1900s melodrama is spoofed, as the heroine is saved from the villain by the hero and a ghost. RECOMMENDATION: Even with a good narrator, the plot is stale and uninteresting, while the puppets required are elaborate and difficult to make. ROYALTY: None. SOURCE: Bradley, Virginia. (1975). Is there an actor in the house? New York: Dodd, Mead. SUBJECTS/PLAY TYPE: Melodrama; Ghosts; Puppet Play.

3155. 7-12. (+) Mattera, John & Barrows, Steve. (Alexander, Karl) **Time after time.** CAST: 4f, 2m, 6u. ACTS: 2. SETTINGS: Room; bank; museum; apartment. PLAYING TIME: NA. PLOT: Leslie John Stephenson, alias Jack the Ripper, uses H.G. Wells' time machine to travel to present day San Francisco. Wells follows him and meets Amy Robbins, a feminist and bank teller. Together they apprehend Stephenson, but not before he has brutally murdered several twentieth century women. After imprisoning Jack in a time warp, H.G. and Amy journey back to 19th century London to live happily ever after. RECOMMENDATION: This shortened version is faithful to the original. Set changes that convey the movement from the 19th to 20th century could cause some staging problems. ROYALTY: $50. SOURCE: Mattera, John & Barrows, Steve. (1983). Time after time. Chicago, IL: Dramatic Pub. Co. SUBJECTS/PLAY TYPE: Time Travel; Jack the Ripper; Adaptation.

3156. 12. (+) Alexander, Ronald. **Time and ginger.** CAST: 3f, 4m. ACTS: 2. SETTINGS: Living room. PLAYING TIME: NA. PLOT: The Davis' daughter is pregnant and doesn't want to get married. Their son wants to experiment with men before he decides his preference. The daughter moves out to live with her boyfriend. The 16 year old son elopes with the girl next door. RECOMMENDATION: This mildly amusing play should be presented by mature audiences for mature audiences; it is not appropriate for school use. ROYALTY: NA.

SOURCE: Alexander, Ronald. (1980). Time and ginger. New York: Dramatists Play Service, Inc. SUBJECTS/PLAY TYPE: Sex; Family; Marriage; Comedy.

3157. 7-12. (+) Fisher, Aileen Lucia. **Time for mom.** CAST: 3f, 5m, Su. ACTS: 1. SETTINGS: Dining room. PLAYING TIME: 10 min. PLOT: Children present Mom with IOU'S for cleaning as her Mother's Day present. RECOMMENDATION: If the stereotype of mothers as house cleaners can be overlooked (or perhaps reworked), this shows nicely the value of one's time as a gift to another. ROYALTY: Free to Plays subscribers. SOURCE: Lucia, Aileen Fisher. (1985). Year- round programs for young players. Boston, MA: Plays, Inc. SUBJECTS/PLAY TYPE: Mother's Day; Playlet.

3158. 7-12. (+) Kelly, Tim J. (Wells, H. G.) **The time machine.** (The time machine) CAST: 7f, 3m, 13u. ACTS: 3. SETTINGS: Sitting room; Land of the Eloi; palace of the Green Porcelain; underground realm of the Morlocks. PLAYING TIME: 90 min. PLOT: The eccentric Mr. Filby invents a time machine. Accompanied on its maiden voyage by his housekeeper, Mrs. Watchett, he travels into the future, meets unusual creatures, and barely escapes them to return to the present. RECOMMENDATION: The special effects are challenging and allow for creativity. ROYALTY: $35. SOURCE: Kelly, Tim. (1977). The time machine. Denver, CO: Pioneer Drama Service. SUBJECTS/PLAY TYPE: Science Fiction; Adventure; Adaptation.

3159. 3-8. (+) Silverman, Eleanor. (Wells, H.G.) **The time machine.** (The time machine) CAST: 1f, 1m. ACTS: 2. SETTINGS: House. PLAYING TIME: 20 min. PLOT: When hippies break in to burglarize the professor's house, they hide in the professor's time machine to avoid detection, and are turned into old people. When the professor demonstrates the machine to the police, he turns the maid into a squaw. All leave as a voice asks what the future holds. RECOMMENDATION: Producers might want to update the hippies and the maid, but this is adequate. ROYALTY: None. SOURCE: Silverman, Eleanor. (1983). Dramatics for children. Metuchen, NJ: Scarecrow Press. SUBJECTS/PLAY TYPE: Science; Inventions; Experiments; Adaptation.

3160. 3-4. (+) Fisher, Aileen Lucia. **Time out for Christmas.** CAST: 1f, 1m, 26u. ACTS: 1. SETTINGS: Playroom. PLAYING TIME: NA. PLOT: Last year's toys do not want Christmas to come because they are afraid they will be forgotten. RECOMMENDATION: This gives information on how Christmas is celebrated around the world. ROYALTY: None for amateur performance. SOURCE: Fisher, Aileen Lucia. (1986). Holiday programs for boys and girls. Boston: Plays, Inc. SUBJECTS/PLAY TYPE: Christmas; Playlet.

3161. 1-12. (+) Kurtz, Jack. **Timmy and the pitiful pink plastic ball.** CAST: 4f, 3m, 2u. ACTS: 1. SETTINGS: Bare stage. PLAYING TIME: NA. PLOT: Timmy is not pleased with the extended Christmas visits of his aunt, uncle, and eight cousins, so he spends more time playing away from home. He helps Brenda, an outcast whose mother is an alcoholic and whose father has run away, to decorate her first Christmas tree. Later, he givers her an old pink ball ornament his family no longer wants. His grandmother, hearing Timmy's story, explains that while most gifts seem inadequate, it is the thought that counts. In an added-on conclusion, Timmy continues to befriend Brenda and invites her to his church's caroling party. RECOMMENDATION: This poignant tale makes a realistic statement about love and generosity. The overriding religious theme makes it best suited for a church production or sermon. ROYALTY: None for the first performance. SOURCE: Kurtz, Jack. (1979). Gargoyles, plastic balls and soup. Boston, MA: Baker's Plays. SUBJECTS/PLAY TYPE: Christmas; Love; Sharing; Reader's Theater.

3162. K-6. (+) Lane, Richard Albert. (Andersen, Hans Christian) **The tinder box.** (The tinder box) CAST: 4f, 5m, 3u. ACTS: 1. SETTINGS: Village inn. PLAYING TIME: NA. PLOT: A wicked witch convinces a soldier to retrieve a tinder box in return for a treasure. However, when threatened by the witch, the soldier keeps the box and uses its magic to rescue a princess from her evil uncle. RECOMMENDATION: While the plot differs from the original, the spirit is retained. ROYALTY: $25. SOURCE: Lane, Richard Albert. (1975). The tinder box. Chicago, IL: Dramatic Pub. Co. SUBJECTS/PLAY TYPE: Folk Tales, Denmark; Adaptation.

3163. 6-9. (+) Denson, Wil. **Tinker autumn.** CAST: 2f, 4m. ACTS: 1. SETTINGS: Clearing. PLAYING TIME: NA. PLOT: The orphaned Peter runs from the sheriff and is hidden by Caitlan. Child Welfare workers decide that Caitlan lives in an environment from which she should be removed. Peter confesses to Caitlan that the sheriff wants to remove him from his land because he is a minor, and Caitlan admits to Peter that she cannot read, but won't enroll in school because she does not want to be laughed at. In a final confrontation with the welfare workers, Caitlan's father and Peter reveal that a judge has stopped the sale of Peter's land because Caitlan's father is going to adopt Peter to work the farm. Caitlan swallows her pride and promises to attend school. RECOMMENDATION: The development of Caitlan's character could lead youngsters to evaluate decisions they have or will have to make. ROYALTY: $35. SOURCE: Denson, Wil. (1985). Tinker autumn. Morton Grove, IL: Coach House Press, Inc. SUBJECTS/PLAY TYPE: School; Children's Rights; Drama.

3164. 1-6. (+) Phillips, D.J. **Tinkerbelle the tiger.** CAST: Su. ACTS: 1. SETTINGS: Living room. PLAYING TIME: 10 min. PLOT: Neighbors and police complain about a tame pet tiger until she apprehends a cat burglar. RECOMMENDATION: This could easily be produced as intended or it could be adapted for the stage, or even used as a cartoon. ROYALTY: Free to Plays subscribers. SOURCE: Phillips, D.J. (1985, May). Tinkerbelle the tiger. Plays: The Drama Magazine for Young People, pp. 52-54. SUBJECTS/PLAY TYPE: Tigers; Comedy; Puppet Play.

3165. 5-6. (+) Gabriel, Michelle. **Tisha B'av.** CAST: 4u. ACTS: 1. SETTINGS: None. PLAYING TIME: 15 min.

PLOT: Four persons discuss the values of the old and the new, of destroying old things and replacing them with new, and of overthrowing people's beliefs and even the people themselves. They talk of the historical persecution of the Jewish people and the Jewish observance of Tisha B'av, a sad day of fasting, but one on which the ideas of building out of destruction, as well as peace and hope coming out of grief, are also present. RECOMMENDATION: This effectively presents the complexity of Tisha B'av in a way which is understandable to young people. ROYALTY: None. SOURCE: Gabriel, Michelle. (1978). Jewish plays for Jewish days. Denver, CO: Alternatives in Religious Education, Inc. SUBJECTS/PLAY TYPE: Tisha B'av; Jewish Drama.

3166. 3-5. (+) Fisher, Aileen Lucia. **To a groundhog on February 2.** CAST: 1f, 1m, Su. ACTS: 1. SETTINGS: None. PLAYING TIME: NA. PLOT: The groundhog is called to determine if spring is near or if winter will prevail for six more months. RECOMMENDATION: This would be simple to perform and produce. ROYALTY: Free to Plays subscribers. SOURCE: Fisher, Aileen Lucia. (1985). Year-round programs for young players. Boston, MA: Plays, Inc. SUBJECTS/PLAY TYPE: Groundhog Day; Choral Reading.

3167. 10-12. (+) Higbee, Rand. **To absent friends.** CAST: 2f, 3m. ACTS: 1. SETTINGS: Hospital room. PLAYING TIME: NA. PLOT: Eric, a high school senior hospitalized after a car accident, is visited by three friends who were in the accident with him. They recount the details of the accident, which include alcohol and excessive speed. During the visit, it becomes apparent that Eric is the only one who survived and he struggles to find a reason. Bruce encourages him to search for and develop his own special talents and Jenny suggests that just his uniqueness is enough reason to live. As the friends leave for the funeral, Eric becomes more positive about his outlook. RECOMMENDATION: The use of humor saves this from didacticism. Acceptance of life's unfairness, making the most of every minute, and appreciating and accepting oneself are some of the themes. Though the messages are clear throughout, the **Twilight Zone** ending is unclear. ROYALTY: $30. SOURCE: Higbee, Rand. (1987). To absent friends. Franklin, OH: Eldridge Pub. Co. SUBJECTS/PLAY TYPE: Death; Alcohol Abuse; Identity; Drama.

3168. K-4. (+) Hall, Margaret. (Lanier, Sydney) **To cover the earth with leather.** (To cover the earth with leather) CAST: 1f, 1m, Su. ACTS: 1. SETTINGS: Throne room. PLAYING TIME: 10 min. PLOT: A king, rising to greet his future bride, stubs his toe and declares that the entire world should be covered with leather to prevent further accidents. The bride gently suggests that, to one who wears shoes, the world already seems to be covered in leather, an idea which both excites and amuses the king. RECOMMENDATION: Short but direct, this Persian flavored fable will entertain. ROYALTY: Free to Plays subscribers. SOURCE: Hall, Margaret. (1988, March). To cover the earth with leather. Plays: The Drama Magazine for Young People, pp. 45-47. SUBJECTS/PLAY TYPE: Shoes; Playlet; Adaptation.

3169. K-3*. (+) Sullivan, Jessie P. **To forgive is to forget.** CAST: 2u. ACTS: 2. SETTINGS: Puppet stage. PLAYING TIME: NA. PLOT: Mortimer and Mathilda teach each other a Bible verse about forgiveness, as they discover that forgiving and being forgiven will make them happy and dispel bad feelings. RECOMMENDATION: The actions of producing a list of grudges and then praying for forgiveness help reinforce the important lesson of Mark 11:25. ROYALTY: None. SOURCE: Sullivan, Jessie P. (1978). Puppet scripts for children's church. Grand Rapids, MI: Baker Book House. SUBJECTS/PLAY TYPE: Forgiveness; Christian Drama; Puppet Play.

3170. 7-12. (+) Banks, Gregory. **To see Christ at Christmas.** CAST: 7f, 7m. ACTS: 1. SETTINGS: Hospital room; waiting room; rehearsal room. PLAYING TIME: NA. PLOT: Bruce Grant and his son, B.J., cannot be convinced by Mrs. Grant and the rest of the family of the importance of God in their lives until Bruce has a heart attack which puts him in the hospital just before Christmas. There, Bruce and B.J. meet faithful Thad, a critically ill little boy whose dying wish is to see Christ at Christmas, and they find God. RECOMMENDATION: The theme of religious salvation is especially appropriate for a church or Christian school. The plot is convincing, and the dialogue is neither contrived nor artificial. Warmly inspirational, the play leaves the audience with a sense of hope and love. ROYALTY: NA. SOURCE: Banks, Gregory. (1987). To see Christ at Christmas. Franklin, Ohio: Eldridge Pub. Co. SUBJECTS/PLAY TYPE: Faith; Christmas; Christian Drama; Drama.

3171. 5-9. (+) Grinins, Tekla A. **To test the truth.** CAST: 7f, 13m, Su. ACTS: 1. SETTINGS: Game show stage. PLAYING TIME: 30 min. PLOT: Three panelists pose as George Washington, and three pose as Abraham Lincoln. Their answers to historical questions reveal which is the real Washington and Lincoln. RECOMMENDATION: Although the intended audience will probably not be familiar with the original TV game show upon which this is modeled, this might be a clever format for enrichment activities if the dialog were updated. ROYALTY: Free to Plays subscribers. SOURCE: Grinins, Tekla. (1976, May). To test the truth. Plays: The Drama Magazine for Young People, pp. 79-82. SUBJECTS/PLAY TYPE: Lincoln, Abraham; Washington, George; Comedy.

3172. K-3. (+) Mahlman, Lewis & Jones, David Cadwalader. (Perrault, Charles) **Toads and diamonds** (Toads and diamonds) CAST: 7f, 1m. ACTS: 1. SETTINGS: Kitchen; forest. PLAYING TIME: 20 min. PLOT: Grace is treated like a slave by her mother and sister. While fetching water, she helps an old woman, who rewards her by making flowers and diamonds fall from her mouth when she speaks. The mother tells the sister to fetch water the next day, hoping that she, too, will be enchanted. The sister refuses to help the old woman and is punished by having toads and snakes fall from her mouth. Grace is evicted from her home, meets a prince who tells her that her diamonds have provided a dowry befitting a princess, and the two marry. RECOMMENDATION: The challenge of creating ugly toads and snakes, as well as flowers and diamonds, will appeal to youngsters. ROYALTY: Free to Plays subscribers. SOURCE: Mahlman, Lewis & Jones, David Cadwalader. (1980). Folk tale plays for puppets. Boston, MA: Plays, Inc. SUBJECTS/PLAY TYPE: Folk Tales, France; Kindness; Adaptation; Puppet Play.

3173. 7-12. (+) Hark, Mildred & McQueen, Noel. A toast for Christmas. CAST: 2f, 6m. ACTS: 1. SETTINGS: Living room. PLAYING TIME: 25 min. PLOT: A movie star couple of the 1940s puts on a front of "Christmas spirit" for reporters while secretly enduring a failing marriage. An inadvertent act of giving rekindles feelings of charity and love, offering hope for future happiness. RECOMMENDATION: The fruits of selfish living are displayed here in all of their unattractiveness, and the moral comes across clearly without being trite. ROYALTY: Free to Plays subscribers. SOURCE: Hark, Mildred and McQueen, Noel. (1982, December). A toast to Christmas. Plays: The Drama Magazine for Young People, pp. 1-9. SUBJECTS/PLAY TYPE: Christmas; Selfishness; Playlet.

3174. 3-12*. (+) Harris, Aurand. A Toby show. CAST: 4f, 3m. ACTS: 3. SETTINGS: Drawing room. PLAYING TIME: NA. PLOT: The Toby character, popular in U.S. traveling theater performances in the 19th and early 20th centuries, acts as both master of ceremonies and as a chief character. The play concerns mistaken identity, an overworked young woman, a cruel stepmother, and Toby, a country handyman who is mistaken for a prince. The real prince flies into the garden in a two-seater airplane and is identified by the stepmother as the handyman. He and Cindy become friends until she discovers who he actually is through the intervention of the Prince's addle-brained Uncle. Toby resumes the role of handyman and stand up comedian. He discovers that Cindy is the true heiress to the estate that her stepmother and stepsisters have been claiming for their own. The prince, who has been dreading the seemingly inescapable necessity of marrying one of the stepsisters is delighted to propose to Cindy even before Toby reveals that she is rich. Toby goes back to being a simple country boy. RECOMMENDATION: The modern setting and the antics of Toby turn the classic Cinderella tale into an effective comedy. Because of the long lines and the need for expert comic timing, this requires an older, skilled cast. ROYALTY: $35. SOURCE: Harris, Aurand. (1978). A Toby show. New Orleans, LA: Anchorage Press, Inc. SUBJECTS/PLAY TYPE: Mistaken Identity; Love; Comedy.

3175. 1-6. (+) Kelly, Tim. (Otis, James) Toby Tyler or ten weeks with a circus. (Toby Tyler or ten weeks with a circus) CAST: 6f, 6m, 5u. ACTS: 2. SETTINGS: Circus grounds. PLAYING TIME: 60 min. PLOT: Toby Tyler runs away from home to work with the circus, and overhears a conversation between Lenita (the circus owner's sinister twin sister), and Olga (the gypsy fortune teller), in which Lenita plots to keep Mrs. Jones (the circus owner) from paying off the mortgage. Toby is caught listening and promises not to tell when he is threatened with an orphanage. The ringmaster is involved in a mishap (planned by Lenita) and Toby is given the job.

When Lenita plans to rob the safe which contains the final mortgage payment, Toby comes to the rescue. RECOMMENDATION: This faithful adaptation is well defined and easy to follow. The development of the characters is excellent and the settings correspond to their particular cast parts. Audience participation is an added attraction. ROYALTY: $25. SOURCE: Kelly, Tim. (1981). Toby Tyler or ten weeks with a circus. Denver, CO: Pioneer Drama Service. SUBJECTS/PLAY TYPE: Circus; Adaptation.

3176. 10-12. (+) Kassin, Michael. Today a little extra. CAST: 1f, 2m. ACTS: 1. SETTINGS: Kosher butcher shop. PLAYING TIME: NA. PLOT: Zalman Abrams, an elderly Jewish butcher, must sell his failing business to a young man, Levine, who does not plan to keep it kosher. During Abrams' last day in the shop, Levine arrives and says he is having some non-kosher meat delivered. He also plans to work Saturdays. Their dialogue, balanced by a visit from a longstanding, widowed customer, reveals the values of a fading Jewish culture. Levine comes to learn the deeper meaning of the word "kosher," and he cancels his delivery and asks Abrams to help him run the business. RECOMMENDATION: The author uses "Yiddish" dialect effectively to set the tone, enhance the atmosphere, and express the characters' values in this simple story of cultural transition. The actors must not exaggerate these speech traits lest an offensive parody result. ROYALTY: $15. SOURCE: Kassin, Michael. (1986). Today a little extra. Boston, MA: Baker's Plays. SUBJECTS/PLAY TYPE: Kashrut; Jewish Values; Drama.

3177. 11-12*. (+) Horovitz, Israel. (Torgov, Morley) Today, I am a fountain pen. (A good place to come from) CAST: 3f, 5m. ACTS: 1. SETTINGS: Home and dry goods store. PLAYING TIME: NA. PLOT: Annie Ilchak, a 15 year old Ukrainian girl, is hired by the Yanover family as a maid so Esther and Moses Yanover can devote their time to operating their dry goods business. Ten year old Irving Yanover and Annie like each other immediately and embark on adventures which get them into trouble together. Double standards present problems for the Yanovers, who refuse to allow Irving to eat bacon, and for the Ilchaks, who hate Annie's Italian boyfriend, Pete, and refuse to acknowledge that opera is mostly Italian. Irving discovers he likes bacon and Annie falls in love with an Italian and becomes pregnant. The parents and children resolve the differences. Irving gets to eat bacon at the Ilchak home, Annie marries the Italian, and, the narrator informs us, each goes on to live a happy life. RECOMMENDATION: This is written for an audience of mature teens and adults. The humorous writing style makes this enjoyable as it describes believable characters with realistic problems. The resolution will leave the audience hungry for a sequel. Happily, there are two more plays which follow this one. A trained stage crew may be required because the staging and lighting are crucial. The actors will need to perfect the timing in the delivery of their lines. ROYALTY: Write to publisher. SOURCE: Horovitz, Israel. (1987). Today, I am a fountain pen. New York, NY: Dramatists Play Service, Inc. SUBJECTS/PLAY TYPE: Family; Standards; Adaptation.

3178. 9-12. (+) Kelly, Tim. **Toga! Toga! Toga!** CAST: 12f, 9m, Su. ACTS: 3. SETTINGS: Living room. PLAYING TIME: 120 min. PLOT: George Brewster, a high school student, inherits a house where he establishes a fraternity, takes in a very odd assortment of boarders to pay the bills, and spends all of his time trying to hide them from the school principal, Miss Woebegone, and the faculty advisor, Miss Butterworth. Rival fraternity brothers sabotage his efforts by arranging for Melissa, who wants to be homecoming queen, to steal the money needed for the house payment. In a series of comical events, Miss Woebegone faints after an encounter with one of the fraternity brothers who is covered with soap. As she is being carried to an ambulance on a stretcher, she falls off and breaks her leg so she spends the rest of the play painfully hobbling around on crutches, determined to get to the bottom of the "scandalous affair." The climax comes as the characters meet at a toga party, the stolen money is recovered, George agrees to move his fraternity house onto campus to make it legal, and the girls plot the beginnings of a sorority. RECOMMENDATION: This has an improbable plot, ridiculous characters and farcical dialogue. However, those looking for a farce might want to consider this with some editing. ROYALTY: $35. SOURCE: Kelly, Tim. (1979). Toga! toga! toga! Denver, CO: Pioneer Drama Service. SUBJECTS/PLAY TYPE: Fraternity; Comedy.

3179. K-6. (+) Carlson, Bernice Wells. **Together or alone.** CAST: 8u. ACTS: 1. SETTINGS: Farm. PLAYING TIME: NA. PLOT: A parent tries to teach his children the importance of sticking together by showing them that seven sticks bound together cannot be broken. But the same sticks separated are easily shattered. RECOMMENDATION: The message that "united we stand, divided we fall" is dramatized with scenes in which siblings fight, a situation with which the audience will identify. ROYALTY: NA. SOURCE: Carlson, Bernice Wells. (1982). Let's find the big idea. Nashville, TN: Abingdon. SUBJECTS/PLAY TYPE: Fable; Unity; Skit.

3180. K-6. (+) Feather, Jean. **Tom and the leprechaun.** CAST: 2m, 5u. ACTS: 1. SETTINGS: Forest clearing. PLAYING TIME: 10 min. PLOT: Tom captures a leprechaun and forces him to reveal the location of his pot of gold. But Tom has forgotten his shovel. Marking the tree with his red handkerchief and securing the leprechaun's promise not to move the pot, Tom frees the leprechaun and goes home quickly for his shovel. Meanwhile, the leprechaun ties red handkerchiefs to all the trees. Tom decides to return to farming and the leprechauns agree to leave the red handkerchief as a reminder to mortals that they shouldn't try to outsmart the leprechauns. RECOMMENDATION: This adaptation of the timeless Irish folk tale is enchantingly faithful to the spirit of the original and uses lively Irish dialogue simple enough for young performers. ROYALTY: Free to Plays subscribers. SOURCE: Feather, Jean. (1989, March). Tom and the leprechaun. Plays: The Drama Magazine for Young People, pp. 41-45. SUBJECTS/PLAY TYPE: St. Patrick's Day; Folk Tales, Ireland; Leprechauns; Comedy.

3181. 7-12. (+) Barton, Dave & Bond, Matt. (Twain, Mark) **Tom Sawyer.** (The adventures of Tom Sawyer). CAST: 11f, 13m, Su. ACTS: 3. SETTINGS: Kitchen; outdoors; street; graveyard; church; courtroom; cave. PLAYING TIME: 90 min. PLOT: Faithful retelling of the original classic. RECOMMENDATION: This musical adaptation maintains the racial stereotyping of the original as well as slang which could be difficult to perform. Because the language is dated, one might suggest revising the script to make it easier to perform and understand. ROYALTY: $60. SOURCE: Barton, Dave, & Bond, Matt. (1975). Tom Sawyer. Denver, CO: Pioneer Drama Service. SUBJECTS/PLAY TYPE: Adventure; Musical; Adaptation.

3182. 5-9. (+) Kelly, Tim J. (Twain, Mark) **Tom Sawyer.** (The adventures of Tom Sawyer.) CAST: 12f, 9m, Su. ACTS: 2. SETTINGS: River, graveyard, schoolhouse, island, house, church, jail. PLAYING TIME: 90 min. PLOT: True to the Mark Twain classic, the play opens with the famous whitewash scene and the friendship/romance of Tom and the new girl, Becky Thatcher. Tom and Huck accidentally witness the graveyard murder of Doc Robinson, rescue the innocent Muff Porter from hanging for the crime, and become the new town heroes. RECOMMENDATION: This would be an excellent period piece for contemporary audiences and actors. Audience recognition helps reinforce the performance. ROYALTY: $35. SOURCE: Kelly, Tim J. (1983). Tom Sawyer. Schulenburg, TX: I.E. Clark. SUBJECTS/PLAY TYPE: Adventure; Comedy; Adaptation.

3183. K-12*. (+) Spencer, Sara. (Twain, Mark). **Tom Sawyer.** (The adventures of Tom Sawyer) CAST: 7f, 13m. ACTS: 4. SETTINGS: Bedroom; street; schoolroom; cemetery; island; church; courthouse; cave. PLAYING TIME: NA. PLOT: This is a faithful retelling of the classic. RECOMMENDATION: This condensed adaptation uses several of the important plots in the book including the murder incident, the Jackson Island adventure, finding buried treasure, Tom and Becky's romance, and some of Tom's mischievous pranks. At times, it even includes direct dialogue from the book. ROYALTY: Write Anchorage Press. SOURCE: Jennings, Coleman A. and Harris, Aurand. (1988). Plays children love, Volume II. New York, NY: St. Martin's Press. SUBJECTS/PLAY TYPE: Adventure; Adaptation.

3184. 3-8. (+) Silverman, Eleanor. (Twain, Mark) **Tom Sawyer.** (The adventures of Tom Sawyer) CAST: 4f, 4m, 1u. ACTS: 4. SETTINGS: House. PLAYING TIME: 30 min. PLOT: Five familiar vignettes are presented: Tom tricking Aunt Polly when she accuses him of eating jam; Aunt Polly trying to get Tom to admit he has played hookey and gone swimming; Tom convincing his friends that whitewashing a fence is fun; Tom falling in love with Becky Thatcher; and Tom playing sick to avoid going to school and ending up losing a tooth. RECOMMENDATION: This could be used in a classroom setting as an introduction to the classic. ROYALTY: None SOURCE: Silverman, Eleanor. (1983). Dramatics for children. Metuchen, NJ: Scarecrow Press. SUBJECTS/PLAY TYPE: Adventure; Adaptation.

3185. 5-9. (+) Thane, Adele. (Twain, Mark) Tom Sawyer, pirate. (The adventures of Tom Sawyer) CAST: 6f, 6m. **ACTS:** 1. **SETTINGS:** Backyard; island. **PLAYING TIME:** 25 min. **PLOT:** Aunt Polly threatens to punish Tom for skipping school. He and two friends leave for Jackson Island to be pirates and return several days later to find Aunt Polly mourning his death and in time to observe their own funeral services. As the funeral procession is about to start, the boys appear. Aunt Polly marches Tom off to the woodshed to chop firewood, but he again avoids punishment by running away. **RECOMMENDATION:** Loosely adapted, this captures the light hearted character of Tom, and contains animated dialogue. None of the splendid irony or satire of the original was chosen by the adapter for inclusion. **ROYALTY:** Free to Plays subscribers. **SOURCE:** Thane, Adele. (1988, October). Tom Sawyer. Plays: The Drama Magazine for Young People, pp. 51-58. **SUBJECTS/PLAY TYPE:** Adventure; Runaways; Adaptation.

3186. 1-5. (+) Sills, Paul. (Grimm Brothers) Tom Tit Tot. (Rumpelstiltskin) CAST: 2f, 2m. **ACTS:** 1. **SETTINGS:** Bare stage, props. **PLAYING TIME:** NA. **PLOT:** A young girl's mother brags that her daughter can spin five skeins of wool in one day, so the king takes the girl for his wife. The only condition of the marriage is that after eleven months of royal living, the girl must spin five skeins of wool a day for the twelfth month. The mother assures the frightened girl that he will forget, but the king remembers. Locked in her work room, the girl sees an "impit" appear, and he agrees to spin the wool if she will be his at the end of the month. Her only release from the deal would come if she guessed his name. Dining with the girl on the last day, the king mentions that he saw an impit spinning wool and singing a song that mentioned his name--Tom Tit Tot. The girl uses the information to free herself from the deal. **RECOMMENDATION:** All four characters have nearly equal amounts of dialogue, so no one will feel left out. **ROYALTY:** NA. **SOURCE:** Sills, Paul. (1981). More from story theatre. New York, NY: Samuel French. **SUBJECTS/PLAY TYPE:** Folk Tales, Germany; Skit.

3187. 7-12. (+) Randolph, Larry. Tomato on Tuesday. CAST: 2f, 1m. **ACTS:** 1. **SETTINGS:** Truck stop restaurant. **PLAYING TIME:** NA. **PLOT:** While eating at a lonely truck stop, an itinerant encourages his teenage waitress to break out of her mold and think of what she really wants out of life instead of just drifting along. **RECOMMENDATION:** This makes its point without preaching, and with a touch of romance to keep the sentimentalists interested. **ROYALTY:** $10. **SOURCE:** Randolph, Larry. (1975). Tomato on Tuesday. Chicago, IL: Dramatic Pub. Co. **SUBJECTS/PLAY TYPE:** Self Awareness; Drama.

3188. 9-12. (+) Dexter, Harriet. (Moliere, Jean Baptiste Poquelin) Too many doctors. (Le malade imaginaire) CAST: 5f, 4m. **ACTS:** 1. **SETTINGS:** Living room. **PLAYING TIME:** 45 min. **PLOT:** Argan is a hypochondriac who keeps three doctors in work and wages. His second wife encourages his dependence on medicines so that she can eventually get all of his money.

Through disguises and deception, Toinette (the impertinent serving girl) proves that Argan's daughters are faithful children and that his second wife is a greedy exploiter. All ends happily as Argan is convinced that all he needs to practice medicine himself is a cap, gown, and medicine bag. **RECOMMENDATION:** Although this version lacks the attack on the law profession, cuts short the music lesson scene, and does not have the sensible brother, its attack on the medical profession remains effective. **ROYALTY:** $15. **SOURCE:** Dexter, Harriet. (1978). Too many doctors. Denver, CO: Pioneer Drama Service. **SUBJECTS/PLAY TYPE:** Hypochondria; Doctors; Greed; Farce; Adaptation.

3189. 9-12. (-) Nolan, Paul T. Too many girls. CAST: 6f, 4m. **ACTS:** 1. **SETTINGS:** Restaurant. **PLAYING TIME:** 30 min. **PLOT:** Clyde, an egotistical high schooler, believes that all girls adore him and dates them all with no consideration for their feelings. He suffers a trauma when none of the girls will go to a school dance with him because of his arrogant boasting and double standards. Finally, Clyde gets a date with Belinda, a girl who originally turned him down. He decides that he must change his tactics and be loyal to one girl in order to get all the others to chase him. **RECOMMENDATION:** This contemporary comedy depicts a young boy who believes in double standards and who does not learn anything from his experiences. The girl who finally goes out with him does so not because she sees any redeeming qualities, but because she believes he is popular and so, of course, desires him. This insulting playlet does not teach anything except that perpetuation of sexism and irresponsibility is cute. **ROYALTY:** $25. **SOURCE:** Nolan, Paul T. (1979). Too many girls. Franklin, OH: Eldridge Pub. Co. **SUBJECTS/PLAY TYPE:** Dating; Comedy.

3190. 7-12. (+) Huff, Betty Tracy. Too many mummies. CAST: 8f, 4m, Su. **ACTS:** 1. **SETTINGS:** Office; museum. **PLAYING TIME:** NA. **PLOT:** An absent minded archaeologist who is almost swindled by his creditor, discovers a priceless sphinx in the museum. When a professor makes the same discovery, he is able to find the financial support to save his museum and eventually propose matrimony to his dedicated assistant. **RECOMMENDATION:** Witty dialogue, funny circumstances, the exaggerated craftiness of the villain, the undying virtue of the heroine, and the appealing confusion of the professor are endearing here. Unexpected role reversed characterizations place a different perspective on this well used plot. **ROYALTY:** Free to Plays subscribers. **SOURCE:** Huff, Betty Tracy. (1985, May). Too many mummies. Plays: The Drama Magazine for Young People, pp. 21-30. **SUBJECTS/PLAY TYPE:** Adventure; Swindlers and Swindling; Mystery; Comedy.

3191. 5-8. (+) Kehret, Peg. Too young for this, too old for that. CAST: 1m. **ACTS:** 1. **SETTINGS:** None. **PLAYING TIME:** NA. **PLOT:** A young boy struggles with the dilemma of being expected to act responsibly, while still being considered too young to have any actual freedom. He finally comes to accept the need for rules and responsibility, but hopes to receive more respect in the future. **RECOMMENDATION:** The theme of growing up with responsibility is clearly evident but told through a child's perspective to make it more interesting to young actors. ROYALTY: NA. SOURCE: Kehret, Peg. (1986). Winning monologs for young actors. Colorado Springs, CO: Meriwether Pub. SUBJECTS/PLAY TYPE: Family Life; Responsibility; Monologue.

3192. 4-6. (+) Bradley, Virginia. **Torko the terrible.** CAST: 3f, 3m, 15u. ACTS: 1. SETTINGS: Room; park; meeting room. PLAYING TIME: NA. PLOT: On the "Day of Strange Happenings" a toy monster comes alive and looks for friends. He learns about friendship and about being himself. RECOMMENDATION: This lengthy play presents the themes of friendship and accepting oneself. The main characters are well defined and costumes and props are manageable. ROYALTY: None. SOURCE: Bradley, Virginia. (1975). Is there an actor in the house? New York, NY: Dodd, Mead. SUBJECTS/PLAY TYPE: Monsters; Magic; Friendship; Fantasy.

3193. 1-4. (+) Cheatham, Val R. **The tortoise, the hare, and friends.** CAST: 9u. ACTS: 1. SETTINGS: Forest. PLAYING TIME: 20 min. PLOT: Fox tries to get everyone to bet on Blue Jay, who is entering the race this year. Fox, however, is betting on the hare. Blue Jay, who has plans of his own, is betting on Tortoise. Fox is outsmarted by Blue Jay, and Tortoise wins again. RECOMMENDATION: This is a fun play which older children who can read would enjoy presenting to younger children. The combination of characters from different stories is interesting. ROYALTY: Free to Plays subscribers. SOURCE: Cheatham, Val R. (1976, October). The tortoise, the hare, and friends. Plays: The Drama Magazine for Young People, pp. 63-70. SUBJECTS/PLAY TYPE: Folk Tale Motifs; Tortoises; Hares; Skit.

3194. 6-12. (+) Schaaf, Albert K. **A touch too much.** CAST: 2f, 3m. ACTS: 1. SETTINGS: Sorcerer's shop. PLAYING TIME: 15 min. PLOT: Heartbroken King Midas has turned his daughter to gold. His search for a cure from his golden touch brings him to Sam, a zany discount sorcerer, and his wife, Minerva, a witch. Minerva mixes a potion which returns the king's daughter to normal, but the problem of the golden touch still remains. Sam decides they need to devalue the king to rid him of his affliction. Midas abdicates the throne, makes his daughter the queen, and becomes a duke. This only reduces his touch to silver. Further devaluation is in order, so Midas signs the official papers to become a commoner. This solves his problem and Midas and his daughter leave the shop happy. RECOMMENDATION: The many puns and witticisms are right on target as the world of business is satirized and finally dismissed as an unhappy place. No business background is needed to understand the concepts involved. ROYALTY: Free to Plays subscribers. SOURCE: Schaaf, Albert. (1976, January). A touch too much. Plays: The Drama Magazine for Young People, pp. 55-61. SUBJECTS/PLAY TYPE: Comedy; Business; Skit.

3195. 9-12. (+) Runnette, Helen V. **Touchstone.** CAST: 3f, 25m, Su. ACTS: 1. SETTINGS: Workroom. PLAYING TIME: 25 min. PLOT: On Christmas Eve, an alchemist is deeply absorbed in his work trying to change a base metal into gold. His servant tries to draw his attention to a group of carolers at his door but he will not listen. After his experiment fails, he decides to search for real gold in peoples' hearts. RECOMMENDATION: This adequately conveys the real meaning of Christmas. Because of its length, difficult speaking parts, and elaborate scenes, props, and costumes, it is better performed by older teenagers. ROYALTY: None. SOURCE: Kamerman, Sylvia E. (1975). A treasury of Christmas plays. Boston, MA: Plays, Inc. SUBJECTS/PLAY TYPE: Christmas; Playlet.

3196. K-6*. (+) Ireland, Vicky. (Aesopus) **The town mouse and the country mouse.** (Aesop's fables) CAST: 3f, 2m, 1u. ACTS: 1. SETTINGS: Large book. PLAYING TIME: NA. PLOT: The country mouse visits the town mouse and discovers the wealth, variety, and excitement of town life. But he realizes that he can only be truly happy in his country home. RECOMMENDATION: This requires adult supervision due to complex lighting and music. The presentation of scenery in a book format (there are sixteen pages, each depicting a scene) is very appealing. ROYALTY: $35. SOURCE: Ireland, Vicky. (1987). The town mouse and the country mouse. New Orleans, LA: Anchorage Press, Inc. SUBJECTS/PLAY TYPE: Mice; Fable; Adaptation.

3197. 2-6. (+) Boiko, Claire. (Grimm Brothers) **The town that couldn't wake up.** (Sleeping Beauty) CAST: 5f, 19m, Su. ACTS: 1. SETTINGS: Street. PLAYING TIME: 35 min. PLOT: Badpenny has cast a spell in which the newborn, Lark Bluebonnet, will, on her 16th birthday, prick her finger on a piece of barbed wire and die. On Lark's 16th birthday, Granny casts a spell which puts the whole town to sleep for 100 years, long after Badpenny has "wrinkled up and fallen to dust." She also sends a "song into the air," which (100 years later) calls Lark's true love, who wakes her and the town with a kiss. RECOMMENDATION: If the hokey western dialect and stereotyped Indian are replaced, this modern musical retelling would be enchanting and easily performed by the older elementary grades for the younger ones. ROYALTY: Free to Plays subscribers. SOURCE: Boiko, Claire. (1987, March). The town that couldn't wake up. Plays: The Drama Magazine for Young People, pp. 23-34. SUBJECTS/PLAY TYPE: Folk Tales, Germany; Western; Parody; Adaptation.

3198. K-1. (+) Pomerance, Charlotte. **Toy tik ka.** CAST: 2u. ACTS: 1. SETTINGS: None. PLAYING TIME: NA. PLOT: In a short rhyme, two readers list some of the meats they enjoy eating. RECOMMENDATION: This can be performed alone, or in combination with **Peculiar** and **Jump Rope Rhyme**, as Bauer recommends. ROYALTY: NA. SOURCE: Bauer, Caroline Feller. (1987). Presenting reader's theater: Plays and poems to read aloud. New York, NY: H.W. Wilson Co. SUBJECTS/PLAY TYPE: Food; Meat; Reader's Theater.

3199. 3-8. (+) Holbrook, Marion. **The toymaker's doll.** CAST: 6f, 5m, 10u. ACTS: 1. SETTINGS: Workshop. PLAYING TIME: NA. PLOT: A poor toymaker becomes wealthy and famous because he can make wind-up dolls that walk. On Christmas Eve, he is so busy making dolls for the burgomaster, he cannot be bothered with children who visit his shop expecting to receive his unsold toys as gifts as they have in the past. His behavior and attitude upset his wife and granddaughter. A mysterious woman visits and prophesies that the toymaker will gladly give away his toys. The toymaker's granddaughter is transformed into a doll when he cannot fill an order from a prince. Realizing the result of his greed, the toymaker breaks the curse by giving all his toys to the children whom he rejected earlier. Once his granddaughter is restored to flesh, he rejoices and abandons his obsession with fame and wealth. RECOMMENDATION: Franz is thought-fully portrayed as a goodhearted man whose priorities are temporarily skewed. The reader sympathizes with his family and along with them, is anxious for him to change. This allows for small children to be a part of the cast and say a short line or two, but older children would be required for the main characters. ROYALTY: SOURCE: McSweeny, Maxine. (1977). Christmas plays for young players. South Brunswick, Canada: A.S. Barnes. SUBJECTS/PLAY TYPE: Christmas; Greed; Wealth; Drama.

3200. 1-6. (+) Zawadsky, Pat. **Toys in the haunted castle.** CAST: 4f, 5m, 1u. ACTS: 2. SETTINGS: Playroom. PLAYING TIME: 60 min. PLOT: Jack, a jack-in-the box, and Janette, a dancing doll, cannot leave the deserted playroom of a haunted castle for the Great Toyland in the sky because they haven't fulfilled their earthly purpose: "To do what you were meant to do, and enjoy it." With the help of two children and an astronaut doll, Jack and Janette discover the meaning of life and escape three mischievous ghosts. RECOMMENDATION: If it weren't for an occasional humorous rhyme from the spooks that haunt the castle, this would be very tedious. The doll characters are brimming with trite sentiments and the theme is not so much developed as it is restated over and over again. Still, young children might find the idea of toys-come-to-life enjoyable. Appropriate as a production by older children for a young audience. ROYALTY: $25. SOURCE: Zawadsky, Pat. (1977). Toys in the haunted castle. Schulenburg, TX: I.E. Clark. SUBJECTS/PLAY TYPE: Ghosts; Haunted Houses; Toys; Drama.

3201. 9-12. (+) Mitchell, Adrian. (Shakespeare, William) **The tragedy of King Real.** (King Lear) CAST: 3f, 4m, 4u. ACTS: 7. SETTINGS: Garden; bunker. PLAYING TIME: NA. PLOT: In this chilling adaptation, the King gives keys to two of his daughters and one of his officers. When turned simultaneously, the keys will trigger a nuclear explosion. The third daughter, who didn't love her father enough, is turned out, along with her faithful lover, who has been turned into a lunatic. The two daughters force their father out of the bunker, trigger the nuclear explosion, and wait the required 40 days before venturing out. In the wasteland, King Real discovers his true daughter and the two reconcile in time to die with each other. The survivors in the bunker kill each other, all except for the last person, who is killed by radioactivity. In symbolic verse, the audience is warned to love the planet earth. RECOMMENDATION: Through rhyme and music, this well preserves the original horror of **King Lear**, as it

modernizes the Armageddon. Some strong language may have to be changed. This will fully involve and greatly affect the cast and audience. ROYALTY: NA. SOURCE: Lowe, Stephen. (1985). Peace plays. New York, NY: Methuen. SUBJECTS/PLAY TYPE: Love; Nuclear War; War; Adaptation.

3202. 2-6. (-) Cavanah, Frances. **The transfiguration of the gifts.** CAST: 2f, 5m, Su. ACTS: 1. SETTINGS: Stable. PLAYING TIME: NA. PLOT: Four children are coaxed by Mary to give the Christ child their simple gifts of hay, pebbles, a wilted flower, and a torn cover. Christ transfigures the gifts into a soft bed, pearls, a new flower, and a warm blanket. The children realize that the value of a gift is based on the feeling in which it was given. RECOMMENDATION: This would be very appropriate for a church program about the spirit of Christmas. ROYALTY: NA. SOURCE: McSweeny, Maxine. (1977). Christmas plays for young players. South Brunswick, Canada: A.S. Barnes. SUBJECTS/PLAY TYPE: Christmas; Values; Drama.

3203. 10-12. (+) Randall, Charles H. & Bushnell, Joan LeGro. **Trapped by a treacherous twin or double trouble.** CAST: 4f, 4m. ACTS: 2. SETTINGS: Drawing room. PLAYING TIME: NA. PLOT: Wealthy Herbert Haverford's mysterious disappearance has left his family in dire circumstances. One son, Noel, is arrested for embezzlement. Noels's evil twin, Yule, threatens the rest of the family with eviction unless Sadie Rose, the love of Noel's life, agrees to marry him. Just when all seems lost, Yule is unmasked as the embezzler, Herbert is restored to his family, and true love wins out. RECOMMENDATION: This has all the hallmarks of a true melodrama with a villain, a pure hearted heroine, a loyal wife, an upright hero, a French maid, a case of amnesia, and a hidden identity. The dialogue is humorous, but it is skillfully written to appear unintentionally so. There is ample opportunity for audience participation if desired. ROYALTY: NA. SOURCE: Randall, Charles H. & Bushnell, Joan Le Gro. (1982). Trapped by a treacherous twin or double trouble. Chicago, IL: Dramatic Pub. Co. SUBJECTS/PLAY TYPE: Christmas; Comedy; Melodrama.

3204. 2-4. (-) Gotwalt, Helen Louise Miller. **A travel game.** CAST: 15f, 14m, 2u. ACTS: 1. SETTINGS: Classroom. PLAYING TIME: 15 min. PLOT: Students play a game in which they recite poems or sing to illustrate points about transportation. RECOMMENDATION: The educational benefits are outweighed by the fact that most of the cast remains on stage for the entire play, the entire cast is required to sing, and the game (which revolves around letters of the alphabet) is boring. ROYALTY: Free to Plays subscribers. SOURCE: Gotwalt, Helen Louise Miller. (1979, April). A travel game. Plays: The Drama Magazine for Young People, pp. 55-60. SUBJECTS/PLAY TYPE: Transportation; Comedy.

3205. 10-12. (+) Wise, William. **Traveler's rest.** CAST: 1f, 1m. ACTS: 1. SETTINGS: Motel room. PLAYING TIME: 60 min. PLOT: Joanne Peterson, on the way home from a meeting with her dead husband's lover, stops at a motel called "Traveler's Rest." When the motel owner,

Andy Milligan, comes to the room to fix the broken light and television, an instant empathy is established between the two lonely people, and they spend the evening sharing stories of their lives--the joys and, gradually, the tragedies. RECOMMENDATION: It is difficult to praise this enough. Its subtle unfolding of the characters' lives and personalities, and the gradual but powerful connection that they establish with each other and with the audience are masterful. School play directors should be aware that there are some frank sexual allusions. ROYALTY: $35. SOURCE: Wise, William. (1979). Traveler's rest. Schulenburg, TX: I.E. Clark. SUBJECTS/PLAY TYPE: Relationships; Marriage; Drama.

3206. 10-12. (+) Koste, Virginia Glasgow. (Baum, Lyman Frank) **Travelin': An odyssey in Oz.** (The wizard of Oz) CAST: 3f, 2m, 1u. ACTS: 2. SETTINGS: None. PLAYING TIME: 75 min. PLOT: Based on the fantasies of Oz, this is a metaphor for the creative process of theater and the process of life. With its message that we must embrace life as a journey, this goes much beyond a mere retelling of the famous story. RECOMMENDATION: The lines are witty, with many allusions to Baum's work. Its positive, upbeat attitude toward enjoying life seems especially good for young adults. However, the many changes in characters, allusions and illusions require experienced actors with musical ability. ROYALTY: $35. SOURCE: Koste, Virginia Glasgow. (1983). Travelin': An odyssey in Oz. I.E. Clark. SUBJECTS/PLAY TYPE: Musical; Oz; Adaptation.

3207. 3-6. (+) Duke's Playhouse Theatre in Education. **Travellers.** CAST: 2f, 3m, 5u. ACTS: 2. SETTINGS: Classroom; playground. PLAYING TIME: 480 min. PLOT: Presented in two half day acts, two weeks apart, this play involves a family of gypsies in England and the problems they encounter because of discrimination against their mobile, non-material way of life. A gypsy wagon breaks down in a school yard and the audience is given the opportunity to see inside the wagon, talk with gypsies and learn about their values and standards. The students help reunite two gypsy brothers, keep the school officials from throwing the gypsies off the school property, and they see first hand how misunderstanding causes prejudice. The story ends happily for one gypsy, who gives up his gypsy life. RECOMMENDATION: The geography, the physical participation of students (i.e., pushing a car) and the topical dated laws in England regarding gypsies would not provide an effective production outside that area. Preparation for this would be difficult (i.e., an authentic gypsy wagon must be provided) and its length makes it too unwieldy for any but the most dedicated civic educators. It is, however, a superb exposition of the untenable treatment of gypsies in Britain. ROYALTY: NA. SOURCE: Duke's Play-house Theatre in Education. (1980). Four junior programmes. London, England: Eyre Methuen. SUBJECTS/PLAY TYPE: Gypsies; Social Commentary; Participation Play.

3208. K-4. (+) Flohr, John W. (Grimm Brothers) **The travelling musicians.** (The Brementown musicians.) CAST: Su. ACTS: 1. SETTINGS: Farm; road; forest; house. PLAYING TIME: NA. PLOT: A group of aging animals who can no longer do their master's rigorous chores seek alternate employment as travelling musicians. When the newly formed vocal group decides to make their debut outside the window of the home of thieves (in hopes of receiving food in return for their performance), they frighten the evil men away and inherit the food, money, and house. RECOMMENDATION: This delightful adaptation is replete with songs, animals, and an amusing plot. Easy and difficult versions of songs are provided as well as other production hints which enable directors to tailor the production to their player's capabilities. ROYALTY: NA. SOURCE: Flohr, John W. & Smith, Robert B. (1984). Music dramas for children with special needs. Denton TX: Troostwyk Press. SUBJECTS/PLAY TYPE: Animals; Folk Tales, Germany; Adaptation.

3209. 6-9. (+) Dias, Earl J. **Treasure at Bentley Inn.** CAST: 5f, 6m. ACTS: 1. SETTINGS: Inn lounge. PLAYING TIME: 30 min. PLOT: The Leslies are thrilled when their chef's excellent reputation begins to improve business, but confusion sets in when word of a legendary treasure, hidden somewhere in the inn, gets out to gangsters. Surprisingly, Miss Pitts, an apparently harmless guest, is the worst of the fortune seekers, but eventually, the Leslies beat everyone to the hidden riches after discovering the final clue in an old diary. RECOMMENDATION: This is predictable but attention-holding. ROYALTY: Free to Plays subscribers. SOURCE: Dias, Earl J. (1987, March). Treasure at Bentley Inn. Plays: The Drama Magazine for Young People, pp. 11-22. SUBJECTS/PLAY TYPE: Treasure; Mystery.

3210. 2-4. (+) Fisher, Aileen Lucia. **Treasure hunt.** CAST: 11f, 11m, 2u. ACTS: 1. SETTINGS: Classroom. PLAYING TIME: NA. PLOT: The teacher has told her students of a treasure, and they guess that the treasure is contained in books. RECOMMENDATION: Many classics are introduced in a witty, engaging way. This is a good way to get parents to read along with their children. ROYALTY: None for amateurs. SOURCE: Fisher, Aileen Lucia. (1986). Holiday programs for boys and girls. Boston, MA: Plays, Inc. SUBJECTS/PLAY TYPE: Books; Reading; Playlet.

3211. 3-8. (+) Silverman, Eleanor. (Stevenson, Robert Louis) **Treasure Island.** (Treasure Island) CAST: 1f, 15m, 1u. ACTS: 11. SETTINGS: Inn; squire's home; ship. PLAYING TIME: 30 min. PLOT: Jim discovers a map revealing pirates' treasure and enlists the help of the Squire and Dr. Livesey to locate it. After a sea voyage and a skirmish with the pirates, Jim and his friends return home with the treasure. RECOMMENDATION: As an introduction to **Treasure Island**, this would work well in the classroom, although it offers only the barest outline of the story. ROYALTY: None. SOURCE: Silverman, Eleanor. (1983). Dramatics for children. Metuchen, NJ: Scarecrow Press. SUBJECTS/PLAY TYPE: Pirates; Adaptation.

3212. 4-8. (+) Bland, Joellen. (Stevenson, Robert Louis) **Treasure Island.** (Treasure Island) CAST: 10m. ACTS: 1. SETTINGS: Home; schooner; stockade. PLAYING TIME: NA. PLOT: Jim overhears information that leads him to a treasure map sought by a group of pirates. Jim and his friends decide to search for the treasure but unknowingly they hire the pirates to help on board ship. When the island is reached, mutiny occurs with battling between the pirates and Jim and his friends. With the help of Ben Gunn, who has been abandoned on the island for years, Jim is able to defeat the pirates and get the treasure. RECOMMENDATION: This follows the original closely. It would require several changes of settings and on more than one occasion Jim narrates the action. Production will require a skilled stage crew and some familiarity with the original. ROYALTY: Free to Plays subscribers. SOURCE: Bland, Joellen. (1978, April). Treasure Island. Plays: The Drama Magazine for Young People, pp. 69-80. SUBJECTS/PLAY TYPE: Treasure; Adventure; Pirates; Adaptation.

3213. 7-12. (+) Caruso, Joseph George. (Stevenson, Robert Louis) **Treasure Island.** (Treasure Island) CAST: 7f, 11m, Su. ACTS: 2. SETTINGS: Inns; ship; woods. PLAYING TIME: 90 min. PLOT: Jim, Auntie Nan, and others hire a ship unknowingly crewed by pirates, to seek the treasure indicated on the map given to Jim by the former pirate and now dead Captain Bones. Once on the island, they are captured by the pirates. RECOMMENDATION: The plot of the original is faithfully followed and the added humor makes this delightful as the audience succumbs to the allure of pirates and buried treasure. ROYALTY: $35. SOURCE: Caruso, Joseph George. (1979). Treasure Island. Denver, CO: Pioneer Drama Service. SUBJECTS/PLAY TYPE: Pirates; Treasure; Adventure; Adaptation.

3214. 3-12*. (+) Harris, Aurand. (Stevenson, Robert Louis) **Treasure Island.** (Treasure Island) CAST: 1f, 12m. ACTS: 1. SETTINGS: Inn; ship; Treasure Island. PLAYING TIME: NA. PLOT: Jim, a serving boy, dreams of adventures on the high seas with ships, pirates and buried treasures. When a pirate with a chest arrives at the Inn, Jim gets the map that shows the way to the treasure and sails in search of it with his friends, the doctor and the squire, and, unbeknownst to them, a band of murderous pirates led by Long John Silver. The pirates kidnap Jim, but he escapes when they reach the island and finds a friend in another pirate, Ben Gunn, who had been ship-wrecked three years before. The pirates recapture Jim and try to kill him but Long John Silver saves his life. Later, when the doctor and squire rout the pirates and recover the treasure, Jim saves the pirate captain. RECOMMENDATION: The swash-buckling pirates and colorful scenes of ships and islands will be delightful for young children (with some language changes) but would be best performed by older students or adults. ROYALTY: $35. SOURCE: Harris, Aurand. (1983). Treasure island. New Orleans, LA: Anchorage Press, Inc. SUBJECTS/PLAY TYPE: Pirates; Treasure; Adventure; Adaptation.

3215. 3-8*. (-) Hotchner, Steve & Hotchner, Kathy. (Stevenson, Robert Louis) **Treasure Island.** (Treasure Island) CAST: 4f, 2m. ACTS: 1. SETTINGS: 19th century London; Treasure Island. PLAYING TIME: NA. PLOT: Jamie, a tomboy, searches for treasure with her uncle, Long John Silver, and his pirate buddies (Red and

Crossbun). They travel to the island, enter a dense jungle and encounter Ben Bulba, the pirate queen. Ghosts (children in the audience) scare the pirates from the treasure, Jamie and the Captain are triumphant, and Long John Silver is spared the hangman's noose. RECOMMENDATION: Too many liberties have been taken with Stevenson's original work, rendering this too confusing to follow. ROYALTY: $25. SOURCE: Hotchner, Steve & Hotchner, Kathy. (1977). Treasure Island. Chicago, IL: Dramatic Pub. Co. SUBJECTS/PLAY TYPE: Pirates; Treasure; Adventure; Adaptation.

3216. 3-6. (+) Schwarz, Ernest J. (Stevenson, Robert Louis) **Treasure Island.** (Treasure Island) CAST: 1f, 5m, 10u. ACTS: 1. SETTINGS: Inn; ship; island. PLAYING TIME: NA. PLOT: After being given a treasure map by the pirate, Billy Bones, young Jim Hawkins becomes involved in a race against pirates for buried treasure. With the help of marooned Ben Gunn, Jim and his shipmates capture pirate Long John Silver. They return to England with the treasure and divide it equally. The fate of Long John Silver is decided upon by the audience, which must choose between taking him back to England or leaving him marooned on the island. RECOMMENDATION: Audience participation and humor makes this appropriate for and appealing to children, even if it is a necessarily very abridged version of the original. ROYALTY: NA. SOURCE: Schwarz, Ernest J. (1979). Pig tales and Treasure Island: Two plays for children. Toronto, Canada: Playwrights Co-op. SUBJECTS/PLAY TYPE: Adventure; Pirates; Treasure; Adaptation.

3217. 6-8*. (+) Way, Brian. (Stevenson, Robert Louis) **Treasure Island.** (Treasure Island) CAST: 1f, 24m. ACTS: 2. SETTINGS: Inn; ship's deck; ship's cabin; island with stockade. PLAYING TIME: NA. PLOT: Jim finds a buried treasure map, and joins a group of seamen on the treasure hunt. After quelling a mutiny and meeting the man who beat them to the gold, Jim and his fellow adventurers return home with a bag of gold. RECOMMENDATION: Producers should be aware that 24 male performers are required, and that the best cast comprises primarily adults. Also, constant fight scenes involving knives and cutlasses might be difficult to stage without a skilled choreographer and countless hours of practice. Some of the old words should be explained in the play program. ROYALTY: $25. SOURCE: Way, Brian. (1977). Treasure Island. Boston, MA: Baker's Plays. SUBJECTS/PLAY TYPE: Adventure; Pirates; Treasure; Adaptation.

3218. K-6*. (+) Sternberg, Pat & Granovetter, Matthew. **The treasure makers.** CAST: 2f, 2m, Su. ACTS: 1. SETTINGS: Dump. PLAYING TIME: NA. PLOT: Determined to prove their trash is treasure, the trashpickers must fight such setbacks as the false arrest of their friend, Sailor Mike, and the domineering attitude of Mrs. Zee, the owner of their property. Through a sculpture contest, in which the trash sculpture wins, Mrs. Zee learns not only that trash can be treasure, but also that Sailor Mike is her brother, believed drowned years ago. RECOMMENDATION: This play uses one uncomplicated set, frequent audience participation (especially through children's drawings), and meaningful songs. It teaches the value of recycling, that truthfulness is a must, and that misunderstandings can result from jumping to conclusions. Especially effective is the use of a mime, whose actions are an integral part of the production. ROYALTY: $25. SOURCE: Sternberg, Pat & Granovetter, Matthew. (1984). The treasure makers. New York, NY: Samuel French. SUBJECTS/PLAY TYPE: Conservation; Recycling; Musical; Comedy.

3219. 2-6. (+) Marshall, Sheila. **A treasure without measure.** CAST: 4f, 9m. ACTS: 1. SETTINGS: Cave. PLAYING TIME: 20 min. PLOT: A crazed scientist invents an enormous machine to regulate the use of television sets in order to take revenge on his former home town friends who never had enough time for him because they were always watching TV. He interrupts broadcasting and announces he must receive a treasure without measure within 24 hours or no more TV. After refusing money and jewelry, the scientist receives a real treasure, an assortment of books. RECOMMENDATION: Book lovers will agree with the final assessment of the importance of reading. This would be excellent to present during Book Week. ROYALTY: Free to Plays subscribers. SOURCE: Marshall, Sheila. (1977, November). A treasure without measure. Plays: The Drama Magazine for Young People, pp. 65-70. SUBJECTS/PLAY TYPE: Reading; Books; Playlet.

3220. 5-8. (+) Gotwalt, Helen Louise Miller. **The tree of hearts.** CAST: 3f, 5m, Su. ACTS: 1. SETTINGS: Garden. PLAYING TIME: 20 min. PLOT: King Valentino orders the palace gardener to develop a special tree for the prince's birthday (February 14th) that will encourage the sickly prince to spend time in the garden to regain his health. If this is not accomplished, the gardener's family will be banished. Two American tourists help design the tree upon which the children of the country attach valentines which tell the prince of their love for him. RECOMMENDATION: In a light hearted manner, this subtly infers that Americans can fix any problem in other countries. But it also expresses values of sharing and friendship. ROYALTY: Free to Plays subscribers. SOURCE: Gotwalt, Helen Louise Miller. (1986). Special plays for holidays. Boston, MA: Plays, Inc. SUBJECTS/PLAY TYPE: Valentine's Day; Playlet.

3221. K-5. (+) Fisher, Aileen. **A tree to trim.** CAST: 3f, 3m. ACTS: 1. SETTINGS: Study. PLAYING TIME: 25 min. PLOT: Mr. Archibald is a "Scrooge-type" author who devotes his professional life to writing about 12th century history. Three children and his secretary persuade him to write a Christmas play for the local orphanage. He writes about a magic Christmas tree that can be trimmed only with wishes that contain the spirit of Christmas. As children try to trim, they and Archibald learn that the true spirit of Christmas lives in our hearts. RECOMMENDATION: Reminiscent of Dickens' classic, this contains excellent dialogue and realistic action. ROYALTY: None. SOURCE: Kamerman, Sylvia E. (1988). The big book of Christmas plays. Boston, MA: Plays, Inc. SUBJECTS/PLAY TYPE: Christmas; Playlet.

3222. 2-6. (+) Osborne, Ron. **The trial of Captain Hero.** CAST: 5f, 3m, 6u. ACTS: 1. SETTINGS: Courtroom. PLAYING TIME: 25 min. PLOT: Captain Hero is on trial for endangering the safety of the public while discharging superhero duties. He is charged with traveling too fast and changing his clothes in a telephone booth. The jury finds him innocent. RECOMMENDATION: Charmingly humorous, the audience acts as the jury. Although the play is lengthy, the steady action and humor will hold interest. However, for the play to be fully appreciated, the audience will need to be able to understand the satire of Superman that is the crux of the humor. ROYALTY: Free to Plays subscribers. SOURCE: Osborne, Ron. (1981, December). The trial of Captain Hero. Plays: The Drama Magazine for Young People, pp. 24-32. SUBJECTS/PLAY TYPE: Superheroes; Trial; Superman; Comedy.

3223. 2-6. (+) Gotwalt, Helen Louise Miller. **The trial of Mother Goose.** CAST: 8f, 11m, Su. ACTS: 1. SETTINGS: Kitchen. PLAYING TIME: 20 min. PLOT: Mother Goose is on trial because the subjects of her poems resent what is written about them. King Cole does not want to be called old or fun-loving; other characters have similar complaints. King Cole threatens to put Mother Goose in the dungeon until children from all parts of the world come to her defense, proving that the characters' flaws are what have endeared them to generations of children throughout the world. RECOMMENDATION: Nursery rhymes come to life in this whimsical situation. For intermediate grades, it could be used as a comic complement to a unit on the historical significance of nursery rhymes. It also could be produced as the combined effort of intermediate and primary classes. ROYALTY: Free to Plays subscribers. SOURCE: Gotwalt, Helen Louise Miller. (1986, April). Plays: The Drama Magazine for Young People, pp. 33-39. SUBJECTS/PLAY TYPE: Nursery Rhymes; Mother Goose; Comedy.

3224. 5-6. (+) Nolan, Paul. **The trial of Peter Zenger.** CAST: 5f, 22m, 1u. ACTS: 1. SETTINGS: Print shop. PLAYING TIME: 40 min. PLOT: Peter Zenger, who runs a little one-man print shop in New York, fights for freedom of the press and disregards threats from the Governor. Even though the court offers Zenger the option to be free if he promises to print no more, he refuses, insisting on the right to publish the truth. Because of his courage, the jurors find Zenger not guilty, in spite of the fact that the verdict will offend the Governor. RECOMMENDATION: Historically accurate, this serves well as a reminder that freedom of the press was not gained without effort, and that it is too precious to take for granted. A Spanish translation (by Alcides and Catherine Rodriguez-Nieto) follows the English version. ROYALTY: NA. SOURCE: Nolan, Paul T. (1988, January/February). The trial of Peter Zenger. Plays: The Drama Magazine for Young People, pp. 44-79. SUBJECTS/PLAY TYPE: Journalism; Zenger, Peter; Playlet.

3225. 4-5. (+) Cheatham, Val R. **The trial of the big bad wolf.** CAST: 2f, 2m, 7u. ACTS: 1. SETTINGS: Courtroom. PLAYING TIME: 15 min. PLOT: The Three

Pigs have charged the wolf with assault and battery, trespassing, and destruction of property. The witnesses against the wolf are the boy who cried wolf, Little Red Riding Hood, and Peter (from **Peter and the Wolf**). The judge releases the wolf. Grandma (from **Little Red Riding Hood**) takes the wolf dancing. RECOMMENDATION: The action and humor here is laudable. ROYALTY: Free to Plays subscribers. SOURCE: Cheatham, Val R. (1981, January). The trial of the big bad wolf. Plays: The Drama Magazine for Young People, pp. 61- 64. SUBJECTS/PLAY TYPE: Animals; Comedy; Folk Tale Characters; Skit.

3226. 5-8. (+) Hamlett, Christina. **The trials and tribulations of fairy tale court.** CAST: 6f, 9m. ACTS: 1. SETTINGS: Courtroom. PLAYING TIME: NA. PLOT: Cinderella is suing the fairy godmother for breach of contract; Jack is suing the bean man for fraud; the Frog Prince is suing the witch because he preferred life as a frog; and the three pigs are being sued by an unhappy customer of their construction business. Each case is resolved by Judge Minerva to the satisfaction of all parties. RECOMMENDATION: This clever courtroom comedy takes the fairy tale characters beyond the well known endings of their stories, and shows what might have happened next in the modern world. The characters are believable and the dialogue is contemporary and fast paced. Recommended for classroom or variety show production. ROYALTY: $20. SOURCE: Hamlett, Christina. (1987). The trials and tribulations of fairy tale court. Franklin, OH: Eldridge Pub. Co. SUBJECTS/PLAY TYPE: Comedy; Folk Tale Characters; Litigation; Skit.

3227. K-3. (+) Havilan, Amorie & Smith, Lyn. **Trick or treat.** CAST: 3f, 1m, Su. ACTS: 1. SETTINGS: Front door; living room. PLAYING TIME: NA. PLOT: On the way to a Halloween party, Polly picks a beautiful yellow flower for her "trick and treat." As her friends warn that Mrs. Mead will be angry, Mrs. Mead forgives and invites the children in for the Halloween party. Once inside she tells them the history of Halloween, the origin of "tricks," the reason for jack-o-lanterns, and a story about witches, broomsticks and black cats. RECOMMENDATION: Ideally suited for very young children, this can be read as a story, performed as a monologue with pantomime, or presented as a play. ROYALTY: NA. SOURCE: Havilan, Amorie & Smith, Lyn. (1985). Trick or treat. Easy plays for preschoolers to third graders. Brandon, MS: Quail Ridge Press. SUBJECTS/PLAY TYPE: Halloween; Tripartite.

3228. 4-8. (+) Winther, Barbara. **Trickster hare's feast.** CAST: 4f, 1m, 11u. ACTS: 1. SETTINGS: Marketplace; rabbit's home. PLAYING TIME: 20 min. PLOT: Although Hare and Elephant agree to share their profits from a day at the marketplace, Elephant reneges. When Hare refuses to be partnered again with Elephant, Elephant plots revenge by sending Lion, Leopard and Hyena to steal Hare's chickens. Hare's quick thinking saves his dinner and his life. RECOMMENDATION: This African trickster tale is entertaining. ROYALTY: Free to Plays subscribers. SOURCE: Winther, Barbara. (1981, April). Trickster hare's feast. Plays: The Drama Magazine for Young People, pp. 49-55. SUBJECTS/PLAY TYPE: Folk Tales, Africa; Comedy.

3229. 3-6. (+) Alexander, Sue. **Tricky gifts.** CAST: 2u. ACTS: 1. SETTINGS: Room. PLAYING TIME: NA. PLOT: A clown is upset because he has no gifts to give his family at Christmas. He tries unsuccessfully to make bowls and candy. Finally, he uses his talents to make people laugh and this is his present. RECOMMENDATION: Simplicity and a clever plot teach the valuable lesson of the giving of one's self. ROYALTY: NA. SOURCE: Alexander, Sue. (1977). Small plays for special days. New York, NY: Seabury. SUBJECTS/PLAY TYPE: Gifts; Christmas; Playlet.

3230. 10-12. (-) Kennedy, Eddie. **The trip.** CAST: 2f, 3m. ACTS: 1. SETTINGS: Hospital waiting room. PLAYING TIME: NA. PLOT: The stress of dealing with a mentally ill young woman climaxes when her mother (who spent a great deal of time with her at the asylum) dies, and family members blame the young woman for the mother's death. RECOMMENDATION: What is a family member's responsibility in the long term care of someone who is ill? How can a family deal with the pressures caused by mental illness or any chronic illness? These are important questions worth exploring. Unfortunately, the play is confusing, relationships between characters are unclear, character motivation is not clearly drawn, characterization is poor, and no resolutions are suggested. ROYALTY: $20. SOURCE: Kennedy, Eddie. (1983). The trip. Chicago, IL: Dramatic Pub. Co. SUBJECTS/PLAY TYPE: Mental Illness; Drama.

3231. 2-5. (+) Schwartz, Stephen & Stein, Anthony. (Keats, Ezra Jack) **The trip.** (The trip) CAST: 8f, 6m, Su. ACTS: 1. SETTINGS: Street. PLAYING TIME: NA. PLOT: Louie is new to the neighborhood and lonely. He fantasizes a return to his old neighborhood on Halloween night. After an imaginary plane ride with his old friends, he is able to face his new situation and begin to make new friends. RECOMMENDATION: Young audiences may enjoy the simple, short and very repetitive songs. The difficulty of leaving old friends and having to make new ones is handled honestly and positively. ROYALTY: $25. SOURCE: Schwartz, Stephen. (1986). The trip. Woodstock, IL: Dramatic Pub. Co. SUBJECTS/PLAY TYPE: Musical; Moving; Friendship; Adaptation.

3232. 9-12. (+) Mercati, Cynthia. **Trixie, the teen detective and the mystery of Gravestead Manor.** CAST: 11f, 7m, 5u. ACTS: 2. SETTINGS: Manor foyer. PLAYING TIME: NA. PLOT: Sheena, Madam Zolga, the Great Linguinis (members of a traveling carnival), an archaeologist and his assistant, two wealthy siblings, two plumbers, a troop of girl scouts, and numerous secret agents come to Gravestead Manor to recover the crown jewels of Muldavia. When it is discovered that the jewels no longer exist, the suspects disperse and Trixie ("Happyvale Heights' most famous teen-age detective") is on to her next mystery. RECOMMENDATION: This parody of the "Nancy Drew" genre is very amusing in all of its absurdity. The bizarre parade of characters, the puns and insults, keep the action rolling and the audience guessing. ROYALTY: $40. SOURCE: Mercati, Cynthia. (1985). Trixie, the teen detective and the mystery of Gravestead Manor. Boston, MA: Baker's Plays.

SUBJECTS/PLAY TYPE: Mystery; Jewels; Haunted Houses; Comedy.

3233. 4-12. (+) Bush, Max. **The troll and the elephant prince.** CAST: 2f, 3m, 2u. ACTS: 1. SETTINGS: Town square. PLAYING TIME: NA. PLOT: The people of Trolltown pay the troll for "protection" from the Zanies. Two strangers show them that the troll has tricked them, and that their fear is the result of self imposed blindness to the outside world. RECOMMENDATION: This has adventure, humor, likeable characters, and holds the interest up to the end. It would be ideal for high school students or amateur theater groups to perform for younger children. ROYALTY: $35. SOURCE: Bush, Max. (1985). The troll and the elephant prince. New Orleans, LA: Anchorage Press, Inc. SUBJECTS/PLAY TYPE: Trolls; Fantasy; Comedy.

3234. 5-6. (-) Fisher, Aileen Lucia. **Trouble in the air.** CAST: 12f, 14m, Su. ACTS: 1. SETTINGS: Bare stage, props. PLAYING TIME: NA. PLOT: Various characters relate historical and modern incidences dealing with air pollution and committees to prevent it. RECOMMENDATION: The information is too dated and too disjointed. ROYALTY: None for amateurs. SOURCE: Fisher, Aileen Lucia. (1986). Holiday programs for boys and girls. Boston, MA: Plays, Inc. SUBJECTS/PLAY TYPE: Air Pollution; Playlet.

3235. K-4. (-) Gotwalt, Helen Louise Miller. **Trouble in tick-tock town.** CAST: Su. ACTS: 1. SETTINGS: Bare stage, props. PLAYING TIME: 12 min. PLOT: Various clocks explain what they do, culminating with the wristwatch. RECOMMENDATION: The language is dated, the allusions too mature, and the message is stupid. ROYALTY: None. SOURCE: Gotwalt, Helen Louise Miller. (1985). First plays for children: A collection of little plays for the youngest players. Boston, MA: Plays, Inc. SUBJECTS/PLAY TYPE: Clocks; Playlet.

3236. 1-6. (+) Boiko, Claire. **Trouble in tree-land.** CAST: Su. ACTS: 1. SETTINGS: Forest. PLAYING TIME: 10 min. PLOT: Willy and Lucy prepare to camp and picnic by building a fire. Willy's attempts to chop a tree down for firewood are stopped by the trees, who brush their needles against him, trip him with their roots, and sweep him away with their branches. In fright, Willy decides to use fire. The trees sway to blow out his matches. They exhort the children to go away. But Lucy leaves litter on the ground, and the trees retaliate by throwing acorns at them as they run away. The Ranger is angry at the mess, cleans up the clearing, and makes the trees happy once again. RECOMMENDATION: The need for conservation is stressed by endowing the trees with human characteristics and emotions, which appeal to children's senses and feelings. ROYALTY: None. SOURCE: Boiko, Claire. (1985). Children's plays for creative actors. Boston, MA: Plays, Inc. SUBJECTS/PLAY TYPE: Arbor Day; Conservation; Ecology; Playlet.

3237. 7-12. (+) Nolan, Paul T. **The trouble with Christmas.** CAST: 4f, 3m. ACTS: 1. SETTINGS: Conference room. PLAYING TIME: 25 min. PLOT: Five students meet on Christmas Eve and decide to lead a drive to ban Santa Claus. After the decision has been reached, Santa Claus drops in and changes their minds. RECOMMENDATION: Although predictable and stilted at times, this does offer a few good insights into the nature of Santa and Christmas. ROYALTY: Free to Plays subscribers. SOURCE: Kamerman, Sylvia E. (1976). On stage for Christmas. Boston, MA: Plays, Inc. SUBJECTS/PLAY TYPE: Christmas; Comedy.

3238. 7-12. (+) Harder, Eleanor & Harder, Ray. (Evans, Greg) **The trouble with Derek.** (Luann comic strip) CAST: 8f, 4m. ACTS: 1. SETTINGS: High school hallway. PLAYING TIME: 40 min. PLOT: When a good looking new boy at school appears to be attracted to Bernice, her friends wonder what Derek sees in her. They also wonder why he stores his gym bag in Bernice's locker and then wants it back several times a day. Derek is moody and demanding, but Bernice is blinded by his good looks. When Derek takes her out in his flashy car and tries to give her some pills, Bernice jumps from the car and dumps Derek's pills in the gutter. Meanwhile, Bernice's friend, Luann, has become worried and talks to a teacher, who suspects what Derek is doing. When Bernice is called to the teacher's office, she learns that Derek had an accident after she left him and might have been killed had she not thrown away the rest of his pills. Bernice is shaken to realize that she was tempted to go along with Derek and is relieved that she resisted. RECOMMENDATION: While the theme here is obvious, it is not belabored. ROYALTY: $15. SOURCE: Harder, Eleanor & Harder, Ray. (1988). The trouble with Derek. Denver, CO: Pioneer Drama Service. SUBJECTS/PLAY TYPE: Drug Abuse; Friendship; Adaptation.

3239. 9-12. (+) Gerrold, David. (Blish, James) **The trouble with Tribbles.** (The trouble with tribbles) CAST: 1f, 17m, Su. ACTS: 1. SETTINGS: Bridge of Enterprise; bar/store; office; briefing room; recreation room; transporter room; corridor. PLAYING TIME: 50 min. PLOT: In this Star Trek episode, Captain Kirk and the crew deal with Klingons and tons of tribbles. RECOMMENDATION: This is exciting, humorous and well recognized. However, the sets, props and the number of scenes make this a very expensive, time consuming production. ROYALTY: None. SOURCE: Kamerman, Sylvia E. (1981). Space and science fiction plays for young people. Boston, MA: Plays, Inc. SUBJECTS/PLAY TYPE: Star Trek; Science Fiction; Space Adventure; Adaptation.

3240. 12. (+) Jacoby, Bruce. **Troubled times.** CAST: 9f, 7m. ACTS: 2. SETTINGS: Newspaper editorial offices. PLAYING TIME: NA. PLOT: This whodunnit mystery addresses, at the university newspaper level, the problems journalists face to publish the truth, and campus issues such as payments to athletes and the autonomy of school newspapers. Did the athlete receive a payment to attend college? And who is the paper's informant? RECOMMENDATION: This is recommended for mature audiences as a realistic depiction of college life and the dilemmas journalists face. The action involves drinking, graphic language, and controversial moral behavior. ROYALTY: $50. SOURCE: Jacoby, Bruce. (1983). Troubled times. Chicago, IL: Dramatic Pub. Co. SUBJECTS/PLAY TYPE: Journalism; College; Athletes; Mystery.

3241. 7-12. (+) Dias, Earl J. **Troy was never like this.** CAST: 3f, 7m, 1u. ACTS: 1. SETTINGS: Palace room. PLAYING TIME: 25 min. PLOT: As a historian relates the Helen of Troy story, the Troy Internal Revenue Service and other modern day conventions interrupt. Finally, Homer throws out all the historical revisionists and insists that the story go on accurately. RECOMMENDATION: This satire demonstrates history, but its humor will be appreciated best by those who know the real story beforehand. ROYALTY: Free to Plays subscribers. SOURCE: Dias, Earl J. (1976, December). Troy was never like this. Plays: The Drama Magazine for Young People, pp. 11-24. SUBJECTS/PLAY TYPE: Helen of Troy; Trojan War; Comedy.

3242. 7-12. (+) Cheatham, Val. **The Truehart Boarding House prospers anew.** CAST: 6f, 3m. ACTS: 1. SETTINGS: Living room. PLAYING TIME: 20 min. PLOT: The villain is exposed as he tries to take advantage of some aging, eccentric stars of the silent screen and the owner of the boarding house where they reside. RECOMMENDATION: This lighthearted play will show off the talents of those portraying the unique characters. ROYALTY: Free to Plays subscribers. SOURCE: Cheatham, Val R. (1980, April). The Truehart Boarding House prospers anew. Plays: The Drama Magazine for Young People, pp. 23-30. SUBJECTS/PLAY TYPE: Swindlers and Swindling; Melodrama.

3243. 9-12. (-) Green, Albert. **A trying ordeal.** CAST: 5f, 3m. ACTS: 1. SETTINGS: Park. PLAYING TIME: 25 min. PLOT: A young girl, immature for her years, tries to understand the world around her as she waits on a park bench for her sister. In the process, she adopts a stranger for a brother. RECOMMENDATION: The confused young girl is very convincing. However, the fairy tale "happily ever after" ending lacks any credibility. ROYALTY: $10. SOURCE: Green, Albert. (1976). A trying ordeal. Schulenberg, TX: I.E. Clark. SUBJECTS/PLAY TYPE: Family; Psychology; Drama.

3244. 3-6. (+) Gabriel, Michelle. **Tu B'Shvat: Little tree learns a lesson.** CAST: 1f, 1m, Su. ACTS: 1. SETTINGS: Outdoors. PLAYING TIME: 20 min. PLOT: The trees talk about the holiday's customs and meanings as themes about self esteem and faith in oneself are delivered. RECOMMENDATION: This has a well done verse format. ROYALTY: None. SOURCE: Gabriel, Michelle. (1978). Jewish plays for Jewish days. Denver, CO: Alternatives in Religious Education, Inc. SUBJECTS/PLAY TYPE: Tu B'Shvat; Self Esteem; Jewish Drama.

3245. 3-6. (+) Kelly, Tim. (Ryan, Tom K.) **Tumbleweeds.** (Tumbleweeds, A comic strip) CAST: 16f, 15m, 2u. ACTS: 2. SETTINGS: Old west town. PLAYING TIME: 120 min. PLOT: In this melodramatic western lampoon, Tumbleweeds (a well meaning dolt) inadvertently becomes a hero who saves Grimy Gulch (the armpit of the West) from Indians and the railroad. The lost troops of Colonel Fluster finally return to Fort Ridiculous,

their mission forgotten, much to the delight of a tour group of young ladies. Throughout, Hildegard Harnhocker relentlessly searches for a husband. Musical lines that advance the story may or may not be sung. RECOMMENDATION: Ideal for hams capable of exploiting the comic devices (dry sarcasm, audience asides, stereotyped characters and low brow situations). Costumes and scenery are simple and fun, but it is helpful if familiar with the Tumbleweeds comic strips. ROYALTY: $60. SOURCE: Kelly, Tim. (1983). Tumbleweeds. Denver, CO: Pioneer Drama Service. SUBJECTS/PLAY TYPE: Western; Musical; Comedy.

3246. 10-12. (+) Cook, Pat. **Tung and Cheek.** CAST: 3f, 4m. ACTS: 2. SETTINGS: Living room. PLAYING TIME: NA. PLOT: Detective Tony Cheek and his sidekick, Squatty, are summoned to the lavish Granville Diamond estate by a mysterious message. The housekeeper assures them that nothing is amiss and that Granville Diamond, the famous scientist, left three days earlier for France. After Tony and Squatty question Granville's blind uncle, Hope Diamond, Tony uncovers a blackboard with "NO HEYP" written on it. As the duo tries to analyze this clue, Honey Diamond, the daughter, mesmerizes them with her beauty. Falling backward onto the couch, Tony and Honey discover Granville Diamond's body under the dust cover. As the plot thickens, the letters on the blackboard are rearranged to spell the real name of everyone in the house. The dynamic pair manage to dodge Uncle Hope's ferocious, near sighted, seeing eye dog, stage a drunken romp through the living room, solve the blackboard's anagram, and unmask the masquerading Granville Diamond, who killed his brainy assistant in an attempt to save face in the scientific world. With the PHONEY revealed, Tony and Honey are free to pursue each other. RECOMMENDATION: The slapstick comedy of Cheek and Squatty mix well with the mystery and its solution. The kisses and lightweight sexual innuendos should be considered when choosing this play, which would also fare well as a college level performance. ROYALTY: $40. SOURCE: Cook, Pat. (1983). Tung and Cheek. Boston, MA: Baker's Plays. SUBJECTS/PLAY TYPE: Comedy; Adventure; Murder; Mystery.

3247. 7-12. (+) Hark, Mildred & McQueen, Noel. **Turkey gobblers.** CAST: 4f, 3m, 1u. ACTS: 1. SETTINGS: Living-dining room. PLAYING TIME: 30 min. PLOT: As the Baldwins prepare Thanksgiving dinner, their teenage daughter watches her boyfriend (on TV) discuss the advantages of eating granola and yogurt. She persuades her parents to forgo the traditional dinner for health food in order to impress her boyfriend, who arrives later. To everyone's relief, they realize the boyfriend was encouraging people to eat health food for breakfast, not dinner, and all sit down to a traditional turkey dinner. RECOMMENDATION: In this simple and straightforward comedy, the characters and dialog are natural and believable, production costs are minimal, and preparation should be easy. ROYALTY: Free to Plays subscribers. SOURCE: Hark, Mildred & Noel McQueen. (1984, November). Turkey gobblers. Plays: The Drama Magazine for Young People, pp. 11-21. SUBJECTS/PLAY TYPE: Thanksgiving; Health Foods; Comedy.

3248. 2-5. (+) Bradley, Virginia. **Turkeys take a dim view of Thanksgiving.** CAST: 2f, 1m, 2u. ACTS: 1. SETTINGS: Room; Turkeyland. PLAYING TIME: NA. PLOT: While reading about the first Thanksgiving, a little girl falls asleep and dreams about the holiday from a turkey's point of view. RECOMMENDATION: Children will enjoy the **Alice in Wonderland** tone of this departure from the traditional Thanksgiving play. ROYALTY: None. SOURCE: Bradley, Virginia. (1975). Is there an actor in the house? New York, NY: Dodd, Mead. SUBJECTS/PLAY TYPE: Thanksgiving; Comedy; Skit.

3249. 9-12. (-) MacMillan, Stuart B. **Turkeys waiting to be plucked.** CAST: 3f, 4m. ACTS: 1. SETTINGS: Employment office. PLAYING TIME: NA. PLOT: A truck driver, chef, and cleaning woman try to find work at a state employment office. The ignorant secretary and the procedure obsessed manager resent these disturbances and make no attempt to match the applicants with available jobs. Mr. Williams, who comes every day to observe the chaos in the office, takes advantage of a staff coffee break to send the job seekers to prospective employers. Upon returning to the office the secretary and manager congratulate themselves for the job placements and the secretary is promoted. RECOMMENDATION: This is overdone, silly, and simplistic; the characters are one dimensional; and the plot seems to wander toward an inevitable conclusion without making any meaningful point. ROYALTY: $15. SOURCE: MacMillan, Stuart B. (1979). Turkeys waiting to be plucked. Chicago, IL: Dramatic Pub. Co. SUBJECTS/PLAY TYPE: Employment Office; Bureaucracy; Comedy.

3250. 2-8. (-) Boiko, Claire. **The turtle who changed his tune.** CAST: 4f, 2m, 12u. ACTS: 1. SETTINGS: House; town square with a teahouse, pond. PLAYING TIME: 15 min. PLOT: A diligent brother finds a magic singing turtle, whose sweet songs earn money which he brings home to his mother. His lazy brother is jealous, steals the turtle, and tries to make it sing. It sings horridly, and rather than give him money, the people run him out of the village and return the turtle to the good brother, who lives happily with the turtle and his mother. RECOMMENDATION: Stilted and unnatural language unduly detracts from the universal plot and theme. ROYALTY: Free to Plays subscribers. SOURCE: Boiko, Claire. (1980, March). The turtle who changed his tune. Plays: The Drama Magazine for Young People, pp. 55-58. SUBJECTS/PLAY TYPE: Diligence; Folk Tales, Japan; Playlet.

3251. K-3. (+) Korty, Carol. **The turtle who wanted to fly.** CAST: 1f, 2m, 5u. ACTS: 1. SETTINGS: None. PLAYING TIME: NA. PLOT: A happy little turtle loves to sing, but most of all wants to fly. Two pigeons give him some of their extra feathers. After he has flown (very badly), a farmer catches him for dinner. Turtle sings as he waits to be cooked and the farmer, his wife, and son dance. The pigeons return and help turtle scuttle to freedom. RECOMMENDATION: This is cheerful, slapstick action. Props can be mimed. ROYALTY: $25. SOURCE: Korty, Carol. (1975). Plays from African folktales. Boston, MA: Baker's Plays. SUBJECTS/PLAY TYPE: Folk Tales, Africa; Turtles; Playlet.

3252. 7-12. (-) Murray, John. **The Tutankhamun murder case.** CAST: 5f, 8m. ACTS: 1. SETTINGS: Living room. PLAYING TIME: 30 min. PLOT: An ancient Egyptian curse strikes down most of the characters in this modern day play that involves archaeologists and the avenging spirit of Khapah Amen, who was wrongly accused of killing King Tutankhamun. An ancient chest that holds the key to the mystery is opened. Amen's spirit is released and inhabits the body of Betty, a young professor's wife. Carl Brooks, the professor, and Dr. Allerton, a noted Egyptologist, disappear into the past, along with other members of the cast, who seek to discover what happened to Allerton and Brooks. The secret is revealed and the "spirits" are put to rest in the final scene. RECOMMENDATION: The living room setting does not convey the mood of mystery and mystique sorely needed to carry off this otherwise unbelievable plot. Many characters are killed in too short a time, leading to confusion about who is who, and drawing attention away from the central question of why. The curse itself is inconsistent: while the first characters disappear into the night, the second's disappearance is heralded by jackals who are blamed for the loss. Although King Tut is an historical figure, this bit of nonsense about his death comes off as just that--nonsense. ROYALTY: Free to Plays subscribers. SOURCE: Murray, John. (1979, October). The Tutankhamun murder case. Plays: The Drama Magazine for Young People, pp. 1-13. SUBJECTS/PLAY TYPE: Mystery; Egypt; Playlet.

3253. 7-12. (-) Nydam, Ken. **TV screen attack.** CAST: 4u. ACTS: 1. SETTINGS: None. PLAYING TIME: NA. PLOT: Rick is apathetic about being with other people, in spite of his mother's pleas to turn off the TV. RECOMMENDATION: As a white angel (good) and black angel (bad) represent Rick's conscience and evil impulses, this gets bagged down in inanity. ROYALTY: NA. SOURCE: Altena, Hans. (1980). The playbook for Christian theater. Grand Rapids, MI: Baker Book House. SUBJECTS/PLAY TYPE: Television; Reader's Theater.

3254. 9-12. (+) Snee, Dennis. **Twain by the tale.** CAST: 5f, 6m, Su. ACTS: 2. SETTINGS: Bare stage with props. PLAYING TIME: NA. PLOT: A compilation of various quotations, sketches, and excerpts from Twain's works, this comprises sixteen segments which include, "A Page from a California Almanac," "The Fable of St. Patrick," "Advice to Little Girls," and "The Legend of Sagenfeld." Several alternative/additional sketches are included at the end, including the selection from **Huckleberry Finn** on curing warts, "When the Buffalo Climbed the Tree," "Cookery Complaints," and the engagement scene between Tom and Becky in **The Adventures of Tom Sawyer.** RECOMMENDATION: This selection of monologues cleverly scans Twain's works, from his witticisms to his novels. Although written to be performed together, the sketches could easily be divided for individual production. At least eleven actors are required, but the roles could be divided, using fresh actors for each segment to allow for greater participation. To ensure full appreciation, the audience should have a basic understanding of Twain and his literary works. ROYALTY: $50. SOURCE: Snee,

Dennis. (1978). Twain by the tale. Boston, MA: Baker's Plays. SUBJECTS/PLAY TYPE: Twain, Mark; Monologue.

3255. K-12. (+) Sabath, Bernard. **Twain plus twain.** CAST: 2f, 4m. ACTS: 4. SETTINGS: Various cities. PLAYING TIME: NA. PLOT: This is a delightful time lapse look at the colorful life of Samuel Clemens. In "Summer Morning Visitor," Sam, having a Southern upbringing and Northern sympathies, is torn between sides during the Civil War. He resolves his dilemma by heading West. In "The Trouble Begins at 8" (five years later), Sam, destitute, meets an old friend who persuades him to travel the lecture circuit. On a cruise two years later ("A Barbarian in Love"), Sam falls in love with a refined lady whose father reluctantly blesses her marriage with the rambunctious Westerner. In "The Loneliest Wayfarer," after many happy years with his family, Sam, now alone, meets a young wayfarer who reminds him of himself many years ago. RECOMMENDATION: The feelings and emotions are transferred from play to play culminating in a fresh, new acquaintance with Mark Twain. The settings are "indicated." Performance could easily be handled by grades 6-12. ROYALTY: $50. SOURCE: Sabath, Bernard. (1983). Twain plus twain. New York, NY: Dramatists Play Service, Inc. SUBJECTS/PLAY TYPE: Twain, Mark; Narrative.

3256. 7-12. (-) Dawson, Elizabeth. **Twas the night after Christmas - 1776.** CAST: 5f, 1m. ACTS: 1. SETTINGS: Sitting room. PLAYING TIME: 35 min. PLOT: On the day after Christmas during the Revolutionary War, the women worry whether they should leave Philadelphia before the British arrive, and whether their husbands are safe. RECOMMENDATION: This presents no history, nor does it discuss the issues of the Revolutionary War. ROYALTY: Free to Plays subscribers. SOURCE: Dawson, Elizabeth. (1976, December). 'Twas the night after Christmas - 1776. Plays: The Drama Magazine for Young People, pp. 65-74. SUBJECTS/PLAY TYPE: Revolution, American; Playlet.

3257. 9-12. (-) Pendleton, Edrie. **Twas the night before Christmas.** CAST: 2f, 3m, Su. ACTS: 1. SETTINGS: Living room. PLAYING TIME: 35 min. PLOT: There is a mix-up in the Christmas gift exchange and 17 year old Bud inadvertently gives his girlfriend the expensive negligee his Dad intended for his Mom. RECOMMENDATION: In this slow production, while the awkwardness of the teenager's plight contains a measure of humor, the dialogue is bereft of any funny material. The characters are neither interesting nor believable. ROYALTY: Free to Plays subscribers. SOURCE: Kamerman, Sylvia E. (1984, December). Plays: The Drama Magazine for Young People, pp. 21- 28. SUBJECTS/PLAY TYPE: Christmas; Comedy.

3258. 9-12*. (+) Pickett, Cecil. (Shakespeare, William) **Twelfth night.** (Twelfth night or what you will) CAST: 2f, 7m, 6u. ACTS: 1. SETTINGS: Bare stage, props. PLAYING TIME: 35 min. PLOT: Twins Viola and Sebastian are shipwrecked and unknown to each other, are alive and well in Illyria. Viola disguises herself as a boy named Cedario and works as a servant to Orsino, the Duke of Illyria. She falls in love with him, but can't flirt because of her male disguise. Orsino is in love with the Countess Olivia, and she is in love with the Duke's servant, Cesario (Viola is disguise). All ends well as Viola wins Orsino's hand in marriage. RECOMMENDATION: Feste and Fabian narrate much of the action to shorten the play and to minimize much of the original dialogue. Clowns change the sets and provide background for the action. The dialogue is a modified Shakespearean style that is easier to understand. ROYALTY: $15. SOURCE: Pickett, Cecil. (1984). Twelfth night. Schulenburg, TX: I.E. Clark. SUBJECTS/PLAY TYPE: Romance; Mistaken Identities; Adaptation.

3259. 10-12. (-) Barefield, J.G. (Shakespeare, William) **Twelfth night, or, what you will.** (Twelfth night, or what you will) CAST: 3f, 11m. ACTS: 2. SETTINGS: Minimal sets, props. PLAYING TIME: NA. PLOT: The original has been abridged to the bare essentials. Twins, Viola and Sebastian, are separated and lost at sea. Both end up on the coast of Illyria where Viola, now disguised as a boy, falls in love with the handsome Duke, Orsino. Sebastian, rescued by a pirate (enemy to Orsino), falls in love with Olivia, the woman Orsino has long loved. Everything ends cheerfully with three happy couples and the twins reunited. RECOMMENDATION: The adapter has unsuccessfully tried to simplify the text without losing the comedic nuances and imagery inherent in all of Shakespeare's works. The omission of various scenes and the modernized dialogue make this disjointed and totally lacking the multi- layered texture of the original. ROYALTY: $35. SOURCE: Barefield, J.G. (1980). Twelfth night, or, what you will. Elgin, IL: Performance Pub. SUBJECTS/PLAY TYPE: Love; Comedy; Adaptation.

3260. 10-12. (+) Sergel, Sherman L. (Rose, Reginald) **Twelve angry women.** (Twelve angry men) CAST: 15f. ACTS: 3. SETTINGS: Jury room. PLAYING TIME: NA. PLOT: Twelve women are jurors in a murder trial. One holds on to her convictions that the defendant has not been proven guilty, though the other 11 think he has. By going over the evidence and asking questions the lawyers didn't, she convinces the others to reluctantly change their minds. RECOMMENDATION: This underscores the importance of the U.S. jury system and could be used as the basis for a high school civics class discussion. The variety of personalities and strong emotions offer challenging roles. ROYALTY: $50. SOURCE: Sergel, Sherman L. (1984). Twelve angry women. New York, NY: Dramatic Pub. Co. SUBJECTS/PLAY TYPE: Juries; Law; Women; Drama.

3261. 5-8. (+) McCallum, Phyllis. (Grimm Brothers) **The twelve dancing princesses.** (The twelve dancing princesses) CAST: 13f, 4m. ACTS: 2. SETTINGS: Throne room; terrace of underground kingdom. PLAYING TIME: 45 min. PLOT: Twelve princesses are spirited away each night and return with their dancing slippers in shreds. The king tries to discover what is happening to them. A handsome soldier, with the help of the wise housekeeper, reveals the secret, as well as the spells and plots of an evil prime minister. The royal kingdom is saved and the soldier is given the loveliest princess as his bride. RECOMMENDATION: Although the cast is large, only five have lines of any length. Roles are stereotypical.

ROYALTY: $20. SOURCE: McCallum, Phyllis. (1978). The twelve dancing princesses. Denver, CO: Pioneer Drama Service. SUBJECTS/PLAY TYPE: Princesses; Magic; Folk Tales, Germany; Adaptation.

3262. 6-9*. (+) Rogers, June Walker & Leslie, Diane. (Grimm Brothers) **Twelve dancing princesses.** (The twelve dancing princesses.) CAST: 22f, 21m, Su. ACTS: 1. SETTINGS: Meadow; bedroom; dance room; hallway. PLAYING TIME: NA. PLOT: A king offers the hand of one of his daughters to the man who can discover how his daughters wear out their shoes every night and explain what has happened to the eleven princes who failed in their attempts to solve the mystery. With magic, a gardener breaks the spell, the princesses are freed from danceland, the gardener is made a prince, and is given the hand of the King's daughter. RECOMMENDATION: Sophisticated language and elaborate musical numbers make this unsuitable for production by a younger audience who would otherwise enjoy the story. Also, since the plot is geared toward a younger audience, it may not appeal to older viewers despite attempts to update it. ROYALTY: $50. SOURCE: Rogers, June Walker. (1976). Twelve dancing princesses. Woodstock, IL: Dramatic Pub. Co. SUBJECTS/PLAY TYPE: Dancing; Folk Tales, Germany; Adaptation.

3263. 4-6. (+) Thane, Adele. (Grimm Brothers) **The twelve dancing princesses.** (The twelve dancing princesses) CAST: 13f, 4m. ACTS: 1. SETTINGS: Anteroom; garden. PLAYING TIME: 30 min. PLOT: Twelve royal sisters sneak away and inexplicably wear out their dancing slippers each night. The noblemen that the King entices to trap the sisters, fail. With the help of a fairy disguised as a cleaning woman, a kind cobbler finds the girls' secret dancing spot and wins the hand of a willing princess. RECOMMENDATION: Although the characters are not well developed, the tale is very pleasant. The costumes and props should be easy to obtain or make, but changes of scenes may be tricky for a young group. The audience will especially enjoy seeing the cobbler's antics when he is rendered invisible to the sisters by a magic cloak. ROYALTY: None. SOURCE: Thane, Adele. (1983). Plays from famous stories and fairy tales. Boston, MA: Plays, Inc. SUBJECTS/PLAY TYPE: Folk Tales, Germany; Shoemakers; Princesses; Adaptation.

3264. 5-8. (+) Wright, Doris G. **The twelve days of Christmas.** CAST: 28f, 26m, 33u. ACTS: 1. SETTINGS: Two thrones. PLAYING TIME: 15 min. PLOT: The King proclaims twelve days of merry making to celebrate the Christmas season. The jester helps the king pick gifts for the Queen; one for each of the twelve days. The Jester is rewarded for his help by his appointment as one of the King's wise counselors. RECOMMENDATION: Language is colloquial but young actors will find it fairly easy to memorize. This is an excellent choice for school and civic entertainment. ROYALTY: None. SOURCE: Kamerman, Sylvia E. (1975). A treasury of Christmas plays. Boston, MA: Plays, Inc. SUBJECTS/PLAY TYPE: Christmas; Comedy.

3265. K-8. (+) Hubert, Paul. **24th century kids.** CAST: 5f, 3m, 5u. ACTS: 1. SETTINGS: Futuristic schoolroom; old fashioned schoolroom. PLAYING TIME: 60 min. PLOT: In this futuristic musical, the students on Planet Earth love their robot teacher, Ms. X, who makes learning fun. The Greenie students on Planet Tweeny don't go to school, but since they want to go, they steal Ms. X. The Earth kids, aided by the nerdy Jeffrey, steal Ms. X back and capture the Greenies. Ms. X explains that though they are from different planets, the students are the same, and she shows them her teaching double, Ms. Y, who will go back to Tweeny to teach the Greenies. RECOMMENDATION: The two themes of cooperation and the universality of people are easily understood. The scores and lyrics are fun and catchy, and the very limited number of lines make this an apt choice for a class production which involves every student. ROYALTY: $70. SOURCE: Hubert, Paul. (1985). 24th century kids. Franklin, OH: Eldridge Pub. Co. SUBJECTS/PLAY TYPE: School; Outer Space; Future; Musical.

3266. 4-7. (+) Bland, Joellen. (Verne, Jules) **20,000 leagues under the sea.** (20,000 leagues under the sea) CAST: 5m. ACTS: 1. SETTINGS: Bare stage. PLAYING TIME: NA. PLOT: Three men tell about an undersea adventure that began two years earlier when the U.S. ship, **Abraham Lincoln**, was sent to investigate a sea monster, reported to be destroying ships. After months at sea, the creature was sighted and pursued. The ship's attack was ineffective and the three men were washed overboard, only to discover that the monster was actually a submarine, in which they were soon imprisoned. The captain of the sub informed the men that they would have to remain aboard since they were now aware of the sub's existence. Reluctantly, they accompanied the moody, irascible captain on his adventures. His brutal attack on a warship convinced the three prisoners that they must escape. They secretly exited the sub into a rowboat just as the sub entered a whirlpool. The play concludes with the viewers pondering the fate of the **Nautilus** and her brilliant but tortured captain. RECOMMENDATION: This captures the excitement and drama of the original, although the transitions between the events described are not smoothly effected and the audience may become confused about times and places. ROYALTY: Free to Plays subscribers. SOURCE: Bland, Joellen. (1978, May). 20,000 leagues under the sea. Plays: The Drama Magazine for Young People, pp. 81-92. SUBJECTS/PLAY TYPE: Reader's Theater; Adventure; Adaptation.

3267. 7-10. (+) McCusker, Paul. **The twilife zone.** CAST: 4f, 5m, 1u. ACTS: 1. SETTINGS: Park bench. PLAYING TIME: NA. PLOT: Joe Davis encounters four individuals who personify stereotypes of Christians: a weak, insecure man dominated by his wife; a fast talking, money hungry Evangelist; and a ranting, religious fanatic. The last character is a dangerous maniac with a gun who believes his destiny is to destroy all the evil things in the world. He explains to Joe that God has told him to kill people who sit in the park and have strange experiences and cry. As he points his gun at Joe's head, the narrator closes the scene by saying Joe has been victimized by Hollywood nonentities, and that there is no escape. RECOMMENDATION: This will generate much discussion about the images of Christianity and how its followers should behave. ROYALTY: NA. SOURCE: McCusker, Paul. (1982). Souvenirs: Comedies and dramas for Christian fellowship. Boston, MA: Baker's Plays. SUBJECTS/PLAY TYPE: Christian Drama; Christian Stereotypes.

3268. 3-5. (+) Spamer, Claribel. **Twinkle. CAST:** 3f, 4m, Su. ACTS: 1. SETTINGS: Sky. PLAYING TIME: 10 min. PLOT: When Santa arrives, Twinkle, the smallest of the stars, tells him what she wants for Christmas. RECOMMENDATION: This well written play considers the meaning of Christmas wishes. ROYALTY: Free to Plays subscribers. SOURCE: Kamerman, Sylvia E. (1975). A treasury of Christmas plays. Boston, MA: Plays, Inc. SUBJECTS/PLAY TYPE: Christmas; Wishes; Playlet.

3269. 2-6. (+) Winther, Barbara. **Two dilemma tales.** CAST: 3f, 5m, 2u. ACTS: 2. SETTINGS: Street of African village. PLAYING TIME: 20 min. PLOT: A grandmother tells two stories. In "The Snore or The Song," two brothers seeking their fortunes spend the night at a village where there can be no noise at night. One of the brothers snores, and to save him from death, the other sings to mask the sound. The villagers are so delighted they give the singer a fortune and let the one who snored live. The snorer feels he is entitled to half the money as a reward for his contribution, and the audience must decide if he is right. In "The Honey Hunter," a father is rescued by his wife, son, and daughter, each of whom has contributed to his rescue, and each of whom demands a part of the father's reward. The audience must decide who deserves the reward. RECOMMENDATION: This will provoke interesting discussions among the audience as they grapple with difficult moral dilemmas. Especially delightful here are the songs in the first story. ROYALTY: Free for amateur performance. SOURCE: Winther, Barbara. (1976). Plays from folktales of Africa and Asia. Boston, MA: Plays, Inc. SUBJECTS/PLAY TYPE: Folktales, Africa; Values; Justice; Playlet.

3270. 7-12. (+) Hoppenstedt, Elbert M. **The two faces of liberty.** CAST: 3f, 6m. ACTS: 1. SETTINGS: Living room. PLAYING TIME: 25 min. PLOT: News of the peace treaty ending the American Revolution has just been received with much joy in Boston. Preparations begin for a celebration while the Citizen's Committee plans revenge against the Loyalists. The Lenkin family, with two brothers who have taken opposite positions in the war, is almost destroyed, but justice and democracy prevail over mob rule and tyranny. RECOMMENDATION: This presents the duality of two issues: respect for the beliefs of others and forgiveness versus hatred and revenge; justice and democracy versus mob rule and tyranny. The struggle is profoundly expressed through the dialogue and the strong characterizations. The family relationships are very dynamic. The time could be changed to World War II or the Vietnam War. ROYALTY: Free to Plays subscribers. SOURCE: Hoppenstedt, Elbert M. (1975, November). The two faces of liberty. Plays: The Drama Magazine for Young

People, pp. 67-76. SUBJECTS/PLAY TYPE: Democracy; Playlet.

3271. 7-12. (+) Murray, John. **Two for the money.** CAST: 8f, 5m. ACTS: 1. SETTINGS: Hotel suite. PLAYING TIME: 35 min. PLOT: When Egbert Q. Puffington is mistaken for French singing idol, Pierre Duval, Egbert's wife, Hazel, becomes infuriated when a young girl gushes over her husband. The resulting comedy of mistaken identities is reminiscent of Oscar Wilde's **The Importance of Being Earnest.** By play's end, identities are unscrambled, all is forgiven, and Egbert is given a chance to be a star himself. RECOMMENDATION: Even though some of the dialogue is dated, this romantic comedy is fast paced and concludes neatly with all the frustrated lovers finding fulfillment. Characters should be played in a flamboyant, exaggerated manner to add to the fun. ROYALTY: Free to Plays subscribers. SOURCE: Murray, John. (1979, February). Two for the money. Plays: The Drama Magazine for Young People, pp. 15- 28. SUBJECTS/PLAY TYPE: Hollywood; Mistaken Identity; Comedy.

3272. 2-8. (+) Schaller, Mary W. **Two horns and a tale.** CAST: 2f, 2m, 14u. ACTS: 1. SETTINGS: Heaven; hell; outside of a post office. PLAYING TIME: NA. PLOT: Inept Will O' Wisp, after graduating from the College of Demonology, is sent to an off-the-map town on Earth's surface as a Tempter. He unwittingly performs a good deed (treason in Hell), is exiled to Earth's surface, and is forced to make a choice between good and evil. RECOMMENDATION: This delightfully funny fantasy, complete with mailboxes and bronze lions that come to life, will entertain younger grades as well as the older grades who probably should produce it. ROYALTY: $25. SOURCE: Schaller, Mary W. (1978). Two horns and a tale. Woodstock, IL: Dramatic Pub. Co. SUBJECTS/PLAY TYPE: Heaven; Hell; Devils; Fantasy.

3273. 7-12. (+) Stahl, Le Roy. **Two shorts, one long.** CAST: 2f, 1m. ACTS: 1. SETTINGS: Office. PLAYING TIME: NA. PLOT: Business is slow for a pair of taxidermists who reminisce about past achievements. Excitement builds when a customer identified as a big game hunter enters the shop. To the disappointment of the taxidermists, the customer is only a newlywed who thinks they can help her stuff the duck she is cooking for dinner. RECOMMENDATION: Based on different understandings of stuffing a bird, this is quite funny. ROYALTY: None. SOURCE: Majeski, Bill. (1981). Easy skits, blackouts and pantomimes. Woodstock, IL: Dramatic Pub. Co. SUBJECTS/PLAY TYPE: Taxidermy; Comedy; Skit.

3274. 8-11*. (+) Bass, Mary Gettys. **Two small fries to go. CAST:** 5f, 3m, Su. ACTS: 1. SETTINGS: Two bedrooms; classroom; lunchroom. PLAYING TIME: NA. PLOT: Each of eight characters voice a personally intriguing question about teenage love. Six of the players, three boys and three girls, enact a series of scenes during which they interact with members of the opposite sex and display the hesitancies, fears, embarrassments, and self doubts of typical young teens and their lack of experience in boy-girl relationships. "Split-screen" and "freeze" techniques, where boy-girl thoughts are spoken aloud (almost simultaneously), create vivid experiences. The other two characters, both girls, present their problems in monologues. RECOMMENDATION: It is likely that teenagers will readily identify with the awkwardness and affectations so common among this age group. ROYALTY: $15. SOURCE: Bass, Mary Gettys. (1987). Two to go. Boston, MA: Baker's Plays. SUBJECTS/PLAY TYPE: Romance; Adolescent Problems; Drama.

3275. 9-12. (+) Whittier, Bert. **The two week one night stand.** CAST: 5f, 5m, Su. ACTS: 3. SETTINGS: Living room. PLAYING TIME: NA. PLOT: When Dr. George Cameron and his wife, Louise, are notified that their family has won an overnight visit from Rex King, a popular TV star, George reluctantly agrees to the visit for the sake of his teenage daughter, Sissy. One guest, however, becomes four when the Cameron's son, Scott, exposes his family and Rex's entourage to a contagious disease and the state health commissioner quarantines the entire household for two weeks. During the quarantine, Lula Mae Stinger, an abrasive gossip columnist, prints a rumor of a romance between Rex and Sissy. Rex's current TV show is abruptly cancelled, but Alex Alexander, the producer, begins plans for a new show. Scott, an electronics enthusiast, is hired as technical advisor, and the family decides to go to Hollywood while Scott works on the pilot. RECOMMENDATION: Although this play centers around cliched characters and a far fetched plot, it has realistic discussions of the lifestyles of famous personalities. The humor could grow stale without strong actors. Scene changes are rather in depth and an alternative arrangement of the acts is offered. This is best left to older high school actors. ROYALTY: $35. SOURCE: Whittier, Bert. (1978). The two week one night stand. Boston, MA: Baker's Plays. SUBJECTS/PLAY TYPE: Show Business; Television Programs; Electronics; Comedy.

3276. 9-12. (-) Norquist, Richard. **A typically atypical day.** CAST: 7f, 2m, 5u. ACTS: 1. SETTINGS: Reception office. PLAYING TIME: NA. PLOT: A reporter is assigned to report on a typical day at the Mayor's office. As the day unfolds, people with various troubles appeal for the Mayor's help, including a woman in labor accompanied by her pet snake, two good natured terrorists, and a fraudulent faith healer. RECOMMENDATION: Despite a 1985 copyright, the characters reflect 1960s humor which is too cliched to be funny. This attempts to be just plain silly, but it does not succeed. ROYALTY: $15. SOURCE: Norquist, Richard. (1985). A typically atypical day. Woodstock, IL: Dramatic Pub. Co. SUBJECTS/PLAY TYPE: Faith Healing; Politicians; Comedy.

3277. 7-12. (+) Sawyer-Young, Kat. **Ugly.** CAST: 1f. ACTS: 1. SETTINGS: None. PLAYING TIME: 1 min. PLOT: Sharon bemoans how foolishly she behaves in front of boys she likes. RECOMMENDATION: Even Sharon has to laugh at the humor of her situation. ROYALTY: None. SOURCE: Sawyer-Young, Kat. (1987). Minute monologues for contemporary teens. Boston, MA: Baker's Plays. SUBJECTS/PLAY TYPE: Dating; Monologue.

3278. 10-12. (-) Freedman, Jeri. **Uncle Duncan's delusion.** CAST: 5f, 3m. ACTS: 1. SETTINGS: Living room. PLAYING TIME: NA. PLOT: Crazy Uncle Duncan and his obsession with the invasion of space aliens wreak havoc for an average American family as they try to entertain guests. Mistaken identities and misunderstandings create chaos and embarrassment as the psychiatrist decides that it is the family, not Uncle Duncan, who is crazy. RECOMMENDATION: Awkward dialogue, an unsympathetic and stereotyped view of a mentally ill person, along with his physical abuse by the "sane" family members, make this unsuccessful. ROYALTY: NA. SOURCE: Freedman, Jeri. (1982). Uncle Duncan's delusion. Boston, MA: Baker's Plays. SUBJECTS/PLAY TYPE: Mental Illness; Comedy.

3279. K-4. (+) Mahlman, Lewis & Jones, David Cadwalader. (Harris, Joel Chandler) **Uncle Remus tales.** CAST: 7u. ACTS: 1. SETTINGS: Peanut patch; pond; campfire-site. PLAYING TIME: 20 min. PLOT: Brer Rabbit is caught stealing Brer Fox's peanuts, but tricks Brer Bear into the trap by convincing him it is really a scarecrow house, and that Brer Fox pays gold pieces to whoever sits in it to keep the thieves away. Then Brer Rabbit and Brer Terrapin keep Brer Fox and Brer Bear from eating them by convincing them that the moon's reflection in the lake is actually the moon, under which lies a pot of gold. When the fox and the bear are safely struggling to get out of the cold water, Terrapin and Rabbit escape. RECOMMENDATION: None of the dialect which can make the Uncle Remus stories so hard to tell has been retained here. However, the cleverness of Brer Rabbit and the interactions of the animals are well preserved. Because of the length of some of the parts, this would have to be produced by older adolescents for youngsters. ROYALTY: Free to Plays subscribers. SOURCE: Mahlman, Lewis & Jones, David Cadwalader. (1980). Folk tale plays for puppets. Boston, MA: Plays, Inc. SUBJECTS/PLAY TYPE: Adaptation; Trickery; Folk Tales, American; Puppet Play.

3280. 7-12. (+) Horovitz, Israel. **Uncle Snake: An Independence Day pageant.** CAST: Su. ACTS: 1. SETTINGS: Bare stage, props. PLAYING TIME: NA. PLOT: With satire and dry humor, a narrator introduces the audience to the thirteen prominent members of the Continental Congress who drafted and signed the Declaration of Independence. The snake represents the unity of the thirteen when they agree to establish independence from Britain. Once the thirteen agree, the snake performs a celebratory snake dance through the streets to a park for a town wide celebration. RECOMMENDATION: Although the humor is occasionally rather brutal and some language is offensive, this introduction to American Independence provides a unique and enlightening view of history. As the bulk of the dialogue rests with the narrator, children may be puppeteers for the dolls which represent each member of the Second Continental Congress. Designed as a kick-off to a Fourth of July parade, stage directions call for an orchestra and a march following the performance, but with a bit of editing, this could easily be scaled into a junior high school performance. ROYALTY: $25.

SOURCE: Horovitz, Israel. (1976). Uncle Snake: An Independence Day pageant. New York, NY: Dramatists Play Service, Inc. SUBJECTS/PLAY TYPE: Continental Congress, Second; Declaration of Independence; Drama.

3281. 9-12. (+) Kelly, Tim. **Under Jekyll's Hyde.** CAST: 9f, 5m. ACTS: 1. SETTINGS: Laboratory. PLAYING TIME: 30 min. PLOT: Dr. Henry Jekyll drinks a concoction to transform himself into Mr. Hyde, his evil side. He attacks a patient and startles Lady Bugg, his fiancee's mother. Lady Bugg's screams draw a crowd, which goes to Mr. Hyde's residence. No one recognizes him as Dr. Jekyll and they accuse Hyde of harming Dr. Jekyll. Hyde and the policeman struggle, Hyde escapes, runs to Jekyll's laboratory, and drinks his concoction to restore his form. The mob returns, amazed that Dr. Jekyll is safe, but he begins to change back to Hyde in front of everyone. Hyde collapses trying to reach his formula, then dies as Dr. Jekyll. During the transformation, Lady Bugg begins to faint and Alice mistakenly gives her the formula which turns her into a creature similar to Mr. Hyde. RECOMMENDATION: This entertaining spoof is ridiculously funny, especially because of silly dialogue, many plays on words, and stereotypical characters. ROYALTY: $15. SOURCE: Kelly, Tim. (1980). Under Jekyll's Hyde. Denver, CO: Pioneer Drama Service. SUBJECTS/PLAY TYPE: Horror; Comedy; Adaptation.

3282. 12. (+) Grote, David. **The undercover lover.** CAST: 4f, 2m, Su. ACTS: 1. SETTINGS: None. PLAYING TIME: 25 min. PLOT: Uyko, who is married to an overbearing woman, Tamanoi, makes a short visit to the country. There he meets a girl named Hanako with whom he has an affair. Hanako follows Ukyo back to the city. Ukyo devises a scheme to visit Hanako without his wife knowing, but it backfires. RECOMMENDATION: Suitable only for very mature audiences, some of the dialogue is particularly degrading to women. ROYALTY: $20. SOURCE: Grote, David. (1978). The undercover lover. Schulenburg, TX: I.E. Clark. SUBJECTS/PLAY TYPE: Farce; Kubuki; Affairs, Extramarital; Comedy.

3283. 7-12. (+) Majeski, Bill. **Undercover romance.** CAST: 16f, 6m. ACTS: 3. SETTINGS: Two offices. PLAYING TIME: NA. PLOT: Blanche Dunwitty is the pseudonym of Ed Barlett, writer of best selling romance novels. His gender is kept secret by his editor for fear women will not buy romance novels written by a man. Complications arise when Blanche must speak at a romance writers' convention. Elaine Hall, a young editor, is selected as a stand-in. An illness in Elaine's family prevents her from going, so Ed attends dressed as Blanche. A rival editor is suspicious, and she plots exposure. Elaine arrives after all, and agrees to make the speech as originally planned. During the speech, the suspicious rival editor tries to tear off "Blanche's" clothes and makes a fool of herself since the speaker is now Elaine. The play concludes with a romance blooming between Elaine and Ed. RECOMMENDATION: Although some of the humor may be a bit silly and the situations somewhat contrived, this slapstick comedy will keep high school students laughing from beginning to end. Especially effective are the twist of plot that sends Ed dressed as a woman to encounter a suspicious rival editor, the inclusion of two satirical romantic playlets within the plot that are acted out as Ed "writes" them, and a subplot which has Ed's landlady and her nosy nephew constantly trying to find out what Ed is "up to." ROYALTY: NA. SOURCE: Majeski, Bill. (1987). Undercover romance. Franklin, OH: Eldridge Pub. Co. SUBJECTS/PLAY TYPE: Imposters & Imposture; Romance; Writers; Comedy.

3284. 3-12. (+) Deverell, Rex. **The underground lake.** CAST: 2f, 4m, 2u. ACTS: 1. SETTINGS: Road; classroom; lake. PLAYING TIME: NA. PLOT: A miserable rich man travelling across the Canadian prairie learns a lesson about greed and prejudice through a tale told by his chauffeur about the people of Overgroundia and the Underground Lake. RECOMMENDATION: This can be performed with a minimal set (one riser) but requires carefully orchestrated pantomime and sound effects to clarify the scene changes. Recommended primarily for its thought provoking theme, this could be used as a springboard for discussion with elementary school audiences. ROYALTY: NA. SOURCE: Deverell, Rex. (1977). The underground lake, the shinbone general store caper, the uphill revival: Three plays by Rex Deverell. Toronto, Canada: Playwrights Co-op. SUBJECTS/PLAY TYPE: Greed; Prejudice; Bigotry; Participation Play.

3285. 1-6. (+) Little, Lynnette. **Unearthly tricks and earthly treats.** CAST: 5f, 2m, 2u. ACTS: 1. SETTINGS: Park. PLAYING TIME: 20 min. PLOT: Crandolf and Zithera (two men from another galaxy) travel to earth to prove their bravery and bring wild boar meat back for their King. Unfortunately, it is Halloween, and, frightened by all the "monsters," they return home with a Big Mac and fries. RECOMMENDATION: The theme that there is a time and place for everyone is well presented here, although racist comments will have to be changed. ROYALTY: Free to Plays subscribers. SOURCE: Little, Lynnette. (1978, October). Unearthly tricks and earthly treats. Plays: The Drama Magazine for Young People, pp. 43-48. SUBJECTS/PLAY TYPE: Halloween; Skit.

3286. 1-4. (-) Fisher, Aileen. **Unexpected guests.** CAST: 6f, 6m. ACTS: 1. SETTINGS: Kitchen-living room. PLAYING TIME: 10 min. PLOT: The Pilgrim women make Thanksgiving dinner and wonder if they've made enough to feed all the Indian guests. When 100, instead of the expected 12 Indians arrive, they are alarmed. But the Indians have also brought food, so the feast is a success. RECOMMENDATION: This might motivate youngsters to think about the Pilgrims. Rhyme interspersed with dialogue effectively livens the otherwise very ordinary actions of preparing a meal. ROYALTY: Free to Plays Subscribers. SOURCE: Fisher, Aileen. (1980, November). Unexpected guests. Plays: The Drama Magazine for Young People, pp. 39-42. SUBJECTS/PLAY TYPE: Thanksgiving; Skit.

3287. 6-12. (+) Hamby, Ray. **Unhand her, you villain.** CAST: 3f, 2m. ACTS: 1. SETTINGS: Home; newspaper office; main street; railroad tracks near a thicket. PLAYING TIME: 30 min. PLOT: A Southern lady and her daughter are left destitute when their husband/father disappears. A newspaper reporter uncovers facts relating to the disappearance. He requests that they go to Ellicott Mills, where the newspaper's editor reveals to the audience that he murdered the gentleman to take over his estate. The reporter catches on to the editor's evil deeds and the daughter shoots the editor. RECOMMENDATION: This has a good balance of dramatic situations and proceeds at a good pace, with the philosophy of an ethical free press nicely intertwined throughout. ROYALTY: $15. SOURCE: Hamby, Ray. (1980). Unhand her, you villain. Denver, CO: Pioneer Drama Service. SUBJECTS/PLAY TYPE: Freedom of the Press; Murder; Melodrama.

3288. 9-12. (+) Kelly, Tim & Nestor, Larry. **Unhappily ever after.** CAST: 11f, 6m. ACTS: 1. SETTINGS: Office. PLAYING TIME: 60 min. PLOT: Characters in fairy tales ask their author to rewrite the endings because they are not living "happily ever after." When the author complies, new problems arise, and he eventually refuses to make any changes. RECOMMENDATION: Focusing on the need for communication and sharing in a relationship, this symbolic play could be especially effective for classes in family living and psychology. It could provide a starting point for student discussion of appropriate ways in which to relate to the world and each other by examining story characters' behavior such as Sleeping Beauty's withdrawal, the Frog Prince's egocentrism, and Cinderella's unending martyrdom. ROYALTY: $50. SOURCE: Kelly, Tim & Nestor, Larry. (1988). Unhappily ever after. Denver, CO: Pioneer Drama Service. SUBJECTS/PLAY TYPE: Family; Dating; Musical.

3289. 1-6. (+) Haugh, Gerry Lynn. **The unhoppy bunny.** CAST: 1f, 8m. ACTS: 1. SETTINGS: Street. PLAYING TIME: 15 min. PLOT: Hilary, a bunny with a long tail, can't hop. Four bunnies, two frogs, and a ballet teacher try, unsuccessfully, to help Hilary. The Easter bunny appears, clips Hilary's tail fur, and with encouragement from her friends, Hilary hops. RECOMMENDATION: Although the implications of trimming Hilary's tail to make her look like the others, and the message that confidence comes from friends are troublesome, this is appealing if taken as lightly as the author intended. The physical comedy as Hilary tries to hop will be especially endearing to performers and audience. ROYALTY: Free to Plays subscribers. SOURCE: Haugh, Gerry Lynn. (1975, March). The unhoppy bunny. Plays: The Drama Magazine for Young People, pp. 47-52. SUBJECTS/PLAY TYPE: Fantasy; Bunnies; Easter; Self Confidence; Skit.

3290. 5-8. (+) Jackson, R. Eugene. **Unidentified flying reject.** CAST: 10f, 4m, 3u. ACTS: 3. SETTINGS: Backyard. PLAYING TIME: 90 min. PLOT: Amateur astronomer Shelley Swoop spots UFO's through her telescope. When aliens appear, Shelley is a believer; others aren't so sure. Soon, all of Smogsville is involved. When Shelley's mother runs for town mayor, the visitors create havoc at a political rally. The town snob withdraws her support of Mrs. Swoop and it appears that she will lose the race. However, another political party decides to back Mrs. Swoop, and Shelley and her friends help the interplanetary visitors on

their way. RECOMMENDATION: The somewhat dated language (wow-wee, far out), the simplistic way in which the plot resolves, and the subplot involving small town politics, are implausible and poorly executed. However, some of the attempted humor may amuse upper elementary viewers, though actual production would be challenging for this age group. ROYALTY: $25. SOURCE: Jackson, R. Eugene. (1982). Unidentified flying reject. Schulenburg, TX: I.E. Clark. SUBJECTS/PLAY TYPE: Politics; Aliens; Comedy.

3291. 9-12. (+) Kelly, Tim J. (Macardle, Dorothy) **The uninvited.** CAST: 6f, 4m. ACTS: 3. SETTINGS: Sitting room. PLAYING TIME: NA. PLOT: A brother and sister buy a house in the country. Shortly after they move in, they feel the place is haunted by the ghost of a woman who was pushed over the cliff outside their door. They befriend Stella, the daughter of the murdered woman, and as they learn more of the tragic story, more ghostly manifestations occur. The action culminates in a seance, in which the whole story comes to light and the spirit is laid to rest. RECOMMENDATION: This entertaining ghost story will be irresistible to fans of the genre. The actors should be physically mature to portray adults convincingly. They will be challenged by the depth of the characterizations. The stage crew will likewise be challenged by the special effects, which involve rather complicated lighting, noises, and a ghost. ROYALTY: $50. SOURCE: Kelly, Tim J. (1979). The uninvited. New York, NY: Dramatists Play Service. SUBJECTS/PLAY TYPE: Ghosts; Occult; Adaptation.

3292. 12. (+) Jory, Jon. **University.** CAST: 5f, 5m, Su. ACTS: 2. SETTINGS: Bare stage. PLAYING TIME: 130 min. PLOT: This includes ten short plays about some of the issues and personal problems that college students face: orientation, dating, athletic competition, and careers as well as the complex issues of sexism, ageism, and abortion. RECOMMENDATION: This work is suitable only for college students or highly sophisticated senior high students because of its language and the topics covered. The cast is expandable to 18 men and 26 women, and not all ten scenes need be included. ROYALTY: $60. SOURCE: Jory, Jon. (1983). University. Woodstock, IL: Dramatic Pub. Co. SUBJECTS/PLAY TYPE: College Life; Dating; Drama.

3293. 7-12. (+) Hicks, John & Dechant, David. **The unlikely undertaking.** CAST: 4f, 8m. ACTS: 2. SETTINGS: Consultation room, preparation room, and state room of a funeral parlor. PLAYING TIME: NA. PLOT: A real "comedy of errors" ensues when a mixup in the crematorium of a funeral parlor coincides with quality inspection. The undertakers are supposed to have cremated an allegedly dead (but really in a coma) opera star, but then mistakenly cremate the Roman Catholic monsignor. Although the famous opera star is saved by the confusion, the funeral parlor receives a terrible rating. RECOMMENDATION: Key issues regarding the little known funeral industry are raised in a thoroughly hilarious way. There are no dull moments. ROYALTY: $50. SOURCE: Hicks, John & Dechant, David. (1985). The unlikely undertaking. Woodstock, IL: Dramatic Pub. Co.

SUBJECTS/PLAY TYPE: Funeral Parlors; Mistaken identity; Death; Comedy.

3294. 4-10. (-) Seale, Nancy. **Unscheduled landing.** CAST: 6f, 2m. ACTS: 1. SETTINGS: Clearing. PLAYING TIME: 25 min. PLOT: A plane crashes, and the five people on board slowly learn that they are dead. RECOMMENDATION: The interesting premise here is unfortunately spoiled by superficial characterizations, poor buildup to the climax, and a trite ending, as all the characters calmly decide that they feel satisfied and that the past doesn't matter. ROYALTY: Free to Plays subscribers. SOURCE: Seale, Nancy. (1983, January/February). Unscheduled landing. Plays: The Drama Magazine for Young People, pp. 13-20. SUBJECTS/PLAY TYPE: Death; Comedy.

3295. 9-12. (-) Magpie Co. **Until ya say ya love me.** CAST: 4f, 4m, 2u. ACTS: 1. SETTINGS: 3 living rooms; drugstore; classroom. PLAYING TIME: NA. PLOT: Fifteen and a half year old Kerry doesn't know whether she wants to go to bed with Jeff (her boyfriend of four dates). Jeff is scared also. Jacko (who owns a van) has "done it" with Cheryl (his girlfriend of five weeks), and gives Jeff the benefit of his wisdom (i.e., a girl can't get pregnant the first time). Kerry's sister (who had to get married) makes Kerry talk to their mother, who refuses to advise Kerry to go onto the pill, and basically refuses to deal with anything. The play ends with Kerry telling Jeff that they need to talk. RECOMMENDATION: Although the topic is valuable, this is too filled with Australian slang, too slow moving, and too didactic to be of interest to American teenaged audiences. ROYALTY: Write to author. SOURCE: Lonie, John. (1985). Learning from life. Sydney, Australia: Currency Press. SUBJECTS/PLAY TYPE: Teenage Pregnancy; Sexual Relations; Drama.

3296. 2-4. (+) Fisher, Aileen. **Up a Christmas tree.** CAST: 3f, 3m. ACTS: 1. SETTINGS: Living room. PLAYING TIME: 15 min. PLOT: The Temple parents tell their children that what they want most for Christmas can't be bought: a pledge not to tease a sister and a promise to practice thrift. RECOMMENDATION: This is musical, imaginative, and rhythmic. ROYALTY: Free to Plays subscribers. SOURCE: Fisher, Aileen. (1988, December). Up a Christmas tree. Plays: The Drama Magazine for Young People, pp. 45-46. SUBJECTS/PLAY TYPE: Christmas; Choral Reading.

3297. 12. (+) Robinette, Joseph. **Up the ivory tower.** CAST: 1f, 2m, Su. ACTS: 2. SETTINGS: Bare stage. PLAYING TIME: NA. PLOT: A young college professor thinks he is going to set the college on fire by being the ultimate teacher. His idealism is challenged throughout as he works toward a tenure decision in his fourth year of teaching. It appears that he will be denied tenure because his standards make some students and colleagues uncomfortable. However, in the end those who have benefitted from his efforts win the day, and he is granted tenure. RECOMMENDATION: The college setting and situations make this appropriate only for a mature audience which could relate to the struggles of a young academic seeking tenure. ROYALTY: $50. SOURCE: Robinette, Joseph. (1981). Up the ivory tower. Chicago, IL: Dramatic Pub. Co. SUBJECTS/PLAY TYPE: College Life; Job Security; Tenure; Comedy.

3298. 10-12. (+) Deverell, Rex. **The uphill revival.** CAST: 4f, 5m, Su. ACTS: 2. SETTINGS: Newsroom; street; motel room; post office; field; dental clinic; fairgrounds. PLAYING TIME: NA. PLOT: The townspeople of quiet little Uphill go wild with excitement following reports of three strange cigar shaped crafts seen swooping down from the sky. After an alien being speaks to them through a nervous, inarticulate, young woman, her pride and their enthusiasm swell until they are ready to give up all they know and love on this earth for a fantasy life on another planet. RECOMMENDATION: This thought provoking drama can be produced with sets and props as simple or as extravagant as time and money allow. Receptive high school audiences might enjoy participating in the final crowd scene, as suggested by the playwright. ROYALTY: NA. SOURCE: Deverell, Rex. (1977). The underground lake, the shinbone general store caper, the uphill revival: Three plays by Rex Deverell. Toronto, Canada: Playwrights Co-op. SUBJECTS/PLAY TYPE: Aliens; Participation Play.

3299. 7-12. (+) Campton, David. **Us and them.** CAST: 6u. ACTS: 1. SETTINGS: None. PLAYING TIME: NA. PLOT: Two groups come on from opposite sides of stage. Their actions are explained by the Recorder who serves as narrator. Both groups decide they want to settle here and agree there is enough room; then they decide to build a fence to mark boundaries. As they consider how high horses can jump and chickens can fly, they decide on a wall instead. They build the wall together. At first they are content, but as they cannot see what is happening on the other side of the wall, they become suspicious. War and disillusionment follow. Each group leaves the area blaming the wall for the strife. RECOMMENDATION: This expressionistic one act play is a fable for our time. Ideally, it would be followed by group discussion. ROYALTY: $20. SOURCE: Campton, David. (1982). Us and them. Woodstock, IL: Dramatic Pub. Co. SUBJECTS/PLAY TYPE: War; International Relations; Relationships; Drama.

3300. K-2. (+) Jacobs, Allan & Jacobs, Leland. **Using subtraction.** CAST: 2u. ACTS: 1. SETTINGS: None. PLAYING TIME: NA. PLOT: Two readers, remembering a lesson on subtraction, list the things they'd like to "take away," such as liver, tattletales, and stomachaches. RECOMMENDATION: This is an amusing piece which should entertain both parents and children. ROYALTY: NA. SOURCE: Bauer, Caroline Feller. (1987). Presenting reader's theater: Plays and poems to read aloud. New York, NY: H.W. Wilson Co. SUBJECTS/PLAY TYPE: Subtraction; Reader's Theater.

3301. 7-12. (+) Murray, John. **The vagabond vampires.** CAST: 4f, 4m, 1u. ACTS: 1. SETTINGS: Living room. PLAYING TIME: 40 min. PLOT: Two vampires attempt to solve a murder mystery to prevent their home (the site of a murder) from being demolished. With the aid of supernatural powers, the night of the murder is re-enacted and the murderer confesses. **RECOMMENDATION:** The comic vampires with their ghoulish humor make this a thoroughly entertaining play, even if the murder mystery lacks suspense. The endless puns will send the audience home groaning happily. **ROYALTY:** None. **SOURCE:** Murray, John. (1979). Fifteen plays for teenagers. Boston, MA: Plays, Inc. **SUBJECTS/PLAY TYPE:** Vampires; Mystery; Comedy.

3302. 10-12. (+) Roschin, Mikhail. **Valentin and Valentina.** CAST: 9f, 9m. ACTS: 3. SETTINGS: Park; apartments; safe. PLAYING TIME: NA. PLOT: This is a translation of Roschin's most well known drama, in which Valentin and Valentina are Russian university students very much in love. Both families object to the relationship because of the youths' age and Valentin's poverty. Valentina's mother especially dislikes love and reminds her daughter to be practical. Valentin and Valentina bribe Valentin's sister with movie money so they can be alone in the apartment. Valentina particularly hates the need to lie and deceive to be together. In Act 2 the existence of love is questioned by the families and friends of the couple. Valentin and Valentina spend time with others but they get back together. They tell Valentin's mother they wish to marry, and she agrees. Valentina agrees to tell her mother but she doesn't. Instead she lies about staying with a girlfriend, when she is really staying with Valentin in a friend's apartment. When her mother and sister confront them, Valentina goes home with them. After much advice from family and friends suddenly supporting their love, the couple is reunited. RECOMMENDATION: The love scenes, although brief, make this difficult for most high school programs. Even without the love scenes, the play comprises many long and sophisticated speeches about love which provide a glimpse of Russian society, but which might be wasted on American adolescents who will probably have difficulty appreciating the historical significance of the 1971 commentary on contemporary Soviet adolescence. ROYALTY: $60. SOURCE: Roschin, Mikhail. (1978). Valentin and Valentina. Chicago, IL: Dramatic Pub. Co. SUBJECTS/PLAY TYPE: Love; Soviet Adolescents.

3303. 1-3. (+) Whittaker, Violet. **A Valentine castle.** CAST: 1f, 1m. ACTS: 1. SETTINGS: Bare stage, props. PLAYING TIME: NA. PLOT: Two children examine a heart shaped castle as they discuss the kinds of love that people have for each other and that God has for mankind. The play ends with each child being given a heart shaped cookie. RECOMMENDATION: By reminding the audience that people get into heaven because God is good, the passage from John 14:1-6 is presented as a logical reason for belief in Jesus. This could be a good vehicle for presenting a religious theme to church groups on Valentine's Day. Directions for the castle and cookie recipe are provided. ROYALTY: NA. SOURCE: Whittaker, Violet. (1984). Puppet people scripts. Grand Rapids, MI: Baker Book House. SUBJECTS/PLAY TYPE: Christian Drama; Love; Puppet Play.

3304. 7-12. (-) Gotwalt, Helen Louise Miller. (Shakespeare, William) **A valentine for Kate.** (The taming of the shrew) CAST: 5f, 4m. ACTS: 1. SETTINGS: Living

room. PLAYING TIME: 35 min. PLOT: Pete Naylor, Shakespeare buff, takes up the challenge to tame ill tempered Kathleen and bring her to the Valentine party at school. Kathleen, who is also a lover of Shakespeare, recognizes what Pete is up to and the taming is a success. RECOMMENDATION: Students familiar with the original taming will recognize the key elements of that play in this one. However, this is a poor substitute, with none of the dramatic energy of the original. Addition-ally, scenes where Kate is physically forced to stay alone with Pete, who also physically forces her onto a couch and removes her coat are totally inappropriate as comedy. This is contrived, insulting and wholly unredeeming. ROYALTY: Free to Plays subscribers. SOURCE: Gotwalt, Helen Louise Miller. (1975, February). A valentine for Kate. Plays: The Drama Magazine for Young People, pp. 15-25. SUBJECTS/PLAY TYPE: Comedy; Theater; Adaptation.

3305. 3-6. (+) Nicholson, Jessie. **Valentine stardust.** CAST: 5f, 3m, 3u. ACTS: 1. SETTINGS: Bakery. PLAYING TIME: 20 min. PLOT: Mr. Starman uses stardust in his baked goods to sweeten people's dispositions. In an attempt to bring tongue-tied Mr. Treut (who can't pop the question) and the eager Miss Prim (who is ready to say yes), together, he bakes a Valentine's cake with the key to Mr. Treut's heart inside so that Miss Prim will be able to say yes without Treut's verbalizing the question. Mr. Starman's wife receives the cake with the key to Mr. Treut's heart. All is resolved when Miss Prim pops the question to Mr. Treut, and Mr. Starman's wife changes into a nice person. RECOMMENDATION: In spite of a few sexist comments, this romance, reminiscent of **A Midsummer Night's Dream**, is better than the usual Valentine's Day fare. ROYALTY: Free to Plays subscribers. SOURCE: Nicholson, Jessie. (1975, February). Valentine stardust. Plays: The Drama Magazine for Young People, pp. 65-72. SUBJECTS/PLAY TYPE: Valentine's Day; Comedy.

3306. 9-12. (+) Way, Brian. **The Valley of Echoes.** CAST: 2f, 2m. ACTS: 1. SETTINGS: Gymnasium. PLAYING TIME: 50 min. PLOT: Clown has lost his laugh. As he leaves, the Echo King informs him that he has used his laugh all up by giving it away, but that he might be able to find it in the Valley of Echoes. King Doublet explains to Clown that once a year, the people, creatures, and insects of the Forest of Fear help one person to pass through the Forest, avoid the Shadow people, and reach the Valley of Echoes. The audience becomes those good creatures who help Clown through the forest until he is surrounded. Frightened, Clown calls to the birds to nest in the treetops to block out the light, and ergo, the shadows. Declared the King of the Forest of Delight, Clown must still cross the icy Mountain of Memories. Again with audience help, he frees Stalag and the Mist People from slavery to the Queen of the Mountain of Memories. Returning to the Valley of Echoes, Clown is rewarded with the return of his laugh. RECOMMENDATION: This endearing adventure reminiscent of **The Wizard of Oz**, draws the audience into the play's physical and emotional action. Production will require skilled adult or young adult performers who can improvise. ROYALTY: $20.

SOURCE: Way, Brian. (1977). The Valley of Echoes. Boston, MA: Baker's Plays. SUBJECTS/PLAY TYPE: Clowns; Laughter; Participation Play; Pantomime.

3307. 7-12. (-) Murray, John. **Valley of evil. CAST:** 5f, 5m. **ACTS:** 1. **SETTINGS:** Valley; forest. **PLAYING TIME:** NA. **PLOT:** Two newlyweds come to the haunted valley to farm. The husband is killed, and the wife, visited by a spirit, is convinced that her husband is merely in a supernatural state of being. She wanders the bogs until a young girl shows her that the ghostly lights are scientifically explainable and the girl's father shows her that her husband was killed by a landslide. **RECOMMENDATION:** This is long, slow, boring, and unsatisfying. **ROYALTY:** Free to Plays subscribers. **SOURCE:** Murray, John. (1978, November). Valley of evil. Plays: The Drama Magazine for Young People, pp. 1-14. **SUBJECTS/PLAY TYPE:** Folklore; Ghost Stories; Playlet.

3308. 9-12. (-) Horrocks, William. **Vandal. CAST:** 1f, 3m. **ACTS:** 1. **SETTINGS:** Schoolyard. **PLAYING TIME:** NA. **PLOT:** Mar, the new kid, tries to impress his pseudo-juvenile delinquent friends by vandalizing their school. The extent of the damage that he does overshadows the gang's previous pranks, which mostly consisted of petty theft and spray painting. The gang censures him for his behavior, and he is left an outsider still. **RECOMMENDATION:** This is an unsuccessful attempt to show how small delinquent acts can get out of hand. No delinquent act should be condoned, and the conclusion, where the gang becomes the "good guys" because Mark has done something "really bad," is reprehensible. Also, the highly stylized and symbolic burning of the gangmembers' possessions (which reflect their media idols) is so symbolic that young audiences may not understand it. **ROYALTY:** NA. **SOURCE:** Doolittle, Joyce. (1984). Eight plays for young people. Edmonton, Canada: NeWest Pub. **SUBJECTS/PLAY TYPE:** Juvenile Delinquency; Vandalism; Gangs; Drama.

3309. 10-12. (+) Heifner, Jack. **Vanities. CAST:** 3f. **ACTS:** 1. **SETTINGS:** Gymnasium; garden; bedroom. **PLAYING TIME:** NA. **PLOT:** This portrays the lives of three graduating senior girls as they move through early adulthood, focusing on how they change from young innocents into experienced adults. They must cope with leaving high school, beginning college, marrying, and finally a reunion ten years later. Through all of their experiences, though, they remain "vain" in their own personal ways. **RECOMMENDATION:** This interestingly juxtaposes two views of the world: through the eyes of teenagers who are ready to conquer the world and through the eyes of adults ten years later, as they are bored and tired with life. It is thought provoking and has material for group discussion. **ROYALTY:** $50. **SOURCE:** Heifner, Jack. (1976). Vanities. New York, NY: Samuel French. **SUBJECTS/PLAY TYPE:** Personality; Life Changes; Comedy.

3310. 9-12*. (+) Caruso, Joseph George & Curnow, Paul. **Vaudeville tonight: A musical revue. CAST:** 2f, 2m, Su. **ACTS:** 2. **SETTINGS:** Bare stage. **PLAYING TIME:** 90 min. **PLOT:** Jim, Sally, Jane, and Ted take us "down memory lane" to a turn of the century musical of "rag" tunes, classic western, minstral, jazz and Irish melodies. These are loosely connected with dialogue about theaters, the Ziegfeld Follies, the Gibson Girls, the "early Western extravaganza," and the Gaelic comedy of New York City. This is a true vaudeville show for all seasons and all ages. **RECOMMENDATION:** Simple boy vs. girl themes connect musical numbers throughout. Some terms and songs may be too dated for some audiences. Actors will need musical accompaniment. **ROYALTY:** $50. **SOURCE:** Caruso, Joseph George and Curnow, Paul. (1983). Vaudeville tonight: A musical revue. Denver, CO: Pioneer Drama Service. **SUBJECTS/PLAY TYPE:** Vaudeville; Musical Revue.

3311. 6-12. (+) Fry, Christopher. **Venus observed. CAST:** 1f, 1m. **ACTS:** 1. **SETTINGS:** Observatory. **PLAYING TIME:** NA. **PLOT:** The Duke attempts to convince Perpetua that she should marry him, by employing an old superstition that involves the use of a mirror. Perpetua coquettishly dodges the Duke's conversation, forcing the Duke to become more and more direct until he thinks he will be required to propose in a traditional way. He asks her if there is some other way that he may know the answer. **RECOMMENDATION:** This study of English culture presents the theme that divine signs are not a basis for decision making, and that people control their own destinies. **ROYALTY:** NA. **SOURCE:** Olfson, Lewy. (1980). Fifty great scenes for student actors. New York, NY: Bantam Books. **SUBJECTS/PLAY TYPE:** Social Customs; Marriage; Scene.

3312. 11-12*. (+) Bennett, Gordon. **Verily. CAST:** 2f, 2m. **ACTS:** 2. **SETTINGS:** Chapel. **PLAYING TIME:** 70 min. **PLOT:** Kim and Ted, internists in a mental hospital, involve two patients, Jerome and Marna, in a psychodrama. Jerome, who suffers from guilt for having betrayed his former employer, believes himself to be Judas Iscariot, who betrayed Jesus. Marna, betrayed by former lovers, believes herself to be Mary Magdalene, whom she sees as having been betrayed by Jesus. In a series of encounters, Marna and Jerome switch back and forth from their assumed roles to their real personalities. Jerome comes to terms with his guilt and appears to be recovering. Marna accepts that Jesus loves her despite her past relationships with men. Ted, an agnostic, is led to accept the possibility of the existence of Christ as a result of his participation in the psychodrama. **RECOMMENDATION:** This is recommended only for the most mature and select of audiences. Its themes of guilt and betrayal set within a mental institution and cast within the framework of sacred Christian Biblical scripture could be potentially offensive. Its appreciation would require both a knowledge of biblical history and a sympathetic mind set for mental illness. The director would need to be skillful to integrate the sometimes adolescent jargon into what is otherwise a very serious dialogue, setting and theme. **ROYALTY:** $25. **SOURCE:** Bennett, Gordon. (1981). Verily. Denver, CO: Pioneer Drama Service. **SUBJECTS/PLAY TYPE:** Personality Disorders; Mental Illness; Grace (Theology); Drama.

3313. 7-9. (+) Majeski, Bill. **The very great grandson of Sherlock Holmes. CAST:** 7f, 4m, 1u. **ACTS:** 2. **SETTINGS:** Office; room. **PLAYING TIME:** NA. **PLOT:** Sherlock Holmes' grandson, Sherwood (a private detective in modern California), is called to prevent the murder of wealthy Harris Creastley. He is aided by Dr. Watson, the grandson of Dr. Watson. Unfortunately, Mr. Creastley is killed by the middle of the second scene. Sherwood Holmes, in a comic fashion, solves the crime. The murderer turns out to be the descendant of the arch criminal, Moriarity. **RECOMMENDATION:** Although loaded with corny jokes, there is some dramatic tension. **ROYALTY:** $35. **SOURCE:** Majeski, Bill. (1976). The very great grandson of Sherlock Holmes. Chicago, IL: Dramatic Pub. Co. **SUBJECTS/PLAY TYPE:** Mystery; Comedy.

3314. 7-12*. (+) DeBoy, David. **Vice as in versa: A full-length comedy. CAST:** 3f, 4m. **ACTS:** 2. **SETTINGS:** Library. **PLAYING TIME:** 90 min. **PLOT:** Percible Nimby and his secretary, Nancy Dunsmore, visit Nimby's Uncle Buck, a rich movie producer who plans to leave all his money to his most manly relative: Nimby or Brad Buckridge. During the visit, Nimby and Nancy accidentally use the magic of a Magoogie doll and switch bodies. Hilarity results when the two try to conceal the change and try to make Nimby appear more "masculine" to his uncle. Mysteriously, Uncle Buck is murdered and a strange man threatens the group with a gun. "Nimby" disarms the man before damage can be done, and they discover he is Uncle Buck in disguise, secretly testing the two men. At the conclusion, the inheritance is to be split evenly between Brad and Nimby, when they decide that the stereotypical male isn't necessarily the most masculine. Using the Magoogie doll again, Nimby and Dunsmore become themselves again and fall in love. **RECOMMENDATION:** Production will be a challenge even for experienced actors due to the male/female impersonations, fast gags, accents, and props required, but done well, this will be a comedy of the highest hilarity. Extremely motivated high school students should be the youngest group to attempt this. **ROYALTY:** NA. **SOURCE:** DeBoy, David. (1987). Vice as in versa: A full-length comedy. Woodstock, IL: The Dramatic Pub. Co. **SUBJECTS/PLAY TYPE:** Inheritances; Mistaken Identities; Masculinity; Comedy.

3315. 10-12. (+) Vernick, Phyllis. (Saki, H.H. Munro) **Vicky. (The open window) CAST:** 2f, 2m. **ACTS:** 1. **SETTINGS:** Living room. **PLAYING TIME:** NA. **PLOT:** Young Humphrey Hubert visits Mrs. Bland and is introduced to vivacious and imaginative Vicky. Humphrey, an incurable `Nerd' and hypochondriac, rapidly falls under the spell of Vicky's flair for ghost stories. Vicki tells him that Mrs. Bland's husband is dead, and when Mr. Bland walks into the house, the poor boy runs out, terrified. Vicky then begins to fabricate an explanation of why Humphrey has left so abruptly. **RECOMMENDATION:** This is easily accessible, is faithful to the original, and does not present any technical challenges to the director. **ROYALTY:** $15. **SOURCE:** Vernick, Phyllis. (1976). Vicky. Chicago, IL: Dramatic Pub. Co. **SUBJECTS/PLAY TYPE:** Ghosts; Adaptation.

3316. 4-6. (-) Gotwalt, Helen Louise Miller. **Vicky gets the vote. CAST:** 5f, 8m. **ACTS:** 1. **SETTINGS:** Living room. **PLAYING TIME:** NA. **PLOT:** A young girl must decide whether to go with her uncle to a ribbon cutting ceremony for a new bridge or cast her vote in the school election. She decides to vote. **RECOMMENDATION:** This is too slow and didactic. **ROYALTY:** Free to Plays subscribers. **SOURCE:** Gotwalt, Helen Louise Miller. (1986). Everyday Plays for Boys and Girls. Boston, MA: Plays, Inc. **SUBJECTS/PLAY TYPE:** Elections; Voting; Playlet.

3317. 6-10. (+) Kelly, Tim J. **Victoria at 18. CAST:** 7f, 2m. **ACTS:** 1. **SETTINGS:** Sitting room. **PLAYING TIME:** NA. **PLOT:** Victoria's mother, ladies-in-waiting, governesses, and government officials adjust to a new Victoria when the young woman moves from her tightly controlled position as Princess to that of Queen. She quickly takes command by defying her dominant mother and conventions of propriety, presaging the strong willed and decisive manner in which she was to rule England. **RECOMMENDATION:** The theme of taking on responsibility and independence is interesting, but the characters are all so predictable and the outcome so obvious, that it may fail to keep the audience's attention. The dialogue has words that may be difficult for younger children to pronounce, and many of the lines are unnatural and stilted. However, this could provoke an interesting discussion of English history. **ROYALTY:** $20. **SOURCE:** Kelly, Tim J. (1978). Victoria at 18. Woodstock, IL: Dramatic Pub. Co. **SUBJECTS/PLAY TYPE:** Victoria, Queen of England; Royalty; Playlet.

3318. 7-8. (+) Bennett, Rowena. **Victory ball. CAST:** 2f, 7m, Su. **ACTS:** 1. **SETTINGS:** None. **PLAYING TIME:** 5 min. **PLOT:** At a victory ball in Mount Vernon, the guests express their gratefulness for Washington's bravery at Valley Forge. **RECOMMENDATION:** This brief choral reading is a simple way to celebrate Washington's birthday. **ROYALTY:** None. **SOURCE:** Kamerman, Sylvia E. (1975). Patriotic and historical plays for young people. Boston, MA: Plays, Inc. **SUBJECTS/PLAY TYPE:** Washington, George; Choral Reading.

3319. 6-12. (+) Dias, Earl J. **Video Christmas. CAST:** 4f, 3m, Su. **ACTS:** 1. **SETTINGS:** Living room. **PLAYING TIME:** 25 min. **PLOT:** The Carson family is chosen to represent the typical American family on a Christmas Eve program. By early afternoon, the family, except Mrs. Carson, is so wrapped up in their problems that there is a state of dissension in the house. Beth is worried about her new dress, Mr. Carson argues with his neighbor, Grandma is obsessed with outshining her rival, and Tom is impatient over his conflicting schedules. Mrs. Carson wonders what happened to their Christmas spirit. A chain of events later in the evening helps the family realize how fortunate they are and how selfish they have been. **RECOMMENDATION:** The theme of family unity is neatly tied together at the end, with family members stating what Christmas means to them. The realistic dialogue and typically petty situations make this both credible and poignant. **ROYALTY:** Free to Plays subscribers. **SOURCE:** Dias, Earl J. (1986, December). Video Christmas. Plays: The Drama Magazine for Young People, pp. 12-20. **SUBJECTS/PLAY TYPE:** Christmas; Family; Playlet.

3320. 9-12. (+) Murray, John. **Video game visitors.** **CAST:** 6f, 4m, 1u. **ACTS:** 1. **SETTINGS:** Office. **PLAYING TIME:** 30 min. **PLOT:** Two aliens from Rockamania help a video game designer uncover a plot from a competing company to steal his video game designs. **RECOMMENDATION:** Humorous and up to date characters who are believable in an absurd sort of way include aliens that are caricatures of typical teenagers. This satirizes the absurdity and humor of teen lifestyles. **ROYALTY:** Free to Plays subscribers. **SOURCE:** Murray, John. (1985, January/February). Video game visitors. Plays: The Drama Magazine for Young People, pp. 1-11. **SUBJECTS/PLAY TYPE:** Video Games; Aliens; Comedy.

3321. 7-12. (+) Kelly, Tim. **Videomania. CAST:** 9f, 8m, 10u. **ACTS:** 3. **SETTINGS:** Family/living room; therapy room; video arcade. **PLAYING TIME:** NA. **PLOT:** When a videogame competition is at held at Happy Hill clinic for sufferers of videomania, the challenger is a robot that blows a fuse at 140,000 points; human Sylvester wins. The patients seem to be in control of themselves, but the two doctors are so involved in cheering Sylvester that they catch the disease. The play ends as they jibber and list the videogame names, just as the patients had done previously. **RECOMMENDATION:** Although the story is simple, timing of the lines can be tricky, much happens in the background, and there are many characters to keep straight. The cast will need to be quite articulate so the audience catches the jokes, which are plays on words. **ROYALTY:** $40. **SOURCE:** Kelly, Tim. (1983). Videomania. Boston, MA: Baker's Plays. **SUBJECTS/PLAY TYPE:** Videogames; Comedy.

3322. 9-13*. (+) Winther, Barbara. **The villain and the toy shop. CAST:** 5f, 9m, 6u. **ACTS:** 1. **SETTINGS:** Toy shop; street. **PLAYING TIME:** NA. **PLOT:** On Christmas Eve, the evil Mr. Glowerpuss threatens to foreclose on the toy shop mortgage unless Caroline agrees to be his bride. With the help of a fairy, the toys in the shop, and the hero, John, the toy shop is saved and Glowerpuss leaves town. **RECOMMENDATION:** This melodrama, with its wonderful character names, would be great fun to produce. **ROYALTY:** Free to Plays subscribers. **SOURCE:** Kamerman, Sylvia. (1978). Onstage for Christmas. Boston, MA: Plays, Inc. **SUBJECTS/PLAY TYPE:** Christmas; Melodrama.

3323. 10-12. (+) Gray, Amlin. (Shakespeare, William) **Villainous company.** (Henry IV) **CAST:** 3m, Su. **ACTS:** 1. **SETTINGS:** None. **PLAYING TIME:** NA. **PLOT:** Hal, the King's son, carouses in taverns with Bardolph and Falstaff and plays at the role of the highway man. He jests with his friends about the duties and responsibilities of the King and swears he will live a life of pleasure while he can. Yet Hal knows where his true allegiance lies as surely as he knows that his friend Falstaff is a coward. When the kingdom is threatened by Hotspur and his men, Hal reverts to his noble origins in time to enter into battle

where he slays Hotspur. Falstaff, meanwhile, fakes death so that he can avoid fighting. **RECOMMENDATION:** This condensation is faithful to Shakespeare's language, and Gray's eye for the dramatic scene makes this a good rendition for young people. Falstaff remains central and the play shows the cruelty and carelessness of his humor as well as the madcap drunken fun. Hal's repudiation of Falstaff at the end of Part II is not included. Among the major scenes are the robbery at Gad's Hill, the confrontation with the King, Falstaff and Hal mocking the King and his son, and the killing of Hotspur. The drama is meant to be produced with three actors playing all the roles, however it could be adapted for a larger cast of up to eighteen. **ROYALTY:** $25. **SOURCE:** Gray, Amlin. (1981). Villainous company. New York, NY: Dramatists Play Service, Inc. **SUBJECTS/PLAY TYPE:** Henry V, King of England; Adaptation.

3324. 11-12*. (+) Nimoy, Leonard. (Stephens, Phillip) **Vincent.** (Van Gogh) **CAST:** 1m. **ACTS:** 2. **SETTINGS:** Bare stage, props; backdrop of slides. **PLAYING TIME:** NA. **PLOT:** Theo recounts the creative passion, mental torment, and suicide of his brother in a two act soliloquy. During the brief life of the brilliant artist, his brother was his best friend, his source of funds, and his companion into the heaven of artistic expression and the hell of mental and emotional despair. Theo describes Vincent's love for humanity, for God, for art and, eventually, for death. He reveals his own anguish at his ultimate inability to help his brother. **RECOMMENDATION:** Nimoy succeeds in expressing the anguish of Van Gogh's life and death in a one actor tour de force. The narrative is simple, believable, and moving. Balanced with sorrow, humor, love, and anger, Theo's words ring true. His shifting emotions and memories are reflected by the backdrop of slides of paintings. Any audience, high school age and older, would be entranced. However, only an unusually gifted high school actor could perform this. Two slide projectors are necessary. **ROYALTY:** $60. **SOURCE:** Nimoy, Leonard. (1984). Vincent. Woodstock, ILL: The Dramatic Pub. Co. **SUBJECTS/PLAY TYPE:** Van Gogh, Vincent; Artists; Adaptation.

3325. 10-12. (+) Phillips, Marguerite Kreger. **Violets for Christmas. CAST:** 4f, 1m. **ACTS:** 1. **SETTINGS:** Office. **PLAYING TIME:** 30 min. **PLOT:** In order to win her husband back, the rich and proud Mrs. Pennington becomes a maid in a shelter for the poor, a few days before Christmas. **RECOMMENDATION:** The marriage theme and some strong language make this suitable only for an older audience. The characters are well presented, but there is much the small cast must do. **ROYALTY:** Free to Plays subscribers. **SOURCE:** Kamerman, Sylvia E. (1975). A treasury of Christmas plays. Boston, MA: Plays, Inc. **SUBJECTS/PLAY TYPE:** Christmas; Comedy; Marriage; Drama.

3326. 7-12. (+) Morse, Jack. **Violets, gladiolas and Arthur's breakfast. CAST:** 1f, 1m. **ACTS:** 1. **SETTINGS:** Cemetery. **PLAYING TIME:** NA. **PLOT:** A widower (of five years) and a widow (of one year), visit their respective spouse's graves and talk with each other about their loneliness after losing their spouses. The play ends on a hopeful note as they plan to meet again next week. RECOMMENDATION: This skillfully written drama very sensitively explores the aftermath of death using symbolic images to avoid becoming morbid. It would be an excellent vehicle for discussions about death as well as symbolism. Arthur's breakfast (from the title) is the meal that the widow prepared for her dead husband, and now must throw away, as a symbol of her ability to let go of the past and go on with the present. ROYALTY: $15. SOURCE: Morse, Jack. (1975). Violets, gladiolas and Arthur's breakfast. Chicago, IL: The Dramatic Pub. Co. SUBJECTS/PLAY TYPE: Coping; Loneliness; Change; Death; Drama.

3327. 7-12. (+) Nord, Myrtle. **A virtue of necessity.** CAST: 1f, 11m. ACTS: 1. SETTINGS: Parlor. PLAYING TIME: 35 min. PLOT: John Jay's decision to join the patriots against the British comes only after he desperately seeks a compromise which would allow him to maintain his loyalty to England. RECOMMENDATION: Jay's dilemma is revealed through his conversations with representatives from England and the colonies at the Continental Congress. Many historical names (Adams, Sullivan, Paine, etc.) come to life as the discussions of revolution unfold in this excellent dramatization. ROYALTY: Free to Plays subscribers. SOURCE: Nord, Myrtle. (1982, April). A virtue of necessity. Plays: The Drama Magazine for Young People, pp. 9-18. SUBJECTS/PLAY TYPE: Jay, John; Revolution, U.S.; Playlet.

3328. 7-12. (+) Martens, Anne Coulter. **Visions of Sugar Plums.** CAST: 4f, 3m. ACTS: 1. SETTINGS: Living room. PLAYING TIME: 30 min. PLOT: A modern day family lets holiday business get in the way of real Christmas spirit, at the expense of 11 year old Kim, who wants them to come to her Christmas program. They realize in time that it is the spirit and not the presents that count. RECOMMENDATION: With the exception of the vast number of lines Kim must memorize, everything is easy, from props to costumes. ROYALTY: Free to Plays subscribers SOURCE: Martens, Anne Coulter. (1988, December). Visions of sugar plums. Plays: The Drama Magazine for Young People, pp. 34-44. SUBJECTS/PLAY TYPE: Christmas; Playlet.

3329. 1-3. (+) Gotwalt, Helen Louise Miller. **A visit to Goldilock's.** CAST: 3f, 2m, 4u. ACTS: 1. SETTINGS: Woods; home. PLAYING TIME: 12 min. PLOT: On the way to visit Goldilocks, the three bears meet three owls who teach them how to be polite when visiting neighbors. The bears follow the advice and enjoy a nice visit with Goldilocks and her parents. RECOMMENDATION: Well written with good songs set to familiar tunes, this includes opportunities for audience participation in songs and pantomime. ROYALTY: Free to Plays subscribers. SOURCE: Gotwalt, Helen Louise Miller. (1960). First plays for children: A collection of little plays for the youngest players. Boston, MA: Plays, Inc. SUBJECTS/PLAY TYPE: Manners; Musical; Skit.

3330. 7-12. (+) Murray, John. **Visiting hours.** CAST: 1f. ACTS: 1. SETTINGS: None. PLAYING TIME: NA.

PLOT: A matronly lady visits a friend in the hospital, who has fallen down a flight of stairs and is now in traction. She proceeds to distress the patient with depressing news while consuming the patient's lunch. RECOMMENDATION: Broad comical pantomime could easily be achieved by having the monologue delivered by a male in woman's clothing. ROYALTY: None. SOURCE: Murray, John. (1982). Modern monologues for young people. Boston, MA: Plays, Inc. SUBJECTS/PLAY TYPE: Hospitals, Pantomime; Monologue.

3331. 8-11. (+) Murray, John. **Visitor from outerspace.** CAST: 8f, 7m. ACTS: 1. SETTINGS: Offices. PLAYING TIME: 35 min. PLOT: In an effort to keep his magazine in business, a photographer fakes a picture of an extraterrestrial, but then he discovers two real aliens, who get married and return to their home planet. RECOMMENDATION: This has the perfect ingredients for a student play: snappy dialogue, simple stage sets, and ordinary clothes for costumes. ROYALTY: Free for amateur performance. SOURCE: Kamerman, Sylvia E. (1981). Space and science fiction plays for young people. Boston, MA: Plays, Inc. SUBJECTS/PLAY TYPE: Aliens; Science Fiction; Comedy.

3332. 3-6. (+) Gotwalt, Helen Louise. **Visitor to Mount Vernon.** CAST: 6f, 10m, Su. ACTS: 1. SETTINGS: Classroom; bus stop. PLAYING TIME: 25 min. PLOT: Freddy brings his red, white and blue teddy bear to school the day his class is to visit Mount Vernon. The class adopts the Patriotic Teddy Bear as a mascot and they take him along. When the tour is over, Freddy discovers that he has lost the bear and is very upset. The bear is found sleeping on George Washington's bed and a photographer takes a picture of the bear with the children. RECOMMENDATION: The Teddy Bear is an endearing character who should captivate the attention while the audience subtly learns about American history. ROYALTY: Free to Plays subscribers. SOURCE: Gotwalt, Helen Louise Miller. (1977, February). Visitor to Mount Vernon. Plays: The Drama Magazine for Young People, pp. 75-82. SUBJECTS/PLAY TYPE: Washington, George; Mount Vernon; Playlet.

3333. 9-12. (+) Harnetiaux, Bryan Patrick. **Vital statistics.** CAST: 2f, 2m. ACTS: 1. SETTINGS: Living room with front door; kitchen and back porch. PLAYING TIME: 35 min. PLOT: Ellie Jensen, a middle aged housewife-horserace "bookie" for the elderly is conducting business on the telephone when Adrian Wyatt walks in. Ellie believes he's an undercover agent for the Feds, but he convinces her that he is merely a census taker. In actuality, he is her 20 year old long-lost illegitimate son, born during the war while her now retired Army sergeant husband was away, and then given up for adoption. When Adrian discloses that he is her son, Ellie at first brushes off the matter as unimportant. Then Adrian recreates his birth which forces his mother to recognize her emotional connection with him. The entrance of Euclid, Ellie's husband, puts her on the defensive until she realizes the two men have met before and that Euclid believes Adrian to be his own illegitimate son from the war. Adrian reveals he's actually Ellie's offspring, but since Euclid already regards him in a fatherly fashion this does not create a crisis and the play ends with the happy reuniting of mother and son. RECOMMENDATION: This is a humorous, light hearted treatment of a delicate subject, one usually fraught with sorrow and negativism. The author keeps the audience in suspense by constantly twisting the plot while adding to the characterization of the players. He does this, layer by layer, until the viewer becomes quite fond of the characters. Despite its brevity, the play has substance. ROYALTY: $15. SOURCE: Harnetiaux, Bryan Patrick. (1985). Vital statistics. Boston, MA: Baker's Plays. SUBJECTS/PLAY TYPE: Illegitimacy; Reunions; Dramatic Comedy.

3334. 7-12. (+) Hatton, Thomas J. **A voice from beyond.** CAST: 5f, 1m. ACTS: 1. SETTINGS: Living room. PLAYING TIME: NA. PLOT: Four college girls share an apartment. Tara does not do her part of the household work. Sandi's sister, Ginger, a senior in high school, visits, and Tara (who is a spiritualist) insists on a seance during which Ginger pretends to be the spirit of Tara's aunt and exhorts Tara to leave the apartment. The roommates are delighted that they have forced Tara to move until an unknown spirit voice communicates with them. RECOMMENDATION: This is a light hearted look at roommate conflicts with an ending that has potential for comical impact. ROYALTY: $15. SOURCE: Hatton, Thomas J. (1982). A voice from beyond. Boston, MA: Baker's Plays. SUBJECTS/PLAY TYPE: Spiritualism; Roommates; Comedy.

3335. 4-6. (+) Fisher, Aileen Lucia. **Voice of liberty.** CAST: 4f, 6m. ACTS: 1. SETTINGS: Living room. PLAYING TIME: NA. PLOT: A family discusses why they are not voting, and the son tells them the story of the Liberty Bell. RECOMMENDATION: This has good historical information not found in classroom history books. ROYALTY: None for amateurs. SOURCE: Fisher, Aileen Lucia. (1986). Holiday programs for boys and girls. Boston, MA: Plays, Inc. SUBJECTS/PLAY TYPE: Liberty Bell; Voting; Playlet.

3336. 7-12. (+) Jones, Elinor. **A voice of my own.** CAST: 5f. ACTS: 1. SETTINGS: None. PLAYING TIME: NA. PLOT: The playwright was inspired to write this after reading **A Room of One's Own**, by Virginia Woolf. In chronological order, 19 women authors--ranging from Sappho to Lillian Hellman--tell how they became authors; if they used male pseudonyms or "anonymous," and why; and how they began to speak for themselves, and why. RECOMMENDATION: In this inspirational, passionate, and informative drama, all of the actresses must be able to sing and one must play the guitar. ROYALTY: $50. SOURCE: Jones, Elinor. (1979). A voice of my own. New York, NY: Dramatists Play Service. SUBJECTS/PLAY TYPE: Women Writers; Drama.

3337. 10-12. (+) Dee, Peter & Welch, John B. **Voices from the high school.** CAST: 14f, 14m, 2u. ACTS: 1. SETTINGS: None. PLAYING TIME: 40 min. PLOT: This is a collection of vignettes about high school students. In the first one, two teenagers with walkman radios cannot hear each other but try to carry on a conversation anyway.

In another, two girls discuss the sexual advances of a boy. There is a conversation between two girlfriends about one's pregnancy, there are two scenes in which friends discuss the deaths of other teenagers, and a teenage boy decides, after reading his first Shakespeare play, to speak only Elizabethan English. The actors move in and out of a group that stays on the stage throughout the play. A member of the group introduces each scene and comments on it. RECOMMENDATION: Although the issues of teen suicide, masturbation, sexuality, and pregnancy are concerns of most teenagers today, some schools may consider this too controversial. ROYALTY: $40. SOURCE: Dee, Peter & Welch, John B. (1982). Voices from the high school. Boston, MA: Baker's Plays. SUBJECTS/PLAY TYPE: Adolescent Problems; Drama.

3338. 5-10. (+) Fisher, Aileen Lucia. **Voting against the odds.** CAST: 3f, 3m. ACTS: 1. SETTINGS: Living room. PLAYING TIME: 20 min. PLOT: Popular but irresponsible Doug, and responsible but not so popular Celia, are running for class president. Two classmates discuss the meaning of voting and the need to examine the candidates. They vote for Celia, the obviously better candidate. RECOMMENDATION: Likable characters in a contemporary setting make this appropriate for a presidential election year. ROYALTY: Free to Plays subscribers. SOURCE: Fisher, Aileen Lucia. (1985, November). Voting against the odds. Plays: The Drama Magazine for Young People, pp. 31-36. SUBJECTS/PLAY TYPE: Voting; Elections; Playlet.

3339. 4-6. (-) Fisher, Aileen Lucia. **Voting day.** CAST: 5f, 5m. ACTS: 1. SETTINGS: Bare stage, signs. PLAYING TIME: NA. PLOT: In this acrostic on the word, "voting," students lament that they are not old enough to vote and discuss why voting is important to them. RECOMMENDATION: The information and wording are dated and incorrect. ROYALTY: None for amateurs. SOURCE: Fisher, Aileen Lucia. (1986). Holiday programs for boys and girls. Boston, MA: Plays, Inc. SUBJECTS/PLAY TYPE: Patriotism; Voting; Choral Reading.

3340. 7-12. (+) Christopher, Jay. **The wackiest resort in the east.** CAST: 12f, 5m. ACTS: 2. SETTINGS: Run-down home being converted into a ski resort. PLAYING TIME: NA. PLOT: A group of girls and their boyfriends try to present the image of a thriving winter resort to a bank executive in order to extend the due date on the mortgage long enough to find a buyer for the home. Their misguided but valiant efforts impress one of the guests, a mild mannered millionaire, who buys the resort for himself and his bride-to-be. RECOMMENDATION: This wacky play is not strong on plot but is full of amusing wisecracks and zany banter. ROYALTY: $35. SOURCE: Christopher, Jay. (1978). The wackiest resort in the east. Elgin, IL: Performance Pub. Co. SUBJECTS/PLAY TYPE: Real Estate; Comedy.

3341. 1-3. (+) Gotwalt, Helen Louise Miller. **Wait and see.** CAST: 2f, 1m, 10u. ACTS: 1. SETTINGS: Dining room. PLAYING TIME: 10 min. PLOT: Little Betsy Button is impatient to see her birthday surprise. Four fairies help her by explaining that the secret to waiting is to spend the time planning a surprise for someone else. RECOMMENDATION: This is a simple production that promotes generosity and selflessness. ROYALTY: Free to Plays subscribers. SOURCE: Gotwalt, Helen Louise Miller. (1980). First plays for children: A collection of little plays for the youngest players. Boston, MA: Plays, Inc. SUBJECTS/PLAY TYPE: Birthdays; Generosity; Skit.

3342. 5-7. (+) **Waiting for Jesus Christ.** CAST: 2m, Su. ACTS: 1. SETTINGS: None. PLAYING TIME: 40 min. PLOT: This service is a compilation of Psalm 100, 1 Corinthians 15:21-26, and 1 Thessalonians 4:16,17. It teaches of the worship icons, the brazen altar, the laver, the altar of incense, the table of the showbread, the golden candlestick, the veil, and the ark of the covenant. RECOMMENDATION: The language is easily recited and the songs are easily learned ("O Come All Ye Faithful," "O Come Emmanuel," and "Come, Thou Long-Expected Jesus"). Pictures of the icons are provided to be made into poster sized drawings or overhead projector overlays. ROYALTY: None. SOURCE: Hendricks, William & Vogel, Cora. (1983). Handbook of Christmas programs. Grand Rapids, MI: Baker Book House. SUBJECTS/PLAY TYPE: Christmas; Dedication Service; Worship Program.

3343. 6-12. (+) Shoemaker, Carole. **Waiting for Uncle Eddie.** CAST: 5f, 4m, 5u. ACTS: 1. SETTINGS: Porch; kitchen. PLAYING TIME: 15 min. PLOT: The nieces and nephews discuss Uncle Eddie, who has become a rich and famous actor and is expected home for a family reunion, his first in many years. Eddie arrives, accompanied by his entourage of photographers, secretary, and public relations people who swarm over the house taking pictures and making disparaging remarks about the poverty of Eddie's family. Eddie doesn't make it to the backyard where his mother and the rest of the family are waiting before leaving. His public relations people make sure the kids on the front porch get autographed pictures. The play ends with a discussion of how the nephews and nieces would behave if they became important. RECOMMENDATION: The theme is timeless but some of the characters' names may need to be updated. ROYALTY: Free to Plays subscribers. SOURCE: Shoemaker, Carole. (1977, December). Waiting for Uncle Eddie. Plays: The Drama Magazine for Young People, pp. 31-38. SUBJECTS/PLAY TYPE: Fame; Playlet.

3344. 9-12. (+) McCusker, Paul. **The waiting room.** CAST: 3f, 4m, 6u. ACTS: 1. SETTINGS: Hospital waiting room. PLAYING TIME: NA. PLOT: A man, waiting at the hospital for his wife to have a baby, encounters other visitors, each waiting for something: a woman and her sister wait to see the woman's suicidal husband, and a man waits for the birth of his first niece. The anxious husband contemplates the length of time which has passed, the poor quality of magazines in the waiting room, and the life of his future child (a daughter he hopes). All is tragically resolved when the daughter is born dead. RECOMMENDATION: The humorous tone set at the beginning turns tragic with the news of the baby's death. The audience is left stunned by the unexpected realism. However, with the closing line that the day has been "business as usual," the audience is made aware of how closely the play has reflected life. ROYALTY: $15. SOURCE: McCusker, Paul. (1984). The waiting room. Boston, MA: Baker's Plays. SUBJECTS/PLAY TYPE: Birth; Death; Hospitals; Drama.

3345. 2-4. (+) Fisher, Aileen Lucia. **Wake up time.** CAST: Su. ACTS: 1. SETTINGS: Bare stage. PLAYING TIME: 3 min. PLOT: The world is exhorted to wake up because it is springtime. RECOMMENDATION: Evenly flowing rhythm and obvious rhymes make this an easily performed choral reading which lends itself to pantomime as well (seeds, trees, roots waking up). It is appropriate for the first day of spring or Earth Day, or to accompany a science lesson on plant growth. ROYALTY: Free to Plays subscribers. SOURCE: Fisher, Aileen Lucia. (1985, April). Wake up time. Plays: The Drama Magazine for Young People, pp. 50. SUBJECTS/PLAY TYPE: Spring; Earth Day; Choral Reading.

3346. K-4. (+) Gotwalt, Helen Louise Miller. **Wake up, Santa Claus.** CAST: Su. ACTS: 1. SETTINGS: Bare stage, props. PLAYING TIME: 15 min. PLOT: Only the children's pleas can wake Santa. RECOMMENDATION: This is a good way to involve many children in acting like animals, clocks, and other noise makers. ROYALTY: None. SOURCE: Gotwalt, Helen Louise Miller. (1985). First plays for children: A collection of little plays for the youngest players. Boston, MA: Plays, Inc. SUBJECTS/PLAY TYPE: Christmas; Playlet.

3347. 7-12. (+) Bradley, Virginia. **Walk up on Christopher.** CAST: 5f, 1m. ACTS: 1. SETTINGS: Room. PLAYING TIME: NA. PLOT: After a visit from a maiden aunt, three young women discover the importance of friendship. RECOMMENDATION: Realistic characters and emotions make this quite successful. ROYALTY: NA. SOURCE: Bradley, Virginia. (1977). Stage eight: One-act plays. New York, NY: Dodd, Mead. SUBJECTS/PLAY TYPE: Family; Friendship; Drama.

3348. 12. (+) Holt, Rochelle Lynn. **Walking into the dawn: A celebration.** CAST: Su. ACTS: 1. SETTINGS: Jungle; cave; tree house; harem tent; attic studio; tenement room. PLAYING TIME: 50 min. PLOT: This is a celebration of women's roles in the world from the dawn of time to women today. It focuses particularly on the two seemingly disparate aspects of the female experience: that some women are tied to the home, symbolized by the various dwellings depicted on stage, while others are movers and shakers, symbolized by the jungle. Although dark thoughts intrude near the end, signified by the howling Hecate, the play concludes by noting that Justice, Peace, Intelligence, Nobility, Wisdom, Rectitude, Devotion, Liberty, Mercy, Intellect, Concord, Gentleness, Clemency, Generosity, etc. are all "feminine" traits and "qualities that embellish man's life." RECOMMENDATION: It is difficult to see how a small high school cast could master the complex dialogue and lengthy, stylized soliloquies. While the author encourages improvisation, the play requires numerous costumes and complex lighting and sound effects. Aside from the physical complexity of the production, this is likely to bore audiences not already attuned to its message. Not without merit as a literary tour de force, this is best left to adult or very mature high school theater groups. **ROYALTY: $60. SOURCE:** Terry, Megan. Two by Terry plus one. (1984). Schulenberg, TX: I.E. Clark. **SUBJECTS/PLAY TYPE:** Women's History; Drama.

3349. 10-12. (+) Lauchman, Richard. **The wall. CAST:** 2m. **ACTS:** 1. **SETTINGS:** Prison cell with window. **PLAYING TIME:** 30 min. **PLOT:** Two condemned criminals, Gestas and Dimas, pass the night before their execution speculating, amid coarse jokes and remembrances, what will happen to them in the morning. Through a window, they see crucifixes being erected. They occasionally peer through a hole into the adjoining cell where a third man is also awaiting execution. This man, they have heard, is the Son of God, has brought dead men to life, and has restored sight to the blind. Dimas is prepared to believe what he has heard, but Gestas dismisses the rumors. At daybreak, despite the disbelief of Gestas, Dimas places his faith in the Man and His "kingdom." **RECOMMENDATION:** The characters in this extremely powerful play are believable, and the well written dialogue maintains a consistently high level of emotional intensity. Its strong, graphic language must be considered within the context of the characters, setting, and tone of the play. The author's technique of allowing the audience to identify the prisoner in the next cell rather than naming him adds a touch of "Hitchcock" drama. **ROYALTY: $10. SOURCE:** Lauchman, Richard. (1978). The wall. Denver, CO: Pioneer Drama Service. **SUBJECTS/PLAY TYPE:** Christ, Jesus; Christian Drama.

3350. 10-12. (+) Milne, Barbara. **The wall hanging. CAST:** 2f, 1m. **ACTS:** 1. **SETTINGS:** Living room. **PLAYING TIME:** NA. **PLOT:** Jane Talbot tells Vladamir and Nina Andreieva that their farm has been sold and the old couple must move into a boarding house. For years, Nina has been deceiving the blind Vladamir that his beloved hive of bees is still alive in a hole in the wall behind a wall hanging. As they prepare to go, Vladamir discovers there are no bees left, and Nina explains they have been dead for many years but she has tried to keep their memory alive for him. At the end, Nina realizes that Vladamir has believed in his bees for so long, he cannot comprehend the reality of their loss. **RECOMMENDATION:** Superb characterization will elicit instant empathy from the audience, as will the portrayal of the elderly as thinking, caring, "real" people. **ROYALTY: $15. SOURCE:** Milne, Barbara. (1982). The wall hanging. Chicago, IL: Dramatic Pub. Co. **SUBJECTS/PLAY TYPE:** Moving; Deception; Elderly; Drama.

3351. 7-9. (+) Fisher, Aileen Lucia. **Walt Whitman's Lincoln. CAST:** 1m, Su. **ACTS:** 1. **SETTINGS:** None. **PLAYING TIME:** NA. **PLOT:** When Walt Whitman hears of Abraham Lincoln's death, he goes to Washington to mourn the man he had so admired, but had never met. Now, he can only hold a sprig of lilac in Lincoln's memory. **RECOMMENDATION:** This cleverly combines the poetry of Walt Whitman with the historical setting of the Civil War and the assassination of Abraham Lincoln. The result is a touching rendition of a familiar event in United States

history. As Whitman tells the story, a chorus answers with poetry. The person playing Whitman has many lines and might use a script. **ROYALTY:** Free to Play's subscribers. **SOURCE:** Fisher, Aileen Lucia. (1985). Year-round programs for young players. Boston, MA: Plays, Inc. **SUBJECTS/PLAY TYPE:** Lincoln, Abraham; Whitman, Walt; Choral Reading.

3352. 10-12. (+) Serpas, Stephen. **Waning crescent moon. CAST:** 1f, 2m. **ACTS:** 1. **SETTINGS:** Backyard. **PLAYING TIME:** NA. **PLOT:** Two friends discuss their plans to leave home. Hal is very anxious since his alcoholic father abuses him. Scooter is reluctant and indecisive. Scooter's mother, Gertie, appears carrying a birthday cake for him even though it isn't his birthday. She suddenly remembers that Hal's father called earlier to tell Hal to come home. They all worry over the consequences. In Hal's absence, Gertie tells Scooter that Hal's hospitalization for mental illness is the reason his father left. This makes Scooter decide that he must make a break and start a new life. He tells Hal his decision when Hal returns. **RECOMMENDATION:** Though not fully developed, each character is unique: Gertie's eccentricities, Hal's relationship with his father, Scooter's mental illness. The play touches on subjects that are relevant to teenagers today: child abuse, mental illness, alcoholism, divorce and abandonment. A high school audience could also relate to the changes and decisions faced by graduating seniors. **ROYALTY:** NA. **SOURCE:** Lamb, Wendy. (1985). The ground zero club and other prize winning plays. New York, NY: Dell Pub. Co. **SUBJECTS/PLAY TYPE:** Adolescent Problems; Decisions; Child Abuse; Drama.

3353. 7-12. (+) Bruce, Mark. **Wanted: Dragon Slayer. CAST:** 1f, 3m. **ACTS:** 1. **SETTINGS:** Road; castle; outside a cave. **PLAYING TIME:** 15 min. **PLOT:** A farm boy longing to be a hero, answers the call of Wizard LaRue to slay a dragon. After he pays his nine dollars for the privilege, the wizards's niece, consumed by guilt, reveals to him that the dragon is not real, but is part of her uncle's money making scheme. To everyone's surprise, there actually is a dragon, the farm boy battles it and wins both self respect and the wizard's niece. **RECOMMENDATION:** This is fast moving and well dotted with humorous one liners and puns. **ROYALTY:** Free to Plays subscribers. **SOURCE:** Bruce, Mark. (1985, October). Wanted: Dragon Slayer. Plays: The Drama Magazine for Young People, pp. 1-8. **SUBJECTS/PLAY TYPE:** Dragons; Comedy.

3354. 1-6. (+) Dunham, Sherrie. **Wanted: One fair damsel. CAST:** 4f, 3m, 1u. **ACTS:** 2. **SETTINGS:** Road. **PLAYING TIME:** 15 min. **PLOT:** A learned damsel uses her intelligence to save a knight from a fierce dragon. She gives the dragon bicarbonate of soda to cure his heartburn (which, of course, has caused him to breathe fire). **RECOMMENDATION:** This cleverly comments on male and female stereotypes. While Henrietta is brave and educated, her brother Gordon mocks his sister's reading habits and exhibits extreme cowardice. In the end, Henrietta saves the knight by outsmarting the dragon rather than cooking some special dish for him like the other more stereotypical women had tried to do. The knight recognizes Henrietta's talents and proposes marriage, but she elects to postpone the wedding so she can pursue her learning. ROYALTY: Free to Plays subscribers. SOURCE: Dunham, Sherrie. (1983, March). Wanted: One fair damsel. Plays: The Drama Magazine for Young People, pp. 54- 58. SUBJECTS/PLAY TYPE: Sex Roles; Skit.

3355. 6-8. (+) Nobleman, Roberta. **The war machine.** CAST: 14u. ACTS: 1. SETTINGS: Room. PLAYING TIME: NA. PLOT: Negotiations between two opposing countries break down and a fight begins which eventually leads to battle. The negotiators are caught trying to dismantle the weapons, but they negotiate a truce because the countries have lost their differences. RECOMMENDATION: The action is to be pantomimed by children portraying happiness and anger. ROYALTY: NA. SOURCE: Nobleman, Roberta. (1979). Mime and masks. Rowayton, CT: New Play Books. SUBJECTS/PLAY TYPE: War; Negotiation; Pantomime.

3356. 1-9. (+) Bauer, Caroline Feller. **Warm ups.** CAST: Su. ACTS: 1. SETTINGS: None. PLAYING TIME: NA. PLOT: This comprises eleven read-aloud exercises, including mimes, cheers, songs, and chants, to help young actors develop reading and listening skills. RECOMMENDATION: The exercises are diverse and provide excellent learning experiences for potential actors. ROYALTY: NA. SOURCE: Bauer, Caroline Feller. (1987). Presenting reader's theater: Plays and poems to read aloud. New York, NY: H.W. Wilson Co. SUBJECTS/PLAY TYPE: Poetry; Mimes; Mental Games; Reader's Theater.

3357. 3-8. (+) Fisher, Aileen Lucia. **Washington marches on.** CAST: 5f, 25m, Su. ACTS: 1. SETTINGS: None. PLAYING TIME: 25 min. PLOT: Biographical briefs of George Washington's life from birth to death include the day Washington was born, two events as a teenager (14 years and 16 years old), inheriting Mount Vernon, the French and Indian War as General Braddock's aide-de-camp, marrying Martha Custis, becoming Commander-in-Chief of the Continental Army during the Revolutionary War, crossing the Delaware, wintering at Valley Forge, winning the battle of Yorktown, farming at Mount Vernon, becoming President, and being eulogized after death. RECOMMENDATION: The person playing Washington has many lines, but the role can be split. The chorus could contain any number of students, so everyone in a class could be included. Using the device of either writing the date on the board or holding up a sign with the appropriate date for each scene helps students to remember the chronology of events. ROYALTY: Free to Plays subscribers. SOURCE: Fisher, Aileen Lucia. (1985). Year-round programs for young adults. Boston, MA: Plays, Inc. SUBJECTS/PLAY TYPE: Washington, George; Revolutionary War, U.S.; Choral Reading.

3358. 9-12. (+) Young, David. **Wasting away.** CAST: 5f, 4m, 9u. ACTS: 1. SETTINGS: Living/dining room; classroom; hospital psychiatric ward; clothing store. PLAYING TIME: NA. PLOT: Rosie, a bright and sensitive teenager, becomes obsessed with her weight after her mother carelessly mentions that her daughter is overweight. For a year, she starves herself, ignoring her parents' and her friends' pleas that she eat. Finally, she is checked into a psychiatric hospital, where her parents realize that her problems stem from their marital problems. RECOMMENDATION: This is an excellent (although stylized) portrayal of anorexia nervosa, its causes, and the need for communication within families. Some of the Australian slang will need to be Americanized, and some of the recorded music which mirrors the play's messages may need to be updated. ROYALTY: Write to author. SOURCE: Lonie, John. (1985). Learning from life. Sydney, Australia: Currency Press. SUBJECTS/PLAY TYPE: Anorexia Nervosa; Drama.

3359. 5-8. (+) Runnette, Helen V. **The way.** CAST: 8f, 9m, 17u. ACTS: 1. SETTINGS: Inn. PLAYING TIME: 25 min. PLOT: A kind innkeeper honors the Baby Jesus on Christmas Eve by opening his doors to anyone who needs a place to rest. American, Dutch, French, Mexican, Peruvian, English, Swedish, and German families arrive and each nationality talks about how Christmas is celebrated in their country. RECOMMENDATION: The purpose and true meaning of Christmas are well presented in this easy to produce, multicultural, highly recommended play. ROYALTY: None. SOURCE: Kamerman, Sylvia E. (1975). A treasury of Christmas plays. Boston, MA: Plays, Inc. SUBJECTS/PLAY TYPE: Christmas; Family; Playlet.

3360. 9-12. (+) Vornholt, John. **Way out.** CAST: 8f, 8m. ACTS: 2. SETTINGS: Living room. PLAYING TIME: NA. PLOT: In the year 2040, Earth has become extremely overcrowded, and it is now a status symbol to rent and inhabit a planet by oneself. The Winthrop family has reached such status on Zanzibar III. The teenagers look upon the move with mixed feelings, especially when things begin to go wrong--water may fall up or down depending on the gravity field, a "domestic management computer" wants to be part of the family, etc. Then (horror of horrors) the Winthrops discover that they have Merloosian neighbors. Although the adults are upset because they have to share the planet, the teenagers are secretly pleased to have friends their own ages and devise several plans to force the families to remain neighbors. At the end, the two families realize the value of neighbors and welcome a third alien family. RECOMMENDATION: Performers will enjoy the creativity of the costuming and props and the humor. The actor who plays the computer is only heard and will have the challenge of putting all acting ability into voice. ROYALTY: $35. SOURCE: Vornholt, John. (1976). Way out. Chicago, IL: Dramatic Pub. Co. SUBJECTS/PLAY TYPE: Computers; Aliens; Future; Neighbors; Comedy.

3361. 9-12. (+) Cable, Howard. (Perrault, Charles) **The way out Cinderella.** (Cinderella) CAST: 5f, 4m. ACTS: 1. SETTINGS: Kitchen; throne room; ballroom. PLAYING TIME: 35 min. PLOT: Instead of being the traditional, overworked stepdaughter, Ella is a housecleaning workaholic. Her stepfamily implores her to go to the ball, as the prince is in search of a bride. When they find out that the prince wants to modernize the ball with disco music, Myrna (fairy godmother) turns Ella into a biker, complete with goggles, helmet, leather jacket, and electric guitar. The rest of the play follows the traditional plot; Ella leaves her shoe at midnight and the prince marries the girl whose foot fits it. RECOMMENDATION: This version has been moved up to the 70s time frame so that teenagers might enjoy the bikers and disco music. ROYALTY: Free to Plays subscribers. SOURCE: Cable, Howard. (1977, February). The way-out Cinderella. Plays: The Drama Magazine for Young People, pp. 19-32. SUBJECTS/PLAY TYPE: Folk Tales, France; Adaptation.

3362. 4-7. (+) Cheatham, Val R. (Baum, L. Frank) **The way out Wizard of Oz.** (The wonderful Wizard of Oz.) CAST: 3f, 1m, 2u. ACTS: 1. SETTINGS: Forest. PLAYING TIME: 15 min. PLOT: This condenses and modernizes the familiar story with clever dialogue and new twists. The tinman is "plasticman" who needs a battery cell (the wicked Witch calls him a "bottle of bleach"); the scarecrow wants to be good looking; the Wizard has a broken wand; and the lion is a lioness who is athletic and believes in equal athletic competition for women. In the happy ending all receive what they want, and even Dorothy returns to Kansas via a non-stop 747 Boeing Balloon with a flight bag and airline ticket in hand. RECOMMENDATION: This is a very clever and humorous play with inventive roles. However, familiarity with the original is needed to appreciate the humor. ROYALTY: Free to Plays Subscribers. SOURCE: Cheatham, Val R. (1978, November). The way-out Wizard of Oz. Plays: The Drama Magazine for Young People, pp. 65-70. SUBJECTS/PLAY TYPE: Fantasy; Comedy; Adaptation.

3363. 7-12. (+) Dias, Earl J. **Way, way down east.** CAST: 3f, 6m. ACTS: 1. SETTINGS: Living room. PLAYING TIME: 25 min. PLOT: Banker Impossible knows that the Ludlow's land is worth a lot to the railroad, and so he threatens to foreclose on the mortgage. Moneybags Ronald and Lily Ludlow (Ronald's girlfriend) foil the scheme by paying off the mortgage and jailing Impossible. RECOMMENDATION: A narrator introduces this as an old fashioned melodrama, and helps to involve the audience as booers and hissers. ROYALTY: Free to Plays subscribers. SOURCE: Dias, Earl J. (1988, October). Way, way down east. Plays: The Drama Magazine for Young People, pp. 21-30. SUBJECTS/PLAY TYPE: Mortgages; Swindlers and Swindling; Melodrama.

3364. 7-10. (+) Huff, Betty Tracy. **Way, way off Broadway.** CAST: 6f, 6m, Su. ACTS: 2. SETTINGS: Cabin; drawing room; railroad tracks. PLAYING TIME: 35 min. PLOT: Daisy, Count von Cliche, Cornball, and an assortment of others act out the story of a country girl duped by a city con artist. The girl does become famous (as promised), but returns to the country because it is the better place to live. RECOMMENDATION: Although disjointed, if over exaggerated, this could be hilarious. ROYALTY: Free to Plays subscribers. SOURCE: Huff, Betty Tracy. (1981, May). Way, way off Broadway. Plays: The Drama Magazine for Young People, pp. 19-32. SUBJECTS/PLAY TYPE: Comedy; Swindlers and Swindling; Melodrama.

3365. 1-5. (+) Boiko, Claire. **The wayward witch.** CAST: 1f, Su. ACTS: 1. SETTINGS: Living room. PLAYING TIME: 15 min. PLOT: Winnie, the wayward, absent minded witch, has a very difficult time performing her witchly arts. One year she sleeps through Halloween altogether. She awakens at Christmas time and, believing it to be Halloween, she goes out to haunt. Instead, she scares some children who believe Santa will be coming down their chimney. She sets off again, determined to find Halloween, but continues to get it wrong, performing her scary arts on Valentine's Day and the Fourth of July. Discouraged, Winnie goes back to bed. Luckily, on the next Halloween, children come to remind her. Still up to her tricks, however, Winnie is rumored to have decided to replace the Easter Bunny. RECOMMENDATION: An enchanting piece of work, the dialogue is designed so that each child has few lines to memorize. This is written in rhyme as an additional memory aid, with many choral lines. ROYALTY: None. SOURCE: Boiko, Claire. (1985). Children's plays for creative actors. Boston, MA: Plays, Inc. SUBJECTS/PLAY TYPE: Halloween; Witches; Playlet.

3366. K-3*. (+) Sullivan, Jessie P. **We can give something to Jesus (Christmas).** CAST: 2u. ACTS: 1. SETTINGS: Puppet stage. PLAYING TIME: NA. PLOT: Mortimer and Mathilda teach each other how to give Jesus a Christmas present by helping others, as they learn Matthew 25:40. RECOMMENDATION: Appropriate especially for Christmas, this provides non-monetary gift ideas. ROYALTY: None. SOURCE: Sullivan, Jessie P. (1978). Puppet scripts for children's church. Grand Rapids, MI: Baker Book House. SUBJECTS/PLAY TYPE: Christmas; Christian Drama; Puppet Play.

3367. 1-5. (+) Boiko, Claire. **We interrupt this program.** CAST: 3f, 10m, Su. ACTS: 1. SETTINGS: Santa's workshop; newsroom; astronomy lab. PLAYING TIME: 25 min. PLOT: A Christmas play is interrupted by a bulletin that an unidentified rocket is heading toward the North Pole. Children from around the world admit that they sent the rocket with gifts for Santa to show their appreciation. RECOMMENDATION: In this clever blend of space and Christmas fantasy, Christmas carols and several solos add to the holiday spirit. The use of children from many different cultures also adds to the value. ROYALTY: Free to Plays subscribers. SOURCE: Kamerman, Sylvia E. (1988). The big book of Christmas plays. Boston, MA: Plays, Inc. SUBJECTS/PLAY TYPE: Christmas; Science Fiction; Musical.

3368. 7-12. (+) Kelly, Tim & Christiansen, Arne. **We like it here.** CAST: 12f, 11m, 2u. ACTS: 2. SETTINGS: Office; classroom; bench; spaceship. PLAYING TIME: 120 min. PLOT: Two aliens whose spaceship experiences technical difficulties, land on the campus of a junior college facing financial ruin. The brother and sister reveal their identities to two students, but also unknowingly, to a fortune seeking family and local sheriff. In the dean's office, fund raising is the topic of discussion. The decision is made to bestow an honorary degree on a famous, although illiterate, ex-student in hopes of a sizable donation. He accepts the degree but fails to donate any money as his revenge. He offers the aliens a chance to appear on his game show. They agree with the intention of donating the money to save the college. Their game show opponents are the fortune seeking family. The aliens lose, yet all is not lost. The boy alien solves an equation that will eliminate pollution. The government agrees to provide funding to the college with the stipulation that the two aliens remain as students. Their leader comes to take them home, but they decide to stay because "they like it here." RECOMMENDATION: This fast moving piece keeps the audience guessing. The setting is easily obtained although some of the costumes may be difficult. ROYALTY: $60. SOURCE: Kelly, Tim & Christiansen, Arne. (1984). We like it here. Denver, CO: Pioneer Drama Service. SUBJECTS/PLAY TYPE: Science Fiction; Comedy; Musical.

3369. 4-6. (-) Fisher, Aileen. **We wanted a hill.** CAST: 3f, 3m, Su. ACTS: 1. SETTINGS: Bare stage. PLAYING TIME: 10 min. PLOT: This describes the building of a hill from rubbish and refuse, and the planting of grass and trees upon it. RECOMMENDATION: In these days of concern over the discovery of long buried toxic wastes, this reading, which describes the building of a hill from just such material, is probably not appropriate. ROYALTY: Free to Plays subscribers. SOURCE: Fisher, Aileen. (1981, April). We wanted a hill. Plays: The Drama Magazine for Young People, pp. 57-59. SUBJECTS/PLAY TYPE: Arbor Day; Choral Reading.

3370. 4-6. (+) Curry, Louise & Wetzel, Chester M. **We would see Jesus.** CAST: Su. ACTS: 1. SETTINGS: Darkened room. PLAYING TIME: 30 min. PLOT: This service is a compilation from the Book of Isaiah and the Gospels according to Saints Matthew and Luke. It covers the announcement of the birth of Christ, the visit of the wise men and the giving of gifts. Christina Rossetti's poem, "What Can I Give Him" is also included. RECOMMENDATION: These readings teach that Christmas is celebrated as the birth of Christ. ROYALTY: NA. SOURCE: Hendricks, William & Vogel, Cora. (1983). Handbook of Christmas programs. Grand Rapids, MI: Baker Book House. SUBJECTS/PLAY TYPE: Christmas; Candlelight Service; Worship Service.

3371. 1-6. (+) Fisher, Aileen. **Wearing of the green.** CAST: Su. ACTS: 1. SETTINGS: None. PLAYING TIME: NA. PLOT: This is a poem about why St. Patrick's Day takes place in March. RECOMMENDATION: The poet employs understandable vocabulary and simple rhymes which could be memorized fairly easily by young children and would add to the festivity of the holiday. ROYALTY: Free to Plays subscribers. SOURCE: Fisher, Aileen. (1985, March). Wearing of the green. Plays: The Drama Magazine for Young People, p. 43. SUBJECTS/PLAY TYPE: St. Patrick's Day; Choral Reading.

3372. 6-12. (+) Pierce, Carl Webster. **Weather or not.** CAST: 1f, 3m. ACTS: 1. SETTINGS: Living room; radio stations. PLAYING TIME: NA. PLOT: Horace and Henrietta try to listen to the evening news, but signals from two different radio stations interfere with each other.

RECOMMENDATION: The humor comes from the juxtaposition of a rapid fire newsman and a laconic weatherman finishing each other's sentences, while discussing totally different subjects. ROYALTY: None. SOURCE: Majeski, Bill. (1981). Easy skits, blackouts and pantomimes. Woodstock, IL: Dramatic Pub. Co. SUBJECTS/PLAY TYPE: Farce; Radio; Comedy; Skit.

3373. K-4. (+) Gotwalt, Helen Louise Miller. **The weatherman on trial.** CAST: 2f, 3m, 20u. ACTS: 1. SETTINGS: Courtroom. PLAYING TIME: NA. PLOT: A jury trial is held to determine the guilt or the innocence of the weatherman, who is accused of creating problems for the children's activities. He is found innocent because, even though he spoils some activities, he allows the plants to grow and nature to exist. RECOMMENDATION: This teaches that sometimes one's inconvenience is another's benefit. ROYALTY: NA. SOURCE: Gotwalt, Helen Louise Miller. (1985). The weatherman on trial. Boston, MA: Plays, Inc. SUBJECTS/PLAY TYPE: Weather; Playlet.

3374. 2-3. (+) Fisher, Aileen Lucia. **The weaver's son.** CAST: 2f, 3m. ACTS: 1. SETTINGS: Workroom-living room. PLAYING TIME: NA. PLOT: Columbus' mother is distraught when the men in the family daydream and the family business slows down. RECOMMENDATION: In this different view of Columbus' childhood, his parents are portrayed as good influences on his future, and the value of dreams and responsibility is underscored. ROYALTY: None for amateurs. SOURCE: Fisher, Aileen Lucia. (1986). Holiday programs for boys and girls. Boston, MA: Plays, Inc. SUBJECTS/PLAY TYPE: Columbus Day; Columbus, Christopher; Playlet.

3375. 7-10. (+) McCusker, Paul. **Wedding invitation.** CAST: 1f, 1m. ACTS: 1. SETTINGS: Bare stage, props. PLAYING TIME: NA. PLOT: Terri refuses to send Donna an invitation to her upcoming wedding because two years earlier, Donna spread rumors about her. Terri's fiance reminds her of the minister's sermon about loving and forgiving even our worst enemies. Terri agrees to invite Donna. RECOMMENDATION: This ends humorously as the tables are turned when Jim finds out that Donna's gossip concerned him, allowing the rather heavy handed message to be softened and more willingly absorbed. ROYALTY: NA. SOURCE: McCusker, Paul. (1982). Souvenirs: Comedies and dramas for Christian fellowship. Boston, MA: Baker's Plays. SUBJECTS/PLAY TYPE: Christian Drama; Forgiveness; Skit.

3376. 7-9. (+) Kehret, Peg. **Wedding woes.** CAST: 1f. ACTS: 1. SETTINGS: None. PLAYING TIME: NA. PLOT: Feeling alone and getting no attention, the little sister pouts about the forthcoming marriage of Elaine, her older sister. Envy and jealousy are disguised with a "pooh-pooh" attitude, as all energies are devoted to Elaine's big day. Dismissing the wedding as a mess, little sister is totally aloof until she is asked by big sister to be a bridesmaid, replete with long gown and flowers. The coming wedding will be glorious! RECOMMENDATION: Walking in the shadow of an older sibling is a familiar experience. The emotions are unforgettable and often difficult to handle, but the accurate and sensitive portrayal in this monologue should provide a satisfying feeling. ROYALTY: NA. SOURCE: Kehret, Peg. (1986). Winning monologs for young actors. Colorado Springs, CO: Meriwether Pub. SUBJECTS/PLAY TYPE: Sibling Rivalry; Monologue.

3377. 3-6. (+) Kittleson, Ole & Turner, Morrie. (Turner, Morrie) **Wee pals.** (Wee pals comic strip) CAST: 18f, 10m, Su. ACTS: 1. SETTINGS: Street; neighborhood; phone booth; home settings. PLAYING TIME: NA. PLOT: Idealistic characters from different religions, races, and backgrounds, live happily together; even the neighborhood bully manages to fit in. Some of the characters include Charlotte, an independent person in a wheelchair; Wellington, a boy from England; and Jerry, a Jewish boy. Unrelated scenes show groups in action (i.e., discussing opening soul-food stands in the neighborhood, a "girls' lib" meeting, etc.) RECOMMENDATION: The humor and songs are very enjoyable and seeing the characters existing together so compatibly is refreshing. Unfortunately, this is not realistic or believable to persons aware of current events. However, the message of tolerance and cooperation is worthwhile. ROYALTY: $60. SOURCE: Kittleson, Ole, & Turner, Morrie. (1981). Wee pals. Chicago, IL: Dramatic Pub. Co. SUBJECTS/PLAY TYPE: Tolerance; Comedy; Musical.

3378. 2-5. (+) Fisher, Aileen Lucia. **The week before Christmas.** CAST: Su. ACTS: 1. SETTINGS: None. PLAYING TIME: 5 min. PLOT: A boy and girl discuss Christmas. The girl is positive and the boy, negative. Then, children appear on the stage, each describing an aspect of Christmas beginning with one of its letters. RECOMMENDATION: The children spell "Christ-mas" as they pantomime a count down of the few days left before the holiday. ROYALTY: Free to Plays subscribers. SOURCE: Fisher, Aileen Lucia. (1985). Year round programs for young players. Boston, MA: Plays, Inc. SUBJECTS/PLAY TYPE: Christmas; Choral Reading.

3379. 1-4. (+) Lahr, Georgiana Lieder. **Welcome, spring!** CAST: 5f, 6m, 16u. ACTS: 1. SETTINGS: Kitchen. PLAYING TIME: 15 min. PLOT: King Winter and Jack Frost kidnap Spring to prolong winter fun. At the pleadings of the squirrels, willows and tulips, they realize what hardships they are causing for others and release spring. RECOMMENDATION: This has enough parts to allow all who want, to perform. The children will enjoy the opportunity to dress up as flowers and animals. ROYALTY: Free to Plays subscribers. SOURCE: Lahr, Georgiana Lieder. (1981, April). Welcome, spring! Plays: The Drama Magazine for Young People, pp. 35-38. SUBJECTS/PLAY TYPE: Spring; Skit.

3380. 9-12. (+) Lippa, Louis. **The welfare lady.** CAST: 3f. ACTS: 1. SETTINGS: Living room. PLAYING TIME: NA. PLOT: Naive but tender hearted Miss Drinkwater has been sent by the welfare office to complete the paperwork for Ms. Bianchi's obviously much needed welfare subsistence. She finds out that Ms. Bianchi's husband, a principled intellect, has not been laid off, but has voluntarily left his place of employment in his initiation of a strike, and will not return to work until the rights of his

coworkers have been guaranteed. In spite of her misgivings, the welfare worker must deny subsistence benefits because the husband has quit his job instead of being laid off. RECOMMENDATION: The frustrating helplessness of people in the face of bureaucracy is poignantly and clearly portrayed in this excellent tragi-comedy. It will spark much discussion and would be especially useful as an introduction to a social studies unit on political activism or politics and government. ROYALTY: $15. SOURCE: Lippa, Louis. (1985). The welfare lady. Chicago, IL: Dramatic Pub. Co. SUBJECTS/PLAY TYPE: Welfare System; Drama.

3381. 7-12. (-) Sodaro, Craig. **Werewolf on the team.** CAST: 10f, 6m, Su. ACTS: 1. SETTINGS: Classroom. PLAYING TIME: 25 min. PLOT: Wolfton High is getting ready for tomorrow's city football championship game and school dance. The star quarterback is injured before the game and the rival school steals the coach's playbook. The school "weakling," who just discovered how to use the mysterious powers of an ancient medallion, becomes the quarterback and wins the game. RECOMMENDATION: This features stereotypical characters, inconsistent appearances and actions, as well as trite dialogue. ROYALTY: Free to Plays subscribers. SOURCE: Sodaro, Craig. (1984, November). Werewolf on the team. Plays: The Drama Magazine for Young People, pp. 1-10. SUBJECTS/PLAY TYPE: Football; Comedy.

3382. 5-9. (+) Fisher, Aileen Lucia. **West to the Indies.** CAST: 3f, 4m. ACTS: 1. SETTINGS: Living room. PLAYING TIME: 15 min. PLOT: The home of Senhora Perestrello (Lisbon, Portugal, 1477), brings together the great navigator, Captain de Andrada, and the young cartographer, Christopher Columbus. Columbus visits to court Felipa Perestrello, and, on this occasion, to share a new map with Captain Andrada that explores a new route west to the Indies. Columbus' aspiring dreams are encouraged by Felipa and her elderly grandfather, who share the vision of seeing Columbus reach the Indies and being cheered as the "Admiral of the Sea." Captain Andrada is more practical and doubts that any ruler would support Columbus' voyage. RECOMMENDATION: Very good historical information is given in an interesting format. The costumes of the 15th century may be difficult, but not impossible. ROYALTY: Free to Plays subscribers. SOURCE: Fisher, Aileen Lucia. (1985, October). West to the Indies. Plays: The Drama Magazine for Young People, pp. 35-42. SUBJECTS/PLAY TYPE: Columbus, Christopher; Playlet.

3383. 6-12. (+) Lee, Jesse. **Westward ho! Ho! Ho!** CAST: 3f, 5m, 1u. ACTS: 1. SETTINGS: Lounge. PLAYING TIME: 30 min. PLOT: Pamela has inherited Bright Star ranch and must take possession by sundown the following day. Ralph Rotten, who owns an adjoining ranch, also wants to own Bright Star and resorts to arson to obtain it. Sam Strong, the newspaper editor, and his Indian friend, Sostoic, try to help Pamela keep her ranch. Ralph Rotten confuses and bullies Sheriff Hem003nghaw into arresting Pamela for impersonating herself, and, Sam, for helping Pamela. Aunt Lucy and Sostoic send smoke signals for help. The U.S. Marshal arrests Ralph Rotten and the Sheriff. Rotten is forced to sell his land to the highest bidder, his own mother. Lucy wins Sam's heart and everyone agrees to help her keep Bright Star ranch. RECOMMENDATION: Complete with the damsel in distress (this time tied to dynamite), caricatured good and bad guys, and modernized jokes, this melodramatic spoof is delightful. ROYALTY: Free to Plays subscribers. SOURCE: Lee, Jesse. (1988, May). Westward ho! ho! ho! Plays: The Drama Magazine for Young People, pp. 19-28. SUBJECTS/PLAY TYPE: Western; Comedy; Romance; Swindlers and Swindling; Melodrama.

3384. 6-12. (+) Hogan, Frank. **Wet paint.** CAST: 1u. ACTS: 1. SETTINGS: Bare stage, props. PLAYING TIME: 20 min. PLOT: Having recently fallen from a ladder, a painter decides that acting is the career for him. Using various voices, he describes the reactions to his decision by his wife, by the cook who serves as his acting coach, and others. While he did not get the first part he auditioned for, he explains that his chances are better now that he has a job painting the theater set. RECOMMENDATION: The painter's role requires an ability to create different accents and voices, as well as to pantomime and sing. ROYALTY: $10. SOURCE: Hogan, Frank X. (1980). Wet paint. Denver, CO: Pioneer Drama Service. SUBJECTS/PLAY TYPE: Acting; Comedy; Monologue.

3385. 6-9. (+) Satchell, Mary. **We've got our rights.** CAST: 8f, 11m, 18u. ACTS: 1. SETTINGS: Park; market; meeting room. PLAYING TIME: 25 min. PLOT: Lynn and her friend, Arty, are sent back in time by the spirits of the Constitution to learn the meaning and importance of the Constitution. At the faltering Constitutional Convention they make "suggestions" that allow the delegates to reach a compromise. They return only after learning to appreciate the rights that are often taken for granted. RECOMMENDATION: In this well developed play with strong parts for Lynn and Arty, textural background material is very solid. ROYALTY: Free to Plays subscribers. SOURCE: Satchell, Mary. (1985, December). We've got our rights. Plays: The Drama Magazine for Young People, pp. 35-45. SUBJECTS/PLAY TYPE: Constitution, U.S.; Drama.

3386. 12. (-) Fowler, Zinita. **What are we going to do with mama?** CAST: 5f, 3m. ACTS: 1. SETTINGS: Porch; sitting room. PLAYING TIME: NA. PLOT: Mama, who is in her late seventies, has become senile. Her son and daughter-in-law can no longer care for her in their home, so they call a family meeting. The other children arrive--a stylish daughter and her "wheeler-dealer" businessman husband, a theatrical daughter with a drinking problem, and a son who lives in a commune. All are shown at their most vulnerable points, and they fight with each other about who "owes" Mama the most. No decision is reached about what to do with her. RECOMMENDATION: This is very unsatisfactory because it is neither enjoyable nor instructive. The characters are too stereotyped and one dimensional. ROYALTY: $15. SOURCE: Fowler, Zinita. (1977). What are we going to do with mama? Chicago, IL: Dramatic Pub. Co. SUBJECTS/PLAY TYPE: Family Relationships; Aging; Senility; Drama.

3387. 3-5. (+) Bradley, Virginia. **What counts at the county fair.** CAST: 1f, 2m. ACTS: 1. SETTINGS: Country road. PLAYING TIME: NA. PLOT: A country bumpkin expects to judge a beauty contest at the county fair, but discovers too late that he is judging the hog contest. RECOMMENDATION: This puppet show which could easily be produced in its entirety by the children, has distinctive characters, and is recommended for use as part of a larger show. ROYALTY: None. SOURCE: Bradley, Virginia. (1975). Is there an actor in the house? New York, NY: Dodd, Mead. SUBJECTS/PLAY TYPE: County Fairs; Comedy; Puppet Play.

3388. 7-10. (+) Kehret, Peg. **What did you learn in school today?** CAST: 1m. ACTS: 1. SETTINGS: None. PLAYING TIME: NA. PLOT: A young boy describes how his parents always ask what he learned in school each day, but they never like his responses. RECOMMENDATION: Both amusing and realistic, this view from a young adolescent should sound familiar to most. ROYALTY: NA. SOURCE: Kehret, Peg. (1986). Winning monologs for young actors. Colorado Springs, CO: Meriwether Pub. SUBJECTS/PLAY TYPE: School; Monologue.

3389. 9-12. (+) Wittenberg, C.H. **What dreams may come.** CAST: 1f, 5m. ACTS: 1. SETTINGS: Room; kitchen; office. PLAYING TIME: 30 min. PLOT: Ham dreams that his father dies. Shortly afterward, Ham's father does die, and Will, Ham's friend, begins to believe in ESP. Very soon after the death, Ham's mother marries his Uncle Claude. A boating accident occurs in which Ham, his mother, and new stepfather are killed. Nineteen year old Ham has willed his sports car, records, and stereo to Will. Will gets the feeling that it was all preordained and had to be acted out by Ham, Ham's mother, and Uncle Claude. Will concludes that Ham had ESP. RECOMMENDATION: The interesting and suspenseful plot are unfortunately marred by an anticlimactic ending. However, the technique of having Will act as narrator and major character is effective and the exposition almost makes up for the weak ending. ROYALTY: Free to Plays subscribers. SOURCE: Wittenberg, C.H. (1975, November). What dreams may come. Plays: The Drama Magazine for Young People, pp. 14-24. SUBJECTS/PLAY TYPE: Suspense; ESP; Mystery.

3390. 8-12. (+) Murray, John. **What happened on Center Street?** CAST: 4f, 5m. ACTS: 1. SETTINGS: Living room. PLAYING TIME: 35 min. PLOT: Vi Meredith finds Professor Allgood dying on Center Street, and his last words are "Club Bannatyne." Vi is hit by the car she attempts to flag down. Two weeks later, her husband goes on a book promotion tour, leaving her at home with a broken leg. The sheriff asks if Vi remembers any more details from the accident, and tells her she may be Professor Allgood's murderer's next target. As the professor's secretary, a new boarder in the community, and Vi's husband all relay conflicting stories, Vi becomes very confused about who is trying to kill her and unsuspectingly welcomes Scott Drake, her neighbor, into her home. The killer actually is Scott, who was trying to steal a valuable and rare book from the professor before he killed him. Ironically, this rare book was mistakenly included in a batch of books that Scott's wife brought to Vi to read while she was recuperating, and Scott is just about to kill Vi and take the book when the sheriff arrives and arrests him. RECOMMENDATION: This fast paced mystery keeps the audience guessing until the last minute as interesting characters, many unusual plot twists, unusually realistic dialogue, and simple but effective settings unfold. ROYALTY: Free to Plays subscribers. SOURCE: Murray, John. (1975, October). What happened on Center Street? Plays: The Drama Magazine for Young People. pp. 13-27. SUBJECTS/PLAY TYPE: Mystery; Playlet.

3391. K-3. (+) Havilan, Amorie & Smith, Lyn. **What I want to be.** CAST: 28u. ACTS: 1. SETTINGS: None. PLAYING TIME: 15 min. PLOT: Twenty-six students recite lines whose key words begin with the letters of the alphabet (A-Z) and identify 26 different careers available to graduating students. RECOMMENDATION: This could provoke discussion about changing values and roles in today's society, provided the director makes an effort to avoid stereotyping in the casting of each role. ROYALTY: NA. SOURCE: Havilan, Amorie & Smith, Lyn. (1985). Easy plays for preschoolers to third grade. Brandon, MS: Quail Ridge Press. SUBJECTS/PLAY TYPE: Careers; Choral Reading.

3392. K-3*. (+) Sullivan, Jessie P. **What is a tithe?** CAST: 2u. ACTS: 1. SETTINGS: Puppet stage. PLAYING TIME: NA. PLOT: As two children discuss tithing, they also learn fractions. RECOMMENDATION: Malachi 3:10 is explained in simple, but effective terms. ROYALTY: None. SOURCE: Sullivan, Jessie P. (1978). Puppet scripts for children's church. Grand Rapids, MI: Baker Book House. SUBJECTS/PLAY TYPE: Tithe; Christian Drama; Puppet Play.

3393. K-5. (+) Bauer, Caroline Feller. (O'Neill, Mary) **What is purple?** (What is purple?) CAST: 5u. ACTS: 1. SETTINGS: None. PLAYING TIME: 2 min. PLOT: Read in parts by five readers, this poem presents several aspects of the color purple. RECOMMENDATION: This lovely, evocative poem would be a good introduction to poetic imagery as it ranges from the purple of eventide, to purple fingernails, to a purple violet opening in the spring. ROYALTY: None. SOURCE: Bauer, Caroline Feller. (1987). Presenting reader's theater: Plays and poems to read aloud. New York, NY: H.W. Wilson Co. SUBJECTS/PLAY TYPE: Choral Reading; Colors; Purple; Adaptation.

3394. K-3. (+) Abisch, Roz & Kaplan, Boche. **What kind of hat?** CAST: 1u. ACTS: 1. SETTINGS: Bare stage. PLAYING TIME: NA. PLOT: A player (or a series of players), with only his or her shadow seen by the audience, dons various hats (e.g., a magician's hat, a baker's hat), and uses simple props made from cardboard and other household items. Speaking in verse, the player asks the audience to guess the kind of hat. RECOMMENDATION: This should generate much enthusiasm in younger children who can "act" with the safety of a sheet between them and the audience. The

construction of props may present a problem for younger children (who are most likely to enjoy this project); reading is necessary, and help from adults or older children will be required. ROYALTY: Free to Plays subscribers. SOURCE: Abisch, Roz & Kaplan, Boche. (1977). The make it, play it, show time book. New York, NY: Walker & Co. SUBJECTS/PLAY TYPE: Hats; Professions; Shadow Play.

3395. K-3. (-) Fisher, Aileen. **What makes Thanksgiving.** CAST: Su. ACTS: 1. SETTINGS: None. PLAYING TIME: 5 min. PLOT: Children spell out Thanksgiving with a rhyme which begins with each of the letters and describes a different aspect of the holiday. RECOMMENDATION: This is too juvenile for older children, yet the vocabulary used is too mature for younger children. ROYALTY: Free to Plays subscribers. SOURCE: Fisher, Aileen. (1983, November). What makes Thanksgiving. Plays: The Drama Magazine for Young People, pp. 80. SUBJECTS/PLAY TYPE: Thanksgiving; Choral Reading.

3396. 3-6. (+) Hark, Mildred & McQueen, Noel. **What, no Santa Claus?** CAST: 1f, 1m, 9u. ACTS: 1. SETTINGS: Living room. PLAYING TIME: 30 min. PLOT: Santa is sick this year and cannot deliver his presents. Mrs. Claus decides to take the sleigh but Santa has his doubts. However, he finally agrees after much persuasion. RECOMMENDATION: With elves and reindeer, this provides a joyful story. ROYALTY: Free to Plays subscribers. SOURCE: Kamerman, Sylvia E. (1978). On stage for Christmas. Boston, MA: Plays, Inc. SUBJECTS/PLAY TYPE: Christmas; Comedy.

3397. 10-12. (-) Fisher, Aileen Lucia. **What now, planet Earth?** CAST: 11f, 13m, 4u. ACTS: 1. SETTINGS: None. PLAYING TIME: NA. PLOT: A panel consisting of a moderator, scientist, librarian, historian, and reporter discuss historical and modern concepts of conservation of earth's natural resources. RECOMMENDATION: The historical statements presented are excellent, but the statements about today's conservation activities are dated and inaccurate. ROYALTY: None for amateurs. SOURCE: Fisher, Aileen Lucia. (1986). Holiday programs for boys and girls. Boston, MA: Plays, Inc. SUBJECTS/PLAY TYPE: Conservation; Playlet.

3398. 7-12. (-) Sullivan, Patricia. **What seems to be the problem?** CAST: 5f, 4m. ACTS: 1. SETTINGS: Hallway. PLAYING TIME: 20 min. PLOT: Two teenagers criticize each other's behavior. Marsha berates John for devoting too much time to basketball and not enough to his schoolwork, and John retaliates. As various other characters appear, they are drawn into the meaningless arguments. When a teacher comes through the hallway, the original students deny that a problem exists. RECOMMENDATION: This has no plot and the hateful, sarcastic dialogue does not enhance its poorly conveyed message. ROYALTY: $20. SOURCE: Sullivan, Patricia. (1977). What seems to be the problem? Franklin, OH: Eldridge Pub. Co. SUBJECTS/PLAY TYPE: Behavior; School; Skit.

3399. 3-6. (+) Fisher, Aileen. **What spells liberty?** CAST: 12u. ACTS: 1. SETTINGS: None. PLAYING TIME: 5 min. PLOT: Children spell out "Lady Liberty," each reciting a short statement of what the letters stand for. RECOMMENDATION: This is easy to present to a PTA meeting or a school open house with room for all to participate. ROYALTY: Free to Plays subscribers. SOURCE: Fisher, Aileen. (1986, October). What spells liberty? Plays: The Drama Magazine for Young People, pp. 46. SUBJECTS/PLAY TYPE: Statue of Liberty; Choral Reading.

3400. 5-8. (+) Bradley, Virginia. **What took you so long?** CAST: Su. ACTS: 1. SETTINGS: Spaceship launch pad. PLAYING TIME: NA. PLOT: The first Earth spaceship lands on Mars, only to find others have beaten them to it. RECOMMENDATION: This brief piece might work if the punch line is tailored to specific audiences (i.e., a group of Boy Scouts, fifth graders, or the football team). ROYALTY: None. SOURCE: Bradley, Virginia. (1975). Is there an actor in the house? New York: Dodd, Mead. SUBJECTS/PLAY TYPE: Comedy; Space Flights; Pantomime.

3401. 6-12. (-) Saigull, Sel. **What was that number?** CAST: 2f, 2m, 1u. ACTS: 1. SETTINGS: Pizza parlor; two homes. PLAYING TIME: 50 min. PLOT: A high school girl dials a wrong number and converses with the college boy who answers the phone. They describe themselves as more attractive than they really are, exchange fake names and phone numbers, and hang up depressed, knowing they can never recontact each other this way. Later, with friends, they analyze the phone call. The girl confesses to the boy that she was the one who called, and they make a date to meet at the pizza parlor the next day. RECOMMENDATION: The dialogue is awkward and tedious, the characters lifeless and flat, and the plot improbable. ROYALTY: $20. SOURCE: Saigull, Sel. (1988). What was that number? Franklin, OH: Eldridge, Pub. Co. SUBJECTS/PLAY TYPE: Dating; Playlet.

3402. 4-10. (+) Kehret, Peg. **What will I be when I grow up?** CAST: 1u. ACTS: 1. SETTINGS: None. PLAYING TIME: NA. PLOT: A youngster ponders several of the many career options open to him. RECOMMENDATION: Short, but with an important message, this could serve as a discussion opener for any age group. ROYALTY: NA. SOURCE: Kehret, Peg. (1986). Winning monologs for young actors. Colorado Springs, CO: Meriwether Pub. SUBJECTS/PLAY TYPE: Careers; Monologue.

3403. 7-12. (-) Bradley, Virginia. **What will you tell us of Christmas?** CAST: Su. ACTS: 1. SETTINGS: Stable with manger. PLAYING TIME: 20 min. PLOT: Through choral readings and pantomime, the Chorus Celestial represents the sacred aspect of Christmas, the Chorus Temporal represents the secular, and the children of Tomorrow represent those who want to learn about Christmas. RECOMMENDATION: The language is stilted and contains words not commonly used. ROYALTY: None. SOURCE: Bradley, Virginia. (1981).

Holidays on stage. New York, NY: Dodd, Mead. SUBJECTS/PLAY TYPE: Christmas; Choral Reading.

3404. 9-12. (-) Hatton, Thomas J. (Chaucer, Geoffrey) **What women want most.** (Wife of Bath) CAST: 2f, 6m. ACTS: 1. SETTINGS: Throne room. PLAYING TIME: NA. PLOT: A knight steals a kiss from a noble maiden and is sentenced to death. Queen Guenivere asks that the knight be spared if he can answer her question "What is it that women want most"? RECOMMENDATION: While this could help to bring Chaucer's tale alive, the dialogue is so ridiculous that students would dismiss it as a waste of time. ROYALTY: $15. SOURCE: Hatton, Thomas J. (1982). What women want most. Chicago, IL: Dramatic Pub. Co. SUBJECTS/PLAY TYPE: Camelot; Arthur, King; Comedy; Adaptation.

3405. 9-12. (+) Emmons, Ron. (Shakespeare, William) **What you will!: A story theatre adaptation of Shakespeare's Twelfth Night.** (Twelfth night or what you will) CAST: 4f, 6m, 7u. ACTS: 1. SETTINGS: Delivery room; ship; inside of a house; outdoors. PLAYING TIME: NA. PLOT: Identical twins, a brother and sister, are separated during a shipwreck. Each thinks the other is dead. The girl, for love of her brother, swears off men and disguises herself as a servant boy but falls in love with her "master," who is taken with another. A series of practical jokes and fortuitous meetings bring the girl, her twin and their sweethearts together. RECOMMENDATION: Recommended for ease of production and minimal props (the actors are the props), this retains much of the humor of the original but in shorter form and with an amusing mix of contemporary and Shakespearean dialogue. ROYALTY: $15. SOURCE: Emmons, Ron. (1987). What you will! A story theatre adaptation of Shakespeare's **Twelfth Night.** Boston, MA: Baker's Plays. SUBJECTS/PLAY TYPE: Comedy; Romance; Adaptation.

3406. 5-8. (-) Majeski, Bill. **Whatever happened to good old Ebeneezer Scrooge?** CAST: 2f, 2m, Su. ACTS: 1. SETTINGS: TV studio; factory; palace. PLAYING TIME: 30 min. PLOT: In this sequel to A Christmas Carol, Scrooge, bankrupt because of his generosity, returns to his old ways. He joins the Seven Dwarves and, although greedy, he never fully becomes his ugly former self. At the end, he falls in love with the dastardly witch of Snow White fame, and the two leave arm-in-arm to find a preacher. RECOMMENDATION: Most of the humor is iconoclastic, as Scrooge disparages such things as charity, honesty, and virtue. Just how a character from Dickens' classic fits in naturally with Snow White and the Seven Dwarves is a puzzlement. Mediocre puns and one liners abound in this vacuous comedy. ROYALTY: Free to Plays subscribers. SOURCE: Kamerman, Sylvia E. (1984, December). Plays: The Drama Magazine for Young People, pp. 12-20. SUBJECTS/PLAY TYPE: Christmas; Scrooge, Ebeneezer; Comedy.

3407. 4-8. (+) Alexander, Sue. **Whatever happened to Uncle Albert.** CAST: 2f, 3m. ACTS: 1. SETTINGS: Living room. PLAYING TIME: NA. PLOT: As George and Mary investigate the disappearance of their Uncle Albert, they find a book of magic spells which indicates that he may have been dabbling in black magic and turned himself into a wolf. **RECOMMENDATION:** A good choice for Halloween, the only difficulty might be growing hair on the two children, who, after reading some of the lines in the magic book, begin to turn into wolves. **ROYALTY:** NA. **SOURCE:** Alexander, Sue. (1980). Whatever happened to Uncle Albert and other puzzling plays. New York, NY: Houghton Mifflin. **SUBJECTS/PLAY TYPE:** Magic; Horror; Mystery.

3408. K-6. (+) Jiminez, Robert. **What's mine is mime.** **CAST:** 1m, 12u. **ACTS:** 4. **SETTINGS:** Park; road. **PLAYING TIME:** 15 min. **PLOT:** Marni the mime gets in trouble for eating the juggler's apple props. On his way to buy more apples, Marni knocks Snake, the street hoodlum, unconscious when he tries to take Marni's money away. Marni is named the hero for aiding in the capture of Snake and receives a reward of money for the good deed. **RECOMMENDATION:** With many chances for each character to ad lib actions, this amusing adventure requires one actor who can juggle. **ROYALTY:** Free to Plays subscribers. **SOURCE:** Jimenez, Robert. (1982). What's mine is mime. Plays: The Drama Magazine for Young People, pp. 54-60. **SUBJECTS/PLAY TYPE:** Circus; Creative Dramatics.

3409. 10-12. (+) Kelly, Tim. **What's new at the zoo.** **CAST:** 3f, 3m. **ACTS:** 1. **SETTINGS:** Wildlife research station; sitting room. **PLAYING TIME:** NA. **PLOT:** A zoologist in Africa convinces his stuffy sister and her friends that "Adam" (his assistant) is an ape and his "assistant" (an ape) is a human. After much confusion, the zoologist goes off into the jungle with his "assistant" to study more about apes. **RECOMMENDATION:** The eccentric professor, old maid sister, and stuffy friends are good natured stereotypes who will keep everyone rolling in the aisles. **ROYALTY:** $15. **SOURCE:** Kelly, Tim. (1982). What's new at the zoo. Boston, MA: Baker's Plays. **SUBJECTS/PLAY TYPE:** Apes; Evolution; Comedy.

3410. 7-12. (+) Nolan, Paul T. **What's zymurgy with you?** **CAST:** 4f, 4m. **ACTS:** 1. **SETTINGS:** Park. **PLAYING TIME:** 30 min. **PLOT:** Tim can't get Janie to notice him until he reads the dictionary and becomes an entertaining user of unique words. **RECOMMENDATION:** Although short on plot, this would tie in to Library Week or might convince children to read. **ROYALTY:** Free to Plays subscribers. **SOURCE:** Nolan, Paul T. (1980, March). What's zymurgy with you? Plays: The Drama Magazine for Young People, pp. 12-22. **SUBJECTS/PLAY TYPE:** Reading; Vocabulary; Library Week; Playlet.

3411. K-3*. (+) Way, Brian. **The wheel.** **CAST:** 2f, 2m. **ACTS:** 1. **SETTINGS:** None. **PLAYING TIME:** NA. **PLOT:** Ned Wheelwright explains a mysterious note which told him not to sell a wheel he had made for a year. Spoke, a sprite-like character, and the audience, help Amos (a potential purchaser of the wheel), Ned, and Martha (Ned's wife), play out a fantasy in which the king learns to dance. Simple articles of clothing from a box transform all the characters into dancers, and magic boots help the king to dance. Another fantasy is played out with

Amos as a pirate, Martha as a sailor, Ned as captain, and children from the audience as pirates and sailors. Spoke tricks Amos into trying to steal the "treasure," symbolized by the wheel. The audience helps release captured sailors. At the end, Ned, Amos, and Martha realize the gift of the wheel is to teach them to share so all will benefit. Amos teaches Ned to make wheels and, as Ned spins them, the three plan to act out wonderful fantasies together. **RECOMMENDATION:** This calls for much active participation from the audience, reminiscent of the kind of audience participation in **Peter Pan.** It would be a very positive first experience with theater for a young child. As long as the cast is capable, the laudable theme of sharing and cooperation will be evident. Some ad-libbing may be necessary to ensure proper response. There is even an opportunity for a very lively chase scene. **ROYALTY:** $20. **SOURCE:** Way, Brian. (1977). The wheel. Boston, MA: Baker's Plays. **SUBJECTS/PLAY TYPE:** Sharing; Cooperation; Envy; Fantasy; Participation Play.

3412. 3-6. (-) Boiko, Claire. **Wheels! A ballad of the highway.** **CAST:** 44u. **ACTS:** 1. **SETTINGS:** Bare stage, props. **PLAYING TIME:** 20 min. **PLOT:** Cars and motorcycles sing and dance their way through a toll booth on the "All American Freeway," get stuck in a traffic jam and, out on the open highway, pass the sea, beach, mountains, and canyons before they watch the sunset over Fort Lauderdale and head home. **RECOMMENDATION:** This is a confusing and self conscious collage of dance, song, pantomime, and "rap." In an age where concern for the environment is a high priority, this play is an anachronism. **ROYALTY:** Free to Plays subscribers. **SOURCE:** Boiko, Claire. (1976, January). Wheels! A ballad of the highway. Plays: The Drama Magazine for Young People, pp. 62-68. **SUBJECTS/PLAY TYPE:** Automobiles; Playlet.

3413. 9-12. (+) Reed, Cory & Kelsey, Stephen. **When death do us part or, how to kill two bards with one stone.** **CAST:** 4f, 4m, 2u. **ACTS:** 1. **SETTINGS:** Living room. **PLAYING TIME:** NA. **PLOT:** Lady Pennington has been murdering people (the milkman, her husband, an old man, and the Stratford-Upon-Avon Lady). The famous detective, Silvius Shylock, and his assistant, Dr. Hawkins, bring her to justice. **RECOMMENDATION:** All of the traditional elements of a Sherlock Holmes mystery, including the final confrontation scene, are brought together, with a touch of Shakespeare added. The comedy lies in the unusual ways in which Shakespearean lines are used. No opportunity is missed to slip in a parody or pun on Shakespeare in this well done comedy. **ROYALTY:** $15. **SOURCE:** Reed, Cory, & Kelsey, Stephen. (1981). When death do us part or, how to kill two bards with one stone. Boston, MA: Baker's Plays. **SUBJECTS/PLAY TYPE:** Shakespeare, William; Holmes, Sherlock; Parody; Comedy.

3414. 4-8. (+) Spamer, Claribel. **When in the course of human events.** **CAST:** 2f, 5m. **ACTS:** 1. **SETTINGS:** Family room. **PLAYING TIME:** 25 min. **PLOT:** Jeb Ryder (saddler apprentice) supports independence from England and hopes to attend Harvard University. His friend, Paul, and father, Edward, oppose independence and believe that John Adams is a traitor. Adams leaves his saddle with Jeb and Paul to be repaired before he rides to Congress to pass the Declaration of Independence. As the two argue over loyalty to England, Paul slashes the saddle girth. The cut is discovered before Adams is hurt, and he uses another saddle. After the Declaration of Independence is signed, Adams reads it. RECOMMENDATION: This illustrates both sides of the American Revolution, making it suitable for either a drama group or a social studies class. ROYALTY: Free to Plays Subscribers. SOURCE: Spamer, Claribel. (1979, April). When in the course of human events. Plays: The Drama Magazine for Young People, pp. 24-32. SUBJECTS/PLAY TYPE: Revolution, U.S.; Declaration of Independence; Playlet.

3415. 5-8. (+) Hamlett, Christina. **When pirates ruled the sea.** CAST: 2f, 3m. ACTS: 1. SETTINGS: Ship cabin. PLAYING TIME: 20 min. PLOT: The captain recounts how his father gambled him away to the Count of Bella Donna, and how, in order to avoid marrying the Count's ugly daughter, he ran away to sea. As he tells his story, various crewmen try, unsuccessfully, to kill him. His ship captures the members of a wedding party on another ship, who turn out to be the Count's relatives. Flotilla, the Captain's betrothed, has run away with another man, and he marries her sister, Lillian. RECOMMENDATION: This is a delightful comedy, filled with pirates, foul play, and romance. ROYALTY: NA. SOURCE: Hamlett, Christina. (1987). Humorous plays for teenagers. Boston, MA: Plays, Inc. SUBJECTS/PLAY TYPE: Pirates; Romance; Comedy.

3416. 2-6. (+) Bauer, Caroline Feller. (Horwitz, Elinor Lander) **When the sky is like lace.** (When the sky is like lace) CAST: 5u. ACTS: 1. SETTINGS: None. PLAYING TIME: NA. PLOT: This nonsensical poem describes what it is like when it is bimulous and the sky is like lace, what you should and shouldn't do, and what happens when you do what you shouldn't. RECOMMENDATION: This delightful classroom reading for older children to present to younger children uses colors, food, and wonderful imagery to evoke happy feelings. ROYALTY: NA. SOURCE: Bauer, Caroline Feller. (1987). Presenting reader's theater: Plays and poems to read aloud. New York, NY: H.W. Wilson Co. SUBJECTS/PLAY TYPE: Feelings; Reader's Theater.

3417. K-5. (+) Ison, Colleen. **When you're scared.** CAST: 5u. ACTS: 1. SETTINGS: Bare stage. PLAYING TIME: NA. PLOT: A narrator illustrates how God can help a person achieve by telling the story of Moses' role in the exodus, Gideon's role in the war against the Midianites, and Jesus' calming of the waters as he and the disciples were crossing to the opposite shore. RECOMMENDATION: Children mime what the narrator says. The narrator will need to be an adult, but any number of any aged children can perform the other parts. Discussion questions are provided at the end. ROYALTY: NA. SOURCE: Ison, Colleen. (1986). Goliath's last stand: And fifteen more easy plays for children. Cincinnati, OH: Standard Pub. SUBJECTS/PLAY TYPE: Bible Stories; Christian Drama; Pantomime.

3418. 1-6. (+) Fisher, Aileen Lucia. **Where is Christmas?** CAST: 1f, 1m, 5u. ACTS: 1. SETTINGS: Bare

stage. PLAYING TIME: 2 min. PLOT: Three eight-line stanzas detail what Christmas isn't, and proclaim that Christmas is in the heart. RECOMMENDATION: Young children could memorize and perform this very short poem with a simple rhyming pattern for many different occasions around the Christmas season. ROYALTY: Free to Plays subscribers. SOURCE: Fisher, Aileen Lucia. (1987, December). Where is Christmas? Plays: The Drama Magazine for Young People, pp. 51. SUBJECTS/PLAY TYPE: Christmas; Choral Reading.

3419. 9-12. (+) Majeski, Bill. **Where it all comes true.** CAST: 9f, 5m, 5u. ACTS: 2. SETTINGS: Hotel lobby. PLAYING TIME: NA. PLOT: The Kaboodle family run a Fantasy Hotel/Hospital in which the Kaboodle twins use their inherited powers in unison to fulfill fantasies, improving the patient's lives. When two criminals, in search of the nonexistent fantasy formula, kidnap one of the twins, the remaining twin tries to fulfill the fantasies on his own, and they get humorously mixed up. In the end, the fantasies are straightened out, the criminals are caught, the patients discover that they like themselves the way they are and, of course, almost everyone finds romance. RECOMMENDATION: This light comedy uses puns, reversals of common sex roles, and silent scenes to create its humor. ROYALTY: $35. SOURCE: Majeski, Bill. (1981). Where it all comes true. Chicago, IL: Dramatic Pub. Co. SUBJECTS/PLAY TYPE: Therapy; Fantasy; Comedy.

3420. K-3. (+) Boiko, Claire. **Where on earth is spring?** CAST: 1f, 11u. ACTS: 1. SETTINGS: Forest. PLAYING TIME: 20 min. PLOT: Spring is late, and the trees and flowers decide that it is because humans have littered and polluted the Earth. The bear challenges the audience to help clean up the Earth. The audience members accept the challenge with their applause, and Spring arrives. RECOMMENDATION: The personification and anthropomorphism will help children to view pollution from the perspective of nature itself. ROYALTY: Free to Plays Subscribers. SOURCE: Boiko, Claire. (1979, March). Where on Earth is Spring? Plays: The Drama Magazine for Young People, pp. 29-32. SUBJECTS/PLAY TYPE: Spring; Environment; Pollution; Participation Play.

3421. 6-12. (+) Raspanti, Celeste Rita. (Cleaver, Vera and Bill) **Where the lilies bloom.** (Where the lilies bloom.) CAST: 9f, 7m, 5u. ACTS: 2. SETTINGS: Mountain home. PLAYING TIME: NA. PLOT: Mary Call does not reveal her father's death in order to keep the family together. She rejects the neighbors and the romance between her older sister and their landlord, Kiser Pease. Kiser turns out to be more honorable than she thought, and his persistence wins him the hand of the oldest sister, along with the opportunity to help the family. RECOMMENDATION: This closely follows the story line and spirit of the well loved original. The dramatic tension created by a plot where children try to survive without help from grown-ups is well developed. ROYALTY: $50. SOURCE: Raspanti, Celeste Rita. (1977). Where the lilies bloom. Woodstock, IL: Dramatic Pub. Co SUBJECTS/PLAY TYPE: Family Life; Survival; Appalachian Mountains; Adaptation.

3422. 4-6. (-) Ross, Laura. **Where there is no north.** CAST: 4f, 8m, Su. ACTS: 4. SETTINGS: Arctic regions. PLAYING TIME: NA. PLOT: Commodore Perry and his party make preparations for his North Pole expedition. RECOMMENDATION: This presents some of the Eskimo culture and beliefs, as well as the complexities of Perry's journey. Especially as part of a unit on the early explorers, it is effective and thought provoking. ROYALTY: None. SOURCE: Ross, Laura. (1975). Mask-Making with pantomime and stories from American history. New York, NY: Lothrop, Lee, & Shepard Co. SUBJECTS/PLAY TYPE: Perry, Robert E.; North Pole, Exploration; Playlet.

3423. 9-12. (+) Nolan, Paul T. **Where you are.** CAST: 3f, 3m. ACTS: 1. SETTINGS: Park. PLAYING TIME: 25 min. PLOT: An elderly couple, feeling sad and old, interact with young people performing tasks the couple had wanted to do in their youth. Some of the children become angry that the older couple have seemingly given up on life. Meanwhile, an artist paints the man and his wife as children pretending to be old. They are distressed at the painting but eventually realize that age itself does not necessarily mean having to feel and act old. RECOMMENDATION: Although the children's "teaching" the old people a lesson about which they really have no knowledge can be perceived as insulting, the message that you're as young as you feel is a worthy one. ROYALTY: Free to Plays subscribers. SOURCE: Nolan, Paul T. (1975, February). Where you are. Plays: The Drama Magazine for Young People, pp. 26-34. SUBJECTS/PLAY TYPE: Aging; Playlet.

3424. 4-6. (+) Martens, Anne Coulter. **Which is witch?** CAST: 5f, 6m, Su. ACTS: 1. SETTINGS: Living room. PLAYING TIME: 30 min. PLOT: In an effort to help her realtor father sell an old house said to be haunted, a strong minded teenager and her timid friend spend an evening there to prove the rumors false. Confusion arises with the appearance of two witches (actually friends disguised as ghosts), the father, and the prospective buyer. After convincing the prospective buyer that the strange occurrences were silly pranks, the teenagers exit, as ghosts of two old men enter. RECOMMENDATION: In contrast to its gloomy setting, this is a light hearted comedy in which mistaken identity causes a chain of humorous events. The characters, though somewhat gullible, are likable and believable. The unconventional characterization of the two witches, and the humor created by the reactions of the older, more conservative witch to the modern ideas of the younger one are strong points. ROYALTY: Free to Plays subscribers. SOURCE: Martens, Anne Coulter. (1980, October). Which is witch? Plays: The Drama Magazine for Young People, pp. 27-38. SUBJECTS/PLAY TYPE: Halloween; Witches; Comedy.

3425. 1-3*. (+) Hoppenstedt, Elbert M. **Which witch is which?** CAST: 4f, 1m, Su. ACTS: 1. SETTINGS: Forest clearing. PLAYING TIME: 20 min. PLOT: Kind Witch Alice's plans to brighten a sick child's Halloween are thwarted by her evil twin sister, Witch Hazel, who steals Alice's broom, intending to frighten the child while pretending to be Alice. To save her friend, Alice steals the Halloween prize, a four-speed broom which is to be awarded to the witch who does the most unusual thing on Halloween night. Although Alice has done the most unusual thing by being kind to a mortal, Hazel takes the credit. She is exposed, and the wizard condemns her to ride the broom forever, while he rewards Alice by turning her into a beloved fairy. RECOMMENDATION: Real dangers and fearful dilemmas give this physical action and emotional appeal. Children will readily identify with the cruel sibling and the fear of being blamed for something unfairly in this simple, yet memorable, play. ROYALTY: Free to Plays subscribers. SOURCE: Hoppenstedt, Elbert M. (1982, October). Which witch is which? Plays: The Drama Magazine for Young People, pp. 37-43. SUBJECTS/PLAY TYPE: Halloween; Witches; Fantasy.

3426. 3-6. (+) Priore, Frank V. **While trolling through the park one day.** CAST: 1f, 3m. ACTS: 1. SETTINGS: Park. PLAYING TIME: 20 min. PLOT: Mayor Bailey's rules and regulations take all the fun out of going to the park until a magical troll helps a little girl to change his mind. RECOMMENDATION: This amusing, light hearted fantasy gently pokes fun at rules, regulations and authority figures. ROYALTY: Free to Plays subscribers. SOURCE: Priore, Frank V. (1984, January/February). While trolling through the park one day. Plays: The Drama Magazine for Young People, pp. 35-40. SUBJECTS/PLAY TYPE: Rules and Regulations; Comedy.

3427. 1-3. (+) Barr, June. **A white Christmas.** CAST: 6f, 6m, 3u. ACTS: 1. SETTINGS: Cloud. PLAYING TIME: NA. PLOT: The Snow King and his Queen, Jack Frost, the North and East Winds, and many snowflakes ensure that earth has a white Christmas. RECOMMENDATION: This allows the younger grades to imagine what snowflakes must endure to produce such a magical effect at Christmas time. ROYALTY: Free to Plays subscribers. SOURCE: Kamerman, Sylvia E. (1975). A treasury of Christmas plays. Boston, MA: Plays, Inc. SUBJECTS/PLAY TYPE: Fantasy; Christmas.

3428. 1-6. (+) Winther, Barbara. **White elephant.** CAST: 3f, 2m, 6u. ACTS: 1. SETTINGS: Courtyard. PLAYING TIME: 25 min. PLOT: A lazy potter and his wife play a joke on a washerman and his wife by telling the king that the washerman and his wife can turn a grey elephant white. Summoned before the king, the washerman and his wife turn the joke around by saying that a giant bathtub made by the potter is needed. The potter and his wife succeed in manufacturing a bathtub after several attempts, learning that hard work pays off. As the elephant's bath is proceeding, a messenger delivers to the king a white elephant as a gesture of friendship from the King of Siam. The king realizes how greedy he has been and rewards the potter and washerman generously. RECOMMENDATION: The dialogue is easy for younger age groups to understand and follow, and it exposes them to the customs of a different culture. ROYALTY: Free to Plays subscribers. SOURCE: Winther, Barbara. (1976, April). White elephant. Plays: The Drama Magazine for Young People, pp. 45-51. SUBJECTS/PLAY TYPE: Folk Tales, Burma; Industriousness; Playlet.

3429. 4-6. (+) Pourchot, Mary Ellen. **White House Christmas.** CAST: 3f, 4m. ACTS: 1. SETTINGS: Sitting room. PLAYING TIME: 20 min. PLOT: President Roosevelt's children want a Christmas tree in the White House, but the President refuses because he is trying to preserve the nation's forests. The children secretly bring the tree in through the window and decorate it for Christmas without the President knowing. The next day they show it to him as a surprise, and he lets them keep it. RECOMMENDATION: This captures the expansive and impressive nature of Theodore Roosevelt. ROYALTY: Free to Plays subscribers. SOURCE: Pourchot, Mary Ellen. (1981, December). White House Christmas. Plays: The Drama Magazine for Young People, pp. 45-53. SUBJECTS/PLAY TYPE: Christmas; Roosevelt, Theodore; Playlet.

3430. 1-3*. (-) Gotwalt, Helen Louise Miller. **The White House rabbit.** CAST: 5f, 8m. ACTS: 1. SETTINGS: Flower bed. PLAYING TIME: 20 min. PLOT: Mr. Rabbit and his friends explain how the annual tradition of rolling eggs on the White House lawn started as a surprise arranged by President Hayes' children. The gardener was alarmed at rabbits in the White House garden but, eventually, Mr. Rabbit was able to convince Mrs. Hayes that the hundreds of colored eggs the rabbits brought could be used in an Easter egg hunt for the children of Washington, D.C. RECOMMENDATION: Suitable for young children still receiving visits from the Easter Bunny, this glimpse into its origins is very interesting. ROYALTY: Free to plays subscribers. SOURCE: Gotwalt, Helen Louise Miller. (1986, March). The White House rabbit. Plays: The Drama Magazine for Young People, pp. 37-42. SUBJECTS/PLAY TYPE: Easter; Skit.

3431. 5-8. (+) Murray, John. **The whitemarsh affair.** CAST: 4f, 4m. ACTS: 1. SETTINGS: Living room. PLAYING TIME: 20 min. PLOT: The home of a female spy for the Continental Army is occupied by British soldiers. In her efforts to alert the Continental Army of impending attack, she gains the admiration of one British aide. Sacrificing his position, he looks the other way as a group escapes to warn the Army. RECOMMENDATION: Good historical points are made by believable characters who bring history alive on a personal level. ROYALTY: Free to Plays subscribers. SOURCE: Murray, John. (1986, January/February). The whitemarsh affair. Plays: The Drama Magazine for Young People, 42-50. SUBJECTS/PLAY TYPE: Revolution, U.S.; Playlet.

3432. 3-7. (+) Willment, Frank. **The whites of their eyes.** CAST: 10f, 9m. ACTS: 1. SETTINGS: Theater stage. PLAYING TIME: 20 min. PLOT: Amidst the confusion of rehearsal, a group of young actors is confronted with creditors. The patriotic play is doomed to failure until Polly wins a phone contest by answering a question about early American history. RECOMMENDATION: This has a flavor of the 1940s and is fast paced with some funny lines. ROYALTY: NA. SOURCE: Kamerman, Sylvia E. (1975). Patriotic and historical plays for young people. Boston, MA: Plays, Inc. SUBJECTS/PLAY TYPE: History, U.S.; Theater; Comedy.

3433. 9-12. (+) Scanlan, Michael. **Who.** CAST: 3f, 2m. ACTS: 1. SETTINGS: None. PLAYING TIME: 30 min. PLOT: Zach, confused about his identity, has adopted a nickname in spite of opposition from his mother, friends, and teacher. Believing that changing names gives one a new start in life, he also renames his girlfriend, Lisa, as Edna, but Lisa insists on using her true name. Still confused and rebellious, Zach defies his mother, who is always proper, and attends the "Who" concert where he is trampled to death in the crowd. Still confused, he wonders what name will be put on his gravestone. RECOMMENDATION: The characters are realistic and well developed as they depict common identity problems of teenagers. ROYALTY: $15. SOURCE: Scanlan, Michael. (1984). Inside/out. Hollywood, CA: Samuel French. SUBJECTS/PLAY TYPE: Identity; Death; Drama.

3434. 6-12+. (+) Campton, David. **Who calls?** CAST: 6f. ACTS: 1. SETTINGS: Kitchen. PLAYING TIME: NA. PLOT: Each member of a household staff is affected differently by the death of the tyrannical Mistress. The Mistress's ill gotten jewels are coveted by all. As the four servants talk, the cook realizes that the housekeeper and the lady's maid have stolen jewels from the corpse and she demands a cut. As they come to an understanding, the bell which calls the servants to the mistress's room rings. The servants try to force the scullery maid to investigate, but she is too terrified to enter the room and returns to the kitchen. The mistress bursts in demanding her jewels and drops dead on the floor, as the bell rings again. RECOMMENDATION: This ghost story dramatizes the relationship between guilt and fear. Although some of the scenes are not believable and the characters are a bit one dimensional, this is suspenseful and may stimulate an awareness in each viewer of his/her own mercenary impulses. ROYALTY: $20. SOURCE: Campton, David. (1980). Who calls? Chicago, IL: Dramatic Pub. Co. SUBJECTS/PLAY TYPE: Ghosts; Mystery; Drama.

3435. 1-6. (+) Fisher, Aileen Lucia. **Who is it?** CAST: 1f, 1m, 12u. ACTS: 1. SETTINGS: None. PLAYING TIME: NA. PLOT: A question and answer format relates information about Benjamin Franklin's life and his contributions to colonial America. RECOMMENDATION: Although brief, this manages to convey many pertinent facts. ROYALTY: Free to Plays subscribers. SOURCE: Fisher, Aileen Lucia. (1985). Year-round programs for young players. Boston, MA: Plays, Inc. SUBJECTS/PLAY TYPE: Franklin, Benjamin; Skit.

3436. 4-6. (+) McCaslin, Nellie. **Who laughs last?** CAST: 5f, 5m, 2u. ACTS: 1. SETTINGS: None. PLAYING TIME: NA. PLOT: The king and queen realize that the court jester is too old because all his jokes are old. The jester and his wife are given a cottage with the promise that they will be financially taken care of. Forgotten by the court, the starving jester and his wife play jokes on the king and queen, making them laugh and reminding them of their promise. RECOMMENDATION: The comedy makes this fun, but does not detract from the serious point about remembering our commitments to care for those among us who cannot care for themselves, and to respect the elderly. ROYALTY: Write the author. SOURCE:

Jennings, Coleman A. and Harris, Aurand. (1988). Plays children love, Volume II. New York, NY: St. Martin's Press. **SUBJECTS/PLAY TYPE**: Comedy; Kindness; Elderly; Playlet.

3437. 4-8. (+) Phend, Julie M. **Who stole the tarts?** **CAST**: 5f, 5m, 5u. **ACTS**: 1. **SETTINGS**: Throne room; garden. **PLAYING TIME**: 20 min. **PLOT**: The Queen of Hearts places the King on a diet and won't allow him to have the tarts she's baked for the ball that evening in honor of their daughter Princess Marianne's sixteenth birthday. The King won't allow Marianne invite the Knave of Hearts to the ball, because the nursery rhyme says he stole the tarts. The thief turns out to be the hungry King himself who, after his discovery, gives his permission for Marianne and the Knave to marry. **RECOMMENDATION**: This delicious extension of the familiar nursery rhyme, with its large cast, also allows for much audience participation. **ROYALTY**: Free to Plays Subscribers. **SOURCE**: Phend, Julie M. (1980, February). Who stole the tarts? Plays: The Drama Magazine for Young People, pp. 31-38. **SUBJECTS/PLAY TYPE**: Nursery Rhymes; Comedy.

3438. K-3. (+) Kennedy, X.J. **Who to pet and who not to.** **CAST**: 1u. **ACTS**: 1. **SETTINGS**: None. **PLAYING TIME**: NA. **PLOT**: The reason for not petting a porcupine is presented with sticky humor. **RECOMMENDATION**: Individually amusing, this can also be presented with others of Bauer's "Animal Antics." **ROYALTY**: NA. **SOURCE**: Bauer, Caroline Feller. (1987). Presenting reader's theater: Plays and poems to read aloud. New York, NY: H.W. Wilson. **SUBJECTS/PLAY TYPE**: Porcupines; Reader's Theater.

3439. 3-6. (+) Winther, Barbara. **Who wears the necklace now?** **CAST**: 13u. **ACTS**: 1. **SETTINGS**: Bare stage, backdrop. **PLAYING TIME**: 20 min. **PLOT**: A Memusi warrior trades his necklace to the Hare for a spearhead. Antelope steals Hare's new necklace. Hare asks fire, water, elephant, termites and hyenas to help him retrieve it, but to no avail. Hare finally tricks Antelope into giving the necklace back, and Antelope is eaten by the hyenas. **RECOMMENDATION**: The repetitions of the Chorus throughout will be entertaining, and the interactions between the Hare and the other characters are fun. This African tale presents some interesting African culture within its universal message about greed. **ROYALTY**: Free to Plays subscribers. **SOURCE**: Winther, Barbara. (1986, May). Who wears the necklace now? Plays: The Drama Magazine for Young People, pp. 32-36. **SUBJECTS/PLAY TYPE**: Animals; Greed; Folk Tales, Africa.

3440. 2-4. (+) Carlson, Bernice Wells. **Who would steal a penny?** **CAST**: 4f, 3m. **ACTS**: 1. **SETTINGS**: Room. **PLAYING TIME**: 10 min. **PLOT**: At a gathering of a coin and stamp club, a girl blames her best friend when a rare penny disappears, and then finds that the coin was merely misplaced. **RECOMMENDATION**: This ends with the line, "What's the big idea?" Audience response is welcomed before the moral, social courtesy, is revealed. **ROYALTY**: None. **SOURCE**: Carlson, Bernice Wells.

(1982). Let's find the big idea. Nashville, TN: Abingdon Press. **SUBJECTS/PLAY TYPE**: Friendship; Courtesy; Skit.

3441. 7-12. (+) Schaaf, Albert K. **Who's minding the store.** **CAST**: 7f, 6m, 2u. **ACTS**: 1. **SETTINGS**: Book department. **PLAYING TIME**: 30 min. **PLOT**: A string of thefts occurs in a department store and a mysterious man claims to know how the thieves are gaining access to the store. The man is revealed to have been living in the department store, and helps catch the thieves. When offered permanent residence in the store, he refuses because he is going to visit his aunt, who resides in the Houston Astrodome. **RECOMMENDATION**: Dual plots occur simultaneously to keep the audience attentive. The part of Miss Werbley, the book department clerk, provides the majority of the humor. **ROYALTY**: Free to Plays subscribers. **SOURCE**: Schaaf, Albert K. (1984, March). Who's minding the store? Plays: The Drama Magazine for Young People, pp. 1-12. **SUBJECTS/PLAY TYPE**: Mystery; Comedy.

3442. 7-12. (+) Seay, James L. (Gilles, Harold J.) **Who's on first.** (Who's on first) **CAST**: 3u. **ACTS**: 1. **SETTINGS**: Baseball park. **PLAYING TIME**: NA. **PLOT**: A reporter interviews the manager of a baseball team, but becomes frustrated as the interview progresses because he cannot understand the manager's responses to his questions, as the manager does a variation on the old "Who's On First" comedy routine. The reporter finally leaves without a news article. **RECOMMENDATION**: The characters can be played by either sex as the success of the play relies on fast line delivery. **ROYALTY**: $15. **SOURCE**: Seay, James L. (1975). Who's on first. Elgin, IL: Performance Pub. Co. **SUBJECTS/PLAY TYPE**: Baseball; Skit.

3443. K-6. (+) Carlson, Bernice Wells. **Who's stronger.** **CAST**: 3u. **ACTS**: 1. **SETTINGS**: Outdoors. **PLAYING TIME**: NA. **PLOT**: The sun and the north wind try to prove who is the strongest by seeing who can make a person take his coat off. The wind tries unsuccessfully to blow it off; the sun succeeds by making the person too hot to wear it. **RECOMMENDATION**: The valuable lesson that "gentle persuasion is stronger than force" is imaginatively presented here. **ROYALTY**: NA. **SOURCE**: Carlson, Bernice Wells. (1982). Let's find the big idea. Nashville, TN: Abingdon. **SUBJECTS/PLAY TYPE**: Fable; Persuasion; Skit.

3444. 9-12. (-) Smith, Larry. **Whodunit.** **CAST**: 3f, 4m. **ACTS**: 1. **SETTINGS**: Room. **PLAYING TIME**: 35 min. **PLOT**: A motley group of characters coincidentally stumbles into a gothic house during a thunderstorm, in which a murder will soon occur. **RECOMMENDATION**: Although this is not a well developed, suspenseful, or even engaging murder mystery, the unsatisfactory climax is redeemed by action filled comic mayhem. Sensitive subjects, such as extra-marital affairs and prostitution, are present. **ROYALTY**: $15. **SOURCE**: Smith, Larry. (1977). Whodunit. Santa Fe Springs, CA: Hunter Press. **SUBJECTS/PLAY TYPE**: Murder; Mystery.

3445. 3-6. (+) Carlson, Bernice Wells. **The whole truth.** **CAST**: 5u. **ACTS**: 1. **SETTINGS**: Jungle. **PLAYING TIME**:

NA. PLOT: A lion asks the other animals if he has bad breath. One says yes and another says no. The lion kills both, one for being nasty and the other for lying. The fox claims he cannot answer because he has a cold, and his life is spared. RECOMMENDATION: "If you can't say something nice, change the subject," is the sage advice wonderfully dramatized here. ROYALTY: NA. SOURCE: Carlson, Bernice Wells. (1982). Let's find the big idea. Nashville, TN: Abingdon. SUBJECTS/PLAY TYPE: Fable; Courtesy; Skit.

3446. 4-8. (+) Kochiss, Joseph P. **Whose mummy are you?** CAST: 8f, 11m. ACTS: 2. SETTINGS: Egyptian reception room. PLAYING TIME: NA. PLOT: An Egyptian teenager and his American friends read an ancient incantation aloud and accidentally revive two mummies: Teppi, a friendly teenage boy; and Kharoom, an evil and angry mummy who wants revenge on Teppi, who caused his death 4,000 years earlier. Kharoom is under the control of a hotel employee, who attempts to manipulate the situation. Kharoom tries to kill the teenagers because they know he is alive, but he is once again "killed" by Teppi. RECOMMENDATION: A clearly preposterous situation is saved by action fast and frightening enough to entertain younger children. Teppi is quite humorous since his part is done entirely in pantomime. The setting is exotic and the characters quirky. ROYALTY: $35. SOURCE: Kochiss, Joseph P. (1980). Whose mummy are you? Chicago, IL: Dramatic Pub. Co. SUBJECTS/PLAY TYPE: Comedy; Mummies; Ancient Egypt; Suspense.

3447. 9-12*. (-) Gregg, Stephen. **Why do we laugh?** CAST: 4f, 4m. ACTS: 1. SETTINGS: Bare stage. PLAYING TIME: NA. PLOT: This follows (although not in chronological order), a couple through their youth, teenage, middle age, and older years. The husband as a youngster asks, "Why do we laugh?" at a situation which is not funny to him. The wife as a young girl answers, "We just do." At the end, it is evident that their essential personalities never changed. The husband has always been sensitive and inquiring, while the wife, seemingly in control of their lives, is not thoughtful and is influenced by convention. RECOMMENDATION: The changes in age are not handled smoothly, as the years fluctuate from one age to another with no pattern. The point of the play is quite opaque, as are the jokes, meaningful comments, and racist/sexist scenes. ROYALTY: NA. SOURCE: Gregg, Stephen. (1983). Why do we laugh? Woodstock, IL: Dramatic Pub. Co. SUBJECTS/PLAY TYPE: Aging; Personality; Drama.

3448. 3-6. (+) Fisk, Dorothea. **Why the lion roars.** CAST: 3f, Su. ACTS: 1. SETTINGS: Bare stage. PLAYING TIME: 15 min. PLOT: A clever rabbit devises a plan to save his animal friends from the lion who is able to disguise his voice as a sheep to trick them. The rabbit convinces the lion that his aunt is dying and that he must go to her to get his fortune. The rabbit has the lion follow him, leads the lion to a beehive, entices the lion to nap, then spreads honey all over him. The bees return and, angered by the loss of their honey, sting the lion. The lion's voice sounds like thunder from that time on. RECOMMENDATION: This ends with a bang.

ROYALTY: Free to Plays Subscribers. SOURCE: Fisk, Dorothea. (1980, January). Why the lion roars. Plays: The Drama Magazine for Young People, pp. 49-52. SUBJECTS/PLAY TYPE: Lions; Folk Tales, Swahili.

3449. K-6. (+) Mahlman, Lewis & Jones, David Cadwalader. (Asbjornsen, Peter C. and Moe, Jorgen) **Why the sea is salt.** (Why the sea is salt) CAST: 2f, 4m, 3u. ACTS: 1. SETTINGS: Ocean floor; cottage in Norway; outside mansion; sea. PLAYING TIME: 15 min. PLOT: A poor man and his wife obtain a magic mill that grinds out wishes if the word "Please" is said, and stops when "Thank You" is said. A greedy brother steals the mill and, not knowing the proper words, causes his own destruction when he turns the sea to salt, and his ship sinks. RECOMMENDATION: The elements of legend and of good triumphing over evil are appealingly presented. ROYALTY: Free to Plays subscribers. SOURCE: Mahlman, Lewis, & Jones, David Cadwalader. (1987, April). Why the sea is salt. Plays: The Drama Magazine for Young People, pp. 38-42. SUBJECTS/PLAY TYPE: Folk Tales, Norway; Adaptation; Puppet Play.

3450. 9-12. (+) Owens, Rochelle. **The widow and the colonel.** CAST: 3f, 2m, Su. ACTS: 1. SETTINGS: Ballroom; sitting room; dining room; porch. PLAYING TIME: NA. PLOT: Martha, a young widow with two young children, and Colonel Washington, a sick and discouraged soldier having an unsatisfying affair with a lovely married woman, are introduced by a common friend who encourages the romance. RECOMMENDATION: Originally written for radio, the lengthy soliloquies might not hold the interest of a contemporary audience. However, audience fascination with the rarely told story of this famous couple may make the play work anyway. ROYALTY: $20. SOURCE: Owens, Rochelle. (1977). The widow and the colonel. New York, NY: Dramatists Play Service, Inc. SUBJECTS/PLAY TYPE: Washington, George; Washington, Martha; Drama.

3451. 6-12. (+) Keeney, C. H. **The widow's might, or, what happened to Henry.** CAST: 3f, 2m. ACTS: 1. SETTINGS: Saloon. PLAYING TIME: 30 min. PLOT: Harriet Highgrade and her innocent daughter, Semura, bravely struggle to retain their saloon and mine after the mysterious death of Henry Highgrade. The evil villain, Rock Bottom, and his not-too-bright accomplice, Penelope Prude, plan to take over after Rock seduces Demura. Their plans are foiled by the plucky widow and Oliver Upright, the town sheriff, using the latest investigative techniques from the correspondence course that Oliver is taking. RECOMMENDATION: Proper costuming and staging are a must. ROYALTY: $5. SOURCE: Keeney, C. H. (1977). The widow's might, or, what happened to Henry. Denver, CO: Pioneer Drama Service. SUBJECTS/PLAY TYPE: Western; Swindlers and Swindling; Comedy.

3452. 2-6. (+) Merten, Elizabeth. **Wiggie in the jungle.** CAST: 2f, 2m. ACTS: 1. SETTINGS: Jungle. PLAYING TIME: NA. PLOT: When a piglet is lost, her encounter with jungle animals produces comic results. RECOMMENDATION: The colorful, whimsical story is easy to produce with sock or hand puppets, and its characters are most appealing. ROYALTY: None. SOURCE: Merten, George. (1979). Plays for puppet performance. Boston, MA: Plays, Inc. SUBJECTS/PLAY TYPE: Pigs; Family; Jungle; Animals; Puppet Play.

3453. K-2. (+) Martin, Judith & Ashwander, Donald. **Wiggle worm's surprise. CAST:** Su. **ACTS:** 1. **SETTINGS:** Bare stage. **PLAYING TIME:** NA. **PLOT:** The wiggle worm comes to cheer up the forest occupants during their midwinter doldrums. When the woodcutters arrive, he tickles the rocks, trees and leaves until they laugh and wiggle. This frightens the woodcutters into leaving the forest, saving the life of Big Tree. **RECOMMENDATION:** This has unlimited parts that could be filled by any size school group and two simple songs the entire cast could sing. **ROYALTY:** $10. **SOURCE:** Martin, Judith & Donald Ashwander. (1977). Wiggle worm's surprise. New Orleans, LA: Anchorage Press, Inc. **SUBJECTS/PLAY TYPE:** Christmas; Winter; Musical; Skit.

3454. 4-8. (+) Boiko, Claire. **The wild Indian and the gentleman's gentleman. CAST:** 7f, 4m. **ACTS:** 1. **SETTINGS:** Parlor. **PLAYING TIME:** 30 min. **PLOT:** Jeremy is the bane of his spinster aunts' existence until he inherits Alfred Bundle, a butler who tames and redirects the mischievous boy's energy. **RECOMMENDATION:** An amusing tale reminiscent of "Dennis the Menace," this will be easily produced. Short musical interludes are included, but the songs are set to familiar tunes. **ROYALTY:** Free to Plays subscribers. **SOURCE:** Boiko, Claire. (1975, May). The wild Indian and the gentleman's gentleman. Plays: The Drama Magazine for Young People, pp. 39-48. **SUBJECTS/PLAY TYPE:** Mischief; Inheritances; Butlers; Comedy.

3455. 10-12. (+) Nolan, Paul T. (O'Keefe, John) **Wild oats.** (Wild oats) **CAST:** 3f, 6m. **ACTS:** 1. **SETTINGS:** Living room. **PLAYING TIME:** 30 min. **PLOT:** Jack Rover, a traveling actor who thinks he is an orphan, is mistaken for Sir Harry Thunder and meets Lady Amaranth. They fall in love and she encourages him to perform for her. The real Sir Harry Thunder, who has been calling himself Dick Buskin, shows up with his father, Sir George Thunder. Neither Jack Rover nor Lady Amaranth knows that Dick Buskin is really Sir Harry, but she knows her Uncle, Sir George. The real Sir Harry tricks everyone so Jack can marry Lady Amaranth, but the plan fails when Sir George's servant, John, finds out about Sir Harry, and Lady Amaranth finds out about Jack. An older woman, Cynthia, appears. Lost for many years, she is really Sir George's first wife and Jack Rover is her son who had been lost at sea. Jack finds his parents, a brother, and a rich wife, and he gets his play ready for performance. **RECOMMENDATION:** The dialog is in the style of the 18th century and there are many quotes from Shakespeare's plays. The plot becomes confusing toward the end but does finally clarify itself. This would be better performed by and for older adolescents because they are more able to identify with the characters and theme. **ROYALTY:** Free to Plays Subscribers. **SOURCE:** Nolan, Paul T. (1980, January). Wild oats. Plays: The Drama Magazine for Young People, pp. 70-80. **SUBJECTS/PLAY**

TYPE: Comedy; Mistaken Identity; Swindlers and Swindling; Adaptation.

3456. 12. (+) McLure, James. (O'Keefe, John) **Wild oats.** (Wild oats) **CAST:** 6f, 23m. **ACTS:** 2. **SETTINGS:** Saloon; farmhouse; desert. **PLAYING TIME:** NA. **PLOT:** Col. Thunder and his faithful Irish-Indian sidekick, Crow, wander the Old West of the 1880s searching for deserters from the seventh cavalry. Thunder's son, Harry, recently expelled from West Point, returns west as "Dick Buckskin," a member of a traveling theatrical troupe. Another member of the group, Jack Rover, is mistaken for Harry by Harry's cousin, Kate, who has recently inherited a small fortune. With the help of many lines from Shakespeare, they fall in love. Mistaken identities and deliberate impersonations multiply. Harry and Jack turn out to be half brothers and all is happily sorted out. **RECOMMENDATION:** Broad humor, hammy asides, and coincidences make this a genuinely funny play for high school and adult audiences. Its necessarily rapid pace and occasionally lengthy, demanding lines put it beyond the abilities of all but the most dedicated and skilled high school casts. **ROYALTY:** NA. **SOURCE:** McLure, James. (1985). Wild Oats. New York, NY: Dramatists Play Service. **SUBJECTS/PLAY TYPE:** Comedy; Mistaken Identity; Swindlers and Swindling; Musical; Adaptation.

3457. 4-6. (+) Thane, Adele. (Andersen, Hans Christian) **The wild swans.** (The wild swans) **CAST:** 4f, 6m. **ACTS:** 1. **SETTINGS:** Cottage; courtyard. **PLAYING TIME:** 25 min. **PLOT:** Princess Elisa must save her three brothers, who have been turned into wild swans by their wicked stepmother. To break the spell, Elisa must weave three flaxen coats from stinging nettles, and toss them over her brothers. A king falls in love with Elisa and asks her to be his queen; she agrees to marry him in one year, provided he does not question her task, for she must keep the reason for her weaving a secret in order to break the spell. At the end of one year, Elisa completes the coats, breaks the spell, and weds the king. **RECOMMENDATION:** Although the production notes suggest rather involved costuming and staging, the play could be produced more simply and still be understood and enjoyed. **ROYALTY:** Free to Plays subscribers. **SOURCE:** Thane, Adele. (1981, January). The wild swans. Plays: The Drama Magazine for Young People, pp. 49-57. **SUBJECTS/PLAY TYPE:** Folk Tales, Denmark; Adaptation.

3458. 1-6. (+) Molter, Alice. (Stokes, Jack) **Wiley and the hairy man.** (Wiley and the hairy man) **CAST:** 1f, 2m, Su. **ACTS:** 1. **SETTINGS:** Bare stage. **PLAYING TIME:** 35 min. **PLOT:** This dramatizes, in poetic form, the tale of Wiley, and how he tricks the hairy man three times, so he won't frighten Wiley again. **RECOMMENDATION:** This unusual verse adaptation has rapid contrapuntal dialogue and pantomime style action, very effective on a bare stage. The emphasis on creative interpretation rather than elaborate staging and costumes makes this an excellent production for theater classes. **ROYALTY:** $20. **SOURCE:** Molter, Alice. (1970). Wiley and the hairy man. Chicago, IL: Coach House Press, Inc. **SUBJECTS/PLAY TYPE:** Folk Tales, American; Comedy; Adaptation.

3459. 3-7. (+) Grinins, Tekla A. **Will the real Abraham Lincoln please stand up?** CAST: 4m, 9u. ACTS: 1. SETTINGS: Game show. PLAYING TIME: 15 min. PLOT: In this takeoff on the old "to Tell the Truth" game show, contestants must identify the real Lincoln. RECOMMENDATION: The facts from Lincoln's life make this appropriate for study of Lincoln or for a Presidents' Day pageant. ROYALTY: Free to Plays subscribers. SOURCE: Grinins, Tekla A. (1977, February). Will the real Abraham Lincoln please stand up? Plays: The Drama Magazine for Young People, pp. 71-74. SUBJECTS/PLAY TYPE: Lincoln, Abraham; Skit.

3460. 1-4. (+) Steinhorn, Harriet & Lowry, Edith. **Will we be free?** CAST: 5f, 4m, 1u. ACTS: 1. SETTINGS: Ghetto courtyard. PLAYING TIME: 10 min. PLOT: Jewish children in a Polish ghetto during World War II discuss how hungry they are, how they look forward to the end of the war, and all the wonderful things they will be able to do when they are free again. The narrator informs the audience that the children all died in the death camp at Treblinka. RECOMMENDATION: This describes, in terms that young children could understand, the hardships of ghetto life. ROYALTY: Free for amateur groups. SOURCE: Steinhorn, Harriet & Lowry, Edith. (1983). Shadows of the holocaust: Plays, readings, and program resources. Rockville, MD: Kar-Ben Copies, Inc. SUBJECTS/PLAY TYPE: World War II; Ghetto Life; Holocaust; Skit.

3461. 4-9. (+) Stockdale, Marina. **William's window.** CAST: 14f, 20m, 16u. ACTS: 2. SETTINGS: Backyard. PLAYING TIME: 60 min. PLOT: Sandy tells her friends that they can enjoy many of Shakespeare's stories by using their imaginations. With Sandy's help, they bring to life scenes from different plays. RECOMMENDATION: The scenes are brief and the plots are explained in the transitional dialogue. The production is very flexible; scenes may be deleted, and doubling is possible for smaller groups. ROYALTY: $25. SOURCE: Stockdale, Marina. (1983). William's window. Schulenburg, TX: I.E. Clark. SUBJECTS/PLAY TYPE: Shakespeare, William; Drama.

3462. K-7. (+) Baldwin, Joseph. (Grahame, Kenneth) **The wind in the willows.** (The wind in the willows) CAST: 17u. ACTS: 2. SETTINGS: Countryside; Toad Hall; dungeon; woods. PLAYING TIME: 75 min. PLOT: Spendthrift, car loving Toad mends his wild and foolish ways with the help and devotion of his faithful friends. Together they rescue Portly Otter and Toad Hall from the mean greedy weasels. RECOMMENDATION: This sparkling adaptation comes to life with much jubilant action sprinkled with humorous lively prose. Since the play is rather long, it is not appropriate for production by the younger grades. ROYALTY: $50. SOURCE: Baldwin, Joseph. (1966). The wind in the willows. Woodstock, IL: Dramatic Pub. Co. SUBJECTS/PLAY TYPE: Animals; Comedy; Adaptation.

3463. 1-6. (+) Hulett, Michael. (Grahame, Kenneth) **The wind in the willows.** (The wind in the willows) CAST: 5u. ACTS: 11. SETTINGS: Riverbank; open road; courtroom; Rat's house; prison; woods; railway; Toad Hall. PLAYING TIME: 90 min. PLOT: The irrepressible Toad becomes involved in a series of adventures which worry his friends, Rat, Mole, and Badger. RECOMMENDATION: This delightful musical adaptation should appeal with its charming song lyrics and minimal audience participation. Although there are a variety of scenes, the settings can be kept simple enough to easily rearrange for each new scene. ROYALTY: $50. SOURCE: Hulett, Michael. (1982). The wind in the willows. Denver, CO: Pioneer Drama Service. SUBJECTS/PLAY TYPE: Animals; Adventure; Musical; Adaptation.

3464. K-6*. (+) Goldberg, Moses. (Grahame, Kenneth) **Wind in the willows.** (The wind in the willows) CAST: 1f, 7m. ACTS: 1. SETTINGS: Rat's house; road; woods; badger's house; Toad Hall; street; jail cell. PLAYING TIME: NA. PLOT: Mole has recently moved in with Rat, who is showing Mole the wonders of the above ground world. They set off for a quiet picnic with Otter when the impetuous Toad sails in, pretending to ride a horse. His equestrian interests soon shift to automobiles, which he buys and wrecks in rapid succession. The other animals, concerned with Toad's violent and destructive pastimes, visit the old Badger for advice, but their problems are soon complicated when the evil weasels kidnap Mole and wreck Toad's family mansion. Badger leads them to a secret passage in Toad Hall and they frighten away the weasels and procure a dubious promise from Toad to choose his hobbies more carefully. RECOMMENDATION: In the process of condensing, there have been some changes from Grahame's original. Due to the 11 fairly substantial scene changes and the in depth characterization, adults would need to be the actors and producers. However, children will enjoy this immensely. ROYALTY: Write to Anchorage Press. SOURCE: Jennings, Coleman A. and Harris, Aurand. (1988). Play children love, volume II. New York, NY: St. Martin's Press. SUBJECTS/PLAY TYPE: Animals; Adventure; Adaptation.

3465. 3-10. (+) Peterson, Liz. (Grahame, Kenneth) **The wind in the willows.** (The wind in the willows) CAST: 12u. ACTS: 1. SETTINGS: Hills; hole. PLAYING TIME: 70 min. PLOT: Animal friends sitting on the riverbank encounter Toad, furiously rowing his boat. Involved with boat racing at the time, Toad's interest switches to gypsy caravans as the season progresses. An unfortunate collision with a motorcar brings about another abrupt change of focus to cars. This passion is Toad's downfall, as he "borrows" a motorcar, frightens some animals, and talks back to the arresting officer. Toad is sent to prison, but the jailor's daughter helps him escape. Beginning to see the error of his ways, Toad wants to go home, but his house has been taken over by weasels and ferrets. With the aid of his friends, Toad defeats the intruders. RECOMMENDATION: Toad, Mole, Water Rat, and Badger all have human characteristics that everyone will recognize. This would be enjoyed by all but, because of its length, would probably best be produced by middle school children. The props could be a problem. The script calls for a cart, a boat, a motorcar, and a caravan with a shaft sturdy enough for Toad to ride. Various members of the cast have songs to sing. ROYALTY: $35. SOURCE: Peterson, Liz. (1984). The wind in the willows. Morton Grove, IL: Coach House Press. SUBJECTS/PLAY TYPE: Animals; Musical; Adventure; Adaptation.

3466. 1-6*. (+) Williams, Guy. (Grahame, Kenneth) **The wind in the willows.** (The wind in the willows) CAST: 3f, Su. ACTS: 1. SETTINGS: Woods; Toad Hall; courtroom; prison cell; inn. PLAYING TIME: NA. PLOT: Toad steals a car and is sentenced to 20 years in prison. Fearful that the Stoats and Weasels will take over Toad Hall, four friends take turns keeping watch, but are overpowered and forced into the night. Meanwhile, Toad escapes prison dressed as a washwoman and reaches Rat's house, plans a secret attack through an underground tunnel, and wins back the Hall. RECOMMENDATION: Although this follows the classic story closely, a noticeable difference is that the descriptive writing in the book is able to create a warmth and charm for the characters and countryside which this play cannot match. Still, the lovable characters come though and make this an enjoyable introduction to the story. This can be presented as a play or as a round the table reading. ROYALTY: NA. SOURCE: Williams, Guy. (1986). The wind in the willows. London: Macmillan Education Ltd. SUBJECTS/PLAY TYPE: Animals; Adventure; Dramascript; Adaptation.

3467. K-10. (-) Foon, Dennis. **The windigo.** CAST: 2f, 2m, 5u. ACTS: 1. SETTINGS: Bare stage. PLAYING TIME: NA. PLOT: This is an adaptation of an Objibway Indian tale about the Windigo, the spirit of hunger. When hunger strikes, Windigo is said to turn a man into a beast who kills and devours his family and friends when they appear, to him, to be giant beavers. Half Sky encounters the Windigo during a harsh winter in which he fails as a hunter to provide for his family; he is able to overcome the spirit. RECOMMENDATION: The symbolism and grimness of this tale make this play inappropriate for the younger children for whom it is intended. It may work as a ghost story for the older ones who will enjoy the frightening aspects of the tale but may not understand the symbolism. ROYALTY: NA. SOURCE: Foon, Dennis. (1978). The windigo. Toronto: Playwright's Co-op. SUBJECTS/PLAY TYPE: Folk Tales, Native American; Supernatural; Drama.

3468. K-8. (+) Barnes, Linda J. **Wings.** CAST: 2f, 2m, Su. ACTS: 1. SETTINGS: None. PLAYING TIME: NA. PLOT: A mother and father bird encourage their baby to use his wings and leave the nest. His initial attempt ends in failure, and the scene shifts to different children who are frustrated in their attempts to "fly" because of societal roles. At the end, the baby bird, now a daddy, encourages his own baby in her attempts to be whatever she wants to be. RECOMMENDATION: The theme of opposing traditional roles for men and women has been done over and over and, although this doesn't shed any new insights on the topic, it does an especially good job of bringing the message to younger children in short, concise, easy to identify scenes. While recommended for elementary and junior high school children, the cast would need to be seventh grade or older. ROYALTY: $10. SOURCE: Barnes,

Linda J. (1974). Wings. Boston, MA: Baker's Plays. SUBJECTS/PLAY TYPE: Stereotypes; Sex Roles; Parable.

3469. 11-12. (+) Kopit, Arthur. **Wings.** CAST: 5f, 4m. ACTS: 1. SETTINGS: Home; hospital; therapy room. PLAYING TIME: NA. PLOT: Mrs. Emily Stilson, a woman in her 70s and a former Wingwalker who has suffered a massive stroke, relates her experiences in the hospital and in therapy from her perspective. RECOMMENDATION: Emily's disorientation and loss of a sense of time and space are created through the use of special lighting techniques and sounds. Emily's speech is garbled, but becomes more comprehensible as she recovers. To emphasize her confusion, Emily's speech may be normal and the doctor's speech garbled. To be successful, great care must be taken to make the audience understand that it is Emily's inner experience that is being presented. This was originally staged as a radio play which means that the use of sounds of all kinds are extremely important. ROYALTY: $50. SOURCE: Kopit, Arthur. (1978). Wings. New York, NY: Samuel French. SUBJECTS/PLAY TYPE: Strokes; Aphasia; Drama.

3470. 2-8. (+) Sroda, Anne. **Wings for the king.** CAST: 1f, 5m. ACTS: 1. SETTINGS: Castle hall. PLAYING TIME: 20 min. PLOT: The bored king offers a bag of gold to the person who helps him fly. He tries different types of wings but none works. Eventually, someone brings the king picture books of far away lands and claims the prize, as the king learns that books are wings to the land of knowledge. RECOMMENDATION: Traditional fairy tale costumes and the opportunity to design their own wings make this delightful presentation one in which all can be involved. ROYALTY: Free to Plays subscribers. SOURCE: Sroda, Anne. (1975, November). Wings for the king. Plays: The Drama Magazine for Young People, pp. 39-44. SUBJECTS/PLAY TYPE: Flight; Reading; Book Week; Playlet.

3471. 3-10. (+) Kehret, Peg. **The winner.** CAST: 1u. ACTS: 1. SETTINGS: None. PLAYING TIME: NA. PLOT: A youngster describes his feelings after his excellent poem loses in a competition to a girl who plagiarized. RECOMMENDATION: Well written, this monologue could open a discussion on creative writing, plagiarism, or fair competition. ROYALTY: NA. SOURCE: Kehret, Peg. (1986). Winning monologs for young actors. Colorado Springs, CO: Meriwether Pub. SUBJECTS/PLAY TYPE: Competition; Writing; Plagiarism; Monologue.

3472. 7-12. (+) Naylor, Phyllis Reynolds. **The winners.** CAST: 3f, 5m, 1u. ACTS: 1. SETTINGS: Bare stage. PLAYING TIME: 12 min. PLOT: At the annual Christmas give-away at Farley's Department Store, the winners choose gifts other than the ones offered, such as no more animal fur coats and access for the handicapped. RECOMMENDATION: Best performed for church groups, the play's message of concern for others is straightforward. ROYALTY: None. SOURCE: Altena, Hans. (1978). The playbook for Christian theatre. Grand Rapids, Michigan: Baker Book House. SUBJECTS/PLAY TYPE: Christmas; Energy Conservation; Skit.

3473. K-4*. (+) Sergel, Kristin. (Milne, A.A.) **Winnie the Pooh.** (Winnie the Pooh) CAST: 2f, 2m, 10u. ACTS: 3. SETTINGS: Bare stage. PLAYING TIME: NA. PLOT: Stuffed animals come to life and enter the stage, discussing newcomers, Kanga and Roo. Kanga is a very maternal being who wants to take care of all the animals by bathing them and enhancing their diet with "strengthening medicine." Roo spots a new playmate in Piglet, to whom Kanga gives a bath before Roo is permitted to play with him. The animals discuss Piglet's plight and how to rescue him. Pooh goes to Rabbit's home where he finds Roo, who has run away from home. After eating too much, Pooh gets stuck trying to leave the rabbit hole, but is freed by the animals and Christopher. Roo is hidden and the animals debate how to rescue Piglet. Pooh exchanges himself for Piglet, reluctantly submits to a bath, and is given the "strengthening formula" which he realizes contains honey. He drinks the entire bottle and asks for more, but Kanga's concern for having enough to give her own child leads her to tell Pooh that she cannot take care of him, after all. RECOMMENDATION: This follows the original closely and includes many of the original lines. The play's emphasis is on the interactions between Kanga and Roo. ROYALTY: Write to The Dramatic Pub. Co. SOURCE: Jennings, Coleman A. and Harris, Aurand. (1988). Plays children love, Volume II. New York, NY: St. Martin's Press. SUBJECTS/PLAY TYPE: Animals; Adaptation.

3474. 7-12. (-) Snelling, Dorothy. **Winning combination.** CAST: 6f, 10m, Su. ACTS: 1. SETTINGS: Classroom; auditorium. PLAYING TIME: 30 min. PLOT: Michael Rowen, successful writer and lecturer, reminisces about high school, where he learned meditation from the school genius, and then used it to pick Penelope, instead of his girlfriend (now wife) as the winner of the beauty contest. He reflects on the basic lesson that "we're all part of the universe and part of each other," so we should make choices that cause the least unhappiness. RECOMMENDATION: This very dated piece is disjointed, makes fun of meditation and Hinduism, and is a lame excuse for a presentation about decision making. ROYALTY: Free to Plays subscribers. SOURCE: Snelling, Dorothy. (1982). Winning combination. Plays: The drama magazine for young people, pp. 19-28. SUBJECTS/PLAY TYPE: Choices; Comedy.

3475. 7-12. (+) Miller, Ev. **Winning season.** CAST: 7f, 8m. ACTS: 1. SETTINGS: Meeting room. PLAYING TIME: NA. PLOT: A citizen's group asks to discuss with the school board the dismissal of three players from the winning basketball team due to a charge of alcohol possession. Two of the parents have hired a lawyer and want the boys reinstated to the team until the trial takes place. The coach disapproves of rule bending and threatens to leave the team. Everyone is upset with the coach, until the mother of one of the boys admits that all three had been drinking. The board still passes the reinstatement, although all know for certain that the rules were broken. RECOMMENDATION: This thought provoking drama's realistic dialogue could lead to discussion of several topics: sports worship, alcohol, or rules. ROYALTY: $15. SOURCE: Miller, Ev. (1983).

Winning season. Elgin, IL: Performance Pub. Co. SUBJECTS/PLAY TYPE: Alcohol; School Sports; Rules; Drama.

3476. K-2*. (+) Balcken, Frances. **Winter carnival.** CAST: 12u. ACTS: 1. SETTINGS: Puppet stage. PLAYING TIME: 15 min. PLOT: The crystal ball has been stolen from the Ice Palace in Winterland; if it is not found, the Palace will melt. The Silver Witch took it because she was angry at not being invited to the Winter Carnival, and when she gets her invitation, all is saved. RECOMMENDATION: Although this will have to be produced by children of at least fifth grade age, it will delight the younger children with its humor and with the lovely names of the characters. ROYALTY: Free to Plays subscribers. SOURCE: Balcken, Frances. (1979, February). Winter carnival. Plays: The Drama Magazine for Young People, pp. 65-69. SUBJECTS/PLAY TYPE: Fantasy; Puppet Play.

3477. 2-6. (+) Wartski, Maureen Crane. **Winter's vacation.** CAST: 2m, 13u. ACTS: 1. SETTINGS: Office. PLAYING TIME: 15 min. PLOT: Chief Weather inventories the elements and discovers that winter is missing. A boy locates winter vacationing in Florida and pleads that winter return. Winter agrees when he discovers that he is not disliked as he had believed, but is cherished by all. RECOMMENDATION: This imaginative approach to teaching children about the seasons uses simple characters and language. Preparing the costumes would be great fun. ROYALTY: Free to Plays subscribers. SOURCE: Wartski, Maureen Crane. (1982, November). Winter's vacation. Plays: The Drama Magazine for Young People, pp. 39-43. SUBJECTS/PLAY TYPE: Seasons; Playlet.

3478. 1-6. (+) Murphy, Helen A. **The wise and clever maiden.** CAST: 1f, 2m, 6u. ACTS: 1. SETTINGS: Courtroom. PLAYING TIME: 20 min. PLOT: A maiden and a farmer have jointly inherited a piece of land. The king awards the land to the farmer, and convinces the maiden to live with him in the palace for one month, at the end of which time she will decide whether to marry him. She decides to return home and chooses the king as the one item she may take home with her as a present. RECOMMENDATION: A delightful romance, this will enchant its audience, while amusing viewers with the clever maiden's doings. The dialogue is simple, but lengthy enough to challenge upper elementary aged children. ROYALTY: NA. SOURCE: Kamerman, Sylvia E. (1987). Plays from favorite folk tales. Boston, MA: Plays, Inc. SUBJECTS/PLAY TYPE: Folk Tale Motifs; Playlet.

3479. 1-6. (+) Winther, Barbara. **The wise man of Baghdad.** CAST: 3f, 3m, 2u. ACTS: 1. SETTINGS: Bare stage, backdrop. PLAYING TIME: 20 min. PLOT: This recounts two folk tales about the clever Persian poet, Abu Nuwas, who died in 810 A.D. In the first story, Abu Nuwas determines which of four likely suspects has stolen Haiji's shoes by having each secretly pull the mint scented tail of his donkey who, he says, will bray at the true thief. Haiji's wife does not touch the tail since she is the thief and doesn't want the donkey to bray. When her hands do not smell like mint, she is exposed. In the second story, Abu borrows a pot from Haiji, who gives him the one with a hole in it hoping that Abu will repair it before bringing it back. Abu does not, but tricks Haiji into believing the pot gave birth to a smaller pot without a hole in it. Haiji loans Abu a better pot in hopes that the miracle will happen again, but Abu keeps the second loan, telling Haiji it died and was thrown in the river. RECOMMENDATION: This effectively captures the mood of the original with its stylized language and dialogue. The poetic justices are satisfying and the exposition just complex enough. ROYALTY: Free to Plays subscribers. SOURCE: Winther, Barbara. (1977, May). The wise man of Baghdad. Plays: The Drama Magazine for Young People, pp. 44-50. SUBJECTS/PLAY TYPE: Nuwas, Abu; Folk Tales, Persia; Playlet.

3480. 7-12. (+) Lieberman, Douglas. (Tenenbaum, Samuel) **The wise men of Chelm.** (The wise men of Chelm) CAST: 5f, 8m, 2u. ACTS: 2. SETTINGS: None. PLAYING TIME: 9 min. PLOT: In Chelm, a place where an angel of god inadvertently deposited heaven's collection of fools, a dark stranger appears with his starving cow. When the Rabbi drops a gold coin beneath the cow, the villagers are convinced that the animal produces money rather than milk. While they wait for the cow's udders to fill with gold, the people of Chelm commit many foolish acts. After many adventures, a blacksmith returns to Chelm with a treasure of 20,000 feathers. He wins the hand of the mayor's daughter and the village is restored to its natural state of happy confusion. RECOMMENDATION: This good humored folk tale of simple (and slightly deranged) Jewish peasants whose wisdom is foolish but hovers on the profound, never sacrifices humanity in the search for a laugh. The play has several musical interludes. Although the audience probably won't go home humming the tunes, the Eastern European flavor compliments the Yiddish dialect of the villagers. Success rests on a critical sense of comic timing. ROYALTY: $50. SOURCE: Lieberman, Douglas. (1985). The wise men of Chelm. Chicago, IL: Coach House Press. SUBJECTS/PLAY TYPE: Folk Tales, Jewish; Wisdom; Foolishness; Adaptation.

3481. K-4. (+) Brown, Abbie Farwell. **The wishing moon.** CAST: 4f, 3m, 9u. ACTS: 1. SETTINGS: Glade on woods' edge. PLAYING TIME: NA. PLOT: Children walk through the woods seeking a fairy who, if captured, will have to grant them their wishes, because it is the time of the "wishing moon." Level headed Belle knows it is better to earn things for yourself and refuses to join in the hunt. The others come upon Busy Bee, a fairy who turns the magic against the greedy children and freezes them. Belle returns and Busy Bee is so impressed by the girl's unselfish nature that she grants Belle's wish that the children be freed. They then leave the woods, with a greater sense of respect for the fairies. RECOMMENDATION: Although didactic, this is still charming. The dialogue is short and rhymed, making it easily memorized by beginning actors. ROYALTY: NA. SOURCE: Brown, Abbie Farwell. (1978). The lantern and other plays for children. New York, NY: Cora Collection Books. SUBJECTS/PLAY TYPE: Fairies; Wishes; Selfishness; Fantasy.

3482. K-4. (+) Gotwalt, Helen Louise Miller. **The wishing stream.** CAST: 2f, 2m, Su. ACTS: 1. SETTINGS: Bare stage, props. PLAYING TIME: 15 min. PLOT: Two brothers and a sister make wishes, but only the sister's is granted because it is for someone else. RECOMMENDATION: This employs the "prop man" to bring things on and off stage, and it uses verse to provide humor and interest. ROYALTY: None. SOURCE: Gotwalt, Helen Louise Miller. (1985). First plays for children: A collection of little plays for the youngest players. Boston, MA: Plays, Inc. SUBJECTS/PLAY TYPE: Wishes; Playlet.

3483. 7-12. (+) Fendrich, Shubert. **The wishing tree.** CAST: 5f, 3m. ACTS: 1. SETTINGS: Shopping mall; employee lounge. PLAYING TIME: 60 min. PLOT: Characters deplore the loss of the magical vision of Christmas which accompanies the loss of childhood, and feel contempt for the haste and materialism which has come to be associated with the holiday season. Each yearns for the financial means to obtain a special gift for another. Nick encourages each to write the wish on a card and attach it to the "wishing tree." In return, unbeknownst to the workers until the surprise Christmas revelation, Mrs. Hotchkiss, the efficient and aloof mall manager, assuages her own holiday loneliness and grief after the death of her husband by granting each of the wishes. Nick is then able to entice Mrs. Hotchkiss' daughter home for a Christmas visit. RECOMMENDATION: An inspiring musical slice of life, this holiday play includes allusions to contemporary movies, songs, and persons which provide a fresh, current appeal for the teenage audience. Care must be taken to ensure that the melodic interludes be performed in a sincere, spirited manner so they do not become gushy or weepy. ROYALTY: $35. SOURCE: Fendrich, Shubert. (1988). The wishing tree. Denver, CO: Pioneer Drama Service. SUBJECTS/PLAY TYPE: Christmas; Comedy; Musical.

3484. 8-12. (+) Brooks, Hindi. **Wising up!** CAST: 8f, 7m. ACTS: 2. SETTINGS: Interior of a group home; alley; room. PLAYING TIME: NA. PLOT: The home for troubled teenagers fights to retain custody of Chico, a Hispanic boy branded retarded by Social Service authorities because of his difficulties with the English language. At the same time, trouble is about to descend on the Lodge in the forms of a teenage prostitute and a drug addict/dealer. The play expresses the sobering message that good intentions and naive love are not always sufficient to mend damaged lives. RECOMMENDATION: Although less tightly crafted than **Making it!**, most of the main characters are well developed. Problems might arise with the two counselors who are amorphous individuals, acted upon rather than acting throughout the play. The heavy topics covered-- suicide, drug addiction, teenage prostitution, racial and ethnic prejudice, betrayal, retardation, and class barriers, among others--will promote much discussion. ROYALTY: $50. SOURCE: Brooks, Hindi. (1986). Wising up! Schulenburg, TX: I. E. Clark. SUBJECTS/PLAY TYPE: Juvenile Delinquency; Drug Addiction; Troubled Teenagers; Drama.

3485. 1-6. (+) Dunham, Sherrie. **The witch and the scarecrow.** CAST: 1f, 5u. ACTS: 1. SETTINGS: Cornfield. PLAYING TIME: 18 min. PLOT: A witch and scarecrow exchange places on Halloween night. The witch encounters a fault finding farmer, while the scarecrow goes for a wild ride with the witch's cat. Both decide that exchanging roles was a terrible idea. RECOMMENDATION: Characterizations of the vain, lazy witch and the scarecrow are interesting and unconventional. ROYALTY: Free to Plays subscribers. SOURCE: Dunham, Sherrie. (1981, October). The witch and the scarecrow. Plays: The Drama Magazine for Young People, pp. 33- 38. SUBJECTS/PLAY TYPE: Halloween; Comedy.

3486. 3-7. (+) Priore, Frank V. **Witch way did they go?** CAST: 4f, 1m. ACTS: 1. SETTINGS: Living room. PLAYING TIME: 20 min. PLOT: Two witches appear at the door of a couple's new home to inform them that they will have to leave because their house has been built on top of the witches' annual meeting place. The couple refuses to leave, and are about to be turned into toads when the wife refuses to become a witch. Just in time, the head witch arrives and announces that the meeting has been moved to a piece of land she has just bought. RECOMMENDATION: This has many one liners which are effective. However, a pentagram drawn on the living room floor may cause problems for some audiences. ROYALTY: Free to Plays subscribers. SOURCE: Priore, Frank V. (1983, October). Witch way did they go? Plays: The Drama Magazine for Young People, 56-60. SUBJECTS/PLAY TYPE: Halloween; Witches; Comedy; Skit.

3487. 2-6. (+) Dye, Sally. **The witch who stole Christmas.** CAST: 14f, 5m, 11u. ACTS: 1. SETTINGS: Large meeting. PLAYING TIME: 20 min. PLOT: Well known fairy tale characters plan a Christmas party, but do not invite the Wicked Witch. When she finds out, she erases Christmas from everyone's mind and eliminates all the Christmas trees and the toy stores. Santa tries to help, but the Witch steals his sleigh. Together, the characters change the witch's spell so that anyone believing in magic will remember Christmas. RECOMMENDATION: This has some funny lines, and is different from the traditional Christmas stories. It would be a good choice for fifth or sixth graders to put on for the younger children. ROYALTY: Free to Plays subscribers. SOURCE: Dye, Sally. (1981, December). The witch who stole Christmas. Plays: The Drama Magazine for Young People, pp. 54-60. SUBJECTS/PLAY TYPE: Folk Tale Characters; Magic; Christmas; Skit.

3488. 11-12*. (-) Pielmeier, John. **A witch's brew.** CAST: 1f, 2m. ACTS: 1. SETTINGS: Basement. PLAYING TIME: NA. PLOT: A brother, sister, and the sister's boyfriend visit after their mother's death. They play a childhood game: eating food in the dark and describing each piece as being a particular body part. As they finish, Jule realizes that what they have just eaten may have been their mother. RECOMMENDATION: This cannibalistic horror tale is so disgusting that it may be inappropriate for any audience. It has no redemptive subplots to alleviate

the horror. ROYALTY: NA. SOURCE: Pielmeier, John. (1984). Haunted lives. New York, NY: Dramatists Play Service, Inc. SUBJECTS/PLAY TYPE: Horror; Death; Cannibalism; Drama.

3489. 9-12. (+) Mauro, Robert. **A witch's tale.** CAST: 1f. ACTS: 1. SETTINGS: Bare stage, props. PLAYING TIME: 10 min. PLOT: A witch explains why she became a psychiatrist, and elaborates on family history, especially her great-great-great-great-great-Grandmother's witch trial in Salem. RECOMMENDATION: This deals with the historical mistreatment of extraordinary women using natural, contemporary language. ROYALTY: Free to Plays subscribers. SOURCE: Mauro, Robert. (1984, October). A witch's tale. Plays: The Drama Magazine for Young People, pp. 52-54. SUBJECTS/PLAY TYPE: Halloween; Women's Rights; Witches; Monologue.

3490. 3-6. (+) Asher, Sandra Fenichel. **Witling and the stone princess.** CAST: 7f, 6m, Su. ACTS: 1. SETTINGS: Throne room. PLAYING TIME: 25 min. PLOT: King Wally's daughters have been turned into stone by the Witch of Wormart and he asks King Stephen, who has three sons, to see if they will save the princesses. Each of the Princes set off to help King Wally; however, the first two, Yawn and Fritter, are easily discouraged. Prince Witling battles the Witch of Wormwood's two curses, ants and ducks, to discover which Princess was eating honey before she was turned into stone. Using the knowledge obtained from bees, he correctly identifies the Princess Amelia, so that the curse is removed, and marriage results. RECOMMENDATION: Based on well known motifs, and using humorously overdrawn characters with under exaggerated dialogue, this might be better acted by older students. ROYALTY: Free to Plays subscribers. SOURCE: Asher, Sandra Fenichel. (1979, January). Witling and the stone princess. Plays: The Drama Magazine for Young People, pp. 41-49. SUBJECTS/PLAY TYPE: Witches; Curses; Folk Tale Motifs; Playlet.

3491. 11-12*. (+) Taylor, Charles G. **Witness.** CAST: 5f, Sm. ACTS: 1. SETTINGS: Bare stage, platforms. PLAYING TIME: 40 min. PLOT: In this modern Passion Play, the narrator dreams that he played major roles (such as Judas, a Roman guard, and a priest) in the last days of Christ. Major episodes from the New Testament are re-enacted. RECOMMENDATION: Some of the burden of memorizing has been taken from the narrator by the creative use of a prerecorded voice-over. Because the narrator plays so many roles, great care must be exercised to ensure that each part is clearly identifiable. The acting is probably best left to adults, for a church group, with time for discussion after the performance. ROYALTY: $15. SOURCE: Taylor, Charles G. (1978). Witness. Schulenburg, TX: I.E. Clark. SUBJECTS/PLAY TYPE: Christ, Jesus; Passion Play; Bible Stories; Christian Drama.

3492. 3-8. (+) Endersby, Clive. (Baum, Frank L.) **The wizard of Oz.** (The wonderful wizard of Oz) CAST: 1f, Su. ACTS: 1. SETTINGS: Bare stage, props. PLAYING TIME: NA. PLOT: Lost in Oz, Dorothy meets Head and Dread, a scarecrow, a tin man, and a lion after she inadvertently kills the wicked witch. On their way to get help from the wizard, they must cross a large piano by stepping on the right keys, weather a rainstorm, counteract their having stepped on a magic spot that shrinks its victims, and flee a vacuum cleaner that tries to suck them up. The wizard tells them they must kill the witch before he will help them. They do, and Dorothy returns home happily, after her friends get what they wanted. RECOMMENDATION: This is faithful to Baum's original, but is quite different than the movie. This would have to be performed by adults and children, as some of the parts are long and the special effects are sophisticated. ROYALTY: NA. SOURCE: Endersby, Clive. (1978). Alice and the wizard of Oz; Two plays for young audiences. Toronto: Playwrights Canada. SUBJECTS/PLAY TYPE: Fantasy; Witches; Adaptation.

3493. 1-7. (+) Hotchner, Stephen. (Baum, Lyman Frank) The wizard of Oz. (The wonderful Wizard of Oz) CAST: 1f, 5u. ACTS: 1. SETTINGS: Land of Oz. PLAYING TIME: 30 min. PLOT: Dorothy is held captive by the Wicked Witch, and the Tin Man, Scarecrow, and Lion ask the audience to help out with various sound effects and to come on stage. The children hold hands and fight off an attack by monkeys. Dorothy discovers the Witch's horror of water and the Witch becomes a puddle when Dorothy throws a bucket of water on her. Dorothy rescues her friends and together they set out to look for the Wizard. RECOMMENDATION: This outstanding play hinges on audience participation. Its depiction of the Wizard as a child shows that children are important people. ROYALTY: $10. SOURCE: Hotchner, Stephen. (1975). The wizard of Oz. Denver, CO: Pioneer Drama Service. SUBJECTS/PLAY TYPE: Adventure; Witches; Adaptation; Participation Play..

3494. K-12. (+) Jackson, R. Eugene. (Baum, Lyman Frank) The wizard of Oz. (The wonderful wizard of Oz) CAST: 6f, 3m, 13u. ACTS: 2. SETTINGS: Plains; cornfield; forest; Emerald City; throne room; castle. PLAYING TIME: 60 min. PLOT: In this faithful adaptation, Dorothy and Toto are swept away from their home in Kansas by a cyclone to a magical land where they meet a lion, scarecrow, tin man, witches, and a wizard. After many adventures, they find a way back to Kansas. RECOMMENDATION: Seven different sets, multiple properties, and simple but specific costumes make this a challenge. Audiences will again be reminded of the values of friendship, cooperation, and belief in others and themselves. Older elementary children should perform this, but all children (and children at heart) will enjoy it. ROYALTY: $35. SOURCE: Jackson, R. Eugene. (1977). The wizard of Oz. Schulenburg, TX; I.E. Clark. SUBJECTS/PLAY TYPE: Adventure; Witches; Adaptation.

3495. 3-6*. (-) Landes, William-Alan & Standish, Marilyn. (Baum, Lyman Frank) The wizard of Oz. (The wonderful wizard of Oz) CAST: 3f, 7m, Su. ACTS: 2. SETTINGS: Forest, ravine; witch's castle; Emerald City; wizard's throne room. PLAYING TIME: 60 min. PLOT: Dorothy and her new found friends help each other against the evil witch. They discover, in the end, that they didn't need the wizard to give them what each was after. RECOMMENDATION: The plays' gymnastics, many

scenes, lighting requirements, high levels of coordination between actors (including choreography), and ad libbing with the audience practically preclude production within a limited budget. This condensed version is apt to fall short of expectations. ROYALTY: $35. SOURCE: Landes, William-Alan & Standish, Marilyn. (1980). The wizard of Oz. Studio City, CA: Players Press. SUBJECTS/PLAY TYPE: Adventure; Witches; Musical; Adaptation.

3496. 1-8. (+) Mahlman, Lewis & Jones, David Cadwalader. (Baum, Lyman Frank) The wizard of Oz. (The wonderful wizard of Oz) CAST: 13u. ACTS: 1. SETTINGS: Puppet Stage with backdrop. PLAYING TIME: 20 min. PLOT: Dorothy and Toto are carried by a cyclone into Munchkinland, where she accidentally kills the Wicked Witch. The Good Witch gives her the Wicked Witch's silver shoes and sends her to the Wizard to discover how to return to Kansas. Scarecrow, the Tin Woodsman, and Cowardly Lion accompany her in hopes of gaining a brain, a heart, and courage. The wizard offers to provide these gifts only if they kill the other Wicked Witch. They do so and return to Oz, only to find that the wizard is a fake, but find that they are able to fulfill their own wishes. RECOMMENDATION: This faithful adaptation can be performed using either simple or elaborate puppets. Due to the number of scene changes, it may be above the production capabilities of younger elementary aged children. ROYALTY: Free to Plays subscribers. SOURCE: Mahlman, Lewis & Jones, David Cadwalader. (1976, February). Plays: The Drama Magazine for Young People, pp. 55-64. SUBJECTS/PLAY TYPE: Adventure; Witches; Adaptation.

3497. 7-12. (+) Martens, Anne Coulter. (Baum, Lyman Frank) The wizard of Oz. (The wonderful wizard of Oz) CAST: 8f, 7m, Su. ACTS: 4. SETTINGS: Oz; wizard's throne room; kitchen. PLAYING TIME: NA. PLOT: This adaptation follows the movie plot line closely. RECOMMENDATION: The director will be challenged by the props, scenery and costuming, but special effects can be produced with good lighting, sound reproductions on record or tape, and a fan for the tornado winds. ROYALTY: NA. SOURCE: Coleman, Jennings & Harris, Aurand. (1988). Plays children love. New York, NY: St. Martin's Press. SUBJECTS/PLAY TYPE: Adventure; Witches; Adaptation.

3498. 3-6. (+) Schwartz, Lynne Sharon. (Baum, Lyman Frank) The wizard of Oz. (The wonderful wizard of Oz) CAST: 6f, 6m, Su. ACTS: 1. SETTINGS: Field; throne room; courtyard; castle parlor. PLAYING TIME: 30 min. PLOT: Dorothy and Toto are carried by a cyclone to Oz, where they make friends with a scarecrow, a tin woodsman, and a lion. Together, they search for the wizard. The wizard proves to be a fake, but he still helps Dorothy's friends and Glinda, the Good Witch, helps Dorothy return to Kansas. RECOMMENDATION: This condensed version preserves the adventurous spirit and fantasy of the original, but the terror of the events is absent. Children who have read the original or seen the famous movie will find this dull in comparison. But, it does tell the story at a primary school acting level. ROYALTY: Free to Plays subscribers. SOURCE: Schwartz,

Lynne Sharon. (1982, April). The wizard of Oz. Plays: The Drama Magazine for Young People, pp. 45-58. SUBJECTS/PLAY TYPE: Adventure; Witches; Adaptation.

3499. K-3. (+) Parson, Nancy. **The wizard of Whiz-Bang.** CAST: 1f, 1m, 4u. ACTS: 1. SETTINGS: Wizard's house and yard. PLAYING TIME: 10 min. PLOT: In spite of his wife's complaints about his messy and poorly compensated vocation, the wizard invents a wonderfully tasting new food, which the neighbors help him name. Since it's cold as ice and smooth as cream they call it ice cream. RECOMMENDATION: The wizard's antics provide enough distraction to mask the obvious ending and make it a surprise. ROYALTY: Free to Plays subscribers. SOURCE: Parsons, Nancy. (1977, March). The wizard of Whiz-Bang. Plays: The Drama Magazine for Young People, pp. 46-48. SUBJECTS/PLAY TYPE: Ice Cream; Inventors; Comedy.

3500. 5-12. (+). Charlton, Peter. **Wolf Boy.** CAST: 1f, 2m, 3u. ACTS: 1. PLAYING TIME: NA. SETTINGS: Bare stage, props. PLOT: In this dramatization of Dr. Itard's famous education of Victor, the "wild boy," Victor is taught the difference between good and bad, as well as how to communicate with sign language. RECOMMENDATION: This asks whether the civilized group is modern man with his desire to make everyone like him, or the unwilling victims of society's desire to uplift the masses. The focus is on this, rather than on the famous work that Dr. Itard pioneered. The part of Victor will require a great deal of acting ability. ROYALTY: Write to author. SOURCE: Lonie, John. (1985). Learning from life. Sydney, Australia: Currency Press. SUBJECTS/PLAY TYPE: Civilization; Itard, John; Drama.

3501. 4-6. (+) Hatton, Thomas. (Aesopus) **Wolf! Wolf! Wolf!** (The boy who cried wolf) CAST: 3f, 2m, 5u. ACTS: 1. SETTINGS: Pasture. PLAYING TIME: 12 min. PLOT: After the wolf tricks a boy into calling wolf twice, the farmers (who have not seen the wolf) say they won't come back until they hear the wolf howl. The wolf, thinking that the entire flock is now a free dinner, is tricked by the boy into howling, and the farmers catch him. RECOMMENDATION: The moral is that it's all right to trick a trickster. ROYALTY: Free to Plays subscribers. SOURCE: Hatton, Thomas. (1983, April). Plays: The Drama Magazine for Young People, pp. 67-73. SUBJECTS/PLAY TYPE: Fable; Wolves; Skit; Adaptation.

3502. 10-12. (+) Murray, John. **The woman who owned the west.** CAST: 9f, 6m. ACTS: 1. SETTINGS: Office; living room of hotel suite. PLAYING TIME: 35 min. PLOT: Aunt Hattie discovers a deed to all the land in the western U.S., which was passed down to her by Native American relatives. She contacts her Senator, a self serving misuser of the office, who tries to discredit her and her claim. Aunt Hattie is not ruffled by the publicity and greed generated by her document, nor is she surprised at government confusion, but she decides to relinquish her claim for the good of all Americans. RECOMMENDATION: This humorous political satire would be a reasonable play for students of the problems of democracy or history classes, or for a larger audience.

ROYALTY: None. SOURCE: Murray, John. (1985). Fifteen plays for today's teenagers. SUBJECTS/PLAY TYPE: Politics; Bureaucracy; Political Satire; Comedy.

3503. 11-12. (+) Goldsmith, Gloria. **Woman- speak.** CAST: 12f. ACTS: 1. SETTINGS: None. PLAYING TIME: 30 min. PLOT: This presents a collage of the thoughts and feelings of American women through a dialogue between a contemporary woman and women from America's past including Abigail Adams, Sojourner Truth, Susan B. Anthony, Margaret Sanger, and Eleanor Roosevelt. RECOMMENDATION: This cerebral play could supplement women's history units. It offers the opportunity for more creative students to design powerful musical and visual backdrops which support the feminist theme. ROYALTY: $15. SOURCE: Goldsmith, Gloria. (1976). Womanspeak. Denver, CO: Pioneer Drama Service. SUBJECTS/PLAY TYPE: Women's History; Drama.

3504. 10-12. (+) Grote, David. (Euripedes) **The women of Troy.** (The Trojan women) CAST: 10f, 3m, Su. ACTS: 1. SETTINGS: Bare stage, backdrop. PLOT: The Greeks have won the Trojan War and all of Troy has been destroyed. The few surviving women are captives and will become slaves. A short and bitter meeting between two survivors, Helen and Hecuba, is detailed. Hecuba has lost her family and her freedom, but learns to accept her fate. RECOMMENDATION: This preserves the original intensity of the Greek drama. ROYALTY: $20. SOURCE: Grote, David. (1981). The women of Troy. Woodstock, IL: The Dramatic Pub. Co. SUBJECTS/PLAY TYPE: Greek Tragedy; Trojan War; Adaptation.

3505. 12. (+) Orr, Mary. **Women still weep.** CAST: 7f. ACTS: 1. SETTINGS: Home library. PLOT: The history of the Lindsey family is related through the deaths of male family members in the Civil War, the Spanish American War, World War I and World War II. The women carry on. However, the latest war in Vietnam takes the life of 18 year old Anne Lindsey, killed by a blow to her head during an anti-war rally at the local high school on the "home front." RECOMMENDATION: This intriguing play is recommended particularly for groups interested in women's issues. ROYALTY: NA. SOURCE: Orr, Mary. (1980). Women still weep. New York, NY: Dramatists Play Service. SUBJECTS/PLAY TYPE: Women; American Military History; Anti-War; Drama.

3506. 3-8. (-) Bradley, Virginia. **Women's lib comes to the hill country.** CAST: 4u. ACTS: 1. SETTINGS: Mountain cabin. PLOT: Now that liberated women are even lazier than the mountain men, they can't be troubled even to leave a burning building. RECOMMENDATION: The stereotypes about women's lib and mountain people are too insulting for this play to be recommended. ROYALTY: None. SOURCE: Bradley, Virginia. (1975). Is there an actor in the house? New York, NY: Dodd, Mead. SUBJECTS/PLAY TYPE: Women's Liberation Movement; Comedy; Puppet Play.

3507. 3-7. (+) Boiko, Claire. **The wonderful circus of words.** CAST: 1f, 3m, 24u. ACTS: 1. SETTINGS: Living room. PLOT: The world of grammar is brought to life in

Jamie's imagination while he does his English homework. The "Flammarian Grammarian" teaches him the basics of sentence composition through a cast of nouns, verbs, adjectives, adverbs, articles and a period, each of which comes forward to embellish an original two-word sentence. RECOMMENDATION: As Jamie develops his sentence into a gripping baseball story, the lesson that grammar makes writing interesting is learned. ROYALTY: Free to Plays subscribers. SOURCE: Boiko, Claire. (1976, November). The wonderful circus of words. Plays: The Drama Magazine for Young People, pp. 47-51. SUBJECTS/PLAY TYPE: Grammar; Skit.

3508. K-12*. (+) Robbins, Norman. **The wonderful story of Mother Goose.** CAST: 6f, 5m, Su. ACTS: 2. SETTINGS: Bare stage, props. PLAYING TIME: NA. PLOT: The Fairy Queen bets her crown that the wicked fairy, Discord, cannot tempt Mother Goose to act only in self interest. Faced with eviction from her home by villain Clarence Creep, the desperately poor and widowed Mother Goose is presented with Priscilla, the goose that lays golden eggs. She shares her fortune, but soon begins to feel lonely, old, ugly, and loved only for her money. Discord offers her eternal youth in exchange for the goose. Mother Goose accepts but, finding that her children loved her for what she was, re-enters the "magic pool" and emerges as she was: old, ugly, and poor. While in the pool, she finds a box containing the will of the late brother of Clarence Creep, deeding the town properties to his son, Colin. Discord is banished from Fairyland, Clarence Creep is disgraced, Priscilla returns to Mother Goose, and Colin and Mother Goose's daughter prepare to marry. RECOMMENDATION: Presented as an English pantomime, this combines fairy tale and burlesque, with strong emphasis on spectacle, song, and dance. Written to be understood on many levels, the dialogue is replete with puns and jokes, audience asides, audience participation, and references to local places and people, celebrities, and recent films. Though actual production should be done by adults, children could be included in smaller parts or in choral or dance troupes. Some British references and jokes may need to be adapted for American audiences and some slapstick humor, such as Mother Goose's striptease, may be deleted. ROYALTY: NA. SOURCE: Robbins, Norma. (1986). The wonderful story of Mother Goose. London: Samuel French. SUBJECTS/PLAY TYPE: Mother Goose; Burlesque; British Pantomime; Musical.

3509. K-6*. (+) Kelly, Tim. (Baum, Lyman Frank) **The wonderful wizard of Oz.** (The wonderful wizard of Oz) CAST: 3f, 2m, Su. ACTS: 2. SETTINGS: Road; forest; palace of Oz; witch's castle. PLAYING TIME: 90 min. PLOT: A faithful adaptation of the well loved story. RECOMMENDATION: This would be good for older students to perform for children. The casting can be flexible (with up to 16 characters of either sex), and the sets and properties are simple. Costuming will be a challenge, with good opportunity for creativity. There are some roles in which younger children could be cast, such as the winged monkeys and the munchkins. ROYALTY: $35. SOURCE: Kelly, Tim. (1977). The wonderful wizard of Oz. Denver, CO: Pioneer Drama Service. SUBJECTS/PLAY TYPE: Adventure; Witches; Adaptation.

3510. 4-6. (+) Newman, Deborah. **The wonderful world of Hans Christian Andersen.** CAST: 7f, 11m, Su. ACTS: 1. SETTINGS: Cobbler's home. PLAYING TIME: 20 min. PLOT: Set in Denmark in 1815, this is the story of a little boy who wants to be a famous writer. He tells his stories to family and friends who encourage him. Abbreviated versions of some Anderson favorites are played as little vignettes in the living room of a cobbler's home. RECOMMENDATION: This is a unique way for children to hear a sampling of several stories. It is an effective presentation of the message that creativity is a rare and valuable part of daily life. ROYALTY: Free to Plays subscribers. SOURCE: Newman, Deborah. (1977, March). The wonderful world of Hans Christian Andersen. Plays: The Drama Magazine for Young People, pp. 39-45. SUBJECTS/PLAY TYPE: Creativity; Writers; Playlet.

3511. 1-6*. (+) Brochu, James & Schalchlin, Steven M. **A wonderful worldful of Christmas.** CAST: 2f, 8m, Su. ACTS: 1. SETTINGS: Mexican hotel; department store exterior; home exterior. PLOT: It's Christmas Eve and Billy and his sister, Janie, cannot mail Billy's letter to Santa Claus because the last mail has already gone. Chester, the Magic Mailman, offers to deliver it and, realizing that Janie doesn't like Christmas and doesn't believe in Santa, he takes them along. They detour to pick up letters in Mexico and Austria and, because it is too late to make it to the North Pole, Santa comes to them. Billy delivers his letter in which he has asked for a special doll to give his sister, a generous act that makes his sister a believer. RECOMMENDATION: This has a nice blend of humor (a la Curly, Larry, and Moe from **The three street Santas**), plenty of singing, a taste of Christmas traditions from Mexico and Austria, and magic. Janie is reminiscent of Scrooge, and her brother's generosity brings back thoughts of **The Gift of the Magi**. ROYALTY: Upon application. SOURCE: Brochu, James & Schalchlin, Steven. (1987). A wonderful worldful of Christmas. New York, NY: Samuel French. SUBJECTS/PLAY TYPE: Christmas, Santa Claus; Musical; Fantasy.

3512. 2-3. (-) Marra, Dorothy Brandt. **"Woof" for the red, white and blue.** CAST: 4f, 1m. ACTS: 1. SETTINGS: Street. PLAYING TIME: 15 min. PLOT: After puppies rip the material that Betsy Ross is planning to use for the flag, she designs the flag from the scraps. RECOMMENDATION: This should be performed by older groups. The imaginative explanation for the flag's design is an amusing twist. Even if it is not true, the scenes do provide genuine insight into the time period. ROYALTY: Free to Plays subscribers. SOURCE: Marra, Dorothy Brandt. (1975, May). "Woof" for the red, white and blue. Plays: The Drama Magazine for Young People, pp. 87-90. SUBJECTS/PLAY TYPE: Ross, Betsy; Flag Day; Comedy; Playlet.

3513. K-3. (-) Berkov, Janet Smith. **The world famous treasure divers.** CAST: 3f, 2m. ACTS: 1. SETTINGS: Beach; underwater coral cave. PLAYING TIME: 10 min. PLOT: Three young adults seek sunken treasure off the coral reef in San Salvador. Warned not to venture into a particular part of the reef, the young divers go, nevertheless. Tony is kidnapped, and brought to the underwater coral cave of Princess Neptune, who wants a companion. She explains that there is no treasure except for a sword that fell off a boat long ago. She gives it to Tony and returns him to his friends. Christopher Columbus's name is on the sword, and they are sure they will be famous. RECOMMENDATION: It is doubtful this will hold the attention of even the youngest viewers. The dialogue is forced and unnatural. ROYALTY: Free to Plays subscribers. SOURCE: Berkov, Janet Smith. (1981, October). The world-famous treasure divers. Plays: The Drama Magazine for Young People, pp. 68-70. SUBJECTS/PLAY TYPE: Adventure; Treasure Hunting; Puppet Play.

3514. 2-12. (+) Lane Carolyn. (Grimm Brothers) **The world of the Grimm Brothers.** (Grimm's Fairy Tales) CAST: 3f, 4m, 4u. ACTS: 1. SETTINGS: None. PLAYING TIME: 45 min. PLOT: Three well known stories are woven together in one act: **King Thrushbeard, The fisherman and his wife,** and **The elves and the shoemaker.** RECOMMENDATION: These are successful because they leave intact the intent and significance of the originals. Since very few resources are needed for production, it seems an ideal choice for a traveling production, but should be produced by the upper grades. ROYALTY: $15. SOURCE: Lane, Carolyn. (1979). The world of the Brothers Grimm. Denver, CO: Pioneer Drama Service. SUBJECTS/PLAY TYPE: Folk Tales, Germany; Adaptation.

3515. 4-8. (+) Kehret, Peg. **World's greatest tinfoil collection.** CAST: 1u. ACTS: 1. SETTINGS: None. PLAYING TIME: NA. PLOT: A youngster explains his attempts to set a world record by saving used tinfoil. RECOMMENDATION: The tenacity displayed by the young collector is admirable and an excellent example. ROYALTY: NA. SOURCE: Kehret, Peg. (1986). Winning monologs for young actors. Colorado Springs, CO: Meriwether Pub. SUBJECTS/PLAY TYPE: World Records; Collections; Monologue.

3516. 4-8. (+) Kehret, Peg. **The worm farm.** CAST: 1u. ACTS: 1. SETTINGS: None. PLAYING TIME: NA. PLOT: A youngster describes his questionably profitable worm farm. RECOMMENDATION: An amusing anecdote, this should evoke humorous memories. ROYALTY: NA. SOURCE: Kehret, Peg. (1986). Winning monologs for young actors. Colorado Springs, CO: Meriwether Pub. SUBJECTS/PLAY TYPE: Worms; Money Making; Jobs; Monologue.

3517. 8-12. (+) Gleason, William. **The worst high school play in the world.** CAST: 7f, 9m, Su. ACTS: 2. SETTINGS: Castle grounds; magician's workshop; woods; Abbey courtyard; inn. PLAYING TIME: NA. PLOT: Ivanka, rightful heir to Saxonia's throne, is abandoned as a baby in the Dark Forest in order to save him from his greedy uncle, Viscera, who wants the throne. He is raised by squirrels, then discovered by a kind friar who educates him and returns him to Saxonia to claim the throne and take a wife. RECOMMENDATION: This incredibly funny takeoff on the classic tale is told through the bizarre device of two narrators who eat their way through the entire narration, growing fatter and fatter. Another hilarious dimension is added by off-stage conversations between the play's director, cast, and stagehands. There is no end of fun. ROYALTY: $50. SOURCE: Gleason, William. (1982). The worst high school play in the world. Chicago, IL: Dramatic Pub. Co. SUBJECTS/PLAY TYPE: Folk Tale Motifs; Parody; Comedy.

3518. 3-8*. (-) Waterhouse, Keith & Hall, Willis. **Worzel Gummidge: A musical.** CAST: 3f, 13m, Su. ACTS: 2. SETTINGS: Field, farmhouse, village cottage, village fete, barn, building interior. PLAYING TIME: NA. PLOT: Crowman creates a live scarecrow, Worzel Hedgerow Gummidge. Mr. Peters' two children, Sue and John, become friendly with Worzel, who wants a wife. Worzel falls in love with money-grubbing Mr. Shepherd's Aunt Sally, an antique wooden dummy. He asks her to marry him, but she refuses because she wants a rich mate. At the village fair, Worzel steals Mr. Peters' new blazer in order to appear more attractive to Aunt Sally. The crowd chases Worzel, but Sue and John help him to escape. He hears Aunt Sally crying because Shepherd intends to sell her to an antique dealer in America, yet she is angered when he asks her to marry him again and threatens to burn him. Sue and John tell the Crowman that Worzel is lovesick and cannot perform his job, causing compassionate Crowman to send Worzel and three other live scarecrows to rescue Aunt Sally from Shepherd's attic. Although Worzel risks his life to free her, she gives all the credit to another. He throws a potato at her and accidentally knocks off Crowman's hat, who threatens to take the case to court; Aunt Sally offers to prosecute. Worzel is sentenced to the rubbish heap, but John and Sue save him by showing his compassion for a robin redbreast and her little ones. RECOMMENDATION: Unfortunately, this clever play stands little chance of appealing to an American audience, due to its plethora of obscure British slang. The lead would also need to be able to speak in an approximation of cockney slang. The plot appears to be for elementary to junior high students, as the vocabulary seems to be aimed at that level. Sexist attitudes portray women as shallow and greedy. Production itself would be difficult because of the acrobatics in several scenes, and the lightning pace. ROYALTY: NA. SOURCE: Waterhouse, Keith & Willis, Hall. (1984). Worzel Gunnidge: A musical. London: Samuel French. SUBJECTS/PLAY TYPE: Romance; Fantasy; Halloween; Scarecrows; Musical.

3519. K-2. (+) Prelutsky, Jack. **The wozzit.** CAST: 9u. ACTS: 1. SETTINGS: None. PLAYING TIME: NA. PLOT: Readers take turns describing the antics of the "wozzit," as it wreaks havoc in a closet. RECOMMENDATION: This is a funny, rhymed comedy. ROYALTY: NA. SOURCE: Bauer, Caroline Feller. (1987). Presenting reader's theater: Plays and poems to read aloud. New York, NY: H.W. Wilson Co. SUBJECTS/PLAY TYPE: Imaginary Creatures; Wozzits; Reader's Theater.

3520. K-6. (+) Martin, Judith & Ashwander, Donald. **Wrap around.** CAST: 3u. ACTS: 1. SETTINGS: None. PLAYING TIME: 10 min. PLOT: One character is trapped in a cylinder of cardboard; a second frees her by unrolling the cardboard, but traps herself as she does; a third frees the second, trapping himself in the same way. The third, however, thinks of a way to free himself without trapping anyone else. RECOMMENDATION: Because of the coordination required in rolling, unrolling and supporting the cardboard, older elementary children or junior high schoolers should perform this for younger students. ROYALTY: NA. SOURCE: Martin, Judith & Ashwander, Donald. (1985). Reasons to be cheerful: A revue for children. New York, NY: The Paper Bag Players, Inc. SUBJECTS/PLAY TYPE: Puzzles; Skit; Musical Revue.

3521. 6-8. (+) Hutson, Natalie Bovee. **The wrongful claim.** CAST: 5f, 3m. ACTS: 1. SETTINGS: Living room. PLAYING TIME: 15 min. PLOT: Melody Lark, a maid, finds out she is eligible for a hefty inheritance from her dead uncle. So do the spoiled son and daughter of Melody's employer, who attempt to cash in by having their friends pose as Melody's long lost parents. Their ruse is discovered, as is a new revelation: another member of the household is actually Melody's long lost sister. Melody and her sister inherit the fortune, and Melody marries her beloved gardener. RECOMMENDATION: The characters of this parody of early melodramas are stereotyped to the extremes of good and evil, adding to the comic flavor. Audiences could have great fun with this if encouraged to cheer and boo. ROYALTY: NA. SOURCE: Hutson, Natalie Bovee. (1984). The wrongful claim. Stevensville, MI: Educational Service, Inc. SUBJECTS/PLAY TYPE: Inheritance; Villains; Parody; Melodrama.

3522. 9-12. (-) Olfson, Lewy. (Bronte, Emily) **Wuthering Heights.** (Wuthering Heights) CAST: 2f, 3m. ACTS: 1. SETTINGS: Kitchen. PLAYING TIME: 30 min. PLOT: Cathy, a young gentlelady, has lived her life in the Wuthering Heights mansion on the moor, raised by servants and a brutal brother. Her closest companion has been Heathcliff, a gypsy who was brought as a baby to Wuthering Heights by Cathy's father and is, in status, somewhere between servant and family. Edgar Linton, a gentleman, asks Cathy to marry him and she accepts, although she doesn't really love Linton. She loves Heathcliff, but doesn't want to marry below her station. Heathcliff overhears her say this and dashes out into a storm to disappear on the moor. Three years later, Cathy, failing in health, returns to Wuthering Heights. Heathcliff returns also, now a wealthy gentleman. Cathy and Heathcliff confess their love and also that they destroyed each other. Heathcliff disappears again while Cathy lapses into delirium. RECOMMENDATION: The original Bronte masterpiece defies abridgement, and none of the original's mood or tragedy are captured, nor are the excellent characterizations of the original even minimally achieved in this adaptation. ROYALTY: Free to Plays subscribers. SOURCE: Olfson, Lewy. (1988, May). Wuthering Heights. Plays: The Drama Magazine for Young People, pp. 65-75. SUBJECTS/PLAY TYPE: Love; Adaptation.

3523. 5-12. (+) Harris, Aurand. **Yankee Doodle.** CAST: 2f, 10m. ACTS: 2. SETTINGS: Bare stage. PLAYING TIME: NA. PLOT: In this musical montage of historical events from Paul Revere to Charles Lindbergh, the movers and shakers of America tell their own stories through singing, dancing, and miming.

RECOMMENDATION: This is a humorous, fast paced whirl through interesting parts of American history, from "the shot heard 'round the world" to the invention of the ice cream cone. Little is required in the way of costuming and scenery, but the cast must be able to sing, mime, and keep up the pace of the musical. ROYALTY: $35. SOURCE: Harris, Aurand. (1975). Yankee Doodle Dandy. New Orleans, LA: Anchorage Press, Inc. SUBJECTS/PLAY TYPE: History, U.S.; Presidents, U.S.; Inventors; Musical.

3524. 4-10. (+) Clapp, Patricia. **Yankee Doodle came to Cranetown.** CAST: 2f, 3m, 1u. ACTS: 1. SETTINGS: Colonial kitchen. PLAYING TIME: 35 min. PLOT: General Washington and his troops bivouac at a farm in upper New Jersey, preparing for a surprise attack on the British, but word arrives that the British are on their way to attack them. The farmer's son, lame from childhood, assists General Washington by riding at night to round up local Minute Men. RECOMMENDATION: Not only is this a valuable history teaching aid, but it also shows that there are many ways in which one can contribute to a cause. ROYALTY: Free to Plays subscribers. SOURCE: Clapp, Patricia. (1976, February). Yankee Doodle came to Cranetown. Plays: The Drama Magazine for Young People, pp. 65-77. SUBJECTS/PLAY TYPE: Washington, George; Revolution, U.S.; Playlet.

3525. 7-12. (+) King, Martha Bennett. **Yankee Doodle comes to town.** CAST: 7f, 8m. ACTS: 3. SETTINGS: Garden. PLAYING TIME: 90 min. PLOT: During the American Revolution, freedom fighters convince Lucy she belongs on the side of the colonists and that, as a printer, her skill is vital to the cause. RECOMMENDATION: Written for the bicentennial of the United States, the point that all people can make contributions in a time of crisis is effectively made. ROYALTY: $20. SOURCE: King, Martha Bennett. (1975). Yankee Doodle comes to town. Chicago, IL: Coach House Press. SUBJECTS/PLAY TYPE: Revolution, U.S.; Drama.

3526. 3-5. (+) Harris, Aurand. **Yankee Doodle dandies.** CAST: Su. ACTS: 3. SETTINGS: Bare stage, props. PLAYING TIME: NA. PLOT: John Chapman tells how he, as Johnny Appleseed, planted his trees, gained the respect of the Indians, and died of pneumonia at the age of 70. Harriet Tubman then appears on stage to tell of the underground railroad and the code of songs which she used to advertise it. Finally, Casey tells the story of "Casey at the Bat." RECOMMENDATION: The scenes use pantomime, poetry, choral reading and music to convey the spirit of the time and are an excellent introduction to each of the famous people or events. ROYALTY: Write to Anchorage Press. SOURCE: Jennings, Coleman A. and Harris, Aurand. (1981). Plays children love. New York, NY: Doubleday Co. SUBJECTS/PLAY TYPE: Appleseed, Johnny; Tubman, Harriet; Playlet.

3527. 1-8. (+) Fisher, Aileen. **Yankee doodle dandy.** CAST: 2f, 6m, Su. ACTS: 1. SETTINGS: Street. PLAYING TIME: 10 min. PLOT: This tells the story of the popular Revolutionary War song, which originated as young American soldiers turned the insulting remarks and taunts from the British into a marching song.

RECOMMENDATION: This may be staged as printed, or expanded to include many extras for movement and expression, such as pantomiming marching, playing musical instruments, carrying flags, and riding horses. The audience can sing and clap. The director might have difficulty coordinating all the movement, but the flexibility makes this particularly useful. ROYALTY: NA. SOURCE: Fisher, Aileen. (1975, November). Yankee doodle dandy. Plays: The Drama Magazine for Young People, pp. 79-81. SUBJECTS/PLAY TYPE: Revolution, U.S.; Creative Dramatics.

3528. 6-9. (+) Boiko, Claire. **Yankees vs. Redcoats.** CAST: 16m, Su. ACTS: 1. SETTINGS: Baseball park. PLAYING TIME: 15 min. PLOT: It is the bottom of the ninth inning of a baseball game between the Yankees and the Redcoats. Patrick Henry is announcing; the Redcoats are leading 2-0. Paul Revere and George Washington lead off the inning with hits, but General Greene strikes out and Benedict Arnold trades himself to the Redcoats. Lafayette pinch hits with two outs and hits a three run home run to win the game for the Yankees. RECOMMENDATION: An ingenious vision of history, this will provide memory aids for young students. ROYALTY: Free to Plays subscribers. SOURCE: Boiko, Claire. (1976, May). Yankees vs. Redcoats. Plays: The Drama Magazine for Young People, pp. 63-66. SUBJECTS/PLAY TYPE: Comedy; Baseball; History, U.S.; Skit

3529. K-8. (+) Sampson, Lu. **A year of poems.** CAST: 12u. ACTS: 1. SETTINGS: None. PLAYING TIME: 10 min. PLOT: This collection of poems summarizes the students' scholastic year. Poem topics include Math, Science, Reading, Grammar and Social Studies. RECOMMENDATION: This excellent resource could be enjoyed by the PTA and student body at the conclusion of the school year. ROYALTY: Free to Plays subscribers. SOURCE: Sampson, Lu. (1983, May). A year of poems. Plays: The Drama Magazine for Young People, pp. 61-65. SUBJECTS/PLAY TYPE: School; Choral Reading.

3530. K-4. (+) Marshall, Sheila L. **The year Santa forgot Christmas.** CAST: 2f, 5m, 4u. ACTS: 1. SETTINGS: Santa's workshop. PLAYING TIME: 15 min. PLOT: Willy, a clumsy elf, knocks Santa down, which causes Santa to forget Christmas. Mrs. Claus and the elf try to help Santa remember by telling him Christmas stories and traditions; nothing works. Finally, Willy uses Santa's sleigh to bring Jean, Billy, and Joey to talk to Santa about Christmas, and his memory returns. Santa takes the children back to their homes as he makes his rounds. RECOMMENDATION: Although it depends on the old ruse of selective amnesia caused by a fall, the children for whom this is written will probably accept it. Because of the religious references, this should be performed in church. ROYALTY: Free to Plays subscribers. SOURCE: Marshall, Sheila L. (1977, December). The year Santa forgot Christmas. Plays: The Drama Magazine for Young People, pp. 51-55. SUBJECTS/PLAY TYPE: Christmas; Musical; Comedy.

3531. 10-12. (-) Fendrich, Schubert & Curnow, Paul. **Yearbook.** CAST: 8f, 6m, Su. ACTS: 2. SETTINGS: Gym. PLAYING TIME: 90 min. PLOT: As Jack and Susan flip through the pages of the high school yearbooks, they reminisce about the activities of their senior year, which ranged from the initial confusion of registration, to the awesome sanctity of graduation day and its somber demand for immediate maturity and vision. The festivities of the homecoming dance and the President's Day Assembly provide opportunities for melodic interludes and a melodramatic rendering of the Gettysburg Address. RECOMMENDATION: Trite, unimaginative dialogue, flat characterization, and contrived plot development plague this disjointed collection of scenes which lacks coordination and an obvious central theme. The overblown pageantry of the spectacle commemorating "The Blue and the Grey," highlighted by the delivery of the Gettysburg Address seems grossly out of context. The musical numbers are melodramatic, often maudlin, and the motives and concerns of the characters are dated. Conflicts dissolve and place no demands upon the intellectual faculties or physical prowess of the actors, who speak and move with apparent lack of purpose. ROYALTY: $60. SOURCE: Fendrich, Schubert. (1982). Yearbook. Denver, CO: Pioneer Drama Service. SUBJECTS/PLAY TYPE: High School; Comedy; Musical.

3532. 6-12. (+) Thane, Adele. (Gilbert, William & Sullivan, Arthur) **The yeoman of the guard.** (Yeoman of the guard, or the merryman and his maid) CAST: 4f, 7m, Su. ACTS: 1. SETTINGS: Tower of London. PLAYING TIME: NA. PLOT: Fairfax has been falsely accused of sorcery by his cousin, who stands to inherit Fairfax's estate if Fairfax dies unmarried. In the last hour before he is to be executed, Fairfax asks his best friend, Sir Richard, to find a bride for him. Sir Richard finds Elsie, a strolling player who needs money, she agrees, and is married to Fairfax. Meanwhile, Phoebe tries to save Fairfax by disguising him as her brother, Leonard. When Fairfax receives a reprieve, Phoebe reluctantly promises to marry the villain in order to keep Fairfax alive, Fairfax decides that he loves Elsie, and Elsie's partner (who also loves her) is a broken hearted man. RECOMMENDATION: Different musical themes are used to characterize each player in the operetta. This non-musical version is true enough to the complex plot of the original, and tries, through lyrics (which could be sung to the original melodies) to provide the transitions and exposition of the original. ROYALTY: Free to Plays subscribers. SOURCE: Thane, Adele. (1975, April). The yeoman of the guard. Plays: The Drama Magazine for Young People, pp. 67-80. SUBJECTS/PLAY TYPE: Operetta; Love; Adaptation.

3533. 7-12. (+) Boiko, Claire. **Yes, yes, a thousand times yes!** CAST: 6f, 4m. ACTS: 1. SETTINGS: Two parlors. PLAYING TIME: 30 min. PLOT: Nell Sweetingood longs for the finer things in life, but lives parsimoniously with Granny. At the ladies' sewing circle, Harry Strongbore (Nell's boyfriend, town marshall, and local hero) arrives with photos of himself. Nell dreams of living in a house of her own with Harry, but finds out that when she and Harry marry, they will, instead, live with Granny and raise hogs. Harry learns that the bank manager is all tied up in town, and leaves to rescue him. Rodney X. Urbane, the bungling apprentice villain to Montague Elegant, tries to compromise Nell and steal the deed to Granny's house. Nell thinks he has come to court her, and gives him the deed. Harry returns to rescue Nell, but the rescue is called off when Rodney proposes to Nell and she accepts. Five years later, Rodney and Nell are visited by Montague Elegant. He is disgusted to learn that the two are happily married, and living a lavish lifestyle. RECOMMENDATION: The broad stock characters in this "campy" melodrama will give young actors great opportunity for hammy acting, and the unusual ending will tickle their funnybones. ROYALTY: Free to Plays subscribers. SOURCE: Boiko, Claire. (1977, January). Yes, yes, a thousand times yes! Plays: The Drama Magazine for Young People, pp. 23- 32. SUBJECTS/PLAY TYPE: Marriage; Comedy; Melodrama.

3534. 9-12. (+) Tobias, Alice. **You bet your vocabulary.** CAST: 1f, 6m, 6u. ACTS: 1. SETTINGS: Game show set. PLAYING TIME: 10 min. PLOT: Contestants in a game show try to define various words and terms. Since no one can define "Pyrrhic victory," a curtain opens to reveal the Greek king, Pyrrhus, who describes the famous battle which was won, but only with severe losses. As the curtain closes, the definition of a pyrrhic victory is given as "with great costs to the winner." RECOMMENDATION: This vocabulary builder/history lesson is certainly more interesting than reading a dictionary or a history text, and would be especially enjoyed by reluctant or poor readers. ROYALTY: Free to Plays subscribers. SOURCE: Tobias, Alice. (1977, May). You bet your vocabulary. Plays: The Drama Magazine for Young People, pp. 79-82. SUBJECTS/PLAY TYPE: Pyrric Victory; Playlet.

3535. 5-8. (+) Bradley, Virginia. **You can't blame women for coming out of the kitchen.** CAST: 1f, 2m, 1u. ACTS: 1. SETTINGS: Breakfast nook. PLAYING TIME: NA. PLOT: After a husband ignores his wife at breakfast, she dresses up in high heels and makeup the next day; he still ignores her. On the third morning, she is disheveled again. Because the newspaper is not at his plate, he looks at his wife for the first time and is shocked. RECOMMENDATION: This short, easy play is suitable for beginners. ROYALTY: None. SOURCE: Bradley, Virginia. (1975). Is there an actor in the house? New York, NY: Dodd, Mead. SUBJECTS/PLAY TYPE: Comedy; Family; Skit.

3536. 6-12. (+) Bruce, Mark. **You can't miss it!** CAST: 1f, 1m, 1u. ACTS: 1. SETTINGS: None. PLAYING TIME: 6 min. PLOT: Two inexperienced tourists with a guidebook to the seven wonders of the modern world expect to see everything pictured in the book in Anytown, U.S.A. The frustrated tour guide has his hands full trying to explain where everything is really located. RECOMMENDATION: This delightful light hearted view of tourists and tour guides would be easy to produce and would provide laughs for a wide audience range. ROYALTY: Free to Plays Subscribers. SOURCE: Bruce, Mark. (1980, February). You can't miss it. Plays: The Drama Magazine for Young People, pp. 63-66. SUBJECTS/PLAY TYPE: Comedy; Tourists; Skit.

3537. 5-8. (-) Bradley, Virginia. **You can't win them all.** CAST: 1f, 3m. ACTS: 1. SETTINGS: Snack bar; cafe;

motel. PLAYING TIME: NA. PLOT: A man, his wife, and child stop by a hot dog stand, look at a map, and ask for directions. The owner gives elaborate directions and sends them on their way. The owner then converts his stand into a cafe. The travelers return, the scene is repeated, and the cafe is converted into a motel. When the travelers realize they've been tricked, they stomp away in anger. The owner turns and winks at audience. RECOMMENDATION: This is best used with creative actors, adept at physical humor. ROYALTY: None. SOURCE: Bradley, Virginia. (1975). Is there an actor in the house? New York, NY: Dodd, Mead. SUBJECTS/PLAY TYPE: Travel; Directions; Comedy; Pantomime.

3538. 8-10. (+) McCoy, Paul S. **You don't belong to me.** CAST: 4f, 3m, 1u. ACTS: 1. SETTINGS: Living room. PLAYING TIME: 30 min. PLOT: Wayne has broken up with his girlfriend because she refuses to let him rule her life by telling her what she can and cannot do. He writes her to apologize; enters the "Girl of my Dreams" contest; and mixes up the letters. Amid family confusion, baffled parents, a sarcastic sister, and an angry ex-girlfriend, Wayne finds out that he has won the contest with the apology letter that was sent by mistake. Of course, Boy finally wins Girl. RECOMMENDATION: There is an implicit contemporary theme on the need for equality in male/female relationships. The writing allows creativity in expanding the characters' actions, making the performance a highly entertaining comedy. Parents would enjoy the play also. ROYALTY: Free to Plays subscribers. SOURCE: McCoy, Paul S. (1984, April). You don't belong to me. Plays: The Drama Magazine for Young People, pp. 24-35. SUBJECTS/PLAY TYPE: Dating; Equal Rights; Comedy.

3539. 9-12. (+) Miller, Kathryn Schultz. **You don't see me.** CAST: 2f, 2m. ACTS: 1. SETTINGS: None. PLAYING TIME: 55 min. PLOT: When a young girl cannot accept her brother's death, she pretends he is invisible to everyone except herself. The conversations she creates help her to finally accept the invisible presence of his love in her life, even though "their team" no longer exists. It is the failure of the camera to take her brother's picture that dramatically forces her to accept the fact that her brother is invisible to her, also. RECOMMENDATION: This presents a brilliant use of photography as a device to develop the theme of coming to grips with the death of a loved one. ROYALTY: $35. SOURCE: Miller, Kathryn Schultz. (1986). You don't see me. Morton Grove, IL: Coach House Press. SUBJECTS/PLAY TYPE: Death; Family; Drama.

3540. 4-8. (+) Kehret, Peg. **You don't want to buy one, do you?** CAST: 1u. ACTS: 1. SETTINGS: None. PLAYING TIME: NA. PLOT: A youngster describes his feelings as a candy, magazine, and raffle ticket salesman. RECOMMENDATION: Feelings of frustration such as those enumerated in this touching monologue, will be easily recognized by children of all ages. ROYALTY: NA. SOURCE: Kehret, Peg. (1986). Winning monologs for young actors. Colorado Springs, CO: Meriwether Pub. SUBJECTS/PLAY TYPE: Fund Raising; Frustration; Monologue.

3541. 7-12. (+) Bradley, Virginia. **You have to stay on the horse.** CAST: 2f, 4m. ACTS: 1. SETTINGS: Living room. PLAYING TIME: NA. PLOT: Josie, a careerwoman, returns home to reconcile with the son she abandoned. She wants him to spend a year with her in Paris, but he refuses because he wants to care for his dying aunt. Josie leaves without telling him of her own terminal disease. RECOMMENDATION: The irony here is quite touching. ROYALTY: NA. SOURCE: Bradley, Virginia. (1977). Stage eight: One act plays. New York, NY: Dodd, Mead. SUBJECTS/PLAY TYPE: Family; Responsibility; Melodrama.

3542. 9-12. (+) Horitz, Tony. **You, me and Mrs. Jones.** CAST: 9f, 10m. ACTS: 1. SETTINGS: Streets. PLAYING TIME: 40 min. PLOT: Two urban teens, Nobody and No-one, search for heroes. They encounter various societal ills of the late 20th century, violent street gangs, religious cults, shallow pop idols, incompetent police, and Mrs. Jones, mother of a street family. By the act of their pilgrimage, they become Somebody and Someone, and learn that a hero may be an ordinary person who shows kindness and generosity to others despite his own difficulties. RECOMMENDATION: This is current and universal, but challenging to perform. The cast may be as large as 19 or as small as six (by doubling or tripling parts). ROYALTY: NA. SOURCE: Horitz, Tony. (1987). You, me and Mrs. Jones. London: Samuel French. SUBJECTS/PLAY TYPE: Heroes; Musical; Comedy.

3543. K-3. (+) Pomerantz, Charlotte. **You tu.** CAST: 2u. ACTS: 1. SETTINGS: None. PLAYING TIME: NA. PLOT: A short poem, included in both English and Spanish versions, ponders the identity of the face in the mirror. RECOMMENDATION: This would be a bilingual treat in an early elementary class also studying Spanish, and will work well with "Reflection" (see review earlier), a pairing chosen by Bauer. ROYALTY: NA. SOURCE: Bauer, Caroline Feller. (1987). Presenting reader's theater: Plays and poems to read aloud. New York, NY: H.W. Wilson. SUBJECTS/PLAY TYPE: Mirrors; Reader's Theater.

3544. 7-12. (+) Powers, Peggy & Robert, Jane. (Grimm Brothers) **You'll find the magic.** (Rumplestiltskin) CAST: 1f, 6m, Su. ACTS: 2. SETTINGS: Castle; throne room. PLAYING TIME: 45 min. PLOT: A poor weaver's daughter must make good on her father's claim that she can spin straw into gold. RECOMMENDATION: Embellished with such fanciful and comic accoutrements as talking clocks and bumbling servants, this sprightly adaptation is comical and nonthreatening. ROYALTY: $50. SOURCE: Powers, Peggy, & Roberts, Jane. (1979). You'll find the magic. Chicago, IL: Dramatic Pub. Co. SUBJECTS/PLAY TYPE: Folk Tales, Germany; Musical; Adaptation.

3545. 5-8. (+) Boiko, Claire. **Young Abe's destiny.** CAST: 2f, 5m, 1u. ACTS: 1. SETTINGS: Backdrop, props. PLAYING TIME: 20 min. PLOT: Childhood friends of Abe Lincoln gather to surprise Abe with birthday gifts. Fortunato and Dr. Fate, both posing as actors lost in the backwoods of Indiana, join the group and speak of their quest for a Presidential candidate for the 1860 election. They hold mock auditions for the children to ascertain which would be most suited for the job. A reluctant Abe undergoes a magical transformation as he repeats the oath of office, and the children, both those in the play and those in the audience, are transfixed by the sincerity and impact of the spectacle. Upon their departure, Dr. Fate and Fortunato off-handedly comment on their anticipated reunion with Abe on the road to Washington. RECOMMENDATION: An excellent follow up for a historical treatment of Abe Lincoln's rise to the Presidency or to commemorate Lincoln's birthday, this blends a factual, realistic portrait of the young Abe with a mystical representation of the forces of Fate. The audience is left with the eerie confirmation that historical events and the nature of man do indeed conform to a perfect plan, or, at least, tend toward an existence beneficial for all men. The part of Abe demands a young actor who can portray a fundamental, earthy earnestness. Fate and Fortunato must be played with care to avoid a descent into the tomfoolery of hocus-pocus. ROYALTY: None. SOURCE: Boiko, Claire. (1985). Children's plays for creative actors. Boston, MA: Plays, Inc. SUBJECTS/PLAY TYPE: Lincoln, Abraham; Playlet.

3546. 10-12. (+) Nash, N. Richard. **The young and the fair.** CAST: 21f. ACTS: 3. SETTINGS: Office; dormitory room; lounge. PLAYING TIME: NA. PLOT: Miss Cantry, the academy founder, hires Fran Morritt, an inexperienced alumna, as personnel director and takes Fran's younger sister, Patty, as a student. Patty finds an immediate friend in her roommate, Lee, who claims to be Protestant rather than Jewish, and feels very guilty about hiding her Jewish heritage. The action revolves around the conflicts that the protagonists have because of the antagonistic Drucilla Eldridge, the spoiled daughter of an influential board member who controls her peers (and the faculty) through intimidation. Each of the protagonists allows her values to be compromised, but later stands up for what is right, in this tale of blackmail, subterfuge, and dishonesty. RECOMMENDATION: The characters and their motivations are clearly drawn. What begins as a light, happy play soon turns into a dark portrayal of the lengths to which fearful people will go to protect themselves. This drama of good and evil has an overdrawn villain or two, but it emphasizes each individual's struggle to make the important decisions in the "small" conflicts of life which develop the patterns of an entire life. ROYALTY: $35. SOURCE: Nash, N. Richard. (1976). The young and the fair. New York, NY: Dramatists Play Service, Inc. SUBJECTS/PLAY TYPE: Honesty; Values; Friendship; Drama.

3547. 7-10. (+) Kelly, Tim J. **Young Dracula, or the singing bat.** CAST: 11f, 7m. ACTS: 2. SETTINGS: Castle. PLAYING TIME: 120 min. PLOT: High school students get lost hiking through Europe, and end up in an isolated castle whose owner, Bill, wants them to stay a few days so he can charge them room and board. The "batty" behavior of Bill's uncle, Dracula, first frightens the young people, but soon they realize Bill really needs money or the bank will foreclose on his castle and replace it with a pickle factory. Inspiration strikes and, at the end, the cast is planning how to employ the entire village and uncle, too, at Draculaland. RECOMMENDATION: Although it requires some technical effects, this appears flexible: it could accommodate a large group of villagers, a dance scene could be added, the number of maids could be enlarged, and it is structured so that groups could be rehearsed separately. The songs are set to familiar tunes. Several characters verge on caricature and would be ideal for young actors who enjoy "hamming it up." ROYALTY: $60. SOURCE: Kelly, Tim J. (1975). Young Dracula, or the singing bat. Denver, CO: Pioneer Drama Service. SUBJECTS/PLAY TYPE: Vampires; Comedy; Musical.

3548. 7-12. (-) Endersby, Clive. **Young King Arthur.** (King Arthur and the knights of the round table) CAST: 2f, 5m, 1u. ACTS: 1. SETTINGS: Cave; throne room; dungeon. PLAYING TIME: NA. PLOT: A bumbling Merlin introduces himself to the audience, tries to make a rock turn into a dragon (but turns it into a dog), and tells the secret of the sword in the stone. Mordred and Kay enter to fight in a joust, as does Gwenivere, disguised as a squire. Arthur, squire of Sir Kay, loses Kay's sword, pulls the sword out of the stone as a replacement, and is declared king by Merlin. Mordred wins the joust through his sister's witchery, takes Arthur prisoner, Arthur is saved by Merlin's magic and Gwenivere's courage, and Mordred is defeated. The dog is made a knight and Arthur is crowned. RECOMMENDATION: This is a confusing hodge-podge of snippets from the original and the author's own imagination. It neither does justice to the original nor does it stand on its own merit. ROYALTY: NA. SOURCE: Endersby, Clive. (1980). Young King Arthur/The adventures of Robin Hood. Toronto: Playwrights Canada. SUBJECTS/PLAY TYPE: Legends, England; Comedy; Adaptation.

3549. K-3. (+) Havilan, Amorie & Smith, Lyn. **Young saint Patrick.** CAST: 2f, 1m, Su. ACTS: 2. SETTINGS: Bare stage, props. PLAYING TIME: 30 min. PLOT: Young Patrick had been kidnapped by Irish raiders on his way to visit his grandfather and, after several years, he escapes and returns home. The action begins when, after spending some time at home, he decides to return to Ireland to spread the word of God. His mother and sister try to dissuade him, but, after his return to Ireland, he becomes a great teacher and legend. RECOMMENDATION: Since the religious theme is central, this is suitable for church, Sunday or parochial school groups. It can be read as a story, or pantomimed with narration. It touches on two of the legends associated with Saint Patrick and Ireland: the shamrock, and the fact that there are no snakes in Ireland. ROYALTY: NA. SOURCE: Havilan, Amorie & Smith, Lyn. (1985). Easy plays for preschoolers to third graders. Cincinnati, OH: Quail Ridge Press. SUBJECTS/PLAY TYPE: St. Patrick's Day; Tripartite.

3550. 10-12. (+) Urdahl, Richard. **Your wife is a what?** CAST: 2m. ACTS: 1. SETTINGS: None. PLAYING TIME: NA. PLOT: Two men compare their relationships with their wives to their relationships with God. One man shows the other that his allegedly close relationship with God is not all it should be because he is overly concerned with earthly affairs. The accused man's defensive attitude proves that his friend is correct. RECOMMENDATION: With a very mature view of man's relationship with God, this would only appeal to deep thinking audiences. Used in a Sunday school setting to be either produced or read aloud, this could foster a discussion on faith and God's relationship with man. ROYALTY: $10. SOURCE: Urdahl, Richard. (1984). Don't listen to us, Lord...we're only praying. Boston, MA: Baker's Plays. SUBJECTS/PLAY TYPE: Psychology; God and Man; Christian Drama.

3551. K-3. (+) Ison, Colleen. **Zaccheus the tax collector.** CAST: Su. ACTS: 1. SETTINGS: Bare stage, props. PLAYING TIME: NA. PLOT: The story of Zaccheus is retold by a narrator, as children act out what is being narrated. The last line tells the audience that Jesus loved everyone. RECOMMENDATION: This is simple and direct, but the narrator will have to be an adult or an older teenager. Discussion questions are provided. ROYALTY: NA. SOURCE: Ison, Colleen. (1986). Goliath's last stand: And fifteen more easy plays for children. Cincinnati, OH: Standard Pub. SUBJECTS/PLAY TYPE: Christian Drama; Skit.

3552. 10-12. (+) Randazzo, Angela. **Zara, or, Who killed the queen of the silent screen?** CAST: 4f, 5m. ACTS: 2. SETTINGS: Beach house. PLAYING TIME: NA. PLOT: Martin James is a modern day writer with an obsession for the silent screen star, Zara St. Cyr, and a determination to solve the mystery of her murder. An ESP experience orchestrated by a male gypsy during a seance puts Martin back into 1925 and allows him to witness the actual murder. The mystery is resolved by a clumsy deus ex machina technique, in which it is revealed that the gypsy is actually an old fan of the actress, who killed her to make her immortal and escape being discovered as a murderer herself. RECOMMENDATION: Zara may be of interest to a mature audience with fond memories of the silent screen or a penchant for **Murder, She Wrote** episodes. However, as a ghost story, it fails to set the proper mood, and the end, where Zara's ghost appears, seems to be more a token nod than a real part of the plot. ROYALTY: $50. SOURCE: Randazzo, Angela. (1985). Zara, or, Who killed the queen of the silent screen? Woodstock, IL: Dramatic Pub. Co. SUBJECTS/PLAY TYPE: Ghosts; Silent Movies; Mystery.

3553. 7-12. (+) DeLong, James R. **Zartan, the grape man.** CAST: 3f, 2m, 20u. ACTS: 2. SETTINGS: Jungle; tree house; cannibal village. PLAYING TIME: NA. PLOT: Professor Schmoo searches the jungle of Jujuba for his former Oxford student, the ape Teecha, now an anthropologist studying Zartan, the Grape Man, a purple missing link. Pursued alternately by a lady pirate and her crew and by the local cannibals, the expedition features Schmoo's assertive daughter, who falls for Zartan. The pirates escape without loot, but are pleased not to have become supper. The daughter pursues the Grape Man into the jungle. The remainder of the expedition, after a taste of the wild man's grape jelly, go ape themselves and disappear into the jungle. RECOMMENDATION: The humor of this exaggerated farce depends on hectic chases, mistaken identities, sight gags, malapropisms, and terrible puns. Most of the latter will be appreciated more by the teacher's generation than by the young adults for whom the play is intended. Colorful and loud, with no discernible plot, the play careens from one gag to the next. The play requires two strong female leads, assorted gorillas, and a strong stomach. Some viewers may object to stereotyping of "natives". ROYALTY: $35. SOURCE: DeLong, James R. (1988). Zartan, the grape man. Franklin, OH: Eldridge Pub. Co. SUBJECTS/PLAY TYPE: Adventure; Pirates; Jungle; Comedy.

3554. 9-12. (-) Boyle, Virginia. !ZAS! CAST: 4f, 3m. ACTS: 1. SETTINGS: Outside. PLAYING TIME: 50 min. PLOT: The sun and moon look down at a group of people of all races, who are working for a tyrant. The workers overpower the tyrant and gain their rights. RECOMMENDATION: This bilingual musical attempts to dramatize the theme of equal rights, especially for migrant workers. However, it is difficult to follow, and too dated in its language, dialogue, and references. ROYALTY: $25. SOURCE: Boyle, Virginia A. (1979). !ZAS! Chicago, IL: Coach House Press. SUBJECTS/PLAY TYPE: Spanish/English Plays; Musical; Drama.

3555. 4-8. (+) Westerhout, Gart. The Zeem dream. CAST: 2f, 2m, 16u. ACTS: 1. SETTINGS: Bedroom; planet Zeem; cave. PLAYING TIME: 15 min. PLOT: Sent to bed early for fighting with Freddie, Stephen and Jennie dream that they are on planet Zeem, where they are captured by the Horrible Hogglewart. Freddie rushes in to save them, they wake, and decide Freddie isn't so bad after all. RECOMMENDATION: An interesting twist on childhood arguments, this clever suspense will challenge and amuse. ROYALTY: Free to Plays subscribers. SOURCE: Westerhout, Gart. (1988, March). The Zeem dream. Plays: The Drama Magazine for Young People, pp. 33-38. SUBJECTS/PLAY TYPE: Arguments; Dreams; Playlet.

3556. 4-8. (+) Satchell, Mary. Zelda's homecoming. CAST: 5f, 4m, Su. ACTS: 1. SETTINGS: Street; classroom; living room. PLAYING TIME: 25 min. PLOT: Judy dislikes the two young immigrants, Zelda and Jake, who are in her class, because she is afraid they will take Lisa's friendship away. When Zelda makes an emotional speech about the Statue of Liberty, Judy accidentally breaks the school's miniature statue, and puts the pieces in Zelda's bag. The pieces are discovered and Zelda doesn't want to go to school the next day, but does. Judy admits breaking the statue, and everyone makes friends with Zelda and Jake. At the end, the cast sings, "Give me your tired, your poor." RECOMMENDATION: This is a very stirring patriotic program. Zelda and Jake's accents should be optional since they may be difficult for younger actors. ROYALTY: Free to Plays subscribers. SOURCE: Satchell, Mary. (1986, November). Zelda's homecoming. Plays: The Drama Magazine for Young People, pp. 41-49. SUBJECTS/PLAY TYPE: Patriotism; Immigrants; Playlet.

3557. 1-4. (+) Bauer, Caroline Feller. Zena and Zach and the sack of gold. CAST: 1f, 2m, 5u. ACTS: 1. SETTINGS: None. PLAYING TIME: 10 min. PLOT: A farmer finds a sack of gold in the forest and tells his wife, who gossips the news through the village. The landowner demands the gold. The farmer's wife tells stories about pancakes in the trees, a fish in an animal trap and a hare in a fish net. The landowner decides she is hallucinating, and the farmer and his wife are able to keep the gold. RECOMMENDATION: With humor and audience participation, this can be a lesson about gossip. It can be either acted or read aloud. ROYALTY: None. SOURCE: Bauer, Caroline Feller. (1987). Presenting reader's theater. New York, NY: H. W. Wilson Co. SUBJECTS/PLAY TYPE: Gossip; Folk Tales, Russia; Reader's Theater.

3558. 11-12. (+) Sharkey, Jack & Reiser, Dave. Zingo!: The carbonated musical. CAST: 6f, 17m, Su. ACTS: 1. SETTINGS: Office/anteroom. PLAYING TIME: NA. PLOT: In this zany musical, two soft drink companies, Zingo and Whang, compete, with Whang plotting to steal Zingo's secret formula, "Culture K." Several couples fall in and out of love, and treachery and deceit run rampant, though everything ends well. RECOMMENDATION: Due to the extensive nature of the musical lyrics, the performing group should be experienced. Adult performers and audiences would probably enjoy this uproarious production more. ROYALTY: $75. SOURCE: Sharkey, Jack & Reiser, Dave. (1986). Zingo!: The carbonated musical. Boston, MA: Baker's Plays. SUBJECTS/PLAY TYPE: Business; Commercials; Comedy; Industrial Espionage; Musical.

3559. K-6. (+) Lewman, Beverly & Smith, Robert B. The zoo story. CAST: Su. ACTS: 1. SETTINGS: Flannel board. PLAYING TIME: 5 min. PLOT: In this musical drama, designed to develop in students the iconic and enactive abilities espoused by Jerome Bruner, a teacher and her students visit a zoo and see a giraffe, an elephant, and a lion. RECOMMENDATION: This is recommended for hyperkinetic and multiply handicapped children who can participate by singing, acting out the parts and drawing scenes. Children learn to sequence events by retelling the story. ROYALTY: NA. SOURCE: Lewman, Beverly & Smith, Robert B. (1984). Music dramas for children with special needs. Denton, TX: Troostwyk Press. SUBJECTS/PLAY TYPE: Zoos; Sequencing Skills; Musical.

3560. 10-12. (+) Kelly, Tim. Zorro's back in town or the curse of Buck Badum. CAST: 6f, 4m, Su. ACTS: 1. SETTINGS: Hotel. PLAYING TIME: 60 min. PLOT: Cinderella-like Alice Sweepup's receipt of the deed to a rich deposit of gold is deceitfully prevented by the town villain and dictator, his fiery "lady," and the wimpy sheriff. Zorro saves the day by returning the deed to Alice, and is revealed as the distant, meek and mild mannered cousin who carried the deed. RECOMMENDATION: The names of the characters reflect their personalities in this fast paced plot. One female character has a singing and dancing act, which must be done poorly. ROYALTY: $25. SOURCE: Kelly, Tim. (1983). Zorro's back in town or The curse of Buck Badum. Denver, CO: Pioneer Drama Service. SUBJECTS/PLAY TYPE: Heroes; Adventure; Zorro; Melodrama.

AUTHOR/ORIGINAL TITLE INDEX

In this index are listed all authors of the plays. If the play was an adaptation of someone else's work, the author and title of the adapted work are also listed in this index. Numbers refer to entries not pages.

CAST INDEX

The cast index is broken down into unspecified, male, and female.
Unspecified casts are first, followed by mixed casts (males and unspecified);
mixed casts (females, unspecified); and mixed casts (females, males,
unspecified). Numbers refer to entries, not pages. S=several; u=unspecified;
f=female; m=male.

9m, Su 2401
9m, 10u 445, 3212
10m, 1u 2677
12m 1977
13m 1996
14m 626
15m, Su 1457
16m, Su 3528
17m, Su 2613
19m 398
23m, Su 2770
30m 1572
Sf, Sm 1353
1f 10, 98, 179, 204, 205, 225, 234, 251, 252, 555, 704, 733, 753, 860, 948, 956, 964, 965, 976, 999, 1061, 1070, 1073, 1075, 1080, 1143, 1326, 1467, 1520, 1522, 1616, 1669, 1755, 1993, 2029, 2040, 2041, 2141, 2175, 2321, 2435, 2446, 2709, 2881, 2889, 2943, 2976, 2986, 3036, 3096, 3126, 3277, 3330, 3376, 3489
1f, Su 491, 1243, 1308, 1765, 3365, 3492
1f, 1u 937, 1361, 2153
1f, 3u 1628, 1835, 2190, 3132
1f, 4u 1484, 2302
1f, 5u 1776, 3485, 3493
1f, 6u 412
1f, 8u 2896
1f, 10u 1463
1f, 11u 3420
1f, 1m 153, 166, 347, 396, 420, 484, 679, 686, 744, 745, 757, 803, 873, 874, 884, 973, 1036, 1037, 1039, 1040, 1042, 1051, 1053, 1055, 1059, 1060, 1065, 1066, 1071, 1072, 1077, 1082, 1083, 1091, 1092, 1094, 1095, 1097, 1098, 1102, 1108, 1111, 1114, 1118, 1125, 1169, 1172, 1190, 1235, 1270, 1297, 1592, 1644, 1654, 1658, 1826, 1872, 1895, 1929, 2059, 2146, 2183, 2244, 2252, 2253, 2330, 2378, 2422, 2430, 2520, 2718, 2729, 2747, 2946, 3043, 3159, 3205, 3303, 3311, 3326, 3375
1f, 1m, Su 1, 36, 92, 253, 1543, 1887, 1890, 1922, 2004, 2196, 2251, 2261, 2267, 2343, 2516, 2828, 2918, 2974, 3166, 3168, 3244, 3418
1f, 1m, 1u 1332, 2568, 2865, 3140, 3536
1f, 1m, 2u 1206, 1323, 2917, 2898
1f, 1m, 3u 59, 1215, 2107, 2699
1f, 1m, 4u 208, 264, 1432, 2522, 3499
1f, 1m, 5u 209, 1474, 2903
1f, 1m, 7u 1429, 1645
1f, 1m, 8u 742, 1175, 2326
1f, 1m, 9u 1752, 2049, 3396
1f, 1m, 11u 240
1f, 1m, 12u 1386, 3435
1f, 1m, 20u 1436
1f, 1m, 21u 927
1f, 1m, 22u 401
1f, 1m, 26u 3160
1f, 1m, 27u 2696
1f, 2m 44, 134, 260, 293, 306, 456, 587, 705, 736, 910, 921, 966, 985, 1032, 1074, 1112, 1136, 1139, 1156, 1165, 1225, 1305, 1420, 1424, 1496, 1536, 1702, 1728, 1844, 1848, 2045, 2204, 2235, 2416, 2537, 2805, 3110, 3176, 3352, 3387, 3488

1f, 2m, Su 114, 291, 341, 850, 967, 2011, 2042, 2144, 2651, 2659, 3297, 3458
1f, 2m, 1u 90, 505, 824, 1352, 1627, 2279, 2286, 2337, 3031, 3041, 3535
1f, 2m, 2u 1580, 1634, 2182, 3144
1f, 2m, 3u 1569, 1713, 1965, 2801, 3500
1f, 2m, 4u 915, 995, 1276, 1724, 2082, 2194, 3139
1f, 2m, 5u 2234, 3251, 3557
1f 2m 6u 2638, 3478
1f, 2m, 8u 819
1f, 2m, 16u 1565
1f, 3m 117, 150, 500, 637, 943, 1067, 1273, 1794, 1941, 2228, 2363, 2384, 2635, 2837, 3308, 3353, 3372, 3426, 3537
1f, 3m, Su 80, 403, 685, 800, 1477, 1564, 1957, 2164, 2424, 2611
1f, 3m, 1u 216, 2110, 2639, 2985
1f, 3m, 3u 357, 1017
1f, 3m, 4u 1455, 2493
1f, 3m, 5u 309, 1385
1f, 3m, 7u 272, 1970, 2900
1f, 3m, 10u 2561
1f, 3m, 13u 2348
1f, 3m, 16u 898
1f, 3m, 24u 3507
1f, 4m 807, 1148, 1198, 1465, 1960, 1972, 2012, 2079, 2221, 2389, 2403, 2627, 2923, 2954, 3151
1f, 4m, Su 531, 1787, 2383, 2386, 2607, 2689
1f, 4m, 1u 5, 120, 1382, 1449, 2893, 3154
1f, 4m, 2u 140
1f, 4m, 3u 2584
1f, 4m, 5u 2078
1f, 4m, 13u 2777
1f, 4m, 16u 2980
1f, 4m, 19u 1380
1f, 4m, 26u 1577
1f, 5m 174, 338, 649, 1493, 1609, 2055, 2489, 2563, 2678, 3389, 3470
1f, 5m, Su 2572, 2656
1f, 5m, 1u 1638, 3136
1f, 5m, 2u 2340
1f, 5m, 3u 1875, 3035
1f, 5m, 8u 938
1f, 5m, 10u 3216
1f, 6m 24, 972, 1694, 311, 1586, 2521
1f, 6m, Su 1514, 3544
1f, 6m, 1u 405
1f, 6m, 6u 2789, 3534
1f, 6m, 9u 2645
1f, 6m, 11u 2686
1f, 6m, 14u 849
1f, 6m, 20u 2579
1f, 7m 1222, 1414, 1650, 2320, 3464
1f, 7m, Su 274, 1140
1f, 7m, 1u 200, 2761
1f, 7m, 10u 1138
1f, 8m 1348, 2266, 2356, 2775, 3289
1f, 8m, 5u 1964
1f, 8m, Su 268, 541, 646, 3003
1f, 9m 289, 691, 2469
1f, 9m, Su 3, 349

5f, 1m 131, 1998, 2157, 3256, 3334, 3347

5f, 1m, Su 2847

5f, 1m, 1u 628, 2167

5f, 2m 91, 542, 570, 579, 1171, 1398, 1539, 1708, 1768, 1862, 1927, 2299, 2408, 2719, 2911

5f, 2m, Su 569, 902, 2295, 2807

5f, 2m, 2u 3285

5f, 2m, 3u 2105, 2867

5f, 2m, 5u 231

5f, 3m 79, 121, 137, 219, 250, 263, 287, 410, 575, 651, 1599, 1600, 1823, 1843, 1940, 1984, 1994, 2020, 2237, 2464, 2536, 2706, 2739, 2960, 3074, 3078, 3243, 3278, 3386, 3483, 3521

5f, 3m, Su 63, 424, 930, 1209, 1542, 2200, 2901, 3141, 3274

5f, 3m, 1u 271, 1195, 1551, 1675

5f, 3m, 3u 2821, 3305

5f, 3m, 5u 3265

5f, 3m, 6u 3222

5f, 3m, 7u 2784

5f, 4m 181, 273, 479, 600, 718, 887, 918, 1639, 1859, 2104, 2138, 2226, 2783, 2937, 2963, 3107, 3188, 3304, 3361, 3398, 3469

5f, 4m, Su 49, 533, 880, 1232, 1371, 2176, 2503, 2786, 2849, 3030, 3556

5f, 4m, 1u 244, 2505, 3460

5f, 4m, 2u 1446

5f, 4m, 3u 1699, 2533

5f, 4m, 5u 3343

5f, 4m, 8u 734

5f, 4m, 9u 1801, 3358

5f, 4m, 10u 475, 891

5f, 5m 185, 389, 737, 934, 1137, 1400, 1411, 1582, 1679, 1700, 1818, 1883, 2035, 2260, 2465, 2501, 2553, 2559, 2594, 2633, 2780, 2853, 2993, 3013, 3039, 3116, 3307, 3339

5f, 5m, Su 17, 55, 390, 406, 885, 890, 1784, 1833, 2543, 2650, 2746, 2938, 2964, 2995, 3275, 3292

5f, 5m, 1u 1988

5f, 5m, 2u 2856, 3073, 3100, 3436

5f, 5m, 4u 480, 2060

5f, 5m, 5u 3437

5f, 5m, 6u 989, 2427, 2664

5f, 5m, 10u 2589

5f, 5m, 15u 2187

5f, 5m, 20u 3102

5f, 6m 40, 81, 300, 554, 619, 639, 764, 811, 909, 1452, 1604, 1943, 1989, 2728, 2732, 2848, 2879, 3065, 3209

5f, 6m, Su 532, 759, 774, 941, 1751, 2179, 2269, 2742, 3254, 3424

5f, 6m, 1u 1740

5f, 6m, 3u 775

5f, 6m, 5u 2023, 2218, 3002

5f, 6m, 6u 536, 2904

5f, 6m, 16u 3379

5f, 7m 269, 2417, 2629, 3026

5f, 7m, Su 66, 446, 990, 1229, 1438, 1479, 2084, 2397, 2679, 2691, 2772, 2914, 2990, 3017

5f, 7m, 1u 207

5f, 7m, 2u 870

5f, 7m, 3u 212, 2771

5f, 7m, 7u 1285

5f, 7m, 8u 1183

5f, 7m, 11u 342

5f, 7m, 16u 2512

5f, 8m 110, 1240, 2442, 2586, 3064, 3085, 3252, 3316, 3430

5f, 8m, Su 978, 1856

5f, 8m, 1u 2922

5f, 8m, 2u 3480

5f, 8m, 4u 2842

5f, 8m, 6u 2297

5f, 8m, 10u 647

5f, 9m 104, 2609, 2597, 2636

5f, 9m, Su 1880, 2393

5f, 9m, 6u 3322

5f, 10m 195, 1472

5f, 10m, Su 1836

5f, 11m 613, 692

5f, 11m, Su 2593

5f, 11m, 2u 857

5f, 12m 2236

5f, 12m, Su 612, 2255

5f, 12m, 8u 2581

5f, 14m 1251

5f, 15m 1374

5f, 15m, Su 1834, 2405

5f, 16m, Su 473, 2768, 2994

5f, 17m, Su 944

5f, 18m 2666

5f, 19m 510

5f, 19m, Su 3197

5f, 20m, 1u 986

5f, 22m, 1u 3224

5f, 25m, Su 3357

6f 42, 1602, 1613, 2634, 3434

6f, 2m 2526, 2854, 3080, 3294

6f, 2m, 1u 1026

6f, 2m, 2u 1607

6f, 2m, 3u 2293

6f, 2m, 7u 674

6f, 2m, 16u 1540

6f, 2m, 20u 2573

6f, 3m 399, 903, 1024, 1680, 2073, 2334, 2432, 2642, 3242

6f, 3m, Su 129, 193, 499, 794, 1019, 1653

6f, 3m, 1u 2259

6f, 3m, 4u 844, 3103

6f, 3m, 13u 3494

6f, 4m 184, 438, 728, 908, 1407, 1673, 1808, 2016, 2127, 3084, 3189, 3291, 3533

6f, 4m, Su 192, 572, 1388, 1483, 1677, 1825, 1914, 3560

6f, 4m, 1u 3320

6f, 4m, 4u 790

6f, 4m, 16u 583

6f, 5m 678, 680, 945, 981, 1234, 1324, 1333, 1739, 1817, 2621, 3007, 3076

6f, 5m, Su 130, 196, 1320, 1528, 1855, 2246, 2800, 3508

6f, 5m, 1u 1370, 2921

6f, 5m, 2u 614

6f, 5m, 6u 2344

6f, 5m, 10u 3199

GRADE LEVEL INDEX

Numbers refer to entries, not pages. *= must be produced by older grade levels.

SUBJECT/PLAY TYPE INDEX

Numbers refer to entries, not pages.

Alphabet 1499, 2696, 3007
Alternative Theater 961
Amazons 96, 97
Ambition 743, 1917
Amos 104
Ananse 107
Ancient Egypt 3446
Ancient India 990
Angels 121, 187, 1297, 2714
Animal Tale 1681, 1749, 2045, 3149
Animal Personification 3464
Animal Rights 2743
Animal Shelter 774
Animal Husbandry 3038
Animal Survival 770
Animals 31, 37, 107, 125, 127, 128, 208, 218, 349, 352, 356,
    453, 475, 769, 782, 913, 920, 1173, 1211, 1233, 1242, 1427,
    1455, 1466, 1566, 1957, 1973, 2060, 2061, 2107, 2242,
    2391, 2429, 2492, 2590, 2602, 2830, 3037, 3111, 3208,
    3225, 3439, 3448, 3462, 3463, 3465, 3466, 3473
Anorexia Nervosa 3358
Ant Hills 35
Ante-Bellum South 1888
Anthony, Susan B. 1234, 2994
Anthropology 190
Anti-Semitism 1099, 1214, 1535, 2178
Anti-War 2929, 3505
Ants 35, 133
Apartheid 1702
Apes 3409
Aphasia 3469
Apostles 1008
Appalachian Mountains 3421
Appearances 2467
Appleseed, Johnny 1340, 1583, 1584, 1585, 1879, 3526
April Fool's Day 147, 608, 1445, 2215, 2992
Arbor Day 1583, 1584, 1585, 1714, 3236, 3369
Archaeology 754
Archery 2612
Architecture 1141
Arguments 3555
Arithmetic 647
Army Regulations 3042
Art 999, 1691, 2096, 2114, 2271, 2304, 2720
Art History 2383
Arthur, King 3404
Artistic Achievement 1919
Artists 448, 1260, 1994, 2975, 3324
Artwork 1065, 1519
Aspirations 1059
Assertiveness 2258
Astrology 42, 593
Astronauts 2015
Athletics 921
Atomic Bomb 461, 2661
Attitudes 106, 294, 377, 1869, 2984
Attucks, Crispus 660, 1278
Auction 2653
Audition 2153

Austen, Jane 2435
Austin, Stephen F. 2254
Australia 1207
Australia 2877
Authors, Adolescent 1680
Automobiles 403, 420, 1424, 3412
Avant-Garde 961, 2421, 2921
Aviation 979
Babies 178
Babysitting 853, 2808
Bakers 191
Bald Eagles 194
Balloons 199
Balls 1998
Bands 2269
Bank Robbery 442, 2548
Banks 2520
Bargains 204
Barnardo school 768
Baseball 445, 1226, 1577, 1764, 2967, 3442, 3528
Basho 380
Basketball 364, 492
Baths 1471
Battle of the Sexes 1180
Beans, Jumping 1597
Bears 30, 156, 221, 352, 2164, 2841, 3117
Bears, Stuffed 3044
Beautification 2674
Beauty 225, 226, 737
Beauty Pageant 1983
Beauty Pageants 1021, 1934
Behavior 396, 664, 1361, 1334, 1494, 1570, 1792, 1891, 3122,
    3398
Beliefs 977, 1279
Ben Gurion, David 1063
Beowulf 1350
Bermuda Triangle 244
Bethlehem 1710
Bethune, Mary McLeod 1914
Betrayal 398, 619
Bets 1439
Bi-Lingualism 2151
Bias 2957
Bible 620, 1443, 1727, 2133
Bible Stories 15, 104, 465, 699, 859, 1194, 1212, 1587, 2248,
    2318, 2778, 3099, 3417, 3491
Bicentennial 2935
Bicycle Safety 195
Bigfoot 270, 1544, 3060
Bigotry 3088, 3284
Bilingual Plays 1242
Billboards 301
Bionic Man 3108
Birds 276, 277, 397, 1361
Birth Control 1603, 2446
Birth 3344
Birthdays 284, 653, 1725, 1950, 2022, 2303, 3341
Bitterness 2149

PLAYING TIME INDEX

All plays for which a time was given in either the play publisher's catalog, or within the text of the play are listed in this index. Numbers refer to entries, not pages.

2911, 2933, 2938, 2952, 2984, 3008, 3009, 3013, 3062,
3105, 3173, 3185, 3195, 3221, 3222, 3237, 3241, 3243,
3270, 3282, 3294, 3319, 3332, 3357, 3359, 3363, 3367,
3381, 3385, 3414, 3423, 3428, 3457, 3490, 3556

30 Minutes   12, 16, 20, 21, 25, 26, 28, 43, 49, 54, 70, 81, 96,
97, 100, 105, 114, 141, 167, 171, 182, 187, 188, 219, 220,
222, 227, 229, 244, 259, 267, 289, 311, 312, 323, 326, 342,
362, 363, 370, 372, 413, 416, 417, 427, 430, 439, 441, 442,
448, 470, 479, 487, 502, 506, 508, 510, 513, 524, 538, 539,
546, 547, 550, 554, 563, 578, 590, 591, 600, 631, 654, 663,
680, 690, 691, 698, 709, 714, 721, 728, 745, 760, 762, 771,
792, 795, 806, 861, 876, 887, 916, 918, 925, 926, 941, 942,
950, 952, 981, 983, 989, 1023, 1129, 1135, 1162, 1167,
1176, 1199, 1203, 1231, 1252, 1254, 1278, 1290, 1291,
1295, 1311, 1315, 1318, 1319, 1321, 1324, 1333, 1339,
1364, 1368, 1381, 1390, 1400, 1401, 1404, 1408, 1409,
1410, 1429, 1446, 1458, 1468, 1489, 1490, 1491, 1497,
1506, 1507, 1517, 1518, 1526, 1531, 1544, 1548, 1549,
1555, 1561, 1589, 1605, 1611, 1612, 1615, 1621, 1622,
1627, 1628, 1634, 1650, 1657, 1664, 1688, 1691, 1708,
1721, 1737, 1738, 1759, 1768, 1778, 1790, 1796, 1805,
1812, 1826, 1840, 1851, 1893, 1900, 1904, 1913, 1914,
1940, 1943, 1975, 1989, 2013, 2019, 2050, 2074, 2091,
2096, 2103, 2104, 2108, 2113, 2114, 2122, 2126, 2166,
2180, 2214, 2224, 2226, 2233, 2237, 2266, 2285, 2299,
2324, 2333, 2349, 2359, 2367, 2382, 2389, 2407, 2426,
2441, 2442, 2452, 2455, 2486, 2489, 2505, 2531, 2544,
2559, 2561, 2564, 2593, 2613, 2682, 2720, 2723, 2724,
2740, 2745, 2754, 2755, 2760, 2790, 2800, 2803, 2806,
2808, 2835, 2854, 2867, 2868, 2875, 2896, 2907, 2914,
2920, 2927, 2928, 2929, 2931, 2935, 2962, 2966, 2995,
3030, 3033, 3035, 3048, 3053, 3058, 3060, 3064, 3074,
3084, 3100, 3120, 3171, 3184, 3189, 3209, 3211, 3247,
3252, 3263, 3281, 3287, 3320, 3325, 3328, 3349, 3370,
3383, 3389, 3396, 3406, 3410, 3424, 3433, 3441, 3451,
3454, 3455, 3474, 3493, 3498, 3503, 3504, 3522, 3533,
3538, 3549

35 Minutes   14, 18, 103, 232, 262, 269, 296, 346, 355, 406,
468, 474, 548, 552, 574, 601, 612, 671, 734, 755, 789, 801,
808, 811, 816, 882, 890, 907, 917, 970, 980, 1031, 1131,
1169, 1258, 1317, 1337, 1349, 1374, 1376, 1402, 1407,
1413, 1414, 1415, 1500, 1528, 1542, 1562, 1675, 1740,
1757, 1806, 1808, 1953, 1964, 1982, 1985, 1986, 2020,
2036, 2076, 2098, 2159, 2209, 2236, 2315, 2346, 2437,
2438, 2449, 2545, 2553, 2566, 2567, 2598, 2605, 2625,
2628, 2657, 2670, 2756, 2798, 2812, 2930, 2940, 2950,
2959, 3019, 3023, 3032, 3078, 3103, 3153, 3197, 3256,
3257, 3258, 3271, 3304, 3327, 3331, 3333, 3361, 3364,
3390, 3444, 3458, 3502, 3524

40 Minutes   13, 47, 161, 223, 297, 344, 425, 520, 571, 741,
1149, 1197, 1238, 1307, 1314, 1338, 1369, 1459, 1532,
1599, 1631, 1791, 1793, 1866, 1867, 1901, 1960, 2117,
2138, 2247, 2249, 2361, 2421, 2469, 2552, 2601, 2619,
2726, 2739, 2886, 2921, 2937, 3085, 3143, 3224, 3238,
3301, 3337, 3342, 3491, 3542

45 Minutes   36, 101, 154, 270, 279, 379, 535, 564, 614, 696,
720, 793, 903, 922, 958, 982, 991, 1000, 1340, 1363, 1422,
1437, 1464, 1466, 1552, 1620, 1679, 1734, 1824, 1883,
1885, 1956, 2046, 2090, 2251, 2291, 2340, 2385, 2500,
2526, 2543, 2582, 2603, 2606, 2643, 2650, 2654, 2661,

2693, 2712, 2764, 2799, 2838, 2870, 2910, 2989, 2998,
3003, 3020, 3028, 3188, 3261, 3514, 3544

50 Minutes   23, 514, 664, 857, 864, 1209, 1617, 1665, 1865,
1870, 1980, 2044, 2087, 2276, 2365, 2517, 2988, 3004,
3239, 3306, 3348, 3401, 3554

55 Minutes   246, 723, 731, 1194, 1391, 1625, 1649, 1695,
1704, 1938, 2245, 2456, 2492, 3539

60 Minutes   1, 22, 31, 53, 56, 61, 63, 128, 130, 137, 164, 172,
196, 218, 235, 286, 302, 307, 349, 352, 415, 446, 503, 573,
584, 599, 623, 689, 740, 774, 780, 782, 850, 865, 901, 912,
928, 1185, 1202, 1335, 1356, 1384, 1428, 1454, 1482, 1556,
1575, 1590, 1614, 1619, 1633, 1651, 1733, 1781, 1916,
2051, 2089, 2099, 2131, 2250, 2277, 2281, 2311, 2329,
2342, 2347, 2357, 2400, 2406, 2420, 2425, 2479, 2532,
2533, 2577, 2608, 2609, 2636, 2656, 2658, 2674, 2717,
2721, 2727, 2736, 2748, 2768, 2821, 2846, 2891, 2972,
3002, 3034, 3102, 3113, 3151, 3175, 3200, 3205, 3265,
3288, 3461, 3483, 3494, 3495, 3560

65 Minutes   29, 1294, 2476, 3106

70 Minutes   17, 276, 821, 1389, 1387, 1388, 1607, 3312,
3465,

75 Minutes   98, 176, 511, 769, 946, 2169, 3206, 3462

80 Minutes   19, 55, 1606

90 Minutes   72, 119, 336, 353, 369, 440, 527, 570, 572, 606,
636, 640, 790, 791, 812, 834, 868, 902, 961, 1013, 1145,
1151, 1158, 1182, 1247, 1279, 1299, 1334, 1343, 1354,
1383, 1406, 1450, 1457, 1501, 1537, 1661, 1680, 1735,
1736, 1875, 1890, 1891, 1925, 1932, 1976, 2062, 2070,
2084, 2139, 2205, 2259, 2332, 2358, 2371, 2417, 2432,
2459, 2460, 2514, 2528, 2592, 2728, 2746, 2772, 2825,
2872, 2878, 2915, 3027, 3146, 3158, 3181, 3182, 3213,
3290, 3310, 3314, 3463, 3509, 3525, 3531

95 Minutes   50

100 Minutes   155, 243, 598, 1160, 1540, 1751

120 Minutes   46, 115, 670, 1012, 1019, 1205, 1260, 1306,
1320, 1456, 1509, 1567, 1579, 1591, 1646, 1652, 1772,
1827, 1831, 2075, 2296, 2519, 2631, 2648, 2757, 2824,
2945, 3178, 3245, 3368, 3547

130 Minutes   3292

135 Minutes   1662

150 Minutes   746

165 Minutes   2523

360 Minutes   309

480 Minutes   2448, 3207